Evangelical scholarship is deeply indebted to Dr. J. Paul Tanner for this contribution to the study of Daniel. Critical evangelical commentaries on this book are rare—and rarer still those that defend a conservative position on the crucial issues of date and authorship. His treatment of the notoriously difficult prophecy of the seventy weeks is a milestone in the history of interpretation of this text. I predict this work will be ranked among the finest expositions of Daniel and will well serve this generation so in need of proper guidance in biblical pedagogy and prophecy.

—Randall Price, Rawlings School of Divinity, Liberty University

Paul Tanner's new commentary will soon take its place among the finest, most thorough and most helpful commentaries ever produced on the book of Daniel. A careful analysis demonstrates that he is definitely committed to the inerrancy of Scripture, a premillennial view of eschatology, a future for Israel in God's kingdom program, and an early date of the book as written by Daniel in the sixth century BC. In spite of this, he interacts fairly, thoroughly and objectively with a broad spectrum of diverse theological approaches. I enthusiastically recommend it.

—Kenneth L. Barker, general editor, *NIV Study Bible*

Every generation or so, a book comes along that becomes a marker of "before X" or "after X." Paul Tanner has written such a book. As a student of Old Testament history and eschatology I have had occasion to give at least passing attention to almost everything written on Daniel in the past one hundred years, and without cavil or hyperbole I judge this work by Tanner—masterful in its use of Hebrew and Aramaic, without peer in the depth and breadth of its citation of relevant resources, and engagingly delightful in the clarity of its literary style—will become the standard in its niche, especially in evangelical scholarship.

—Eugene H. Merrill, Dallas Theological Seminary

Daniel is a challenging book to study, but it is an important one. Paul Tanner handles the book's issues in a solid way so that its message is made clear. Views are treated fairly and well surveyed. Your understanding of Daniel will be richly enhanced through Tanner's treatment of the text.

—Darrell Bock, Dallas Theological Seminary

The evangelical world has long needed a commentary of this magnitude. Dr. Tanner has produced a truly monumental work that will serve Bible teachers for many years to come. Unlike many commentators, he interacts with many other evangelical scholars. He also presents his case with sound reasoning and avoids dogmatic statements where the biblical text is ambiguous. The technical but indispensable interaction with the Hebrew is kept separate from the commentary sections, so as not to bog down those who cannot read the original text. Several supplemental studies address pertinent texts outside of Daniel, including biblical theology, devotional thoughts with insightful applications, and select bibliographies (e.g., the Daniel 7 sources alone total eight pages!). If you can only own one commentary on Daniel, this is it.

—Rick Griffith, Singapore Bible College

Dr. Tanner provides a solid argument for his theological position throughout his commentary, and does so while interacting sufficiently with opposing views, both messianic and non-messianic. This provides the reader with the latest treatment of all the chapters, especially the most difficult ones. This includes the harmony between chapters 2, 7, and 8 with a thorough exploration of the four kingdoms, with the fourth to reappear in the unprecedented time of the tribulation. It is here that the difficult details of chapter 11 are explained, spanning the intertestamental period, but also shown to ultimately point to the work of the antichrist in the tribulation. The treatment of chapter 9 consistently provides the umbrella for the repeated mention of the final establishment of God's kingdom for his people. All this is accompanied by rich application and devotional implications for each section.

—Imad N. Shehadeh, Jordan Evangelical Theological Seminary

DANIEL

EVANGELICAL EXEGETICAL COMMENTARY

DANIEL

J. Paul Tanner

LEXHAM ACADEMIC

Daniel
Evangelical Exegetical Commentary

Lexham Academic, an imprint of Lexham Press
1313 Commercial St., Bellingham, WA 98225
LexhamPress.com

English quotations from Daniel for this commentary are the author's own translation, unless otherwise indicated.

LXX refers to a reading accepted in both Gk traditions.

ISBN 9781683593096

Library of Congress Control Number: 2019951230

Lexham Editorial Team: Derek R. Brown, Russell Meek, Steven Tsoukalas
Cover Design: Brittany Schrock
Typesetting: ProjectLuz.com

To Linda . . . my precious wife
with whom I have had the privilege of sharing the
joyous adventure of life and ministry.
To you, my darling, I dedicate this most ambitious labor of love.

Contents

Acknowledgements

There are many I wish to thank who have contributed directly and indirectly to helping make this commentary possible. I am deeply grateful to my professors at Dallas Seminary under whom I first studied the biblical languages, and especially Dr. Kenneth Barker, the advisor for my ThM thesis. During my PhD studies at the University of Texas, I was privileged to study Aramaic under Dr. Aaron Bar-Adon, which fueled my intense interest in the book of Daniel. I am very appreciative of Dr. Roy Zuck, former editor of *Bibliotheca Sacra*, and Dr. Ron Youngblood, former editor of the *Journal of the Evangelical Theological* Society, both of whom encouraged me in the publication of various journal articles I wrote pertaining to the book of Daniel. I am thankful to Mr. Dave Semmelbeck, president of BEE World, for consenting to my working on this commentary in addition to my regular duties with our ministry. There are also many unnamed faithful prayer warriors that have lifted me in prayer over the several years that I was engaged in researching and writing this commentary. Not least among these are the men in my Thursday morning men's Bible study group in Tyler, TX, all of whom (in my opinion) exceed *David's mighty men*! Naturally I am grateful to Dr. William Barrick and Dr. H. Wayne House, editors of this commentary series, for entrusting to me the task of writing this commentary on the book of Daniel. Finally, but most important of all, there is my beautiful and faithful wife, Linda, who has served as my constant encourager and partner in prayer to see this commentary finished and made available to faithful teachers and pastors who will proclaim its truths to those of their generation.

Commentary Editors

Editors' Preface

The Bible is true in everything it intends to teach. At the same time, it is not always clear—which means it is not always obvious what it intends to teach, thus the need for commentary. The Evangelical Exegetical Commentary intends to help scholars, pastors, and laypeople understand Scripture in order to inform their understanding of God, motivate them to faithful action, and encourage their faith. We have recruited some of the best evangelical scholars to explore the meaning and application of the various books of the Old and New Testaments. Experts in the best sense of the word, they are doing their scholarship in the service of the church. They share a high regard for the Bible as God's Word, having honed their skills in biblical scholarship over decades of study.

The present commentary series is, first of all, *evangelical*. As the title of the series suggests, our contributors write from an evangelical perspective. While evangelicalism can be defined and exemplified in more than one way, evangelicals are united in recognizing the primary authority of Scripture for our knowledge of God and as a guide to faithful living.

The Evangelical Exegetical Commentary is also *exegetical*. The emphasis is on the original meaning of the text, starting with a close reading of the original languages in their original context. The biblical books, after all, were not written directly to us today, but to the faithful who were contemporary with the authors. Still, the fact that the church recognizes these books as canonical means that though they may not have been written *to* us, they were written *for* us.

Our hope and prayer, as editors and as contributors, is that these commentaries will help you so understand Scripture to inform your minds but also to stimulate your imaginations, to fire your emotions with faith, and to cultivate faithful obedience of God.

Tremper Longman III, General Editor

David T. Lamb, Senior Old Testament Editor

JoAnna M. Hoyt, Assistant Old Testament Editor

Andreas J. Köstenberger, Senior New Testament Editor

Benjamin L. Gladd, Assistant New Testament Editor

Abbreviations

2 Bar.	*2 Baruch (Syriac Apocalypse)*
ABD	*Anchor Bible Dictionary.* Edited by David Noel Freedman. 6 vols. New York: Doubleday, 1992
ABR	*Australian Biblical Review*
ABRL	Anchor Bible Reference Library
abs.	absolute (form)
acc.	accusative
AcPB	*Acta Patristica et Byzantina*
AD	anno Domini ("in the year of our Lord"); reference to years since the birth of Christ
adj.	adjective
'Ag.	*Aggadat*
AJSL	*American Journal of Semitic Languages and Literature*
Akk.	Akkadian
AJP	*American Journal of Philology*
AJT	*American Journal of Theology*
ANE	Ancient Near East
ANET	*Ancient Near Eastern Texts Relating to the Old Testament.* Edited by James B. Pritchard. 3rd ed. Princeton: Princeton University Press, 1969
ANRW	H. Temporini and W. Haase (eds.), *Aufstieg und Niedergang der römischen Welt* (Berlin/New York: de Gruyter)
AnSt	*Anatolian Studies*
Ant.	*Antiquities of the Jews* (by the first-century AD Jewish historian Josephus)
AOAT	Alter Orient und Altes Testament
appr.	approximately
Aram.	Aramaic
AS	*Aramaic Studies*
ATR	*Australian Theological Review*
AUSS	*Andrews University Seminary Studies*
AUSSJ	*Anderews University Seminary Student Journal*
AYBD	*The Anchor Yale Bible Dictionary*
b. Bat.	*Baba Batra* in the Babylonian Talmud
b. Sanh.	Tractate *Sanhedrin* in the Babylonian Talmud
BA	*Biblical Archaeologist*
BASOR	*Bulletin of the American Schools of Oriental Research*

BBR	*Bulletin for Biblical Research*
BC	"before Christ"; reference to the years preceding the birth of Christ
BDAG	Danker, Frederick W., Walter Bauer, William F. Arndt, and F. Wilbur Gingrich. *Greek-English Lexicon of the New Testament and Other Early Christian Literature*. 3rd ed. Chicago: University of Chicago Press, 2000 (Danker-Bauer-Arndt-Gingrich)
BDB	Brown, Francis, S. R. Driver, and Charles A. Briggs. *A Hebrew and English Lexicon of the Old Testament*
BECNT	Baker Exegetical Commentary on the New Testament
Ber.	*Bereshit*
BETL	Bibliotheca Ephemeridum Theologicarum Lovaniensium
BH	Biblical Hebrew
BHS	*Biblia Hebraica Stuttgartensia*. Edited by Karl Elliger and Wilhelm Rudolph. Stuttgart: Deutsche Bibelgesellschaft, 1983
Bib	*Biblica*
BAram.	Biblical Aramaic
BKC	*Bible Knowledge Commentary*
BL	Bauer, H. and P. Leander, *Grammatik des Biblisch-Aramäischen*. Halle: Niemeyer, 1927
BR	*Biblical Research*
BRev	*Bible Review*
BSac	*Bibliotheca Sacra*
BT	*The Bible Translator*
BZ	*Biblische Zeitschrift*
BZAW	Beihefte zur *ZAW*
ca.	about, approximately
CAD	*Chicago Assyrian Dictionary*
CAL	Comprehensive Aramaic Lexicon Project (online: cal1.en.huc.edu)
C. Ap.	*Contra Apion* (or "Against Apion," a work by Josephus)
CBQ	*Catholic Biblical Quarterly*
CBQMS	Catholic Biblical Quarterly Monograph Series
CD	The Cairo (Geniza text of the) *Damascus* (*Document*)
cf.	compare
C^G	A Hebrew fragment from the manuscripts in the Cairo Genizah collection
chap.	chapter
chaps.	chapters
ClPh	*Classical Philology*
CNS	*Cristianesimo nella storia*
ConBNT	Coniectanea neotestamentica or Coniectanea biblica: New Testament Series
ConBOT	Coniectanea biblica, Old Testament

const.	construct
CP	*Classical Philology*
CT Levi	Testament of Levi from the Cairo Genizah
CTJ	*Conservative Theological Journal*
CTR	*Criswell Theological Review*
CurBS	*Currents in Research: Biblical Studies*
Cy	*Cyropaedia* (by Xenophon)
D	Damascus Document
DBL	*Dictionary of Biblical Languages with Semantic Domains: Hebrew*. J. A. Swanson. Oak Harbor: Logos Research Systems, 1997.
DBSJ	*Detroit Baptist Seminary Journal*
DCH	*Dictionary of Classical Hebrew*. Edited by David J. A. Clines. 9 vols. Sheffield: Sheffield Phoenix Press, 1993–2014
def.	definition
DJD	Discoveries in the Judaean Desert of Jordan
DSD	*Dead Sea Discoveries*
DSS	Dead Sea Scrolls
DTT	*A Dictionary of the Targumim, the Talmud Babli and Yerushalmi, and the Midrashic Literature*. Compiled by Marcus Jastrow. New York: G. P. Putnam's Sons, 1886
East. Aram.	Eastern Aramaic
EANEC	Explorations in Ancient Near Eastern Cultures
EBC	*The Expositor's Bible Commentary*
Ech. Rab.	*Echa Rabba* (Lamentations Rabbah)
Edd.	Editions
EDNT	*Exegetical Dictionary of the New Testament*. Edited by Horst Balz and Gerhard Schneider. ET. 3 vols. Grand Rapids: Eerdmans, 1990–1993
e.g.	for example
esp.	especially
En.	*Enoch* (e.g., *1 En.*)
Eng.	English
ETL	*Ephemerides Theologicae Lovanienses*
ETS	Evangelical Theological Society
ExpTim	*Expository Times*
EvJ	*Evangelical Journal*
EvQ	*Evangelical Quarterly*
FAT	Forschungen zum Alten Testament
ff.	following (usually refers to "following verses")
fig.	figurative
fn	footnote
fp	feminine plural
fs	feminine singular

GBA	*A Grammar of Biblical Aramaic*. Franz Rosenthal. Porta Lingarium Orientalium 5. 7th ed. Göttingen: Harrassowitz, 2006
Gk.	Greek
GKC	*Gesenius' Hebrew Grammar.* Edited by Emil Kautzsch. Translated by Arther E. Cowley. 2nd ed. Oxford: Clarendon, 1910
gl.	gloss (a word or remark inserted in the text for explanation or clarification)
GJ	*Grace Journal*
GTJ	*Grace Theological Journal*
HALOT	*The Hebrew and Aramaic Lexicon of the Old Testament.* Ludwig Koehler, Walter Baumgartner, and Johann J. Stamm. Translated and edited under the supervision of Mervyn E. J. Richardson. 4 vols. Leiden: Brill, 1994–1999
HAR	*Hebrew Annual Review*
Heb.	Hebrew
Hen	*Henoch*
HeyJ	*Heythrop Journal*
HDR	Harvard Dissertations in Religion
HTS	*Harvard Theological Studies*
HUCA	*Hebrew Union College Annual*
HvTSt	*Hervormde Teologiese Studies* (South Africa)
HW	*Hebräische Wortforschung* (FS W. Baumgartner; VTSup 16, 1967)
IBHS	*An Introduction to Biblical Hebrew Syntax*. Bruce K. Waltke and Michael O'Connor. Winona Lake, IN: Eisenbrauns, 1990
IBRLR	*IBR Library Review*
IDB	*The Interpreter's Dictionary of the Bible.* Edited by George A. Buttrick. 4 vols. New York: Abingdon, 1962
idem	the same
i.e.	that is
IEJ	*Israel Exploration Journal*
impf.	imperfect
impv.	imperative
incl.	including
inf.	infinitive
Int	*Interpretation*
IOS	*Israel Oriental Society*
IOSOT	*International Organization for the Study of the Old Testament*
ISBE	*The International Standard Bible Encyclopedia*, ed. Geoffrey W. Bromiley. 4 vols. Grand Rapids, MI: Eerdmans, 1979–88
JAH	*Journal of Ancient History*
JAJ	*Journal of Ancient Judaism*

JANES(CU)	*Journal of the Ancient Near Eastern Society of Columbia University*
JAOS	*Journal of the American Oriental Society*
J. Aram.	Jewish Aramaic
JATS	*Journal of the Adventist Theological Society*
JBL	*Journal of Biblical Literature*
JBQ	*Jewish Biblical Quarterly*
JECS	*Journal of Early Christian Studies*
Jeph.	Jephet Ibn Ali (the Karaite commentator on Daniel)
JESOT	*Journal for the Evangelical Study of the Old Testament*
JETS	*Journal of the Evangelical Theological Society*
JHebScr	*Journal of Hebrew Scriptures*
JHS	*Journal of Hellenic Studies*
JJS	*Journal of Jewish Studies*
JNES	*Journal of Near Eastern Studies*
JNSL	*Journal of Northwest Semitic Languages*
JPhil	*Journal of Philology*
JQR	*Jewish Quarterly Review*
JSem	*Journal for Semitics*
JSJ	*Journal for the Study of Judaism in the Persian, Hellenistic and Roman Periods*
JSJSup	*Supplements to Journal for the Study of Judaism*
JSOT	*Journal for the Study of the Old Testament*
JSP	*Journal for the Study of the Pseudepigrapha*
JSS	*Journal of Semitic Studies*
JTI	*Journal of Theological Interpretation*
JTS	*Journal of Theological Studies*
JTVI	*Journal of the Transactions of the Victoria Institute*
Jub.	*Jubilees* (OT Pseudepigrapha)
Kenn.	Kennicott, critical apparatus
lit.	literally
LNTS	Library of New Testament Studies
LSJM	Liddell, Henry George, Robert Scott, Henry Stuart Jones. *A Greek-English Lexicon*. 9th ed. with revised supplement. Oxford: Clarendon, 1996
LXX	The Septuagint (the Greek translation tradition of the Old Testament)
Macc	Maccabees (books found among the Apocrypha)
Mart. Ascen. Isa.	*Martyrdom and Ascension of Isaiah*
masc.	masculine
MH	Mishnaic Hebrew
Midr.	*Midrash*
mp	masculine plural
ms	masculine singular
MSJ	*The Master's Seminary Journal*

MS(S)	manuscript(s)
MT	Masoretic Text (the Hebrew text of the OT as found in the *Biblia Hebraica Stuttgartensia* edition)
NAC	The New American Commentary series
NASB	New American Standard Bible
NET	The NET Bible translation (available on the Internet at www.bible.org)
NETS	*A New English Translation of the Septuagint*. Edited by Albert Pietersma and Benjamin G. Wright. New York: Oxford University Press, 2007
NGTT	*Nederduitse gereformeerde teologiese tydskrif* (formerly, *Dutch Reformed Theological Journal*; now *Stellenbosch Theological Journal* [*STJ*])
Nat.	*Naturalis Historia* (Pliny the Elder)
NICOT	The New International Commentary on the Old Testament
NIDNTTE	*The New International Dictionary of New Testament Theology and Exegesis*. Edited by Moisés Silva. Grand Rapids: Zondervan, 2014.
NIDOTTE	*New International Dictionary of Old Testament Theology and Exegesis*. Edited by Willem A. VanGemeren. 5 vols. Grand Rapids: Zondervan, 1997
NIV	New International Version
NKJV	New King James Version
NLT	New Living Translation
NT	New Testament
NTS	*New Testament Studies*
OP	Old Persian
OrS	*Orientalia Suecana*
OT	Old Testament
OTA	*Old Testament Abstracts*
OTE	*Old Testament Essays*
OtSt	*Oudtestamentische Studiën*
perf.	perfect
PJBR	*Polish Journal of Biblical Research*
pl.	plural
poss.	possibly
prep.	preposition
pron.	pronoun, or pronominal
PRSt	*Perspectives in Religious Studies*
Prud	*Prudentia*
Ps.-Sa.	Pseudo-Saadia
ptc.	participle
PTMS	Pittsburgh Theological Monograph Series
PTR	*Princeton Theological Review*
r.	reigned (indicating years of a king's reign)

RA	*Revue d'Assyriologie et d'archéologie orientale*
Rab.	*Rabbah*
RB	*Revue biblique*
RefR	*Reformed Review*
ResQ	*Restoration Quarterly*
RevExp	*Review and Expositor*
RevQ	*Revue de Qumran*
RJ	Rabbi Isaac Jerusalmi, *The Aramaic Sections of Ezra and Daniel*
RTR	*Reformed Theological Review*
Syr.	Syriac
Sanh.	*Sanhedrin* (in the Talmud)
SBJT	*The Southern Baptist Journal of Theology*
SBLSP	*Society of Biblical Literature Seminar Papers*
SBS	Stuttgarter Bibelstudien
Scr	*Scripture*
SBLSCS	Septuagint and Cognate Studies published by the Society of Biblical Literature
sg.	single, singular
SJOT	*Scandinavian Journal of the Old Testament*
Sok.	Sokoloff, M. *A Dictionary of Jewish Palestinian Aramaic of the Byzantine Period*. 2nd ed. Baltimore: Johns Hopkins University Press, 2003.
SPB	Studia Post Biblica
ST	*Studia theologica*
Stim	*Stimulus*
STJ	*Stulos Theological Journal*
StudBibT	*Studia biblica et theologica*
suff.	suffix
SVTQ	*St. Vladimir's Theological Quarterly*
Syh	The Syro-Hexapla Greek manuscript of Daniel
TA	*Tel Aviv*
Tanch. tol.	The Midrashic Commentary *Tanchuma tôlᵊḏôṯ*
TAPA	*Transactions of the American Philological Society*
TAPS	*Transactions of the American Philosophical Society*
TDNT	*Theological Dictionary of the New Testament.* Edited by Gerhard Kittel and Gerhard Friedrich. Translated by Geoffrey W. Bromiley. 10 vols. Grand Rapids: Eerdmans, 1964–1976
Tg.	Targum
Tg. Neb.	*Targum of the Prophets*
Tg. Onq.	*Targum Onqelos*
TGUOS	Transactions of the Glasgow University Oriental Society
Them	*Themelios*
TJ	*Trinity Journal*
TLZ	*Theologische Literaturzeitung*
Tg. Neof.	*Targum Neofiti*

TWOT	*Theological Wordbook of the Old Testament.* Edited by R. Laird Harris, Gleason L. Archer Jr., and Bruce K. Waltke. 2 vols. Chicago: Moody Press, 1980
ThViat	*Theologia Viatorum*
TynBul	*Tyndale Bulletin*
TZ	*Theologische Zeitschrift*
UF	*Ugarit-Forschungen*
v., vv.	verse(s)
vb	verb
V^S	A Hebrew variant in unpublished manuscripts cited in Strack, *Grammatik des Biblishch-Aramäischen*, 6th ed., 1921.
Vg.	Latin Vulgate
vv.	verses
viz.	namely
VSS	versions
VT	*Vetus Testamentum*
VTSup	Vetus Testamentum Supplements
WW	*Word and World*
WUNT	*Wissenschaftliche Untersuchungen zum Neuen Testament*
ZA	*Zeitschrift für Assyriologie*
ZAC	*Zeitschrift für Antikes Christentum/Journal of Ancient Christianity*
ZAW	*Zeitschrift für die alttestamentliche Wissenschaft*
ZNW	*Zeitschrift für die neutestamentliche Wissenschaft und die Kunde der älteren Kirche*
ZPEB	*Zondervan Pictorial Encyclopedia of the Bible.* Edited by Merrill C. Tenney. 5 vols. Grand Rapids: Zondervan, 1975

Introduction

General Introduction

The book of Daniel, undoubtedly one of the most unique books in the Bible, has fascinated Christian readers throughout the centuries. In the initial setting of the book, Daniel and his Jewish compatriots are brought to the city of Babylon following the siege of Jerusalem and deportation of a select group of Jewish youths at the hands of Nebuchadnezzar, an invading Babylonian general. The book consists of two primary parts: court tales in chaps. 1–6 and visions given to Daniel in chaps. 7–12. Despite being numbered among the Jewish exiles, Daniel and his friends experience incredible interventions of the Lord while living in pagan Babylon. God in his sovereignty cares for his covenant people, uses Daniel to interpret kingly dreams and explain divine signs, and delivers Daniel and his friends from those out to harm them. Daniel is even elevated to high positions of service in the government of both Babylon and Medo-Persia. In the latter part of the book, Daniel is given a series of visions (chaps. 7–12) revealing sufferings and persecution yet to come for the Jewish people. Yet hope is held out that ultimately Gentile kingdoms will all give way to a kingdom set up by the God of heaven that will be ruled by "One like a son of man," namely, the Lord Jesus Christ.

The stories and visions, while they make for entertaining reading, also provide significant revelation about God and his sovereign control of the nations of the world, the rise of the end-times antichrist, and the divine plan for history that culminates in the kingdom of God being entrusted to the Messiah. The book is thus rich in biblical theology. In fact, Daniel is probably *the* most foundational book in the Old Testament for New Testament eschatology.

Despite the crucial role that the book of Daniel plays in the canon of Scripture, it is at the same time one of the most controversial books of the Old Testament, being under heavy attack by critical scholars who dispute its trustworthiness and contradict the very teachings in it that the church has traditionally believed. While the traditional conservative evangelical understanding of the book of Daniel has been that the historical person Daniel wrote it in the sixth century BC (and thus much of the book consists of predictive prophecy), critical scholars deny Danielic authorship and the book's historical claims, choosing instead to believe that the book for the most part was written "after the fact" by an unknown author (or authors) living during the reign of the second-century BC Seleucid king Antiochus IV Epiphanes. The following quotation typifies such a skeptical approach:

> The observation that the book contains many historical inaccuracies is the most important clue for the fact that the book originated in the second century. These inaccuracies are explained once it is realized that the writer wrote about the events of her own period, the second century.[1]

Nevertheless, the accusation of historical inaccuracies does not hold up to a careful examination of the evidence, and the second-century BC Antiochene theory of the book (and the resulting interpretation imposed on the text) fails in the light of careful exegesis. For too long, critical scholars have dominated the discussion of Daniel. I hope this commentary will fill a much-needed gap, providing evangelical pastors and teachers with a full-orbed commentary that provides the technical details regarding manuscripts and translation issues, commentary resting on careful exegesis and consistent application of hermeneutics, and yet with pastoral concerns and applicational insights befitting those who wish to live in submission to God's revealed Word. Throughout the process of study and writing, this author has felt the conviction for writing this commentary "as unto the Lord" ... being accountable to him while desirous only of his honor.

Place in the Canon

In the Hebrew Bible—with its three primary divisions of the Torah, the Prophets, and the Writings—the book of Daniel is not classified under the Prophets (נביאים) but under the Writings (כתובים). Harrison explains: " ... the book was placed in this part of the Hebrew canon because Daniel is not called a *nāḇî* ("prophet") but rather a *ḥōzeh* ("seer") and a *ḥāḵām* ("wise man"). None but the works of the *nᵉḇî'îm* were put in the second part of the Jewish canon, the third being reserved for the heterogeneous works of seers, wise men, and priests.[2] Although the NT does refer to Daniel as a prophet (Matt 24:15), he was not a prophet in the same sense as other OT prophets. Harrison points out, "In ancient Israel the prophet was primarily a mediator between God and the nation, speaking to the people on behalf of God. He was in effect a spokesman for the Lord."[3] Although Daniel did have night visions and interpreted dreams as OT prophets often did, he did not have this mediatorial role (despite the fact he interceded in prayer on behalf of his nation). Pentecost (1323) adds, "God did not deliver a message through

1. M. Nel, "A Literary-historical Analysis of Daniel 2; Two Powers in Opposition," *Acta Theologica* 22 (2002): 78.

2. R. K. Harrison, "Daniel, Book of," in *ISBE*, 1:860.

3. Ibid.

Daniel publicly to the nation Israel." Daniel was primarily a statesman at a heathen court.

Despite this clarification, we should point out that in the Qumran material, Daniel is referred to as a prophet. Di Lella (25–26) observes,

> In 4Q174, col. ii, line 3, however, we find this expression: .... *'š]r ktwb bspr dny'l hnby'*, '... a]s it is written in the Book of Daniel the prophet.' These words are then followed by quotations of Dan 12:10 and 11:32. This Qumran text is to be dated ca. 30–1 B.C. It seems, from this evidence, that the Essenes of the Qumran community considered Daniel as one of the prophets .... .

Similarly, Josephus referred to Daniel as a prophet and called his writings prophecies (*Ant.* 10.11.7). In the Talmud, however, Daniel is spoken of as weightier than "all the wise men of the peoples" (*b. Yoma* 77a) but not as a prophet.[4]

Finally, in the Greek OT canon (and in contrast to the Hebrew Bible), the book of Daniel is generally grouped with the prophets (typically following Ezekiel). Goswell suggests this is undoubtedly due to the visionary character of chaps. 7–12, in which Daniel receives visions depicting future events, and concludes, "As a result of the placement of the prophetic books at the end of the canon (culminating with Daniel), the Greek canon points to an eschatological hope centered on the kingdom of God as the dominant theology of Scripture."[5]

Texts and Versions

The Hebrew-Aramaic Composition

The book of Daniel (like the book of Ezra) was written in more than one language. About half of the book (1:1–2:4a; 8:1–12:13) was written in Hebrew, while the remainder (2:4b–7:28) was written in Aramaic (the KJV refers to this as "Syriack" in Dan 2:4).

Hebrew was the language of God's covenant people, the Jews, whereas Aramaic was the *lingua franca* of the Gentile world in Daniel's day. One possible explanation for the use of the two languages is that Aramaic is used

4. Similarly, in medieval rabbinic literature (e.g., Kimchi and Maimonides) Daniel is denied being a prophet, though Abarbanel considered him to be one. So A. Pinker, "A Dream of a Dream in Daniel 2," *JBQ* 33 (2005): 233–34. Cf. L. Ginzberg, "Daniel," in *The Jewish Encyclopedia*, 12 vols., ed. C. Adler et al. (New York: Funk and Wagnalls, 1901–1906), 4:428.

5. G. Goswell, "The Canonical Position(s) of the Book of Daniel," *ResQ* 59 (2017): 133. Cf. J. M. Scheetz, "Daniel's Position in the Tanach, the LXX-Vulgate, and the Protestant Canon," *OTE* 23 (2010): 178–93.

when the book focuses on Gentile powers, and Hebrew is used when the book focuses on God's covenant people (Israel) and their future.[6]

The Aramaic language takes its name from the Aramean people, or the people of Aram. As a place name, Aram is found in Old Akkadian writings at least as early as the middle of the third millennium BC, referring to the region of the Tigris north of Elam and east of Assyria.[7] Accordingly, Aramaic is typically divided into several dialects based on chronological and geographic principles, the first being "Old" or "Ancient" Aramaic. Greenspahn explains the second phase of Aramaic,

> The next period of Aramaic is dominated by what is called Official, Imperial, or Standard Literary Aramaic because it served as the official administrative language of the Persian Empire from the sixth to the fourth centuries, although it may have begun to spread somewhat earlier, under the Assyrians and Babylonians. This is also the dialect found in the Bible, although some scholars assign the book of Daniel to a later category. …
>
> … After Judah fell to the Babylonian king Nebuchadnezzar, the Hebrews adopted the Aramaic form of what had originally been the Phoenician alphabetic script for purposes of writing Hebrew (it is important to distinguish between a language and a script) … .
>
> … When Persia, which defeated Babylonia in 539 B.C., adopted Aramaic for official administrative purposes, the language's importance grew dramatically. Eventually, the Persian Empire stretched from Egypt to India, ensuring Aramaic's widespread use and prominence. Official sponsorship also created a kind of standardization, something which did not begin to wane until the encroachment of Greek under Alexander the Great and then, many centuries later, Arabic.[8]

Commenting on the Aramaic of Daniel, Harrison notes, "… Official Aramaic was employed increasingly by Assyrian government officials between 1100 and 600 BC, becoming the language of diplomacy in the Persian period, even though royal inscriptions were still being inscribed in Old Persian at

---

6. For a survey of various views explaining the presence of the two languages within the book, see A. E. Portier-Young, "Languages of Identity and Obligation: Daniel as Bilingual Book," *VT* 60 (2010): 98–115. Though some have speculated that Daniel 1 and 7 might be translated texts, H. J. M. van Deventer, "Testing-Testing, Do We Have a Translated Text in Daniel 1 and 7?," *JNSL* 32 (2005): 91–106 has concluded that neither text is, in fact, a translation, but rather, both were composed originally in the language in which they now appear.

7. W. S. Lasor, "Aramaic," in *ISBE*, 1:229.

8. F. W. Greenspahn, *An Introduction to Aramaic*, 2nd ed. (Atlanta: Society of Biblical Literature, 2003), 6–7.

that time."[9] Since the Aramaic of the book of Daniel is quite in keeping with Official Aramaic, there is nothing about the text itself that would suggest the book had not been composed in the sixth century BC. Harrison adds, "When the vocabulary of Daniel is examined, nine-tenths of it can be attested immediately from West Semitic inscriptions, or papyri from the 5th cent. B.C. or earlier."[10] Hebrew terms and expressions in Daniel are also characteristic of the sixth century BC, and do not suggest a late date for the book.[11] (See further comments under "Date" and "Authorship.")

The Question of an Aramaic Original

Critical scholars sometimes postulate that chaps. 1 and 7–12 were originally written in Aramaic and only later translated into Hebrew. For an introductory discussion, see Collins (12–13). However, the lack of any supporting Aramaic manuscripts for these chapters renders such a suggestion highly suspect. Of greater significance is the fact that four of the Qumran fragments for the book of Daniel do reflect the same Hebrew/Aramaic sections, which strongly argues that this was the nature of the original autograph. VanderKam and Flint write,

> The four scrolls that preserve material from the relevant sections (1QDan[a], 4QDan[a], 4QDan[b], and 4QDan[d]) support the same transitions from Hebrew to Aramaic and back again. Although the reasons for having Hebrew and Aramaic sections in the same book are complex, the scrolls show us that Daniel existed in this form very early on and was thus most likely compiled in Hebrew and Aramaic.[12]

9. Harrison, "Daniel," 1:860.

10. Ibid.

11. Some Hebrew terms were thought to be evidence of late linguistic usage: (1) S. R. Driver (508) once regarded *malkûṯ* ("royal power," "reign") as such. These terms were "actually used in all periods of the Hebrew language, and represent a noun pattern found in Akkadian as early as the 18th cent. B.C." (Harrison, "Daniel, Book of," 860). (2) *āmar lᵊ* ("command to") was formerly thought to be a late literary form. Yet this also occurs in Deut 9:25; Josh 22:33; 1 Sam 30:6, as well as in the postexilic works (Neh 9:15, 22).

12. J. VanderKam and P. Flint, *The Meaning of the Dead Sea Scrolls* (San Francisco: HarperCollins, 2002), 138. This conclusion is also supported by the research of E. Ulrich, "The Text of Daniel in the Qumran Scrolls," in *The Book of Daniel: Composition & Reception*, ed. J. J. Collins and P. W. Flint, VTSup 83:2 (Leiden: Brill, 2001), 579.

Presence of Foreign Loanwords

In addition to the Hebrew and Aramaic sections of the book, there are a number of foreign *loanwords* in the book.

A. Akkadian loanwords

There are some twenty-one words in the Aramaic section of Daniel thought to be of Akkadian origin. These are identified in the commentary by Collins (18):

> These are ארגון (purple), אשף (enchanter or prognosticator), אתון (furnace), היכל (temple), זִו (radiance or splendor), זכו (innocence), זמן (time), חשח (needing), כרבלה (hat), כרסא (throne), מנא (mina), נולי (dunghill), סגן (prefect), עדן (time), פחה (governor), פחר (potter), פרזל (iron), פרס (half-shekel), שׁיזב (rescue), שׁגלה (concubine), תלת (triumvir).[13]

Their presence, however, has no particular bearing on the dating of the book, as Kitchen has pointed out:

> The vocabulary analysis already mentioned would indicate that practically all of these 21 words are either attested in Imperial Aramaic well beyond Daniel, or have a long history prejudicial to their entering Aramaic only in the sixth century BC (or later) or occur already in Old Aramaic or West Semitic, or in Hebrew outside Daniel (ruling out special usage there). In other words, the Akkadian loan-words are probably simply part of the multicoloured fabric of Aramaic, and have no real bearing on the date of the language of Daniel within the sixth to the second centuries BC.[14]

B. Old Iranian loanwords (mostly Old Persian dialect)

Noonan has identified some twenty-three Old Iranian loanwords, mostly found in the court narratives of the Aramaic portion of the book. He writes,

> There are 23 old Iranian loanwords in the book of Daniel: אֲדַרְגָּזַר (a financial official), אַזְדָּא ("certain, known"), אֲחַשְׁדַּרְפַּן ("satrap"), אַפֶּדֶן ("columned palace, audience hall"), גְּדָבַר ("treasurer"), דָּת ("law"), דְּתָבַר ("judge"), הַדָּבַר ("assistant, aide"), הַדָּם ("limb"), הַמְנִיכָא ("necklace"), זְמָן ("time"), זַן ("kind, type"), כַּרְבְּלָה (a type of pointed cap), נֶבְרְשְׁתָּא ("lamp"), נְדַן ("sheath"), סַרְבָּל (a type of trousers), סְרַךְ (a chief official), פַּטִּישׁ (a type of leg wrappings),

13. Collins (18) adds: "Two other terms of Akkadian origin, מלצר (superintendent) and בירה (fortress), are found in the Hebrew section of Daniel at 1:11 and 8:2."

14. K. A. Kitchen, "The Aramaic of Daniel," in *Notes on Some Problems in the Book of Daniel*, ed. D. J. Wiseman et al., 31–79 (London: Tyndale, 1965), 35.

> פַּרְתְּמִם (an official of the royal court), פַּתְבַּג ("food allowance"), פִּתְגָם ("decree"), רָז ("secret, mystery"), and תִּפְתָּי (an official, perhaps a guard supervisor).[15]

Some of these are attested in the Targums. Harrison notes, "About half of the Persian loan words occur in Official Aramaic, and in general can be found in sixth- to fifth-century BC literary sources."[16] He concludes, "... all the Persian loanwords in Daniel are specifically Old Persian (which is found on inscriptions from the 6th and 5th cent. BC), indicating that the Aramaic of Daniel in this area is certainly pre-Hellenistic rather than Maccabean."[17] Furthermore, the ratio of distinct Old Iranian loanwords to the number of distinct lexemes in the book of Daniel is higher than that of the books of Ezra-Nehemiah and Esther. Noonan points out the significance of this observation:

> One could try to explain the high percentage of Old Iranian loans in the book of Daniel as a late literary creation. It is unlikely, however, that someone writing so long after the fact would be capable of inventing such a literary creation. Much of the Old Iranian terminology found in Daniel would have been forgotten during the Hellenistic period, as indicated by the fact that the Greek translators of Daniel did not know what to do with many of the book's Old Iranian loans.[18]

---

15. B. J. Noonan, "The Presence and Significance of Foreign Loanwords in the Book of Daniel" (paper presented at Evangelical Theological Society annual meeting, Baltimore, November 20, 2013), 1.

16. Harrison, "Daniel," 1:861.

17. Ibid., 1:865. Although Collins does not agree with Harrison on this point, he does concede that the failure of the Greek translators to fully understand many of these Old Iranian terms is a significant point in regard to the dating of the book. Collins writes (19): "This observation does not necessarily require a pre-Hellenistic date for any part of the extant text of Daniel, but it does weigh against the theory that the whole book originated in the second century." Kitchen, "The Aramaic of Daniel," 43, points out that Old Persian loanwords date to a period prior to 300 BC. Noonan (The Presence and Significance of Foreign Loanwords in the Book of Daniel), 5 following a technical discussion of phonological changes in Old Iranian that confirms Kitchen's argument, concludes, "In sum, phonological evidence demonstrates that Daniel's Iranian loanwords belong typologically to Old Iranian rather than Middle Iranian. This means that they must have been borrowed before the collapse of the Achaemenid Empire (i.e., prior to ca. 300 BC) as Kitchen argues. It is quite likely that the book of Daniel's Iranian loanwords were borrowed earlier rather than later during the time of the Achaemenid Empire because the above phonological changes took place over time."

18. Noonan, "Presence and Significance," 6.

C. Greek loanwords

Within the book of Daniel, at least four possible Greek loanwords have been identified: כָּרוֹז (*kārôz*, "herald"), סוּמְפֹּנְיָה (*sûmpōnyâ*, "tambour"; Qere סוּפֹּנְיָה, *sûpōnyâ*), פְּסַנְטֵרִין/פְּסַנְתֵּרִין (*pᵊsantērîn*, or *pᵊsanṭērîn*), a stringed musical instrument), and קִיתָרֹס (*qîṯārîs*, a type of lyre or zither).[19] In addition, the word שַׂבְּכָא (*śabbᵊḵāʾ*, "trigon") is thought to be related to Greek σαμβύκη (*sambukē*, a small arched-type harp). All these terms occur in chap. 3 of Daniel. (For further discussion, see comments on Greek words under "Linguistic Objections to the Traditional Date and Authorship," and the commentary at Dan 3:1–7.)

As with the case of Akkadian loanwords, it is not surprising to find Greek words in Daniel. This is certainly no indication of a late dating of the book. Waltke notes, "Greek words are now attested in the Aramaic documents of Elephantine dated to the fifth century B.C."[20]

Fragments from Qumran

The book of Daniel must have enjoyed some degree of popularity among the inhabitants of Qumran. As of this date, we now have eight small fragments for the book of Daniel.[21] VanderKam and Flint describe the Qumran finds:

> A total of eight Daniel scrolls were discovered at Qumran: two in Cave 1, five in Cave 4, and one in Cave 6. None is complete due to the ravages of time, but between them they preserve text from eleven of Daniel's twelve chapters. This does not mean that the book lacked the final chapter at Qumran, since Dan. 12:10 is quoted in the *Florilegium* (4Q174), which tells us that it is "written in the book of Daniel the Prophet" (frag. 1–3 2.3–4). All eight manuscripts were copied in the space of 175 years, ranging from about 125 BCE (4QDan[c]) to about 50 CE (4QDan[b]).[22]

---

19. Note that *HALOT*, 1902d takes כָּרוֹז (*kārôz*) to be Old Persian in origin.
20. B. K. Waltke, "The Date of the Book of Daniel," *BSac* 133 (1976): 324.
21. In addition to these eight fragments of Daniel, a few other fragments have been found making apparent reference to the book of Daniel, namely, 4Q243-245. See J. Collins and P. Flint, "243-245. 4Qpseudo-Daniel[a-c] ar," in *Parabiblical Texts, Part 3*, ed. G. Brooke et al., 95-164, DJD 22 (Oxford: Clarendon, 1996); and L. DiTommasso, "4Q*Pseudo-Daniel*[a-b] (4Q243-4Q244) and the Book of Daniel," *DSD* 12 (2005): 101-33.
22. VanderKam and Flint, *Meaning*, 137. Cf. P. W. Flint, "The Daniel Tradition at Qumran," in *The Book of Daniel: Composition & Reception*, ed. J. J. Collins and P. W. Flint, VTSup 83:2 (Leiden: Brill, 2001), 329–67.

Significantly, none of the apocryphal additions to Daniel appear in the Qumran fragments.[23] In 1QDan[b] and 4QDan[d], for example, Dan 3:23 is simply followed by 3:24, not the Prayer of Azariah and the Song of the Three Young Men as in the Greek Septuagint. Furthermore, the eight surviving fragments reveal no major disagreements against the MT, though they do have some minor textual variants.[24]

The Qumran fragments for the book of Daniel consist of the following:[25]

1) 1QDan[a] (1:10–17; 2:2–6)[26]
   1QDan[b] (3:22–30)
2) 4QDan[a] (1:16–20; 2:9–11, 19–49; 3:1–2; 4:29–30; 5:5–7, 12–14, 16–19; 7:5–7, 25–28; 8:1–5; 10:16–20; 11:13–16)[27]
   4QDan[b] (3:22–30; 5:10–12, 14–16, 19–22; 6:8–22, 27–29; 7:1–6, 11?, 26–28; 8:1–8, 13–16)
   4QDan[c] (10:5–9, 11–16, 21; 11:1–2, 13–17, 25–29)
   4QDan[d] (3:8–10?, 23–25; 4:5–9, 12–16; 7:15–23)
   4QDan[e] (9:12–17)
3) pap6QDan (8:16–17?; 8:20–21?; 10:8–16; and 11:33–36, 38)[28]

---

23. For an introductory treatment of the apocryphal additions to Daniel, see D. A. deSilva, "Additions to Daniel: 'Let Them Know That You Alone Are God,'" in *Introducing the Apocrypha*, by D. A. DeSilva (Grand Rapids: Baker, 2002), 222–43.
24. Ulrich, "Text of Daniel," 575–79, lists all the differences of significance.
25. This list is drawn from Ulrich, "Text of Daniel," 574.
26. The original work on 1QDan[a] and 1QDan[b] was published by D. Barthelemy and J. T. Milik, "Discoveries," in *Qumran Cave 1*, DJD 1 (Oxford: Clarendon, 1955), 150–52. The plates were published subsequently by J. C. Trever, "Completion of the Publication of Some Fragments from Cave I," *RevQ* 19 (1965): 323–36. The Daniel fragments appear on plates v and vi.
27. The analysis and publication of the fragments from Cave 4 was entrusted to F. M. Cross of Harvard. In 1956 he reported, "... a sizeable proportion of the book of Daniel is extant in three relatively well preserved MSS"; "Editing the Manuscript Fragments from Qumran: Cave 4 of Qumran (4Q)," *BA* 19 (1956): 83–86. In the late 1980s and onward, several articles were published by E. Ulrich (a student of Cross) on other MSS from Cave 4. See "Daniel Manuscripts from Qumran: Part 1: A Preliminary Edition of 4QDan[a]," *BASOR* 268 (1987): 17–37; "Daniel Manuscripts from Qumran: Part 2: Preliminary Editions of 4QDan[b] and 4QDan[c]," *BASOR* 274 (1989): 3–31"; and "Orthography and Text in 4QDan[a] and 4QDan[b] and in the Received Masoretic Text," in *Of Scribes and Scrolls*, ed. H. W. Attridge, J. J. Collins, and T. H. Tobin, 29–42 (Lanham, MD: University Press of America, 1990).
28. Published by M. Baillet, J. T. Milik, and R. de Vaux, *Les 'Petites Grottes' de Qumran*, DJD 3 (1962; repr., Oxford: Clarendon, 2003), see plate xxiii.

Pictured above: A portion of 4QDan^c from the Dead Sea Scrolls Digital Library http://www.deadseascrolls.org.il/explore-the-archive/manuscript/4Q114–1

Those who date the book of Daniel in the second century BC find the fragments from Qumran to be rather significant. Cross, for instance, writes,

> One copy of Daniel is inscribed in the script of the late second century B.C.; in some ways its antiquity is more striking than that of the oldest manuscripts from Qumrân, since it is no more than about a half century younger than the autograph of Daniel. It is thus closer to the original edition of a biblical work than any biblical manuscript in existence, unless it be the Rylands Fragment of John from the first half of the second century A.D.[29]

Of course Cross presumes that the original autograph of Daniel dates to the second century BC. Other scholars, however, find the evidence to point in the direction of a much earlier date for the book. First, if it is true that 4QDan^c dates to 125 BC, as DSS scholars have argued, and the original autograph was penned about 164 BC, this raises a serious question.[30] This hardly allows for enough time for the book to have been read, accepted as canonical, distributed, and finally to have gained the popularity that it obviously had at Qumran.[31] Hasel makes this very point:

> It seems very difficult to perceive that one single desert community should have preserved such a significant number of Daniel manuscripts if this book had really been produced at so late a date.

29. F. M. Cross, *The Ancient Library of Qumran & Modern Biblical Studies*, rev. ed. (Grand Rapids: Baker, 1961), 43. Cf. F. M. Cross and S. Talmon, eds., *Qumran and the History of the Biblical Text.*

30. Ulrich, "Text of Daniel," 574, regards 4QDan^c and 4QDan^e as the earliest fragments, dating them as "late 2nd or early 1st c. BCE." Flint, "The Biblical Tradition at Qumran," 330, dates 4QDan^c to "late 2nd c. BCE" and 4QDan^e as simply "2nd c. BCE."

31. That the book of Daniel was accepted as canonical at Qumran is evidenced by the fact that 4QFlorilegium employs the quotation formula, "which is written in the book of Daniel the prophet."

> The large number of manuscripts in this community can be much better explained if one accepts an earlier origin of Daniel than the one proposed by the Maccabean hypothesis of historical-critical scholarship, which dates it to the second century B.C.[32]

Compounding this difficulty for the second-century BC view of Daniel is that several non-biblical writings have surfaced at Qumran that either allude to or refer to various themes or subjects from the book of Daniel. This, too, argues for a much longer time span between the original autograph of Daniel and these other writings of the intertestamental period.

The eight manuscript fragments of the book of Daniel found at Qumran are significant. First, they attest to the reliability of the transmission of the Hebrew text. Second, they confirm the originality of the dual Hebrew/Aramaic use of languages. Third, they suggest that the apocryphal additions to the book of Daniel were not original. Fourth, they point to a date for the book of Daniel much earlier than the mid-second century BC (and thus before the time of Antiochus IV Epiphanes). There is nothing about the Qumran fragments that would negate a sixth-century date its composition.

Greek Translations

Ideally it would be helpful to be able to compare *the* Greek Septuagint text (LXX) with the present critical edition of the Hebrew Bible (MT).[33] Unfortunately, such an ideal Greek text does not exist for Daniel. Instead, we have two quite differing Greek traditions, each represented by several Greek manuscripts.[34] These are the "Old Greek" tradition (OG) and another most

32. G. F. Hasel, "New Light on the Book of Daniel from the Dead Sea Scrolls," *Ministry* (1992): 11; repr. from *Bible and Spade* 24 (2011).

33. The standard critical text of the Hebrew Masoretic edition is still *Biblia Hebraica Stuttgartensia* (ed. Elliger and Rudolph, 1983, with Daniel edited by W. Baumgartner). This edition is based primarily upon the Leningrad Codex $B19^{A}$ (dated to 1008–1009 AD). An updated edition of Daniel in *Biblia Hebraica Quinta* is expected by 2020. The editing of Daniel has been assigned to A. Gianto of the Pontifical Biblical Institute of Rome.

34. In addition to the two primary Greek traditions (OG and Th), there are also fragments representing other efforts to translate Daniel into Greek. A. M. D. Bledsoe, "The Relationship of the Different Editions of Daniel: A History of Scholarship," *CurBS* 13 (2015): 180, explains, "Two additional fragmentary Greek editions of the book of Daniel have also been identified. These are Aquila and Symmachus. Aquila's text is a slavishly literal translation of the MT. It is known primarily from Origen's Hexapla, but is also quoted several times by patristic authors. It is associated with a second-century CE person, who was said to be a proselyte to Judaism and student of the famous Rabbi Akiba (Epiphanius, *De mens.* 15; Irenaeus, *Haer.* 3.24). Symmachus, on the other hand, offers a much freer translation of the MT (yet certainly influenced

often referred to as Theodotion (Th or θ)—though there is considerable debate as to whether the historical person of Theodotion translated it.[35] In the commentary, these will be referred to as LXX^{O} and LXX^{θ}. Before using the Greek translation to supplement our study of the Hebrew-Aramaic text of Daniel, we must first know more about these two Greek traditions, the manuscripts that lie behind them, and the relationship that they have to one another. G. J. Swart summarizes the challenge this quest poses:

> What is disputed, however, is whether this Theodotion really was the translator of the Greek version bearing his name (cf. Schmitt 1992:1–29, who argues that the characteristics of this translation of the book of Daniel differ from those of other materials attributed to Theodotion; Jobes & Silva 2000:286–87; and Di Lella 2001:593–97), and whether and to what extent the translator of Th used the OG in preparing his version (cf. McLay 1996:15).[36]

What we can be more certain of is that the early church gave preference to the Theodotion tradition, thinking it to be much closer to the original Hebrew-Aramaic text. Jerome, writing near the end of the fourth century, confessed:

> The Septuagint version of Daniel the prophet [Jerome means the OG] is not read by the Churches of our Lord and Saviour. They use Theodotion's version, but how this came to pass I cannot tell. Whether it be that the language is Chaldee, which differs in certain peculiarities from our speech, and the Seventy were unwilling to follow those deviations in a translation; or that the book was published in the name of the Seventy, by someone or other not familiar with Chaldee, or if there be some other reason, I know not; this one thing I can affirm—that it differs widely from the original, and is rightly rejected.[37]

---

by the OG and Theodotionic editions) in an elegant Greek style (see Metzger 1993). This work is credited to a person of the late second century CE, who was either an Ebionite Christian (Eusebius, *Eccl. hist.* 6.17 and Jerome, *Vir. ill.* 54) or a Samaritan converted to Judaism (Epiphanius, *De mens.* 16)."

35. Theodotion (d. ca. AD 200) was a Hellenistic Jewish scholar who in the latter half of the second century AD translated the Hebrew Bible into Greek. His Greek translation formed one column of Origen's *Hexapla*. There is debate as to whether he was revising the Septuagint or working from a parallel tradition of Hebrew MSS that have not survived.

36. G. J. Swart, "Divergences Between the OG and Th Versions of Daniel 3: Evidence of Early Hellenistic Interpretation of the Narrative of the Three Young Men in the Furnace," *AcPB* 16 (2005): 107.

37. Jerome, "Preface to Daniel," quoted in Collins, 3–4.

For a helpful, up-to-date description of the various Danielic manuscripts, their relationship to one another, and a summary of the scholarly efforts to explain the developments underlying the various traditions (Hebrew, Aramaic and Greek), see A. M. D. Bledsoe, "The Relationship of the Different Editions of Daniel: A History of Scholarship."

A. The Old Greek Tradition (OG)

Segal has described OG this way:

> The Old Greek (OG) translation of Daniel is a relatively free translation of its Hebrew-Aramaic *Vorlage*. This free approach is reflected in phenomena such as different word order and sentence structure, lack of one-to-one correspondence between the words in the source and target languages, interchanges of active and passive verbal forms, and the influence of Greek syntax.[38]

There are three primary witnesses to the OG tradition:

1. Codex Chisianus (MS 88)

This manuscript (sometimes referred to as Chigi) is variously dated to the ninth–eleventh centuries AD and was finally published in 1772.[39] Collins (4), however, believes that it attests not the original OG but Origen's Hexaplaric recension. Jobes and Silva point out that the Chigi MS (88) has two distinctives: "it is one of the few manuscripts that include the Hexaplaric signs, and it is the only Greek manuscript that preserves the Old Greek (rather than the Theodotionic) version of Daniel in its entirety."[40]

2. The Syro-Hexapla (Syh)

This MS is in Syriac rather than Greek, although it is a witness to the OG.[41] Collins (4) states that this was made by the Monophysite bishop Paul of

38. M. Segal, "Daniel 5 in Aramaic and Greek and the Textual History of Daniel 4–6," in *IOSOT Congress Volume Stellenbosch 2016*, ed. L. C. Jonker, G. R. Kotzé, and C. M. Maier, 251-84, VTSupp 177 (Leiden and Boston: Brill, 2017), 252.

39. Codex Chisianus was referred to as MS 88 in both Rahlfs' edition (1935) and Ziegler's edition (1954) of the Septuagint but was incorrectly numbered as 87 by H. B. Swete. Tischendorf dated MS 88 in the eleventh century. It was first published by Simon de Magistris in 1772 in Rome as *Daniel secundum LXX ex tetraplis Origenis nunc primum editus e singulari Chisiano codice.*

40. K. H. Jobes and M. Silva, *Invitation to the Septuagint*, 2nd ed. (Grand Rapids: Baker, 2015), 56.

41. Regarding the Syriac translation of Daniel, see R. A. Taylor, "The Peshitta of Daniel: Questions of Origin and Date," in *VI Symposium Syriacum: 1992, University of Cambridge, Faculty of Divinity, 30 August–2 September 1992*, ed. R. Lavenant (Roma: Pont. istituto orientale, 1994), 31–42; idem, "The Peshitta of Daniel," in *Monographs of the Peshitta Institute* 7 (Leiden: Brill, 1994); and idem, "The Book of

Tella in AD 616–617, and published in 1788.[42] McLay notes, "The Syh is an extremely literal translation of Origen's Hexapla into Syriac."[43] By this he means the fifth column of the Hexapla, not the work in its entirety. He adds, "One notable feature of 88 and Syh is the extent of their agreement. Ziegler refers to them as 'sister manuscripts.'"[44]

3. Fragments from MS 967

This is an incomplete but nevertheless significant witness to the OG. Papyrus 967 dates to the early third century AD (perhaps even second century) and was discovered in Aphroditopolis in Egypt in 1931 (Collins, 4). Its leaves are found today in three different locations.[45] McLay concludes, "The only extant pre-hexaplaric manuscript of Daniel is papyrus 967, which was discovered in 1931 and required 46 years and the efforts of four editors before it was fully published."[46]

Until 1999, the primary edition of the OG had been that of J. Ziegler (1954, 1968). However, it was based on MS 88, Syh, and one portion of papyrus 967 (namely, the Chester Beatty fragments). Unfortunately, this edition of Ziegler was lacking some of the crucial manuscript evidence, as the Cologne and Barcelona fragments of 967 were not available to him at the time. Yet there are a number of variants between 967 and Ziegler's text.[47] Furthermore, McLay contends that there are instances where the reading of 967 should be accepted over Ziegler's text. He concludes, "There is no doubt that 967 is the more faithful witness to the original OG text."[48] Naturally,

---

Daniel in the Bible of Edessa," *IBRLR* 6 (2008) 21–35. The Syriac text is available in a nineteenth-century facsimile edition published by A. M. Ceriani. Based on his analysis of the Syriac Peshitta, Taylor concludes, "The Peshitta Old Testament is a primary version of the Hebrew Bible and not a daughter version based on the Septuagint, in spite of certain assertions to the contrary in the secondary literature. The Syriac translators of the book of Daniel based their work on a Hebrew-Aramaic source text." ("The Book of Daniel in the Bible of Edessa," *Aramaic Studies* 5 [2007], 243.) For a helpful introduction to the Syriac Bible, see S. Brock, *The Bible in the Syriac Tradition*, 2nd rev. ed., Gorgias Handbooks 7 (Piscataway, NJ: Gorgias, 2006).

42. Note that Goldingay (xxvi), however, dates it to the ninth century AD.

43. R. T. McLay, *The OG and Th Versions of Daniel*, SBLSCS 43 (Atlanta: Scholars Press, 1996), 6–7.

44. Ibid., 7.

45. In addition to the Chester Beatty fragments of MS 967 (located in Dublin), there also exist the Cologne and Barcelona fragments.

46. McLay, *The OG and Th Versions of Daniel*, 7.

47. See R. T. McLay, "A Collation of Variants from 967 to Ziegler's Critical Edition of *Susanna, Daniel, Del et Draco*," *Textus* 18 (1995): 121–34.

48. McLay, *The OG and Th Versions of Daniel*, 7. McLay (241) goes so far as to call 967 the most reliable extant witness to the OG, though he confesses that 967 has (like 88 and Syh) suffered some corruption from Th and correction toward MT.

Rahlfs' 1935 edition of the Septuagint was even more deficient for OG, since none of the fragments of papyrus 967 had been published at that time.[49]

Fortunately, an excellent new edition of Ziegler appeared in 1999 under the editorial hand of Olivier Munnich, which provides scholars with a more complete standard critical edition for not only OG but Th as well, taking into account all known manuscripts.[50] With this, we are in good position to evaluate the Septuagintal readings, though many questions remain about the relationship they have to MT.

B. Theodotion (Th or θ)

The common theory has been that Theodotion made his translation of the Old Testament into Greek about AD 180–181 (so Collins, 10). The earliest mention of Theodotion comes from the end of the second century AD by Irenaeus (lived ca. AD 120–202), who makes a passing comment about him in regard to the virgin birth prophecy from Isa 7:14. He states, "'Behold, a young woman shall conceive, and bring forth a son,' as Theodotion the Ephesian has interpreted, and Aquila of Pontus, both Jewish proselytes."[51] This does not necessarily mean, however, that the textual tradition given us by Theodotion comes from the latter second century AD. Collins claims that because "the version of Daniel attributed to him was already known to New Testament authors, scholars posited a pre-Christian 'proto-Theodotion' whose work was allegedly taken up by the second-century author."[52] In other words, Theodotion (rather than providing an entirely new translation) may

49. The initial publication of papyrus 967 (containing fragments of chaps. 3–8) was that of F. G. Kenyon, *The Chester Beatty Biblical Papyri* (London: Walker, 1937). Subsequent publications of other portions were provided by A. Geissen, *Der Septuaginta-Text des Buches Daniel 5–12 sowie Esther 1–2, 15*, PTA 5 (Bonn: Habelt, 1968); W. Hamm, *Der Septuaginta-Text des Buches Daniel Kap. 1–2 nach dem Kölner Teil des Papyrus 967*, PTA 10 (Bonn: Habelt, 1969); idem, *Der Septuaginta-Text des Buches Daniel Kap. 3–4*, PTA 21 (Bonn: Habelt, 1977); and R. Roca-Puig, "Daniele: Due semifogli del codice 967: P. Barc. inv. nn. 42 e 43," *Aegyptus* 56 (1976): 3–18.

50. Ziegler, *Septuaginta*, 16/2, "Susanna, Daniel, Bel et Draco," rev. ed. (1999).

51. Irenaeus, *Against Heresies*, III.21.1. in *The Ante-Nicene Fathers*, vol. 1, ed. Alexander Roberts and James Donaldson (1867; reprint, Grand Rapids: Eerdmans, 1981), 451.

52. Collins, 10. Cf. Collins (9 nn. 78 and 79) for examples of readings thought to be Theodotionic in Matthew and Revelation. Jobes and Silva (*Invitation*, 28) also point out a reference to Dan 6:23 in Heb 11:33, noting, "Although the author of Hebrews is otherwise heavily dependent on the LXX/OG, this passage reflects Theodotion's rendering: '[God] shut the mouths of the lions' (*enephraxe ta stomata tōn leontōn*), rather than the Old Greek which says, 'God saved me from the lions' (*sesōke me ho theos apo tōn leontōn*)."

have merely been passing on a Greek tradition that had been in existence for two or more centuries.[53]

The primary witnesses to "Theodotion" are Codex Vaticanus (B), Codex Alexandrinus (A), Origen's Hexaplaric recension, and the Lucianic recension (*L* = G^L).[54] The 1999 critical text of Ziegler is the standard edition for Th (though Rahlfs' edition is also good, being based on A, B, and *L*).

C. Drawing Conclusions About Th and OG

If OG is older than Th (and scholars even debate this point), the question still remains as to whether or not Th is merely a recension (or revision) of the former. Most scholars have assumed this to be the case.[55] Before commenting further on that, however, it would be wise to point out some of the challenges raised by using the Greek text for text-critical purposes in regard to the Hebrew-Aramaic text:

1. We have two differing traditions of the Greek text (OG and Th), and there is still no scholarly consensus regarding the relationship between them.

2. Chapters 4–6 of Daniel in the OG appear to be quite different than the other chapters of OG, which may suggest that the Greek translator was working with an entirely different Vorlage.[56]

---

53. A. Schmitt, *Stammt der sogennante θ'–Text bei Daniel wirklich von Theodotion?* Mitteilungen des Septuaginta-Unternehmens 9 (Göttingen: Vandenhoeck & Ruprecht, 1966) has argued that the characteristics of Daniel-Theodotion do not fit those found in materials otherwise attributed to Theodotion.

54. Lucian was a presbyter from Antioch (d. AD 312). For a helpful discussion of Origen's Hexaplaric Recension, see Jobes and Silva, *Invitation*, 39–46, and N. F. Marcos, *The Septuagint in Context: Introduction to the Greek Versions of the Bible*, trans. W. G. E. Watson (Leiden: Brill, 2000), 204–20.

55. S. P. Jeansonne, *The Old Greek Translation of Daniel 7–12*, CBQMS 19 (Washington, DC: Catholic Biblical Association of America, 1988) and D. O. Wenthe, "The Old Greek Translation of Daniel 1–6" (Ph.D. diss., Univ. of Notre Dame, 1991) have argued that Th is a revision of OG (in which the reviser had as one of his goals adjusting the translation toward the contemporaneous Hebrew text), but McLay has called into question Jeansonne's approach and statistical sampling. Schmitt has also argued against Th being a revision of the OG text (and that Th in Daniel cannot be ascribed to Theodotion).

56. Ulrich, however, came to very different conclusions than McLay. Bledsoe, "The Relationship of the Different Editions of Daniel," 184, explains, "Ulrich suggests, then, that chs. 4–6 in the OG 'appear to be woven from the same fabric as the OG translation of 1–[3] and 7–12', and OG Daniel, as a whole, 'seems to be a consistent, unified document with a consistent translation technique' (Ulrich 1999: 45; see also Montgomery 1927: 36–37; Meadowcroft 1995: 263). Thus, the differences in OG chs.

McLay assumes that chaps. 4–6 represent an alternative *Vorlage* than chaps. 1–3 and 7–12 (which supports Albertz's contention that chaps. 4–6 may be from a different translation).[57] McLay concludes, "Therefore, our working hypothesis is that the *Vorlage* of OG was very close to MT except in chaps. 4–6 and the end of chapter 3 where OG has differences due to the long addition in the text."[58]

3. Finally, although OG for the most part closely adheres to the MT, there is the problem of evaluating variant readings in the OG as against the MT. McLay's comments in this regard are quite insightful. He posits,

> There are three basic options: 1) Does the OG reflect a different *Vorlage* or a misunderstanding of the *Vorlage*? 2) Is the reading merely a dynamic rendering or does it in some way reflect the TT [translation technique] of the translator? 3) Is there evidence of theological *Tendenz* on the part of the translator, which motivated the rendering? Only with a balanced assessment of the TT of the whole book/unit in question can the text-critic begin to evaluate each possible variant and whether it originates from a differing *Vorlage*.[59]

How then are we to evaluate OG and Th, and the relationship between them? McLay suggests three options:

> There are at least three ways by which we could characterize Th's relation to OG. 1) It could be a completely independent translation. 2) It could be a recension in the way that it is generally understood. That is, Th had the OG and proto-MT before him and copied OG as long as it formally reproduced the *Vorlage*. In certain cases Th standardized the terminology, though not always consistently, and Th introduced corrections to the OG where it departed from his proto-MT *Vorlage*. These corrections may have resulted from Th's perception that OG translated incorrectly or too freely. 3) Another way to view their relationship is that Th did have both proto-MT and OG (or may have been familiar with OG), but that Th translated his *Vorlage* more or less independently and employed OG occasionally or when confronted with difficult passages.[60]

4–6 were made early on at the Aramaic level, and were later translated into Greek (Ulrich 1999: 45; see also Montgomery 1927: 248)."

57. R. Albertz, *Der Gott des Daniel*, SBS 131 (Stuttgart: Katholisches Bibelwerk, 1988). Collins (6–7) provides a helpful summary of the complicated and inconsistent translation of chaps. 4–6 in OG.

58. McLay, *The OG and Th Versions of Daniel*, 12.

59. Ibid., 9.

60. Ibid., 15.

Based on his intensive studies, McLay opts for the third possibility. Elsewhere, he states that "... the Theodotion text in Daniel is an independent translation and not a revision of the Old Greek."[61] Furthermore, he is of the opinion that the text of OG has been corrupted through harmonization to MT and Th.[62] If this were true, it would then require that the original OG text be disentangled as much as possible from the latter corrupted form, a task which would obviously be nearly impossible to do. Based on McLay's sampling of five passages, he concluded that both the OG and Th were attempting to give a faithful rendition of "a text virtually identical to MT," though OG tends to be more of a dynamic translation in contrast to the formal equivalence in Th.[63]

Thus, there is need of a great deal more work before we can confidently speak of the relationship of OG and Th, as well as their reliability for emending the readings of the MT. If McLay is correct, however, Th should be given due respect as a vital witness itself and not merely seen as a revision of the OG text. Furthermore, Th should certainly be regarded as the more reliable witness for chaps. 4–6 in particular.

Selected Bibliography (Texts and Versions)

Albertz, R. *Der Gott des Daniel.* SBS 131. Stuttgart: Katholisches Bibelwerk, 1988.

Baillet, M., J. T. Milik, and R. de Vaux. *Les 'Petites Grottes' de Qumran.* DJD 3. 1962. Repr., Oxford: Clarendon, 2003.

---

61. Ibid., xv. In contrast to McLay, however, Collins (11) asserted that Th is "better read as a correction of the older translation to conform more closely to the Hebrew-Aramaic. The difference between such a correcting revision and a fresh translation with an eye on the OG does not, however, appear to be either clear-cut or very significant."

62. Ibid., 14. See McLay's *Appendix* (245) for a list of the possible borrowing between OG and Th that he discovered in his studies.

63. Jobes, *Invitation to the Septuagint*, 2nd ed., 306, has concluded that "θ' Daniel appears to be a more literal rendering of the Hebrew than OG Daniel." For further discussion, see A. A. Di Lella, "The Textual History of Septuagint-Daniel and Theodotion-Daniel," in *The Book of Daniel: Composition & Reception*, ed. J. J. Collins and P. W. Flint, 586–607, VTSup 83:2 (Leiden: Brill, 2001). Yet Swart—in his comparative study of OG and Th in Daniel 3—faults McLay's conclusions, since the latter only did a limited sampling of text (vv 11–20). Swart, "Divergences Between the OG and Th Versions of Daniel 3," 118, concluded: "The complexity of the relation between OG and Th in the diverse parts of this story cannot be explained merely in terms of recension versus independent translation, but demands a more complex explanation. It seems that we are compelled to postulate a scenario where both OG and Th independently revised an existing Greek version of Daniel 3 which contained the additions – that is, the Prayer of Azariah (vv.26–45), the Song of the Three Youths (vv.52–90) and the link text common to both versions (vv.24–25; vv.46–51; and, probably, parts of v.91)."

Barthelemy, D., and J. T. Milik. *Qumran Cave 1*. DJD 1. Oxford: Clarendon, 1955.

Bledsoe, A. M. D. "The Relationship of the Different Editions of Daniel: A History of Scholarship." *CurBS* 13 (2015): 175–90.

Braverman, J. *Jerome's Commentary on Daniel: A Study of Comparative Jewish and Christian Interpretations of the Hebrew Bible*. CBQMS 7. Washington, DC: Catholic Biblical Assoc. of America, 1978.

Brock, S. *The Bible in the Syriac Tradition*. 2nd rev. ed. Gorgias Handbooks 7. Piscataway, NJ: Gorgias Press, 2006.

Ceriani, A. M. *Codex syro-hexaplaris ambrosianus*. Monumenta sacra et profana 7. Milan: Bibliotheca Ambrosiana, 1874.

Collins, J. J., and P. W. Flint. "243-245. 4Qpseudo-Daniel[a-c] ar." In *Parabiblical Texts, Part 3*, ed. G. Brooke, et al., 95–164. DJD 22. Oxford: Clarendon, 1996.

Collins, J. J., P. W. Flint, and C. Vanepps, eds. *The Book of Daniel: Composition and Reception*. 2 vols. Leiden: Brill, 2000–2001.

Cross, F. M. *The Ancient Library of Qumran & Modern Biblical Studies*. Rev. ed. Grand Rapids: Baker, 1961.

———. "Editing the Manuscript Fragments from Qumran: Cave 4 of Qumran (4Q)." *BA* 19 (1956): 83–86.

Cross, F. M., and S. Talmon, eds. *Qumran and the History of the Biblical Text*. Cambridge, MA: Harvard University Press, 1975.

deSilva, D. A. "Additions to Daniel: 'Let Them Know That You Alone Are God.'" In *Introducing the Apocrypha*, by D. A. DeSilva, 222–43. Grand Rapids: Baker, 2002.

Di Lella, A. A. "The Textual History of Septuagint-Daniel and Theodotion-Daniel." In *The Book of Daniel: Composition & Reception*, ed. J. J. Collins and P. W. Flint, 586–607. VTSup 83:2. Leiden: Brill, 2001.

DiTommaso, L. "4Q*Pseudo-Daniel*[a-b] (4Q243–4Q244) and the Book of Daniel." *DSD* 12 (2005): 101–33.

Flint, P. W. "The Daniel Tradition at Qumran." In *The Book of Daniel: Composition & Reception*, ed. J. J. Collins and P. W. Flint. 329–67. VTSup 83:2. Leiden: Brill, 2001.

Ginzberg, L. "Daniel." In *The Jewish Encyclopedia*, 12 vols., ed. C. Adler et al., 4:427–28. New York: Funk and Wagnalls, 1901–1906.

Goswell, G. "The Canonical Position(s) of The Book of Daniel." *ResQ* 59 (2017): 129–40.

Greenspahn, F. W. *An Introduction to Aramaic*. 2nd ed. Atlanta: Society of Biblical Literature, 2003.

Hasel, G. F. "New Light on the book of Daniel from the Dead Sea Scrolls." *Ministry* (January 1992): 10–13. Repr. from *Bible and Spade* 24 (2011).

Irenaeus. *Against Heresies*. In *The Ante-Nicene Fathers*. Vol. 1, ed. A. Roberts and J. Donaldson. 1867. Repr., Grand Rapids: Eerdmans, 1981.

Jeansonne, S. P. *The Old Greek Translation of Daniel 7–12*. CBQMS 19. Washington, DC: Catholic Biblical Association of America, 1988.

Jerome. "Preface to Daniel." In *Patrologia Latina* 28, col. 1357, ed. J. Migne.

———. *The Principal Works of St. Jerome*. Translated by W. H. Fremantle. Nicene and Post-Nicene Fathers, Series 2, 6. 1892. Repr. Grand Rapids: Eerdmans, 1983.

Jerusalmi, I. *The Aramaic Sections of Ezra and Daniel; A Philological Commentary*. 2nd ed. Cincinnati, OH: Hebrew Union College, 1978.

Jobes, K. H., and M. Silva. *Invitation to the Septuagint*. 2nd ed. Grand Rapids: Baker, 2015.

Kitchen, K. A. "The Aramaic of Daniel." In *Notes on Some Problems in the Book of Daniel*, ed. D. J. Wiseman et al., 31–79. London: Tyndale, 1965.

Mansoor, M. *The Dead Sea Scrolls*. 2nd ed. Grand Rapids: Baker, 1983.

Marcos, N. F. *The Septuagint in Context: Introduction to the Greek Versions of the Bible*. Trans. W. G. E. Watson. Leiden: Brill, 2000.

McLay, R. T. "A Collation of Variants from 967 to Ziegler's Critical Edition of *Susanna, Daniel, Del et Draco*." *Textus* 18 (1995): 121–34.

———. *The OG and Th Versions of Daniel*. SBLSCS 43. Atlanta: Scholars Press, 1996.

———. "The Old Greek Translation of Daniel IV–VI and the Formation of the Book of Daniel." *VT* 55 (2005): 304–23.

Noonan, B. J. "The Presence and Significance of Foreign Loanwords in the Book of Daniel," Paper presented at Evangelical Theological Society annual meeting, Baltimore, November 20, 2013.

Pinker, A. "A Dream of a Dream in Daniel 2." *JBQ* 33 (2005): 231–40.

Portier-Young, A. E. "Languages of Identity and Obligation: Daniel as a Bilingual Book." *VT* 60 (2010): 98–115.

Rösel, M. "Enhanced and Revised: The Old Greek Edition of the Book of Daniel." In *Septuagint, Sages, and Scripture; Studies in Honour of Johann Cook*, ed. by R. X. Gautheir, G. R. Kotzé, and G. J. Steyn, 279–93. Leiden: Brill, 2016.

———. "Theology After the Crisis: The Septuagint Version of Daniel 8–12." In *Text-Critical and Hermeneutical Studies in the Septuagint*, ed. J. Cook and H.-J. Stipp, 207–19. Leiden: Brill, 2012.

Scheetz, J. M. "Daniel's Position in the Tanach, the LXX-Vulgate, and the Protestant Canon." *OTE* 23 (2010): 178–93.

Schmitt, A. "Die griechische Danieltexte (<<θ'>> und o') und das Theodotionproblem." *BZ* 36 (1992): 1–29.

———. *Stammt der sogennante ϑ'–Text bei Daniel wirklich von Theodotion?* Mitteilungen des Septuaginta-Unternehmens 9. Göttingen: Vandenhoeck & Ruprecht, 1966.

Segal, M. "Daniel 5 in Aramaic and Greek and the Textual History of Daniel 4–6." In *IOSOT Congress Volume Stellenbosch 2016*, ed. L. C. Jonker, G. R. Kotzé, and C. M. Maier, 251-84. VTSupp 177. Leiden and Boston: Brill, 2017.

Smith-Christopher, D. L. "Daniel." In *Introduction to Apocalyptic Literature, Daniel, and the Minor Prophets*. New Interpreter's Bible 7. Abingdon Press, 1996.

Swart, G. J. "Divergences Between the OG and Th Versions of Daniel 3: Evidence of Early Hellenistic Interpretation of the Narrative of the Three Young Men in the Furnace." *AcPB* 16 (2005): 106–20.
Taylor, R. A. "The Book of Daniel in the Bible of Edessa." *Aramaic Studies* 5 (2007): 239–53.
———. "The Book of Daniel in the Bible of Edessa." *IBRLR* 6 (2008): 21–35.
———. "The Peshitta of Daniel." In *Monographs of the Peshitta Institute* 7. Leiden: E. J. Brill, 1994.
———. "The Peshitta of Daniel: Questions of Origin and Date." In *VI Symposium Syriacum: 1992, University of Cambridge, Faculty of Divinity, 30 August–2 September 1992*, ed. R. Lavenant, 31–42. Roma: Pont. istituto orientale, 1994.
Trever, J. C. "The Book of Daniel and the Origin of the Qumran Community." *BA* 48 (1985): 81–102.
———. "Completion of the Publication of Some Fragments from Cave I." *RevQ* 19 (1965): 323–36.
Ulrich, E. "Daniel Manuscripts from Qumran: Part 1: A Preliminary Edition of 4QDan[a]." *BASOR* 268 (1987): 17–37.
———. "Daniel Manuscripts from Qumran: Part 2: Preliminary Editions of 4QDan[b] and 4QDan[c]." *BASOR* 274 (1989): 3–31.
———. "Double Literary Editions of Biblical Narratives and Reflections on Determining the Form to be Translated." In *The Dead Sea Scrolls and the Origins of the Bible*, 34–50. SDSSRL. Grand Rapids: Eerdmans, 1999.
———. "Orthography and Text in 4QDan[a] and 4QDan[b] and in the Received Masoretic Text." In *Of Scribes and Scrolls*, ed. H. W. Attridge, J. J. Collins, and T. H. Tobin, 29–42. Lanham, MD: University Press of America, 1990.
———. "The Text of Daniel in the Qumran Scrolls." In *The Book of Daniel: Composition & Reception*, ed. J. J. Collins and P. W. Flint, 573–85. VTSup 83:2. Leiden: Brill, 2001.
Van Deventer, H. J. M. "Testing-Testing, Do We Have a Translated Text in Daniel 1 and 7?" *JNSL* 32 (2005): 91–106.
VanderKam, J., and P. Flint. *The Meaning of the Dead Sea Scrolls*. San Francisco: HarperCollins, 2002. (See esp. 137–38 for the Daniel fragments.)
Waltke, B. K. "The Date of the Book of Daniel." *BSac* 133 (1976): 319–29.
Wenthe, D. O. "The Old Greek Translation of Daniel 1–6." Ph.D. diss. University of Notre Dame, 1991.
Wesselius, J. W. "The Literary Nature of the Book of Daniel and the Linguistic Character of Its Aramaic." *Aramaic Studies* 3 (2005): 241–83.
Ziegler, J. *Septuaginta: Vetus Testamentum Graecum 16/2: Susanna, Daniel, Bel et Draco*. Revised by O. Munnich. Göttingen: Vandenhoeck & Ruprecht, 1999.

Unity and Literary Structure[64]

Introduction

To determine the message of the book of Daniel, it is first necessary to understand the composition and design of the book as a whole. However, many critical scholars have questioned the book's unity and authorship. Although there are exceptions, critical scholars generally maintain that chaps. 7–12 were written after the earlier chapters by an author living at the time of Antiochus IV Epiphanes in the second century BC.[65] Many also say that the author's purpose was to encourage his fellow Jews who were suffering persecution under Antiochus. This is said to be the controlling purpose of the book, and the other material (particularly chaps. 1–6) is then explained in some secondary way.

Thus Beyerle, who distinguishes the court tales in chaps. 1–6 from the visions in chaps. 7–12, argues that these major blocks arose from different social settings. "If the text is taken as a starting-point, the court-tales and visions—representing two different genres—go back to different social settings (*Sitze im Leben*): the court-tales reflecting the fate of Jews in the diaspora, and the visions offering examples of persecuted, pious Jews in Jerusalem."[66]

64. The following material in this section on unity and literary structure is taken from J. Paul Tanner, "The Literary Structure of the Book of Daniel," *BSac* 160 (2003): 269–82. Used by permission. Slight modifications have been made to adapt to the formatting style of this commentary.

65. One common argument for the late dating of Daniel is the claim that these chapters are representative of apocalyptic literature, a literary genre that did not arise until well after the sixth century BC. Not all critical scholars, however, are convinced that these chapters should be properly labeled as apocalyptic genre. P. R. Davies, "Eschatology in the Book of Daniel," *JSOT* 17 (1980): 33–53, for instance, has argued that chaps. 8–12 are not apocalypses but are visions that demonstrate eschatology. Other scholars see apocalyptic elements even in the earlier portions of the book. R. Albertz, "The Social Setting of the Aramaic and Hebrew Book of Daniel," in *The Book of Daniel: Composition and Reception*, ed. J. J. Collins and P. W. Flint, 171–204, VTSup 83 (Boston: Brill, 2001), 191, has argued that chaps. 2–7, comprising "the original Aramaic apocalypse," should be dated to the reign of Antiochus III and that subsequently the "Hebrew author wished to make full use of the older apocalypse during the ongoing rebellion against Antiochus IV Epiphanes (about 165 BC) by supplementing it with new apocalyptic instructions of topical interest (chaps. 8, 9, and 10–12)."

66. S. Beyerle, "The Book of Daniel and Its Social Setting," in *The Book of Daniel: Composition and Reception*, 211.

Not all critical scholars have rejected the book's unity, two exceptions being Otto Eissfeldt and H. H. Rowley.[67] Rowley in particular has argued strongly for the unity of the book, though he also seeks to explain the entire book in light of Antiochus and the Maccabean revolt (the whole composition having been written, he says, in the second century BC). But most critical scholars have rejected the idea of a single author and a unified composition of the book.[68] For them chaps. 7–12 are primary, and the author of these chapters added chaps. 1–6 to the book.[69] The implication of such an approach, of course, is that the purpose and meaning of chaps. 1–6 are now different from what they originally were.

For those who reject the authorship of the book by Daniel in the sixth century BC, theories abound as to how and when the final composition came into being. Collins (38) suggests that the Hebrew-Aramaic text of Daniel evolved through five stages.[70]

(1) The individual tales of chaps. 2–6 were originally separate, although the form in which they first circulated is unknown.
(2) There was probably an initial collection of 3:31–6:29, which allowed the development of two textual traditions in these chapters.[71]
(3) The Aramaic tales were collected, with the introductory chap. 1, in the Hellenistic period.

---

67. O. Eissfeldt, *The Old Testament: An Introduction*, trans. P. R. Ackroyd (New York: Harper & Row, 1965), 517–29; and H. H. Rowley, *The Servant of the Lord and Other Essays on the Old Testament,* 2nd ed. (Oxford: Blackwell, 1965), 249–80. Cf. R. H. Pfeiffer, *Introduction to the Old Testament* (New York: Harper, 1941), 764.
68. More recently J.-W. Wesselius, "Discontinuity, Congruence and the Making of the Hebrew Bible," *SJOT* 13 (1999): 24–77, has differed from prevailing critical opinion by asserting that the entire book was composed as a whole just before the beginning of the Hasmonean revolt, rather than by the redaction of preexisting texts.
69. A number of studies have stressed the literary stages in the growth of the court tales of the book of Daniel. For example, J. Gammie, "The Classification, Stages of Growth, and Changing Intention in the Book of Daniel," *JBL* 95 (1976): 191–204; idem, "On the Intention and Sources of Daniel i–xi," *VT 31* (1981): 282–92; J. J. Collins, "The Court-Tales in Daniel and the Development of Apocalyptic," *JBL* 94 (1975): 218–34.
70. L. L. Grabbe, "A Dan[iel] for All Seasons: For Whom Was Daniel Important?" in *The Book of Daniel: Composition and Reception*, ed. J. J. Collins and P. W. Flint, 229–46, VTSup 83:1 (Leiden: Brill, 2001), 229–46, presents a similar theory on the composition of Daniel.
71. Collins' (37) rationale for separating Dan 3:31–6:28 from the larger Aramaic section of the book is that the Old Greek translation of these chapters significantly differs from that of the Masoretic text and Theodotion's Septuagint. Collins (37) says this is evidence of a different Semitic *Vorlage,* which suggests, he believes, that this material once circulated as an independent document.

(4) Daniel 7 was composed in Aramaic in the early years of Antiochus Epiphanes's persecution of the Jews before the desecration of the temple. Chapters 1–7 may have circulated briefly as an Aramaic book.
(5) Between 167 and 164 BC the Hebrew chaps. 8–12 were added, and chapter 1 was translated to provide a Hebrew frame for the Aramaic chapters. The glosses in 12:11–12 were added before the rededication of the temple.

Others have proposed alternative theories, but as Henze has put it, "It is clear, then, that the textual history of the court tales differs significantly from that of the apocalyptic visions."[72] Yet the bifurcation of material based on literary genre alone (i.e., apocalyptic visions in chaps. 7–12 versus narrative stories in chaps. 1–6) fails to justify a redactional composition of the book stemming from different eras. As some scholars have pointed out, even the court tales in the first half of the book have apocalyptic themes within them.[73]

Conservative evangelicals, however, insist on the unified authorship of the book by the historical person Daniel who lived in the sixth century BC.[74] This, however, does not imply that all agree on the book's literary structure or the author's controlling purpose for writing. In general most scholars (both critical and evangelical) see ten primary units to the composition of the

72. M. Henze, "The Narrative Frame of Daniel: A Literary Assessment," *JSJ* 32 (2001): 5–24. Cf. L. Wills, *The Jew in the Court of the Foreign King: Ancient Jewish Court Legends* (Minneapolis: Fortress, 1990).

73. T. A. Boogaart, "Daniel 6: A Tale of Two Empires," *RefR* 39 (1986): 106–12. Summarizing M. Nel, "Literêre genre van die Daniëlverhale," *In die Skriflig* 35 (2001): 591–606, on the literary genre of the stories in Daniel, C. T. Begg, *OTA* 25 (2002): 304, writes, "He concludes that there is no consensus regarding the classification of the genre of the stories and that the lack of an agreed-on system for the classification of genres impedes the discussion."

74. For a general evangelical treatment of the book's unity, historicity, and early dating see R. K. Harrison, *Introduction to the Old Testament* (Grand Rapids: Eerdmans, 1969), 1106–27; G. L. Archer Jr., "Daniel," in *The Expositor's Bible Commentary*, ed. F. E. Gaebelein, 12 vols., (Grand Rapids: Zondervan, 1985), 7:3–157; see esp. 4–6, 12–26; and Waltke, "The Date of the Book of Daniel," 319–29. Several evangelical studies involving linguistic analysis have demonstrated that Daniel's Aramaic and Hebrew clearly antedate the state of the languages in the second century. See G. L. Archer Jr., "The Aramaic of the 'Genesis Apocryphon' Compared with the Aramaic of Daniel," in *New Perspectives on the Old Testament*, ed. J. B. Payne, 160–69 (Waco, TX: Word, 1970); idem, "The Hebrew of Daniel Compared with the Qumran Sectarian Documents," in *The Law and the Prophets*, ed. J. H. Skilton (Philadelphia: Presbyterian and Reformed, 1974), 470–81; K. A. Kitchen, "The Aramaic of Daniel," in *Notes on Some Problems in the Book of Daniel* (London: Tyndale, 1965), 31–79; and E. M. Yamauchi, "The Greek Words in Daniel in the Light of Greek Influence in the Near East," in *New Perspectives on the Old Testament*, 170–200.

book, corresponding to the chapter divisions, with chaps. 10–12 forming one complete vision (and hence one unit). Historically the tendency has been to see a major division at the end of chap. 6, with chaps. 1–6 describing "court tales" from the life of Daniel and chaps. 7–12 recording a series of visions given personally to Daniel.[75]

Such a division (though thematically correct) suffers from the linguistic observation that all the material in 2:4–7:28 is written in Aramaic, whereas the other material is in Hebrew. Why would the author deliberately choose to write a significant portion of the book in Aramaic, and why would he choose to break the material following chap. 7? To understand the structural composition of the book, this linguistic division must be taken into account. Two significant studies, one by Lenglet and one by Gooding, question the traditional division of the book after chap. 6, and both of them rely on the paralleling of key motifs between chapters.

Lenglet's Concentric Structure for Chapters 2–7

In 1972 Lenglet wrote that chaps. 2–7 were a literary unit, not only because of the commonality of Aramaic but also because they were carefully composed in a concentric structure.[76] He observed that there was a paralleling relationship between chaps. 2 and 7, 3 and 6, and 4 and 5, based on similar thematic concerns.

75. Regarding "court tales" as a specific literary genre see R. D. Patterson, "The Key Role of Daniel 7," *GTJ* 12 (1991): 248: "Such stories have as their central plot an account of the heroic exploits of a godly exile in a foreign court. This person's godly walk and wisdom prove his worth in various tests. He then rises to such personal prominence that he is able to improve the well-being of his people or even effect their deliverance. These narratives customarily include such elements as: (1) a specific test involving faith, morality, or compromise of covenantal standards, (2) the friendliness of some resident court official, (3) besting the foreigners in contests or conflict, and (4) an unexpected extraordinary resolution to a besetting problem." Elsewhere Patterson has argued on the basis of comparing "court tales" from the first and second millennia BC that the material in Dan 1–6 must predate the Hellenistic or late Persian periods ("Holding on to Daniel's Court Tales," *JETS* 36 [1993]: 445–54).

76. A. Lenglet, "La structure littéraire de Daniel 2–7," *Bib* 53 (1972): 169–90.

Lenglet's Concentric Structure for Daniel 2–7

A	B	C	C'	B'	A'
Four-fold Period-ization of Gentile Powers to Rule Over Israel	Divine Deliv-erance of Those Faithful to God (From Furnace)	Divine Hum-bling of Babylo-nian King (Nebu-chad-nezzar)	Divine Hum-bling of Babylo-nian King (Belshaz-zar)	Divine Deliv-erance of Those Faithful to God (From Lion's Den)	Four-fold Period-ization of Gentile Powers to Rule Over Israel
Chapter 2	Chapter 3	Chapter 4	Chapter 5	Chapter 6	Chapter 7

This structural understanding corresponds well with the Aramaic boundaries of the book. Yet it must be observed that chap. 7 is not merely a duplication of chap. 2. Chapter 7 seems to focus again on the general scheme of four kingdoms, but it goes further in presenting new aspects (the "little horn") as well as developing further some of the matters only lightly treated in chap. 2 (e.g., the messianic role). Nevertheless, Lenglet's scheme is quite plausible.

Furthermore, it is doubtful that the Aramaic portion of Daniel is merely late material incorporated into a document comprising the latter chapters of the book (an argument also used to assert their historical unreliability). The affinity of the Aramaic portion with known fifth-century Aramaic documents argues for its early composition. Fox writes,

> Recent studies on the Aramaic of Daniel indicate that it is closely akin to the fifth-century Imperial Aramaic of Ezra and the Elephantine papyri, but very different from the later Palestinian derivations of Imperial Aramaic witnessed by the Genesis Apocryphon and the Targum of Job found among the Dead Sea Scrolls. It now appears that "the Genesis Apocryphon furnishes very powerful evidence that the Aramaic of Daniel comes from a considerably earlier period than the second century B.C." Of the fragments of Daniel that have been found at Qumran, the points in the book where the language changes from Hebrew to Aramaic are attested. This means the present structure of Daniel, with its changes between Aramaic and Hebrew, is very ancient. With its early variety of Aramaic, Daniel is certainly earlier than the Aramaic found in the Dead Sea Scrolls. For these reasons, no one today should assert that Daniel is dependent on Ben Sira: the early Aramaic in Daniel precludes such a possibility. So

Gooding's Paralleling Structure for Daniel 1–12

Chapters 1–5	Chapters 6–12
Chapter 1 The refusal to eat the king's impure food, though Daniel and his friends are vindicated.	Chapter 6 The refusal to obey the king's command to refrain from praying, though Daniel is vindicated.
Two Images	**Two Visions of Beasts**
Ch 2 – Nebuchadnezzar's dream-image	Ch 7 – The four beasts
Ch 3 – Nebuchadnezzar's golden image	Ch 8 – The two beasts
Two Kings Disciplined	**Two Writings Explicated**
Ch 4 – The discipline and restoration of Nebuchadnezzar	Ch 9 – The prophecy in the book of Jeremiah.
Ch 5 – The 'writing on the wall' and the destruction of Belshazzar.	Ch 10–12 – The 'writing of truth' and the eventual destruction of 'the king' (11:36–45)

discoveries since Nöldeke's day make his suggestion that "Daniel" used Ben Sira highly suspect.[77]

Gooding's Paralleling Structure

Writing in 1981, Gooding took notice of Lenglet's work but suggested a radically different pattern for the entire book. "Further observation suggests that the pattern is deliberate, that the book's ten component parts were intentionally arranged in two groups of five each, with chap. 5 forming the

77. D. E. Fox, "Ben Sira on OT Canon Again: The Date of Daniel," *WTJ* 49 (1987): 344–45.

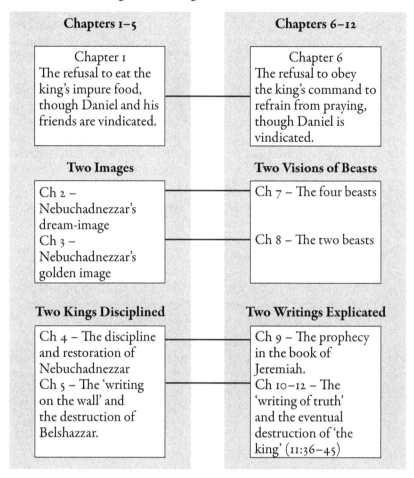

climax of the first group, and chaps. 10–12 the climax of the second."[78] For him the turning point of the book is at the end of chap. 5 rather than the end of chap. 7 (or chap. 6, according to the traditional view). Gooding's theory has the advantage of being more intricate, for there are not only binding relationships within each of the two cycles but also relationships between the paralleling members of each cycle.

Although the horizontal relationships between the corresponding pairs are not readily apparent in each case from the above diagram, to his credit Gooding does endeavor to explain them in his article. In support of his view he notes that the vessels of the temple, mentioned in chap. 1, appear again at the climax to group 1 in chap. 5, which tends to bind the entire series together as a unit. The second group demonstrates the progressive deterioration in the attitudes of the Gentile emperors toward God.

> But just as Nebuchadnezzar's idolatrous and unsatisfactory treatment of the divine vessels in Group 1 led on to Belshazzar's immeasurably worse treatment of those vessels, so Darius' temporary banning of prayer to Israel's (and anybody else's) God in Group 2 heads a progression that gets steadily worse until the ultimate horror, when the king of 11:36ff exalts himself above every god, the God of Israel included. ... It rightly forms the climax of Group 2 as Belshazzar's impiety formed the climax of Group 1.[79]

Thus in Gooding's view the fifth item in each group forms a marked climax, and his structural understanding influences his concept of the book as a whole. "The total message of the book, then, is nothing less than a survey, part historical and part prophetic, of the whole period of Gentile imperial rule from Nebuchadnezzar's first assault upon Jerusalem and the removal of its Davidic king until the abolition of all Gentile imperial power and the setting up of the Messianic kingdom."[80]

Some might disagree with Gooding's structure by noting that chap. 6 is a "court tale" just like chaps. 1–5, thus casting doubt on a major break after chap. 5. In support of Gooding's theory, however, is that chap. 5 brings to a close the Babylonian era, whereas chap. 6 opens the Medo-Persian era. Although the Babylonian Empire appears again in chap. 8, the emphasis in the remainder of the book falls on kingdoms after Babylon. Furthermore, Gooding's theory properly couples chaps. 4 and 5, for both stress royal discipline, and chap. 5 utilizes elements that had been narrated in chap. 4 (i.e., the humbling of Nebuchadnezzar's pride). This close association of chaps. 4

---

78. D. W. Gooding, "The Literary Structure of the Book of Daniel and Its Implications," *TynBul* 32 (1981): 43–79.

79. Ibid., 57.

80. Ibid., 68.

and 5, however, does not *prove* Gooding's overall scheme, for Lenglet's theory also maintains this connection between chaps. 4 and 5.[81]

In Gooding's seemingly plausible theory, several weaknesses may be noted. First, his view does not explain the Aramaic section in chaps. 2–7. He rather cursorily dismisses this matter when he states, "As O. Eissfeldt ... has said, 'An explanation of the double language which is entirely satisfactory has not yet been proposed by anyone.'"[82] However, it is difficult to believe that the author had no purpose in composing these chapters in Aramaic; the issue calls for further attention.

Second, Gooding's reason for seeing a parallel between chaps. 4 (the humbling of Nebuchadnezzar) and 9 (Jeremiah's prophecy) is not convincing. He says they have a common theme of "God's discipline on pride."

Third, Gooding's contention that chap. 5 (on the destruction of Babylon's final ruler) and chaps. 10–12 (on the destruction of the last Gentile ruler) are parallel is unconvincing. "But while in chapter 5 the end concerned is the end of the first Gentile power to destroy Jerusalem and suppress the Judaean kings, the end in chaps. 10–12 is that of the last Gentile power; it is in fact nothing less than The End, preceded by an unprecedented time of trouble and accompanied by the resurrection of the dead (12:1–2)."[83]

Gooding's proposed relationship is not compelling because one could just as easily posit a certain parallel between chaps. 7 and 10–12. In the latter case both culminate with the "beast" (the antichrist) that is destroyed. "Parallels" can easily be found, and one must not make more of them than is legitimate. A similar situation exists between chaps. 1 and 6 (which Gooding says are parallel). He observes, "In chapter 1 Daniel refuses to take part in unclean Gentile practice; in chapter 6 he refuses to abstain from Jewish religious practice."[84] While this is true, the deliverance theme is a stronger motif behind chap. 6, thus suggesting that a better parallel could be found between chaps. 3 and 6 (as Lenglet has called for). However, of benefit in Gooding's scheme (as in Lenglet's) is that chap. 2 parallels chap. 7. Whereas the similarity is obvious (a series of four kingdoms), Gooding has helpfully highlighted the differences as well. Chapter 2 uses the imagery of a man, whereas chap. 7 that of animals. He concludes,

> The pairing of these two chapters, then, with their striking similarities and yet more striking differences, seems to be aimed at

---

81. For more on the close association between chaps. 4 and 5 see W. H. Shea, "Further Literary Structures in Daniel 2–7: An Analysis of Daniel 4," *AUSS* 23 (1985): 193–202; idem, "Further Literary Structures in Daniel 2–7: An Analysis of Daniel 5, and the Broader Relationships within Chapters 2–7," *AUSS* 23 (1985): 277–95. Shea argues for a chiastic structure to each of those two chapters.

82. Gooding, "Literary Structure," 54.

83. Ibid., 63.

84. Ibid.

> calling attention to the fact that there are two different ways of looking at, and estimating the character of, Gentile imperial rule, its strengths and weaknesses. And it is surely a sign of balanced judgment on the part of our author to show that Gentile governments are from one point of view man-like, humane, majestic, but plagued with the weakness of incoherence, and at the same time to show from another point of view that Gentile governments are basically amoral, self-seeking, cruelly destructive, animal-like power-blocs.[85]

A Proposal: An Overlapping Structure

In the traditional approach to the book of Daniel a major break occurs after chap. 6, thus dividing the material between the "court tales" in the first six chapters and the visions given to Daniel in the last six chapters. Lenglet, however, says the major break comes after chap. 7, based on the concentric arrangement of chaps. 2–7.[86] Gooding, on the other hand, asserts that the major break falls after chap. 5, based on the theory of an intricate paralleling structure between chaps. 2–5 and chaps. 6–12. Of these three views, only Lenglet's coincides with the linguistic division of the book, that is, the Aramaic section in chaps. 2–7 in contrast to the Hebrew section in chaps. 8–12. Because the linguistic division is a highly significant factor, Lenglet's theory is more convincing than the other two. But it is not enough simply to divide the book into two major parts after chap. 7. The structure of the book is more complex than this, for the book seems to have an overlapping structure. Two major divisions—chaps. 2–7 and chaps. 7–12—overlap. Thus chap. 7 belongs to both halves.

						Visions Given to Daniel			
	Concentric Structure Establishing God's Sovereignty Over Gentile Empires					**Vision 1**	**Vision 2**	**Vision 3**	**Vision 4**
Historical Setting	**A** Dream: Four-Part Image	**B** Refusal to Worship Image	**C** Humbling of King Neb.	**C'** Humbling of King Bel.	**B'** Refusal to Stop Praying	**A'** Four Beasts	Ram & Goat	70 Weeks	Final Vision Antiochus — Antichrist
1	2	3	4	5	6	7	8	9	10–12
H	*Aramaic*						*Hebrew*		

85. Ibid., 61.

86. More recently Albertz, "Social Setting," 178, has defended the division of the book based on languages and has argued that the well-thought-out structure of Dan 2–7 makes it highly probable that this stands as a literary unit.

Three reasons support this view of an overlapping structure. (1) It takes into account the linguistic division of the book. (2) It recognizes Lenglet's observation of the concentric structure for chaps. 2–7. (3) It recognizes that chap. 7 initiates a series of four visions given to Daniel. While such reasons alone are enough to support this structure, four additional matters confirm this theory.

The Temporal Perspective of the Book

Chapters 2–6 are primarily (though not exclusively) historical, the focus being on God's dealing with kingdoms in Daniel's lifetime.[87] Chapters 8–12 are primarily future-oriented, the focus being on matters that went beyond the lifetime of Daniel (viz., the days of Antiochus IV Epiphanes and the more distant future period of the antichrist). Chapter 7, however, belongs to both. It reiterates the succession of ancient Gentile kingdoms; yet it provides more detail about the "latter days" when the antichrist will arise.

The Dating Notices in the Book

The way in which dates are noted in chaps. 7–10 differs from the way they are noted in chaps. 1 and 2. Chapters 1 and 2 have only these two notices: "In the third year of the reign of Jehoiakim king of Judah" (1:1); and "Now in the second year of the reign of Nebuchadnezzar" (2:1).

But in chaps. 7–10 a date notice heads every major unit in the section. "In the first year of Belshazzar king of Babylon, Daniel saw" (7:1). "In the third year of the reign of Belshazzar the king a vision appeared to me" (8:1). "In the first year of Darius the son of Ahasuerus ... I, Daniel, observed" (9:1–2). "In the third year of Cyrus king of Persia a message was revealed to Daniel" (10:1).

This seems to be significant because chaps. 2–7 are not strictly arranged chronologically (chap. 6 concerns the time of Darius, while chap. 7 relates to the earlier time of Belshazzar's kingdom), whereas the visions of chaps. 7–12 are arranged in precise chronological order.

The Concluding Motifs in Each Unit

The concluding motifs in each of the ten units of the book seem to place an emphasis on chap. 7. In chaps. 1–6 each chapter ends with either Daniel being

87. Chapter 2, of course, is not merely historical, because the imagery of the statue does have futuristic elements, namely, the feet of iron and clay, as well as the (messianic) "kingdom" that will put an end to all Gentile kingdoms. However, the emphasis of the chapter is on the historical past, because the dream was given to Nebuchadnezzar to help him understand that his kingdom was not an eternal kingdom but rather one kingdom in a chain of others, all of which would eventually give way to a kingdom established by God. In contrast, chap. 7 is a vision given to Daniel, and the emphasis is not on Babylon's role but on the far distant future when the rule of antichrist will be surpassed by the kingdom given to the "Son of man."

honored or God being exalted and praised (and in several cases, simultaneously both are honored). Chapter 2, for instance, concludes with both an exaltation of Daniel and the honoring of God. "Then King Nebuchadnezzar fell on his face and did homage to Daniel, and gave orders to present to him an offering and fragrant incense. The king answered Daniel and said, 'Surely your God is a God of gods and a Lord of kings and a revealer of mysteries, since you have been able to reveal this mystery'" (2:46–47).

Chapter 6 has similar motifs. "Then Darius the king wrote to all the peoples ... 'I make a decree that in all the dominion of my kingdom men are to fear and tremble before the God of Daniel; for He is the living God and enduring forever, and his kingdom is one which will not be destroyed, and his dominion will be forever. He delivers and rescues and performs signs and wonders in heaven and on earth, who has also delivered Daniel from the power of the lions'" (6:25–28).

Similar constructions occur in 1:18–21; 3:28–30 (in this case, Daniel's three friends were exalted); 4:36–37; and 5:29–30. In chaps. 8–12, however, the concluding paragraph of each unit generally emphasizes a much different motif, namely the opposition and defeat of a future ruler who will martyr many saints (8:23–27; 9:27; 11:44–45).[88] In each case this future ruler is the antichrist (except 8:23–27, which seems to portray Antiochus IV Epiphanes as a type of the antichrist). Chapter 7 seems unique in that both motifs—the exaltation of God and the opposition and defeat of the future ruler—appear in the concluding paragraph. "He [the 'little horn'] will speak out against the Most High and wear down the saints of the Highest One ... and they will be given into his hand for a time, times, and half a time. But ... his dominion will be taken away, annihilated and destroyed forever. Then the sovereignty, the dominion, and the greatness of all the kingdoms under the whole heaven will be given to the people of the saints of the Highest One; his kingdom will be an everlasting kingdom, and all the dominions will serve and obey him" (7:25–27). Thus chap. 7 belongs to both the preceding chapters and the following chapters.

The "Person" of Narration

In chaps. 1–6 the stories are consistently narrated from the third person in regard to Daniel. An example of this is in 1:8. "But Daniel made up his mind that he would not defile himself with the king's choice food." Daniel's thoughts and actions are described in the third person, as though the stories are being narrated by an imaginary author. Exceptions to this (e.g., 2:27–45) occur in passages that appear as quotations of Daniel's speech.

---

88. Daniel 11:36–12:4 seems to stand as the last major unit of the book, with 12:5–13 constituting an epilogue to the book (Daniel's response to the vision). Thus 11:44–45 can rightfully be viewed as part of the concluding unit to chaps. 10–12.

In chaps. 8–12, however, the material is narrated from the first-person perspective.[89] "In the third year of the reign of Belshazzar the king a vision appeared to me, Daniel. ... And I looked in the vision" (8:1). In general, the remainder of the book is narrated in the first person (though the introduction to the final unit [10:1–3] quickly shifts from the third person to the first). Chapter 7, however, is technically in the third person, though in practicality it is in the first. That is, the whole chapter is presented as a summary of Daniel's vision, in which the vision is communicated from the perspective of the first person. "In the first year of Belshazzar king of Babylon Daniel saw a dream and visions in his mind as he lay on his bed; then he wrote the dream down and related the following summary of it. Daniel said [shift to first person], 'I was looking in my vision by night, and behold, the four winds of heaven were stirring up the great sea'" (7:1–2).

It is understandable that the narration of chap. 7 would continue in the first person so long as it is being presented as a summary of his vision. One would expect that once Daniel's report was completed, the narration would shift back to the third person. This, however, does not happens. Instead, the narration continues in the first person, as seen in 7:28. "At this point the revelation ended. As for me, Daniel, my thoughts were greatly alarming me and my face grew pale, but I kept the matter to myself."

Chapter 8 immediately opens in the first person. That this is unusual can be demonstrated from the observation of how chap. 2 is narrated. That chapter has a long section in the first person throughout 2:27–45, because this is presented as reported speech (i.e., a quotation of what Daniel said to the king). Immediately following this, however, the text (as expected) returns to the third person. "Then King Nebuchadnezzar fell on his face and did homage to Daniel and gave orders to present to him an offering and fragrant incense" (v. 46). The remaining verses of the chapter (vv. 47–49) continue in the third person. Thus chap. 7 is unique in how it utilizes the person of narration.

Obviously then, Dan 7 stands out as unique in the book. Through these numerous literary techniques the author was highlighting this chapter for the readers' attention. In some instances it is linked with chaps. 2–6 while in other instances with chaps. 8–12. Thus chap. 7 is a "hinge" chapter to the book. "Its central location and close correspondence with the two major portions make it evident that Daniel 7 is in many respects the key that unlocks the door to the problem of the unity, as well as the understanding, of the book."[90]

---

89. In defense of the unity of the book in spite of the change of person, see Z. Stepanovic, "Thematic Links Between the Historical and Prophetic Sections of Daniel," *AUSS* 27 (1989): 121–27; idem, "Daniel: A Book of Significant Reversals," *AUSS* 30 (1992): 139–50.

90. Patterson, "The Key Role of Daniel 7," 252.

Implications of the Literary Structure

What implications does this view have for the message and purpose of the book of Daniel? To answer this, the emphasis of the two major sections of the book should be noted, taking into account the overlap. Thus, one must look for the rationale behind chaps. 2–7 and then for chaps. 7–12.

The first major section (chaps. 2–7) emphasizes the Gentile nations under whom Israel is being disciplined. This would explain why these chapters were written in Aramaic, the *lingua franca* of the Gentile world in Daniel's day. Since the general context of the whole book is the theological reason for Israel's exile (see chap. 9 in this regard), chaps. 2–7 pertain to the Gentile nations in their relationship to Israel's exile. Israel's discipline would not be a mere seventy years but rather a discipline spanning the complete course of history up to the second coming of Christ. Only when Christ returns, the antichrist is defeated, and Messiah's kingdom is formally established will Israel's discipline be lifted. Until then she will be dominated by Gentile kingdoms. In the final analysis God's discipline on Israel will be removed and believing Israel will be allowed to enjoy Messiah's kingdom. In light of what is revealed in the opening and concluding chapters of this section, chaps. 2–7 depict the role, character, and succession of the Gentile nations of the world under whom Israel is being disciplined before Messiah's kingdom. These chapters affirm that these Gentile kingdoms have the right of world sovereignty (under God's authority) until God is pleased to establish the messianic kingdom, and that no adversary can successfully oppose him (2:44; 4:3, 34–35; 5:21; 6:26; 7:14, 27).

The second major section (chaps. 7–12) more particularly addressed the nation of Israel, which explains the shift back to Hebrew after chap. 7. Each of Daniel's four visions emphasizes the future ruler who will stand in opposition to Israel and who will be bent on persecuting her. This is the antichrist, who will serve as God's final means of his discipline on Israel (though in chap. 8 he is typified by Antiochus). Foolishly, Israel will initially put her trust in him (9:26–27) but will eventually suffer much at his hands. As a tool to grasping how utterly despicable and wrathful he will be toward Israel, the book of Daniel highlights the historical figure of Antiochus IV Epiphanes, who emulates what the eventual antichrist will be and do, thus serving as a biblical type of the antichrist. The motif of suffering at the hands of the future antichrist thus undergirds chaps. 7–12.

Daniel 7 thus serves as a hinge to both major sections of the book. What has been introduced in chaps. 1–6 is reiterated in chap. 7 (the role of Gentile kingdoms and their subjection to God's sovereignty and eventual kingdom), and what is highlighted in chap. 7 (the "little horn" that comes out of the fourth beast, the antichrist) is played out in the remaining chapters of the book. Through such literary techniques the author carefully focused the readers' attention on chap. 7. This chapter is the most beautiful expression of God's ultimate purpose of good, not only for Israel but also for all peoples. "I kept looking in the night visions, and behold, with the clouds of heaven

One like a Son of Man was coming, and He came up to the Ancient of Days and was presented before him. And to him was given dominion, glory and a kingdom, that all the peoples, nations, and men of every language might serve him. His dominion is an everlasting dominion which will not pass away; and his kingdom is one which will not be destroyed" (7:13–14).

A certain gloom is present in the book of Daniel; Israel had been exiled in Babylon because of her covenant unfaithfulness, but in addition she must endure God's hand of discipline throughout history. Yet her hope, as well as the hope of all peoples and nations, is on the kingdom to be given to the Lord Jesus Christ at the end of the ages. To receive this consolation, one must be properly related to the person for whose glory it is being given (to be a kingdom subject, one must have faith in the King himself). His kingdom (not Nebuchadnezzar's or that of any other ruler throughout Gentile history) is the only one that really matters. As Nebuchadnezzar himself confessed, "His kingdom is an everlasting kingdom, and his dominion is from generation to generation" (4:3).

Thus the purpose of the book of Daniel could be stated this way: "To demonstrate that God is sovereignly in control of the nations under whom Israel is being disciplined until the time comes when He will bring in Messiah's kingdom, and that Israel will ultimately be restored and blessed in this kingdom after she has first undergone tribulation and sufferings imposed by the antichrist."[91]

Selected Bibliography (Unity and Literary Structure)

Albertz, R. "The Social Setting of the Aramaic and Hebrew Book of Daniel." In *The Book of Daniel: Composition and Reception*, ed. J. J. Collins and P. W. Flint, 171–204. VTSup 83:1. Leiden: Brill, 2001.

Arnold, B. T. "The Use of Aramaic in the Hebrew Bible: Another Look at Bilingualism in Ezra and Daniel." *JNSL* 22 (1996): 1–16.

Beyerle, S. "The Book of Daniel and Its Social Setting." In *The Book of Daniel: Composition and Reception*, ed. J. J. Collins and P. W. Flint, 205–28. VTSup 83:1. Leiden: Brill, 2001.

Boogaart, T. A. "Daniel 6: A Tale of Two Empires." *RefR* 39 (1986): 106–12.

Breed, B. "A Divided Tongue: The Moral Taste Buds of the Book of Daniel." *JSOT* 40 (2015): 113–30.

91. B. Breed, "A Divided Tongue: The Moral Taste Buds of the Book of Daniel," *JSOT* 40 (2015): 113 (abstract). Breed has shown how the theme of God's sovereignty pertains to both parts of the book: "Whereas Daniel 1–6 focuses on moral aspects of authority and loyalty, Daniel 7–12 emphasizes the moral dimension of authority as framed by concerns with sanctity and liberation. Both parts of the book of Daniel concern themselves with the sovereignty of Yhwh, but their distinct moral frameworks reveal different understandings of the pressing problems facing Yhwh's sovereignty and the appropriate response of the faithful."

Collins, J. J. "The Court-Tales in Daniel and the Development of Apocalyptic." *JBL* 94 (1975): 218–34.
Davies, P. "Eschatology in the Book of Daniel." *JSOT* 17 (1980): 33–53.
Eissfeldt, O. *The Old Testament, An Introduction*. Translated by P. R. Ackroyd. New York: Harper & Row, 1965. Esp. 517–29.
Gammie, J. "The Classification, Stages of Growth, and Changing Intention in the Book of Daniel." *JBL* 95 (1976): 191–204.
———. "On the Intention and Sources of Daniel I–VI." *VT 31* (1981): 282–92.
Gooding, D. W. "The Literary Structure of the Book of Daniel and Its Implications." *TynBul* 32 (1981): 43–79.
Grabbe, L. L. "A Dan(iel) for All Seasons: For Whom Was Daniel Important?" In *The Book of Daniel: Composition and Reception*, ed. J. J. Collins and P. W. Flint, 229–46. VTSup 83:1. Leiden: Brill, 2001.
Henze, M. "The Narrative Frame of Daniel: A Literary Assessment." *JSJ* 32 (2001): 5–24.
Lenglet, A. "La structure littéraire de Daniel 2–7." *Bib* 53 (1972): 169–90.
Nel, M. "Literêre genre van die Daniëlverhale." *In die Skriflig* 35 (2001): 591–606. See review and summary: C. T. Begg, *OTA* 25 (2002): 304.
Patterson, R. D. "Holding on to Daniel's Court Tales." *JETS* 36 (1993): 445–54.
———. "The Key Role of Daniel 7." *GTJ* 12 (1991): 245–61.
Pfeifer, R. H. *Introduction to the Old Testament*. New York: Harper, 1941.
Rowley, H. H. "The Unity of the Book of Daniel." In *The Servant of the Lord and Other Essays on the Old Testament*, (1952): 249–80, 2nd ed. Oxford: Blackwell.
Shea, W. H. "Further Literary Structures in Daniel 2–7: An Analysis of Daniel 4." *AUSS* 23 (1985): 193–202.
———. "Further Literary Structures in Daniel 2–7: An Analysis of Daniel 5, and the Broader Relationships Within Chapters 2–7." *AUSS* 23 (1985): 277–95.
Tanner, J. P. "The Literary Structure of the Book of Daniel." *BSac* 160 (2003): 269–82.
Taylor, R. A. *Interpreting Apocalyptic Literature: An Exegetical Handbook*. Handbooks for Old Testament Exegesis. Grand Rapids: Kregel Academic, 2016.
van Deventer, H. J. M. "Another Look at the Redaction History of the Book of Daniel, or Reading Daniel from Left to Right." *JSOT* 38 (2013): 239–60.
Waters, B. V. "The Two Eschatological Perspectives of the Book of Daniel." *SJOT* 30 (2016): 91-111.
Wesselius, J.-W. "Discontinuity, Congruence and the Making of the Hebrew Bible." *SJOT* 13 (1999): 24–77.
———. "The Literary Nature of the Book of Daniel and the Linguistic Character of its Aramaic." *AS* 3 (2005): 241–83.
Wills, L. *The Jew in the Court of the Foreign King: Ancient Jewish Court Legends*. Minneapolis: Fortress, 1990.
Woodard, B. L., Jr. "Literary Strategies and Authorship in the Book of Daniel." *JETS* 37 (1994): 39–53.

Date and Authorship

The issue of the date and authorship of Daniel is without doubt the most controversial subject of study today pertaining to the book of Daniel. Historically, the Hebrew and Christian tradition has consistently attributed the authorship of the book to the prophet Daniel who wrote in the latter part of the sixth century BC. The reference to the third year of Cyrus in Dan 10:1, about 536/35 BC, is the last mentioned event involving the person of Daniel, and this would suggest that the book was written shortly after this final vision given to Daniel.

Yet the traditional position has not gone unchallenged. In the third century AD, a Neoplatonic philosopher and skeptic named Porphyry (ca. AD 234–ca. 305), asserted in a work entitled *Against the Christians* that the book of Daniel was not written in the sixth century BC but rather in the Maccabean age (second century BC), with the purpose of encouraging the Jewish people who were being persecuted by Antiochus IV Epiphanes, a Seleucid king holding power over the land of Judah at that time. His work has not survived, but his comments on Daniel have been preserved in the writings of early church fathers such as Jerome. All scholars agree that the book of Daniel makes reference to personages and events after Daniel's own day (e.g., Alexander the Great and Antiochus IV Epiphanes). Porphyry's presupposition was that predictive prophecy was not possible and that only someone living in the second century BC could have had knowledge of all the events recorded in the book of Daniel.

Since the rise of liberal Christianity and biblical criticism in the eighteenth century, critical scholars have consistently denied the traditional date and authorship of the book of Daniel. Although not all critical scholars hold to the same view of the authorship of the book, they are united in their opinion that the final writing (or redaction) of the book took place around 165/64 BC as the reign of Antiochus IV Epiphanes was drawing to a close. This date is normally chosen for the book since Antiochus is clearly spoken of in Dan 11:21–35. In addition, critical scholars take the position that the author of the book referred to the death of Antiochus in 11:40–45, but did so in error (historical documents reveal that he did not die in the land of Judah), which suggests to them that the final author wrote this material shortly before Antiochus died. Had he written after the death of Antiochus (so they say), he would not have made such a mistake about his death. (Most conservative scholars believe that 11:40–45 does not refer to Antiochus but rather to a future ruler.)

The whole issue is not merely an academic discussion, as there is a lot riding on the verdict. If the book purports to be written by Daniel in the sixth century BC, but in reality is *vaticinium ex eventu* (prophecy after the fact), then this calls into question the integrity of the Bible and its trustworthiness. B. W. Anderson is representative of those critical scholars who take the second-century BC position. Yet a careful reading of his comments also reveals a denial of predictive prophecy and an outright attack on the integrity of Scripture. He states, "The author of Daniel spoke to the people of the day *in the guise of a writing* that was predated in the Babylonian period, as though one were looking forward into the future rather than backward from the present" (emphasis mine).[92] His statement implies that the author deliberately sought to mislead his readers. Furthermore, Anderson has no sympathy for those taking the early date of the book, even mocking those who would believe in predictive prophecy. He has asserted:

> Some people have been misled by the author's portrayal of incidents and visions experienced by Daniel during the Babylonian Exile. Supposing that the book of Daniel was written during the Exile, they have regarded it as a prophetic preview of several centuries of future history and, indeed, of the divine program for a future that still lies ahead. Thus the book has become a happy hunting ground for those who are fascinated by 'biblical prophecy' and who look for some mysterious blueprint of the future hidden in its pages.[93]

Another critical scholar, Di Lella, holds that the second-century author(s) merely used erroneous traditions for the sake of communicating the true concern, namely, a theological message. For him, the accounts are midrashic tales or edifying stories (1–6) and apocalyptic visions (2:13–45; 7–12). He then accuses conservatives of misrepresenting God's Word: "… the so-called conservative also does the Word of God a huge disservice by insisting that the book does in fact deal with real persons and events of the seventh and sixth centuries BC, as if the authors of Daniel intended to write history."[94]

Yet the book clearly portrays the sixth-century BC Daniel as its author. The phrase "I, Daniel" occurs in several places (e.g., 8:1, 27; 9:2; 10:2; 12:5). Near the close of the book, Daniel is the one responsible for its care and preservation: "But as for you, Daniel, conceal these words and seal up the book until the end of time; many will go forth, and knowledge will increase" (12:4, NASB). Even though in some portions of the book Daniel is referred

---

92. B. W. Anderson, *Understanding the Old Testament*, 4th ed. (Englewood Cliffs, NJ: Prentice-Hall, 1986), 619.

93. Ibid., 618-19.

94. Di Lella (61). He also refers to the accounts as "pious romances," similar to other Jewish works like Susanna, Bel and Dragon, and others. He writes (61), "In general, the principal theme of these religious romances is the serious problem that faced Israel as God's holy people living in a pagan environment, and the intention of the authors was to dramatize, often with great imagination and ingenuity, the truth that the almighty and omniscient God of the Fathers will protect and rescue the current Israel of faith from disaster and will raise up wise and stalwart men and women who will overwhelmingly confound the wisdom and might of the Gentiles."

to in the third person, this is not uncommon for ancient writers. Xenophon authored *Anabasis* even though he used the third person to refer to himself. The same is true of Caesar's *Gallic Wars*.

The position taken in this commentary is that the prophet Daniel, shortly after 536/35 BC, wrote the book bearing his name in its entirety. Aside from the issue of predictive prophecy, critical scholars raise a number of objections to the traditional position of the date and authorship. These will now be considered and answered. Finally a defense of the traditional position will be positively set forth.

Objections to the Traditional Date and Authorship of Daniel

Most of the objections are based on what some have perceived as historical inaccuracies in the book. In addition, linguistic, theological, and literary objections have also been raised.

Alleged Historical Inaccuracies

1. Daniel 1:1 and the Issue of the Third Year of Jehoiakim

Daniel 1:1 reports that Nebuchadnezzar's attack on Jerusalem was in the third year of Jehoiakim, in contradiction to Jer 25:1 and 46:2 which indicate that it occurred in Jehoiakim's fourth year.

Anderson is quick to charge the author with a mistake in his historical facts:

> The book begins with a glaring historical error, for Nebuchadnezzar did not take Jerusalem in the third year of King Jehoiakim (606 BCE), and it was Jehoiakim's son—Jehoiachin—who was borne away to captivity (see II Kings 24). The author did not have the history of the Persian empire straight, as is shown by confusion about the sequence of kings (see Dan. 5:31; 9:1) and the telescoping of historical periods (11:2). These and other errors indicate that the writer was looking back over four centuries of history from a time when memories were blurred or distorted by popular views. After all, his purpose was not to give a correct history, after the manner of Thucydides or Herodotus, but to proclaim a religious message to embattled fellow Jews.[95]

While it is true that Daniel gives a different year than Jeremiah for Nebuchadnezzar's attack, this does not necessarily indicate a historical error or contradiction. One must take into account that calendar systems and methods of dating were different in the ANE from that used today (for them, a year did not begin on January 1). Furthermore, there was not a uniform system used throughout the ANE or even within Israel itself. To Thiele (whose work has been refined by McFall) we are greatly indebted for giving

95. Anderson, *Understanding the Old Testament*, 622–23.

us a much better understanding of dating methods used by ancient Israel.[96] There are two major issues that have to be taken into account in regard to the dating of ancient kings in Israel and the ANE. First, there is the matter of the beginning month of the year, whether Nisan in the spring of the year (March-April) or Tishri in the autumn of the year (September-October). So, a regnal year of a king's reign could be based on Tishri to Tishri, or Nisan to Nisan. Second, distinction must be made between an "accession year" and a "non-accession year" of a king's reign. Finegan explains,

> In the non-accession-year system the year in which the ruler comes to the throne is counted as his first year regardless of how many days or months remain in that year, and his second year begins with the first new year's day (Tishri 1 or Nisan1) after his accession; ... In the accession-year system the year in which the king comes to the throne is called his accession year and for the purpose of counting his years of reign, his first official year is that which begins with the new year's day after his accession.[97]

These factors proved to be the key to Thiele's success in reconciling the chronological data of the kings of the northern kingdom (Israel) with that of the southern kingdom (Judah). This was complicated by the fact that the counting system could and did change over the years, especially for the northern kingdom. McFall writes,

> An important factor affecting the form of the biblical report is that two major source documents were used by the writer of kings. His two sources were the "Chronicles of the Kings of Judah" and the "Chronicles of the Kings of Israel." The most significant difference between these two documents was that they used two distinct calendars to record each other's history. Neither side recognized the other's calendar and so each wrote up the other's history using its own calendar.[98]

Further refining the work of Thiele and McFall, R. Young has persuasively shown that Jeremiah used Tishri years and non-accession reckoning for the last years of the Judean monarchy (consistent with 2 Kings and Ezekiel).[99]

---

96. E. R. Thiele, *The Mysterious Numbers of the Hebrew Kings*, 3rd rev. ed. (Chicago: University of Chicago Press, 1983); L. McFall, "A Translation Guide to the Chronological Data in Kings and Chronicles," *BSac* 148 (1991): 3–45.
97. J. Finegan, *Handbook of Biblical Chronology*, rev. ed. (Peabody, MA: Hendrickson, 1998), 247.
98. McFall, "A Translation Guide," 6.
99. R. C. Young, "When Did Jerusalem Fall?" *JETS* 47 (2004): 21–38 (see esp. 33–37 for the chronology of Jeremiah). Finegan, however, drew a different conclusion: "Nisan years are also employed in Jeremiah, Ezekiel, Haggai and Zechariah

The collapse of Josiah's reign began in the summer of 609 BC with the Babylonian attack upon the remnant of Assyria's forces based at Haran. Finegan elaborates,

> British Museum Tablet No. 21901 records that in his sixteenth year (610/609 BC) Nabopolassar drove Ashur-uballit out of Haran; in the near year (609/608) between Duzu (June/July) 609 and Ululu (Aug/Sept) 609 Ashur-uballit and "a large army of Egypt" tried to reconquer Haran. ... The death of Josiah in his own thirty-first year, in his ill-fated attempt at Megiddo, is therefore to be dated in the seventeenth year of Nabopolassar and in the month of Duzu/Tammuz (June 25–July 23) 609 BC.[100]

Following Josiah's death, his son Jehoahaz reigned briefly for three months. Finegan notes, "The reign of Jehoahaz began, therefore, in Tammuz and ended three months later in Tishri (Sept 21–Oct 19) 609 B.C."[101] Jehoahaz's reign was cut short because Pharaoh Necho deposed him and installed Eliakim, another son of Josiah, in his place. Pharaoh also changed the name of Eliakim to Jehoiakim. Since Jehoiakim's reign began sometime *in* the month of Tishri, he had a long accession year of about eleven months until his first regnal year began the next Tishri 1 (Sept. 10, 608 BC).

The next important step is to identify the correct time of Nebuchadnezzar's siege of Jerusalem following the Battle of Carchemish. Young points out, "From the Babylonian Chronicles, it is known that Jehoiakim was installed by Necho in Tishri of 609, and the Battle of Carchemish occurred in the 605n/605t time frame."[102] That is, the Battle of Carchemish occurred in the summer of 605 BC with Nebuchadnezzar's invasion of Jerusalem coming immediately afterward in August of that year as the Babylonian general hastily pursued Pharaoh Necho in his retreat to Egypt. According to Merrill, however, Nabopolassar (up until that time the king of Babylon) died on August 15, 605 BC, and Nebuchadnezzar—having only recently laid siege to Jerusalem as described in Dan 1:1—had to return at once to Babylon to secure his place as the next king.[103] Thus, Nebuchadnezzar left off his pursuit

---

for the Hebrew kings and likewise for the rulers of Babylon and Persia" (*Handbook of Biblical Chronology*, 247).

100. Finegan, *Handbook of Biblical Chronology*, 252.

101. Ibid., 253. R. C. Young, "Tables of Reign Lengths from the Hebrew Court Recorders," *JETS* 48 (2005): 246, concurs that Jehoiakim's reign began in Tishri of 609 BC.

102. Young, "When Did Jerusalem Fall?," 33. "605n/605t" designates that time period between Nisan of 605 BC and Tishri of 605 BC. For a detailed examination of the historical events concerning the Neo-Babylonian Empire in relation to Judah and Egypt between 607–598 BC, see M. K. Mercer, "Daniel 1:1 and Jehoiakim's Three Years of Servitude," *AUSS* 27 (1989): 179–92.

103. E. H. Merrill, *Kingdom of Priests*, 2nd ed. (Grand Rapids: Baker, 2008) 463.

Nebuchadnezzar's Siege of Jerusalem in 605 BC
Reconciling Dan 1:1 with Jer 25:1

	Jeremiah Non-Accession Year Dating	**Daniel** Accession Year Dating
• Tishri 1 609 BC (Sept 21) • Jehoiakim's Reign Began—Tishri 609	1st Regnal Year	Accession Year
• Tishri 1 608 BC (Sept 10)	2nd Regnal Year	1st Regnal Year
• Tishri 1 607 BC (Sept 29)	3rd Regnal Year	2nd Regnal Year
• Tishri 1 606 BC (Sept 19) • Nebuch.'s Siege of Jerus—Aug 605 • Nebuch. Crowned King—Sept 605	4th Regnal Year	3rd Regnal Year
• Tishri 1 605 BC (Oct 7)		

of Necho and returned to Babylon on September 7, 605 BC.[104] The month Tishri for that year began shortly afterwards on October 7, 605 BC.[105] Thus, if Jeremiah was using a Tishri system with non-accession year dating (as Young has demonstrated), Jeremiah was correct that Nebuchadnezzar laid siege to Jerusalem in the fourth year of Jehoiakim's reign. Apparently then, Daniel—in contrast to Jeremiah—must have been employing accession-year dating for Jehoiakim. Perhaps this was because Daniel (who wrote from Babylon) employed the accession-year standard used by the Babylonian scribes. Young writes,

> In Jer 25:1, the fourth year of Jehoiakim coincided with the "first year" (הַשָּׁנָה הָרִאשֹׁנִית, *haššānâ hārašōnîṯ*) of Nebuchadnezzar. Thiele, following Tadmor, pointed out that הַשָּׁנָה הָרִאשֹׁנִית (*haššānâ hārašōnîṯ*) refers not to Nebuchadnezzar's first full year, but to his accession year, in keeping with standard Babylonian accession-year counting.[106]

104. Josephus preserves an account of Nebuchadnezzar's return to Babylon that derived from the writings of the Babylonian historian Berossus (see *C. Ap.*, 1.135–38).
105. Finegan, *Handbook of Biblical Chronology*, 254.
106. Young, "When Did Jerusalem Fall?," 34.

In conclusion, both Jeremiah and Daniel seem to have reckoned the beginning of the new year from Tishri 1, but Jeremiah (following Judean practice) used non-accession-year dating whereas Daniel (following Babylonian practice) used accession-year dating.[107] Although we cannot prove that Daniel reckoned Jehoiakim's reign in this way, there is nothing improbable about this proposal. If true, this demonstrates that there is no necessary conflict between Jeremiah and Daniel, and thus no historical inaccuracy in Daniel's account.

2. *Daniel's Reference to Darius in 5:31—Confusion with Darius I*

Some have thought that Daniel's reference to Darius in 5:31 and in chap. 6 reflects the author's mistake in placing Darius I (r. 522–486 BC) before Cyrus (539–530 BC) and in making Xerxes (another Persian king, r. 486–465 BC) the father of Darius I (cf. 9:1); a mistake that would tend to point to a Maccabean author who was less familiar with sixth-century history.[108] Daniel's reference to Darius as a Mede (5:31; 9:1) is also considered a blunder. (For discussion of the identity of Darius the Mede, see below.) Regarding Darius the Mede, Rowley felt forced to conclude, "We are compelled to recognize that he is a fictitious creature."[109]

In response, one can say it is an assumption on the part of critical scholars that the author's reference to "Darius" must be linked with the Persian king Darius I. Quite clearly the author was not speaking of Darius I but of "Darius the Mede," a contemporary of Cyrus. Admittedly, presently-known extrabiblical sources do not mention a "Darius the Mede," but that does not prove he never existed. Either he bore the same name as Darius I (history knows of several men named Darius), or the word "Darius" is something of an honorific title (like Caesar) or a throne name.[110] Furthermore, if the author had indeed written in the Maccabean era, it would be unlikely that he would have made such a blunder, as he certainly had access to books like Ezra and Nehemiah (see esp. Ezra 4:1–23).

---

107. This explanation has been defended elsewhere by F. F. Bruce, "The Chronology of Dan 1:1," in *The Climax of the Ages: Studies in the Prophecy of Daniel*, ed. F. A. Tatford, 229–36 (London: Marshall, Morgan, and Scott, 1953), 242. Bruce acknowledges others before him who took this same position, including R. D. Wilson, *Studies in the Book of Daniel* (New York: Revell, 1917).

108. For discussion by critical scholars, see Collins (30–32) and Di Lella (35–36).

109. H. H. Rowley, *Darius the Mede and the Four World Empires in the Book of Daniel: A Historical Study of Contemporary Theories* (1959; repr., Eugene, OR: Wipf and Stock, 2006), 59.

110. W. F. Albright, "The Date and Personality of the Chronicler," *JBL* 40 (1921): 112, fn 19, once suggested that "Darius" was a title or throne name for Gubaru: "It seems to me highly probable that Gobryas [Gubaru] did actually assume the royal dignity, along with the name 'Darius,' perhaps an old Iranian royal title, while Cyrus was absent on an Eastern campaign."

Furthermore, the book of Daniel does not present this Darius as ruling over the Persian Empire but of being *made king* over the kingdom of the Chaldeans or as having received the kingdom (see Dan 5:31; 9:1 for further discussion). This may imply another authority had bestowed the honor on him (in contrast to the Persian king Darius I).[111]

Some have suggested that Daniel held to the idea of a Median kingdom as the successor to Babylon and then objected to the idea of there ever being a separate Median kingdom. Anderson states, "Strictly speaking, the idea of a Median kingdom between the Babylonian and Persian regimes is a historical inaccuracy." He adds in regard to the Medes,

> ... they never established themselves as imperial successors to the Babylonians. Rather, their leader, Astyages, was vanquished by Cyrus, who established the Persian empire as the successor to Babylonia.[112]

Actually, the problem is only imaginary. The author never stated there was a Median kingdom between those of Babylonia and Persia (Darius is simply said to be of Median descent).

3. Belshazzar and the Question of the Last King of Babylon

Daniel recorded Belshazzar as the last Babylonian king, whereas in contemporary cuneiform writings it was Nabonidus who occupied the Babylonian throne (ca. 555–539 BC). Anderson remarks, "Actually Belshazzar never reigned as king of Babylon, and the statement that he was the son of Nebuchadnezzar (5:2, 11) is a glaring error." Anderson admits that Nabonidus went away and that Belshazzar ruled in his place. In a similar vein, Di Lella (50) writes, "... for a period of ten years of Nabonidus' reign Belshazzar was appointed crown prince or coregent with his father, but he never became king in the strict sense because he could not preside at the celebration of the New Year Festival, which was the climax of the Babylonian cultic year."

In response, the truth is that Nabonidus was plagued with political troubles in other parts of his realm and thus had to appoint his son Belshazzar as co-regent so he could travel away from the city to deal with these threats. He campaigned in Syria and North Arabia for a decade while the Babylonian priesthood gradually simmered down. The mention in Dan 5:29 of Daniel being made a third ruler in the kingdom correctly accounts for the co-regency

---

111. Critical scholars have objected to the notion of this Darius being a viceroy to a higher authority on the basis that no viceroy would have dared to issue a decree to the inhabitants "in all the earth" (6:25, KJV). In response, the word translated "earth" can just as well be translated "land," thus giving it a more *local* sense. The Aramaic *ʾăraʿ* (like its Hebrew cognate *ʾereṣ*) may mean "land" rather than "earth" in its largest sense (cf. 2:35; 4:20). Both the NIV and ESV translate *ʾăraʿ* in Dan 6:25 as "earth" (NRSV has "the whole world"), although the NASB and NET have "land."

112. Ibid.

of Nabonidus and Belshazzar his son. Furthermore, Harrison shows evidence that Nabonidus had indeed entrusted the kingship to Belshazzar:

> The name Belshazzar has long been known from cuneiform sources, but instead of describing him as king the texts spoke of him predominantly as *mar šarri*! (i.e., son of the king, crown prince), since Nabonidus was the actual king of Babylon. Nevertheless, one document, the so-called 'Persian Verse' account of Nabonidus, does in fact state that Nabonidus had entrusted the kingship to his son Belshazzar, and that he himself made his dwelling in Teima in Arabia.[113]

In addition, Belshazzar functioned as king in Babylon:

> The cuneiform evidence also supports the view that Belshazzar did exercise regal functions. Oaths were taken in the name of both Nabonidus and Belshazzar; Belshazzar granted leases and issued commands. Both the names of Belshazzar and Nabonidus are mentioned in connection with the payment of the royal tribute.[114]

4. *Daniel 5:2 and Nebuchadnezzar as the "Father" of Belshazzar*

In Dan 5:2 Nebuchadnezzar is called the father of Belshazzar, although historically Nabonidus was the father of Belshazzar. Admittedly, Belshazzar was actually the grandson of Nebuchadnezzar, as his father Nabonidus married the daughter of Nebuchadnezzar (Nitocris) to gain the throne. Yet this alleged problem arises from a false reading of Western concepts into ANE terminology. The term "father" (אָב, *ʾaḇ*) is being used in the common oriental manner to describe an ancestor (here, a forefather). Archer explains, "... it should be understood that *ʾāḇ* ('father') was also used in both Hebrew and Aramaic to refer to a grandfather (Gen 28:13; 32:9) or even to a great grandfather (1 Kings 15:10–13)."[115] The mention in Dan 5:29 of Daniel being made a third ruler in the kingdom supports this understanding of *ʾaḇ* ('father'), as this bears witness to the co-regency of Belshazzar with his biological father, Nabonidus.

5. *The Question of Darius the Mede as a Historical Figure*

Critics claim that there is no historical person known as Darius the Mede (Dan 5:31, Aram. 6:1) and that such a reference in Daniel is a complete fabrication without historical basis. This is a slightly different argument than objection number two above. This situation is not about confusion with the Persian king Darius but about the fact that there is no historical confirmation

113. Harrison, "Daniel," 1:863.

114. Ibid.

115. Archer, "Daniel," 7:16.

of any so-called Darius the Mede.[116] Di Lella (36) boldly charges, "... 'Darius the Mede' is a literary fiction in the Book of Daniel."

In response, we must admit that as of this time, the historical documents make no mention of a "Darius the Mede," and the records make it clear the Babylonian kingdom under Nabonidus and Belshazzar was conquered by armies led by Cyrus the Great in 539 BC. Nevertheless, the lack of proof at the current time for Darius the Mede is not proof that Daniel erred in this regard. Several theories have been put forward as possible explanations to resolve the tension, though no theory has gained consensus.

In pursuit of a reliable resolution, we naturally turn first to available source material. Details of Babylon's fall are well documented from such historical sources as the Nabonidus Chronicle,[117] the Cyrus Cylinder,[118] and the writings of Berossus (a third-century BC Babylonian priest and historian), though only fragments and scattered quotations remain of Berossus' work. In addition, we have the accounts of the Greek historians—Herodotus (ca. 484–425 BC) who wrote his *Histories*, and Xenophon (ca. 430–354 BC) who authored *Cyropaedia*. Finally, the Harran Stele[119] provides a valuable piece of evidence regarding the status of the Medes (written shortly before Babylon's fall, about 542–540 BC).

In one way or another, all the theories presented in this discussion share the common denominator that "Darius" was another name or title for someone of Median descent. Except for the theory that Darius the Mede was actually Cyrus himself (see option "a" below), most of these theories assert that Cyrus appointed a high-ranking Mede to rule as viceroy over Babylon while he himself returned to dwell in one or more of his royal cities in Persia as the ultimate ruler of the Persian Empire. There is possible evidence to this effect. Archer explains,

> In Daniel 9:1 it is asserted that Darius the Mede was *made* king (*homlak*) over the realm of the Chaldeans. This term indicates that he was invested with the kingship by some higher authority than himself, which well agrees with the supposition that he was installed as viceroy in Babylonia by Cyrus the Great. Similarly, in

116. L. Grabbe, "Another Look at the *Gestalt* of Darius the Mede," *CBQ* 50 (1988): 213, has argued that Darius the Mede of the book of Daniel is not a single individual at all, but only an imaginary figure, something of an amalgamation of several individuals (Darius I included) whose characteristics "are only the inherited clichés of folk-tradition about the Persians." That is, in Grabbe's estimation, Darius is a figure a confused author (writing centuries later and not well acquainted with Persian history) contrived based on traditions and folklore that had come down to him.

117. *ANET*, 305–7.

118. *ANET*, 315–16.

119. *ANET*, 562–63.

Dan. 5:31 we are told that Darius "received" (*qabbēl*) the "kingdom" (*malkūtā*).[120]

Furthermore, it is doubtful that the author was confusing "Darius the Mede" with the famous Persian king, Darius I the Great (522–486 BC).[121] Not only was this latter Darius clearly regarded as a Persian, but it is also well known that Darius Hystaspes was fairly young when he began his rule.

The historical development of the Persian Empire would easily allow for a viceroy of Median descent, for the Medes and Persians were very closely linked. Initially the Medes were the dominant power, but eventually the Persians came to dominate. Merrill explains,

> ... in time Cyaxares (625–585) overthrew the Scythians and the Assyrians, establishing Median control over all of northern Mesopotamia and Iran. He also reduced Persia to submission, setting up Cambyses as governor over that province.[122]

But the domination of the Medes eventually gave way to the Persians as a result of the rise in power of Cyrus II the Great (ruler of Anshan), the conqueror of Babylon in 539 BC. Cyrus actually descended from both groups, his father being a Persian and his mother a Mede.[123] Exactly how and when this shift in power took place, however, is a matter of scholarly debate. Some hold that the Medes were conquered and made subservient to Persia *before* the fall of Babylon, while others hold that the Medes continued to be the dominant partner until *after* Babylon's fall. (This is not a minor point of contention, as will be pointed out in consideration of option "e" below, since Xenophon [contradicting Herodotus] maintained that there was a Median king named Cyaxares II that still ruled over the Medes at the time of Babylon's fall.) The following diagram illustrates these relationships:

---

120. Archer, *A Survey of Old Testament Introduction*, 366. Despite Archer's comments, the verb הָמְלַךְ (*homlak*) does not prove that Darius was made king by a higher authority. See translation notes for Dan 9:1 for discussion of this point.

121. Archer ("Daniel," 7:17) points out that the fall of Babylon was well-known information, such that a second-century author would not have made such blunders. "Herodotus (1.191) states that it was Cyrus, in command of a combined Medo-Persian army, who captured Babylon by the stratagem of diverting the channel of the Euphrates and slipping into the city at night by means of the riverbed. His work was published in the middle of the fifth century BC. Writing in the early fourth century, Xenophon related in his *Cyropaedia* (7:20) how Cyrus engineered the surprise attack through the skillful leadership of his generals Gadatas and Gobryas and thereby took control of all Babylon."

122. Merrill, *Kingdom of Priests*, 491.

123. According to Herodotus, Cyrus the Great was actually a descendant of the Median king Astyages. The granddaughter of Astyages (Mandane) married the Persian vassal of her father (Cambyses I), and to this marriage was born Cyrus II (the Great).

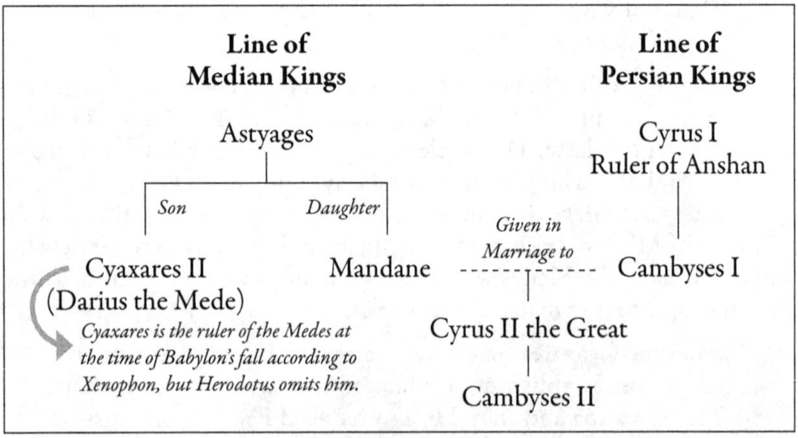

What we do know is that Cyrus II was able to unify several Persian tribes and eventually helped bring about the merger of empires of the Medes and Persians. The resulting union, however, was a kingdom in which both the Medes and the Persians played an important part. Clines explains,

> Because Cyrus remained respectful of Median culture, made Median Ecbatana one of his royal residences, and often appointed Medes to high positions in his provincial government, his kingdom became known as that of the "Medes and Persians" (cf., e.g., Dnl. 5:28; 6:8,15; Est. 10:2).[124]

Thus it is entirely possible that a Mede was appointed to rule over Babylon after the armies of Cyrus conquered the city in 539 BC. We know from extrabiblical documents that the Medes played an active part in the capture of Babylon and that a Mede by the name of Ugbaru or Gubaru (sometimes referred to as Gobryas) was in charge of Cyrus' forces and led the capture of the city.[125] Much speculation has been made about this Ugbaru/

---

124. D. J. A. Clines, "Cyrus," in *ISBE*, 1:846. In his commentary on Daniel (in *EBC*, 7:18), Archer elaborates on the cooperative empire that emerged from the defeat of the Medes by the Persians. He notes, "The *Encyclopaedia Britannica* article on 'Media' (1969 ed., 15:68) remarks, 'In the new empire they [the Medes] retained a prominent position; in honor and war they stood next to the Persians ... many noble Medes were employed as officials, satraps and generals.' It would not, therefore, be surprising for Cyrus to appoint as viceroy over the newly conquered Babylonian domain a trusted lieutenant who was a Mede."

125. An account of the fall of Babylon is contained in the Nabonidus Chronicle, a translation of which is provided in Pritchard, *ANET*, 305–7. In Cyrus' attack upon the province of Babylonia, the city of Sippar fell and two days later the city of Babylon fell: "The 14th day, Sippar was seized without battle. Nabonidus fled. The 16th day, Gobryas (*Ugbaru*), the governor of Gutium and the army of Cyrus entered

Gubaru, with attempts to link him to Daniel's "Darius the Mede." (Some regard these as one and the same individual, while others as separate individuals.) Whether or not this might be "Darius," Cyrus certainly had strong links to the Medes, and they did play a significant role in the capture of Babylon. That Ugbaru/Gubaru was a Mede himself is most likely from the fact that he had been "governor of Gutium." The Guti were a mountainous people of ancient Mesopotamia who lived primarily around Hamadân, which had been the capital of the Median Empire known as Ecbatana. Cyrus himself had close connections with Ecbatana and the Guti people (i.e., the Medes), as Hayden points out: "Cyrus captured the city from Astyages (548 BC), ... Cyrus and other Persian kings used to spend the two summer months there yearly, owing to the comparative coolness of the climate."[126]

Hence, it is entirely reasonable that Cyrus may have appointed a Mede to be king of Babylon or (if option "e" is correct) simply turned the rule of Babylon over to the Median king (Cyaxares II, his uncle) after conquering it. We may not be certain as to *why* Daniel calls him "Darius the Mede," but having a king or ruler of Median descent should not be surprising.[127] Although there is no historical evidence outside the Bible for a person by this name, this may be an alternative designation or throne name for someone else (or "Darius" may have been an honorific title like Caesar).[128] The following are the more prominent suggestions that have been made as to the identity of this "Darius the Mede":

Babylon without battle. Afterwards Nabonidus was arrested in Babylon when he returned (there).... In the month of Arahshamnu, the 3rd day, Cyrus entered Babylon, green twigs were spread in front of him—the state of 'Peace' (*šulmu*) was imposed upon the city. Cyrus sent greetings to all Babylon. Gobryas, his governor, installed (sub-) governors in Babylon.... In the month of Arahshamnu, on the night of the 11th day, Gobryas died" (306). In this text, the governor of Gutium (here translated Gobryas, the name by which the Greek historian Xenophon referred to him; see *Cyropaedia*, iv.6, vii.5, 26–30) is referred to as Ugbaru and at some points Gubaru. This official (a Mede) died very shortly after the capture of Babylon.

126. R. E. Hayden, "Ecbatana," in *ISBE*, 2:11.

127. Even though the Medes are thought to have been conquered by the Persians in 550 BC, there is evidence for a king of the Medes after this date. Harrison, "Daniel," 1:863, points out: "...it is known that in the tenth year of Nabonidus (546 BC), a cuneiform text at Harran referred specifically to the 'king of the Medes.'"

128. Archer ("Daniel," 7:18) writes, "This viceroy was given the title of *Dārᵉyāwēš* which apparently meant 'The Royal One,' from *dara* (which is attested in Avestan Persian as a term for 'king')." Archer also writes concerning the famous king Darius having a personal name: "...we should take note of the fact that even the later Darius, son of Hystaspes (*Wištāspa*), bore the personal name of *Spantadāta* (cf. F. W. König, *Relief und Inschrift des Königs Dareios I* [Leiden: Brill, 1938], p. 1)." (Ibid., 7:19).

A. Darius the Mede Might Be an Alternative Name for Cyrus. D. J. Wiseman, J. M. Bulman, B. Colless, J. Baldwin, and G. R. Law take this position.[129] In this case, the text (6:28) may be translated: "So Daniel prospered during the reign of Darius, even the reign of Cyrus the Persian."[130] Harrison points out that Cyrus was related to the Medes. "He was evidently about sixty-two years of age when he became king of Babylon, and according to inscriptions he appointed many subordinate governors."[131] Hence, "Darius the Mede" would be an alternative title to "Cyrus the Persian." McDowell states, "In the Harran Stele and other sources, Cyrus is called king of the Medes. Also, in Theodotion's ancient text of Bel and the Dragon, the king who sends Daniel to the lions' den is Cyrus of Persia; in the Book of Daniel, it is Darius the Mede."[132]

This position is not without its problems. Inscriptions do not mention Cyrus as the son of Ahasuerus. Furthermore, why call him Cyrus the Persian in one place and Darius the Mede in another? (If it were a matter of being Cyrus the Persian and Darius the Persian, it might be a bit more believable.) Also, Daniel makes a clear distinction between Darius of Median descent (9:1) and Cyrus who was the king of Persia (10:1)—and these in such close proximity! That Cyrus was sixty-two years old (see 5:31) is also subject to question, since Cyrus died six years later leading troops into battle (would a sixty-eight year old king be leading troops into battle?).[133] As noted in a preceding footnote, Cyrus was more likely less than forty at the time of the

129. D. J. Wiseman et al., *Notes on Some Problems in the Book of Daniel* (London: Tyndale, 1970), 12–14; J. M. Bulman, "The Identification of Darius the Mede," *WTJ* 35 (1973): 247–67; B. E. Colless, "Cyrus the Persian as Darius the Mede in the Book of Daniel," *JSOT* 56 (1992): 113–26; Baldwin, 26–32, 141; and G. R. Law, *Identification of Darius the Mede* (Pfafftour, NC: Ready Scribe, 2010), 185.

130. Wiseman, *Notes on Some Problems*, 12, explains the retranslation: "Such a use of the appositional or explicative Hebrew *wāw* construction has long been recognized in I Chronicles 5:26 ('So the God of Israel stirred up the spirit of Pul king of Assyria, even the spirit of Tiglath-pileser king of Assyria') and elsewhere."

131. Harrison, "Daniel," 1:863. Harrison's claim that Cyrus was about age sixty-two at the time of the conquest of Babylon has been called into question by others, as there is dispute about the date of his birth. Most sources give either 600 BC or 575 BC as Cyrus' birth year. Cuneiform evidence suggests another possibility for 576 BC, but, again, more sources seem to favor a standard number at 575 BC for his birth. Therefore, a conclusive answer is not yet fully clear. If the 575 BC date proves correct, then Cyrus would have been less than forty years old at the time of the conquest of Babylon.

132. J. McDowell, *Daniel in the Critics' Den: Historical Evidence for the Authenticity of the Book of Daniel* (San Bernardino, CA: Here's Life, 1979), 72.

133. "Following this decree in 538 Cyrus continued to maintain and even expand his magnificent empire. He died in 530 in combat against the Massagetae in the Jaxartes River valley in central Asia" (Merrill, *Kingdom of Priests*, 492).

conquest of Babylon. Even though Wiseman tries to show evidence that Cyrus was *also* known as a king of the Medes, it is doubtful that he would be referred to as such. McDowell argues, "Cyrus came from Persia, not Media, and Persia under Cyrus had overthrown the Median rulers and conquered not only Media but also Elam, the third important province in that area."[134]

Finally, the expression in Dan 9:1 that Darius "was made king over the kingdom of the Chaldeans" (NASB) does not fit Cyrus (cf. 5:31). Archer explains, "*Homlak̠* is a causative passive that strongly suggests that he was appointed king by some higher authority."[135]

B. DARIUS THE MEDE MIGHT BE IDENTIFIED AS UGBARU/GUBARU (MENTIONED IN *ANET*), WHO WAS APPOINTED BY CYRUS TO RULE OVER BABYLON.[136] This is the position of W. H. Shea, J. D. Pentecost, and E. H. Merrill.[137] In this case, emphasis is put on the fact that Babylon refers to a small portion of the Medo-Persian Empire. According to this position, Ugbaru conquered Babylon on October 12, 539 BC, but Cyrus entered shortly afterwards on October 29. Cyrus then appointed Ugbaru to rule in Babylon on his behalf. Darius was simply another name for Ugbaru.

Complicating this theory is that the Nabonidus Chronicle mentions both an Ugbaru and a Gubaru. Some take these to be variant spellings of the same name, and that this person is also the same as Gobryas in the Greek sources. Others differentiate Ugbaru and Gubaru (see view "c" below).

Mercer summarizes the position equating Darius with Ugbaru:

> The evidence in favor of the identification of Ugbaru as the vassal king of Babylon can be summarized as follows. First, the change of Cyrus' titulary from "King of Babylon, King of Lands" to simply "King of Lands" and then back to "King of Babylon, King of Lands"

134. McDowell, *Daniel in the Critics' Den*, 74.

135. Archer, "Daniel," 7:18. Archer's point, however, is not as convincing as it might at first seem. See commentary at Dan 9:1 for an alternative explanation of the passive verb form *homlak̠*.

136. Both names Ugbaru and Gubaru appear in *ANET*, and there is debate as to whether these are two different individuals or whether they are one and the same.

137. W. H. Shea, "Darius the Mede: An Update," *AUSS* 20 (1982): 229–47; Pentecost, 1347; and Merrill, *Kingdom of Priests*, 492, fn 35. Merrill (497, fn 52) writes, "It seems best, without going into the debate here, to accept Shea's identification of Darius the Mede with Gubaru, governor of Gutium, who as the head of the Persian army conquered Babylon." Although Shea, "Darius the Mede in His Persian-Babylonian Setting," *AUSS* 29 (1991): 235–57, temporarily abandoned this position in favor of the theory that Darius the Mede was actually Cyrus, he nevertheless returned to affirm it in "Nabonidus Chronicle: New Readings and the Identity of Darius the Mede," *JATS* 7 (1996): 1–20 and again in "The Search for Darius the Mede (Concluded), or, The Time of the Answer to Daniel's Prayer and the Date of the Death of Darius the Mede," *JATS* 12 (2001): 97–105.

> during a fourteen-month period following the fall of Babylon suggests the throne was vacant or that someone else was "King of Babylon" during the interim period in which Cyrus is called simply "King of Lands" (William H. Shea, "An Unrecognized Vassal King of Babylon in the Early Achaemenid Period," *AUSS* 9 [1971]:105–28, esp. Table II, pp. 107–8). Assuming that the throne of Babylon would not be left vacant at such a crucial period in Cyrus' reign, the most logical choice for the position of "king of Babylon" would be Ugbaru, the governor of Guti, who captured Babylon. Second, the mere mention of Ugbaru in the Nabonidus Chronicle suggests his royalty because of the extreme paucity of nonroyal personages in the Babylonian Chronicles (Shea, "An Unrecognized Vassal King," pp. 147–52). Finally, the record of Ugbaru's death suggests that he was king because with only one exception, all the death dates in the Babylonian Chronicles refer to royalty (Shea, "An Unrecognized Vassal King," pp. 152–54).[138]

Evaluation: Ugbaru was indeed the conqueror of Babylon, and his victory is recorded in *ANET* (306). However, there is a question as to how long he reigned. The Nabonidus Chronicle indicates that Ugbaru died on the night of the eleventh day of the month Arahshamnu, whereas earlier in the same passage Cyrus is said to have entered Babylon on the third day of Arahshamnu.[139] Yet it is not clear from the passage whether Ugbaru died a few days after Cyrus' entry (i.e., Nov. 6, 539 BC), or if he died in the month Arahshamnu a year later. If the former is the case, it is hard to see how the reference to Darius the Mede could be equated with Ugbaru, since Daniel seems to speak of his reign (6:28; 9:1), although Ugbaru did not live long enough to really have a "reign" (a few weeks?). If he died approximately a year later, this would be more realistic. In either case, Ugbaru had been the governor of Gutium (and is thought by some to be the Gobryas mentioned in the *Cyropaedia* of Xenophon).

c. Darius the Mede Might Refer to Another Official Named Gubaru (Different from Ugbaru) Who Was Appointed by Cyrus to Rule Babylon. J. C. Whitcomb, B. K. Waltke, and G. L. Archer prefer this view.[140] According to this position, Ugbaru and Gubaru were not confused names for the same individual but actually different individuals.

---

138. M. Mercer, "An Historical, Exegetical, and Theological Study of Daniel 11:26–12:4" (Th.D. diss., Dallas Theological Seminary, 1987)," 15–16, fn 18.

139. Arahshamnu is sometimes spelled Marcheswan—so D. W. Thomas, *Documents from Old Testament Times* (1958; repr., New York: Harper & Row, 1961), 82, or Araḫ Samna (so Wikipedia).

140. J. C. Whitcomb, *Darius the Mede: A Study in Historical Identification* (Grand Rapids: Eerdmans, 1959); Waltke, "The Date of the Book of Daniel," 327–28; and Archer, *A Survey*, 367.

Ugbaru was the governor of Gutium who helped conquer Babylon. However, when Cyrus entered the city on Oct 29, 539 BC, he appointed another individual named Gubaru to rule (Ugbaru either suffered from wounds in battle or had incurred a fatal illness and died shortly thereafter on November 6).[141] Gubaru seems to have held this position for fourteen years, as Archer brings forth evidence of Gubaru's existence and rule long after the fall of Babylon: "A Gubaru appears as the governor of Babylonia and of Ebir-nari (the western domains under Chaldean sovereignty) in tablets dated from the fourth to the eighth year of Cyrus (535–532 BC) and even as late as the fifth year of Cambyses (525 BC)."[142]

In response, Harrison has pointed out the weakness to this view: "To date, however, there is no specific evidence which would show that he was a Mede, a descendant of Ahasuerus, or a man who was about sixty years of age."[143] Furthermore, in the records mentioned by Archer, he is called a "governor," not a king. Also, the fact that this Gubaru lived considerably longer after Babylon's fall raises a question, since Dan 5:31 indicates Darius was already about the age of sixty-two at the time he began to reign.

Grabbe also argues against the likelihood of Ugbaru and Gubaru being different individuals:

> Shea has given a useful discussion of the question; as he points out, the signs for *ug* and *gu* are actually not very different in the neo-Babylonian script. More important is that the scribe who copied the text seems to have been unsure of the reading on his original in at least one case because he did not complete the writing of the sign (iii 15). Other than the question of orthography,

141. Harrison, "Daniel," 2:17: "The Nabonidus Chronicle mentioned two persons connected with the fall of Babylon, namely Ugbaru and Gubaru, and faulty tr. of the Chronicle since 1882 has tended to confuse their identities. It was on the basis of this misunderstanding that scholars such as H. H. Rowley assumed that they were actually one person, the Gobryas of Xenophon's *Cyropaedia*, who died after the fall of Babylon in 539 BC. The tr. of the Chronicle by Sidney Smith in 1924, however, distinguished between Ugbaru and Gubaru, and it is now apparent that the former, who was governor of Gutium and an ally of Cyrus, took a prominent part in the capture of Babylon and then died shortly afterward, presumably of wounds sustained in the battle. Whereupon the other victorious leader Gubaru, who with Ugbaru was apparently responsible for diverting the river Euphrates so that his soldiers could capture the city by infiltrating along the dried-up river bed, was appointed by Cyrus as the governor of Babylon." A. T. Clay, "Gobryas," *JAOS* 41 (1921): 466, suggested that Gubaru had held a "high command in the army of Nebuchadrezzar."

142. Archer, "Daniel," 7:18.

143. Harrison, "Daniel," 1:863.

> there is little to lead one to postulate two different individuals in the context.[144]

D. Darius the Mede Might Be the Same as Cambyses II (Cyrus' Son). This was the position of C. Boutflower.[145] Cambyses II ruled Persia from 530–522 BC. Cambyses had connections to Babylon (participating each spring in the annual New Year Festival), but he did not live there. Miller (172) further points out:

> A serious problem with this view is the age of Cambyses. Daniel records that Darius the Mede was sixty-two years old when he began to rule over Babylon (5:31), but Cambyses would have been much younger than this in 539 B.C. Cambyses also could not be considered of Median descent because both of his parents were Persian.

E. Darius the Mede Might Have Been a Throne Name for Cyaxares II, the Median King. This was a position advocated by Calvin, then later in the nineteenth century by C. F. Keil and O. Zöckler, in the early twentieth century by W. S. Auchincloss, and defended more recently by S. Hirsch and S. Anderson.[146] The theory stems from the thesis that the two primary Greek historians, Herodotus and Xenophon, have contradictory accounts regarding the accession of Cyrus and the existence of a Median king at the time of Babylon's fall. While mainline scholarship has historically leaned on Herodotus' *Histories*, Hirsch and Anderson maintain that it is actually the account of Xenophon's *Cyropaedia* that preserves the more accurate record, at least in regard to these matters. Most notably, Herodotus claimed that Cyrus overthrew the previous Median king (Astyages) in a coup prior to the conquest of Babylon and indicated that Astyages had no male heir (*Histories*, 1.109). This would have made Cyrus king over both the Medes and the Persians prior to the conquest of Babylon. Xenophon, on the other hand, described a Median king, Cyaxares II (omitted by Herodotus), who

---

144. Grabbe, "Another Look," 206.

145. C. Boutflower, *In and Around the Book of Daniel* (1930; repr., Grand Rapids: Kregel, 1977).

146. Calvin, 1:347–48, 2:140–41; Keil, 192–200; Zöckler, 35–36; W. S. Auchincloss, "Darius the Median," *BSac* 66 (1909): 536–38; S. W. Hirsch, "1000 Iranian Nights: History and Fiction in Xenophon's *Cyropaedia*," in *The Greek Historians: Literature and History: Papers Presented to A. E. Raubitschek*, ed. M. H. Jameson (Saratoga, CA: ANMA Libra, 1985), 63–85; idem, *The Friendship of the Barbarians: Xenophon and the Persian Empire* (Hanover, NH: University Press of New England, 1985); S. D. Anderson, "Darius the Mede: A Reappraisal" (a revision of Ph.D. dissertation, Dallas Seminary, May 2014); and S. D. Anderson and R. C. Young, "The Remembrance of Daniel's Darius the Mede in Berossus and Harpocration," *BibSac* 173 (2016): 315–23.

was the actual head of government at the time Cyrus led the Medo-Persian armies on campaigns of conquest.

Anderson marshals a great deal of evidence to show that Xenophon has preserved a more reliable account concerning the succession of Median rulers and their relationship to Cyrus and the fall of Babylon. He maintains that the major witnesses supporting Herodotus consist of cuneiform propaganda texts produced by the government of Cyrus. If, then, the account of Xenophon is given serious consideration, Cyrus did not conquer the Medes and assume rule over their kingdom prior to his conquest of Babylon. Rather, Astyages the Median king had a male heir, Cyaxares II, who actually ruled over the Medes and the Persians, while Cyrus did not gain full power until Cyaxares II died sometime *after* Babylon's fall. When Babylon was conquered, the rule of this realm was given to Cyaxares II, with Darius apparently being his throne name. Arguments favoring the account of Xenophon over Herodotus include the following considerations:[147]

- Herodotus incorrectly relates there was only one king of Babylon at the time that it fell to Cyrus. He calls this king Labynetus, apparently his version of Nabonidus. Xenophon, without giving the names, correctly states there were two Babylonian kings (*Cyropaedia* 4.6.3, 5.2.27, 5.4.12), a father and a son, and it was the son who was in the city when it was captured.
- Both Herodotus and Xenophon relate how the forces of Cyrus took the city by the stratagem of diverting the Euphrates River that flowed through the city, and both agree that Babylon was observing a festival on the night the city was taken. Xenophon, however, adds a detail that is not found in Herodotus: that the king reigning there was slain the night the city was taken, a statement that is corroborated by Dan 5:31.
- Xenophon has an extensive history of Ugbaru/Gubaru (Greek Gobryas), governor of Gutium and leader of Cyrus' forces in the capture of Babylon. Ugbaru is also known from the Nabonidus Chronicle,[148] where, in agreement with the *Cyropaedia*, he leads the army that captures Babylon. Herodotus never mentions this name, a curious deficiency given the importance of Ugbaru in the capture of the city and prior events.
- Xenophon states that Cyrus was the son of a Persian king (1.2.1). As an important part of Herodotus' tale of the upbringing of Cyrus, he states that although Cyrus' mother Mandane was the daughter of Astyages, Astyages gave Mandane in marriage to someone not

147. The bullet points are quoted from Wikipedia contributors, "Cyropaedia," *Wikipedia: The Free Encyclopedia*, http://en.wikipedia.org/wiki/Cyropaedia (accessed 25 February 2015).

148. Pritchard, *ANET*, 306b.

of "suitable rank," so that any son born to Mandane could not claim a royal heritage (1.107). In this important matter the Cyrus Cylinder agrees with Xenophon against Herodotus. In the Cylinder, Cyrus states that he is "son of Cambyses, great king, king of Anshan, grandson of Cyrus, great king, king of Anshan, descendant of Teispes, great king, king of Anshan, of a family (which) always (exercised) kingship."[149]

- The Harran Stele[150] is a document from the court of Nabonidus that gives events in his various regnal years. In the entry for his year 14 or 15, corresponding to 542–540 BC,[151] Nabonidus speaks of his enemies as the kings of Egypt, the Medes, and the Arabs. The *Cyropaedia* presents the king of Media as the senior partner and Cyrus the king of Persia as the junior or lesser partner until after the conquest of Babylon. During this time the Medes were stronger than the Persians (1.5.2). This fits with Nabonidus mentioning the king of Media as his enemy, without mentioning his subordinate, whom the *Cyropaedia* supplies as Cyrus, king of Persia. According to Herodotus and the current consensus, there was no independent Median kingdom at this time, Cyrus having conquered the Medes many years previously. C. J. Gadd, following the consensus view, stated that the Harran Stele provides an example of the title "king of the Medes" being applied to Cyrus, without his being named.[152] But in all other cuneiform inscriptions from the time of Cyrus, every reference to him before the capture of Babylon designates him as either "King of Anshan" or "King of Persia," never "king of the Medes." The relevant texts are "The Verse Account of Nabonidus,"[153] The Cyrus Cylinder,[154] and the Nabonidus Chronicle.[155] If these texts are read without *a priori* assumptions, the natural understanding would be that the king of the Medes mentioned in the Harran Stele is not Cyrus, king of Persia.
- Archaeological evidence supports the *Cyropaedia's* picture of relations between the Medes and the Persians. According to Herodotus, who was apparently following the later Persian propaganda of the Nabonidus Chronicle, Cyrus rose up in rebellion against his grandfather Astyages, king of Media, and conquered the Medes, who were then subject to Cyrus from that

149. Ibid., 316.
150. Ibid., 562–63.
151. P.-A. Beaulieu, *The Reign of Nabonidus, King of Babylon 556–539 B.C.* (New Haven, CT: Yale Univ. Press, 1996), 32.
152. C. J. Gadd, "The Harran Inscriptions of Nabonidus," *AnSt* 8 (1958): 77.
153. Pritchard, *ANET*, 312–15.
154. Ibid., 315–16.
155. Ibid., 305–7.

> point on. The *Cyropaedia*, in contrast, presents both kingdoms as partners, with the Medes being the senior partners and equal with the Persians right up to the death of Cyaxares II, son of Astyages, about two years after the conquest of Babylon. After the death of Cyaxares the two kingdoms were merged peaceably under Cyrus. Archaeological evidence, such as the stairway reliefs at Persepolis, shows no distinction in official rank or status between the Persian and Median nobility. Although Olmstead followed the consensus view that Cyrus subjugated the Medes, he nevertheless wrote, "Medes were honored equally with Persians; they were employed in high office and were chosen to lead Persian armies."[156]

Thus, by giving priority to Xenophon's *Cyropaedia*, the individual known as "Darius the Mede" in the book of Daniel is none other than Cyaxares II, the son of Astyages and maternal uncle of Cyrus the Great. He was the heir and rightful king of the Medes, and would have been older than Cyrus so as to fit the description of being "sixty-two years of age" (Dan 5:31). He received the kingdom (or "was made king," Dan 9:1) in the sense that after Cyrus led the armies of the Medes and Persians in conquest of Babylon, he turned over the rule of it to Cyaxares II and by doing so, honored him.

Summary and Conclusions

Until the mid-nineteenth century, Jerome's opinion prevailed—namely, that Darius the Mede was the maternal uncle of Cyrus the Great, the son of the Median king Astyages. This would be Cyaxares II, as identified by Xenophon. With the discovery of Akkadian inscriptions (primarily in the nineteenth century), scholarly opinion began to shift in favor of Herodotus' account (namely, that Astyages had no male heir and Cyrus had conquered and subjected the Medes prior to the defeat and fall of Babylon). Over the past half century, the dominant evangelical position has been that Darius was historical but that no one theory is provable, while most critical scholars have simply regarded Darius the Mede as a fictional or historically inaccurate character.

More recently, the account of Herodotus has been called into question and even the reliability of existing inscriptions ("Dream Text of Nabonidus" [Sippar Cylinder], Cyrus Cylinder, "The Verse Account of Nabonidus," and the Nabonidus Chronicle) has been challenged, as they tend to be propagandistic. Scholars such as S. W. Anderson, having carefully reviewed all the data, have concluded that the claim that Cyrus overthrew Astyages and became king of Media-Persia well before the fall of Babylon (as Herodotus maintained) is inaccurate. Instead, Xenophon's viewpoint is more reliable: Cyrus did not conquer and rule the Medes prior to Babylon's fall but that the two powers combined their forces for mutual benefit and that the Medes were ruled by Astyages' son, Cyaxares II. Once Babylon was conquered, the

156. A. T. Olmsted, *History of the Persian Empire* (Chicago: University of Chicago Press, 1948), 37.

rule of Babylon was entrusted to Cyaxares II, known in Daniel as "Darius the Mede" (the latter being perhaps his throne name, a practice common among ancient near Eastern kings).[157]

Although the older views embraced by evangelicals (views "a" – "d") are possible, they each have serious weaknesses as pointed out in the discussion. Cyrus and his son Cambyses were not likely to be referred to as "Medes" nor were they considered sons of Ahasuerus (Dan 9:1). As for Ugbaru/Gubaru, they either did not live long enough to have had a rule at Babylon (view "b") or had no known identity as a Mede or a noble standing by which they would have been readily received as king (view "c").

View "e"—that Darius the Mede was a throne name for Cyaxares II, a Median king who continued to rule over Babylon until he died roughly a couple of years after Babylon's fall in 539 BC—has more to commend it. In weighing the evidence, Anderson contends:

> Herodotus and Ctesias give an elaborate and legendary tale of Cyrus' origins, whereas Xenophon and Aeschylus are matter-of-fact. The four major cuneiform texts which support Herodotus—the Cyrus Cylinder (maybe), the Verse Account (maybe), the Nabonidus Chronicle, and the Dream Text—also lay out an elaborate story, and all four originate from the same official source and have the same propagandistic purpose. Berossus, Harpocration, and the Harran Stele, by contrast—three highly credible sources completely independent of one another—support Xenophon by means of a passing reference for no other purpose than to note a pertinent fact. It is these latter texts which have the mark of historical fidelity, since there is no concocted story or need to support a bias, only a mention of a known fact that is part of a larger but unstated history.[158]

---

157. For example, the name of the last king of Persia, Darius III (r. 336/5–330 BC), was originally Artašata and called Codomannus by the Greeks.

158. Anderson, *Darius the Mede*, 122. Aeschylus, mentioned in this quotation, was a Greek author of numerous plays who wrote the tragedy *The Persians*, about 472 BC. Significantly, his work predates that of both Herodotus and Xenophon, and thus he wrote independent of either of them. One of the lines in his play supports the idea that Cyrus did not conquer the rebellious Medes as Herodotus indicated, but rather was preceded by two Median kings. The line reads, "For the Mede was the first leader of [our] host; And another, his son, completed this work, For [his] mind directed his passion. And third from him was Cyrus, a fortunate man; When he ruled, he established peace for all his own." The first Mede referred to cannot be Cyaxares I, for he did not establish a Medo-Persian kingdom. Hence, the two Median kings preceding Cyrus must be Astyages and his son, Cyaxares II, thus supporting Xenophon's account.

The Cyaxares theory, as maintained by Anderson and Hirsch, is not without its problems.[159] At this time, the consensus of scholarship still sides with Herodotus and the major inscriptions and cuneiform texts that support the notion of Cyrus' conquest and subordination of the Medes prior to Babylon's fall. Furthermore, even if the historicity of Cyaxares II proves true, there is still no extrabiblical mention of him as "Darius the Mede." Yet, with the publication of Anderson's work, the scholarly world will now need to (1) be more cautious about its reliance upon Herodotus' account of Cyrus; (2) give greater consideration to Xenophon; and (3) take seriously the notion that there was an historical king of the Medes named Cyaxares II (the son of the Median king Astyages) who might be equated with the biblical Darius the Mede.

In addition to what has been said about the Cyaxares theory in preceding material, two supportive points will be made in closing. First, the Harran Stele of Nabonidus (*ANET*, 562), which dates from the period shortly before the fall of Babylon in 539 BC, witnesses to the existence of a king of the Medes independent of the Persians and that the Medes—not Persia—at this time were the primary threat to Babylonia. In the inscription, Nabonidus is reported to have stated, "the king of Egypt, the Medes and the land of the Arabs, all the hostile kings, were sending me messages of reconciliation and friendship." This works against the view that Cyrus had conquered the Medes long before Babylon's fall and had become their king. Second, we have a very noteworthy reference by the first-century Jewish historian Josephus that lends weight to the fact that not only did Astyages have a son to succeed him as king, but that this son was indeed Darius. For the source of his information, Josephus relied upon the work of the Babylonian priest and historian, Berossus, whom he held in high esteem and frequently quoted. Berossus wrote a three-volume work entitled *Babyloniaca* (*History of Babylonia*) around 290–278 BC. Although it is no longer extant and only

---

Of some interest is a statement made by Valerius Harpocration, a second-century AD lexicographer in regard to the "daric" coin. In his entry for "daric," Harpocration wrote, "But darics are not named as most suppose, after Darius the father of Xerxes, but after a certain other more ancient king" (cited in Anderson and Young, "The Remembrance of Daniel's Darius the Mede," 319). This statement attests to a king named Darius who predates Darius Hystaspes.

159. Law, *Identification of Darius the Mede*, 63, points out, "Another problem for the Cyaxares (II) theory is that the narrative of Xenophon does not place Cyaxares (II) in or about Babylon either before or after its fall to Cyrus.... According to Xenophon's story, Cyrus again meets Cyaxares (II) after the fall of Babylon. Cyrus tells Cyaxares (II) that a palace is ready for him whenever he wants to visit Babylon (a detail which must be told Cyaxares (II) because he has not been to Babylon). And so in this story, Cyaxares (II) stays in Media, and Cyrus appoints the satraps in Babylon."

fragments remain today, we have a number of quotations and references to it in both Josephus and Eusebius.[160] In his *Antiquities*, Josephus writes:

> And this is the end of the posterity of king Nebuchadnezzar, as history informs us; but when Babylon was taken by Darius, and when he, with his kinsman Cyrus, had put an end to the dominion of the Babylonians, he was sixty-two years old. He was the son of Astyages, and had another name among the Greeks.[161]

This is in complete harmony with Xenophon's account that names Cyaxares II as that son of Astyages and probably the most likely candidate at this time for Daniel's "Darius the Mede."

6. The Lack of Confirmation for Nebuchadnezzar's Disease

In addition to the lack of historical confirmation for Nebuchadnezzar's disease in Neo-Babylonian sources, Di Lella (52) argues that the whole account has an appearance of artificiality. He points out that there are several striking parallels between Nebuchadnezzar's praise account and Old Testament phraseology, which gives one the impression that he has been made to speak like a pious Jew (Dan 4:3 with Ps 145:5, 13; Dan 4:35 with Isa 45:9; and Dan 4:37 with Ps 101:5).[162]

While it is true that the account of Nebuchadnezzar's disease is not confirmed by historical records of that period, it is not difficult to see that this kind of thing would have been kept from historical records, for it would have been highly insulting to the monarch and his family. There are numerous examples from ANE history where historical facts have been kept from record where they distracted from a sovereign's glory. Harrison, however, points out that the issue is not entirely lacking of historical reference: " ... three centuries after the time of Nebuchadnezzar a Babylonian priest named

160. One section of Berossus' *Babyloniaca* has survived in an Armenian translation of the first volume of the *Chronicle* of Eusebius. In this, the following statement is made: "Cyrus at first treated him [Nabonidus] kindly, and, giving a residence to him in Carmania, sent him out of Babylonia. (But) Darius the king took away some of his province for himself" (cited from Anderson and Young, "The Remembrance of Daniel's Darius the Mede," 318). Anderson and Young point out that others have suggested an alternative translation, but even then the mention of Darius the king remains, and that at the time of Babylon's fall.

161. Josephus, *Ant.* 10.11.4 in W. Whiston, *The Works of Josephus: Complete and Unabridged*, 248.

162. A similar charge is made in regard to "Darius the Mede," who utters a beautiful prayer that reflects purely Jewish thought and devotion (Dan 6:27–28). Di Lella (52) remarks, "But the humility and piety, the monotheism and praiseworthy sentiments attributed to Nebuchadnezzar, a Babylonian polytheist, and to Darius the Mede, whose very existence cannot be proved, are the stuff not of history but of religious folklore and fiction."

Berossus preserved a tradition that Nebuchadnezzar became ill suddenly toward the end of his reign, which was mentioned by Josephus as well as by the 2nd cent. BC writer Abydenus."[163]

Some critical scholars suggest that the madness episode in Daniel is wrongly ascribed to Nebuchadnezzar (Nabonidus being the true victim) based on the discovery at Qumran of a document known as the "Prayer of Nabonidus." Anderson, for example, makes this attack:

> ... 'The Prayer of Nabonidus,' a story similar to that of Daniel 4 is told of Nabonidus, rather than Nebuchadnezzar. This seems to suggest an older tradition in which Nabonidus was regarded as the father of Belshazzar (see Dan. 5:2).[164]

Cross concurs: "The change of names, as well as the development of the elaborate details of Nebuchadnezzar's theriomania, is best attributed to the refracting tendencies of oral transmission, in this case the shift of a legend from a lesser to a greater name."[165]

The dissimilarity of the accounts, however, argues against such a view.[166] Certainly such a switch would have been exposed by those close to the author's own time.

7. The Term "Chaldean" Used in a Non-Ethnic Sense

The term "Chaldean" appears in Daniel in both an ethnic sense as well as a specialized sense (indicating a group of "wise men").[167] Since the latter case is not found elsewhere in the OT or in inscriptions, this supposedly points to a late date of composition. Critics allege that this term (Chaldean) for Nebuchadnezzar's ethnicity could not have become specialized to indicate a class of soothsayers until a much later time (i.e., it would only have carried an ethnic connotation in Nebuchadnezzar's day). Note, however, that the author was aware of the ethnic use of the term, for in Dan 5:30 Belshazzar is referred to as the king of the Chaldeans (cf. 3:8).

Archer points out that Herodotus (vol. 1, sec 181–183; fifth century BC) "refers to the Chaldeans in such a way as to imply that they were speedily

---

163. Harrison, "Daniel," 2:15. Abydenus was a Greek historian who wrote *History of the Chaldeans and Assyrians*.

164. Anderson, *Understanding the Old Testament*, 625, fn 16.

165. Cross, *Ancient Library of Qumran*, 167–68.

166. See the remarks of Harrison, "Daniel," 2:16.

167. According to Anson Rainey, "Chaldea, Chaldeans," in *Encyclopaedia Judaica* (Jerusalem: Keter, 1971), 5:330, the ethnic sense of "Chaldean" is first attested in extrabiblical literature during the reign of Ashurnasirpal II or III (883–859 BC), though Chaldeans are mentioned in the Bible as early as Gen 11:28, 31 (cf. Job 1:17). For a discussion of the possibility that Moses was aware of the ethnic sense of the Chaldeans in his day, see William D. Barrick, "'Ur of the Chaldeans'" (Gen 11:28–31): A Model For Dealing With Difficult Texts," *MSJ* 20 (2009): 7–18.

put into all the politically strategic offices of Babylonia as soon as they had gained control of the capital. If this was the case, then 'Chaldean' may have early come into use as a term for the priests of Bel-Marduk."[168]

Harrison adds,

> However, Herodotus (ca. 450 BC) in his *Persian Wars* consistently spoke of the Chaldeans in an ethnic manner, referred to them as priests, and accepted some of their traditions as going back to the early days of Cyrus. Furthermore, from the 10th cent. BC, Assyrian annals used the term *Kaldu* to describe the 'Sea-land' of earlier inscriptions and the people inhabiting that area. The latter were also mentioned in inscriptions from Ashurbanipal II (883–859 BC) and Adadnirari III (811–783 BC), as well as being referred to by Isaiah (23:13; 43:14). The usage of 'Chaldean' in Daniel thus conforms with normal Near Eastern practices in this respect.[169]

Archer provides a technical explanation for the evolution of the term Chaldean as a soothsayer priest. He understands these to be two homonyms, "one of which is the ethnic designation *kašdu* (as it was spelled in Babylonian cuneiform) and the other is a *kaš-du*, which resulted from a modification of an earlier *kal-du*."[170]

8. The Brevity of Reference to the Persian Rulers in Dan 11:2

Only a brief reference is made to the Persian rulers in Dan 11:2 (in contrast to the Seleucid rulers), which supposedly suggests that the author was not familiar with the Persian period and hence wrote long afterwards.

Anderson charges that it is precisely because the author was writing from the Maccabean period that Dan 11:2 is sketched in only one verse: "The author's backward glance from the Maccabean period also explains why historical knowledge about the period before the rise of Alexander is blurred, and why historical information becomes more exact and detailed as one comes closer to the time of writing."[171] Anderson also claims that the text makes a historical blunder in that " ... ten Persian kings (not three) succeeded Cyrus."[172]

Such criticisms are insubstantial if one considers them from the standpoint of the author's purpose. He is brief in his reference to the Persian period not because he is unfamiliar with Persian history but because the main purpose of the chapter is to focus on Antiochus IV Epiphanes (11:21–35), who serves as a type of the antichrist (11:36–45). It is not his purpose to give a full

168. Archer, *A Survey*, 382.
169. Harrison, "Daniel" 1:864.
170. Archer, "Daniel," 7:14.
171. Anderson, *Understanding the Old Testament*, 629.
172. Ibid.

account of the Persian period but to move quickly to the Hellenistic period, for it is that period which gave rise to Antiochus. The fact that of forty-five verses in the chapter, over half of them deal precisely with Antiochus and the antichrist (of whom Antiochus is a *type*), argues for this view.

Furthermore, the text does not say there were only three Persian kings who succeeded Darius the Mede. It only points out the fourth (probably Xerxes I in 480 BC), because of his significance regarding the hostility between Persia and Greece, furthering their clash. Notice that the text (Dan 11:2) calls attention to this: "he will arouse the whole *empire* against the realm of Greece." Xerxes I (r. 486–465 BC), the fourth Persian king, was famous for his assault upon Greece.[173] This set the stage for the attack by Alexander the Great upon Persia, which in turn set the stage for the Seleucid dynasty and the coming of Antiochus IV. The point was never to list all Persian kings between Daniel's day and the coming of Alexander the Great.

9. Dan 2:1 and the Placement of Nebuchadnezzar's Dream in the "Second Year"

At first glance this verse appears to clash with chap. 1 (see vv. 5, 18–19), as Daniel did not enter the king's service as a "wise man" for three years.[174]

The first year of Nebuchadnezzar's reign was considered his "accession year," lasting from September 605 BC (when he ascended the throne) until Nisan (March/April) of 604 BC. Then the year after that would be regarded as his first official or "regnal year," counting from Nisan of 604 until Nisan of 603 BC, according to Babylonian practice. (Although the practice of the Judean kings was to count Tishri to Tishri, the Babylonians counted their regnal years from Nisan to Nisan.) The "second year" then is probably a reference to a time late in his *second regnal year*, which would technically be sometime in his third actual year of rule. Knowing that a part of a year could also be counted as a "year," this would allow for the training program to have been completed by this point. Hence, although the text indicates the dream took place in the second year of Nebuchadnezzar's reign, this was probably *after* the "three-year" training program that Daniel went through.

---

173. R. E. Hayden, "Xerxes," in *ISBE*, 4:1161, describes the assault of Xerxes I upon Greece: "Xerxes' preparations included digging a canal near Athos and having a bridge built over the Hellespont by Phoenician and Egyptian engineers. ... After being delayed by the Greeks at Thermopylae, the Persians pushed on to Athens and burned the city. Later that year the Persian fleet suffered a disastrous defeat at Salamis ... Xerxes withdrew from Greece, leaving the army in the hands of his general Mardonius. In 479 the Greeks defeated the Persian army at Plataea and, on the same day, the Persian fleet at Mycale."

174. See Di Lella (48) for this charge. He assumes the date of 606 BC for Dan 1:1, though 605 is the more commonly accepted date.

10. Dan 9:1 and the Reference to Darius the Mede as a "Son of Ahasuerus"

The problem raised here is the identification of "Ahasuerus" as the father of Darius the Mede. Not only is there uncertainty about the identity of Darius the Mede, but his having a father named Ahasuerus is also questioned. There is a king known as Ahasuerus in the Bible (see Esther), but he is universally regarded as Xerxes I (r. 486–465 BC), who would certainly not have been the father of a ruler in Daniel's day. Critics are quick to charge that the author of Daniel has blundered in assigning "Ahasuerus = Xerxes I" as the father of Darius the Mede, seeing that Xerxes I came later than "Darius the Mede."

Critics, however, must admit that it is only their assumption that the reference to Ahasuerus is the Persian king Xerxes I. In actuality, it is possible that there is another historical figure with the name Ahasuerus (or a throne name as such) who could have been the father of Darius the Mede. If so, he would have been one of the Medes.

The Median rulers in proximity to Daniel were Cyaxares and Astyages, as Merrill explains:

> The Median throne remained vacant from 653 to 625 because of Scythian domination of northwest Iran, but in time Cyaxares (625–585) overthrew the Scythians and the Assyrians, establishing Median control over all of northern Mesopotamia and Iran. He also reduced Persia to submission, setting up Cambyses as governor over that province. Cyaxares was succeeded by his son Astyages (585–550), whose daughter would be the mother of the great Cyrus II.[175]

Some have theorized that the Ahasuerus mentioned in Dan 9:1 might have been the Median king Cyaxares (r. 625–585 BC).[176] Yet Josephus preserves a tradition that Ahasuerus was another name for the Median king Astyages (the father of Cyaxares II according to Xenophon).[177] However, there is no conclusive evidence at this time for either of these suggestions, and it is best to remain open-minded for the time being.

Even though we have no definitive evidence for this "Darius the Mede" or of "Ahasuerus," we should be cautious to conclude they did not exist (or that the author has confused them). (See the earlier discussion under point #5 regarding "Darius the Mede" as a throne name for Cyaxares II.) Belshazzar and Sargon (Isa 20:1) were once thought to be fabrications, but archaeology has since turned up inscriptions proving their existence. Critical scholars

---

175. Merrill, *Kingdom of Priests*, 491.

176. Mentioned (but not necessarily affirmed) in K. L. Barker, "Ahasuerus," in *ZPEB*, 1:82.

177. In the account of the first-century historian Josephus we are told that "Babylon was taken by Darius, and when he, with his kinsman Cyrus, had put an end to the dominion of the Babylonians, he was sixty-two years old. He was the son of Astyages, and had another name among the Greeks" (Josephus, *Ant.*, 10.10.4).

once assumed Daniel's mention of Belshazzar to be completely unhistorical on the basis of what was known from extrabiblical historical sources. Archer notes, "After the discovery of oath tablets in Neo-Babylonian cuneiform dating from the twelfth year of Nabonidus (543 BC) and associating Belshazzar, his son, with him on an equal footing ... , it became startlingly apparent that the writer of Daniel was much more accurately informed about the history of the 540s in Babylonia than Herodotus was in 450 B.C."[178]

11. The Question of the Title "Kng of Kings" in Dan 2:37 Being Anachronistic

Driver (28) claimed that the use of this title was anachronistic since it was characteristic of Persian kings who came after Nebuchadnezzar's time. However, this title is equivalent to the Akkadian title *sar sarrani*, which is used as early as the reign of Tukulti-Ninurta I (1244–1208 BC).

12. Dan 1:2 and the Question of Jehoiakim's Removal to Babylon

Anderson has pointed out that in Dan 1:2, it was not Jehoiakim who was borne away to captivity but rather his son Jehoiachin several years later (cf. 2 Kgs 24).[179]

Indeed, Jehoiakim was not taken into captivity in 605 BC. If one reads the text closely, however, Dan 1:2 does not say that Jehoiakim was borne away to captivity. The text states, "The Lord gave Jehoiakim king of Judah into his hand, along with some of the vessels of the house of God; and he brought *them* to the land of Shinar, to the house of his god, and he brought the vessels into the treasury of his god" (NASB emphasis added). Anderson has assumed that the word "them" refers to the king and other nobles. However, the following phrase ("to the house of his god") is pointing out the temple at Babylon (probably the temple to Marduk) to which the "them" are taken. This would refer, then, to the vessels from the Jewish temple, which were removed to Babylon and brought to the Babylonian temple. The reference is not to the king at all.

Linguistic Objections to the Traditional Date and Authorship

1. Persian Words

There are some twenty-three words of probable Persian origin in the court narratives of the Aramaic section of the book.[180] This is not surprising if Daniel was written around 536 BC when the Persian Empire had replaced the Babylonian Empire. As discussed earlier ("Presence of Foreign Loanwords"), K. A. Kitchen and B. J. Noonan have pointed out that the failure of the Greek translators to adequately render these terms (writing at a time and location when such terms would not have been familiar to them) argues

178. Archer, "Daniel," 7:16.

179. Anderson, *Understanding the Old Testament*, 622.

180. For a list of Persian words in the book of Daniel, see the earlier section of the "Introduction" under "Presence of Foreign Loanwords." Cf. Archer ("Daniel," 7:21, including fn 3).

for a dating of the book prior to 300 BC. Even if someone argues that the Aramaic chapters were written early and the other chapters later (multiple authorship and editing), the word אַפַּדְנוֹ (*appadnô* from Persian *apadâna*) occurs in Dan 11:45.

2. Greek Words

A number of musical instruments mentioned in the book of Daniel are from Greek words. Critical scholars sometimes point to this as indicative of an origin in the Hellenistic period, long after the time of Daniel (see Dan 3:5, 7, 10, 15). Hartman and Di Lella (13) represent this position, saying "the Greek names for the musical instruments in 3:5 probably do not antedate the reign of Alexander the Great (336–323 B.C.)." P. W. Coxon was even bolder when he said, "the Greek loans seem to provide the strongest evidence in favour of the second century B.C."[181] How, then, could such words have been part of the vocabulary of a person writing in sixth-century BC Babylon? E. Yamauchi has conclusively shown that musical instruments known by these terms not only existed, but that there is abundant evidence of cross-cultural contact between the Aegean and the Near Eastern worlds well before Alexander the Great that would have facilitated the spread of such cultural items.[182] Yamauchi's work has been confirmed more recently by I. Young.[183] In addition, Walvoord has pointed out, "It has now been proved that one hundred years before Daniel, Greek mercenaries served in the Assyrian armies under the command of Esarhaddon (683 BC) as well as in the Babylonian army of Nebuchadnezzar."[184] Certainly the infusion of Greek musical instruments and cultural terms into the Ancient Near East was possible well before the time of Alexander the Great.

---

181. P. W. Coxon, "Greek Loan-Words and Alleged Greek Loan Translations in the Book of Daniel," TGUOS 25 (1973–74): 24-40.

182. E. M. Yamauchi, *Greece and Babylon: Early Contacts Between the Aegean and the Near East* (Grand Rapids: Baker, 1967), and subsequently in an updated work, "Greece and Babylon Revisited," in *To Understand the Scriptures: Essays in Honor of William H. Shea*, ed. D. Merling (Berrien Springs, MI: Institute of Archaeology/ Siegfried H. Horn Archaeological Museum, 1997), 127–35. Yamauchi's 1967 work shows pictures of cylinder seals with musical instruments inscribed.

183. I. Young, "The Greek Loanwords in the Book of Daniel," in *Biblical Greek in Context: Essays in Honour of John A. L. Lee*, ed. J. K. Aitken and T. V. Evans (Leuven-Paris-Bristol: Peeters, 2015), 247–68.

184. Walvoord, 23. Cf. E. M. Yamauchi, "Daniel and Contacts Between the Aegean and the Near East Before Alexander," *EvQ* 53 (1981): 38–40; also C. Engel, *The Music of the Most Ancient Nations Particularly of the Assyrians, Egyptians, and Hebrews*, 2nd ed. (1870; repr., Charleston, SC: Nabu Press, 2014), 303, for evidence of Assyrian bas-reliefs picturing captives being led away into captivity carrying musical instruments.

Here are a few of the Greek terms used for musical instruments (see Dan 3:5):

- lyre, zither = קִיתְרוֹס (*qîṯrôs*) [Gk. κίθαρις, *kitharis*]

  "The first of these can be identified without difficulty with one of the numerous Near Eastern precursors of the Greek *kithára*, such as the elaborate harp uncovered by Sir Leonard Woolley at Ur."[185] Commenting on the antiquity of the word, Yamauchi notes, "It is found in Homer's *Odyssey* (eighth cent. B.C.) and in Herodotus (fifth cent. B.C.)."[186]

- trigon = סַבְּכָא (*sabbᵊḵāʾ*) [Gk. σαμβύκη, *sambukē*]

  "The sakbut was another variety of chordophone similar to or derived from the *sabitu* or seven-stringed lyre of the Akkadians."[187]

- psaltery (stringed instrument) = פְּסַנְתֵּרִין (*pᵊsantērîn*) [Gk. ψαλτηριον, *psaltērion*]

  "The 'psaltery' was the Persian-Arabic *santir*, an early variety of dulcimer represented on first-millennium B.C. Assyrian reliefs and elsewhere."[188]

- tambour = סוּמְפֹּנְיָה (*sûmpōnyâ*) [Gk. συμφωνία, *sumphōnia*; or τύμπανον, *tumpanon*]

  The correct identification of this term is the most disputed of the group. According to Harrison, "The term *sûmpōnyāʾ*, formerly rendered 'dulcimer' (RSV 'bagpipe'; NEB 'music') apparently is not an instrument at all, but a musical notation having the meaning of 'in ensemble' or its general equivalent."[189]

Archer points out that this term "does not occur in extant Greek literature until the time of Plato (ca. 370 BC), at least in the sense of a musical instrument."[190] However, since we only have one-tenth of the significant Greek literature of the classical period, we lack sufficient data for timing the precise origin of any particular word or usage in the development of the Greek vocabulary. On the other hand, the term may be neither a bagpipe nor "musical notation," but another type of instrument (perhaps a "tambour"). Dyer has argued at length that the term refers to an instrument like a drum:

185. Harrison, "Daniel," 1:864.
186. Yamauchi, *Greece and Babylon*, 18.
187. Ibid.
188. Ibid.
189. Ibid.
190. Archer, *A Survey*, 387.

A final proposal is to identify סוּמְפֹּנְיָה as a musical instrument but to reject its association with the Greek word συμφωνία. Instead, according to this view, it should be identified with the Greek word τύμπανον, to be translated "drum."[191]

In any case, the matter of musical instruments with Greek names is certainly not a proof of late dating for Daniel. Harrison writes,

> Despite the fact that the instruments superficially appear to have Greek names, they are all in fact of specific Mesopotamian origin ... What is evident, however, is that the Near Eastern peoples had enjoyed a prolonged tradition of music and singing for many centuries before the Greeks began to influence life in that area from the 7th cent. B.C. onward, and that the various genuine musical instruments in Daniel had already claimed familiar precursors long before that period.[192]

Archer adds,

> ... the inscriptions of Sargon II (722–705) back in the Assyrian period refer to Greek captives from Cyprus and Ionia sold into slavery ... . It is therefore evident that Greek mercenaries and slaves served in the Babylonian and Assyrian periods, some of whom were undoubtedly versed in Greek music and musical instruments.[193]

More recently, B. J. Noonan has built a strong case that the Greek loanwords in Daniel, rather than suggesting a late date of composition, actually argue for an early date. Had the material been written in the latter Hellenistic period (when Attic Greek was in vogue), we would have expected the author to have spelled the words in accordance with phonological characteristics of Attic Greek. Yet he does not.[194] Noonan explains the significance of this observation:

---

191. C. H. Dyer, "The Musical Instruments in Daniel 3," *BSac* 147 (1990): 434.

192. Harrison, "Daniel," 1:864. Cf. J. C. Waldbaum, "Early Greek Contacts with the Southern Levant, ca. 1000–600 B.C.: The Eastern Perspective," *BASOR* 293 (1994): 67–78; and W.-D. Niemeier, "Archaic Greeks in the Orient: Textual and Archaeological Evidence," *BASOR* 322 (2001): 11–32.

193. Archer, "Daniel," 7:21. Pentecost (1325) adds, "However, archaeology has revealed that commerce existed between Greece and Babylon even *before* Daniel's day. This would explain the presence of Greek words. And the Persian words in the book were from an official or literary form of the Persian language which was in wide use throughout the Near East. (Wiseman et al., *Notes of Some Problems in the Book of Daniel*, 23–27, 35–50)."

194. B. J. Noonan, "Presence and Significance," 9–10 presents at least three examples: (1) "The vocalization of biblical Aramaic כָּרוֹז indicates that it is a loan from Aeolic or Doric Greek κᾶρυξ rather than Attic-Ionic κῆρυξ. Original ᾱ (cf. Linear B *ka-ru-ke*)

> In sum, at least three of the Greek loanwords in the book of Daniel exhibit phonological characteristics that set them apart as non-Attic. This is strong evidence for a date of borrowing before Alexander the Great because Aramaic speakers should have borrowed the Attic forms if they had adopted them during the Hellenistic period. Hence, the evidence indicates that the book of Daniel's Greek loanwords were borrowed earlier rather than later, and the burden of proof remains on those who argue that they are insignificant for dating purposes or must have been borrowed late.[195]

In addition to the Greek musical terms, there is another Aramaic word in the text mistakenly attributed to Greek: "satrap" (pl. אֲחַשְׁדַּרְפְּנַיָּא, *ʾăḥašdarpᵊnayyāʾ*). Harrison clarifies, "Thus the term 'satrap,' once thought to be Gr., is now known to have been derived from the old Pers. *Kshathrapan*, which also occurred in the cuneiform texts as *satarpanu*, from which the Gr. form emerged."[196]

Theological Objections to the Traditional Date and Authorship

1. Advanced Theology

Sometimes critics charge that Daniel's theology is too advanced for the sixth-century BC period. Supposedly, the frequent references to angels, the reference to the resurrection of the dead, the last judgment, and the Messiah necessitate a late postexilic date for the book.

This is a weak argument, for angels are attested elsewhere in the Old Testament and throughout Israel's history. Although critics acknowledge this, they insist that it occurs in a much more developed form in Daniel than in books such as Ezekiel or Zechariah (is this proof?). Resurrection is attested to in Ps 16:10 and Isa 26:19, both of which certainly predate Daniel.

2. The lack of use of the term "Lord" (יְהוָה, Yahweh)

Critics argue that this term was commonly used in biblical literature of the sixth century BC, and therefore its absence in the book of Daniel suggests a later date. Use, however, is determined by the author's content of material and purposes in writing. Furthermore, the term יְהוָה (Yahweh), though rare in Daniel, is found in Dan 9:2, 4, 8, 10, 13–14, 20.

---

is preserved in all Greek dialects with the exception of Attic-Ionic, in which it becomes *η*"; (2) "Biblical Aramaic פְּסַנְטֵרִין/פְּסָנְתֵּרִין uses נ rather than ל, indicating a borrowing from an unattested Arcadian or Doric **ψαντήριον* rather than Attic *ψαλτήριον*. In Arcadian and Doric, the consonant cluster *λτ* becomes *ντ*"; and, (3) "Biblical Aramaic קִיתָרֹס represents a final –ς rather than a vowel and clearly comes from Ionic or Aeolic *κιθάρις* rather than Attic *κιθάρα*."

195. Ibid., 13.

196. Harrison, "Daniel," 2:18.

Literary Objections to the Traditional Date and Authorship

1. Daniel as Apocalyptic Literature

Critical scholars often claim that Daniel belongs to a distinctive literary type known as "apocalyptic literature," which appeared prolifically in Israel during the Maccabean era.[197] Hence, for them, a date of 168–134 BC would seem more plausible.[198] Collins (33) refers to the book as "historical apocalypse" and claims that it is "characterized by *ex eventu* [meaning 'after the fact'] prophecy of history and by eschatology that is cosmic in scope and has a political focus."[199]

That portions of the book of Daniel might be classified as "apocalyptic literature," however, does not automatically lead to the conclusion that it must be dated to the Maccabean era of the second century BC. One could argue, for instance, that Ezekiel also has apocalyptic elements, but scholars do not date this book as late as the Maccabean era.[200] Furthermore, some critics trap themselves in their own arguments, as Anderson appears to do:

> We have seen that prophets tried to account for the sufferings of the present age in the context of a covenant with Yahweh and had called Israel to repent. But apocalyptic writers knew that the sufferings of Israel—or other peoples—cannot be explained on the basis of sin—that is, a failure in human responsibility.[201]

Anderson is attempting to link Daniel with "apocalyptic writers" in contrast with the "prophets" on the issue of sin and repentance, and yet Daniel in chap. 9 is acknowledging the nation's sin and need for repentance (the very fact that Anderson claims apocalyptic writers do not do).

---

197. J. J. Collins, *Apocalypse, Prophecy, and Pseudepigraphy* (Grand Rapids: Eerdmans, 2015), 57, argues that there are "significant differences between the apocalypses of the Hellenistic and early Roman periods and the canonical prophetic writings" and that Daniel is representative of the former. In his opinion, "Resurrection is atypical to postexilic prophecy, whereas it is central to the latter apocalypses" (61). Hence, Collins argues that the element of *resurrection* found in Dan 12:2 is indicative of its place in later apocalyptic literature. For a helpful introduction to apocalyptic literature from an evangelical perspective, see R. A. Taylor, *Interpreting Apocalyptic Literature*, Handbooks for Old Testament Exegesis (Grand Rapids: Kregel Academic, 2016). He discusses six features of Jewish apocalyptic texts (65), seven common themes (73), and provides a helpful annotated bibliography regarding key works on apocalyptic literature (108–16).

198. Di Lella (62–71) spends an entire chapter discussing Daniel's resemblance to apocalyptic literature.

199. Cf. J. J. Collins, *The Apocalyptic Imagination: An Introduction to Jewish Apocalyptic Literature*, 2nd ed. (Grand Rapids: Eerdmans, 1998).

200. Lawrence Boadt, "Ezekiel," in *AYBD*, 2:714, concludes that the book of Ezekiel was written during "the decade or so after 585."

201. Anderson, *Understanding the Old Testament*, 621.

2. *The Absence of Daniel's Name in Ben Sira's Work*

Ben Sira wrote his book (known as *Ecclesiasticus* or *Sirach* or *The Wisdom of Ben Sira*) in Hebrew about 190–180 BC with a long section (see Sir 44–49) devoted to the "Praise of the Fathers."[202] Since the name of Daniel is missing (in contrast to other major prophets who are listed), some claim that the book of Daniel had not yet been written at the time Ben Sira wrote. This would suggest (supposedly) a date of writing for the book of Daniel after 180 BC.

However, other "notables" such as Job, Ezra, and Mordecai are also not listed in the same section. The author's agenda in writing was to recount a number of the famed champions in the history of the nation, but he was selective (not exhaustive) in doing so. His purpose was not to list all the books of the canon and their authors. That Daniel was not highlighted does not prove the book did not exist at that time. Furthermore, since Daniel was in the third division of the Hebrew canon (in contrast to the other prophets), it is not surprising that his name was not present in Ben Sira's work. In fact, most of the books belonging to the third division of the Hebrew Bible (the Writings) are not mentioned (though Nehemiah is). The fact that Daniel is mentioned several times in the book of Ezekiel (14:14, 20; 28:3)—a book that even critical scholars acknowledge as having been written in the sixth century BC—is also a weighty objection to the argument based on Ben Sira's work. (See under "A Defense of the Traditional Date" for discussion of the passages from Ezekiel.) Other studies have shown that the work of Ben Sira must have been written subsequent to that of the book of Daniel.[203]

A Defense of the Traditional Date and Authorship of Daniel

Having considered and responded to a number of the objections to the traditional date and authorship of the book of Daniel, several positive arguments supporting the traditional view will now be considered.

1. The Testimony of Christ—Matt 24:15

In Dan 12:11 reference is made to an "abomination of desolation" that would be carried out in the latter days. The Lord Jesus in his Olivet Discourse made the comment, "Therefore when you see the ABOMINATION OF DESOLATION which was spoken of through Daniel the prophet, standing in the holy place (let the reader understand), then those who are in Judea must flee" (Matt

202. For discussion of the date of writing for Ben Sira, see A. A. Di Lella, "Wisdom of Ben Sira," in *ABD*, 6:932. The earliest known manuscripts of Ben Sira are those found at Qumran. P. C. Beentjes, *The Book of Ben Sira in Hebrew*, VTSup 68 (Atlanta: SBL, 2006), 6, notes, "Fragments of the Book of Ben Sira recovered from Qumran have been dated either in the second half of the 1st Century BCE (2Q18) or in the first half of the 1st Century CE (11QPs[a])."

203. For discussion, see Fox, "Ben Sira on OT Canon Again."

24:15–16, NASB). Jesus did not say "which was spoken of in the book of Daniel" but rather "which was spoken of through Daniel the prophet." This reflects his opinion that (1) Daniel the prophet authored these words from the final chapter of the book, and (2) this final section of Daniel was not fulfilled in the second century BC person of Antiochus IV.

2. Evidence from Qumran Discoveries

a. Qumran Fragments of Daniel

Portions of Daniel have surfaced among the documents from Qumran, i.e., the Dead Sea Scrolls, which would strongly suggest a date well before the Maccabean era. Harrison states,

> Fragments from 1Q, along with some complete scrolls of Daniel from other caves, have testified to the popularity of the work at Qumrân. A florilegium recovered from 4Q spoke, like Mt. 24:15, of 'Daniel the prophet,' furnishing eloquent second-century BC testimony to the way in which the book was revered and cited as Scripture. Since all the Qumrân fragments and scrolls are copies, the autograph of Daniel and other OT canonical works must of necessity be advanced well before the Maccabean period if the proper minimum of time is allowed for the book to be circulated and accepted as Scripture.[204]

Admittedly, not all would agree with Harrison's dating of Florilegium (4Q174), although his point remains concerning documents found at Qumran.[205] For instance, the oldest Daniel fragment found at Qumran (4QDan[c]) has been dated about 125 BC.[206] To insist on a late date for the book of Daniel around 165–164 BC means that the book must have been quickly read and approved by the Jewish scribes and priests, copies were then made, and then these copies found their way to the Qumran community where they were recopied, all by no later than 125 BC. Such a hypothesis is difficult to believe.

---

204. Harrison, "Daniel," in 1:861. He adds, "When 1Q was excavated, two of the three fragments of Daniel recovered from the site proved to be related paleographically to the large Isaiah MS (1QIsa[a]). Since the book of Isaiah comes from a time several centuries prior to the earliest date to which 1QIsa[a] can be assigned on any grounds, it follows that the autograph of Daniel also must be several centuries in advance of the Maccabean period."

205. J. Milgrom, "Florilegium: A Midrash on 2 Samuel and Psalms 1–2," in *The Dead Sea Scrolls: Hebrew, Aramaic, and Greek Texts with English Translations*, ed. J. H. Charlesworth, 248–63 (Tübingen: Mohr Siebeck, 2002), 248, dates the Florilegium much later: "Paleographically, the manuscript of 4Q174 is dated early in the first century C.E."

206. VanderKam and Flint, *The Meaning of the Dead Sea Scrolls*, 137.

b. An Early 1 Enoch Document Referring to Daniel

The consensus of scholarship is that *1 Enoch* is a composite work, originally written in Aramaic (or possibly part in Aramaic and part in Hebrew).[207] Chapters 1–36, the Book of the Watchers, is considered one of the oldest portions. Regarding the date of these chapters, Charlesworth has summarized the conclusions of scholars participating in the Enoch Seminar:

> ... the members of the Enoch Seminar agreed on the probable date of the earliest composition among the books of Enoch. The consensus is now that the Book of the Watchers was composed by the early Hellenistic period. ... Thus, the writings now called the books of Enoch originated before 200 B.C.E., and conceivably as early as the end of the fourth century B.C.E.[208]

Significantly, *1 En.* 14:18–22 clearly refers to Dan 7:9–10. The question, however, is which came first? Was Daniel dependent on *1 Enoch*, or was *1 En*och dependent on Daniel? Beckwith uses this to argue that *1 Enoch* was referencing Dan 7, and therefore Daniel must pre-date *1 Enoch*.[209] If he is correct, then (1) Daniel cannot have been written during the Maccabean period (about 165 BC) as critical scholars have suggested; and (2) the book of Daniel must contain predictive prophecy. Yet the matter is disputed. Rowland has argued that Daniel came later and drew upon *1 Enoch*.[210] Henze, on the other hand, contends that both Daniel and *1 Enoch* drew upon a common source.[211]

The following is the passage in question from *1 Enoch* (with parallel words and phrases in bold):[212]

---

207. E. Isaac, "1 (Ethiopic Apocalypse of) Enoch: A New Translation and Introduction," in *The Old Testament Pseudepigrapha*, vol. 1, Apocalyptic Literature and Testaments, ed. J. H. Charlesworth, 5–108 (Garden City, NY: Doubleday, 1983), 6.

208. J. H. Charlesworth, "Summary and Conclusions: The Books of Enoch or 1 Enoch Matters: New Paradigms for Understanding Pre-70 Judaism," in *Enoch and Qumran Origins*, ed. G. Boccaccini, 436–54 (Grand Rapids: Eerdmans, 2005)," 436. Some scholars would even date the Book of the Watchers to the fourth or third centuries BC; cf. G. Boccaccini, *The Origins of Enochic Judaism* (Turin: Zamorani, 2002).

209. R. Beckwith, "Early Traces of the Book of Daniel," *TynBul* 53 (2002): 77–79.

210. C. Rowland, "Dating the Apocalypses," in *The Open Heaven: A Study of Apocalyptic in Early Judaism and Christianity*, 248–67 (1982; repr., Eugene, OR: Wipf & Stock., 2002), 258. H. S. Kvanvig, "Throne Visions and Monsters: The Encounter Between Danielic and Enochic Traditions," *ZAW* 117 (2005): 255–58, drew the same conclusion.

211. M. Henze, "Enoch's Dream Visions and the Visions of Daniel Reexamined," in *Enoch and Qumran Origins: New Light on a Forgotten Connection*, ed. G. Boccaccini, 17–22 (Grand Rapids: Eerdmans, 2005), 19.

212. Translation by E. Isaac, in Charlesworth, *The Old Testament Pseudepigrapha*, 21. Among the finds from Qumran is Aramaic fragment 4Q204 (4QEn^c) containing portions of the Book of the Watchers. Unfortunately col. VI stops with *1 Enoch* 14:16.

> And I observed and saw inside it a **lofty throne**—its appearance was like crystal and its **wheels** like the shining sun; and (I heard?) the voice of the cherubim; and from beneath the throne were issuing streams of **flaming fire**. It was difficult to look at it. And the Great Glory was sitting upon it—as for **his gown**, which was shining more brightly than the sun, it was **whiter than any snow**. None of the angels was able to come in and see the face of the Excellent and the Glorious One; and no one of the flesh can see him—the **flaming fire was round about him, and a great fire stood before him**. No one could come near unto him from among those that surrounded **the tens of millions** [Gk: μυρίαι μυριάδες] (that stood) before him.[213]

Dan 7:9–10:

> I continued observing until **thrones** were set up, and the Ancient of Days took his seat. **His garment** was like **white snow**, and the hair of his head was like pure wool. His throne *appeared as* **flames of fire**, *with* its **wheels** as burning fire. [10]**A river of fire was streaming and going forth from him**. Many thousands were ministering to him, and many **tens of thousands** [LXX$^{\theta}$ μύριαι μυριάδες] were standing before him.

That *1 Enoch* drew from Daniel is favored by the fact that these verses (*1 En.* 14:18–22) do not merely have casual similarities to Dan 7 but are a *conflation* of Ezekiel's vision of God's throne (Ezek 1) and Dan 7:9–10. If the author of *1 En.* 14:18–22 drew upon the vision of Ezek 1 (note throne, wheels, expanse like crystal, cherubim), then most likely he was also drawing upon Dan 7:9–10 as source material. (There is no evidence that the author of Daniel and the author of *1 Enoch* both drew from a third source.) Hence, recognizing *1 En.* 14:18–22 as an *intentional conflated reading* supports that the author of *1 Enoch* is drawing upon existing sources (a point that Rowland failed to consider sufficiently), therefore indicating that Daniel is the older of the two. Given the dates currently assigned to *1 Enoch*, this suggests that Daniel is pre-Maccabean and even much earlier than the second century BC.

3. Evidence of Persian Loanwords from the Sixth Century BC

Harrison further points out, " ... all the Persian loanwords in Daniel are specifically Old Persian (which is found on inscriptions from the 6th and

---

213. R. H. Charles, *The Book of Enoch* (London: SPCK, 1917), 42, translated the numbered multitude in the last verse, "ten thousand times ten thousand (stood) before him" (contrast Isaac's "tens of millions"). In the Greek translations this is the same expression.

5th cents. BC), indicating that the Aramaic of Daniel in this area is certainly pre-Hellenistic rather than Maccabean."[214]

4. Acceptance into the Jewish Canon

If Daniel had indeed been a second-century BC work by an author attempting to disguise the book as written in the sixth century BC, it is extremely unlikely that the Jews would have allowed this to slip by unnoticed into the Hebrew canon. Certainly they would have given it the utmost scrutiny before accepting it as the word of God.

5. Comparison with Literary Material of the First and Second Centuries BC

a. Ecclesiasticus (ca. 200–180 BC)

This writing would furnish us with a fair sample of the type of Hebrew current at the time Daniel was written according to the late-date theorists. Nevertheless, Ecclesiasticus exhibits later linguistic characteristics than Daniel, being somewhat rabbinical in tendency. Archer writes, "Israel Lévi in his Introduction to the Hebrew text of Ecclesiasticus (1904) lists the following: (a) new verbal forms borrowed mainly from Aramaic, (b) excessive use of the *hiphil* and *hithpael* conjugations, and (c) peculiarities of various sorts heralding the approach of Mishnaic Hebrew."[215]

b. The Hebrew Documents from Qumran (1st century BC)

Archer, in his comparative study of the book of Daniel with certain other documents from Qumran, concluded, "'The Manual of Discipline' (1QS), 'The War of the Children of Light Against the Children of Darkness' (1QM), and 'The Thanksgiving Psalms' do not show any distinctive characteristics in common with the Hebrew chapters of Daniel."[216] He cites a number of examples of later Hebrew morphology, syntax, and vocabulary appearing in 1QS and 1QM as contrasted with Daniel.[217]

---

214. Harrison, "Daniel" 1:865.

215. Archer, *A Survey*, 391.

216. Archer, "The Hebrew of Daniel," 470–81.

217. Archer ("Daniel," 23–24, fn 6) elaborates, "Morphological examples are, first of all, an Aramaic-type third singular masculine suffix after a plural noun, such as *yômôy* instead of the regular *yāmāyw* ('his days') used by Daniel. Similarly, the Aramaic-type *'alēhôn* ('upon them') in 1QS 3:25 instead of the earlier *'alēhem* is invariably used in Daniel. As for the masculine plural nouns, at least twenty-five times the Aramaic *în* is used in place of the Hebrew *îm* in the eleven columns of 1QS. Daniel has only one such example—*hayyāmîn* ('the days'), in 12:13. Already the later first plural pronoun *'ānû* is beginning to show up in sectarian Hebrew (1QS 1:25 and 1QM 3:6), but never in Daniel or, indeed, in the rest of the OT (except for a Kethiv reading in Jer 42:6)." Archer continues the discussion, providing further examples with verbal forms.

c. *The Genesis Apocryphon (1QapGen) and the Job Targum (11QtgJob)*

These Aramaic documents (third- to first-century BC) show considerable variance from the Aramaic chapters of Daniel. According to its editors (N. Avigad and Y. Yadin), the Apocryphon was probably composed in the third century BC.[218] Archer notes, "linguistic analysis indicates that in morphology, vocabulary, and syntax, the Apocryphon shows a considerably later stage of the Aramaic language than do the Aramaic chapters of Daniel."[219] Additional studies of biblical Aramaic syntax have shown that the Aramaic of Daniel bears the mark of Official Aramaic and is earlier than the second century BC.[220] In a more recent study, Machiela (who acknowledges the Aramaic of Daniel as earlier than that of the Apocryphon) has come to a similar conclusion:

> Together, the above points make clear that a relative date of the Genesis Apocryphon's Aramaic to the 1st cent. BCE on linguistic grounds break down significantly under scrutiny. ... the most compelling support for a significantly earlier date comes from other Aramaic texts found at Qumran. A number of these date to the 2nd cent. BCE based on paleography and radiocarbon

---

218. N. Yadin and Y. Avigad, *A Genesis Apocryphon: A Scroll from the Wilderness of Judaea* (Jerusalem: Magnes, 1956).

219. Archer, "Daniel," 7:23. Cf. Archer, "The Aramaic of the Genesis Apocryphon." Archer's work built on that of earlier scholars who had reached the same conclusion. See P. Winter, "Das aramäische Genesis-Apokryphon," *TLZ* 4 (1957): 258–62; and E. Y. Kutscher, "The Language of the 'Genesis Apocryphon,'" in *Aspects of the Dead Sea Scrolls,* Scr. Hier. 4, 2nd ed. (Jerusalem: Magnes Press, 1965), 1–35. These studies were in contrast to the work of H. H. Rowley, "Notes on the Aramaic of the Genesis Apocryphon," in *Hebrew and Semitic Studies Presented to Godfrey Rolles Driver*, ed. D. W. Thomas and W. D. McHardy, 116–29 (Oxford: Clarendon, 1963), 129, who concluded that, "[o]n linguistic grounds there is nothing to preclude a date in the second century BC, since there is nothing that would require any long interval between the date of the Aramaic of Daniel and the language of the Genesis Apocryphon." Yet Rowley's conclusions were tainted by his earlier studies in which he had argued for a relatively late second-century BC date for the Aramaic of Daniel. Cf. H. H. Rowley, *The Aramaic of the Old Testament* (Oxford: Oxford University Press, 1929).

220. P. W. Coxon, "The Syntax of the Aramaic of Daniel: A Dialectical Study," *HUCA* 48 (1977): 107–22, and idem, "The Distribution of Synonyms in Biblical Aramaic in the Light of Official Aramaic and the Aramaic of Qumran," *RevQ* 9 (1978): 497–512. For a summary of Coxon's conclusions, see G. Hasel, "The Book of Daniel and Matters of Language: Evidences Relating to Names, Words, and the Aramaic Language," *AUSS* 19 (1981): 223–24. Cf. K. Kitchen, "The Aramaic of Daniel." For a more recent study of the verbal system in the Aramaic of Daniel, see T. Li, *The Verbal System of the Aramaic of Daniel: An Explanation in the Context of Grammaticalization* (Leiden: Brill, 2009).

> measurement, or are datable to this period on other grounds, and yet are written in an Aramaic that does not differ substantially from that of the Apocryphon. Given the culmination of evidence, it seems time to adjust the linguistic *terminus post quem* of the Genesis Apocryphon from the 1st cent. BCE to at least the early 2nd cent. BCE.[221]

Further complicating the relationship of Aramaic Daniel to the Genesis Apocryphon is the dating of the Job Targum (11QtgJob).[222] R. I. Vasholz has demonstrated that the Job Targum (11QtgJob) is earlier than the Genesis Apocryphon (1QapGen). He concludes that "11QtgJob is at least a century older than the Genesis Apocryphon" and "may originally have been composed in the late third century or early second century B.C."[223] Furthermore, based on a comparative study of 11QtgJob and Daniel, Vasholz has demonstrated that the book of Daniel is even older than 11QtgJob.[224] He concludes "that the evidence now available from Qumran indicates a pre-second-century date for the Aramaic of Daniel."[225]

6. Ezekiel's Mention of Daniel—Ezek 14:14, 20; 28:3

The book of Ezekiel, which is dated even by critical scholars to a period much earlier than the second century BC, mentions the person of Daniel.[226] Critical scholars sometimes try to dodge this observation by claiming that this Daniel could not refer to Ezekiel's contemporary but to the old Canaanite hero

221. D. A. Machiela, *The Dead Sea Genesis Apocryphon: A New Text and Translation with Introduction and Special Treatment of Columns 13–17* (Leiden: Brill, 2009), 140.
222. For discussion of specific linguistic traits of 1QapGen and 11QtgJob, see Machiela, *The Dead Sea Genesis Apocryphon*, 138–39.
223. R. I. Vasholz, "Qumran and the Dating of Daniel," *JETS* 21 (1978): 319.
224. R. I. Vasholz, "A Philological Comparison of the Qumran Job Targum and Its Implications for the Dating of Daniel" (Ph.D. dissertation, University of Stellenbosch, 1976).
225. Vasholz, "Qumran and the Dating of Daniel," 320. He lists the technical linguistic phenomena substantiating his conclusion that biblical Aramaic, and hence the book of Daniel, is older than 11QtgJob.
226. The name "Daniel" has a slight variant spelling in Ezekiel than in the book of Daniel, but this is no more than a stylistic variation. In the book of Daniel it is spelled דָנִיֵּאל (*dāniyyē ̓ l*), while in the book of Ezekiel it appears as דָנִאֵל (*dāni ̓ēl*) without the consonant *yōḏ*. There are other men in the OT with the name Daniel (1 Chr 3:1; Ezra 8:2; Neh 10:7), yet the spelling is always the same as that in the book of Daniel: דָנִיֵּאל (*dāniyyē ̓ l*).

Dan'el whose story appears in the Ugaritic legend of Aqhat many centuries earlier.[227]

That argument, however, is most unlikely in light of the character of the "Dan'el" of the Ugaritic legend. The point of the Ezekiel passages is to highlight three men well-known for their righteousness before Yahweh, namely, Job, Noah, and Daniel. Archer ("Daniel," 7:5) notes that "a careful reading of the Aqhat epic reveals that Dan'el, the father of Aqhat, was a dedicated idol-worshiper, occupied with blood sacrifices to El, Baal, and other pagan gods for weeks at a time." Block, in a detailed discussion of the problem, likewise rejects equating Ezekiel's "Daniel" with the Canaanite Dan'el from the legend of Aqhat:

> ... this interpretation is not as convincing as it appears. The weight of the orthographic evidence should not be overestimated since *dnyʾl* and *dnʾl* are variant spellings of the same name, and the fuller form *Da-ni-èl* is attested in the eighteenth-century B.C. Mari Letters. Furthermore, every member of Ezekiel's audience would have known that even though Noah and Job were not Israelites, the God they worshiped was Yahweh (Gen. 8:20–21; Job 1:6ff.; 42:1ff.). Too little is known about the Ugaritic Dan'el to impose him on Ezekiel, and what is known would hardly have fit his definition of piety. While the hero of the Aqhat story may have gained a reputation as a just ruler, he is a pagan, worshiping a foreign god, much more at home with the Canaanites and more like Ezekiel's audience than the people of Yahweh as the prophet envisions them.[228]

There is no other Daniel that the prophet Ezekiel could have had in mind than the man carefully portrayed in the book of Daniel as a model of integrity and righteousness. This strongly bears witness to the fact that Daniel was well known to Ezekiel as a historical figure (they were both exiles in Babylon) and that this Daniel was the author of the book bearing his name.

7. Implications of the Roman Empire in Daniel's Series of Empires

The series of empires must include the Roman Empire, thus pushing the scope of reference well past the Maccabean period. In Dan 2 and Dan 7 a

---

227. For a detailed discussion, see J. Day, "The Daniel of Ugarit and Ezekiel and the Hero of the Book of Daniel," *VT* 30 (1980): 174–84. H. H. P. Dressler, "The Identification of the Ugaritic Dnil with the Daniel of Ezekiel," *VT* 29 (1979): 152–61; and idem, "Reading and Interpreting the Aqht Text: A Rejoinder to Drs J. Day and B. Margalit," *VT* 34 (1984): 78–82, however, argues persuasively that the Ugaritic Dan'el cannot be the figure intended by Ezekiel. For an evaluation and rebuttal to both Day and Dressler, see D. Wallace, "Who is Ezekiel's Daniel?" (<https://bible.org/article/who-ezekiels-daniel>).

228. D. I. Block, *The Book of Ezekiel, Chapters 1–24*, NICOT (Grand Rapids: Eerdmans, 1997), 448.

series of empires are listed. Critical scholars claim that the third empire in the series is Media and the fourth the Hellenistic kingdoms, thus excluding the Roman Empire. Conservatives, however, believe that Media was meant to be coupled with Persia and viewed as one empire (the second), with the result being that the series must include the Roman Empire as the fourth. Since the Roman Empire essentially came into renown after the time of Antiochus IV Epiphanes, reference to it creates a great difficulty for critical scholars. By their own reasoning, they are forced to conclude that the book was written about 165 BC, but this predates the Roman Empire's rise to power. If the Roman Empire is in view in Dan 2 and Dan 7, then critical scholars are forced to conclude that the book of Daniel has predictive prophecy, the very thing they are unwilling to admit.

a. Archer has pointed out that the wordplay at Belshazzar's feast in the handwriting on the wall argues strongly against a view of an empire of Media distinct from Persia. He writes, "The only possible inference is that the author who wrote these words believed that imperial power was taken from the Babylonians under Belshazzar and given over directly and immediately to the Persians, who at the time of the capture of Babylon were already merged with the Medes in a single domain" ("Daniel," 25).

b. The symbolism of chaps. 7 and 8 points unmistakably to the identification of the second kingdom as Medo-Persia and the third as Greece, which would imply that the fourth must be Rome.

1) Chapter 7 depicts the third kingdom dividing into four parts, which must be an allusion to Alexander's Hellenistic Empire that was divided among his four generals following his death. There is no historical evidence for Persia being divided into four parts.

2) Dan 8:20–21 views Media and Persia as one entity.

c. In Dan 6 Darius regards himself as bound to the law of the Medes *and Persians*, which would not have been necessary for a Median king (and which argues that these two realms had merged and were viewed as one).

8. The Author's Acquaintance with Sixth-Century BC Customs and Events

a. Harrison points out, "... the author was sufficiently well informed about 6th cent. B.C. life in Babylonia to represent Nebuchadnezzar as being able to formulate and change Babylonian law with absolute sovereignty (2:12, 13, 46), while showing that Darius the Mede was powerless to alter the rigid laws of the Medes and Persians (6:8, 9)."[229]

b. Harrison also notes, "... he was quite correct in recording the change from punishment by fire in the time of the Babylonians (Ch. 3) to punishment

229. Harrison, "Daniel" 14.

by being thrown into a lion's den under the Persians (Ch. 6), since fire was sacred to the Zoroastrians."[230]

c. In Dan 8:2 the city of Shushan is described as being in the province of Elam back in the time of the Chaldeans. Archer writes,

> But from the Greek and Roman historians we learn that in the Persian period Shushan, or Susa, was assigned to a new province which was named after it, Susiana, and the formerly more extensive province of Elam was restricted to the territory west of the Eulaeus River. It is reasonable to conclude that only a very early author would have known that Susa was once considered part of the province of Elam.[231]

9. Linguistic Arguments for an Early Date of Daniel

a. We have abundant use in Daniel of the particle אֲשֶׁר (*'ăšer*), which had become more rare in the Maccabean period and had essentially dropped out of Mishnaic Hebrew that flourished in the first to fourth centuries AD (see Dan 1:4, 8 [2x], 10 [2x], 11, 18, 20 [2x]; 8:2, 6, 20, 21, 26; 9:1, 2, 6, 7 [2x], 8, 10, 11, 12 [3x], 14, 15, 18, 21; 10:1, 7, 11, 12; 11:4, 24, 38, 39; 12:1, 6, 7).[232] In contrast, we have no occurrences in Daniel of שֶׁ (*še*) (or שֶׁל, *šel*), which critical scholars normally regard as indicative of a late-dated work, as in Ecclesiastes, Song of Solomon, and the Psalms (by their reckoning). However, these forms are attested in earlier biblical literature (as in Judges, for example).

b. While Mishnaic Hebrew lost the נָה (*nâ*) suffix for the second and third feminine singular verb forms, we do have יַעֲמֹדְנָה (*ya'ămōḏ^e nâ*, with the נָה suffix) in Dan 8:22. This suggests that the Hebrew of Daniel is earlier than the Mishnaic period.

c. Kutscher argues that ירושלים, *ye rûšālayîm* (mostly with *yōḏ* before the final *mēm*), in the DSS (Isa^a) is late, whereas the form without *yōḏ* is characteristic of standard Biblical Hebrew.[233] Notice that in Dan 1:1 we have the earlier form יְרוּשָׁלַםִ, *ye rûšālaim* (cf. 9:2, 7, 12, 16, 25), bearing witness that Daniel is not late. (Cf. יְרוּשְׁלֶם, *ye rûš^e lem*, in Dan 6:11 Heb.)

---

230. Ibid.

231. Archer, *Old Testament Introduction*, 379–80; Archer's fn 4: "Cf. Strabo 15:3, 12; 16:1, 17; Pliny. *Natural History*. 6.27."

232. Admittedly, the relative particle אֲשֶׁר (*'ăšer*) is also observed in some of the fragments of Ben Sira (see, for example, Manuscript B, 37:12–15, in Beentjes, *The Book of Ben Sira*, 155), which indicates that it could still be found in Hebrew literature as late as 180 BC.

233. E. Y. Kutscher, *A History of the Hebrew Language*, ed. R. Kutscher (Jerusalem: Magnes, Hebrew University, 1984), 94.

Selected Bibliography (Date and Authorship)

Albright, W. F. "The Date and Personality of the Chronicler." *JBL* 40 (1921): 104–24.

Anderson, B. W. *Understanding the Old Testament*. 4th ed. Englewood Cliffs, NJ: Prentice-Hall, 1986.

Anderson, S. D. *Darius the Mede: A Reappraisal*. Grand Rapids: Amazon/ CreateSpace, 2014.

———, and R. C. Young. "The Remembrance of Daniel's Darius the Mede in Berossus and Harpocration." *BSac* 173 (2016): 315–23.

Archer, G. L. "The Aramaic of the Genesis Apocryphon Compared with the Aramaic of Daniel." In *New Perspectives on the Old Testament*, ed. J. B. Payne, 160–69. Waco, TX: Word, 1970.

———. "Daniel." In *The Expositor's Bible Commentary*, 12 vols., ed. F. E. Gaebelein, 7:3–157. Grand Rapids: Zondervan, 1985.

———. "The Hebrew of Daniel Compared with the Qumran Sectarian Documents." In *The Law and the Prophets*, ed. J. Skilton, 470–81. Nutley, NJ: Presbyterian and Reformed, 1974.

———. *A Survey of Old Testament Introduction*. 4th ed. Chicago: Moody, 2007.

Auchincloss, W. S. "Darius the Median." *BSac* 66 (1909): 536–38.

Barker, K. L. "Ahasuerus." In *ZPEB*, 5 vols., ed. Merrill C. Tenney, 1:82. Grand Rapids: Zondervan, 1975.

Beaulieu, P.-A. *The Reign of Nabonidus, King of Babylon 556–539 B.C.* New Haven, CT: Yale University Press, 1996.

Beckwith, R. "Early Traces of the Book of Daniel." *TynBul* 53 (2002): 75–82.

Beentjes, P. C. *The Book of Ben Sira in Hebrew*. VTSup 68. Atlanta: SBL, 2006.

Bledsoe, A. M. D. "The Relationship of the Different Editions of Daniel: A History of Scholarship." *CurBS* 13 (2015): 175–90.

Block, D. I. *The Book of Ezekiel, Chapters 1–24*. NICOT. Grand Rapids: Eerdmans, 1997.

Boadt, L. "Ezekiel, Book of." In *ABD*, 6 vols., ed. D. N. Freedman, 2:711–22. New York: Doubleday, 1992.

Boccaccini, G. *The Origins of Enochic Judaism*. Turin: Zamorani, 2002.

Boutflower, C. *In and Around the Book of Daniel*. Society for Promoting Christian Knowledge, 1930. Repr.; Grand Rapids: Kregel, 1977.

Bruce, F. F. "The Chronology of Daniel 1:1." In *The Climax of the Ages: Studies in the Prophecy of Daniel*, ed. F. A. Tatford, 229–36. London: Marshall, Morgan, and Scott, 1953.

Bulman, J. M. "The Identification of Darius the Mede." *WTJ* 35 (1973): 247–67.

Charles, R. H. *The Book of Enoch*. London: SPCK, 1917.

Charlesworth, J. H. "Summary and Conclusions: The Books of Enoch or 1 Enoch Matters: New Paradigms for Understanding Pre-70 Judaism." In *Enoch and Qumran Origins*, ed. G. Boccaccini, 436–54. Grand Rapids: Eerdmans, 2005.

Clay, A. T. "Gobryas." *JAOS* 41 (1921): 466–67.

Clines, D. J. A. "Cyrus." In *ISBE*, 4 vols., ed. G. W. Bromiley, 1:845–49. Grand Rapids: Eerdmans, 1988.

Colless, B. E. "Cyrus the Persian as Darius the Mede in the Book of Daniel." *JSOT* 56 (1992): 113–26.

Collins, J. J. *Apocalypse, Prophecy, and Pseudepigraphy*. Grand Rapids: Eerdmans, 2015.

———. *The Apocalyptic Imagination; An Introduction to Jewish Apocalyptic Literature*. 2nd ed. Grand Rapids: Eerdmans, 1998.

———. *Daniel with an Introduction to Apocalyptic Literature*. Grand Rapids: Eerdmans, 1984.

Coxon, P. W. "The Distribution of Synonyms in Biblical Aramaic in the Light of Official Aramaic and the Aramaic of Qumran." *RevQ* 9 (1978): 497–512.

———. "Greek Loan-Words and Alleged Greek Loan Translations in the Book of Daniel." TGUOS 25 (1973–74): 24-40.

———. "The Syntax of the Aramaic of Daniel." *HUCA* 48 (1977): 107–22.

Day, J. "The Daniel of Ugarit and Ezekiel and the Hero of the Book of Daniel." *VT* 30 (1980): 174–84.

Di Lella, A. A. "The Wisdom of Ben Sira." In *ABD*, 6 vols., ed. D. N. Freedman, 6:931–45. New York: Doubleday, 1992.

Dressler, H. H. P. "The Identification of the Ugaritic Dnil with the Daniel of Ezekiel." *VT* 29 (1979): 152–61.

———. "Reading and Interpreting the Aqht Text: A Rejoinder to Drs J. Day and B. Margalit." *VT* 34 (1984): 78–82.

Dyer, C. H. "The Musical Instruments in Daniel 3." *BSac* 147 (1990): 426–36.

Engel, C. *The Music of the Most Ancient Nations Particularly of the Assyrians, Egyptians, and Hebrews*. 2nd ed. 1870. Repr.; Charleston, SC: Nabu, 2014.

Finegan, J. *Handbook of Biblical Chronology*. Rev. ed. Peabody, MA: Hendrickson, 1998.

Fox, D. E. "Ben Sira on OT Canon Again: The Date of Daniel." *WTJ* 49 (1987): 335–50.

Gadd, C. J. "The Harran Inscriptions of Nabonidus." *AnSt* 8 (1958): 35–92.

Grabbe, L. L. "Another Look at the *Gestalt* of Darius the Mede." *CBQ* 50 (1988): 198–213.

Harrison, R. K. "Daniel, Book of." In *ISBE*, 4 vols., ed. G. W. Bromiley, 1:850–66. Grand Rapids: Eerdmans, 1979.

———. "Daniel, Book of." In *ZPEB*, 5 vols., ed. M. C. Tenney, 2:12–21. Grand Rapids: Zondervan, 1975.

Hasel, G. "The Book of Daniel and Matters of Language: Evidences Relating to Names, Words, and the Aramaic Language." *AUSS* 19 (1981): 211–25.

Hayden, R. E. "Ecbatana." In *ISBE*, 4 vols., ed. G. W. Bromiley, 2:10–11. Grand Rapids: Eerdmans, 1982.

———. "Xerxes." In *ISBE*, 4 vols., ed. G. W. Bromiley, 4:1161–62. Grand Rapids: Eerdmans, 1988.

Henze, M. "Enoch's Dream Visions and the Visions of Daniel Reexamined." In *Enoch and Qumran Origins: New Light on a Forgotten Connection*, ed. G. Boccaccini, 17–22. Grand Rapids: Eerdmans, 2005.

Hirsch, S. W. "1000 Iranian Nights: History and Fiction in Xenophon's *Cyropaedia*." In *The Greek Historians: Literature and History: Papers Presented to A. E. Raubitschek*, ed. M. H. Jameson, 65–85. Saratoga, CA: ANMA Libra, 1985.

———. *The Friendship of the Barbarians: Xenophon and the Persian Empire.* Hanover, NH: Univ. Press of New England, 1985.

Isaac, E. "1 (Ethiopic Apocalypse of) Enoch: A New Translation and Introduction." In *The Old Testament Pseudepigrapha*, vol. 1, Apocalyptic Literature and Testaments, ed. J. H. Charlesworth, 5–108. Doubleday: Garden City, NY, 1983.

Kitchen, K. A. "The Aramaic of Daniel." In *Notes on Some Problems in the Book of Daniel*, ed. D. J. Wiseman et al., 31–79. London: Tyndale Press, 1965.

Kutscher, E. Y. *A History of the Hebrew Language.* Jerusalem: Magnes, Hebrew University, 1984.

———. "The Language of the 'Genesis Apocryphon.'" In *Aspects of the Dead Sea Scrolls.* Scripta Hierosolymitana IV, 2nd ed., ed. C. Rabin and Y. Yadin, 1–35. Jerusalem: Magnes, Hebrew University, 1965.

Kvanvig, H. S. "Throne Visions and Monsters: The Encounter Between Danielic and Enochic Traditions." *ZAW* 117 (2005): 249–72.

Law, G. R. *Identification of Darius the Mede.* Pfafftour, NC: Ready Scribe, 2010.

Lawrence, P. "Who Wrote Daniel?" *Bible and Spade* 28 (2015): 4–11.

Li, T. *The Verbal System of the Aramaic of Daniel: An Explanation in the Context of Grammaticalization.* Leiden: Brill, 2009.

Lucas, E. C. "Daniel Resolving the Enigma." *VT* 50 (2000): 66–80.

Machiela, D. A. *The Dead Sea Genesis Apocryphon: A New Text and Translation with Introduction and Special Treatment of Columns 13–17.* Leiden: Brill, 2009.

McDowell, J. *Daniel in the Critics' Den: Historical Evidence for the Authenticity of the Book of Daniel.* San Bernardino, CA: Here's Life Publishers, Inc., 1979.

McFall, L. "A Translation Guide to the Chronological Data in Kings and Chronicles." *BSac* 148 (1991): 3–45.

Mercer, M. K. "Daniel 1:1 and Jehoiakim's Three Years of Servitude." *AUSS* 27 (1989): 179–92.

———. "An Historical, Exegetical, and Theological Study of Daniel 11:26–12:4." Th.D. diss., Dallas Theological Seminary, 1987.

Merrill, E. H. *Kingdom of Priests.* 2nd ed. Grand Rapids: Baker, 2008.

Milgrom, J. "Florilegium: A Midrash on 2 Samuel and Psalms 1–2." In *The Dead Sea Scrolls: Hebrew, Aramaic, and Greek Texts with English Translations*, ed. J. H. Charlesworth, 248–63. Tübingen: Mohr Siebeck, 2002.

Niemeier, W.-D. "Archaic Greeks in the Orient: Textual and Archaeological Evidence." *BASOR* 322 (2001): 11–32.

Noonan, B. *Foreign Words in the Hebrew Bible: Linguistic Evidence for Foreign Contact in Ancient Israel (Linguistic Studies in Ancient West Semitic).* Winona Lake, IN: Eisenbrauns, forthcoming.

———. "The Presence and Significance of Foreign Loanwords in the Book of Daniel." Evangelical Theological Society annual meeting, Baltimore, MD, November 20, 2013.

Olmsted, A. T. *History of the Persian Empire*. Chicago: Univ. of Chicago Press, 1948.

Pritchard, J. B., ed. *ANET.* 3rd ed. Princeton, NJ: Princeton University Press, 1969.

Redditt, P. L. "The Community Behind the Book of Daniel: Challenges, Hopes, Values, and Its View of God." *PRSt* 36 (2009): 321–39.

Rowland, C. "Dating the Apocalypses." In *The Open Heaven: A Study of Apocalyptic in Early Judaism and Christianity*, 248-67. NY: Crossroad, 1982. Repr.; Eugene, OR: Wipf & Stock, 2002.

Rowley, H. H. *The Aramaic of the Old Testament*. Oxford: Oxford University Press, 1929.

———. *Darius the Mede and the Four World Empires in the Book of Daniel: A Historical Study of Contemporary Theories*. 2nd ed. Cardiff: Univ. of Wales, 1964.

———. "Notes on the Aramaic of the Genesis Apocryphon." In *Hebrew and Semitic Studies Presented to Godfrey Rolles Driver*, ed. D. W. Thomas and W. D. McHardy, 116–29. Oxford: Clarendon, 1963.

Shea, W. H. "Darius the Mede: An Update." *AUSS* 20 (1982): 229–47.

———. "Darius the Mede in His Persian-Babylonian Setting." *AUSS* 29 (1991): 235–57.

———. "Nabonidus Chronicle: New Readings and the Identity of Darius the Mede." *JATS* 7 (1996): 1–20.

———. "The Search for Darius the Mede (Concluded), or, The Time of the Answer to Daniel's Prayer and the Date of the Death of Darius the Mede." *JATS* 12 (2001): 97–105.

Stepanovic, Z. "Daniel: A Book of Significant Reversals." *AUSS* 30 (1992): 139–50.

———. "Thematic Links Between the Historical and Prophetic Sections of Daniel. *AUSS* 27 (1989): 121–27.

Thiele, E. R. *The Mysterious Numbers of the Hebrew Kings*. 3rd rev. ed. Chicago: University of Chicago Press, 1983.

Valenta, D. M. "The Book of Daniel in Recent Research Part 1." *CurBS* 6 (2008): 330–54.

VanderKam, J., and P. Flint. *The Meaning of the Dead Sea Scrolls*. San Francisco: HarperCollins, 2002. (See esp. 137–38 for the Daniel fragments.)

Vasholz, R. I. "A Philological Comparison of the Qumran Job Targum and Its Implications for the Dating of Daniel." Ph.D. dissertation, University of Stellenbosch, 1976.

———. "Qumran and the Dating of Daniel." *JETS* 21 (1978): 315–21.

Waldbaum, J. C. "Early Greek Contacts with the Southern Levant, ca. 1000–600 B.C.: The Eastern Perspective." *BASOR* 293 (1994): 67–78.
Waltke, B. K. "The Date of the Book of Daniel." *BSac* 133 (1976): 319–29.
Whitcomb, J. C. *Darius the Mede: A Study in Historical Identification.* Grand Rapids: Eerdmans, 1959.
Wiseman, D. J., et al. *Notes on Some Problems in the Book of Daniel.* London: Tyndale, 1970.
Yadin, N., and Y. Avigad. *A Genesis Apocryphon: A Scroll from the Wilderness of Judaea.* Jerusalem: Magnes, 1956.
Yamauchi, E. M. "Daniel and Contacts Between the Aegean and the Near East Before Alexander." *EvQ* 53 (1981): 37–47.
______. *Greece and Babylon: Early Contacts Between the Aegean and the Near East.* Grand Rapids: Baker, 1967.
______. "Greece and Babylon Revisited." In *To Understand the Scriptures: Essays in Honor of William H. Shea*, ed. D. Merling, 127–35. Berrien Springs, MI: Institute of Archaeology/Siegfried H. Horn Archaeological Museum, 1997.
Young, I. "The Greek Loanwords in the Book of Daniel." In *Biblical Greek in Context: Essays in Honour of John A. L. Lee,* ed. J. K. Aitken and T. V. Evans, 247–68. Leuven: Peeters, 2015.
Young, R. C. "Tables of Reign Lengths from the Hebrew Court Recorders." *JETS* 48 (2005): 225–48.
———. "When Did Jerusalem Fall?" *JETS* 47 (2004): 21–38.

The Historical Context for the Book of Daniel

Introductory Comments

The following section provides a basic overview of the historical developments related to the book of Daniel. The Assyrian period will be briefly examined first, as it sets the stage for Babylon's rise to power. During the power struggle between Assyria and Babylon, the land of Judah was caught in the crossfire, which led to Nebuchadnezzar's siege of Jerusalem in 605 BC and the first deportation of Jews (including Daniel) to Babylon. The crucial years between 609 and 586 BC will be examined in detail, for it is during these years that further deportations of the Jewish people were carried out, culminating in the destruction of Jerusalem in 586 BC. The attack and conquest of Babylon by the armies of the Persian king Cyrus in 539 BC will then be examined, and highlights of the Persian Empire will be noted. Because much of the prophetic material in Daniel relates to the conquest of Persia by Alexander the Great, which gave rise in turn to the Seleucid Empire in Syria, highlights of the Hellenistic period will also be noted. Of particular importance will be the second-century BC Seleucid ruler, Antiochus IV Epiphanes, the infamous persecutor of the Jewish people. Finally, Rome's rise to power in the first and second centuries BC served to bring about the collapse of the Seleucid Empire and set the stage for New Testament events.

The Assyrian Background

For nearly three hundred years prior to Daniel's time, Assyria dominated the Middle East. This period is generally termed the Neo-Assyrian Period (900–612 BC). Assyria's expansionist tendencies were fueled by the desire to establish vassal states and enact tribute from them. During this time, outlying areas (e.g., Syria) made repeated attempts to rebel against Assyria. The Babylonians were also suppressed by Assyria during this period, despite attempts to gain their independence. The grip of Assyria was strengthened under the reign of Tiglath-pileser III (745–727 BC). His forces invaded Israel during the period 734–732 BC (2 Kgs 15:29), and he annexed Damascus in 732. About this time disturbances arose in Babylonia following the death of Nabû-naṣir (Nabonassar) in 734 BC, which led to Tiglath-pileser taking a more direct hand in the affairs of Babylon:

> ... Tiglath-pileser himself marched to defeat the usurper and lay the tribal lands waste. He took over personal rule in Babylon in 729, participating in the New Year Festival under his native name of Pul(u) (so 2 K. 15:19; 1 Ch. 5:26).[234]

Under Shalmaneser V (r. 727–722 BC), Assyria instigated a three-year siege against the city of Samaria (capital of the northern kingdom of Israel), which resulted in the fall of Samaria in 722 BC and the deportation of thousands of Israelites.[235] This marked the collapse of the northern kingdom, predicted by Isaiah, as discipline from Yahweh for years of covenant unfaithfulness (cf. Deut 28–30).

Under the Assyrian king Sennacherib (705–681 BC), Nineveh's importance rose. Previously, Nineveh shared the splendor of other royal cities of Assyria—Asshur, Nimrûd (Calah), and Khorsabad. Under Sennacherib it became the capital of the land and one of the architectural wonders of the world.[236] During Sennacherib's reign the Babylonians again attempted to throw off the yoke of Assyria. The Babylonian king, however, was defeated along with his allies by Sennacherib near Kish in 703 BC. According to

---

234. D. J. Wiseman, "Assyria," in *ISBE*, 1:335.

235. There is some confusion as to whether the actual fall of Samaria took place under Shalmaneser V or his son Sargon II (r. 722–705 BC). Sargon II claims to have taken the city, but many scholars feel he may have been simply taking credit for an achievement of his father. In discussing the problem, Grayson concludes, "The most attractive solution to the problem is that Samaria fell in 722 BC, the year of Shalmaneser V's death and the accession of Sargon II. Thus the leading of the Israelites into exile by the Assyrians was probably carried out during the reign of Sargon II (721–705 BC). Consequently, references to Shalmaneser (Gk. *Enemessaros*) in the book of Tobit (1:2, 13, 15, 16), in connection with events during the exile of the people of Samaria at Nineveh, actually relate to the period of Sargon II" ("Shalmaneser," in *ABD*, 5:1155).

236. C. T. Fritsch, "Nineveh," in *ISBE*, 3:539.

Wiseman, "Sennacherib plundered Babylon, deported 208,000 prisoners to Nineveh, and set up a young friend Bēl-ibni as ruler."[237] Resistance to Assyria continued, until eventually Sennacherib had to sack the city of Babylon itself (ca. 689 BC). At this time, the statue of the god Marduk (the national god of Babylon) was carried off to Assyria. These events fueled Babylonia's hatred for Assyria, which continued for another eighty years or so until Babylon eventually defeated Assyria late in the seventh century BC.[238]

Babylon's Rise to Power

During the years 651–648 BC, under the reign of the Assyrian king Ashurbanipal (669–ca. 627 BC), the Babylonians unsuccessfully rebelled against Assyria.[239] However, Assyria was weakening, especially during the reign of Ashurbanipal's sons, when Assyria began losing territory. Phraortes the Mede attacked the Assyrians,[240] and by 626 BC the Chaldean Nabû-apla-usur (Nabopolassar) had won independence for Babylon and was recognized there as king, though not accepted or recognized by Assyria.[241] Nabopolassar was important, not only for his eventual conquest of Nineveh but also as the father of Nebuchadnezzar[242] the Babylonian king of the book of Daniel. Under Nabopolassar, a new dynasty had begun, generally referred to as the Neo-Babylonian or Chaldean Period.

---

237. Wiseman, "Assyria," 1:336.

238. Under Esarhaddon (r. 681–669 BC), there was some improvement in the relationship. Upon taking the throne, Esarhaddon restored Babylon (an eleven-year project), which won over the Babylonians, and eventually returned the statue of Marduk to Babylon in a great ceremonial procession.

239. J. Oates, *Babylon*, rev. ed. (London: Thames and Hudson Ltd., 1986), 127, observes, "Assurbanipal left a further and perhaps more important legacy to the modern world. A library, collected at Nineveh under his personal direction and discovered there by British excavators in 1853, has provided modern scholars with undoubtedly the world's single most important collection of cuneiform tablets.... including the Epic of Gilgamesh and the Creation Epic, the 'Babylonian Genesis.'"

240. The Medes were heirs to Elamite power in western Iran. Oates reports, "... they had been welded into a single kingdom by an able ruler, Huvakshatra, known to Herodotus as Cyaxares. In 614 Cyaxares marched on Nineveh; Nimrud was sacked, the walls of Assur breached and that city captured and looted" (*Babylon*, 127). Nebuchadnezzar seems to have maintained friendly relations with the Medes, as there is little mention of trouble on the eastern frontier.

241. Wiseman, "Assyria," 1:338. A mysterious ruler by the name of Kandalanu appeared as king of Babylon during the years 647–627 BC.

242. Sometimes spelled Nebuchadrezzar, but both spellings are used as legitimate alternative forms in the Old Testament. See D. J. Wiseman, *Nebuchadrezzar and Babylon*, Schweich Lectures (Oxford: Oxford University Press, 1985), 2–5, for discussion.

Nabopolassar gained further territory from the Assyrians. By 614 BC Asshur fell, and by 612 the Medes and Babylonians marched up the Tigris to Nineveh. In fulfillment of the book of Nahum, Nineveh fell to the combined forces of the Medes, the Umman-Manda (apparently a reference to the Medes and perhaps the Scythians and/or Cimmerians) and the Babylonians in 612 BC.[243] A remnant of the Assyrian forces attempted to withdraw west of the Euphrates River, hoping to be supported by their Egyptian allies under Pharaoh Neco II. This led to the defeat of the Assyrians and Egyptians at Harran (609 BC) and of the Egyptians at Carchemish in 605 BC.[244] These victories established Babylon as the dominant world power of that day and set the stage for Judah's exile to Babylon.

Judah's Exile to Babylon

In the aftermath of Nebuchadnezzar's great victory at Carchemish in 605 BC, the small kingdom of Judah became a victim in a major international shakeup. To appreciate this development, however, it is best to back up and examine the reign of Josiah, Judah's last great king.

Chronological Factors

The following chart lists the kingships of Judah in this period:[245]

---

243. For a brief account of Nineveh's fall at the hands of the king of Akkad and Cyaxares, king of the Umman-manda, see Pritchard, *ANET*, 304–5. The exact identity of the Umman-manda is still debated, and the term is not necessarily limited to one particular people group. In general, it appears to have been used for the peoples to the east and northeast of Nineveh, inhabiting the territory of the Medes and even up through the Caucasus Mountain range. W. F. Albright, "The Seal of Eliakim and the Latest Preexilic History of Judah, with Some Observations on Ezekiel," *JBL* 51 (1932): 86–87, identified the Umman-manda as the Medes. For a more up-to-date and extended discussion, see S. F. Adali, *The Scourge of God: The Umman-manda and Its Significance in the First Millennium BC*, State Archives of Assyria Studies (Helsinki: Neo-Assyrian Text Corpus Project, 2011). In his chapter on "Etymology" (15–34), Adali proposes that the term Umman-manda means "troops of the (distant) terrain." In his final chapter ("Emerging patterns," 169-71), Adali suggests that the Cimmerians and Medes were designated as Umman-manda in Assyrian and Babylonian texts due to the fact that "they came from a distant land in the east."

244. The victory of Babylon at Carchemish (605 BC) was led not by Nabopolassar himself but by his energetic son Nebuchadnezzar. This marked the end of Assyria for good.

245. From McFall, "A Translation Guide," 45.

The Last Kings of Judah Before the Exile

NAME	COREGENT	BECAME KING	DIED
Josiah		Sep 641–Sep 640	ca. July 609
Jehoahaz		July 609	ca. Oct 609
Jehoiakim		Oct 609	9 Dec 598
Jehoiachin	Sept 608*	Dec 598–Apr 597**	After Apr 561
Zedekiah		Apr 597–Aug 586	ca. Aug 586

* McFall notes that Thiele failed to consider Jehoiachin's coregency.
** McFall uses Mar 597 (not Apr 597).

A. Judah under Josiah (יֹאשִׁיָּהוּ, yō'šiyyāhû)—641/640–July 609 BC

Josiah reigned thirty-one (accession) years according to 2 Kgs 22:1 (= 2 Chr 34:1).[246] McFall concludes, "Josiah became king between September 641 and September 640 B.C. and died during Tammuz (25 June–23 July) 609 B.C."[247] The chronology of this period is quite reliable due to extrabiblical materials and two rather firm dates:

1) 2 Adar (15/16 March), 597 BC, Nebuchadnezzar captured Jerusalem and took Jehoiachin prisoner to Babylon.[248]
2) 9 Tammuz (18 July), 586 BC, the nineteenth year of Nebuchadnezzar, when Jerusalem fell.[249]

These dates can be confirmed by contemporary tablets of the Babylonian Chronicle now in the British Museum.[250]

Josiah was considered one of the "good" kings of Judah (he did "right" in the sight of Yahweh). In his eighth year (Sept. 633–632 BC), the Scriptures tell us that he began to seek the God of his father David (see 2 Chr 34:3). In his twelfth year (Sept. 629–628 BC), he began to purge the land of evil and idolatry. During his eighteenth year, the book of the Law was found, which

246. According to accession-year dating, the year in which a king comes to the throne is termed his accession year, and his first official year is that which begins with the new year's day after his accession; cf. E. R. Thiele, *A Chronology of the Hebrew Kings* (Grand Rapids: Zondervan, 1977), 87.

247. McFall, "A Translation Guide," 38.

248. Thiele, *The Mysterious Numbers*, 173.

249. Ibid., 189. Despite the popularity of the 586 BC date for the fall of Jerusalem, not all scholars support this date. Some prefer a date of 587 BC. In defense of the latter, see R. C. Young, "When Did Jerusalem Fall?" He concludes, "Jerusalem fell in the fourth month (Tammuz) of 587 BC" (38). Wishing to leave this an open question for now, the more commonly accepted date of 586 BC will be used in this commentary.

250. Cf. D. J. Wiseman, *Chronicles of Chaldaean Kings (626–556 B.C.) in the British Museum* (London: British Museum, 1956).

had been neglected during the previous evil reigns of Manasseh and Amon. These events led to a reform effort during Josiah's reign to turn the nation back to Yahweh.

Under Josiah's reform effort, the southern kingdom of Judah experienced some measure of revival and return to Yahweh. Unfortunately, this reform was somewhat superficial (more of an outward cleansing), though Josiah did right in the sight of Yahweh (2 Kgs 22:2) and was credited with removing much of the occultic movement in the land (2 Kgs 23:24) and attempting to turn the nation back to the Word of God (2 Kgs 23:25). Linked with Josiah's reform movement was the prophetic and preaching ministry of the prophet Jeremiah. Despite these measures, God's judgment was already settled in light of the nation's disobedience to the Mosaic law and particularly on account of the evil reign of Manasseh of Judah. The time was ripe for the southern kingdom to be taken away into exile (Deut 28:41, 65), just as the northern kingdom had earlier experienced in 722 BC. This judgment was hastened by the death of Josiah, and the advent of the international power struggle that enveloped Judah.

During Josiah's reign, a fierce competition for control of the Middle East broke out between the three major empires of the day, namely Egypt, Assyria, and Babylon. As Assyria's domination of the Middle East was nearing an end, Babylon and Egypt attempted to grab what power they could. Nineveh had fallen in 612 BC, thus marking the virtual demise of Assyria. However, with a remnant of the Assyrian army still surviving, the struggle continued on and even shifted westward, closer to Judah itself. In 609 BC Pharaoh Necho II of Egypt, in response to an urgent appeal from Aššur-uballiṭ of Assyria, marched northward through Judah on his way to Harran to deliver his ally from an approaching Babylonian military force.[251] Josiah, however, attempted to intervene against the Egyptian force and was killed (2 Kgs 23:29). Pentecost (1326) elaborates:

> In 609 BC the Assyrians sought the help of Egypt, and Pharaoh Neco II led an army from Egypt to join Assyria. Josiah, the king of Judah, hoping to incur favor with the Babylonians, sought to prevent the Egyptians from joining Assyria and met the Egyptian army at Megiddo. Josiah's army was defeated and he was killed in this attempt (2 Kings 23:28–30; 2 Chron. 35:24).

B. Judah under Jehoahaz[252] (יְהוֹאָחָז, yᵊhôʾāḥāz)*—July 609–October 609 BC*

Upon the death of Josiah, Jehoahaz was made king by "the people of the land" (2 Kgs 23:30) but shortly thereafter removed by Pharaoh Necho of Egypt (2 Kgs 23:31 = 2 Chr 36:2). In fact, he was taken away into exile to

251. Merrill, *Kingdom of Priests*, 459.

252. Jehoahaz was also known as Shallum (שַׁלֻּם, *šallum*; see Jer 22:11). In 2 Chr 36:2 he is called Joahaz (יוֹאָחָז, *yôʾāḥāz*).

Egypt (2 Chr 36:4; 2 Kgs 23:33; Jer 22:10–12). He reigned three months in Jerusalem. McFall adds,

> ... Thiele noted that the reign of Jehoahaz began in Tammuz (25 June–23 July) of 609 and ended three months later in September/October. Because Jehoahaz's three months spilled over into the next new year, Jehoiakim had an accession year lasting about 11 months.[253]

C. Judah under Jehoiakim (יְהוֹיָקִם, y^əhôyāqim)—October 609–9 December 598 BC

Jehoiakim was twenty-five years old when he became king, and he reigned eleven (accession) years (2 Kgs 23:36 = 2 Chr 36:5). McFall states, "Jehoiakim became king about October 609 and Thiele noted that Jehoiakim died on 9 December 598 BC."[254] According to 1 Chr 3:15, he was the second son of Josiah. His given name was Eliakim (אֶלְיָקִים, *ʾelyāqîm*), but he was given the throne name of Jehoiakim (יְהוֹיָקִם, *yəhôyāqim*) by Pharaoh Necho of Egypt.

Jehoiakim was the ruling king of Judah when Nebuchadnezzar invaded Jerusalem in 605 BC when Daniel and his friends were taken away into exile in Babylon. Although placed on the throne by Pharaoh Necho of Egypt, Jehoiakim was made subject to Babylon, as the following account explains.

Following the capture of Nineveh in 612 BC by Nabopolassar (with help from the Medes), the Assyrians were forced to retreat to Harran. Nabopolassar, however, took Harran and in 609 repelled the Assyrians and their Egyptian allies who attempted to recapture Harran, driving them westward across the Euphrates River.[255] Thus Egypt still held sway over Syro-Palestine during the years 609 to 605 BC. During this period, Jehoiakim remained subject to Pharaoh Necho of Egypt as an Egyptian vassal state, forced to pay heavy tribute. In 605, however, Nebuchadnezzar (the commanding general of the Babylonian forces at the time) turned to the last remaining Assyrian stronghold, Carchemish. In that year Nebuchadnezzar defeated Assyria at Carchemish once and for all, and he forced Egypt to withdraw from northern

253. McFall, "A Translation Guide," 38–39. These events can be correlated with the *Babylonian Chronicle* now in the British Museum. Thiele observes, "These tablets give a year-by-year account of the interesting events that were then taking place. For the year 609 BC, the seventeenth year of Nabopolassar, father of Nebuchadnezzar, the account is that in the month of Tammuz, July, of that year a great Egyptian army went with Assur-uballit, king of Assyria, against the city of Harran which was near the Euphrates, and the attack continued to the month of Elul, September. That would give Jehoahaz a reign of three months in 609 before Necho returned and placed Jehoiakim on the throne in Tishri of 609. That was the commencement of Jehoiakim's accession year" (*A Chronology of the Hebrew Kings*, 68).

254. McFall, "A Translation Guide," 39.

255. Merrill, *Kingdom of Priests*, 462–63.

Syria.[256] Nebuchadnezzar then pursued the Egyptian forces toward Egypt. It was at this time that he laid siege to Jerusalem, forced the Jews to pay tribute, and took prisoners, including Daniel. From 605 BC onward, Jerusalem was subject to Babylon and incorporated into the Babylonian Empire. Tribute that previously went to Egypt now went to Babylon. It was also at this time that his father Nabopolassar died unexpectedly (on Aug. 15/16, 605 BC) and Nebuchadnezzar had to rush back to Babylon (by Sept. 7, 605 BC). He remained in Babylon until the turn of the year.

For the next three years (605–602 BC) Jehoiakim remained a loyal subject of Babylon.[257] But then he attempted to rebel (2 Kgs 24). Merrill writes,

> He then rebelled for some unexpressed reason;[258] retribution was swift and sure (2 Kings 24:1–2). Nebuchadnezzar sent troops from Babylonia and from some of his western vassal states such as Aram, Moab, and Ammon, and forced Jehoiakim to submit. The chronicler says that Nebuchadnezzar went as far as to bind Jehoiakim with shackles in order to take him as a prisoner of war to Babylon (2 Chron. 36:6). Apparently he relented but as punishment stripped the temple of many of its sacred articles and took them to his own pagan temples in Babylon. Thereafter until his death in 598 Jehoiakim remained in subservience to the Babylonian overlord.[259]

---

256. Further information is supplied from the *Babylonian Chronicle*. Thiele reports, "According to the Babylonian account, Nebuchadnezzar inflicted a crushing defeat on an Egyptian army at Carchemish in 605, beat it into 'nonexistence,' and then 'conquered the whole of the Hatti-country'" (*A Chronology of the Hebrew Kings*, 68).

He adds, "The Babylonian account for that year states further that Nabopolassar, after twenty-one years on the throne, died on the eighth day of the month of Ab, August 16, and that Nebuchadnezzar returned to Babylon 'and on the first day of the month of Elul he sat on the royal throne in Babylon,' September 17, 605" (ibid., 69; quote from Wiseman, *Chronicles of Chaldaean Kings*, 67, 69). An additional account of Nebuchadnezzar's exploits at Carchemish and following has been recorded by the ancient Babylonian historian Berossus in his *History of Babylonia* (pub. ca. 290–278 BC), and subsequently preserved by Josephus (*Ant.* X.11.1; and *C. Ap.*, i.19). See Bruce, "The Chronology of Dan 1:1," 240, for a copy and discussion of interpretation.

257. Merrill does point out, however, that Nebuchadnezzar's first campaign after succeeding his father was in his first regnal year (604 BC). "At that time he plunged deep into Palestine and took the Philistine city of Ashkelon" (*Kingdom of Priests*, 464).

258. Fn 60 from Merrill: "Malamat ('Last Kings,' 142–43) associates Jehoiakim's rebellion with the Babylonian conflict with Egypt in the winter of 601/600 BC, which is attested to by a letter written in Aramaic from the town of Saqqarah. For the letter, see William H. Shea, 'Adon's Letter and the Babylonian Chronicle,' *BASOR* 223 (1976): 61–62."

259. Merrill, *Kingdom of Priests*, 464.

In 601 BC, Nebuchadnezzar engaged Necho II in a great battle near the border of Egypt, a contest that appears to have ended in a draw (with both sides incurring heavy losses). This indecisive outcome tempted Judah to free herself from Babylon and seek an alliance with Egypt. In 599–598 BC, Nebuchadnezzar marched into northern Syria (his sixth year). Before the Babylonians could take Jerusalem, however, Jehoiakim died (ca. Dec. 598 BC).[260]

D. Judah under Jehoiachin[261] *(*יְהוֹיָכִין, yᵊhôyāḵîn*)—December 598–March/April 597* BC

According to 2 Chr 36:9, Jehoiachin became king at age eight, although 2 Kgs 24:8 states that he was eighteen years old and reigned three months.[262] McFall understands the ten-year difference to refer to a coregency of Jehoiachin with his father:

> Jehoiachin became coregent in September 608 B.C. and was king from 21 Marcheswan to 10 Nisan (= 9 December 598 to 22 April 597 B.C.). Consequently Jehoiachin concluded his reign on 22 April 597 B.C. The exact date of Jehoiachin's kingship can be given with some degree of accuracy because extrabiblical evidence indicates that Nebuchadnezzar captured Jerusalem on 15/16 March, 597 B.C.[263] Jehoiachin was deported to Babylon on

---

260. Oates reports that after Nebuchadnezzar sent troops to besiege Jerusalem, Jehoiakim died, perhaps in the siege but certainly before the main Babylonian army arrived (*Babylon*, 129).

261. He is also called Jeconiah and Coniah, כָּנְיָהוּ, *konyāhû* (Jer 22:24).

262. The NIV translates 2 Chr 36:9 as "eighteen" rather than "eight," although most Hebrew manuscripts have "eight." Either we have a textual problem here, or the ten-year difference refers to coregency.

263. Nebuchadnezzar's attack upon Jerusalem in 597 BC is confirmed by the Babylonian records. Thiele reports, "The Babylonian record for Nebuchadnezzar's seventh year, 598/97, is also of unusual interest. That record reads, 'In the seventh year, the month of Kislev, the king of Akkad mustered his troops, marched to the Hatti-land, and encamped against [i.e., besieged] the city of Judah and on the second day of the month of Adar he seized the city and captured the king. He appointed there a king of his own choice [lit., heart], received its heavy tribute and sent [them] to Babylon'" (*A Chronology*, 69).

He adds (ibid., 69–70), "This is a striking confirmation from a contemporary Babylonian document of the biblical record of 2 Kings 24:10–17. According to his own account, Nebuchadnezzar started against Jerusalem in the month of Kislev, the ninth month of the Babylonian and Hebrew year. That month began on December 18, 598 B.C., so Jehoiachin must have been on the throne during the last days of 598. Jerusalem was taken on the second of Adar, the last month of the Babylonian year, which was on March 16, 597. So the three-month reign of Jehoiachin can be set with complete certainty as 598–597 B.C."

> 22 April 597 B.C., and this day marked the end of Jehoiachin's reign of three months and 10 days. Working back from this day places the commencement of Jehoiachin's reign in the early days of December and consequently Jehoiakim must have died on or around 9 December 598 B.C., which confirms the prophecy of Jeremiah 36:30 that his dead body would be exposed to the frost of the night.[264]

Hence, in March/April of 597 BC Nebuchadnezzar took Jerusalem from Jehoiachin and set up Zedekiah as king (another son of Josiah). Jehoiachin, together with his family, leading state and military officials, craftsmen, and troops, were taken captive to Babylon (a second deportation). The total number of captives at this time was 10,000 (2 Kgs 24:14), and the prophet Ezekiel was also taken in this deportation of 597 BC. Although Jerusalem was spared, a heavy tribute was taken, including the treasures from Solomon's temple and the royal palace (2 Kgs 24:13). Jehoiachin remained a captive in Babylon for many years, but was eventually released from prison on April 2, 561 BC (2 Kgs 25:27–30).[265]

*E. Judah under Zedekiah (*צִדְקִיָּהוּ*, ṣidqiyyāhû)–April 597–August 586 BC*

With Jehoiachin deported to Babylon, his uncle Zedekiah was made king of Judah (2 Kgs 24:17–20). His reign of eleven years culminated in a major rebellion against Babylon. As a result, Nebuchadnezzar laid siege to Jerusalem one final time (which lasted for thirty months) and eventually destroyed the city, the fall coming on July 18, 586 BC. At this point Daniel had been in Babylon for almost nineteen years and was serving as an important official in Nebuchadnezzar's court. Not only was Jerusalem destroyed, but the temple of Solomon (which had been built about 960 BC) was completely destroyed. This was the lowest point in the nation's history (see Lamentations) and must have come as very disheartening news to Daniel and his companions in Babylon. The prophet Jeremiah lived through all these terrible events in Jerusalem and witnessed the destruction of 586 BC.

To summarize, there were three major deportations of Jews to exile in Babylon:

---

264. McFall, "A Translation Guide," 39. McFall contends that 2 Chr 36:9 is not a textual problem but that Jehoiachin had a coregency of ten years. In reference to 2 Kgs 24:8 which mentions that he was eighteen when he became king, McFall notes, "Here and in 2 Kings 8:16 and 24:18...the RSV translated the verb מלך 'he became king' contrary (but not necessarily incorrect) to its usual practice of translating it 'he began to reign'" (40).

265. The Babylonian Chronicle, which correlates much of the historical events, breaks off at 594–593 BC (a missing section) and does not pick up again until 557–556 BC.

1) 605 BC This deportation was limited to a number of the nobility and leading youths of the city. Daniel and his companions were taken at this time.
2) 597 BC In response to the rebellion of Jehoiakim and Jehoiachin, about 10,000 captives were taken to Babylon, including Ezekiel (Ezek 1:1–3; 2 Kgs 24:8–20; 2 Chr 36:6–10).
3) 586 BC Zedekiah's rebellion brought on the final siege, which culminated in 586 BC with the city and temple being destroyed and many Jews being killed. Many more who were not killed were deported to Babylon (2 Kgs 25:1–7; Jer 34:1–7; 39:1–7; 52:2–11).

Highlights of the Babylonian Period

The Neo-Babylonian Empire, founded by Nabopolassar of Babylon, reached its zenith under his son, King Nebuchadnezzar. His rule began in 605 BC and lasted for some forty-three years, until 562 BC.[266] He is famous for the hanging gardens of Babylon (one of the seven wonders of the ancient world) as well as for his destruction of Jerusalem in 586 BC. He was succeeded by his son Amēl-Marduk (Evil-Merodach) in early October 562 BC. During his reign, Daniel enjoyed great favor with the king, and King Jehoiachin (who held the claim to the Davidic throne) was kept in prison at Babylon. Following Nebuchadnezzar's death, Jehoiachin was released. Thiele explains,

> According to the Babylonian records, Nebuchadnezzar ended his reign and Amēl-Marduk began his reign in early October, 562, which would bring the twelfth month of his accession year at the very time indicated in the biblical account. The release of Jehoiachin on the twenty-seventh day of the twelfth month, just before the beginning of the new year's festivities, would be a fitting time for the release of political prisoners placed in custody by the previous ruler.[267]

The Neo-Babylonian Empire (as mighty as it was) turned out to be rather short-lived, from Nabopolassar's rise in 627 BC until its defeat by

266. Thiele, *A Chronology*, 69 comments on the certainty of the chronology: "Two eclipses establish beyond question 605 as the year when Nebuchadnezzar began his reign. The first took place on April 22, 621, in the fifth year of Nabopolassar, which would make 605 the year of his death in his twenty-first year, and the year of Nebuchadnezzar's accession. The second eclipse was on July 4, 568, in the thirty-seventh year of Nebuchadnezzar, which again gives 605 as the year when Nebuchadnezzar began to reign. No date in ancient history is more firmly established than is 605 for the commencement of Nebuchadnezzar's reign. The year 605 BC can thus be accepted with all certainty as the year when the first attack of Nebuchadnezzar on Jerusalem was made, and as the year when Daniel was taken to Babylon and when the seventy-year captivity in Babylon began (Jer. 25:9–12)."
267. Ibid., 70.

Cyrus of Persia in 539 BC. The succession of Babylonian kings for this period is provided in the following chart:[268]

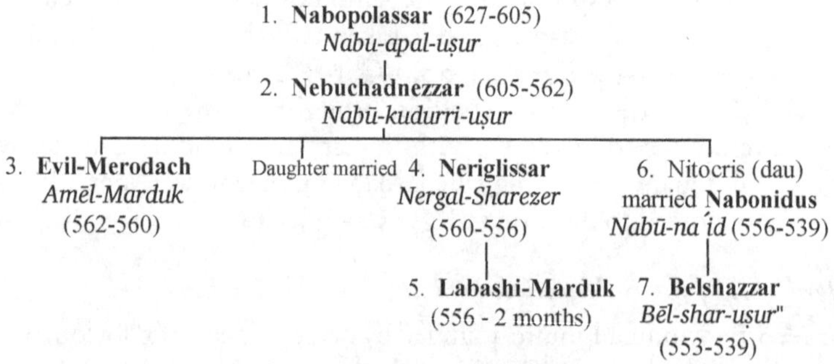

During the final phase, Nabonidus and Belshazzar served as co-rulers. However, Nabonidus remained away from Babylon for much of this time. Anderson explains,

> Nabonidus came to the throne of Babylon (556–539). He was an unpopular king, especially with the priests of Marduk, who hated him for constructing a rival sanctuary to the moon god Sin. Nabonidus went off on a distant expedition to Tema in Arabia, and, after conquering the city, established it as his royal residence.[269]

Cyrus' Conquest of Babylon and the Persian Empire

The end of the Neo-Babylonian Empire came in 539 BC when the armies of Cyrus captured the city of Babylon. The background to this is helpful for understanding the merger of the Medes and Persians into a force powerful enough to defeat Babylon.

The Medes and the Persians shared a common heritage, as Merrill explains:

> Both were descendants of Aryan tribal folk who had moved south to the Urartian plateau from Russia and by 1000 BC had settled in the vicinity of Lake Urmia in what is now extreme northwestern Iran. Gradually the Medes moved east and occupied west Irán south of the Caspian Sea, and the Persians migrated far to the southeast and settled in southwest Iran toward the Persian Gulf.[270]

Basically, the Medes occupied what is today northern Iran, while the Persians occupied southern Iran. Much of their territory was under the control of Assyria (to the west) while that empire dominated the ancient

268. Adapted from *The Bible Knowledge Commentary, Old Testament*, 1:1326.

269. Anderson, *Understanding the Old Testament*, 469.

270. Merrill, *Kingdom of Priests*, 490. For this Merrill cites Ghirshman, *Iran*, 90–96.

Near East. Furthermore, the Medes were pressured by the Scythians to the north (what would be lower Russia today around the Caucasus mountain range between the Black Sea and Caspian Sea), and the Scythians dominated northwest Iran until about 625 BC. About this time, with the weakening of Assyria (keep in mind that Nabopolassar asserted his authority in Babylon against Assyria in 626), the Medes began to gain power and become more daring in their attempts at expansion. They were led by Cyaxares the Mede and initially dominated the Persians to the south, as Merrill explains:

> ... in time Cyaxares (625–585) overthrew the Scythians and the Assyrians, establishing Median control over all of northern Mesopotamia and Iran. He also reduced Persia to submission, setting up Cambyses as governor over that province. Cyaxares was succeeded by his son Astyages (585–550), whose daughter would be the mother of the great Cyrus II.[271]

The Medes attempted to expand northwestward (especially toward Lydia, modern-day western Turkey), but any southwestern expansion was curtailed by the newly formed empire of Babylon, especially under Nebuchadnezzar. As it turned out, the Medes joined forces with the emerging Babylonians to overthrow Assyria.[272] In 612 BC the Babylonians and Medes combined forces to capture Nineveh, which proved to be a deathblow for the Assyrian Empire. From 612 until 550, the Medes and Babylonians seem to have respectfully tolerated each other. Yet in the progress of time, the Babylonians and Medes became bitter foes.

With the death of Cyaxares in 585 BC, the Median throne passed to his son Astyages. His daughter (Mandane) gave birth to Cyrus II, who would eventually become the great ruler of the whole Persian Empire (known as Cyrus the Great). If Herodotus' account is correct, Cyrus had a Persian father and a Median mother.[273]

---

271. Merrill, *Kingdom of Priests*, 491.

272. Merrill mentions that this alliance between Nabopolassar of Babylon and Cyaxares of Media may have been confirmed by a marriage linking their families (ibid., 462, citing Wiseman, *Chronicles of the Chaldaean Kings*, 14). A. R. Millard, "Medes; Media," in *ISBE*, 3:298 writes, "After Median troops had sacked the ancient capital of Asshur, Cyaxares made alliance with Babylon, and one of his princesses married the crown prince Nebuchadnezzar (who built the 'Hanging Gardens' of Babylon to counter her pining for the Median hills, according to Berossus, *apud* Josephus *CAp* i.19 [141])."

273. There are conflicting traditions about Cyrus' origin. D. J. A. Clines, "Cyrus," in *ISBE*, 1:846, points out, "Various stories concerning the birth and early history of this famous figure were of course in circulation in the ancient Near East, and of course may contain genuine historical information. According to the best-known of them, as told by Herodotus (i.108–122), Cyrus was the offspring of the marriage of Cambyses, the Persian vassal of the Median king Astyages, and Mandane, daughter

Initially, Cyrus was a vassal of his grandfather Astyages, ruling a region called Anshan (present-day south-central Iran). According to one version of history, he eventually led a rebellion against the Median capital. He unified several Persian tribes around him and even made an alliance with Nabonidus of Babylonia. This culminated with a march against Ecbatana (the Median capital), in which Cyrus took Astyages prisoner and made Media itself a Persian province in 550 BC. In doing so, Cyrus laid claim to all Median territories. (For an alternative version of history that understands the Medes to have remained independent until after Babylon's fall, see under "Date and Authorship" the discussion of Darius the Mede as Cyaxares II. The alternative version takes the view that Cyrus did not conquer and subject the Medes, but rather united their armies to fight against common foes.)

Regardless of which view is taken of Cyrus in regard to the Medes, certainly the Persians and Medes from this point on were moving in the direction of a common empire composed of both Medes and Persians. Median influence in the new realm was substantial, as Millard points out:

> Cyrus made the Median capital Ecbatana (modern Hamadân) his capital, a position it retained beside Persepolis and Susa until Alexander's conquest (cf. Ezr. 6:2). Moreover, he adopted the system of government set up by Median kings and retained Medes in high office.[274]

The Persians came to dominate the Medes (regardless of some uncertainty of the exact time this took place). Their resulting merger helps explain the vision of the ram in Dan 8:3: "Then I lifted my eyes and looked, and behold, a ram which had two horns was standing in front of the canal. Now the two horns *were* long, but one *was* longer than the other, with the longer one coming up last" (NASB). The text tells us in 8:20 that the ram with the two horns represents the kings of Media and Persia. The horn that was longer and that came up last was Persia. Media's power was a mere seventy-five years, but Persia dominated the ANE for over two hundred years.

Cyrus was famous not only for establishing the Persian Empire that dominated the Medes but also for his conquest of Babylon. Although Babylon was thought to be impregnable, the handwriting on the wall at the feast of Belshazzar (Dan 5) was God's certain verdict: "your kingdom has been divided and given over to the Medes and Persians." That very night (Oct. 12, 539 BC), Babylon was captured by the armies of Cyrus, a historical fact well confirmed by extrabiblical sources. Merrill summarizes the outcome:

---

of Astyages.... A different story was told by the historian Ctesias, a court physician to the later Persian king Artaxerxes II (404–358 BC). According to his account, Cyrus was the son of a Persian bandit and a shepherdess; he rose to a place of honor in the Median court and eventually led a successful revolt against Astyages."

274. Millard, "Medes; Media," 3:299.

> Many Babylonian provinces, such as Elam, fell away to Persia, and in 539 Cyrus sent an army under his general Gubaru to invest Babylon itself. The city fell without a struggle, and Cyrus immediately made it the capital of yet another Persian satrapy, Babirus, which included Syria, Phoenicia, and Palestine within its jurisdiction.[275]

The conquest of Babylon by Cyrus fulfilled the words of Isaiah the prophet uttered about 150 years beforehand:

> Thus says the LORD to Cyrus His anointed, whom I have taken by the right hand, to subdue nations before him, and to loose the loins of kings; to open doors before him so that gates will not be shut: I will go before you and make the rough places smooth; I will shatter the doors of bronze, and cut through their iron bars. ... For the sake of Jacob My servant, and Israel My chosen one, I have also called you by your name; I have given you a title of honor though you have not known Me. (Isa 45:1–4 NASB)

Even though extrabiblical sources do not mention a "Darius the Mede," Cyrus' respect and esteem for the Medes suggests that an appointment of a Mede as king of Babylon is entirely plausible. (See the discussion of Darius the Mede under the earlier section "Objections to the Traditional Date.")

Following the conquest of Babylon, Cyrus ordered a decree to permit the Jews to return to Jerusalem to rebuild the temple and city that had been destroyed by Nebuchadnezzar in 586 BC. This too had been foretold in the prophecies of Isaiah: "It is I who says of Cyrus, 'He is My Shepherd! And he will perform all My desire.' And he declares of Jerusalem, 'She will be built,' and of the temple, 'Your foundation will be laid'" (Isa 44:28 NASB). Even the fulfillment of this decree was recorded afterwards by Ezra:

> Now in the first year of Cyrus king of Persia, in order to fulfill the word of the LORD by the mouth of Jeremiah, the LORD stirred up the spirit of Cyrus king of Persia, so that he sent a proclamation throughout all his kingdom, and also put it in writing, saying, "Thus says Cyrus king of Persia, 'The LORD, the God of heaven, has given me all the kingdoms of the earth, and He has appointed

---

275. Merrill, *Kingdom of Priests*, 492. Herodotus attributed the fall of the city to the diverting of the Euphrates into the depression near Aqar Quf. This permitted the Persian troops to enter the city along the riverbed. Nabonidus was later captured in Babylon where, according to Xenophon, he was killed (though Josephus, *Ap.* 1.20.153, reports that Cyrus did not kill Nabonidus that night but deported him to Carmania). Cyrus entered Babylon in triumph after his army, under the command of Ugbaru (or possibly Gubaru, governor of Guti), took the city. Cyrus forbade looting, appointed a ruler over Babylon, and left undisturbed the religious institutions and civil administration.

> me to build him a house in Jerusalem, which is in Judah. Whoever there is among you of all his people, may his God be with him! Let him go up to Jerusalem which is in Judah, and rebuild the house of the LORD, the God of Israel, He is the God who is in Jerusalem.'" (Ezra 1:1–3)

This decree was issued in 538 BC, and Daniel (who had been taken as a captive to Babylon as a youth in 605 BC) was too old to return to Jerusalem by this time. He chose to remain and finish out his years in Babylon under the rule of the Medes and Persians. No doubt he rejoiced over the return to Jerusalem and to hear that the foundation of the temple had been re-laid.[276] As for Cyrus, he continued expanding his empire and died in combat about the year 530 BC. He had well established the mighty Persian Empire, assuring a Persian king for the next two hundred years.

Alexander and the Hellenistic Period

The mighty Persian Empire dominated the ancient Near East from 539 to 333 BC. There were wars with Greece (which kept Persia from advancing on Europe), but Persia remained the unrivaled superpower of the known world. All of this came to a crashing halt, however, in the fourth century BC when a youthful Alexander the Great stepped onto the stage of history.[277] Following Alexander's victory at Issus, his destiny to dominate the world seemed certain. Beitzel explains,

> As a twenty-year-old claimant to the Macedonian throne in 334 BC, Alexander set out with a mere 35,000 troops on a much more ambitious mission: Alexander intended to demolish the mighty Persian Empire. Having won a narrow victory near Troy, Alexander liberated the province of Caria and the city of Side before turning inland to winter at Gordion. In the spring, Alexander marched south through the Cilician Gates, through which the apostle Paul would later pass, and re-entered the Cilician plains. In October 333 BC, the Macedonian's army collided with the Persian forces of Darius III at Issus ... in one of the most pivotal battles of biblical antiquity. Classical historians Diodorus Siculus and Plutarch relate perhaps with some exaggeration how that with the loss of only 450 soldiers, Alexander's

276. The temple in Jerusalem was not actually completed until 516/515 BC (as a result of the ministry of the prophets Haggai and Zechariah). Hence it is doubtful that Daniel lived to hear of its completion.

277. "Alexander the Great (336–323), son of Philip II of Macedon, was born in 356 and was taught by the philosopher Aristotle who was himself the star pupil of Plato" (Di Lella, 38).

disciplined army killed some 110,000 Persians and captured even Darius's wife and family.[278]

This victory at Issus allowed the Macedonian army under Alexander to sweep south, first taking Egypt and eventually the heart of Persia. In 331 BC (only a couple of years after the battle at Issus), Alexander had his final encounter with Darius III at Gaugamela (not far from present-day Mosul in Iraq), just east of the Tigris River. With amazingly incredible speed, he conquered the world that had long been ruled by Persia. No wonder the book of Daniel (7:6) describes him as a speedy leopard with four wings on its back!

The significance of Alexander's conquest of the Persian Empire was that Greek customs, language, and influence were spread throughout the known world west of India. This included the land of Judah, thus setting the stage for the Maccabean revolt many years later.

Almost as quickly as he came to power, Alexander left the stage of history. He died very suddenly in 323 BC, a mere thirty-two years old. Since there was no clear successor to his throne, a power play ensued for control of his empire. By the year 301 BC Alexander's empire, the most extensive the world had ever known, was divided between four of his generals:

1)	Ptolemy I	Egypt, Lebanon, and Coele-Syria (lower Syria and Judah)
2)	Seleucus I	Phrygia as far as the Indus (including Syria and Babylon)
3)	Lysimachus	Thrace and Bithynia
4)	Cassander	Macedonia

The rise of Alexander and the division of his kingdom into four realms was envisioned symbolically in Dan 8:8: "Then the male goat [Greece] magnified himself exceedingly. But as soon as he was mighty, the large horn [Alexander] was broken; and in its place there came up four conspicuous horns [his generals] toward the four winds of heaven" (my interpretation in brackets).

The most important of these, as far as Judah was concerned, were the realms of Ptolemy and Seleucus. The successors of Seleucus I ruled Syria until Pompey made it a Roman province in 64 BC. Unfortunately, Judah was caught between the Ptolemies of Egypt and the Seleucids of Syria, sometimes ruled by one and sometimes by the other. The strife between the Ptolemies and the Seleucids is clearly foretold in Dan 11. One of the rulers who emerged from the Seleucid line was the notorious Antiochus IV Epiphanes, a prominent figure in the book of Daniel (see 8:9–14, 23–26; 11:21–35). Antiochus

278. B. J. Beitzel, *The Moody Atlas of Bible Lands* (Chicago: Moody, 1985), 150. For a detailed biography of Alexander's life and exploits, see I. Worthington, *Alexander the Great: Man and God* (Harlow, UK: Pearson Education Limited, 2004).

IV ruled Syria (and Palestine) during the years 175–164 BC. The references in Daniel speak so clearly of him that critical scholars insist the book had to have been written *after* his time in power.

In the years 168–167 BC, Antiochus carried out a most despicable act of defiling the temple and the Jewish religion and then went on to severely persecute those who resisted his attempts to Hellenize the country of Judah. Upon Antiochus' return from his second Egyptian campaign in 168 BC, he took measures to communicate that no attempts at insurrection would be tolerated.

Such opposition to Hellenism and Seleucid authority could only be interpreted as sympathy for Egypt, for only from Egypt could the rebels hope to receive support for their liberation movement. Therefore, upon reaching Jerusalem, Antiochus had the walls of the city torn down, slaughtered thousands of Jews, and sold many more into slavery (2 Macc 5:11–16). In addition, he himself entered the holy of holies.

Yet this was not the full extent of his atrocities. In December of 167 BC Antiochus issued his persecutory decrees in an attempt to force the Jews to transgress their commandments. McCullough describes some of his offensive actions:

> Here the Jewish ritual was prohibited (1 Mac 1:45–6), and the sacred precincts were formally given over, on the fifteenth of Chislev, 167 BC, to the worship of Zeus Olympios (1 Mac 1:54; 2 Mac 6:2), whose Aramaic designation may have been 'Lord of heaven' (b`l šmyn). The main structure of the temple seems to have been left intact, as well as the altar of burnt offering, although upon the latter a small pagan altar was erected (1 Mac 1:59; 4:44). It is generally assumed that this pagan object is the 'desolating sacrilege' of 1 Mac 1:54 (cf Dan 11:31).[279]

The religious persecution not only involved a complete abomination of the temple and the altar, but copies of Torah were burned, and Sabbath keeping and circumcision were forbidden. Furthermore, the Jews were forced to celebrate the king's birthday every month and to participate in the festal procession in honor of Dionysus. High places and altars on which swine and other animals were to be sacrificed were erected throughout Judah, and inspectors were appointed by the king to make sure these measures were carried out.

These offensive measures prompted the Maccabean revolt, recorded in the books of 1 and 2 Maccabees. This revolt eventually succeeded, and by 164 BC the temple was renovated and rededicated. Antiochus died (supposedly in late 164 BC) while attempting to plunder temples in the eastern part of

---

279. W. S. McCullough, *The History and Literature of the Palestinian Jews from Cyrus to Herod* (Toronto: University of Toronto Press, 1975), 115.

his empire.[280] The temporary relief from Seleucid dominion would be short-lived, for by 64 BC Pompey marched into the area, leading the armies of Rome in victory over both Syria and Judah. With the coming of the Roman Empire, the fourth beast of Daniel had come: "I kept looking in the night visions, and behold, a fourth beast, dreadful and terrifying and extremely strong; and it had large iron teeth. It devoured and crushed, and trampled down the remainder with its feet" (Dan 7:7 NASB). Rome would rule for the next five hundred years, until AD 476, but during the midst of her rule the promised Messiah would come.

Judah Under the Roman Empire

Although Rome had already emerged on the world scene prior to 64 BC, it was Pompey's conquest of Syria and the land of Judah in the years 64–63 BC that brought Roman rule to bear upon the eastern Mediterranean regions.

Following Pompey's conquest of Syria in 64 BC, in which he deposed its king and reconstituted it as a Roman province, he moved southward in 63 BC to establish Roman supremacy over Phoenicia and Coele-Syria (which included Judah). At that time in Judah a civil war was raging, with one faction supporting the Pharisees and another the Sadducees. Pompey chose to back the Pharisaic faction led by Hyrcanus II (the Jewish high priest who had also been appointed as king by his mother, Alexandra Salome). The armies of Pompey and Hyrcanus II laid siege to Jerusalem, and three months later the city fell. In the process, some twelve thousand Jews died. Pompey himself entered the temple but subsequently ordered its cleansing and restored the high priesthood to Hyrcanus II (Josephus, *Ant.*, 14.4).

Taking sides with Pompey and Hyrcanus II was an Idumaean named Antipater. (Idumaea was a territory southeast of Judah between the Dead Sea and the Gulf of Aqaba—what had once been the territory of the Edomites.) By 49 BC civil war between Pompey and Julius Caesar broke out, which eventually brought both men to Egypt. Although Pompey was shortly assassinated, Caesar subsequently became involved in the internal conflicts of Egypt. Siding with Cleopatra against her brother Ptolemy XIII, Caesar was nearly defeated and killed at Alexandria in 47 BC. Coming to his rescue was Antipater I, and for this he was made the first Roman procurator of Judah, with the right to collect taxes. Although Julius Caesar was later assassinated in 44 BC and Antipater was poisoned in 43 BC, the political standing

280. The exact date of Antiochus' death is debated. Some would place it in the spring of 163 BC, but Collins (390) writes that his death was known in Babylon in December 164 BC (cf. Sachs and Wiseman, "A Babylonian King List," 202–12). J. Whitehorne, "Antiochus," in *ABD*, 1:271, concurs: "Antiochus meanwhile, after quelling the revolt of Artaxias of Armenia (165 BC), had invaded Elymais (Elam), where he was foiled in an attempt to sack the temple of Artemis (Aphrodite in some accounts). He withdrew to Tabae in Persia and died there in late 164 B.C. of consumption."

achieved by Antipater set the stage for first-century Judah (later designated by the Romans as Palestine).

Antipater I had a son named Herod who, following his father's assassination, went to Rome. According to Josephus, Herod was elected "king of the Jews" by the Roman senate in 40 BC. Upon his return to Judah he married Mariamne, the Hasmonean princess (which he hoped would legitimize his claim to the throne). A three-year power conflict ensued, but by 37 BC Herod had captured Jerusalem and secured his position of power. History would know him as "Herod the Great," the evil tyrant who sought to murder the baby Jesus (Matt 2) at Bethlehem. He would also be remembered for his many building projects, the most significant being the renovation and enlargement of the Jerusalem temple complex. Since Herod died in 4 BC, most scholars conclude that Jesus was born about 5 BC. One of Herod the Great's sons, Herod Antipas (tetrarch of Galilee and Perea), later had John the Baptist murdered and participated in the trial of Jesus along with Pontius Pilate, the Roman prefect over Judah. As a result of their rulings, Jesus was crucified in AD 33, fulfilling Dan 9:26, "Now after the sixty-two weeks, the Messiah will be cut off and have nothing" (NASB).

Some three decades later the Jews rebelled against their Roman occupiers in the first Jewish-Roman War of AD 66–73. This resulted in the utter destruction of Jerusalem and the Jewish temple in AD 70, events that also fulfilled Dan 9:26, "As for the city and the sanctuary, the people of the coming prince will destroy them. But his [or its] end will come speedily like a flood. Until the end of the war that has been decreed there will be destruction" (NET). Rome mightily crushed the Jewish rebellion, with thousands being killed and thousands more led away into slavery.

Yet, remarkably, another Jewish rebellion took place in AD 132–136 known as the Bar Kokhba Revolt. In this uprising many of the Jews had come to believe that a man known as Simon Bar Kokhba was the Jewish messiah. Again the Romans brutally put down the revolt. The Roman historian Cassius Dio reported that 580,000 Jews were killed, and fifty fortified towns and 985 villages razed. More significantly, the Romans changed the name of Jerusalem to Aelia Capitolina, installed a statue of Jupiter at the former temple site, prohibited Jews from entering Jerusalem, and exiled or sold into slavery most of the surviving Jews. Jesus himself had predicted the destruction of Jerusalem in AD 70 (see Luke 21:20–24) and indicated that these revolts would lead to the expulsion of the Jews from the land: "They will fall by the edge of the sword and be led away as captives among the nations. Jerusalem will be trampled down by the Gentiles until the times of the Gentiles are fulfilled" (Luke 21:24 NET). Although the Roman Empire would eventually collapse by AD 476, the long exile of Jews from the land of Judah would continue until modern times.

The following chart provides a summary of the major historical periods and empires related to the book of Daniel:

The World Empires of the Ancient Near East In Relation to the Book of Daniel				
Assyrian Empire ca. 900–612 BC	Babylonian Empire ca. 612–539 BC	Medo-Persian Empire 539–331 BC	Hellenistic Empires (Origins with Greece) 331–64 BC	Roman Empire 64 BC – AD 476
722 - Northern Kingdom of Israel exiled by Assyria 701 - Isaiah predicts Babylonina invasion (Isa 39:6) 612 - Ninevah sacked by Medes & Babylonians	Daniel in Babylon 605–abt. 535 BC **Nabopolassar** (r. 627–650) **Nebuchadnezzar** (r. 605–562) 605 - Daniel exiled to Babylon 597 - Secon Babylonian deportation (Ezekiel) 586 - Babylonians destory Jerusalem and the Temple	**Cyrus the Great** (r. 559–530) 539 - Cyrus the Great conquers Babylon 538 - Cyrus' decree permitting Jews to return to Judah 516 - Jewish Temple rebuilt in Jerusalem 444 - Nehemiah rebuilds Jeru.	**Alexander** (d. 323) Lysimachus Cassander Ptolemy Seleucus Antiochus IV (r. 175–164) 331 - Alexander the Great defeats Persia 323 - Alexander dies in Babylon 301 - Seleucus becomes the ruler of Syria, Babylonia and more 167 - Antiochus IV Epiphanes desecrates the Jewis Temple 167- 164 The Maccabean revolt	**Julius Caesar** (r. 49–44) 64 - Pompey conquers Syria (64) and Judah (63) 44 - Julius Caesar killed 37 - Herod the Great becomes king of Judah ca. 5 BC - Messiah Jesus is born AD 70 - Romans destroy Jerusalem and the Temple

Selected Bibliography (The Historical Context)

Adali, S. F. *The Scourge of God: The Umman-manda and Its Significance in the First Millennium* BC. State Archives of Assyria Studies. Helsinki: Neo-Assyrian Text Corpus Project, 2011.

Albright, W. F. "The Seal of Eliakim and the Latest Preexilic History of Judah, with Some Observations on Ezekiel." *JBL* 51 (1932): 77–106.

Anderson, B. W. *Understanding the Old Testament*. 4th ed. Englewood Cliffs, NJ: Prentice-Hall, 1986.

Beitzel, B. J. *The Moody Atlas of Bible Lands*. Chicago: Moody, 1985.

Clines, D. J. A. "Cyrus." In *ISBE*, 4 vols., ed. G. W. Bromiley, 1:845–49. Grand Rapids: Eerdmans, 1979.

Fritsch, C. T. "Nineveh." In *ISBE*, 4 vols., ed. G. W. Bromiley, 3:538–41. Grand Rapids: Eerdmans, 1986.

Girshman, R. *Iran*. Hamondsworth: Penguin, 1954.
Grayson, A. K. "Shalmaneser." In *ABD*, 6 vols., ed. D. N. Freeman, 5:1155. New York: Doubleday, 1992.
Malamat, A. "The Last Kings of Judah and the Fall of Jerusalem." *IEJ* 18 (1968): 137–56.
McCullough, W. S. *The History and Literature of the Palestinian Jews from Cyrus to Herod*. Toronto: University of Toronto Press, 1975.
McFall, L. "A Translation Guide to the Chronological Data in Kings and Chronicles." *BSac* 148 (1991): 3–45.
Merrill, E. H. *Kingdom of Priests*. 2nd ed. Grand Rapids: Baker, 2008.
Millard, A. R. "Medes; Media." In *ISBE*, 4 vols., ed. G. W. Bromiley, 3:297–99. Grand Rapids: Eerdmans, 1986.
Oates, J. *Babylon*. Rev. ed. London: Thames and Hudson Ltd., 1986.
Sachs, A. J. and D. J. Wiseman. "A Babylonian King List from the Hellenistic Period." *Iraq* 16 (1954): 202–12.
Sack, R. H. "Nebuchadnezzar II and the Old Testament History Versus Ideology." In *Judah and the Judeans in the Neo-Babylonian Period*, ed. O. Lipschits and J. Blenkinsopp, 221–33. Winona Lake, IN: Eisenbrauns, 2003.
Shea, W. H. "Adon's Letter and the Babylonian Chronicle." *BASOR* 223 (1976): 61–64.
Thiele, E. R. *A Chronology of the Hebrew Kings*. Grand Rapids: Zondervan, 1977.
———. *The Mysterious Numbers of the Hebrew Kings*. 3rd rev. ed. Chicago: Univ. of Chicago Press, 1983.
Wiseman, D. J. "Assyria." In *ISBE*, 4 vols., ed. G. W. Bromiley, 1:332–41. Grand Rapids: Eerdmans, 1979.
———. *Chronicles of Chaldaean Kings (626–556 B.C.) in the British Museum*. London: British Museum, 1956.
———. *Nebuchadrezzar and Babylon*. Schweich Lectures. Oxford: Oxford Univeristy Press, 1985.
Worthington, I. *Alexander the Great: Man and God*. Harlow, England: Pearson Education Limited, 2004.

The Religious Context of the Babylonian Exile

Part of the agreement between Yahweh and Israel was that the nation would commit herself to remain faithful to the Mosaic covenant. According to Deut 28–30, if she obeyed and remained faithful to the covenant stipulations, God would bestow his blessings; if she disobeyed, however, God would bring curses. These curses would come in various levels of severity, but prolonged disobedience would eventuate in exile from the land of promise. Yahweh directly forewarned Israel of this in Deut 28:36–37, "The LORD will bring you and your king whom you shall set over you to a nation which neither you nor your fathers have known, and there you shall serve other gods, wood and stone. And you shall become a horror, a proverb, and a taunt among all the people where the LORD will drive you" (NASB).

Throughout her history Israel embraced the deities of other nations in direct violation of the Ten Commandments. Although God gave ample time for repentance, this tendency to idolatry persisted. Therefore exile eventually came, first to the northern kingdom of Israel in 722 BC (by the Assyrians) and then to the southern kingdom of Judah in 586 BC (by the Babylonians). One purpose of the exile was to impress upon God's covenant people how revolting idolatry was to the Holy Creator God. In effect, God was saying, "If you like idolatry and the worship of other gods so much, then I will plunge you into a society that is totally given to this, so that you will see how repugnant this is to me." The discipline worked its intended effect, for after the Babylonian exile the nation did not revert to idolatry again.

To appreciate the culture into which Daniel and the other Jewish exiles were placed, one must understand some of the religious aspects of Babylon. Although Assyria and Babylon existed as political and military rivals for much of ANE history, the two had much in common in their religion. Much of the Assyro-Babylonian religion was derived from the earlier Sumerian culture. In contrast to Israel's strict monotheism, Assyro-Babylonian religion held to a vast pantheon of deities. Furthermore, these deities were often (supposedly) struggling with one another. There were mythological accounts of both creation and a universal flood, but creation was not the result of a spoken word by a single deity (as with Israel's God, Yahweh).

Central to Mesopotamian religious practice was the belief that man was created in order to serve the gods. The list of their deities is so long that it is simply not possible to list them all here (over 3,000 deities are known from god lists or theophoric personal names). Furthermore, many of their functions and attributes would overlap at times. However, it may prove helpful to highlight the three major cosmic deities, the three astral deities, and a few of the other prominent deities.

The three cosmic deities:

1. Anu
Anu (meaning "heaven") was the father and king of the gods, the heavens personified. Although in theory he was the supreme deity among the gods, he was in practicality rather passive. His consort was variously Antu or Ishtar, and his chief city was Uruk. Supposedly the demons derived their origin from him.

2. Enlil
Enlil (meaning "lord wind") represented the atmosphere, wind, and storm. He practically functioned as the chief deity. He also possessed the "tablets of destiny" which determined the destiny of the world. His city was Nippur.

3. Ea
Ea was lord of the subterranean sweet-water ocean, and was god of wisdom, sorcery, arts, crafts, and culture, and the source of all secret magical knowledge.

The three astral deities:

1. Sin
Sin represented the moon. His principal city was Ur, but he was also worshiped at Harran in northern Mesopotamia. The last king of the Neo-Babylonian empire, Nabonidus (father of Belshazzar), attempted to make Sin the highest god.

2. Šamaš
Šamaš represented the sun and was god of justice and equity (as well as judge of the gods).

3. Ishtar
Ishtar was the most important female deity, and the functions and characteristics of other goddesses were often assimilated into her. She was particularly viewed as the goddess of love and fertility, but also of war. Ishtar was highly popular at Babylon, and one of the notable archaeological discoveries from the ruins of Babylon has been the Ishtar Gate (a major gate of the city dedicated to her). She later became the most important goddess throughout western Asia, known as the Aramean Northwestern Semitic Astarte. She was often represented riding on her sacred beast, the lion.

Other prominent deities:

1. Adad
Adad was the god of thunder and rainstorm (Hadad was his prominent West Semitic counterpart). He could either be beneficent by enabling vegetation and life to flourish, or destructive through flooding.

2. Ashur
Ashur became the national god of Assyria, understood as a deified form of the city Aššur.

3. Marduk (= biblical "Bel")
Marduk is one of the primary deities of interest for a study of the book of Daniel, for it was Marduk who was chosen as the national god of Babylonia. As such, he assumed the functions accorded to other deities and came to have the prominent place of honor in Babylonia.[281] As son of Ea, he was god of magic and incantation. Babylon was his chief city, and his temple (named

281. According to P. W. Gaebelein, Jr., "Marduk," in *ISBE*, 3:244, Marduk's rise to supremacy over other deities occurred early in her history, over 1000 years before the days of Nebuchadnezzar: "Upon the political ascendancy of Hammurabi of Babylon (*ca.* 1750 B.C.), Marduk the god of Babylon became supreme among the older Sumerian gods as creator and ruler—a position formerly enjoyed by Enlil but affirmed for Marduk in the Code of Hammurabi (*ANET*, pp. 163–180) and the Creation Epic (*ANET*, pp. 60–72)." In the *Enuma Elish* epic of creation, Marduk serves as the real hero. This story was recited on the fourth day of the New Year Festival at Babylon.

Esagila) was located there. Daniel and his friends would have witnessed the worship of Marduk firsthand.

4. Nabu (Hebrew = Nebo)
Another key deity was Nabu, god of Borsippa, who was Marduk's son. Nabu was popularized greatly in the first millennium BC as the Babylonian deity of wisdom. The name Nebuchadnezzar may mean "O (god) Nabû, protect my offspring (or firstborn son)."[282] Nabu also played a role in the Babylonian New Year festival.

Not only was Assyro-Babylonian religion extremely polytheistic, but it was very superstitious. Adherents believed that numerous demons attacked people with distress and diseases. Hence, people felt that it was through appeasement of the deities that they could avoid bad fate. Service to the deities, divination, and magic were a way of life. In addition, the promotion of the local religious cult was considered highly important. In the religious cult, the king stood as head of the cult, although in practice the various functions of the cult were delegated to others. Horsnell notes,

> The ancient Babylonians believed that kingship came down from heaven and was bestowed by the gods. Thus the king ruled by divine sanction. ... He was the head of the cult, the foremost servant of the gods, bearing the ultimate responsibility for correctly perpetuating the cult and for building and restoring the temples of his realm.[283]

Although temples were erected to other gods at Babylon, Marduk was the primary god worshiped there.[284] At least for much of his life, Nebuchadnezzar fulfilled his expected role as king of being the leader of the cult. In an ancient inscription, Nebuchadnezzar gives praise to Marduk and prays to him:

> I have made ... the city of Babylon to the foremost among all the countries and every human habitation; its name I have [made/

---

282. Wiseman, *Nebuchadrezzar and Babylon*, 2–5, has a good discussion on the meaning of Nebuchadnezzar's name, although there has been some confusion and disagreement on the exact meaning. He points out, "The meaning of the name formerly given as 'O Nabû, protect the boundary' is now more likely to be interpreted as 'O Nabû, protect my offspring.'" A. van Selms, "The Name Nebuchadnezzar," in *Travels in the World of the Old Testament, FS M. A. Beek*, ed. M. S. H. G. Heerma van Voss et al., 223–29 (Assen: Van Gorcum, 1974), 225, has suggested, "Nabu, protect the crown prince."

283. M. J. A. Horsnell, "Religions of the Biblical World: Assyria and Babylonia," in *ISBE*, 4:88.

284. Although the major temple of Babylon was the temple of Marduk situated at the center of the city, other temples existed for Gula, Shamash, Adad, Belit Nina, and Ishtar of Agade. See the city map of Babylon in Oates, *Babylon*, 148.

> elevated] to the (most worthy of) praise among the sacred cities. … The sanctuaries of my lords Nebo and Marduk (as a) wise (ruler) …
>
> … (Trusting in the power of my lords Nebo and Marduk, I organized [my army] for a[n expedition] to the Lebanon. …
>
> O Marduk, my lord, do remember my deeds favorably as good [deeds], may (these) my good deeds be always before your mind (so that) my walking in Esagila and Ezida—which I love—may last to old age. May I (remain) always your legitimate governor (*šakanakku*), may I pull your yoke till (I am) sated with progeny, may my name be remembered in future (days) in a good sense, may my offspring rule forever over the black-headed.[285]

How humbling it must have been for Nebuchadnezzar, king of Babylon and head of the cult of Marduk, to honor Daniel's God:

> But at the end of that period I, Nebuchadnezzar, raised my eyes toward heaven, and my reason returned to me, and I blessed the Most High and praised and honored Him who lives forever; For His dominion is an everlasting dominion, and His kingdom endures from generation to generation. All the inhabitants of the earth are accounted as nothing, but He does according to His will in the host of heaven and among the inhabitants of earth; and no one can ward off His hand or say to Him, 'What have You done?' (Dan 4:34–35 NASB)

Mesopotamian religion held that man was created in order to serve the gods. Hence, the image of the god was important (as the deity was considered to be present in its image). When the image was carried off to war, the deity remained absent until its return. During festival times the image was carried through the streets in solemn procession.

The focal point of religious life in Babylon centered on the temple of the deity, of which there were several in Babylon. The primary temple, of course, was the temple for Marduk named Esagila. A major temple complex would typically have a ziggurat, i.e., a great, man-made, multi-staged mountain of earth and brick up to 90 meters. Describing the temple, Horsnell remarks,

> The temple was the deity's dwelling place, where he was present on earth to provide blessing for city and people and to be approached by the priesthood and rulers. Here many of the cultic rituals, and especially the daily service (Akk. *dullu*), were carried out.[286]

There would be priests and temple staff for carrying out the daily offerings and animal sacrifices.

Once a year, in the springtime, an important festival was held—a New Year Festival to honor the chief deity of the city. This "akitu festival" was held

---

285. From the so-called Wadi-Brisa Inscription, published in Pritchard, *ANET*, 307.

286. Horsnell, "Religions of the Biblical World," 4:89.

during the first eleven days of the month Nisan (about the time of Israel's Passover). On the second day of the festival, "the *šešgallu*-priest prayed to Marduk, extolling the god's victories and seeking his favor for Babylon, its people, and the temple Esagila."[287] Also during this festival, the god Nabû, Marduk's son, would arrive from neighboring Borsippa. On the tenth day of the festival, the king of Babylon would accompany Marduk, i.e., his image, and lead a procession from Esagila through Babylon.

In the Bible Marduk is referred to as Bel (בֵּל, *bēl*) meaning "lord," and Nabû is termed Nebo (נְבוֹ, *nᵉḇô*). In Isa 46 the prophet proclaimed over a hundred years before Daniel the superiority of Yahweh over the gods of Babylon (even before they were ever taken into exile). "Bel has bowed down, Nebo stoops over; their images are consigned to the beasts and the cattle" (Isa 46:1; cf. Jer 50:2; 51:44). Isaiah went on to declare that Babylon would be judged by Yahweh and that his covenant people would be delivered from Babylon. Mocking Babylon's reliance upon occultic measures, Yahweh (speaking through Isaiah the prophet) challenged Babylon:

> But evil will come on you which you will not know how to charm away; ... Stand fast now in your spells and in your many sorceries with which you have labored from your youth; perhaps you will be able to profit, perhaps you may cause trembling. You are wearied with your many counsels; let now the astrologers, those who prophesy by the stars, those who predict by the new moons, stand up and save you from what will come upon you. (Isa 47:11–13 NASB)

Babylon's reliance upon the occult would do her no good in the day when God visited her in judgment. That day would come in Daniel's own lifetime when the Medo-Persian forces under Cyrus would interrupt Belshazzar's feast to capture the city and terminate the Neo-Babylonian Empire.

In contrast to Israel, who could look to the revealed word of God for instruction about life, the future, and the supernatural, Babylon relied on supernatural information supplied through occult channels. One means was through divination (a technique of communication with the gods) by which the Babylonians sought to know the will of the gods and destinies they had determined for the people. Through this information they could hope to avoid disasters and choose more favorable outcomes. There were various means for the practice of divination, and numerous manuals were compiled to assist the divination specialists.[288] Dream divination was also

287. Ibid.

288. Oates, *Babylon*, 178, states, "A great variety of techniques were used in divination, including the observation of animals' entrails, oil in water, smoke from incense, the behavior of birds and other animals, and celestial and other natural phenomena." Regarding the importance of those who practiced divination, she goes on to say: "Indeed its senior practitioners were men of influence, held in high esteem in their

practiced for interpreting the content of dreams.[289] It would not have been unusual for Nebuchadnezzar (see Dan 2) to summon his court for the interpretation of his dream. At times, an individual might even sleep in a temple in hopes of receiving an enlightening dream from the deity. The Babylonians passionately studied astrology, the observation of celestial phenomena, in hopes of detecting omens that might affect the nation, and Babylon became the most celebrated center for divination based on astrology.[290] Magic was also a popular practice.

Horsnell states,

> Magic and divination were closely related. Divination sought to know the will of the gods and the fate of people through the interpretation of omens, while the art of magic (conjuration or exorcism) sought to ward off evil forces that unfavorable omens indicated were about to invade people's lives with sickness and disasters.[291]

---

own society. They were consulted on all important occasions both by private individuals and officers of state. The army was always accompanied by a diviner."

289. Dreams were highly esteemed, and some were even regarded as revelation from the gods. Archaeologists have recovered a well-preserved, cuneiform, baked-clay cylinder on which Nabonidus (555–539 BC) has recorded his famous dream in which he is instructed by the gods to undertake the restoration of the temple of the moon-god in Harran: "At the beginning of my reign the gods let me see a dream: in it there stood both Marduk, the Great Lord, and Sin, the light of heaven and earth." This is known as the Nabonidus Cylinder of Sippar, a translation of which is provided in Oates, *Babylon*, 132. Cf. A. L. Oppenheim, "The Interpretation of Dreams in the Ancient Near East: With a Translation of an Assyrian Dream-Book," *TAPS* 46 (1956): 179–373.

290. H. Ringgren, *Religions of the Ancient Near East* (Philadelphia: Westminster, 1973), 95, writes, "In course of time observations of the heavenly bodies are developed to an astrological system. The planets are each connected with a god, and their course in heaven is assigned significance for events on earth. The starry sky is sometimes called 'the book of heaven' (*šiṭir šamê*), i.e., a writing which reveals the intentions of the gods. ... We do not know for certain when and where the theory arose that a man's life depends on the position of the stars at the moment of birth, which led to the establishment of the horoscope, but there is much to suggest that it was precisely in Babylonia, where the oldest known horoscopes come from 410 B.C." From the time of Nabonassar (r. 747–734 BC), the Chaldaeans accurately recorded the times of the motion of the stars. In fact, the very term Chaldaean came to signify "astronomer." Oates, *Babylon*, 115, reports the functioning of an astronomical observatory in Babylon as early as the reign of Marduk-apla-iddina II (= biblical Merodach-Baladan, 721–710 BC).

291. Horsnell, "Religions of the Biblical World," 4:90.

Selected Bibliography (The Religious Context)

Gaebelein, P. W. "Marduk." In *ISBE*, 4 vols., ed. G. W. Bromiley, 3:244. Grand Rapids: Eerdmans, 1986.
Horsnell, M. J. A. "Religions of the Biblical World: Assyria and Babylonia." In *ISBE*, 4 vols., ed. G. W. Bromiley, 4:85–95. Grand Rapids: Eerdmans, 1988.
Schneider, M. J. *An Introduction to Ancient Mesopotamian Religion*. Grand Rapids: Eerdmans, 2011.
Oates, J. *Babylon*. Rev. ed. London: Thames and Hudson Ltd., 1986.
Ringgren, H. *Religions of the Ancient Near East*. Philadelphia: Westminster Press, 1973.
van Selms, A. "The Name Nebuchadnezzar." In *Travels in the World of the Old Testament, FS M. A. Beek*, ed. M. S. H. G. Heerma van Voss et al., 223–29. Assen: Van Gorcum, 1974.
Wiseman, D. J. *Nebuchadrezzar and Babylon*. Schweich Lectures. Oxford: Oxford University Press, 1985.

Purpose and Message of the Book

The Primary Theme

The primary *theme* of the book of Daniel is the revelation of Israel's future in relation to the Gentile kingdoms (now that the nation has gone into exile in Babylon), and God's exaltation of Daniel as a channel through whom He reveals his will.

The Primary Purpose of the Book

The primary *purpose* is to establish that God is sovereignly in control of the nations under whom Israel is being disciplined, and that Israel will ultimately be restored and blessed in Messiah's kingdom after she has first undergone tribulation and sufferings imposed by the antichrist.[292]

Secondary Purposes of the Book

1. To portray Daniel's personal dedication to God. This would have been a good example to the other deportees of how to live in a pagan society.
2. To portray through Daniel's example the mighty power of prayer.

---

292. For a helpful study of the book's message, see L. P. Bruce, "Discourse Theme and the Narratives of Daniel," *BSac* 160 (2003): 174–86. He concludes (186) that the coherent message of the book is "that only God is truly sovereign and that He will establish an eternal kingdom."

3. To emphasize God's sovereign authority over Gentile nations and how he establishes and deposes kings and empires to serve his purposes.
4. To give an example of God's faithfulness to his covenant people, even in times of discipline.
5. To outline graphically the prophetic period known as "the times of the Gentiles" (cf. Luke 21:24). The book traces the course of Gentile powers during the period in which Israel was and is being disciplined by Gentiles.

   Pentecost (1327) elaborates, "Daniel outlines the history of the times of the Gentiles and describes past and future empires that occupy Palestine and rule over Israel until the Messiah returns."
6. To reveal God's long-range plan of redemption through Messiah and especially to reveal Israel's future deliverance and the blessings she will enjoy in the coming millennial kingdom.

An Outline of the Book of Daniel

I. THE HISTORICAL SETTING: God's Elevation of Daniel and His Friends in the Courts of Babylon (1:1–21)
- A. Nebuchadnezzar's Siege of Jerusalem and the Deportation to Babylon (1:1–2)
- B. Nebuchadnezzar's Attempt to Reprogram Daniel and His Friends (1:3–7)
- C. Daniel's Resolve Not to Compromise His Faith (1:8–16)
  - 1. Daniel's decision and his appeal to the head of the court officials (1:8–10)
  - 2. Daniel's creative proposal of an alternative (1:11–13)
  - 3. The successful outcome of the test (1:14–16)
- D. God's Elevation of Daniel and His Friends (1:17–21)
  - 1. God's reward for the four Hebrew youths (1:17)
  - 2. The examination by the king (1:18–20)
  - 3. Daniel's longevity of service (1:21)

II. THE ARAMAIC SECTION: The Demonstration of God's Sovereignty over the Gentile Nations That Israel Was Being Subjected to (2:1–7:28)
- A. Nebuchadnezzar's Dream of the Four-Part Image and the Eventual Establishment of Messiah's Kingdom (2:1–49)
  - 1. The inability of the Babylonian "wise men" to interpret the king's dream (2:1–13)
    - a. Nebuchadnezzar startled by a divinely given dream (2:1–3)
    - b. The first response of the Chaldeans (2:4–6)
    - c. The second response of the Chaldeans (2:7–9)

d. The third response of the Chaldeans (2:10–13)
2. Daniel's intercession and prayer (2:14–23)
a. Daniel's intercession with the king (2:14–16)
b. Daniel's prayer with his friends (2:17–18)
c. Daniel's praise in response to God's revelation of the mystery (2:19–23)
3. Daniel presented to King Nebuchadnezzar (2:24–30)
a. Daniel's approach to Arioch (2:24)
b. Daniel's appearance before Nebuchadnezzar (2:25–26)
c. Daniel's witness to King Nebuchadnezzar (2:27–28)
d. Daniel's humility in announcing the king's dream (2:29–30)
4. Daniel reveals the dream and its interpretation (2:31–45)
a. Daniel's declaration of the dream (2:31–35)
b. Daniel's interpretation of the dream (2:36–45)
(i) The 1st kingdom = Babylon (2:37–38)
(ii) The 2nd kingdom = Medo-Persia (2:39a)
(iii) The 3rd kingdom = Greece (2:39b)
(iv) The 4th kingdom = Rome (2:40)
(v) The feet and toes = a kingdom in the distant future (2:41–43)
(vi) The everlasting kingdom set up by God (2:44–45)
5. Nebuchadnezzar's response to Daniel's disclosure (2:46–49)
a. Nebuchadnezzar's adoration (2:46–47)
b. Daniel's rewards (2:48)
c. Daniel's loyalty to his friends (2:49)

B. God's Deliverance of Daniel's Three Friends Who Refuse to Worship the Image of Gold (3:1–30)
1. Nebuchadnezzar's decree demanding worship before the statue of gold (3:1–7)
a. The making of the statue (3:1)
b. The dedication of the statue (3:2–3)
c. The king's decree (3:4–6)
d. The compliance with the king's command (3:7)
2. The Jews are accused of defying the king's orders (3:8–12)
a. The accusers (3:8)
b. Recollection of the king's edict (3:9–11)
c. The charges against the Jews (3:12)
3. Nebuchadnezzar's angry interrogation of Daniel's three friends (3:13–18)
a. Nebuchadnezzar's interrogation (3:13–15)
b. The courage and faith of Daniel's three friends (3:16–18)
4. Nebuchadnezzar's wrathful order to throw the three into the furnace (3:19–23)
a. The king's furious reaction (3:19–20)

b. The three youths cast into the furnace (3:21–23)
5. God's divine protection upon the three in the furnace (3:24–27)
a. Nebuchadnezzar's horrified response (3:24–26a)
b. Their emergence from the furnace (3:26b–27)
6. Nebuchadnezzar's decree to honor the God of Heaven (3:28–30)
a. Nebuchadnezzar's acknowledgment (3:28)
b. Nebuchadnezzar's decree (3:29)
c. Exaltation of Daniel's three friends (3:30)
C. God's Humbling of Nebuchadnezzar, to Whom is Revealed the Dream of the Great Tree (4:1–37)
1. An introduction to Nebuchadnezzar's decree made after his humbling (4:1–3)
2. Nebuchadnezzar's dream and the search for an interpreter (4:4–9)
a. The reception of the dream (4:4–5)
b. The appearance of the Babylonian wise men (4:6–7)
c. The appearance of Daniel before the king (4:8–9)
3. Nebuchadnezzar's disclosure of the dream to Daniel (4:10–18)
a. The bountiful tree (4:10–12)
b. God's judgment against "the tree" (4:13–17)
c. Nebuchadnezzar's instruction to Daniel (4:18)
4. Daniel's interpretation of Nebuchadnezzar's dream (4:19–27)
a. Daniel's initial reaction of shock (4:19)
b. The interpretation, Part I: Nebuchadnezzar's prior blessedness (4:20–22)
c. The interpretation, Part II: Seven years of judgment (4:23–25)
d. The interpretation, Part III: Future grace (4:26)
e. Daniel's advice for the king (4:27)
5. Nebuchadnezzar's pride and the fulfillment of the dream (4:28–33)
a. Nebuchadnezzar's prideful boasting (4:28–30)
b. God's judgment on Nebuchadnezzar (4:31–33)
6. Nebuchadnezzar's restoration and humble praise for God (4:34–37)
a. Nebuchadnezzar's restoration (4:34–36)
b. Conclusion (4:37)
D. God's Humbling of Belshazzar, to Whom is Revealed the Handwriting on the Wall (5:1–30)
1. Belshazzar's insolence at the Feast (5:1–4)
a. Belshazzar's feast (5:1)
b. The sacrilegious use of the temple vessels (5:2–4)
2. Belshazzar's perplexity upon seeing the inscription (5:5–9)

a. The inscription written on the wall (5:5–6)
b. The Babylonian wise men summoned (5:7–9)
3. The queen mother's recommendation to call in Daniel (5:10–12)
4. Belshazzar's offer to reward Daniel for interpreting (5:13–16)
5. Daniel's response to Belshazzar (5:17–28)
a. Daniel's confrontation of Belshazzar's arrogance (5:17–24)
b. Daniel's explanation of the meaning of the inscription (5:25–28)
6. The outcomes of Belshazzar's feast (5:29–31)
a. The end of Belshazzar's reign (5:29–30)
b. The beginning of Darius' reign (5:31)

E. God's Deliverance of Daniel, Who Refuses to Forego Prayer (6:1–28)
1. The conspiracy against Daniel (6:1–9)
a. Daniel's rise in Darius' administration (6:1–3)
b. The attempt to defame Daniel (6:4–5)
c. The manipulation of Darius to entrap Daniel (6:6–9)
2. Daniel's detection, condemnation, and sentencing (6:10–18)
a. The test of Daniel's faith (6:10)
b. The accusation against Daniel (6:11–15)
c. The sentencing of Daniel to the lions (6:16–18)
3. Daniel's deliverance and the punishment of his enemies (6:19–24)
a. Darius' concern for Daniel (6:19–20)
b. Daniel's deliverance (6:21–23)
c. The destruction of Daniel's enemies (6:24)
4. Darius' testimony to God's sovereignty (6:25–28)
a. Darius' decree (6:25–27)
b. Daniel's favor in the Medo-Persian period (6:28)

F. Daniel's Vision of the Four Beasts from the Sea and the Eventual Establishment of Messiah's Kingdom (7:1–28)
1. The visions given to Daniel (7:1–14)
a. Vision of the four beasts (7:1–8)
b. Vision of judgment before the Ancient of Days (7:9–14)
2. The interpretation of the visions given to Daniel (7:15–28)
a. Daniel's reaction to the visions and inquiry to understand (7:15–16)
b. A summary explanation of the visions for Daniel (7:17–18)
c. Further elaboration of the fourth beast in response to Daniel's inquiry (7:19–25)
d. The eventual victory and establishment of Messiah's kingdom (7:26–28)

III. THE HEBREW SECTION: The Revelation of God's Plan to Ultimately Rescue Israel, but Not Until She Has First Suffered at the Hands of Both Antiochus and the Antichrist (8:1–12:13)

- A. The Vision of the Ram and the Goat: Anticipated Persecution by Antiochus (8:1–27)
  - 1. The vision given to Daniel at Susa (8:1–14)
    - a. Introduction to the vision (8:1–2)
    - b. The ram with the two horns: Medo-Persia (8:3–4)
    - c. The male goat: Greece and its division into four parts (8:5–8)
    - d. The "Small Horn" and his hostility against Israel (8:9–14)
  - 2. Gabriel gives Daniel insight about the vision (8:15–27)
    - a. The encounter with Gabriel (8:15–19)
    - b. Gabriel's explanation of the vision (8:20–26)
    - c. Daniel's alarm over the vision (8:27)
- B. The Vision of the 70 "Weeks" Prophecy: God's Time-table for Israel (9:1–27)
  - 1. Daniel's observation from Jeremiah's prophecy (9:1–2)
  - 2. Daniel's prayer: National confession and petition for mercy (9:3–19)
    - a. Daniel's humility before God (9:3–4)
    - b. Confession of the nation's sin and God's righteous judgment (9:5–14)
    - c. Petition for God's mercies and the restoration of Jerusalem (9:15–19)
  - 3. God's response to Daniel's prayer (9:20–27)
    - a. Gabriel's appearance to give Daniel insight (9:20–23)
    - b. Revelation of the seventy "weeks" prophecy (9:24–27)
- C. The Final Vision: Sufferings from Antiochus and Antichrist, but Then Rescue (10:1–12:13)
  - 1. Preparation of Daniel for the vision (10:1–11:1)
    - a. The occasion of the vision (10:1–3)
    - b. The vision of the "man dressed in linen" (10:4–9)
    - c. The visitation of the angel to give Daniel understanding regarding the "latter days" (10:10–11:1)
  - 2. Predictions of the near future—now historically fulfilled (11:2–35)
    - a. From the time of the Persian Empire to Antiochus IV (11:2–20)
      - (i) Origins of the conflict between the Ptolemies and Seleucids during the Persian period (11:2–4)
      - (ii) Conflict between the Ptolemies and Seleucids prior to Antiochus III (11:5–9)

(iii) Seleucia's eventual domination under Antiochus III (11:10–20)

b. During the reign of Antiochus IV (11:21–35)

(i) Antiochus' rise in power (11:21–24)

(ii) Antiochus' rivalry with Egypt (11:25–28)

(iii) Antiochus' persecution of the Jews after the second Egyptian campaign (11:29–31)

(iv) The Jewish uprising against Antiochus: The Maccabean revolt (11:32–35)

3. Predictions of the distant future—reserved for the "end times" (11:36–12:4)

a. The antichrist of the "end times" (11:36–45)

(i) A description of the antichrist (11:36–39)

(ii) The military campaigns of the antichrist leading up to Armageddon (11:40–45)

b. Implications for the Jewish remnant living in the days of the antichrist (12:1–4)

4. The question about the duration of the "distress" (12:5–7)

5. Daniel's concern about the final outcome (12:8–12)

6. God's special promise for Daniel in the resurrection (12:13)

Commentary Bibliography

Allen, J. *Daniel Reconsidered; The Key to the Divine Timetable.* Cookstown, Northern Ireland: Kingsbridge, 2013.

Anderson, R. A. *Signs and Wonders: A Commentary on the Book of Daniel.* ITC. Grand Rapids: Eerdmans, 1984.

Archer, G. L., Jr. "Daniel." In *EBC,* 12 vols., ed., Frank E. Gaebelein, 3:3–157. Grand Rapids: Zondervan, 1985.

Baldwin, J. G. *Daniel: An Introduction and Commentary.* TOTC 23. 1978. Repr.; Downers Grove, IL: InterVarsity, 2009.

Bentzen, A. *Daniel.* 2nd ed. Tübingen: Mohr, 1952.

Buchanan, G. W. *The Book of Daniel.* Mellen Biblical Commentary, Old Testament Series 25. Lewiston, NY: Edwin Mellen, 1999.

Calvin, J. *Daniel.* Geneva Series of Commentaries. 1st English transl., 1570. Repr., 2 vols. Carlisle, PA: Banner of Truth, 1995.

Campbell, D. *Daniel: God's Man in a Secular Society.* Grand Rapids: Discovery House Pub., 1988.

Carpenter, E. "Daniel." In *Ezekiel, Daniel.* Cornerstone Biblical Commentary 9. Carol Stream, IL: Tyndale House, 2010.

Charles, R. H. *A Critical and Exegetical Commentary on the Book of Daniel.* Oxford: Clarendon, 1929.

Collins, J. J. *Daniel.* Hermeneia. Minneapolis, MN: Fortress, 1993.

Constable, T. L. "Notes on Daniel." 2015 ed. http://www.soniclight.com/constable/notes/pdf/daniel.pdf (accessed 20 October 2015).

Culver, R. D. "Daniel." In *The Wycliffe Bible Commentary*, ed., C. F. Pfeiffer and E. F. Harrison, 769–800. Chicago: Moody, 1962.
DeHaan, M. R. *Daniel the Prophet*. Grand Rapids: Zondervan, 1947.
Driver, S. R. *The Book of Daniel*. 5th ed. CBC. London: Cambridge University Press, 1922.
Feinberg, C. L. *Daniel: The Man and His Visions*. Chappaqua, NY: Christian Herald Books, 1981.
Ferguson, S. B. *Daniel*. Preacher's Commentary 21. Nashville: Thomas Nelson, 2002.
Gaebelein, A. C. *The Prophet Daniel: A Key to the Visions and Prophecies of the Book of Daniel*. 14th ed. New York: Our Hope, 1911.
Ginsburg, H. L. *Studies in Daniel*. Texts and Studies of the Jewish Theological Seminary of America 14. New York: Jewish Theological Seminary of America, 1948.
Goldingay, J. *Daniel*. WBC 30. Waco, TX: Word, 1989.
Goldwurm, H. *Daniel: A New Translation with a Commentary Anthologized from Talmudic, Midrashic and Rabbinic Sources*. 2nd ed. Brooklyn, NY: Mesorah, 1980.
Gowan, D. E. *Daniel*. AOTC. Nashville: Abingdon, 2001.
Hartman, L. F., and A. A. Di Lella. *The Book of Daniel*. AB 23. Garden City, NY: Doubleday, 1978.
Hill, A. E. "Daniel." In *EBC*, rev. ed., 10 vols., ed. T. Longman III and D. E. Garland, 8:19–212. Grand Rapids: Zondervan, 2008.
Hippolytus. *Commentaire sur Daniel*. Edited by Gustave Bardy. Translated Maurice Lefèvre. SC 14. Paris: Cerf, 1947. See below on T. C. Schmidt regarding Hippolytus.
Ironside, H. A. *Lectures on Daniel the Prophet*. 1920. Repr.; Grand Rapids, Kregel, 2005.
Jeffrey, A. "The Exegesis of the Book of Daniel." In *IBC*, 6:341–59. Nashville: Abingdon, 1956.
Jephet ibn Ali. *A Commentary on the Book of Daniel*. Edited by D. S. Margoliouth. Oxford: Clarendon, 1889. Repr.; Cambridge: Cambridge University Press, 2013.
Jerome. *Jerome's Commentary on Daniel*. Translated by G. L. Archer. Grand Rapids: Baker Book, 1958.
Keil, C. F. "Biblical Commentary on the Book of Daniel." In vol. 9: *Ezekiel, Daniel*. Translated M. G. Easton. Commentary on the Old Testament. 10 vols. 1884. Repr.; Grand Rapids: Eerdmans, 1975.
Kelly, W. *Notes on the Book of Daniel*. 7th ed. New York: Loizeaux Bros., 1943.
Kennedy, G. *Daniel*. IB 6. New York: Abingdon-Cokesbury, 1956.
Lacocque, A. *The Book of Daniel*. Trans. D. Pellauer. Atlanta: John Knox, 1979.
Leupold, H. C. *Exposition of Daniel*. 1949. Repr.; Grand Rapids: Baker, 1969.
Longman, T. *Daniel*. NIVAC. Grand Rapids: Zondervan, 1999.
Lucas, E. C. *Daniel*. AOTC 20. Downers Grove, IL: InterVarsity, 2002.

———. "Daniel." In *ZIBBC*, 5 vols., ed. J. H. Walton, 4:518–75. Grand Rapids: Zondervan, 2009.
MacArthur, J. *The Future of Israel (Daniel 9:20–12:13)*. Chicago: Moody, 1991.
MacRae, A. A. *The Prophecies of Daniel*. Singapore: Christian Life, 1991.
Mastin, B. *Daniel: An Exegetical and Critical Commentary*. ICC. New York: Bloomsbury T & T Clark, forthcoming.
Miller, S. R. *Daniel*. NAC 18. Nashville, TN: Broadman & Holman, 1994.
Montgomery, J. A. *A Critical and Exegetical Commentary on the Book of Daniel*. ICC. Edinburgh: T & T Clark, 1927.
Newsom, C. A., with B. W. Breed. *Daniel A Commentary*. OTL. Louisville, KY: Westminster John Knox, 2014.
Pace, S. *Daniel*. Smyth & Helwys Bible Commentary. Macon, GA: Smyth & Helwys, 2008.
Pentecost, J. D. "Daniel." In *The Bible Knowledge Commentary, Old Testament*, ed. J. F. Walvoord and R. B. Zuck, 1323–75. Wheaton, IL: Victor, 1985.
Phillips, J. *Exploring the Book of Daniel*. John Phillips Commentary. Grand Rapids: Kregel, 2003.
Pierce, R. W. *Daniel*. Teach the Text Commentary. Grand Rapids: Baker, 2015.
Porteous, N. W. *Daniel, a Commentary*. 2nd ed. Philadelphia: Westminster, 1979.
Pusey, E. B. *Lectures on Daniel the Prophet*. 1864. Repr.; Minneapolis, MN: Klock & Klock Christian Publishers, 1978.
Schmidt, T. C., and N. Nicholas. *Hippolytus of Rome: Commentary on Daniel and 'Chronicon.'* Gorgias Dissertations 67. Gorgias Studies in Early Christianity and Patristics. Piscataway, NJ: Gorgias, 2017.
Seow, C. L. *Daniel*. Westminster Bible Companion. Louisville, KY: Westminster John Knox, 2003.
Sevener, H. A. *God's Man in Babylon: The Visions and Prophecies of Daniel*. Charlotte, NC: Chosen People Ministries, 1994.
Slotki, J. J. *Daniel-Ezra-Nehemiah*. Soncino Books of the Bible. London: Soncino, 1978.
Smith-Christopher, D. L. "Daniel." In NIB, 7:19–152. Nashville: Abingdon, 1996.
Steinmann, A. E. *Daniel*. Concordia Commentary. St. Louis, MO: Concordia, 2008.
Strauss, L. *The Prophecies of Daniel*. Neptune, NJ: Loizeaux Bros., 1969.
Talbot, L. T. *The Prophecies of Daniel*. 3rd ed. Wheaton, IL: Van Kampen, 1954.
Tanner, J. P. *A Commentary on the Book of Daniel*. BEE World Course on the Book of Daniel. Colorado Springs, CO: BEE World, 2015.
Theodoret (of Cyrus, Syria). *Theodoret of Cyrus: Commentary on Daniel*. Translated by R. C. Hill. Atlanta: SBL, 2006.
Towner, W. S. *Daniel*. IBC. Atlanta: John Knox, 1984.
Tregelles, S. P. *Remarks on the Prophetic Visions in the Book of Daniel*. 5th ed. London: Samuel Bagster and Sons, 1864.
Wallace, R. S. *The Lord is King: The Message of Daniel*. Downers Grove, IL: InterVarsity, 1979.

Walvoord, J. F. *Daniel*. John Walvoord Prophecy Commentaries. Revised and edited by P. E. Rawley and C. H. Dyer. Chicago: Moody, 2012.

———. *Daniel: The Key to Prophetic Revelation.* Chicago: Moody, 1971.

Whitcomb, J. C. *Daniel.* Chicago: Moody, 1985.

Widder, W. L. *Daniel.* Hearing the Message of Scripture 23. Grand Rapids: Zondervan, forthcoming.

Wood, L. *A Commentary on Daniel.* 1973. Repr.; Eugene, OR: Wipf and Stock, 1998.

Young, E. J. *The Prophecy of Daniel.* Grand Rapids: Eerdmans, 1949.

Zöckler, O. "Daniel." In vol. 7: *Ezekiel, Daniel and the Minor Prophets.* Translated, enlarged and edited by J. Strong, aided by G. Miller. Lange's Commentary on the Holy Scriptures. 12 vols. 1870. Repr.; Grand Rapids: Zondervan, 1960.

Part I:
The Historical Setting

God's Elevation of Daniel and His Friends in the Courts of Babylon (1:1–21)

The book of Daniel, undoubtedly one of the most unique books in the entire Bible, has fascinated Christian readers throughout the centuries. The book focuses on a Hebrew man named Daniel who was taken into exile in Babylon but providentially became an important political leader in the courts of Gentile kings as an interpreter of dreams and one to whom Yahweh revealed important visions regarding his nation's future.

Daniel was probably only a young teenage boy growing up in Judah when his country was suddenly besieged by Babylon in 605 BC. Daniel and many other choice young men of Judah were forcibly taken into exile to Babylon at that time. There, Daniel would spend the rest of his life. In the course of time, he rose to become a very prominent official in the courts of Babylon. While serving under the powerful Babylonian king Nebuchadnezzar, he would hear the sad news how the city of Jerusalem and the temple of Yahweh were destroyed in 586 BC. Daniel would go on to live a long life, even living to see Babylon's overthrow at the hands of the Medes and Persians in 539 BC. Through all his days, however, Daniel remained faithful and true to the God of heaven. As a result, God used Daniel in extraordinary ways ... to interpret dreams and to explain visions that God gave him.

Daniel 1 provides the setting for the entire book. We are told how Daniel came to Babylon (1:1–2), how Nebuchadnezzar attempted to *reprogram* Daniel and his friends for service to Babylon (1:3–7), how Daniel remained true to God and refused to compromise his faith (1:8–16), and how, as a result, God elevated Daniel and his friends to places of prominence in the Babylonian court (1:17–21). In particular, chap. 1 introduces the series of court tales that comprise the first half of the book (chaps. 1–6). These court tales revolve around the tension that Daniel and his fellow Jews in exile faced regarding the issue of their loyalty to Israel's God, Yahweh, and their submission to the authority of Gentile rulers who did not recognize Yahweh's divine rule. The court tales resolve the tension of foreign rulers in respect to Yahweh's divine sovereignty. Breed elaborates,

> Court stories were popular presumably because they provided storytellers with apposite narrative materials for resolving pressing social and political problems. For diasporic Jews, these problems

> involved the tension between their belief in a sovereign God and their experiences of Gentile kings announcing and enacting their own sovereignty, often in direct conflict with the presumed will of the Jewish God. ... Thus the imagined resolution for the court stories in Daniel comprises the Gentile king's recognition of both the limitations on his own sovereignty and the ultimate sovereignty of YHWH.[1]

A. Nebuchadnezzar's Siege of Jerusalem and the Deportation to Babylon (1:1–2)

The book opens with a short account of the historical circumstance that led to Daniel and his friends being exiled to Babylon. A Babylonian general named Nebuchadnezzar successfully laid siege to Jerusalem. (See "The Historical Context" for a fuller account of the historical details provided in the introductory matters.) Nebuchadnezzar had just defeated the Egyptians at the Battle of Carchemish in the summer of 605 BC and was pursuing Pharaoh's army southward in the direction of Egypt. This brought him right through the land of Judah, which up until that time had been a vassal state of Egypt under Pharaoh Necho II.

Textual Notes

1.a. The quiescent א in נְבוּכַדְנֶאצַּר is sometimes absent and the name written נְבוּכַדְנֶצַּר (e.g., Dan 1:18; Ezra 1:7). Quite frequently (esp. in Jeremiah and Ezekiel), the name is spelled נְבוּכַדְרֶאצַּר, with a ר instead of a נ (e.g., Jer 21:2). That we have numerous examples of both spellings testifies that both were considered acceptable. The Babylonian form was *Nabû-kudurri-uṣur* (so BDB, 613), a theophoric name honoring the god Nabu (see "The Religious Context" in introductory matters for elaboration).

2.a. Some MSS have יהוה instead of אֲדֹנָי (note יהוה אדני in Kenn. 245). The form אֲדֹנָי in *BHS* emphasizes God's sovereignty, which is significant to the context.

Translation

1:1 In the third year of the reign of King Jehoiakim of Judah, King Nebuchadnezzar of Babylon came to Jerusalem and laid siege to it. **2** Then

1. B. W. Breed, "A Divided Tongue: the Moral Taste Buds of the Book of Daniel," *JSOT* 40 (2015): 117.

the Lord delivered[2] King Jehoiakim of Judah into his hand along with[3] some[4] of the vessels of the house of God. He brought them[5] to the land of Shinar[6] to the house of his god, and then he put the vessels in the temple treasury[7] of his god.

---

2. The word translated "delivered" is lit. "gave" from the Heb verb נָתַן (*nāṯan*), but contextually it has the sense of *handing* or *giving one over* (see BDB, 679). Cf. 1 Kgs 14:16.
3. Regarding the translation of the *waw* as "along with," see B. T. Arnold, "Word Play and Characterization in Daniel 1," in *Puns and Pundits: Word Play in the Hebrew Bible and Ancient Near Eastern Literature*, ed. S. B. Noegel, 231–48 (Bethesda, MD: CDL Press, 2000), 234. He argues that the verb *nāṯan* governs not only the first clause, but the next phrase as well, *ûmiqṣāṯ kᵊlê ḇêṯ-hāʾĕlōhîm*, taking the *waw* as a *waw*-of-accompaniment.
4. Regarding מִקְצָת (*miqṣāṯ*), Goldingay (4–5, fn 2d) discusses possible translations "part of the extremity," "the costliest of" and "all of." T. J. Meek, "Translation Problems in the Old Testament," *JQR* 50 (1959–60): 45–46, argues that here *miqṣāṯ* means "all the utensils," though it is obvious from 2 Kgs 24:13 that Nebuchadnezzar did not take all the utensils at the time of the 605 BC siege. Yet מִקְצָת (*miqṣāṯ*), from the noun קְצָת (*qᵊṣāṯ*) can have the partitive sense "some of" as in Neh 7:69. Montgomery (118) adds, "The partitive use of מקצת is common in the Talmud, s. Jastrow, *s.v.*" Nebuchadnezzar did not take all of the temple vessels, as is clear from other passages (2 Kgs 24:13; Jer 52:17–23).
5. The word "them" (suffix on וַיְבִיאֵם, *wayᵊḇîʾēm*) refers to the temple vessels, which is clear from 2 Chr 36:6–7. Collins (127 fn 6) points out, "θ′, G, and Vg. read neuter here (i.e., the vessels, not the king)."
6. I.e., the land of Babylonia. LXX^{O} makes the point clear by its translation εἰς Βαβυλῶνα (*eis babulōna*), in contrast to LXX$^{\theta}$'s εἰς γῆν Σεννααρ, *eis gēn Sennaar* (on the significance of the word choice, see comments under biblical theology). Shinar was once thought to be connected with ancient Sumer, but philological studies have more recently shown that to be unlikely. R. Zadok, "The Origin of the Name Shinar," *ZA* 74 (1984): 240–44, has related Shinar to a name for Babylonia and its foreign rulers used by the Hittites and others in the Late Bronze Age. A Hittite source (the "Telepinus Declaration") indicates Mursili I made a campaign against *Bābili* (Babylon), and yet a Neo-Hittite document reports a campaign by the same king though using the name ^{uru}*Ša-an-ḫa-ra* (Shinar).
7. The Heb (בֵּית אוֹצַר אֱלֹהָיו, *bêṯ ʾôṣar ʾĕlōhāyw*) is literally "the treasure house of his god." See Neh 10:39 where בֵּית הָאוֹצָר (*bêṯ hāʾôṣār*) means a treasury at the temple (having storerooms; cf. 1 Kgs 7:51). LXX$^{\theta}$ rendered this rather literally as τὸν οἶκον θησαυροῦ τοῦ θεοῦ αὐτοῦ (*ton oikon thēsaurou tou theou autou*), "the house of the treasury of his god" (i.e., "treasure house"), whereas LXX^{O} was more theological, τῷ εἰδωλίῳ αὐτοῦ (*tōi eidōliōi autou*), "his idol temple."

Commentary

1:1 Jehoiakim came to the throne of Judah in October of 609 BC following King Josiah's death at the hands of the Egyptian Pharaoh, Necho II.[8] (For details, see introductory matters, "The Historical Context.") In the following years, Judah remained a vassal state of Egypt, with the burden of annual tribute. When the Babylonians defeated the Egyptians at Carchemish in 605 BC, they pursued them southward (thus driving them back to Egypt). This naturally brought the Babylonians to Judah, where they quickly advanced on the capital at Jerusalem and laid siege to it (in the summer of 605 BC but before Nabopolassar's death on 15/16 Aug). Probably their motive in laying siege to Jerusalem was to make Judah a Babylonian vassal state and so prevent Egypt from pushing northward again.

Regarding the supposed discrepancy with Jer 25:1, which places the siege in Jehoiakim's fourth year, see the introduction regarding alleged historical inaccuracies under "Objections to the Traditional Date and Authorship." There is no actual discrepancy because Jeremiah and Daniel were using different methods of reckoning the years. Although both Jeremiah and Daniel seem to have reckoned the beginning of the new year from Tishri 1, Jeremiah (following Judean practice) used non-accession year dating, whereas Daniel (following Babylonian practice) used accession year dating.

1:2 Verse 2 makes the point that Jerusalem's fate was not merely a matter of being the victim of an international power struggle between Babylon and Egypt. The Lord was in control of this situation, and he purposely allowed the Babylonians to afflict His chosen people. The text says, "Then the *Lord* gave ... into his hand." Here, "hand" is a metonymy of cause for effect, i.e., the power or authority of the person (cf. BDB, 390 2). There are two different Hebrew words that are both translated by the same English word

8. Necho II reigned as the Egyptian Pharaoh for approximately fifteen years (610–595 BC). Upon coming to the throne, he inherited a rather strong and reunited Egypt from his father. In his foreign affairs, he chose (like his father) to support the Assyrian Empire that was crumbling due to the assaults of Babylon and Media. Shortly after coming to power, Necho marched in 609 BC through Syria to help the last Assyrian king, Aššur-uballit, against the Babylonians. As he passed through Judah, however, King Josiah came out to oppose him, thus forcing Necho to do battle. In the process, King Josiah was killed (2 Kgs 23:29; 2 Chr 35:20–24). Yet the Egyptian army had been slowed, and the delay helped the Babylonians to destroy unaided Assyria. Upon his return to Egypt, Pharaoh Necho replaced Josiah's son Jehoahaz with another of his sons, Jehoiakim. Jehoiakim was required to pay tribute to the Pharaoh as a token of his loyalty to Egypt (2 Kgs 23:31–35; 2 Chr 36:1–4). Egypt thus laid claim to Judah and would hold sovereignty over her until Nebuchadnezzar attacked Judah in 605 BC.

"Lord."[9] One is God's personal name, יְהוָה (Yahweh), and the other is the Hebrew word *ʾăḏōnāy*. The latter word is used here stresses God's *sovereignty*. The point is that the Lord, the one who is sovereign over everything, is the One who *delivered* (lit., gave) Jehoiakim into the power or authority of Nebuchadnezzar (cf. 2 Chr 36:14–17). Nebuchadnezzar's victory was not due to his brilliance or military might.

At the time of the 605 BC siege, Nebuchadnezzar allowed Jehoiakim to remain on the throne of Judah (though as a vassal to Babylon). Yet he took *some* (not all) of the temple vessels and brought them to Babylon, where he placed them in one of the treasury rooms of the temple of his god (see further discussion under "Biblical Theology Comments"). Kalimi and Purvis clarify that each of the three invasions of Jerusalem by Nebuchadnezzar resulted in removal of some of the temple utensils with the third and final temple plundering occurring in 586 BC when Zedekiah was dethroned (2 Chron 36:18).[10] According to 1 Kgs 24:1, Jehoiakim remained loyal for three years but then rebelled against Babylon. He finally died in 598 BC, following which his son Jehoiachin briefly ruled in his place.

Biblical Theology Comments

Why would the Lord do such a thing to his covenant people Israel, allowing Nebuchadnezzar to so easily overrun Jerusalem and ransack the temple built in Solomon's day? Did he not love them? Was he not a God faithful to his covenant? The Lord had certainly defended Jerusalem in Hezekiah's day when the much larger Assyrian army of King Sennacherib had besieged it (2 Kgs 19). Centuries earlier Yahweh had entered into a formal covenant relationship with the nation of Israel at Mt. Sinai (cf. Exod 19). He agreed to faithfully care for them, provided they agree to keep the terms of his covenant, also referred to as the Mosaic law. Later, Yahweh clarified that obedience to this covenant (the Mosaic law) would be essential for his blessings.

A similar elaboration of the blessings and curses is recorded for us in Deut 28–29. Note, for instance, Deut 28:1–2 and v. 15:

> And it will be that if you indeed obey the LORD your God, being careful to observe all his commandments that I am giving you today, that he will elevate you above all the nations of the earth. And all these blessings will come to you in abundance if you obey the LORD your God.

---

9. In many English translations, these words are distinguished by the use of capital letters. The Hebrew word for Yahweh (יְהוָה, God's personal name) is usually represented by "LORD" (small caps), whereas the word אֲדֹנָי (*ʾăḏōnāy*) is spelled "Lord" (lower case).

10. I. Kalimi and J. D. Purvis, "King Jehoiachin and the Vessels of the Lord's House in Biblical Literature," *CBQ* 56 (1994): 449–57.

> ... But if you pay no attention to the LORD your God and are not careful to keep all his commandments and statutes I am relating to you today, then all these curses will come and overtake you. (NASB)

If the people obeyed the law, then Yahweh would pour out his blessings on them. On the other hand, if they disobeyed his law, he would discipline them (they would receive curses). These *curses* could be things like withholding rain upon the land (necessary for growing crops). Moreover, if they continued in disobedience, Yahweh would send harsher forms of discipline. Hopefully, this harsher discipline would be sufficient to prompt the people to turn back in repentance and obey Yahweh. If it did not, however, Yahweh would have to send an even harsher form of discipline. He even warned them that continued disobedience and rebellion (particularly for idolatry) would ultimately result in Yahweh removing them from the land of promise altogether (see Deut 28:36–37, 41; 29:22–28).[11]

This is exactly what was happening in Dan 1:1–2 in the year 605 BC. Israel had been in the land of promise for over 800 years.[12] Although there were a few periods when the nation was relatively obedient (e.g., under King David), most of this time was marked by continued disobedience and giving themselves over to idolatry. They were becoming more like the idolatrous pagans than the pagans were becoming like the people of God.

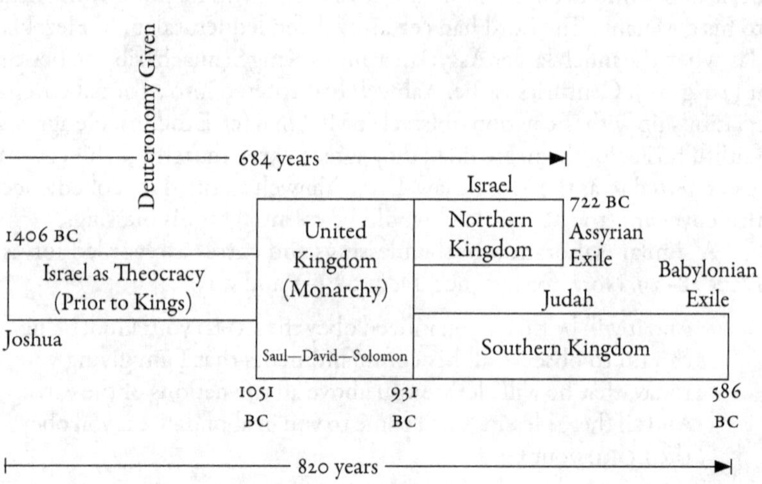

11. The "land of promise" refers to the land of Canaan Yahweh had promised to the descendants of Abraham by covenant as an everlasting possession many centuries earlier (cf. Gen 15:18–21; 17:8; 26:3–4).

12. After being led out of Egypt in 1446 BC (cf. 1 Kgs 6:1), the Hebrews entered the land of promise (i.e., Canaan) in 1406 BC. Regarding the 1446 BC date for the Exodus, see J. P. Tanner, "Old Testament Chronology and Its Implications for the Creation and Flood Accounts," *BSac* 172 (Jan 2015): 36–38.

In 722 BC God sent Assyria to afflict his people and lead away the Northern Kingdom of Israel into exile. This should have been a serious wake-up call to the Southern Kingdom of Judah. God gave them over 100 years of grace, but even the Southern Kingdom refused to truly repent and turn back to faithfully obeying the Mosaic Law. Finally, God said, "That's enough," and he decided that the Southern Kingdom of Judah would also have to depart the land of promise. Nebuchadnezzar and his Babylonian army were merely the agents of God to bring about the curse of exile Yahweh had forewarned the people about in Deut 28–29. The discipline of exile would take place in stages, beginning in 605 BC, and continuing through 586 BC. Obviously, this was a harsh judgment from Yahweh, but there was good reason for doing so. Israel had been chosen to be a light to the nations to lead them out of darkness and idolatry, and yet they had perverted that responsibility.

Following Nebuchadnezzar's successful siege of Jerusalem, he plundered the Jewish temple at Jerusalem. This was the temple that had been built under King Solomon about the year 960 BC (cf. 1 Kgs 6:1; 6:38). The Babylonians then took some of the vessels that were used in the temple ministry back to their capital in the land of *Shinar*, an ancient name for the area of Babylon (cf. Zech 5:11). The use of the term *Shinar* is significant.[13] Baldwin (78) explains,

> The land of Shinar is a deliberate archaism. ... Shinar, site of the tower of Babel (Gn 11:1–9; cf. 10:10), was synonymous with opposition to God; it was the place where wickedness was at home (Zc 5:11) and uprightness could expect opposition.

Ironically, God sent disobedient Judah to the very place known for wickedness and idolatry, for there they would learn just how repulsive an idolatrous civilization could be. Upon arrival in Babylon, the temple vessels from Jerusalem were then placed in the Babylonian temple that had been constructed to the honor of pagan deities worshiped by the Babylonians. Several pagan temples existed in Babylon, but chief among these was the temple of Marduk, the *national god* of Babylon. Even many of the walls of the city had bricks ornamented with the depiction of Marduk as a hybrid dragon creature.

Placing the temple vessels from Jerusalem in the temple of Marduk held symbolic significance, for it was the Babylonians' way of proclaiming that their god was superior to the God of Israel. The Babylonians attributed their success to their deity, and from their perspective Marduk was the champion god. Little did they realize that Marduk was no god at all and that Israel's God (Yahweh, the only true God) had purposely allowed the Babylonians to do this to his covenant people. He was disciplining them for their sinfulness

13. The Hebrew text of Dan 1:2 uses the term *Shinar* (Heb., *šinʿār*) rather than the term "Babylon."

and rebellion against him. Furthermore, Yahweh did not feel slighted that these impotent Babylonian gods were being credited with superiority over him. Yahweh knew that he alone is God, and in due time he would also act to destroy and discredit these idols (cf. Isa 46:1–2). Dumbrell elaborates how the choice of the term Shinar (and its association with Babel) serves the theological purposes of the book:

> ... the use of the phrase in Gen. 11:2 of the Babel incident is important. In Dan. 1 Nebuchadnezzar's monochrome policy for his empire of one language, one common culture, one educational base etc., all emanating from the 'land of Shinar', recalls vividly Gen. 11. We have previously noted that the book of Daniel is the account of the clash of two imperiums, world power structures of one form or another, and the kingdom of God. We are left in no doubt by the laconic conclusion to Dan. 1 ('Daniel continued until the first year of King Cyrus' – i.e. Daniel lived through the entire exile and saw the downfall of Babylon), which imperium will prevail.[14]

Finally, the removal of the temple vessels by Nebuchadnezzar, on three occasions no less (Dan 1:2; 2 Kgs 24:10–17; and 2 Kgs 25:13–17), was a temporary, not permanent, allowance by Yahweh. The Chronicler is careful to point out that the vessels would eventually find their way back to the postexilic temple, allowing the Yahweh worship system to be resumed in continuity with the nation's past:

> For the Chronicler, to stress the fact that Nebuchadnezzar had removed the vessels in the time of Jehoiachin, and that they had not been physically violated, was also to underscore the assertion that the sacred vessels were in Babylon awaiting the time when God would give attention to them and bring them back. The importance of this was also stressed by Ezra: when Sheshbazzar led the returning exiles to Zion he brought with him "the vessels of the house of the Lord which Nebuchadnezzar had carried away from Jerusalem" (Ezra 1:7; see also 5:13–15; 6:5). ...
>
> The purpose of stressing continuity in the use of the same vessels was to demonstrate that the holiness of Zerubbabel's temple was not less than that of Solomon's.[15]

---

14. W. J. Dumbrell, *Covenant and Creation: A Theology of the Old Testament Covenants* (Exeter, UK: Paternoster, 1984), 201–2.

15. Kalimi and Purvis, "King Jehoiachin and the Vessels of the Lord's House," 455. P. R. Ackroyd, "The Temple Vessels—a Continuity Theme," in *Studies in the Religion of Ancient Israel*, ed. by B. W. Anderson, VTSup 23 (Leiden: Brill, 1972), 166–81, writing in a similar vein, insists that the rebuilding of the temple itself was not enough to restore the worship system. More was needed to reestablish continuity with the past. He states (ibid., 178), "Thus the restoration of the temple includes the

Application and Devotional Implications

The words, "the Lord delivered King Jehoiakim of Judah into his hand," have a very grave sound to them. They remind us that the Lord God is completely sovereign to do exactly as he wishes, but they also remind us that—though he is a God of love and amazing grace—he is nevertheless a God who holds his people accountable and disciplines them according to his wise judgment. Furthermore, we are reminded by this (and other passages) that God holds both nations and individuals accountable to him. The abiding principle from this passage is that God can and does give his children into the hand of someone (or something) on account of rebellion against his authority. This may bring pain in the immediate future, yet the purpose is not to simply punish for the sake of making one suffer. Rather, God, as a perfect and loving Father, always designs discipline with a purpose. He always acts out of love, and whenever he disciplines us it is for our own good—that we might derive some benefit from it.

The principle of God's discipline is still true for new covenant believers today. We are reminded from Heb 12:6 that those whom the Lord loves, he disciplines. This same passage goes on to say, "All discipline for the moment seems not to be joyful, but sorrowful; yet to those who have been trained by it, afterwards it yields the peaceful fruit of righteousness" (Heb 12:11, NASB). Just as Judah's discipline at the hands of Nebuchadnezzar—though sorrowful for a moment—was intended to cure her of the problem of idolatry, so God's disciplinary actions unto his covenant children today are meant to bring about good in our lives, particularly that he might cultivate a more righteous character in us. Holiness may be a word that seems out of fashion in today's modern society, yet God's basic desire for our lives has not changed in time. The apostle Peter reminds us, "Like obedient children, do not comply with the evil urges you used to follow in your ignorance, but, like the Holy One who called you, become holy yourselves in all of your conduct, for it is written, 'You shall be holy, because I am holy'" (1 Pet 1:14–16, NET). If we harden our hearts against the Lord, we may be setting ourselves up for God's discipline. That is why it is so important to turn from sin quickly and not allow sin and rebellion to build up in our lives.

B. Nebuchadnezzar's Attempt to Reprogram Daniel and His Friends (1:3–7)

Shortly following Nebuchadnezzar's siege of Jerusalem, his father (Nabopolassar, r. 626–605 BC) died in Babylon, and Nebuchadnezzar hastily returned to

---

bringing back of the vessels, and with them the guarantee that there is a direct link with the earlier worship of the community." He adds (ibid., 180), "Thus across the disaster of the exile, in which the loss of the temple might seem to mark an irreparable breach, there is a continuity established which enables the later worshipper to know, through the actual vessels in use, that he stands with his ancestors in the faith."

secure the throne and be crowned the next Babylonian king. He brought with him several choice young Hebrew men, including Daniel, Hananiah, Mishael, and Azariah, to be trained for diplomatic service in the empire.

The Bible does not tell us about the journey they had to make from Jerusalem to Babylon. Undoubtedly, this was a sad and miserable time for these young Jewish captives. The journey from Jerusalem to Babylon would have amounted to roughly 1,100 km (ca. 680 miles), if we assume that they marched along one of the northern trade routes through Damascus that connected to Mari and then down the Euphrates River.

As they neared the end of their long and arduous journey, the glorious specter of the ancient city of Babylon began to appear on the horizon. Babylon was a city larger, more fortified, and more ornate than anything the Hebrew youths had ever seen. Through the city ran the mighty Euphrates River, the lifeline of Mesopotamia. As they drew closer, there was a large bridge for them to cross before entering one of the many glorious gates of the city. Just imagine how intimidating the scene must have been for these Hebrew youths!

Walking across the bridge that spanned the Euphrates, thousands of Babylonians would have been lining the tops of the city walls. Probably they were laughing and hurling insults at the "conquered" Hebrews. From the crowds, someone might have yelled "Foolish Hebrews! Now you'll learn to trust in Marduk!" Daniel had not chosen to be here. He was only the victim of circumstances, powerless in himself to change what was happening. From this point on, his life would never be the same. He was forced to leave behind his parents and family, his beloved Jerusalem, and the Hebrew culture with its focus upon the worship of Yahweh at the beautiful temple of Solomon. These things he would never see again. For the rest of his life he would be a resident of Babylon. Probably only a young man of fifteen years at the time, he now faced the daunting challenge of remaining faithful and true to the God of the Bible while living in the midst of an idolatrous and pagan civilization.

The main point of vv. 3–7 is to show how Daniel and his friends were uniquely chosen and put through a regimen of training that would prepare them for governmental service within the Babylonian Empire. Their training, however, was meant to strip them of their national and religious affections, and to conform them to the pagan worldview of the Babylonians. In essence, they were being reprogrammed to think and act like the world.

Textual Notes

3.a. LXX$^{\theta}$'s transliteration of אַשְׁפְּנַז as Ασφανεζ is understandable, but LXX^{O}'s Αβιεσδρι raises questions (except Pap. 967, Ασπανες). *BHS* points out that LXX^{O} might be thinking of אָבִיעֶזֶר, which it has in v. 11 in place of הַמֶּלְצַר. Collins (127) considers אַשְׁפְּנַז an Old Persian term meaning "innkeeper" (Goldingay [5] "guest-master or the like"), but the versions understood this as a personal name. Αβιεσδρι, then, is an attempt to Hebraize the term.

3.b. Instead of מִבְּנֵי יִשְׂרָאֵל, LXX$^{\theta}$ has τῶν υἱῶν τῆς αἰχμαλωσίας Ισραηλ, "of the sons of the captives of Israel," apparently adding αἰχμαλωσίας to clarify they were from the exiles, and perhaps a gloss under the influence of Dan 2:25. LXX^{O} has τῶν υἱῶν τῶν μεγιστάνων τοῦ Ισραηλ, "of the sons of the great ones of Israel." R. H. Charles (12) attempted to argue from LXX$^{\theta}$ for an emendation *gōlat* after *bᵊnê*, and to assert that only two groups (not three) were in view by translating, "from the children (of the exile of) Israel, both of the royal seed and of the nobles." See Josh 9:23 for a case of ו ... ו meaning "both ... and." M. Stone ("A Note on Dan i. 3," 69–71), has refuted Charles's emendation and translation. However, see my translation note below for a third option, namely the *explicative* use of the conjunction ו on מִזֶּרַע.

4.a. מְאוּם (*mᵊʾûm*, "blemish, defect") occurs elsewhere only in Job 31:7. However, the Q reading מוּם, without the quiescent א, is fairly frequent (same meaning), and a number of MSS have מוּם in Dan 1:4. This can be used of a physical or moral blemish, and the presence of such excludes one from priestly service (Lev 21:17, 18, 21, 23).

7.a. The second וַיָּשֶׂם is lacking in both LXX^{O} and LXX$^{\theta}$, and in the Vg. The translators may have had a Heb MS with the second וַיָּשֶׂם but felt it unnecessary for Gk, and perhaps to make it consistent with the sentence construction for the following names.

7.b. Daniel's new name appears as בֵּלְטְשַׁאצַּר in *BHS*, but a few MSS have variations: –שצר, –אשצר, or –שצאר. Both LXX^{O} and LXX$^{\theta}$ have Βαλτασαρ at 1:7, but this is identical to the spelling in Dan 5 of the Babylonian king named Belshazzar.

Translation

1:3 The king commanded[16] Ashpenaz, the chief of his court officials,[17] to

16. Lit., "he said," but contextually the translation "commanded" is appropriate (coming from a king).

17. Older translations such as the KJV refer to Ashpenaz as "the master of his eunuchs," which might imply that he had been emasculated (cf. ESV, "his chief eunuch"). The Hebrew term *sārîs*, however, can mean either "eunuch" (Isa 56:3) or "court official" (without any reference to sexual impotence). Goldingay (5) indicates that "סריס comes from Akk. *ša-reši* 'he who is the head.'" The same term is used in Gen 37:36 and 39:1 to describe Potiphar, who was a married man. There is no reason, therefore, to insist that Ashpenaz was a eunuch, though that remains a possibility (so Goldingay, 5). *HALOT* (770) suggests "state official" in the Babylonian court for *sārîs* in Dan 1:3, 7, 11, 18. Interestingly, both LXX traditions rendered this as ἀρχιεταῖρος (*archietairos*), a word LSJM gives the meaning "chief friend, companion." The use of the Gk term in 2 Sam 16:16 suggests that the emphasis is on a very trusted person, perhaps one's *confidant*. If the LXX helps with the understanding of *sārîs*, then "eunuch" is not the main idea.

bring in some of the sons of Israel, that is,[18] some of the royal family and the nobility[19]— **4** young men[20] in whom there was no defect and who were good-looking, who had comprehension in all manner of wisdom, who had gained much knowledge[21] and were very discerning, and who had the ability[22] for serving[23] in the king's royal court—and to teach them the literature[24] and language of the Chaldeans.[25] **5** And the king appointed for them a daily ration[26] from the food served to the king and from the wine which he drank,[27] and *appointed* them to be trained[28] for three years, at the end[29] of *which time* they might serve the king. **6** Now among the sons of Judah

18. *BHS* has *waw* before מִזֶּרַע (*mizzera'*), which could be translated "*and* from the royal family." However, the Hebrew *waw* can be understood as "explicative" (namely, that is)—so Goldingay (5)—or "emphatic" (even, especially). The NET chose to render this as a relative clause ("who were of royal and noble descent"). The conjunction is even missing in some Heb MSS. The explicative use makes the best sense, indicating the specific ones of the sons of Israel that were chosen.
19. Heb פַּרְתְּמִים (*partᵉmîm*) is an Old Persian term (*fratama*). So BDB, 832. LXX$^{\theta}$ transliterated it, but LXX^{O} translated by the word ἐπιλέκτων (*epilektōn*), meaning "the choicest." See Esth 1:3 and 6:9 in the sense "nobles" of the empire.
20. Goldingay (5) asserts that יְלָדִים (*yᵉlāḏîm*) "covers males from birth to marriage."
21. The translation "gained much knowledge" is an attempt to render MT's "knowers of knowledge" (יֹדְעֵי דַעַת, *yōḏᵉ'ê ḏa'aṯ*).
22. The Heb word כֹּחַ (*kōaḥ*) normally means "strength, power," but see BDB, 470 1b for the nuance of ability or efficiency. Cf. NET's "who were capable of."
23. Heb לַעֲמֹד בְּהֵיכַל הַמֶּלֶךְ (*la'ămōḏ bᵉhêḵal hammeleḵ*) is literally "to stand in the royal palace of the king," but the word *stand* implies service to the king. See BDB, 764 1e for the nuance of עָמַד ('*āmaḏ*) as standing before another for the purpose of service or attending to (though usually עָמַד ('*āmaḏ*) is followed by לִפְנֵי (*lip̱nê*) as in 1 Kgs 10:8; 12:8).
24. Heb. סֵפֶר (*sēp̱er*), a collective sg, is translated γράμματα (*grammata*) in both LXX, meaning not only "letters" but "documents" (LSJM, 358 III 2). The English word "literature" captures the point.
25. "Chaldeans" (כַּשְׂדִּים, *kaśdîm*) is an older term for the Babylonians, used here in an ethnic sense.
26. דְּבַר־יוֹם בְּיוֹמוֹ (*dᵉḇar-yôm bᵉyômô*) is lit., "the thing of a day in its day," that is, a daily ration (since food ration is the context).
27. Lit., the wine of his drink.
28. The verb לְגַדְּלָם (*lᵉgaddᵉlām*) means to be or become great in the Qal, but here the Piel form means "to raise, bring up" with the implication of *educating* the one being brought up (so *HALOT*, 179). LXX^{O}'s ἐκπαιδεῦσαι (*ekpaideusai*) reinforces this understanding (ἐκπαιδεύω [*ekpaideuō*] means to "bring up from childhood or train thoroughly"; LSJM, 515).
29. קְצָת (*qᵉṣāṯ*) can have a partitive sense (as in 1:2) or refer to the *end* of something (here, a period of time). BDB (892 3) and most translations opt for the latter. Goldingay (5 fn 5d), however, goes with the partitive option: "and some of them,"

were Daniel, Hananiah, Mishael, and Azariah. 7 Then the head of the court officials gave[30] them *new* names. To Daniel he gave the name Belteshazzar, to Hananiah *the name* Shadrach, to Mishael *the name* Meshach, and to Azariah *the name* Abednego.

Commentary

1:3–4 *The selection of the candidates.* In vv. 3–4, we are introduced to the criteria by which Nebuchadnezzar chose candidates for diplomatic service within his empire. In order to govern such a large diverse empire, Nebuchadnezzar saw the practical wisdom of recruiting and training individuals from different ethnic groups of his realm to serve within his state department. Such individuals, of course, would have to be loyal to the king and committed to the goals of the empire. This could be achieved by taking qualified men at an early age, giving them a thorough education in Babylonian ways, and training them in the procedures of court life.

The choice and preparation of the candidates was entrusted to one of the king's confidants, Ashpenaz, whom the text describes as "the chief of his court officials." As far as the Babylonians were concerned, Hebrew young men were needed for diplomatic service (just as were men from other ethnic groups) and thus were included along with many others. Verses 3–4 tell us the qualifications by which all the candidates were chosen.

According to our text in Dan 1, the first qualification was that they needed to be of "royal and noble descent," i.e., they needed to be related to the royal family or to be from the nobility of the land. Second, they had to have the right "look" physically. The idea of "no blemish" (KJV) means no physical defect.[31] The Hebrew word translated blemish (מְאוּם, *mᵊʾûm*) occurs in an alternate form in Lev 21:17–23 in which men with *physical defects* were disqualified for priestly service. It was not enough, however, that they be free of physical defect. Positively, they had to even be "good-looking" (lit., "those good in appearance"). Thus, a premium was placed upon physical condition and appearance. Those with physical handicaps would have been discriminated against. Third, the candidates had to be of superior mental acumen. Three phrases are used to describe the mental ability required, thus stressing the importance that was placed on this particular qualification. The main point is that the young men had the ability to comprehend knowledge because they were intelligent and discerning. Finally, the candidates had to have "the ability for serving in the king's royal court" (lit., "the ability to

---

feeling constrained to be consistent with v. 2 and to treat the 3mp suffix in line with וּלְלַמְּדָם (*ûlălammᵊḏām*) and וּלְגַדְּלָם (*ûlgaddᵊlām*).

30. The unusual verb for "naming" (*wayyāśem*)—twice in v. 7—sets the stage for the wordplay at v. 8.

31. Goldingay (5 fn 4b) thinks מְאוּם (*mᵊʾûm*) can connote either physical or moral defect here, but it is not convincing that the Babylonians would have been so scrupulous about morality.

stand in the palace of the king"). This would refer to the proper manner of court behavior, how to conduct oneself properly in the presence of the king and to relate to others at the royal court.

Those who could meet these qualifications were to be taught the literature and language of the Chaldeans. Here "Chaldean" probably means "Babylonian" in general, rather than the technical sense that it has in Dan 2–5 of a special class of wise men or priests. The Babylonian language was a form of Akkadian known as Neo-Babylonian. This was a language written in cuneiform and made up of various combinations of wedge-shaped characters that were commonly engraved on clay tablets with a small tool called a stylus.

While much of this literature would have been of an historical and legal nature, an extensive amount would have been religious, including omen texts, magic, sorcery, occultic practices, and the science of astrology. The Mosaic law had banned the *practice* of such occultic techniques (Deut 18:10–12; cf. 1 Sam 28:3–25). To read and study this material was not forbidden, but Daniel and his friends would have needed a strong walk with God and a biblical mindset to retain the ability to think critically when engaged in this type of study. Evidently, their esteem for God's Word protected them during this time of indoctrination.

Reflecting back on vv. 3–4, the qualifications presented here may seem at first glance to be rather exemplary. The king wanted those of noble extraction who were outstanding physically and mentally. Deeper reflection on these verses, however, reveals that they do not reflect God's value system. Nebuchadnezzar's qualifications smacked of *elitism* and *humanistic* standards, an environment in which everyone was aspiring to be humanly the best. What was noticeably absent was any esteem for devotion to Yahweh God and a corresponding moral lifestyle based on his standards of righteousness. In the sovereignty of God, however, Daniel and his three friends met Nebuchadnezzar's criteria and were thus elevated to important positions of influence within the realm. As we shall see, because of their devotion to God and his Word, Yahweh not only took them through this intensive time of training, but even elevated them above their peers.

1:5 *The king's regimen for the candidates.* According to v. 5, the king specified both their period of training as well as the diet they were to observe. Their diet would now consist of the same food the king ate, as well as the wine that he drank.[32] His motivation was probably to ensure that they had the finest

32. The NET has translated the food as "royal delicacies." The Hebrew word is פַּת־בַּג (*paṯ-bag*). According to Hartman (130), this is derived from the Old Persian word, *patibaga*, a technical term designating a government-supplied "portion, ration" of food. Collins (127 fn 20) agrees and adds, "The word passed into Greek as ποτίβαζις. The stress is probably not on the quality of the food, but in this case (being the same as the king ate), it was obviously of high quality. LXX translated פַּת־בַּג (*paṯ-bag*) by the word τράπεζα (*trapeza*), meaning "table."

provisions so as to become as strong and healthy as possible. Despite what might have been a valid motivation, however, such a diet reflected a lifestyle in which godly values were ignored. For the Hebrew youths, the diet meant defilement (note v. 8), though we are not told specifically what the nature of the violation was. Perhaps this involved a violation of the Old Testament dietary laws (see Lev 11 and Deut 14:3–21 for a prohibition against eating "unclean" foods). Another possibility is that these foods were considered "defiled" because they were the product of pagan sacrificial use. According to Exod 34:15, God's people were forbidden to eat foods that had been sacrificed or offered to pagan deities or idols. In Babylon, food was served to idols and later eaten by the king's court:

> The image was fed, in a ceremonial fashion accompanied by music, from offerings and the produce of the temple land and flocks. When the god was 'eating', he was, at least in later times, hidden from human view, even the priests, by linen curtains surrounding the image and his table. ... When the god had 'eaten', the dishes from his meal were sent to the king for consumption. What was not destined for the table of the main deity, his consort, his children or the servant gods was distributed among the temple administrators and craftsmen. The quantities of food involved could be enormous.[33]

The king specified that the period of training be three years. Young (42) notes that such a period was attested in other ANE cultures:

> Plato, *Alcibiades* 1:121, states that the education of Persian youths began in their 14th year, and Xenophon, Cy., 1, 2 mentions the 16th or 17th years as the close. The [Persian] Avesta says that a student for holy training should go to a master for three years.

In Daniel's case, though this pertains to Babylonian culture, it is quite conceivable that the trends would have been similar. This could be a further support that Daniel was about age fourteen to sixteen when he was taken to Babylon. At the end of this training, he was expected to be ready for service to the king.

1:6–7 *The assignment of new names.* It was quite common in Hebrew culture to give theophoric names to one's children, i.e., part of the name would have the word "God" in it or an abbreviated reference to "Yahweh" (his personal name). Furthermore, names nearly always had a special meaning, usually honoring God. The Hebrew word for God was אֵל (*ʾēl*), and the name "Daniel," for instance, had the word *ʾēl* suffixed at the end. The Hebrew verb דִּין (*dîn*), from which we get "Dan," means "to judge," and thus the name Daniel means, "God is my judge." Such names were meant to give glory to Israel's

33. Oates, *Babylon* (London: Thames and Hudson Ltd, 1986), 175.

God, and the same was true of Daniel's three friends. Why then were their names changed? The new names (though the meanings are not entirely clear to us) were based on the names of Babylonian deities, and thus the young men had a new identity (as it were) in relation to the gods of Babylon. Yet renaming the young men was also intended to demonstrate *domination* over them, as Chia points out:

> The naming of the subject, as in the creation story, carries with it a notion of domination and lordship over the subject. The naming or re-naming, in biblical literature is also a sign of inferior, subordinate and dependent status; Eliakim was renamed by Pharaoh Neco as Jehoiakim (2 Kg. 23:34), and Mattaniah was changed to Zedekiah by Nebuchadnezzar (2 Kg. 24:17).[34]

The following chart explains the meaning of the original names as well as the meaning of the new names:

Hebrew Name		**New Name Given**	
Daniel	"God is my judge"	Belteshazzar	Meaning uncertain, but possibly "protect his life!" [implying, "May Bel protect his life!"][35]
Hananiah	"Yahweh has been gracious"	Shadrach	Uncertain, but Archer suggests the meaning "The command of Aku," a Sumerian or Elamite moon-god.[36]
Mishael	"Who is what God is?"	Meshach	Uncertain, but Archer suggests the meaning "Who is what Aku is?"[37]
Azariah	"Yahweh has helped"	Abednego	Possibly: "Servant of (the god) Nebo"

34. P. Chia, "On Naming the Subject: Postcolonial Reading of Daniel 1," in *The Postcolonial Biblical Reader,* ed. R. S. Sugirtharajah, 171–85 (Oxford: Blackwell, 2006), 181.

35. *HALOT* (1834–35) admits that the precise meaning of Belteshazzar cannot now be determined (both LXX traditions transliterated as Βαλτασαρ, *Baltasar*). The etymology is certainly Akkadian. *HALOT* lists three suggestions: (1) *balāṭ-šarri-uṣur*—"protect the life of the king!"; (2) *balāṭsu-uṣur*—"protect his life" (that of the king); or (3) *Bēlēt-šarra-uṣur*—"may Belet protect the king."

36. G. Archer, "Daniel," in *EBC*, 34.

37. Ibid.

The new names were meant to erase the previous identity of each of the young men and to associate them more closely with Babylonian culture and religion. Babylonian allegiance was expected to follow their new identity and enlightened education. Renaming them was the quintessential attack on their heritage and faith. How degrading this must have been for these young men so committed to the true God of heaven.

Application and Devotional Implications

As we reflect over these verses in Dan 1:3–7, what we really see are the kinds of values that the Babylonian society cherished. This is a reflection of Satan's deceitful plan to mold us according to the "world's value system"—a cheap substitute for God's plan to mold us into the image of Christ. Notice the characteristics behind the qualifications:

1. Elitist attitude – People were valued based upon their family status (belonging to royalty or at least the nobility). This tended to promote an attitude that others were "second-class citizens," and that "lesser people" should serve the more deserving. The real truth, however, is that all humans are sinners in need of the saving grace of God. No one is better than another based upon earthly relationships or social status. The Lord Jesus Christ was humble. He came to serve others, not to be served by them. How pride can so easily deceive us! We must be careful that we not think more highly of ourselves than we ought.

2. Humanistic aspirations – The Babylonian value system underscored the importance of physical appearance and intellectual superiority. The message was "aspire to be humanly the best you can." Consider, though, what was *not* considered important: godliness, humility, an understanding of the Word of God, acknowledgment of one's weaknesses and a reliance upon the Lord. The Bible reminds us that God looks upon the *heart* (1 Sam 16:7)—it is the heart of man that God considers the most important.

3. An ungodly lifestyle – For those with no sensitivity to God, they are not concerned about what pleases him. The "food issue," however, was important, because it was a matter of obedience to God, even though others may have seen it as a relatively harmless practice. Daniel and his three friends were concerned about living a godly life. Yahweh was their Lord, and they wanted to do the things that pleased him.

All of these things spoke of the Babylonian value system that permeated their society. The "world" always operates on a different value system than God's. Furthermore, the "world" wants to impose its value system upon those of us who are believers. Ultimately, it is Satan who seeks to propagate *the world's value system*. In Rom 12:2, however, we are told, "Do not be conformed to this present world, but be transformed by the renewing of your mind, so that you may test and approve what is the will of God—what is good and well-pleasing and perfect" (NET). Therefore, the way that we resist conformity to this world is by allowing God to renew our minds, and he will do this as we are seriously engaged in the study of his Word (and taking it to heart). When our minds and hearts are stayed upon the Word, we develop sensitivity to God's values. Then the Holy Spirit works to produce the image of Christ in us.

C. Daniel's Resolve Not to Compromise His Faith (1:8–16)

The previous paragraph revealed how the king had appointed a special food regimen for the young men. For most of the Gentiles participating in the program, the diet posed no special problem. In fact, they probably considered themselves blessed that they had it so good. They would be eating well! For Daniel and his Hebrew friends, however, the diet was indeed a problem—either because it involved unclean foods (according to the Mosaic Law) or because the food and drink had previously been sacrificed to idols (and both of these problems could have been true). Although the entire training program was built on humanistic values and a thoroughly pagan education, the Hebrews could still participate without disobeying God. The food issue, however, would have meant a clear-cut act of disobedience before God. Therefore, Daniel and his friends were faced with two important decisions: (1) whether they would be faithful to God regardless of the consequences, and (2) how they would handle the situation and communicate their beliefs to their Babylonian superiors.

The main point of this paragraph is to show how Daniel's decision to obey God was met by God's faithfulness to act on his behalf. God made a way for Daniel to obey God and yet still remain in the training program.

Textual Notes

11.a. BDB (576) regards מֶלְצַר (*melṣār*) as a Babylonian title of questionable meaning, perhaps "guardian" (compare *DBL*, 4915: "guardian, steward, overseer"). LXX$^{\theta}$ attempts to transliterate the word as Αμελσαδ, apparently taking the Hebrew ר as ד (KJV translated as a personal name, "Melzar"). LXX^{O} treats it as a personal name, Αβιεσδρι (and assumes he is speaking to the same person as in v. 3). West Syriac Codex Ambrosianus (of the Peshitta) has *mnṣr* = מְנַצַּר. Goldingay (6 fn 11a) indicates that it is probably Akk., from a root *nṣr* equivalent to BH נצר (= "watch, guard, keep"). Collins' (144) derivation is similar, but from Akk. *maṣṣaru* (root *nṣr*). S. Paul adds that מֶלְצַר is "itself a loan-word from the Akkadian *maṣṣaru/maṣṣartu*, 'watcher, supervisor'" ("Mesopotamian Background of Daniel 1–6," 62). *HALOT* (594) gives the meaning "overseer," an official under Ashpenaz. Collins (144) points out that the Jewish commentators Saadia, Ibn Ezra, and Rashi all treat it as a title.

12.a. A few MSS support the spelling הזֵּרְעֹנִים, conforming to v. 16 (though 1QDan[a] has זרעים at v. 16). BDB (283) lists both roots זֵרֹעַ and זֵרְעֹן (each meaning "vegetable"), although the latter is only attested in Dan 1:16. Jastrow (414) indicates that MH does have the root זֵרָעוֹן (with a pl. form זֵרְעוֹנִים).

15.a. Missing in a few MSS, as well as LXX$^{\theta}$. LXX^{O} inserts ἄλλων ("the other young men").

16.a. 4QDan[a] adds את (sign of the acc.) before יין (compare v. 10).

16.b. See note above at 12.a. regarding the spelling זֵרְעֹנִים (with נ). 1QDan[a] has זרעים at v. 16.

Translation

1:8 Yet Daniel resolved[38] that he would not defile himself with the king's food or the wine[39] that he drank, and sought *permission* from the head of the court officials that he might not defile himself. **9** Now God had given[40] Daniel favor[41] and compassion[42] before the head of the court officials. **10** The head of the court officials replied to Daniel, "I am fearful of my lord, the king, who appointed your food and drink, for[43] why should he see your

---

38. BDB (963 2c) indicates that שִׂים לֵב (*śîm lēḇ*) with עַל (*ʿal*) means "intend" (lit., "set his heart on"), and thus the translation of "purpose" or "resolve" is contextually appropriate. Arnold ("Word Play and Characterization," 236) points out the wordplay with *wayyāśem* in v. 7 (twice). According to him, "the narrator uses this word play to dramatize Daniel's surpassing faithfulness in the face of unprecedented oppression. The irony is that he uses the same verb, albeit in different phrasal idioms, to denote both Daniel's faith and Nebuchadnezzar's persecution."

39. Lit., "the wine of his drink" (as in v. 5).

40. The use of *nātan* in this verse must be seen in contrast to its earlier use in v. 2. Though God *gave* Jehoiakim and the temple treasures into the hands of Nebuchadnezzar, He *gave* favor and compassion to Daniel.

41. Perhaps "favor" is a suitable translation for חֶסֶד (*ḥeseḏ*), though the word more often has the meaning "loyal love" in the OT (with a sense of strong devotion, as Prov 20:6), often being used of God's loyal love towards those with whom he is in covenantal relationship (esp. in the Psalms: e.g., Pss 32:10; 33:22). So this is a strong statement in v. 9, but the idea is that God's loving loyalty and compassion were upon Daniel, which led to God extending this favorable attitude into the heart of the head of the court officials. A similar situation involving חֶסֶד (*ḥeseḏ*) is observable in Ezra 7:27–28. In the book of Ruth, humans can certainly exercise חֶסֶד (*ḥeseḏ*) to one another, as both Ruth and Boaz did.

42. The NET takes חֶסֶד וּלְרַחֲמִים (*ḥeseḏ ûlᵊraḥămîm*) as a hendiadys (made the overseer "sympathetic"), which is possible but not necessary.

43. אֲשֶׁר (*ʾăšer*) has a causal force here, so that the phrase אֲשֶׁר לָמָּה יִרְאֶה (*ʾăšer lāmmâ yirʾeh*) means "for why should he see?" For לָמָּה (*lāmmâ*) meaning "why?" see Gen 4:6. *IBHS*, 324 (§18.3.c), however, argues that לָמָּה (*lāmmâ*) can be used in a quasi-rhetorical way, and when preceded by a relative pronoun, can simply mean "otherwise."

faces more dejected[44] than the young men who are about your age? Then you might cause me to forfeit[45] my head to the king." **11** Daniel then spoke to the overseer[46] whom the head of the court officials had appointed over Daniel, Hananiah, Mishael, and Azariah, **12** "Test your servants for ten days, and let[47] them give us some vegetables to eat and water to drink. **13** Then let our appearance be observed in your presence[48] and the appearance of the young men who ate the king's food. Deal with your servants just as you see *fit*." **14** So he listened to them regarding this matter and tested them for ten days. **15** At the end of the ten days, their appearance was observed as better and healthier[49] than all the young men who ate the king's food. **16** So the overseer continued[50] to remove their food and the wine they drank and was giving them vegetables *instead*.

---

44. BDB (277 1) assigns the meaning "dejected" to זָעֵף (*zā'ap̄*). *DCH* (III:126–27) indicates two roots: (1) be angry, enraged; or (2) be thin or wretched-looking (so Dan 1:10). The NASB translates as "haggard," which means to have a wild or worn look as from sleeplessness, grief, or illness. The NET translates as "malnourished." Notice Gen 40:6 where *zā'ap̄* is paralleled with "sad," which tends to support the translation "haggard" or "dejected." Goldingay (6 fn 10b) writes, "here presumably Ashpenaz refers to their looking 'out of sorts.'"

45. "To lose my head" is an attempt to convey the thought of וְחִיַּבְתֶּם אֶת־רֹאשִׁי (*wᵉḥiyyab̄tem 'et̲-rō'šî*), although NET prefers not to make the issue of capital punishment so explicit ("endanger my life"). Similarly, Collins (128 fn 31) remarks, "It is not clear whether this implies the threat of capital punishment," and appeals to a comment by F. M. Cross "that the expression regularly means 'be liable (to penalty)' in the Samaria papyri." The verb חוב (*ḥûb̄*) means to "be guilty" in the Qal but "inculpate" in the Piel (so BDB, 295). *HALOT* (295) indicates that *ḥûb̄* means "to make guilty" in the Piel, and with ראשׁ (*rō'š*), *ḥûb̄* means "to endanger one's life." Yet note the noun חוב (*ḥôb̄*) meaning "a guilt, obligation." This leads to the sense of "I would obligate my head" to the king. LXX^{O}'s κινδυνεύσω τῷ ἰδίῳ τραχήλῳ (*kinduneusō tōi idiōi trachēlōi*, "I will put my own neck in danger") could easily be understood as life threatening, and NIV's "the king would then have my head" reflects this understanding.

46. See the textual note above (v. 11) for מֶלְצַר (*melṣār*) as a title.

47. The verb וְיִתְּנוּ (*wᵉyittᵉnû*) is a jussive in meaning, expressing a request for permission. Translate "let ... them give."

48. For לְפָנֶיךָ (*lᵉp̄āneykā*), see BDB (816 II.4) where with the prep. ל (*l*) is "the most general word for *in the presence of, before*."

49. Although the basic meaning of בָּרִיא (*bārî'*) is "fat," this has other connotations. *TWOT* (279a) notes, "While always retaining this original connotation it occurs with various nuances. It is used to describe healthy human beings (Dan 1:15), animals (Gen 41:2), and vegetation (Gen 41:5)."

50. The participle נֹשֵׂא (*nōśē'*) can express continual action in the past (past progressive), which accounts for the words "continued to" in order to bring this out (so Goldingay, 6). The same is true of וְנֹתֵן (*wᵉnōt̲ēn*), "was giving."

Commentary

1:8–10 *Daniel's decision and his appeal to the head of the court officials*. Arnold points out how the word-play at the beginning of v. 8 (*wayyāśem*)—in light of its earlier use in v. 7—sets the stage for the remainder of the book:

> The irony of the word play is that the Babylonians think they have changed Daniel's character, but the narrator knows otherwise. They succeeded in changing all the circumstances of his life, and the name change in verse 7 represents Daniel's complete transformation, at least from the Babylonian perspective. But the inner resolve and dedication revealed by the word play in verse 8 is the narrator's full portrait of Daniel and transcends even the description of his impressive personal and intellectual skills in verses 3–4. It is his commitment to God that sets Daniel apart, and prepares the reader for the continued conflict between aggressive world powers and God's servants.[51]

These verses focus on Daniel and the decision that he made. It is clear from v. 12 and following that all four of the young men were in this together ("Test your servants"). Daniel appears to have been the leader among them as well as the spokesman to the authorities. Yet the decision was a mutual one made by all four young men. To some people, this whole situation might not seem so significant. What would be so bad about eating the food that the king apportioned?[52] In fact, Jesus later declared all foods "clean," and we have the liberty (now) to eat what once had been forbidden (see Mark 7:19). Considering that Daniel and his friends were probably just teenagers at the time of this test, this was probably a tough decision for them to face.

51. Arnold, "Word Play and Characterization," 248.

52. For a discussion of the difficulty of eating the king's food, see D. Soesilo, "Why Did Daniel Reject the King's Delicacies?," *BT* 45 (1994): 440–44. Some scholars conclude that this was a ritual issue while others consider it a moral one. Baldwin attempts to argue that "covenant significance" was involved. She writes (92), "Those who had thus committed themselves to allegiance accepted an obligation of loyalty to the king." Similarly, G. Goswell, "The Ethics of the Book of Daniel," *ResQ* 57 (2015):131, noting the reference to פַּת־בַּג (*pat̲-bag*) again at Dan 11:26 near the end of the book ("those who eat his *choice food* will destroy him"), concludes, "Such rebellion against the king of the south in 11:26 is reprehensible because the rebels eat from the king's table and their eating is a symbol of political covenant and subservience (cf. 1 Sam 20:26–34; 2 Sam 9:9–13; 19:27–29; 2 Kgs 25:27–30). To eat the king's food is tantamount to a pledge of unqualified loyalty. ... By means of this dietary regimen, the king seeks to impose a binding political commitment on his subjects." Yet there is no specific mention in the Daniel text that this was the issue behind their refusal, and this theory fails to explain why a vegetarian diet was sufficient to solve the dilemma. The text is far more interested in highlighting the concern of the youths to be obedient to God than on what the exact point of defilement was.

The truth is that every decision to obey God always involves the opportunity to have done otherwise. Furthermore, when we obey God, we have acted in faith (for it is usually more convenient, or at least more enticing, not to obey). Therefore, when the text tells us "Yet Daniel resolved that he would not defile himself," we must understand that this was a choice of faith, in which obedience to God became more important than what might have been momentarily more convenient or beneficial for him.

As we reflect upon Daniel's decision to obey, we would do well to consider his life from the broader perspective. Daniel was a person whom God greatly used, and he was a person to whom God revealed marvelous truths. What we must be careful to see is the relationship between his obedience and the resulting use God made of his life. Charles Feinberg (21) has said, "If we are to gain the most from the study of this book, we must bear in mind that the visions and truths in this book were revealed to a spiritually minded man who was separated from the sin and degradation of his day." Daniel is a good model for how we ought to have a sensitivity to God and a desire to please him in every decision we make. One of the benefits in studying the Bible is that it not only teaches us what is right and wrong but lets us see this fleshed out in the lives of men and women who were faithful, who had convictions and lived by them. Godly men and women live with convictions, and they stick by them even when this puts them at odds with the world and its value system. Convictions are the "truths" we are committed to live by, regardless of whether others agree with us and regardless of what price we have to pay for keeping them.

What Daniel had resolved in his heart was one thing; how he would handle the situation was another. Think for a moment how Daniel might have responded: (1) he could have planned an escape from Babylon and run away; or, (2) he could have acted defiantly and simply told the authorities he would not obey their rules. Verse 8, however, tells us that he "sought *permission* ... that he might not defile himself." That is, he sought permission from the human being in charge not to defile himself. We learn from this that obeying God is only one side of the coin, for we are also responsible as to *how* we obey God before others. Daniel's obedience toward God was balanced by *a respect for authority*. While we live in this world, we will often be in situations where we are placed under the authority of non-believers. God still expects us to honor them; and we honor God by honoring the lines of authority that he has permitted to exist (cf. Rom 13:1–7; 1 Tim 2:1–2; 1 Pet 2:13–15).

Daniel and his friends certainly took a risk in making an issue of the king's diet. Probably they were also prepared to pay the consequences of their choice. (We should keep in mind that there are times when we must suffer for choosing to obey God.) In this particular case, however, God honored their obedience. Verse 9 says, "God had given Daniel favor and compassion before the head of the court officials" (words reflecting a fulfillment of 1 Kgs 8:50; cf. Ps 106:46). One of the wonderful things about being a believer (a child of God) is that we are never left alone. We cannot see God visibly, but he often works in his own sovereign and mysterious ways on our behalf. He can even turn the hearts of unbelievers to do his will and accomplish his purposes. This truth is echoed in Prov 21:1, "The king's heart is like channels of water in the hand of the LORD; He turns it wherever He wishes" (NASB). This is exactly what God did in the case of the head of the court officials who were over Daniel. Rather than being wrathful and vindictive toward Daniel, God caused him to be favorably disposed toward him—to be sympathetic toward him. Without a doubt, God used Daniel's *respectfulness* as part of the process.

The head official's initial reaction was one of hesitation. In his opinion, the king's diet would lead to better health and appearance, but another diet was bound to be less beneficial. He was concerned that the effects would even show up in their countenance: "Why should he see your faces more dejected." The word translated "dejected" is a rather rare Hebrew word, זָעֵף (*zā ʿap̱*), probably suggesting that the proposed diet would even result in a sullen look on their faces (see the use in Gen 40:6 in support of this interpretation). The head official realized that such consequences could even mean the loss of his own life, as he would be held responsible for what had happened.

1:11–13 *Daniel's creative proposal of an alternative.* Though Daniel had favor in the eyes of the head official, initially the response was not so favorable. Often God does not allow "answers to prayer" to come so quickly or so easily, as was the case here. Through delay we learn to persevere in prayer and in faith. In just such a time, however, God enabled Daniel to come up with some *creative thinking*: a short-term test for ten days in which the Hebrew young men would eat vegetables and water. This proposal was apparently not presented to the head official directly but to the "overseer" (or *guardian*—see the textual note above, v. 11, for מֶלְצַר, *melṣār*, as a title) who had been placed over them. Whether or not he relayed the proposal to the head official immediately, we do not know. Most likely the head of the court officials was involved in approving the arrangement at some point, in light of what we were told in v. 9. The idea of eating only vegetables and water may not have been as restrictive as one might think. The word translated "vegetables" is from the Hebrew word *zērōa ʿ*, which has the basic idea of that which grows from "seed" (*zera ʿ*). This would include not only vegetables but fruits, grains, and bread made from grains (so Goldingay, 6). This would have been quite a healthy diet. The test, then, was simple: if after ten days the Hebrew youths looked fine, they could be allowed to continue the alternative diet.

1:14–16 *The successful outcome of the test.* The overseer permitted the test, and after ten days there was a noticeable outcome. In fact, rather than looking dejected (or "haggard"), their appearance was better and their bodies healthier in comparison with the others.[53] Hence, they were allowed to con-

---

53. The NET translation for v. 15 is quite good ("their appearance was better and their bodies were healthier"). The NASB states that "they were fatter than all the youths," but that is not really the point. The Hebrew is *ûbrî ʾê bāśār* (lit., "ones fat of flesh").

tinue the alternative diet (presumably with the commander's knowledge and authorization).

Application and Devotional Implications

Most of us will never find ourselves in the same kind of situation that Daniel and his three friends did. The dietary laws do not apply today (as mentioned above), and it is very unlikely that any of us would be in a king's training program in which we were expected to eat food that had been sacrificed to idols. Nevertheless, we can learn from the way Daniel handled the situation. Most of us, at one time or another, are confronted with situations in which we are asked or tempted to compromise our faith. For instance, we may live in a culture in which business deals are sealed in a bar where alcoholic beverages are consumed, and we may be expected to go along with this "lifestyle" (or risk losing out on the deal). Or, we might live in a culture where bribes are expected in order to secure someone's approval or to finalize a transaction. Or, young people (wanting to make friends) might be expected to compromise themselves morally to be accepted as part of the group. Since we live in a world that generally does not accept God's value system, there are many ways that each of us are being challenged all the time to make these kinds of moral choices. Will we be obedient (like Daniel), or will we compromise our walk with God for the sake of some temporal goal? Furthermore, how will we communicate our moral values and beliefs to others who are not Christians?

What we learn from these verses is that we should not only be obedient to God, but we should wisely relate our convictions to unbelievers—and in particular we should show respect for authority in the process. The principle at work here is this: *do not offend unnecessarily.* That does not mean that we should never take a clear stand for righteousness. Certainly we should. We may need to do as Martin Luther did and declare, "Here I stand, I can do no other." Yet there are many times when we can respond in situations *with respect* and without exhibiting a "better than you" attitude. Conviction does not excuse us from acting with sensitivity, tact, and respect. Daniel had clearly made up his mind that he would be obedient to the Lord, but he went about it in a courteous way. That is especially important to do when relating to those whom God has put in authority over us. Remember: God honors an approach in which, while committed to God's will, we still honor authority.

D. God's Elevation of Daniel and His Friends (1:17–21)

Chapter 1 began on the dismal note that Jerusalem was besieged by the Babylonian army under the command of Nebuchadnezzar, but it ends on the

---

Though the adjective *bārîʾ* can mean "fat" in reference to humans (see Judg 3:17), the expression in this context is probably metaphorical for "healthy, well-nourished" (cf. Ps 73:4).

more positive note that God worked through all these circumstances to bless and elevate these faithful Hebrew youths in the courts of Babylon. After the early trial involving the issue of diet, the next three years passed with little comment. The Hebrew youths were allowed to continue their vegetarian diet, and apparently they applied themselves diligently to succeeding in the king's special program. Their obedience to God did pay off, and God was glorified through them.

Textual Notes

20.a-a. *BHS* suggests reading חכמָה וּבִ׳ (with *waw*, and not in construct). LXX has conjunctive καὶ.

20.b. *BHS* suggests הָאַשָּׁפִים be read with initial *waw*, as some MSS have. So LXX with καὶ.

Translation

1:17 Now as for these four young men, God gave them knowledge and understanding[54] in all *the Chaldean*[55] literature[56] and *in* wisdom. Daniel even gained understanding into every *kind of* vision[57] and dreams. **18** At the end of the period[58] that the king ordered[59] for them to be brought[60] in, the head of the court officials brought them before Nebuchadnezzar. **19** The king spoke with them and there was not found among any of them *such* as Daniel, Hananiah, Mishael, or Azariah. So they entered[61] the king's service. **20** And *as for* every

54. הַשְׂכֵּל (*haśkēl*), translated here as a noun ("understanding"), is actually a Hiphil inf. abs. verb. See *IBHS*, 592 (§35.3.3b) for an inf. abs. used in an accusative role as a direct object. Cf. Jer 3:15; Job 34:35.

55. The word "Chaldean," though not in the Heb text, is supplied here in light of v. 4. The king had assigned them to study the literature and language of the Chaldeans.

56. MS 88 and Syh translate סֵפֶר (*sēp̄er*) as "scribal skill" (γραμματικῇ τέχνῃ, *grammatikēi technēi*) rather than "literature." However, τέχνῃ (*technēi*) is not found in Pap. 967 or LXX$^{\theta}$.

57. Most translations put "vision" in the plural, although חָזוֹן is singular in the Heb. This word does not occur in the plural in biblical usage.

58. Lit., "at the end of the days," that is, the days that had been specified by the king (so, a *period* of time).

59. Lit., "said, spoke," but contextually (since he was the king), this is understood as an order.

60. Although the verb לַהֲבִיאָם (*lahăḇîʾām*) is in the Hiphil, it makes for smoother English to translate this with the passive voice.

61. "Entered the king's service" is a translation of וַיַּעַמְדוּ לִפְנֵי הַמֶּלֶךְ (*wayyaʿamdû lip̄nê hammeleḵ*), which literally is "and they stood before the king." Although the verb עָמַד (*ʿāmad*) followed by לִפְנֵי (*lip̄nê*) may simply mean to be in one's presence (as when Moses stood before Pharaoh, Exod 9:10), it can sometimes have the connotation of

matter of wisdom *and*[62] understanding which the king sought from them, he found them ten times[63] better[64] than all the magicians and conjurers[65] who were in all his kingdom.[66] **21** So Daniel continued on until the first[67] year of Cyrus the king.

Commentary

1:17 *God's reward for the four Hebrew youths*. Verse 17 summarizes God's blessing and reward upon the Hebrew youths who were obedient to him. The text tells us, "God gave them knowledge and understanding in all *the Chaldean* literature and *in* wisdom." The key thought here is upon what

---

being there to serve (Gen 41:46; Num 16:9) or in submission and ready to receive orders (Deut 4:10). The latter fits the context of Dan 1 better.

62. The Hebrew text lacks the conjunction, reading the first word in the phrase as a construct ("wisdom of understanding"). A number of other versions (Theodotion, the Syriac, the Vg., and the Sahidic Coptic) all have the conjunction. According to Collins (128 fn 53), 4QDan[a] probably reads חכמה בינה (*ḥḵmh ḇynh*).

63. Lit., "ten hands" (עֶשֶׂר יָדוֹת, *ʿeśer yāḏôṯ*). BDB (390c 4c) indicates this is a special use of יָד (*yāḏ*) in regard to time. *IBHS*, 287 (§15.4.b) notes that multiplicative expressions involve a number plus another word conventionally rendered "time."

64. Lit. "over" (עַל, *ʿal*), meaning higher or superior to.

65. The terms "magicians" (הַחַרְטֻמִּים, *haḥarṭummîm*) and "conjurers" (הָאַשָּׁפִים, *hāʾaššāp̄îm*) will be discussed further in the commentary. The term הָאַשָּׁפִים (*hāʾaššāp̄îm*) has been translated in various ways: (1) "conjurers" (NASB); (2) "enchanters" (NIV, ESV, NRSV); and (3) "astrologers" (NKJV, NET). The translation "conjurer" was chosen here because that is the common lexical meaning given in BDB (80b), *HALOT* (96), *NIDOTTE* (1:566), and *DCH* (1:418). *TWOT* (80 #181) lists all three meanings. There is some uncertainty about the precise meaning of the term. In contrast to most English translations, Goldingay (6) regards them as two asyndetic foreign words that interpret each other and so translates "the diviners (the chanters) in all his realm." Despite his appeal to Dan 5:15, this conclusion is not so obvious.

66. Collins (129) thinks v. 20 was originally longer, drawing some support from the apparent lacuna (missing gap) of 4QDan[a]. He states, "Cross suggests בכל מלכותו [ויכבדם המלך ויראם ב]כל ד[בר] במלכותו. MS 88 and Syh expand 'and the king honored them and appointed them rulers, and showed them to be wise beyond all his own people in affairs in his whole land and kingdom.' Syh marks this passage with obeli to indicate that it is not in the Hebrew." Yet 4QDan[a] (even if there is a lacuna) does not necessarily prove to be a superior reading to MT.

67. Cyrus' *first year* in control of Babylon would be 539 or 538 BC. Daniel actually lived beyond the first year of Cyrus, as is clear from 10:1. The purpose of the statement in 1:21 is merely to say that Daniel's life spanned the entire period of the neo-Babylonian empire, in which he had just gained an official government position. His life span also included the early years of the Persian control of Babylon. However, by that time his age was so advanced that he probably died sometime in the 530s BC.

God did: He gave them these special gifts. This should not be taken to mean that the young men did not seriously apply themselves in their studies and training. Quite obviously they did. In the final analysis, however, God gave them their success.

God enjoys rewarding his children for their obedience. In 1 Sam 2:30 we are told, "those who honor Me, I will honor" (NASB). How God chooses to honor his children, however, is his prerogative. We should keep in mind that God is *the rewarder* (we do not pick the rewards), and we must learn to accept the gifts that he chooses to give according to his sovereign will. This passage does not mean to imply that obedient believers will always have earthly success, that obedience will always lead, for example, to promotion in school, government or business. There will be times when we are hopeful of some special attainment, but God may not allow us to have that which we have desired (even when the goal may have been good, and we have been walking obediently with the Lord). We can and will be disappointed at times. Yet we must respond maturely and realize on such occasions that God has not ordained such gifts or crowning success for us. God may choose to reward us in this earthly life, or He may choose to reward us in the resurrection.[68] We must let him be the judge of what is best and what fits in most appropriately with his sovereign purposes.

Returning to Daniel, we should also notice carefully the nature of the reward that the young men received. Their reward did *not* come in the form of being set free or being allowed to return to Jerusalem (things that they might have humanly wished for). Their faithfulness to God paid off in ways that really mattered. In this case, they were equipped for their God-given mission in Babylon. Observe the process that led to the outcome:

The Process				**The Outcome**
1 Knowing what God desires	2 Inner conviction to obey	3 Wise implementation	4 Endurance (time)	God distinguished them by granting them what they needed to succeed in His mission for them

The word translated "understanding" (Heb הַשְׂכֵּל, *haśkēl*)— translated "skill" by the NET—informs us that God gave them a special ability for *comprehending* the Babylonian literature in which they studied. The things that Nebuchadnezzar had desired (wisdom, knowledge, understanding—recall v. 4), these God gave the four Hebrew young men. Daniel, however, was

68. The subject of rewards receives much more emphasis in the New Testament. A few key passages are: 2 Cor 5:9–10; 1 Cor 3:12–15; 4:3–5; and Rev 22:12. All Christians will one day stand before the "judgment seat of Christ," and knowing this should be an incentive for us to live a life pleasing to the Lord.

singled out for further distinctive honors. He had understanding about (i.e., he discerned) every kind of vision, as well as dreams. This statement prepares us for the remainder of the book in which we see Daniel's unique role of interpreting dreams and receiving visions.

Daniel's honor must also be seen in light of the emphasis put on dreams and visions in Babylonian culture (this will be further explained under 2:1–13). In Babylon, great stress was put upon the "understanding" of dreams and visions, though the techniques used for their discernment were entirely occultic. The "wise men" who surrounded the king had a highly developed methodology for interpreting dreams and visions. Significantly, Daniel was gifted by God for dealing with such phenomena, yet he did not have to rely on the occultic methods that the king's advisors typically did.

We should take notice that this special ability for discerning dreams and visions was not given to all four young men, but only to Daniel. God was very selective in terms of the human instrument he used for this (it was not something every believer could do). We should also keep in mind that although God did on occasion speak through dreams, most dreams were never intended as revelation from God. As is true today, dreams are typically the result of the brain putting together thoughts and images during one's sleep (usually in some ridiculous way!). There are several times in the Old Testament, however, where God supernaturally interceded with a divinely given dream, even at times with unbelievers (cf. Gen 41:1–8). Visions, in contrast, were only given to believers (usually Old Testament prophets). The New Testament includes very few cases of God using dreams (only a few times in Matthew's Gospel, e.g., Matt 1:20–2:22; 27:19), and none beyond the Gospels. There are some instances in which God gave visions in the New Testament, but after the Gospels these are infrequent and usually limited to one of the apostles (e.g., Acts 16:9) or to someone God was using in an exceptional way to advance the gospel. In light of these observations, *believers today* should not be overly occupied with trying to interpret dreams, as though they were divinely given, especially for the purpose of seeking divine guidance. (This does not rule out, however, that God might choose to convey some spiritual insight to unbelievers through a dream.) Similarly, visions seem to have been limited to extraordinary situations after the day of Pentecost (usually involving an apostle), which should caution us from seeking or expecting them today.[69] God can certainly do this if he chooses to, but our reliance should primarily be upon the revealed Word of God handed down to us from the apostles.

1:18–20 *The examination by the king.* The three years that the king had specified for their education and training (recall v. 5) had now passed. At this

69. Care should be taken to distinguish dreams and visions from the gift of prophecy in the New Testament. The latter was a spiritual gift given by the Holy Spirit and not limited to the apostles.

point, Ashpenaz, the commander of the officials, formally presented the candidates to the king. According to v. 19, King Nebuchadnezzar personally conversed with each of them. Based on his personal interviews, it was apparent that these four Hebrew young men outclassed all the others who had gone through the king's training. At one point, they faced the possibility of being eliminated from the program, yet now we are told that they "entered the king's personal service"—a reminder that God was faithful to see them through.

Not only did these four successfully complete the program at the top of their class, but they even excelled over all the others in the realm who served as "magicians and conjurers" (not just the other young trainees). Why, though, were Daniel and his friends compared to magicians and conjurers? Because these were two classes of dignitaries that officially served in the royal courts of Babylon as advisors to the king. (In most cultures today, we would not think of magicians and conjurers as official government employees.) The term "magicians" is the Hebrew word חַרְטֻמִּים, *ḥarṭummîm*.[70] According to Archer (37), "… a *ḥarṭōm* was probably a diviner, one who used some sort of inscribed chart or magical design (possibly imposed on a chart of the stars) in order to arrive at an answer to questions put to him." The term "conjurers" (NIV = enchanters; NET = astrologers) is the Hebrew word אַשָּׁפִים (*ʾaššāpîm*) a term, according to Harman (131), derived from the Akkadian word *āšipu*, meaning "incantation priest." With their spells and incantations, they were believed to be able to communicate with the spirit world. Miller (72) elaborates on the function of these two types of court officials:

> Supposedly in touch with the world of the spirits and the gods, these individuals were the advisers to the king on virtually every matter. They employed rites and spells intended to heal, exorcise demons, or counter an evil spell placed upon the sufferer. Omens were studied in order to understand the future, and astrology played an important part in this activity. Techniques, such as examining a sheep's liver (hepatoscopy), also were employed

---

70. On the proposed Egyptian background of the term *ḥarṭummîm*, see T. O. Lambdin, "Egyptian Loanwords in the Old Testament," *JAOS* 73 (1953): 150–51; and compare H.-P. Müller, "חַרְטֹם, (*ḥarṭōm*)," in *TDOT*, 5:177), who notes (178), "The term is applied to Egyptian mantics and magicians in two narrative complexes, Gen. 41 and Ex. 7f. … In a third complex, Dnl. 1f.; 4f., … it stands for Babylonian mantics. … The Demotic Egyptian magician became a mantic specializing in dreams because magic also served to prevent bad dreams of their fulfilment, and perhaps also because the *ḥr-tb* dealt with dream books." For a discussion of a "mantic" as a practitioner of divination in order to predict the future, see esp. R. G. Wooden, "The Book of Daniel and Manticism: A Critical Assessment of the View That the Book of Daniel Derives from a Mantic Tradition" (Ph.D. diss., Univ. of St. Andrews, 2000), 1–26.

> in decision-making (cf. Ezek 21:21). Dream interpretation was another function of these wise men as may be observed from ancient sources and the Book of Daniel itself.

Both of these officials (magicians and conjurers) served in important positions to the king. In the Babylonian culture, determining the will of the gods or the outcome of certain events was highly significant. The king thus relied on these officials to help him in making decisions through their access to occultic knowledge. The point of v. 20, however, is probably not to restrict the comparison of Daniel and his three friends to these two particular classes of occultic advisors. Rather, these two are representative of all types of advisors to the king (of which there were other types as well—compare Dan 2:2). Hence, through the wisdom and understanding with which Daniel and his three friends were able to advise the king, they were "ten times better" (i.e., far better) than all other types of "wise men" that were found in the Babylonian realms.[71] The latter sought their "wisdom" through occultic channels (a way which God strongly condemned—see Deut 18:9–14), but this was vastly inferior to the wisdom that God was able to give to those who sought him and walked with him.

1:21 *Daniel's longevity of service.* The point of v. 21 is not to specify how long Daniel "lived." The NASB renders this verse, "Daniel continued until the first year of Cyrus the king." In this context, Daniel had just been elevated to a position in the personal service of the Babylonian king (v. 19). Daniel served in an official governmental capacity throughout the reign of Nebuchadnezzar (who died in 562 BC) and even longer under other Babylonian kings. Eventually, the Babylonian Empire was defeated at the hands of Cyrus the Great, king of Persia, in 539 BC. (In this context, the "first year of Cyrus" does not represent the year in which he became the king over the Persians and the Medes, but the year in which his kingship was extended to include Babylon, traditionally understood as 539 BC.) Daniel was still serving the Babylonian Empire when it fell to the Persians in 539 BC. In fact, we learn from Dan 10:1 that Daniel was even living at the time of the third year of Cyrus' reign (ca. 536 BC). So, the point of v. 21 is to indicate that Daniel not only received an appointment to official capacity in the king's personal service but that he outlasted (by God's grace) the Babylonian Empire. As the following chapters reveal, there were many trials, temptations, plots, and intrigues during these many years, but God saw him through every one. Thus, he outlived his Babylonian masters. This would mean that he served in the Babylonian courts for over sixty years (though with probable interruptions) and lived to see King Cyrus of Persia issue the decree permitting the Jews

71. By stating that the Hebrew young men were "ten times better" than the magicians and conjurers, we may have a subtle allusion to the ten plagues in Exodus by which Moses demonstrated Yahweh's supremacy over the occult in Egypt.

to return to the land (cf. Ezra 1:1–3). Daniel lived to see God's faithfulness with Israel begin to be worked out.

Biblical Theology Comments

Chapter 1 opened with the startling news that Yahweh's holy people and holy temple had been invaded, in what—at first glance—might appear to be a defeat for him. Nations of that time had their *protector gods*, and Yahweh was allowing his ability to serve as Israel's protector to come into question. Furthermore, the changing of the names of his "representatives" marked them as no longer the property of Yahweh but rather of the Babylonian deities (at least in the eyes of the Babylonians). In what might at first seem to be disheartening, the events show Yahweh as all the more superior to pagan deities.

De Bruyn has provided a very insightful article using an approach of cognitive linguistics and the concept of a deity's sacred "space" to show how Yahweh reversed what seemed to be his defeat into his victory in Marduk's own camp. This begins with eating a non-Marduk diet. He writes,

> Marduk is suddenly challenged by Yahweh from within Marduk's own city. The challenge comes through what we can describe in terms a cognitive approach as a 'clash of foods or battle of the banquet'. Daniel and his friends refuse to eat the food coming from Nebuchadnezzar's table. Within a cognitive linguistic frameset, eating vegetables is a way for Daniel and his friends to set themselves apart as vessels through which Yahweh can act inside Marduk's god-space. By narrating the fact that Daniel and his friends prefer a different diet, the author establishes a base of operation for Yahweh within Marduk's god-space.[72]

The battle culminates with Nebuchadnezzar's examination and affirmation of the superiority of Yahweh's representatives.

> Yahweh again is victorious, seeing that, as vessels of Yahweh, Daniel and his friends are found to be wiser and more intelligent, not only than all the other young men; they are also proven to be wiser and even more astute than Nebuchadnezzar's (and thus Marduk's) own counsellors.[73]

The lesson is that if Yahweh can invade Marduk's own "god space" and show himself superior there, he can certainly protect his people who have to live out the days of their exile in the land of Marduk.

---

72. J. J. De Bruyn, "A Clash of Gods: Conceptualising Space in Daniel 1," *HTS* 70 (2014): 5.
73. Ibid.

Application and Devotional Implications

The emphasis of this final paragraph in Dan 1:17–21 is upon the many ways God blessed and honored these four young men from Judah who had acted obediently before him. In fact, their decision to be obedient to God paved the way for a long life of faithful service to God (especially for Daniel), a task for which God had uniquely equipped them. When we consider that they were only teenagers at the time, this truly is remarkable.

As stated earlier, the ways and time by which God chooses to reward our obedience to him is entirely a matter of his sovereign choice (and that will vary from one individual to the next). We can be assured that God will reward us for being obedient to him, whether immediately in very tangible ways or whether in the distant future. In any case, obedience to God does pay off. The question for us, then, is this: how can we, too, live a lifetime of faithful service for God? The important issue here is *devotion to God*, from which obedience results. Devotion to God is something that even a teenager can experience, yet it is something that all of us have to maintain and nourish (regardless of our age or maturity). Devotion to God develops in proportion to the degree that we are "God-centered" in our lives. It is futile for us to expect that devotion and obedience will take place in our lives apart from being "God-centered." Listen to the advice of Jerry Bridges:[74]

> **The Practice of Godliness**
> The practice of godliness is an exercise or discipline that focuses upon God. From this Godward attitude arises the character and conduct that we usually think of as godliness. So often we try to develop Christian character and conduct without taking the time to develop God-centered devotion. We try to please God without taking the time to walk with him and develop a relationship with him. This is impossible to do.

As Bridges wisely advises, we must take the time to *develop a relationship* with the living God. Otherwise, devotion and obedience will never really develop in our lives. What are you doing to develop a God-centered devotion? Are you taking regular time to be alone with God? Are you communing with him in prayer and actively studying his Word?

It is sometimes easy to excuse ourselves in our thought life and actions because of the world we live in. If we are not careful, we begin to define our standards in relation to the world rather than in relation to God himself. We can be lulled into thinking that as long as our standard is just a little bit better than the world's, we may think we are pleasing God (cf. Titus 2:11–13).

74. J. Bridges, *The Practice of Godliness* (Colorado Springs: NavPress, 1983), 18.

Selected Bibliography (Daniel 1)

Ackroyd, P. R. "The Temple Vessels—a Continuity Theme." In *Studies in the Religion of Ancient Israel*, ed. G. W. Anderson, 166–81. VTSup 23. Leiden: Brill, 1972.

Arnold, B. T. "Word Play and Characterization in Daniel 1." In *Puns and Pundits: Word Play in the Hebrew Bible and Ancient Near Eastern Literature*, ed. S. B. Noegel, 231–48. Bethesda, MD: CDL, 2000.

Breed, B. W. "A Divided Tongue: The Moral Taste Buds of the Book of Daniel." *JSOT* 40 (2015): 113–30.

Bruce, F. F. "The Chronology of Daniel 1:1." In *The Climax of the Ages; Studies in the Prophecy of Daniel*, ed. F. A. Tatford, 229–36. London and Edinburgh: Marshall, Morgan, and Scott, 1953.

Chia, P. "On Naming the Subject: Postcolonial Reading of Daniel 1." In *The Postcolonial Biblical Reader*, ed. R. S. Sugirtharajah, 171–85. Oxford: Blackwell, 2006.

De Bruyn, J. J. "A Clash of Gods: Conceptualising Space in Daniel 1." *HTS* 70 (2014): 1–6.

Dumbrell, W. J. *Covenant and Creation; A Theology of the Old Testament Covenants*. Exeter, UK: Paternoster, 1984.

Fewell, D. N. *Circle of Sovereignty: A Story of Stories in Daniel 1–6*. Sheffield: Almond, 1988.

Gardner, A. E. "The Eating of 'Seeds' and Drinking of Water by Daniel and Friends: An Intimation of Holiness." *ABR* 59 (2001): 53–63.

Goldingay, J. "Nebuchadnezzar = Antiochus Epiphanes?" *ZAW* 98 (1986): 439.

Goswell, G. "The Ethics of the Book of Daniel." *ResQ* 57 (2015): 129–42.

Kalimi, I., and J. D. Purvis. "King Jehoiachin and the Vessels of the Lord's House in Biblical Literature." *CBQ* 56 (1994): 449–57.

Meek, T. J. "Translation Problems in the Old Testament." *JQR* 50 (1959–60): 45–54.

Mercer, M. K. "Daniel 1:1 and Jehoiakim's Three Years of Servitude." *AUSS* 27 (1989): 179–92.

Oates, Joan. *Babylon*. Rev ed. London: Thames and Hudson Ltd, 1986.

Paul, S. M. "The Mesopotamian Babylonian Background of Daniel 1–6." In *The Book of Daniel: Volume 1, Composition and Reception*, ed. J. J. Collins and P. W. Flint, 55–68. Leiden, Boston: Brill, 2001.

Smith-Christopher, D. L. "Hebrew Satyagraha: The Politics of Biblical Fasting in the Post-Exilic Period (Sixth to Second Century B.C.E.)." *Food and Foodways* 5 (1993): 269–92.

Soesilo, D. "Why Did Daniel Reject the King's Delicacies? (Daniel 1:8)." *BT* 45 (1994): 441–44.

Stone, M. "A Note on Daniel i.3." *ABR* 7 (1959): 69–71.

Tanner, J. P. "Old Testament Chronology and Its Implications for the Creation and Flood Accounts." *BSac* 172 (Jan 2015): 24–44.

Wooden, R. G. "The Recontextualization of Old Greek Daniel 1." In *Of Scribes and Sages: Early Jewish Interpretation and Transmission of Scripture*,

Volume 1: Ancient Versions and Traditions, ed. C. A. Evans, 47–68. Library of Second Temple Studies 50. London: T&T Clark, 2004.

Zadok, R. "The Origin of the Name Shinar." *ZA* 74 (1984): 240–44.

Part II: The Aramaic Section

The Demonstration of God's Sovereignty Over the Gentile Nations to Which Israel Was Being Subjected (2:1–7:28)

This chapter initiates a major section of the book, extending from 2:1 through 7:28. Beginning in 2:4b, the language changes from Hebrew to Aramaic (and remains so to the end of chap. 7). Scholars have wrestled with the question of why this large section was written in Aramaic rather than in Hebrew. Furthermore, they have sought to understand how this issue relates to the literary structure and the purpose of the book as a whole. Probably chaps. 2–7 are intended as a literary unit, and the Aramaic language serves to underscore this conclusion, though chap. 7 probably serves as a "hinge chapter" (belongs to both 2–7 and 7–12). See the section on "Unity and Literary Structure" in the introductory material for a defense and elaboration of this position.

This first major section (chaps. 2–7) emphasizes the Gentile nations that Israel was being disciplined by and subjected to (during the Babylonian exile and the long history following it). It would be natural for these chapters to be written in Aramaic since that was the *lingua franca* of the Gentile world in Daniel's day. Only when Christ returns, the antichrist is defeated, and Messiah's kingdom is formally established (all major themes within the book) will Israel's discipline be lifted. In light of what is revealed in the opening and concluding chapters to this section, it is fair to say that chaps. 2–7 depict the role, character, and succession of the Gentile nations of the world under whom Israel is being disciplined prior to Messiah's kingdom. These chapters affirm that these Gentile kingdoms have been allowed temporal rule (under God's authority) until God is pleased to establish the everlasting messianic kingdom, and that no adversary can successfully oppose him (note esp. 2:44; 4:3, 34–35; 5:21; 6:26; and 7:14, 27).

In regard to chaps. 2 and 7 that open and conclude the section, though similar there is a noticeable difference. In chap. 2, God's revelation comes to a pagan king in the form of a dream, whereas in chap. 7 it comes to righteous Daniel in the form of a vision. The question might be asked: Why should God's revelation come to King Nebuchadnezzar at all? In this manner, not only is the truth revealed, but also God is clearly seen as the victor. He is supreme to the Babylonian religious system, and this clarifies that the deportation seen in 1:1–2 does not represent a defeat of Yahweh, the God worshiped by Daniel and the other captives.

The unity of chaps. 2–7 is underscored by the literary structure binding these chapters. There is an intentional paralleling of themes between certain chapters. For example, chaps. 2 and 7 depict a succession of Gentile kingdoms that will arise and have dominion over Israel. In the case of both, the Gentile kingdoms are eventually replaced by Messiah's kingdom. Likewise, there is a parallel of chap. 3 with chap. 6 (refusal/deliverance themes), and chap. 4 with chap. 5 (arrogance and humbling of a Babylonian king). The result is a concentric structure, as the following chart reveals:

Literary Structure of Daniel 2–7

Nebuchadnezzar's Dream of the Four-Part Image	**Refusal to Worship the Image of Gold**	**Nebuchadnezzar's Dream of the Tree**	**Belshazzar's Feast**	**Daniel's Refusal to Stop Praying**	**Daniel's Vision of the Four Beasts**
Gentile Powers and Messiah's Kingdom	Deliverance from the Furnace	Humbled for His Pride by Animal-like Madness	Humbled for Arrogant Defiance by Defeat of Babylon	Deliverance from the Lions	Gentile Powers and Messiah's Kingdom
Chap 2	Chap 3	Chap 4	Chap 5	Chap 6	Chap 7

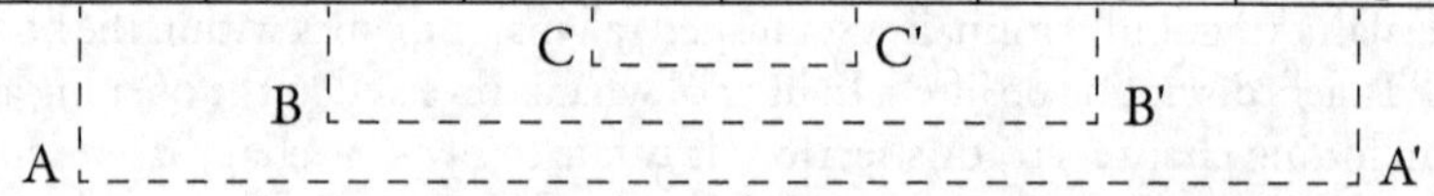

A. Nebuchadnezzar's Dream of the Four-Part Image and the Eventual Establishment of Messiah's Kingdom (2:1–49)

This chapter focuses upon the dream that God gives to Nebuchadnezzar. Yet the significance of the dream is found not just in its interpretation but also in how the interpretation comes about. The Babylonian "wise men" were supposedly experts in the interpretation of dreams, yet the king's request leaves them totally discredited—they cannot meet the demand of the king to state both the dream and its interpretation. Daniel's God, on the other hand, is glorified, as He reveals the dream and its interpretation to Daniel. Thus the successful siege against Jerusalem in chap. 1 does not mean that the God of Judah is weak and inferior to the gods of Babylon. Furthermore, the interpretation of the dream shows that not only Babylon but also all the subsequent Gentile kingdoms are but momentary "earthly powers" that will ultimately be subdued and replaced by the kingdom to be established by the one true God of heaven.

1. The Inability of the Babylonian "Wise Men" To Interpret the King's Dream (2:1–13)

The first thirteen verses provide the setting for the court tale of chap. 2. The king has a dream, and he demands that the wise men of Babylon reveal to him the dream and its interpretation. They, however, cannot meet the king's demand.

Textual Notes

Note: Most of the text critical notes in *BHS* concern minor details of spelling and pointing.

9.a. Pap. 967, MS 88, and Syh add "and explain its interpretation." No Heb MS support.

9.b. The Qere has a ד inserted: הִזְדְּמִ׳, and a number of MSS have הִזְדַּמִ׳. Hitpaʿal of זְמַן.

Translation

2:1 In the second year of his reign,[1] Nebuchadnezzar had dreams.[2] His mind[3]

1. Lit., "the reign of Nebuchadnezzar," but the pronoun "his" is used in translation for better English.
2. The Heb text contains a cognate accusative, "Nebuchadnezzar dreamed dreams" (cf. Joel 3:1). The NET renders this "was in a dream state," whereas the NASB and NIV simplify to "Nebuchadnezzar had dreams." For discussion of the cognate accusative, see *IBHS*, 166–67 (§10.2.1f-g). The cognate accusative can be used comparatively, or to intensify the action. For the latter, see Ps 14:5, "they dreaded with dread," i.e., they were overwhelmed with dread. The latter case may suggest that Nebuchadnezzar did not merely have a dream; he had an overwhelming (or unusual) dream (or, he was baffled by his dream). In light of v. 28, this should be understood as one dream (cf. GKC, 400 [§124o]: "in some few cases the plural is used to denote an indefinite singular").
3. Lit., "spirit" (רוּחַ, *rûaḥ*). For the sense of "mind," see BDB, 925 #6.

was troubled[4] and he could not sleep.[5] **2** The king gave orders[6] to summon the magicians, conjurers,[7] sorcerers,[8] and Chaldeans in order to tell the king his dream. So they came and stood before the king. **3** The king told them, "I had an unusual dream, and my mind is troubled to understand the dream." **4** The Chaldeans replied to the king (in Aramaic),[9] "O king, live forever! Tell your servants the dream, and we will declare its interpretation." **5** The king answered and said to the Chaldeans, "My decision[10] is firm.[11] If you do not make known to me the dream and its interpretation, you will be dismembered[12]

---

4. פָּעַם (*pāʿam*) means to "thrust, impel" in the Qal but "to be disturbed, troubled" in the Niph (Ps 77:5) and Hithp. The basic idea is "beating" (note Judg 5:28 where the cognate noun פַּעַם, *pāʿam*, is used of a horse's hoofbeat). From the idea "beaten" is derived the idea of "troubled, agitated."

5. MT's נִהְיְתָה (*nihyᵊṯâ*) would be a Niph Perf 3fs from הָיָה (*hāyâ*), "be, become." BDB (Niph 3) gives the meaning "be done, finished, gone," but only in Daniel. *BHS* proposes נָדְדָה from נְדַד (*nᵊḏaḏ*, "retreat, flee, depart, stray;" BDB, 622), which Collins (148 fn 6) supports (cf. Dan 6:19). A similar situation is found in Esth 6:1, "the king could not sleep" (שְׁנַת הַמֶּלֶךְ נָדְדָה, *šᵊnaṯ hammeleḵ nāḏᵊḏâ*). Yet this requires a significant emendation lacking MS support. LXX has ἐγένετο (*egeneto*), which supports נִהְיְתָה (*nihyᵊṯâ*). Others have speculated that this might be from a root הָוָה (*hāwâ*), since Hebrew has the nouns הֹוָה (*hōwâ*, "ruin, disaster") and הַוָּה (*hawwâ*, "chasm, fig. destruction"). Translators struggle with how to render this clause. Literally it seems to be "his sleep was done on him." So "his sleep left him" would be the idea, i.e., he could not sleep (contra Collins, who argues MT must mean "he fell asleep again"). The NET "he suffered from insomnia" captures the sense of the clause.

6. Lit., "said."

7. Regarding magicians and conjurers, see note and commentary to Dan 1:20.

8. See commentary on Dan 2:2 for discussion of the terms translated "sorcerers" and "Chaldeans."

9. The following words and on through 7:28 are written in Aramaic rather than Hebrew. The word ארמית (*ʾrmyt*) is missing in the extant text of 1QDan[a]. However, Collins (148 fn 11) points out "there is still sufficient space for ארמית (*ʾrmîṯ*) in the lacuna at the end of the preceding line." For further discussion as to whether ארמית (*ʾrmîṯ*) is part of the narrative or a marginal gloss, see B. A. Mastin, "The Reading of lQDan[a] at Daniel II 4," *VT* 38 (1988): 341–46, who argues that it is not a gloss.

10. Lit., "the word from me" (מִלְּתָא מִנִּי, *millᵊṯāʾ minnî*).

11. The Aramaic text reads "the word/matter from me is *ʾazdâ*," a Persian loanword. *ʾazdâ* basically means "public knowledge, publicly known" but carries the implication that something has been "decided" (thus "firm" or "decisive," coming from the king). The KJV translated the clause "the thing is <u>gone</u> from me," thinking (mistakenly) that the verb was derived from a root *ʾăzad* (= *ʾăzal*) meaning "to go away" (BDB, 23c).

12. Lit., הַדָּמִין תִּתְעַבְדוּן (*haddāmîn tiṯʿaḇḏûn*) means "limbs you will be made." הַדָּם (*haddām*) is a Persian loanword for "limb" (cf. 2 Macc 1:16). Cf. J. Makujina, "Dismemberment in Dan 2:5 and 3:29 as an Old Persian Idiom," *JAOS* 119 (1999):

and your house turned into rubble.[13] **6** But, if you declare the dream and its interpretation, you will receive from me gifts, a reward,[14] and great honor. Therefore[15] declare to me the dream and its interpretation." **7** They replied a second time saying, "Let the king state the dream to his servants, and we shall declare its interpretation." **8** The king answered, saying, "I know for certain that you are *trying to* buy time, inasmuch as[16] you have seen that the decision from me is firm. **9** That if you do not make known to me the dream, there is just one decree *for* you.[17] For you have agreed together to issue me a false and misleading report, until the situation might change. Therefore tell me the dream, so that I may know that you are able to declare its interpretation." **10** The Chaldeans replied before the king saying, "There is no one in the world[18] who is able to declare *such a* thing to the king, inasmuch as no great[19] king or ruler has asked such a thing of any magician, conjurer, or Chaldean. **11** The thing the king asks is difficult,[20] and there is no other who can declare it before the king except *the* gods,[21] whose dwelling is not

---

309–12, who argues that *haddāmîn tiṯʿaḇḏûn* in Dan 2:5 and 3:29 is a loan translation from Old Persian used to convey dismemberment.

13. For נְוָלִי (*nᵊwālî*), BDB (1102) gives the meaning "refuse-heap." The etymology is uncertain. Jastrow (887) gives the meaning "dunghill." Hartman (138) suggests "ruins," and NET translates "reduced to rubble." A similar use is found in Ezra 6:11.

14. Regarding נְבִזְבָּה, *nᵊḇizbâ* (cf. Dan 5:17), *HALOT* (1924) notes, "etymology is uncertain, perhaps to be related to Akk." BDB (1102) gives the meaning "reward" and RJ (48) "gift."

15. Goldingay (33) objects to the meaning "therefore" for לָהֵן (*lāhēn*) and takes it as an adversative ("now"). *HALOT* (1907–8) understands two roots לָהֵן (*lāhēn*), one meaning "therefore" (Dan 2:6, 9) but a second as an adversative particle, "but, yet," (so Dan 2:30; Ezra 5:12). Collins (148 fn 18) points out that the adversative use is supported by Pap. 967, whereas the Vg. has "therefore." Also note that LXX^{O} translates לָהֵן (*lāhēn*), as "therefore" in v. 9.

16. RJ (50) suggests the translation "inasmuch as" for כָּל־קֳבֵל, *kol-qŏḇēl* (and in v. 10), though BDB (1110) suggests reading this as כִּלְקֳבֵל (*kᵊlāqŏḇēl).*

17. The Aramaic text has "one is your law/decree," implying that only one fate awaited them.

18. Lit., "dry land" (יַבֶּשְׁתָּא, *yabbešᵊtāʾ*) meaning "the earth" (*HALOT*, 1887); best understood and translated here as "world."

19. The NET has "no king, regardless of his position and power." In the Aramaic text, however, "regardless of his position" translates the one adjective *raḇ*, which more likely *modifies* "king"; hence "no great king." The word "power" is the adjective *šallîṭ* ("having mastery, ruling"), probably used substantivally here for "ruler" (so LXX^{O} and LXX$^{\theta}$). The idea is that "no great king or ruler has asked" something like this.

20. *HALOT* (1893) indicates that יַקִּיר (*yaqqîr*) can mean (1) "difficult" (so Dan 2:11), or (2) "honorable" (so Ezra 4:10).

21. The LXX^{O} has "except for angels," though LXX$^{\theta}$ has "the gods" (*theoi*). Collins (149) translates "divine beings."

with mankind." **12** Wherefore the king became furiously angry[22] and gave orders to destroy all the wise[23] men of Babylon. **13** So a decree went out, and the wise men were about[24] to be slain. And Daniel and his friends were *also* sought[25] so they could be slain.

Commentary

2:1–3 *Nebuchadnezzar startled by a divinely given dream.* Chapter 2 opens with the announcement that Nebuchadnezzar had a most unusual dream in the second year of his reign. Some critical scholars have questioned the historicity of the book because of this statement. Daniel appears to have already completed his training from chap. 1 and to have been elevated to the status of a "wise man" of the realm. Yet if the training was to have been three years (so 1:5), how could this dream take place in only the second year of King Nebuchadnezzar? This is not necessarily a contradiction, as some have charged. There are at least two possible explanations. The first is that the events of chap. 2 actually took place while Daniel was still in his training program (so Wood, 49–50). The strength of this position is that it treats the training program as lasting a full three years, rather than parts of years. However, it would demand that Daniel was not with his three friends when the king tested them in 1:18–19 (since he would have already been elevated as "ruler over the whole province of Babylon" according to 2:48).

A better solution (and one favored by most Bible scholars) is that the events of chap. 2 occurred after the training program. In this case, chap. 2 follows chap. 1 chronologically, which is what we would expect apart from evidence to the contrary. Also, it would be extremely unlikely that Daniel would have been made "ruler over the whole province of Babylon" while still in the training program (2:48). Then, tension of the "second year" can be resolved by assuming that accession-year dating is involved and that a part of a year is counted as a year. An accession year (according to Babylonian reckoning) is that part of a year from the time a man first becomes king

---

22. The Aramaic "became angry and very furious" is properly understood as a hendiadys: "he became furiously angry" (so Collins, 149 fn 37; and NET).
23. "The wise men" (Aram. חַכִּימַיָּא, *ḥakkîmayyāʾ*) is a general, all-inclusive term to describe the various advisors to the king, whether magicians, conjurers, sorcerers, or Chaldeans. Daniel was also considered one, though he did not practice occultic techniques.
24. The words "were about to be slain" reflect the one Aramaic participle *miṯqaṭṭᵊlîn* (Hitpeʿel of *qṭl*). The temporal sense of the participle is best rendered as a *futurum instans* (participle of the immediate future = about to be). See GKC, 359–60 (§116p).
25. The Aram. verb *ḇᵊʿô* ("seek") is technically in the *active* voice, but the impersonal active plural of the Aram. verb can function like a passive (so NET). Some translations may have "they (the king's agents) sought Daniel and his friends." The final verb of the sentence (Hitpeʿel inf. const.) favors the NET translation.

until the following Nisan (March-April).[26] Then official regnal years are counted from Nisan to Nisan. The following chart shows that it is possible to have completed the training program before the end of the king's second *official year*:[27]

Year of Training	Year of King's Reign	Date
First	Accession year	From Sept 605 (the time Nebuchadnezzar assumed the throne) to Nisan 604 BC
Second	First year	Nisan 604–603 BC
Third	Second year	Nisan 603–602 BC

If the dream was near the end of the second official year, there could have conceivably been nearly thirty months for the training program (which may meet the criteria of "three years").

Hanson reports that in the ancient world in general, "The extant data show that dreams and visions were nearly always considered meaningful or significant."[28] Being a miraculously given dream by Yahweh God made it all the more perplexing, intriguing, and troubling. Because of the unusual nature of the dream, the king could not sleep and consequently summoned the "wise men" of Babylon to come to his aid. Four categories are specified.[29] For the first two (magicians and conjurers), see comments on 1:18–20. The third category is the "sorcerers" (מְכַשְּׁפִים, *mᵊkaššᵊpîm*). According to Leon

26. D. N. Freedman, "The Babylonian Chronicle," *BA* 19 (1956): 53, confirms the Babylonian practice of an accession year that precedes Nisan: "Nabopolassar died on Aug. 16, 605. On receiving the news, Nebuchadrezzar hurried back to Babylon to be crowned king on Sept. 7, 605. From then until the following April is designated his 'accession-year.' Then in April, 604, during the *akitu* or New Year's Festival, the official 'first year' of his reign began."

27. This chart is adapted from Miller, 76.

28. J. S. Hanson, "Dreams and Visions in the Graeco-Roman World and Early Christianity," in *Aufsteig und Niedergang der römishen Welt*, ed. H. Temporini and W. Haase, Part II, Vol. 23.2 (Berlin: Walter de Gruyter, 1980), 1396.

29. For an insightful article surveying various types of divination used in the ANE for acquiring divine knowledge, see H. Hoffner, "Ancient Views of Prophecy and Fulfillment: Mesopotamia and Asia Minor," *JETS* 30 (1987): 257–65. In addition to people who functioned as prophets and oracles, Hoffner highlights five major types of divination: (1) extispicy (the examination of the entrails of a sacrificial sheep by a trained specialist called a *bârû*, "seer"); (2) astrology (especially noting the time of the disappearance of the old moon, its reappearance, its relation to the sun, and other data on eclipses); (3) augury (observing the movements and behavior of birds); (4) kleromancy (using lots, sometimes attached to small animals); and (5) oneiromancy (reporting or interpreting symbolic elements of dreams).

Wood (50), this likely refers to the religious group from Akkadian texts known as *kashshapu*, who used herbs, charms, and various potions, and was considered to be in league with evil forces. In essence, they practiced witchcraft, which was strongly forbidden by the Bible because it opened one's life to demonic influence or possession (Exod 7:11; 22:18; Deut 18:10; Isa 47:9,12; Jer 27:9). The fourth category is that of the "Chaldeans" (כַּשְׂדִּים, *kaśdîm*). The Bible seems to use this term in three different senses. One is the ethnic sense (see 5:30) to describe the group of people known as the *kaśdîm*. Their origin is uncertain, but they lived among the swamps and lakes along the lower parts of the Tigris and Euphrates rivers and eventually came to dominate the larger region (what is lower Iraq today). "The tribal territory covering the southern marshes and coastal plains of ancient Iraq bordering the Persian Gulf was called by outsiders 'Chaldean land' (*māt Kaldu*) after the name of the tribes inhabiting the area."[30]

Dan 2:2, however, seems to employ the word *kaśdîm* in a more restricted sense of experts/priests in the Chaldean religion. They had numerous functions, one of which was astrology. Whitcomb (36–37) illustrates how diligent their efforts were in studying the celestial bodies: "the Babylonian astronomer Naburimannu (ca. 500 BC) was able to calculate the length of the year at 365 days, 6 hours, 15 minutes, 41 seconds—only 26 minutes and 55 seconds too long!" Their interest in the celestial bodies, however, was for the purpose of ascertaining the outcome of future events (which made it evil, since they opened themselves up to satanic deception).

Sometimes the term "Chaldeans" could be applied in a general way to all the occult practitioners of Babylon, as seems the case in the following verses. These various religious *experts* made up what was known as the "wise men" (חַכִּימַיָּא, *ḥakkîmayyā'*) of Babylon. They were not rulers per se but important court officials who relied upon the occult for supernatural power and information. One of their main purposes was to use this information to advise the king. All of these practices were forbidden by God's Word (Deut 18:10–11).

One of their "skills" was the interpretation of dreams, and records indicate that this had become a highly developed discipline in the ancient Near East. This would explain why the king summoned these men following his

---

Of further help in understanding Mesopotamian divination practices is J. N. Lawson, "'The God Who Reveals Secrets': The Mesopotamian Background to Daniel 2.47," *JSOT* 74 (1997): 61–76 (esp. 65–69). He mentions some techniques not covered by Hoffner, e.g., lecanomancy (the observation of oil on water), and libanomancy (the observation of smoke from incense). He also added an important aspect to the discussion: "However, and of specific importance to the idea of divine revelation, it was *not only* the omens that were revealed by the gods, *but also* the very knowledge required to interpret them" (69). That is, the *knowledge to interpret* also came from the gods.

30. D. J. Wiseman, "Chaldea; Chaldeans; Chaldees," in *ISBE*, 1:630.

dream. Dream manuals had even been composed with elaborate instructions on proper interpretation.[31] Baldwin (87) writes,

> These experts in dreams worked on the principle that dreams and their sequel followed an empirical law which, given sufficient data, could be established. The dream manuals, of which several examples have come to light, consist accordingly of historical dreams and the events that followed them, arranged systematically for easy reference. Since these books had to try to cover every possible eventuality they became inordinately long; only the expert could find his way through them, and even he had to know the dream to begin with before he could search for the nearest possible parallel. The unreasonable demands of the king and the protests of the interpreters in verses 3–11 are in keeping with his character and the known facts concerning dream books.

2:4–6 *The first response of the Chaldeans.* The record of their response (beginning in v. 4) indicates that it was "in Aramaic." Most likely this note refers not to their immediate response, as though they actually addressed the king in Aramaic, but is used as a signal to the reader that the text is switching to Aramaic (which will continue through 7:28). Aramaic had been used for several centuries prior to the Neo-Babylonian Empire and was used by the Babylonians themselves. While it is possible that the "wise men" would have addressed the king that day in Aramaic, it may simply mean that the record preserved for us in the Bible is in Aramaic. Perhaps they actually spoke to the king in a Semitic Babylonian dialect, as Wiseman has suggested.[32]

The Chaldeans begin by asking to be told the dream. This was the standard practice in Babylon: the dream is related and then an "interpretation" is proclaimed. The king, however, did the unexpected. He demanded that they tell him *both* the dream and its interpretation. He knew they could just invent an interpretation if he were to tell them the dream (which suggests he was skeptical of them from the outset). If they really had supernatural abilities, then they ought to be able to also state the contents of the dream itself (so the king reasoned). Failure to do so would result in their dismemberment—being torn limb from limb. Also, their homes would be reduced to rubble (Aram. *nᵊwālî*)—i.e., the homes would be completely destroyed. On the other hand, if they could meet the king's request, they would be amply rewarded. They would receive "gifts" (plural) and a "reward" (singular). The singular "reward" (*nᵊḇizbâ*) suggests a very special gift, perhaps known to

31 A. L. Oppenheim, "The Interpretation of Dreams in the Ancient Near East," *TAPS* 46 (1956): 179–373; idem, "New Fragments of the Assyrian Dream-Book," *Iraq: British School of Archaeology in Iraq* 31 (1969): 153–65. Interpretation of dreams was done through consulting texts or relying upon "the oral tradition of the masters."

32. Wiseman, "Chaldea, Chaldeans," 180.

them at the time but unknown to us today (but no doubt enticing). They would also be given "great honor," i.e., public recognition and fame.

2:7–9 *The second response of the Chaldeans.* Though they were flattered by the honors the king promised, they no doubt were trembling and in utter fear at the fate that awaited them for their failure. Rather than challenging the king, however, they simply requested that he tell them the dream. That did not profit them anything, for the king saw right through their tactics, and accused them of "attempting to buy time." Perhaps they hoped that given some time, he would calm down and act more rationally. But this only made him all the more angry. He angrily announced that there was only one thing that was going to happen to them. Literally the text says, "one is your *decree* (דָּתְכוֹן, *dāṯkôn*)," i.e., there is no alternative for them other than what the king had already decreed would happen to them. Then he accused them of conspiring together against him to lie. Yet Nebuchadnezzar held to his demand: they must tell him the dream so that he could be confident they had the ability to declare the right interpretation.

What made the king so insistent to act this rashly about a "mere dream"? Probably the dream itself had terrified the king and left him fearful. Although he did not understand the details of the dream, the very thought of a stone destroying a statue that he saw in his dream (2:35) may have been regarded by him as a kind of divine omen that he would be assassinated or his kingdom overthrown. Hence, he wanted to be absolutely certain of the interpretation.

2:10–13 *The third response of the Chaldeans.* They dared not ask again what the dream was, so now they attempted to reason with the king by making three points. First, they tried to point out the impossibility of what the king was asking (no man on earth could do this). Second, they tried to point out that "wise men" have never been asked to do such a thing, even by "great kings and rulers." Third, the king's request was so "difficult" (יַקִּירָה, *yaqqîrâ*) that only the gods (such as those worshiped by the Babylonians) could do this. But gods do not live with mankind, so there is no way to know what they think. This last point is an amazing confession on the limitation of their arts. The whole point to their magical arts, rituals, and astrology was to learn the will of the gods and the outcome of earthly events. Now they confess that their system does not work. Wooden remarks, "It was not, then, a failure of other professionals to have mastered the correct body of knowledge and skills; it was a failure of the very professions themselves to be able to deliver what was expected."[33] This sets the stage for the demonstration by the true

---

33. R. G. Wooden, "The Witness of Daniel in the Court of the Kings," in *'You will be my Witnesses': A Festschrift in Honor of the Reverend Dr Allison A Trites on the Occasion of His Retirement*, ed. R. G. Wooden, T. R. Ashley, and R. S. Wilson, 30–52 (Macon, GA: Mercer University Press, 2003), 36.

God of heaven that he can and does reveal knowledge to man. He can do what they claim is impossible.

Verses 10–11 point out the limitations to human wisdom and knowledge, even when aided by occultic techniques. In every stage of history, man is insufficient to understand the universe around him (especially the spiritual realm). No matter how advanced science becomes, there is a limit to man's knowledge. Man needs *special revelation* from God, and if he is willing to listen to God, he can have the answers to life's most significant questions. Campbell (25–26) writes,

> ... there *are* absolute answers because God has revealed them. If men persist in rejecting God's revelation, they have only themselves to blame if they continue in uncertainty and confusion.

But there is a principle in Scripture that governs what is revealed to us by God: if we respond positively to the light that has been given us, more light will be given (cf. Matt 13:10–12, 16–17; Heb 5:12–14). We must remember that if we do not respond positively to the light that God gives us, and if we do not apply the Word to our lives and begin to mature, then we have no right to expect God to show us more spiritual truth.

In v. 12, the king's anger reaches a boiling point and begins to explode. The translation "got furiously angry" accurately captures the sense of the Aramaic text.[34] In fact, he did not even wait to see if they could come up with the dream; he just ordered all the "wise men of Babylon" to be slain. Apparently this even included all the recent *trainees* who were to become "wise men," since Daniel and his friends were sought out for execution (v. 13).

Biblical Theology Comments

As pointed out in the commentary (see Dan 2:1–3 above), the "wise men" of Babylon were not rulers per se but important court officials who relied upon the occult for supernatural power and information. As religious experts, they advised the king on a host of matters and helped guide him in making important decisions related to his rule.

What took place in the courts of Babylon, however, was a stark manifestation of satanic darkness. Human government had been ordained by God, initially having the responsibility for safeguarding human life (Gen 9:6). In the course of time, Satan sought to propagate his diabolical plot to usurp God's authority by influencing and taking control of human governments. This soon led to corrupt rulers exemplified by bloodthirsty tyrants like Nimrod (Gen 10:8–12). Idolatry became the hallmark of pagan kingdoms on the earth, augmented by all sorts of occultic practices that further entrenched human society in Satan's quest to dominate God's created order.

---

34. Cf. Gen 40:2 where the same term *qᵊṣap̱* ("wrath") is used of Pharaoh. But Dan 2:12 has בְּנַס וּקְצַף שַׂגִּיא (*bᵊnas ûqᵊṣap̱ śaggîʾ*), lit., he "became angry and very furious," but here understood as a hendiadys "became furiously angry."

Israel, however, had been created as a light to the world, designed to operate under God's commandments and reveal to the world the one true God and his holy ways. Israel was not to follow the satanic practices of the other nations:

> When you enter the land which the LORD your God gives you, you shall not learn to imitate the detestable things of those nations. There shall not be found among you anyone who makes his son or his daughter pass through the fire, one who uses divination, one who practices witchcraft, or one who interprets omens, or a sorcerer, or one who casts a spell, or a medium, or a spiritist, or one who calls up the dead. For whoever does these things is detestable to the LORD; and because of these detestable things the LORD your God will drive them out before you. You shall be blameless before the LORD your God. For those nations, which you shall dispossess, listen to those who practice witchcraft and to diviners, but as for you, the LORD your God has not allowed you *to do* so. (Deut 18:9–14, NASB)

In the courts of Babylon, Daniel and his friends found themselves in contest with the very evil that God had commanded his nation to avoid. Theologically, then, the success of Daniel in Babylon was not merely a demonstration that Nebuchadnezzar had not taken Israel captive because of his greater military power, but to show that Israel's God—the creator God—was more powerful than Satan and all those who operated by the occultic practices he propagated. This momentary triumph would eventually be overshadowed by Jesus' victory over Satan at the cross.

Application and Devotional Implications

Throughout these verses, Nebuchadnezzar grew more and more angry, until he totally lost control in v. 12—he "got furiously angry." This shows us the very possible outcome for any of us, when the anger of man is not under the control of the Spirit of God. All of us have become angry at one time or another, and we know how destructive this is—not only to others but to ourselves as well. No one wins when anger rules. Yet the good news is that we do not have to be dominated by anger; it does not have to control us.

Notice the contrast between Nebuchadnezzar (as anger takes over him) and Daniel who trusts in God. Nebuchadnezzar totally lost his regard for human life. Verse 13 indicates that he even issued a formal decree (*dāṯ*) ordering the death of the "wise men." It is one thing to be disappointed in their inability to help him; it is quite another to have them destroyed. Yet when anger took over, rational thinking quickly disappeared. Human life suddenly meant nothing to him. Perhaps he did not stop to consider that in the process he was also destroying his own reputation. A wise leader (even among unbelievers) is respected, but Nebuchadnezzar was acting like an animal that no one could respect. In contrast stands young Daniel, who does not explode in anger when he hears of the king's decree—nor does he panic. This portrays for us what God is able to achieve in the life of a believer: a life of a *calm spirit*, not ruled by anger. Galatians 5:20 teaches us that "outbursts of anger" are one of the deeds of the flesh. The believer *filled with the Spirit* does not do that (which is why we need to walk in the power of the Spirit and not allow the flesh to be in control).

2. Daniel's intercession and prayer (2:14–23)

In contrast to the section mentioning the explosive anger of King Nebuchadnezzar, this section portrays the controlled reaction of Daniel as he and his friends took the matter before the Lord in prayer.

Textual Notes

16.a-a. The MT has עַל וּבְעָה ("entered and sought"), but LXX$^{\theta}$ only has ἠξίωσεν ("he requested"). LXX^{O}, on the other hand, not only lacks a verb for "entered" but adds an adverb "quickly": εἰσῆλθε ταχέως ("he entered quickly").

Translation

2:14 Then Daniel responded prudently[35] to Arioch,[36] the commander[37] of the king's guard, who had gone forth to slay the wise men of Babylon. **15** He

---

35. Lit., "he returned counsel and discretion" (הֲתִיב עֵטָא וּטְעֵם, *hătîḇ ʿēṭāʾ ûṭᵊʿēm*). NET correctly understands עֵטָא וּטְעֵם (*ʿēṭāʾ ûṭᵊʿēm*) to be a hendiadys and translates "spoke with prudent counsel" (contrast Collins, 149, "responded with good counsel and prudence"). Goldingay (33 fn 14a) admits "the two nouns are near synonyms, like other pairs in this chapter." The point is that Daniel responded tactfully with words of discretion (which showed great maturity on his part). To "respond prudently" captures the main idea.

36. Arioch (Aram. אַרְיוֹךְ, *ʾaryôḵ*) is an ancient name. Cf. Gen 14:1; Jdt 1:6. Collins (158) notes, "Various etymologies have been proposed: Sumerian *eri-aku* (servant of the moon god) is no longer accepted. Delcor says it is 'certainly Hurrian' because a similar name, *A-ri-wu-uk*, is attested at Mari. More recently it has been identified as the Old Persian name *Ariyauka*, and this is plausible at least for Daniel and Judith."

37. The official is termed רַב־טַבָּחַיָּא (*raḇ-ṭabbāḥayyāʾ*). For טַבָּח (*ṭabbāḥ*), BDB (371) suggests "guardsman," whereas *HALOT* (1883) gives "executioners" or "bodyguard." Admittedly, it is very difficult to know which nuance is correct in this instance. The versions are mixed: NIV "the commander of the king's guard," NASB "the captain of the king's bodyguard," NRSV "the king's chief executioner," and NET "in charge of the king's executioners." Both LXX^{O} and LXX$^{\theta}$ have ἀρχιμαγείρῳ (*archimageirōi*, dat. of ἀρχιμαγείρος, *archimageiros*) for which LSJM (253) gives the meaning "chief cook" or "title of a great officer in Oriental courts." The root μάγειρος (*mageiros*) means "cook, butcher." Despite this, Josephus (*Ant.* 10.10.3) used the word σωματοφύλαξ (*sōmatophulax*, "bodyguard") in his summary of this story in Daniel. Commentators

said to Arioch, the king's officer,[38] "Why is *this* decree from the king so urgent?"[39] Arioch then informed Daniel about the matter. **16** So Daniel went in[40]

---

are likewise divided. Collins (149) translates "chief of the royal executioners," though he acknowledges (158), "By the neo-Babylonian period, however, the title had lost its etymological meaning and had become the court title of a high official." Goldingay (30) has "the royal chief of police." He notes (33 fn 14c), "etymologically 'slaughter-men,' which is just what they were on this occasion! But elsewhere the word simply means 'guard/police.'" Montgomery (155) remarks, "'Executioners' ('butchers') is simple and appropriate enough here; s. Pr., citing use of the root in Akk. = 'execute,' and so Kön., *Hwb*." (Pr = commentary by J. D. Prince, 1899).

The root does occur frequently in BH, טָבַח (*ṭāḇaḥ*), to "slaughter, butcher, slay" (BDB, 370), and in MH (Jastrow, 516), "to prepare a feast, esp. to slaughter and dress meat, to cook." רַב־טַבָּחַיָּא (*raḇ-ṭabbāḥayyāʾ*) may have been a technical expression for a royal official, the exact meaning of which we cannot assuredly know today. We do have a similar expression in BH, רַב־טַבָּחִים, *raḇ-ṭabbāḥîm* (see 2 Kgs 25:8; Jer 39:9; 52:12; and compare Gen 39:1) where it has the sense of being an important official, "captain of the guard" (he was on a foreign mission for the king, but not as an executioner). Perhaps, then, the NIV's "the commander of the king's guard" is a reasonable translation (and would be consistent with LXX^{O}, LXX$^{\theta}$ and Josephus). In any case, as "head" (רַב, *raḇ*), he need not have performed the executions himself; he was in charge of those who did.

38. The translation "officer" translates the Aram. adj. שַׁלִּיטָא, *šallîṭāʾ*, meaning one who is powerful or mighty (*HALOT*, 1996).

39. The word translated "urgent" is from the Aram. root חֲצַף (*ḥăṣap̱*). The meaning according to *HALOT* (1879) is "harsh," and this is the translation given by the NIV. Both meanings are possible, however. Note Dan 3:22 where the notion of "urgent" is contextually better (even the NIV translates it "urgent" in that case). LXX$^{\theta}$'s ἀναιδής (*anaidēs*; LSJM, 105: "lacking in restraint, intemperate") seems to have the idea of being *rash*, which supports the translation "urgent." LXX^{O}, on the other hand, has πικρῶς (*pikrōs*; LSJM, 1404: "harshly, bitterly, vindictively"), which favors "harsh." The translation of *ḥăṣap̱* as "harsh" stresses the *severity* of the king's action, whereas "urgent" emphasizes the temporal aspect. Since the word can incorporate both ideas, perhaps the translation "decisive" would be better. Yet "urgent" is a good choice, and Daniel's request in the next verse for more "time" may suggest the temporal aspect is dominant in v. 15.

40. Did Daniel actually enter into the king's presence and speak with him? In light of v. 25, that would seem surprising. Some manuscripts (the Greek LXX$^{\theta}$ and Syriac) omit the words "went in and," and just say that Daniel sought from the king. Goldingay (34) thinks that if Daniel had actually gone into the king's presence, the text would have included the words "before the king" (קֳדָם מַלְכָּא, *qŏḏām malkāʾ*) as in vv. 24–25. But see the use of the Aram. verb עֲלַל (*ʿălal*; "go, come in, enter") in Dan 4:4–5 (Eng. vv. 7–8) without the qualifying words קֳדָם מַלְכָּא (*qŏḏām malkāʾ*), though entering the king's presence is clearly the case.

and requested of the king that he might grant[41] him time,[42] that he might make known the interpretation to the king. **17** Then Daniel went off to his quarters[43] and informed his friends, Hananiah, Mishael, and Azariah, about the matter **18** so that they might seek[44] compassion[45] before the God of heaven concerning this mystery, that[46] Daniel and his friends might not be put to death along with the rest of the wise men of Babylon. **19** Then the mystery was revealed to Daniel in a night vision. So Daniel blessed the God of heaven, **20** saying,[47] "Let[48] the name of God[49] be blessed

---

41. Aram. נְתַן (*nᵊṯan*) ordinarily means "give, allow" (BDB, 1103d2). Heb. נָתַן (*nāṯan*) is very flexible and in addition to the common meaning "give" can also be used "of (gracious) bestowals of various kinds: give = grant" (so BDB, 678d 1d). Hence, NET translates "grant" for Dan 2:16.

42. The word translated "time" in v. 16 is זְמָן (*zᵊmān*), whereas the word for "time" in v. 8 was עִדָּן(*ʿiddān*). *ʿiddān* in v. 8 means either "time (as *duration*)" or "a definite *period* of time" (BDB, 1105). Normally Aram. *zᵊmān* (in most of the eleven times it occurs in Daniel) means "a specified or appointed time," which could imply that Daniel—in contrast to the Babylonian wise men—was requesting an appointment with the king (a "hearing"), not that he might be given *more time*. Compare ESV: "requested the king to appoint him a time." However, to insist on such a nuance in the case of v. 16 is difficult. Tomasino, although acknowledging that the various cognate forms of *zᵊmān* "mean a point in time when an event occurs," goes on to say, "It can also refer to a predetermined period of time, as in 2:16, where Daniel requests a period of time to determine the meaning of the king's dream; and 7:12, where the existence of three human empires was allowed to continue for a period of time" (A. Tomasino, "זמן," *NIDOTTE*, 1:1114). Compare Heb *zᵊmān* in Neh 2:6, where Tomasino (1:1115) argues, "The context demands that the time refers not to a set date, but to a predetermined duration."

43. Lit., "to his house" (לְבַיְתֵהּ, *lᵊḇayṯēh*), but this need not mean his own building. His place of residence is the idea.

44. LXX^{O} expands, νηστεία̣ν καὶ δέησιν, *nēsteian kai deēsin* ("by fasting and supplication").

45. The translation "mercy" is not the best rendering of Aram. רַחֲמִין, *raḥămîn* (so Goldingay, 34 fn 18a). *HALOT* (1981) suggests "compassion" (so BDB, 1113a). Compassion stresses the *deep tender feelings* of God that they hoped would be touched by their prayers.

46. For this use of דִּי (*dî*), see BDB, 1088 3c, meaning "that" after verbs of asking.

47. Lit., "Daniel answered and said" (עָנֵה דָנִיֵּאל וְאָמַר, *ʿānēh ḏāniyyēʾl wᵊʾāmar*).

48. Regarding לֶהֱוֵא (*lehĕwēʾ*), the verb הֲוָא (*hăwāʾ*) is a Peʿal imperfect 3ms (here jussive), with ל as the preformative of the third person (so RJ, 4). Hence, "let ... be."

49. LXX^{O} adds the word "great," τὸ ὄνομα τοῦ κυρίου τοῦ μεγάλου (*to onoma tou kuriou tou megalou*), "the name of the *great* Lord." 4QDan[a] supports the addition of "great." MT and LXX$^{\theta}$ simply have "God." The phrase "the name of God" is more literally "His name, that of God" (שְׁמֵהּ דִּי־אֱלָהָא, *šᵊmēh dî-ʾĕlāhāʾ*), with the 3ms suffix on שֻׁם (*šum*). אֱלָהָא (*ʾĕlāhāʾ*, with def. article) is not unusual in biblical Aramaic (see, for

from one end of eternity[50] to the other, for wisdom and power are his.[51] **21** It is he who changes the times and eras,[52] deposing kings and setting up *other* kings. He gives wisdom to wise men and knowledge to those with understanding. **22** He reveals the deep and hidden things. He knows what is in the darkness, and light dwells with him. **23** To you, O God of my fathers, I praise and glorify[53] you, for you have given me wisdom and power. Now you have made known to me what we[54] have asked from you; you have made known to us[55] this matter of the king."

Commentary

2:14–16 *Daniel's intercession with the king.* Suddenly Daniel and his three friends were caught up in a major crisis within the kingdom. Although these four men were not practitioners of the occult (as were the other advisers to the king), they were regarded as "wise men" of the court, and thus the king's decree affected them just as it did the others. In this paragraph we see how men of God respond maturely in times of crises.

In contrast with the king's violent explosion of anger (v. 12), Daniel reacts with calmness and rational thinking. This is a mark of a believer under the control of the Holy Spirit and one who understands how the sovereignty of God works. Thus, Daniel did not try to lead a coup against the king or incite

---

example, Dan 5:26). Goldingay (34 fn 20b) views שְׁמֵהּ דִּי־אֱלָהָא (*šᵊmēh dî-ʾĕlāhāʾ*) as a surrogate for Yahweh.

50. "From one end of eternity to the other" is an attempt to capture the force of מִן־עָלְמָא וְעַד־עָלְמָא, *min-ʿolmāʾ wᵊʿaḏ-ʿolmāʾ* (lit., "from perpetuity even unto perpetuity"). BDB (1106) notes that this phrase is used "of limitless time both past and future."

51. Regarding דִּי לֵהּ (*dî lēh*) = "his," see BDB, 1098c 4b.

52. Goldingay (34 fn 21a) points out that there is not a great deal of difference between עִדָּן (*ʿiddān*) and זְמַן (*zᵊman*), though he prefers the translation "era" for the latter (as "season" can convey the wrong idea). עִדָּן (*ʿiddān*) can refer to a specific period of time, such as a year (so Dan 7:25), while זְמַן (*zᵊman*) can be used of the "age" or "period" in which one lives (Dan 7:25). Yet such distinctions cannot always be pressed (e.g., Dan 7:12).

53. There is very little difference between יְדָא (*yᵊḏāʾ*) and שְׁבַח (*šᵊḇaḥ*). They both have the basic meaning of "praise." *NIDOTTE* (4:26) indicates that BH שׁבח (*šābaḥ*) can also mean to "glorify" and NET uses that translation for שׁבח (*šābaḥ*).

54. The verb הוֹדַעְתַּנִי (*hôḏaʿtanî*) has a 1cs suffix ("caused *me* to know"), whereas the following verb, בְעֵינָא (*ḇᵊʿênāʾ*), is in the 1cp ("what *we* have asked"). NET translates the latter "what *I* requested from you," taking the plural subject as an editorial plural. Though possible, this is a bit speculative, and most major translations stick with the grammatical plural. The same editorial plural applies to the final verb of the sentence, הוֹדַעְתֶּנָא, *hôḏaʿtenāʾ*.

55. MT's הוֹדַעְתֶּנָא (*hôḏaʿtenāʾ*) does have the 1cp suffix ("us"), but LXX$^{\theta}$ and S have the singular. Was this an effort by the latter to reconcile with הוֹדַעְתַּנִי (*hôḏaʿtanî*)?

a rebellion (knowing that the king was God's appointed authority—cf. 1 Tim 2:1–2; Rom 13:1–2). Instead, he approached the king's representative, Arioch, who was either in charge of the king's bodyguard or perhaps the executioners that had been ordered to carry out the decree (see textual note above on v. 14). Significantly, he did not try to defy Arioch or denounce the king. Instead, he spoke with "prudent counsel," i.e., tactfully using words of discretion and sought to know why the action was so urgent. Daniel's respectful approach to Arioch gained him some cooperation and even made it possible for Daniel to get a message to the king (though there is some uncertainty whether or not Daniel actually appeared before the king himself—see textual note above on 2:16). Daniel requested of the king time in order that he might declare the interpretation of the king's dream (probably their conversation *implied* that he would also declare the dream, as the king demanded). Unlike the other Chaldeans, Daniel's request was not a stall tactic, as though he was trying to bargain for time (recall 2:8 and see the translation note at 2:16 for "time"—זְמָן, *zᵊmān*). The king must have already had respect for Daniel as a man of integrity and great wisdom (1:19–20). Apparently Daniel's request of the king for time was granted, in light of the following episode when he meets with his friends.

2:17–18 *Daniel's prayer with his friends.* In these verses we see another wise action on the part of Daniel: he sought the fellowship of other believers who could pray with him. The use of their original Hebrew names (contrast 3:13) reminds us of their godly heritage and identification with the true God of heaven. We now see them acting in a godly and mature way, though they were still but young men. But Daniel did not inform his friends of this news that they might feel sorry for themselves or turn to complaining. He informed them *for the purpose* that they might seek God's compassion upon them.[56] His motive was not to confront his friends with bad news, but to lead them in the proper way to respond to a crisis, i.e., by prayer. Daniel also recognized that it was not ultimately the information itself that must be sought, but God's compassion on them. It would be the compassionate favor of God that would make possible the revelation of the king's dream. Although the king had found Daniel and his friends "ten times better" than the Babylonian wise men (1:20), not even that made them equal to the challenge now before them.

As they turned to God for compassion, they prayed to "the God of heaven." Although this expression had been used on rare occasions for the true God as early as Gen 24:7, it became a rather common way of referring to him during the exile and the postexilic period.[57] This expression may have seemed quite appropriate for the Jews during this time when they were living

---

56. The infinitive construct with the *lamed* preposition (*lᵊmiḇʿēʾ*) following the main verb "he informed" (*hôḏaʿ*) signals a purpose clause. Translate: "he informed his friends about the matter, so that they might seek compassion."

57. See Ezra 1:2; 6:10; 7:12, 21; Neh 1:5; 2:4; and Ps 136:26.

among the Gentiles and wanted to distinguish their God from the multitude of deities worshiped by the Gentiles. In contrast to the Babylonian wise men who worshiped the starry heaven and sought to determine the future by supernatural knowledge through astrological means, Daniel's God was the Creator of the heavens and the one holding all the stars and celestial bodies in place.

The specific compassion from God that they sought concerned the "mystery." The term "mystery" (רָז, *rāz*) is regarded by BDB as a Persian loanword meaning something *secret*.[58] What had been shown King Nebuchadnezzar was a *secret* known only to the true God of heaven, and no occultic gimmick in the world could discover what this was about. Yet God could choose to *reveal* it, and knowing this prompted them to pray to that end.

2:19–23 *Daniel's praise in response to God's revelation of the mystery.* Daniel did not have the ability in himself to *figure out* what the king had seen, much less to interpret it. Only by a revelation from God could Daniel know this. That night (in a "night vision") God revealed it all to Daniel. The natural human tendency would be to immediately run to Arioch exclaiming that he now had the answer. That he first took time to thank and worship God speaks volumes of his character. Apparently Daniel's prayer recorded in vv. 20–23 was uttered in the presence of the other three. The use of the plural pronouns in v. 23 (e.g., "You have made known to <u>us</u> the king's matter") indicates he was not alone. If Daniel was not with the others when the night vision came, he soon gathered them all together. Praise for God can sometimes be a private affair, but it is especially appropriate when uttered in the presence of others (cf. Ps 22:22–25).

Scholars have noticed the prayer's resemblance to hymns of thanksgiving found in the Psalter and have sought to analyze its function accordingly.[59] Such analyses have often been extended to include the study of other poems/

---

58. Hartman (139) suggests that Aramaic *rāz* is related conceptually to Hebrew *sôḏ* (which designates both a "council" and the secret decisions or counsel that comes from it—see BDB, 691c). God holds council in heaven and is able to reveal to his prophets the decisions that are made there (e.g., Amos 3:7; Jer 23:18, 22).

59. Noteworthy studies include those of W. S. Towner, "The Poetic Passages of Daniel 1–6," *CBQ* 3l (1969): 317–26 and "Daniel's Praise (Daniel 2.20–23)," in J. W. Watts, *Psalm and Story: Inset Hymns in Hebrew Narrative*, JSOTSup 139 (Sheffield: Sheffield Academic Press, 1992), 145–54. For the semantic and thematic links of Daniel's prayer in 2:20–23, see esp. Watts, 146–47. Concerning the resemblance of Daniel's prayer to that of an individual psalm of thanksgiving, Towner points out (319), "Not only is the situation of the speaker one in which thanksgiving is appropriate; not only does the word 'thanks' (*mehôdē'*) appear in the prayer; but also it exhibits many of the usual formal features of a thanksgiving psalm: the call to praise and extol, the account of the distress from which relief has been obtained, the description of the deliverance obtained, and formulae of praise."

benedictions found in chaps. 1–6, namely Dan 4:1–3 (Eng.), 4:34–35 (Eng.), and 6:25–27 (Eng.), though the latter three passages lack the element of thanksgiving found in 2:23. Critical scholars tend to see these as later assertions made by a final redactor attempting to weave together narrative and poetic material (with various stereotyped liturgical phrases) with the aim of emphasizing *theologically* the eternality of God's kingdom. Towner, for example, writes,

> ... these three liturgically formulated passages bear closest resemblance to the hymn *Gattung* of Israelite religious poetry. In all three poems there is stress on the world rule of God, praise of him as Creator and All-wise, and the typical hymnic celebration of his eternality.[60]

The prayers then serve to support important thematic notions contained in the narratives:

> In all four cases, the prayers focus the point of the narratives roughly as follows: God's decision to allow evil its hour of ascendancy will be vindicated before the eyes of all the nations when good ultimately triumphs; this vindication will come about because of God's own transcendent power and endurance; to this fact the evil powers of the world will themselves be obliged at last to testify.[61]

One need not hold to a redactionary perspective of the book's composition, however, to appreciate the role that Daniel's prayer and the other benedictions play in regard to the narrative development. Clearly the focus of Daniel's praise was for God's *wisdom* (*ḥoḵmâ*) and power (*gᵉḇûrâ*). Notice how these terms are repeated in both v. 20 and v. 23. In fact, the prayer is carefully structured around these concepts:

A Praise for God who possesses wisdom and power (20)
  B God's power: He controls human thrones (21a)
  B' God's wisdom: He has all understanding and reveals hidden knowledge to men (21b-22)
A' Praise for God who dispenses His wisdom and power (23)

This *wisdom* and *power* should be seen in regard to the dream and its revelation about the future kingdoms (vv. 31–45). God's power is illustrated by his complete control over the events of history. Verse 21 indicates that "He changes times and eras, deposing some kings and establishing *other* kings." The words "times" (עִדָּנַיָּא, *ʿiddānayyāʾ*) and "seasons" (זִמְנַיָּא, *zimnayyāʾ*) are near synonyms. They look at the "appointed times" of history (i.e., when events will occur), as well as the "periods or epochs" of history (i.e., the stages

60. Towner, "The Poetic Passages of Daniel 1–6," 321.
61. Ibid., 322–23.

and duration of things).[62] Archer (43) states, "God determines when in history events are to take place and how long each process or phase in history is to endure." Both aspects (when and the duration/period) are illustrated by Jer 25:11–12 and the seventy years of captivity God decreed for Judah. Because God controls the times and eras, he intervenes especially in the establishing and deposing of earthly kings. This was often seen in Israel's earlier history (1 Samuel–2 Kings), though other civilizations had similar beliefs. On the famous Cyrus Cylinder (an inscription on a clay cylinder recording a decree of King Cyrus), we find the claim that Marduk deposed Nabonidus and raised up Cyrus as king in his place. The reality is that Yahweh (and he alone) has the power to do this.

God's *wisdom* is seen in his infinite knowledge and understanding of everything, and by his ability to reveal that to men of his choosing. Verse 22 ("light dwells with him")[63] reflects God's omniscience—his complete awareness of all that exists, and of all that can happen and will happen.[64] He knows the end from the beginning. What would otherwise remain unknowable and hidden (i.e., in the darkness), God has seen fit to reveal to Daniel. Job 12:22 states, "He reveals the deep things of darkness, and brings deep shadows into the light" (NET).

Daniel's prayer in 2:20–23 serves primarily for the characterization of God, for he is the source of wisdom and power over both sage and king (the point toward which both the story and book are driving). Secondarily, however, the prayer characterizes Daniel himself, as Watts has pointed out:

> His first reaction to the revelatory vision is praise and thanksgiving, expressed with complete trust that a positive outcome to his dangerous situation will now be forthcoming. Daniel is thus cast as a model of piety, which matches the narrative's depiction of him through his prayer (2.19), witness (vv. 27–28), and self-effacement (v. 30), and in which he is also characterized as a model Israelite sage (v. 14).[65]

The statement "He gives wisdom to the wise" (v. 21) is full of irony. The *wise men* of Babylon had nothing to offer the king, whereas the man who sought God's wisdom (Daniel) was made truly wise. Such is the case for

---

62. Within the book, Dan 7:12 provides an example of the latter aspect of an appointed period of time. Cf. footnote to translation of עִדָּנַיָּא (*ʿiddānayyā*ʾ) and זִמְנַיָּא (*zimnayyā*ʾ) in v. 21.

63. There is a tradition preserved in *Midr. Lam. Rab.* 36 that "Light" is a name of the Messiah. The context here, however, does not favor such an interpretation.

64. Wood (61) remarks, "To say that light thus dwells with God means that He has it constantly. The overall thought of the verse is suggested to Daniel by God's revelation, just given, bringing 'light' on the 'darkness' of the 'deep and hidden' dream of the king."

65. Watts, "Daniel's Praise," 148.

those of us today who know the true source of wisdom—a wisdom not of this world (cf. 1 Cor 1:18–25).

Application and Devotional Implications

The true character of a person is revealed in a time of crisis. Baldwin (89) notes, "The ability to keep calm under severe shock and pressure, to think quickly and exercise faith in a moment of crisis, these are aspects of *prudence* and *discretion* seen in Daniel here (14; *cf.* Phil. 4:7)."

Notice carefully the admirable qualities that we see in Daniel:

a. He had the grace to guard his speech and refrain from making any unwise and inappropriate comments (vv. 14–15).
b. He demonstrated great boldness and faith (v. 16).
   He had the boldness to seek an audience with the king and the faith to believe that God would do the "impossible."
c. He faced the crisis by seeking fellowship and prayer with other believers (vv. 17–18).
d. Once God revealed the dream to him, he took time to thank and worship God rather than immediately head off to "take care of the business" (vv. 19–23).

This picture of wise Daniel is not given that we might merely admire and applaud him. Rather, this is meant for our own edification—that we might desire to be like him. Daniel is not some Olympic champion whose feats are unattainable. He is an example of what God can do with any person who yields his life to him and seeks after the Lord with all heart. Remember, God is not limited in what he can do with any one of us. It is only our unbelief and hardness of heart that limits God.

3. Daniel Presented to King Nebuchadnezzar (2:24–30)

In this section, the young "lad" Daniel gains an audience with Nebuchadnezzar, arguably the most powerful man on earth at the time. Daniel uses the opportunity not to bring glory to himself but to testify of and honor the God of heaven.

Textual Notes

24.a. 4QDanᵃ and some MSS have only one עַל, not two. Perhaps this was a case of haplography, writing once what should have been written twice. Granted, the prep. עַל following the verb עַל seems odd. Normally we might expect "brought before" (קדם) as in 5:13, or "brought to" (לְ) as in 6:11. Yet given the limited data to examine, there is no reason to reject MT's עַל עַל-אַרְיוֹךְ, unless the text originally had לְאַרְיוֹךְ, without the second עַ (cf. 2:14, 15). Collins (150 fn 64) points out, "4QDanᵃ has a lacuna after עַל and may have originally read עַל [לאריו]ךְ (so Cross)." Note the same verb עַל in 2:16.

24.b. The verb אֲזַל is missing in some MSS, LXX, and Vg. Though it is not essential to the sentence syntactically and seems redundant in light of the preceding verb עַל, it is difficult to explain how it came to be inserted in the text had it not originally been there.

25.a. For גְּבַר, LXX^{O} has ἄνθρωπον σοφὸν ("a wise man"), an addition perhaps prompted by the fact the "wise men" of Babylon had been ordered put to death.

25.b. Instead of בְּנֵי גָלוּתָא ("sons of the exile"), 4QDan^{a} has "the Jews." Both LXX traditions, however, have the word αἰχμαλωσίας ("captivity," i.e., exile).

28.a. MT has וְהוֹדַע, Hap'el perf 3ms of יְדַע. 4QDan^{a}, however, has מהודע, a ptc., perhaps to align with the preceding ptc. גָּלֵא. Yet both LXX^{O} and LXX$^{\theta}$ have a participle followed by an aorist vb., reflective of MT.

29.a. The Qere has אַנְתְּ for the Kethib אַנְתְּה, yet both are acceptable forms. See Dan 2:37, 38 with אַנְתְּה.

29.b. In place of MT's רַעְיוֹנָךְ (sg. noun) some MSS have a pl. noun ־נַיִךְ (as does 4QDan^{a} רעיוניך). The plural seems a superior reading (cf. the pl. form רַעְיוֹנַיִ in the next verse, plus the pl. רַעְיֹנֹהִי "his thoughts" in Dan 4:16, and note the pl. διαλογισμοί in LXX$^{\theta}$).

Translation

2:24 On account of this,[66] Daniel went to Arioch, whom the king had appointed to destroy the wise men of Babylon. He came and said to him, "Do not destroy the wise men of Babylon. Bring me before the king, and I shall declare the interpretation to the king." **25** Arioch then hurriedly[67] brought Daniel before the king and said to him, "I have found a man among the exiles[68] of Judah who can make known the interpretation to the king."

---

66. For the prepositional use of קֳבֵל (*qŏḇēl*) and the phrase כָּל־קֳבֵל דְּנָה (*kol-qŏḇēl dᵊnâ*), see BDB, 1110 2a, "because of this, therefore."

67. בְּהִתְבְּהָלָה (*bᵊhiṯbᵊhālâ*) is a Hitpe'el infinitive const. with prep ב (*bᵊ*), in this case used substantively: in haste.

68. Lit., "the sons of the exile" (בְּנֵי גָלוּתָא, *bᵊnê gālûṯā'*).

26 The king said[69] to Daniel, whose name was Belteshazzar,[70] "Are you able[71]
to make known to me the dream I had in a vision and its interpretation?"
27 Daniel answered before the king, saying, "*As for* the mystery which the
king asks about, neither wise men, conjurers, magicians, nor diviners[72] are
able to make *this* known to the king. **28** However, there is a God in heaven
who reveals mysteries and has made known to King Nebuchadnezzar what
will come to pass[73] in the latter days.[74] This is your dream and[75] the vision of
your head *while* upon your bed. **29** As for you, O king, *while* on your bed
your thoughts turned[76] to what would come to pass after this,[77] and the

---

69. Lit., "the king answered and said" (עָנֵה מַלְכָּא וְאָמַר, *ʿānēh malkāʾ wəʾāmar*).

70. The Aram. text gives Daniel's new name as *bēlṭəšaʾṣṣar* (recall 1:7), though the Greek manuscripts have Βαλτασαρ (so the king's name in 5:1). Scholars are uncertain about the meaning of *bēlṭəšaʾṣṣar*, although the prefix *bēl* suggests that the name is meant to honor the god Bel (otherwise known as Marduk). Note Dan 4:8. One possibility is that the name means (or suggests) "May Bel protect his life." Collins (141) states, "The etymology is Akkadian: *balaṭ-su-uṣur*, 'protect his life,' or *balaṭ-šar-uṣur*, 'protect the life of the prince.'"

71. Goldingay (34) suggests that the force of the question is more emphatic: "are you *really* able?" He bases this on the Aramaic construction *haʾîṯayik kāhēl* (the particle *ʾîṯay* followed by a participle), appealing to Muraoka (*Emphatic Words*, 81).

72. The word translated "diviners" is the Aram. *gāzərîn* (גָּזְרִין), from the verb *gəzar* ("to cut, determine"), and appears here in Daniel for the first time. It may be somewhat *limiting* to translate this as "astrologers" (though astrology could be included in their functions). "Determiners of fate" may better capture the idea (BDB, 1086), which would refer to those who used various forms of divination (including astrology) to determine the outcome of an event or what awaited a person. The NIV, NET, and NASB all translate as "diviners" (so Collins, 161). For a helpful discussion about divination at Babylon, see Oates, *Babylon*, 178–80. She notes, "A great variety of techniques were used in divination, including the observation of animals' entrails, oil in water, smoke from incense, the behavior of birds and other animals, and celestial and other natural phenomena" (178).

73. "What will come to pass" is a translation of לֶהֱוֵא (*lehĕwēʾ*), lit., "what is to be." See translation comments at 2:20.

74. בְּאַחֲרִית יוֹמַיָּא (*bəʾaḥărîṯ yômayyāʾ*). Lit., "in the latter days" or "in the end of days." For explanation, see commentary for 2:28.

75. Goldingay (34 fn 28b) takes the *waw* in חֶלְמָךְ וְחֶזְוֵי (*ḥelmāḵ wəḥezwê*) as explicative: "your dream, the vision that came into your head."

76. סְלִקוּ (*səliqû*), lit., "came up, went up, ascended" (see *HALOT*, 1938, and compare BH סָלֵק (*sālēq*) in Ps 139:8. Most translations render this "turned to" (so NIV, NET, and NASB).

77. The translation "what will come to pass after this" is a literal rendering of לֶהֱוֵא אַחֲרֵי דְנָה (*lehĕwēʾ ʾaḥărê ḏənâ*). The text is not clear what the demonstrative pronoun דְּנָה (*dənâ*) actually refers to. NET rendered the whole expression simply "future things" and NIV "things to come." The remainder of the chapter will clarify

revealer of mysteries has made known to you what will come to pass. **30** But as for me, this was not revealed to me on account of *any* wisdom there is in me more than any other living person, but in order that the interpretation might be made known to the king and that you might know the thoughts in your mind."[78]

Commentary

2:24 *Daniel's approach to Arioch.* Arioch had been given the unpleasant duty of having to slay the wise men of Babylon. So it must have been something of a relief for Arioch when Daniel came to him with the good news that he could interpret the king's dream. We should note carefully, however, that Daniel's first words were not a boast of being able to tell the dream but a concern for the pagan wise men whose lives were in danger. "Do not destroy the wise men of Babylon," he pleaded. We do not know how well Daniel personally knew these men or what relationship he might have had to them. Daniel's likely disdain for their occultic practices and refusal to engage in their arts might have aroused their contempt for him (and certainly their suspicions). Nevertheless, Daniel had compassion on these men who were lost and did not know Yahweh. Their welfare was of more concern to him than his own personal success and reward.

2:25–26 *Daniel's appearance before Nebuchadnezzar.* Though Daniel was the real hero in this crucial hour, Arioch took advantage of the situation to promote himself before the king: "I have found a man."[79] With these words, Arioch attempted to gain the credit for himself, as though the king should be indebted to him. He wanted to enhance his standing through Daniel's success and perhaps even to get some of the reward the king had spoken about (v. 6). Arioch is what we might call a "glory grabber," a person out to promote himself, especially taking the credit that rightfully belongs to others. As Christians, we must always be careful not to let pride control us. Our desire should be fixed on seeing that the glory goes to the Lord, for whatever God does through us is by his grace and not just for our own credit (cf. 1 Cor 15:9–11).

---

that it is a broad sketch of history from Nebuchadnezzar's own time until the inauguration of the messianic age.

78. Lit., "the thoughts of your heart." Both the NIV and NASB translate לִבְבָךְ (*libbāḵ*) as "your mind," since both the Heb. and Aram. word for "heart" can often refer to that inner part of man where thoughts are processed.

79. M. Segal, "From Joseph to Daniel: The Literary Development of the Narrative in Daniel 2," *VT* 59 (2009): 125–26, argues that Arioch's presenting of Daniel to the king in v. 25 stands as a contradiction, since Daniel had previously appeared to the king requesting time in v. 16. Yet v. 25 is not insinuating that "Arioch needs to present him, indicating that Nebuchadnezzar does not know of Daniel at all" (Segal, 126). Rather, the point of v. 25 is to emphasize Arioch's vainglory.

In v. 26 we see Daniel standing before King Nebuchadnezzar with the king putting the crucial question to him: "Are you able to disclose the dream?" The text, at this point, reintroduces Daniel with the words "whose name was also Belteshazzar." Since we had already been told this in 1:7, what need was there for this repetition? To the original readers, it would have been an additional reminder that the famous Jewish ruler in the courts of Babylon, whom they knew as Belteshazzar, was none other than the biblical Daniel.[80] Yet there may be a further purpose in this context. "Belteshazzar" is how the king thought of him, and the name (with the prefix "Bel") associated Daniel with the supreme Babylonian deity Bel, otherwise known as Marduk (see the textual note at 1:7 and the translation note for 2:26).[81] The mention of the name Belteshazzar is important because it sets the stage for what is about to happen as Daniel honors and glorifies not Bel/Marduk but the true God of heaven. The king and all other Babylonians may call him by the name Belteshazzar, but his real identity is with Yahweh, who was about to manifest his power before the king (the name Daniel means *God is my judge*).

2:27–28 *Daniel's witness to King Nebuchadnezzar.* The king was anxious to know if Daniel could indeed tell the dream and its interpretation, but Daniel delayed this matter. He knew in this crucial moment that he had the king's attention, and so he used the golden opportunity to bear witness for the Lord. Notice that his witness had two aspects, one negative and the other positive. He first denies the ability of the Babylonian wise men to accomplish the king's demand, and then he affirms that his God is able to do this.

There were several occult practitioners among the wise men of Babylon, and Daniel mentions three specific types in v. 27. Conjurers and magicians were discussed earlier (see 1:18–20).[82] Now he adds a new category, namely

---

80. See similar statements about the name Belteshazzar in 4:8, 19; 5:12; and 10:1, as well as the king's use of this name in 4:9, 18.

81. P. W. Gaebelein, Jr., "Marduk," in *ISBE*, 3:244, reports, "Upon the political ascendancy of Hammurabi of Babylon (*ca.* 1750 BC), Marduk the god of Babylon became supreme among the older Sumerian gods as creator and ruler – a position formerly enjoyed by Enlil but affirmed for Marduk in the Code of Hammurabi (*ANET*, pp. 163–180) and the Creation Epic (*ANET*, pp. 60–72)."

82. The word translated here as "conjurers" (Aram. אָשְׁפִין, *ʾāšᵉp̄în*) was rendered by LXX$^{\theta}$ as μάγων (*magōn*, pl. of μάγος, *magos*), from which we get the term *magi* (see Matt 2:1). In the context of Daniel, they were clearly occult practitioners who used religious and magical arts, including astrology. The *magi* of Matt 2:1 may have come from the regions of Babylonia. For a helpful study regarding the Chaldeans, the Magi, and the development of astrology in Mesopotamia, see E. M. Yamauchi, "The Episode of the Magi," in *Chronos, Kairos, Christos: Nativity and Chronological Studies Presented to Jack Finegan*, ed. J. Vardaman and E. M. Yamauchi, 15–40 (Winona Lake, IN: Eisenbrauns, 1989), 23–32. Cf. T. Maalouf, "Were the Magi from Persia or Arabia?" *BSac* 156 (1999): 423–42, for a helpful study on the background of the

the "diviners" (גָּזְרִין, *gāzᵊrîn*). They functioned as "determiners of fate" who used several forms of divination—not merely astrology—in their pursuits (see translation note above for v. 27). Regardless of their specialty for discerning one's fate or interpreting dreams, they were powerless to do anything. Over a century earlier, the prophet Isaiah had announced the downfall of Babylon and the inability of her occult specialists to do anything to help her: "Persist in trusting your amulets and your many incantations, which you have faithfully recited since your youth! Maybe you will be successful—maybe you will scare away disaster. You are tired out from listening to so much advice. Let them take their stand—the ones who see omens in the sky, who gaze at the stars, who make monthly predictions—let them rescue you from the disaster that is coming upon you!" (Isa 47:12–13, NET; cf. 44:25). With this comment about the occult practitioners in Dan 2:27, Daniel was denouncing the polytheistic religion of Babylon. Sometimes before the truth can be seen, false beliefs must first be exposed and discredited.

In v. 28 Daniel boldly announced the God who was able to help the king, calling him the "God in heaven." Part of the reason the king had this dream was for this God to make known to him what would happen "in the latter days" (NIV "in days to come"; NET "the times to come"). This phrase "in the latter days" deserves careful attention. In the Aramaic text this is בְּאַחֲרִית יוֹמַיָּא (*bᵊʾaḥărîṯ yômayyāʾ*), which is exactly equivalent in meaning to the Hebrew phrase בְּאַחֲרִית הַיָּמִים (*bᵊʾaḥărîṯ hayyāmîm*) occurring thirteen times elsewhere.[83] Although the phrase can sometimes be used to refer to an indefinite time in the future (e.g., Deut 31:29), it primarily refers to the far distant future, especially when Messiah will reign. The noun אַחֲרִית (*ʾaḥărîṯ*) means "after-part, end" (BDB, 31a), and thus the phrase literally means "in the end of days." BDB (31b) defines this as "a prophetic phrase denoting the final period of the history so far as the speaker's perspective reaches; the sense thus varies with the context, but it often = the ideal or Messianic future."[84] A study of the phrase in the OT shows that it typically refers to events still to come, or what we would think of as events in conjunction with Messiah's second coming.[85] It is used, for instance, in Isa 2:2–4 and Mic 4:1 to describe

---

term "magi." He concludes, rather uniquely, that the *magi* of Matt 2:1 were wise men from Arabia.

83. בְּאַחֲרִית הַיָּמִים (*bᵊʾaḥărîṯ hayyāmîm*) occurs in Gen 49:1; Num 24:14; Deut 4:30; 31:29; Isa 2:2; Jer 23:20; 30:24; 48:47; 49:39; Ezek 38:16; Hos 3:5; Mic 4:1; and Dan 10:14.

84. Also in the DSS, the phrase is used with reference to the messianic age (1QSa 1:1; 4 QpIsa[a] 7.3.22; CD 6:11; 4QFlor 1:2, 12).

85. This phrase should not be confused with what is said in Heb 1:2, that God has spoken to us now "in these last days," even though the Greek text of that verse (ἐπ' ἐσχάτου τῶν ἡμερῶν τούτων, *ep' eschatou tōn hēmerōn toutōn*) is essentially the same as the LXX for Dan 2:28. The emphasis of Hebrews is upon the contrast of the old covenant (which expired with the death of Christ on the cross) and the inauguration

the time of Jerusalem's restoration in the messianic kingdom when "the law will go forth from Zion," when "nation will not lift up sword against nation," and "never again will they learn war" (which cannot fairly be said to describe the present age). Quite frequently it describes the time when Israel as a nation will repent and be regathered to the land to enjoy messianic blessing (Deut 4:30; Jer 23:20, noting the mention of Messiah's reign in 23:5–8; 30:24, noting the mention of regathering and Messiah's reign in 30:9–10; and Hos 3:5), the time when Gog will invade the land of Israel (Ezek 38:16), or the time of the tribulation, antichrist, and resurrection of OT saints (Dan 10:14, introducing the prophecies of chaps. 10–12).

Not everything about the king's dream will pertain to the "latter days," for (as seen in Dan 2:31–45) the events of the dream begin with Nebuchadnezzar and stretch to the ending of Gentile powers and setting up of a kingdom by the God of heaven (2:44). However, the climactic part of the king's dream is the latter part of this spectrum (particularly the kingdom of God), and thus Daniel tells him that God has made known to him what will happen "in the latter days."

2:29–30 *Daniel's humility in announcing the king's dream.* Before informing the king of the specifics of the dream, Daniel tells him, "your thoughts turned to what would come to pass after this." The words "after this" refers to the broad sketch of history from Nebuchadnezzar's time until the inauguration of the messianic age, as the remainder of the chapter clarifies. Rather than referring to God by name, Daniel calls him the "revealer of mysteries" (or *secret things, rāzayyā*ʾ, recall v. 18). Nebuchadnezzar should meditate upon that virtue of Daniel's God, for it marks him out as unique in contrast to all the powerless Babylonian deities. Daniel stopped short of saying that Yahweh was the only god who existed. Nebuchadnezzar's first need was to consider Yahweh as superior to the Babylonian deities (comp. v. 47). In v. 30, however, Daniel clarifies that the disclosure of the dream and its interpretation (already clear in Daniel's mind) was not due to any special wisdom found in him. Walvoord (59) wisely remarks, "Daniel's answer is a masterpiece of setting the matter in its proper light and giving God the glory." In contrast to Nebuchadnezzar in his anger, Daniel was a man who could react calmly in a crisis; in contrast to self-exalting Arioch, Daniel was a man whose first desire was to give the Lord all the credit and glory.

Application and Devotional Implications

Daniel was faithful at this crucial moment to witness to a man who was lost and headed toward an eternity without Christ. Even though Nebuchadnezzar

---

of the new covenant. Hence, the old covenant cultic regulations, sacrifices and priesthood are no longer appropriate. The contexts of Heb 1:2 and Dan 2:28 are quite different (since Hebrews primarily has this shift of covenants in view). Even the book of Hebrews views the kingdom as something still to come (12:25–29; cf. 2:5).

was the most powerful person on earth at that time in history, Daniel had the faith and courage to testify to him. Although he said it tactfully and kindly, Daniel had said something quite disparaging about the gods worshiped by the Babylonians (an act that could have cost him his life). Being a faithful witness, though, is what we are all called to be.

Sometimes we may feel too timid to approach an important person in our society and confront them with the truth. Two things should be kept in mind, however, that will help us be faithful and courageous like Daniel:

1) No matter how important that person might be in our culture, they are only human and subject to God just like everyone else.
2) Their eternal destiny depends upon the decision they make about Jesus Christ. Often, Christians tend to overlook them and forget to remember that they need to hear the truth and the gospel.

We need to witness with our lives, but we also need to witness with our words.

4. Daniel reveals the dream and its interpretation (2:31–45)

This section falls into two distinct paragraphs. In the first paragraph (vv. 31–35), Daniel declares Nebuchadnezzar's dream to him, as the king had requested. In the second paragraph (vv. 36–45), Daniel gives the interpretation of the king's dream, as it was revealed to him by God (recall v. 19). The dream concerned a symbolic depiction of successive Gentile kingdoms that would rule and have authority over Israel until finally being destroyed and replaced by a kingdom from heaven. This dream parallels the vision given directly to Daniel in chap. 7.

Textual Notes

33.a. Qere and several MSS have ־הֵין

34.a. *BHS* proposes inserting מטורה (see v. 45 מִטּוּרָא "from the mountain"). Both LXX^{O} and LXX$^{\theta}$ have ἐξ ὄρους, but this may just be an attempt to harmonize with v. 45.

35.a. אִדְּרֵי is in the pl., but 4QDan[a] has sg. (so LXX^{O} and LXX$^{\theta}$).

38.a. Qere is דָּיְרִין, but see Dan 3:31, 4:32 and 6:26 with the medial א.

39.a. Qere is אֲרַע for אֲרַעא, but this is not the definite article but א of direction (BDB, 1083).

39.b. Qere has תְּלִיתָאָה for Kethib תְּלִיתָיָא.

40.a. Qere has רְבִיעָאָה for Kethib רְבִיעָיָה, but compare the Kethib/Qere רְבִיעָאָה/רְבִיעָיָא at 7:23.

40.b-b. Lacking in LXX^{O}, LXX$^{\theta}$ and Vg., but attested in 4QDan[a].

41.a. The word "toes" is omitted in LXX^{O} (Pap. 967) but is found in LXX$^{\theta}$. Collins (151) notes, "There is a lacuna in 4QDan^{a} at this point, but there does not seem to be enough room for the full MT text." Yet "toes" is clearly present at the beginning of v. 42.

43.a. *BHS* has no conjunction prefixed to דִּי, but a number of MSS do, along with LXX^{O}, Vg., and the Qere reading וְדִי.

45.a. Rather than MT's אִתְגְּזֶרֶת, a few MSS have הת־ as in v. 34.

Translation

2:31 "You, O king, were watching and behold, a single great statue[86]; that statue, which was enormous and of exceeding splendor, [87] was standing before[88] you, and its appearance was terrifying.[89] **32** As for that statue, its head was of pure gold, its breast and arms of silver, its belly and thighs of bronze, **33** its legs of iron, and its feet partly of iron and partly of clay.[90] **34** You continued watching as[91] a stone was cut out without hands, and it

86. The noun צְלֵם (*ṣəlēm*) can mean an idol (for worship) or a statue, but in this context a statue is in view.

87. The words זִיוֵהּ יַתִּיר (*zîwēh yatîr*), translated "impressive ... appearance" by the NET, are more literally "its splendor (or brightness) excessive." The emphasis could either be on its dazzling appearance (so NIV) or its extraordinary brightness (so Collins, 151; Goldingay, 31). Either option would fit the context.

88. Usually when one stands before a king, it is in a position of subjection and readiness to obey (recall 1:19). The irony here is that the statue signifies the sovereign will of the Lord God over history that Nebuchadnezzar is powerless to defy. He has no choice but to submit to God's will.

89. The verb דְּחִיל (*dəḥîl*) at the end of v. 31 is a Peʿal pass. ptc. of דְּחַל (*dəḥal*), which properly means "was terrifying" (or "fearsome"—so Collins, 151). NET has "caused alarm," though both the NIV and NASB render it as "awesome," but the parallel use with "trembling" in Dan 5:19 suggests that *fear* is the basic nuance (so *HALOT*, 1850).

90. Goldingay (35 fn 33b), after pointing out that "clay" (*ḥăsap̱*) means *baked clay* rather than the raw material, translated as "pottery." Cf. חֲסַף דִּי־פֶחָר, *ḥăsap̱ dî-peḥār*, in v. 41. *HALOT* (1879) gives the meaning "molded clay," but notes this is a "loanword < Akk. *ḫaṣbu(m)* ... potter's clay, sherd." Baked clay, though hard, is also brittle and fragile. Most translations render this simply as "clay," though the NIV has "baked clay."

91. Although BDB (1105) indicates that עַד דִּי (*ʿaḏ dî*) means "until," Goldingay (35) argues that here it does not mean "until" but "as" (see BL, 79i). *HALOT* (1943c) also rejects the meaning "until" in this construction. Yet in Dan 6:25 (Aram), עַד דִּי (*ʿaḏ dî*) does mean "until." LXX's ἕως (*heōs*) can mean either "until" or "while, as long as" (LSJM, 752).

struck the statue on its feet of iron and clay, and it crushed[92] them. **35** Then
they were crushed together[93]—the iron, the clay, the bronze, the silver, and
the gold—and they became as chaff from a threshing floor in the summer;
and the wind carried them away and no trace[94] of them was found. But the
stone that struck the statue became a great mountain and filled the whole
earth. **36** This was the dream; now we will tell its interpretation before the
king. **37** You, O king, are the king of kings[95] to whom the God of heaven has
given sovereignty,[96] power, might, and honor. **38** And wherever the sons of
men, the beasts of the field, and the birds of heaven dwell, He has made you
to rule *over* them all. You are the head of gold. **39** Now after you another
kingdom will arise, one inferior[97] to you, and then another, a third kingdom
of bronze, which shall rule *over* all the earth. **40** Then there will be a fourth
kingdom as strong as iron. Inasmuch as iron crushes and smashes everything
and as iron which breaks in pieces, it will crush and break all others.[98] **41** In

---

92. Although the verb הַדֱּקֶת (*haddēqet̲*)—Hap'el perf of *dᵊqaq*—can mean "break in pieces" (see BDB, 1089a), the meaning "crushed" may be more accurate (so *HALOT*, 1855). Cf. Dan 7:23 where the same verb is used in conjunction with another verb meaning "tread down": "it will devour the whole earth and tread it down and crush it."

93. *HALOT* (1869d) suggests that כַּחֲדָה (*k̲aḥăd̲â*) means "together," and both the NASB and NIV translate it "at the same time." The idea is that all the materials of the statue were crushed *at the same time*, probably looking at the climactic moment of the statue's destruction when the "stone" struck it. Contrast Goldingay (35) who suggests that *k̲aḥăd̲â* means "suddenness" (all at once) more than simultaneity—but his examples are not convincing. NET translates "without distinction," with this footnote, "For the meaning 'without distinction' see the following: F. Rosenthal, *Grammar*, 36, §64, and p. 93; E. Vogt, *Lexicon linguae aramaicae*, 60."

94. Despite Goldingay's preference to translate אֲתַר (*'ăt̲ar*) as "place," *HALOT* (1829) indicates that אֲתַר (*'ăt̲ar*) can mean (1) trace; or (2) place, location. *HALOT* assigns Dan 2:35 to the first, "trace." Hence, "no trace was found."

95. Nebuchadnezzar is also referred to as "king of kings" in Ezek 26:7, "For thus says the Lord GOD, 'Behold, I will bring upon Tyre from the north Nebuchadnezzar king of Babylon, king of kings, with horses, chariots, cavalry and a great army'" (NASB).

96. מַלְכוּתָא (*malk̲ût̲ā'*) can be translated "sovereignty" (NET), "dominion" (NIV), or "kingdom" (NASB). The definite form of מַלְכוּ (*malk̲û*) occurs in Dan 2:44 with the clear sense of "kingdom" (cf. 2:39). *HALOT* (1917) indicates that מַלְכוּ (*malk̲û*) can mean (1) kingship, sovereignty; (2) reign; or (3) kingdom, realm. Goldingay (32) translates "royal authority."

97. Regarding אֲרַעא (*'ăra''*), the root אֲרַע (*'ăra'*) is a fem. noun meaning "earth," with final א of direction. Hence, (lit.) "to the earth," i.e., downward (so Leupold, 115). With the following prep מִן (*min*), this expresses the idea of being "inferior" (so *HALOT*, 1826b).

98. Some would prefer to put "all others" (כָּל־אִלֵּין, *kol-'illên*, lit., "all these") with the preceding: "and as iron which breaks all these [metals] in pieces" (so NET and Collins, 151). Goldingay (35 fn 40.d-d), however, argues that it properly goes with

that you saw the feet and the toes partly of potter's clay and partly of iron, so it will be a divided kingdom. But it will have in it some of the strength of iron, inasmuch as you saw the iron mixed with baked clay.[99] **42** As the toes of the feet *were* partly of iron and partly of clay, so part[100] of the kingdom will be strong, and part will be fragile.[101] **43** And[102] in that you saw the iron mixed with baked clay, they will be a mixture in the seed of men, but they will not adhere[103] with one another, as the iron will not mix with the clay.
44 And in the days of those kings, the God of heaven will set up a kingdom that will never be destroyed, nor will this kingdom be left for another people. It will crush and put an end to all these kingdoms, but it will endure forever.
45 Inasmuch as you saw that a stone was cut out from the mountain—not with human hands—and that it crushed the iron, bronze, clay, silver, and the

---

the final two verbs. Cf. Dan 7:7, 23. In light of the statement in 7:23 ("it will devour all the earth"), the words "all others" is best placed with the final clause. Plus, this better preserves the parallelism of the verse: "iron crushes and smashes everything ... it will crush and break all others." The point is that the fourth kingdom will crush and break the countries of the world that exist at that time.

99. The expression at the end of v. 41 (חֲסַף טִינָא, *ḥăsap̱ ṭînāʾ*) is translated "baked clay." טִין (*ṭîn*), like חֲסַף (*ḥăsap̱*), also means "clay." See note at v. 33 for חֲסַף, *ḥăsap̱*. For the combination, *HALOT* (1884) suggests "earthenware." The translations struggle with the best way to render this: "common clay" (NASB), "wet clay" (NET). The NIV and NRSV simply put "clay" without making a distinction from the simple form חֲסַף (*ḥăsap̱*). The first word (חֲסַף, *ḥăsap̱*) is properly a "clay vessel" or "potsherd," whereas the second (טִינָא, *ṭînāʾ*) indicates the "wet clay" from which it came—a contrast to the previous strong metals.

100. Although קְצָת (*qᵉṣāṯ*) means "end" (comp. BH קָצֶה, *qāṣeh*, "end, extremity"), the partitive use of the preceding מִן (*min*) gives it the sense "part of" in parallel with מִנַּהּ (*minnah*) in the following clause (so BDB, 1111; *HALOT*, 1971d; and RJ, 75).

101. תְבִירָה (*ṯᵉḇîrâ*) is a Peʿil pass. ptc. from the verb תְּבַר (*tᵉḇar*) meaning to "break" (corresponding to BH שָׁבַר, *šāḇar*). Both the NASB and NIV translate this "brittle" (so Collins, 152). *HALOT* (2004b) gives the sense "breakable, fragile," and RJ (75) indicates the ptc. is used adjectively with the sense "fragile, breakable." Something that is brittle is obviously easily breakable, yet the translation "fragile" gets more directly to the point.

102. See textual note at 2:43a, preferring the Qere reading וְדִי (*wᵉḏî*).

103. דְּבֵק (*dᵉḇēq*) means to "cling" (BDB, 1087a). *HALOT* (1848b) suggests "cling to, stick together" for the Peʿal ptc. Both the NASB and NET use the word "adhere," as this seems appropriate in this context. If mixing "in the seed of men" refers to *intermarriage*, the verb דְּבֵק (*dᵉḇēq*) might be a slight pun, as the corresponding BH דָּבַק (*dāḇaq*) was used of the first marriage (Gen 2:24) for the man and woman who were to "cleave" to one another.

gold, the great[104] God has made known to the king what will come about in the future.[105] The dream is certain, and its interpretation trustworthy.

Commentary

2:31 *The frightening statue.* In his dream, the king had seen a large statue.[106] The image seems to have had a very bright luster, probably due to its predominantly metallic composition. Its appearance caused the king to be alarmed (i.e., it frightened him), probably due to its immense size and unusual composition of varying materials. This statue may be related to various "royal statues" utilized in ancient Mesopotamia. Seow explains,

> The dream revolves around a statue, the Aramaic word here (*ṣalmāʾ*) being a cognate of the Akkadian term used for images erected to represent the presence of gods and kings. Since kingship is at issue, it is likely that a royal statue is meant, although in this case it is not the statue of an individual king but apparently a composite symbol of political power, represented by various regimes. They were placed in the temple in various postures before divine images to represent the constant pious presence of the king before the deity, or they were placed in other public places, notably in vanquished territories, to remind the populace of the king's majesty and power.[107]

2:32–33 *The composition of the statue.* Daniel's description of the statue begins with the head and then proceeds downward until it reaches the feet. The head is of fine gold, whereas the feet are a mixture of iron and clay. In between are the chest and arms of silver, the belly and thighs of bronze, and the legs of iron.[108] Several things should be observed. First, the metals composing the statue are put in order of decreasing value (starting with gold and continuing

---

104. Contrast with "great" in Dan 2:10. No *great* king or ruler ever made such a request for having his dream explained in this way, but the *great* God of heaven was able to provide the dream and its interpretation.

105. The translation "in the future" is lit., "after this" (אַחֲרֵי דְנָה, *ʾaḥărê ḏᵊnâ*). That is, "after this *time*." Most translations have "in the future" (contrast NRSV "hereafter"—so Collins, 152).

106. The Aram. term for "statue" is *ṣᵊlēm*, equivalent to the Heb. *ṣelem*. Although this Semitic root can mean either "idol" or "statue," in this context it clearly means "statue" (God would not have presented this as an idol to be worshiped).

107. C. L. Seow, "From Mountain to Mountain: The Reign of God in Daniel 2," in *A God So Near: Essays on Old Testament Theology in Honor of Patrick D. Miller*, ed. B. A. Strawn and N. R. Bowen, 355–74 (Winona Lake, IN: Eisenbrauns, 2003), 365.

108. The word translated "bronze" (Aram. *nᵊḥāš*) can mean either copper or bronze (*HALOT*, 1929). The KJV mistakenly translated *nᵊḥāš* as "brass." Brass, however, is not attested that early in history, whereas bronze (an alloy of copper and tin) was

to the iron/clay mixture). Second, the materials are listed in order of increasing hardness (gold is the most pliable, whereas iron is the strongest). These qualities will reflect something about the kingdoms they represent. Third, the fifth and final material is unique in regard to the others. It is not a pure metal but rather a composite of metal and clay (which do not easily blend or adhere to one another). Also, it shares the same metal as the fourth part, namely iron (which probably suggests there is a close connection between what is symbolized by the "legs" and the "feet"). The last stage is made of hard iron and brittle (yet fragile) baked clay.

2:34–35 *The smashing stone that destroys the statue.* The statue, however, did not last forever, for a stone eventually destroyed it. This stone was *associated with* a certain "mountain," being "cut out" from the mountain.[109] This mountain should not be equated with the mountain that results from the stone (v. 35). The mountain from which the stone is cut out (v. 34) depicts the sphere of *origin* for the stone, not its result.

Not only was the stone cut out from this mountain, but also it was cut out "without human hands." Its origin and power were not from any human source, but rather divine. We should also note that the stone struck the statue precisely on its feet. Normally, a deathblow would be rendered to the head or chest, but in this case the point of assault is at the feet. Since the statue represents successive kingdoms, this would imply that it is during the days of the final kingdom (symbolized by the feet) that the statue is destroyed.

Although the statue speaks of successive kingdoms, there is a sense in which they represent one entity, for they are crushed all at the same time. The deathblow rendered to the "feet" spells the end for the entire entity of kingdoms, i.e., human rule. The parts of the statue are destroyed "all at the same time," that is, decisively and completely, not gradually. As a result, they became like chaff from a summer threshing floor. A threshing floor was usually an open area outside a city gate which would get a good breeze that was freely available to all for threshing wheat.[110] In the summer months (the normal time for harvesting the wheat), the wheat would be tossed up in the air so that the wind would carry away the worthless chaff. Hence, with the destruction of the statue we finally see the true value of what the statue symbolized: the parts were worthless in value before God. That no trace of them was left (v. 35) suggests that they will be totally done away with (removed),

---

commonly used in Daniel's day and earlier. Herodotus (*Hist.* 1:181) described the lavish use of bronze in Babylonia, including the bronze-gated temple of Bel.

109. The words "from the mountain" are not contained in the Aramaic text of Dan 2:34, but they are found in v. 45 when the dream is interpreted. Both LXX$^{\theta}$ and LXX^{O} add the Greek words ἐξ ὄρους (*ex orous*, "from a mountain") after "stone" in v. 34, but this is probably an attempt to harmonize with v. 45.

110. "Threshing floor" is a translation of אִדַּר (*ʾiddar*), which is equivalent in meaning to BH גֹּרֶן (*gōren*). A good illustration of the latter is found in Hos 13:3.

no longer to interfere with God's plan for history. This is a stronger point than saying that the "stone" will simply *have dominion* over the statue.

The "stone," however, has a different outcome. It *becomes* a great mountain that fills the earth.[111] The imagery of a "mountain" is sometimes used in Scripture to depict a *kingdom* (cf. Isa 2:1–4). Thus, God's plan for history will culminate in a universal kingdom that stems from the powerful "stone." The thought of "kingdom" prepares us for the interpretation now to be revealed in vv. 36–45.

Orientation to vv. 36–45. Daniel's interpretation of the king's dream clarifies that the statue is a symbolic depiction of various kingdoms that will come into power, beginning with that of Nebuchadnezzar. Such a symbolic technique was not unusual in the ancient world.[112] Miller (93) notes that Hesiod (in *Works and Days,* ca. 700 BC) employed gold, silver, bronze, and iron to represent eras in human history—not to suggest, however, that Daniel 2 is in any way dependent on Hesiod. In Daniel 2 these kingdoms have one thing in common. They represent the Gentile powers that dominate over God's chosen people Israel, beginning with the Babylonian exile brought on by Nebuchadnezzar himself.[113]

---

111. Regarding the filling of the whole earth, E. F. Siegman ("Stone Hewn from the Mountain," *CBQ* 18 [1956]: 371) notes, "The phrase, 'fill the whole earth,' is rare in the OT and is used only of the glory of Yahweh (Nm 14,21; Is 6,3; Hb 2,14; Ps 71 [72],19), or of His knowledge (Is 11,9), or of His spirit (Wis 1,7)."

112. For a survey of various Near Eastern prototypical schema of successive kingdoms in an effort to discern if Dan 2 might have borrowed from these, see G. Hasel ("The Four World Empires of Daniel 2 against Its Near Eastern Environment," *JSOT* 12 [1979]: 17–30). He concludes that Dan 2 is distinct, with no evidence found of borrowing. At one time it was widely believed that the four-empire scheme originated in Persia (see J. S. Swain, "The Theory of the Four Monarchies," *ClPh* 35 [1940]: 1–21), from which D. Flusser has argued for the Persian influence on both the Sibylline Oracles and Daniel 2 and 7 ("The Four Empires in the Fourth Sibyl and in the Book of Daniel," *IOS* 2 [1972]: 148–75). Yet E. Lucas has shown more recently that the four-empire scheme in Dan 2 and 7 is not dependent on Persian sources ("The Origin of Daniel's Four Empires Scheme Re-examined," *TynBul* 40 [1989]: 185–202). In particular Lucas (199) notes, "The inclusion of ten kings in the fourth empire in Daniel 7 has no parallel in either the Sibylline or Persian texts, so influence from them seems unlikely."

113. Possibly Israel's exile into Babylon is the beginning of what Christ later referred to as "the times of the Gentiles" (see Luke 21:24), a long period of history when Israel would be disciplined and subjected to Gentile nations. Bock, however, suggests, "More likely 'the times of the Gentiles' is a general way to describe the current period in God's plan, when Gentiles are prominent but that will culminate in judgment on those nations" (D. L. Bock, *Luke 9:51–24:53*, BECNT [Grand Rapids: Baker, 1996], 1681).

Various interpretative approaches to the symbolism. Although all scholars agree that the components of the statue represent various kingdoms, they do not always agree as to which kingdoms are intended.[114] There are three main interpretative issues at stake:

1) Which four primary kingdoms are intended?
2) How do the "toes and feet" relate to the fourth kingdom? Is this a fifth and separate kingdom? Or is it simply part of the fourth kingdom?
3) What kind of kingdom does the God of heaven set up and when is it established?

Although there are minor variations concerning the interpretation of the first four kingdoms, the differences primarily boil down to one of two schemes.[115] Most evangelicals today, regardless of their eschatological viewpoint, and virtually all the early church fathers interpret the first four kingdoms as beginning with Babylon and extending to the Roman Empire.[116]

114. For an excellent overview of the history of interpretation of the successive kingdoms and the fulfillment of the smiting stone, see G. Pfandl, "Interpretations of the Kingdom of God in Dan 2:44," *AUSS* 34 (1996): 249–68. See also H. H. Rowley, *Darius the Mede and the Four World Empires in the Book of Daniel* (Cardiff: University of Wales Press, 1959).

115. Other than the two major schemes outlined here, other suggestions have been made for the four kings/kingdoms. Yet none of these has succeeded in gaining a significant following. B. D. Eerdmans, writing in 1931, identified the four as Nebuchadnezzar and his three dynastic successors, Amil-Marduk, Nergalsarusur, and Nabunaid ("Origin and Meaning of the Aramaic Part of Daniel," in *Actes du XVIIIe congrès international des orientalistes Leiden 7–12 Septembre 1931* [Leiden: Brill, 1932], 198–202.) Seow, in his commentary (45–46), has suggested the four kings of Dan 2 represent Nebuchadnezzar, Belshazzar, Darius, and Cyrus (the only kings mentioned by name in Daniel) or some variation on this sequence. More recently, G. Goswell has argued that the two visions (Dan 2 and 7) "provide an outline of the whole course of human history, such that the four kingdoms in Dan 2 and 7 represent *all* kingdoms (irrespective of their number) that will rise and fall during the historical process" ("The Visions of Daniel and Their Historical Specificity," *ResQ* 58 [2016]: 129).

116. Regarding the early church, Pfandl (251) notes, "Thus Cyril of Jerusalem (301–386) could say: That this fourth kingdom 'is that of the Romans has been the tradition of the Church's interpreters.' This tradition was continued by John Chrysostom (344–407) and Jerome (345–413), who wrote in his commentary on Daniel: 'Now the fourth kingdom, which clearly refers to the Romans, is the iron empire which breaks in pieces and overcomes all others.'" Cf. Irenaeus, *Haer.* 26.1. In addition, Josephus, the Jewish historian, affirmed the fourth kingdom as Rome (*Ant.* 10.11.7). Several statements in the Jewish Talmud also affirm the fourth kingdom as Rome (*b. Šebu.* 20; *b. ʿAbod. Zar.* 2b; *b. Yoma* 77a; *Meg.* 11a; *Qidd.* 72a).

Critical scholars, on the other hand, agree that Babylon is the first kingdom but insist the fourth is Greece (not Rome).[117] In keeping with this, they typically view the *significance* of Daniel 2 in terms of the second-century BC Seleucid king Antiochus IV Epiphanes.[118]

Among modern-day evangelicals, R. Gurney, "The Four Kingdoms of Daniel 2 and 7," *Them* 2 (1977): 39–45, is an exception. He takes an early dating of the book of Daniel yet attempts to argue that the successive kingdoms are Babylon, Media, Persia, and Greece, and that all of these along with the kingdom prophesied in Dan 2:44 were fulfilled by the time of Christ's first advent. Yet his theory fails to account for the ten horns of the fourth beast in Dan 7 (Greece?), as well as for the fact that 8:20 depicts "the kings of Media and Persia" as representing one stage (and which thus sheds light on Dan 2 and 7).

J. Walton, "The Four Kingdoms of Daniel," *JETS* 29 (1986): 25–36, adopts the basic thesis of Gurney and attempts to make a few refinements to this view. He concludes (36), "The ten horns of the fourth empire would be the ten independent states that had arisen from Alexander's empire by the last quarter of the third century BC. The little horn would represent the Seleucid overlords of Palestine, dating from the reign of Antiochus the Great and continuing during the time of Antiochus Epiphanes. The three displaced horns would represent the conquests of Antiochus the Great. The kingdom of God is left open to be interpreted in any number of different ways." Yet Walton's view is unconvincing, for it fails to satisfy the stipulation of Dan 2:44 that "in the days of those kings the God of heaven will set up a kingdom which will never be destroyed."

Seow ("From Mountain to Mountain," 367) takes these, not as successive kingdoms but successive reigns, and interprets them as Nebuchadnezzar, Belshazzar, Darius the Mede, and Cyrus the Persian.

D. B. Armistead ("The Images of Daniel 2 and 7: A Literary Approach," *STJ* 6 [1998]: 63–66, though claiming to be an evangelical, holds to the general critical interpretation regarding the successive kingdoms and affirms that such passages as the "little horn" in Dan 7 and the 70 weeks prophecy in 9:24–27 pertain to Antiochus IV. Though he takes an essentially preterist interpretation of the book, he nevertheless tries to argue (65) that "the symbolic nature of apocalyptic language allows the reapplication of these visions" to subsequent periods and even the eschaton. Hence, he can conclude (66), "The symbolic nature of apocalyptic language also allows Jesus to apply the prophecy of the defilement of Jerusalem by the Greeks (Dan. 9:27) to the destruction of Jerusalem by the Romans (Mat. 24:15)." I contend, however, that his interpretation of Dan 7 and Dan 9 do not hold up to close exegetical examination.

117. A clear presentation of the view of the four kingdoms in critical scholarship is presented in M. J. Gruenthaner, "The Four Empires of Daniel," *CBQ* 8 (1946): 72–82, 201–12.

118. M. Nel, "A Literary-Historical Analysis of Daniel 2: Two Powers in Opposition," *AcT* 22 (2002): 89. Typical of many critical scholars, Nel denies any prophetic validity to Dan 2 and skeptically concludes, "Daniel 2 does not contain any reference to a

	Critical Scholars	Evangelicals
Head of fine gold	Babylon	Babylon
Breast & arms of silver	Media	Medo-Persia
Belly & thighs of bronze	Persia	Greece
Legs of iron	Greece	Rome

The evangelical position has been the historic Christian interpretation throughout the centuries, including the early church (e.g., Jerome).[119] The critical position stems from a bias against the Bible. Since critical scholars reject the traditional authorship of the book by Daniel and attribute it to an unknown author/editor about 165 BC during the Maccabean period, they cannot hold to Rome being the fourth kingdom.[120] Rome did not come to power until after 165 BC, and therefore to admit Rome as the fourth kingdom would be to admit that the Bible records true prophecy (which their presuppositions do not allow them to do). Whether one dates the Roman Empire from its conquest of Carthage (146 BC), from Pompey's conquest of Syria-Palestine (63 BC), or from Octavian being renamed Augustus as the first Roman Emperor (27 BC), clearly Rome did not become a dominant world

---

messiah, or any prophecies concerning the end of time (Reeves 1999:20). The narrator encourages the readers of her day—the victims of Antiochus' vicious prosecution of Jews who tried to remain loyal to their religion and culture—with the comfort that God is determining what is going to happen. The essence of her encouragement is found in the words attributed to Nebuchadnezzar (v. 47)."

119. Though the historic Christian position has affirmed Rome as the fourth kingdom, the interpretation of the exact historic outworking of the fourth beast has varied. J. Walton ("The Four Kingdoms of Daniel," 28) explains: " three positions ... are commonly held among evangelicals today, all of which posit Rome as the fourth empire: (1) The fourth empire and the ten horns are all in the past, and the kingdom of God is represented and fulfilled in the church. Fulfillment is viewed as complete. This view is at least as old as Augustine. (2) The fourth kingdom is still in power through the continued influence (political, religious, cultural, etc.) of the Roman empire, but the ten-horns stage is still future. An early proponent of this view is Jerome, and it seems to be the most popular view, historically speaking. But it is held by very few today because of the historical difficulties. (3) The fourth kingdom is over, and we are now in a prophetic gap that will end when a ten-nation confederacy reconstitutes the Roman Empire."

120. Critical scholars rejecting Danielic authorship and embracing the Maccabean theory include J. A. Montgomery (ICC), Hartman and Di Lella (AB), and J. J. Collins (Hermeneia). Goldingay (WBC) takes the four components not as kingdoms but as kings and concludes that these are Nebuchadnezzar, Belshazzar, Darius the Mede, and Cyrus the Persian.

empire until after 165 BC. Therefore, critical scholars (rejecting any prophecy about Rome) contend that Greece must be the fourth and final kingdom.

Evangelical Christians, however, have rightfully rejected the conclusions of critical scholars and included the Roman Empire for the following reasons:

1) Historically, there was no independent kingdom of Media that followed Babylon. Instead, Babylon was conquered by the Persian king Cyrus the Great who ruled over the joint empire of the Medes and Persians.[121]
2) In Dan 5:28 the handwriting on the wall declared that Babylon would be given over to the Medes and Persians—not merely to the Medes.
3) Dan 6:8 refers to "the law of the Medes and Persians" (attesting that they were viewed by the author of Daniel as one empire).
4) In Dan 8 two animals are used to symbolize Gentile kingdoms, a ram with two horns and a shaggy goat. The latter is identified by the text itself as Greece (8:21), while the ram (one entity) represents Media and Persia (v. 20).[122]

The correct interpretation, then, is that the first kingdom is Babylon (with Nebuchadnezzar as its head), and this would be followed by Medo-Persia, Greece, and the Roman Empire. The other major interpretative issues will be dealt with in the course of the commentary.

---

121. Collins (166) tries to build a case that in Greek and Roman historiography Media was recognized as a separate empire from Persia, but he concedes that it never ruled over the Jews. Also, both 2 Chr 36:22–23 and Ezra 1:1–4 testify that Cyrus (the conqueror of Babylon) was a Persian king. Hence, there never was an independent Media that ruled *between* Babylon and Persia. E. C. Lucas ("A Statue, a Fiery Furnace and a Dismal Swamp," *EvQ* 77 [2005]: 295–96), while admitting there was no independent kingdom of Media between Babylon and Persia, nevertheless contends that the second kingdom is Media. He does this by arguing for Media as a dominant superpower that followed Nebuchadnezzar as an individual rather than Babylon as a kingdom: "With Nebuchadnezzar's death Babylon went into a fairly sharp decline, and for about a decade Media was clearly the dominant superpower of the region" (295). The problem with his argument is that elsewhere in the kingdom list of Dan 2:37–45, even though each symbol may represent both the king and corresponding kingdom, it does include the kingdom. Hence, the head of gold does not merely represent Nebuchadnezzar but also the Neo-Babylonian Empire. The second kingdom, then, must represent the kingdom that follows Babylon, not merely Babylon's first king.

122. Observe that the shaggy goat (Greece) in Dan 8 is characterized by four horns (v. 8), which is parallel to the leopard in chap. 7 that has four heads (representing the four generals of Alexander the Great). Since the first beast in Dan 7 is Babylon and the third is Greece, the second must be Medo-Persia (a perfect correlation with Dan 8 in which the ram precedes Greece).

2:36–38 *The 1st Kingdom = Babylon*. Daniel had correctly described the dream itself (vv. 31–35), and in v. 36 he announced that he was now going to reveal its interpretation, all in striking similarity to what Joseph had once done in the foreign court of Pharaoh.[123] In vv. 37–38, he reveals to the king that the head of the statue symbolizes the Babylonian Empire and its great king, Nebuchadnezzar. In this dream (as we will also find true in the vision of chap. 7), each part of the statue represents both the kingdom and the king associated with it, as the king was considered to be the embodiment of the kingdom. Notice in v. 39 that another "kingdom" arises after the first.

Although Nebuchadnezzar was not the first Babylonian king (his father Nabopolassar founded the Neo-Babylonian Empire and ruled from 627–605 BC), he was by virtue of his lengthy forty-three year reign the

---

123. Several scholars have made comparative studies with Joseph, who also served as a Hebrew dream revealer in the court of a foreign king (Gen 41). See S. Niditch, and R. Doran, "The Success Story of the Wise Courtier: A Formal Approach," *JBL* 96 (1977): 179–93; R. Gnuse, "The Jewish Dream Interpreter in a Foreign Court: The Recurring Use of a Theme in Jewish Literature," *JSP* 7 (1990): 29–53; idem, *Dreams and Dream Reports in the Writings of Josephus: A Traditio-Historical Analysis* (Leiden: Brill, 1996), 86–92, 131–33, 193–94; M. S. Rindge, "Jewish Identity under Foreign Rule: Daniel 2 as a Reconfiguration of Genesis 41," *JBL* 129 (2010): 85–104; and Philpot, J. M. "Was Joseph a Type of Daniel? Typolocial Correspondence in Genesis 37–50 and Daniel 1–6." *JETS* 61 (2018): 681-96.

Niditch and Doran attempted a comparative analysis of similar narratives based on plot analysis and identification of common motifs. They identified Gen 41 and Dan 2 as belonging to the same basic narrative type but concluded (190): "In its present form, Dan 2 contains two action motifs and one character motif foreign to the type. These are the actions of prayer or supplication to God, the answering of the prayer, and the presence of the divine helper, God. While Joseph does say that his ability to interpret comes from God, he does not really interact with God in Gen 41. In contrast, Daniel asks for mercy and for help from God (2:17, 18), he receives help (2:19), and he then praises his helper (2:20–23)."

Rindge (88–89) lists eighteen similarities between the plot structures of Gen 41 and Dan 2. He goes on to state (90), "In addition to these specific similarities there is the more patent one of a Jew serving in the court of a foreign king. Parallels also exist between the assignment of characters in Genesis 41 and Daniel 2. In each narrative, the characters can be categorized into one of four groups: the ruler (Pharaoh/Nebuchadnezzar); the magicians and those who fail to interpret the dream; the interpreter of the dream (Joseph/Daniel); and the person who functions as an intermediary between the ruler and the interpreter (cupbearer/Arioch)." Yet the dissimilarities of the two accounts highlight Daniel as the superior of the two, especially Nebuchadnezzar's demand for not only the interpretation of his dream but the content of it as well. Note also Daniel's piety as evidenced by his prayer in Dan 2:17–23, whereas Joseph is never depicted as one who prays.

greatest of the Babylonian kings. Furthermore, he was the king at the time of the exile of Judah. So, he is the "head of gold."

Daniel begins by calling Nebuchadnezzar "the king of kings," and in doing so he honored Nebuchadnezzar as being one of the great kings of the earth. The same designation had been given to Nebuchadnezzar by the prophet Ezekiel (see Ezek 26:7). Hence, it was appropriate for Nebuchadnezzar to be represented as the "head of gold." However, not only does gold reflect the quality of Nebuchadnezzar's rule in comparison to the rulers which followed, but Nebuchadnezzar had a special taste for gold. In the temple to Marduk in Babylon, the inner shrine was embellished with gold. Oates writes,

> Of this inner cella Nebuchadnezzar says that he 'covered its wall with sparkling gold, I caused it to shine like the sun.' Here, according to Herodotus, was the great sitting figure of Marduk, all of gold on a golden throne, supported on a base of gold, with a golden table standing beside it. I was told by the Chaldeans that to make all this more than 22 tons of gold were used. Outside the temple is a golden altar.[124]

Daniel spoke frankly and boldly to this eminent king by confronting him with the truth that it was not Marduk or any other Babylonian god that gave Nebuchadnezzar his kingship. Rather it was "the God of heaven" (*ʾelāh šᵊmayyāʾ*). His kingdom (or sovereignty[125]), the power that he exercised, and the resulting honor/glory that he enjoyed had been given to him by the God Daniel worshiped. It was common in the ancient Near East for kings to claim that their god(s) had given them their kingship. Archaeologists have unearthed an inscription written by Nebuchadnezzar himself in which he attributed his kingship to Marduk. Part of this inscription reads,

> [from] the Upper Sea [to] the Lower Sea ... which Marduk, my lord, has entrusted to me, I have made ... the city of Babylon to the foremost among all the countries and every human habitation.[126]

The extent to which Nebuchadnezzar had been given authority and dominion is described in Dan 2:38 as "wherever the sons of men, the beasts of the field, and the birds of heaven dwell." The reference to the beasts and birds has striking parallels to the initial granting of dominion to mankind

---

124. Oates, *Babylon*, 157.

125. The Aram. word *malkûṯāʾ* (root *malkû*) can mean kingdom, kingship, or sovereignty (*HALOT*, 1917).

126. This is from the so-called Wadi-Brisa Inscription recorded in J. B. Pritchard, *ANET*, 307. The date of this inscription is not given, though it concerned an expedition made into Syria. In another inscription known as the Cyrus Cylinder, the Persian King Cyrus boasted, "I am Cyrus, king of the world, great king, legitimate king, king of Babylon, king of Sumer and Akkad ... whose rule Bel and Nebo love, whom they want as king to please their hearts" (316).

in Gen 1:28: "Be fruitful and multiply and fill the earth and subdue it, and have dominion over the fish of the sea and over the birds of the heavens and over every living thing that moves on the earth" (ESV). Man had been assigned the task of ruling over all things as God's representative. Merrill has suggested a link between these two passages:

> Clearly, Nebuchadnezzar, even as a fallen and unbelieving pagan king, could enjoy the grace of God who allowed him to participate in the dominion mandate. He may have been the golden head of an image of human design (Dan. 2:38), but the image of human government is nonetheless suggestive of mankind created to be the image of God and to rule for Him on the earth.[127]

Thus, the privilege of being God's representative ruler—even though he was a pagan king—did not excuse Nebuchadnezzar from being accountable to the ultimate sovereign of the universe.

2:39a *The 2nd Kingdom = Medo-Persia.* In contrast to Babylon, the next two kingdoms are discussed in only one verse each. The brevity of their treatment is made up for by the fact that they receive much more attention in chaps. 7 and 8. Nebuchadnezzar was not told when or how, but he did know that his kingdom would not last forever. It would be replaced by another kingdom. Historically, Nebuchadnezzar was blessed by God to rule from 605–562 BC and was followed briefly by his son Evil-Merodach (= *Amēl-Marduk*), then two sons-in-law, and finally by his grandson Belshazzar (553–539). Nevertheless, when Cyrus the Great conquered Babylon in 539 BC by a combined army of the Medes and Persians (cf. Isa 45:1–4), the Neo-Babylonian Empire—made famous by Nebuchadnezzar—came to an end.

At the time of this dream, Nebuchadnezzar did not know what kingdom or king would replace his own kingdom; he only knew that it was to be "inferior" to his own. In what sense was the Medo-Persian Empire *inferior* to that of Babylon? It certainly was not in terms of geographical extent or duration (the Persian Empire, as it came to be known, was actually larger and lasted far longer). Some have thought it might be inferior in terms of inner unity, and others that it was more corrupt morally (so Calvin). Perhaps a preferable option would be in regard to the authority enjoyed by the king. Nebuchadnezzar had unfettered power, but during the Persian Empire the king was restricted in his authority, for he could not annul a law once he had made it (cf. Dan 6:8).[128]

---

127. E. Merrill, "A Theology of Ezekiel and Daniel," in *A Biblical Theology of the Old Testament*, ed. R. B. Zuck, 365–95 (Chicago: Moody Press, 1991), 389.

128. G. Archer took the view that the superiority of Babylon to Persia was to be found in terms of the power of the ruling despot. He wrote (47), "From Nebuchadnezzar's standpoint the restriction on the monarch's authority to annul a law once he had made it (6:12) was less desirable than his own unfettered power."

2:39b *The 3rd Kingdom = Greece.* The third kingdom is that made famous by Alexander the Great of Greece when he conquered Darius III (the last of the Persian kings) at Gaugamela in 331 BC. This could also be called the Hellenistic Empire. Following Alexander's untimely death in 323 BC, his kingdom was eventually parceled out among four of his generals, each of whom spread Hellenistic culture and the Greek language to their realms. At the end of v. 39 we are told that this third kingdom would "rule all the earth." Up until this time, the territory conquered by Alexander the Great was the most extensive realm under the power of one king, as Alexander virtually ruled over the entire civilized world.

2:40 *The 4th Kingdom = Rome.* "Iron" was a fitting metal to be associated with Rome, as the Roman legions were noted for their ability to crush all resistance with an iron heel. Although there are some technical difficulties to translating v. 40, the point seems to be that the fourth kingdom will crush and break the countries of the world that exist at that time (comp. 7:23). Rome could virtually take whatever she wanted, and most countries were powerless to resist her might.

Although Rome ascended in power gradually, Pompey brought Rome's influence upon Judah in 63 BC:

> ... in 63, Pompey, on his own initiative and without relying upon the Senate's approval, made his own settlement of the East. He founded client states, reorganized Judaea, established colonies and claimed Syria for Rome. In large measure, subsequent Roman policy in the East was based upon this systematic adjustment.[129]

2:41–43 *The Feet and Toes.* Up until this point there is general agreement among evangelicals concerning the identity of the successive kingdoms. Beginning with v. 41, however, there is more debate. Since the "feet" are said to be made partly of iron, the question arises as to what connection (if any) this part has to the "legs of iron." Some think that the legs and feet all refer to the same kingdom, and thus refer to the ancient empire of Rome. Others, however, think that despite the commonality of iron, there is a distinctive difference between the legs and the feet. The latter usually take the position that the "feet" (and toes) look at a kingdom still to come in the future, though having a connection with the ancient Roman Empire.[130] This

129. M. Bunson, *Encyclopedia of the Roman Empire*, rev. ed. (New York: Facts On File, 2002), 441.

130. Those who adhere to the Maccabean date of the book, and who interpret the fourth kingdom as Greece, will generally understand the "feet and toes" as an extension of that empire. They see the iron and clay as representing two divisions of that empire, with the iron denoting the stronger Seleucid kingdom, and the clay as denoting the weaker Ptolemaic kingdom.

said, there seems to be three possibilities for the chronological fulfillment of the "feet":

1) This kingdom exists during the lifetime of the ancient Roman Empire and is merely an extension of it. (Thus the fulfillment of the "feet" must come before the end of the Roman Empire.) Note: Historically, the Roman Empire splintered into two parts. The western empire came to an end in AD 476, while the eastern empire lasted until AD 1453.
2) This kingdom immediately follows the Roman Empire, and thus we must look for an historical fulfillment in the past but *after* the Roman Empire.
3) This kingdom does *not* immediately follow the fourth kingdom of Rome, and there is an unspecified *gap of time* that must be understood between the demise of the fourth kingdom (Rome) and the "feet/toes."

In an attempt to solve this interpretative problem, we should follow careful hermeneutical rules. We should first look to see if the text itself interprets the symbolism. If not, then we look for hints from the immediate context, then for hints from the broader biblical context, and finally from the historical context (is there a historical correlation?).

Since the text does not interpret the symbolism of the feet/toes, we next look for any hints from the immediate context. First, the element of iron suggests that the "feet" must have some connection to the fourth kingdom (since each metal speaks of a different kingdom), although the mixed components or iron and clay suggest that this kingdom is somehow distinct from the fourth kingdom of Rome. Second, the kingdom represented by the feet/toes is likely a confederacy of nations/kings that exist simultaneously, since v. 44 tells us that God will set up an everlasting kingdom "in the days of those kings" (not "in the days of *the last of* those kings"). Third, when this everlasting kingdom is set up by God, these Gentile kingdoms will end ("it will crush and put an end to all these kingdoms"). This third observation alone would effectively eliminate possibilities 1 and 2 above. The most devastating argument against the position that the kingdom represented by the "feet/toes" is to be found in the ancient Roman Empire, is the fact that there was no kingdom set up by God in the past that "crushed" and "put an end" to Gentile kingdoms. If one says that the kingdom is that established by Christ in his first coming, one faces the very serious problem that this kingdom (Christianity? the church?) did not "put an end" to the ancient Roman Empire. The western portion of the Roman Empire lasted until AD 476, and the eastern portion even longer.

Next, we must turn to the broader biblical context. If the "feet/toes" is a confederacy of kings that exist simultaneously (and it seems so in light of v. 44), then how many kings comprise this confederacy? The most logical conclusion would be a number suggested by the "toes" of the feet, namely ten.[131] Some scholars have tried to argue that it is reading too much into the symbolism to appeal to the ten toes. However, notice that the text itself mentions the "toes" twice in these verses (v. 41 and again in v. 42). If the author is only concerned with the feet of mixed iron and clay, why repeatedly refer to the toes? Probably they do have some significance. So, the repeated reference to the toes argues for ten kings comprising this confederacy. Yet, there is probable confirmation of this in light of chap. 7. We have already pointed out that chap. 2 and chap. 7 parallel one another (see notes on 2:1–13). In 7:23–24, we are specifically told that the ten horns represent ten kings that come out of the last kingdom. Furthermore, the Bible goes on in the book of Revelation to reveal that these ten horns (= ten kings) are a confederacy of ten kings that will rise up in the future just before the second coming of Christ and be in league with "the beast" (Rev 17:12). Looking at the historical context, it would be very difficult to claim that a confederacy of ten kings existed during the time of the Roman Empire or immediately following it.

In conclusion, the best interpretation (in light of the points above) is to regard the "legs" as representing the ancient Roman Empire and the "feet/toes" as a confederacy of ten kings still to come in the future. Since the "feet/toes" are partly of iron, then this future kingdom probably has some connection to the ancient Roman Empire (most likely, in light of 7:24, the future kingdom arises *out of* the same general geographical location as the ancient kingdom).

This conclusion would imply that there is a gap of time between the fourth kingdom (Rome) and the final phase of that kingdom, i.e., the confederacy of ten kings. However, the concept of a gap of time or a "jump forward" in time is not that unusual in Scripture, nor should it be casually rejected. Consider Isa 41:25–42:9, for example, in which case we have two prophecies back to back. The first, Isa 41:25–29, predicts that God will raise up Cyrus (which is fulfilled in the sixth century BC).[132] The second, Isa 42:1–9, predicts the coming of "My Servant," who is obviously the Lord Jesus Christ (Matthew quotes Isa 42:1–4 in Matt 12:18–21). So, there is a gap, as regards historical events, of over 500 years between Isa 41:29 and the next verse, Isa 42:1. Even within the book of Daniel, there is an obvious gap of time between Dan 11:2 (referring to the Persian king Xerxes I, r. 486–465 BC) and 11:3

---

131. Some might accept the idea of "ten" (as implied by the ten toes) but treat this as a round number (implying that it might not be exactly ten kings—note Miller, 99). I prefer a literal ten, because there is no evidence or reason to assume that a round number is meant (even if the Bible sometimes uses round numbers). Also, to make this a round number would mean that we would need to do the same at 7:24 (if the "three" mentioned in 7:24 are literal, it would follow that the "ten" are also literal). The same logic applies to the "ten" in Rev 17:12.

132. In Isa 44:28–45:1, the Lord again prophesies of Cyrus, and this time even calls him *by name* (though Isaiah himself lived long before Cyrus even stepped on the stage of history).

(referring to Alexander the Great, r. 331–323 BC). Later, I will demonstrate that there is also a gap of time in 9:26–27 and again at 11:36.

So how will this future kingdom (a confederacy of ten kings) be characterized? Like Rome of the past, this future kingdom will be "like iron," i.e., it will be tough and brutal—undoubtedly very strong militarily. Yet it will also be "partly of clay and partly of iron." That is, it will be inherently weak or "fragile" (the word תְּבִירָה, *tᵉḇîrâ*, can mean fragile or brittle, thus easily breakable). Just as iron and clay do not mix, so this future kingdom will be weak in that it will not be cohesive—it will be a divided kingdom (v. 41). The words in v. 43, "they will be a mixture in the seed of men, but they will not adhere with one another," have been interpreted in different ways. Quite a few take it as implying intermarriage for the purpose of unifying the subjects of the kingdom.[133] Others, however, understand this to refer to a failed attempt to bring different people groups together to form this confederation (i.e., they will not mix well).[134] Similarity of the verb "will be mixed" (מִתְעָרְבִין *miṯʿārᵉḇîn*) to the verb in Ezra 9:2 (הִתְעָרְבוּ, *hiṯʿārᵉḇû*, usually translated "intermingle") might favor the view of intermarriage, but it is difficult to be certain which view is correct. More insight on this latter kingdom will be given in the commentary on chap. 7.

2:44–45 *The Kingdom set up by God.* These verses are clear that God will eventually set up a kingdom of his own, which undoubtedly refers to the same kingdom given to the "son of man" in 7:13–14. In both passages the kingdom is described in the same way, as being "everlasting" (*ʿālam*) and which "will not be destroyed" (*lōʾ tiṯḥabbal*). The time of this kingdom's establishment is said to be "in the days of *those kings*." Young (78) holds that "those kings" refers to all four preceding kingdoms, with the fourth one (i.e., Rome) representing the others. This leads him to the conclusion that this kingdom in 2:44 is established at the time of the ancient Roman Empire and, hence, at Christ's first coming. From this he suggests that this kingdom is a spiritual kingdom (now) in which Christ reigns in the hearts of believers, i.e., those comprising the church.[135]

---

133. So Collins (170) and Goldingay (36).

134. So Wood (71), Miller (98), and Montgomery (177). Young (77) understands that intermarriage may be part of the explanation, but not intermarriage alone.

135. Young defines the kingdom as "the sphere of His reign or sovereignty among men" (79), but also argues that this kingdom is "in the hands of the same people, the true Israel of God, the Church" (78). Some teachers try to defend the notion that the kingdom has already come by saying that the kingdom is internal and mystical. They base this on Christ's statement "For the Kingdom of God is <u>within you</u>" (KJV). A closer look at this passage (Luke 17:20–21), however, reveals that Christ is not saying this at all. First, "within you" is a poor translation, and the words are better translated "among you" or as the NASB puts it "the kingdom of God is in your midst." Second, Christ is not referring to the inner spiritual realm of the disciples but to

There are several problems with the view that the kingdom spoken of in Dan 2:44 was established at Christ's first coming (and any equation of this kingdom with the church). First, the nearest antecedent to "in the days of those kings" would be not the "legs" (Rome) but the "feet/toes," i.e., the future confederation of kings (which we have already shown to come about shortly before Christ's second coming). Second, the Roman Empire of the past was not terminated by Christ's first coming or the founding of the church.[136] Notice carefully that v. 44 says that God's kingdom will not merely "break in pieces" (or "crush") but will even "bring about *the demise* of all these kingdoms."[137] The Roman Empire continued long after the first century AD. Third, the parallel revelation about this kingdom in chap. 7 (see esp. vv. 25–27) indicates that it is not established until *after* the time of the "little horn" (which even Young correctly identifies as the "antichrist" who arises shortly before Christ's second coming).[138]

Scripture often portrays the "kingdom of God" as being established at the second coming of Christ (cf. Matt 25:31; Luke 21:27,31; Rev 11:15). Although there is a sense in which the kingdom is *now*, i.e., during this church age, it seems that Scripture puts the emphasis on the *formal* establishment of the kingdom that will come about at our Lord's return in glory.[139] It is this latter idea of the kingdom that Dan 2:44 speaks about—that formal inauguration of the kingdom at Christ's return.

The "stone cut from a mountain" certainly represents the Lord Jesus Christ.[140] He is the One who "smashes" the Gentile kingdoms. Ps 2:8–9 states,

---

himself. He was in the midst of the nation of Israel at that time. This is made clear by the verses that follow in which he predicts that the time is coming when he will not be with them.

136. One cannot say that the church broke the power of pagan Rome either. Christianity was not the decisive factor that broke up the Roman Empire. Rather it was internal decay and political conditions.

137. The Aram. word translated "bring about the demise" is the Haph'el form of *sûp̱*, which *HALOT* (1938) defines as "put an end to something, completely annihilate."

138. Young, 158, 163.

139. The present aspect of the kingdom is seen in such passages as Col 1:13 (we have been transferred to the kingdom of his beloved Son) and Rev 1:6 (he has made us to be a kingdom of priests). This pertains to our *citizenship* and the *function* that we have in the world. However, the formal establishment of the kingdom awaits the second coming when Christ conquers the nations and brings them into submission. In the meantime, we can speak of the "heavenly kingdom" in which Christ exercises "all authority" from the right hand of the Father (cf. 2 Tim 4:18). For further insights on the present aspect of the kingdom, see my article, "James's Quotation of Amos 9 to Settle the Jerusalem Council Debate in Acts 15," *JETS* 55 (2012): 65–85.

140. Regarding the stone imagery and its association with the promised Messiah, one should compare Isa 8:11–15; 28:16–17; Zech 3:9; and Ps 118:22–23 (and compare Luke 20:17–18, esp. the comment "on whomever it falls, it will scatter him like dust").

"Ask me, and I will give you the nations as your inheritance, the ends of the earth as your personal property. You will break them with an iron scepter; you will smash them as if they were a potter's jar" (NET). The clear allusion in Rev 19:15 to Ps 2:9 strengthens the view that Dan 2:44–45 is fulfilled at the second coming of Christ (Rev 19:11–16 describes the return of Christ). Daniel 2:35 tells us that the "stone" became a large mountain that filled the entire earth. This signifies that Christ's kingdom will be worldwide in scope (cf. Ps 72:8–11).

Biblical Theology Comments

Although the time of the kingdom suggested by Dan 2:44 coincides with the second coming of Christ, another important question is the form or nature that this kingdom will take. Some holding to an amillennial theology (who deny a physical rule of Christ on earth following his return) would even agree with this conclusion about the timing of the kingdom, but they understand the nature of the kingdom differently—as that which will exist in heaven. As they would see it, Christ returns, the nations are judged, and eternity starts (the kingdom of God takes place in the eternal state). Most amillennialists, however, tend to stress the kingdom as "now"—between the two advents of Christ—and as that which continues forever.

Those holding to a premillennial theology (who believe that Christ's return will be followed by his physical rule on earth for 1,000 years) see this kingdom of Dan 2:44 as *beginning* with the "millennium" (a word meaning 1,000 years). The "kingdom" and the "millennium," however, are not exactly the same thing. Messiah's kingdom *begins* with the millennium but continues past this period and on into the eternal state in which Christ continues to rule. Thus, the millennium is only part (or a phase) of the kingdom of God. This author prefers the premillennial view as that which best accounts for all the biblical data.[141] Christ will return in glory at a time when the final human kingdom is active (a confederacy of kings represented by the "feet/toes" in league with the antichrist). Christ will put an end to this kingdom (and thus to human government), and then his kingdom will commence with his personal rule on earth for 1,000 years (Rev 20:1–4) and will continue into the new creation (Rev 21). Thus his kingdom will "endure forever."

Prior to the book of Daniel, there was already abundant revelation about Messiah's kingdom. Genesis 49:10 prophesied of one who would come from the tribe of Judah and who would receive the obedience of the peoples. David

141. For some discussion on the various millennial positions, see R. P. Lightner, *The Last Days Handbook; A Comprehensive Guide to Understanding the Different Views of Prophecy*, rev. ed. (Nashville: Thomas Nelson Publishers, 1998); P. N. Benware, *Understanding End Times Prophecy; A Comprehensive Approach* (Chicago: Moody, 1995); D. Bock, ed., *Three Views on the Millennium and Beyond* (Grand Rapids: Zondervan, 1999); and S. J. Grenz, *The Millennial Maze; Sorting Out Evangelical Options* (Downers Grove, IL: Intervarsity, 1992).

was promised that one of his descendants would have an eternal throne/kingdom (2 Sam 7:12–13). David went on to reflect on Messiah as world ruler in Ps 2. Isaiah compared Messiah's kingdom of the "last days" to a mountain and declared that warfare would be absent (Isa 2:1–4). He also predicted that Messiah would govern the earth with a righteous rule (9:6–7).

The premillennial view of the kingdom receives further support from the imagery of the stone becoming a mountain and filling the whole earth (Dan 2:35). If the kingdom represented by the mountain is fulfilled in heaven (as some amillennialists argue), why would this verse describe it as filling *the earth*? The fact that the kingdom is still future and yet fills the earth is best accounted for by a premillennial view of the kingdom.

The dream of Nebuchadnezzar in chap. 2 is relatively straightforward. There is a series of kingdoms, each following the other, until at the culmination of history the Lord God of heaven replaces all human kingdoms with a kingdom of his own making. In subsequent visions, however, additional details will be added to show that this plan of history is far more complex and will ultimately involve a "showdown" with a particular king. Blaising explains:

> There is thus a progression in the complexity of the pattern in Daniel's visions from the relatively simple image of a collision (Dan. 2) to a narrated pattern of an antagonist who is destroyed by God. The antagonist is gradually shown to be a blasphemer who exalts himself as a god.[142]

Yet with Daniel chap. 2, the foundation of God's kingdom plan is laid, on which further revelation will be added in subsequent chapters of the book of Daniel.

Application and Devotional Implications

Daniel ended his presentation to the king by saying, "The dream is certain, and its interpretation trustworthy." There will always be those in universities who analyze history and posit theories as to where it is going. Yet the only correct view of history is the biblical one. What God revealed to Nebuchadnezzar in this dream was only a sketch of where history was going, yet it was entirely correct in every detail that it provided. The fulfillment of this revelation based on the statue has not been completed. However, believers can take consolation in the fact that the kingdoms symbolized by this statue did come to pass one by one. God knew beforehand that Babylon would be succeeded by Medo-Persia, Medo-Persia by Greece, and Greece by the Roman Empire. God even had the power to reveal this to King Nebuchadnezzar, using Daniel as a guide. If these aspects of the dream were literally fulfilled, then certainly the prediction about the kingdom to be set up "in the days of those kings" (Dan 2:44) will also be literally fulfilled.

---

142. C. Blaising, "The Day of the Lord and the Seventieth Week of Daniel," *BSac* 169 (2012): 133.

Somehow in the future, there is going to arise a confederacy of kings that has a connection to the ancient Roman Empire. This confederation is going to be personally destroyed by Christ (the smiting stone). Then, following the second coming, God will set up a new kingdom in which Christ will rule over the earth. This is not just a "maybe"—something that might happen in the future. This is certain and reliable: it will happen.

If this is where history is headed—culminating in a kingdom ruled by Christ—how should that affect the way we live now? The King himself has already been here once and told us how he wants us to live and what we should be living for. Our individual purpose in life ought to be defined in terms of this goal for history. We need to ask ourselves: in what ways are we living for this kingdom now? If we are living for his kingdom, then we ought to seek (through the Holy Spirit's enabling) to be the kind of people he wants us to be—utterly faithful to him and holy. We also ought to be faithful to the Great Commission that he has called us to be a part of. Each of us has a role to play. Being convinced of the certainty of his kingdom does influence the way we live for him today.

5. Nebuchadnezzar's response to Daniel's disclosure (2:46–49)

Not only did Daniel correctly disclose the king's dream and its interpretation, but the king was convinced that he had spoken the truth. In fact, the king was so impressed he immediately sought to honor Daniel and the God whom Daniel served.

Textual Notes

48.a. Rather than שִׂגְנִין, some MSS have סִגְנִין. However, although the latter is amply attested in later Rabbinic literature (e.g., סִגְנִין in *Tg. Neb.*, Judg 8:30), it does not occur in BAram. Yet שִׂגְנִין occurs thirteen times in BAram. and is assuredly the correct reading.

Translation

2:46 Then King Nebuchadnezzar fell *prostrate* on his face and paid homage[143] to Daniel, and he gave orders[144] to present an offering[145] and incense to him. **47** The king replied to Daniel, saying, "Truly your God is a God of gods and Lord of kings, and a revealer of mysteries, seeing that you were able to

143. See "Additional Exegetical Comments" at the end of the section for extended discussion regarding the verb סְגִד (*sᵊgiḏ*).

144. Being the words of the king, the verb אֲמַר (*ʾămar*, "to say") can be translated "commanded, gave orders."

145. The Aram. noun מִנְחָה (*minḥâ*) can mean "gift, offering" (BDB, 1101). In Heb, מִנְחָה (*minḥâ*) can mean a gift, a tribute, an offering (of any kind), or specifically a grain offering. The following נִיחֹחִין (*nîḥōḥîn*, "incense") suggests an offering is in view.

reveal this mystery." **48** Then the king promoted[146] Daniel and gave him many great gifts, and made him ruler[147] over the entire province of Babylon and chief prefect[148] over all the wise men of Babylon. **49** Then Daniel made a request of the king, and he appointed Shadrach, Meshach, and Abednego over the administration of the province of Babylon, while Daniel was at the king's court.[149]

Commentary

2:46–47 *Nebuchadnezzar's adoration*. For the king to hear young Daniel give such a startling and accurate presentation of the dream and its interpretation must have left him filled with awe. He also realized that Daniel had done something that none of his Babylonian "wise men" had been able to do. So amazed was Nebuchadnezzar at this spectacle that he actually got down on his hands and knees before Daniel and fell on his face before him. The text does not tell us who else might have been present and observing at this time. For a Babylonian king to have prostrated himself before one of the Jewish captives—and a young one at that—is almost too remarkable to believe. Yet the text tells us that Nebuchadnezzar really did that. This need not mean, however, that the king was worshiping Daniel and should probably not be understood that way (see "Additional Exegetical Comments" for discussion on the verb סְגִד, *sᵊgîḏ*, translated above as "paid homage"). Had he actually "worshiped" Daniel, this would have created significant theological tension for Daniel in *authoring* this account, for how could a strict monotheist as Daniel fail to object or at least comment upon such an act? Notice in the next verse, however, that Nebuchadnezzar goes on to give glory to God himself.

---

146. The verb רְבָה (*rᵊḇâ*) means "to make great, make high" (*HALOT*, 1977). RJ (78) suggests translating "to promote" (i.e., he put him in a high position).

147. Goldingay (36) tries to make a case that Nebuchadnezzar did not actually make Daniel a ruler and translates "would have made him governor." He argues that וְהַשְׁלְטֵהּ (*wᵊhašlᵊṭēh*) "in part expresses a possible, not an actual act." He cites Exod 9:15 and 1 Sam 13:13 in support of his theory, but in both cases the sentence begins with the particle כִּי (*kî*) which expresses conditionality, unlike the syntactical situation we have in Dan 2:48.

148. The Aram. text says that the king made him "chief prefect" (רַב־סִגְנִין, *raḇ-signîn*). סִגְנִין (*signîn*) means "prefect or governor," and according to Collins (172), the title is derived from Akkadian *šaknu*, "prefect." Daniel's authority over the province of Babylon included authority over the "wise men" themselves.

149. Lit., the Aram. text has "was at the gate of the king," which is an idiom for "the royal court" (*HALOT*, 2010c). Goldingay (36) adds "'gate'–i.e., originally where the king's servants awaited his call (Esth 2:19; 21; 3:2–3)." This custom is explained by Xenophon (*Cyr.* 8.1.6), who writes that Cyrus required "that men of rank and honor should be in attendance continually at the palace gates. ... That custom is still in force, and to this day the Asiatics under the Great King wait at the door of their rulers" (cited in Collins, 172–73).

E. J. Young (81) comments on a historical situation recorded by Josephus that may shed some light:

> In the *Antiq.* (11:8:5) Josephus records that Alexander the Great bowed before the high priest of the Jews, and when asked by his general, Parmenio, as to the meaning of his action, replied, "I do not worship the high-priest, but the God with whose high-priesthood he has been honored."

However we choose to interpret the king's actions, it is nevertheless remarkable that a Babylonian king would humble himself before another man like this, especially since this young man was not only a foreigner, but a Jew from among the captives. Even a special offering and fragrant incense offerings were made to Daniel (v. 46b).

Having greatly esteemed Daniel, the king next turned to acknowledge Daniel's God. He does not mention his personal name (i.e., Yahweh), but says, "your God is a God of gods and Lord of kings." The expression "God of gods" (אֱלָהּ אֱלָהִין, *ʾĕlāh ʾĕlāhîn*) is a Semitic superlative expression equivalent to "the greatest god of all." Furthermore, Nebuchadnezzar acknowledges that he is the "Lord of kings," i.e., greater than all kings (himself included). Rindge has pointed out the contrast between Nebuchadnezzar's response to his dream being revealed with the similar situation regarding Pharaoh in Gen 41:

> The response of Pharaoh and Nebuchadnezzar following the interpretation of their dream is also telling. Although both rulers affirm the interpreter and God, there is a marked difference in the quality of these affirmations. Pharaoh does acknowledge that God is the one who has revealed both the interpretation and the pragmatic proposal to Joseph. Yet such recognition serves merely as a prelude to praising Joseph as one who has more discernment and wisdom than anyone else (41:39). Conversely, Nebuchadnezzar confesses that Daniel's God is "god of gods and lord of kings" (אֱלָהּ אֱלָהִין וּמָרֵא מַלְכִין, *ʾĕlāh ʾĕlāhîn ûmārēʾ malḵîn*) (2:47).[150]

We must understand that Nebuchadnezzar is not confessing a personal faith in Yahweh God alone. As a polytheist, he could say this. While this does amount to an acknowledgment that Daniel's God is supreme, it is not the same as saying that his God is the only deity. As a result, Nebuchadnezzar remained in spiritual darkness and without eternal life. Much later in history, the Lord Jesus would say, "And this is eternal life, that they may *know* Thee, the only true God, and Jesus Christ whom Thou hast sent" (John 17:3). What was really needed was for Nebuchadnezzar to come to *personally know* the one true living God. Fortunately, Nebuchadnezzar's spiritual journey was not over with, and at least he had taken a step in the right direction (i.e., he is at a point where he begins to give serious consideration to the true God).

150. Rindge, "Jewish Identity under Foreign Rule," 94.

Nebuchadnezzar is saying that Daniel's God is supreme over all other gods as well as human kings. Lastly (v. 47b), Nebuchadnezzar mentions the matter that really captured his attention, namely that Daniel's God is a "revealer of mysteries." While these acknowledgments are remarkable in and of themselves, his humility seems to have only been a temporary attitude (in chap. 3 he misapplies the lesson learned).

2:48 *Daniel's rewards*. The king had promised wonderful rewards for the man who could state his dream and correctly interpret it (see Dan 2:6). Now he fulfills his word. Daniel is elevated to a high position and given great gifts. Although he is just a young man, he is even allowed to rule the entire province of Babylon (probably meaning the province that included the capital city of Babylon). The word for "made him ruler" is the Aramaic verb שְׁלֵט (*šᵊlēṭ*). Wood (76) thinks Daniel may have even been given the title "satrap":

> The Babylonian empire was divided into provinces, each with a head, called in 3:2 a "satrap" (*ʾăḥashdarpᵉnayya*ʾ). Daniel apparently was made "satrap" over the province of Babylon proper, a position of high responsibility for one not yet having reached his twentieth year.

Whatever his title might have been, it is astonishing that a Jew of the captivity would rise to so prominent a political position. This must be attributed to the sovereignty of God. Most likely this would have taken place before the second deportation of Jewish exiles in 597 BC and certainly before the third one following 586 BC. God tempered his discipline on Judah by actually putting a man of God in a high political position who could bring God's grace upon these exiles that entered the province of Babylon.

In addition to ruling the province of Babylon, Daniel was also elevated over the other "wise men" of Babylon. Verse 48 tells us that he was made chief prefect (רַב־סִגְנִין, *raḇ-signîn*).[151] From what we already know of Daniel's purity of devotion to Yahweh, he undoubtedly did not join with the "wise men" in their occultic practices. He did not need their tactics to be a good counselor to the king, yet they were under his authority. Since none of them had been able to do what he did (reveal the king's dream), it is not surprising that the king put him in charge of all the "wise men." Miller (104) notes, "It was reasonable for the king to desire an administrator and a chief adviser who had the wisdom of the gods at his disposal." In reality, Daniel had much more to offer than this.

2:49 *Daniel's loyalty to his friends*. Daniel was no egotist, selfishly looking after his own skin. Earlier, in v. 28, Daniel credited the God of heaven for his ability to interpret the king's dream. Now he thinks of his three friends,

---

151. Notice in Dan 4:6 that Daniel is called *raḇ-ḥarṭumayyāʾ* ("chief of the magicians").

requesting the king allow them to help as administrators of the province he was to govern. The four of them had gone through a lot together: they had all been taken as captives in 605 BC, had braved the three years of training together, faced the recent crisis together, and had jointly sought God's compassion in prayer. Daniel was not about to be content with his own good fortune but looked after their interests as well. Apparently they lived away from the king's palace, as v. 49 closes by saying that Daniel was at the royal court. In addition to his titles and responsibilities, he had the privilege of being very near the king and having access to him.

Biblical Theology Comments

That Daniel alone was able to declare Nebuchadnezzar's dream and its interpretation resulted not only in the exaltation of the true God of heaven but also in the discrediting of the Babylonian wise men. Wooden remarks,

> ... the view presented in the book is that the *raison d'être* of the professions of the diviners was without foundation. In distinction from them, Daniel is portrayed as a person who received divine revelations directly from his God, and not as a diviner who read the indirect messages sent by gods through various phenomena. In his role as the receptor of direct revelations, Daniel served as a witness to the uniqueness of the God of Israel.[152]

God certainly does not need to prove himself to anyone, though at times he has intervened in history to demonstrate that he (and he alone) is the only true God by doing what no other can. Just as Daniel alone could announce and interpret the king's dream (and that only because God had revealed it to him), so there are other unique moments in history when God chooses to do what no other can. This had been demonstrated earlier, for instance, when Elijah challenged the prophets of Baal and the people witnessed "the God who answers by fire" (1 Kgs 18:24).

God's unmatchable power was seen later in the days of Isaiah when God challenged the idols to a contest of declaring things still to come (Isa 41:21–24). They, of course, could not meet the challenge, but God put his reputation on the line by prophesying first of the coming of Cyrus (41:24–29) and second of one called "My Servant" upon whom God would put his Spirit and who would bring forth justice to the nations (42:1–7). Even greater still, God demonstrated he can do what no other can in resurrecting the Lord Jesus from the grave.

Though the nations continued to worship idols and false deities (as even Nebuchadnezzar himself did), such trinkets of Satan were no match for the true and living God. Nebuchadnezzar would go through a painful process in coming to realize this. Yahweh alone is God eternal who dwells

152. Wooden, "The Witness of Daniel in the Court of the Kings," 32.

on high, and he will not give his glory to another, nor his praise to graven images (Isa 42:8).

Application and Devotional Implications

Although Daniel lived long before the days of the New Testament and the coming of Christ, he remarkably demonstrated a spiritual maturity very much in keeping with what we learn from the New Testament. Phil 2:3–4 says, "Do nothing from selfish ambition or conceit, but in humility count others more significant than yourselves. Let each of you look not only to his own interests, but also to the interests of others" (ESV).

In Dan 2:49, Daniel's consideration of the welfare of his friends exemplifies this spirit. He was loyal to his fellow believers, and he was obviously thinking of their interests, not just his own. He may also have been motivated by a desire to see godly men appointed to significant political places of service, knowing that this would certainly benefit the other people of God living in captivity in the Babylonian Empire.

In today's fast-paced world, many people are looking to advance in rank, prestige, power and wealth. They can be so busy thinking about their own personal world that they fail to think about the needs of others around them. One of the areas that desperately needs much attention is the concern for the development and advancement of spiritual leaders. There are young people that have been called by God to serve him vocationally in Christian ministry. Yet they need the opportunity to be trained for service and to get a good Christian education to help prepare them for their life of serving the Lord. Is there someone like this that you could be helping to get his or her education and go on to enter into a significant place of service for the sake of Christ? Is there something you could do to encourage this person or to help provide for him/her financially as he/she seeks to serve the Lord? Remember the principle of Matt 10:42: "And whoever gives one of these little ones even a cup of cold water because he is a disciple, truly, I say to you, he will by no means lose his reward." Help someone else, and you will probably find a greater blessing returning to you.

Additional Exegetical Comments

Comments on סְגִיד *(sᵊgîḏ) and Nebuchadnezzar's Prostration to Daniel in Dan 2:46*

The verb סְגִיד (*sᵊgîḏ*) means "to pay homage to" (*HALOT*, 1937) and is translated that way by the NASB and NET. The NIV renders this "paid honor." The NRSV, however, translates this as "worshiped." The verb סְגִיד (*sᵊgîḏ*) occurs eleven times in Daniel chap. 3, where the NASB, NIV, NKJV, and NRSV all translate it "worship" (i.e., worship of Nebuchadnezzar's statue), though the NET translates it "pay homage to" in chap. 3. Collins (152) translates סְגִיד (*sᵊgîḏ*) in 2:46 as "worship," but Goldingay (32) translates it as falling "prostrate before." The latter remarks (36) that "it is used in the papyri of prostration before a man." Both LXX traditions rendered this by προσκυνέω (*proskuneō*), but this has a range of meanings (to kiss, bow before, serve, or to worship). Προσκυνέω (*proskuneō*), for instance, is used in Gen 18:2 of Abraham bowing himself to the ground before his guests, hence "to make obeisance." סָגַד (*sāgad̲*) occurs four times in BH (Isa 44:15, 17, 19; 46:6). In Isa 44:17 it is used of "falling down before": "he *falls* down before it and worships it" (the word "worship" is a translation of יִשְׁתַּחוּ, *yištaḥû*). The fact that a separate word was used to express the activity of worshiping would suggest that סָגַד (*sāgad̲*) does not necessarily convey that meaning, at least not always.

B. A. Mastin includes some helpful insights about סְגִיד (*sᵊgîd̲*) from extra-biblical sources:

> … in line 13 of *The Words of Aḥiqar* סְגִד is used to tell how Aḥiqar does obeisance to Esarhaddon, and סגדוהי (line 10), unless it also is a verbal form, is a cognate noun meaning 'courtier'. Similarly S. R. Driver, who cites II Sam 14_{33} $18_{21,28}$ 24_{20}, notes that in the Targums this word is used of obeisance done to a human superior; of the four examples which he gives three refer to the behavior of men in the presence of a king and one (II Sam 18 21) to the respect shown Joab by a messenger whom he sends. Thus סְגִד is by no means invariably employed as a cultic term.[153]

Despite this admission about סְגִיד (*sᵊgîd̲*), Mastin goes on (82) to contend that the cumulative effect of the various terms in Dan 2:46 argues that "a cultic interpretation of some kind seems essential," i.e., worship is being given. In his article Mastin attempts to argue, though, that what Nebuchadnezzar is doing can be understood in light of the ancient practice of "Benefactor-Cult."[154] He writes (85), "in the world in which the author of Daniel lived a benefactor could be treated like this without impiety, and Nebuchadnezzar is simply expressing in an extravagant way his great gratitude for the very considerable service which Daniel has done him by interpreting his dream." Supposedly (in Mastin's thinking) the author's purpose in portraying Nebuchadnezzar in this way was to develop his theology of the

153. B. A. Mastin, "Daniel 2:46 and the Hellenistic World," *ZAW* 85 (1973): 81. In this quotation, Mastin references A. Cowley, *Aramaic Papyri of the Fifth Century B.C.* (Oxford: At the Clarendon Press, 1923) 212, 220; C.-F. Jean and J. Hoftijzer, *Dictionnaire des Inscriptions Sémitiques de l'Quest* (Leiden: E. J. Brill, 1965) 190; and Driver, *The Book of Daniel*, 31.

154. In explaining this concept, Mastin quotes M. P. Charlesworth, "Some Observations on Ruler-Cult, Especially in Rome," *HTR* 28 (1935): 8–16, who wrote that "from the earliest times in Greece there was a feeling that to a person who had saved you or helped you in distress you ought in gratitude to pay the highest honors you could, such honors as you would offer to a god. … To a Greek sacrifices, altars, precincts, etc., are a perfectly normal way of expressing gratitude for benefits and of showing honor to a benefactor."

subjection of the nations to Israel. He writes (91), "Nebuchadnezzar is then presumably the type of those who will bow down to Israel after the death of Antiochus Epiphanes." Yet Mastin's theory is not convincing, as (1) he presumes a second-century BC date for this portion of Daniel (as though the author thought and wrote from a Hellenistic perspective); and (2) the practice he appeals to, though evidenced in the Greco-Roman world, cannot be casually assumed for an earlier Mesopotamian setting. Moreover, what we see happening in v. 46 is not an act on the part of an ordinary Babylonian citizen, but of the king himself.

The translation "pay homage to" in v. 46 is more likely than "worship." Nebuchadnezzar may have done this as a way of recognizing that Daniel was Yahweh's representative, for in v. 47 he gives glory to Daniel's God. Though begging to differ, Mastin acknowledged the interpretation of Bevan (77) who wrote, "the king's homage, though ostensibly paid to Daniel, is in reality paid to Daniel's God (v.47)."[155]

Selected Bibliography

Armistead, D. B. "The Images of Daniel 2 and 7: A Literary Approach." *STJ* 6 (1998): 63–66.
Benware, P. N. *Understanding End Times Prophecy; A Comprehensive Approach*. Chicago: Moody, 1995.
Blaising, C. A. "The Day of the Lord and the Seventieth Week of Daniel." *BSac* 169 (2012): 131–42.
Bock, D. L. *Luke 9:51–24:53*. BECNT. Grand Rapids: Baker, 1996.
———, ed. *Three Views on the Millennium and Beyond*. Grand Rapids: Zondervan, 1999.
Brooke, G. J. "Qumran Pesher." *RevQ* 10 (1981): 483–503.
Bunson, M. *Encyclopedia of the Roman Empire*, rev. ed. New York: Facts On File, Inc., 2002.
Davies, P. R. "Daniel Chapter 2." *JTS* 27 (1976): 392–401.
Eerdmans, B. D. "Origin and Meaning of the Aramaic Part of Daniel." In *Actes du XVIIIe congrès international des orientalistes Leiden 7–12 Septembre 1931*, 198–202. Leiden: Brill, 1932.
Finkel, A. "The Pesher of Dreams and Scriptures." *RevQ* 4 (1963–64): 357–70.
Flusser, D. "The Four Empires in the Fourth Sibyl and in the Book of Daniel." *IOS* 2 (1972): 148–75.
Freedman, D. N. "The Babylonian Chronicle." *BA* 19 (1956): 50–60.
Ginsberg, H. L. "'King of Kings' and 'Lord of Kingdoms.'" *AJSL* 57 (1960): 71–74.
Glasson, T. F. *Greek Influence on Jewish Eschatology*. London: SPCK, 1961.
———. "'Visions of Thy Head' (Daniel 2[28])." *ExpTim* 81 (1969–70): 247–48.

155. Likewise, Jerome (33) saw v. 47 as epexegetical of v. 46 when he wrote, "And so it was not so much that he was worshipping Daniel as that he was through Daniel worshipping the God who had revealed the holy secrets."

Gnuse, R. K. *Dreams and Dream Reports in the Writings of Josephus: A Traditio-Historical Analysis*. Leiden: Brill, 1996.

———. "The Jewish Dream Interpreter in a Foreign Court: The Recurring Use of a Theme in Jewish Literature." *JSP* 7 (1990): 29–53.

Goswell, G. "The Visions of Daniel and Their Historical Specificity." *ResQ* 58 (2016): 129–42.

Grelot, P. "Ariok." *VT* 25 (1975): 711–19. [French]

Grenz, S. J. *The Millennial Maze; Sorting Out Evangelical Options*. Downers Grove, IL: InterVarsity, 1992.

Gruenthaner, M. J. "The Four Empires of Daniel." *CBQ* 8 (1946): 72–82, 201–12.

Gurney, R. J. M. "The Four Kingdoms of Daniel 2 and 7." *Them* 2 (1977): 39–45.

Hanson, J. S. "Dreams and Visions in the Graeco-Roman World and Early Christianity." In *Aufsteig und Niedergang der römishen Welt*, ed. H. Temporini and W. Haase, Part II, Vol. 23.2. 1395–1427. Berlin: Walter de Gruyter, 1980.

Hasel, G. F. "The Four World Empires of Daniel 2 against Its Near Eastern Environment." *JSOT* 12 (1979): 17–30.

Hoffner, H. A. "Ancient Views of Prophecy and Fulfillment: Mesopotamia and Asia Minor." *JETS* 30 (1987): 257–65.

Horgan, M. P. *Pesharim: Qumran Interpretations of Biblical Books*. CBQMS 8. Washington: Catholic Biblical Association of America, 1979.

Hunter, E. C. D. "Nebuchadnezzar's Dream in Daniel 2." In *Leshon Limmudim; Essays on the Language and Literature of the Hebrew Bible in Honor of A. A. MacIntosh*, ed. D. A. Baer and R. P. Gordon, 218–35. London and New York: Bloomsbury T&T Clark, 2013.

Klingbeil, G. A. "'Rocking the Mountain': Text, Theology, and Mission in Daniel 2." In *'For You Have Strengthened Me': Biblical and Theological Studies in Honor of Gerhard Pfandl in Celebration of His Sixty-fifth Birthday*, ed. Martin Proebstle, 117–39. St. Peter am Hart, Austria: Seminar Schloss Bogenhofen, 2007.

Kruschwitz, R. B., and P. L. Redditt. "Nebuchadnezzar as the Head of Gold: Politics and History in the Theology of the Book of Daniel." *PRS* 24 (1997): 399–416.

Lattey, C. "Sovereignty and Realm in Dan. 2, 44." *Bib* 4 (1923): 91–94.

Lawson, J. N. "'The God Who Reveals Secrets': The Mesopotamian Background to Daniel 2.47." *JSOT* 74 (1997): 61–76.

Lightner, R. P. *The Last Days Handbook; A Comprehensive Guide to Understanding the Different Views of Prophecy*, rev. ed. Nashville: Thomas Nelson, 1998.

Löwinger, S. "Nebuchadnezzar's Dream in the Book of Daniel." In *Ignace Goldziher Memorial Volume*, ed. S. Löwinger and J. Somogyi, 1:336–52. Budapest: Globus, 1948.

Lucas, E. C. "The Origin of Daniel's Four Empires Scheme Re-examined." *TynBul* 40 (1989): 185–202.

———. "A Statue, a Fiery Furnace and a Dismal Swamp; A Reflection on Some Issues in Biblical Hermeneutics." *EvQ* 77 (2005): 291–307.
Maalouf, T. T. "Were the Magi from Persia or Arabia?" *BSac* 156 (1999): 423–42.
Makujina, J. "Dismemberment in Dan 2:5 and 3:29 as an Old Persian Idiom, 'To Be Made into Parts.'" *JAOS* 119 (1999): 309–12.
Mastin, B. A. "Daniel 2 46 and the Hellenistic World." *ZAW* 85 (1973): 80–93.
———. "The Reading of lQDan[a] at Daniel II 4." *VT* 38 (1988): 341–46.
McAllister, R. "Clay in Nebuchadnezzar's Dream and the Genesis Creation Accounts." *JATS* 18 (2007): 121–28.
Mendels, D. "The Five Empires; A Note on a Propagandistic *Topos*." *AJP* 102 (1981): 330–37.
Millard, A. "Incense—The Ancient Room Freshener: the Exegesis of Daniel 2:46." In *On Stone and Scroll; Essays in Honor of Graham Ivor Davies*, ed. J. K. Aitken, K. Dell, and B. A. Mastin, 111–22. Berlin: de Gruyter, 2011.
Momigliano, A. "The Origins of Universal History." In *The Poet and the Historian*, ed. R. E. Friedman, 133–54. Chico, CA: Scholars, 1983.
Muraoka, T. *Emphatic Words and Structures in Biblical Hebrew*. Jerusalem/Leiden: Magnes/Brill, 1985.
Nel, M. "A Literary-Historical Analysis of Daniel 2; Two Powers in Opposition." *AcT* 22 (2002): 77–97.
Newton, B. W. *Aids to Prophetic Enquiry*. 3 vols. London: Nisbet, 1848–49.
Niditch, S., and R. Doran. "The Success Story of the Wise Courtier: A Formal Approach." *JBL* 96 (1977): 179–93.
Olojede, F. "Daniel 'More than a Prophet'? Images, Imagery, Imagination, and the *Mashal* in Daniel 2." *OTE* 27 (2014): 945–59.
Oppenheim, A. L. "The Interpretation of Dreams in the Ancient Near East with a Translation of an Assyrian Dream-Book." *TAPS* 46 (1956): 179–373.
———. "New Fragments of the Assyrian Dream-Book," *Iraq* 31 (1969): 153–65.
Pfandl, G. "Interpretations of the Kingdom of God in Daniel 2:44." *AUSS* 34 (1996): 249–68.
Pinker, A. "A Dream of a Dream in Daniel 2." *JBQ* 33 (2005): 231–40.
Rindge, M. S. "Jewish Identity under Foreign Rule: Daniel 2 as a Reconfiguration of Genesis 41." *JBL* 129 (2010): 85–104.
Rowley, H. H. *Darius the Mede and the Four World Empires in the Book of Daniel.* Cardiff: University of Wales Press, 1959.
Rundgren, F. "An Aramaic Loanword in Daniel." *OrS* 25–26 (1976–77): 45–55.
Segal, M. "From Joseph to Daniel: The Literary Development of the Narrative in Daniel 2." *VT* 59 (2009): 123–49.
Seow, C. L. "From Mountain to Mountain: The Reign of God in Daniel 2." In *A God So Near; Essays on Old Testament Theology in Honor of Patrick D. Miller*, ed. B. A. Strawn and N. R. Bowen, 355–74. Winona Lake, IN: Eisenbrauns, 2003.
Siegman, E. F. "The Stone Hewn from the Mountain." *CBQ* 18 (1956): 364–79.
Stevenson, W. B. "The Identification of the Four Kingdoms in the Book of Daniel." *TGUOS* 7 (1934–35): 4–8.

Swain, J. W. "The Theory of the Four Monarchies." *ClPh* 35 (1940): 1–21.
Tanner, J. P. "James's Quotation of Amos 9 to Settle the Jerusalem Council Debate in Acts 15." *JETS* 55 (2012): 65–85.
Towner, W. S. "The Poetic Passages of Daniel 1–6." *CBQ* 31 (1969): 317–26.
Venter, P. M. "The Function of Poetic Speech in the Narrative in Daniel 2." *Hervormde Teologiese Studies* 49 (1993): 1009–20.
Wallace, R. "Tyrant, Kingdom, and Church." *Int* 15 (1961): 431–38.
Walton, J. H. "The Four Kingdoms of Daniel." *JETS* 29 (1986): 25–36.
Watts, J. W. "Daniel's Praise (Daniel 2.20–23)." In *Psalm and Story: Inset Hymns in Hebrew Narrative*, 145–54. JSOTSup 139. Sheffield: Sheffield Academic Press, 1992.
Wooden, R. G. "The Witness of Daniel in the Court of the Kings." In *'You will be my Witnesses': A Festschrift in Honor of the Reverend Dr Allison A Trites on the Occasion of His Retirement*, ed. R. G. Wooden, T. R. Ashley, and R. S. Wilson, 30–52. Macon, GA: Mercer University Press, 2003.
Yamauchi, E. M. "The Episode of the Magi." In *Chronos, Kairos, Christos: Nativity and Chronological Studies Presented to Jack Finegan*, ed. J. Vardaman and E. M. Yamauchi, 15–40. Winona Lake, IN: Eisenbrauns, 1989.

B. God's Deliverance of Daniel's Three Friends Who Refuse to Worship the Image of Gold (3:1–30)

Daniel 3 is one of the best-loved stories from the Old Testament with its wonderful testimony of God's power to deliver from the fiery furnace for the sake of three Hebrews who refused to compromise their worship of God. The narrative presents a basic conflict between Nebuchadnezzar's call to worship a statue—an idol—and Yahweh's strict prohibition against worshiping idols.

Though it is a great "faith chapter" of the Bible, Daniel 3 also furthers God's divine dealing with Nebuchadnezzar, humbling him until he finally comes to see himself before the one and only creator God who alone is to be worshiped. In this sense, Dan 2–4 is a progressive account of Nebuchadnezzar's journey to faith in the God of heaven. Critical scholars, on the other hand, see the purpose of the chapter (supposedly written in Hellenistic times) not as a faithful historical record, but rather as a "court tale" meant to encourage those suffering under the persecutions of Antiochus IV, the second-century BC Seleucid ruler.[156]

The text does not indicate at what specific time this event occurred in Nebuchadnezzar's reign (see textual note for 3:1a regarding the additional words in the LXX text indicating that this took place in his eighteenth

---

156. G. T. M. Prinsloo, "Daniel 3: Intratextual Perspectives and Intertextual Tradition," *AcPB* 16 (2005): 75–76. He writes (76), "The purpose of the tales is to emphasize that it is possible to advance in a hostile, gentile world without compromising the principles of Jewish religion."

year).[157] Strangely in this chapter, nothing is said about Daniel himself, only his three friends. Numerous suggestions have been offered to explain this, though the actual reason remains unknown.[158] As for Daniel's three Hebrew friends, W. H. Shea even claims to have found their names (in slightly different form) on an ancient Babylonian list of officials comprising the court of Nebuchadnezzar.[159]

Structurally, the chapter develops along the lines of two parallel units, 3:1–18 and 3:19–30. Each moves to its own climax with a pronouncement of which God is worthy to be worshiped; the first pronouncement by the three Hebrew youths (vv. 16–18) and the second by Nebuchadnezzar (vv. 28–29). Brensinger has provided a helpful analysis of the development:

> In 3:1–18, the golden statue erected by King Nebuchadnezzar, though intended to serve as a rallying point for all of his subjects, becomes instead a test for Shadrach, Meshach and Abednego. This initial unit reaches its climax in v. 18, when the three Jewish administrators refuse to yield to Nebuchadnezzar's demands and will not worship his gods. ... Like the first unit, 3:19–30 begins by describing an object of escalating controversy. In this case, the furnace of burning fire, though initially intended to function as the consequence for deviant behavior in 3:1–18, becomes instead a test for the God of Shadrach, Meshach and Abednego. This unit reaches its climax in v. 29, when Nebuchadnezzar offers his final pronouncement and, in contrast to the earlier refusal of Shadrach, Meshach and Abednego, worships their God.[160]

The structure can be diagrammed as follows:[161]

---

157. W. Shea, "Daniel 3: Extra-biblical Texts and the Convocation on the Plain of Dura," *AUSS* 20 (1982): 29–52, seeks to build a case that the scene depicted in Dan 3 occurred in 594 BC.

158. Z. Ron, "Rescue from Fiery Death," *JBQ* 41 (2013): 26, points out that "the Talmud explains that God manipulated events so that Daniel would be out of the country during the fiery furnace episode in order to focus on Hananiah, Mishael and Azariah, thus showing that they merited a miraculous deliverance even without the help of Daniel." Cf. *b. Sanhedrin* 93a.

159. Shea, "Daniel 3." For a translation of the list, which appears on a prism found in Babylon, see Pritchard, *ANET*, 307–8. Shea associates Hananiah with Hanuna, Abednego with Ardi-Nabu, and Mishael with Mushallim-Marduk.

160. T. L. Brensinger, "Compliance, Dissonance and Amazement in Daniel 3," *EvJ* 20 (2002): 8.

161. Adapted from Brensinger, 8.

Unit One	Recurring Components in Daniel 3	Unit Two
3:1	Description: Object of Contention	3:19
3:2	Instructions: Orders from the King	3:20
3:3–7	Compliance: Orders Followed	3:21–23
3:8–15	Dissonance: Orders Thwarted	3:24–27
3:16–18	Pronouncement: Worship and the Gods	3:28–29
(3:30)	Promotion: Advancement of the Hebrew Youths	3:30

1. Nebuchadnezzar's decree demanding worship before the statue of gold (3:1–7)

The opening scene of chap. 3 depicts King Nebuchadnezzar's order for the building of a statue of gold, and a call for all his subjects to bow before it at the sound of music.

Textual Notes

1.a. Both LXX^{O} and LXX^{θ} add the words Ἔτους ὀκτωκαιδεκάτου ("in the eighteenth year") at the beginning of the sentence. Apparently the Greek translators wanted to indicate that the events of chap. 3 took place at the time of the destruction of Jerusalem and the temple (Aug. 586 BC). Although 2 Kgs 25:8 and Jer 52:12 indicate the destruction took place in Nebuchadnezzar's nineteenth year, the difference may simply be a matter of how the years are being reckoned (e.g., the issue of accession years and regnal years). There are no Hebrew MSS, however, that include the chronological notice, and there is no compelling reason to believe that these events would have occurred in conjunction with Jerusalem's destruction.

3.a–a. These words are not present in LXX^{O} and LXX^{θ}. Note their earlier occurrence in the verse.

5.a. The Qere reading is קַתְרוֹס, although some MSS in Strack have קַתְרֹס (similarly, vv. 7[a], 10[b], 15[a]).

5.b. A C^{G} fragment reads שַׂבְּכָא rather than סַבְּכָא; note that שַׂבְּכָא appears in vv. 7, 10, and 15.

5.c. פְּסַנְתֵּרִין (same in vv. 10 and 15) appears in a slightly variant form פְּסַנְטֵרִין in v. 7, the latter being the form listed in BDB, 1108c.

5.d. The form סוּמְפֹּנְיָה occurs again in v. 15, but in v. 10 the Kethib reading is סִיפֹּנְיָה (and some MSS have an ending ־יא).

Translation

3:1 King Nebuchadnezzar made a statue of gold, its height *being* sixty

cubits[162] and its width six cubits.[163] He set it up in the plain of Dura[164] in the
province of Babylon. **2** Then King Nebuchadnezzar sent *word to* assemble
the satraps, the prefects, the governors, the counselors, the treasurers, the
law officials, the police magistrates, and all *other* officials of the provinces to
come to the dedication of the statue that King Nebuchadnezzar had erected.
3 So the satraps, the prefects, the governors, the counselors, the treasurers,
the law officials, the police magistrates, and all other officials of the provinces
assembled for the dedication of the statue that King Nebuchadnezzar had
erected. They were standing before the statue that Nebuchadnezzar had
erected.[165] **4** Then the herald[166] loudly proclaimed: "You are commanded,
O people, nations, and *men of every* language,[167] **5** when you hear the sound
of the horn, the flute, zither, trigon, stringed instrument, tambour,[168] and all

162. Assuming a length of eighteen inches for the standard cubit, the image would be ninety feet high (or 27.4 m).

163. Six cubits would be about nine feet in width (or 2.74 m).

164. LXX$^{\theta}$ transliterated Dura (דּוּרָא, *dûrāʾ*) as a place-name, Δεϊρα (*Deira*), though LXX^{O} translated this as περιβολου (*peribolou*, meaning "encircling, enclosure"). Cf. E. M. Cook, "In the Plain of the Wall," *JBL* 108 (1989): 115–16, who argues that LXX^{O} should be translated "in the plain of the wall in the city of Babylon" (taking מְדִינַת, *mᵊḏînaṯ*, as "city" rather than "province"). He concludes (116), "The wall spoken of, of course, would be Nimit-Enlil, the great outer wall of Babylon built by Nebuchadnezzar, famous in antiquity and described in detail by Herodotus (1.178–82). This prominent feature of ancient Babylon thus forms part of the local color of the narrative of Daniel; the author wishes us to imagine representatives of 'all peoples, nations, and tongues' (Dan 3:4) gathered to worship the golden image in the plain between the outer wall—the wall *par excellence—and* the city proper." Yet few scholars have concurred with this suggested understanding of דּוּרָא (*dûrāʾ*).

165. Both LXX$^{\theta}$ and LXX^{O} are missing the words "that Nebuchadnezzar had erected" (but notice the duplication of the clause in the sentence).

166. The Aram. term for "herald" is כָּרוֹז (*kārôz*). The older lexicon BDB (1097d) regarded this as a Greek loanword, although the newer *HALOT* (1902d) takes it to be Old Persian in origin. Both LXX$^{\theta}$ and LXX^{O} transliterated it by the Greek word κῆρυξ (*kērux*). (But the Greek term and its cognates may be of oriental origin).

167. The translation "*men of every* language" is literally "tongues" (לִשָּׁנַיָּא, *liššānayyāʾ*). The point is that all the various language groups of the realm participated in this ceremony.

168. Aram. סוּמְפֹּנְיָה (*sûmᵊpōnᵊyâ*). There is debate as to whether this is an instrument or a musical notation. For discussion, see the introductory notes on Greek terms under "Linguistic Objections to the Traditional Date and Authorship," and the following commentary. Some have argued that it is a type of drum (identified with the Gk. word τύμπανον, *tumpanon*). The lexicons and most translations view it as some type of pipe instrument.

sorts of music, you must fall down and prostrate yourselves in homage[169] to the statue of gold that King Nebuchadnezzar has erected. **6** And whoever does not fall down and prostrate himself in homage, immediately he will be cast into the midst of the furnace[170] of blazing fire. **7** Therefore, at the very moment they heard the sound of the horn, the flute, zither, trigon, stringed instrument, tambour,[171] and all sorts of music, all the peoples, nations, and *men of every* language prostrated *themselves* in homage to the statue of gold that King Nebuchadnezzar had erected.

Commentary

3:1 *The making of the statue.* In chap. 2 the king had seen a huge "statue" in his dream that was made of various metals, the head being made of gold. Now in chap. 3, we see him ordering a statue to be made all of gold. The Aramaic term for "statue," צְלֵם (*ṣᵊlēm*), is the same in both chapters, and we can presume that the statue the king had seen in his dream became the inspiration for the statue of gold that he ordered made (though not at God's instruction). In chap. 2 the dream of the huge statue was intended to communicate that God would ultimately judge and destroy the idol-worshiping

169. The words "prostrate yourself in homage" are a translation of the one Aram. word תִסְגְּדוּן (*tisgᵊdûn*) from the vb. root סְגִד, *sᵊgid* (see translation comments at Dan 2:46). The NASB, NKJV, NIV, and NRSV all translate it "worship" in this context, although Goldingay (63) translates it "bow prostrate before" and *HALOT* (1937b) suggests "to pay homage to." The NET translates "pay homage to." The question must remain open whether they only had to bow before it, or to actually worship it. Dan 3:28 may imply that worshiping the statue was part of the king's command. Yet it is hard to believe that the same word in 2:46 means that Nebuchadnezzar *worshiped* Daniel. Goswell, "Ethics of the Book of Daniel," 134, remarks, "This terminology picks up its previous use in 2:46 (RSV 'King Nebuehadnezzar ... did homage [סגד] to Daniel'), and it is best understood to refer to the act of obeisance, as does the same term in the Targum for 2 Sam 14.33; 18:21, 28 and 24:20 (each verse describing people bowing down before a human superior)."

170. The word for "furnace" (אַתּוּן, *ʾattûn*) appears to be an ancient Babylonian loanword. Cf. S. A. Kaufman, *The Akkadian Influences on Aramaic*, Assyriological Studies Series 19. (Chicago: University of Chicago Press, 1974), 110. J. B. Alexander, "New Light on the Fiery Furnace," *JBL* 69 (1950): 375–76, reports a text (in the Nies Babylonian Collection at Yale University) that in effect is a royal decree by Rim-Sin, king of Larsa, a contemporary of Hammurabi, king of Babylon, ordering the death of a slave by burning in a furnace as a form of punishment. In the text, the word translated "furnace" is *utûnum*. Alexander suggests that the author of Daniel has correctly recorded a practice used some 1200 years earlier than Nebuchadnezzar.

171. Although *BHS* lacks וסומפניא (*wᵊsûmᵊpōnᵊyâ*)—perhaps a "tambour," a type of drum instrument—it does appear in many medieval Hebrew MSS, the Syriac Peshitta, some LXX MSS, and Vg. Note that it does appear in the list of vv. 5, 10, and 15.

empires. The interpretation of the dream by Daniel, however, had revealed Nebuchadnezzar in a rather exalted manner. He was the *head of gold* and the king of kings, and the empires that followed would be inferior to his.

Nebuchadnezzar appears to have let his honored status go to his head, his pride prompting him to glorify himself. In doing so, he was distorting the message that God had intended. Based on the dream of the statue, Nebuchadnezzar decided to make a statue for his subjects to bow down to and pay homage to. That he made it all of gold suggests that this was an egotistical attempt to glorify himself, whereby he took his God-given authority and turned to exalting himself (insulting the God who had given him authority and who was to ultimately establish his own kingdom). If he had some other purpose in mind by building the statue, we are not told. Goswell, however, has suggested that this act was more than just prideful boasting:

> The king's action is to be understood as an attempt to prevent the vision becoming reality, namely the replacement of his kingdom by subsequent kingdoms. God had revealed that he would "set up (קים) a kingdom which shall never be destroyed," (2:22) but Nebuchadnezzar's reaction is to "set up (קים) an image." In other words, God's effective rule as King over all the nations (the substance of the dream in ch. 2) is resisted by Nebuchadnezzar, who seeks to ensure the loyalty of his subjects and to bolster the strength of his kingdom by commanding that they prostrate themselves before the golden image that symbolises his glorious empire (and is not an idol as such).[172]

Did he intend the statue to serve as an idol to one of the Babylonian deities?[173] Most commentators do not think so.[174] It is very possible that the requirement to do homage before the statue represented a loyalty check for the king's subjects (especially if he felt any threats against his rule).

Regarding the composition of the statue, most likely it was not made of solid gold but was goldplated (cf. Isa 40:19; Jer 10:4). It need not have been made of solid gold in order to be called a statue of gold. In Exod 38:30 the altar is called a "bronze altar," yet we know from Exod 27:1–2 that it was only overlaid with bronze. Other than being covered with gold, we do not know what the statue looked like. (Was it like Nebuchadnezzar? Was it like some

---

172. Goswell, "The Ethics of the Book of Daniel," 133.

173. The Aram. *ṣᵊlēm* can mean either "statue" or (idolatrous) "image." This is the same term for the "statue" that Nebuchadnezzar saw in his dream in chap. 2. *HALOT* (1964d) gives the meaning as "statue," although the Hebrew equivalent *ṣelem* normally means "image." In this context, "statue" is probably the best translation.

174. Archer (7:51), however, contends that the statue would have had a connection to pagan deities: "It is far more likely that the statue represented Nebuchadnezzar's patron god, Nebo (or Nabu). Prostration before Nebo would amount to a pledge of allegiance to his viceroy, *Nabu-kudurri-uṣur*, i.e., Nebuchadnezzar."

Babylonian deity?). What we are told is that its size was sixty cubits high and six cubits wide. Some translations render this in other measurements (e.g., 90 ft. x 9 ft. or 27 m. x 2.7 m.). Yet the dimensions based on the number six are probably intentional. Baldwin (101) notes, "The Sumero-Akkadian number system was mainly sexagesimal, as opposed to the decimal system rigidly adhered to in Egypt." The proportions of the measurements would have made the figure look quite bizarre and distorted. However, the height given might have included a base on which it stood, in which case the figure itself was smaller.

While the height of this statue was quite imposing, it was not beyond reason. The Colossus at Rhodes (one of the seven wonders of the ancient world) was even higher. Rhodes was an island trade center in the Aegean Sea. A bronze statue thirty-two meters high (105 ft.) of the sun god Helios was erected at the mouth of Mandrákion harbor to commemorate the end of Demetrius' long siege against Rhodes (ca. 305 BC). This statue took twelve years to build (ca. 294–282 BC).

The location of the statue is said to be in the plain of Dura (*dûrāʾ*). This could be a *place name* (so most translations), or it could indicate the type of place in which it was erected.[175] Even if Dura was a place name, we still are not able to locate the site precisely. There were several places with compounded names that included the element *dur*. One strong possibility is Tolul Dura that has been identified by J. Oppert. Young (85) notes,

> The archaeologist Oppert ... declared that S. S. E. of Hillah, at a distance of about 12 miles, there were some mounds called Tolul Dura (the mounds of Dura). One of these, known as el-Mokhattat, consisted of a rectangular brick structure 45' square and 20' in height, which according to Oppert, may have formed the pedestal of a colossal image.[176]

3:2–3 *The dedication of the statue.* Nebuchadnezzar decided to have an elaborate dedication ceremony for his new statue, during which the important officials of his realm would be in attendance. The following officials were included:

1) satraps (אֲחַשְׁדַּרְפְּנַיָּא, *ʾăḥašdarpᵉnayyāʾ*): This is a Persian loanword, which according to Wood (81) means "protector of the realm."

---

175. The Babylonian term *dûru* means a "wall." This could refer to an enclosed or walled place (a fortress?), or perhaps described the terrain—a broad area enclosed by mountains round about. Apparently the Greek translators were divided. LXX$^{\theta}$ transliterated it *deira*, whereas LXX^{O} translated it *peribolou* (meaning "circuit, enclosure"). For further discussion, see "Dura" in the revised *ISBE* (1:996); D. J. Wiseman, *Nebuchadrezzar and Babylon* (Oxford: Oxford University Press, 1985), 111; and E. M. Cook, "In the Plain of the Wall," 115–16.

176. Young refers to J. Oppert, *Expédition scientifique en Mésopotamie*, I (1863), 238ff.

These were apparently the rulers over the primary provinces of the empire (cf. 6:1).

2) prefects (סִגְנַיָּא, *signayyā'*): This is an Assyrian loanword from Akk. *šaknu*. Most likely the prefects were high-ranking officials directly responsible to the satraps (so Archer, 156–57). The term may have had a general meaning for one having "jurisdiction over." Recall that Daniel was made "Chief Prefect" (רַב־סִגְנִין, *raḇ-signîn*) over the wise men of Babylon in 2:48.
3) governors (פַּחֲוָתָא, *paḥăwāṯā'*): This is also an Assyrian loanword from Akk. *bēl pihāti* ("lord of an administrative district"). These were probably the administrators over smaller regional districts. In the postexilic period, the area of Judah was ruled by a *peḥāh*, governor (Mal 1:8).
4) counselors (אֲדַרְגָּזְרַיָּא, *'ăḏargāzᵊrayyā'*): This is a Persian loanword that means a counselor within the king's court (*HALOT*, 1807), or a royal "advisor" (so NIV).
5) treasurers (גְּדָבְרַיָּא, *gᵊḏāḇᵊrayyā'*): This is a Persian loanword (cf. Aram. *gizbar*, *HALOT*, 1843d—one who is a supervisor of the treasury—from Old Persian *ganzabara*).
6) judges (דְּתָבְרַיָּא, *dᵊṯāḇᵊrayyā'*): This is a Persian loanword for one who is a judge or law official, or someone versed in the law (*HALOT*, 1856d).
7) magistrates (תִּפְתָּיֵא, *tip̱tāyē'*): *HALOT* (2008) suggests that the term means police officer or magistrate.

In addition to the seven specifically mentioned authoritative figures who were invited to the dedication, there were also lesser figures referred to as "all the other provincial authorities" (*kōl šilṭōnê mᵊḏînāṯā'*). Obviously the ceremony was a gathering of the "who's who" of the land, and people would be closely watching all these dignitaries. In looking over the list above, we can see that several of the terms are Persian in origin. This is not a problem for Danielic authorship, since our sixth century BC Daniel is known to have lived on into the Persian period and may have written the book at that time when Persian words were commonly used.[177]

H. Avalos has explored the comedic function of the enumerated lists in Dan 3 (i.e., the lists of officials and lists of instruments), in which the repeated lists serve to belittle the mindless actions of the pagan Babylonians in contrast to the mindset of the three Hebrew youths. Regarding the first enumerated list of officials, he notes,

> ... the lengthy list is not meant simply to provide the reader with an accurate descriptive analysis. The lengthy list emphasizes the mindlessness of the entire Chaldean bureaucracy. Indeed, the list

177. For a list of words in Daniel of Persian origin, see "Introductory Matters" ("Texts and Versions"; "Presence of Foreign Loanwords").

> seems careful not to omit the most minor official. ... The four mechanical iterations of a lengthy list of musical instruments in vv 5,7,10, and 15 mirror the mechanistic behavior of the pagans before the image. ... Indeed, as soon as the instruments sound, the pagans genuflect *en masse* before a lifeless image without a second thought.[178]

The three pious Jews, however, stand in stark contrast. Avalos points out (586), "Their response (vv 16–18) informs us that they are only impressed with the true God, the only one being capable of intervening in human affairs."

3:4–6 *The king's decree.* Once the royal officials were all assembled, the "herald" (*kārôz*) loudly proclaimed the king's command that *everyone* was to obey upon hearing the music.[179] The sound of musical instruments was to be the signal to bow down before the image. The following instruments were used on this occasion:

1) horn (קֶרֶן, *qeren*): In both Greek versions this is translated as σάλπιγξ (*salpigx*), meaning a trumpet. This term could also refer to an animal's horn (cf. Josh 6:4–6). It was apparently some type of instrument that made a sound (music?) by blowing in it, but distinguished from the following term.
2) flute (מַשְׁרוֹקִי, *mašrôqî*): This refers to some type of pipe instrument, which might be comparable to the modern flute. The term comes from the root *sᵊraq*, meaning "to play a pipe, whistle, or hiss" (*HALOT*, 2002c). Both Greek versions translated this as συριγξ (*surigx*), meaning a pipe or anything like a pipe.
3) zither (קִיתְרוֹס, *qaytᵊrôs*): This is one type of lyre, and the term itself is a loanword from Greek κἴθάρις (*kitharis*). In Homer and Herodotus, the *kithara* was a triangular shaped lyre with seven strings. A "zither" is an instrument with strings stretched across a soundboard and played with a plectrum or the fingers. The translation "zither" is suggested by *HALOT* (1970c), NIV, NET, and Collins (176).
4) trigon (שַׂבְּכָא, *śabbᵊkāʾ*): This term is also a Greek loanword, rendered by both Greek versions as σαμβύκη (*sambukē*). The *sambukē* was a

---

178. H. Avalos, "The Comedic Function of the Enumerations of Officials and Instruments in Daniel 3," *CBQ* 53 (1991): 585. By "comedic," the author looks at the satirical elements of the story. M. Nel "Daniel 3 as Satirical Comedy," *NGTT* 53 (2012): 218 defines *satire* as "the poetic ridiculing of vices or follies of institutions and individuals by way of irony, sarcasm, etcetera with the purpose of changing readers' or listeners' perspective of these institutions or individuals by exposing their vices or follies."

179. The command was for "O peoples, nations, and *men of every* language group," which is a rather common formula for all the subjects of the realm regardless of ethnicity or language (cf. 3:7, 29; 4:1; 6:25).

triangular musical instrument with four strings, i.e., a triangular shaped lyre.[180]

5) stringed instrument (פְּסַנְטֵרִין, *pᵊsanṭērîn*): This term is a Greek loanword from ψαλτήριον (*psaltērion*). Mitchell notes, "The *psalterion* was literally something plucked, from the Greek verb *psallein*, 'to pluck.'"[181] *HALOT* (1958b) indicates that the Arabic *sanṭūr* or *sanṭīr* is derived from this, a stringed instrument, triangular in shape, rather like a dulcimer harp. However, it would not have looked like the modern-day harp.
6) tambour (סוּמְפֹּנְיָה, *sûmᵊpōnᵊyâ*): This is also thought to be a Greek loanword from either συμφωνία (*sumphōnia*) or τύμπἄνον (*tumpanon*). This is the most disputed term in the group. The NASB translates as "bagpipe" (which is too confusing with the modern Scottish bagpipe), and the NIV as simply "pipes." *HALOT* (1938a) gives the meaning "double-barreled flute, sackbut." Some scholars have questioned it being an instrument at all. According to Harrison, "The term *sûmpōnyā*', formerly rendered 'dulcimer' (RSV 'bagpipe'; NEB 'music') apparently is not an instrument at all, but a musical notation having the meaning of 'in ensemble' or its general equivalent."[182] Archer points out that this term "does not occur in extant Greek literature until the time of Plato (ca. 370 BC), at least in the sense of a musical instrument."[183] However, since we only have one-tenth of the significant Greek literature of the classical period, we lack sufficient data for dating the precise origin of any particular word or usage in the development of the Greek vocabulary. On the other hand, the term may be neither a pipe/bagpipe nor "musical

---

180. Mitchell, "And the Band Played on … But What Did They Play on? Identifying the Instruments in Nebuchadnezzar's Orchestra." *BRev* 15 (1999): 36, agrees that it had a triangular shape and adds, "At the same time, references in musical contexts mention strings, sometimes 'many strings,' and indicate that the instrument had a high pitch. So some kind of small harp is a reasonable guess."

181. Ibid. Mitchell understands the *pᵊsanṭērîn* to be a "lyre," but of a different type than the *qayṯᵊrôs*. He provides ample evidence that in the Mediterranean world and the ANE, several different types of lyres were used.

182. R. K. Harrison, "Daniel, Book of," in *ISBE*, 1:864. B. J. Noonan, "The Presence and Significance of Foreign Loanwords in the Book of Daniel," paper presented at Evangelical Theological Society annual meeting, Baltimore, Nov. 20, 2013, 12, defends the meaning "musical harmony." Similarly, F. W. Galpin, *The Music of the Sumerians* (Cambridge: Cambridge University Press, 1937), 67–69, saw it as an orchestra (i.e., of many instruments in accord), though other scholars like M. Ellenbogen, *Foreign Words in the Old Testament* (London: Luzac, 1957), 122 and S. B. Finesinger, "The Musical Terms of the Old Testament," *HUCA* 3 (1926): 21–77 have understood it to be a musical instrument.

183. Archer, *A Survey of Old Testament Introduction*, 368.

notation," but another type of instrument altogether. Dyer has argued at length that the term refers to an instrument like a drum:

> A final proposal is to identify *sûmpōnyâ* as a musical instrument but to reject its association with the Greek word *sumphōnia*. Instead, according to this view, it should be identified with the Greek word *tumpanon*, to be translated "drum."[184]

Mitchell gives a lengthy discussion of *sûmpōnyâ* and also concludes that this term is derived from the Greek *tumpanon* and should be understood as a "tambour," a kind of handheld drum (like a tambourine without the jingles).[185]

The chart on the following page summarizes the Aramaic names of the musical instruments, their Greek translation, lexical definitions, and English translations from various versions.

Although there continues to be debate about the precise identification of these instruments, several of the names are obviously Greek loanwords. Some critical scholars have used this observation to attack the traditional belief of a sixth-century BC Daniel as the author, suggesting instead a date for the author in the Hellenistic period. However, it is very reasonable that Greek musical instruments and terms could have spread to the Orient long before the conquests of Alexander in the fourth century BC.[186] Terms such as *kitharis* have been found in Homer's writings from a very early period. We also know of Greek mercenaries and Greeks being sold as slaves before Daniel's day, either of which could have brought these terms and instruments to the Orient.

When the instruments and music were heard, all the subjects were first to fall down. Then they were to *do homage to* the statue (the Aramaic term is סְגִד, *sᵊgid*). Whatever nuance of meaning *sᵊgid* has (see translation note above for v. 5), it seems clear from the use of this same term in 3:28 that this

---

184. C. H. Dyer, "The Musical Instruments in Daniel 3," *BSac* 147 (1990): 434. Greek and Aramaic terms in Dyer's original article have been transliterated. Cf. T. C. Mitchell and R. Joyce, "Musical Instruments in Nebuchadnezzar's Orchestra," in D. J. Wiseman, ed., *Notes on Some Problems in the Book of Daniel* (London: Tyndale, 1965), 26; T. C. Mitchell, "And the Band Played On," 32–39; and J. G. Westenholz, Y. Maurey, and E. Seroussi, eds., *Music in Antiquity: The Near East and the Mediterranean* (Berlin/Boston: Walter de Gruyter GmbH, 2014).

185. Mitchell, "And the Band Played on," 39. According to Mitchell, the notion that *sûmpōnyâ* might have been derived from the Greek *tumpanon* was first suggested by Mitchell and Joyce, "The Musical Instruments in Nebuchadnezzar's Orchestra," 25–26.

186. For documentation of inscriptions and conquests that evidence contact with Greek culture in the Assyrian, Neo-Babylonian, and Persian periods, see E. Yamauchi, "Daniel and Contacts Between the Aegean and the Near East Before Alexander," *EvQ* 53 (1981): 37–47. For further discussion, see "Linguistic Objections to the Traditional Date and Authorship" in the "Introductory Matters."

type of action was only appropriate for Yahweh God. To do this before Nebuchadnezzar's statue would amount to a violation of the first two of the Ten Commandments (Exod 20:1–6). This, then, became a serious challenge for the Hebrews in attendance. To make the matter even more serious, the king commanded that anyone not obeying his order would be cast into a furnace of blazing fire (v. 6).[187] Furnaces for manufacturing bricks (kilns) have been used in Babylonia (modern-day lower Iraq) from ancient times, and this author has witnessed many of them in his travels there in days past. Kilns would have also been needed for smelting the ore for the gold plating as well as for making lime.[188] Baukal's suggestion is very plausible:

> It may have been the furnace used to make the metal used in the giant image; this would explain its close proximity to the statue. The production of metals such as bronze would have required the conduction of some type of furnace to achieve the temperatures necessary to smelt the ore and produce liquid metal that could be cast into shapes.[189]

The thought of being cast into such a furnace would have been terrifying. Joyce Baldwin (103) reports that temperatures in these kilns could reach as high as 1000 degrees centigrade.

---

187. The penalty of death by burning was an ancient practice, attested centuries earlier in the law code of Hammurabi (e.g., §§25. 110), as reported in Montgomery (196). Cf. F.-A. Beaulieu, "The Babylonian Background of the Motif of the Fiery Furnace in Daniel 3," *JBL* 128 (2009): 273–90, who documents three specific cases where people were executed by being thrown into a burning furnace as punishment for breaking certain laws. T. L. Holm, "The Fiery Furnace in the Book of Daniel and the Ancient Near East," *JAOS* 128 (2008): 85–104, provides a helpful detailed study concerning burning as a form of punishment in the ANE (see esp. 88–92). Though burning as a form of punishment is well attested, Holm documents that there is very little evidence for burning *in a furnace*. Other than the example of Rim-Sin (see textual note for "furnace" at v. 6), Holm (91) does acknowledge another: "A second occurrence (and the only other that this author is able to find) of throwing someone into a furnace in Mesopotamia is in the Middle Assyrian edicts concerning the regulation of the harem (Middle Assyrian Palace Decrees). Edict 19 from the time of Aššur-rēša-iši (ca. 1132–1115 B.C.E.) threatens witnesses who fail to inform on those who are breaking the rules of the harem with being thrown into an oven: *lū sinnilta lū aʾīla āmerāna ana libbi utūne ikarrurūšunu*: 'Whether a woman or a man, they shall throw the eyewitness into the oven.'" Holm finds far more evidence of burning in a furnace in ancient Egyptian literature, which leads him to conclude (incorrectly, I believe) that this court tale more likely had its origin in Egypt than Mesopotamia.

188. For discussion on the possible types of furnaces used in ancient Mesopotamia and the technical aspects of design, operation, fuels, and combustion, see C. E. Baukal, "The Fiery Furnace," *BSac* 171 (2014): 148–71.

189. Baukal, "The Fiery Furnace," 154.

Aram.	Translit.	LXX	BDB	*HALOT*	NASB	NKJV	NRSV	NIV	NET
קֶרֶן	*qeren*	σάλπιγξ trumpet	horn	horn (1973)	horn	horn	horn	horn	horn
מַשְׁרוֹקִי	*mašrôqî*	συριγξ pipe, flute	pipe	pipe (1924)	flute	flute	pipe	flute	flute
קִיתְרוֹס	*qayṯᵊrôs*	κιθάρα lyre	lyre, zither	zither (1970)	lyre	harp	lyre	zither	zither
שַׂבְּכָא	*śabbᵊkāʾ*	σαμβύκη small arched harp	trigon	a four-stringed harp (1984)	trigon	lyre	trigon	lyre	trigon
פְּסַנְטֵרִין	*pᵊsanṭērîn*	ψαλτήριον stringed instrument, psaltery	stringed instru-ment	triangular shaped stringed instrument, like dulcimer (1958)	psaltery	psaltery	harp	harp	harp
סוּמְפֹּנְיָה	*sûmpōnyâ*	συμφωνία musical concord, harmony, band, drum	bagpipe, double-pipe, Pan's pipe	double-barreled flute, sackbut (1938)	bagpipe	"in sym-phony with"	drum	pipe	pipes

3:7 *The compliance with the king's command.* Undoubtedly the music would have heightened and intensified the emotions on this occasion, even deadening one's ability to think clearly. Like a mass gathering at a football game with thousands in attendance, the dynamic of the crowd would have been most compelling. Verse 7 indicates that the masses readily complied with the king's command, but as we see in v. 12 Daniel's friends did not go along with the masses. Their allegiance to Yahweh God was not for sale at any price, even if it meant their own martyrdom. What a stark contrast they were to King Nebuchadnezzar's other subjects.

Biblical Theology Comments

This passage exemplifies the tension believers face when a demonstration of their loyalty to the state is demanded. As Christians, we are responsible for being good citizens of whatever government we might find ourselves under, and we are to subject ourselves to the authorities of such governments (Rom 13:1–7). Hence, the apostle Paul wrote, "Render to all what is due them: tax to whom tax is due; custom to whom custom; fear to whom fear; honor to whom honor" (Rom 13:7, NASB). Paying taxes, observing various customs, and even honoring pagan rulers are entirely appropriate observances (though not always pleasurable). However, there are lines that we as believers do not cross, and "we must obey God rather than men" (Acts 5:29). Hence, we do not submit to doing evil or violating God's commands, and above all else we do not worship anything or anyone other than our Lord—even if we must suffer for doing what is right as a result (1 Pet 3:13–17).

Early Christians had to face intimidating issues arising from Roman culture, such as the imperial cult and the demand of Caesar worship. Thousands in the early centuries had to make the choice of whether or not to demonstrate their loyalty to the Roman Empire by renouncing their worship of Jesus and indulging in the pagan practice of sacrificing to Roman gods such as Jupiter. In the future tribulation, believers will face the challenge (at the peril of their lives) of whether or not to receive the mark of the beast and to worship the image of the beast (Rev 13:14–18). (The demand to worship Nebuchadnezzar's statue almost seems like a foreshadowing of that future event.) Loyalty to the state has its limits, and the faithful believer must know when to be the good citizen and when to draw the line.

Application and Devotional Implications

In chap. 1 we read that these same three Hebrew youths had already had their faith challenged (in regard to consuming the king's food and drink). In that case, they had to face the issue of whether they would compromise God's commandments or not. Now their faith was put to a far more serious test. In polytheistic Babylon, they had not been forbidden from worshiping the god(s) of their own choosing. The Hebrews had been free to worship Yahweh God. In this instance, however, they were being forced to *broaden* their religion. They could still worship Yahweh ... as long as they were willing to *also* bow before the king's statue and do homage to it. The music was blaring away and the crowd was yelling. It was so compelling to just fall in line with the others. How easily these young Hebrews could have rationalized by saying, "Well, everyone is doing it!"

For those of us who are believers in the Lord Jesus Christ, this issue touches the very core of our being. Jesus himself said, "I am the way, and the truth, and the life; no one comes to the Father, but through Me" (John 14:6, NASB; cf. Acts 4:12). The bedrock of our faith is that there is one and only one God—the God of the Bible. The world may worship or follow other (so-called) gods, but as Christians we know that there is only one true God—the triune God we know as the Father, Son, and Holy Spirit. We reject any other suggestion, and we will not concede that there is any other god—not even for a moment. There is no such thing as *multiple ways to God*. There is only one way, and that is through Jesus our Lord. The reason that we have this confidence is (1) because of the miraculous ministry of our Lord Jesus while He was on earth, and (2) because of his resurrection from the dead. Furthermore, He is the only one that gives hope to our souls. On one occasion when the Lord Jesus asked the twelve if they also wanted to stop following him as some disciples had done, Peter replied to him, "Lord, to whom shall we go? You have words of eternal life. We have believed and have come to know that You are the Holy One of God" (John 6:68–69, NASB).

Our faith is not for sale at any price, and we will not worship or bow down to any other god. Someone has said that life is not worth living, if we are not willing to die for something. If we have not discovered anything in life worth dying for, then there is nothing of any real substance to our life. Are you willing to die for your faith in the Lord Jesus Christ? Do you give a clear testimony to others that your allegiance belongs to him alone? If you are suffering for your faith in Christ today, remember his promise: "Blessed are you when people insult you and persecute you and say all kinds of evil things about you falsely on account of Me. Rejoice and be glad because **your reward** is great in heaven, for they persecuted the prophets before you in the same way" (Matt 5:11–12; NET). Cowards are not rewarded, only heroes of the faith.

2. The Jews are accused of defying the king's orders (3:8–12)

Textual Notes

8.a-a. The words כָּל־קֳבֵל דְּנָה are lacking in LXX$^{\theta}$, Syr., and Pap. 967. The inclusion in MT could be a case of dittography with v. 7.

9.a-a. The words לִנְבוּכַדְנֶצַּר מַלְכָּא are lacking in LXX^{O} which reads instead κύριε βασιλεῦ, "lord king." LXX$^{\theta}$, however, reflects MT: βασιλει Ναβουχοδονοσορ (with "king" twice).

10.a. In place of the Kethib וְסִיפֹּ־, the Qere is וְסוּפֹּ־, thus conforming to v. 5.

10.b-b. LXX$^{\theta}$ omits the words יִפֵּל וְיִסְגֻּד לְצֶלֶם דַּהֲבָא, but they are reflected in LXX^{O}.

12.a. Instead of the Kethib לֵאלָהָיךְ (pl. "to your gods"), the Qere is לֵאלָהָךְ (sg. "to your god"). LXX$^{\theta}$ (τοῖς θεοῖς) reflects the plural. LXX^{O} is singular but more interpretative: τῷ εἰδώλῳ, "to your idol."

Translation

3:8 Now[190] at that time *certain* Chaldeans[191] came forward and maliciously accused[192] the Jews. **9** They spoke up and said[193] to King Nebuchadnezzar, "O king, live forever! **10** You, O king, issued a decree that every man who hears the sound of the horn, the flute, the zither, the trigon, the stringed instrument, the tambour, and all sorts of music must fall down and prostrate himself in homage to the statue of gold. **11** And whoever does not prostrate himself in homage will be cast into the midst of the furnace of blazing fire. **12** There are *certain* Jews[194] whom you have appointed over the administration[195] of the province of Babylon, *namely* Shadrach, Meshach, and Abednego. These men have not paid attention[196] to you, O king. They do not serve

---

190. The words כָּל־קֳבֵל דְּנָה (*kol-qŏḇēl dᵉnâ*) are not reflected in some versions (see textual note), and their presence in the MT could be a case of dittography with v. 7. Hence the NIV does not include them. RJ (82) suggests the translation "thereupon," but this sounds archaic in English. Other English versions render this "now" (NET), "therefore" (ESV), or "for this reason" (NASB).

191. Lit., "Chaldean men" (גֻּבְרִין כַּשְׂדָּאִין, *guḇrîn kaśdāʾîn*).

192. The translation "maliciously accused" is an attempt to render וַאֲכַלוּ קַרְצֵיהוֹן (*waʾăḵalû qarṣêhôn*), an idiomatic expression that literally means "they ate their pieces." *HALOT* (1974) notes that Akk. *karṣu* means "something pinched off." Goldingay (64) translates the idiom as "denounced" and points out that this is "an Akk. expression for 'accusing'" (see *CAD* A, 1:255–56). Collins (17) translates as "slandered," and NET has "brought malicious accusations against."

193. עֲנוֹ וְאָמְרִין (*ʿănô wᵉʾāmᵉrîn*, lit., "they answered and said,") is a common Aramaic idiom occurring repeatedly in this chapter. The translation "they spoke up and said" captures the point.

194. Lit., "Jewish men" (גֻּבְרִין יְהוּדָאיִן, *guḇrîn yᵉhûḏāʾyin*). Notice the similarity with גֻּבְרִין כַּשְׂדָּאִין (*guḇrîn kaśdāʾîn*) in v. 8.

195. עֲבִידָה (*ʿăḇîḏâ*) basically means "work, service," but BDB (1105a) suggests the translation "administration" in the case of Dan 3:12.

196. The verb שִׂים (*śîm*) normally means "to set, place." Yet in combination with the prep. עַל (*ʿal*) and the noun טְעֵם (*ṭᵉʿēm*) it can have the meaning "to have regard for" (*HALOT*, 1986) or "to pay attention to" (RJ, 84; so NIV).

(*worship*)[197] your gods, nor do they prostrate themselves in homage to the statue of gold that you have erected."

Commentary

3:8 *The accusers.* The text tells us that "certain Chaldeans" came forward to accuse the Jews. The term "Chaldeans" (כַּשְׂדָּאִין, *kaśdāʾîn*) appeared in Dan 2:2 in a list of occult practitioners (see commentary on 2:2). In that case, the term was used in the sense of experts/priests in the Babylonian religion (one of their functions being astrology—note the NIV's translation "astrologers" at 3:8). Some commentators, however, feel that the term has the ethnic sense here in 3:8 (equivalent to "Babylonians," as in 5:30).[198] While either nuance is possible in this case, there is no reason to abandon the meaning the term had in chap. 2 (in light of the close relationship of chap. 3 to chap. 2), namely that of experts/priests in the Babylonian religion. In fact, that makes perfectly good sense in this context. Despite the fact that Daniel and his three friends had been something of "saviors" to the *wise men* of Babylon (they literally saved their necks), there was probably still a lingering resentment at these "foreigners" who had been appointed over them. These Chaldeans had been made to look like fools when their occultic tactics could not help them identify the king's dream and interpretation. It is not hard to imagine that they would have been looking for an opportunity to "get even" with these despised foreigners.

Verse 8 also tells us that these Chaldeans "brought malicious accusations against" the Jews. This is a translation of a Semitic idiom, which literally means "to eat their pieces" (וַאֲכַלוּ קַרְצֵיהוֹן, *waʾăkalû qarṣêhôn*). This is sometimes translated "denounce" or "slander," but "maliciously accuse" reflects the sentiment accurately. Their attitude toward these Jews resembles that exhibited by Haman, who sought to destroy all the Jews in the days of Esther and King Ahasuerus. He maliciously exclaimed to Ahasuerus, "There is a certain people scattered abroad and dispersed among the peoples in all the provinces of your kingdom. Their laws are different from those of every other people, and they do not keep the king's laws, so that it is not to the king's profit to tolerate them" (Esther 3:8, ESV).

3:9–11 *Recollection of the king's edict.* Before stating their specific charges, the accusers first reminded the king of his own edict. They began their address to the king with the standard court protocol, "O king, live forever," a formality no doubt with little sincerity behind it. Verses 10–11 are essentially a restatement of 3:5–6. Those who refused to bow down and prostrate themselves in homage to the statue at the sound of the music were to be thrown alive into

197. The verb פְּלַח (*pᵊlaḥ*) means "to pay reverence to, to serve (a deity)" (BDB, 1108c). Yet it also connotes a person, deity or thing which one worships. See the discussion to follow under "Additional Exegetical Comments."

198. See, for example, Young (88) and Wood (85).

the furnace of blazing fire. (Regarding the musical instruments mentioned in v. 10, see the commentary at 3:4–6.)

3:12 *The charges against the Jews*. The Chaldeans began by identifying the violators of the king's edict as "*certain* Jews." Actually, their ethnic makeup was immaterial, and did not need to be pointed out. The fact that the Chaldeans called the king's attention to this reflects their prejudice against this unique people. Even though the Bible does not always portray the Jews in a favorable way (e.g., 1 Thess 2:14–16; Rev 3:9) and holds them partly accountable (with Gentiles) for the crucifixion of the Lord Jesus Christ (Acts 2:22–23), it is still true that God has a special role for them in history. One such contribution is that the Messiah would come from this line. Satan knows this, and he is the one who ultimately stands behind the attempts to destroy both the Jews and Messiah Jesus (Esth 3:6; Matt 2:13–16; Rev 12:4, 13).

The Chaldeans also underscored the fact that these three specific Jews had been given their positions by the king himself—"whom you have appointed over the administration of the province of Babylon."[199] They were probably trying to stress the fact that the king had been gracious to these Jews, so as to malign the three young men as being unappreciative and rebellious. Then three specific charges are brought against them (not all of which were true). First, the Chaldeans charged, "These men have not paid attention to you." From what we have observed thus far in the book, Daniel and these three young men had paid attention and shown the highest respect for the king (2:37, 49). They also sought to be obedient and respectful to others whom the king had appointed over them (e.g., 1:8, 12–13). So, this first charge was false. Yet from Nebuchadnezzar's perspective their refusal appeared differently, as Pace (100) has pointed out:

> The actions of the three young men of Dan. 3 threaten Nebuchadnezzar himself, for by not serving the deities that sanction his rule, give him prosperity, and protect his very life, they denigrate the king's royal standing. The author shows that for Nebuchadnezzar, their refusal is not only a religious act; it is a thoroughly political one—namely disloyalty to the state.

Goswell finds further reason in the words "*your* gods" why the loyalty of the three youths became suspect:

> The expression "they do not serve your gods" (instead of "our gods") also makes the king the target of their action; and their different religious affiliation from the king, like their foreign ethnicity ("certain Jews"), neither of which is normally a problem in the multi-ethnic and multi-religious empire of the Babylonians,

---

199. In the Aram. text, the verb "appoint" (מַנִּיתָ, *mannîṯā*) is in the 2nd person, masculine singular.

> becomes a further reason to suspect their loyalty. As noted by Fewell, the cleverly crafted speech "turns political betrayal into personal betrayal."[200]

As Christians, we are also commanded by Scripture to respect governing authorities. In Rom 13 we read,

> Let every person be subject to the governing authorities. For there is no authority except from God, and those that exist have been instituted by God. Therefore whoever resists the authorities resists what God has appointed, and those who resist will incur judgment. For rulers are not a terror to good conduct, but to bad. Would you have no fear of the one who is in authority? Then do what is good, and you will receive his approval, for he is God's servant for your good. (Rom 13:1–4, ESV)

Daniel and his three friends fulfilled this principle in their day.

The second and third charges, however, were true: "They do not serve [*worship*] your gods, nor do they prostrate themselves in homage to the statue of gold that you have erected." Although the charges were true, it was a case of obeying God rather than man (cf. Acts 4:19–20). God had specifically revealed his will in regard to this (Exod 20:1–5), so these three godly young men had to disobey the king.

Application and Devotional Implications

Even though it was true that the three young Jewish believers had not served the king's gods or worshiped his statue, they had actually obeyed Yahweh God. They had a pure heart in this particular situation and had acted righteously. As we reflect upon what happened, however, we should realize that their antagonists had not acted righteously. They were not accusing the Jewish youths because they wanted to defend Babylonian religion. That is, they were not motivated by a sincere zeal to defend the deities worshiped by Babylonians, nor the king's statue. This was only an excuse to land the Jewish youths in trouble.

The real motivation behind the accusers was the prejudice they had against these Jewish exiles, and this was fired by the envy they had toward them for being appointed to high positions in the king's administration. *Envy* drove them to commit harm against God's people. We should all learn a lesson here about the dangers of envy. The New Testament teaches us, "Let us not become conceited, provoking one another, envying one another" (Gal 5:26, ESV). Being envious of other people has no place in the Spirit-filled life, and if we are envying others, we are not filled with the Spirit.

---

200. Goswell, "The Ethics of the Book of Daniel," 135.

Additional Exegetical Comments

Regarding פְּלַח (*pᵊlaḥ*) in Dan 3:12:

According to BDB (1108c), Aramaic פְּלַח (*pᵊlaḥ*) means "to pay reverence to" or "to serve (deity)." *HALOT* (1957) indicates that *pᵊlaḥ* means "to serve God," and the substantival use (ptc.) means "servant, labourer." For the latter usage, see Ezra 7:24—those who were "servants of the house of God," i.e., the temple. A crucial exegetical question is whether *pᵊlaḥ* means more than simply serving or honoring. The corresponding word in BH (פָּלַח, *pālaḥ*) does not have a religious connotation.In BH פָּלַח (*pālaḥ*) means "to cut, slice, or cleave" (e.g., 2 Kgs 4:39) or "to plough (land)." The latter would have the idea of cleaving the soil (hence, ploughing), and so to cultivate a field (see for example, Ps 141:7). Isbell (*TWOT*, 1059) explains how the physical task of cleaving something open came to have a religious connotation:

> The original meaning of the root was "to cleave [open]" or "divide in two." From this meaning was derived the idea of cultivating a field and ultimately of cultivating (i.e. working hard at) the worship of a deity, hence the idea of service or worship of a deity. In Biblical Hebrew, the root is used only in the sense of cleave or split, and apparently did not develop into a term for religious service, as is the case in Aramaic.

Whether or not the religious connotation in Aramaic was merely an internal development is difficult to say. *HALOT* (1957) points out that there is an Akkadian word *palāḫu* meaning "to fear, respect, venerate" that could explain an etymological development in Aramaic. Certainly in later Talmudic Aramaic, the meaning of *pᵊlaḥ* as "worship" is clearly attested (e.g., *Sanh.* 102[b]; cf. Jastrow, 1178).

That *pᵊlaḥ* can mean *more than* "serve, honor," is demanded by the use of the same verb in Dan 3:17. There the three Hebrew youths declared to the king, "our God whom we worship (פָּלְחִין, *pālᵊḥîn*) is able to deliver us." They clearly were not trying to say that they were temple *servants* of Yahweh, seeing that they were in Babylon. Also, they were not merely affirming that they honored or paid reverence to Yahweh God. They undoubtedly meant they "worshiped" him, and this is confirmed by the following verse in which they boldly testified, "we will not worship (פָּלְחִין, *pālᵊḥîn*) your gods." Here they were speaking about the deities worshiped by the Babylonians, not the statue of gold itself.

In conclusion, פְּלַח (*pᵊlaḥ*) in biblical Aramaic does indeed have the connotation "to worship" a deity. The three Hebrew youths were being accused in 3:12 of two things: (1) of not *worshiping* the Babylonian deities; and (2) of not paying homage to the statue of gold. Almost all English Bibles translate פְּלַח (*pᵊlaḥ*) in 3:12 literally ("will not serve your gods"), but "serving a god" connotes the worship of it.

3. Nebuchadnezzar's angry interrogation of Daniel's three friends (3:13–18)

Textual Notes

13.a. If the passive verb הֵיתָיו is repointed to הַיְתִיו (active, as in Dan 5:3), this could be translated "they brought these men before the king" (so NET).

15.a. Though L (B19[A]) has דֵּי, several MS editions have דִּי (relative pron. "who").

15.b. Rather than the plural יְדָי in L ("my hands"), the editor proposes reading יְדִי ("my hand") as a few MSS have. Notice יְדָךְ in v. 17 (sg, "your hand"). However, both LXX[O] and LXX[θ] have the pl, χειρῶν μου ("my hands").

16.a-a. The MT reads לְמַלְכָּא נְבוּכַדְנֶצַּר, with an *ʾaṯnāḥ* separating the title from the name. *BHS* puts a note suggesting that the words be reversed, so as to avoid a discourteous address in speaking to the king by his name without his title (as NASB, "they said to the king, 'O Nebuchadnezzar …'"). Yet there is no need for the reversal, as the problem can be remedied by relocating the *ʾaṯnāḥ* after נְבוּכַדְנֶצַּר (so NET). We have the same construction לְמַלְכָּא נְבוּכַ־דְנֶצַּר in Dan 2:28 which is obviously read "King Nebuchadnezzar" (despite the occasional word order נְבוּכַדְנֶצַּר מַלְכָּא as in 3:1). But placing the *ʾaṯnāḥ* after וְאָמְרִין (so NIV) is unlikely, as this would have the vocative begin with the prep. לְ.

18.a. Instead of the Kethib לֵאלָהָיִךְ (pl. "to your gods"), the Qere is לֵאלָהָךְ (sg. "to your god") … similar to v. 12. Again, LXX[θ] (τοῖς θεοῖς) reflects the plural, and LXX[O] is singular but more interpretative: τῳ εἰδώλῳ, "to your idol."

Translation

3:13 Then Nebuchadnezzar in furious rage[201] commanded to bring Shadrach, Meshach, and Abednego *to him*.[202] Then these men were brought before the king. **14** Nebuchadnezzar said[203] to them, "Is it true,[204] Shadrach, Meshach,

---

201. Lit., "in anger and fury (or wrath)," בִּרְגַז וַחֲמָה (*birgaz waḥămâ*). This hendiadys could be rendered "in a furious rage" (so Goldingay, 64), or as the NET "in a fit of rage."

202. The words "to him" are not in the Aramaic text but are implied by the context.

203. Lit., "Nebuchadnezzar answered and said." The construction עָנֵה וְאָמַר (*ʿānēh wᵊʾāmar*) seems to be a common stylistic technique of the author without implying that both words be translated (note Dan 2:5, 8; 3:26).

204. BDB (1109c) gives the meaning of הַצְדָּא (*haṣdāʾ*) as "purpose," but *HALOT* (1963b) indicates צְדָא (*ṣᵊdāʾ*) means "truth." With the interrogative ה, the sense is "Is it true?" So Collins (177). LXX[O] rendered this διὰ τί (*dia ti*, "why?"), but LXX[θ]

and Abednego that you do not serve my gods or prostrate yourselves in homage to the statue of gold that I had set up? **15** Now if you are *indeed*[205] ready, when you hear the sound of the horn, flute, zither, trigon, string instrument, tambour, and all sorts of music, then you must fall down and do homage to the statue I made. But if you will not prostrate yourselves in homage, immediately you will be thrown into the midst of the furnace of blazing fire. And what god is there who can deliver you out of my hands?[206] **16** Shadrach, Meshach, and Abednego answered King Nebuchadnezzar, "We do not need to give you a reply[207] concerning this matter. **17** If our God whom we serve [*worship*] is able to deliver us,[208] from the furnace of burning fire and out of your hand, O king, He will deliver us. **18** But if not, let it be known to you, O king, that *indeed*[209] we will not serve [*worship*] your gods or prostrate ourselves to do homage to the statue of gold that you have set up."

Commentary

3:13–15 *Nebuchadnezzar's interrogation.* This whole scene begins with Nebuchadnezzar in a fit of "furious rage." He certainly is in no frame of mind to think clearly and make rational decisions. His temper is out of control, and he is filled with arrogance ("what god is there who can deliver you?"). Nebuchadnezzar was in a difficult situation himself. He had given a strict order and certainly expected no one to defy him. Although he had stipulated that the penalty would be death in the blazing hot furnace, this was probably

---

has εἰ ἀληθῶς (*ei alēthōs*, "is it true"). Other suggestions have been made (including a proposed Persian etymology connecting this with *ʾzd*). However, *ṣᵊḏāʾ* meaning "true" has been found on an ancient ostracon reported by M. Lidzbarski (see Montgomery, 207, for details).

205. Goldingay (66) indicates that the particle עֲתִידִין (*ʿăṯîḏîn*) in v. 15 indicates an emphatic sense. He translates (64), "If you are indeed now ready." Note the play on this in v. 18.

206. The Aramaic text literally says "from my hands," but hand is a metonymy for power. The exertion of one's power often emanates from the hand, and thus the hand is a symbol of one's power. It is perfectly acceptable to translate "from my power" (so NET).

207. The Aramaic is lit., "to return a word to you." The verb root is *tûḇ* ("return, go back"), which is equivalent to Hebrew *šûḇ*. In the Aram. Hapʿel stem, *tûḇ* means "give back, bring back, send back." When it is combined with *piṯgām* ("command, word, affair") as an object, however, *tûḇ* means "to answer" (as in Ezra 5:11).

208. Verse 17 is extremely difficult to translate, as witnessed by the great variation among the versions. For a more detailed analysis, see the discussion in the "Additional Exegetical Comments" section. Observe that the Masoretes placed an *ʾaṯnāḥ* following לְשֵׁיזָבוּתָנָא (*lᵉšêzāḇûṯanāʾ*), thereby breaking the initial conditional clause at that point (as the translation above reflects).

209. The particle אִיתַיְנָא (*ʾîṯayᵊnāʾ*) in v. 18 is emphatic, balancing the use of the particle עֲתִידִין (*ʿăṯîḏîn*) in v. 15 (see above).

hastily said so as to assert his authority. Now his authority was being put to the test. On the other hand, he could not possibly have forgotten the three young Jewish men that he had once found so superior to his own "wise men" (Dan 1:19–20) and whom he himself had appointed to high positions at Daniel's request (2:49). Rather than immediately killing them, the king gave them an opportunity to escape their fate of death. The king asked them if the charges of not serving his gods and doing homage to the statue of gold were true. He also gave them opportunity to comply by falling down and worshiping the statue when the music sounded again, once more asserting the penalty of death by severe burning.

At the end of v. 15, however, his arrogance emerges, "And what god is there who can deliver you out of my hands?" In saying this, he seems to have forgotten the encounter he so recently had with Daniel's God (chap. 2). Daniel had given the king an opportunity to understand that there was another god, the God of heaven, Yahweh Elohim, who could not only give the king a symbolic dream but could even reveal its interpretation to one of his prophets. Nebuchadnezzar had certainly realized that this God had done something more remarkable than what any of his Babylonian gods could have done. Yet it seems that he had not come to grips with the power of this God of heaven. Young (90) wisely remarks, "Had he paused to reflect, he would have realized that the God of the Jews was unlike his own deities, but rage does not reflect; instead, it threatens."

3:16–18 *The courage and faith of Daniel's three friends.* The first thing that the three said to Nebuchadnezzar was "We do not need to give you a reply concerning this matter." There was no denial of what they had done, nor was there any "excuse making" for what they had done. Neither was there any apology for what they had done. There was no need to do so. They had made a brave decision, and they were ready to stand behind their decision even if it meant the cost of their lives. Their words should not be construed as being disrespectful to the king, as they were simply being frank and firm. Furthermore, their reply is probably aimed at the king's final statement, i.e., they did not feel that they had to defend God's ability to deliver.[210]

Verse 17 has occasioned a great deal of diversity in translation and interpretation (see the section on "Additional Exegetical Comments"). Though this is undoubtedly a conditional statement about what God is able to do,

---

210. R. L. Heller, "'But if not …' *What*? The Speech of the Youths in Daniel 3 and a (Theo)logical Problem," in *Thus Says the Lord: Essays on the Former and Latter Prophets in Honor of Robert R. Wilson*, ed. J. J. Ahn and S. L. Cook, 244–55 (London: T & T Clark, 2009), 248, understands דְּנָה פִּתְגָם (*dᵊnâ pitgām*)—which he translates as "this decree"—to refer to the king's indictment against them, though Collins (187) as the offer of reprieve. Yet Goldingay (71) thinks it is the king's rhetorical question to which they refer in light of their following words, since they do respond to the offer of reprieve in v. 18 (so Newsom, 110).

we should not think that they were questioning God's *power* (as though he might lack the power to deliver them). In fact, the end of v. 17 indicates their affirmation of God's ability to deliver them. Their statement—couched in a conditional clause, just as the king had done in v. 15 with them—was a clear rebuttal to the king's own claim. The king claimed no god could deliver (*šêzib̲*) them "from my hands" (*min yᵊd̲āy*), but they bravely asserted that their God could deliver (*šêzib̲*) them "from your [the king's] hand" (*min yᵊd̲āk̲*). Coxon concludes,

> The confession mirrors the faith of the Confessors. If their God is able to save, all well and good, but even if it proved impossible for Him to intervene on their behalf they would still refuse to commit idolatry. At all costs they intend to respect the commandment against idolatry.[211]

Since they did not know what Yahweh Elohim might do in their case, they went on to say in v. 18 that even if God should choose not to deliver them, they would remain faithful to him and not serve Nebuchadnezzar's gods or give homage to his statue.

Application and Devotional Implications

For three young believers so far away from their homeland, Daniel's three friends displayed remarkable courage and faith before Nebuchadnezzar, the most powerful man on earth at that time. They well knew the king would have no hesitation about committing them to the burning furnace. Yet they were prepared to die, if necessary, for the sake of being faithful to the one true God of heaven. They had given up their right to life, and they were focused on trying to obey and please their Lord (cf. Acts 20:22–24).

In an interesting article revealing how the Dan 3 story was utilized in the early church, W. D. Tucker has demonstrated the difference in how it was preached before Constantine's conversion to Christianity (AD 312) as compared to afterwards.[212] Prior to Constantine's conversion, imperial intolerance of Christianity had led to massive persecution, including burnings, beheadings, and being thrown to the lions (especially with Septimus's edict in AD 202 outlawing conversion to Christianity). Hence representative examples before AD 312 (e.g., Hippolytus and Origen) developed a martyrdom theology of what it meant to be faithful under imperial persecution. Witness Origen's *Exhortation to Martyrdom* in AD 235, following which, in

---

211. P. Coxon, "Daniel 3:17: A Linguistic and Theological Problem," *VT* 26 (1976): 408.

212. W. D. Tucker, "The Early *Wirkungsgeschichte* of Daniel 3: Representative Examples," *JTI* 6 (2012): 295–306. For other examples of Dan 3 in the NT and early Christian literature, see J. W. van Henten, "Daniel 3 and 6 in Early Christian Literature," in *The Book of Daniel: Composition and Reception,* ed. J. J. Collins and P. W. Flint, 1:149–69 (Leiden: Brill, 2001).

AD 253, Valerian ordered all Christian clergy to sacrifice to the Roman gods and subsequently issued an edict that failure to do so would be punishable by death. This all changed once Christianity became the empire's official religion. Hence, before AD 312, preaching focused on political loyalties (and disloyalties) and one's willingness to die for Christ, whereas after this date preaching shifted to a focus—emulating that of the three faithful Hebrew youths—on individual piety and the pursuit of virtue.

Yet the courage and bravery of these three young men is not the only lesson we learn from this episode. We should also reflect on their understanding of God's will as they made their decision. They knew that their God could intervene to deliver his people, if he chose to do so. The exodus event, when the Hebrews came out of Egypt, supremely demonstrated this. Yet, they also realized that God does not always choose to deliver his people, and even when we (as believers) do not know what God might do for us, we must stand ready to do our part and be faithful to him. Elsewhere, the Bible clearly teaches that God may allow his own children (who are so precious to him) to be martyred for his sake. Jesus comforted his disciples whom he prepared for suffering with these words:

> And do not fear those who kill the body but cannot kill the soul. Rather fear him who can destroy both soul and body in hell. Are not two sparrows sold for a penny? And not one of them will fall to the ground apart from your Father. But even the hairs of your head are all numbered. Fear not, therefore; you are of more value than many sparrows. (Matt 10:28–31, ESV)

God is free in his sovereignty to decide as he pleases, and he is under no obligation to prove that to anyone. Whether he chooses to demonstrate that or not, our role is to be obedient and accept the outcome. One thing we can be sure of: he is a loving God, he knows every possible fact by which to base his decisions, and he will do what is perfectly wise. We might not understand his ways (now), but we can trust him by faith.

In Acts 12 the Lord allowed James to be slain but miraculously caused Peter to be freed from jail. The Lord could have caused both brothers to have been freed, but he did not. As we mature in the Christian life, we realize that we will often not know what the Lord is going to do for us nor why he chooses to do what he does. Part of growing in maturity involves learning to trust him when we do not know.

Additional Exegetical Comments

Verse 17 is extremely difficult to understand and to translate.[213] The following is a sample of various proposals:

---

213. For a more detailed and technical discussion, see Coxon, "Daniel 3:17," 400–409.

> NASB: "If it be *so,* our God whom we serve is able to deliver us from the furnace of blazing fire"
>
> NIV: "If we are thrown into the blazing furnace, the God we serve is able to save us from it"
>
> NET: "If our God whom we are serving exists, he is able to deliver us from the furnace of blazing fire"
>
> NJPS: "for if so it must be, our God whom we serve is able to save us from the burning fiery furnace"
>
> Goldingay (64): "If our God, whom we honor, exists, he is able to rescue us from the red-hot blazing furnace"
>
> Collins (177): "If our God, whom we worship, is able to save us, he will save us from the furnace of fire"

The proposal by Collins probably comes the closest to a literal translation. However, it obviously raises a theological problem. Were the Jewish youths uncertain of God's ability to save (i.e., deliver) them that they would say "<u>If</u> our God is able to save us"? The Greek translations tried to alleviate the difficulty by avoiding the conditional element altogether:

> LXX$^{\theta}$: ἔστιν γὰρ θεός, ᾧ ἡμεῖς λατρεύομεν, δυνατὸς ἐξελέσθαι ἡμᾶς
> *estin gar theos, hō hēmeis latreuomen, dunatos exelesthai hēmas*
> "For there is a God, whom we serve, able ... "
>
> LXX^{O}: ἔστι γὰρ θεὸς ἐν οὐρανοῖς εἷς κύριος ἡμῶν, ὃν φοβούμεθα, ὅς ἐστι δυνατὸς
> *esti gar theos en ouravois heis kurios hēmōn, hon phoboumetha, hos esti duvatos*
> "For there is a God in heaven, our one Lord, whom we fear, who is able ... "

In the Aramaic text, however, there is certainly a conditional clause initiated by the particle הֵן (*hēn*, "if"), because it is used again at the beginning of v. 18 as the alternative condition: "But if (*hēn*) not .... " Jerome (Latin *Vulgate*) tried to escape the difficulty by emending the text from *hēn* to *hā* ʾ, the latter being equivalent to the Hebrew *hinnēh* ("Behold!")—thus, "Behold, our God is able to save us." But there is no textual support for this, and it faces the same problem of the presence of *hēn* at the beginning of v. 18. So, we must understand this as a true conditional statement.

In solving the problem, we need to examine the combination of the first two words of v. 17, הֵן אִיתַי, *hēn ʾîṯay*. This phrase occurs here and also in v. 15 and Ezra 5:17. The case in Ezra 5:17 is not exactly parallel, because it is immediately followed by the particle *dî*, and thus translated "if it be <u>that</u> ..."[214]

214. For a more technical discussion against the view that *hēn ʾîṯay* contains the whole protasis within itself ("if it be so"), see Coxon, "Daniel 3:17," 404.

The case in Dan 3:15 is more helpful, as the pronominal subject on אִיתַי (*ʾîṯay*), namely אִיתֵיכוֹן (*ʾîṯêḵôn*), indicates that the subject of the condition follows, and then a subsequent word (in this case, an adjective) completes the thought—thus, "now if you are ready." This is parallel in structure to v. 17, except the latter verse does not have an adjective completing the thought, but rather a participle.

Further help is provided by examining the Hebrew equivalent, *ʾim yēš*, which occurs twenty-one times in the OT. In some cases this can be rendered "if there is," but only when no subject of the conditional clause is expressed (e.g., Prov 23:18; Job 33:23; Jer 5:1; Lam 1:12; and Ps 7:4). But Dan 3:17 does have an expressed subject, and hence this is not a suitable parallel.

In several verses, however, we do find *ʾim yēš* followed by a subject, and then subsequently by a participle—the same structure as Dan 3:17 (see Gen 24:42, 49; 43:4; and Judg 6:36). In these cases, *yēš* serves as an equative verb, the participle completes the thought, and the subject after *ʾim yēš* is the one doing the action. This would lead to the conclusion that Dan 3:17 should be translated:

> If our God whom we serve is able to deliver us, from the furnace of burning fire and out of your hand, O king, He will deliver us. But if not, let it be known ...[215]

Finally, in the Aramaic text, the words and syntax used by the youths echo the words and syntax that had been used by the king in v. 15. In that earlier verse, the king had used הֵן אִיתַי, (*hēn ʾîṯay*) followed by an action (be "ready"), and had concluded his thought with the verb *šêzib̲* ("save, deliver") combined with *min yᵊd̲āy* ("out of my power"). Hence, their choice of words was purposely formulated to echo the king's own words. Once we recognize this, we realize *why* they are using the words they do in v. 17; we must not try to understand the statement in isolation but rather see it in light of the preceding context. Thus, they are not questioning God's ability to save/deliver them. It is the king who thinks there is no one able to deliver them

215. The footnote to the NET objects to this translation on the basis of the short relative clause ("whom we serve") standing between the verb "is" and the completing construction "able to deliver." However, the subject itself ("our God") stands between the two, thus revealing that this is really no problem. The relative clause simply modifies "God," and this is the logical place (in Aramaic) to place it. Coxon, "Daniel 3:17," also argues for this translation and shows that the syntactical construction has an emphatic function here to give prominence to the subject. Though the separation of *ʾîṯay* from the participle is unusual, he counters (406), "First a comparative study of *ʾîṯay* reveals that while the structure is an unusual one, examples may be found where it is separated from its participle by intervening words" (citing in defense Targum Deut 29:4 and Aḥiqar, i 159). He also demonstrates a parallel in Akkadian usage. Lucas, "A Statue, a Fiery Furnace and a Dismal Swamp," 292, comes to a similar conclusion as is reflected in my translation.

from his power. The youths know that he is greatly mistaken, but they couch their words in a form similar to his, so that their response parallels the way he had put his demand to them. The conditional element, however, is only for the purpose of making a fitting response to the king and clarifying that they will not bend the knee to his statue or serve his gods. The issue in Dan 3:17 is not a matter of whether God exists or not (as the NET and Goldingay suggest), nor a matter of whether or not they will be thrown into the furnace (as the NIV suggests).[216]

4. Nebuchadnezzar's wrathful order to throw the three into the furnace (3:19–23)

Textual Notes

19.a. MT has 3mp form אֶשְׁתַּנּוּ, but the Qere reads אֶשְׁתַּנִּי (sg.) in concord with sg. צְלֵם.

21.a-a. LXX^{O} and LXX$^{\theta}$ list only three garments in contrast to four in MT.

21.b. The Qere reading is פַּטְּשֵׁיהוֹן (as well as Strack's ed. and a few MSS).

22.a-a. These words are lacking in LXX^{O} and LXX$^{\theta}$.

23.a. The LXX tradition inserts additional deuterocanonical material at this point, namely the Prayer of Azariah, a description of the furnace heated and the descent of the Angel of Yahweh, and finally the Song of Praise. These additional texts comprise sixty-eight verses (see Collins, 195, for translation and textual comments).

Translation

3:19 Then Nebuchadnezzar was filled with rage, and his facial expression[217]

---

216. In contrast to the interpretation taken here, Heller, "'But if not …' *What?*," 245–55, in a technical discussion presenting the various translation options for the protasis and apodosis clauses of vv. 17–18, concludes that the subject of the negated protasis of the second clause is the proposed ultimatum and threat of the youths' execution itself (see esp. 252). Heller attempts to argue against what he perceives to be logical and theological problems with alternative interpretations, yet he fails to consider how the response of the youths is deliberately cast in similar wording to that of Nebuchadnezzar himself.

217. Lit., "the expression of his face was altered." The word translated "expression" is צְלֵם (*ṣᵊlēm*, "statue, image"), used elsewhere in the chapter for the statue (of gold). So we have a wordplay: Nebuchadnezzar's image/statue was brilliantly golden, but the image of his face was distraught, reflecting his rage within.

was changed toward Shadrach, Meshach, and Abednego. He gave orders[218] to heat up the furnace seven times more than what was customary[219] to heat it. **20** He ordered some of the strongest men[220] in his army to bind Shadrach, Meshach, and Abednego for casting *them* into the furnace of blazing fire. **21** Then these men were bound with their trousers,[221] their coats,[222] their caps,[223] and their *other* garments, and they were cast into the midst of the furnace of blazing fire. **22** Therefore, because the command[224] of the king was so urgent[225]

---

218. עָנֵה וְאָמְרִין, *ʿānô wᵊʾāmᵊrîn* (lit., "he answered and said"), a common idiom in Daniel meaning "he spoke up and said" (see note at 3:9), but the present context is one of speaking a command. Hence, "he gave orders."

219. חֲזֵה, *ḥăzēh* ("see, behold") as a pass. ptc. has the sense of "seemly," hence "appropriate." *HALOT* (1872c) suggests "proper, customary."

220. The words "some of the strongest men" is an attempt to render לְגֻבְרִין גִּבָּרֵי־חַיִל (*lᵊgubrîn gibbārê-ḥayil*), lit., "to men, mighty of strength." In BH, גִּבּוֹרֵי הַחַיִל (*gibbôrê haḥayil*) means "mighty men of valor" (or valiant warriors). See Josh 1:14; 2 Kgs 24:14. LXX^{O} rendered these words ἄνδρας ἰσχυροτάτους (*andras ischurotatous*), "very strong men." Goldingay (66) discusses the superlative construction, rendering this "the strongest men in his army."

221. The exact meaning of the articles of clothing mentioned here is rather uncertain. They are foreign loanwords, though their exact origin is not known (possibly Persian). For example, the first term, סַרְבָּלֵיהוֹן (*sarbālêhôn*, translated "their mantles" by the NET) may mean either a type of coat, or long baggy oriental trousers (like a type of Persian pantaloon). The meaning "mantle" is supported by Talmudic and targumic usage, as well as by Rashi and Ibn Ezra. On the other hand, the meaning "trousers" is supported by LXX$^{\theta}$, Vg., and Symmachus. The LXX^{O} translated it ὑποδήματα (*hupodēmata*), a sandal or type of boot. Regarding LXX$^{\theta}$'s σαραβαροις (*sarabarois*), Collins (188) points out that σαραβαρα (*sarabara*) were "loose trousers worn by the Scythians in the work of fourth-century B.C.E. comic poet Antiphanes (201)." The NASB, as well as Goldingay (66) and Collins (177), translates סַרְבָּלֵיהוֹן (*sarbālêhôn*), "their trousers."

222. The meaning of פַּטִּישֵׁיהוֹן, *paṭṭîšêhôn* (Qere פַּטְּשֵׁיהוֹן, *paṭṭᵊšêhôn*), is also uncertain. The NIV and NET render as "trousers," and NASB as "coats." Neither LXX^{O} nor LXX$^{\theta}$ render it at all (they have only three items, not four). *HALOT* (1956b), though noting that פְּטִישָׁא (*pᵊṭîšāʾ*) means "trousers" in Jewish Aramaic (see Jastrow, 1155), refrains from giving a lexical definition and admits the meaning cannot be identified. Goldingay (64) simply transliterates, "pattishin."

223. כַּרְבְּלָתְהוֹן (*karbᵊlātᵊhôn*), thought to be a loanword from Akkadian, is translated "turbans" by NET and NIV. *HALOT* (1901–2) has "caps" but notes that this head-dress is probably a particular type of cap. Both LXX^{O} and LXX$^{\theta}$ translated this by the Greek word τιάρα (*tiara*), a particular type of Persian head-dress (LSJM, 1789).

224. Lit., "word" (Heb מִלָּה, *millâ*). Coming from the king, however, it is authoritative.

225. See textual note to Dan 2:15. The term *ḥăṣap* can also mean "harsh" (so *HALOT*, 1879d).

and the furnace was heated so excessively,[226] *as for* these men who brought up Shadrach, Meshach, and Abednego, the flame of the fire slew them. **23** Yet these three men, Shadrach, Meshach, and Abednego, fell into the midst of the furnace of blazing fire all bound up.[227]

Commentary

3:19–20 *The king's furious reaction*. Even in chap. 2 we had seen Nebuchadnezzar as a man prone to anger and often reacting irrationally (recall 2:12–13). He was angry upon hearing of the insubordination of the three Hebrew youths (3:13), and now in 3:19 we see his anger totally out of control over their refusal to serve his gods or give homage to the image.[228] His whole facial expression reflected his extreme anger (see textual note to v. 19). There is a wordplay in the Aramaic text. The three youths would not change their mind about worshiping his statue/image (Aram. *ṣᵊlēm*), and as a result the "expression" (lit. "image," Aram. *ṣᵊlēm*) of Nebuchadnezzar's face was changed. Wood (90) captures the emotions that flared:

> Prior to that moment, he had displayed a face apparently of interest, ready to pardon these men, if they could present a proper defense; but now he reddened in his wrath. High emotion may be imagined flashing from his eyes, as he thundered horrifying orders, now to be noted.

As a result, the king ordered the furnace heated *seven times* above what was customary. This may have been some type of proverbial expression (cf. Prov 24:16; 26:16) or idiomatic expression (= "as hot as possible") or simply hyperbole.[229] In any case, the furnace was now far hotter than necessary to burn someone alive.

---

226. According to RJ (88), the adj. יַתִּירָא (*yattîrāʾ*) is used adverbially, meaning "excessively." He notes, "the ending *–ā*, mostly unstressed, the remnant of an ancient accusative ending, used adverbially."

227. Lit., "being bound" (מְכַפְּתִין [*mᵊkappᵊṯîn*], a Paʿel pass. ptc. of כְּפַת, *kᵊpaṯ*).

228. Coxon (see "Nebuchadnezzar's Hermeneutical Dilemma," 87–97) attempts to present a more sympathetic assessment of Nebuchadnezzar, who as the Babylonian "king of justice," had an obligation to see that justice prevailed according to the accepted law code of Babylonia. Coxon sees more of the villainy found in the conniving Chaldeans that set up the three Jewish youths than in Nebuchadnezzar who in the final analysis becomes their deliverer. He asserts (96), "In Daniel 3 Nebuchadnezzar is inveigled by the clever dispositions of 'certain Chaldaeans' into the unenviable position of judging Shadrach, Meshach and Abednego for forthright blasphemy and *lèse-majesté*."

229. In defense of the notion that "seven times hotter" cannot be taken literally, see Baukal, "The Fiery Furnace," 162–64. Baukal has calculated that a temperature of this magnitude would be equal to that of the sun's surface.

3:21–23 *The three youths cast into the furnace.* The soldiers chosen to carry out the execution were not just average troops. The Aramaic text suggests that these were some of the bravest and strongest of the king's "valiant warriors" (see textual note to v. 21). It may not have been necessary to have men of this caliber to bind and throw the Hebrews into the furnace, but they certainly provide a stark contrast in the story: the fire of the furnace does no harm to the Hebrew youths who are bound, whereas Babylon's "crack troops" are destroyed by the fire without being bound and without even entering the furnace. Several times the text reminds us that the three Hebrews were "bound" (vv. 20, 21, 23 and 24), assuring us that they were unable to save themselves.

As they went into the blazing furnace, they did so still fully clothed. The terms for their clothing are of uncertain meaning (see textual notes above on v. 21) but seem to have included their outer attire, headgear, and other articles of clothing. The text mentions these because such garments would normally have caught fire immediately (this will highlight the miraculous nature of the event). The satirical aspect magnifies God's power to deliver his servants. As Nel has observed:

> The king's reaction is dominated by the references to the fiery furnace, with the fire symbolizing the king's fury and rage ... The furnace is red-hot (vv. 20, 21, 23, 26) but the fire does not consume the Jews (vv. 24, 25, 26, 27). The clothing of the three Jews is described in an alliterative list while the bounding of them is described in verses 20, 21, 23 and 24, in contrast to their being unbound (v. 25), indicating that the king's will is not done even though he tries his very best ... The scene creates an atmosphere of absurdity and humour.[230]

The urgency of the king's command and the exceedingly hot furnace were a dangerous combination. Perhaps in their haste to obey the king's urgent command, they did not take proper precautions in approaching the furnace. As a result, the men who brought up those to be punished were actually slain by the flames themselves (v. 22). Apparently, they had to get very close to the furnace door in order to push the Hebrews in (which they succeeded in doing), but they underestimated the danger of the flames (not being accustomed to having the furnace heated this hot). Although we don't have a detailed description of the type of furnace that was being used, it apparently had some type of door near the top, because the text indicates that the three Hebrew youths "fell" (נְפַלוּ, *nᵊpalû*) into the midst of the furnace (v. 23). Perhaps when the soldiers opened the upper door the flames shot out and killed them as they pushed the Hebrews in. Then the three Hebrews fell to the lower part of the furnace. The last word of v. 23 (*mᵊkappᵊtîn*, "being

230. Nel, "Daniel 3 as Satirical Comedy," 225.

bound") reminds us that they were still securely tied up as they fell inside the furnace, and thus unable to do anything to deliver themselves.

Following v. 23 the Greek versions add material not found in the Aramaic text of Daniel. While this material is interesting, it should not be regarded as "Scripture," being additions that were made subsequent to the original writing of Daniel. Wood (92) summarizes the nature of this material:

> At this point the Septuagint version inserts extra information, which is commonly and correctly taken to be apocryphal. Included first is a prayer of one of the young men, Azariah, covering twenty-two verses, which expresses praise to God and requests deliverance from, and punishment upon, Israel's enemies. Then follow six verses of description which tell of the special heating of the furnace and the descent of the Angel of the Lord, who "smote the flame of the fire out of the oven, and made the midst of the furnace as though a wind of dew had gone hissing through it." Finally a song rendered by the three from the furnace occupies forty verses. This is a song of praise for the deliverance effected by the Angel.

Application and Devotional Implications

Anger is not an easy thing to control, even for believers indwelt by the Spirit of God. Not all anger is sin (cf. Eph 4:26), but anger that results from the "flesh" is sinful and wrong. In Nebuchadnezzar's case, his anger was totally out of control (which probably was not rare for Assyrian/Babylonian kings). He had probably come to rely on anger (and harsh, merciless actions) as the way of getting the results he wanted. Unfortunately for him, he was the one who suffered. As is often the case, he probably ran high blood pressure and found little inner peace. Furthermore, operating angrily inevitably led to poor decisions and foolish actions. Walvoord (90) writes,

> ... he lost his temper! That is always the mark of a little man. His furnace was hot, but he himself got hotter! And when a man gets full of fury, he gets full of folly. There is no fool on earth like a man who has lost his temper.

There is a principle here for us to live by: For a wise man, there is greater value in self-control than in conquest (cf. Prov 16:32; Jas 3:2). Anger turns men into fools, but this sinful bad habit needs to be (and can be) brought under the control of the Holy Spirit.

5. God's divine protection upon the three in the furnace (3:24–27)

Textual Notes

26.a. The Kethib reading is עִלָּיָא, but the Qere is עִלָּאָה. Same situation in Dan 3:32; 5:18, 21.

Translation

3:24 Then King Nebuchadnezzar was startled[231] and hastily[232] arose. He spoke up to his ministers,[233] "Were not three men cast into the midst of the fire, all bound up?"[234] They replied to the king, "Certainly, O king." **25** He exclaimed, "Behold I see four men loosed and walking about in the midst of the fire, unharmed.[235] The appearance of the fourth is like a son of the gods."[236] **26** Then Nebuchadnezzar approached the door of the furnace of blazing fire. He called out, "Shadrach, Meshach, and Abednego, servants of the Most High God, come out! Come here!" Then Shadrach, Meshach, and Abednego, came forth from the midst of the fire. **27** The satraps, prefects, governors, and ministers of the king gathered around and saw these men, that the fire had no power over their bodies, nor had the hair of their heads been singed, nor had their trousers[237] been affected.[238] Not even the smell of fire remained[239] on them.

---

231. The word translated "startled" (תְּוַהּ, *tᵊwah*) means not only to be "startled, amazed" but also has the element of *fear* to it (so Goldingay, 66). *HALOT* (2005) adds that the word also includes the nuances of "horrified" or "frightened." In Jewish Aramaic, we find תְּהְוָא (*tihwāʾ*), meaning "anxiety, fear, horror." BDB's "be startled, alarmed" (1117d) remains a good lexical choice. Compare NIV "in amazement" and NASB "was astounded."

232. "Hastily" is an attempt to smoothly render the inf. const. בְּהִתְבְּהָלָה (*bᵊhitbᵊhālâ*). See the use of this word in Dan 2:25.

233. The translation "ministers" may suffice (so NET), although the exact meaning of הַדָּבַר (*haddābar*) is uncertain (NIV gives "advisors" and NASB "high officials"). It is perhaps a Persian loanword, and *HALOT* (1857) gives the meanings "high-ranking royal officials, state counselors." This word did not appear in the list of officials in Dan 3:2, but it does appear in v. 27 alongside other top-ranking rulers of the land. Its placement in the list of v. 27, however, suggests that it is not a *general* category, but a specific office of high rank. It apparently was not clear to the Greek translators. LXX$^{\theta}$ translated it μεγιστᾶσιν, *megistasin* ("great men"), and LXX^{O} translated it φίλοις, *philois* ("friends, dear ones"). Recall v. 2, where the word אֲדַרְגָּזַר (*ʾădargāzar*) was translated "counselors" (NIV, "advisors").

234. For "bound up," see comments at 3:23.

235. The translation "unharmed" is lit., "and injury there was not on them" (וַחֲבָל לָא־אִיתַי בְּהוֹן, *waḥăbāl lāʾ-ʾîtay bᵊhôn*).

236. The Aramaic text is דָּמֵה לְבַר־אֱלָהִין, *dāmēh lᵊbar ʾĕlāhîn*, "like a son of (the) gods" (so NIV and NASB). The KJV rendered this (wrongly) "the Son of God." Coming from the lips of a polytheistic pagan king, it probably had the meaning "like a divine being." See further discussion in the commentary.

237. See comments at 3:21 regarding סָרְבָּלֵיהוֹן (*sārᵊbālêhôn*).

238. Lit., "been changed" (Peʿal perf of שְׁנָא, *šᵊnāʾ*).

239. Lit., "the smell of fire had not passed [עֲדָא, *ʿădāʾ*, 'pass on, pass away'] on them."

Commentary

3:24–26a *Nebuchadnezzar's horrified response.* Apparently the furnace must have had some type of door at the lower portion (in addition to the upper opening), because the king and his cohorts were able to see inside. What the king saw was not only amazing, but even frightening.[240] Not only were the Hebrews alive and unbound, but there were also now four individuals in the blazing fire. To make sure he had not overlooked something, the king asked his "ministers" to confirm that only three men had been thrown into the fire, and they quickly affirmed this was so. There had been no mistake about the number of men put into the furnace. With the furnace as hot as it was, one would have expected the bodies to have charred and been consumed rather quickly. Instead the king saw (v. 25) the four men unbound and even walking about in the midst of the fire, totally unharmed. The miracle, however, was more than the fact that the fire did not kill them. Baukal points out,

> Shadrach, Meshach, and Abednego were not only saved from the conflagration, but also from asphyxiation, CO poisoning, and possibly from other toxic fumes generated during the combustion process. This further heightens the magnitude of this spectacular miracle.[241]

One can only imagine the exhilarating feeling that the Hebrew youths must have had as they walked about in the fire without being harmed, for surely they were conscious and aware of what was taking place—not to mention any conversation they might have had with the fourth individual.

But who was the fourth individual? Obviously he was not an ordinary human being, though he may have appeared in human form to them. The older KJV had "the Son of God."[242] Newer translations like the NIV and NASB, however, have "a son of the gods." The issue is not merely a christological one—whether he was the preincarnate Christ or not—but a matter of whether Nebuchadnezzar recognized him as the Messiah, Son of God. Coming from the lips of a polytheistic pagan king, it is doubtful that Nebuchadnezzar would have recognized him this way. Linguistically, however, the translation "Son of God" is inaccurate.[243] The Aramaic should be

---

240. See translation note above at v. 24 regarding the meaning of "startled" (Aram. *tᵉwah*).

241. Baukal, "The Fiery Furnace," 170.

242. The NKJV retains the translation "Son of God," but adds a footnote, "Or, a son of the gods."

243. The translation "Son of God" would be *bar ʾĕlāhāʾ* in Aramaic (having the singular form of "god"), but our text has *bar ʾĕlāhîn* (with the plural form "gods"). In Hebrew, the plural form *ʾĕlōhîm* can mean either "God" or "gods," but the same phenomenon does not hold true in Aramaic (especially in Daniel). Normally in the Aramaic section of Daniel, if "God" is meant, we find the singular form (as in 3:26 with *ʾĕlāhāʾ*—cf. the singular form of God in vv. 28 and 29). We could also compare

translated "like a son of the gods," probably meaning that Nebuchadnezzar took him to be some kind of divine being without really grasping who or what he was. That Nebuchadnezzar calls him a *mal'aḵ* in v. 28 (normally translated "angel") does not necessarily prove that the king took him to be an "angel." Montgomery notes, "Also the term 'angel' was appropriate to common WSem. diction as expressing an appearance-form of Deity."[244]

Jewish tradition has typically taken the fourth individual to be an "angel," and the Talmud even asserted that it was the archangel Gabriel (*Pes.* 118a,b).[245] In the preponderance of Christian tradition, however, the fourth individual has been understood as none other than the preincarnate Lord Jesus Christ.[246] Collins (190) comments regarding Hippolytus, who is believed to have written one of the earliest commentaries on Daniel: "Hippolytus wonders how Nebuchadnezzar recognized him and saw here a prefiguration of the recognition of Christ as Son of God by the Gentiles." In the book of Daniel we find both angels and Messiah referred to (assuming, for instance, that "one like a son of man" in Dan 7:13 is a Messianic prophecy).

Rather than being just a "mighty angel," the fourth individual could be more specifically "the Angel of Yahweh" mentioned elsewhere in the Old Testament, and thus we have a theophany here in v. 25.[247] This could lead to the conclusion that the fourth individual was God himself, appearing in human form.[248] More specifically, it is possible that Jesus Christ (who has always existed) would appear at times prior to his incarnation at Bethlehem as "the Angel of Yahweh" (cf. Josh 5:13–15). If this is Christ appearing in Dan 3:25, then we might want to refer to this more specifically as a Christophany.

Even if the fourth individual is not "the Angel of Yahweh," it is still possible to regard this as an Old Testament appearance of the preincarnate

---

2:47 when Nebuchadnezzar proclaimed, "Your God (singular *'ĕlāhăḵôn*) is a god (singular *'ĕlāh*) of gods (plural *'ĕlāhîn*)."

244. Montgomery, 214. The LXX^{O} may have followed the "angel" interpretation, as they rendered *ḇar 'ĕlāhîn* by the Greek *angelou theou* ("angel of God").

245. Note that Gabriel appears in the book of Daniel at 8:16 and again at 9:21.

246. LXX$^{\theta}$ translated the Aramaic into Greek as ὁμοία υἱῷ θεοῦ (*homoia huiōi theou*), "like the son of God." (Note the use of the singular "God" by LXX$^{\theta}$.) In early church history there were exceptions to the christological interpretation. P. J. Botha, "The Interpretation of Daniel 3 in the Syriac Commentary Ascribed to Ephrem the Syrian," *AcPB* 16 (2005): 41–42, in his study of the commentary attributed to Ephrem the Syrian, points out that the author understood the fourth individual as one of the persons of the Trinity, but most likely the Holy Spirit.

247. A "theophany" is a visible manifestation of God during the Old Testament period.

248. W. Broomall, "Theophany," in *Baker's Dictionary of Theology*, 520, points out that the deity of this unique angel is proved by the fact that he (1) is identified as God (Gen 16:7,13); (2) is recognized as God (Judg 6:22–24); (3) is described in terms befitting the deity alone (Josh 5:15 cf. Exod 3:2–6); (4) calls himself God (Gen 31:11–13); and (5) speaks with divine authority (Judg 2:1–5).

Christ. The Lord Jesus Christ was certainly active prior to his incarnation. A common point in both John 1:1–3 and Col 1:16–17 is that Christ was directly involved in creation; indeed "all things have been created by (or through) him." So there is no logical reason why he could not have been the one to appear with the three youths in the furnace (cf. 1 Cor 10:4).

In conclusion, the fourth individual in the furnace was probably understood by Nebuchadnezzar to be some type of *divine being* (whose true identity he did not recognize), and v. 25 should be translated "like a son of *the* gods." There is a high probability, however, that this individual was none other than the preincarnate Christ. Feinberg (47) wisely remarked, "Whenever His children are in the fiery furnace of trials for His name's sake, He is there. Christ never sends forth His sheep unless He goes on before them."

Astounded by what he saw, the king moved closer for a better look (v. 26). Then he called out to the three youths to come out, addressing them as "servants of the Most High God."[249] Though this was a very honorable way to refer to them (and to their God), this does not mean Nebuchadnezzar had had some type of conversion. Young (95) points out that Greeks referred to Zeus as "the Most High." We should also recall Dan 2:47 where the king told Daniel that his God was a "god of gods." It probably does indicate that the king viewed the true God of heaven in an exalted way and as someone quite special. Walvoord (92) remarks, "Nebuchadnezzar was not disavowing his own deities but merely recognizing on the basis of the tremendous miracle which had been performed that the God of Israel was higher."

3:26b–27 *The emergence from the furnace.* Just imagine how it must have appeared to everyone to see the three Hebrews emerging from this blazing furnace looking quite normal (but with smiles on their faces). Nebuchadnezzar was not the only witness to this miracle, for the text tells us that the highest rulers and officials of the empire were there as witnesses. Nel comments on the satirical nature of this moment:

> The officials inspect the three's bodies and hair, clothes and smell (v. 27b). It is as though they have to make absolutely certain that the men are unharmed, a humorous picture as if the officials are examining the Jews for lice.[250]

For those who were not there on that day or who could not have been close enough to observe what happened, they would have received a highly credible report about the miracle, coming as it was from such astute dignitaries. Three crucial observations were noted: (1) their bodies had been unharmed—not even the hair on their head was singed; (2) their *sarbālêhôn*

---

249. The Aram. for "God most high" is אֱלָהָא עִלָּיָא, *'ĕlāhā' 'illāyā'* (comparable to Heb. *'ēl 'elyôn* in Gen 14:20).

250. Nel, "Daniel 3 as Satirical Comedy," 225–26.

(סַרְבָּלֵיהוֹן, "their trousers")[251] had not been damaged—implying that the rest of their clothing was undamaged; and (3) they did not even have the smell of smoke on them. There was no way to account for this other than that a divine miracle had occurred. Furthermore, Nebuchadnezzar's presumptuousness about his kingdom glory has been corrected and his ego deflated to a point of realizing the greatness of the sovereignty of the Hebrews' God. Nel remarks,

> What initial readers would have heard is that heathen kings are not as all-powerful as they (and their subjects) think, but that they are subject to the authority of the Jews' God. The tale is humorous in order to demonstrate the foolishness of a heathen king in thinking that he can decide about the fate of God's people, the Jews. They would laugh at the Babylonian king who never learns his lesson because the next tale finds the king driven from society and living with the wild animals as a lunatic because he did not confess the rule of the Most High over human sovereignty (4:22).[252]

Application and Devotional Implications

Although we cannot prove that the fourth individual in the furnace with the Hebrew youths was the Lord Jesus Christ, this was probably the case. Over a hundred years before Daniel's time, Isaiah the prophet had penned these words, "Fear not, for I have redeemed you; I have called you by name, you are mine. When you pass through the waters, I will be with you; and through the rivers, they shall not overwhelm you; when you walk through fire you shall not be burned, and the flame shall not consume you. For I am the Lord your God, the Holy One of Israel, your Savior" (Isa 43:1b–3a, ESV). As Christians today, we do not have a blanket promise from God that no harm will ever befall us. We have no right to claim that we will never be hurt. But what we do have a right to claim is our Savior's promise that we do not have to fear because he will be with us. Whatever we have to go through, he will be with us right in the midst of it. We can at least be freed from fear. When we come to the end of our lives, we will have the joyful recollection of those trying moments in life when our path seemed so painfully difficult. Yet we will remember with glad countenance how comforting we found the closeness of his presence in those times. As we reflect on the fact that he never abandoned us but instead made his presence more deeply felt, those will be our fondest memories and the trophies we cherish the most.

251. See translation comment for Dan 3:21.

252. Nel, "Daniel 3 as Satirical Comedy," 226.

6. Nebuchadnezzar's decree to honor the God of Heaven (3:28–30)

Textual Notes

28.a. The Greek translators apparently felt that "gave their bodies" was too abrupt and needed clarification. LXX$^{\theta}$ added εἰς πυρ, "to the fire;" while LXX^{O} added εἰς ἐμπυρισμόν, "to burning." Hebrew MSS lack such words.

29.a. אֱלָהּ (so B19[a]) should have the *mappiq*: אֱלָהּ, as we see in Dan 2:18, 19, 23, 28 etc. Several MS edd have אֱלָהּ.

29.b. The Kethib reading is שְׁלָה or שֵׁלָה, while the Qere is שָׁלוּ. The latter occurs in Dan 6:5 where there is no text critical problem.

30.a. LXX$^{\theta}$ adds, καὶ ἠξίωσεν αὐτοὺς ἡγεῖσθαι πάντων τῶν Ιουδαίων τῶν ὄντων ἐν τῇ βασιλείᾳ αὐτοῦ: "and deemed them worthy to govern all the Judeans who were in his kingdom." But there is no support for this addition in the Hebrew MSS.

Translation

3:28 Nebuchadnezzar exclaimed, "Blessed be the God of Shadrach, Meshach, and Abednego, who has sent His angel and rescued[253] his servants who trusted in Him. They defied[254] the king's command and gave up their bodies, so as[255] not to serve or give homage to any god except their God. **29** So I decree[256] that anyone—*no matter what* people, nation, or tongue—who utters a malicious statement[257] against the God of Shadrach, Meshach, and Abednego, shall be

---

253. *HALOT* (1993) indicates that שֵׁיזִב (*šêziḇ*) is a loanword from Akk. *šūzubu, ušēzib* meaning "rescue." A different word, נְצַל (*nᵊṣal*, "to rescue, deliver") is used in Dan 3:29, though they are very similar in meaning.

254. שַׁנִּיו (*šannîw*, Pa'el perf. of שְׁנָא, *šᵊnāʾ*) has a basic meaning "to change" (BDB, 1116c; and note Dan 3:27). That nuance obviously does not fit with this verse. The translations vary: NASB "violating;" NET "ignoring;" ESV "set aside;" NRSV "disobeyed; and NIV "defied." *HALOT* (1999) indicates that in the Pa'el, שְׁנָא (*šᵊnāʾ*) can mean "to violate an order." Hence, NIV's "defied" is perhaps the best option (so Collins, 178 and Goldingay, 65). LXX^{O} translated שְׁנָא (*šᵊnāʾ*) by the Greek word ἀθετέω (*atheteō*), "to set aside, deny, refuse (a request)," which would be close in meaning to "defy."

255. RJ (92) indicates that דִּי לָא (*dî lāʾ*) has a telic function in this case: "in order that … not."

256. Lit., "from me has been given a command" (וּמִנִּי שִׂים טְעֵם, *ûminnî śîm ṭᵊʿēm*). Defending the notion that the idiom is of Old Persian origin for issuing a decree, see J. Makujina, "On the Possible Old Persian Origin of the Aramaic טעם שים, 'to Issue a Decree,'" *HUCA* 68 (1997): 1–9.

257. The word שָׁלוּ, *šālû* (Qere; see textual note), means "negligence" (*HALOT*, 1994). With the verb אֲמַר (*ʾămar*, "to say, speak"), this would have the idea of *speaking negligently*, and thus of "speaking against" (so NIV) or saying something "offensive"

dismembered[258] and his house reduced to rubble,[259] since there is no other god who is able to deliver like this." **30** Then the king promoted[260] Shadrach, Meshach, and Abednego in the province of Babylon.

Commentary

3:28 *Nebuchadnezzar's acknowledgment.* Nebuchadnezzar's response in vv. 28–30 shows some progress in his own spiritual understood, although it comes short of true faith and personal salvation. First, when he said, "Blessed is the God," he used the singular form of god, thus indicating he understand the biblical concept of God as being monotheistic (though he himself remained a polytheist). But it is "the God of Shadrach, Meshach, and

(so NASB). BDB (1115c) adds that it could possibly be read שִׁלָּה (*śillâ*). *HALOT* (1987), in discussing שִׁלָּה (*śillâ*), indicates that this root means "to utter abuse" (perhaps "blaspheme"). Collins (178) relates it to Akk. *šillatu*—as had G. R. Driver, "Studies in the Vocabulary of the Old Testament Texts," *JTS* 31 (1930): 282–83, before him—and translates it "who blaspheme." S. M. Paul, "A Case Study of 'Neglected' Blasphemy," *JNES* 42 (1983): 292, argues forcefully for the meaning "blaspheme" in the case of Dan 3:29: "What should be emphasized is that Akk. *šillatu* is part of the 'Akkadian stock of terms for sinful speech.' Such improper speech when directed against God is blasphemy and when uttered against a human being is slander, insolence, impudence, effrontery." Yet he may be overly reliant on drawing the parallel to Akk. *šillatu*.

Both the LXX^{O} and LXX^{θ} translated *šāluh/šālû* as "blasphemy" (LXX^{O} using the verb form, and LXX^{θ} the noun form). However, in discussing the classical usage of the word group for βλασφημέω (*blasphēmeō*), *NIDNTTE* (1:515) notes, "But the Gk. word group is often used of ill-speaking more generally, i.e., slanderous language that defames or damages someone else's reputation." Seen in this light, the LXX choice of βλασφημία (*blasphēmia*) is understandable. In summary, *šāluh/šālû* probably means something like "malicious statement," closely related to the classical meaning of βλασφημία (*blasphēmia*).

258. Lit., "shall be made into limbs" (הַדָּמִין יִתְעֲבֵד, *haddāmîn yiṯʿăḇēḏ*).

259. "Reduced to rubble," נְוָלִי יִשְׁתַּוֵּה (*nᵊwālî yištawwēh*). The noun נְוָלִי (*nᵊwālî*) means "refuse-heap" (BDB, 1084c). Cf. Dan 2:5. LXX^{O} understood it in the sense of one's house being "confiscated," and LXX^{θ} rendered it εἰς διαρπαγήν (*eis diarpagēn*), "for plundering."

260. The word translated "promoted" is the Hapʿel perf. of the root צְלַח (*ṣᵊlaḥ*), "cause to prosper, make successful." This would probably have included a *promotion* in rank but could also have meant other forms of prosperity such as material reward. The two Greek traditions took the liberty to elaborate on this verse, describing them as leaders and rulers. The LXX^{O}, for instance, reads, "and deemed them worthy to be leaders of all the Jews in his kingdom." Hence, the LXX tradition saw this primarily in terms of promotion as leaders.

Abednego," not his own god.[261] Nevertheless, he credits this God with rescuing the three Hebrews by sending "His angel" to help them (his interpretation of the event). Second, the king takes notice of their faith. They "trusted in him." Apparently their faith made an indelible impression upon the king, and he felt compelled to comment upon it. Third, the king took note of the courage that stemmed from their faith in God. They were willing to defy the king's edict (even at the point of death), because it was more important for them to obey God than man—even if that man were the most exalted king on earth. Fourth, the king witnessed their dedication—their worship of God was not for sale at any price, and they would not compromise on this fundamental matter.

In saying these things, the king was making a tacit admission that he had been wrong in v. 15 when he said, "what god is there who can deliver you out of my hands?" Also, in saying these things, he was acknowledging his *respect* for them personally. He did not see these "believers" as cowards but as courageous heroes. Their faith had been severely put to the test, but they had remained faithful, and in so doing they had gained the admiration of this pagan king (and thus another seed was sown in his heart).

3:29 *Nebuchadnezzar's decree.* According to v. 29, the king even went so far as to issue an edict calling on all the subjects of his empire to respect this God of heaven. (Notice that this chapter begins with one decree and ends with another.) He did not forbid them to worship their Babylonian deities, but they were not allowed to utter malicious statements about "the God of Shadrach, Meshach, and Abednego." To do so would bring severe punishment: dismemberment and loss of home and property. Nebuchadnezzar was clearly beginning to see the uniqueness of the God of the Bible, for he even admitted (v. 29b) that no other god could deliver the way this God had done. (Marduk and Ishtar might have felt insulted by that remark.)

Brensinger insightfully points out how the climactic pronouncement found in vv. 28–29 forms a fitting contrast and to that in vv. 16–18:

> The contrast between the two pronouncements, however, is indeed significant. In unit one, Shadrach, Meshach and Abednego refuse to worship the gods of Nebuchadnezzar, alluding instead to the primacy of their God (vv. 16–l8). In unit two, Nebuchadnezzar elevates the God of Shadrach, Meshach and Abednego, alluding to the inadequacy of his gods (vv. 28–29). As a result, the same "peoples, nations and tongues" who were previously instructed to bow down to the golden statue are now threatened if they utter so much as a word against the God of these Jews. True to form,

261. The phrase "their god" is אֱלָהֲהוֹן (*ʾělāhăhôn*), which involves the singular form of אֱלָה (*ʾělāh*) with a 3rd person pl. pron. suffix (but this is an *anticipatory pronoun*, and the following list of names clarifies the pronoun's antecedent—and thus "their" does not need to be translated).

> Nebuchadnezzar is still giving orders, but the rules of the game have undergone a thorough reversal.[262]

3:30 *Exaltation of Daniel's three friends.* Finally, these three young men were rewarded (v. 30). Literally the text says, "the king caused them to prosper." At the very least, this would have included restoration to the positions they had been given in Dan 2:49. Perhaps they received other rewards in the form of material gain. In any case, they would continue as prominent officials in the Babylonian Empire.

A comparison can be drawn between the events of this chapter and things that the Bible foretells in regard to the future reign of the antichrist. Just as Nebuchadnezzar erected a statue and demanded his subjects to bow before it, so the "Beast" (the antichrist) will do in a similar way during the period of the great tribulation prior to the second coming of Christ (see Rev 13:15). Like Shadrach and his friends, the believers of that time will stand true to God and refuse to worship the Beast or his image (Rev 14:9–11).

Application and Devotional Implications

Nebuchadnezzar not only marveled at the power of God, but also at the *trust* that his devotees had put in him. The king had probably never seen anything like this among those who worshiped the Babylonian deities. Oh, there were those who would have been devoted to these deities and done great deeds of service, but none who experienced a personal love relationship and a life of faith. Even if God had not delivered the three Hebrew youths, there still would have been glory to God, because the unbelieving world would have been confronted by the love of believers for their God. What a powerful testimony this was unto Nebuchadnezzar, and this ought to be a lesson to us today. When the unbelieving world witnesses our faith in action, it grabs their attention and causes them to consider (perhaps even desire) how they might know God in a personal way. Every day we face decisions—some small, some large—but we face decisions in which we can either choose the way of faith, or we can make *mere human choices*. The world may mock our morals and value system, but witnessing our faith in action is what will grab their attention and perhaps even lead to their own personal faith in the Lord Jesus Christ. After all, it certainly got Nebuchadnezzar's attention.

Selected Bibliography

Alexander, J. B. "New Light on the Fiery Furnace." *JBL* 69 (1950): 375–76.

Astour, M. C. "Greek Names in the Semitic World and Semitic Names in the Greek World." *JNES* 23 (1964): 193–201.

Avalos, H. "The Comedic Function of the Enumerations of Officials and Instruments in Daniel 3." *CBQ* 53 (1991): 580–88.

262. Brensinger, "Compliance, Dissonance and Amazement in Daniel 3," 14.

Baukal, C. E., Jr. "The Fiery Furnace." *BSac* 171 (2014): 148–71.
Beaulieu, P. A. "The Babylonian Background of the Motif of the Fiery Furnace in Daniel 3." *JBL* 128 (2009): 273–90.
Botha, P. J. "The Interpretation of Daniel 3 in the Syriac Commentary Ascribed to Ephrem the Syrian." *AcPB* 16 (2005): 29–53.
Brensinger, T. L. "Compliance, Dissonance and Amazement in Daniel 3." *EvJ* 20 (2002): 7–19.
Broomall, W. "Theophany." In *Baker's Dictionary of Theology*, ed. E. F. Harrison, 520–21. Grand Rapids: Eerdmans, 1960.
Cook, E. M. "In the Plain of the Wall." *JBL* 108 (1989): 115–16.
Cook, S. A. "The Articles of Dress in Dan iii, 21." *JPhil* 26 (1899): 306–13.
Coxon, P. "Daniel 3:17: A Linguistic and Theological Problem." *VT* 26 (1976): 400–409.
———. "Nebuchadnezzar's Hermeneutical Dilemma." *JSOT* 66 (1995): 87–97.
De Bruyn, J. J. "Daniel 3, Contesting Space for Clashing Images." *JSem* 23 (2014): 37–52.
Deventer, H. J. M. van. "'We Did Not Hear the Bagpipe': A Note on Daniel 3." *OTE* 11 (1998): 340–49.
Driver, G. R. "Studies in the Vocabulary of the Old Testament Texts." *JTS* 31 (1930): 275–84.
Dyer, C. H. "The Musical Instruments in Daniel 3." *BSac* 147 (1990): 426–36.
Eichorn, D. E. "Sanhedrin 93a and the Third Chapter of Daniel." *Central Conference of American Rabbis Journal* 16 (1969): 24–25.
Ellenbogen, M. *Foreign Words in the Old Testament.* London: Luzac, 1957.
Engel, C. *The Music of the Most Ancient Nations Particularly of the Assyrians, Egyptians, and Hebrews.* 2nd ed. London: John Murray, 1870; reprint, Nabu Press, 2014.
Finesinger, S. B. "Musical Instruments in OT." *HUCA* 3 (1926): 21–77.
Galpin, F. W. *The Music of the Sumerians.* Oxford: Clarendon, 1937.
Goswell, G. "The Ethics of the Book of Daniel." *ResQ* 57 (2015): 129–42.
Heller, R. L. "'But if not …' *What*? The Speech of the Youths in Daniel 3 and a (Theo)logical Problem." In *Thus Says the Lord: Essays on the Former and Latter Prophets in Honor of Robert R. Wilson*, ed. J. J. Ahn and S. L. Cook, 244–55. London: T & T Clark, 2009.
Henten, J. W. van. "Reception of Daniel 3 and 6 in Early Christian Literature." In *The Book of Daniel: Composition and Reception,* ed. J. J. Collins and P. W. Flint, 1:149–69. Leiden: Brill, 2001.
Holm, T. L. "The Fiery Furnace in the Book of Daniel." *JAOS* 128 (2008): 85–104.
Kaufman, S. A. *The Akkadian Influences on Aramaic.* Assyriological Studies Series 19. Chicago: University of Chicago Press, 1974.
Lesley, M. "Illusions of Grandeur: The Instruments of Daniel 3 Reconsidered." In *Music in Antiquity; The Near East and the Mediterranean*, ed. J. G. Westenholz, Y. Maurey, and E. Seroussi, 201–12. Berlin/Boston: Walter de Gruyter GmbH, 2014.

Lucas, E. C. "A Statue, a Fiery Furnace and a Dismal Swamp; A Reflection on Some Issues in Biblical Hermeneutics." *EvQ* 77 (2005): 291–307.

Makujina, J. "On the Possible Old Persian Origin of the Aramaic טעם שים, 'to Issue a Decree.'" *HUCA* 68 (1997): 1–9.

Mastin, B. A. "The Text of Daniel 3:16." In *Leshon Limmudim; Essays on the Language and Literature of the Hebrew Bible in Honor of A. A. MacIntosh*, ed. D. A. Baer and R. P. Gordon, 236–49. London and New York: Bloomsbury T&T Clark, 2013.

Mitchell, T. C. "And the Band Played On … But What Did They Play On? Identifying the Instruments in Nebuchadnezzar's Orchestra." *BRev* 15 (1999): 32–39.

Nel, M. "Daniel 3 as Satirical Comedy." *NGTT* 53 (2012): 218–28.

Noonan, B. J. "The Presence and Significance of Foreign Loanwords in the Book of Daniel." Paper presented at Evangelical Theological Society annual meeting, Baltimore, Nov. 20, 2013.

Paul, S. M. "Dan 3:29: A Case Study of 'Neglected' Blasphemy." *JNES* 42 (1983): 291–94.

———. "The Mesopotamian Babylonian Background of Daniel 1–6." In *The Book of Daniel: Composition and Reception*, ed. J. J. Collins and P. W. Flint, 55–68. Vol. 1. Leiden, Boston: Brill, 2001.

Polin, C. C. J. *Music of the Ancient Near East*. New York: Vantage, 1954.

Prinsloo, G. T. M. "Daniel 3: Intratextual Perspectives and Intertextual Tradition." *AcPB* 16 (2005): 70–90.

Ron, Z. "Rescue from Fiery Death: Daniel Chapter 3 and Genesis Chapter 38." *JBQ* 41 (2013): 24–27.

Sanders, B. G. "The Burning Fiery Furnace." *Theology* 58 (1955): 340–45.

Shea, W. H. "Daniel 3: Extra-biblical Texts and the Convocation on the Plain of Dura." *AUSS* 20 (1982): 29–52.

Swart, G. J. "Divergences Between the OG and Th Versions of Daniel 3: Evidence of Early Hellenistic Interpretation of the Narrative of the Three Young Men in the Furnace." *AcPB* 16 (2005): 106–20.

Tucker, W. D. "The Early *Wirkungsgeschichte* of Daniel 3: Representative Examples." *JTI* 6 (2012): 295–306.

Wiseman, D. J. *Nebuchadrezzar and Babylon*. Oxford: Oxford University Press, 1985.

Werner, E. "Musical Instruments." In *The Interpreter's Dictionary of the Bible*, ed. G. A. Buttrick et al. New York/Nashville: Abingdon Press, 1962, 3:469–76.

Yamauchi, E. M. "Daniel and Contacts between the Aegean and the Near East before Alexander." *EvQ* 53 (1981): 37–47.

———. "Greek Words." In *New Perspectives on the Old Testament*, ed. J. B. Payne, 170–200. Waco, TX: Word, 1970.

C. God's Humbling of Nebuchadnezzar, To Whom is Revealed the Dream of the Great Tree (4:1–37)

Orientation. Daniel chap. 4 provides one of the Bible's greatest lessons about pride, particularly for those who look at their own accomplishments and give themselves all the credit. As a point of reference, God uses the great Babylonian king, Nebuchadnezzar, as an object lesson. In this case, the story ends happily, for this king actually humbles himself beneath the mighty hand of God. It is helpful at this point to recall the diagram on the *literary structure* of chaps. 2–7 that was introduced in the orientation to chap. 2. According to the literary structure, chaps. 4 and 5 form the innermost parallel of the concentric arrangement. This serves to highlight these chapters for comparison. In both cases we have a story involving a prideful Babylonian king, Nebuchadnezzar in chap. 4 and Belshazzar in chap. 5. The first is humbled for his pride through an animal-like madness, while the latter is humbled for his arrogant defiance by defeat at the hand of the Medes and Persians. The first learns his lesson and goes on to recover, while the latter is punished and never recovers.

Shea has also argued that chap. 4 is carefully composed in a chiastic structure, which I present here with slight modification.[263]

A Prologue (1–3): Post-fulfillment Proclamation (Poem 1)
- B Dream Reception (4–7)
  - C Dialogue I: King to Daniel (8–9)
    - D Dream Recital (10–17)
      - E Dialogue II: King's Encouraging Remarks to Daniel (18–19a)
      - E' Dialogue II: Daniel's Encouraging Remarks to the King (19b)
    - D' Dream Interpretation (20–26)
  - C' Dialogue II: Daniel to the King (27)
- B' Dream Fulfillment (28–33)

A' Epilogue (34–38): Post-fulfillment Restoration (Poem II)

At the center comes the king's confession that the Babylonian wise men—in contrast to Daniel—are incompetent aids to the king, as they had no ability to interpret his dream. At the polar extremes comes the king's praise of Yahweh God and his acknowledgment of God's everlasting kingdom as that which is most important and which will surely be established.

---

263. W. Shea, "Further Literary Structures in Daniel 2–7: An Analysis of Daniel 4," *AUSS* 23 (1985): 202.

Dating. The Bible does not provide a precise date when this incident took place in the life of Nebuchadnezzar. One of the Greek translations (LXX^{O}) adds an additional comment at the beginning of Dan 4:4 (4:1 in the Aramaic text) that this took place "in the eighteenth year" of Nebuchadnezzar's reign, a date that would correspond with the fall of Jerusalem in 586 BC. (A similar chronological notation is found in the Greek texts at Dan 3:1.) This addition, however, is undoubtedly a fabrication and receives no support from either the Masoretic text or the other primary Greek translation (LXX$^{\theta}$). Evidently, the translators of LXX^{O} sought to connect Nebuchadnezzar's madness with the destruction of Jerusalem, as though the madness came upon him as a judgment by God for destroying the holy city. More likely is the suggestion that the events of chap. 4 took place in the latter years of Nebuchadnezzar's reign. We know from extrabiblical sources that Nebuchadnezzar had a lengthy reign, from 605 BC to 562 BC. Miller (127–28) reasons:

> ... clues in the text point to the close of Nebuchadnezzar's reign. For example, his building operations seem to have been concluded (4:30), there was peace throughout the empire (4:4), and possible allusions to the king's illness by Abydenus (second century BC) and Berossus (the third century BC Babylonian priest) suggest a time late in Nebuchadnezzar's life.[264]

If the illness began a year after the dream (4:29) and the illness lasted probably seven years (v. 32), and if an interval of time was needed for Nebuchadnezzar's reign after his cure (at least a year?), then the dream must have taken place no later than the thirty-fourth year of his reign (i.e., *ca*. 571 BC).

Historicity. More challenging than the date itself is the question of the story's historicity. Critical scholars almost universally deny that any such event like this ever happened to King Nebuchadnezzar, seeing that we know nothing of him having a long mental illness from extrabiblical records, much less that he personally came to praise the God of the Bible.[265] The lack of such

264. Abydenus' account, though disputed, is preserved by Eusebius (*Praep. ev.* 9.41.1; see Montgomery, 221 for a reproduction). Regarding Berossus, see Josephus, *C. Ap.* 1.20.

265. Often, appeals are made to Akkadian literature in support of a non-literal understanding of Nebuchadnezzar's experience as recorded in Dan 4:33 (Eng.). M. Henze, *The Madness of King Nebuchadnezzar: The Ancient Near Eastern Origins and Early History of Interpretation of Daniel 4*, JSJSupp 61 (Leiden: Brill, 1999), 3, for example, argues that Nebuchadnezzar's madness "is modeled on a trope we find in the mythic lore of the ancient Near East, the notion of the wild man," with Gilgamesh's friend, Enkidu, being a principal example of that trope (stories of those who lived outside civilized urban centers). C. B. Hays, "Chirps From the Dust: The Affliction of Nebuchadnezzar in Dan 4:30 in Its Ancient Near Eastern Context," *JBL* 126 (2007): 305–25, has argued that Nebuchadnezzar's affliction is best understood in the context of netherworld imagery, and that the type of animal imagery found in the Daniel passage frequently symbolized those who were afflicted by divine powers.

information, however, is not conclusive proof against the biblical account. The fact of the matter is that the Babylonian Chronicles (from which we get much of our historical information) only cover the period 605–594 BC, and this is followed by a large gap in the records, so the records for most of the reign of Nebuchadnezzar are not extant (especially the latter part of his reign when this is most likely to have occurred).[266]

Critical scholars, on the other hand, expend a great deal of effort in trying to identify the sources they think originally lay behind the present biblical account.[267] They have long suspected that traditions about Nabonidus (r. 556–539 BC), rather than Nebuchadnezzar, underlie the account in Dan 4. Cuneiform discoveries document that Nabonidus was absent from Babylon for several years, as he sojourned in Teima in the Arabian Desert. Critical scholars, therefore, reasoned that it was Nabonidus who must have had good reason to be away from his capital at Babylon, and that he would have been the more likely king for the Dan 4 story. Among the finds at Qumran, archaeologists have discovered the *Prayer of Nabonidus* (known as 4QPrNab) which some have used as "proof" for this theory.[268] "This document purports

---

For Hays, the animals function simply as metaphors, and hence the animal images in 4:30 express suffering, lending detail and poignancy to Nebuchadnezzar's condition. H. Avalos, "Nebuchadnezzar's Affliction: New Mesopotamian Parallels for Daniel 4," *JBL* 133 (2014): 498, contra Hays, has attempted to show that "a group of magico-medical Mesopotamian texts collected by Wilfred G. Lambert and known as the dingir.šà.dib.ba incantations do provide clear evidence that a primal earthly status could result from the curse of a deity" upon a human being. In response to these suggested theories, I would point out that we ought to be able to find some confirming remark in regard to them in Daniel's interpretation of the dream (vv. 24–26), yet it is precisely here that nothing more than a literal judgment upon the king is mentioned.

266. In 1912 S. Langdon published fifty-two building inscriptions belonging to Nebuchadnezzar. Yet Langdon noted that after 590 BC, "we have scarcely anything but palace inscriptions with little to say about the religious interests of the king." Cited in P. Ferguson, "Nebuchadnezzar, Gilgamesh, and the 'Babylonian Job,'" *JETS* 37 (1994): 322. For the original work in German, see S. H. Langdon, *Die neubabylonischen Königsinschriften, Vorderasiatische Bibliothek* 4 (Leipzig: Hinrichs, 1912).

267. See Collins (216–21) for a good example of discussion on sources and redaction from a critical viewpoint. In addition to the *Prayer of Nabonidus*, critical scholars have also sought to find source material in the book of Abydenus, *Concerning the Assyrians*, which was reported by Eusebius.

268. For the official publication of the *Prayer of Nabonidus*, see J. J. Collins, "Prayer of Nabonidus," in *Qumran Cave 4.XVII: Parabiblical Texts, Part 3*, ed. G. J. Brooke, et al., 83–93, DJD 22 (Oxford: Clarendon, 1996). For a more recent attempt to connect Nabonidus with Dan 4 on the basis of the *Prayer of Nabonidus* (and other extrabiblical accounts regarding him), see C. A. Newsom, "Why Nabonidus?: Excavating Traditions from Qumran, the Hebrew Bible, and Neo-Babylonian Sources," in *The*

to give 'the words of the prayer which Nabonidus, king of Babylon, the great king, prayed when he was stricken with an evil disease by the decree of God in Teman" (Collins, 217). Admittedly, there are certain interesting parallels. Nabonidus was smitten for seven years, and a Jewish *diviner* instructed him to recount these things in prayer to give honor to the name of God. Apparently, the Qumran account included a dream that the king saw, although the extant fragments do not include Nabonidus' confession of the Most High God. What is lacking, however, is the crucial matter of the king becoming like a *beast* of the field. Coxon—who rejects Nabonidus' long absence from the capital as the basis for the story of Nebuchadnezzar's "madness"—admits that "there is no evidence that Nabonidus suffered from fever or mental disorder."[269] These studies, while interesting, should be flatly rejected.[270] The biblical account explicitly names King Nebuchadnezzar as

---

Dead Sea Scrolls: Transmission of Traditions and Production of Texts, ed. S. Metso, H. Najman, and E. Schuller (Leiden; Boston: Brill, 2010), 57–79. Utterly rejecting the historicity of the court narratives of Daniel, she not only sees Nabonidus behind the story of Dan 4 but of most of the early chapters. She concludes (60), "Thus of the five core chapters (Daniel 2–6), four have a significant claim to have been originally composed about Nabonidus and his son Belshazzar." In her opinion, material originally pertaining to Nabonidus was transferred to the more famous figure of Nebuchadnezzar in the actively redacted Daniel tradition.

269. P. W. Coxon, "Another Look at Nebuchadnezzar's Madness," in *The Book of Daniel in the Light of New Findings*, ed. A. S. van der Woude, 211–22, BETL 106 (Leuven: Leuven University Press, 1993), 217. Coxon favors another theory as to what gave rise to the biblical account of Nebuchadnezzar (which he regards as a "fictional tale"). He believes that behind this story lie certain mythological legends. In particular "the primary influence on the shaping of the story is mythical and the model that excited the imagination of its author was Enkidu, first encountered in the Gilgamesh Epic (GE) as the savage brute chosen by the gods to challenge the overwhelming authority of the hero Gilgamesh" (218). He goes on to say that "Older versions of the early Enkidu confirm the picture of a wild, animal-like creature who was hairy, unclothed and ate grass" (219). Hence, on account of Nebuchadnezzar's brazen defiance of the Most High, "he is forced to assume the role of the early Enkidu, the primordial savage-man whose habitat was the steppe and whose company the wild asses" (221).

270. More recently, A. Steinmann, "The Chicken and the Egg: A New Proposal for the Relationship between the *Prayer of Nabonidus* and the *Book of Daniel*," *RevQ* 20 (2002): 557–70, has argued for strong internal evidence that the Prayer of Nabonidus is probably a composition based upon Dan 4. He writes, "This internal evidence includes apparent borrowing of language not only from *Dan* 4, but also from *Dan* 2, 3 and 5 as well as attempted theological corrections of *Daniel* toward a strict monotheism. It is likely, therefore, that the *Prayer* is actually the composition of a Palestinian Jew who was attempting to fill in the historical gap between the reign of Nebuchadnezzar (*Dan* 4) and the fall of Babylon to the Persians (*Dan* 5)," 557.

the central figure in this story, and there is no solid proof casting doubt on the historicity of this biblical story.

Granted that this story of Nebuchadnezzar really did take place and is historically reliable, we stand amazed that such a king as he would ever reveal this to his subjects publicly. Assyrian and Babylonian kings typically exaggerated their greatness and personal achievements rather than calling attention to their defects and weaknesses. So much of the story is told in the first person by Nebuchadnezzar; would it not have been greatly embarrassing to the king to recount this to his subjects?[271] The opening decree (Dan 4:1–3) provides further insight. At the end of v. 2 the king says, שְׁפַר קָדָמַי לְהַחֲוָיָה (*šᵊpar qoḏāmay lᵊhaḥăwāyâ*), which the NET translates, "I am delighted to tell you." The verb *šᵊpar* means, "to please, seem good to" (*HALOT*, 2001). In other words, he did not tell this story reluctantly; it was quite pleasing to him to do it—he actually wanted to do this. In my opinion, there is only one satisfactory explanation for this: in the process of his humiliation by God, the heart of this man was truly changed, and he personally came to faith in the God of heaven (see further comments at vv. 34–37). In making this story public, the king accomplished two things: (1) he provided a clear explanation to all his subjects why he was absent from his throne (which over a seven-year period would have become noticeable to all), and (2) it was his opportunity to glorify the true God of heaven who had dealt so mercifully with him—despite his immense pride—patiently bringing the king to faith and a true, heart-felt praise for the God of the Bible. Most likely, Nebuchadnezzar was an older man and near the end of his reign when his illness ended. He probably thought carefully what he could do to honor God for all that God had done for him. What greater honor could he have rendered than to declare his story to all his subjects and point them (they being steeped in idolatry) to the one true God of heaven? In doing so, he became one of the truly great men of history—a man rescued by the grace of a loving God.

If this thesis is correct about Nebuchadnezzar, it would be helpful to back up for a moment and trace his spiritual journey in chaps. 2–4.

---

271. T. Meadowcroft, "Point of View in Storytelling: An Experiment in Narrative Criticism in Daniel 4," *Did* 8 (1997): 30–42, points out that although the chapter is fundamentally told in the first person (autobiographical), a large block (vv. 19–33 Eng.) is related in the third person. He argues that the chapter has a deliberate shift of "point of view" at v. 19, thereby allowing "the retelling of the dream, its interpretation, and the delicate problem of its interpretation all to be viewed through the eyes of Daniel" (35). He concludes (38), "In the process the attitude of the narrator or implied author toward King Nebuchadnezzar becomes more evident, and the inclusion of more than one standpoint within the story prevents readily over-identification with the author of the epistle that opens ch. 4." While the text does display a shift in point of view to Daniel for vv. 19–33, Meadowcroft seems overly concerned that the purpose is for insuring Nebuchadnezzar's perspective does not control the proper evaluation of his experience and judgment.

1. Chap. 2: Daniel's interpretation of the dream about the great image

   He learned that the God of the Hebrews was all-powerful (controlling all history), all wise, and could reveal mysteries no other god could make known.

2. Chap. 3: The deliverance of Shadrach, Meshach, and Abednego

   He learned that the true God was Lord of nature and history and could by his miracle-working power override the will of the mightiest earthly potentates and deliver his servants from death.

3. Chap. 4: His humiliation to the state of a beast of the field.

   Finally, Nebuchadnezzar really began to understand his weakness and folly before the Lord God Almighty. At last he realized his utter dependence on God for his reason, his power, and his very life. He saw that he was but an instrument in the hands of the omnipotent God, the true Sovereign of the universe who ordered all history by his own decree. Hence, he came to terms with the primary lesson of the book—the absolute sovereignty of God and his faithfulness to his covenant people.[272] The implication is that he personally put his faith in this God and became a worshiper of the God of heaven.

1. An introduction to Nebuchadnezzar's decree made after his humbling (4:1–3)

Note: The verse numbering of this chapter is different than the original text. Dan 4:1–3 in English versions is Dan 3:31–33 in the Aramaic text.[273]

Textual Notes

31.a. [Eng. 4:1a] LXX^{O} lacks vv. 31–33 (Eng. 4:1–3), though LXX$^{\theta}$ has them.

272. Credit goes to Archer, "Daniel," 59, for these observations. Burkholder, "Literary Patterns and God's Sovereignty in Daniel 4," *Direction* 16 (1987): 45–54, has shown how the imagery and some of the parallel structures sharpen the theme of God's sovereignty in Daniel 4.

273. In the original Aramaic text, the verse numbers of chap. 4 differ from those in our modern English Bibles. In the English Bible, we find 4:1–37. In the original Aramaic, however, 4:1–3 (in our English Bibles) is really the end of chap. 3. Thus, 4:1 Eng. = 3:31 Aram., 4:2 Eng. = 3:32 Aram., etc. Then 4:4 Eng. = 4:1 Aram. As a result, chap. 4 of the Aramaic ends at 4:34. The present verse numbering came from the medieval chapter division of the Latin Vulgate (generally attributed to the thirteenth-century archbishop Stephen Langton). In this commentary, verse references will refer to English numbers.

31.b. [Eng. 4:1b] A few MSS add שְׁלַח ("he sent") following מַלְכָּא, while a few other MSS (including Syriac) have added כְּתַב ("he wrote").

31.c. [Eng. 4:1c] Regarding the Qere reading דָּיְרִין, see note at 2:38a.

Translation

4:1 [Aram. 3:31] "King Nebuchadnezzar, to all peoples, nations, and *men of every* language[274] in all the earth:[275] May your prosperity[276] abound. **2** I am pleased[277] to declare the signs and wonders which the Most High God has done for me. **3** How great are His signs and how mighty are His wonders. His kingdom is an everlasting kingdom, and His dominion is throughout all generations."[278]

Commentary

4:1 The initial verse is typical of decrees uttered by oriental kings, being something of a standard greeting. It is worded almost exactly the same as that by Darius in Dan 6:25. The NET chose the translation "in all the land," which would be somewhat restrictive. The Aramaic אֲרַע, *ʾăraʿ* (like Heb. אֶרֶץ, *ʾereṣ*) can mean either "land" or "earth" (as in Gen 1:1), and the NASB's translation "in all the earth" (similarly NIV) is probably correct. When we examine the ancient cuneiform documents of Assyrian, Babylonian, and Persian kings, they typically regarded themselves as kings "of all the earth"—their empires embraced most (but not all) the known civilized world and they boasted beyond their measure. From the famous Cyrus cylinder, for example, we find the following grandiose boast:

> I am Cyrus, king of the world, great king, legitimate king, king of Babylon, king of Sumer and Akkad, king of the four rims (of the earth), son of Cambyses (*Ka-am-bu-zi-ia*), great king, king of

---

274. Lit., "tongues" (וְלִשָּׁנַיָּא, *wəliššānayyāʾ*). The added words "men of every" bring out the concern for all language groups.

275. Aram. אֲרַע, *ʾăraʿ* (like Heb. אֶרֶץ, *ʾereṣ*) can mean "earth" or "land." NET takes it as "land" (the land of Babylon), but most Eng. versions translate it "earth." Assyrian and Babylonian kings regarded themselves as kings of all the earth (see Pritchard, *ANET*, 316 concerning Cyrus).

276. Verse 31 is literally "May your שְׁלָם (*səlām*) increase (or abound)." Aram. *səlām*, like Heb. *šalôm*, generally means "peace," but also means one's "welfare, health, or prosperity." We could paraphrase this by saying, "May your health and good fortune abound!" Cf. Goldingay (77), "Peace and prosperity be yours."

277. Lit., "it seemed good before me" (שְׁפַר קֳדָמַי, *šəpar qoḏāmay*).

278. Lit., "and His dominion *is* with a generation and a generation" (וְשָׁלְטָנֵהּ עִם־דָּר וְדָר, *wəšālṭānēh ʿim-dor wəḏor*), i.e., with all generations (from one generation to the next).

> Anshan, descendant of Teispes ... whose rule Bel and Nebo love, whom they want as king to please their hearts.[279]

Having wished for their good welfare and fortune (שְׁלָמְכוֹן, *šᵊlomḵôn*—see translation note at v. 2), Nebuchadnezzar said that he found it pleasing to declare the signs and wonders that God had done for him (see comments above under *Orientation*). To tell his story risked a certain embarrassment, especially for a Babylonian king, but he felt compelled to tell it.

4:2–3 The expression "signs and wonders" (אָתַיָּא וְתִמְהַיָּא, *ʾāṯayyāʾ wᵊṯimhayyāʾ*), though involving miraculous deeds of God, probably has in mind the distressing discipline that God had brought upon Nebuchadnezzar, just as it did when God brought the plagues (also called "signs and wonders") upon Pharaoh to coerce him into yielding to God's will (see Exod 7:3; Deut 6:22). Nebuchadnezzar was about to tell his subjects how he had to be disciplined by God (though in the final analysis it would be a good thing, for he would be a changed man). These signs/wonders were indeed great and mighty (v. 3), because they powerfully brought the king to his knees.

Nebuchadnezzar had spent a lifetime building one of the world's great kingdoms, but he had failed to see his kingdom in proper perspective with God's kingdom. In v. 3 he declares, "His kingdom is an everlasting kingdom, and His dominion is throughout all generations." This reflects a proper perspective of God's kingdom and rule. Two crucial observations need to be made. First, this confession about God's kingdom is strikingly similar to Ps 145:10–13 (ESV):

> All your works shall give thanks to you, O LORD, and all your saints shall bless you! They shall speak of the glory of your kingdom and tell of your power, to make known to the children of man your mighty deeds, and the glorious splendor of your kingdom. Your kingdom is an everlasting kingdom, and your dominion endures throughout all generations. The LORD is faithful in all his words and kind in all his works.

Dan 4:3b is almost a direct reference to the last two lines quoted above (even more similar in the original Aramaic and Hebrew). It may be that Nebuchadnezzar was familiar with this Davidic psalm and had come to appreciate its truth. Second, v. 3b is strikingly similar to the latter part of v. 31. These observations lead to the conclusion that Nebuchadnezzar did not come to acknowledge this truth until *after* his humbling and illness and that v. 31 reflects the correct chronological sequence of events. Thus, vv. 1–3 are really a viewpoint that Nebuchadnezzar had come to *after* the experience recorded in chap. 4. He uses that to introduce his story, so that in vv. 4–37 he is actually backing up to tell us (the readers) how he had come to view God's kingdom this way. It is entirely possible that Daniel had ministered

---

279. Pritchard, *ANET*, 316.

to him somewhere in the process (near the end of his illness? shortly after his restoration?) with the words from Ps 145 above, and that by the grace of God Nebuchadnezzar came to faith and fully trusted in this revelation about God's kingdom.

Biblical Theology Comments

Nebuchadnezzar's appreciation for "God's kingdom," of course, needs to be seen in light of the progressive revelation of the *kingdom theme* in Daniel. We recall how in Dan 2:44 the prophecy was made that God would eventually ("in the days of those kings") set up a kingdom that would never be destroyed. This looks forward to the future establishment of the *kingdom of God* that will come about *after* the Gentile kingdoms have run their course. Now Nebuchadnezzar is beginning to see that history centers around the development of God's kingdom, not his own. More insight about this coming kingdom will be given in 7:13–14, and this must all be seen in light of Jesus' ministry in which he preached, "Repent, for the kingdom of God is at hand." As pointed out in chap. 2, it seems that the full realization of this kingdom will come about with Jesus' second coming (though God is certainly ruling and orchestrating history in every age).

Application and Devotional Implications

In keeping with the fact that God is the creator of the entire universe, he is also its rightful ruler and king. As v. 3 states, "His dominion is throughout all generations." Day in and day out, the Lord diligently and perfectly exerts his rule over his creation. Because he has purposed to allow evil to dwell in his universe, there are times when we who dwell on earth may have trouble recognizing the exercise of his rule over the world we live in. God does allow Satan and the hordes of demons that have aligned themselves with him to have a certain amount of freedom to operate in this same sphere in which we dwell. Yet at every precise moment, God is consciously and carefully extending his rule—never allowing "the darkness" to go further than he permits and never allowing "the evil side" to frustrate his purposes and plans. God ensures that the promises and principles of his Word remain valid in every generation. The forced submission of Nebuchadnezzar into recognizing Yahweh God as the rightful ruler is a reminder to us that no earthly ruler will ever thwart his will or cause his kingdom plan to fail. The fact that we who are born-again believers in the Lord Jesus have been "rescued from the domain of darkness and transferred to the kingdom of His beloved Son" (Col 1:13) is a great comfort, for now we are part of an everlasting kingdom that will assuredly prevail and come to full fruition at the return of our Lord.

2. Nebuchadnezzar's dream and the search for an interpreter (4:4–9)

Dan 4:4 marks the beginning of chap. 4 in the Aramaic text of Daniel (see note with 4:1). The NET includes the following helpful information:

The Greek OT (LXX) has the following addition: "In the eighteenth year of Nebuchadnezzar's reign he said." This date would suggest a link to the destruction of Jerusalem in 586 BC. In general, the LXX of chapters 4–6 are very different from the MT, so much so that the following notes will call attention only to selected readings. In Daniel 4 the LXX lacks sizable portions of material in the MT (e.g., vv. 3–6, 31–32), includes sizable portions of material not in the MT (e.g., v. 14a, parts of vv. 16, 28), has a different order of some material (e.g., v. 8 after v. 9), and in some instances is vastly different from the MT (e.g., vv. 30, 34). Whether these differences are due to an excessively paraphrastic translation technique adopted for these chapters in the LXX, or are due to differences in the underlying *Vorlage* of the LXX, is a disputed matter. There is a growing trend in modern scholarship to take the LXX of chapters 4–6 much more seriously than was the case in most of earlier text-critical studies that considered this issue.

Textual Notes

1.a. [Eng. 4:4a] LXX^{O} has some additional words not found in MT: Ἔτους ὀκτωκαιδεκάτου τῆς βασιλείας Ναβουχοδονοσορ, "In the eighteenth year of the reign of Nebuchadnezzar." This temporal notation is lacking in LXX$^{\theta}$. See comments above on the introduction to Dan 4:4–9.

1.b. [Eng. 4:4b] LXX$^{\theta}$ omits reference to the "palace," whereas LXX^{O} reads instead, ἐπὶ τοῦ θρόνου μου, "upon my throne."

3.a. [Eng. 4:6a] LXX^{O} lacks vv. 6–9 (Aram. 3–6), though they are present in LXX$^{\theta}$.

4.a. [Eng. 4:7a] Qere is עָלִּין (Peʿal ptc. mp of עֲלַל).

4.b. [Eng. 4:7b] Qere is כשׂדאי (same situation as Dan 2:5).

5.a. [Eng. 4:8a] A C^{G} fragment and a few MSS read בשׁם, yet the MT makes perfectly good sense as is.

6.a. [Eng. 4:9a] One MS has חֲזִי rather than חֶזְוֵי. The latter is a masc. pl. noun (construct) of חֵזוּ, meaning a "vision, appearance." The problem is that חֶזְוֵי does not make good sense in this context, for this would mean that the king was demanding that Daniel tell him both the visions he had seen *and* the interpretation (which of course is not the case). חֲזִי, on the other hand, makes better sense. This would be the masc. sg. imperative of חֲזָה ("see, behold"). See further discussion in the translation note below.

Translation

4:4 [Aram. 4:1] I, Nebuchadnezzar, was at ease[280] in my home and flourishing[281] in my palace. **5** I beheld a dream that frightened me. The things I imagined[282] *while* on my bed and the visions in my head were alarming[283] me. **6** So I issued a command[284] to bring before me all the wise men of Babylon, so that[285] they could make known to me the interpretation of the dream. **7** When the magicians,[286] the conjurers, the Chaldeans, and the diviners[287] had entered, I told them the dream. Yet they did not make known to me its interpretation. **8** Eventually Daniel came before me—he whose name is Belteshazzar after the name of my god[288] and in whom is a spirit of the holy gods[289]—and I told him the dream. **9** "O Belteshazzar, chief of the magicians,

---

280. שְׁלֵה (*šᵊlēh*) means to be "calm, at east" (*HALOT*, 1994). Goldingay (80), however, thinks שְׁלֵה (*šᵊlēh*) suggests being prosperous rather than relaxed. RJ (94) suggests "carefree," which may be closer to the point. His kingdom was secure, and he was living in a time when he could feel at ease.

281. The words "living luxuriously" are a translation of Aram. רַעְנַן (*raʿănan*), which basically means "flourishing." The idea should not be limited, however, to financial prosperity (as NET's translation "prosperous" might imply). *HALOT* (1983) suggests the meaning "happy, fortunate." Hebrew has a similar adjective (*raʿănān*), "luxuriant, fresh." Most often, this was used of trees and plants, and hence to be "leafy" (thus, *thriving*). The more general translation "flourishing" seems more suitable in v. 4, as it allows wider application—not just financial prosperity but probably political and military stability as well. The idea is that most everything seemed to be going well for the king. (Take note, then, of the irony—he was flourishing like a leafy tree, but in the dream he is a *cut-down tree*.)

282. "Things I imagined" is one word in Aram. (הַרְהֹרִין, *harhōrîn*), a word meaning "fancy, imagining" (BDB, 1090d). Cf. RJ (95) "imaginings." The context concerns fearful things the king was imagining in his mind.

283. יְבַהֲלֻנַּנִי, *yᵊḇahălunnanî* (Paʿel impf. of בְּהַל, *bᵊhal*) is best understood as a past progressive impf. and translated "were alarming me" or "kept alarming me" (so NASB).

284. Lit., "from me a command has been made" (וּמִנִּי שִׂים טְעֵם, *ûminnî śîm ṭᵊʿēm*). Cf. Dan 3:10.

285. Telic use of דִּי, *dî* (cf. Dan 3:28).

286. For the translation and understanding of magicians, conjurers, and Chaldeans, see Dan 1:20; 2:2, 10.

287. For comments and translation of גָּזַר (*gᵊzar*), see translation note at Dan 2:27.

288. Regarding the meaning of the name *Belteshazzar*, see the notes to Dan 1:7. More commonly this name is thought to be an abbreviated form of a theophoric name, although some scholars have regarded it as more of a paronomasia (based on similar sounds) than a strict etymology.

289. Aram. רוּחַ־אֱלָהִין קַדִּישִׁין (*rûaḥ-ʾĕlāhîn qaddîšîn*). Some prefer to translate as "a spirit (or 'the Spirit') of the holy God" (referring to the true God of heaven). The NET is probably correct, however, in translating: "spirit of the holy gods," given that

I know that a spirit of the holy gods *resides* in you, and no mystery[290] baffles[291] you. Consider[292] my dream that I have seen, and declare its interpretation!"

Commentary

4:4–5 *The reception of the dream.* Nebuchadnezzar begins his testimony by recounting his situation at the time he received this dream from God. He was very much "at ease" (i.e., *calm*, perhaps even carefree), and he was "flourishing" (see translation note on v. 4). The purpose of v. 4 is to bring out the king's false sense of security. This was probably at a point in his career when he had

---

the remark came from a polytheistic king. For further discussion, see "Additional Exegetical Comments" at the end of this section.

290. On the term "mystery" (*rāz*), see commentary at Dan 2:18.

291. "Baffles" is a translation of אָנֵס (*ʾānēs*), which literally means "to oppress" (*HALOT*, 1818). That which is very difficult or oppressive is that which baffles; cf. RJ (97), "to be too difficult, baffle."

292. The NET's translation "Consider" is based on a slight emendation of the MT, as commentators struggle with how to translate the latter part of v. 9. The MT has חֶזְוֵי (*ḥezwê*), "the visions of," whereas the emended reading is חֲזִי, *ḥăzî* ("Behold," or "Consider"—understood as a impv. ms verb from חֲזָה, *ḥăzâ*). The latter understanding was proposed years ago by Montgomery (228). He defended emending the text as follows: "But the simplest emendation is to read *ḥăzî* 'behold!' This use of חזי appears in the papp. *APO* pap. I, l. 23, pap. 54, l. 7 (s. Cowley *AP* index), the ostrakon in *APA* no. M, col. I, l. 4, col. 2, ll. I. 3 (Lidz., *Eph.*, 2, 236 *ff.*). This was early confused with the word for 'vision,' and Θ felt bound, exceptionally, to insert 'hear.'" Emending the text is favored by many scholars, because the MT would literally read, "The visions of my dream which I saw and its interpretation, declare! [impv.]." This presents a problem, since Nebuchadnezzar himself states the dream and only asks Daniel for the interpretation. The emended reading finds some support from LXX$^{\theta}$ which rendered this as *akouson* (= Heb. *šəmaʿ*, "Hear!"), "Hear my dream … ." Because the proposed emendation is of a very minor nature, it is certainly possible—even the conservative E. J. Young (101) accepted it. It is also favored by Montgomery (228), Collins (208, 223), Goldingay (80), NIV, NET, and NRSV. If the MT is allowed to stand (favored by NASB and NKJV), the king's words would need to be understood in light of the context (i.e., even though he mentions the dream *and* its interpretation, he is really only expecting the interpretation). This is not unreasonable in light of the larger context of the book. Nebuchadnezzar already knows that Daniel can declare both, so he only needs the interpretation. Furthermore, earlier in v. 7 he only expected the interpretation from the other wise men. Finally, we might point out that had the author wished to say "Behold" (or "Consider"), he might have used the demonstrative particle *hāʾ* (as he did in Dan 3:25), or *ʾălû* (as in Dan 4:7). However, we do have a Hebrew parallel with חֲזֵה, *ḥăzēh* (impv. ms of חָזָה, *ḥāzâ*) in Isa 33:20—"Look at Zion!" (cf. Isa 48:6). One final point: the copyist's eye might have glanced at חֶזְוֵי (*ḥezwê*) at the beginning of v. 7, which caused him to erroneously write the same in v. 6. All things considered, the emended reading is slightly preferred.

succeeded in military conquests, his kingdom had become stable, material riches were flowing into his treasury, and he was enjoying the fruits of his many building projects for which he would become famous.[293] Ferguson reports an occasion of Nebuchadnezzar's boasting as found in his Building Inscription Number 9 that illustrates the sentiment found in v. 4:

> The palace, the seat of my royal authority, a place of union of mighty peoples, abode of joy and happiness, the place where proud ones are compelled to submit, I rebuilt upon the bosom of the wide world. ... My royal decisions, my imperial commands, I caused to go forth from it.[294]

Ferguson adds,

> The king proudly asserted that he made his palace to be gazed at in astonishment by everyone. It was "bursting with splendor. Luxuriance, dreadfulness, awe, gleaming majesty surrounded it." He boasted that he made Babylon into a fortress, strong like a mountain. He says, "I made the dwelling-place of my lordship glorious."

Just when he seemed to have all that his heart longed for, God sent him a dream that would lead to a *shaking up* of his little world. As a result of the visions in his dream, Nebuchadnezzar—who normally would have felt so secure behind the massive walls for which Babylon was famous—was left terrified and deeply troubled.[295]

4:6–7 *The appearance of the Babylonian wise men*. As noted in chap. 2, the Babylonians commonly sought interpretations for their dreams, and the royal court was full of *experts* who specialized in the interpretation of dreams (for which dream manuals had been carefully composed). Thus it is not surprising that the king (v. 6) issued a command (טְעֵם, *tᵉʿēm*) for the wise men of Babylon to be brought in. No explanation is given as to why he did not immediately turn to Daniel for help (rather than calling all the wise men). Notice carefully in v. 6 that the purpose was that the "interpretation" (פְּשַׁר, *pᵉšar*) might be made known—not the dream *and* the interpretation, as in

293. In addition to the many notable temples in Babylon and the famous Ishtar Gate, we could also mention the Hanging Gardens of Babylon that Nebuchadnezzar had built for one of his wives.

294. P. Ferguson, "Nebuchadnezzar, Gilgamesh, and the 'Babylonian Job,'" 324. Ferguson draws on the 1912 work of S. H. Langdon for his quotations (*Die neubabylonischen Königsinschriften*, Vorderasiatische Bibliothek 4 [Leipzig: Hinrichs, 1912], 95, 119, 121).

295. It is difficult to know if "imaginings" (*harhōrîn*) and "visions" (*ḥezwê*) refer to the same thing or to two different experiences.

chap. 2. So, in came the wise *men*, and the king told them the dream (see Dan 1:20; 2:2, 10, 27 regarding the categories of wise men).

The NET indicates that the wise men were unable to disclose the interpretation to the king, as though they were not capable of interpreting the dream. The Aramaic text, however, is literally translated "they did not make its interpretation known to me" (without necessarily commenting on their ability or lack thereof).[296] Based on what we know of Babylonian dream interpretations, we would have expected them to have rendered a verdict on the meaning of the dream (not to do so would be a tacit admission that they lacked the skill to do so). However, in this particular case, the NET's translation "they were unable to disclose its interpretation" is probably justified. In Dan 4:18, the king notifies Daniel that the wise men "were not able to make known the interpretation," and the words "not able" (לָא־יָכְלִין, *lāʾ yōḵlîn*) are explicit in the text. At the very least, the king's opinion is that they were unable to interpret the dream.

4:8–9 *The appearance of Daniel before the king.* The opening words of v. 8 are עַד אָחֳרֵין (*ʿaḏ ʾāḥŏrên*), meaning "eventually" or "at last" (NET has "later"). Daniel did not appear before the king at the same time as the other wise men, though we are not told why.[297] This need not imply that he was not *called* until the king had first spoken to the wise men. Certainly King Nebuchadnezzar would not have forgotten his earlier experience with Daniel recorded in chap. 2. That was too dramatic an event to have easily been forgotten, no matter how much time might have passed. A more likely suggestion is that all the wise men were called at the same time, but Daniel was delayed in coming immediately. Possibly the delay was even purposed by God. Wood (105) states, "The reason could have been that such a delayed appearance of Daniel would give time for the deficiency of the other wise men to show itself once more, which in turn would make his true interpretation all the more impressive."

In recounting the story, the king paused to remind his readers that Daniel had been renamed Belteshazzar "according to the name of my god." Certainly this name, however derived (see 1:7), associated Daniel with Babylonian false gods. The subjects of the empire would most likely have known Daniel by this pagan name, and thus the comment was useful to the

296. The verb מְהוֹדְעִין (*mᵊhôḏᵊʿîn*) is a Hapʿel ptc. of the root *yᵊdaʿ* ("know"), which has the causative nuance "make known," i.e., *inform*. Literally, this means "they did not inform me." The reason *why* they did not inform the king could either be because they were not able to interpret the dream or because they chose not to inform him (realizing that the dream had a negative message and that disclosing it might be offensive to the king). The grammar, however, leaves either option possible, and this must be decided contextually.

297. LXX^{O} omits vv. 6–9 [Aram. 3–6], which concern the calling of the wise men and Daniel's late appearance. The deletion may have been an attempt to solve the difficulty of Daniel's late arrival.

original readers/hearers. The queen in Dan 5:12 also offered a similar name clarification. By the end of chap. 4, the king will realize how unfitting such a name was for Daniel.

The king also points out that there was something else unique about Daniel: "in whom there is a spirit of the holy gods." This comment has elicited a great deal of discussion. Some commentators would translate this differently, most notably by using the singular "God" rather than "gods." Thus, some prefer the translation, "in whom is a spirit/Spirit of the Holy God," as though Nebuchadnezzar meant the true God. The translation "gods/God" reflects the plural *ʾĕlāhîn*. In Hebrew the general word for "God" (i.e., the God of the Bible) is *ʾĕlôhîm*, which is grammatically plural. It can be translated "God" (sg.) or "gods" (pl.) depending on the context.[298] But this parallel does not imply that *ʾĕlāhîn* in the Aramaic passages of Daniel should be rendered in the singular. It should be translated by the plural "gods," and the NET has correctly translated the phrase. (For a defense of this position, see "Additional Exegetical Comments" at the end of this section.) At the time of the dream, the king appraised Daniel as being someone special—someone having a sort of *divine spirit* within him (i.e., very spiritual)—who was amply qualified for the task of interpreting dreams.[299] This was similar to his assessment of the fourth person in the furnace with Shadrach, Meshach, and Abednego—"the appearance of the fourth is like that of a god" (3:25). Nebuchadnezzar could not correctly explain Daniel's unique ability, but he was sure that Daniel was very spiritual and had some sort of divine help.

Verse 5 indicates that Nebuchadnezzar told Daniel the dream he had. In v. 6 the king acknowledges Daniel's uniqueness: (1) he had a spirit of the holy gods; and (2) no mystery (or secret) baffles him. Daniel used the word translated "mystery" earlier in 2:27 when he introduced his interpretation to the king, and the king's use of it here confirms that he did remember that earlier experience with Daniel.

---

298. Some scholars would explain this strange use of the plural as being a "plural of intensification," magnifying how absolute is the Creator God of the Bible (so T. E. Fretheim, "אֱלֹהִים," *NIDOTTE* 1:405–06). Ross, however, indicates that "the plural form of the word, a specialized use of the plural to signify his majestic potentialities, adds to the emphasis on his sovereign power" (A. Ross, *Creation and Blessing* [Grand Rapids: Baker, 1988], 105).

299. B. Becking, "'A Divine Spirit is in You': Notes on the Translation of the Phrase *rûaḥ ʾelāhîn* in Daniel 5,14 and Related Texts," in *The Book of Daniel in the Light of New Findings*, ed. A. S. van der Woude, 515–32, BETL (Leuven: Leuven University Press, 1993), 518, takes אֱלָהִין (*ʾĕlāhîn*), in the expression רוּחַ־אֱלָהִין (*rûaḥ-ʾĕlāhîn*), as a "genitivus qualitatus" and translates "a divine spirit," though he thinks the phrase is meant to express an intentional ambivalence.

Regarding the difficult translation problem at the end of 4:9 ("Consider my dream that I have seen"), see the translation notes above at v. 9. Whether or not one accepts the emended reading over the MT, it is clear that the king had already related the dream to Daniel (v. 8), just as he had to the other wise men (v. 7). Only the interpretation was expected.

Application and Devotional Implications

In the commentary to vv. 4–5, it was pointed out that Nebuchadnezzar seems to have had a false sense of security. He was "at ease" and "flourishing." His kingdom was coming along just fine, and God's kingdom did not matter to him. Probably he could pat himself on the back for having done such a good job of ruling the Babylonian Empire. He had fought hard (literally!) to get where he was—often by brutality and oppression of others—and he fully expected to enjoy the fruit of his efforts. Just when everything seemed to be going right for him, however, the picture suddenly changed.

God decided he would shake King Nebuchadnezzar's world up a bit. Yet God did so graciously, for before administering discipline he sent the king a dream to warn him and give him an opportunity for repentance. Actually, it was grace that God did anything at all in Nebuchadnezzar's life. He could easily have just let Nebuchadnezzar continue straight down the path he was plodding, headed straight for hell. Yet, as we discover many times in the Bible, God loves sinners and yearns to save them from their sinful lifestyles and meaningless existence. Despite all that he had, Nebuchadnezzar was really a poor man, leading an empty life. He might not have realized it, but that was who he was, and God knew it. God wanted him to have more—to know him (the true God), to experience his fellowship, and to learn of his sovereign ways over all mankind.

At certain times in our lives, God may have to take us through a lot to get our attention. We may not like what we experience at the time, but it may be the very best thing for us. The real goal of life is not being "at ease" and "flourishing." Rather, it is in intimately knowing God. What is your chief goal at this moment in your life? Are you mainly concerned about "your kingdom"—what you are achieving, where you are headed? Jesus says to all of us, "seek first His kingdom and His righteousness, and all these things will be added to you" (Matt 6:33, NASB). We need to frequently ask ourselves if we are doing that.

Additional Exegetical Comments

Dan 4:8: "a spirit of the holy gods"

The translation of Dan 4:8 (Aram. v. 5) is indeed difficult, especially the phrase דִּי רוּחַ־אֱלָהִין קַדִּישִׁין בֵּהּ (*ḏî rûaḥ ʾĕlāhîn qaddîšîn bēh*). Should אֱלָהִין (*ʾĕlāhîn*) be translated "gods" or "God"? Should רוּחַ (*rûaḥ*) be translated "spirit" or "Spirit"? Commentators are split on these questions, and we even find both critical scholars and conservatives opting for the translation "God."[300] Various lines of support are offered in defense of the translation "God":

(1) Montgomery has attempted to set forth a case that there is evidence of the plural *ʾĕlāhîn* being used for the singular "God" in extra-biblical Aramaic papyri (and paralleled in Akkadian with *ilâni*).[301] While this should be considered, it does not prove that this is how the plural *ʾĕlāhîn* should be understood in Dan 4:8. At best, it only makes it possible.

(2) Theodotion (LXX^{θ}) rendered the phrase *pneuma theou hagion*, "the Holy Spirit of God" (sg.). Jerome, in the Latin Vulgate, quite deliberately rejected Theodotion's translation in favor of the plural "gods." But this is only Jerome's interpretative opinion, and not necessarily better than that of scholars today.

(3) Some have pointed out that this phrase in Daniel is quite similar to a Hebrew phrase in Gen 41:38 in Pharaoh's question about Joseph: *ʾăšer rûaḥ ʾĕlōhîm bô*. The NET translated this, "in whom the Spirit of God is present." The NASB, on the other hand, has "in whom is a divine spirit." Since Gen 41:38 could be argued either way, it cannot be used as solid proof for the correct interpretation and translation of Dan 4:8.

(4) Taking *ʾĕlāhîn* as singular "God," though followed by a plural adjective "holy" (*qaddîšîn*), is not a problem (so they say), since we find a similar parallel in Hebrew usage. Josh 24:19 has *ʾĕlōhîm qᵊḏōšîm hûʾ*, "He is a holy God," though *holy* (*qᵊḏōšîm*) is in the plural. While this observation is true, when the Hebrew *Elohim* (pl.) is meant to be understood as the true God, a singular adjective is *normally* used (cf. Neh 8:6; Ps 7:10 [Heb. v. 9]). Thus, to cite Josh 24:19 is not sufficient, for the general rule is to have a singular adjective if *Elohim* is intended as "God" rather than "gods."

What is far more persuasive is how the Aramaic *ʾĕlāh* (sg.) and *ʾĕlāhîn* (pl.) are used in the book of Daniel. A careful study of the usage of these terms *in Daniel* indicates that *ʾĕlāhîn* in 4:8 should be taken as a true plural, "gods."

(1) Daniel consistently refers to the true God by the singular *ʾĕlāh*. This is seen in such phrases as "the God of heaven" (*ʾĕlāh šᵊmayyāʾ*) in 2:37, "God Most High" (*ʾĕlāhāʾ ʿillāyʾā*) in 5:18 (cf. 5:21), "the God [*ʾlāhāʾ*] in whose hand is your life-breath" in 5:23, "my God" (*ʾĕlāhî*), and in several places where God alone is referred to (e.g., 5:26).

300. Representatives of this position include such conservative scholars as Young (99) and Wood (106), as well as critical scholars like Montgomery (155, 214) and Collins (208, 222).

301. See Montgomery (153) for details. For instance, he claims that the plural אלהין (*ʾĕlāhîn*) is found construed with a singular verb (e.g., *APO* pap. 56, l. I), while in the subsequent text אלהין = "God."

(2) Elsewhere in Daniel, when Nebuchadnezzar referred to Daniel's God, he used the singular *ʾĕlāh*, not the plural *ʾĕlāhîn*. See 2:47; 3:26, 28, 29; and 4:2 (Eng.).
(3) General references to Daniel's God are in the singular (6:23 [Eng. 22]).
(4) In all other cases where the plural *ʾĕlāhîn* is used in Daniel, the translation "gods" seems appropriate (see 2:11; 3:25; and 5:11).
(5) When blasphemous Belshazzar speaks to Dan in 5:14, he uses the similar expression "a spirit of the gods [*ʾĕlāhîn*] is in you," but we can be sure he is not acknowledging that there is only one true God.
(6) Finally (and perhaps most convincing) in cases where adjectives are used and the true "God" (sg.) is the subject, the adjective will be singular (not plural as in 4:8). A good case in point is 6:27 (Eng. 26) where we have הוּא אֱלָהָא חַיָּא (*hûʾ ʾĕlāhāʾ ḥayyāʾ*), "He is the <u>living</u> God." Similarly, we have אֱלָהּ רַב (*ʾĕlāh rab*), "the great God," in 2:45.

Since אֱלָהִין (*ʾĕlāhîn*) should be translated "gods," it follows that רוּחַ (*rûaḥ*) should be translated "spirit."

3. Nebuchadnezzar's disclosure of the dream to Daniel (4:10–18)

Now that Daniel has been brought into Nebuchadnezzar's presence, the king carefully describes the details of his dream.

Textual Notes

7.a-a. [Eng. 4:10a-a] The words וְחֶזְוֵי רֵאשִׁי are lacking in the LXX tradition. Note בְּחֶזְוֵי רֵאשִׁי in v. 10, which reads more smoothly with the prep. ב.

9.a. [Eng. 4:12a] The Kethib reads יְדֻרוּן (3mp of דור), although the Qere is יְדוּרָן (3fp). The subject (צִפֲּרֵי) occurs in both the fem. and masc., which accounts for the confusion. Note that צִפֲּרֵי take a 3fp verb in Dan 4:18 (albeit the verb שְׁכַן, "to dwell"), in support of the Qere.

9.b. [Eng. 4:12b] The Kethib reading is יִתְּזִין (Hitpeʿel impf. of זון), whereas יִתְּזָן is supported by C^G and V^S. Yet יִתְּזִין is the expected reading. Rosenthal (50) notes, "The hiṯpᵊʿel shows germination of the preformative *t*, and either *ī* or *ā* after the first consonant of the root: יִתְּזִין 'obtains food' D 4:9." Cf. Greenspahn (113).

13.a. [Eng. 4:16a] Elsewhere in Daniel, the determinative form of אֱנָשׁ is אֲנָשָׁא (e.g., 2:38), hence the Qere reading אֲנָשָׁא (rather than Kethib אֱנוֹשָׁא).

14.a. [Eng. 4:17a] A few MSS have וּבְמ׳ ("and by the command of") rather than וּמֵאמַר, perhaps in parallel to בִּגְזֵרַת at the beginning of v. 14. (Observe כְּמֵאמַר in Ezra 6:9.) Notice the NET translation: "This announcement is <u>by</u> the decree of the sentinels; this decision is <u>by</u> the pronouncement of the holy ones." The first two clauses parallel one another.

14.b. [Eng. 4:17b] C^G and some MSS read עַל rather than עַד, and so Collins (210). This is supported by Dan 2:30, עַל־דִּבְרַת דִּי, "in order that." The assimilated form עדבר is attested in Aram. papyrus.

Translation

4:10 [Aram. 4:7] "I was looking[302] in[303] the visions of my mind[304] *while lying* on my bed, and behold, *there was* a tree in the midst of the earth[305] of great height. **11** The tree grew large and became strong until its height reached to the sky and its visibility[306] to the end of the earth.[307] **12** Its foliage was beautiful and its fruit abundant, and on it *there was* food *enough* for all. Under it the animals[308] of the field could[309] find shade, and in its branches the birds of the sky could nest.[310] All creatures[311] could subsist[312] *eating* from it. **13** I continued looking in the visions of my mind *while lying* on my bed,

---

302. חָזֵה הֲוֵית (*ḥāzēh hăwêṯ*) is a common expression in Daniel (13x) meaning "was looking" or "kept looking."

303. Reading בְּחֶזְוֵי רֵאשִׁי (*bᵊḥezwê rē'šî*) as in v. 10 (Aram.).

304. Lit., "head" (רֵאשִׁי, *rē'šî*), but this is a metonymy for the *mind* associated with the head.

305. Verse 10 could be translated "a tree in the midst of the earth" (so NASB). Aram. *'ăra'* can mean either "land" (so NET) or "earth." See commentary on Dan 4:1. The translation "earth" seems more suitable to the universal message that chap. 4 conveys.

306. The meaning of חֲזוֹת (*ḥăzôṯ*) is not entirely clear, seeing that the word only occurs here and in v. 17 (Aram.). BDB (1092d) suggests "sight, visibility," and RJ (97) "appearance." *HALOT* (1873) mentions two primary views: (1) the tradition that this is derived from חזה (*ḥzh*), hence "visibility, appearance"; and (2) the suggestion by Gesenius that this relates to the branches, and thus the *crown* of the tree. Jewish Aramaic does have חָזוּתָא (*ḥāzûṯā'*), "appearance" (Jastrow, 442). LXX^O translated κὰι ἡ ὅπασις αὐτοῦ (*kai hē hopasis autou*), "and his appearance." LXX^θ has καὶ τὸ κύτος αὐτοῦ (*kai to kutos autou*), "and its span (or extent)." Collins (208) wrongly understands κύτος (*kutos*) as "trunk," a meaning it can have but which is improbable in this context.

307. See comment above on v. 10 regarding "earth/land." In either case, this seems to be hyperbole (but it is a dream, not reality).

308. Aram. has literally "the beasts of the field" (*ḥēywaṯ bārā'*); the NET translation "wild animals" captures the point accurately.

309. תַּטְלֵל (*taṭlēl*) and the following imp. verbs are translated as "potential imperfects" (*could*).

310. Lit., "dwell" (דור, *dûr*), but as applied to birds the translation "nest" is more suitable.

311. Lit., "all flesh" (כָּל־בִּשְׂרָא, *kol-biśrā'*).

312. For זון (*zûn*), *HALOT* (1864) suggests the meaning "to live from, subsist on." Adding the word "eating" clarifies (BDB, 1091b gives the meaning "feed").

and behold, an *angelic* watcher,[313] a holy one from heaven, was descending.
14 He was loudly[314] proclaiming as follows: 'Cut down the tree and cut off
its branches! Strip off its leaves and scatter its fruit! Let the animals flee from
under it and the birds from its branches! **15** Only leave the stump[315] with its

---

313. The expression "watcher, a holy one from heaven" (עִיר וְקַדִּישׁ מִן־שְׁמַיָּא, *'îr wᵊqaddîš min-šᵊmayyā'*) refers to an angel. LXX$^{\theta}$ merely transliterated this (ιρ, *ir*), whereas LXX^{O} gave an interpretative translation "an angel" (ἄγγελος, *angelos*). Aram. *'îr* is commonly thought to be related to the Heb. verb *'ûr*, "to awake, rouse oneself" (BDB, 734d), though BH does not use the term *'îr* of a "watcher" (= angel). *HALOT* (1946) indicates that *'îr* is derived from "awake," hence, a watcher, meaning an angel. In Mishnaic Hebrew, *'îr* means a "watcher" or "angel" (Jastrow, 1075a). According to *HALOT* (1946), Aquila and Symmachus translated *'îr* by the Greek term *egrēgoros*, "watcher, wakeful one" (from *egeirō*, "to awaken, wake up").

Despite its commonly understood meaning of "watcher," R. Murray, "The Origin of Aramaic *'îr*, Angel," *Or* 53 (1984): 303–17, has attempted to defend a suggestion originally put forward by M. Dahood that *'îr* originally stemmed from a verb *'yr* meaning "protect," from which possible noun forms (*'ār* or *'ēr*) would have derived in the sense of "guardian." He posits (315), "... *'ār*/*'ēr* was adopted in Aramaic, where we find it vocalized *'îr* and soon understood as 'one who keeps awake.' ... On the hypothesis we have been considering, *'ār*/*'ēr* 'guardian' did not have to move far afield to become *'îr* the unsleeping 'watcher', but the development was part of a far greater spiritual migration." The weakness in Murray's argument is the very little convincing evidence he musters in support of a Heb. verb *'yr* meaning "protect." He appeals to יָעִיר (*yā'îr*) in Deut 32:11 and Job 8:6.

Against Murray stands the evidence from the Greek and Aram. versions of *1 Enoch*. In the Aram. fragments of *1 Enoch*, עִיר (*'îr*) is used of a "heavenly watcher," an angelic being, but is translated εγρήγορος (*egrēgoros*) in the Greek version, which argues for the fact that *'îr* originally stemmed from a verb meaning "to awaken" and hence "to be watchful." We find it, for example, in 4Q204 Col. vi:8: במלי קושטא וחזיה ומוכח לעירי שמ[יא, "with words of justice and of vision and to admonish the heav[enly] Watchers." Yet the term עירי in the Aram. fragment is rendered ἐγρηγόρους (*egrēgorous*) in the Greek version. The term עירין (*'îrîn*) is also found in the *Genesis Apocryphon* (e.g., 1QapGen Col. ii:1: חשבת בלבי די מן עירין הריאתא, "I thought in my heart that the conception was [the work] of the Watchers"). Quite rightly the NASB translated עִיר (*'îr*) as "an *angelic* watcher" (adding the word "angelic" to clarify the meaning).

314. Lit., "proclaiming with strength" (*qārē' bᵊḥayil*).

315. The construct עִקַּר שָׁרְשׁוֹהִי (*'iqqar šoršôhî*) is lit., "the stump of its roots." *HALOT* (1953) indicates that the two words combined may have a singular meaning, "main root" or "taproot." The NET renders this "the stump and its taproot." Although the tree is chopped down, enough of it remains (especially the lower stump and main root) that *life* is still left in it.

roots in the ground, yet with a band of iron and bronze *around it*,[316] in the grass of the field. Let him be drenched with the dew of the sky, and along with the animals, let his portion be the grass of the earth. **16** Let his mind[317] be changed from *that of* man, and let him be given a mind of an animal. Then let seven periods of time [years][318] pass by[319] him. **17** This decree[320] is by the decision[321] of the watchers, and this verdict[322] by a command of the holy ones, in order that the living might know that the Most High rules over

---

316. The words "around it" are not in the Aram. text (but perhaps implied). The verse itself is difficult to understand, and some scholars (e.g., Collins) feel that part of the original text may even have been lost. Goldingay (80) presumes that v. 12b pertains to Nebuchadnezzar and translates, "a band ... around him." The NET adds the following note, "The function of the *band of iron and bronze* is not entirely clear, but it may have had to do with preventing the splitting or further deterioration of the portion of the tree that was left after being chopped down. By application it would then refer to the preservation of Nebuchadnezzar's life during the time of his insanity."

317. Lit., "his heart" in the Aram. (*libbēh*).

318. The words "seven periods of time" is a translation of שִׁבְעָה עִדָּנִין, *šiḇʿâ ʿiddānîn*. The word *ʿiddān* can refer to time in general or to a definite period of time such as a year (see BDB, 1105c2). This is the same word that appears in Dan 7:25 ("time, times, half a time"), where it undoubtedly refers to three and one-half years (cf. comments at Dan 7:25). LXX^{O} translated 4:16 as ἑπτὰ ἔτη (*hepta etē*), "seven years," and this is the probable intention—note that LXX$^{\theta}$ left it more general as "seven times" (ἑπτὰ καιροὶ, *hepta kairoi*). In Josephus' account of this portion of Daniel (*Ant.*, X. 217; emphasis added), he understood *ʿiddānîn* to mean "seven years." He stated, "For the king spent the forementioned period of time in the wilderness, none venturing to seize the government *during these seven years* (παρὰ τὴν ἑπταετίαν, *para tēn heptaetian*), and, after praying to God that he might recover his kingdom, he was again restored to it." Hence, Collins (212) is quite correct in translating *ʿiddānîn* as "Seven years will pass."

319. The words "by him" (*ʿălôhî*) are more literally "over him" in Aram. (so vv. 23, 25, 32).

320. *HALOT* (1961) suggests the translation "decree" for פִּתְגָם (*piṯgām*) in the case of Dan 4:14. BDB (1109) "command, word, affair."

321. גְּזֵרָה (*gᵊzērâ*) is a noun derived from the verb גְּזַר (*gᵊzar*), meaning "to cut, determine." *HALOT* (1844) suggests "decree, resolution," and RJ (100) suggests it can also mean "decision."

322. Regarding the noun שְׁאֵלָה (*šᵊʾēlâ*), BDB (1114b) suggests the meaning "affair," RJ (100) a "question, problem," and *HALOT* (1989) "request, question." Montgomery, however, shows the derivation from שְׁאֵל (*šᵊʾēl*) "to ask." He states (237), "But 'שׁ = 'the thing asked about,' and so the 'decision' upon it. In Targ. to Jer. 12¹ שאילת דינין tr. Heb. משפטים. Further, form II, I of Akk. *šaʾālu* is used of mutually asking questions and so of coming to a decision; hence Shamash is *muštalum* 'decider'; and the derivative *šitultu* = 'Berathung, Entscheidung.'" [Entscheidung, "decision"]. Hence שְׁאֵלָה

the realm[323] of mankind, and He gives it to whom He wills. He will set over it the lowliest[324] of men.' **18** This is the dream that I, Nebuchadnezzar, saw. Now you, Belteshazzar, declare its[325] interpretation, inasmuch as none of the wise men of my kingdom are able to make known to me the interpretation. But you are able, for a spirit[326] of the holy gods is in you."

Commentary

4:10–12 *The bountiful tree.* Earlier, Nebuchadnezzar had related the content of the dream to the other wise men of Babylon (v. 7). Now he relates it to Daniel. The dream contained two essential parts. The first was the tree, and the second was the individual whose *mind is changed*. The tree seems to represent both Nebuchadnezzar and his kingdom. In v. 22 Daniel says, "It is you, O king." However, the leaving of a stump indicates that his kingdom is not completely cut off (v. 26). As in the case of the parts of the statue in chap. 2, the symbolism is fluid enough to pertain to both the king and the kingdom over which he rules.

The metaphor of a tree as representing a *kingdom* is rooted in Hebrew tradition (Ezek 31:3; cf. Isa 2:12–13). In the Ezekiel passage, Assyria was likened to a great cedar in Lebanon. Note especially the common elements in Ezek 31:5–6 (NASB): "Therefore its height was loftier than all the trees of the field and its boughs became many and its branches long because of many waters as it spread them out. All the birds of the heavens nested in its boughs, and under its branches all the beasts of the field gave birth, and all great nations lived under its shade."

The point of this imagery in both Ezekiel and Daniel is to portray the extensiveness of the kingdom and those who are reliant upon and benefit from it . In Matt 13:31–32 the Lord Jesus told a parable of a mustard seed becoming a huge tree, such that "the birds of the sky come and nest in its branches." Most likely this was an allusion to Dan 4:12. Unlike the case of

---

(*šᵊʾēlâ*) in this context is close in meaning with גְּזֵרָה (*gᵊzērâ*). "Verdict" captures the point well.

323. Technically מַלְכוּת (*malkûṯ*) is sg., but some translations (NET, NIV) translate as plural in order to capture the intended idea (contrast NASB, "the realm of mankind"). BDB (1100) gives the general meaning "royalty, reign, kingdom," but BDB #3 is "realm." The point is that the Most High God exercises His sovereign authority over the entire *realm* of mankind.

324. The phrase "lowliest of human beings" is "a low one of men" in Aram. (*šᵊp̱al ʾănāšîm*). However, the words in construct convey the notion of a superlative and thus should be translated "the lowliest (or most lowly) of men" (so Collins, 210). The word "men" (*ʾănāšîm*) is Heb. rather than Aram. (*šᵊp̱al* can be either Heb. or Aram.).

325. The Qere reading is *pišrēh* ("its interpretation"), in contrast to the Kethib *pišrēʾ* ("the interpretation").

326. Regarding the phrase "a spirit of the holy gods," see the "Additional Exegetical Comments" at the end of the previous section pertaining to v. 8.

Nebuchadnezzar, the Lord Jesus' kingdom will not have its branches chopped off (i.e., authority removed in discipline). The point of his parable can be deduced from the intended contrast between the starting size and the final product. Messiah's kingdom, though its beginning was small and obscure, will become large and significant in due time. It began with a handful of common fishermen but will spread through all the earth to include men and women from every tribe and people and tongue.

Miller is probably correct in suggesting that the tree was located "in the middle of the earth" (rather than "middle of the land" as in the NIV and NET). He notes (132), "The tree evidently was centrally located in order to symbolize its position of supreme importance in relation to the rest of the earth." The belief that Babylon was situated at the middle of the earth is reflected in ancient documents, as Ferguson has noted:

> A quarter of a millennium before Nebuchadnezzar an ancient treatise on the topography of Babylon identified the city as the "link of heaven and the underworld." A. R. George sees this as attributing to the city a position at the middle point of the cosmos.
>
> The only known Mesopotamian map of the world probably dates from just a few generations before Nebuchadnezzar. It depicts Babylon as a large rectangle located near the center of the earth. All the other kingdoms are small circles that revolve around it.[327]

Furthermore, its visibility (v. 11b) extended to the end of all the earth (see translation note to v. 10). Ferguson (citing Langdon) has pointed out that "In his building inscriptions Nebuchadnezzar describes his kingdom as encompassing 'all the lands, the entire inhabited world ... kings of far-off mountains and remote *nagû*.'"[328] This is hyperbolic language, to be sure, but not inappropriate for a dream.

---

327. Ferguson, "Nebuchadnezzar, Gilgamesh, and the 'Babylonian Job,'" 323. For A. R. George, see "The Cuneiform Text Tin tirki Babilu and the Topography of Babylon," *Sumer* 35 (1979): 231. Regarding Babylon in ancient cartography, see W. Horowitz, "The Babylonian Map of the World," *Iraq* 50 (1988): 153–54; "The Babylonian Map of the World," in *Mesopotamian Cosmic Geography* (Winona Lake, IN: Eisenbrauns, 1998), 20–42.

328. Ferguson, "Nebuchadnezzar, Gilgamesh, and the 'Babylonian Job,'" 323. Cf. Langdon, *Neubabylonischen Konigsinschriften*, 146, II 17–33, III 2–7; 206, line 17. Even the notion of the tree reaching to the sky has parallels in Babylonian literature. Ferguson notes, "the king's father Nabopolassar leaves an inscription about the restoration of Etemenanki ('The House of the Foundation of the Heavens and the Earth,' 324). He claims that he and his sons made its summit in Babylon 'rival or equal to the heavens.'" For this, Ferguson cites Langdon, *Konigsinschriften,* 60, I 36, 62, I 44. Nebuchadnezzar made a similar claim (147, II 8)].

Verse 12 depicts how blessed this kingdom was and what a blessing it was to many. The shade it provided probably looks at the "protection" and "security" it gave to those who submitted to its authority. In light of Jer 27:6–8, the reference to "wild animals" (lit., "beasts of the field") may refer to the lesser countries and territories that were brought under the dominion of the Babylonian kingdom. It is difficult to know if there is any intended distinction between the wild animals, the birds, and "all creatures" (lit., "all flesh"). In summary, vv. 10–12 are meant to depict the general blessed status that Nebuchadnezzar and his kingdom enjoyed prior to God's discipline against him.

4:13–17 *God's judgment against "the tree."* Beginning in v. 13, the mood of the revelation changes. There is a shift from blessing to judgment. Inaugurating the revelation of this judgment, "an angelic watcher, a holy one from heaven," descends to make the announcement. The term itself for "watcher" (Aram. *ʿîr*) is rather obscure, only occurring in the Bible in Dan 4 (see translation notes above to v. 13). The NIV's translation "messenger" fails to retain the important nuance of the word. Most likely it is related to the Hebrew verb *ʿûr*, meaning "to awake; to arouse oneself." *HALOT* (1946) explains the connection: to be awake meant that one was suitable to serve as a "watcher," which became a fitting term for the angels. In literature of the intertestamental period, the term "watcher" was used of angels.[329] This was especially true in *I Enoch* (see 12:1–6; 20:1–7; and 39:12–14), but also in *Jubilees* and *XII Testaments*.[330] The word also appears later in the *Genesis Apocryphon* from Qumran cave I, where it is used as a term for an angel. In *I Enoch*, it was used of the evil fallen angels who had transgressed their domain as described in Genesis 6 (see *I Enoch* 12:1–6). Enoch was instructed, "Enoch, scribe of righteousness, go and make known to the Watchers of heaven who have abandoned the high heaven, the holy eternal place, and have defiled themselves with women" (12:4).[331] The idea of angels being called "watchers" was quite appropriate.[332] They were to *watch over* the activities of human beings, and when instructed, to carry out divine missions for the Lord God. Hence, we read in *I Enoch* 20:1, "And these are the names of the holy angels

---

329. For a helpful discussion of the "watcher" concept in Jewish literature of the Hellenistic and early Roman periods, see Collins (224–26). Wood (109) points out that this expression was used in the Bun-Dehesh, a commentary on the Zendavesta of the Zoroastrians: "Ormuzd has set four *watchers* in the four parts of the heavens, to keep their eye upon the host of the stars."

330. In *Jub* 4:15 we read of angels of the Lord, referred to as "watchers," who initially came down to teach humanity and perform judgment and righteousness on the earth.

331. Quotations from *I Enoch* are taken from J. H. Charlesworth, *The Old Testament Pseudepigrapha*, Vol 1.

332. One might think of Ps 121:4, "Look! Israel's protector does not sleep or slumber!" The angels were to be like their Lord in keeping watch.

who watch: Suru'el, one of the holy angels—for (he is) of eternity and trembling. Raphael, one of the holy angels, for (he is) of the spirits of man." In this latter case, the "watchers" are holy angels, not fallen ones. The adjective "holy" (קַדִּישׁ, *qaddîš*) in Dan 4:13 clarifies that this *angelic watcher* is indeed one of the holy angels.[333]

This *angelic watcher* makes a loud proclamation (v. 14). Such an action is frequently made by angels in the book of Revelation (e.g., Rev 10:1–3), thus underscoring the divine authority with which he speaks. His announcement was that the tree was to be cut down and its branches, leaves, and fruit removed. Also the animals and birds were to flee. This action is probably what would have frightened the king, and most likely even he himself would have perceived that evil was about to befall him.

Ferguson calls attention to the Wadi Brissa inscription recorded by Nebuchadnezzar as his troops marched westward to conquer Lebanon in which the mighty cedars of Lebanon are repeatedly mentioned. He notes,

> Nebuchadnezzar calls Lebanon "the lush, green mountain forest of Marduk." Twice in the inscription he boasts that he felled the mighty cedars with his own clean hands.[334]

On the inscription, Nebuchadnezzar stands beside one of the trees with something in his hand. Ferguson points out (328): "In column 4, directly to the left of the tree, the king states: 'With my own clean hands I felled (the mighty cedars).' It seems reasonable, then, to assume that this engraving portrays the king in the very act of chopping down a cedar." In column 6, "the king boasts that he made the city into a mountain-high fortress. He goes on to state that he gathered all men to its shadow for their well-being, prosperity and blessing. His kingdom reached the ends of the earth, and he raised the city of Babylon to the summit." Ferguson concludes (328),

> This inscription clearly shows how totally obsessed Nebuchadnezzar was with the mighty cedars of Lebanon. It is little wonder that he dreamed about them. There would have been no more vulnerable point for God to speak to Nebuchadnezzar about his pride than through the metaphor of the great tree. He would have

333. Although the term *qaddîš* is used in Dan 7:18, 21 to refer to God's people (i.e., saints), the precise subject must be determined by context. That he "descends from heaven" in 4:13 makes clear that this is an angel, not a human "saint." In support of this, I. Fröhlich, "Stars and Spirits: Heavenly Bodies in Ancient Jewish Aramaic Tradition," *AS* 13 (2015): 120, points out, "The fact that the Holy Ones are normally heavenly beings has long been recognized. An extensive body of evidence from Qumran texts proves that the beings called Holy Ones were usually understood as heavenly beings." Collins (314) makes reference to 1QM 1:16; 10:11–12; 12:1, 4, 7; 15:14; 1QS 11:7–8; 1QH 3:21–22; 10:35; 1QDM 4:1; 1QSb 1:5; 1Q 36:1; 1QapGen 2:1; 11Qmelch 1:9; and 4Q181 1:3–6.

334. Ferguson, "Nebuchadnezzar, Gilgamesh, and the 'Babylonian Job,'" 327.

> had little problem in identifying the sheltering, nourishing tree with his own kingdom."

Since we have limited historical records from the latter part of Nebuchadnezzar's reign, we really do not know what kind of "disruption" might have gone on within his kingdom. Was there a rebellion? Was there a famine or other natural disasters? We simply do not know. The text seems to suggest that the kingdom itself (not just Nebuchadnezzar as an individual) was disrupted or negatively affected.

Verse 15, however, indicates that the divine judgment would not be complete and irreversible. The stump (or stump and taproot) would be left in the ground (see translation note to v. 15). That is, the tree still had life left in it and had the potential to return to its flourishing state once again. As in the case of the stump of Isa 6:13 (cf. 11:1), a ray of hope remained for Nebuchadnezzar and his kingdom. The purpose of the band of iron and bronze is not clear in v. 15, but most likely signified some sort of *protection* put on the kingdom while the king himself was rendered unfit to rule.

The latter part of v. 15, along with v. 16, concerns King Nebuchadnezzar himself. The imagery shifts from that of the tree to that of an animal-like creature. He would even eat like an animal. The term translated "grass" (עֲשַׂב, *ʿăśaḇ*) can also mean other forms of herbage.[335] Goldingay (78) translates this as "plants" to indicate that his diet was not necessarily limited to grass. His mind (lit., "heart") would also be changed from that of a man to that of an animal. Archer (7:61) summarizes the meaning of the Aramaic word *lᵊḇaḇ*:

> the word for 'mind' is *lᵊḇaḇ* (lit., 'heart,' a term that in Scripture refers to the inner self as the seat of moral reflection, choice of the will, and pattern of behavior). It includes not only the mental processes but also the feelings, affections, and emotions, along with all the motivational factors leading to decisions and responses to life situations.

The king's heart (including his mental reasoning) was the very source of his pride, and it is there that God touched him.

The length of punishment is prescribed in v. 16 as "seven periods of time" (שִׁבְעָה עִדָּנִין, *šiḇʿâ ʿiddānîn*). (See translation notes to v. 16 and 7:25.) A certain specified period for his punishment was intended, and this would have been most likely measured in years. While acknowledging that *ʿiddān* is sometimes used in a general sense for "time," it can be used of a definite period of time such as a "year," and that is the most likely meaning in 4:16.[336] The context (in which the interpretation is given in v. 32) argues for an

335. *HALOT* (1954) offers the meaning "plants, grass, herbage" for *ʿăśaḇ* and makes reference to the Akkadian verb *ešēbu*, meaning "to grow luxuriantly."

336. In Dan 2:8 and 3:5 it pertains to a general sense of time. Goldingay (81) admits that the Akk. equivalent has the meaning of "year" in the Harran inscription.

understanding as "years."[337] As will be argued in the case of 7:25, the term *ʿiddān* undoubtedly means "year" in that context. Hartman (172) points out that in giving the explanation of the dream in 4:32, Daniel would have used the unambiguous word for "years" if *ʿiddānîn* did not also have this meaning. God ordained that Nebuchadnezzar was to be punished by having his *dignity* and *kingly pride* taken away for seven years.

In v. 17 the reason is stipulated for this punishment upon Nebuchadnezzar. Before stating the reason, the text first explains the announcement/decision is by the decree of the "watchers" and "holy ones." These terms are used in a *parallelism*, and thus are to be equated. The terms are the same as those in v. 13, though they are now expressed in the plural. This seems to refer to an *angelic council* that stood before Yahweh God (cf. Gen 1:26; Ps 82:1; 1 Kgs 22:18–23; Job 1:6–12; 2:1–6). The NET's translation ("by the decree of the sentinels; ... by the pronouncement of the holy ones") would signify that the angels merely *announced* the heavenly decision. Other translations (e.g., NASB's "the decision is a command of the holy ones") would indicate that the angels somehow may have been involved in the making of the decree. The latter part of v. 17 tends to favor the former idea (the decision was God's, and the angels concurred with the divine decree)—and this is the understanding of most commentators.

In the final part of v. 17, we see that this heavenly decision was not merely to punish Nebuchadnezzar, but that he (and others[338]) might learn a valuable two-part lesson. The first is that "the Most High rules over the kingdom of mankind, and He gives it to whom He wills." The point was clear to Nebuchadnezzar: he needed to humble himself before the one who granted him the authority to be king. The second part of the lesson was that "He will set over it the lowliest of men." The word "lowliest" in this context does not mean the most *unworthy*, but the most *humble*. Without doubt, God has a special regard for humility (Ps 138:6). God is never impressed by those who deceive themselves into thinking they are something (cf. Isa 57:15). The translation given by the NET (and most other translations) is to render the verb tense as though this is a *timeless truth*. The verb יְקִים, *yəqîm* (often translated "He establishes"), could also be translated "He will establish (or will set over)"—future tense. The first makes it sound like a general principle, which is really not true. God does not *generally* establish humble men as kings. History is full of kings who for the most part were self-centered, prideful rulers. The second option (as future tense) looks to the future when God will establish a ruler over the realm of mankind who is indeed the

---

337. Collins (228) points out, "The expression is understood as 'years' in the OG, Josephus, Jerome, and the medieval Jewish commentators but some patristic authors take it as 'season.'"

338. The NET's "those who are alive" is actually one word in the Aramaic: חַיַּיָּא, *ḥayyayyāʾ*. The adjective *ḥay* is in the plural ("the living ones"), and thus refers to more people than just Nebuchadnezzar.

lowliest of men, namely the Lord Jesus Christ (cf. Zech 9:9–10; Matt 11:29; Phil 2:8).[339] Even if one takes the latter part of the verse as a general principle, this virtue is seen most sublimely in Jesus Christ.

4:18 *Nebuchadnezzar's instruction to Daniel.* Following his recounting of the dream, Nebuchadnezzar then turned to Daniel and told him to tell the interpretation. The main lesson of the dream in v. 17, which Nebuchadnezzar himself stated, was already apparent and needed no interpretation. The symbolism of the tree and the animal-like behavior, however, did need interpretation. The king admitted before Daniel that the other wise men of the royal court were not able (*lo ʾ yōḵlîn*) to declare the interpretation, and then expressed his confidence that Daniel was able to do so, because he had "a spirit of the holy gods" in him. The king's understanding of Daniel's ability may have been faulty, but he at least recognized that Daniel had a way of receiving divine help to interpret dreams.[340] (Recall Dan 2:26 where the king asked Daniel *if he were able* to interpret his dream.) Nebuchadnezzar recognized that Daniel was different than the other wise men, and he knew the reason was due to the God Daniel worshiped.

339. B. T. Viviano, "The Least in the Kingdom: Matthew 11:11, Its Parallel in Luke 7:28 (Q), and Daniel 4:14," *CBQ* 62 (2000): 41–54, has observed that the phrase "lowliest of men" (שְׁפַל אֲנָשִׁים, *šᵊp̱al ʾănāšîm*) stands out in the chapter because (1) it is the only element of the dream that does not get repeated in the interpretation (comp. 4:25 and 4:32); and (2) the phrase is in Heb. rather than Aram. (though he admits that *šᵊp̱al* can be either Heb. or Aram.). He concludes (52), then, that this is a *title* pointing in a Christological direction and is the most proximate OT influence on the formulation of Matt 11:11, that "the one who is least in the kingdom of heaven is greater than" John the Baptist. He also observes (51), "that the Vg. translation gives *humillimum hominem,* 'the basest man.' This supports the OG translator's decision to take the phrase as one referring to an individual person, as singular rather than plural."

340. R. G. Wooden, "Changing Perceptions of Daniel: Reading Daniel 4 and 5 in Context," in *From Biblical Criticism to Biblical Faith: Essays in Honor of Lee Martin McDonald*, ed. W. H. Brackney and C. A. Evans, 9–23 (Macon, GA: Mercer University Press, 2007), has helped put the king's assessment of Daniel's abilities in proper context. He argues that the assessment coming from the lips of Babylonian figures in chaps. 4 and 5 must be balanced by a broader contextual reading. Wooden states (20), "when we come to chapters 4 and 5, we have been prepared to understand the divine source of Daniel's abilities. They are not merely impressive human feats, ... ; they have an immediate divine origin. ... By prefacing chapters 4 and 5 with the information from 1:17 and the prayer in 2:20–23, the editors of the stories make it clear that Daniel acts with divine revelation. He was not merely a diviner; he was much more like a prophet, from the Jewish point of view."

Biblical Theology Comments

The appearance of the *angelic* watcher to the king in a dream at night in Dan 4:13 is not necessarily unusual. In this case, the angel's mission was to announce impending judgment facing the king. A study of angels in the Bible reveals that they served a number of different purposes. Among other things, they would speak for God (Gen 16:9–11), convey God's will to humans (Gen 16:9), bring encouragement (Jud 6:12), give direction (2 Kgs 1:3), and do things that would graciously benefit men (Gen 24:7). Though in the OT we do see cases in which they enacted God's judgment (e.g., 2 Sam 24:16; 1 Chron 21:12), only rarely do we see them *announcing* impending judgment from God. Yet such an activity is clearly observed in the NT, especially in regard to "Babylon's" coming judgment (Rev 14:8–9; 18:21).

A bit odder is the statement in Dan 4:17 that "This decree is by the decision of the watchers, and this verdict by a command of the holy ones." Nowhere else in Scripture do we find a clear example of an angelic council that collaborates to make decisions of judgment upon mankind. We do, however, have an example of angels attending a heavenly court in which they participate and dialogue with God about divine decisions. This is seen in the prophecy of Micaiah against Ahab, king of Israel (1 Kgs 22:19–23). Yet here the angels are not acting independently of the Lord, and the final decision is his (note v. 23 – "the Lord has proclaimed disaster against you"). This strengthens the conclusion in Dan 4:17 that the decision to bring judgment upon Nebuchadnezzar may have been made in a heavenly court attended by angels, but the final verdict was God's.

Application and Devotional Implications

One of man's weaknesses is his faulty thinking that he has to impress others that he is great. Genuine humility is not always seen as an *absolute credential* for leadership. Too often the tendency in leaders is to try to impress others rather than to be a person of humility, or to be consumed with receiving "glory" in the eyes of men. In God's economy, however, humility is right up there at the top of the list. God (who is greater than all) is not impressed by puny little earthlings who think they are something when they are not. He is impressed by people who are genuinely humble.

God also showed all mankind what true humility would look like, for the Lord Jesus Christ was the perfect model of godly humility. Jesus is undoubtedly the "lowliest" of all men who have ever lived, in that he has been the most humble. Philippians 2:6 tells us that Jesus did not consider equality with God as something that had to be *grasped* or tightly clung to. He could let go of all his royal privileges to come to earth and become a sacrifice for sins. That took humility. One could also think of his illustration of washing the feet of the twelve before he was crucified. When he had finished, he told them:

> You call me Teacher and Lord, and you are right, for so I am. If I then, your Lord and Teacher, have washed your feet, you also ought to wash one another's feet. For I have given you an example, that you also should do just as I have done to you. Truly, truly, I say to you, a servant is not greater than his master, nor is a messenger greater than the one who sent him. If you know these things, blessed are you if you do them. (John 13:13–17, ESV)

Just as God wanted Nebuchadnezzar to realize a lesson about humility, so he desires that all of us realize this lesson. The position we have (whatever it is) has been given to us by God. With that position, we should be humble and stand ready to serve the needs of others—not seek glory itself. Are you serving others today, or are you serving yourself?

4. Daniel's Interpretation of Nebuchadnezzar's Dream (4:19–27)

In the previous paragraph Nebuchadnezzar carefully explained the details of the dream to Daniel, being confident that Daniel would be able to give the correct interpretation. Beginning with v. 19 and running through v. 33, the "point of view" shifts from Nebuchadnezzar to Daniel.

In vv. 19–27 Daniel does indeed interpret the details of the dream for the king. This paragraph has three parts: the first (v. 19) records Daniel's initial reaction of shock upon hearing the dream; the second (vv. 20–26) is the actual interpretation of the dream; and the third (v. 27) is Daniel's advice for the king in light of what has been predicted. The second part (vv. 20–26) is obviously the longest and is broken down into three subsections. In each of these sub-sections, Daniel restates a part of the dream and then gives the corresponding interpretation. The first subsection (vv. 20–22) deals with Nebuchadnezzar's blessedness up until the present time; the second (vv. 23–25) deals with the seven years of judgment awaiting him; and the third (v. 26) deals with the grace of having his kingdom restored after the discipline.

Textual Notes

16.a. [Eng. 4:19a] Rather than the Kethib reading פִּשְׁרֵא ("the interpretation"), the Qere is פִּשְׁרֵהּ ("its interpretation"), conforming to פִּשְׁרֵהּ at the end of the verse.

17.a. [Eng. 4:20a] Rather than לְכָל־אַרְעָא, a number of MSS read לסוף כל ארעא, "to the end of the earth" as in v. 8 (Eng. v. 11).

21.a. [Eng. 4:24a] Rather than the 3ms verb form מְטָת, a few MSS read the 3fs מְטַת. Note the fem noun גְּזֵרַת that stands as the subj. Two MSS have מטית (מְטִיַת or מְטָיַת).

24.a. [Eng. 4:27a] Rather than the Kethib חֲטָיָךְ (sg. form), read with Qere חֲטָאָךְ (pl.). Note the form חטאיך from the Cairo Geniza. For discussion, see Montgomery (242).

Translation

4:19 [Aram. 4:16] Then Daniel (whose name was Belteshazzar) was momentarily[341] appalled.[342] His thoughts were terrifying him. The king responded,[343] "Belteshazzar, do not let the dream and its[344] interpretation terrify you." Belteshazzar replied, "My lord,[345] *if only*[346] the dream were for those who hate you and its interpretation for your adversaries. **20** The tree that you saw that grew large and became strong, whose height reached to the sky and its visibility to all the earth, **21** whose foliage was beautiful and its fruit abundant and on which *there was* food *enough* for all, under whose branches the animals of the field used to dwell[347] and the birds of the sky used to nest[348] in its branches—**22** it is you, O king! You have become great and strong, and your greatness has increased and reached the heavens, and your dominion[349] to the end[350] of the earth. **23** And *as for the fact* that the king saw an *angelic* watcher,[351] a holy one, coming down from heaven and saying, 'Chop down the tree and destroy it, but leave the stump with its roots in the ground, yet with a band of iron and bronze, in the grass of the field, and let him be drenched with the dew of the sky, and his portion be with the animals of the field, until seven periods of time [years] pass by him'—**24** this is the interpretation, O king. That which has come upon my lord, the king, is by decree of the Most

---

341. Lit., "for a while" (כְּשָׁעָה חֲדָה, *kᵊšāʿâ ḥăḏâ*). KJV translates, "was astonished for <u>one</u> <u>hour</u>." But the Aram. text does not indicate the time so specifically. The word *šāʿâ* means "a moment, a short space of time" (*HALOT*, 2001).

342. The NIV translation "perplexed" could be misleading, as this may suggest there was some confusion on Daniel's part. But the point is that he understood and was alarmed at the fate awaiting the king.

343. Lit., "answered and said." Yet this is redundant in Eng., and thus shortened (and so throughout).

344. Reading with the Qere פִּשְׁרֵהּ (*pišrēh*).

345. NET's translation "Sir" is perhaps weak. The Aram. מָרְאִי (*mārᵊʾî*) literally means "lord" (so *HALOT*, 1922), and can be used of superiors such as kings, and even of God himself (as in Dan 5:23). The word appears again in v. 24, where NET translates it "my lord."

346. The words "if only" are added (so NET, NIV, and NASB), as contextually this is better understood as a hypothetical wish rather than a real wish.

347. Understanding תְּדוּר (*tᵊḏûr*) as a customary impf.: "used to dwell."

348. Lit., "dwelling" (יִשְׁכְּנָן, *yiškᵊnān*), and taking the verb as a customary impf.

349. Aram. *šālṭānāḵ* means "your dominion" (i.e., the extent of your rule).

350. The MT reads לְסוֹף אַרְעָא (*lᵊsôp̄ ʾarʿāʾ*), "to the end [sg.] of the earth." LXX^{θ}, S, and Vg. read the pl., "ends."

351. For עִיר וְקַדִּישׁ (*ʿîr wᵊqaddîš*), see translation notes at Dan 4:13 [Eng.], and the commentary for this verse.

High. **25** You are about to be driven out[352] from human society,[353] and your dwelling place shall be with the animals of the field. They will give you grass to eat[354] like cattle, and you will be drenched with the dew of the sky. Seven periods of time *[years]* shall pass by for you, until you come to realize[355] that the Most High rules over the realm[356] of mankind and gives it to whomever He wills. **26** Now in that they said to leave the stump and roots of the tree, your kingdom will be restored[357] to you as soon as[358] you come to realize that *the God enthroned in* heaven[359] rules. **27** Therefore, O king, may my advice be pleasing to you. Break away from your sins by dealing righteously[360] and

---

352. The verb טָרְדִין (*ṭārdîn*), though grammatically an active ptc., is properly translated as a passive. Rosenthal (56, § 181) explains, "The 3. masc. pl. and the masc. pl. of the participle frequently express an impersonal subject and thus substitute for a passive construction."

353. Lit., "from mankind" (*min ʾănāšā ʾ*). NET's "rom human society" captures the point well.

354. According to *HALOT* (1885), טְעֵם (*ṭᵊʿēm*) means "to give to eat."

355. "Come to realize" translates the one Aram. word, תִנְדַּע (*tinda ʿ*), meaning to "know, learn, understand" (*HALOT*, 1888). NET's "understand" and NASB's "recognize" tend to be slightly more passive than NIV's "acknowledge." There is slight difference between *understanding* that "the Most High rules over" all and *acknowledging* this truth. The main point seems to be that Nebuchadnezzar had to come to recognize this truth.

356. For מַלְכוּת (*malkûṯ*) as "realm," see the translation note at 4:17 (Eng.).

357. The words "will be restored" are not actually a verb in the Aram. text, but a rendition of the adjective קַיָּמָה (*qayyāmâ*) meaning, "enduring." Hence, "your kingdom will endure until you recognize." The point is that his kingdom would stay intact during this time of judgment and be safe-guarded by God.

358. This combination ,מִן־דִּי *min-dî* (preposition and relative particle), though causal in Dan 3:22 and Ezra 5:12, has the force "as soon as, insofar as" in this context (so *HALOT*, 1852). RJ (105) suggests "as soon as, after, until."

359. In the previous verse (as well as 4:17) the king was to recognize that "it is the Most High who rules." Now in v. 26, he substitutes "heaven" for "Most High"—until you understand that heaven rules. "Heaven" (שְׁמַיִן, *šᵊmayin*) is a reference to God who rules from his throne in heaven (metonymy of adjunct for subject). Hence, the words "the God enthroned in" are supplied in the translation in italics to bring out the point. Cf. Luke 15:21, "I have sinned against heaven and in your sight."

360. The translation "dealing righteously" is an attempt to render the noun צִדְקָה (*ṣiḏqâ*), which BDB (1109) defines as "right doing." This would be the Aram. equivalent to the Heb. term for "righteousness." The NIV simply translates "by doing what is right," and the NASB "by doing righteousness." Collins (212) tries to connect this with almsgiving: "to atone for your sins by almsgiving and for your iniquity by mercy to the poor." This receives some support from a statement in *TDNT* (2:485) that in Judaism צדקה came to have the sense of "benevolent activity" and even almsgiving. Cf. *HALOT* (1963), "correct practice, charity." Justification for this understanding

from your iniquities by being merciful to those who are oppressed.[361] Perhaps your prosperity will be prolonged."

Commentary

4:19 *Daniel's initial reaction of shock.* For a brief moment Daniel stood there, appalled at what he had heard. Was he appalled because he did not understand the dream? The NIV's "greatly perplexed" might infer that he was confused, but this was not the case. The reason for his reaction of shock is clarified by the following words: "his thoughts were terrifying him." This word "terrifying" (from Aram. בְּהַל, *bᵊhal*) means that Daniel was frightened by what he had heard. Daniel understood right away what the dream signified, and the interpretation terrified him. The context indicates that Daniel personally cared about the king, and thus any misfortune for the king was a real concern to Daniel. Furthermore, we can well imagine that Daniel might be greatly concerned about any political repercussions that might eventuate from this, and especially for his people who were living in exile in Babylonia.

Nebuchadnezzar could sense Daniel's astonishment and emotional reaction of fear and tried to calm Daniel (notice that the king is still calling Daniel by his Babylonian name, Belteshazzar). We can sense that the king appreciates his faithful servant, Daniel. Young (106) remarks, "By his previous courage and steadfast adherence to principle, Dan. has won the confidence and respect of the king." Conversely, Daniel's respect for the king was shown in two ways. First, Daniel called him "my lord" (מָרְאִי, *mārᵊʾî*).[362] Second, he told the king that he wished the dream and its interpretation were for the king's enemies. In saying this, he was giving a word of comfort in a critical moment. Even though the king faced a difficult future, Daniel was indicating that he stood loyally by him. Daniel's reaction could have been to think that this pagan misfit of a king was merely getting what he deserved,

---

arises from the parallelism with בְּמִחַן עֲנָיִן (*bᵊmiḥan ʿănāyin*), "by being merciful to the poor/oppressed" (yet see below on עֲנָיִן, *ʿănāyin*). Nevertheless, most English translations give it a more general rendering, one that would call for the king to rule over his subjects in a righteous and fair way (avoiding corruption and overly harsh measures).

361. The word translated "oppressed" is Aram. עֲנָיִן, *ʿănāyin* (masc. pl. adj. of *ʿănāy*). BDB (1107b) gives the meaning as "poor, needy," but *HALOT* (1952) suggests "miserable." The translation "the oppressed" might be more suitable, however, as the Heb. adj. *ʿānî* can mean "poor, afflicted, humble." There were many in Nebuchadnezzar's kingdom that were oppressed and afflicted (and *poor* as a result), and much of this was the fault of Nebuchadnezzar's harsh policies and overly-ambitious building projects.

362. The Qere reading; Kethib is *mārʾî.*

and to be delighted in what was about to happen. Being mature in the Lord, however, Daniel did not hastily take delight in God's discipline that befell the king and was able to see himself in a more noble role of being a friend and spiritual witness to the king.

4:20–22 *The interpretation part I: Nebuchadnezzar's prior blessedness.* Verses 20–21 essentially repeat 10–12. Daniel merely restated the main points of the first part of the dream. Beginning in v. 22, however, he gave the interpretation of what the tree itself signified. He began by saying, "it is you, O king." The words almost seem to be an echo of what Nathan the prophet said to David: "you are the man" (*ʾattāh hāʾîš*)—though without such confrontational force. God had allowed Nebuchadnezzar's kingdom to expand, so that (figuratively) it "reached to the sky." This depicts Nebuchadnezzar at the peak of his political power, dominating the world scene. His authority—his dominion, the extent of his rule—reached to the ends of the earth (at least over most of the civilized world). At this particular time in history, Nebuchadnezzar's kingdom was the undisputed superpower of its day, stretching across all Mesopotamia as far as the Mediterranean and including even Egypt. It was God's sovereign permission that had allowed this kingdom to come about and for Nebuchadnezzar to be the man to rule over it all. Truly it was a great kingdom to rule over, and Nebuchadnezzar was very blessed. God reminded him of this so that he would realize what was being taken away from him, and that the Lord was the one who controlled human kingdoms and those who ruled over them.

4:23–25 *The interpretation part II: Seven years of judgment.* In this second phase of the interpretation, the same pattern is followed: Daniel restates a part of the dream (v. 23) and then follows that with the interpretation (vv. 24–25). The restatement of the dream in v. 23 began by recalling parts of vv. 13–14. Not all the actions from v. 14, however, are restated, and in fact, Daniel seems to summarize them in v. 23a by saying, "and destroy it" (וְחַבְּלוּהִי, *wᵊḥabbᵊlûhî*). This verb (root *ḥăḇal*) was not used earlier when Nebuchadnezzar recounted the dream. However, it appears in Dan 2:44 in regard to God's kingdom: "the God of heaven will raise up an everlasting kingdom that will not be destroyed" (תִּתְחַבַּל, *tiṯḥabbal*). Using this verb in 4:23 draws a deliberate contrast between God's kingdom, which will not be destroyed, and Nebuchadnezzar's kingdom, which can be destroyed.

Beginning in v. 24, Daniel relates the interpretation of the cutting down of the tree, the metal band, the animal-like behavior, and the seven periods of time. First, however, he clarified that the decision to carry all this out came from "the Most High." Earlier in v. 17 it was said to be by decree/decision of the watchers/holy ones (i.e., holy angels). This is not a contradiction. God (the Most High) issued the decree, and the holy angels affirmed and announced it. Again in v. 24, Daniel called the king "my lord," showing his respect for the king, even in the light of pronouncing judgment.

The judgment would affect especially the king, for he was to be driven out from human society and dwell among the wild animals.[363] (This will be explained more in v. 33.) He would even behave like a wild animal, being fed grass (or perhaps herbage/vegetation—see commentary to v. 15). Becoming "damp with the dew of the sky" probably indicates that he would spend his nights out in the fields and thus be covered with dew by morning. He would carry on in this state for "seven times," i.e., seven years (see commentary on v. 16). Though it would be for seven years, his punishment would continue until he recognized that the Most High exercised his authoritative rule over the realm of mankind and had the right to give it to whomever he wanted.

The punishment was appropriate for Nebuchadnezzar: he lost control of his kingdom because he lost control of himself (and thus, acting like a beast, he was allowed to live with beasts). Archer (7:63) remarks, "This prolonged humiliation would teach him to respect God's sovereignty over the affairs of men and to realize that he, like all earthly rulers, held authority only by permission of the Almighty in heaven above."

4:26 *The interpretation part III: Future grace.* Lastly, Daniel explained the leaving of the stump and roots of the tree. The fact that the tree was not *completely* removed gave hope of a restoration in the future when the punishment would be over with. This was a word of grace, for his kingdom would *endure* (see translation notes on v. 26). The point is that his kingdom would stay intact during this time of judgment and be safeguarded by God, allowing the possibility for him to be restored again to his throne and in his right mind. Yet it would be necessary for him to recognize that it is heaven (i.e., the Lord God upon his heavenly throne) that rules, before any such restoration could take place.[364] Who served as the official ruler, then, while the king was incapacitated during these seven years? One possibility would be that the king's son (Amel-Marduk) ruled over the country during this period, thus allowing the government to continue functioning.[365] We do

363. Ferguson, "Nebuchadnezzar, Gilgamesh, and the 'Babylonian Job,'" 325, points out that the portrayal of the king's humiliation has close parallels with the Mesopotamian picture of the primordial man, Enkidu, found in the Gilgamesh epic, a work with which Nebuchadnezzar would certainly have been quite familiar. Ferguson concludes (326), "There would have been no plainer way to tell an educated Babylonian he would be humbled than to inform him that he was going to become like Enkidu." For a similar study along these lines, see J. A. Garrison, "Nebuchadnezzar's Dream: An Inversion of Gilgamesh Imagery," *BSac* 169 (2012): 172–87.

364. See translation notes on מִן־דִּי (*min-dî*) above.

365. D. J. Wiseman, "Babylonia 605–539 B.C.," in *The Cambridge Ancient History III:2*, rev. ed. (Cambridge: Press Syndicate of the University of Cambridge, 1991), 240, mentions some contracts signed by Amel-Marduk before Nebuchadnezzar's death that could indicate a period of co-regency. He also remarks, "Later tradition

know that this Amel-Marduk served as king *after* Nebuchadnezzar for at least two years (562–560 BC; cf. Jer 52:31–32).

4:27 *Daniel's advice for the king.* Verse 26 concluded the interpretation for the king. The final element of this paragraph (v. 27) concerns the advice that Daniel himself gave to Nebuchadnezzar: "Break away from your sins by dealing righteously and from your iniquities by being merciful to those who are oppressed. Perhaps your prosperity will be prolonged." (See translation notes to v. 27 for the choice of "oppressed" rather than "poor.")

Other scholars, perhaps influenced by the LXX translations, have differed, viewing this as a call for almsgiving. (For a more technical discussion, see the additional exegetical comments at the end of this unit.)

The word translated "break away" is פְּרֻק, *pᵊruq*.[366] This is parallel to the Heb. *pāraq*, and we have a couple of good examples that help us understand its concrete meaning. The first comes from Gen 27:40 involving the imagery of a yoke: "When you grow restless, you will tear off (*pāraqtā*) his yoke from your neck" (NET). The second example comes from Exod 32:2, when Aaron was collecting gold for the calf idol: "Tear off (*pārᵊqû*) the gold rings which are in the ears of your wives, your sons, and your daughters, and bring them to me" (NASB). In both examples, the idea of "separating from" is fundamental to the meaning of the verb. Therefore, the translation "break away" in Dan 4:27 is substantiated. Daniel is not advising the king to *atone for* his sins, but to *part from them* (i.e., to cease doing the sins he had been doing).

In breaking away from his sins, the king was to "deal righteously." In the Aramaic text, this is one word (בְּצִדְקָה, *bᵊṣidqâ*—with a prefixed preposition *bᵊ*). In the history of Judaism, the word *ṣidqâ* (Heb. *ṣᵊdāqâ*) came to have the sense of "benevolent activity" and even specifically of almsgiving.[367] Yet it is doubtful that *ṣidqâ/ṣᵊdāqâ* carried that kind of nuance at such an early stage as that of Daniel.[368] This is a common Old Testament term meaning "righteousness," and Daniel's advice was for the king to break from his sins *by dealing righteously* (i.e., with the subjects of his kingdom). In Old Testament Israel, this was always to have been the king's responsibility. We read of David, for example: "David reigned over all Israel; he guaranteed justice [*mišpāṭ ûṣᵊdāqâ*] for all his people" (2 Sam 8:15).

The king was not only to break away from his sins by *dealing righteously*, but also by "being merciful to the oppressed." The word עֲנָי (*ʿănāy*) is better translated "oppressed" (NIV, ESV) than "poor" (NASB, NET)—see translation

---

supposed that Amel-Marduk acted as regent during his father's illness and that there was confusion at the time of a handover to a successor."

366. The verb appears here as a Peʿal impv. ms of *pᵊraq*. BDB (1108d) gives the meaning "tear away, break off" for this root. *HALOT* (1959), however, gives the meaning "remove, wipe away [sins]," which could suggest a different idea.

367. *TDNT*, 2:485.

368. See BDB (842) for the various lexical options of *ṣᵊdāqâ* in the Old Testament.

note to v. 27—though the two words are closely related. Nebuchadnezzar, in all his zeal to build massive cities, temples, and palaces, had harshly oppressed many people—using them as cheap labor and paying only meager wages. They were oppressed and living in poverty, while he himself enjoyed the luxuries of his palace. Daniel was keenly aware of these social injustices and beckoned the king to change all this by being merciful to his subjects.

The advice that Daniel offered the king required a great deal of courage on his part. Archer (7:64) writes,

> Daniel needed real courage to inform his royal master that his rule was marred by the sin of oppression and callousness toward the poor and disadvantaged among his people. Daniel's candor might have cost him his high office or even his life.

If the king were to heed Daniel's advice, it would be better for him: "Perhaps your prosperity will be prolonged." This fell short of an absolute promise, but it did suggest that this was a likely outcome for the king. The noun translated "prosperity" (שְׁלֵוָה, *šᵉlēwâ*) only occurs here in Daniel, but the related adjective *šᵉlēh* was seen earlier in v. 4, where it was used to describe the king "at ease" in his palace prior to the dream. In regard to that flourishing and sense of security that he had previously enjoyed, God was quite willing to extend to him this blessedness in life. But he could not continue to enjoy that while oppressing his subjects and failing to uphold righteousness in the land. What he enjoyed (power and a luxurious lifestyle) was not evil in and of itself, but *how* he obtained it was obnoxious to God. In the same spirit whereby God would one day show how much he loved the world by giving his Son to die on the cross for all mankind (John 3:16), even now he showed his care and compassion for every one of those poor, oppressed members of Nebuchadnezzar's kingdom.

The prolonging of the king's prosperity was conditioned upon breaking from his sinful ways of oppressing his subjects. Does this mean that the judgment could actually have been averted altogether had Nebuchadnezzar listened to Daniel's advice? Scholars are divided on this issue. Young (108–9), for example, argues that the judgment would not have been averted, but only that the time until the judgment would have been delayed. Miller (139), on the other hand, states, "Daniel seems to have held out to the king the genuine possibility of foregoing this judgment, demonstrating God's willingness to forgive." It is hard to be dogmatic on this issue, though the fact that judgment does not fall immediately (there is a twelve-month wait according to v. 29) may indicate that true repentance might have averted the judgment of God. Of course, God knew exactly what Nebuchadnezzar would do, and he knew that judgment would indeed come. This question should not distract us from seeing the main issue of v. 27, namely God's compassion on the subjects of Nebuchadnezzar and his concern for *righteous dealings* within the kingdom.

Biblical Theology Comments

According to Dan 4:26, Nebuchadnezzar would be under discipline until he recognized that it is "heaven that rules." As pointed out in the translation note for this verse, the word "heaven" is a metonymy for God, who inhabits and rules from heaven. This is evident in light of the parallel statement in v. 17: "the Most High rules over the realm of mankind."

The Scriptures repeatedly emphasize that God is an active ruler over his created order, and therefore earthly kings are expected to govern in accordance with his laws and principles. They may choose to violate his will (and obviously do), but this does not go undetected. God tolerates their disobedience to a certain limit (provided his purposes are not thwarted in any way), and yet he is certainly capable of intervening at any time (and often does). The point is that God is not passive in his divine jurisdiction, and he remains firmly in control at all times. This is pointedly brought out in Ps 33:10–11:

> The LORD brings the counsel of the nations to nothing; he frustrates the plans of the peoples. The counsel of the LORD stands forever, the plans of his heart to all generations. (ESV)

To this could be added Ps 66:7:

> He rules forever by his power, his eyes watch the nations— let not the rebellious rise up against him. (NIV)

As God sovereignly rules over the nations, his holy angels are commissioned to carry out his will (Ps 103:19–20):

> The LORD has established his throne in the heavens, and his kingdom rules over all.
> Bless the LORD, O you his angels, you mighty ones who do his word, obeying the voice of his word! (ESV)

The pride of man often puffs itself up, and earthly rulers are frequently guilty of thinking more highly of themselves than they should. Nebuchadnezzar—like all men—needed to learn that God (and God alone) was the absolute sovereign ruler of the world.

Application and Devotional Implications

In his efforts to build Babylon into the world's premier city (a monument to himself), Nebuchadnezzar had undoubtedly inflicted great pain and suffering on other people in the process through forced labor, heavy taxation, military inscription, etc. Rather than abusing people to build his own monuments, God called upon him to have compassion on the needs of individuals under his authority.

There is a lesson for all of us here. Some people use positions of authority to serve their own interests, but a true leader is concerned for the needs and interests of those whom he/she represents. What about the people around you, and especially those who might be under your area of responsibility?

Do you know their needs, and do you take time to find out how you might be of help to them?

Yet it is not enough to "not oppress" others. God wants us to be men and women of mercy—really caring for people. He wants us to treasure people more than projects and human needs more than deadlines. We are to be agents of mercy unto those who are hurting in this world. We will never be able to right every wrong in the whole world, but we can be merciful to those in our own sphere of influence. In this fast-paced, "hardly a free moment" kind of world, God calls us to take notice of others and help those who are struggling. It is not easy, and there is a fierce temptation to excuse oneself by saying "I just don't have time." Yet it is important to our Lord. He wants us to do the kinds of things that uphold righteousness, and he delights to see us extending mercy. Since he is like that, no wonder he wants his people to be like that.

Additional Exegetical Comments

The translation and interpretation of v. 27 is complex. One example is that of Hartman (170), who suggests the following translation: "atone for your sins by good deeds, and for your misdeeds by kindness to the poor; then you will have lasting happiness." Similarly, Collins (212) translates, "to atone for your sins by almsgiving and for your iniquity by mercy to the poor." Such translations could easily lead to a theology of salvation by works and thus need careful evaluation.

The ideas of "atoning for sins" and "almsgiving" arise from the LXX translations. For example,

The LXX$^{\theta}$ translation:	τὰς ἁμαρτίας σου ἐν ἐλεημοσύναις λύτρωσαι *tas hamartias sou en eleēmosunais lutrōsai*

This *could be* translated: "atone for your sins by alms" (or perhaps, "redeem your sins"). The word translated *alms* is the fem. pl. form of ἐλεημοσύνη (*eleēmosunē*), which means "pity, mercy, kind deed," and often in a specific sense of "alms, charity." The word translated *atone for* is the Greek verb λύτρωσαι (*lutrōsai*), aorist inf. of λυτρόω (*lutroō*). This could be translated "atone" but basically means to *release* (on payment of ransom). According to *TDNT* (4:332), "On 4 occasions λυτροῦσθαι is used for פרק in the Aram. sense 'to loose' (Ps. 7:2; 136:24; Lam. 5:8; Da. 4:24)." In light of these observations, it may be that the LXX translators were not thinking of "atonement" in the NT sense of that word, nor were they necessarily thinking of "alms" (since this Greek word need not have that specific nuance). In any case, the LXX translations have had an influence on the understanding and translation of Dan 4:27.

It is better, however, to rely not on the LXX translations for an understanding of this verse but also upon the lexical evidence of the Aramaic terms and their Hebrew equivalents. Hence, *ṣiḏqâ* should not be seen as *almsgiving*, but as "righteousness," "upholding righteousness," or "dealing righteously." Wood (117) agrees,

> Such translations as "well-doing" or "almsgiving" (Jerome) are not satisfactory. Again, post-Old Testament writings carry this secondary meaning, but in the time of the Old Testament, the corresponding Hebrew word was used definitely for the concept "righteousness."[369]

Thus, Daniel was advising the king to break from his sins, not to atone or redeem his sins. This conclusion makes the best lexical sense of the terms employed, fits the context well, and avoids any serious theological difficulties. In no way should this verse be used to teach salvation by good deeds. Scripture is clear that one's personal salvation from sin is *by grace, through faith* (Eph 2:8–9).

5. Nebuchadnezzar's Pride and the Fulfillment of the Dream (4:28–33)

Textual Notes

30.a. [Eng. 4:33a] MT כִּנְשְׁרִין, "as eagles" (from root נְשַׁר) is understood differently by LXX$^{\theta}$, which translated ὡς λεόντων, "as lions" ("until his hair lengthened like that of lions"). Although LXX^{O} translated the first simile "like wings of an eagle" (ἀετοῦ), LXX^{O} translated the second simile "like those of a lion" (λέοντος). There is some speculation that the reading of λεόντων in LXX$^{\theta}$ stemmed from confusion with LXX^{O}'s insertion of λέοντος in the second simile. This is possible, because in the second simile, כצפרין ("as birds") could easily be mistaken for ככפרין, "as lions" (cf. Heb. כְּפִיר, "young lion"), which explains how the reading "lions" entered the translation.

369. Wood points out that Tob 12:9 and 14:11 show a near equation between "righteousness" and "almsgiving." Hartman (173) adds, "In later Judaism, which laid great stress on charity to the poor (Tobit 4:7–11; 12:8*f*; Sir 3:29–4:10; 29:8–13), Hebrew *ṣᵊdāqāh* and the corresponding Aramaic *ṣidqāh* and Greek *dikaiosynē* frequently have the meaning of 'almsgiving' (Matt 6:1; II Cor 9:9)."

Translation

4:28 [Aram. 4:25] Now all this happened to Nebuchadnezzar the king. **29** At the end of twelve months, he was walking on *the walls*[370] *of* the royal palace[371] of Babylon. **30** The king uttered these words:[372] "Is this not[373] Babylon the great[374] that I have built as a royal residence[375] by my mighty strength[376] and for the honor of my majesty?"[377] **31** While the word was still in the mouth[378]

---

370. The words "on the walls of" are not in the Aram. text but have been added for clarification. Note that LXX^{O} has the additional words ἐπὶ τῶν τειχῶν τῆς πόλεως (*epi tōn teichōn tēs poleōs*), "on the walls of the city."

371. Literally, the Aram. text has the genitive construct "the palace of the kingship" (*hêḵal malḵûṯāʾ*). Most translations (including NASB and NIV) regard this as an *attributive genitive* and thus translate "the royal palace." Compare *bēt mamlāḵâ* in Amos 7:13. *HALOT* (1859) notes that *hêḵal* is a loanword from Akk. *ekallu* and from Sumerian *e-gal*, and can mean either "palace" or "temple" (note LXX$^{\theta}$'s translation ἐπὶ τῷ ναῷ τῆς βασιλείας).

372. Lit. "spoke ... and said" (וְאָמַר ... עָנֵה, *wᵊʾāmar ... ʿānēh*).

373. B. Mastin, "The Meaning of *hălāʾ* at Daniel IV:27," *VT* 42 (1992): 234–47, discusses the options of translating הֲלָא (*hălāʾ*) as an asseverative particle ("Surely") rather than the more customary rendering of introducing a rhetorical question ("Is this not?"). He concludes (247), "the rendering 'Surely this is great Babylon!' is to be preferred at Dan. iv 27. This suits the context well, and *hălāʾ* has the denotation "behold" or "surely" in Targum Jonathan, B. Sanhedrin, and, possibly, 4QtgJob." Mastin admits that both BDB (1089) and *HALOT* (1857) understand it rhetorically (having the force *nonne*), as do most Eng. translations (see NLT for an exception).

374. The NASB renders בָּבֶל רַבְּתָא (*bāḇel rabbᵊṯāʾ*) as "Babylon the great." Both LXX^{O} and LXX$^{\theta}$ translate as Βαβυλὼν ἡ μεγάλη, "Babylon the great," which is the exact wording found in Rev 17:5 (cf. Rev 14:8; 16:19; 18:2).

375. "Royal residence" (so NASB and NIV) is a translation of the Aram. *bêṯ malḵû* ("house of royalty"). Taking *malḵû* as an attributive genitive, the expression is properly translated "royal residence."

376. The Aram. בִּתְקַף חִסְנִי (*biṯqap̱ ḥisnî*) is literally "by the strength of my might." Both the NET and the NIV understand this as a nominal hendiadys, meaning, "by my mighty strength (or power)." Contrast the NASB: "by the might of my power."

377. The Aram. לִיקָר הַדְרִי (*lîqār haḏrî*) is literally "for the honor (or glory) of my majesty." This also could be a nominal hendiadys (as *biṯqap̱ ḥisnî*), translated "for my majestic honor" (so NET; Goldingay, "for my kingly honor" [79]). *yᵊqār* can mean "dignity" or "honor" (*HALOT*, 1893). According to Sokoloff, *A Dictionary of Jewish Palestinian Aramaic*, 2nd ed. (Ramat-Gan, Israel: Bar Ilan Univ. Press, 2003), 244, the verb *yqr* was used in later Palestinian Aramaic with the meaning "to honor someone."

378. The words בְּפֻם מַלְכָּא (*bᵊpum malkāʾ*) are literally "in the mouth of the king." The NIV renders this "on his lips" (and similarly NET). The point is the same.

of the king, a voice came down[379] from heaven, "To you it is declared,[380] O Nebuchadnezzar the king, *that* your right to rule[381] has been removed. **32** You will be driven[382] away from mankind, and your dwelling place will be with the beasts of the field. You will be fed grass like cattle, and seven periods of time *[years]*[383] will pass over you until you recognize that the Most High is ruler over[384] the realm[385] of mankind, and He gives it to whomever He wills." **33** At that very moment[386] the word concerning Nebuchadnezzar was fulfilled. He was driven away from mankind, he began to eat[387] grass like cattle, and his body was drenched with the dew of the sky, until his hair had grown long like eagles' *feathers* and his nails like *the claws of* birds.[388]

Commentary

4:28–30 *Nebuchadnezzar's prideful boasting.* The mysterious dream of Nebuchadnezzar had been rightfully interpreted by Daniel. God had warned the king beforehand that he would be humbled and made to understand that

---

379. For the use of נְפַל, *nᵊpal* ("fall") in the sense "to come down," see *HALOT*, 1932.

380. The words "it is declared" are a translation of the plural Peʿal active ptc. אָֽמְרִין (ʾ*āmᵊrîn*). Rosenthal (56 [§181]) explains the basis for a passive translation: "The 3. masc. pl. and the masc. pl. of the participle frequently express an impersonal subject and thus substitute for a passive construction." Comp. Dan 3:4, לְכוֹן אָֽמְרִין (*lᵊkôn* ʾ*āmᵊrîn*), "you are commanded."

381. Lit., "the kingdom has been taken from you" (מַלְכוּתָה עֲדָת מִנָּךְ, *malkûtâ* ʿ*ădāt minnāk*). Yet *malkû* might be better rendered "kingship" or "sovereignty" (so *HALOT*, 1917). What the king temporarily lost was his "right to rule." Note the NIV "royal authority," the NASB "sovereignty," and NET "kingdom."

382. The words "driven from" are a translation of the active ptc. טָֽרְדִין (*ṭārᵊdîn*). For explanation, see note above for ʾ*āmᵊrîn.*

383. Regarding "seven periods of time" as seven years, see the translation comments at Dan 4:16 (Eng.).

384. The translation of the prep. *bᵊ* as "over" is appropriate here. *HALOT* (1830) points out that *šᵊlēṭ bᵊ* means "to rule over." Recall Dan 2:38, *hašlᵊṭāk bᵊkollᵊhôn*, "he has made you to rule over all of them."

385. For "realm" (*malkût*), see comments at Dan 4:17 (Eng.).

386. The Aram. בַּהּ־שַׁעֲתָא (*bah-šaʿăṯāʾ*) means "at that very moment," i.e., immediately (RJ, 106).

387. The verb יֵאכֻל (*yēʾkul*) is a Peʿal impf. of ʾ*ăkal*. If this is classified an *incipient past impf.* (stressing the commencement and continuing phases of the activity), then it could be translated "he began to eat" (compare NASB, "began eating"). Cf. Waltke and O'Connor, *IBHS*, 503–4 (§31.2.c).

388. Regarding the ending to Dan 4:33 and the difficulties in translating the two similes, see the textual note to this verse above. Words like "feathers" and "claws" have to be presumed to make a sensible translation. Even then, comparing the king's long hair to the feathers of eagles is admittedly a difficult comparison, which may help explain the differences with the LXX tradition.

"it is heaven that rules," and that God puts men in places of ruling according to his choosing (v. 25). Verse 28 tells us that what Daniel had foretold is exactly what came to pass. Yet it did not happen immediately. Instead, twelve months passed by after Daniel's interpretation of the dream before God began to act (v. 29). Perhaps the king was beginning to think that there was no danger of judgment from God or that it had only been a silly, meaningless dream to begin with. If so, he was very wrong. The God of heaven does not forget his word. Daniel had expressed that there was hope for the king, provided he truly repent (v. 27). God had given the king twelve months in which to repent and acknowledge the God of the Bible as the true ruler of mankind. Unfortunately, the king did not avail himself of God's grace, and the opportunity passed him by.

According to Dan 4:29–30, it was a moment of prideful boasting that became the occasion for God's judgment. One evening he was taking a stroll on the rooftop of his royal palace and started boasting in his heart over the city he had built up to be the most awe-inspiring city of the world in that day. He referred to his city as "Babylon the great" and then made three prideful claims about it (v. 30). First, he claimed to have built it himself as his personal "royal residence." From his perspective, Babylon was first and foremost *his* dwelling place. He saw the city's purpose primarily for his personal benefit and luxury rather than seeing himself as a servant to his people. Second, he claimed to have built it by his own "mighty strength." Even though the city was really built by the sweat of thousands of his subjects (probably including slave labor and foreign captives), he viewed the city as a reflection of his mighty strength and gave himself the credit for its accomplishment. Third, he saw the city's purpose as being for "the honor of his majesty." This was self-centered thinking to believe that the architectural grandeur of the city was intended for his personal honor. This was not only an insult to the God of heaven, but it even violated his own religious beliefs, for as a worshiper of Babylon's patron deity, Marduk, the city was meant to be for Marduk's honor and glory. From an earlier part of his reign, Nebuchadnezzar wrote,

> ... [from] the Upper Sea [to] the Lower Sea ... which Marduk, my lord, has entrusted to me, I have made ... the city of Babylon to be the foremost among all the countries and every human habitation; its name I have [made/elevated] to the (most worthy of) praise among the sacred cities. ... The sanctuaries of my lords Nebo and Marduk (as a) wise (ruler) ... always.[389]

In another inscription Nebuchadnezzar extolled his palace: "In Babylon, my dear city, which I love, was the palace, the house of wonder of the people, the bond of the land, the brilliant place, the abode of majesty in Babylon."[390]

389. From the so-called Wadi-Brisa Inscription, cited in Pritchard, *ANET*, 307.
390. From the East India House Inscription (vii, 34), cited in Montgomery (244).

Of course, Babylon was indeed a spectacular architectural achievement, and Nebuchadnezzar was its greatest builder. The walls and gates of the city alone made Babylon a wonder to behold. Miller (140) summarizes,

> Babylon was a rectangularly shaped city surrounded by a broad and deep water-filled moat and then by an intricate system of double walls. The first double-wall system encompassed the main city. Its inner wall was twenty-one feet thick and reinforced with defense towers at sixty-foot intervals while the outer wall was eleven feet in width and also had watchtowers. Later Nebuchadnezzar added another defensive double-wall system (an outer wall twenty-five feet thick and an inner wall twenty-three feet thick) east of the Euphrates that ran the incredible distance of seventeen miles and was wide enough at the top for chariots to pass. The height of the walls is not known, but the Ishtar Gate was forty feet high, and the walls would have approximated this size. A forty-foot wall would have been a formidable barrier for enemy soldiers.[391]

We might mention that most of the bricks taken out of Babylon in various archaeological excavations have the name "Nebuchadnezzar" inscribed on them. Nebuchadnezzar was also responsible for many of the pagan temples of the city, and perhaps most significantly for the famous Hanging Gardens of Babylon, one of the seven wonders of the ancient world. Accounts of this are found in the remaining fragments of the Babylonian historian Berossus:

> ... he himself magnificently decorated the temple of Bel and the other temples with the spoils of war; he also restored the originally existing city and fortified it with another one, and, in order that besiegers might no longer be able to divert the course of the river and direct it against the city, he surrounded the inner city with three walls and the outer one with three, those of the inner city being of burnt brick and bitumen, while those of the outer city were of brick alone. After walling about the city in this

391. Herodotus further describes the city (*Hist.* 1.178–83). Of particular interest are Herodotus' comments about the bitumen used to cement the bricks and the numerous "brass" gates: "Then they set to building, and began with bricking the borders of the moat, after which they proceeded to construct the wall itself, using throughout for their cement hot bitumen, and interposing a layer of wattled reeds at every thirtieth course of the bricks. On the top, along the edges of the wall, they constructed buildings of a single chamber facing one another, leaving between them room for a four-horse chariot to turn. In the circuit of the wall are a hundred gates, all of brass, with brazen lintels and side-posts. The bitumen used in the work was brought to Babylon from the Is, a small stream which flows into the Euphrates at the point where the city of the same name stands, eight days' journey from Babylon. Lumps of bitumen are found in great abundance in this river" (1.179, G. Rawlinson translation).

> remarkable way and adorning the gate-towers as befitted their sacred character, he built, where his father's palace was, another palace adjoining it, of the height of which and its magnificence in other respects it would perhaps be extravagant of me to speak, except to say that in spite of its being so great and splendid it was completed in fifteen days. In this palace he erected retaining walls of stone, to which he gave an appearance very like that of mountains and, by planting on them trees of all kinds, he achieved this effect, and built the so-called hanging garden because his wife, who had been brought up in the region of Media, had a desire for her native environment.[392]

Another testimony to Babylon's grandeur is that two hundred years later Alexander the Great planned to make the city the headquarters of his vast domain.

4:31–33 *God's Judgment on Nebuchadnezzar*. At the very time that Nebuchadnezzar was puffed up in pride, God chose that moment to cause his judgment to fall (v. 28). The first step was hearing a voice from heaven announcing the judgment. In whatever way the voice was manifested (perhaps by an angel?), the point is that it was a clear and unmistakable revelation from God. Before there was any change in his behavior, there was first the hearing of God's pronouncement upon him (so he would fully understand his fault). His "kingdom," that is, his sovereign right to rule, was being taken away. By God's grace, the kingdom itself was being preserved and would still be waiting for him following the completion of the discipline.

Nebuchadnezzar would enter into a state of living like a beast of the field. In one sense, this state was temporal, but it was also conditional, for it would not be lifted until he recognized that the God "Most High" was the *true* ruler over mankind and was the one to bestow the right of ruling on whomever he wished. This discipline upon the king was temporal, for it would only last for "seven periods of time." The expression "periods of time" is one word in Aramaic, namely עִדָּנִין, *ʿiddānîn*. As explained in the translation note to Dan 4:16 (Eng.), this really means *seven years*. For seven long years the king was to live and behave like an animal.

The term "zoanthropy" is used to describe the mental disorder in which a patient imagines himself to be a beast and acts like one. As Wood (121) has pointed out, it might be more appropriate to label his disorder as "boanthropy," in which the one afflicted behaves like an ox. R. K. Harrison reports

392. Berossus, Book 3, *History of Chaldaea* (cited in Josephus, *Ant.* x.224–26, Loeb Classical Library ed., 281–83). Berossus was a Chaldean priest of Bel who wrote about 290 BC. His three-volume history of ancient Babylonia (originally written in Greek) has been lost, but portions remain in citations by such men as Josephus and Eusebius.

that he observed a young man with a similar affliction in a British mental institution in 1946. Harrison describes his behavior as follows:

> His daily routine consisted of wandering around the magnificent lawns with which the otherwise dingy hospital situation was graced, and it was his custom to pluck up and eat handfuls of the grass as he went along. ... He never ate institutional food with the other inmates, and his only drink was water. ... The writer was able to examine him cursorily, and the only physical abnormality noted consisted of a lengthening of the hair and a coarse, thickening condition of the fingernails. Without institutional care, the patient would have manifested precisely the same physical conditions as those mentioned in Daniel 4:33.[393]

Even the king's hair was like eagles, and his nails like those of birds. Archer (7:66) explains, "Most particularly the hair of his head and his body, becoming matted and course, looked like eagle feathers; his fingernails and toenails, never cut, became like claws."

Critical scholars have often scoffed at this account, pointing out that there is no historical evidence for it.[394] While it is true that we do not have any evidence for this in extrabiblical literature, two things can be said in response: (1) official annals commissioned by ancient monarchs were primarily used as political propaganda and were written to exalt the reputation of the king and the nation over which he ruled (exaggeration was not uncommon, and weaknesses were deliberately omitted); and (2) in the official court records for Nebuchadnezzar's rule, we are missing many of the tablets covering the years of Nebuchadnezzar's reign (esp. after 594 BC). Thus, there may actually be evidence, but we simply do not have the data available to us today. We can only presume that during this seven-year period the king's true state of affairs was kept a secret known only to a select few and that the administration of his realm was carried out by trusted high-up officials. Assuming this to be the case, it must be a credit to the sovereignty of God that power-grabbing opportunists did not seize Nebuchadnezzar's kingdom during this time.

Biblical Theology Comments

The primary theological point of the previous section (Dan 4:19–27) is that God actively rules over the realm of mankind with absolute sovereignty. A

393. R. K. Harrison, *Introduction to the Old Testament* (Grand Rapids: Eerdmans, 1969), 1116–17.

394. Collins (232–34) exemplifies the skepticism of many scholars. He treats this chapter as a fictional account, in which most of the details have been transformed from another source known as the "Prayer of Nabonidus" (4QPrNab), an Aramaic fragment discovered at Qumran. His explanation is that the king in view was originally Nabonidus, and that the king's absence from the throne was linked with Nabonidus' absence from Babylon.

corollary to this truth is that he "gives it to whomever He wishes" (v. 32), i.e., he appoints human rulers. Though it may be tempting to think that men attain to high positions of power as a result of their own actions (whether good or bad), the truth is that God determines who rules and who does not. Rom 13:1 states, "there is no authority except from God, and those which exist are established by God" (NASB). Hence, Jesus could respond to Pilate's intimidating inquiry, "You would have no authority over Me, unless it had been given you from above" (John 19:11, NASB).

Though it may baffle us as to why God would allow a Hitler or a Stalin to be entrusted with the reins of power, it is neither confusing to God nor contradictory to his righteous ways. God has his reasons—and we can trust him—for what he does and what he allows. Obviously evil is allowed to operate in the fallen world we live in, and that will continue until the Lord Jesus returns. Prov 29:2 states, "When the righteous increase, the people rejoice, but when a wicked man rules, people groan" (NASB). For those who would use their power to oppress and persecute Christians, history has shown repeatedly that the church grows the fastest when persecution is the severest. Fortunately, in his mercies, God is also free and capable of deposing whomever He wishes.

Application and Devotional Implications

The problem with Nebuchadnezzar was that he tended to measure himself by himself (rather than measuring himself by God). He looked around at all the architectural achievements that had been accomplished under his reign, and then he considered the extensive boundaries of his empire. Adding it all up, he concluded that he was really great and worthy of glory. What folly! Man's efforts can certainly seem impressive, especially when viewed from the short-term perspective. But put them in eternal perspective, and the picture suddenly looks different. In the course of time, the Babylonian kingdom came and went. The fabled city of Babylon eventually crumbled to dust and rubble.

Pride is basically a failure to see ourselves in proper perspective before God. Pride often manifests itself in *self-applause*—attributing one's successes to one's own efforts and failing to properly give God the credit. When we do this, we rob God of the glory he deserves. We are reminded in both the Old and New Testaments that "God is opposed to the proud, but gives grace to the humble" (Prov 3:34; 1 Pet 5:5). Who wants to have God *opposed* to him? The alternative is far better—the grace of God upon us. We have a choice to make: grace, or God in opposition to us. Humility keeps *grace* coming down the pipeline. Pride, on the other hand, not only cuts off the flow of grace but also causes God to stand opposed to us.

6. Nebuchadnezzar's Restoration and Humble Praise for God (4:34–37)

Textual Notes

32.a. [Eng. 4:35a] Read with the Qere וְדָיְרֵי, as the Pe'al ptc. takes a י infix.

32.b. [Eng. 4:35b] Cairo Geniza and a number of MSS read כְּלָא ("as nothing") rather than MT's כְּלָה. This is reflected in the following translation.

32.c-c. [Eng. 4:35c-c] The duplication of the words וְדָאְרֵי אַרְעָא are regarded by some as a case of dittography and therefore omitted (so Collins, 212, and Newsom, 127), but are retained by most English versions (so NET, NASB, and NIV).

33.a. [Eng. 4:36a] Some would emend the noun הַדְרִי to a verb form הַדְרֵת, corresponding to ἦλθον in LXX$^{\theta}$. Yet, see the translation note for v. 36 (Eng.) favoring the MT.

33.b-b. [Eng. 4:36b-b] The MT, as it stands, is problematic. With this pointing, it literally reads "and over my kingdom, she/it was established," with the verb הָתְקְנַת as a Hupʿal perf. 3fs. This could be resolved by emending the preposition to וַעֲלַי (with 1cs suff. = "over me") or (less intrusively) by repointing the verb to הָתְקְנֵת (Hupʿal perf. 1cs) = "I was reestablished (or reinstated)." The latter is favored in the translation.

Translation

4:34 [Aram. 4:31] "Now at the end of the appointed time[395] I, Nebuchadnezzar, lifted my eyes to heaven,[396] and my sanity[397] began returning[398] to me. I blessed the Most High, and I praised and glorified the One who lives forever, for His dominion is an everlasting dominion, and His kingdom extends from one generation to the next.[399] **35** All the inhabitants of the earth are accounted as nothing. He does according to His will, with the army of heaven or the inhabitants of the earth. And there is no one who can stay[400] His hand or say to Him, 'What have You done?' **36** At that time my sanity began

---

395. Lit., "at the end of the days," וְלִקְצָת יוֹמַיָּה (*wəliqṣāt yômayyâ*).
396. That is, *the God of* heaven (a metonymy). See translation note at Dan 4:26 (Eng).
397. NET favors the translation "sanity" for the root מַנְדַּע (*mandaʿ*). *HALOT* (192c) indicates that it means "understanding;" and RJ (107) "knowledge, reason." LXX$^{\theta}$ translated αἱ φρένες μου (*hai phrenes mou*), "my mind/wits/senses."
398. Taking the imperfect verb יְתוּב (*yətûḇ*) as incipient past impf. (see Waltke and O'Connor, *IBHS*, 503–4 (§31.2c).
399. Lit., the Aram. reads "with a generation and a generation" (עִם־דָּר וְדָר, *ʿim-dār wədār*), i.e., "with all generations." I have adopted the translation of the NET, "extends from one generation to the next."
400. According to *HALOT* (1914), the verb מְחָא (*məḥāʾ*) means "to strike" (e.g., to strike on the arm, and thus to hinder). RJ (109) suggests "to stay." Cf. NET "slap," NASB "ward off," and NIV "hold back."

returning to me. Now as for[401] my kingly glory,[402] my majesty[403] and my splendor returned to me, my ministers[404] and nobles began seeking me, I was reinstated over my kingdom, and surpassing greatness was added to me. **37** Now I, Nebuchadnezzar, praise, extol, and glorify the King of heaven, for all His works are true and His ways just, and He is able to humble those who walk in pride."

Commentary

4:34–36 *Nebuchadnezzar's restoration.* Beginning with v. 34, the account is expressed in the first person. Despite the humiliation he endured and the deranged mind he must have experienced, Nebuchadnezzar still retained a measure of sanity, for the text tells us that he "lifted his eyes to heaven." The emphasis is not upon the direction of his glance but upon the change of heart by the king. This would imply that he humbly sought the true God of heaven and his mercy. In light of the stipulations in v. 32, we can also assume that he did indeed acknowledge the Most High as ruler over human governments and the one who decides on those who are to rule on earth. In view of his *right action*, his "sanity" (i.e., his wits or senses) returned to him.

All the misery and anguish that the king had to go through stands in stark contrast to the joy of heart and overflowing praise that characterized him afterward. Even this shows the goodness of God, for those who are willing to part with their prideful ways and humble themselves before God are often found with newfound joy of heart. When we do what is right in the eyes of God, we discover more joy and freedom, not less. Consequently, the king's praise for the true God is recorded for us in vv. 34–35. Notice that the text does not merely say he thanked God. His response is much deeper than that. It tells us that he extolled, praised, and glorified him. Although we should be somewhat cautious in our conclusions, these actions do seem to speak of a transformed and redeemed heart of a saint. Therefore, we may very well assume that Nebuchadnezzar himself became a true believer in the

401. Here, ל (*lᵊ*) topicalizes its object, "and as for" (so Newsom, 127). Cf. GKC, 458 (§143e); and Goldingay, 79, 81.

402. Taking מַלְכוּתִי (*malkûṯî*, "royalty, reign, kingdom") as a genitive of attribute, "kingly glory."

403. Retaining the reading of the MT, הַדְרִי, *haḏrî* (masc. noun with 1cs suff.). Some (e.g., NET) emend to a verb form הַדְרֵת, *haḏrēṯ* ("I returned," or NET "I was restored"), reading with Rashi and LXX$^{\theta}$ (ἦλθον, *ēlthon*). Yet the textual support is not strong for הַדְרֵת (*haḏrēṯ*); and the verb הדר (*hdr*) meaning "to return" is very rare. Furthermore, Goldingay (81) points out, "Th (ἦλθον) presupposes הדרת or more likely, takes as 1 s vb הדר (see *DTT*), 'I returned (to the honor of my kingship).' But the form is EA, and MT seems to be taking up the phrasing from v 27." (Note הַדְרִי, *haḏrî*, in Dan 4:27 where it was used with יְקָר, *yᵊqār*.)

404. For הַדָּבָר (*haddāḇar*), see translation notes at Dan 3:24.

same God as Daniel and will one day stand with Daniel in the kingdom of God that will be given to the Son of Man.[405]

When Nebuchadnezzar said, "His dominion is an everlasting dominion, and His kingdom extends from one generation to the next," he was confessing how temporal his own kingdom was in light of God's eternal rule. He no longer saw himself as the one having "mighty strength" who acted for his "majestic honor" (v. 30). Rather, he and all inhabitants of the earth were as *nothing* in comparison to God (a thought closely reflecting Isa 40:17). The Most High was absolutely sovereign and thus did according to his will (v. 35). This was true in regard to both the "army of heaven" as well as those who inhabited the earth. The expression "army of heaven" probably means the angelic forces that have access to heaven, in light of the paralleling with "the inhabitants of the earth." Furthermore, Nebuchadnezzar confessed that no one could hinder him ("stay His hand") or even had the right to question God in what he does.[406] The God of heaven does not operate by the dictates of man. How awful it would be to have man who is sinful and malicious controlling God who is holy and infinitely good.

Not only did Nebuchadnezzar gain a joyful heart of praise, but God even exalted him more than he had been before. In regard to his kingly glory, his majesty and splendor returned to him (v. 36). Furthermore, his ministers (see 3:24 for comments on *haddāḇar*, a Persian loanword) and nobles began seeking him out again. During the seven years that the king was incapacitated, most officials obviously did not meet with the king to discuss state matters. Now that his sanity (i.e., understanding, *manda*ʿ) was restored, he could once again meet with them and discuss official affairs. Verse 36 closes by pointing out that Nebuchadnezzar became even greater

405. Although many biblical scholars have denied that Nebuchadnezzar was truly converted (including Calvin and Keil), others have affirmed that this is likely what took place—so Young, 114; Wood, 128; Miller, 144; and Walvoord, 111–12.

406. In a Babylonian document dating from about 1200 BC called *Ludlul Bēl Nēmeqi* ("I will praise the Lord of Wisdom," that is, Marduk), there is an opening line reminiscent of Dan 4:35: "whose hands the heavens cannot hold back." Ferguson notes the remarkable similarities the document has with Dan 4, suggesting that Nebuchadnezzar—who would have likely known about such hymns to his god—might have borrowed from its literary pattern to communicate to his countrymen what he had learned from the true God. Ferguson, "Nebuchadnezzar, Gilgamesh, and the 'Babylonian Job,'" 329–30, writes: "Like Daniel 4 it opens and closes with a doxology and confession of the deity's sovereignty to show mercy or judgment. It also contains affirmations of his god's universal kingship. ... As in Daniel 4, the speaker announces his intention to provide people with instruction in worship and to present his situation as a public example of his god's ability to punish and restore. The person's situation is associated with a terrifying dream, as in Dan 4:5. The author repeatedly stresses that four classes of dream interpreters and omen experts could not help him."

than before (lit., "surpassing greatness was added to me"). This seems reminiscent of Job's experience: "The LORD blessed the latter days of Job more than his beginning" (Job 42:12). This also teaches us something very important about the *grace* and the *goodness of God*. He is incredibly enthusiastic about bestowing grace. Yes, he may discipline us and take us through fiery trials that he deems necessary, but in the end he longs to shower us with tokens of his goodness. Ps 34:8 says, "O taste and see that the LORD is good." Even Nebuchadnezzar discovered this truth about the God of heaven. Although we do not know at what point in his reign these events would have happened, it is worth pointing out that Nebuchadnezzar reigned for forty-three long years (605–562 BC). He must have had quite a few years left after his humbling in order for there to have been enough time to have experienced the "surpassing greatness."

4:37 *Conclusion*. The last verse of the chapter is a touching finale to the difficult lesson that the king had to learn. In saying that he praised, exalted, and glorified the King of heaven, Nebuchadnezzar made clear that he had learned who the true king was: Yahweh God of heaven. Furthermore, he confessed that he had learned the main lesson: "He is able to humble those who walk in pride." Notice carefully that this chapter does not simply teach that pride is wrong but that God *humbles* the proud. Thus, God is actively at work in the affairs of this world, although his ways of doing so and his timing may not be so apparent to those of us who abide here.

Biblical Theology Comments

There is probably not a more exquisite expression of the sovereignty of God in the entire Bible than that coming from the lips of Nebuchadnezzar in 4:34–35:

> His dominion is an everlasting dominion, and His kingdom extends from one generation to the next. [35]All the inhabitants of the earth are accounted as nothing. He does according to His will, with the army of heaven or the inhabitants of the earth. And there is no one who can stay His hand or say to Him, "What have You done?"

With Nebuchadnezzar's confession, a sub-climax of the court tales is achieved regarding the tension that has been building throughout chaps. 1 to 4 pertaining to Nebuchadnezzar's power and Yahweh's cosmic sovereignty. Breed explains,

> Thus Daniel attempts to resolve diasporic theological tension by repeatedly claiming that YHWH, the cosmic sovereign, rules over temporal sovereigns (Dan. 2.27–28, 46–47; 3.17–18, 29, 32–33; 4.33–34 [ET 36–37]). YHWH has chosen to give limited temporal sovereignty to foreign empires—so long as the foreign kings are open to learning about YHWH's sovereignty. Nebuchadnezzar's

kingdom is restored when he recognizes YHWH's rule in Dan. 4.31–34 (ET 34–37).[407]

The outworking of God's sovereign rule in history deserves elaboration, especially as it relates to the Lord Jesus. On the one hand, he himself is God and Creator. Colossians 1:16 states, "by Him all things were created, *both* in the heavens and on earth, visible and invisible" (NASB). Yet the authority he exercises does not rest merely on his role as Creator but as Redeemer. Because he has voluntarily gone to the cross in obedience to the Father, he is the *recipient* of ruling authority. Hence, before exhorting the disciples to the task of the Great Commission, he announces to them, "All authority in heaven and on earth has been given to Me" (Matt 28:18, ESV). Perhaps we could say that he rules out of well-deserved honor rather than inherent self-identity, with this honor connected to his resurrection and ascension to the Father's right hand. Peter thus declared on the Day of Pentecost: "Let all the house of Israel therefore know for certain that God has made him both Lord and Christ, this Jesus whom you crucified" (Acts 2:36, ESV). Likewise the Apostle Paul declared that God (in response to the crucifixion event) "highly exalted Him" and that one day "every tongue will confess that Jesus Christ is Lord" (Phil 2:9–11). The point is clear, then, that the awesome sovereignty of God depicted in Dan 4:34–35 is meant to be eternally entrusted to the Lord Jesus Christ. Looking to the future, as the tribulation scene comes to a close and the second coming of Christ draws near, the angel of the seventh trumpet shouts in joyful anticipation, "The kingdom of the world has become *the kingdom* of our Lord and of His Christ; and He will reign forever and ever" (Rev 11:15, NASB). Then, the Lord Jesus will use the sovereign authority entrusted to him to bring this world into full submission to her Creator.

Application and Devotional Implications

Fortunately for Nebuchadnezzar, he did not remain a "beast" forever. By God's kindness, he tasted the grace of God (which must have been a radically new experience for him, in that he had never been dealt with in grace by the uncaring Babylonian deities). In the aftermath of it all, Nebuchadnezzar came to see whose kingdom really mattered. Nebuchadnezzar's kingdom was only a temporal kingdom of short-term duration. He should have known on the basis of God's revelation to him in chap. 2 that his kingdom would one day be replaced by another. Now, at last, he saw it so much more clearly and thus confessed, "His dominion is an everlasting dominion, and His kingdom extends from one generation to the next" (4:34).

Many of us easily get caught up in building our own little kingdoms. When we do that, we fail to really see the purpose for which God made us.

---

407. Breed, "A Divided Tongue," 118.

We do not realize our own potential as humans, until we realize that it is not our kingdom that matters, but God's. So, how about you? Are you wrapped up in building your own kingdom, or do you see God's kingdom as the true goal? When we are living for "His kingdom" (and helping to further that), then we find our true fulfillment in life, and God brings out the full potential for which he created us.

Selected Bibliography

Avalos, H. "Nebuchadnezzar's Affliction: New Mesopotamian Parallels for Daniel 4." *JBL* 133 (2014): 497–507.

Ball, C. J. "Daniel and Babylon." *Exp* 8 (1920): 235–40.

Basson, A. "'A King in the Grass': Liminality and Immersion in Daniel 4:28–37. *JSem* 18 (2009): 1–14.

Becking, B. "'A Divine Spirit Is in You': Notes on the Translation of the Phrase *rûaḥ ʾelāhîn* in Daniel 5,14 and Related Texts." In *The Book of Daniel in the Light of New Findings*, ed. A. S. van der Woude, 515–32, BETL. Leuven: Leuven University Press, 1993.

Bledsoe, A. M. D. "The Identity of the 'Mad King' of Daniel 4 in Light of Ancient Near Eastern Sources." *CNS* 33 (2012): 743–58.

Breed, B. W. "A Divided Tongue: The Moral Taste Buds of the Book of Daniel." *JSOT* 40 (2015): 113–30.

Burkholder, B. "Literary Patterns and God's Sovereignty in Daniel 4." *Direction* 16 (1987): 45–54.

Cason, T. S. "Confessions of an Impotent Potentate: Reading Daniel 4 through the Lens of Ritual Punishment Theory." *JSOT* 39 (2014): 79–100.

Charlesworth, J. H. *The Old Testament Pseudepigrapha*. Vol 1, *Apocalyptic Literature and Testaments*. Garden City, NY: Doubleday, 1983.

Coxon, P. W. "Another Look at Nebuchadnezzar's Madness." In *The Book of Daniel in the Light of New Findings*, ed. A. S. van der Woude, 211–22. BETL 106. Leuven: Leuven University Press, 1993.

———. "The Great Tree of Daniel 4." In *A Word in Season: Essays in Honour of William McKane*, ed. J. D. Martin and P. R. Davies, 91–111. JSOTSup 42. Sheffield: JSOT, 1986.

Cross, F. M. "Fragments of the Prayer of Nabonidus." *IEJ* 34 (1984): 260–64.

Di Lella, A. A. "Daniel 4:7–14: Poetic Analysis and Biblical Background." In *Mélanges bibliques et orientaux en l'honneur de M. Henri Cazelles*, ed. A. Caquot and M. Delcor, 247–58. AOAT 212. Kevelaer, Germany: Butzon & Bercker, 1981.

Ferguson, P. "Nebuchadnezzar, Gilgamesh, and the 'Babylonian Job.'" *JETS* 37 (1994): 321–31.

Freedman, D. M. "The Prayer of Nabonidus." *BASOR* 145 (1957): 31–32.

Fröhlich, I. "Stars and Spirits: Heavenly Bodies in Ancient Jewish Aramaic Tradition." *AS* 13 (2015): 111–27.

Gadd, C. J. "The Harran Inscriptions of Nabonidus." *AnSt* 8 (1958): 35–92.

———. "The Kingdom of Nabu-na'id in Arabia." In *Akten des vierundzwanzigsten international Orientalischen-Kongresses München*, ed. H. Franke, 132–34. Wiesbaden: Deutsche Morgenländische Gesellschaft, 1959.

Garrison, J. A. "Nebuchadnezzar's Dream: An Inversion of Gilgamesh Imagery." *BSac* 169 (2012): 172–87.

Gladd, B. L. "The Use of *Mystery* in Daniel." In *Hidden but Now Revealed; A Biblical Theology of Mystery*, ed. G. K. Beale and B. L. Gladd, 29–46. Downers Grove, IL: IVP Academic, 2014.

Gowan, D. E. *When Man Becomes God: Humanism and Hybris in the Old Testament*. PTMS 6. Eugene, OR: Pickwick Publications, 1975.

Hartman, L. F. "The Great Tree and Nabuchodonosor's Madness." In *The Bible in Current Catholic Thought*, ed. J. L. McKenzie, 75–82. New York: Herder & Herder, 1962.

Hays, C. B. "Chirps from the Dust: The Affliction of Nebuchadnezzar in Dan 4:30 in Its Ancient Near Eastern Context." *JBL* 126 (2007): 305–25.

Henze, M. *The Madness of King Nebuchadnezzar: The Ancient Near Eastern Origins and Early History of Interpretation of Daniel 4*. JSJSupp 61. Leiden: Brill, 1999.

———. "Nebuchadnezzar's Madness (Daniel 4) in Syriac Literature." In *The Book of Daniel: Composition and Reception*, ed. J. J. Collins and P. W. Flint, 550–71. Leiden: Brill, 2001.

Jacobs, Naomi. "When the King Is the Other: Nebuchadnezzar's Hibernian Cousin." In *The 'Other' in Second Temple Judaism: Essays in Honor of John J. Collins*, ed. D. Hartlow, 132–44. Grand Rapids: Eerdmans, 2011.

Mastin, B. A. "The Meaning of *hălāʾ* at Daniel IV:27." *VT* 42 (1992): 234–47.

Mazani, P. "Nebuchadnezzar's Deficits in Daniel 4:27 and His Responses to Divine Prompting." *JATS* 24 (2013): 59–74.

Meadowcroft, T. "Point of View in Storytelling: An Experiment in Narrative Criticism in Daniel 4." *Did* 8 (1997): 30–42.

Murray, R. "The Origin of Aramaic *ʿîr*, Angel." *Or* 53 (1984): 303–17.

Newsom, C. A. "Now You See Him, Now You Don't; Nabonidus in Jewish Memory." In *Remembering Biblical Figures in the Late Persian and Early Hellenistic Periods*, ed. D. V. Edelman and E. ben Zvi, 270–82. Oxford: Oxford University Press, 2013.

———. "Why Nabonidus?: Excavating Traditions from Qumran, the Hebrew Bible, and Neo-Babylonian Sources." In *The Dead Sea Scrolls: Transmission of Traditions and Production of Texts*, ed. S. Metso, H. Najman and E. Schuller, 57–79. Leiden: Brill, 2010.

Oppenheim, A. L. *The Interpretation of Dreams in the Ancient Near East, with a Translation of an Assyrian Dream Book*. TAPS 46. Philadelphia: American Philosophical Society, 1956.

Shea, W. H. "Further Literary Structures in Daniel 2–7: An Analysis of Daniel 4." *AUSS* 23 (1985): 193–202.

Thomas, D. W. "Some Observations on the Hebrew word רַעֲנָן." In *Hebräische Wortforschung* (Festschrift to W. Baumgartner), ed. B. Hartmann, et al., 387–97. VTSuppl 16. Leiden: E. J. Brill, 1967.

Viviano, B. T. "The Least in the Kingdom: Matthew 11:11, Its Parallel in Luke 7:28 (Q), and Daniel 4:14." *CBQ* 62 (2000): 41–54.

Wiseman, D. J. "Babylonia 605–539 B.C." In *The Cambridge Ancient History*, ed. J. Boardman, I. Edwards, E. Sollberger, & N. Hammond, 229–51. The Cambridge Ancient History. Cambridge: Cambridge University Press, 1992.

Wooden, R. G. "Changing Perceptions of Daniel: Reading Daniel 4 and 5 in Context." In *From Biblical Criticism to Biblical Faith; Essays in Honor of Lee Martin McDonald*, ed. W. H. Brackney and C. A. Evans, 9–23. Macon, GA: Mercer Univ. Press, 2007.

D. God's Humbling of Belshazzar, to Whom is Revealed the Handwriting on the Wall (5:1–30)

The handwriting on the wall at Belshazzar's feast comprises one of the most well-known stories of the book of Daniel. The story has formed the basis for countless poems, plays, and music scores throughout history. In these, Belshazzar's hubris has been used to decry the tyranny of ungodly regimes that have defied the moral standards of a holy God. Following a survey of the story in art and literature, Liptzin states:

> Down the many centuries, the fiery symbols of the Book of Daniel—Mene, Mene, Tekel, Upharsin—have been hurled by literary spokesmen at tyrants and tyrannical systems, and have brought hope and comfort to oppressed groups and national entities, including Jewish communities under the heels of brutal conquerors from Belshazzar to Hitler. These symbolic words remain an eternal affirmation of divine justice that humbles the proud and uplifts the lowly.[408]

Orientation. Following the introduction in chap. 1, the first major section of the book of Daniel consists of chaps. 2–7, emphasizing the Gentile nations under which Israel was being disciplined (and how God exercised his sovereignty over them). This, in turn, consists of two halves: chaps. 2–4 and chaps. 5–7, all of which are arranged in a concentric structure.[409] Consequently, chap. 4 is seen to parallel chap. 5. Chapter 4 records the divine humbling of the Babylonian king (Nebuchadnezzar), and this is paralleled in chap. 5 with

408. S. Liptzin, "Belshazzar's Folly," in *Biblical Themes in World Literature*, 273–81 (Hoboken, NJ: Ktav, 1985), 281.

409. For further discussion, see the section on "Unity and Literary Structure" in the introductory matter.

the divine humbling of another Babylonian king (Belshazzar). Thus, Daniel chap. 5 is a turning point in the first major section of the book, both from a literary perspective as well as a historical perspective. Chaps. 2–4 dealt with King Nebuchadnezzar, but now the narrative jumps forward at least twenty-three years to the time of Belshazzar, Nebuchadnezzar's grandson.

Chaps. 4 and 5 are similar in that both are concerned with Babylonian kings whose pride must be humbled before the God of heaven. The nature (and extent) of the humbling, however, is different. In chaps. 2–4, God progressively dealt with Nebuchadnezzar, revealing more about himself and sovereignly bringing the king to a point of praise for the true God. Obviously, God could have dealt accordingly with each king thereafter—humbling them until at last they praised him. By the end of chap. 4, however, the point had sufficiently been made as to who truly rules over human affairs. There is no need to demonstrate this again (at least in the same way), and judgment is allowed to fall upon Babylon so as to advance the revelation of the successive Gentile powers.

From a literary standpoint, chap. 5 is also developed in a chiastic structure, though different from that of chap. 4.

A Banquet Setting (1–9)

1. Belshazzar's Insolence at the Banquet (1–4)
2. The Handwriting on the Wall (5–6)
3. Offers and Honors Made to the Wise Men (7–8)
4. Outcome for Belshazzar: Alarm (9)

B Queen's Speech in Regard to Nebuchadnezzar (10–12)

Commends Daniel's role during rule of Nebuchadnezzar

C Belshazzar's Speech (13–16)

Admission of wise men's failure and offer of rewards to Daniel

B` Daniel's Speech in Regard to Nebuchadnezzar (17–21)

Decline of rewards and recounts lesson learned by Nebuchadnezzar

A` Banquet Conclusion (22–30)

1. Belshazzar's Insolence at the Banquet Rebuked (22–24)
2. Handwriting on the Wall Interpreted (25–28)
3. Honors Bestowed on Daniel (29)
4. Outcome for Belshazzar: Slain (30)

Although my analysis of the structure differs from that of Shea, he does correctly point out the commonality of the three inner sections of the chiasm:

> Thus, there are two common themes which run throughout all three of the passages in the central section of this narrative: There is, first of all, reference to the time of Nebuchadnezzar; and then, connected with that in each instance is the idea that Daniel was a competent interpreter of mysteries during Nebuchadnezzar's reign and should also be able to function in a similar capacity at this present time.[409]

Heading up the center section (Belshazzar's speech, vv. 13–16) is the initial statement of v. 13a, "Then Daniel was brought in before the king." Hilton (also recognizing the centrality of this statement in the chapter's structure) points out, "The significance of the structure in our story is that it highlights the key elements: the writing on the wall at the beginning and end of the chapter, and Daniel at the centre."[410] Also in the central section is the king's admission that the wise men and conjurers of the court were unable to read or interpret the inscription. In this regard, the central section of chap. 5 echoes the same message found in the central section of chap. 4. At the polar ends, however, chap. 5 spells the doom of insolent Belshazzar who does not give praise to God (in contrast to Nebuchadnezzar who did).

Finally, a few comments are in order regarding the historical situation. As mentioned above, at least twenty-three years have now passed since Nebuchadnezzar's rule ended in 562 BC. See the following chart of Nebuchadnezzar's descendants).[411]

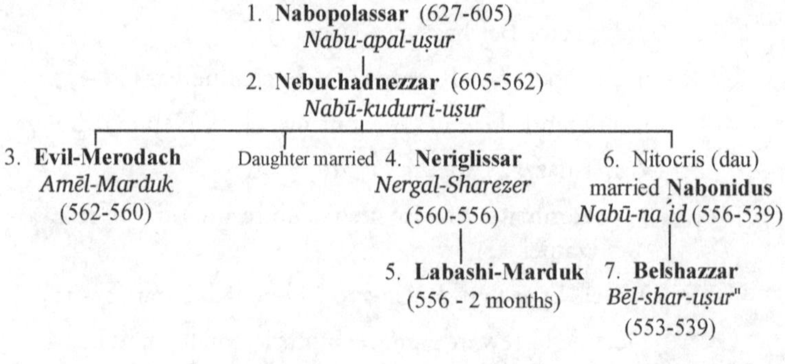

409. W. H. Shea, "Further Literary Structures in Daniel 2–7: An Analysis of Daniel 5, and the Broader Relationships Within Chapters 2–7," *AUSS* 23 (1985): 286.
410. M. Hilton, "Babel Reversed—Daniel Chapter 5," *JSOT* 66 (1995): 105.
411. Adapted from a chart in *The Bible Knowledge Commentary, Old Testament*, ed. J. F. Walvoord and R. B. Zuck (Wheaton, IL: Victor, Scripture Press Publications, 1985), 1:1326.

During this time, several family members of Nebuchadnezzar have sat on the throne (see the "Historical Context" in the "Introductory Matters" for more details). At the time chap. 5 took place, Belshazzar was not the sole ruling king. Rather, his father, Nabonidus, was the primary ruling king and Belshazzar served as co-ruler over Babylon (albeit in a subordinate position).[412] Nabonidus, history informs us, spent several years away from Babylon in both Harran and Arabia.[413] Regarding the latter, he conquered the city of Teima in Arabia (strategically situated at the junction of two important trade routes). He slaughtered the inhabitants and then repopulated the city. For reasons that are not entirely clear (though there is some evidence that he had offended and alienated himself from the religious priests of Babylon), he spent ten years away from Babylon living in Teima, during which time his son Belshazzar was entrusted with the daily administration of Babylon.[414] We should also keep in mind that Daniel had been in Babylon for at least sixty-six years, which probably indicates that he was in his eighties at the time of the events recorded in chap. 5.

We also know from extrabiblical sources that it was in the year 539 BC that this feast occurred and Babylon fell to the combined armies of the Medes and Persians under the command of Cyrus. During the years leading up to this climactic event, Cyrus had been leading his armies against the Babylonian Empire. As recorded in the Nabonidus Chronicle, Cyrus had already conquered the neighboring cities to Babylon of Sippar and

412. According to W. G. Lambert, "Nabonidus in Arabia," in *Proceedings of the Fifth Seminar for Arabian Studies*, 53–64 (London: Seminar for Arabian Studies, 1972), 53, "From the framework established by the abundant dated administrative, economic and legal texts, confirmed by astronomical data, and subject to checks of various kinds, it is known that Nabonidus became undisputed king by the end of June 556 B.C."

413. T. Fish, "Texts Relating to Nabonidus," in *Documents from Old Testament Times*, ed. D. W. Thomas, 89–91 (New York: Harper & Row, 1958), 89, informs us, "Nabonidus had ties with far away Harran where his mother became high priestess of the Moon-god. His piety towards his mother and her god partly explains his piety towards both the city and the god of Harran. He protests his devotion to the deities of Akkad, but he offended local susceptibilities by introducing into Babylon deities who did not belong there."

414. P.-A. Beaulieu, *The Reign of Nabonidus, King of Babylon 556–539 B.C.* (New Haven, CT: Yale University Press, 1989), 178–85, has concluded that religion was only one factor that led Nabonidus to take up residence in Teima. He was a player on the world political stage, and his excursion into northern Arabia served to further Babylonian military imperialism in the west and take control of the important caravan trade routes, thereby gaining control of the vast wealth of the region. For further analysis of original documents pertaining to Nabonidus and his lengthy absence in Teima, see Lambert, "Nabonidus in Arabia," 53–64; and C. J. Gadd, "The Harran Inscriptions of Nabonidus," *AnSt* 8 (1958): 58–59.

Akkad.[415] Now his advance had brought him within only a few kilometers of Babylon itself.

Thus, the feast of Daniel 5 was no ordinary feast. The Babylonian Empire was in the process of crumbling. Belshazzar's father, Nabonidus, had attempted to lead an assault against the Medo-Persian forces of Cyrus but had been defeated and had to flee to Borsippa.[416] At the time of this feast, Babylon was surrounded by the troops of Ugbaru, a general under Cyrus. Perhaps Belshazzar and the citizens of Babylon felt secure behind the massive walls of the city, having enough food and provisions to outlast a siege of several years. Yahweh God, however, had other plans for Belshazzar and Babylon.

1. Belshazzar's insolence at the Feast (5:1–4)

In the Old Greek version (LXX^{O}) of Dan 5, there is a brief preface prefixed to the chapter. While it recounts some of the elements of the main story, it also offers a few differing details. The preface reads:

> Baltasar the king gave a great reception on the festival day of the consecration of his palace, and of his leading citizens he invited 2000 men. On that day Baltasar became inflated with arrogance from the wine, and haughtily praised all the gods of the nations made of molten metal or carved by hand which were in his palace, but he did not give praise to the God Most High. During that same night there appeared fingers like human fingers, and they inscribed in the plaster of the palace wall opposite the lamp-stand, "*Mane phares thekel.*" The interpretation of these words is *mane*, numbered, *phares*, taken away, *thekel*, placed.[417]

Pannkuk argues that this Preface must have derived from a longer independent version of the narrative, and (since several variant details cannot be traced back to the OG or the MT) he suggests that "the source from which the Preface derives was a third, parallel edition of the narrative."[418] Though such a thesis is difficult to prove, it is interesting to note that the king's

415. See Pritchard, *ANET*, 306.

416. This detail comes from the historical account given by the Chaldean historian Berossus, which is preserved in the writings of Josephus (see *C. Ap.* 1:20).

417. This translation is from L. M. Wills, *The Jew in the Court of the Foreign King: Ancient Jewish Court Legends*, HDR 26 (Minneapolis: Fortress, 1990), 121–22. The Preface is attested in Papyrus 967, the Syro-Hexapla, and Codex Chisianus (ms. 88).

418. J. L. Pannkuk, "The Preface to Old Greek Daniel 5: A Formal Approach," *VT* 57 (2016): 215–16. Related to this discussion is the case that Ulrich has made for the MT and OG versions of Daniel 5 representing parallel editions that stemmed from a shorter version of the story (see E. Ulrich, "The Parallel Editions of the Old Greek and Masoretic Text of Daniel 5," in *A Teacher for All Generations: Essays in Honor of James C. VanderKam*, ed. E. F. Mason et al., 201–17, JSJSup 153 [Leiden: Brill, 2012], 208–9).

banquet was "on the festival day of the consecration of his palace." Wills sees in this reference an association being made to the New Year's *akitu* Festival, which would explain why a banquet was being held at a time when the city was under assault.[419]

Textual Notes

1.a. Belshazzar's name appears as בֵּלְשַׁאצַּר here, but two MSS read בֵּלְאשַׁצַּר in conformity with Dan 5:30, 7:1, and 8:1. A few MSS have בלשצר. Both LXX^{O} and LXX$^{\theta}$ have βαλτασαρ.

3.a. LXX$^{\theta}$ has ἠωέχθησαν (passive), which would presuppose an Aram. הֵיתַיו (Hupʿal perf. 3mp). However, this lacks Aram. MS support, and MT reads fine as is.

3.b. LXX$^{\theta}$ adds "and silver" (καὶ τὰ ἀργυρᾶ), probably in an attempt to conform to v. 2.

3.c. In contrast to MT's plural verb (הַנְפִּקוּ), LXX$^{\theta}$ has sing ἐξήνεγκεν (and similarly S and Vg).

3.d-d. דִּי־בֵית אֱלָהָא is lacking in Vg., and בֵית is lacking in LXX$^{\theta}$ and S.

Translation

5:1 King Belshazzar[420] held[421] a great banquet for a thousand[422] of his nobles, and he was drinking[423] wine in the presence of the thousand. **2** Upon tasting the wine,[424] Belshazzar gave a command to bring in the vessels of gold and

---

419. Wills, *The Jew in the Court of the Foreign King*, 123–24.

420. The NET offers the following note about Belshazzar being "king": "As is clear from the extra-biblical records, it was actually Nabonidus (ca. 556–539 BC) who was king of Babylon at this time. However, Nabonidus spent long periods of time at Teima, and during those times Belshazzar his son was *de facto* king of Babylon. This arrangement may help to explain why later in this chapter Belshazzar promises that the successful interpreter of the handwriting on the wall will be made *third* ruler in the kingdom. If Belshazzar was in effect second ruler in the kingdom, this would be the highest honor he could afford."

421. Lit., "made" (עֲבַד, *ʿăbad*), yet it is obvious that the king himself did not do the menial work or preparations.

422. Goldingay (100) suggests taking the whole phrase לְרַבְרְבָנוֹהִי אֲלַף (*ləraḇrəḇānôhî ʾălap*) as determinative in light of Dan 7:24 ("ten horns") and translates "his thousand nobles." His point may be well taken, but most Eng. versions have "a thousand of his nobles."

423. In this case the ptc. שָׁתֵה (*šāṯēh*) should be given its durative force, i.e., continual drinking.

424. Some translations (e.g., NET) prefer rendering בִּטְעֵם חַמְרָא (*biṭʿēm ḥamrāʾ*), "while under the influence of the wine." Literally, this is "at the taste (*biṭʿēm*) of the wine" (cf. NASB, "when Belshazzar tasted the wine"). Commenting on the use of

silver that Nebuchadnezzar his forefather[425] had taken out of the temple which was in Jerusalem, so that[426] the king, his nobles, his wives,[427] and his concubines might drink from them. **3** Then they brought[428] in the vessels of

---

ṭᵊʿēm in Dan 5:2, *HALOT* (1885) indicates a preference for the aspect of "tasting the wine": "Da 5_2 either 'under the influence of the wine' (KBL; NRSV; REB), or rather 'at the tasting of the wine, through the flavor of the wine, with the enjoyment of the wine', following Semitic *ṭaʿm* taste (AHw. 1385b)." Several English Bible translations (e.g., NRSV, NEB), however, take the liberty to render the expression "under the influence of" (so Collins, 236), but not NASB or NIV. LXX$^{\theta}$ translated the Aramaic quite literally: ἐν τῇ γεύσει τοῦ οἴνου (*en tēi geusei tou oinou*), "at the taste of the wine," although LXX^{O} was a bit more interpretative: καὶ ἀνυψώθη ἡ καρδία αὐτοῦ (*kai anupsōthē hē kardia autou*), "and his heart was raised up." An appeal to Esth 1:10 is not convincing, as the terminology is quite different: *kᵊṭôḇ lēḇ ... bayyāyin* ("while the heart ... was merry [lit., *good*] with wine").

425. Lit., "father" (אַב, *ʾaḇ*), but as in Hebrew, the term can refer to one's literal father or even grandfather (e.g., Gen 28:13), just as *ʾēm* ("mother") can also mean "grandmother" (1 Kgs 15:10). See *NIDOTTE* (1:219–23) for discussion. Hence, even though Nebuchadnezzar was the grandfather of Belshazzar rather than his father, the author of Daniel is not incorrect in referring to him as the *ʾaḇ* of Belshazzar. Most Eng. translations render *ʾaḇ* as "father," but "forefather" makes the issue clear.

426. The impf. verb וְיִשְׁתּוֹן (*wᵊyištôn*) is a good example of a "final imperfect" verb, and thus should be translated "so that they might drink" (cf. 2 Sam 9:1).

427. The words "his wives and his concubines" is a translation of the Aram. שֵׁגְלָתֵהּ וּלְחֵנָתֵהּ (*šēgᵊlāṯēh ûlḥēnāṯēh*). Although the same translation is given by the NIV and NASB, Goldingay (99) prefers "his consorts, and his mistresses." Both terms are foreign loanwords, and thus difficult to translate with precision. *HALOT* (1415) regards *šēgal* as a loanword from Akk. *ša ekalli* ("queen"), and gives the lexical meaning as "royal wife, concubine" (*HALOT* mentions the studies of W. G. Lambert, "An Eye-Stone of Esarhaddon's Queen and Other Similar Gems," *RA* 63 (1969): 66, who argued for the meaning "royal consort"). Note that in the Hebrew text of Neh 2:6, we have the queen of Artaxerxes referred to as *šēgal*. LXX$^{\theta}$ translated *šēgal* as *pallakai* ("young girl, concubine")—note that the verb *pallakeuō* means "to be a concubine." *lᵊḥēnāh*, on the other hand, is a loanword from Akk. *laḫḫinatu* (*HALOT*, 1908–09), referring to a woman who has duties in a session of the court, though *HALOT* suggests the meaning "concubine" for *lᵊḥēnāh*. LXX$^{\theta}$ translated *lᵊḥēnāh* as *parakoitoi* (one who lies beside). Undoubtedly, Belshazzar had a large harem (in typical oriental fashion), and perhaps with our limited knowledge, the best we can say is that these two terms refer to various members of his harem, including some of his concubines, though one may have had a higher status than the others.

428. The verb הַיְתִיו (*hayṯîw*) is a Hapʿel perf., but LXX$^{\theta}$ translates with the passive verb ἠνέχθησαν (*ēnechthēsan*), reading instead הֵיתַיו, *hêṯayû* (Hupʿal perf.). Since it is only the pointing that makes the difference, the passive is possible. However, most Eng. translations regard this as an active form.

gold[429] that they had taken from the temple, the house of God in Jerusalem, and the king, his nobles, his wives, and his concubines drank[430] from them. **4** They drank the wine and praised the gods of gold and silver, bronze, iron, wood, and stone.

Commentary

5:1 *Belshazzar's feast.* Critical scholars have attacked the historicity of this chapter on numerous matters, especially in regard to the naming of Belshazzar as king of Babylon.[431] Extrabiblical literature consistently refers to Nabonidus as the king of Babylon rather than Belshazzar.[432] However, we do have clear evidence that Belshazzar was the son of Nabonidus: "(O Moon god) preserve me, Nabonidus, king of Babylon, from Sin. To me give the gift of long life, and as regards Belshazzar, my first born son, my dear offspring, put in his heart reverence for thy high divinity."[433]

Furthermore, Young (116) cites evidence from the *Persian Verse Account of Nabonidus* to show that Nabonidus had also entrusted the rule of Babylon to Belshazzar in his absence: "He freed his hand; he entrusted the kingship (ip-ta-kid-su sharru-tam) to him. Then he himself undertook a distant campaign."[434]

Thus, there is sufficient evidence to demonstrate that the father and son shared a *joint-regime* in which Belshazzar occupied the subordinate position. As a result, official documents would be dated according to Nabonidus, but the book of Daniel made reference to Belshazzar, because this was the man in Babylon that the Jews actually had to deal with and whose royal word could affect them.

The hosting of great banquets was typical of oriental kings, especially of Persian kings (note Esth 1). "According to Ctesias and Dinon, the Persian king 'used to dine in company with 15,000 men and 400 talents were

---

429. The NET has added the words "and silver" (Aram. *wᵊḵaspāʾ*) in light of LXX$^{\theta}$ (καὶ τὰ ἀργυρᾶ, *kai ta argura*), and similarly Vg. Verse 2 does have "the vessels of gold and silver," and the NET understands that the words were accidentally dropped from the Aram. text of v. 3 due to homoioteleuton (writing once what should have been written twice).

430. Regarding the verb form אִשְׁתִּיו (*ʾištîw*) in v. 3 with a prosthetic א, P. W. Coxon, "A Philological Note on אשתיו Dan 5 3f.," *ZAW* 89 (1977): 275–76, has shown that this does not constitute evidence of late borrowing in the Aramaic of Daniel but rather is an eastern feature of Official Aramaic.

431. For example, see H. H. Rowley, "The Historicity of the Fifth Chapter of Daniel," *JTS* 32 (1931): 12–31.

432. See, for example, Pritchard, *ANET*, 312.

433. Fish, "Texts Relating to Nabonidus," 90.

434. Cf. S. Smith, *Babylonian Historical Texts, Relating to the Downfall of Babylon*, (London: Mathuen & Co., Ltd., 1924), 83–91; and M. J. Gruenthaner, "The Last King of Babylon," *CBQ* 11 (1949): 416–19.

expended on the dinner.'"[435] Both Herodotus (*Hist.* 1.191) and Xenophon (*Cyr.* 5.15) report that the capture of Babylon was partly aided by the fact that the Babylonians were celebrating a festival when "the citizens drink and make merry the whole night long" (so Xenophon). So, the idea of a banquet for a thousand nobles is no exaggeration at all. This particular banquet would have taken place on October 12, 539 BC.[436] The king set the tone for the evening by drinking wine before them (the durative force of the participle [שָׁתֵה, *šāṯēh*], "was drinking," is probably intended to stress the ongoing activity until they reached a state of inebriation).

In light of the historical circumstances, two significant questions immediately surface. First, if the armies of the Medes and Persians had already conquered the neighboring cities of Sippar and Akkad, and if the Babylonian army led by Belshazzar's father, Nabonidus, had already suffered a defeat in the territory to the north of Babylon, why would Belshazzar have been holding a banquet at this crucial time when the enemy forces were surrounding their walls? Second, why would Belshazzar have chosen this occasion to bring out the vessels from the Jewish temple to use them for drinking wine?

Regarding the first question, we must admit that we do not know why Belshazzar would have called for a banquet at a time when everyone knew the armies of Cyrus had them surrounded.[437] The Babylonians may have been observing a customary feast that simply happened to fall at this time, and there are some indications of this in the accounts of Xenophon and Herodotus.[438] On the other hand, it may be that Belshazzar (knowing of Nabonidus' defeat at Sippar about eighty km. to the north), may have felt

435. Cited in Collins (244), as reported by Athenaeus, *Deipn.* 4.146e.
436. Beaulieu, *The Reign of Nabonidus*, 230. According to the Nabonidus Chronicle, Babylon fell on the sixteenth day of Tašritu of the seventeenth year of Nabonidus, which would be October 12, 539 BC. For the text, see Thomas, *Documents from Old Testament Times*, 82.
437. A. Wolters, "Belshazzar's Feast and the Cult of the Moon God Sîn," *BBR* 5 (1995): 199–206, has attempted to bolster the case that Belshazzar's feast is to be understood as occurring at the time of the fall *akītu* festival in honor of the Babylonian moon-god *Sîn*, and in doing so builds upon the theory set forth earlier by Beaulieu in *The Reign of Nabonidus.* According to this theory, Belshazzar's festival was held on the eve of the seventeenth of Tašritu when the fall *akītu* festival in honor of the moon god Sîn would have begun.
438. See Xenophon, *Cyr.* 7.5.15; and Herodotus, *Hist.* 1.191. Observe the following selection from this portion of Herodotus: "But, as it was, the Persians came upon them by surprise and so took the city. Owing to the vast size of the place, the inhabitants of the central parts (as the residents at Babylon declare) long after the outer portions of the town were taken, knew nothing of what had chanced, but as they were *engaged in a festival*, continued dancing and reveling until they learnt the capture but too certainly. Such, then, were the circumstances of the first taking of Babylon."

that he and the other Babylonians were perfectly safe behind the massive walls of Babylon, and thus called for the banquet to build morale and flaunt the threat of the enemy. Since the Euphrates River ran through the city (a plentiful water supply) and they had ample provisions to outlast any siege, they may have felt invincible to Cyrus' attack against them.[439]

5:2–4 *The sacrilegious use of the temple vessels.* The second question raised above concerns the decision to bring out the vessels that had been taken from the Jewish temple in Jerusalem many years earlier. These "vessels" (Aram. מָאנֵי, *mā'nê*) were most likely a type of silver or gold goblet, since they were used for drinking purposes. If these vessels had been taken in the first Babylonian deportation of 605 BC (as Dan 1:2 implies), then nearly sixty-six years had passed since they were removed to Babylon. It is amazing that Belshazzar would even know of their existence. Furthermore, what prompted him to bring them out for use on this particular night? The fact that Belshazzar called for their use suggests that he knew something about the history of the Jewish exile and their worship of the one God, Yahweh. Most likely he also knew some of the events pertaining to his grandfather Nebuchadnezzar and how he had come to a personal faith in this God (recall Nebuchadnezzar's public testimony recorded in 4:1–3, 37). He may very well have known about the dream of Nebuchadnezzar and the prediction that Babylon would be overthrown by another kingdom (2:39). In light of what Belshazzar did with these temple vessels, it seems that he purposely had them brought out just to make a point that he himself scoffed at these matters, thus reinforcing the message he sought to convey that the Medes and Persians were not to be feared.

Verses 2–3 twice state that these "gold and silver vessels" had formerly been in the temple in Jerusalem. This is to emphasize the point that these vessels had been used in the worship and service of the true God of heaven. To bring these vessels out and use them in any manner would have been a sacrilegious act specifically aimed at defying the true God of heaven. Yet, Belshazzar even went a step further by using them for drinking purposes, in what probably became a drunken orgy. Rather than being used for the worship and adoration of the true God, the vessels were instead used to exalt the deities and idols of Babylon. Verse 4 indicates that they praised "the gods of gold and silver, bronze, iron, wood, and stone." This is a way of saying that they praised the Babylonian idols that were made of such materials. Ironically, this was also an accurate appraisal of Babylon's deities. They were worth nothing more than these perishable materials, in contrast to the Most High God whose kingdom is an everlasting kingdom (4:2–3). (For the names and descriptions of some of the false gods of Babylon, see "The Religious Context of the Babylonian Exile" in the "Introductory Materials.")

---

439. Regarding the provisions for outlasting a siege, see Herodotus, *Hist.* 1.190; and Xenophon, *Cyr.* 7.5.13.

Belshazzar was not simply making an innocent mistake. Rather, he was knowingly and openly defying the Most High God. Now it remained to be seen if Yahweh would respond to Belshazzar's challenge. Not only would he (as the rest of the chapter demonstrates), but he had already answered the challenge before Belshazzar even came to the throne. About 150 years earlier Yahweh had spoken through Isaiah the prophet as to what he would do with idolatrous Babylon (see Isa 46:1–2; 47:1–15). Some fifty years earlier, he had also spoken through Jeremiah about Babylon's judgment (see Jer 50:1–2, 18; 51:7–8, 11, 41b–44, 57–58). The following words from Isa 47:1, 8, 11 (NASB) were directed at proud and self-confident Babylon:

> Come down and sit in the dust, O virgin daughter of Babylon;
> Sit on the ground without a throne, O daughter of the Chaldeans!
>
> Now, then, hear this, you sensual one, Who dwells securely,
> Who says in your heart, "I am, and there is no one besides me."
>
> But evil will come on you which you will not know how to charm away;
> And disaster will fall on you for which you cannot atone;
> And destruction about which you do not know will come on you suddenly.

All this was prophesied long before Belshazzar acted so arrogantly and defiantly. Perhaps Belshazzar thought he was communicating a message that the gods of Babylon (and he as their earthly representative) would protect them. If so, how greatly he underestimated the power of the true God.

Application and Devotional Implications

Belshazzar was what we might call a "hard-hearted man." By his actions at the banquet, he was showing just how much he disregarded the true God of heaven and how much contempt he had for him. He did not merely choose not to trust in Yahweh Elohim (though his grandfather Nebuchadnezzar had done so), but he made a point to go out of his way to mock and ridicule the Most High God ... even to openly defy him. Sadly, he lived a life of walking in darkness in bondage to sin. His excess drinking was only one of his many personal problems (cf. Prov 20:1). Thus, he paid a heavy price for his contempt of God: he lived in spiritual darkness and ultimately faced God's judgment. How do we react to a guy like Belshazzar? It is easy to just say, "Well, he got exactly what he deserved!" When we consider him in light of the broader context of Scripture, however, we are reminded that God even loves men like Belshazzar. God even saves and changes men as evil as Belshazzar. Think for a moment what he did with the life of the apostle Paul: once a persecutor of Christians, but eventually Christianity's greatest advocate. The wonderful thing about the gospel message of the cross is that God uses it to gloriously change sinners into redeemed and godly saints. We see men like Belshazzar around us even in today's world, but let us not think they are beyond the hope of the gospel. Let us be ready with compassionate hearts to share the love of Christ with them.

2. Belshazzar's perplexity upon seeing the inscription (5:5–9)

Textual Notes

5.a. The Kethib reading (נְפַקוּ) has the difficulty of a masc. verb with a fem. subject. Read instead the Qere נְפַקָה, fem. pl. of נְפַק.

6.a. זִיוֺהִי שְׁנֹוהִי is awkward. Collins (236) suggests that rather than שְׁנוֹהִי (Peʿal perf. 3mp with 3ms suff.), the text should read שְׁנַיִן עֲלוֹהִי (Peʿal perf. 3mp) as found in v. 9. Otherwise, Goldingay (101) regards the suffix on שְׁנוֹהִי as an anomalous indirect object; cf. GKC, 369 (§117x).

6.b. חֲרַץ is only attested in the OT in Dan 5:6. 4QDan[a] reads חלצה for חרצה, in what is apparently an attempt to conform to BH חָלָץ ("loins"). However, חֲרַץ is well attested in extrabiblical Aramaic literature and there is no reason to doubt its authenticity.

7.a. 4QDan[a] adds "dream interpreters," as do MS 88 and Syh (but Pap. 967 lacks both "dream interpreters" and Chaldeans).

7.b. MT has the adjective form תַּלְתִּי, though V^S (Strack) reads as a noun, תָּא- (similarly Cairo Geniza וְתִלְתָּא). As an adjective, it is used substantively, meaning "third (ruler), i.e. triumvir" (BDB, 1118; so RJ, 114), whereas the noun תְּלַת means "a third part." LXX^{θ} translated this by the Greek adj. τρίτος ("a third"). On the meaning, *HALOT* (2006) indicates that this was "traditionally a triumvir, a man of the third rank ..., or the ruler of the third part of the empire" (cf. Collins, 236, "have the authority of a triumvir in the kingdom"). Most Eng. translations understand this to mean the third highest ruler of the kingdom.[440] For further discussion, see commentary at 5:7.

8.a. The Qere is עָלִּין (see Dan 4:4 for the same Kethib-Qere reading for עלל).

8.b. Rather than "the wise men of the king," some MSS read "the wise men of Babylon (בָבֶל)." *BHS* editor proposes מַלְכוּתָא = "the wise men of the kingdom." However, MT's reading is not problematic; they are "the king's wise men," as it is their duty to serve him.

8.c. The Qere reading פשרה ("its interpretation" rather than "the interpretation") is supported by some MSS and favored by Collins (236). Similarly, Dan 4:18 (see translation note to v. 18 Eng.).

---

440. So R. P. Dougherty, *Nabonidus and Belshazzar*, Yale Oriental Series, Researches 15 (New Haven, CT: Yale University Press, 1929), 196.

Translation

5:5 At that moment, the fingers of a human hand appeared[441] and were writing on the plaster of the royal[442] palace wall, near[443] the lampstand.[444] The king was watching the back[445] of the hand that was writing. **6** Then the brightness[446] of his countenance changed, while his thoughts were alarming him, the joints of his loins[447] were giving way,[448] and his knees were knocking

441. The Aram. word נְפַק (*nᵊpaq*) actually means "to come forth" (*HALOT*, 1932).
442. Taking דִּי מַלְכָּא (*dî malkāʾ*) as a genitive of attribute.
443. Aram. קֳבֵל (*qŏḇēl*) can mean "that which is in front, in full view, opposite" (*HALOT*, 1966). With the *lamed* preposition, it can mean "over against." This is the same word that was used in Dan 5:1 and translated "in front of" by the NET. The NIV translates 5:5 as "near the lampstand," which probably captures the point.
444. Aram. נֶבְרַשְׁתָּא (*neḇraštāʾ*) is a loanword from Old Persian *nibrāza*, meaning "burning brightly, lamp" (*HALOT*, 1925). It is translated "lampstand" by the NIV, NASB, and NET.
445. The word "back" is not in the Aram. text. Instead, we have פַּס יְדָה (*pas yᵊḏâ*), lit., "palm of the hand." However, Goldingay's explanation (101) is helpful: "פס usually refers to the palm—which would be hardly visible during writing, even to someone below it (Bentzen)—but essentially it denotes the hand itself as opposed to the lower arm and hand, effectively referring here to the back of the hand or knuckles."
446. Literally, the verse says, "Then the king, his *zîw* changed." Aram. זִיו (*zîw*) is from Akk. *zīmu(m)*, meaning "face, facial features, appearance" (*HALOT*, 1864). The meaning in Aram. can be "radiance, brightness," referring to one's countenance. LXX$^{\theta}$ translated *zîw* by the Greek word *morphē* ("form, appearance"), and LXX^{O} by a similar word *horasis* ("appearance"). Perhaps the translation "the brightness of his countenance changed" would capture both ideas. Compare NET's "all the color drained from the king's face."
447. חֲרַץ (*hăraṣ*) is a hapax, the meaning of which is uncertain. Whatever the meaning of the phrase in which it occurs (most likely an idiom), there appears to be a deliberate wordplay with Dan 5:12, 16. For further discussion, see "Additional Exegetical Comments" at the end of this section.
448. Lit. "were loosening" (Hitpaʿal ptc. of שְׁרָא, *šᵊrāʾ*). The same word was used earlier in Dan 3:25 of the young men walking about in the fire whose bonds were "loosed." Cf. 11Q10 (Col. xxxii.5), which speaks of the onager (wild ass) being "untied." Regarding the Hitpaʿal ptc. of שְׁרָא (*šᵊrāʾ*) in Dan 5:6, *HALOT* (2002) offers the nuances "to be loosened, shake, shudder" (though offering no support for "shake, shudder"). Take note of the wordplay involving שְׁרָא (*šᵊrāʾ*) and קְטַר (*qᵊṭar*), which occur together again in Dan 5:12, 16 in the sense "loosening of knots," i.e., explaining problems or riddles.

together. **7** The king loudly[449] summoned[450] the conjurers,[451] the Chaldeans,[452] and the diviners.[453] Then the king proclaimed to the wise men of Babylon, "Anyone who can read this inscription[454] and declare to me its interpretation will be clothed in purple and have a golden collar[455] placed about his neck and be third ruler in the kingdom." **8** So[456] the king's wise men all came in, but they were not able to read the inscription or make known its interpretation to the king. **9** Then King Belshazzar was greatly alarmed and visibly shaken.[457] Even his nobles were perplexed.

---

449. Lit., "with strength" (בְּחַיִל, *bᵊḥayil*).

450. Lit., "called ... to bring in" (קָרֵא... לְהֶעָלָה, *qārēʾ ... lᵊheʿālâ*). The Hapʿel of the verb *ʿălal* means "to bring in."

451. On the meaning of "astrologers" (אָשְׁפַיָּא, *ʾāšpayyāʾ*), see the commentary on Dan 1:20.

452. For "Chaldeans," (כַּשְׂדָּיֵא, *kaśdāyēʾ*), see the commentary on Dan 2:5. These were experts/priests in the Chaldean religion, especially making use of astrology. Both LXX^{O} and LXX$^{\theta}$ transliterated as Χαλδαίους (*chaldaious*).

453. The word translated "diviners" is the Aram. גָּזְרִין (*gāzᵊrîn*). See the translation note for Dan 2:27.

454. MT is clear throughout the chapter (vv. 7, 8, 15, 16, 17, 26) that the king demanded they both read the text and interpret it. OG, however, assumes they could read it and were only challenged to interpret it. M. Segal, "Daniel 5 in Aramaic and Greek and the Textual History of Daniel 4–6," in *IOSOT Congress Volume Stellenbosch 2016*, ed. L. C. Jonker, G. R. Kotzé, and C. M. Maier, 251–84, VTSupp 177 (Leiden: Brill, 2017), 263, explains, "Throughout the chapter, OG consistently replaces MT's double formulation with the expression ὑποδείκνυμι/ἀπαγγεῖλαι τὸ σύγκριμα τῆς γραφῆς 'relate the meaning of the writing,' without mentioning the need to actually read the writing."

455. Aram. הַמְנִיךְ (*hamnîḵ*), which *HALOT* (1860–61) regards as a Persian loanword from *hamyānak*. Broader cognate usage indicates possible meanings of "armband," "neckband," or "neck ornament," though *HALOT* gives the meaning "necklace" for Aram. *hamnîḵ*. Goldingay suggests that this is "a Persian word perhaps denoting a collar on the garment rather than a chain" (101). Most likely, it had some significance of importance in the Babylonian culture.

456. The *BHS* editor proposes that the first five words of v. 8 be deleted or transposed before v. 7b, since the previous verse makes clear that the wise men had already come before the king. Yet this proposal is unnecessary. The adverb אֱדַיִן (*ʾĕḏayin*) functions similarly to Heb. אָז (*ʾāz*), which though often indicating *temporal transition* ("then"), can sometimes be used of *logical transition* in the reporting of narrative. The translation "so" captures this idea in Dan 5:8. The point of v. 8 is not that they next came before the king (again). Rather this is a summary statement: though they came before the king, they could not read and interpret what had been written.

457. The Aram. text for "visibly shaken" (וְזִיוֹהִי שָׁנַיִן עֲלוֹהִי, *wᵊzîwōhî šānayin ʿălôhî*) is virtually the same as that found earlier in 5:6, which the NET had translated "all the color drained from the king's face." The point may be that his facial countenance

Commentary

5:5–6 *The inscription written on the wall.* How quickly the mood of Belshazzar's banquet changed. In a miraculous act, God caused a human hand to appear and write letters on the wall of the royal palace. The inscription appeared *near* the lampstand, i.e., in the illumination of the lampstand. (Some translations, like NASB, have "opposite the lampstand.") The letters appeared on the wall quite near the lampstand, where they could best be seen. The written inscription was not merely something seen in a *vision* by the king alone, for it was clearly visible later when the wise men arrived, and later still when Daniel was brought in.[458]

Arnold points out how the verb translated "appeared" (נְפַק, *nᵉp̄aq*) underscores the irony by use of a subtle wordplay. The same verb appeared in the Hapʿel stem in vv. 2–3 in the sense "taken" but in the Paʿel in v. 5 in the sense "appeared." He explains,

> The purpose of the wordplay is clear. The two occurrences of the *haphel* (vv. 2 and 3) emphasize the arrogant blasphemy of Nebuchadnezzar. Then the paronym in v. 5 subtly, and without mentioning God directly, introduces the divine reaction to human insolence. This skillful use of *nĕpaq* uses irony to contrast the arrogance of human rebellion with the omnipotence of God's response. Nebuchadnezzar may have exercised his royal power in capturing the sacred vessels, but now God exercises his divine prerogative in bringing the blasphemy to an end.[459]

The hand itself signified a certain irony for the king. Daniel brings this out later in vv. 23–24: "But the God in whose hand are your life-breath and your ways, you have not glorified. Then the hand was sent from Him and this inscription was written out" (NASB).

Belshazzar's purpose as a king on earth (whether he realized it or not) was to bring glory to the one true God. This God held Belshazzar in his hand, so to speak. Belshazzar was nothing more than a puny king in the hand of the all-powerful Sovereign of the universe. In this moment of judgment, the Babylonian deities (in contrast) were unable to speak out or even raise so much as a finger to help him. Since Belshazzar did not recognize the One in whose hand his life rested, God sent a hand to spell out the divine judgment for Belshazzar.

---

showed even more alarm. Note the NASB translation, "his face grew *even* paler."

458. M. Segal, "Rereading the Writing on the Wall," *ZAW* 125 (2013): 167, has argued that only the king saw the handwriting, yet his position is unconvincing. How could the Babylonian wise men be invited to read and explain the inscription if it was not visible to them?

459. B. T. Arnold, "Wordplay and Narrative Techniques in Daniel 5 and 6," *JBL* 112 (1993): 482.

The Aramaic word in v. 5 for plaster is גִּיר (*gîr*), which can also mean "whitewash," suggesting that the walls of the palace were coated in a whitewashed plaster.[460] Montgomery, citing the results of the archaeological work of Robert Koldewey at Babylon, reports the following observations:

> In the southern part of the area lies the largest room of the castle, the throne hall of the Babylonian kings. In every respect it is distinguished from all the other halls, and there can be no doubt that it was the chief royal audience chamber. "If one would localize anywhere the ill-fated banquet of Belsh., it could be found with greatest warranty in this enormous room," which is 17 m. wide by 52 long. In the centre of one of the long sides, opposite the entrance, is a niche, in which the throne must have stood. And the explorer notes that the walls were covered with white plaster.[461]

To this Larue provides a further description of the room:

> On the external facade, against a background of dark blue glazed bricks, were tall columns of yellow glazed bricks topped with bright blue Ionic capitals with double volutes linked by palmettos. A frieze of white rosettes ran above the columns and the entire pattern was framed with a border of glazed squares of alternating yellow, black and white. Other motifs reconstructed by the Germans [archaeologists] out of the thousands of fragments of shattered tile included scorpions, serpents, panthers, lions and mythological monsters. The interior of the throne room appears to have been relatively simple. The roof was constructed of cedar and the windowless walls were whitewashed. ... The doorways had thresholds of bronze and traces were found of cedar doors covered with bronze.[462]

Seeing this miraculous site of the hand writing on the wall of the palace obviously had a strong impact upon Belshazzar. Verse 6 suggests that his facial countenance drastically changed, he was mentally shaken, and he apparently lost the strength to stand. (For further discussion, see "Additional Exegetical Comments" at the end of this section.) He was completely unnerved at the sight of this spectacle!

5:7–9 *The Babylonian wise men summoned.* Belshazzar realized immediately that this situation was beyond his understanding, so he sought spiritual help.

---

460. LXX$^{\theta}$ translated *gîr* by the Greek word κονίαμα (*koniama*), meaning "stucco, plaster, whitewashing." The masculine form *koniatēs* means one who is a "plasterer, whitewasher."

461. Montgomery, 253. He cites R. Koldewey, *The Excavations at Babylon* (London: Macmillan, 1914), 104.

462. G. A. Larue, *Babylon and the Bible* (Grand Rapids: Eerdmans, 1969), 57–58.

Not surprisingly, he turned not to those who were truly spiritual (like Daniel) but to the practitioners of the Babylonian occult system, notably those who were skilled in dream interpretations and astrology (see the translation notes to v. 7).[463] To anyone who could read and interpret the inscription, the king offered a threefold reward.

Purple was the color of royalty in antiquity and thus signified a great elevation in the rank and status of the person.[464] The golden collar about the neck (see translation note above to v. 7) probably signified a special distinction in Babylonian culture as an award by the king.[465]

The third part of the reward was the offer to make the person a "third ruler in the kingdom." Technically, the Aramaic text says that he will be made a תַּלְתִּי (*taltî*), which some would relate to the noun *tᵊlaṯ* meaning "a third part." Miller (157–58) notes that there are three primary views concerning the significance of this. First, in the view of Montgomery, the word *ṯaltî* lost its numerical significance and acquired a different connotation.[466] Miller (157) explains,

> Montgomery argues that the term is reminiscent of Akkadian *šalšû*, which was a title meaning "Thirdling" or "Triumvir," similar to Hebrew *šālîš*. The Akkadian term eventually came to designate simply an official, having lost any numerical sense. Therefore the terms in Daniel may simply represent a high official.

Since the "wise men" were already high officials, this argument seems weak. Hence, a second view proposed is that the term *ṯaltî* refers to a triumvir

---

463. M. Broida, "Textualizing Divination: The Writing on the Wall in Daniel 5:25," *VT* 62 (2012): 1–13, tries to build a case that the writing on the wall involved an appropriation of Mesopotamian techniques of mantic writing. In doing so, the Mesopotamian diviners are supposedly beaten at their own game, as it were. She writes (13), "Just as Moses and Aaron's prowess in Pharaoh's court served to demonstrate God's mastery of Egyptian magic, so God's use [of] Mesopotamian mantic writing was meant to show the superiority of Jewish deity as well as Jewish scribe."

464. For evidence of this among the Persians, see Esth 8:15; 1 Esd 3:6; Xenophon, *Anab.* i, 5,8. Among the Medes, see Xenophon, *Cyr.* i,3,2; ii,4,6. During the Greek period, note 1 Macc 10:20 and 14:43.

465. Montgomery (254) indicates that this golden collar (or necklace) in Persian culture was worn by Persians of rank (*Anab.* i,5,8; 8,29) and was presented by the king as a special compliment (*Anab.* i, 2,27; Herodotus, *Hist.* iii, 20; ix, 80; 1 Esd 3:6). According to *Cyr.* xiii, 5,18, the decoration could be worn only when presented by the king.

466. Montgomery, 254. Similarly Gruenthaner, "The Last King of Babylon," 420–21. Goldingay (99), more recently, also argues that the term may have lost its original numerical value and translates "a Deputy." Yet against Montgomery, see W. H. Shea, "Nabonidus, Belshazzar, and the Book of Daniel: An Update," *AUSS* 20 (1982): 138–39.

who would rule one-third of the kingdom equally with two other persons, namely Belshazzar and Nabonidus.[467] Against this view is the question of Belshazzar having the authority to make such an offer, given that his father Nabonidus was the highest ruler whom one would expect to be consulted.

A third view is that the one able to give the interpretation would be promoted to the third-highest position in the kingdom, namely just after Nabonidus and Belshazzar.[468] This view is reflected in the translation of the NIV, NASB, and NET. In light of what we know about the historical situation, this view would make the most sense.

Despite the worldly attractive rewards offered by Belshazzar, none of the Babylonian "wise men" were able to read or to make known the meaning of the inscription. Why was this? First, even if these were Aramaic words (which both the Babylonians and the Hebrews understood), we do not know what script they were written in. Second (and more importantly), the real issue was the significance of the words. Seeing isolated words without a context would be extremely difficult to make sense of, as they did not even form a complete sentence. Most likely they did not have the vowel pointing, either, which further complicated one's ability to make sense of them.

Finally, that the Babylonian wise men could not read and explain the inscription serves as a polemic against their idolatrous system. What they cannot do despite all their knowledge of Mesopotamian divination texts, the worshiper of Yahweh (Daniel) is able to do, thereby demonstrating the superiority of Yahweh to the gods of Babylon. In this regard, the story is quite similar to that in chap. 2. Segal explains,

> … both stories concern knowledge that is beyond the reach of the wise men, yet fully accessible to Daniel, who is endowed with divine wisdom. This contrast is intended to demonstrate the superiority of divinely inspired knowledge over and above the extensive educational training of Mesopotamian scribes and scholars in Antiquity. Both stories assert that there are situations in which divine wisdom trumps any human or earthly knowledge, which is by definition limited, and therefore favor the prophetic revealed word over the scholastic training that royal courtiers received.[469]

Application and Devotional Implications

The king's revelry and mockery of God by using the temple vessels must have seemed very funny to Belshazzar as he stood laughing and drinking wine in front of the guests at the banquet. Naturally, the audience laughed along with him. What a contrast we see in Dan 5:6 after the king saw the handwriting on the wall: "Then the brightness of his countenance changed,

467. Lacocque, 92, advocates this position.

468. So Dougherty, *Nabonidus and Belshazzar*, 196.

469. Segal, "Rereading the Writing on the Wall (Daniel 5)," 174.

while his thoughts were alarming him, the joints of his hips were giving way, and his knees were knocking together." The fear of God had suddenly fallen on this man, as he encountered the supernatural power of the Living God. Of course there are thousands of people who act just as belligerently as Belshazzar did but who never see a comparable demonstration from God. If God wanted, he could use his incredible power to silence all his critics and mockers. Normally, he does not do that. He much prefers to manifest his grace to people like Belshazzar. The love of God is absolutely amazing, and we see it perfectly displayed in what the Lord Jesus Christ did for us on the cross. Though he (the King of glory) was whipped, spat upon, and finally crucified, he was willing to go through it all just to demonstrate that God loves sinners. What grace!

Additional Exegetical Comments

The proper translation and interpretation of קִטְרֵי חַרְצֵהּ מִשְׁתָּרַיִן (*qiṭrê ḥarṣēh mištārayin*) in Dan 5:6 is difficult. At the heart of this is the word חֲרַץ (*ḥăraṣ*), an OT hapax. The translations vary:

> KJV: "the joints of his loins were loosed" (similarly Collins, 236)
> NKJV: "the joints of his hips were loosened"
> NASB: "his hip joints went slack"
> NIV: "his legs became weak" (cf. Goldingay, 99, "his body went weak")
> NRSV: "his limbs gave way" (so ESV; cf. Hartman, 181, "his legs gave way")
> NET: "the joints of his hips gave way"

According to BDB (1093d), *ḥăraṣ* means "loins." *HALOT* (1880) suggests "hip" but offers no evidence to support this nuance. (*HALOT* is followed by *DBL Aramaic*, #10284 while RJ, 114 and *TWOT*, 1021 admit both meanings. Cf. Keil, 182, who understood it as the "thighs.") The meaning "loins," however, is well attested in extrabiblical Aramaic literature. *CAL* mentions several examples: *EchR [1]* 53:25, *TN* Exod 12:11, and *CT Levi ar b D.9*. Cf. Sok. (215) for more examples. There is also one example from Qumran (4Q214 f2:6) with the meaning "loins." As for the translations, LXX^{O} omitted the phrase, while LXX^{θ} rendered it οἱ σύνδεσμοι τῆς ὀσφύος αὐτοῦ διελύοντο (*hoi sundesmoi tēs osphuos autou dieluonto*), "the bonds (or sinews/ligaments) of his loins were loosening (or weakening)." So the nuance of "loins" is clearly attested, despite the ambiguity of the phrase as a whole.

Wolters argues against the meaning "hip" or "thigh" in favor of a unique interpretation of the king's inability to control bodily wastes:

> ... the problematic phrase *qiṭrê ḥarṣēh* in Dan 5:6 refers to the sphincter muscles of the bladder and anus. This interpretation fits the usual meaning of Aramaic *ḥăraṣ* (= Hebrew *ḥălāṣayim*), namely "loins" (often associated in the Bible with the reproductive organs), and does not require recourse to the otherwise

> unattested meanings of "hip" or "thigh." ... The loss of sphincter control would then be described as the "loosening of the knots" situated in the lumbar region or "loins."[470]

Newsom (170), however, is probably correct in dismissing Wolters' suggestion: "As appealing as that interpretation is in some respects, ch. 5 otherwise does not have the bawdy style that fits such a narrative detail." More likely, the king's reaction reflects an ancient Near Eastern literary convention in which the recipient of disturbing news exhibits fear that expresses itself by bodily weakness or possibly shaking.[471] P. Shalom offers an example made in response to the Assyrian king Esarhaddon: "(When) he [the king] heard my [Esarhaddon's] royal message which burns the enemies like a flame ..., his hips collapsed ..., his heart was seized (by fear) ..., his legs trembled ... his countenance looked bad."[472]

I have suggested the rather literal translation "the joints of his loins were loosened, i.e., gave way." Goldingay's explanation (101) is probably correct: "he lost the strength to stand." Though using different terms, the concept of *loss of support* is reflected in Isa 21:3, Ezek 21:12 (Eng. 21:7), Nah 2:11 (Eng. 2:10), and Ps 69:24 (Eng. 69:23). The latter is particularly interesting: "Make their <u>loins</u> (מָתְנֵיהֶם, *motnêhem*) shake continually."

The expression *qiṭrê ḥarṣēh mištārayin* in Dan 5:6 may very well be an idiomatic expression whose exact meaning escapes us today, just as the similar wordplay involving שְׁרָא (*šᵊrāʾ*) and קְטַר (*qᵊṭar*) in 5:12, 16 is an idiom for resolving difficult problems. In any case, it is a psychosomatic reaction of fear upon seeing the hand writing on the wall. Collins (246–47) has noted the irony, "The sudden transformation of the king from arrogant luxury to physical dissolution has a comic effect."

3. The Queen Mother's recommendation to call in Daniel (5:10–12)

Textual Notes

10.a. A few MSS read עֲנָת, which is to be preferred (being the proper form for the 3fs).

12.a. *BHS* editor suggests pointing these participles as infinitives (hence, מְפַשַּׁר and מְשָׁרֵא, respectively). The latter receives some support from Vg. and Vˢ. Emerton,[473] however, argues that this "looks suspiciously like a conscious or unconscious attempt by a scribe to introduce an easier reading." He then

470. A. Wolters, "Untying the King's Knots: Physiology and Wordplay in Daniel 5," *JBL* 110 (1991): 119.

471. For examples of this literary feature, see D. R. Hillers, "A Convention in Hebrew Literature: The Reaction to Bad News," *ZAW* 77 (1965): 86–90.

472. P. Shalom, "Decoding a 'Joint' Expression in Daniel 5:6, 16," *JANES* 23 (1993): 122.

473. J. A. Emerton, "The Participles in Daniel v. 12." *ZAW* 72 (1960): 263.

draws an analogy to biblical Hebrew, where the participle can "denote the action as such, or the abstract idea of a certain action or condition, with no reference to the agent." On this basis, Emerton defends the pointing as participles and translates "interpretation" and "loosing" respectively.

12.b. The Qumran MS 4QDan^{a} has the additional words וכתבא יקרא ("and he will read the writing"), which Collins (238) accepts and includes in his translation. He remarks, "In 4QDan^{b} the preceding word ends in א, so Ulrich reconstructs יתקר[א וכת]בא יקרא. MT omits וכתבא יקרא by homoioteleuton. Alternatively, the phrase could be added in the 4Q manuscripts by analogy with 5:7, 17 (so Ulrich)." Noticeably, however, neither LXX^{O} and LXX$^{\theta}$ have these words.

Translation

5:10 On account of what the king and his nobles had said,[474] the queen

474. Lit., the Aram. says "on account of the words of the king and his nobles." The NET ("Due to the noise caused by the king and his nobles") implies that they were talking so loudly, the queen heard them and came to the banquet hall (cf. NIV, "hearing the voices of the king and his nobles"). While this is a possibility, another interpretation could be that their words were *reported* to the queen, on account of which she came in. The previous verses do not substantiate that they were yelling. What is called to the reader's attention are the lavish gifts that the king offered the wise men, about which the nobles were no doubt jabbering. The words "had said" are used in the translation as a result of the classification of מַלְכָּא (*malkāʾ*) in the construct מִלֵּי מַלְכָּא (*millê malkāʾ*) as a *subjective genitive*. The king and his nobles are the ones who uttered the words, i.e., they had spoken.

mother[475] herself[476] entered the banquet room.[477] She[478] said, "O king, live forever! Do not let your thoughts alarm you. Do not let this dim[479] your countenance. **11** There is a man in your kingdom in whom is a spirit[480] of the holy

---

475. Technically, the Aram. has "the queen" (*malkᵊṯāʾ*), though the NET is probably correct in translating this "queen mother." Most commentators since the time of Josephus have understood this to be a reference to the wife of Nebuchadnezzar, and thus the grandmother of Belshazzar. (Note: not all historians regard Belshazzar as a descendant of Nebuchadnezzar, but the words of v. 11 imply that he was. If so, then Belshazzar's father Nabonidus may have married a daughter of Nebuchadnezzar named Nitocris, for Nabonidus himself was not a son of Nebuchadnezzar.) Josephus called her Belshazzar's grandmother, using the Greek word *mammē* (*Ant.* 10.11.2). Collins (248) offers support that the Aram. *malkâ* can mean both "queen" and "queen mother," based on a parallel with Greek usage. In Arrian, *Anab.* 2.12 (second cent. BC), both the mother and the wife of Darius were given the same title of *basilissa* by Alexander. Thus, she is the "queen mother," though this leaves open the question as to whether she is the wife of Nebuchadnezzar and grandmother to Belshazzar (so Josephus, Collins, 248, and Young, 122), or whether she is the wife of Nabonidus and mother of Belshazzar—possibly named Nitocris (so Miller, 160). Regarding Nitocris' identity, Shea, "Nabonidus, Belshazzar, and the Book of Daniel: An Update," 137, sounds a note of caution: "Herodotus tells us that Nitocris was the last great queen of the Neo-Babylonian empire (*Histories*, I: 185– 188), but his description of her includes so much legendary material that it is difficult to tell whether he was referring to Nabonidus' wife or mother in this case." Yet Dougherty, *Nabonidus and Belshazzar*, 39–44, 53–63, 69–70, presents a convincing case that Nitocris was the wife of Nabonidus and the mother of Belshazzar.

476. The word "herself" is added, following Goldingay (101) who observes the emphatic position of *malkâ* at the beginning of the sentence.

477. בֵּית מִשְׁתְּיָא (*bêṯ mištᵊyāʾ*) is literally, "the house of the feast," i.e., a banquet room or feasting hall (Collins, 236).

478. Lit., "The queen mother."

479. The translation "Do not let this dim your countenance!" is an attempt to render the Aram. וְזִיוָךְ אַל־יִשְׁתַּנּוֹ (*wᵊzîwāyḵ ʾal-yištannô*), which literally means "and your countenance, let it not be changed." On "countenance" (Aram. *zîw*), see the translation note to Dan 5:6.

480. The expression "a spirit of the holy gods" (Aram. *rûaḥ ʾĕlāhîn qaddîšîn*) is the same expression found earlier in Dan 4:5 (Eng. 4:8). See the "Additional Exegetical Comments" on Dan 4:8 (Eng.), in which the conclusion was reached that *ʾĕlāhîn* should be understood as a true plural, "gods." In contrast, Wood (141) thinks this is a reference to the "Spirit of the holy God" and suggests that the queen mother probably had even become a true believer. Collins (249) takes note of the view of the early church as reported by Jerome: "all the authorities, except Symmachus, who follows the Chaldean original (*veritatem*), render 'the spirit of God.'"

gods. In the days of your grandfather,[481] illumination,[482] insight, and wisdom like the wisdom of the gods were found in him. King Nebuchadnezzar your grandfather—your grandfather the king[483]—appointed him chief of the magicians,[484] conjurers, Chaldeans, *and* diviners. **12** Because an extraordinary spirit, knowledge, insight for interpreting[485] dreams and declaring riddles, and resolving difficult problems[486] were found in him—in *this* Daniel whom the king named Belteshazzar—let Daniel therefore be summoned, and he will make known the interpretation."

---

481. Aram. *ʾab̲* ("father"), but see translation note to Dan 5:2.

482. The word translated "illumination" is Aram. נַהִירוּ (*nahîrû*), which can mean either "illumination" (*HALOT*, 1927) or "insight" (BDB, 1102, lists both). One can compare a similar noun *nəhôr* in Dan 2:22 meaning "light."

483. The words "your father the king" (*ʾăb̲ûk̲ malkāʾ*) are present in the MT at the end of v. 11 but omitted from the NET and NIV. They are included, however, in the NASB, NKJV, and ESV. The words seem unnecessary and are missing from LXX$^{\theta}$ and the Syriac. R. Taylor, "The Book of Daniel in the Bible of Edessa," *Aramaic Studies* 5 (2007): 244, has argued for omitting them: "Most exegetical attempts to account for the phrase are not convincing. It probably originated as a secondary scribal gloss. The absence of this phrase in the Peshitta probably points to the correct reading."

484. Three of these four terms appeared in Dan 5:7 (see the translation notes to 5:7 for comments). The first is the Aram. term *ḥarṭummîn*, which first appeared in 1:20 (see the commentary on 1:20)—a *ḥarṭom* was probably a diviner, one who used some sort of inscribed chart or magical design (possibly imposed on a chart of the stars) in order to arrive at an answer to questions put to him.

485. Although the MT has pointed the verb מְפַשַּׁר (*məpaššar)* as a Paʿel ptc., the NET has chosen to vocalize this differently as an infinitive (מִפְשַׁר, *mip̄šar*)—following Collins (236)—and regards it as epexegetical to the noun שָׂכְלְתָנוּ (*śok̲lət̲ānû*). (Observe the infinitive forms in v. 16.) This results in the translation "skill (lit., insight) *to interpret* dreams." However, if the noun שָׂכְלְתָנוּ (*śok̲lət̲ānû*) is regarded as in construct with מפשר (*mp̄šr*), seeing this as a ptc. is not a problem. We could then take the ptc. substantively and classify it as a genitive of purpose, "insight for the purpose of interpretation." The result, then, is the same. Related to this discussion is what one does with וְאַחֲוָיַת (*waʾaḥăwāyat̲*). BDB (1092) takes this as a noun, yet *HALOT* (1871) regards this as an Apʿel inf. If the latter, this could influence one's understanding of מפשר (*mp̄šr*). Goldingay (101), however, opts to view them as ptcps.: "מפשר 'interpreting' and משרא 'resolving' need to be understood as verbal nouns, like אחוית 'explaining'; this may not involve emending them, if the ptpl can denote the action as such, without focusing on an agent: so Emerton, *ZAW* 72 (1960) 262–63, noting that Syr, Th do not support emendation."

486. The translation "resolving difficult problems" (NET "decipher knotty problems") renders the Aram. מְשָׁרֵא קִטְרִין (*məšārēʾ qiṭrîn*), which literally means "the loosening (or untying) of knots." This is an idiomatic expression for *solving difficult problems*. Goldingay (99) translates "resolving enigmas."

Commentary

5:10 Apparently the scene in the banquet hall created quite a stir, and word quickly spread throughout the palace. The queen mother—either the grandmother of Belshazzar (who had been the wife of Nebuchadnezzar) or the mother of Belshazzar (and thus the wife of Nabonidus)—had not been present during the feast and drinking activities. (See the translation note to v. 10 on the explanation of "queen mother.") Either she heard the loud voices from the banquet hall, or possibly someone brought word to her about the spectacular phenomenon that was taking place and all that was being said. In either case, she quickly came to the banquet hall to see for herself. Upon entering, she gave the king the typical oriental greeting, "O king, live forever," as a public display of her respect (though from the perspective of the narrator this may be uttered in irony).

5:11 Noticing how shaken and upset the king was, she sought to calm him by calling to his attention that there was a man in the kingdom who could be of help. One might wonder why the king himself had not thought to call Daniel earlier (especially since according to v. 7 he had called for others among the "wise men"). The most logical solution is that Daniel had probably been out of active government service for some time. The time of this scene was the year 539 BC, and if Daniel had come to Babylon in 605 BC at age fifteen (in Nebuchadnezzar's first deportation), then he would have been about eighty-one years old by now. Furthermore, Belshazzar had begun to reign in 553 BC as part of a joint-regime with his father Nabonidus. This was fifty-two years after Daniel's arrival in Babylon, which would mean Daniel was probably at least sixty-seven years old when Belshazzar began to reign. Being this old in 553 BC, possibly he was never part of Belshazzar's administration, which might suggest that Belshazzar was not familiar with Daniel (notice how Belshazzar addresses Daniel in vv. 13–14).[487]

---

487. An alternative theory is that Belshazzar was familiar with Daniel's role in the days of Nebuchadnezzar and that the queen mother's counsel—though diplomatically stated—is actually a rebuke of the king. H. J. M. Van Deventer, "Would the Actually 'Powerful' Please Stand? The Role of the Queen (Mother) in Daniel 5," *Scriptura* 70 (1999): 248, concludes, "It is significant that the queen mother in Daniel 5 is not named. Her power is derived from her very high social standing, in fact the highest social standing a woman could obtain, albeit through personal ingenuity. As indicated the queen mother acts in the narrative world along the lines of the female rebuker. It is noteworthy that the narrator chooses the queen mother for this part. According to the societal set-up she was placed in a role from which rebuke is expected and, indeed, accepted. It is, after all, not one of 'his' concubines that rebukes the king. The queen mother's social standing explains her conduct in this court tale."

5:12 The queen mother began by pointing out that Daniel had within him "a spirit of the holy gods" (recall Dan 4:8), i.e., he was a spiritual man with some special connection to the deities. (This should not be translated or understood as a reference to "the Spirit of the holy God"—see "Additional Exegetical Comments" to Dan 4:8.) She then referred to the days of Belshazzar's grandfather, Nebuchadnezzar (lit., "father"), when Daniel actively served him. The queen mother then spoke of the insight, discernment, and wisdom that Daniel had displayed in Nebuchadnezzar's day (probably thinking of the things recorded in Daniel chaps. 2 and 4). Accordingly, Nebuchadnezzar had appointed Daniel "chief" (*raḇ*) over the other "wise men"—the occult practitioners in the royal court.

Once again in v. 12 the queen mother points out the excellent qualities possessed by Daniel that qualified him to interpret dreams, explain riddles, and solve difficult problems. Up until this point, the queen mother has not mentioned his name, but now she does. Even though his Babylonian name was Belteshazzar (which Nebuchadnezzar had given to him), she also knew and even referred to him first by his true name, Daniel. This was the name that reflected his relationship to the true God of the Bible (Daniel = "God is my judge"). Nebuchadnezzar had apparently come to respect Daniel's original name (see Dan 4:8), and the queen mother herself associated him with his original name. Thus, she uttered her advice: "Now summon Daniel, and he will make known the interpretation."

Wolters has pointed out the subtle wordplay in the Aramaic text of Dan 5:12 (and 5:16) with 5:6.[488] In the earlier verse, the king was described with the words *qiṭrê ḥarṣēh mištārayin*, "the knots/joints of his loins were loosening (giving way)." In contrast, Daniel is introduced by the words *mᵊšārē᾽ qiṭrîn*, "loosening knots" (i.e., explaining problems/riddles). Both phrases have the words שְׁרָא (*šᵊrā᾽*) and קְטַר (*qᵊṭar*). Wolters sees this as an example of dramatic irony involving double entendre, as though the sovereign Yahweh is mocking the arrogant Belshazzar (and his psychosomatic reaction of fear) by the competency of his prophet, Daniel. He writes,

> The difference in context thus clearly separates the untying of knots in v. 6 from that in vv. 12 and 16, but the identity of vocabulary binds them together. It is the interplay between difference and identity that makes the wordplay work.[489]

Application and Devotional Implications

Applicational thoughts for this section have been combined with the following section. See "Application" at the end of the section for Dan 5:13–16.

---

488. A. Wolters, "Untying the King's Knots," 118.

489. Ibid., 121.

4. Belshazzar's Offer to Reward Daniel for Interpreting (5:13–16)

Textual Notes

14.a. A few MS Editions (plus S and Arabic versions) add קַדִּישִׁין ("holy"). However, this does not appear in LXX$^{\theta}$, which simply has πνεῦμα θεοῦ ("a spirit of a god"). More likely, the addition was due to a harmonization with the phrase רוּחַ אֱלָהִין קַדִּישִׁין in Dan 5:11.

16.a. One MS reads חֶלְמִין ("dreams") rather than פִּשְׁרִין ("interpretations") due to the awkwardness of פִּשְׁרִין לְמִפְשַׁר ("to interpret interpretations"). However, the MT is fine as is once we recognize this as a cognate accusative; cf. Jon 1:10; *IBHS*, 167 (§10.2.1g). Translate: "you are able to render interpretations."

Translation

5:13 Then Daniel was brought in before the king. The king said to Daniel, "Are you *that* Daniel who is one of the exiles[490] of Judah, whom the king, my forefather,[491] brought from Judah? **14** Now I have heard about you that there is a spirit of the gods[492] in you and that you have[493] illumination, insight, and surpassing wisdom. **15** The wise men *and*[494] conjurers were brought before me that they might read this inscription in order to make known to me its interpretation, but they were not able to declare the interpretation of the message.[495] **16** But I myself[496] have heard about you, that you are able to render[497] interpretations and to solve difficult problems. Now if you are able to read the inscription and make known to me its interpretation, you will be

490. The Aram. בְּנֵי גָלוּתָא (*bᵉnê gālûṯāʾ*) literally means "sons of the deportation," i.e., the exiles (see *HALOT*, 1845).

491. Lit., "father" (אַב, *ʾaḇ*). See translation note at Dan 5:2.

492. For "a spirit of the gods," see commentary for Dan 4:8 (and "Additional Exegetical Comments" at the end of that section).

493. Literally, הִשְׁתְּכַחַת בָּךְ (*hištᵉkaḥaṯ bāḵ*) means "have been found in you." The verb שְׁכַח (*šᵉḵaḥ*) is in the Hithpe'el stem, with a passive nuance. "You have" is a smoother English translation.

494. The NET adds the following note: "The Aramaic text does not have 'and.' The term 'astrologers' is either an appositive for 'wise men' (cf. KJV, NKJV, ASV, RSV, NRSV), or the construction is to be understood as asyndetic (so NET, NASB, NIV, and the translation above)."

495. Lit., "the word" (מִלְּתָא, *millᵉṯāʾ*).

496. The independent personal pronoun אֲנָה (*ʾănâ*), being placed at the beginning, is probably emphatic: "I myself have heard."

497. Taking פִּשְׁרִין לְמִפְשַׁר (*pišrîn lᵉmipšar*) as a cognate accusative (see textual note above).

clothed with purple *and have* a golden necklace about your neck, and you will rule as one of three in the kingdom."[498]

Commentary

5:13 The king did not waste any time in summoning Daniel to his presence, and apparently Daniel was not too far away at the time (since he arrived rather quickly). Although the queen mother had pointed out the fact of Daniel's promotion to *chief* (רַב, *raḇ*) of the wise men, the king made no mention of this when he addressed Daniel. Instead, the king pointed out the matter of Daniel's association with the Judean exiles—a fact the queen mother had not commented on. Perhaps it was the recognition of Daniel's Hebrew name, דָּנִיֵּאל, *dāniyyēʾl* (which was easily identifiable as a foreign name and connected him with the God of the Hebrews). Thousands of these Jews who had been taken captive by Nebuchadnezzar were still living in the realm, and undoubtedly Belshazzar was familiar with them in general. By acknowledging in v. 13 that Daniel was "from Judah" (מִן־יְהוּד, *min-yᵊhûḏ*), the king was certainly aware that he was now talking face-to-face with a man (renowned for having a spirit of the gods) that represented the deity whose temple vessels he had desecrated. One suspects that Belshazzar must have been highly anxious at this moment, as he waited to hear from the representative of the deity he had made mockery of.

5:14–16 Belshazzar continued in v. 14 with his elaboration of what he knew about Daniel. He acknowledged that Daniel possessed a "spirit of the gods," omitting the word "holy" in regard to gods.[499] Belshazzar's wording of Daniel's spiritual qualifications (v. 14) seems to be a summary of what the queen mother had said to him previously (vv. 11–12). The king also acknowledged to Daniel that the wise men of the court (חַכִּימַיָּא, *ḥakkîmayyāʾ*) had seen the inscription but had not been able to declare its interpretation. Although several categories of wise men had been listed in v. 7, the king only refers to the conjurers (אָשְׁפַיָּא, *ʾāšᵊp̄ayyāʾ*) here in v. 15. Perhaps this was done for the sake of brevity. Finally, in v. 16 Belshazzar acknowledged what he had heard about Daniel in regard to his ability to make interpretations and solve difficult problems. Interestingly, Belshazzar extended the same offer of the three rewards to Daniel that had been offered to the other wise men of Babylon. Nebuchadnezzar had rewarded Daniel in days past because of how amazingly God had worked through Daniel (recall 2:48). This offer of reward, however, came in a very different context—from the lips of a king who deliberately mocked and ridiculed the God of glory.

---

498. Regarding the translation and interpretation of the various rewards in this verse, see the translation notes and commentary to Dan 5:7.

499. A few manuscript editions plus the Syriac and Arabic versions add the word "holy" (*qaddîšîn*), though this is missing from the MT. Most likely the addition was due to a harmonization with רוּחַ אֱלָהִין קַדִּישִׁין (*rûaḥ ʾĕlāhîn qaddîšîn*) in Dan 5:11.

Application and Devotional Implications

One of the amazing things about this segment of the story is that the queen mother is found actually praising and promoting Daniel to the king. What prompted her to speak so favorably of Daniel? After all, he was a Jewish exile, while she was of the Babylonian nobility. Furthermore, he was most likely a frail old man by this time, probably having been in virtual retirement during the years of Belshazzar's reign. Nevertheless, she spoke with such confidence about him: "Now summon Daniel, and he will make known the interpretation."

We do not know the true spiritual condition of the queen mother. In fact, we are not altogether certain if this was Nebuchadnezzar's wife or the mother of Belshazzar. We have no reason to believe that she came to faith in Yahweh Elohim, although that remains a possibility. Yet regardless of the motives by which she acted, the significant thing is that God was working in and through this woman's testimony. She commended Daniel, and that was key to Daniel having an audience with the king. This is nothing less than the sovereignty of God at work to give Daniel a golden opportunity to be God's spokesman.

There is a verse in the book of Proverbs that seems appropriate in regard to this story in Daniel, namely Prov 16:7. "When a man's ways are pleasing to the LORD, He makes even his enemies to be at peace with him" (NASB). Now this is not a universal law that will always be manifested. We cannot claim that Christians who live godly lives will always experience peace and kindness from their enemies. We have to take into account other verses like John 15:18–19 (NASB):

> If the world hates you, you know that it has hated Me before it hated you. If you were of the world, the world would love its own; but because you are not of the world, but I chose you out of the world, because of this the world hates you.

Thus, what Prov 16:7 is really trying to tell us is that though we cannot expect all unbelievers to favor us (at times, they may even hate us), God can sovereignly control those whom we might expect to oppose us, and he can even direct their hearts to be favorably disposed towards us. He did this with the queen mother in Daniel 5, and he still does this today. So, while we need to be prepared to be hated by the world, we can nevertheless take comfort in knowing that God is sovereign and can supernaturally intercede in our affairs to cause others to act favorably toward us when that is needed to give us an opportunity to serve God and glorify him.

5. Daniel's response to Belshazzar (5:17–28)

Daniel was not enamored with King Belshazzar's offer of rewards, but he knew that God had a divine mission for him. Now was a time for courteous but bold declaration of God's imminent judgment upon Babylon.

Textual Notes

17.a. לְמַלְכָּא is lacking in LXX$^{\theta}$ (though some MSS in the LXX$^{\theta}$ tradition do have τῷ βασιλεῖ), but 4QDan[a] retains it.

17.b. The reading וּפִשְׁרֵהּ ("its interpretation" rather than "the interpretation") is supported by 4QDan[a], LXX$^{\theta}$, Vg., and S.

19.a. The Qere reading is without the א: זָיְעִין. Cf. Heb. זוּעַ ("tremble, quake").

19.b. MT מַחֵא is normally taken as an Ap'el ptc. of חֲיָה ("to let live, keep alive"). LXX$^{\theta}$ rendered this as ἔτυπτεν, impf. 3s from τύπτω ("to smite"), reading BH מחה or Aram. מחא. Yet the idea "allowing to live" balances the previous "slaying" in the sentence.

20.a. *BHS* editor proposes וִיקָרֵהּ (with suffix), "and <u>his</u> honor/glory," which is supported by LXX^{L} (Lucianic), S, and Vg. Most Eng. translations insert "his."

21.a. Rather than MT's passive form שַׁוִּי (Pe'il perf. 3ms = "was made like"), the Qere reading is שַׁוִּיו (Pa'el perf. 3mp). Goldingay (102) takes this as an impersonal plural and translates, "became like." Most Eng. translations, however, accept the passive Pe'il (LXX$^{\theta}$ has the passive ἐδόθη).

Translation

5:17 Then Daniel replied to[500] the king, "Keep[501] your gifts for yourself and give your presents[502] to someone else. Nevertheless, I will read the inscription for the king and make known its interpretation. **18** As for you, O king, the Most High God bestowed on Nebuchadnezzar your forefather the kingdom, greatness, honor, and majesty.[503] **19** Because of the greatness that He bestowed on him, all the peoples, nations, and *men of every* language[504] would tremble in fear[505] before him. Whom he wished, he would slay; and whom

---

500. Lit., "Daniel answered and spoke before the king."
501. Lit., "let them be for you" (לָךְ לֶהֶוְיָן, *lāḵ lehewyān*).
502. The Aram. word וּנְבָזְבְּיָתָךְ, *ûnᵊḇāzᵊbᵊyāṯāḵ* ("your presents") has caused some confusion. LXX$^{\theta}$ seems to have regarded this as two separate words (*ûnᵊḇizbāṯ baytāḵ*), translating as καὶ τὴν δωρεὰν τῆς οἰκίας σου (*kai tēn dōrean tēs oikias sou*), "and the gift of your <u>house</u>." The Qumran document 4QDan[a] has נבזבתך (*nbzbtk*, without the *yod*). BDB proposes that נְבִזְבָּה (*nᵊḇizbâ*) is a Persian loanword, but *HALOT* (1924) indicates that the "etymology is uncertain, perhaps to be related to Akk."
503. It is possible to understand these last four words as two pairs, each pair representing a hendiadys (so Goldingay, 100; and Hartman, 185). Understanding this as a double hendiadys, then, would yield the translation "royal authority" and "glorious splendor."
504. The translation "*men of every* language" is literally "tongues" (לִשָּׁנַיָּא, *liššānayyā'*). Cf. Dan 3:4.
505. Lit., the Aram. has "were trembling (ptc.) and fearing (ptc.)," הֲווֹ זָאֲעִין וְדָחֲלִין (*hăwô zā'ă'în wᵊḏāḥălîn*). The NET takes this as a hendiadys: "trembling with fear."

he wished, he spared.[506] Whom he wished, he exalted; and whom he wished, he brought low. **20** But when his mind[507] became haughty and his spirit had become arrogant so that[508] he acted presumptuously, he was deposed from his royal throne,[509] and the honor[510] was taken away from him. **21** Then he was driven out from mankind, his mind[511] became like[512] that of an animal, he dwelt[513] with the wild donkeys, as cattle he was given grass to eat, and his body was drenched with dew from the sky, until he came to understand that the Most High God is ruler over the realm of mankind,[514] and He appoints over it whomever He wishes. **22** But you, his grandson,[515] Belshazzar, have

---

506. The NET correctly translates מַחֵא (*maḥēʾ*) as "spared" (or "allowed to live"), understanding this as a Hap'el ptc. of *ḥāyâ* (or *ḥăyāʾ*). LXX$^{\theta}$ (and similarly Vg) translates *maḥēʾ* as ἔτυπτεν (*etupten*), "he smote whom he wished." LXX$^{\theta}$ took the verb as a form of the root *mᵊḥāʾ* ("to smite") rather than *ḥăyâ*. The remainder of the verse, however, indicates that opposites are probably in view (e.g., exalt / bring low). Thus "spared" would be the expected opposite of "slayed."
507. NET translates לִבְבֵהּ, *libbēh* ("his heart") as "his mind." In light of its use in v. 21 (where the "mind" is clearly in view), it is best to translate both instances the same. Where he became haughty (in his mind) is where God afflicted him (having a mind like an animal).
508. The infinitive לַהֲזָדָה, *lahăzāḏâ*, with *lamed* preposition expresses result. Cf. *IBHS*, 606–7 (§36.2.3d).
509. Taking "his kingdom" in the genitive construct as a genitive of attribute = "his royal throne."
510. Possibly "his throne," if the alternative reading is accepted (see the textual note to this word above). Most Eng. translations do have "his throne" rather than "the throne."
511. Lit., "heart," but לְבַב (*lᵊḇaḇ*) can mean the "mind," and that is clearly in view in this verse.
512. Heb. עִם (*ʿim*) can mean "like" (see BDB, 767d).
513. The translation "dwelt with" suggests that this clause has a verb, though it does not. Lit., the Aram. reads "his dwelling place (noun מְדוֹרֵהּ, *mᵊḏôrēh*) *was* with the wild donkeys." The equative verb is implied.
514. Technically מַלְכוּת (*malkûṯ*) is singular, but some translations (NET, NIV) translate as plural ("over human kingdoms") in order to capture the intended idea (contrast NASB, "the realm of mankind"). BDB (1100) gives the general meaning "royalty, reign, kingdom," but BDB's #3 is "realm." Cf. Dan 4:17 (Eng.). The point is that the Most High God exercises his sovereign authority over the entire *realm* of mankind. The NET takes אֲנָשָׁא (*ʾănāšāʾ*) as an attributive genitive ("human kingdoms").
515. For the translation "grandson" (lit., "his son"), see translation note at Dan 5:2 for "father" (אַב, *ʾaḇ*).

not humbled yourself,[516] although[517] you knew all this. **23** Rather, you have exalted yourself against the Lord[518] of heaven, and the vessels of His temple[519] they have brought before you.[520] Then you and your nobles, *along with* your wives and your concubines, drank wine from them, and you praised the gods of silver and gold, bronze, iron, wood, and stone, which neither see nor hear nor understand[521] *anything*! But as for the God in whose hand is your breath and your entire fate,[522] you have not glorified Him![523] **24** Then the back of the hand was sent from Him, and this inscription was written."

Commentary

5:17 *Daniel's refusal of the king's rewards.* The tone of Daniel's response may almost seem rude at first reading. Josephus' account of the story reflects a softer reply: "Then Daniel begged him to keep his presents—for, he said, that which was wise and divine could not be bought with gifts but freely benefited those who asked for help—and said that he would explain the writing to him."[524] Rather than being rude, Daniel was probably trying to be *clear* with the king. He was there only to speak the truth and refused the rewards, so that he would not be under any obligation that would interfere with him being less than truthful. One thing is evident: Daniel was not motivated by such earthly treasures. At this stage of his life, he could see the limited value these offered. It takes a man of genuine godly character to pass up the glitter of worldly desires, but that is precisely what Daniel did. Furthermore, for him the rewards were wrong because of the context in which they were offered—a context of belittling the God whom he loved and served.

516. Lit., "brought low your heart."
517. Goldingay (102) objects to the concessive use of כָּל־קֳבֵל דִּי, *kol-qŏḇēl dî* ("although"), even though most translations (e.g., NASB, NIV, NET, NRSV) render it that way. More often it is "causal" (e.g., 5:12; 6:4).
518. "Lord" in this verse is not Yahweh or Adonai, but מָרֵא (*mārēʾ*). The term was used of Nebuchadnezzar in Dan 4:24 (Aram. 4:21).
519. Lit., "house," but the same term was used in Dan 1:2 of the temple (house of God) that was plundered.
520. NET translates "You brought before you the vessels," though the verb is in the 3rd mas pl. From the context it is clear that Belshazzar was the one authorizing this.
521. Adding the word "anything" (though not actually in the Aramaic) completes the thought expressed by the ptc. יָדְעִין (*yoḏʿîn*, lit., "they do not know/understand"). Alternatively, NET translates "cannot ... comprehend."
522. Lit. the text reads "and all your ways" (וְכָל־אֹרְחָתָךְ, *wᵉḵol-ʾōrᵉḥāṯāḵ*). Yet "ways" is a metonymy for his life experiences. Note Goldingay (100), "your whole destiny."
523. The pronoun is emphatic, being placed at the beginning of the clause: "Him you have not glorified."
524. Josephus, *Ant.* 10.11.3 (§241).

5:18–21 *The reminder of Nebuchadnezzar's experience in being humbled.* Beginning in v. 18, Daniel turns the king's attention to the consideration of God's discipline upon Nebuchadnezzar, his grandfather. Even though God knew beforehand how Nebuchadnezzar would behave as king, He still allowed him to have a *full taste* of earthly greatness: "a kingdom, greatness, honor, and majesty." God had allowed Nebuchadnezzar to realize "greatness" far beyond what Belshazzar was then experiencing, for the Babylonian kingdom had been eroding for some time, as Cyrus (leading the combined armies of Persia and Media) continued to grow in power. Yet in Nebuchadnezzar's day, he had enjoyed a much superior and almost unrivaled power (cf. Jer 27:5–7). God had allowed Nebuchadnezzar to be an absolute monarch over many peoples, nations, and language groups—doing virtually whatever he wished (v. 20). It would be hard for almost any human being to have this much power and still view himself rightly before God, and not surprisingly Nebuchadnezzar was swept away in pride. Yet God is sovereign, and just as He allowed Nebuchadnezzar to have greatness, so He took it all away from him until he learned his lesson. Verse 21 recounts the period that Nebuchadnezzar had to dwell as an animal and with the animals. The verse even stipulates that his dwelling place was with the *wild donkeys* (עֲרָדַיָּא, *ʿărāḏayyāʾ*). There was no specific reference to these animals in Dan 4:25, only that the king dwelt among the "animals of the field" (חֵיוַת בָּרָא, *ḥêwaṯ bārāʾ*). The wild donkey was known as being difficult to tame (cf. Job 39:5–8), which would have been appropriate in regard to Nebuchadnezzar himself.

All men, even rulers, must recognize who the true ruler is and must humbly submit themselves before him as Lord. Nebuchadnezzar was a grand illustration that no matter who you are or how much you have going for you, you cannot escape the consequences of the sin of pride. As Daniel spoke about Nebuchadnezzar, the implication was apparent that Belshazzar was behaving the same way, and even worse. But some people learn very little from history. Belshazzar certainly had not learned much.

5:22–24 *Daniel's rebuke of Belshazzar.* Previously, Daniel had referred to Nebuchadnezzar as Belshazzar's *forefather* (אַב, *ʾaḇ*), by which he meant his *grandfather*.[525] Now, he called Belshazzar the "son" (בַּר, *bar*) of Nebuchadnezzar. Once again, it is the closeness of relationship that is stressed, as Belshazzar was technically the *grandson*. This is not an error on the part of the author; rather, it shows the flexibility of the language. More importantly, Daniel confronted Belshazzar with the fact that he knew these things about Nebuchadnezzar, and yet did not humble himself. Belshazzar was not so removed in time from Nebuchadnezzar that these things would have escaped his knowledge. Miller (163) explains:

> Belshazzar served as chief officer during the administration of King Neriglissar in 560 BC according to Babylonian historical

525. See translation note to Dan 5:2.

> texts. This means that the king was old enough to fill a high position in government only two years after Nebuchadnezzar's death (562 BC). Since Nabonidus was an official in Nebuchadnezzar's administration, Belshazzar would have lived in Babylon and would have observed personally the last years of the great king's reign.

Belshazzar had no excuse for what he did. He had an advantage over Nebuchadnezzar in that he had the example of Nebuchadnezzar before him. Being a foolish man, this example failed to curb his pride. Thus, there would be no reprieve for him.

Daniel also points out that Belshazzar had not merely exalted himself. More pointedly, he exalted himself *against* the "Lord of heaven." The word translated "Lord" is not the personal name of God (i.e., Yahweh). Rather, this is the Aramaic word *mārēʾ* (מָרֵא), which is a term indicating both respect and high position of authority. Daniel had used this same term while speaking to Nebuchadnezzar in Dan 4:24—"my lord, the king" (*marʾî malkāʾ*). Yet Nebuchadnezzar was only a "lord" of the earthly kingdom of Babylon; Daniel's God is "Lord of heaven."[526] The use of this phrase underscored the authority of the one he was defying and the extent to which he had overstepped his bounds. The word translated "exalted yourself" (הִתְרוֹמַמְתָּ, *hiṯrômamtā*, Hitpoʿlel of *rûm*) is the same as that used in 11:36 of "the king" who exalts and magnifies himself above every god, which in that context is a reference to the future antichrist.

Belshazzar did not merely drink wine from some vessels used for religious purposes. Daniel pointed out (v. 23) that these were the vessels of "His temple," i.e., the temple of "the Lord of heaven." Belshazzar's sin had been extremely offensive. With these vessels, Belshazzar praised the gods made of various earthly materials (cf. Deut 4:28; Ps 115:4–8)—inanimate gods, as it were, and in contrast did not glorify the God in whose hand was his breath—that is, the living God. Not only was Belshazzar's very breath in God's hands (i.e., he controlled whether Belshazzar lived or died), but so was his "fate"—or as Goldingay (100) puts it, *his whole destiny*. Belshazzar's self-exaltation and sacrilegious defiance had caused God to send forth the hand making the inscription. Without a doubt, the inscription could hardly be anything less than words of judgment against Belshazzar.

---

526. Referring to the God of the Bible as "Lord of heaven" might have been a deliberate insult to the Babylonian deities. In the famous Cyrus Cylinder, Marduk was viewed as the "great lord." Part of the inscription reads, "Marduk, the great lord, a protector of his people/worshipers, beheld with pleasure his (i.e. Cyrus') good deeds and his upright mind (lit.: heart) (and therefore) ordered him to march against his city Babylon" (Pritchard, *ANET*, 315).

Textual Notes

25.a. With the double appearance of מנא, the question is raised if this is a case of dittography. In contrast to MT stands LXX$^{\theta}$'s μανη θεκελ φαρες (reflecting singular מנא), and so Josephus (*Ant.* 10.11.3), Jerome, and Vg. Yet S agrees with MT. Furthermore, there is the question if these are nominal or verbal forms, and finally how these terms should be translated. Kraeling reports, "Bauer accepts the idea (which goes back as far as Berthold, 1806) that the text of v. 25 originally had only the three words מנא תקל פרס."[527] However, an original reading מנא מנא in v. 25 is quite reasonable, as a single appearance of מנא in v. 25 in some manuscripts could be explained as an attempt to harmonize with the singular מנא in v. 26.

25.b. In contrast to MT's וּפַרְסִין (either plural or dual), LXX$^{\theta}$ has a singular form φαρες. De Guglielmo has argued that the original must have been singular and was changed to a plural by a later copyist.[528]

Translation

5:25 "Now this is the inscription which was written: 'MENE, MENE,[529] TEQEL, and PHARSIN.'[530] **26** This is the interpretation of the words: *As for* MENE[531]—God has numbered your kingdom and put an end to it. **27** *As*

527. E. G. Kraeling, "The Handwriting on the Wall," *JBL* 63 (1944): 14.

528. A. de Guglielmo, "Dan. 5:25—An Example of a Double Literal Sense," *CBQ* 11 (1949): 202–6.

529. LXX$^{\theta}$ has MENE only once (transliterated μανη in Greek), and similarly Vg. However, there is no reason to reject the doubling of MENE in MT, the repetition probably being for emphasis. Cf. discussion on this issue in the textual note above for v. 25. Kraeling, "The Handwriting on the Wall," 16, has noted, "The possibility of a twofold *menē,* furthermore, is demonstrated by the Mishnaic phrase מנה מנה ופרס, in which מנה actually occurs with פרס. Geiger called attention to it in 1867. It is found (Eduyoth 3, 3; Hullin 9, 2) in a saying of Dossa ben Harkhina who lived at the time of the destruction of the temple."

530. LXX$^{\theta}$ has the singular form φαρες (*phares*), whereas the Aram. form *parsîn* is in the plural, though *HALOT* (1959) recognizes this may be a dual form, as does Goldingay (102). Apparently, LXX$^{\theta}$ is attempting to conform PHARSIN of v. 25 to the singular *pᵉrēs* of v. 28. Some translations (e.g., the NASB) render the word in v. 25 as UPHARSIN, but the initial U is simply a connective ("and") joining the words TEQEL and PHARSIN.

531. The NET adds the following note: "The Aramaic term מְנֵא (*méne'*) is a noun referring to a measure of weight. The linkage here to the verb 'to number' (Aram. מְנָה, *ménah*) is a case of paronomasia rather than strict etymology. So also with תְּקֵל (*téqel*) and פַּרְסִין (*farsin*)."

for TEQEL—you have been weighed on the balances[532] and found lacking. **28** As for PERES[533]—your kingdom has been divided and given to the Medes and Persians."

Commentary

5:25–28 Following the confrontation with Belshazzar, Daniel interpreted the inscription on the wall. The inscription consisted of four words, each of which signified an aspect of the judgment that was to fall on Belshazzar and his kingdom. The four words are often explained as either simple noun forms or passive participle forms, which literally mean something like "numbered, numbered, weighed, and divided."[534] An interesting theory was espoused in an article published in 1886 by Clermont-Ganneau, suggesting that the three terms referred to weights or monetary values.[535] Montgomery explains:

> Acc. to this view we would have a series of money values: the *mn*ʾ = Heb. *māneh*, Gr. *mna*, *i.e.*, the mina, or Bab. talent; *teqel* would be the correct Aram. equivalent for *šeqel*; while the discovery of

532. The word for "balances" (מֹאזַנְיָא, *mōʾzanyāʾ*) seems to have been a commonly shared Semitic term. J. Shepherd notes, "Several ANE languages have a term for scales that seem to be related. Ugar. *mznm*; Arab. *mīzān/mawāzin*; Aram. *mōʾzanyāʾ/mōʾznēʾ*. Possibly also related are the Akk. *zibānītu*, scales, and the Egyp. *wdn*, heavy" (*NIDOTTE*, 2:829).

533. In v. 28 we find the singular form פְּרֵס (*pᵉrēs*), in contrast to the plural form פַּרְסִין (*parsîn*) in v. 25. There seems to be a double wordplay here. The verb *pᵉras* means to "break in two, divide"; yet the similar sounding proper noun *pāras* means "Persia, Persians."

534. Miller (165) argues the case that these words are passive participle forms. Normally the passive participle form would have a *hîreq-yôḏ* infix. Hence, we would expect *mᵉnîʾ* rather than the MT *mᵉnēʾ* (and similarly for *tᵉqēl* and *pᵉrēs*). Miller, however, points out that the syllables are accented in the MT, which may have produced the changed vowels. Collins (250), on the other hand, argues that these are noun forms: "The words are vocalized as nouns 'after the pattern of the simplest Aram. noun-form *qetēl*; the most natural form for the narrator to choose if he wished them to be non-committal'"—citing C. C. Torrey, "Notes on the Aramaic Part of Daniel," *Transactions of the Connecticut Academy of Arts and Sciences* 15 (1909): 277.

535. C. Clermont-Ganneua, "Mene, Tekel, Peres, and the Feast of Belshazzar," trans. R. W. Rogers, *Hebraica* 3 (1887): 87–102 (originally published in French in *Journal Asiatique*, 1886, 36ff.—mentioned by Montgomery, 263). Others have built on this theory to suggest alternative explanations. O. Eissfeldt, following a suggestion of P. Haupt, understood the terms to mean a mina, a shekel, and half-minas. He then explained the mina as representing Nebuchadnezzar, the shekel as Belshazzar, and the half-minas as Media and Persia; O. Eissfeldt, "Die Menetekel-Inschrift und ihre Deutung," *ZAW* 63 (1951): 109. For a more recent interpretation along the line of a weight system, see K. P. Kirchmayr, "Mene-tekel-uparsin," *VT* 60 (2010): 483–86.

the word *prs* on an Ass. weight as equal to a half-mina (s. Clerm.-Gann.), which mng. *prs* has in the Talmud, appeared to clinch the discovery.[536]

While many have accepted this theory of monetary weights in general, it suffers one significant flaw, as W. H. Brownlee has pointed out: "There is one fatal weakness to this method of interpreting the handwriting on the wall: It is not so interpreted in the Book of Daniel itself!"[537] So, if the words had any correlation to monetary weights or values, the text itself does not make that point, thus casting doubt on the theory.[538]

What is certain is that each of the terms in v. 25 is taken up and explained in vv. 26–27 by interpreting them in light of their related verb forms.[539] Hence, the term *mᵊnēʾ* is explained by the verb *mᵊnâ*, meaning to "number, count." So, the interpretation of *mᵊnēʾ* is that God *has numbered* (*mᵊnâ*) Belshazzar's kingdom (i.e., the years of his reign) and decided to put an end to it. The repetition of the word *mᵊnēʾ* probably serves to underscore the certainty of the matter (cf. Gen 41:32). No extension of time would be granted Belshazzar.

Likewise, the term *tᵊqēl* was to be understood in light of the verb *tᵊqal*, meaning to "weigh." God had *weighed* Belshazzar in the "scales" as it were, had found him "lacking" or "deficient," and thus rejected him. Collins (252) points out that "The motif of weighing the actions of people is common in eschatological contexts: *1En* 41:1; *2En* 52:15; *T. Abraham* 13:10 (of individuals); *4 Ezra* 3:34 (of nations)." The biblical concept is rooted in 1 Sam 2:3, "The LORD is a God of knowledge, and with Him actions are weighed" (NASB).

Finally, the term *pᵊrēs* was to be understood in light of the verb *pᵊras*, meaning to "divide, break in two." This term is distinguished from the first two, in that it appears in the plural (or dual) in v. 25 as *parsîn* but in the singular *pᵊrēs* in v. 28. There may be a reason for listing it in two different ways.

536. Montgomery, 263 (Hebrew and Greek terms have been transliterated from the original quotation).

537. W. H. Brownlee, *The Meaning of the Qumran Scrolls for the Bible* (New York: Oxford University Press, 1964), 41.

538. Some scholars, like R. B. Chisholm, *Handbook on the Prophets* (Grand Rapids: Baker, 2002), 302, take the position that the words meant literally "a mina, a mina, a shekel, and half-shekels," but the key to their significance lies in the fact that they *sound like* certain verbs. For example, mina *sounds like* the verb *mᵊnāh*, meaning "to number."

539. F. Zimmermann, "The Writing on the Wall," *JQR* 55 (1964–65): 205–7, argues against understanding the three words disjunctively as three sentences (counted, weighed, and divided): "The truth of the matter is, however, that the words should be read as one *sentence* as any oracle, and the meaning of מְנֵא תְּקֵל פְּרֵס would be: *set* or *appointed is the Persian trap*." His theory is not convincing because he has to presume an error occurred in the transmission (whether in the oral transmission or in being misvocalized). Theoretical possibility is not proof.

It is clear from v. 28 that *pᵊrēs* is related to the verb *pᵊras*, meaning to "divide, break in two." But the plural/dual form *parsîn* may have a connection to the final clause of v. 28, "and it has been given to the Medes and Persians (*pārās*)." "Thus, we see the word in two different forms, because there is a double play-on-words involved."[540] As Montgomery (263) points out, "Here a balanced phrase is obtained by finding a double paronomasia in the mystic word, *i.e.*, *division* and *Persia*." Not only was Belshazzar's kingdom to be *divided* or *broken in two*, but it was also going to be conquered and fall into the hands of the *Persians* (the dominant people of the Medo-Persian army). Indeed, that very night the forces of the Persian Cyrus the Great would march into Babylon victoriously.

Application and Devotional Implications

Belshazzar, in all his haughty arrogance, illustrates what the book of Proverbs calls a fool and a scoffer. As a fool, he stands opposite the wise son who willingly listens to godly counsel and realizes his need for instruction in life. After rehearsing the earlier experience of King Nebuchadnezzar (who had to be severely disciplined for his pride), Daniel boldly turned to King Belshazzar and declared to him, "But you, his grandson, Belshazzar, have not humbled yourself, although you knew all this. Rather you have exalted yourself against the Lord of heaven" (Dan 5:22–23a). In doing so, Belshazzar has played the fool who now has to pay the price for his refusal to receive instruction.

Belshazzar is also a "scoffer." Prov 13:1 states, "A wise son *accepts his* father's discipline, but a scoffer (לֵץ, *lēṣ*) does not listen to rebuke" (NASB). Like Belshazzar, even we as believers can fall into the trap of *knowing—but not humbling*. The text says Belshazzar "knew all this" but could not bring himself to act humbly. He scoffed in the face of truth. There are times when we all need "rebuke" in some form or fashion, because rebuke correctly and wisely given is good for us. Life has many hidden pits that we can fall into, and there are many ways in which we can be taken advantage of by evil. To listen to truth and respond appropriately is a virtue that will benefit us. Belshazzar, then, is a good reminder to us of our need to listen and act wisely in light of what we know to be true rather than arrogantly pushing the truth away.

6. The outcomes of Belshazzar's feast (5:29–31)

The last three verses of the chapter give us a glimpse of the final moments of the Babylonian Empire. Ironically, Daniel was honored, while Belshazzar

540. De Guglielmo, "Dan. 5:25," 202–6, argues that the original form in v. 25 was not a plural form *parsîn* but a singular form (since the explanation in v. 28 has the singular) and that a later copyist, recognizing the double wordplay, changed it to a plural accordingly.

lost all honor. The king was slain, and a Mede known as Darius replaced him as ruler over Babylon.

Textual Notes

6:1.a. [Eng. 5:31] LXX$^{\theta}$ has Καὶ Δαρεῖος ὁ Μῆδος in agreement with MT. Witnesses to LXX^{O}, however, differ. Pap. 967 has Ξέρξης ὁ τῶν Μήδων βασιλεὺς ("Xerxes who was king of the Medes"), whereas MS 88 and Syh read *καὶ* Ἀρταξέρξης ὁ τῶν Μήδων ("Artaxerxes of the Medes"), both being perhaps a vain attempt to make sense of the text due to a struggle to properly identify "Darius the Mede." The closest known Artaxerxes would be the Persian king, Artaxerxes I Longimanus (r. 465–424 BC), son of Xerxes I of Persia. These LXX^{O} readings are undoubtedly an attempt at harmonization with Dan 9:1, where Darius is said to be "the son of Ahasuerus" (but of Median descent). The LXX^{O} translator, knowing that the name Ahasuerus is used in Esth 1:1 (whom most scholars equate with Xerxes I, r. 486–465 BC), is apparently attempting to understand the Darius of Daniel as the son of the Ahasuerus of Esther (= Xerxes I). The son of the Ahasuerus of Esther would be Artaxerxes I Longimanus. Obviously LXX^{O} is in serious error. Not only would the dating of Artaxerxes be far too distant from the lifetime of Daniel, but the Darius of Daniel is a Mede, not a Persian monarch (cf. Dan 9:1; 11:1; Jer 50:1–2, 41–43; 51:11, 28).

6:1.b-b. [Eng. 5:31b-b] For Darius' age, LXX$^{\theta}$ has *ὢν ἐτῶν ἑξήκοντα δύο*, "being sixty-two years old," which reflects MT. LXX^{O}, on the other hand, chose a more paraphrastic translation, *πλήρης τῶν ἡμερῶν καὶ ἔνδοξος ἐν γήρει*, "full of days and esteemed in old age."

Translation

5:29 Then Belshazzar gave the command,[541] and they clothed Daniel in purple and *placed* a golden collar about his neck, and they publicly announced concerning him that he would be third ruler[542] in the kingdom. **30** That *very*

541. Lit., "Then Belshazzar spoke (i.e., commanded)."

542. For discussion of שַׁלִּיט תַּלְתָּא (*šallîṭ taltāʾ*), see commentary for Dan 5:7. Collins (240) translates "a triumvir," while Goldingay (100) has "as a Deputy."

night Belshazzar, the Chaldean king,[543] was slain. **31** [Aram. 6:1][544] So Darius the Mede received[545] the kingdom, *being*[546] sixty-two years of age.

Commentary

5:29–30 *The end of Belshazzar's reign.* Despite Daniel's refusal of Belshazzar's rewards (v. 17), the king still ordered him to be so honored, though this may have all been done in mockery of Daniel and his God. According to v. 30, Belshazzar died that very night. The king thought he was so secure behind the massive walls of Babylon, but that night (Oct. 12, 539 BC) a general of Cyrus named Ugbaru (or Gobryas) took the city with hardly a battle. Nabonidus (father of Belshazzar) had already been defeated in a previous battle and had sought refuge in the neighboring city of Borsippa, but Belshazzar (who had remained in Babylon) was slain by the forces of Cyrus. Details of Babylon's fall are well documented in the Nabonidus Chronicle (*ANET*, 305–7), the Cyrus Cylinder (*ANET,* 315–16), Herodotus' *Histories* (fifth cent. BC),

---

543. NET translates "the Babylonian king." Lit., the Aram. text has בֵּלְאשַׁצַּר מַלְכָּא כַשְׂדָּיָא (*bēlʾšaṣṣar malkāʾ kaśdāyāʾ*), "Belshazzar, the Chaldean king." In this case, "Chaldean" is obviously being used in the ethnic sense rather than the more technical sense of priests in the Chaldean religion (see commentary on Dan 2:2 for more discussion).
544. Dan 5:31 in our English versions is verse 6:1 in the Aramaic text.
545. A lot of discussion has gone into how best to render the verb קַבֵּל (*qabbēl*) in Dan 6:1 (Aram.). Both BDB and *HALOT* offer the basic definition "to receive." Likewise, both LXX^{O} and LXX$^{\theta}$ translate קַבֵּל (*qabbēl*) by the Greek verb παραλαμβάνω (*paralambanō*), meaning "to receive" ("*receive from* another, esp. of persons succeeding to an office, etc."; *LSJM*, 1315). Yet Montgomery (267), Goldingay (102), and Miller (167) all argue against the idea that in Dan 6:1 it means to receive from another higher authority (such as from God or Cyrus); instead, the think it simply means he succeeded Belshazzar. NET simply translates "Darius the Mede took control of the kingdom." Yet the other usage of קַבֵּל (*qabbēl*) in Daniel suggests the nuance of receiving something from another cannot be so quickly ruled out (see 2:6; 7:18). If the pointing הָמְלַךְ, *homlak̲* (Hophal, "was made king") can be maintained in 9:1, then the possibility certainly exists that the kingdom was entrusted to Darius by a person of superior authority. Yet see the discussion at 9:1 for a different understanding of the Hophal.
546. Many English versions add the word "about" in view of the prep כְּ (*kᵊ*) prefixed to בַר (*b̲ar*), but both Goldingay (102) and Montgomery (267) argue against this. Rosenthal, *GBA*, 34 (§78), notes, "כְּ may also be used in a temporal sense: כְּבַר שְׁנִין שִׁתִּין וְתַרְתֵּין 'as (a man) sixty-two years old' D 6:1." Since sixty-two is a rather exact number, it would be inconsistent to add the word "about" to this. Furthermore, LXX$^{\theta}$ did not insert a word meaning "about" but simply translated ὢν ἐτῶν ἑξήκοντα δύο (*ōn etōn hexēkonta duo*) as "being sixty-two years old." The point is that he was sixty-two years old.

Xenophon's *Cyropaedia* (ca. 434–355 BC), and the writings of Berossus (a third cent. BC Babylonian priest and historian). Though Belshazzar certainly died that night, as Dan 5:30 plainly states, according to Berossus, Cyrus did not execute Nabonidus but deported him to Carmania.[547] On the Cyrus Cylinder, Cyrus boasts that he took the city of Babylon without a battle, aided by the Babylonian deity, Marduk:

> Marduk, the great lord, a protector of his people/worshipers, beheld with pleasure his (i.e., Cyrus') good deeds and his upright mind (lit.: heart) (and therefore) ordered him to march against his city Babylon. ... He made him set out on the road to Babylon ... going at his side like a real friend. His widespread troops—their number, like that of the water of a river, could not be established—strolled along, their weapons packed away. Without any battle, he made him enter his town Babylon ..., sparing Babylon ... any calamity.

Further details are provided from the Nabonidus Chronicle (*ANET*, 306):

> The 14th day, Sippar was seized without battle. Nabonidus fled. The 16th day, Gobryas (*Ugbaru*) the governor of Gutium and the army of Cyrus entered Babylon without battle. Afterwards Nabonidus was arrested in Babylon when he returned (there). ... In the month of Arahshamnu, the 3rd day [= Oct 29, 539 BC], Cyrus entered Babylon, green twigs were spread in front of him—the state of "Peace" (*šulmu*) was imposed upon the city. Cyrus sent greetings to all Babylon. Gobryas, his governor, installed (sub-) governors in Babylon. ... In the month of Arahshamnu, on the night of the 11th day [= Nov 6, 539 BC], Gobryas died.

The Greek historian Herodotus confirms the account that the city was taken without a bloody battle of storming the walls but by a sneak attack through the Euphrates riverbed that ran through the middle of Babylon. Archer (7:70) summarizes:

> Unknown to them, Cyrus's resourceful commander, Ugbaru (referred to in the Chronicle as governor of Gutium), had diverted the waters of the Euphrates to an old channel dug by a previous ruler ... suddenly reducing the water level below the river-gates. Before long the Persian besiegers would come wading in at night and clamber up the river-bank walls before the guards knew what was happening.

Making their way as quickly as possible to the palace, the invaders located Belshazzar and put him to death. This account is preserved for us in Xenophon's *Cyropaedia* (see the "Excursus" at the end of this section).

547. This information from Berossus is preserved in Josephus, *C. Ap.* 1.20.153.

5:31 *The beginning of Darius' reign*. The last verse of chap. 5 ("So Darius the Mede received the kingdom, being sixty-two years of age") is actually v. 1 of chap. 6 in the Aramaic. The identification of Darius the Mede has proven to be one of the more perplexing verses of the book, as we have no record in secular history about any such person by that name. Not surprisingly, critical scholars have seized this issue to attack the integrity of the book, claiming that Darius was a purely fictitious character or that the author clearly made an historical error (so Rowley, Di Lella, Montgomery, and Collins). Collins (32), for example, takes the position that the author has confused this person with Darius I, the famous Persian king (r. 522–486 BC). He then uses this to assert that the true author or editor "must have lived long after the fall of Babylon when these events were a matter of distant memory."

Most conservative scholars, on the other hand, believe that there really was a person known as Darius the Mede but that we cannot be certain today who this really was, as his name is not attested outside the Bible. Nevertheless, several suggestions have been made to identify Darius the Mede. (For a more complete discussion, see section "5" of "Alleged Historical Inaccuracies" under "Objections to the Traditional Date and Authorship" in the "Introduction" to the book.) The chart below summarizes the different views taken by conservative scholars, as well as the representatives of each view. Some scholars are rather non-committal about identifying Darius the Mede (e.g., Young and Goldingay), while still others believe that it could be either view A or C in the chart below and are content to leave it at that (e.g., Walvoord and Miller). For sake of convenience, the letters in the left-hand column designating each view correspond to the same letters and views presented in the "Introductory Matters."

A further clue to Darius' identity is given in Dan 9:1: "In the first year of Darius son of Ahasuerus, who was of Median descent, who had been made king over the kingdom of the Chaldeans." Once again he is associated with the Medes (a people mostly dwelling in what is today northern Iran), but the words "who had been made king" raises the question of who entrusted the rule of Babylon to him. There is no doubt that Cyrus led a combined army of Medes and Persians in the conquest of Babylon, but the exact political alignment at that time and the resulting events from the conquest are not as certain as we would like. As discussed in the "Introductory Matters," Herodotus tends to paint a different picture than Xenophon (both being Greek historians, not Persian, and both writing quite some time after the events took place).

The account provided by Herodotus holds that Cyrus conquered and subjected the Medes (under their last king, Astyages) to the Persians *prior to* the conquest of Babylon and that Astyages had no male heir. Thus Cyrus was ruler over both Media and Persia prior to the fall of Babylon in 539 BC. Xenophon, on the other hand, indicates that the Medes were not conquered by the Persians prior to the fall of Babylon and that Astyages did have a son named Cyaxares II who became the king of the Medes and was still in power in 539 BC. According to Xenophon, the Medes and the Persians—being under the rule of the Median king Cyaxares II—combined their armies under the command of Cyrus for the purpose of conquering Babylon (which they did). Following the victory, the right of ruling over Babylon was given to Cyaxares II, the Median king and rightful ruler over the Medes and Persians.

The Identification of "Darius the Mede" in Daniel

	Description of the View	Adherents
A	An alternative name for Cyrus the Great	D. J. Wiseman, J. M. Bulman, B. Colless, Joyce Baldwin
B	Another name for Ugbaru/ Gubaru,[548] the commander under Cyrus at the time of Babylon's fall	Wm. H. Shea, E. Merrill, J. D. Pentecost
C	Another name for Gubaru (distinct from Ugbaru) whom Cyrus appointed to rule over Babylon	R. D. Wilson, W. F. Albright, J. C. Whitcomb, B. Waltke, G. Archer, L. Wood
D	An alternative name for Cambyses II (son of Cyrus the Great)	C. Boutflower
E	A throne name for Cyaxares II, the Median king and son of Astyages	C. F. Keil, S. W. Hirsch, S. Anderson

Josephus made a statement that tends to support the version of Xenophon. He remarked, "Now Darius (Δαρείῳ), who with his relative Cyrus (Κύρου) put an end to the Babylonian sovereignty, was in his sixty-second year when he took Babylon; he was a son of Astyages (Ἀστυάγους) but was called by another name among the Greeks."[549]

So, according to Josephus, Astyages was *not* the last Median king, and (in contradiction to Herodotus) he did have a son who ruled over Media after him. This assertion is further confirmed by Jerome in his early commentary on Daniel (61): "Darius was sixty-two years old, and that, according to what we read, the kingdom of the Medes was more sizable than that of the Persians, and being Cyrus's uncle, he naturally had a prior claim, and ought

548. According to view "B," Ugbaru and Gubaru are one and the same person.

549. Josephus, *Ant.* x.248. If Josephus was correct, then Cyrus the Great would have been related to Darius, both being descendants of Astyages, king of Media. In fact, Cyaxares II (Darius) would have been Cyrus' uncle, since Cyrus' mother (Mandane) was the sister of Cyaxares II.

to have been accounted as successor to the rule of Babylon." Since Astyages was not Cyrus' uncle but rather his grandfather, this statement can only mean that Astyages had a son (Cyrus' uncle, since his father had married Astyages' daughter, Mandane), which would harmonize with Xenophon's account. In fact, according to Xenophon, Cyrus eventually married the daughter of Cyaxares (*Cyr.* viii.5.28), thereby having a double relationship with the Medes. (See the chart in the "Introductory Matters" showing these various relationships.)

But why the different names—Cyaxares according to Xenophon and Darius according to Daniel? Keil (200), after a very technical linguistic discussion of all the names and terms, offers a plausible explanation: "Xenophon has communicated to us the Median name and title of the last king; Daniel gives, as it appears, the Persian name and title which Cyaxares, as king of the united Chaldean and Medo-Persian kingdom, received and bore."

The theory that Darius the Mede is none other than Cyaxares II, the last Median king and son of Astyages, has been defended at length more recently by S. Anderson.[550] Although not without its problems, this view has much to commend it, particularly if the details of Xenophon's historical account can be substantiated. Until then we need to remain open-minded, but at least we can say that the mention of Darius the Mede is no historical blunder on Daniel's part.

Biblical Theology Comments

Once again the absolute sovereignty of Yahweh God is displayed. In chap. 4 God's sovereignty was seen in the way he humbled Nebuchadnezzar. Now in chap. 5 God's sovereignty extends even further to deposing Belshazzar and removing Babylonian independence altogether. God not only determines which kings will rule but when nations and kingdoms will rise and when they will fall. Ps 47:8 declares, "God reigns over the nations; God sits on his holy throne" (ESV). How applicable are the words of Ps 66:7 in regard to Belshazzar, since Yahweh God is the one "who rules by his might forever, whose eyes keep watch on the nations—let not the rebellious exalt themselves" (ESV).

Application and Devotional Implications

In Dan 5:30 we read, "That *very* night Belshazzar, the Chaldean king, was slain." His life was suddenly and unexpectedly over. He had been warned by Daniel that despite his arrogant delusion of power, he did not possess the ability to determine the length of his days on earth. That power belonged to the God he had so flippantly belittled: "But as for the God in whose hand is your breath and your entire fate, you have not glorified Him!" (v.

550. S. D. Anderson, *Darius the Mede: A Reappraisal* (Grand Rapids: Amazon/CreateSpace, 2014).

23). Belshazzar had been entrusted with much as ruler over the Babylonian Empire. He could have used that position of influence for the sake of the Lord God. Instead, he wasted his life away, and in a drunken moment even defied God through a blasphemous act. A wasted life is always sad, no matter whom it involves.

Each of us is given one life, for which we are responsible to use wisely and for the glory of God. Ps 90:12 admonishes us, "Teach us to number our days, that we may present to You a heart of wisdom" (NASB). The point is that we need to grasp our mortality, and then use the days we have for living wisely unto Yahweh our God. How are you doing with the life that has been given you? Do you stop to think that your "life breath" is daily in the hands of God? He could take that from you at any moment, should he so desire. But he lets you live so that you will know him in an ever-deepening love relationship and in so doing will serve him from the heart as a gift back to God. Are you numbering your days? Have you paused lately to take stock of your life and assess what you might need to change in your life? You may not be squandering your life and defying God (as Belshazzar did), but are you using your life as wisely as possible? Remember, you and I are not promised unlimited *tomorrows*. So, whether we have few or many left, it is imperative that we realize how precious they are and that we not postpone any decision to live our days for him. How do you want the remainder of your life to turn out?

Excursus: Xenophon's Account of Cyrus' Capture of Babylon (*Cyr.* 7.5.15–34)

[15] At last the ditches were completed. Then, when he heard that a certain festival had come round in Babylon, during which all Babylon was accustomed to drink and revel all night long, Cyrus took a large number of men, just as soon as it was dark, and opened up the heads of the trenches at the river. [16] As soon as that was done, the water flowed down through the ditches in the night, and the bed of the river, where it traversed the city, became passable for men.

[17] When the problem of the river was thus solved, Cyrus gave orders to his Persian colonels, infantry and cavalry, to marshal their regiments two abreast and come to him, and the rest, the allies, to follow in their rear, drawn up as before. [18] They came, according to orders, and he bade his aides, both foot and horse, get into the dry channel of the river and see if it was possible to march in the bed of the river. [19] And when they brought back word that it was, he called together the generals of both infantry and cavalry and spoke as follows:

[20] "My friends," said he, "the river has made way for us and given us an entrance into the city. Let us, therefore, enter in with dauntless hearts, fearing nothing and remembering that those against whom we are now to march are the same men that we have repeatedly defeated, and that, too, when

they were all drawn up in battle line with their allies at their side, and when they were all wide awake and sober and fully armed; [21] whereas now we are going to fall upon them at a time when many of them are asleep, many drunk, and none of them in battle array. And when they find out that we are inside the walls, in their panic fright they will be much more helpless still than they are now.

[22] "But if any one is apprehensive of that which is said to be a source of terror to those invading a city—namely that the people may go up on the house-tops and hurl down missiles right and left, you need not be in the least afraid of that; for if any do go up upon their houses, we have a god on our side, Hephaestus. And their porticoes are very inflammable, for the doors are made of palm-wood and covered with bituminous varnish which will burn like tinder; [23] while we, on our side, have plenty of pine-wood for torches, which will quickly produce a mighty conflagration; we have also plenty of pitch and tow, which will quickly spread the flames everywhere, so that those upon the house-tops must either quickly leave their posts or quickly be consumed.

[24] "But come, to arms! and with the help of the gods I will lead you on. And do you, Gadatas and Gobryas, show the streets, for you are familiar with them. And when we get inside the walls, lead us by the quickest route to the royal palace."

[25] "Aye," answered Gobryas and his staff, "in view of the revelry, it would not be at all surprising if the gates leading to the palace were open, for all the city is feasting this night. Still, we shall find a guard before the gates, for one is always posted there."

"We must lose no time, then," said Cyrus. "Forward, that we may catch the men as unprepared as we can."

[26] When these words were spoken, they advanced. And of those they met on the way, some fell by their swords, some fled back into their houses, some shouted to them; and Gobryas and his men shouted back to them, as if they were fellow-revellers. They advanced as fast as they could and were soon at the palace. [27] And Gobryas and Gadatas and their troops found the gates leading to the palace locked, and those who had been appointed to attack the guard fell upon them as they were drinking by a blazing fire, and without waiting they dealt with them as with foes. [28] But, as a noise and tumult ensued, those within heard the uproar, and at the king's command to see what the matter was, some of them opened the gates and ran out. [29] And when Gadatas and his men saw the gates open they dashed in pursuit of the others as they fled back into the palace, and dealing blows right and left they came into the presence of the king; and they found him already risen with his dagger in his hand. [30] And Gadatas and Gobryas and their followers overpowered him; and those about the king perished also, one where he had

sought some shelter, another while running away, another while actually trying to defend himself with whatever he could.

[31] Cyrus then sent the companies of cavalry around through the streets and gave them orders to cut down all whom they found out of doors, while he directed those who understood Assyrian to proclaim to those in their houses that they should stay there, for if any one should be caught outside, he would be put to death.

[32] While they were thus occupied, Gadatas and Gobryas came up; and first of all they did homage to the gods, seeing that they had avenged themselves upon the wicked king, and then they kissed Cyrus's hands and his feet with many tears of joy.

[33] And when day dawned and those in possession of the citadels discovered that the city was taken and the king slain, they surrendered the citadels, too. [34] And Cyrus at once took possession of the citadels and sent up to them guards and officers of the guards. As for the dead, he gave their relatives permission to bury them. He furthermore ordered the heralds to make proclamation that all Babylonians deliver up their arms; and he ordered that wherever arms should be found in any house, all the occupants should be put to the sword. So they delivered up their arms and Cyrus stored them in the citadels, so that they might be ready if he ever needed them for use.

Selected Bibliography (Daniel 5)

Alfrink, B. "Darius Medus." *Bib* 9 (1928): 316–40.

Anderson, S. D. *Darius the Mede: A Reappraisal.* Grand Rapids: Amazon/ CreateSpace, 2014.

Anderson, S. D., and R. C. Young. "The Remembrance of Daniel's Darius the Mede in Berossus and Harpocration." *BibSac* 173 (2016): 315–23.

Arnold, B. T. "Wordplay and Narrative Techniques in Daniel 5 and 6." *JBL* 112 (1993): 479–85.

Beaulieu, P.-A. *The Reign of Nabonidus, King of Babylon 556–539 B.C.* New Haven, CT: Yale University Press, 1989.

Beck, J. "*More than 'Troubling':* The Meaning of בהל in the Book of Daniel." Paper presented at the annual meeting of the Society of Biblical Literature. Baltimore, MD, November 2013.

Becking, B. "'A Divine Spirit Is in You': Notes on the Translation of the Phrase *rûaḥ ʾᵉlāhîn* in Daniel 5,14 and Related Texts." In *The Book of Daniel in the Light of New Findings*, ed. A. S. Van der Woude, 515–32. BETL. Leuven: Leuven University Press, 1993.

Broida, M. "Textualizing Divination: The Writing on the Wall in Daniel 5:25." *VT* 62 (2012): 1–13.

Brownlee, W. H. *The Meaning of the Qumran Scrolls for the Bible.* New York: Oxford University Press, 1964.

Boutflower, C. "The Historical Value of Daniel v and vi." *JTS* 17 (1915–1916): 43–60.

———. "'Belshazzar the King' (Dan. V. 1)." *ExpT* 36 (1924–1925): 526–27.
Bruyn, J. J. de. "Daniel 5, Elohim and Marduk: The Final Battle." *OTE* 26 (2013): 623–41.
Bulman, J. M. "The Identification of Darius the Mede." *WTJ* 35 (1972–1973): 247–67.
Clay, A. T. "Gobryas." *JAOS* 41 (1921): 466–67.
Clermont-Ganneau, C. "Mene, Tekel, Peres, and the Feast of Belshazzar." Trans. R. W. Rogers. *Hebraica* 3 (1887): 87–102. [Orig. pub. in French in *Journal Asiatique*, 1886].
Colless, B. E. "Cyrus the Persian as Darius the Mede in the Book of Daniel." *JSOT* 56 (1992): 113–26.
Coxon, P. W. "A Philological Note on אשתיו Dan 5 3f." *ZAW* 89 (1977): 275–76.
Dougherty, R. P. *Nabonidus and Belshazzar*. Yale Oriental Series, Researches 15. New Haven, CT: Yale University Press, 1929.
Eissfeldt, O. "Die Menetekel-Inschrift und ihre Deutung." *ZAW* 63 (1951): 105–14.
Emerton, J. A. "The Participles in Daniel v. 12." *ZAW* 72 (1960): 262–63.
Fish, T. "Texts Relating to Nabonidus." In *Documents From Old Testament Times*, ed. D. W. Thomas, 89–91. New York: Harper & Row, 1958.
Gadd, C. J. "The Harran Inscriptions of Nabonidus." *AnSt* 8 (1958): 58–59.
Galling, K. "H. H. Rowley, *Darius the Mede*...." *ZDMG* 95 (1941): 148–50.
Grabbe, L. L. "Another Look at the *Gestalt* of Darius the Mede." *CBQ* 50 (1988): 198–213.
Gruenthaner, M. J. "The Last King of Babylon." *CBQ* 11 (1949): 406–27.
Guglielmo, A. de. "Dan. 5:25—An Example of a Double Literal Sense." *CBQ* 11 (1949): 202–6.
Hillers, D. R. "A Convention in Hebrew Literature: The Reaction to Bad News." *ZAW* 77 (1965): 86–90.
Hilton, M. "Babel Reversed—Daniel Chapter 5." *JSOT* 66 (1995): 99–112.
Kirchmayr, K. P. "Mene-tekel-uparsin." *VT* 60 (2010): 483–86.
Koldewey, R. *The Excavations at Babylon*. London: Macmillan, 1914.
Kraeling, E. G. "The Handwriting on the Wall." *JBL* 63 (1944): 11–18.
Lambert, W. G. "An Eye-Stone of Esarhaddon's Queen and Other Similar Gems." *RA* 63 (1969): 65-71.
———. "Nabonidus in Arabia." In *Proceedings of the Fifth Seminar for Arabian Studies*, 53–64. London: Seminar for Arabian Studies, 1972.
Larue, G. A. *Babylon and the Bible*. Grand Rapids: Eerdmans, 1969.
Liptzin, S. "Belshazzar's Folly." In *Biblical Themes in World Literature*, 273–81. Hoboken, NJ: Ktav, 1985.
Millard, A. "Daniel and Belshazzar in History." *BAR* 11 (1985): 73–78.
Pannkuk, J. L. "The Preface to Old Greek Daniel 5: A Formal Approach." *VT* 57 (2016): 213–26.
Paul, S. "Decoding a 'Joint' Expression in Daniel 5:6, 16." *JANES* 23 (1993): 121–27.

Polaski, D. C. "*Mene, Mene, Tekel, Parsin*: Writing and Resistance in Daniel 5 and 6." *JBL* 123 (2004): 649–69.

Rabinowitz, J. J. "A Legal Formula in the Susa Tablets, in an Egyptian Document of the Twelfth Dynasty, in the Aramaic Papyri, and in the Book of Daniel." *Bib* 36 (1955): 74–77.

Robinson, A. C. "Darius the Median." *JTVI* 54 (1922): 1–30.

Rowley, H. H. "The Belshazzar of Daniel and of History." *Exp* 9 (1924): 182–95, 255–72.

———. *Darius the Mede and the Four World Empires in the Book of Daniel.* Cardiff: University of Wales Press, 1964.

———. "The Historicity of the Fifth Chapter of Daniel." *JTS* 32 (1931): 12–31.

Segal, M. "Daniel 5 in Aramaic and Greek and the Textual History of Daniel 4–6." In *IOSOT Congress Volume Stellenbosch 2016*, ed. L. C. Jonker, G. R. Kotzé, and C. M. Maier, 251–84. VTSupp 177. Leiden and Boston: Brill, 2017.

———. "Rereading the Writing on the Wall (Daniel 5)." *ZAW* 125 (2013): 161–76.

Setio, R. "Fantasy in Apocalyptic Daniel 7." *AJT* 27 (2013): 185–207.

Shea, W. H. "Darius the Mede." *AUSS* 20 (1982): 229–47.

———. "Darius the Mede in His Persian-Babylonian Setting." *AUSS* 29 (1991): 235–57.

———. "Further Literary Structures in Daniel 2–7: An Analysis of Daniel 5, and the Broader Relationships Within Chapters 2–7." *AUSS* 23 (1985): 277–95.

———. "Nabonidus, Belshazzar, and the Book of Daniel: An Update." *AUSS* 20 (1982): 133–49.

———. "Nabonidus Chronicle: New Readings and the Identity of Darius the Mede." *JATS* 7 (1996): 1–20.

———. "The Search for Darius the Mede (Concluded), or, the Time of the Answer to Daniel's Prayer and the Date of the Death of Darius the Mede." *JATS* 12 (2001): 97–105.

———. "An Unrecognized Vassal King of Babylon in the Early Achaemenid Period." *AUSS* 9 (1971): 51–57, 99–128; 10 (1972): 88–117, 147–78.

Smith, S. *Babylonian Historical Texts, Relating to the Downfall of Babylon.* London: Methuen & Co., 1924.

Soesilo, D. H. "Belshazzar's Scales: Towards Achieving a Balanced Translation of Daniel 5." *BT* 40 (1989): 426–32.

Sparks, H. F. D. "On the Origin of Darius the Mede." *JTS* 47 (1946): 41–46.

Steinmann, A. "The Chicken and the Egg: A New Proposal for the Relationship between the *Prayer of Nabonidus* and the *Book of Daniel*." *RevQ* 20 (2002): 557–70.

Taylor, R. "The Book of Daniel in the Bible of Edessa." *Aramaic Studies* 5 (2007): 239–53.

Ulrich, E. "The Parallel Editions of the Old Greek and Masoretic Text of Daniel 5." In *A Teacher for All Generations: Essays in Honor of James*

C. VanderKam, ed. E. F. Mason et al., 201–17. *JSJSup* 153. Leiden: Brill, 2012.

Van Deventer, H. J. M. "Another Wise Queen (Mother): Woman's Wisdom in Daniel 5:10–12." *TV* 26 (2000): 92–113.

———. "Would the Actually 'Powerful' Please Stand? The Role of the Queen (Mother) in Daniel 5." *Scriptura* 70 (1999): 241–51.

Whitcomb, J. H. *Darius the Mede*. Grand Rapids: Eerdmans, 1959.

Wilson, R. D. "Darius the Mede." *PTR* 20 (1922): 177–211.

Wiseman, D. J. *Notes on Some Problems in the Book of Daniel*. London: Tyndale, 1970.

Wolters, A. "Belshazzar's Feast and the Cult of the Moon God Sîn." *BBR* 5 (1995): 199–206.

———. "The Riddle of the Scales in Daniel 5." *HUCA* 62 (1991): 155–77.

———. "Untying the King's Knots: Physiology and Wordplay in Daniel 5." *JBL* 110 (1991): 117–22.

Zimmermann, F. "The Writing on the Wall." *JQR* 55 (1964–65): 201–7.

E. God's Deliverance of Daniel, Who Refuses to Forego Prayer (6:1–28)

Although no date is given at the beginning of this chapter, the event probably took place in the first year of Darius the Mede, when he was establishing the administration for the newly created province of Babylonia. Cyrus the Great had led the combined armies of the Medes and Persians in victory against Babylon, and Daniel would certainly have been on hand to witness Cyrus' entrance to Babylon on Oct 29, 539 BC. Very possibly he would even have had opportunity to have met him, though we have no record of that. Subsequently, the governance of Babylonia was entrusted to Darius the Mede. Only later did Cyrus take over the rule of Babylon himself, presumably after the death of Darius the Mede (cf. Dan 6:28).

The chapter's recounting of the miraculous deliverance of Daniel from a den of lions is similar in theme to that of chap. 3.[551] Lesley explains:

551. For a more complete list of the shared motifs and textual similarities of Dan 3 and 6, see M. Segal, "The Old Greek Version and Masoretic Text of Daniel 6," in *Die Septuaginta: Orte und Intentionen. Proceedings of the Fifth International Wuppertal Symposium on the Septuagint*, ed. S. Kreuzer, M. Meiser, and M. Sigismund (Tübingen: Mohr Siebeck, 2016), 419–22. Yet for Segal, the similarities are due to an editing of Dan 6 so as to harmonize it with Dan 3. In a subsequent article, he writes, "I suggest that this specific detail of the story in Dan 6, as reflected in OG, was adjusted in MT so as to harmonize it with Dan 3. These three details demonstrate that OG Dan 6 at times presents a more original version of the story, which has been altered in the MT edition due to harmonization or assimilation with the parallel story in chapter 3"; M. Segal, "Harmonization and Rewriting of Daniel 6 from the Bible to Qumran," in *Hā-'îsh Mōshe: Studies in Scriptural Interpretation in*

> The story of Shadrach, Meshach and Abednego in Dan 3 is strikingly similar to Dan 6, the story of Daniel in the lions' den: in both stories, officials of Judean descent (מִבְּנֵי יְהוּדָה; Dan 1:6) in a foreign court are denounced for disobeying a royal decree demanding idolatrous worship—an offense punishable by death. The officials remain faithful to their God, and are consequently sent to die: Daniel in the lions' den and Shadrach, Meshach and Abednego in a furnace. With divine help they survive, precipitating the king to outlaw blasphemy against their God.[552]

In both cases, we witness miraculous deliverance of God's faithful servants. Brensinger, however, points out the contrasting tests of faith between these two chapters: "If in chapter 3 Shadrach, Meshach and Abednego were pressured to do what their faith prohibited, Daniel is now pressured to refrain from doing what his faith requires."[553]

As true as the deliverance motif may be in these chapters, de Bruyn argues for a more theocentric motivation to the chapter's message in regard to what he terms "sacred space":

> Protection is indeed a major theme in these stories, but instead of interpreting protection simply as an act of the God of Israel on behalf of the faithful—as most scholars do—this article postulates that the author uses the theme of protection to indicate the capability of the God of Israel to act outside the land of Israel. Furthermore, in terms of a body-spatial framework, it could be argued that in each of these stories in Daniel 1–6 protection is the consequence of the Israelite God being victorious after he was challenged by foreign powers outside the land of Israel. Or protection is the means by which the author demonstrates the victory of the God of Israel when challenged by foreign powers.[554]

While de Bruyn's point is a helpful corrective—putting the emphasis upon God's victorious capability rather than simply the deliverance of the faithful—even this does not go far enough. As the conclusion to the chapter will show, this is a step forward in establishing the primacy and certitude of God's enduring kingdom. The point is that the omnipresent Yahweh Elohim is free to break into the *god space* of the Medes and Persians at will to demonstrate his power and proclaim his kingdom intentions—and this while "his city" lies in shattered ruins.

---

the Dead Sea Scrolls and Related Literature in Honor of Moshe J. Bernstein, ed. B. Y. Goldstein, M. Segal, and G. J. Brooke, 256–79 (Leiden and Boston: Brill, 2018), 269.

552. Lesley, "Illusions of Grandeur," 207.

553. Brensinger, "Compliance, Dissonance and Amazement in Daniel 3," 18.

554. J. J. de Bruyn, "Daniel 6: There and Back Again—A Deity's Tale," *HTS Teologiese Studies* 71 (2015): 4.

1. The conspiracy against Daniel (6:1–9)

The chapter opens with a plot being hatched against Daniel that will land him in deep trouble with King Darius and that the plotters hope will lead to his death.

Textual Notes

2.a-a. [Eng. 6:1a-a] LXX$^{\theta}$ agrees with MT (120 satraps), but LXX^{O} has ἑκατὸν εἴκοσι ἑπτὰ (127 satraps), mistakenly relating this Darius son of Ahasuerus to the Ahasuerus (= Xerxes I) of Esther. Cf. Esth 1:1, 2, 9.

5.a-a. [Eng. 6:4a-a] These words are lacking in LXX$^{\theta}$, and Collins (256) omits them as being an erroneous duplication. There is no reason to omit them, however. Though they may sound overly repetitious to a modern reader, the repetition is deliberate, underscoring Daniel's integrity. English versions retain the words, as there is no reason to doubt the MT at this point.

Translation

6:1 [Aram. 6:2] It pleased Darius to appoint over the kingdom 120 satraps[555] that they might be over[556] the whole kingdom. **2** And over them *were* three chief ministers[557] (one of whom was Daniel), that these satraps might be accountable[558] to them, so that the king might not suffer harm.[559] **3** Now this Daniel was distinguishing himself above the chief ministers and the

---

555. NET offers the following note regarding "satraps": "This is a technical term for an official placed in charge of a region of the empire." The word itself (Aram. אֲחַשְׁדַּרְפְּנַיָּא, *ʾăḥašdarpᵉnayyāʾ*) means "protector of the kingdom" (Miller, 177). These satraps were answerable to a supervisor, who in turn answered to Darius. For further insight, see the commentary on Dan 3:2.

556. For the preposition בְּ (*bᵉ*) in the sense of "over," see Dan 4:14 (Eng. 4:17).

557. The Aram. for "chief ministers" is סָרְכִין (*sārᵉḵîn*), translated "commissioners" in the NASB, "supervisors" in the NET, and "administrators" in the NIV. *HALOT* (1940) gives the meaning "high official (of the king)" for סְרַךְ (*sᵉraḵ*), and BDB indicates that this was a loanword from Persian *sār*, "head, chief." Hence the idea "chief minister" is a good English equivalent. LXX$^{\theta}$ translated as τακτικοὺς (*taktikous*), which generally means one "fit for ordering or arranging, esp. in war" (LSJM, 1753).

558. Lit., "giving them the report" (טַעְמָא, *ṭaʿmāʾ*), apparently an idiomatic expression meaning "to give an account" (so *HALOT*, 1885).

559. Both the NIV and NASB translate as "might not suffer loss." The verb נָזִק (*nāziq*) means "to suffer injury" (BDB, 1102c) or "to come to grief" or "suffer harm" (*HALOT*, 1929). This was translated by LXX$^{\theta}$ as ἐνοχλῆται (*enochlētai*), from ἐνοχλέω (*enochleō*), meaning "to trouble, annoy." Goldingay (120–21) adds "... Akk. *nazāqu* suggests 'troubled/worried' (*CAD*; H. L. Ginsberg, 'Lexicographical Notes,' *HW* 81)." The purpose of the three "chief ministers" was to ensure that the king did not have to worry about matters in his kingdom. This could certainly include protecting his financial interests but need not be limited to that.

satraps, for he had an extraordinary spirit. The king was even intending to appoint him over the entire kingdom. **4** Then the chief ministers and the satraps were seeking to find some pretext[560] against Daniel with respect to governmental affairs.[561] But they were unable to find any pretext or corrupt dealings,[562] inasmuch as he was trustworthy, and no negligence[563] or corruption was found in him.[564] **5** Then these men concluded,[565] "We will not find any pretext against this Daniel unless we find[566] *something* concerning him with the law of his God." **6** Then these chief ministers and satraps, conspiring

---

560. The word "pretext" (so NET) is a good translation for Aram. עִלָּה (*ʿillâ*). BDB suggests "ground of accusation" (1106c). LXX$^{\theta}$ translated as πρόφασιν (*prophasin*), which means a "motive or cause alleged, whether truly or falsely" (LSJM, 1539); LSJM category #2 is a "falsely alleged motive (or cause), pretext, pretence, excuse."

561. The Aram. text מִצַּד מַלְכוּתָא (*miṣṣad malkûtāʾ*) means literally "concerning the kingdom." Although *ṣad* normally means "side," when used in combination with the prep מִן (*min*), it means "concerning" (so *HALOT*, 1963). "Concerning the kingdom" implies the *administrative or governmental affairs* of the kingdom.

562. The words "corrupt dealings" translate שְׁחִיתָה, *šᵊḥîtâ*, a Peʿil ptc. (passive) of שְׁחַת (*šᵊḥat*), meaning something corrupted or bad (*HALOT*, 1992). They were not able to come up with any "pretext" (see note above) or any *evidence* of corruption, and thus nothing that they could use to damage Daniel's reputation.

563. Aram. שָׁלוּ (*šālû*). S. M. Paul, "The Mesopotamian Background of Daniel 1–6," in *The Book of Daniel: Composition and Reception*, ed. J. J. Collins and P. W. Flint, 1:55–68 (Leiden, Boston: Brill, 2001), 56–57, although admitting the possibility of translating as "negligence," opts for the translation, "improper speech." He states, "However, in its present context the term may also reflect Akkadian *šillatu*, and thus the two nouns שלו and שחיתה would be the cognate equivalents of Akkadian *arnu u šillatu*, 'crime and/or improper speech.' ... The two substantives would thereby constitute a merism—in both speech and deed Daniel remained a loyal and trustworthy servant to his king." However, the meaning "negligence" for שָׁלוּ (*šālû*) is clearly attested in BAram. (Ezra 4:22; 6:9), and most English translations opt for this nuance (exceptions: ESV and NKJV translate as "error").

564. The preposition עֲלוֹהִי (*ʿălôhî*) is very flexible in meaning. Here, it probably means "in him" (comp. 3:28) or "concerning him" (comp. 5:29).

565. Lit., "were saying" (אָמְרִין, *ʾāmᵊrîn*).

566. Lit., "unless we find (something) concerning him in/with the law of his god." The perf. verb הַשְׁכַּחְנָה (*haškaḥnâ*) follows the conjunction לָהֵן (*lāhēn*). This is equivalent to a Hebrew exceptive clause, in which case the perf. verb refers to a yet future situation. Cf. GKC, 500 (§163c). Collins (256) renders the final phrase "in the law of his god" as "in his religious practice," which captures the point quite well.

together,[567] approached the king and said[568] to him, "O King Darius, live forever! 7 All the chief ministers of the kingdom, the prefects,[569] the satraps, the ministers,[570] and the governors have consulted together[571] in order to establish a royal edict[572] and to make binding[573] a prohibition. Anyone who

---

567. The words "conspiring together, approached" is an attempt to translate a single word in Aram., namely the verb הַרְגִּשׁוּ (*hargišû*) from the root רְגַשׁ (*rᵉgaš*). This is one of the most difficult translation problems in the book and has received considerable attention in the commentaries. The NET translation ("came by collusion") is probably accurate, although perhaps a bit awkward. See the "Additional Exegetical Comments" at the end of this unit for a detailed discussion in support of the translation chosen here.

568. Lit., "and thus were saying to him" (וְכֵן אָמְרִין לֵהּ, *wᵉkēn ʾāmᵉrîn lēh*).

569. For "prefect" (סִגְנַיָּא, *signayyāʾ*) see translation note at the first use of the term in Dan 2:48.

570. For "ministers" (הַדָּבְרַיָּא, *haddāḇᵉrayyāʾ*) see translation note at the first use of the term in Dan 3:24. The exact meaning of this high-ranking official is difficult to pin down, leading to a wide diversity in the translations (NASB "high officials"; NIV "advisors"; NET and ESV "counselors").

571. The verb אִתְיָעַטוּ (*ʾiṯyāʿaṭû*) from the root יְעַט (*yᵉʿaṭ*, "to advise") is in the Ithpaʿal stem, having a reciprocal notion—took counsel together (so *HALOT*, 1892).

572. Lit., "a statute of the king" (קְיָם מַלְכָּא, *qᵉyām malkāʾ*), but understanding "king" as a genitive of attribute. There is debate as to whether "the king" (*malkāʾ*) should go with "edict" (*qᵉyām*) as a genitive construct, or whether it should stand independently and serve as the subject of the infinitive. The NET has opted to view it in construct with *qᵉyām* and translate it as genitive of attribute: "royal edict" (not "edict of the king"). Collins (256), on the other hand, takes "the king" as the subject of the infinitive לְקַיָּמָה (*lᵉqayyāmâ*) and translates, "that the king should enact an ordinance." There are two factors in support of the option "royal edict": (1) it would be a bit unnatural for the subject of the infinitive (in this case, *malkāʾ*) to be separated from the infinitive by having the object (*qᵉyām*) stand between them; and (2) several versions (LXX$^{\theta}$, Vg., and Syriac) view *malkāʾ* as part of a genitive construct with *qᵉyām*. There is some understandable motivation for taking *malkāʾ* as the subject of the infinitive, namely that it more clearly specifies the king as the one who issues/establishes the edict rather than his officials. Otherwise, the sentence reads, "All the chief ministers ... have taken counsel with each other ... to establish a royal edict ... ." All things taken into consideration, however, it seems more reasonable to take *malkāʾ* as part of the genitive construct with *qᵉyām*, as this commentary has opted for. It is too unnatural as the subject of the infinitive. In doing this, however, we should take the context into consideration and realize that they are only making a proposal to the king, not ordering him what to do (cf. Esth 1:19; 3:9; and Ezra 4:11–14).

573. S. M. Paul, "Dan 6,8: An Aramaic Reflex of Assyrian Legan Terminology," *Bib* 6 (1984): 109–10, has argued that the correct legal nuance of תַּקָּפָה (*ṯaqqāpâ*), being an interdialectal semantic equivalent of the Assyrian verb *dunnunu*, is to "make valid and binding," not "to issue a strong prohibition" or "to make strong a prohibition."

seeks a petition[574] from any god or man during *the next* thirty days (except from you, O king) shall be thrown into a den of lions. **8** Now therefore, O king, issue the prohibition and sign[575] the written decree, which cannot be changed according to the law of the Medes and Persians, *and* which cannot be annulled."[576] **9** Consequently[577] King Darius signed the written decree and the prohibition.

Commentary

6:1–3 *Daniel's rise in Darius' administration*. This Darius is the one mentioned at the end of chap. 5, namely Darius the Mede. He should not be confused with Darius I Hystaspes (otherwise known as Darius the Great), the famous Persian king who ruled 522–486 BC (cf. Hag 1:1; Zech 1:1). As explained in the previous unit, the rule of Babylonia was turned over to Darius the Mede following Cyrus' conquest of Babylon in October of 539 BC. Although the exact identification of Darius the Mede still awaits confirmation, this may have been an alternative or throne name for him (and thus different from the name he might be known by in historical documents). One attractive suggestion—consistent with the account of Xenophon—is that Darius the Mede is a name for the final Median king, Cyaxares II, son of Astyages.[578] Some critical scholars (e.g., Collins, 264; Montgomery, 269) feel that the author of the book made a historical blunder, confusing the king with Darius I of Persia, a king noted for his organization of satrapies. Yet Dan 6:28 indicates that the author was not confusing Darius with the

574. "Seeks a petition" is a rather literal rendering of Aram. יִבְעֵה בָּעוּ (*yib̲ʿēh b̲āʿû*). The noun *b̲āʿû* can mean either "prayer" or "petition" (*HALOT*, 1836). Hence, "anyone who prays to any god" is also legitimate (so NET). By use of the verb בְּעָא (*bᵊʿaʾ*) and its cognate בָּעוּ (*bāʿû*), the author is building on a wordplay begun initially in v. 5 [Aram.] and that will come to fruition in vv. 12–14 [Aram.]. See commentary at v. 11 [Eng.].

575. Goldingay's note (121) on רְשַׁם (*rᵊšam*) is of interest: "Or perhaps תרשם denotes 'put your seal to.'" Cf. Esth 8:8. However, the root *rᵊšam* usually refers to something written. In Dan 5:24, the verb *rᵊšam* refers to the *inscription* that had been written.

576. According to BDB (1105b2), עֲדָא (*ʿăd̲āʾ*) means "to pass on, away." *HALOT* (1943–44) suggests a secondary meaning, "to be annulled." The final part of the sentence (דִּי־לָא תֶעְדֵּא, *dî-lāʾ t̲eʿdēʾ*) is not in LXX$^{\theta}$. LXX^{O} omits the whole reference to "the law of the Medes and Persians" in this verse and elsewhere in the chapter, and the binding status of the law remains not because of any such law of the Medes and Persians, but because the king himself has confirmed it.

577. RJ (129) suggests that כָּל־קֳבֵל דְּנָה (*kol-qŏb̲ēl dᵊnâ*) has the equivalent force of "consequently."

578. For a more complete discussion and evaluation of views, see Section "5" of "Alleged Historical Inaccuracies" under "Objections to the Traditional Date and Authorship" in the "Introductory Matters" to the book.

Persian kings: "So this Daniel prospered during the reign of Darius and the reign of Cyrus the Persian."

Others have objected to the idea of the kingdom being divided up into 120 satrapies. According to Herodotus, the Persian Empire was divided into twenty satrapies.[579] We should note carefully, however, that Dan 6:1 does not state that Darius divided the kingdom into 120 satrapies, only that he appointed 120 satraps. It is known from Greek historians such as Xenophon that the term "satrap" could be applied to lower officials. It is indeed possible that some of the satraps governed geographical territories, while others may have had other administrative duties. Yet even if there were 120 satrapies, this should not be considered unreasonable. The Babylonian Empire prior to Cyrus' conquest had been quite extensive, and undoubtedly there would have been some larger and some smaller satrapies. Esther 1:1 indicates that Ahasuerus (i.e., Xerxes I) reigned over 127 provinces (Heb מְדִינָה, *mᵊḏînâ*).

That Darius the Mede appointed the 120 satraps and placed them in authority over the whole kingdom certainly suggests that Darius wielded great power. This would tend to support the thesis that Darius was not subservient to Cyrus at this time (as argued by Anderson in his dissertation equating Darius the Mede with Cyaxares II).[580] This should be compared with the note we have in the famous Nabonidus Chronicle describing the conquest of Babylon and that indicated that "Gobryas, his governor, installed (sub-)governors in Babylon."[581] Yet that Gobryas—a Mede at that, having served as governor of Gutium—is said to have died about a week following the fall of Babylon and thus cannot be Darius the Mede.

Above the 120 satraps were the three supervisors (סָרְכִין, *sārᵊḵîn*), which probably means something like "chief ministers" (see translation note above). Daniel was one of these, though he would already have been an old

579. Herodotus, *Hist.* 3.89. For a discussion of Old Persian inscriptions that provide lists of satrapies belonging to the Achaemenian Empire during the reigns of Darius and Xerxes, see G. Cameron, "The Persian Satrapies and Related Matters," *JNES* 32 (1973): 47–56.

580. Anderson, *Darius the Mede*.

581. Pritchard, *ANET*, 306. Two crucial questions arise from a study of the Nabonidus Chronicle. First, is this information truly reliable, or has it been embellished to glorify Cyrus and the Persians? (Anderson argues that it is propagandistic.) Second, what else is said about Gobryas in this same account? A few lines earlier, Gobryas is said to have been "the governor of Gutium" (a Median territory) who entered Babylon with Cyrus. Also, this same Gobryas died "on the night of the 11th day" (approximately a week later). He is obviously not Darius the Mede, but what relationship did he have to Darius and to Cyrus? In Xenophon's *Cyropaedia* (see esp. Book 5), Gobryas is a Median general distinct from King Cyaxares, the latter being the uncle of Cyrus (and Cyrus is subservient to Cyaxares the Median king).

man.[582] The satraps were organized such that each of them was accountable to one of these three chief ministers, so that the king's interests might not incur damage. Undoubtedly this would have included the protection of the financial interests of the king, making sure that taxes and tribute were properly channeled to the king. But it probably applied to other matters, such as ensuring the protection of territory due to uprisings.

One could reasonably ask why Daniel would have been chosen for such an exalted position if he were already a man at least in his eighties (keep in mind that he first came to Babylon as a young man in 605 BC). Yet "bringing him out of retirement" at this time would have been a wise thing to do by the new rulers: (1) he had a long experience and wide acquaintance with the Babylonian government; (2) he had a reputation for honesty and integrity in service; (3) he was known to be a "spiritual" man and an interpreter of dreams and visions; and (4) his successful prediction at Belshazzar's feast had undoubtedly become known to Cyrus the Great and/or Darius the Mede.

As old as he may have been, Daniel soon began distinguishing himself above the other two supervisors and the satraps. The participial form of the verb *nᵉṣaḥ* (to "distinguish oneself") in v. 3 probably has a continual (or iterative) nuance in this context. Thus, he was distinguishing himself time and time again, because there was an "extraordinary spirit" (*rûaḥ yattîrāʾ*) in him. This is the same phrase that was used by the queen mother in chap. 5 to describe him. Miller (178) states, "This 'exceptional spirit' may refer to his good attitude or abilities, but possibly the king recognized that Daniel was in touch with the gods and thus possessed great wisdom." Of course, Daniel's real secret was that he had become a godly man as a result of many years of walking with the God of heaven and because God's hand was uniquely upon him. It did not take Darius very long to observe that Daniel was unique, and thus he sought to elevate him over the whole kingdom.[583] Whether the king had hinted his intentions to others or the other high officials simply suspected as much, Daniel soon became the object of a political power play. It is amazing how the unbelieving world can be so hostile and resentful of God's people gaining influence and authority.

6:4–5 *The attempt to defame Daniel.* The other two supervisors appear to have collaborated with some of the satraps (probably not all of them, but maybe only those closer to Babylon itself) to find a *pretext* (עִלָּה, *ʿillâ*) against

582. Dan 6:2 indicates "one of whom" was Daniel (חַד־מִנְּהוֹן, *ḥaḏ-minnᵉhôn*). The KJV, however, stated that he was "first" among the three. Yet Aram. *ḥaḏ* (though it can mean the ordinal "first" in some contexts) probably indicates the cardinal "one" here. Verse 3 seems to suggest that Daniel had not yet been elevated above the others.

583. For a discussion of the possibility of Daniel as governor of Babylon, see W. H. Shea, "A Further Note on Daniel 6: Daniel as 'Governor,'" *AUSS* 21 (1983): 169–71. Shea works on the premise (faultily I believe) that Darius the Mede was the Gubaru mentioned in the Nabonidus Chronicle.

Daniel. They were looking for some motive or cause (even though falsely alleged) that they could bring against Daniel regarding how he handled the administrative matters of the kingdom. As hard as they looked, however, they could not find any pretext or any evidence of corruption in Daniel. The reason was simple: "Daniel was trustworthy" (מְהֵימַן, *mᵊhêman*). He was a reliable man, one who could be counted on to do what was right and not stoop to foul play of any kind. Here was a man of integrity, who because he was first and foremost committed to pleasing God, could be trusted by others to do what was right.

Daniel's antagonists soon realized they were not going to come up with anything that they could use to defame him. Yet they did get the idea that they might land him in trouble in another way, namely on religious grounds. Everyone was aware that Daniel was a religious man—and quite different from those who followed the Babylonian religion. If they could somehow bring his religious practice in conflict with the state, their attack would be successful.[584]

Obviously, the resentment toward Daniel was strong. Since Daniel was Jewish, others in the administration who were race conscious resented his elevation in government, especially the idea that he might be promoted to a rank next to the king himself. Possible reasons for this would include: (1) for those who operated by graft and corruption, Daniel's honesty would have hampered their conduct; and, (2) apparently the Jews in exile in Babylonia were still looked upon as an inferior race (or were at least resented). Yet, there is also a root cause behind the problem. As a Jew, Daniel was one of God's chosen people—a nation he had purposed to work through in special ways throughout history. For instance, through this people have come the Scriptures and the Messiah (according to the flesh). Furthermore, there are many biblical promises that God has made to this people, and God's Word and integrity hinge on fulfilling these promises. Likewise, in this age God is primarily working through the church, composed of all who believe in Jesus Christ regardless of ethnic background. As we examine the Scriptures, we see that throughout history Satan has had a special hatred for the Jewish people and for Christians. In Daniel's day, Satan aimed his hatred for God toward God's covenant people, and thus Daniel himself became a victim of this satanic opposition.

God had Daniel in this position for a special reason. Not only was he a capable administrator for the kingdom, but he was in this high position to help carry out God's covenant program. From God's perspective, this was a significant time, which accounts for the satanic opposition. Notice several important events going on about this same time during 539–38 BC. On Oct.

584. The word for "law" in v. 5 (Aram. דָּת, *dāṯ*) need not be limited to a meaning such as the "Mosaic law," as though that in itself was what they found objectionable. Collins (265) suggests, "The word דת is a Persian loanword and is used in the general sense of 'religious practice.'"

29, 539, Cyrus entered Babylon, and it is very possible (maybe even probable) that Daniel met him at this time. If so, he may even have shared with him the prophecy of Isa 44:28–45:7 in which God predicted the coming of Cyrus (*by name!*) about 150 years before he conquered Babylon. Since Daniel was appointed to a very high position within Darius' administration, Cyrus certainly would have known of him.

According to Dan 9:1–3, the first year of Darius was a time of intensive Bible study and prayer for Daniel. He would have realized through his study of Bible prophecy (especially Jer 25:11) that the time was drawing near for God to act again on Israel's behalf. Of key importance is Cyrus' decree made during his first year of rule, recorded for us in Ezra 1:1–4. This decree granted official permission to the Jews to return to their land and to rebuild the temple (key steps forward in God's covenant program). If this decree was made in Cyrus' first *regnal year*, then it was proclaimed during the period Mar./Apr. 538 – Mar./Apr. 537, and most likely after the events recorded in Dan 6. One cannot help but wonder if Daniel, in his position of authority and influence, had counseled Cyrus to make the decree permitting the return and rebuilding of the temple at Jerusalem. Furthermore, could this hostility against Daniel as recounted in chap. 6 really be Satan's attempt to eliminate Daniel before he could share prophetic details with Cyrus and influence him in the furthering of God's covenant program? If these things are true (though admittedly we have no historical confirmation), then Dan 6 is not merely about his faith in facing a severe trial. It is also about God's covenant program being preserved in the face of satanic opposition.

6:6–9 *The manipulation of Darius to entrap Daniel.* A conspiracy was hatched against Daniel, and as a result the other two supervisors and (representatives of) the satraps came to the king. Verse 6 uses the verb רְגַשׁ (*rᵊgaš*) to describe their approach to the king, a verb indicating that they approached the king with conspiracy in mind (see the "Additional Exegetical Comments" at the end of this unit for a detailed discussion of this word).

According to v. 7, they presented a proposal for a royal edict to be established by the king that would prohibit anyone from praying or making petition to any deity or man other than to the king himself for a thirty-day period. They also proposed a penalty for violation of the edict, namely being thrown into a den of lions. At this time in history, lions were common to this part of the world and were often captured to be used for sport and hunting purposes, as is well-attested by Assyrian and Babylonian sculptures and cylinder seals. Most likely this proposal was portrayed to the king as some kind of test of loyalty to his new government and would have subtly appealed to his pride.[585]

585. J. Walton, "The Decree of Darius the Mede in Daniel 6," *JETS* 31 (1986): 279–86, doubts that the intent of the statute was to prohibit prayer to all deities, given the polytheistic nature of the realm, as this would prohibit the religious practice of every subject and would have risked the wrath of all deities. Instead, Walton contends that

With a limited time duration, it would have only been a brief interruption in the regular worship of the citizens of the realm. Archer (79) writes,

> The suggested mode of compelling every subject in the former Babylonian domain to acknowledge the authority of Persia seemed a statesmanlike measure that would contribute to the unification of the Middle and Near East. The time limit of one month seemed reasonable. After it the people could resume their accustomed worship.

Surely the king must have noticed Daniel's absence among these officials, but probably he did not suspect that their motive was to entrap Daniel. Yet they had actually lied to the king in saying that "all the chief ministers" had counseled together to make the proposal, for Daniel had clearly been left out. This lie eventually came back to haunt them. According to v. 8, they urged the king to sign the edict (perhaps implying that he put his seal to it), thus making it unable to be changed or annulled, in keeping with the laws of the Medes and the Persians (cf. Esth 1:19; 8:8). This was a strict policy that laws, once enacted, could not be changed or annulled. For an illustration of this custom, we have a passage from Diodorus Siculus in reference to Darius III of Persia (reigned 336–330 BC). Having passed a sentence of death on one Charidemus, "immediately he repented and blamed himself, as having greatly erred; but it was not possible to undo what was done by royal authority."[586]

The proposal seemed reasonable to the king, and thus he signed it into law (v. 9). Observe that by referring to this as a law of "the Medes and the

---

Darius was setting himself up as the sole mediator for prayers for a thirty-day period. The problem comes with Walton's attempt to connect Darius with Zoroastrianism. He writes (285): "While it would certainly not eliminate syncretism nor depose the Magi from their powerful position, it would make a statement concerning the stand of the king, throwing his support to orthodox Zoroastrianism." Supposedly by this he would be giving a good example of honoring Ahura Mazda to all Iranians. Even more troublesome are the contradictory comments at the end of his article (286): "Of course we cannot prove that Darius the Mede was an orthodox Zoroastrian, since we do not know who he was. But there is evidence that Cyrus was a loyal worshiper of Ahura Mazda. On the other hand, there are statements in Cyrus' inscriptions that would seem to separate him from the doctrines of Zarathustra." Then he quotes statements from the Cyrus cylinder in which Cyrus honors the gods Bel, Nebo, and Marduk. The whole view, then, is highly speculative and lacks any positive evidence that Darius the Mede had any leanings whatsoever toward Zoroastrianism. Furthermore, when Dan 6:7 is examined closely, the injunction did not merely concern petitions to gods, but even to other men. So the restriction was aimed at temporarily halting petitions of all kinds, not in making Darius the "sole mediator."

586. *Diod.* 17.30, cited in Montgomery (270) on the basis of a quote from S. Bocharti, *Hierozoicon: sive de animalibus S. Scripturae*, 2 vols. (Leipzig: Libraria Weidmannia, 1794), I:748.

Persians," our author did not think of a Median Empire that was separate from Persia but saw these as a joint kingdom (though apparently ruled initially by a Median king according to Xenophon's account). Critical scholars contend (mistakenly) that Media stood as a separate empire between Babylonia and Persia, a point important to their interpretation of the prophecy of the successive kingdoms in chaps. 2 and 7.

Application and Devotional Implications

"But they were unable to find any pretext or corrupt dealings, inasmuch as he was trustworthy, and no negligence or corruption was found in him" (v. 4 Eng.). What a powerful statement about the character of Daniel. It is a wonderful thing for a man or woman to have a good reputation in the eyes of others, because this does not come easily. A few verses from Proverbs are especially relevant here. First, "A good name is to be chosen rather than great riches, and favor is better than silver or gold" (Prov 22:1, ESV). A *good name* means a good reputation, and this is so precious that the Bible says it is worth more than earthly riches. When people thought of Daniel, they could say, "Now, there is a man with a *good name*." Second, "The integrity of the upright guides them, but the crookedness of the treacherous destroys them" (11:3, ESV). Daniel was a man of integrity. Even his enemies could not find any grounds of accusation against him. He was a man of integrity, because he followed the Lord God in his life and put all his trust in him. This integrity was the result of his walk with God.

Daniel was not only an honest government employee, but he was competent in his work as well. How refreshing it is to find a man in business or politics who has integrity blended with skill and diligence (cf. Eph 6:5–8). There can be a temptation when working in the midst of dishonest workers to begin operating just like them. As Christians, our focus must stay on our true master, the Lord Jesus Christ. He wants us to be trustworthy, and we each have a responsibility to maintain a testimony before the eyes of the world of being faithful. Daniel was a model of a stewardship faithfully discharged (cf. Prov 20:6; 1 Cor 4:2).

Additional Exegetical Comments

Dan 6:7 [Eng. 6] – הַרְגִּשׁוּ - *hargišû*

The difficulty of translating the word הַרְגִּשׁוּ (*hargišû*) in Dan 6:6 (Eng.) is apparent from the widely varying translations in Bibles and commentaries. Consider the following survey:

KJV: "assembled together to the king"
NKJV: "thronged before the king"
NJPS: "came thronging in to the king"
NASB: "came by agreement to the king"
NIV: "went as a group to the king"
NET: "came by collusion to the king"
Goldingay (119): "mustered to see the king"

Collins (256): "went in a throng to the king"

The Aramaic verb *hargišû* occurs here as a Hapʿel perf. of the root רְגַשׁ (*rᵊgaš*). According to BDB (1112d), the meaning in this stem is "shew tumultuousness, come thronging." For this verse, *HALOT* (1979) suggests the meaning "to enter in a crowd." The versions (LXX$^{\theta}$, LXX^{O}, Vg., and Syriac) are not particularly helpful, because of the three times that *rᵊgaš* occurs in this chapter (cf. vv. 12, 16), they typically translate with a different word each time. In the case of Dan 6:6, LXX$^{\theta}$ translated *hargišû* by the Greek *parestēsan* (aorist of *paristēmi*), meaning that they stood by the king. LXX^{O}, on the other hand, translated by the Greek *prosēlthosan* (aorist of *proserchomai*), meaning that they came forward (or approached) the king. Both Greek translations say little more than that these officials came to the king without clarifying in what manner or with what motive they did so.

All the lexical ideas offered by BDB and *HALOT* also seem to have problems. To come *tumultuously* to the king would suggest that they came making a lot of commotion. The problem with this idea (unless it can clearly be substantiated) is that it would seem out of keeping with proper court etiquette.[587] On the other hand, to come *thronging* to the king (crowding upon? cf. *HALOT*'s "to enter in a crowd") lacks solid lexical support.

Although there is no other biblical data outside this chapter for Aramaic *rᵊgaš*, we do have the biblical Hebrew verb *rāgaš* to compare.[588] In Ps 64:3 (Eng. 2) we have a derivative form of *rᵊgaš* in parallel with the noun *sôḏ* (BDB, 691c: "counsel; 2b = secret counsel"):

"Hide me from the conspiracy of (*missôḏ*) the wicked;
from that noisy crowd (מֵרִגְשַׁת, *mērigšaṯ*) of evildoers" (NIV)

In light of the parallelism, the translation "noisy crowd" may not be best (the NASB has "from the tumult").[589] The parallelism might suggest a meaning more in line with "conspiracy, plotting."

We have another biblical example from Ps 2:1:

"Why do the nations rage (רָגְשׁוּ, *rāḡšû*),
and the peoples plot in vain?"

The word "plot" is a translation of *yehgû* (יֶהְגּוּ, from *hāgâ*), meaning "moan, growl, utter, speak, muse" (BDB, 211d), although BDB's category 3b is "imagine, devise." So, in this context we find *rāgaš* paralleled with a word

587. Despite the tension with the idea of a *noisy crowd*, Goldingay (121) favors this nuance. After a lengthy discussion about *rᵊgaš*, he concludes, "The vb suggests a group acting by agreement but with the bustle that a crowd inevitably makes."

588. Sokoloff, *A Dictionary of Jewish Palestinian Aramaic*, 516 does have an entry for רגש, though the examples are from a much later period. He gives the meanings "to feel, perceive, be aware of," though it is doubtful that any of these lexical meanings would fit the context for Dan 6:6.

589. The LXX translated as *plēthous*, "great number, multitude."

suggesting "plotting, devising a plot." Thus, both these biblical examples (Pss 64:3 and 2:1) exhibit *rāgaš* in parallel with words suggesting "conspire, plot." This idea should be considered because it fits the context of Dan 6:6 quite well.

Bowling similarly concludes in *TWOT* (2:833): "*rāgaš* and its derivatives have been translated by such ideas as 'tumult' (KB, AV) or 'noisy throngs' (BDB). However, contextual parallels ('to plot' Ps 2:1; 'secret plot' Ps 64:2; 'sweet converse' Ps 55:14) indicate that ideas such as 'conspire' (RSV) are probably correct."

Montgomery, writing in the 1920s, also came to similar conclusions. After a long discussion of the translation problem in Dan 6:6, he concludes, "Our vb. הרגשו then may be taken as mng. 'they acted in concert, harmony,' here practically, 'in conspiracy.'" If this idea is correct, then the NET translation "came by collusion" (secret cooperation for an illegal or deceitful purpose) is on the mark. However, because "collusion" may be an unfamiliar term to some readers, I suggest the translation "conspiring together, they approached the king."[590]

2. Daniel's detection, condemnation, and sentencing (6:10–18)

Textual Notes

11.a. [Eng. 6:10a] Although MT points as a pronoun הוּא, both Goldingay (121) and Collins (256) repoint as the verb הֲוָא before the participle בָּרֵךְ. The 3ms Peʿal perf. verb הֲוָא (or הֲוָה) is used several times in Daniel with a following ptc. to express continual action (as in 5:19; 6:4; and even at the end of v. 11). Given that (1) Daniel characteristically uses the equative verb הֲוָא/הֲוָה before participles, and (2) some manuscript editions have the alternative verb form הֲוָה instead of הוּא in 6:11, the verb form הֲוָא is preferable. Translate: "He would kneel."

13.a. [Eng. 6:12a] MT gives the plene spelling קְרִיבוּ. However, this should be קְרֵבוּ, as in Dan 3:8, and many other MSS. One fragment from the Cairo Geniza has קְרַבוּ.

13.b-b. [Eng. 6:12b-b] The words עַל־אֱסָר ("about prohibition") are lacking in LXX^{O} and LXX$^{\theta}$. However, 4QDan^{b} supports the reading with על אסרא (with def. article).

15.a. [Eng. 6:14a] 4QDan^{b} has לזבאותה (rather than MT's לשיזבותה), but Collins (258) regards this as a "probable scribal error." Note that the verb *šêziḇ* occurs again at the end of v. 16 [Aram. v. 17].

---

590. Also of interest is Jerome's Latin translation. "Jerome translates *surripuerunt* and explains, 'It was well said that they privily withdrew [or 'went surreptitiously'] for they did not come right out with what they were aiming at, but contrived their plot against a private enemy on the pretext of honoring the king'" (Collins, 266).

15.b. [Eng. 6:14b] The plural construct form would not be מֶעָלֵי שִׁמְשָׁא as *BHS* has, since a suffix would prompt a vowel change. Hence a few MSS have מֶ', and one MS has מַעֲ'. Cf. *DTT* (1903): "*Pl.* constr. מֶעָלֵי, מֵי', מַעֲ'.—מ' שמשא. *sunset.*"

16.a-a. [Eng. 6:15a-a] The words הַרְגִּשׁוּ עַל־מַלְכָּא ו are lacking in LXX^θ. However, they are found in 4QDan^b.

18.a. [Eng. 6:17a] MT has the plural construct form וּבְעִזְקָת. Although LXX^θ has the singular δακτυλίῳ (which implies a singular construct form וּבְעִזְקַת), LXX^O supports MT with the plural δακτυλίοις.

19.a. [Eng. 6:18a] The meaning of the hapax וְדַחֲוָן is a *crux interpretum* (see translation notes for discussion). One proposed solution has been to emend the text to וּלְחֵנָן, fem. pl. of לְחֵנָה, "concubines." In fact, one MS for Dan 6:18 [Aram. 19] reads לְחֵנָה (also note the use of *lᵊḥēnâ* in Dan 5:2–3, 23). The form is possible, although we would normally expect a חֵי infix, i.e., לְחֵינָן, as found in the Targum to 1 Kgs 11:3 (וּלְחֵינָן) and similarly in *Tg. Onkelos Gen* 25:6 and *Tg. Job* 19:15. Others have argued for "concubine" on the basis of the Arabic *daḫay* (دحى), meaning "an outstretched mat" in an obscene sense. Yet further tension to this proposed emendation is caused by the singular Hapʿel verb הַנְעֵל that follows. If the text was intended to say, "and concubines were not brought before me," we would have expected a plural Hupʿal perf. form of עֲלַל, namely הֻעַלוּ, as we have in Dan 5:15 ("the wise men and conjurers were brought before me," הֻעַלּוּ קֳדָמַי חַכִּימַיָּא אָשְׁפַיָּא). Hence, the emendation is doubtful.

Translation

6:10 When Daniel realized[591] that the written decree had been issued, he entered his house, where the windows in his upper room[592] were open toward Jerusalem. Then three times daily he would kneel on his knees, pray and offer praise to his God, just as[593] he had been doing previously.[594] **11** Then those

591. Lit., "knew."

592. *HALOT* (1948) gives the meaning "roof-chamber" for עִלִּי (*ʿillî*). The NIV has "upstairs room," and NET has "upper room." Not knowing the exact architecture, "upper room" is a more flexible rendering. Was this a small chamber with windows situated on a flat roof?

593. For the sense "just as" for כָּל־קֳבֵל דִּי (*kol-qŏḇēl dî*), see Dan 2:45.

594. מִן־קַדְמַת דְּנָה (*min-qaḏmaṯ dᵊnâ*) is lit., "from before this," but the sense is that of "previously" (so RJ, 129).

men,[595] conspiring together,[596] came and found Daniel making petition and imploring the favor[597] of his God. **12** So they approached the king and spoke to him about the prohibition:[598] "O king, did you not sign a prohibition that any man who seeks a petition from any god or man for a period of[599] thirty days—except from you, O king—would be thrown into a den[600] of lions?" The king replied, "The matter is certain, according to the law of the Medes and Persians, which cannot be annulled." [601] **13** Then they answered the king, "Daniel, from *among* the exiles[602] of Judah, has not paid attention to you, O king, nor to the prohibition which you signed. Three times daily he presents

---

595. Although גֻּבְרַיָּא (*guḇrayyāʾ*) means "men," the NET has rendered this "officials who had gone to the king." The NET has taken the liberty to expand the translation for sake of clarity. In the context, these men are clearly those administrative officials who had earlier urged the king to issue the royal edict (see vv. 6-9).

596. The translation "conspiring together, came," is an attempt to render the Aram. verb הַרְגִּשׁוּ (*hargišû*) from the root רְגַשׁ (*rᵉgaš*). See the translation note to Dan 6:6 [Eng.] and the additional exegetical comments at the end of the previous section for fuller discussion. They not only came as a group, but they came by way of a plot and with evil motives. The corresponding Heb. verb *rāḡaš* is used this way in Ps 2:1 (note the parallelism with "devise a vain thing"), and the Heb. noun *rigšāh* is used similarly in Ps 63:2 (the parallelism being "the plots of evil men").

597. The final phrase, וּמִתְחַנֵּן קֳדָם אֱלָהֵהּ (*ûmiṯḥannan qŏḏām ʾĕlāhēh*), is lit., "imploring favor before his God." As in BH, the related noun *ḥēn* means "grace, favor," and the corresponding verb means to implore God for his grace or favor. Thus, the *help* that Daniel seeks is that which comes from the grace of God.

598. The NET omits the words "about the prohibition/edict" (עַל־אֱסָר, *ʿal-ʾĕsār*; cf. v. 7). Although this phrase is lacking in both LXX traditions and the Syr, it is present in the MT and probably should be retained (it is easier to understand how a LXX translator might have left it out—redundancy?—than a copyist would have added it). As pointed out in the textual notes, the phrase is attested in 4QDan^b with the א suffix (על אסרא).

599. Lit., "until thirty days" (עַד־יוֹמִין תְּלָתִין, *ʿad-yômîn tᵉlāṯîn*).

600. Instead of "den of lions," it might be preferable to translate this "lion pit." It is not a natural *den* for lions but rather a special pit that was constructed for purposes of torture. *HALOT* (1841) suggests "pit" for Aram. גּוֹב (*gôḇ*). Most translations, however, retain the traditional "den of lions."

601. Rather than the translation "which cannot be changed" (so NET), it would be slightly more preferable to translate דִּי־לָא תֶעְדֵּא (*dî-lāʾ ṯeʿdēʾ*) as "which cannot be annulled" (so *HALOT*, 1944). The verb עֲדָא (*ʿăḏāʾ*) has a basic meaning "to be taken (or removed)." See, e.g., the use of *ʿăḏāʾ* in Dan 7:12.

602. Lit., "from the sons of the exiles" (מִן־בְּנֵי גָלוּתָא, *min-bᵉnê gālûṯāʾ*).

his petition."[603] **14** When the king heard this report,[604] he was very grieved[605] and set his mind on how he might deliver Daniel. Even until sunset,[606] he was seeking *a way* to rescue him. **15** Then those men, conspiring together,[607] approached the king and said to him, "Be mindful,[608] O king, that it is a law of the Medes and Persians that any prohibition or statute that the king establishes[609] cannot be changed." **16** Then the king gave the command,[610] and they brought Daniel and threw *him* into the den of lions. The king then said to Daniel, "Your God whom you continually serve[611] is able[612] to rescue you."

---

603. Aram. בָּעֵא בָּעוּתֵהּ (*bāʿēʾ bāʿûṯēh*) is a cognitive accusative with the sense "presents his petition." Recall Dan 6:8 [Aram.].

604. Lit., "heard the word" (מִלְּתָא שְׁמַע, *millᵊṯāʾ šᵊmaʿ*).

605. בְּאֵשׁ עֲלוֹהִי (*bᵊʾēš ʿălôhî*), lit., "it was evil/bad on him." Rosenthal (*GBA*, 36 [§82]) suggests "it grieved him," though Goldingay (121) and *HALOT* (1831) prefer "displeased." Whether "displeased" or "grieved," the context makes it clear that it was not Daniel that the king was upset with but rather those who had duped him. This should be contrasted with the phrase טְאֵב עֲלוֹהִי (*tᵊʾēḇ ʿălôhî*), "very pleased/glad," in Dan 6:23 [6:24 in Aram.]. The syntax is precisely the same, thus highlighting the contrast. The sound of Daniel's voice after the night of internment in the lion pit reversed the king's emotional distress.

606. Lit., "until the goings (in) of the sun" (עַד מֶעָלֵי שִׁמְשָׁא, *ʿaḏ meʿālê šimšāʾ*), i.e., until sunset.

607. For the translation "conspiring together, approached," see translation notes to Dan 6:6 [Eng.].

608. Lit., "Know" (דַּע, *daʿ*, from the root *yᵊḏaʿ*).

609. יְהָקֵים (*yᵊhāqêm*) is the habitual use of the impf.

610. Lit., "said," but contextually it is clear that what the king said was regarded as an order.

611. The verb is פְּלַח (*pālaḥ*). Although it is correctly translated "serve," this does not have reference to *labor*, as such, but is virtually synonymous with "worship." To serve a god (or idol) would be to reverence it, treating it as deity. Notice how *pālaḥ* is used in Dan 3:18 in parallel with the verb *sᵊgiḏ* (to worship or do homage to). The latter is translated "and regarding the statue of gold that you set up, we will not <u>worship</u> (it)."

612. Some translations (e.g., NIV and NRSV) render the verb יְשֵׁיזְבִנָּךְ (*yᵊšêzᵊḇinnāḵ* from the root *šêziḇ*) as a jussive, "May He rescue you." Some might prefer a jussive, thinking it is too much for a pagan king to assert outright that Daniel's God would rescue him. But as Goldingay (121) and Hartman (195) have pointed out, the presence of the letter *nun* before the suffix makes a jussive unlikely; cf. Rosenthal, *GBA*, 44 (§108). It seems best, then, to regard this as an impf. verb, which could be classified as a potential impf.: "Your God *is able* to rescue you." In either case, the text seems to infer that the king had some regard for Daniel's God as one who could do such miracles. It is of course possible that Daniel had witnessed to the king on prior occasions, perhaps even telling him the story of his three friends who were

17 Then a stone was brought and placed over the opening[613] of the den. The king sealed it with his signet ring and with the signet rings[614] of his nobles, so that nothing could be changed regarding Daniel. **18** Then the king went off to his palace, but he spent the night going hungry, and no entertainment[615] was brought in to him, and he was unable to sleep.[616]

Commentary

6:10 *The test of Daniel's faith.* Word that the king had signed a new decree prohibiting the worship of any other god or man for thirty days quickly reached the ears of Daniel. This was like a two-edged sword for Daniel. On the one hand, it represented an attack by his fellow pagan officials against his faith in the true living God. On the other hand, it was a divine test to see if Daniel would be faithful in the face of persecution. Driver (71) insightfully points out, "It is not, as with his three companions in ch. iii., a question of a positive sin which he will not commit, but of a positive duty which he will not omit." Based on an overall understanding of Scripture, it is also true that Satan was the behind-the-scenes instigator of this diabolical scheme. At this

---

delivered from the burning furnace. If so, the king could have had such a confidence in Daniel's God, even though he himself worshiped other deities (so Jerome).

613. Lit., "mouth" (Aram. פֻּם, *pum*).

614. Aram. "the signet rings." The pointing of the MT is for the plural construct form (–*qāṯ*). LXX$^{\theta}$, however, has the singular form, δακτυλίῳ (*daktuliōi*; similarly, Vg.), implying an Aramaic form –*qaṯ*.

615. As pointed out in the textual note for this verse, the hapax דַּחֲוָן (*ḏaḥăwān*) is a *crux interpretum*, and the exact meaning is simply not able to be determined with our present knowledge. Suggested translations have included "table," "food," "instruments of music," "dancing girls," "perfumes," and "concubines." As argued in the textual note, emending the text from וְדַחֲוָן (*wᵊḏaḥăwān*) to וּלְחֵנָן (*ûlᵊḥēnān*), meaning "concubines," is doubtful, despite how contextually appropriate such a suggestion might be. Following the lead of Montgomery (278) and Collins (258), the NET and ESV have chosen to translate *ḏaḥăwān* as "diversions," deliberately leaving the meaning vague. Medieval Jewish commentators Saadia and Rashi suggested the meaning "tables" (i.e., feast tables), implying foods for the king's pleasure. If this were correct, it would amplify the previous clause that stated he had spent the night going hungry. In MHeb, *daḥăwānôṯ* does mean "tabletops" (see *t. Kelim, B. Metzi'a* 5:3). LXX$^{\theta}$ translated the word by the Greek ἐδέσματα (*edesmata*, pl. of *edesma*), "meats" or "foods," which would have the same implication as "tables." LXX^{O} omits the clause. Ibn Ezra took the meaning to be musical instruments (Aram. *dᵊḥāʾ* means "push," "thrust"— striking the strings?). There is an Arabic word, *duḫān* (to "smell"), that could support the idea of "perfumes," but that is too presumptive. All things considered, the simple translation "entertainment" (so NASB and NIV) is a suitable translation, broad enough to capture the gist of any of the specific suggestions made by others (cf. Montgomery, 278: "'diversions' is good because it is non-committal").

616. Lit., the Aram. reads "his sleep fled from him."

point, Daniel had to make a choice what he would do, knowing full well what the consequences of disobeying the king's decree would mean.

One should keep in mind that Daniel is an elderly man at this time, probably in his eighties. This is not the first time that he has had to make hard choices in light of his faith. Experiences such as that recorded in Daniel 1 served to build the character of Daniel over the years, even as an oak tree gains strength with each passing year. Godly men want to finish the race well, and thus it is no surprise to find Daniel opting to faithfully continue as a man of prayer. Prayer, after all, was a core part of his being, not something to flippantly be set aside. This was the avenue for the real strength in his life. Young (135) remarks, "The higher the task to which God calls a man, the more does he feel the need of prayer."

Daniel's living quarters had an upper room (or roof chamber). Upper rooms with ample windows and adorned with lattice were common in the hot environment of the Middle East. Such an elevated room allowed for better ventilation and what comforting breeze there might be (cf. 2 Sam 18:33; 1 Kgs 17:19).[617] Obviously Daniel could have chosen a less conspicuous place to pray, for he was quite confident that his enemies would be watching him. Yet he wanted to maintain his testimony before them; his love and worship of the true God were not something negotiable.

The text adds that the windows were opened toward Jerusalem. The significance of this relates back to Solomon's prayer at the dedication of the Jerusalem temple (see esp. 1 Kgs 8:27–30, 46–50). In this prayer, Solomon looked ahead to the days when the Jewish people would be taken away into exile because of their sins (cf. Deut 4:25–31; 28:64–68). Yet, if while they were in exile they would humble themselves, repent, and pray toward the place where their temple had once stood, God would forgive them and restore them from captivity (cf. Deut 30:1–3). Daniel was being faithful to do this. Goswell correctly points out, "What Daniel is modeling is not the pious practice of daily prayers *per se* but unbending loyalty to God's kingship and rule, as demonstrated by his earnest concern for the fate of the Jerusalem temple (= God's palace)."[618]

Although the Jerusalem temple lay in ruins (destroyed by the Babylonians in 586 BC), Daniel continued this practice in hopes that someday his people would be allowed to return and rebuild Jerusalem. (Dan 9:1–19 gives us a glimpse of the content of his prayers.) Knowing that the seventy years of exile had nearly run its course (see Jer 29:10, 14), Daniel was motivated to pray all the more. That he prayed three times a day may not have been peculiar

617. Such a room was known in Heb. as an עֲלִיָּה (*ʿăliyyâ*), from the verb עָלָה (*ʿālâ*) meaning "to go up." The word is similar in Aram.: *ʿillî*.

618. Goswell, "The Ethics of the Book of Daniel," 138–39.

to him but perhaps reflected a custom (at least in the eastern Diaspora).[619] Such a practice was not commanded in Scripture, though precedence for this can be found in Ps 55:17.

Finally, we should take note that elderly Daniel continued his prayers before God while "kneeling on his knees" (literal translation of the Aramaic). One's bodily position does not ultimately determine how God receives the prayer, and one could certainly pray while sitting or standing. Yet there is something about the posture of kneeling that beautifully reflects the humility of the petitioner. From this position, one innately senses his frailty and unworthiness before Almighty God, as though saying to him, "I am in need of you and your grace, and it is enough for me to be 'your servant.'"

6:11–15 *The accusation against Daniel.* According to v. 11, Daniel's antagonists came to his personal quarters looking for him. The first verb (translated "conspiring together, came;" cf. the NET "came by collusion") implies that a devious plot underlay their visit.[620] This would have come as no surprise to Daniel, and the way he handled the situation is exemplary. Notice first that he did not try to retaliate against them with a vindictive spirit. Also, he did not rationalize the situation or attempt to compromise his godly responsibility. It might have been tempting for him to dodge this difficulty by merely ceasing his prayers for one month, or he could have found a way to pray privately beyond the eye of any onlookers. That he did not do these things suggests that his paramount concern was in being a faithful witness to the unsaved, not in being "politically correct." He could do this because he had no shame in the Lord or of his Word (cf. Matt 10:32–33).

Observing Daniel, they found him "making petition and imploring the favor of his God." Arnold points out how the author has utilized the verb translated "making petition" (בְּעָא, *bəʿāʾ*) in making a wordplay throughout the chapter (including its cognate noun בָּעוּ, *bāʿû*). The word has a primary meaning "to search for" (as in Dan 2:13) but secondarily means "to request compassion and grace from a deity or king." Arnold explains:

> … we are suggesting the narrator has used the primary meaning *bĕʿāʾ* in v. 5 in a deliberate and calculated fashion in order to create a paronym in vv. 8 and 12–14, where the word is used in its secondary meaning of "make petition." The point of the wordplay becomes clear when Daniel ignores the royal decree. After he learned that the decree had been issued, he went home to his upper chamber, where the opened windows faced Jerusalem, and as was his custom, he prayed three times, giving thanks to his God.

---

619. See Collins (268–69) for a survey of various customs related to fixed times for prayer.

620. For fuller discussion, see the translation note to Dan 6:11 above, and compare the "Additional Exegetical Comments" to Dan 6:1–9.

> After his enemies found Daniel *praying* ("seeking" his God, v. 12), they reminded the king of his royal decree regarding anyone who *makes a petition* ("seeks," v. 13) to any god or man for thirty days. In v. 14, they proudly announce that Daniel *makes his petition* three times a day. Daniel's enemies find what they are *seeking* when he defies the royal decree and *makes petition* to his God.[621]

The characterizing wordplay contrasts Daniel with his antagonists. Daniel's *seeking* of God ultimately upends their *seeking* to frame him.

Armed with their discovery about Daniel, the antagonists rushed off to inform the king. Before reporting Daniel's violation of the king's decree, they first prompted the king to acknowledge his own prohibition (v. 12). He did so, and even affirmed that it was impossible to be annulled, being a law of the Medes and Persians (see v. 8). With this, the trap was now fully set. According to v. 13, they not only accused Daniel of violating the king's command, but they cast him in the worst possible light they could. They reminded the king that Daniel was one of the captives from Judah, i.e., he was a foreigner who had been forcibly brought to Babylon against his will, thus implying he was untrustworthy. We observe that they fail to say anything about Daniel's long history of loyal service in the realm of Babylon (he had already been there at least sixty-six years), and they say nothing of his present position in which he had admirably served. Furthermore, they tried to portray Daniel's disobedience as a personal affront to the king. He "pays no attention to you, O king," they charged, hoping to raise the king's ire all the more.

Verse 14 reflects that their report was upsetting to the king, but not for the reasons they presented. The fact that the king immediately wanted to seek Daniel's rescue indicates that his displeasure was not with Daniel but with the other nobles who had accused Daniel. He realized that they had duped him into condemning Daniel, when in reality Daniel was one of the most competent and loyal members in his service. They had not really urged this thirty-day law to honor the king (or to provide a loyalty check), but only to rid the court of a rival they envied.

Since the text indicates the king kept seeking a way to rescue Daniel until "late afternoon" (or sunset), this implies that he was obligated to act that day. Hence, v. 15 seems to indicate that the antagonists came back later in the day to insist on the implementation of the penalty against Daniel. In v. 12, the king had confessed that each law of the Medes and Persians could not be "annulled" (from the verb עֲדָא, *ʿăḏāʾ*). When they confront the king in v. 15 about this policy, however, they use a different verb. They tell the king that such laws cannot be "changed" (from שְׁנָא, *šᵉnāʾ*), lest he thought he could bring about Daniel's rescue by somehow changing the law or its

621. Arnold, "Wordplay and Narrative Techniques in Daniel 5 and 6," 484.

application to Daniel. Try as he could, not even the king could rescue Daniel from their malicious intent.

6:16–18 *The sentencing of Daniel to the lions.* Lions were commonly kept by Assyrian, Babylonian, and Medo-Persian monarchs for sporting purposes. They could also be used for torture, and the thought of live humans becoming a meal for these ferocious, hungry lions would have been harrowing. Amazingly, the king (v. 16) sought to console Daniel by telling him that the God whom he served *continually* was able to rescue him. The word "continually" reflects the king's acknowledgment that Daniel worshiped this God unceasingly, and no earthly power could deter him from that. This admission indicates Daniel's testimony had not been in vain. Furthermore, that the king regarded Daniel's God as actually able to rescue him probably reflects something of his own understanding about Yahweh. While he still remained a pagan king (as far as we know), his positive assessment of Daniel's God most likely indicates that he had learned of the miraculous power of Yahweh from Daniel himself. In particular, this would have included the story of God rescuing Shadrach, Meshach, and Abednego.

Not only was a stone placed over the opening to the lion pit, but it was marked by both the official seal of the king and that of his nobles. Perhaps the seal was made in wax and affixed to ropes or chains that had been used to secure the stone in place. In any case, the purpose was to make sure that no one tampered with the only way out for Daniel. Only when they returned in the morning to view the results could the seals be broken.

Waiting was not easy for Darius. Verse 18 indicates that this whole affair had troubled him so much that he cared nothing for normal entertainment that evening, not even his royal meal. Not only did he go to bed hungry, but he could not even get to sleep that night—tossing and turning all night in deep concern over Daniel's welfare.

Biblical Theology Comments

Theologically, this passage is rich in regard to the biblical practice of prayer. Several features of Daniel's prayer life are highlighted: (1) kneeling; (2) facing Jerusalem (on account of being in exile); (3) giving of thanks; and (4) engaging in prayer at least three times daily.

Although kneeling is not required for prayers to be effective, there are several examples of this in Scripture. When Solomon prayed at the time of the temple dedication, he "knelt on his knees in the presence of all the assembly of Israel and spread out his hands toward heaven" (2 Chron 6:13, NASB). When Jesus prayed at Gethsemane, "He knelt down and *began* to pray" (Luke 22:41). When Peter healed Tabitha, he knelt down and prayed (Acts 9:40). Following the Apostle Paul's farewell message to the elders at Ephesus (20:17–38), we read that "he knelt down and prayed with them all" (v. 36). Also, at his farewell departure with the disciples at Tyre, we are told that they knelt down on the beach and prayed (21:5). Kneeling reflects a worshipful attitude and one's humility before the Lord. Ps 95:6 states, "Oh come, let us worship and bow down; let us kneel before the LORD, our Maker!" (ESV). Of course a person could physically kneel to pray and yet his heart be far from the Lord. So it is important that the one who prays is also "kneeling" in the heart.

Application and Devotional Implications

Prayer was fundamental to Daniel's life. Twice in this one paragraph we are told that Daniel had a habit of praying three times each day. Furthermore, when the antagonists came looking for him, he did not put on a show of prayer just for this occasion. Verse 10 indicates that he continued this spiritual discipline "as he had been doing previously." Prayer had become a carefully developed habit in the life of this octogenarian. As with any believer, such a commitment to prayer does not come easily. I suspect that Daniel also had had those moments in his life, particularly as a younger man, when he struggled to be consistent in this area of his walk with God. Certainly it was not any easier for him than it is for busy Christians today. Yet when we take a moment to reflect, we have to admit that Daniel is one of the spiritual giants of the Bible. If we truly aspire to greater spiritual heights ourselves, there is no escaping the fact that prayer must take center place in our lives. And as we seek to grow in this area, let us not think that prayer is a mere drudgery to be endured. Indeed, those who truly partake of prayer discover its richness: it is nothing less than communion with God himself. If we want to be a "Daniel," then we must also be on our knees, as he made a habit of doing.

3. Daniel's deliverance and the punishment of his enemies (6:19–24)

Textual Notes

20.a. [Eng. 6:19a] 4QDan[b] omits the verb יְקוּם. The impf. form of the root קום does appear awkward in past tense narration (both LXX[O] and LXX[θ] translate with aorist verbs). Montgomery (279) mentions a possible parallel of בֵּאדַיִן ... יְקוּם to BH אָז plus the impf., which can be used to express past time (e.g., Exod 15:1). However, בֵּאדַיִן is frequently used in Daniel and almost always followed by a verb in the perf. (not the impf.) for expressing past tense narration. Goldingay (122) thinks the impf. may be used to throw more emphasis on the verb אזל that follows. Notice should be made of the phrase וְקָם בְּהִתְבְּהָלָה in Dan 3:24 with similar wording but having the perf. form קָם (with אֱדַיִן at the beginning of the sentence). Despite the peculiarity, יְקוּם should be translated past tense.

21.a-a. [Eng. 6:20a-a] The words עָנֵה מַלְכָּא וְאָמַר לְדָנִיֵּאל are lacking in LXX[θ] but are found in 4QDan[b].

22.a. [Eng. 6:21a] Although MS L (B19[a]) has the spelling דָנִיֵּאל, many MSS Edd. have 'ֵ-.

Translation

6:19 Then the king arose at dawn,[622] at the first light of day,[623] and went in haste[624] to the den of lions. **20** When he approached the den, he called to Daniel with a troubled voice.[625] The king said[626] to Daniel, "O Daniel, servant of the living God, has your God whom you continually serve been able to rescue you from the lions?" **21** Then Daniel replied to[627] the king, "O king, live forever! **22** My God has sent His angel, and He has shut the mouth of the lions. They have not harmed me, inasmuch as I was found *to be* innocent before Him. And also before you, O king, I have committed no treacherous

---

622. Although the word שְׁפַרְפָּרָא (*šᵊp̱arpārāʾ*) only occurs here in BAram. (meaning "dawn, daybreak," *HALOT*, 2002), we do find it with prep כְּ (*kᵊ*) in *Tg. Isa* 58:8 as כִּשְׁפַרְפָּרָא (*ḵišp̱arp̱ārāʾ*), "like the dawn" (as well as the Aram. Targum to Isa 62:1; Job 3:4; 7:4; Lam 2:19; and in an appendix at the end of the book of Esther [10:3] in both Aram. Targums). S. M. Paul, "Daniel 6:20: An Aramaic Calque on an Akkadian Expression," *Scriptura* 87 (2004): 315 notes, "שְׁפַרְפָּרָא ... appears in Syriac, שַׁפְרָה and שֶׁפְּרָה, meaning Aurora, and is the interdialectal etymological equivalent of Arabic سفر (*safara*), 'to shine,' referring to the dawn."

623. The words "at the first light of day" are actually a translation of one word in Aram., בְּנָגְהָא (*bᵊnoḡhāʾ*). *HALOT* (1926) suggests the word נֹגַהּ (*nōḡah*) literally means "brightness." There is a corresponding Heb. word, נֹגַהּ (*nōḡah*), with the same meaning, derived from the Heb. verb *nāḡah*, "to shine." So, the idea seems to be that of the first bright light of the dawn. Paul, "Daniel 6:20," 316, contends that *bᵊnoḡhāʾ* is not a gloss "but rather an Aramaic calque on the Akkadian expression, *ina/ana mimmû šēri ina namāri,* 'When the first light of dawn shone,' which occurs several times in the Gilgamesh epic, tablets VI:88; VIII:1, 64, 90, 206; XI:48, 97, which is comprised of the Akkadian verb, *namāru,* 'to dawn, shine brightly,' and the noun, *šēru* (= נֹגַהּ) 'daybreak, daylight.'"

624. See Dan 2:25 for a similar use of בְּהִתְבְּהָלָה (*bᵊhiṯbᵊhālâ*, an inf. const. form of בְּהַל, *bᵊhal*). The alternative reading in 4QDan[b] at 6:19 (אתבהלה) is wrong. Goldingay (120) translates "agitatedly" based on the meaning for *bᵊhal* in the Paʿel stem, "alarm, dismay."

625. Although LXX[θ] translates עֲצִיב (*ʿăṣîḇ*) as ἰσχυρᾷ (*ischura*, "strong, mighty") and LXX[O] as μεγάλῃ (*megalēi*, "great"), *HALOT* (1952) correctly defines *ʿăṣîḇ* as meaning "troubled, sad."

626. The Aram. literally reads, "the king spoke up and said to Daniel." For stylistic reasons, this was rendered "he said."

627. The Aram. has "with," though Goldingay (122) contends that *ʿim* can be used for speaking "to" someone (based on parallels in Syriac).

act."[628] **23** Then the king was overjoyed[629] and gave an order to bring Daniel up from the den. So Daniel was taken up from the den. No injury was found on him, because he had trusted in his God. **24** At the king's command,[630] they brought those men who had maliciously accused[631] Daniel and threw[632] them into the den of lions, along with their children and their wives. They had not even reached the bottom of the den before the lions overpowered them and crushed[633] all their bones.

Commentary

6:19–20 *Darius' concern for Daniel.* The king's actions demonstrate the obvious concern he had for Daniel's welfare. He appears to have even had a glimmer of hope that Daniel might have survived, though his "troubled voice" betrays his intuition that this was most unlikely. The fact that Daniel is held in high esteem by the king is evidenced by (1) his coming to the lion pit at the earliest possible moment, (2) the haste by which he went there, (3) the "troubled voice" by which he spoke, and (4) his address to Daniel as "the servant of the living God." The latter expression is quite remarkable from the lips of Darius in light of the numerous times that the Scriptures refer to the God of the Bible as "the living God" (e.g., Josh 3:10; Deut 5:26; 1 Sam 17:26, 36; Jer 23:36). In the apocryphal writing "Bel and the Dragon," Daniel confronts King Cyrus that only the God of the Bible (not Bel) is the "living God."[634] He is a living God in contrast to the worthless idols that can do nothing for themselves or others (cf. Isa 44:9–20). Although there is insufficient evidence to conclude that Darius truly believed in Yahweh

---

628. The translation "treacherous act" (Aram. חֲבוּלָה, *hăḇûlâ*) can mean either a "hurtful act" or a "crime" (so *HALOT*, 1868). This corresponds to the accusation against Daniel in 6:13. NASB translates "crime," the NET "harm," and the NIV "wrong."

629. The expression טְאֵב עֲלוֹהִי (*tᵊʾēḇ ʿălôhî*), translated "joyful," is the reverse of the king's reaction in Dan 6:14, בְּאֵשׁ עֲלוֹהִי (*bᵊʾēš ʿălôhî* ["grieved"]). The NIV translation "overjoyed" captures well the sense of שַׂגִּיא טְאֵב עֲלוֹהִי, *śagîʾ tᵊʾēḇ ʿălôhî* (lit., "was exceedingly glad").

630. Lit., "then the king spoke" (וַאֲמַר מַלְכָּא, *waʾămar malkāʾ*).

631. Lit., the Aram. is translated "had eaten the pieces of," a figurative expression for *maliciously accusing* someone (used earlier in Dan 3:8). The NET adds the note, "Although figurative, the literal Aramaic expression is ironic, in that the accusers who had 'eaten the pieces of Daniel' are themselves devoured by the lions."

632. The NET translates with passive verbs: "they were brought and thrown," adding this note: "Aramaic active impersonal verb is often used as a substitute for the passive."

633. For the Hapʿel of דְּקַק (*dᵊqaq*), BDB (1089) suggests "to break in pieces," but *HALOT* (1855) "to crush."

634. For a helpful introduction to the apocryphal account, see J. J. de Bruyn, "Dining in the Lions' Den—Bel and the Dragon, Verses 28–42 (Old Greek/Theodotion)," *Verbum et Ecclesia* 36 (2015): 1–9.

God alone, his words seem to indicate that he had at least come to a point of esteeming Daniel's God (probably as a result of Daniel's life and witness).

6:21–23 *Daniel's deliverance.* Daniel's calmness in the situation is reflected in his reply with the standard greeting of respect for royalty, "O king, live forever!" (cf. Dan 2:4; 3:9; 5:10; 6:6). Then he added that God had sent "His angel" to protect him during the night. This expression, "His angel" (מַלְאֲכֵהּ, *mal'ăḵēh*), is the same form as occurred in 3:28, suggesting that the same one who protected the three youths in the furnace was the one who protected Daniel in the lions' den (see comments on 3:25).[635] The words of Ps 34:7 are appropriate at this point: "The angel of the LORD encamps around those who fear Him, and rescues them."

Daniel also explained to the king that his survival was nothing less than a divine declaration of his "innocence" (v. 22). Daniel's name meant "God is my judge," and so his deliverance from the lions' pit was his vindication. It is not that Daniel was sinless, but innocent of the trumped-up charges against him, especially any insinuation that he had insolently paid no attention to the king's orders (recall v. 13).

That the king was "overjoyed" upon discovering Daniel's safety further underscores his high esteem for Daniel. After being lifted from the lion's den (apparently through an opening in the top), "no injury" (NIV, "no wound") was found on him. Such a status was *prima facie* evidence of God's supernatural working. Darius (and all others) had encountered a miracle, and this may have drawn him closer to personal faith in Yahweh—though the text does not make this obvious. The end of v. 23 adds the reason for this miracle: "he [Daniel] had trusted in his God." This probably reflects back to the moment that Daniel made a conscious decision to continue his practice of prayer (see 6:10), not just the time when he was placed in the lion's den. At a crisis moment in his life, he decided *by faith* to remain faithful to Yahweh. For this, God rewarded him with a miraculous deliverance. As Heb 11:33 puts it, he "by faith ... shut the mouths of lions."[636]

6:24 *The destruction of Daniel's enemies.* King Darius knew what Daniel's antagonists had done and how they had attempted to dupe the king himself in the process. Therefore, he called for them to be brought forth and

635. "His angel" may be a shortened form for "the angel of Yahweh," commonly found in the OT. Frequently, the angel of Yahweh speaks and acts as God (see Gen 16:7; 22:11; Exod 3:2; Isa 37:36). In Judg 6:11–14 Gideon's visitor is called "the angel of Yahweh" in v. 11 and then simply "Yahweh" in v. 14 (cf. Josh 5:13–6:2 regarding the "commander of the host of Yahweh").

636. For other examples of Dan 6 in the NT and early Christian literature, see J. W. van Henten, "Daniel 3 and 6 in Early Christian Literature," in *The Book of Daniel: Composition and Reception*, ed. J. J. Collins and P. W. Flint, 1: 149–69 (Leiden: Brill, 2001).

thrown to the lions. We need not think that every supervisor and satrap of the kingdom was punished. The text only says that "those men who maliciously accused Daniel" were punished.[637] More startling is the inclusion of the children and wives in the punishment.[638] We should not conclude, however, that God commended such stern action in this case. Rather, this was Darius' choice and a reflection of Persian custom. The ancient Greek historian Herodotus tells an account of how one Intaphernes and his family were subjected to a similar fate by the Persian King Darius (not the same Darius as in Dan 6):

> … he laid hands on Intaphernes, his children, and all his near kindred; strongly suspecting that he and his friends were about to raise a revolt. When all had been seized and put in chains, as malefactors condemned to death, the wife of Intaphernes came and stood continually at the palace-gates, weeping and wailing sore. So Darius after a while, seeing that she never ceased to stand and weep, was touched with pity for her, and bade a messenger go to her and say, "Lady, king Darius gives thee as a boon the life of one of thy kinsmen - choose which thou wilt of the prisoners." Then she pondered awhile before she answered, "If the king grants me the life of one alone, I make choice of my brother." Darius, when he heard the reply, was astonished, and sent again, saying, "Lady, the king bids thee tell him why it is that thou passest by thy husband and thy children, and preferrest to have the life of thy brother spared. He is not so near to thee as thy children, nor so dear as thy husband." She answered, "O king, if the gods will, I may have another husband and other children when these are gone. But as my father and my mother are no more, it is impossible that I should have another brother. This was my thought when I asked to have my brother spared." Then it seemed to Darius that the lady spoke well, and he gave her, besides the life that she had asked, the life also of her eldest son, because he was greatly pleased with her. But he slew all the rest.[639]

The way in which the lions ferociously attacked the bodies of Daniel's accusers is not recorded for the sake of shock but to once again demonstrate the miraculous nature of what happened. These were not lions that just happened not to be hungry one night. They were hungry killers, and Daniel's survival underscores the miraculous nature of God's intervention.

---

637. LXX^{O} attempts to soften the implication by limiting the revenge to "those two men" (*hoi duo anthrōpoi ekeinoi*) rather than MT's "those men."

638. For examples of other biblical accounts where family members were included in divine punishment, see Num 16:23–33 and 2 Chron 21:12–15.

639. Herodotus, *Hist.* 3.119 (George Rawlinson translation).

Application and Devotional Implications

It is rather easy for those of us who are Christians to read these verses and rejoice in the great miracle that God did in Daniel's case. How could it be that a human being could be lowered into a pit filled with hungry lions and yet escape unharmed? Truly Yahweh preserved Daniel alive. Yet we must remember that it is not always God's purpose to spare his own children of hardship and even martyrdom. In Acts 12:1–2 we read, "About that time King Herod laid hands on some from the church to harm them. He had James, the brother of John, executed with a sword." This was James, one of Jesus' twelve. In the very same chapter we discover that though Peter is arrested and about to be killed as well, the Lord miraculously delivered him. Certainly the Lord could have delivered both men, if He had so desired. We learn from this that what God intends for one of his children is not necessarily what he intends for another. For each of us, God has a separate plan and purpose. For Daniel, God had a purpose in delivering him (the miracle provided a mighty testimony to Darius). Yet all of us must be willing to accept what the Lord brings our way. That may be a debilitating disease or terminal illness. That may be prosperity or financial limitation and struggle. We must beware the danger of comparing ourselves to others. What God intends for another (whether blessing or distress) is not necessarily what he intends for any one of us. We may or may not be delivered "from the lions' den," but the important thing is that we remain faithful and give a good testimony before all.

4. Darius' testimony to God's sovereignty (6:25–28)

The chapter ends similarly to chap. 4, with the king of Babylon testifying to the sovereignty of the God worshiped by Daniel.

Textual Notes

26.a. [Eng. 6:25a] Compare Dan 2:38 for the Qere reading דָּיְרִין.

27.a. [Eng. 6:26a] The Qere reading is זָיְעִין (comp. 5:19).

29.a. [Eng. 6:28a] Though MS L reads פַּרְסָיאָ, the K is פָּרְסָיָא and the Q is פָּרְסָאָה.

Translation

6:25 Then King Darius wrote to all the peoples, nations, and *men of every* language[640] throughout the whole earth[641]: "May your prosperity

---

640. The translation "*men of every* language" is literally "tongues" (לִשָּׁנַיָּא, *liššānayyāʾ*). The point is that all the various language groups of the realm participated in this ceremony.

641. The NASB and NET translate בְּכָל־אַרְעָא (*bᵊkol-ʾarʿāʾ*) "in all the land," whereas the NIV and ESV have "in all the earth." Goldingay (120), however, translates "in all the world," and Collins (258) "the whole earth." *ʾarʿāʾ* can mean either "earth" or

abound![642] **26** A decree has been made before me that in all the dominion of my kingdom, men are to tremble[643] and fear before the God of Daniel, for He is the[644] living God and enduring forever. His kingdom is one which will not be destroyed, and His dominion is forever.[645] **27** He rescues, delivers, and performs signs and wonders in the heavens and on the earth. He has rescued Daniel from the power[646] of the lions." **28** So this Daniel prospered in the reign of Darius and[647] in the reign of Cyrus the Persian.

Commentary

6:25–27 *Darius' decree.* Critical scholars are quite skeptical of the historicity of this account (cf. Collins, 272–73), but given that we do not have a precise identification for Darius the Mede, a more cautious approach is in order. If Darius the Mede is not the same as the Persian king Cyrus (as seems

---

"land" (as BH *ʾereṣ*). The translation "land" could be understood as a more restricted area, i.e., the *land* (or region) of Babylonia, rather than the whole earth. (This could have a bearing on how one understands the relationship between Cyrus and Darius the Mede, and the political situation of their day.) Wood (175) takes the translation *in all the earth* as "a hyperbole customary to kings of the day."

642. See translation note at Dan 4:1 [Aram. 3:31] for an explanation of שְׁלָם, *šᵊlām*. Lit., the Aram. reads "may your *šᵊlām* abound." Aram. *šᵊlām* (like BH *šālôm*) means more than simply "peace." The word includes the concern for the total welfare of another. The oriental sense is, "May everything be well with you!"

643. The words "tremble" and "fear" are participles. The syntactical construction involves the particle דִּי (*dî*) followed by לֶהֱוֺן (*lehĕwōn*; prep לְ, *lᵊ*, on the equative verb הֲוָה, *hăwâ*), followed in turn by a ptc. This type of construction is used to form a purpose clause (for other examples, see Dan 6:3; Ezra 6:10; 7:25). The sentence could be translated, "made a decree *for the purpose that* men might tremble and fear."

644. The article is absent in LXX (θεὸς ζῶν, *theos zōn*) and 4QDan[b] but present in MT and Syr.

645. Lit., "until the end" (עַד־סוֹפָא, *ʿad-sôpāʾ*). The nuance, however, is "forever," as is clear from the usage of the same phrase in Dan 7:26. The "little horn" out of the fourth beast is destroyed *forever*. This last sentence in 6:26 [Eng.] is strikingly similar to 2:44 (cf. 4:3, 34).

646. Lit., "from the hand" (*min-yad*). Quite commonly, "hand" is a metonymy for the "power" derived from the hand.

647. Those who equate Darius the Mede with Cyrus the Great take the conjunction *waw* as explicative (GKC, 484–85, §154*a*N): "in the reign of Darius, that is, Cyrus the Persian." (So J. Baldwin, J. M. Bulman, B. Colless, and D. J. Wiseman.) Regarding Darius the Mede, see commentary at Dan 5:31. Further discussion is found in section 5 of "Alleged Historical Inaccuracies" under "Objections to the Traditional Date and Authorship" in the "Introduction" to the book. This view (equating Darius with Cyrus) is very problematic. Cyrus was not regarded as a Mede (even though his mother was a Mede), and in the book of Daniel he is referred to elsewhere as "Cyrus king of Persia."

probable), then it is certainly possible that Darius could have espoused the outlook recorded in vv. 25–27.

The introduction to the decree does appear to be a rather stereotypical way for a king to initiate a royal decree. Note that most of the wording in Dan 6:25 is identical to the introduction that Nebuchadnezzar gave his decree as recorded in 4:1. The reverence and fear to be accorded Daniel's God is similar to the esteem given to Nebuchadnezzar himself in 5:19. Yet the reasons are different. According to 6:26, it is because he is the "living God" and endures forever (see comments on 6:20 for "living God"). Darius adds that this reverence and fear of Daniel's God is also because "His kingdom" will not be destroyed, and his dominion is forever. The issue of God's kingdom is a prominent topic of the book of Daniel. Thinking back to chap. 2, God had revealed to Nebuchadnezzar that a series of earthly kingdoms (beginning with Babylon) would come and go. In the final analysis, however, "the God of heaven will set up a kingdom that will never be destroyed, nor will this kingdom be left for another people" (2:44). This kingdom is the goal of history. The expression "not be destroyed" (*lāʾ tiṯḥabbal*) is precisely the same in 2:44 and 6:26. In 4:3 [Eng.] Nebuchadnezzar even came to a point of confessing that "His kingdom" lasts forever and "His dominion" continues from generation to generation, using terms strikingly similar to those in 6:26. (These ideas about the enduring nature of his kingdom and dominion will be reiterated again in 7:14.) Hence, Darius' confession about God's kingdom and authority in 6:26 must be considered in this light. Although the emphasis of Dan 6 has not been upon God's kingdom, apparently Darius had learned something about this from Daniel. The miracle, then, of Daniel's rescue from the lions' den served to convince Darius that this *kingdom teaching* was true. Notice that following Darius' confession about God's kingdom and authority in v. 26, he refers to God's signs and wonders in v. 27, particularly Daniel's rescue. Knowing that God had severely humbled Nebuchadnezzar to bring him to the point of professing God's kingdom to come, it may be that Darius readily (and wisely) professed this kingdom.

6:28 *Daniel's favor in the Medo-Persian period.* The chapter ends on the note that Daniel "prospered" during the reign of Darius and Cyrus the Persian. The word translated "prospered" (הַצְלַח, *haṣlaḥ*) means *political success* in this context (as it did in 3:30). According to 6:1–3, Darius had already promoted Daniel to being one of the three chief ministers (or commissioners) to which the 120 satraps reported and was being considered for appointment "over the entire kingdom." Thus, v. 28 assures us that Daniel, a man at least in his eighties by that time, continued to enjoy political success in the new administration established by the Medes and Persians following the overthrow of Babylon. According to 10:1, Daniel lived on to see at least the third year of Cyrus (ca. 536/35 BC). Ironically, Belshazzar had offered political advancement to Daniel in return for interpreting the writing on the wall (5:16), though Daniel turned down the reward he offered. (He could not accept a reward from someone who had so insulted the honor and glory of his God.)

God, in his grace, gave Daniel an extremely high political position anyway, and that after Belshazzar had been slain.

Biblical Theology Comments

According to Dan 2:44, Daniel revealed to Nebuchadnezzar that the God of heaven would eventually set up a kingdom that would never be destroyed, nor would it be turned over to another people. Following his humbling in chap. 4, Nebuchadnezzar acknowledged God's kingdom plan when he declared, "His dominion is an everlasting dominion, and His kingdom extends from one generation to the next" (4:34). Darius the Mede echoed the same general truth (6:26). This sets the stage for further revelation of God's kingdom plan by means of a vision given to Daniel in chap. 7. With this vision, several major contributions will be made to the developing kingdom theology, including the fact that the kingdom will be entrusted to "One like a Son of Man" (7:13) and that the kingdom will be preceded by a great persecutor of God's people.

Application and Devotional Implications

Reflecting back on chap. 6, we see that Daniel nearly lost his job—which for him was a prominent political position in the Medo-Persian province of Babylon. Yet he did not try to save his job by "hiding his faith." No job on earth was worth having to compromise his faith or damage his testimony before his unbelieving associates. In the end, not only was he rescued and remained alive, but the Lord graciously took care of the matter of his job as well. "Job security" is something that can easily govern what we do and say, even at the expense of more important values we profess to believe in. Whatever the risk we may face, however, we can be sure that the Lord is going to be faithful to us. Our circumstances may not be the same as Daniel's, and our outcome may not exactly mirror his. Yet, in one way or another, God is going to be faithful to us. The psalmist declared, "I was once young, now I am old. I have never seen a godly man abandoned, or his children forced to search for food" (Ps 37:25). The "living God" who endures forever is going to care for us and remain faithful to us, and thus we must find our security in him.

Selected Bibliography (Daniel 6)

Arnold, B. T. "Wordplay and Narrative Techniques in Daniel 5 and 6." *JBL* 112 (1993): 479–85.

Boutflower, C. "The Historical Value of Daniel v and vi." *JTS* 17 (1915–1916): 43–60.

Cameron, G. "The Persian Satrapies and Related Matters." *JNES* 32 (1973): 47–56.

de Bruyn, J. J. "Daniel 6: There and Back Again—A Deity's Tale." *HTS Teologiese Studies* 71 (2015): 1–8.

———. "Dining in the Lions' Den—Bel and the Dragon, Verses 28–42 (Old Greek/Theodotion)." *Verbum et Ecclesia* 36 (2015): 1–9.

Dempsey, D., and S. Pace. "A Comparison of Darius, Pharaoh, and Associates." *PRSt* 43 (2016): 203–14.
Montgomery, J. A. "The 'Two Youths' in the LXX to Dan. 6." *JAOS* 41 (1921): 316–17.
Paul, S. M. "Dan 6,8: An Aramaic Reflex of Assyrian Legal Terminology." *Bib* 6 (1984): 106–10.
———. "Daniel 6:20: An Aramaic Calque on an Akkadian Expression." *Scriptura* 87 (2004): 315–16.
———. "The Mesopotamian Babylonian Background of Daniel 1–6." In *The Book of Daniel: Composition and Reception*, vol. 1, ed. J. J. Collins and P. W. Flint. Leiden, Boston: Brill, 2001. 55–68.
Polaski, D. C. "*Mene, Mene, Tekel, Parsin*: Writing and Resistance in Daniel 5 and 6." *JBL* 123 (2004): 649–69.
Segal, M. "Harmonization and Rewriting of Daniel 6 from the Bible to Qumran." In *Hā-'îsh Mōshe: Studies in Scriptural Interpretation in the Dead Sea Scrolls and Related Literature in Honor of Moshe J. Bernstein*, ed. B. Y. Goldstein, M. Segal, and G. J. Brooke, 265–79. Leiden: Brill, 2018.
———. "The Old Greek Version and Masoretic Text of Daniel 6." In *Die Septuaginta: Orte und Intentionen. Proceedings of the Fifth International Wuppertal Symposium on the Septuagint*, ed. S. Kreuzer, M. Meiser, and M. Sigismund. Tübingen: Mohr Siebeck, 2016. 404–28.
Shea, W. H. "A Further Note on Daniel 6: Daniel as 'Governor.'" *AUSS* 21 (1983): 169–71.
Van der Toorn, K. "In the Lions' Den: The Babylonian Background of a Biblical Motif." *CBQ* 60 (1998): 626–40.
Van Deventer, H. J. M. "Literary Lions with Real Bite: Re-examining the Intertextual Rhetoric in Daniel 6." *OTE* 28 (2015): 832–46.
Van Henten, J. W. "Reception of Daniel 3 and 6 in Early Christian Literature." In *The Book of Daniel: Composition and Reception*, ed. J. J. Collins and P. W. Flint, 1:149–69. Leiden: Brill, 2001.
Walton, J. "The Decree of Darius the Mede in Daniel 6." *JETS* 31 (1986): 279–86.
Wills, L. M. *The Jew in the Court of the Foreign King: Ancient Jewish Court Legends*. HDR 26. Minneapolis: Fortress, 1990.

F. Daniel's Vision of the Four Beasts from the Sea, and the Eventual Establishment of Messiah's Kingdom (7:1–28)

Chapter 7 of Daniel is the final chapter written in Aramaic. As explained in the introduction to Dan 2:1–13, these chapters depict the role, character, and succession of the Gentile nations of the world under whom Israel is being disciplined prior to Messiah's kingdom. This explains why they are written in the dominant language of the Gentile world at that time, namely Aramaic. Yet, chap. 7 is also a *hinge chapter* to the book. Collins is correct in stating, "Daniel 7 serves as a linking chapter by which the two halves of the book are interlocked."[648] Although it forms a literary unit with chaps. 2–6, at the same time it has a vital link to chaps. 8–12, being the first of four visions given directly to Daniel. Thus, what appears at first to be chronological disorder—chap. 7 reverts to the first year of Belshazzar—can easily be explained by the author's rather obvious purpose of grouping the four visions of Daniel together. The first one (i.e., the one recorded in chap. 7) was given in the first year of Belshazzar, and hence it is placed first in the sequence. The following chart should clarify the chronological confusion:

Chronology of the Visions in Daniel 7–12

Chapter 7	Chapter 8	Chapter 9	Chapters 10–12
1st Vision	2nd Vision	3rd Vision	4th Vision
First Year of Belshazzar	Third Year of Belshazzar	First Year of Darius	Third Year of Cyrus
553 BC	550 BC	539–538 BC	536–535 BC

As a hinge chapter to the book, chap. 7 is also related to the preceding chapters. In fact, Lenglet has demonstrated that chaps. 2–7 are carefully arranged in a concentric structure such that chap. 7 parallels chap. 2.[649] The similarities between these two chapters are rather obvious: (1) both chapters portray a sweep of successive Gentile powers in four stages beginning with the kingdom of Babylon; (2) both culminate in Gentile powers being replaced by the kingdom of God which triumphs over them; and, (3) both chapters elaborate more on the fourth kingdom than the first three. In spite of these parallels, however, Campbell (106) points out that there is a difference of perspective between these chapters:

> The vision of chapter 2 was seen by a pagan king and therefore portrayed history as man would view it, each empire having at least some intrinsic value. The vision of chapter 7, however, was given to a man of God, and to him God reveals the nations of history as they really are inwardly. They are portrayed as God sees them—wild, ferocious beasts, continually fighting and devouring one another.

As in chap. 2, the main focus of chap. 7 falls on the fourth kingdom in the series. Yet chap. 7 adds crucial details in regard to the fourth kingdom not found in chap. 2. For instance, chap. 7 provides revelation about the "little horn" that arises out of the fourth kingdom and his persecution of the saints of God. Furthermore, although both chap. 2 and chap. 7 portray the series of kingdoms being ultimately replaced by the kingdom of heaven, it is

648. J. J. Collins, *The Apocalyptic Vision of the Book of Daniel* (Ann Arbor, MI: Scholars Press, 1977), 15.
649. A. Lenglet, "La structure littéraire de Daniel 2–7," *Bib* 53 (1972): 169–90.

chap. 7 that provides explicit revelation about "one like a son of man" who receives the kingdom. Chap. 7 then becomes the springboard to show how the kingdom of God will be implemented through the intercession of "one like a son of man," the ultimate victory over the final earthly opponent to God's rule (the little horn), and the righteous saints resurrected and rewarded in the kingdom of God. Though interpreting the details differently, Rabbe concurs with this strategic role that Dan 7 plays in the book's structure:

> The final judgment comes when the "little horn" meets his end after persecuting Israel (11:45–12:1). Daniel's people, "all who are found written in the book" (12.1), are delivered. The resurrection takes place with some receiving "everlasting life" and others receiving "everlasting contempt" (12.2). It is clear that this two-fold division of people is the result of the judgment depicted in chapter 7, since the "book(s)" of judgment is only mentioned in 7:10 and 12:1. Also, only in 7:25 and 12:7 do we find the phrase "a time, (two) times, and a half a time" (*ʿiddān weʿiddānîn ûpelag ʿiddān*, 7:25; *môʿēd môʿădîm wāḥēṣî*, 12:7).
>
> Therefore, Daniel 7 serves as a pivot or hinge in the book's present structure. It recalls the kingdoms of chapter 2 and concludes the Aramaic section of 2–7. It stresses the final judgment and thus anticipates chapter 12.[650]

Most scholars agree that the vision of beasts in chap. 7 was intended to portray successive kingdoms, yet they differ on the identification of the kingdoms in view.[651] In general, critical scholars interpret the four beasts as Babylon, Media, Persia, and Greece, with the little horn representing Antiochus IV Epiphanes of the second century BC.[652] Even Goldingay (157) has adopted this position, denying that Daniel himself received this vision as predictive prophecy:

---

650. P. R. Raabe, "Daniel 7: Its Structure and Role in the Book," *HAR* 9 (1985): 273.

651. K. Hanhart, "The Four Beasts of Daniel's Vision in the Night in the Light of Rev. 13.2," *NTS* 27 (1980–1981): 582–83, is an exception. He holds that the vision in Dan 7 is *not* parallel to the image in Dan 2, but rather that the four beasts of Dan 7 represent contemporaneous powers operative at the time of Antiochus IV. For him, the lion represents Egypt, the bear Persia, the leopard Rome, and the anonymous beast Syria (under the imagery of a trampling war elephant commonly utilized by Syria).

652. In contrast to the vast majority of critical scholarship, R. J. Korner, "The 'Exilic' Prophecy of Daniel 7: Does It Reflect Late Pre-Maccabean or Early Hellenistic Historiography?" in *Prophets, Prophecy, and Ancient Israelite Historiography*, ed. M. J. Boda and L. M. W. Beal, 333–53 (Winona Lake, IN: Eisenbrauns, 2013), has argued that the "little horn" of chap. 7 is to be equated with Ptolemy I Soter (323–282 BC) rather than Antiochus IV, and that Dan 7 functions as a symbolic history of Judean events in the early Hellenistic period.

> Dan 7 presents itself as a dream experienced by Daniel c. 550 B.C., ... it is more likely a quasi-predictive vision deriving from the period on which it focuses and to which it is especially relevant (that of the king symbolized by the small horn) than an actual predictive vision from the sixth century. It thus presupposes actions by Antiochus IV against Jerusalem such as 1 Macc 1:29–40, ... Its date is thus mid-167 B.C.

A major problem, however, for critical scholars who attempt to interpret Daniel 7 in light of Antiochus IV Epiphanes and the Maccabean uprising is that Antiochus' defeat did not result in a realization of the promised kingdom of God. Hence, Walker (who adheres to the Antiochene thesis) is forced to confess "that this author was mistaken in his expectations for the future."[653]

Evangelicals, on the other hand, generally take the beasts to represent Babylon, Medo-Persia, Greece, and Rome, with the little horn representing the future antichrist.[654] Still others prefer to refrain from identifying specific kingdoms. Longman (190), for example, counsels,

> The best way to view the imagery of Daniel 7 is not in terms of four specific evil empires, but as four kingdoms symbolically representing the fact that evil kingdoms (of an unspecified number)

653. W. O. Walker, "Daniel 7:13–14," *Int* 39 (1985), 179. Elsewhere he acknowledges, "Even at its best, the Maccabean state could not be regarded as the true kingdom of 'the saints of the Most High,' and it could be argued that the eventual situation of the Jews in Palestine became worse than it had been under the Seleucids" (181).

654. There are exceptions, of course, among evangelicals. R. Gurney, "The Four Kingdoms of Daniel 2 and 7," *Them* 2 (1977): 39–45, holds that the four kingdoms are Babylon, Media, Medo-Persia, and Greece. He differs from critical scholars, however, in holding to a sixth century BC date for the book. Gurney is forced to take the position that Media is contemporaneous with the Babylonian Empire, and he has no good argument for identifying the ten horns. J. Walton, "Daniel's Four Kingdoms," *JETS* 29 (1986): 36, holds to the same four kingdoms as Gurney but attempts to explain the ten horns as follows: "The ten horns of the fourth empire would be the ten independent states that had arisen from Alexander's empire by the last quarter of the third century BC. The little horn would represent the Seleucid overlords of Palestine, dating from the reign of Antiochus the Great and continuing during the time of Antiochus Epiphanes. The three displaced horns would represent the conquests of Antiochus the Great." The scheme suggested by Gurney and Walton faces several problems, not the least of which is that the ram and goat in chap. 8 (with the horn of the goat replaced by four horns) are parallel to the second and third creatures of chap. 7. Yet the ram is interpreted in the text (8:20) as "the kings of Media and Persia" (one entity). Furthermore, the "ten horns" suggested by Walton (independent states that he lists on p. 32) do not satisfy the textual detail of 7:24 of being "ten kings," not to mention that Rev 17 interprets them as ten contemporaneous kings in the future Great Tribulation.

> will succeed one another from the time of the Exile to the time of the climax of history, when God will intervene and once and for all judge all evil and bring into existence his kingdom.[655]

This author holds to the general evangelical view for reasons that will be presented in the commentary to follow.

Numerous attempts have been made to attribute the symbolic imagery of Dan 7 with borrowing from mythological literature of the ancient Near East.[656] Hill (134) points out, "The picture of 'beasts rising out of the sea' is typically connected with the Babylonian creation myth, *Enuma Elish*, in which the gods bring order out of chaos ..., or the Canaanite mythology that pits Baal against Yam. ... Likewise the background for the imagery of the throne scene in the vision has been tied to the Baal cycle of Ugaritic mythology."[657] However, there is no need to go to such extreme speculation

---

655. Longman's view is unconvincing. The parallel account in Dan 2 clearly indicated that Babylon and successive kingdoms to it were in view, a situation likewise demanded by 7:15 ("These great beasts ... are four kings who will arise from the earth"—and *kingdoms*, as 7:23 substantiates). Furthermore, Dan 8 builds on the vision of chap. 7 by clearly identifying two of these (8:20–22).

656. A typical example would be G. R. Beasley-Murray, "The Interpretation of Daniel 7," *CBQ* 45 (1983): 44–58. For a survey of how the motifs and imagery in Dan 7:2–14 have been understood (and the sources lying behind them), see J. Eggler, *Influences and Traditions Underlying the Vision of Daniel 7:2–14: The Research History from the End of the 19th Century to the Present* (Fribourg, Germany: University Press; Göttingen: Vandenhoeck & Ruprecht, 2000). H. Kvanvig, *Roots of Apocalyptic: The Mesopotamian Background of the Enoch Figure and of the Son of Man* (Neukirchen-Vluyn, Germany : Neukirchener, 1988), tries to argue that the background imagery for Dan 7 was to be found in the seventh-century BC Mesopotamian work, "Vision of the Underworld," rather than the Babylonian creation myth, *Enuma Elish*, but Kvanvig's theory has been debunked by J. J. Collins, "Stirring up the Great Sea; the Religio-Historical Background of Daniel 7," in *The Book of Daniel in the Light of New Findings*, ed. A. S. Van der Woude, 121–36, BETL 106 (Louvain: Leuven University Press, 1993), who argues in favor of Canaanite myths (namely fourteenth-century BC Ugaritic texts) as the more likely background source material.

657. J. H. Walton, "The Anzu Myth as Relevant Background for Daniel 7?" in *The Book of Daniel: Composition and Reception*, ed. J. J. Collins and P. W. Flint, 1:69–89 (Leiden: Brill, 2000), has conducted a comparative study of Dan 7 with three representative exemplars from ANE literature, namely *Baal and Yamm*, *Enuma Elish*, and the *Anzu* myth. He concluded (85) that Daniel was written in the chaos and conflict genre but that Dan 7 is not highly dependent upon any one of these in particular but rather draws upon the genre in general in developing its own unique production. According to Walton (88), Dan 7 "ought to be recognized as an informed and articulate literary mosaic whose author has assimilated and mastered a wide spectrum of literary traditions in order to transform them to his own theological

(especially when verification is virtually impossible), given that symbolic dreams are not unusual in the Bible (for example, Joseph's dreams in Genesis). In addition, Goldingay (152–53) wisely cautions, "Tracing the development of ideas and motifs that appear in a text does not in itself explain their significance there, ... the sea and the animals stand here not for otherworldly cosmic or cosmogonic chaos forces, but for historical ones."[658]

---

will and purpose." Yet the fact that the beasts of Dan 7 arise from the sea hardly amounts to an equivalent motif with the mythological accounts, and Walton has failed to substantiate—despite the author's use of hybrid creatures commonly seen in the Assyrian-Persian world—that the author was consciously recasting these pagan myths for his own purposes. The beasts in Dan 7 have a much different purpose as representing successive kingdoms. Furthermore, several of Walton's conclusions are highly questionable (e.g., he follows J. Day in equating the champion figure—"one like a son of man"—with Michael, 80).

For a helpful discussion of intertextuality (i.e., Daniel drawing upon ANE literary source materials) and chaos and conflict genre, see C. Barnes, "The Surprising Ascension of the Son of Man," (paper presented at national conference of ETS, Atlanta, Nov. 18, 2015). Though he argues that Daniel has drawn upon such source material (*Enuma Elish* being the more likely candidate), he is careful to point out important contrasts, especially in regard to the "son of man" (21): "While the one like the son of man stands in the place of the typical hero from chaos and conflict genre, the one like the son of man does not do battle with the small horn, nor any of the beasts. This is, perhaps, the greatest point of intentional conflict between Dan 7 and chaos and conflict literature. The one like the son of man possesses few of the characteristics of the stereotypical heroes of chaos and conflict genre. Instead of a lengthy epithet chronicling superior strength and non-human characteristics the champion of Daniel's vision is human in appearance. His victory is not won through superhuman strength, as with Marduk, nor is his victory based on cunning or divine instruments, as with Ninurta and Baʿal. Instead, the one like the son of man inherits the effortless victory which flows from the sovereign judgment of the Ancient of Days."

More on intertextuality regarding Daniel (and especially in relation to Isaiah) can be found in G. B. Lester, *Daniel Evokes Isaiah: Allusive Characterization of Foreign Rule in the Hebrew-Aramaic Book of Daniel*, LHBOTS 606 (London: Bloomsbury T&T Clark, 2015); and A. Chou, *I Saw the Lord: A Biblical Theology of Vision* (Eugene, OR: Wipf & Stock, 2013).

658. Even a critical scholar of the stature of Hartmann cautions against imposing a reliance of the author on ANE mythological literature (212): "... there is no need here to look for any direct borrowing from ancient mythological literature, such as the Babylonian epic *Enuma Elish*. Our author could easily have derived his idea of monsters coming up out of the sea from the Bible, which knows of such sea monsters of Canaanite mythology. ... But essentially the four monstrous beasts of Dan 7:3–7 are *ad hoc* creations of the author, who gives them the characteristics that make them 'each different from the others' for the purpose of symbolizing the four

E. C. Lucas, after a survey and evaluation of various proposals for the imagery (including Babylonian, Canaanite, Ugaritic, birth omens—e.g., *Shumma Izbu*—and astrological ideas), concluded that the imagery of Dan 7 (and Dan 8) more likely had its essential background in the OT itself. He states,

> The use of this animal imagery, and in particular its rather bizarre nature, may well be a result of the author's acquaintance with Mesopotamian *Mischwesen* and birth-omens. In our view this is only a secondary influence. Overall, we would agree with Day's conclusion that, "the fundamental basis for the four types of beast is drawn from Hos. 13:7–8, with some influence from ancient near-eastern *Mischwesen*."[659]

Though Lucas concluded that the OT itself best accounts for the background of Dan 7–8, he did, however, allow for a relevant contribution of Mesopotamian influence:

> ... we have also argued that there is evidence of Mesopotamian influence in the visions. The phrase 'the four winds of heaven' and the imagery of the beasts arising out of the turbulent sea in Daniel 7:2f. suggests influence from *Enūma Eliš*. We see here a polemical allusion to the Babylonian New Year ceremony and its mythology.[660]

Finally, a comment about the structure of the chapter is appropriate. The chapter divides into two major sections, the first (vv. 1–14) outlining the visions seen by Daniel, and the second (vv. 15–28) providing selected interpretation of details. This can be depicted by the following diagram:

Visions		**Interpretation**	
The Beasts vv. 1–8	Judgment Before the Ancient of Days vv. 9–14	General vv. 15–18	Specifically in Regard to the 4th Beast vv. 19–28
7 :1–14		7:15–28	

successive kingdoms of men; for, as he is told by the heavenly spirit who explains his dream-vision to him, these four beasts represent 'four kingdoms' (vs. 17)."

659. E. C. Lucas, "The Source of Daniel's Animal Imagery," *TynBul* 41 (1990): 183. *Mischwesen* is a German term for a "hybrid creature." In addition to the passage from Hos 13:7–8, Lucas points out (182) that "in the OT Nebuchadnezzar is referred to as a lion (e.g. Jer. 4:7; 49:19; 50:17) and his armies as eagles (Jer. 49:22; Ezek. 17:3)." Regarding J. Day, see *God's Conflict with the Dragon and the Sea: Echoes of a Canaanite Myth in the Old Testament* (Cambridge: Cambridge University Press, 1985), 157.

660. Lucas, "The Source of Daniel's Animal Imagery," 185.

1. The Visions given to Daniel (7:1–14)

The first half of the chapter focuses on laying out the essence of the vision that Daniel saw, first by a series of four beastly creatures depicting successive empires having dominion over Israel, and then by a judgment scene depicting the victorious outcome of God's people as the kingdom of God is entrusted to "one like a son of man."

a. Vision of the four beasts (7:1–8)

Textual Notes

1.a. Compare בֵּלְשַׁאצַּר in Dan 5:1. Both LXX^{O} and LXX$^{\theta}$ have Βαλτασαρ.

1.b-b. LXX$^{\theta}$ omits רֵאשׁ מִלִּין, and this is apparently absent in 4QDan^{b}, as there does not appear to be enough room (so Collins, 274). LXX^{O}, however, has εἰς κεφάλαια λόγων (translated in NETS as "a summary of the account"). Cf. *LSJM* (944): κεφάλαια λόγων = sum, gist of the matter (citing Pindar, *Pythia* 4.116).

2.a-a. In contrast to MT's עָנֵה דָנִיֵּאל וְאָמַר, LXX$^{\theta}$ has ἐγὼ Δανιηλ. Yet the phrase in MT is common in Aram. Daniel, thus arguing for its originality. ἐγὼ Δανιηλ is also lacking in LXX^{O} and Vg.

2.b-b. The phrase בְּחֶזְוִי עִם־לֵילְיָא is lacking in LXX$^{\theta}$ but is attested in 4QDan^{b}. Cf. v. 13.

4.a-a. In contrast to MT's "and on two feet as a man," LXX^{O} has "and on two human feet" (καὶ ἐπὶ ποδῶν ἀνθρωπίνων); similarly LXX$^{\theta}$.

5.a. Although *BHS* shows the form הֳקִמַת (rather than הֳקִימַת, the expected form for the Hupʿal perf., as in v. 4), a close look at the Leningrad codex (B19^{a}) reveals that the text has הֳקִימַת with the י partially rubbed out. Goldingay's comment (144) that L's reading is "apparently another mixed form" stands corrected.

6.a. The Kethib reading has the plural form, גַּבַּיהּ, whereas the Qere is singular, גַּבַּהּ. The word in question is גַּב (*gab̲*), which can mean either "back" or "side." The plural form would tend support the translation "sides." However, Goldingay (144) points out that the plural form can sometimes be "defectively" written, as in the case of the Qere reading שִׁנַּהּ in v. 5 ("teeth") rather than the Kethib form, שִׁנַּיהּ. Hence, the Qere form גַּבַּהּ could still mean "sides."

7.a. The Kethib reading has the plural form, בְּרַגְלַיהּ, "with its feet." The Qere, on the other hand, has the singular form, בְּרַגְלַהּ, "with its foot." Both LXX^{O} and LXX$^{\theta}$ have a plural form.

8.a. There is a Kethib-Qere reading for both בֵּינֵיהוֹן and אֶתְעֲקַרוּ in v. 8. In both cases the option is between a masc. form and a fem. form. The root issue is what gender to ascribe to the word for "horn" (קֶרֶן), to which they refer. Although both BDB (1111) and *HALOT* (1973) indicate this to be a fem. noun, some regard this as "common" (either masc. or fem.). However, notice the adjective קַדְמָיָתָא following מִן־קַדְמַיָּא in v. 8. קַדְמָיָתָא, modifying קֶרֶן is fem. Therefore, the Qere readings should be accepted (בֵּינֵיהֵן and אֶתְעֲקַרָה respectfully).

Translation

7:1 In the first year of Belshazzar king of Babylon, Daniel beheld[661] a dream and[662] *had* visions in his mind[663] *while* on his bed. Then he wrote down the dream *in which* he related the gist of the matter.[664] **2** Daniel said,[665] "I was observing in my vision during[666] the night, and behold, the four winds of heaven[667] were stirring[668] up the great sea. **3** Then four great beasts, different from one another, were coming up from the sea. **4** The first one was like a lion but had wings of an eagle. I continued observing until its wings were

661. Lit., the Aram. reads "he envisioned *in* a dream" (Aram. חֲזָה, *ḥăzâ*, "to see, behold" by vision).

662. Goldingay (143) suggests we have *waw explicative* with וְחֶזְוֵי, *wᵊḥezwê* ("had a dream, a vision which ...").

663. Lit., "visions of his head" (וְחֶזְוֵי רֵאשֵׁהּ, *wᵊḥezwê rēʾšēh*).

664. The translation "the gist of the matter" is an attempt to render the notoriously difficult phrase רֵאשׁ מִלִּין (*rēʾš millîn*, lit., "head of words"). Several commentators have observed that *rēʾš millîn* in v. 1 is balanced by *sôpāʾ dî millᵊtāʾ* in v. 28 ("the end of the word/matter"), as though these similar phrases seem to open and close the account. Thus, Goldingay (142) translates *rēʾš millîn* "the beginning of the account" (similarly Hartman, 205, and Montgomery, 283–84). Yet the phrases are not precisely parallel (the first lacks *dî*, with *millîn* being plural). Turning to the translations, LXX^{θ} omits the phrase, while LXX^{O} renders this εἰς κεφάλαια λόγων (*eis kephalaia logōn*). Although the Greek literally translates "into heads of words," LSJM (944) notes that κεφάλαια λόγων together can mean "sum, gist of the matter" (citing Pi. *P* 4.116). Hence, the NET translation, "in summary fashion."

665. Lit., the Aram. is "answered and said."

666. The word "during" is a translation of the preposition עִם (*ʿim*), which normally is translated "with." Yet a temporal nuance is occasionally found, as in Ps 72:5 ("while the sun"). Cf. Dan 3:33 and 4:31 [Aram.].

667. The NET prefers the translation "sky" rather than the more commonly used "heavens." Aram. *šᵊmayin* (like Heb. *šāmayim*) can mean either "sky" or "heavens."

668. The words "stirring up" translate the Hapʿel ptc. מְגִיחָן (*mᵊgîḥān*, verbal root *gûaḥ*). The LXX^{θ} seems to prefer the intransitive meaning "to break forth" in light of their translation by the Greek verb *prosballō* ("to strike, dash against"; LSJM, 1504). However, *HALOT* (1843), in agreement with most modern translations, prefers the transitive meaning for *gûaḥ* of "churn up, stir up" (cf. Goldingay, 144).

plucked off. Then[669] it was lifted up from the ground, was made to stand on two feet as a man, and was given the mind[670] of a man. **5** Then behold,[671] another beast (a second one) appeared, resembling a bear. It was reclining[672] on one side, and three ribs[673] were in its mouth between its teeth. It was told,[674] 'Arise, devour much meat!' **6** After this, I continued observing, and behold, another one, like a leopard, and on its back[675] it had four wings of

---

669. It seems preferable to translate the conjunction *waw* as "then" and to make this a separate sentence. The "pulling off" (from מְרַט, *mᵊraṭ*, "to tear off, pluck off") looks at the divine judgment imposed upon Nebuchadnezzar, whereas the "lifting up" and being "made to stand" portray God's grace in restoring him. This makes a better transition from judgment to restoration.
670. Lit., "heart of a man." Aram. לְבַב (*lᵊḇaḇ*), normally rendered "heart," can also mean "mind," and the latter is emphasized in this context.
671. Lit., "and behold" (but in light of the transition, "then behold" is more appropriate).
672. Translators struggle with how best to translate the verb הֳקִמַת (*hŏqimaṯ*), Hupʿal perf. of *qûm*, whose root meaning is to "arise, stand" and in the Hupʿal "made to stand." Hartman (205), for example, translates "It raised one end upright" and comments, "It seems more natural to understand this of an animal standing only on its hind legs, a position which a bear often assumes, rather than to understand it of an animal raising its two right legs or its two left legs." Goldingay (144) admits this is doubtful. Rather than "standing," the imagery is rather of a bear that is reclining on one side. *HALOT* (1969) indicates that the Hupʿal means "to be set up." Hence, the position of "standing" is not the point. The bear is "set up" on one side, and the best way to capture the imagery in translation is to say that it was "reclining on one side."
673. Hartman (205) vainly tries to argue for the translation "tusks" instead of "ribs" for Aram. עִלְעִין (*ʿilʿîn*). He writes, "R. Frank (*CBQ* 21 [1959], 505*f*) has shown that Arabic *ḍalaʿ*, 'rib,' is used at times metaphorically of a 'tusk' or large tooth." Yet his case is seriously weak. First, the meaning "ribs" is the commonly accepted meaning of Aram. *ʿilʿîn*, and that meaning is perfectly acceptable in this context. (That is a much stronger argument than relying on an Arabic derived meaning.) Second, Hartman opts for this supposed metaphorical meaning "tusks" simply on the basis that he sees no good reason why three ribs would be in the mouth of the bear. Yet this rationale fails, for if "eating" depicts military conquest in the symbolism, then ribs in its mouth would quite logically look at conquered enemies (i.e., they have already been devoured).
674. Lit., "and thus they were saying to it."
675. The noun גַּב (*gaḇ*) can mean "back" or "side." Most Eng translations opt for "back," but *HALOT* (1841) suggests "sides." The Kethib reading גַּבַּיַּהּ (*gabbayyah*) is plural, which would favor "sides." However, the Qere reading גַּבַּהּ (*gabbah*) is singular, favoring "back." Furthermore, the LXX$^{\theta}$ translation ὑπεράνω αὐτῆς, *huperanō autēs* ("above it") would correspond better to the "back" than "sides" (similarly, LXX^{O}'s ἐπάνω αὐτοῦ, *epanō autou*).

a bird.[676] Also the beast had four heads, and it was given dominion. **7** After this, I continued observing in the night visions, and behold, a fourth beast … dreadful, terrifying,[677] and exceedingly strong. It had large iron teeth[678] *with which it* devoured and crushed, and the rest it trampled with its feet. It was different from all the beasts that *were* before it, and it had ten horns. **8** While I was contemplating the horns, behold, another horn—a little one—came up among them, and three of the former horns were uprooted[679] from it.[680] And behold, on this horn *were* eyes like the eyes of a man and a mouth speaking boastfully."[681]

Commentary

7:1–3 *Introduction to the first vision.* The vision given to Daniel in chap. 7 is dated to the first year of King Belshazzar. Although Belshazzar's historicity was questioned by earlier scholars, the discovery of documents about Nabonidus has confirmed that Belshazzar was his first-born son (see commentary at Dan 5:1 for evidence). Furthermore, the so-called Verse Account of Nabonidus (first made available in 1924) provided firm evidence that Nabonidus appointed Belshazzar as his co-regent. This document states:

> … when the third year was about to begin—he [Nabonidus] entrusted the "Camp" to his oldest (son), the first-born [Belshazzar], the troops everywhere in the country he ordered

676. Or "bird-like wings" (so NET).

677. Although אֵימְתָן (*ʾêmᵊṯān*) means "terrible" (so BDB, 1080a; *HALOT*, 1811), the translation "terrifying" is more to the point (so RJ, 140). Cf. the use of this adjective in *Tg. Hab* 1:7 ("dreaded").

678. The NET has "two large rows of iron teeth," based on the pointing of the word "teeth" (שִׁנַּיִן, *šinnayin*), the *dual* number (rather than pl.). However, Rosenthal (24) concedes, "In such nouns, the dual may be used for the pl.," as we have in the case of *qarnayin ʿăśar* ("ten horns") in Dan 7:7. Furthermore, the fem. pl. form *šinnayyah* in Dan 7:19 favors the simpler *plural* rendering "large iron teeth" in v. 7.

679. The Hitpeʿel verb form אֶתְעֲקַרָה (*ʾeṯʿăqarâ*; Qere reading), from the root עֲקַר (*ʿăqar*) means "be rooted up" (BDB, 1107d) or "be plucked out" (*HALOT*, 1953). It is equivalent to Heb. עָקַר (*ʿāqar*). The latter is used in Zeph 2:4 in the sense of militaristic conquest.

680. The NET translation of מִן־קֳדָמַיַהּ (*min-qŏḏāmayah*) is "to make room for it." Although *qŏdām* itself means "before," in this type of construction with the prep *min*, it can simply mean "from it." Note similar constructions in Dan 2:6 and 2:15. Hence, the idea is that "three former horns were uprooted from it" (the translation "make room" obscures the point—as though more room were needed for the "small horn").

681. Lit., "speaking great (things)." Although Goldingay (145) does not see this description as "unequivocally negative" (and thus opts for the translation "making great statements"), the context favors the understanding that the little horn utters "great boasts" (notice a similar thought in v. 11, which contributes to his judgment and destruction).

> under his (command). He let (everything) go, entrusted the kingship to him and, himself, he started out for a long journey.[682]

Since Nabonidus began to rule in 556 BC, the reference to his "third year" would thus be about 553 BC. This would apparently be the "first year of Belshazzar" mentioned in Dan 7:1. God may have chosen the outset of wicked Belshazzar's reign to grant the vision to Daniel, since it would be at the end of his reign that the predicted judgment upon Babylon would fall, and the Medo-Persian Empire would take its place.

The visions appeared to Daniel at night in his dreams. Hill (147) points out, "In the OT the word 'vision' (Heb. *ḥāzôn*; GK 2606) is associated with receiving revelation from God (e.g., Isa 1:1; Na 1:1)." This was not merely a dream, but one in which God controlled the content in such a way as to reveal his truth to Daniel. According to v. 2, he saw the four winds of the heaven (or sky) stirring up the great sea. As in Dan 8:8, the four winds of heaven represent the various points of the compass, and thus the agitation of the sea seems to come from all directions.[683] The word translated "winds" (רוּחֵי, *rûḥê*), however, can also mean "spirits." Although the imagery is indeed of four winds, the flexibility of the term itself indicates that angelic beings are behind this agitation of the sea (cf. the use of *rûḥôṯ* in Zech 6:5). Since "the great sea" is often used in the OT to refer to the Mediterranean Sea in particular, some have suggested that meaning here (so Archer, 85; and Goldingay, 160).[684] If this is the point, the Mediterranean's proximity to Israel would suggest that the troubled waters are impacting the covenant nation.[685]

---

682. Pritchard, *ANET*, 313.

683. Cf. Dan 11:4; Jer 49:36; Ezek 37:9; and Zech 2:6.

684 Aram. *yammā ʾ rabbā ʾ* is equivalent to Heb. *hayyāmmâ haggāḏôl*, which refers to the Mediterranean in such passages as Num 34:6; Josh 15:12; and 1QapGen 21:16. P. M. Casey, *The Solution to the Son of Man Problem*, LNTS 343 (London: T&T Clark, 2007), 82, has defended the Mediterranean interpretation, and his arguments are summarized by A. Angel, "Short Note: The Sea in 4Q541 7.3 and in Daniel 7:2," *VT* 60 (2010): 475: "First, the Mediterranean was the largest sea with which the Jews were acquainted and so it was natural for them to call it the great sea. Second, the OT uses the equivalent Hebrew phrase הים הגדול (the great sea) to refer to the Mediterranean and an Aramaic text contemporary to Daniel (lQapGen 21.16) uses the phrase ימא רבא to refer to the Mediterranean. Thus 'the great sea' is to be identified with the Mediterranean and not the chaos sea." Angel, however, argues against this on the basis of a reading in 4Q541 7.3 ("and the great sea will be silenced"), which he identifies as the mythological chaos sea. Yet Angel fails to see that other Qumran texts do equate "the great sea" with the Mediterranean, and thus to cite 4Q541 7.3 alone is insufficient to prove his case.

685. H. Macumber, "A Monster without a Name: Creating the Beast Known as Antiochus IV in Daniel 7," *JHebScr* 15 (2015): 18, objects: "Although this term might be interpreted as the Mediterranean Sea, this is unlikely since three of the four

In any case, the agitation of the sea reflects the turmoil going on among the nations (cf. Isa 17:12–13; Jer 46:7–8). Taken together, the imagery suggests God's providential action through angelic beings of arousing the chaotic nations of the world in such a way to impact the covenant nation of Israel (cf. Rev 7:1; 9:14–15). This is appropriate, since the vision goes on to depict the Gentile powers that have dominion over Israel (and afflict her) during her time of chastisement by God.

Four beasts are said to arise from this "sea." In Dan 7:17, however, they are said to arise "from the earth." These statements are not in conflict, since the sea merely depicts the chaotic scene from which these Gentile nations arise. The truth is that they are *earthly* empires. Lacocque (whose view of Dan 7 at this point relies on Canaanite mythology) goes too far in seeing an intentional allusion of the chaotic waters of the sea in Dan 7 to the waters of Gen 1:2:

> There is doubtlessly an intertextual relationship between Dan 7:1ff. and Gen 1:2, which evokes an ominous watery and dark abyss from which, one can surmise, only terrible monsters can emerge. The Danielic scene describes the ultimate victory over the last enemy and the inauguration of the "new" creation (that is, a creation at last freed from the threat of chaos).[686]

The link with Gen 1:2 is not convincing, and, furthermore, there is little evidence that the creation account in Gen 1 refers to a conquest of chaos.[687]

The bizarre nature of these "beasts" is quite startling upon first consideration to the Western mind. In the Ancient Near East, however, people were very accustomed to seeing hybrid creatures in their artwork and religious symbolism. Thus, any distortion of appearance would not have seemed so strange, and it would have been immediately perceived as due to intended symbolism.

7:4 *First beast: Like a lion.* The first beast is said to be "like a lion" and yet have the wings of an eagle. According to vv. 17, 23, each beast represents a king and kingdom, and virtually all scholars agree that this first beast symbolizes the Neo-Babylonian Empire. In light of the parallelism with the image of chap. 2, we would expect this. Just as the image in chap. 2 had a head of gold (which depicted the grandeur of its majesty), so the first beast is symbolized by the king of beasts (the lion) and the king of birds (the eagle). Furthermore,

---

kingdom [*sic*] associated with the beasts are not located near it." Yet this overlooks the fact that the issue is the sea's proximity to Israel, not the origin of the beasts.

686. A. Lacocque, "Allusions to Creation in Daniel 7," in *The Book of Daniel: Composition & Reception*, VTSup 83:2, ed. J. J. Collins and P. W. Flint, 114–31 (Leiden: Brill, 2001), 128.

687. Cf. David Tsumura, *Creation and Destruction: A Reappraisal of the Chaoskampf Theory in the Old Testament*, rev. ed. (Winona Lake, IN: Eisenbrauns, 2005).

Babylon has been symbolized elsewhere in the OT as a lion (Jer 4:7; cf. 49:19, 22; 50:17, 44), as well as being compared to an eagle (Ezek 17:2–3, 12; cf. Deut 28:49; Jer 48:40; 49:22; Hab 1:8). Finally, Babylon was famous for its processional way (after entering the Ishtar Gate) that was ornamented with some 120 lions in glazed-brick relief (the lions were symbols of Ishtar).

Despite Babylon's initial grandeur and majesty, Dan 7:4 says that its "wings were plucked off." The wings depict the greatness of the kingdom—that which elicited the pride of the all-powerful kingdom—and particularly as manifested in the life of her great king, Nebuchadnezzar. His military conquests and architectural achievements brought him fame beyond all others of his day. The plucking of the wings would then refer to the humbling of Nebuchadnezzar in chap. 4 by the sovereign hand of God. (This could not be Babylon's defeat by Medo-Persia because the same verse also speaks of the "lifting up" that followed the plucking.)

Once God had humbled Nebuchadnezzar, however, he was "lifted up from the ground" and "made to stand on two feet like a human being and a human mind was given to it." This depicts the king's restoration, once he recognized that heaven rules (see especially 4:34). He went from being an animal-like being to human-like. That is, he rightly saw himself as just a mere man, and he saw that it was God's kingdom that really mattered (and endured forever), not his own.

7:5 *Second beast: Like a bear*. God allowed the Babylonian Empire to be ruled by several kings following Nebuchadnezzar, until finally she was conquered in 539 BC by the combined forces of the Medes and Persians. Hence, evangelicals are almost unanimous in interpreting the bear as Medo-Persia. Critical scholars, on the other hand, consistently deny this interpretation, preferring to interpret the second beast as only Media, with the third beast representing Persia. Nevertheless, the evidence overwhelmingly favors the Medo-Persian view. Consider the following points:

(1) Daniel 5:28 predicted that Babylon would be replaced by the Medes and the Persians, not merely the Medes.
(2) Chapter 6 with its reference to the "law of the Medes and Persians" (6:8, 12, 15) views these two peoples as forming *one* empire.
(3) In chap. 8 (see vv. 3, 20) Media and Persia are viewed as *one power* under the figure of a two-horned ram.
(4) In chap. 8 the kingdom that follows Medo-Persia is Greece (represented by a male goat). The four horns of this goat (Greece) in chap. 8 parallel the four heads of the third beast in chap. 7, thus confirming that the latter represents Greece, not Persia.
(5) The interpretation of the critical scholars leaves Rome out of the picture (as this would be to admit predictive prophecy), but they still face the dilemma of the clear reference to Rome in Dan 9:26 (the people who destroy "the city," Jerusalem, in AD 70).

(6) The fact that Darius is said to be a Mede in Dan 5:31 indicates his race; it does not establish that the empire that follows Babylon was Media (alone). As pointed out elsewhere, the Medes and the Persians had combined their armies in several military endeavors prior to and including that of 539 BC.

(7) The details of chap. 7 do not favor the interpretation of critical scholars:

  (a) The fact that the third beast is a leopard (7:6) implies swiftness, and this characterizes the campaign of Alexander the Great more than Persia.

  (b) The ten horns connected with the fourth beast are difficult to reconcile with the political leaders following Alexander or with the Seleucid dynasty.

One could debate the rationale for depicting Medo-Persia as a bear. (Technically, the second beast is not a bear but is said to "resemble a bear.") Although the figure of a bear could stress its *ferociousness* and *power*, more likely the figure is meant to highlight its *appetite* in light of the remaining details in v. 5.[688] The Persian Empire could never be content with its huge domain, and its appetite for conquest led her into repeated conflict with Greece. Hence, the "three ribs in its mouth" probably are meant to signify three crucial conquests that helped solidify the power of the Medo-Persian kingdom.[689] Their identity is not stated, but a reasonable suggestion would be (1) Lydia (in western Asia Minor) in 546 BC, Babylon in 539 BC, and Egypt (by Cambyses) in 525 BC.[690] Finally, the bear-like beast is told to "Arise; devour much meat" (v. 5).

7:6 *Third beast: Like a leopard.* In contrast to Babylon, the Medo-Persian Empire lasted much longer, just over 200 years. The third beast represents the

---

688. Walvoord, 192, remarks that this second empire was "powerful like a bear, ferocious (Is 13:17–18), but less majestic, less swift, and less glorious."

689. Most commentators view the three ribs as three conquests, but other suggestions have been made as to their identity. Walvoord, *Prophecy Knowledge Handbook*, 231, suggests that this "probably referred to the three provinces of Babylonia, Persia, and Media" which were reduced to a single realm, as had Jerome many centuries ago. Pentecost, "Daniel," 1350, mentions another possibility: the preceding kingdoms of Egypt, Assyria, and Babylon. Less likely is the suggestion of Hartman (212), who asserts they symbolize three Babylonian kings known to the author: Nebuchadnezzar, Evil-Merodach, and Belshazzar. Two of these were never affected by Medo-Persia.

690. The inclusion of Lydia in the three conquests is not insignificant. Lydia at that time controlled western Asia Minor (including significant cities like Ephesus and Sardis), had abundant gold reserves, and formed a natural buffer with the Greek and Macedonian realms—a strategic position militarily to the Medes and Persians.

Grecian empire founded by Alexander the Great and the Hellenistic kingdoms that resulted from the breakup of his empire. The animosity between Greece and Persia had been fomenting for many years. As early as the reign of Darius the Great (522–486 BC), trouble between the two erupted. The cities of Ionia (present-day western Turkey) revolted against Persia, and this was thought to be at the encouragement and participation of the Athenians. This in turn led to Persian expeditions against Greece in 492 BC and again in 490. The latter resulted in the famous Battle of Marathon in the fall of 490 BC, in which a much smaller Athenian army routed the Persian forces. Following Darius' death in 486 BC, his son Xerxes (the biblical Ahasuerus) came to the throne (r. 485–465 BC). In the early fall of 480 BC, Xerxes brought a huge army and naval force against Greece to avenge the humiliation suffered earlier at Marathon. Although the invasion brought extensive suffering and misery to Greece, it was not a Persian victory at all.[691] Xerxes' great navy was smashed before his very eyes at Salamis (to the west of Athens). His army, on the other hand, was nearly blocked by the Spartans at the pass of Thermopylae and was defeated in 479 BC at Plataea, northwest of Athens. Xerxes was able to keep his army intact, but he returned home without the victory he set out to achieve. As a result of these hostilities, the Greeks never forgave the Persians. This long-standing animosity helped provoke Alexander the Great to invade Persia many years later.

The third beast in Dan 7:6 is not only likened unto a leopard but is said to have on its back "four wings like a bird." This emphatically underscores the *tremendous speed* by which Alexander carried out his conquest of the Persian Empire. In 336 BC at the mere age of twenty, he took the throne of Macedon. In 334 BC he set out to conquer Persia. Following an initial defeat of the Persian army at the Battle of Issus in 333 BC, Alexander was able to advance southward and lay claim to Egypt. By 331 BC he achieved a decisive victory over the Persians at the Battle of Arbela. In the aftermath, he burned Persepolis in retaliation for the Persians having burned Athens in 480 BC. In three to four years he had conquered all of Persia, an empire that had taken centuries to build.

The third beast is also said to have had four heads, which looks at the division of Alexander's kingdom into four parts following his untimely death. Despite his incredible achievement in conquering Persia, Alexander's taste of victory was short-lived. In 323 BC, yet thirty-three years old, he died in Babylon. A long struggle ensued from 323–301 BC as to who would reign in his place. During this time his infant son was murdered, which led to a rivalry among his generals for power. Following Cassander's overthrow of Antigonus in 301 BC at the Battle of Ipsus, Alexander's kingdom was parceled out to four of his generals:

---

691. See E. M. Yamauchi, *Persia and the Bible* (Grand Rapids: Baker, 1996), 194–226, for a helpful discussion of Xerxes' invasion of Greece and an evaluation of classical sources. It is true that the Persians burned and destroyed Athens itself in 480 BC.

(1) Lysimachus: Thrace and Bithynia (much of Asia Minor)
(2) Cassander: Macedonia and Greece
(3) Seleucus: Syria, Babylonia, and the lands to the east
(4) Ptolemy: Egypt, Palestine, and Arabia Petrea

7:7–8 *Fourth beast: Dreadful with iron teeth.* Conservative evangelicals are virtually unanimous in identifying the fourth and final beast as the Roman Empire.[692] In contrast to Greece, which acquired its power rapidly under Alexander, the Roman Empire acquired dominion gradually (from about 241 BC with Rome's victory over Carthage until the height of its power in AD 117). Alexander conquered by the rapidity of his troop movements, whereas Rome conquered by the ruthless crushing of other peoples ("it devoured and crushed, and the remainder it trampled with its feet"). In 64/63 BC Pompey conquered Syria and Palestine, bringing these biblical lands into the folds of Rome.

Several important observations should be made concerning this fourth beast:

(1) The fourth kingdom is differentiated from the previous three in that it is not likened to any specific animal but is simply described as being "dreadful, terrible, and very strong" (v. 7). There is no animal fierce enough to portray this kingdom. Also, its uniqueness calls attention to the emphatic role it plays in this chapter, as Macumber points out: "the final beast stands out due to its lack of name and specific corporality that hinders one's abilities to classify and identify it."[693]
(2) The kingdom portrayed by the fourth beast comes about in successive stages. According to Dan 7:24a, the ten horns arise *after* the fourth beast. Then Dan 7:24b indicates that the "little horn" arises *after* the ten.
(3) The kingdom portrayed by the fourth beast has both a near and a remote fulfillment:
    (a) The "fourth beast proper" is the historic Roman Empire of the past (paralleling the fourth part of the image in Dan 2). Note that the element of *iron* is common to the fourth part of the image in chap. 2 and the fourth beast in chap. 7 (the latter had large iron teeth).
    (b) However, the book of Revelation makes clear that the ten horns and the "little horn" will arise in the yet distant future, being reserved for the period known as the great tribulation (Rev 13, 17, and 19; see esp. 17:12).

692. Even the consensus of Jewish opinion favors the idea of the fourth beast being Rome. Goldwurm (199) notes, "The *midrashim* consistently lists the four kingdoms as Babylon, Persia, Greece, and Rome."
693. Macumber, "A Monster without a Name," 22.

(c) Therefore, the symbolism of the fourth beast has its fulfillment over a vast expanse of time. Furthermore, there is a *gap of time* between the initial entry of the fourth beast and the final aspects represented by the ten horns and the little horn.[694]

(d) Despite the fact that the fourth beast has the additional features of the ten horns and the "little horn" (with a time gap involved), there is a strong connection between the historic Roman Empire and the eventual fulfillment in the great tribulation.

i) The text refers to this as one beast (7:3, 17).

ii) Daniel 7:24 specifically says that "ten kings will arise from that kingdom." The preposition מִן (*min*) before "that kingdom" seems to indicate the geopolitical realm as the source from which the ten kings arise. (See Dan 7:3, 17 for a similar use of the preposition: "from the sea" and "from the land.")

This suggests that the future phase of the fourth beast—that involving both the ten kings and the little horn—will arise out of the territories and/or political spheres that once constituted the ancient Roman Empire. This conclusion will be confirmed for us in Dan 9:26, where we are told: "As for the city and the sanctuary, the people of the coming prince will destroy them." Since the Romans destroyed the city of Jerusalem and its temple in AD 70, it stands to reason that "the coming prince" arises from what once constituted the Roman people. (I will argue later that the "little horn" of Dan 7 and the "coming prince" of 9:26 are one and the same.)

In his vision, Daniel was particularly drawn to consider the horns on the head of the fourth beast (v. 8). This was apparently a key factor that made this fourth beast different from the preceding three. In Scripture, a horn is seen to be symbolic of power (1 Kgs 22:11; Zech 1:18–21), particularly the power of a reigning ruler (Ps 132:17; Ezek 29:21).[695] Indeed, according to Dan 7:24, the horns are clearly symbolic of kings. Verse 8 calls attention to the "little horn" that came up among the ten horns. As he arises, three of the horns among the ten are "uprooted from it." This imagery of "uprooting" denotes violent

---

694. The idea of there being a "time gap" involved in the fulfillment of the symbol should be seriously entertained for at least three reasons: (1) in Dan 8:9 the "small horn" comes out of one of the four horns. This involves a time lapse between Seleucus I in 312–280 BC and Antiochus Epiphanes (the "small horn") in 175–164 BC; (2) a time gap is involved in the "Seventy Weeks" prophecy of Dan 9:24–27; and (3) some OT verses refer to both the first coming and second coming of Christ in one broad sweep, even though separated by nearly 2000 years (e.g., Isa 61:1–2).

695. For discussion of the metaphorical uses of the Heb. word קֶרֶן (*qeren*), translated "horn," see M. L. Brown, "קֶרֶן," *NIDOTTE*, 3:990–92.

militaristic overthrow.[696] Although the latter horn is described as "little" in v. 8, this is not a true indication of his power (or perhaps it was only applicable initially). In v. 20, it is said that his "appearance was more formidable than the others." This "little horn" appears to be a symbol of the future antichrist who will arise in the great tribulation prior to Christ's return in glory (see further discussion on vv. 19–25).[697]

Daniel 7:8 indicates that he "had eyes like the eyes of a man." Wood (188) makes the following suggestion:

> Eyes are symbolic of insight, intelligence, prudence. The significance here is that the Antichrist will be characterized by unusual mental ability. He will be clever, shrewd, knowledgeable—able to solve problems and give advice, which others will find wise.

On the other hand, the eyes like the eyes of a man may reflect not his mental ability, but the prideful attitude that drives his actions (cf. Isa 2:11; 5:15). This would parallel his "boastful speaking" that is highlighted at the end of the verse. Then again, calling attention to this aspect of his being may be intended to deliberately contrast him with the Lord Jesus Christ, for in Rev 1:14 his eyes are said to be "like a fiery flame," i.e., able to see right into the souls of men and rightfully judge them (cf. Rev 2:18; Dan 10:6). Despite his enormous power (and even satanic energizing), the antichrist is really nothing more than a man; he is not a match for the Lord Jesus.

Finally, Dan 7:8 tells us that he has a mouth that speaks arrogant things. That is, he is an arrogant boaster (cf. 7:11; Rev 13:5). Apparently, his boasting

---

696. The Aramaic word translated "uprooted" is equivalent to Heb. עָקַר (*ʿāqar*). The latter is used in Zeph 2:4 in the sense of militaristic conquest.

697. The antichrist interpretation is very ancient, affirmed by the majority of early church fathers and witnessed in the Epistle of Barnabas as early as AD 90–135. It was still affirmed by Jerome and Augustine about AD 400. Alternative interpretations are almost too numerous to mention. Most critical scholars view the "little horn" as a reference to Antiochus IV Epiphanes. Jewish views vary (cf. Goldwurm, 202). Rashi understood him to be the Roman general Titus who destroyed the temple in AD 70. Abarbanal and Malbim, on the other hand, viewed the symbol as a reference to the papacy. Naturally, one's view of the ten horns is affected by his view of the "little horn." Hence, Hartman (213), for example, takes the ten horns as ten successive kings who ruled during the Seleucid period. His interpretation breaks down, however, when it is observed that he must make Antiochus IV both the "little horn" and the last of the ten horns. Furthermore, Antiochus was not responsible for the uprooting of three other kings. Conservative amillennial scholars differ in their interpretations. Many, including Young (150), take the "little horn" as the antichrist of the future, but have differing opinions about the ten horns. Young (149), for instance, does not take the number "ten" literally (he considers it a symbol of completeness), and thus concludes that these are "a number of kingdoms" that follow the ancient Roman Empire in succession.

will even extend to claims of divinity, so that he demands the worship of mankind. Second Thessalonians 2:4 states that he "opposes and exalts himself above every so-called god or object of worship, so that he takes his seat in the temple of God, displaying himself as being God" (NASB; cf. Dan 11:36). As a result, "the whole earth was amazed and followed after the beast; they worshiped the dragon because he gave his authority to the beast; and they worshiped the beast" (Rev 13:3–4, NASB).

Biblical Theology Comments

Daniel 7:1–8 surveys several empires that Israel would be subjected to in the course of her history. Each of these would be known as a mighty *conqueror* of other nations. Like a ravenous beast, each would be hungry for conquest as well as the acquisition of power and fortune. Israel, rather than being ruled by a Davidic king (as the Lord had spoken in 2 Sam 7), would be ruled by ruthless pagan nations. The first of these (Babylon) was, of course, the empire that carried the southern kingdom away into exile out of the land. Yet even when the Babylonian exile came to an end as a result of Cyrus' proclamation, Israel continued to be subjected to foreign powers. She was made to drink the bitter dregs of the Deuteronomic curses (Deut 28–29). Consider a few of the statements from Deut 28 and 29 (ESV):

> The LORD will bring a nation against you from far away, from the end of the earth, swooping down like the eagle, a nation whose language you do not understand, a hard-faced nation who shall not respect the old or show mercy to the young. It shall eat the offspring of your cattle and the fruit of your ground, until you are destroyed; it also shall not leave you grain, wine, or oil, the increase of your herds or the young of your flock, until they have caused you to perish. They shall besiege you in all your towns, until your high and fortified walls, in which you trusted, come down throughout all your land. And they shall besiege you in all your towns throughout all your land, which the LORD your God has given you. (28:49–52)
>
> And the LORD will scatter you among all peoples, from one end of the earth to the other, and there you shall serve other gods of wood and stone, which neither you nor your fathers have known. And among these nations you shall find no respite, and there shall be no resting place for the sole of your foot, but the LORD will give you there a trembling heart and failing eyes and a languishing soul. (28:64–65)
>
> But to this day the LORD has not given you a heart to understand or eyes to see or ears to hear. (29:4)

All this happened to Israel on account of her unfaithfulness to the Mosaic covenant. Yet even to this day the grand saga of Israel's blindness continues, her sin compounded by her rejection of Messiah Jesus. Although Israel is back in the land today, her spiritual blindness still persists, and what awaits her is the deception of the "little horn" and the suffering he will ultimately bring on her.

Application and Devotional Implications

Each of the kingdoms portrayed in the series had at least one powerful and notable leader, though far from being godly. Of all the atrocious rulers that rise to power, the "little horn" that springs from the fourth beast is the most powerful and self-aggrandizing of all. One of his notable characteristics is that he has "a mouth speaking boastfully" (Dan 7:8). He is a champion boaster, we might say. A person who boasts of himself before others obviously has a huge ego and is extremely self-centered. One of the qualities that the Spirit of God desires to bring about in our lives, as Christians, is that of humility, which, in turn, should lead to being "other-centered." For such a person, *boasting* has no place. When we truly fathom what God has done by the cross to bring us to himself, there is no room left for boasting (1 Cor 1:26–31). If I am of any significance at all, it is in being a "new creation" in Christ. Yet, the Lord Jesus gets all the credit for this accomplishment. Hence, the Apostle Paul could say, "But far be it from me to boast except in the cross of our Lord Jesus Christ, by which the world has been crucified to me, and I to the world" (Gal 6:14, ESV). So let us be careful to refrain from boasting of ourselves before others. This is what the antichrist loves to engage in, but it is not for those wanting to live Spirit-filled lives.

b. Vision of judgment before the Ancient of Days (7:9–14)

The description of the night visions seen by Daniel in the opening paragraph of chap. 7 continues in vv. 9–14, but the emphasis now shifts to a heavenly setting where one called "the Ancient of Days" sits to administer judgment. There are striking similarities of vocabulary between Dan 7:9–4 and both *1 Enoch* 14:18–25 and *The Book of Giants* (4Q530 col. ii, 17–18), clearly evidencing dependency of one upon the other (though scholars debate the direction involved).[698]

698. For a presentation and comparison of these texts, see H. S. Kvanvig, "Throne Visions and Monsters: The Encounter Between Danielic and Enochic Traditions," *ZAW* 117 (2005): 251–58; and R. E. Stokes, "The Throne Visions of Daniel 7, *1 Enoch* 14, and the Qumran *Book of Giants* (4Q530): An Analysis of Their Literary Relationship," *DSD* 15 (2008): 340–58. For a discussion of similarities and differences between Dan 7:9–10 and *1 En.* 14:18–25, see I. Fröhlich, "Stars and Spirits: Heavenly Bodies in Ancient Jewish Aramaic Tradition," *AS* 13 (2105): 116–17. For a helpful cataloging of the textual and contextual differences between Dan 7:9–10 and *The Book of Giants* (4Q530 col. ii, 16–20), see J. L. Angel, "The Divine Courtroom Scenes of Daniel 7 and the Qumran *Book of Giants*: A Textual and Contextual Comparison," in *The Divine Courtroom in Comparative Perspective*, ed. A. Mermelstein and S. E. Holtz, 25–48 (Leiden, Boston: Brill, 2015), 31–33. If it could be determined that *1 En.*

The judgment is first negative (against the "little horn" of the fourth beast), and then positive (in favor of "one like a son of man"). Just as the dream of the image in Dan 2 culminated with the establishment of God's kingdom, so the vision of the four beasts is followed by the establishment of an eternal kingdom entrusted to "one like a son of man." Chapter 7, however, provides more detail about both the fourth kingdom (especially in regard to the persecutor "the little horn") and God's kingdom that follows. Hill (137) points out that the shift of scene is accompanied by a shift in the language and style as well, from prose to short phrases presented in poetic parallelism.

Textual Notes

10.a. Aramaic would expect the pl. form, אַלְפִין (so Qere), which is attested in *Tg. Onq.* Exod 38:26.

13.a. Although the prep. עִם (*ʿim*, "with") is well attested for the Aram. text, it is worth pointing out that LXX^{O} renders the phrase ἐπὶ τῶν νεφελῶν ("upon the clouds"), whereas LXX$^{\theta}$ has μετὰ τῶν νεφελῶν ("with the clouds").[699] The verse is quoted or alluded to frequently in the NT, sometimes using ἐπὶ τῶν νεφελῶν ("upon the clouds")—so Matt 24:30; 26:64—but at other times μετὰ τῶν νεφελῶν ("with the clouds"), as in Mark 14:62; Rev 1:7.[700]

14:18–25 was dependent upon Dan 7:9–10, this would have significant implications for the dating of the book, seeing that Nickelsburg dates *1En.* 12–16 between 300 and 250 BC; G. W. Nickelsburg, *1 Enoch 1: A Commentary on the Book of 1 Enoch, Chapters 1–36; 81–108*, Hermeneia (Minneapolis: Fortress, 2001), 230; cf. J. H. Charlesworth, "A Rare Consensus among Enoch Specialists: The Date of the Earliest Enoch Books," *Hen* 24 (2002): 225–34).

The Book of Giants (4Q530 col. ii, 15–19) is particularly striking:

> Then [ʿ]Ohyah, his brother, acknowledged and said in front of the Giants: I also saw something amazing in my dream this night: The Ruler of the heavens came down to earth, and thrones were erected and the Great Holy One sa[t down. A hundred hun]dreds were serving him, a thousand thousands [were ...] him, [and ten thousand times ten thousand be]fore him were standing. And behold, [book]s were opened and the sentence was proclaimed. And the sentence [... in a book] was [wri]tten, and recorded in an inscription [...] for all the living and the flesh. (F. G. Martīnez and E. J. C. Tigchelaar, *The Dead Sea Scrolls: Study Edition (Translations)*, 2 vols. [Leiden: Brill, 1997–1998], 2:1063)

699. For discussion of the scholarly debate concerning the translation "with" versus "upon," see T. Longman, "The Divine Warrior: The New Testament Use of an Old Testament Motif," *WTJ* 44 (1982): 295–97.

700. H. D. Zacharias, "Old Greek Daniel 7:13–14 and Matthew's Son of Man," *BBR* 21 (2011): 453–54, 464, assumes Matthew's preference for ἐπὶ is due to his acquaintance with a textual tradition similar to the throne vision preserved in LXX^{O}-Dan

13.b-b. Rather than MT's "he came to the Ancient of Days," LXX^{O} has ὡς παλαιὸς ἡμερῶν παρῆν, "he came *like* the Ancient of Days." For this and other reasons, Reynolds argues that LXX^{O} presents a more openly messianic portrait of "one like a son of man" than that found in MT and LXX$^{\theta}$.[701]

Translation

7:9 "I continued observing until thrones were set up,[702] and the Ancient of Days[703] took His seat. His garment was like white snow, and the hair of His

---

7, and that the peculiarities of the LXX^{O} version of Dan 7:13–14 as found in Pap. 967 helped shape Matthew's portrait of the Son of Man.

701. B. F. Reynolds, "The 'One Like a Son of Man' According to the Old Greek of Daniel 7,13–14," *Bib* 89 (2008): 70–80. He concludes (90), "This figure is more closely aligned with the Ancient of Days. He is described as having arrived like the Ancient of Days, appearing with the clouds, receiving service due a divine figure, and having those standing before the Ancient of Days approach him. While the 'one like a son of man' is similar to the Ancient of Days, there is no indication of equivalency or identification. In fact the giving of authority to the 'one like a son of man' implies that the son of man figure's status is different from that of the Ancient of Days." Earlier, L. T. Stuckenbruck, "'One like a Son of Man as the Ancient of Days' in the Old Greek Recension of Daniel 7,13: Scribal Error or Theological Translation?" *ZNW* 86 (1995): 268–76, argued that the second ὡς in Dan 7:13 more likely resulted from a translator's theological intention rather than scribal error. On the bearing that LXX^{O}'s reading might have had upon the Christian interpretation that equated the "Ancient of Days" and "one like a son of man," see B. G. Bucur, "The Son of Man and the Ancient of Days: Observations on the Early Christian Reception of Daniel 7," *Phronema* 32 (2017): 2–6.

702. Most translations render רְמִיו (*r^emîw*) as "were set up," assuming that the thrones are associated with God and serve in the administration of divine judgment. The KJV, on the other hand, renders v. 9, "I beheld till the thrones were cast down." Montgomery (300) explains that this translation "goes back to the Jewish comm. (also Polanus, Geier, etc.), who interpreted it by הוטלו 'were removed,' Ra., A Ez.; or הושלכו 'were cast down,' Ps Sa.; Sa., 'cast away,' so Jeph., the thrones being understood as those of the beasts."

703. The expression "Ancient of Days" (עַתִּיק יוֹמִין, *ʿattîq yômîn*) only occurs here as a title (cf. Ps 55:20 [Heb.], which refers to God as "the one who sits enthroned from of old"). Most assume this to be a reference to God (though Jephet views him an angel, and ibn Ezra specifically as being Michael). Although *ʿattîq* appears here in Aram. as an adj., עָתֵק (*ʿāṯēq*) occurs frequently in BH as a verb with the meaning "move, proceed, advance." *TWOT* (708) notes, "Its Akkadian cognate *etēqu* is a common verb meaning 'to pass along, advance.'" Hence, it can have the sense of "old, ancient" (= to be *advanced* in years). Other meanings are derived from this, as in the case of Ps 6:8 [Heb.], "his eye has *wasted away*" (עָֽתְקָה, *ʿāṯ^eqâ*), i.e., grown old and thus weak. Finally, the adj. form *ʿattîq* does occur in BH in 1 Chr 4:22 in the sense of "ancient." Such a reference to God as the "Ancient of Days" is appropriate in this

head was like pure[704] wool. His throne *appeared as*[705] flames of fire, *with* its wheels as burning fire. **10** A river of fire was streaming and going forth from Him.[706] Many thousands[707] were ministering[708] to Him, and many tens of thousands[709] were standing[710] before Him.[711] The court[712] sat in judgment, and *the* books were opened. **11** Then I continued observing on account of

---

context, since wisdom and being qualified to judge are associated with advancing age in ANE culture (cf. Sir 25:3–5).

704. Rather than the more traditional translation as an adjective meaning "clean, pure" (so NASB, ESV), the NET has "lamb's wool," presuming that נְקֵא (*nᵉqēʾ*) means "lamb." In defense of the translation "lamb," compare the Syr. *neqyaʾ* ("a sheep, ewe"), and consult M. Sokoloff, "*ʿămar nĕqēʾ*, 'Lamb's Wool' (Dan 7:9)," *JBL* 95 (1976): 277–79. In defense of the traditional understanding, cf. BH verb *nāqâ* ("be clean") and BH adj. *nāqî* ("clean, free from"). Seeing that both LXX traditions translate *nᵉqēʾ* by the Greek *katharon* ("clean"), however, argues in favor of the meaning "clean, pure," rather than "lamb."

705. Lit., "His throne flames of fire," without any verb (כָּרְסְיֵהּ שְׁבִיבִין דִּי־נוּר, *korsᵉyēh šᵉḇîḇîn dî-nûr*). The NET translates "His throne was ablaze with fire, and the NIV, "his throne was flaming with fire." Fire is often associated with the presence of God in Scripture (Exod 3:2; 19:16–18; Deut 33:2).

706. The combination of the prep מִין (*mîn*) preceding the prep. קֳדָם (*qŏḏām*) with the 3ms suff. will either mean "before Him" (as in 4:19; 5:19) or "from Him" (as in 2:6; 5:24), rather than "from before Him." Notice that later in the same verse the author uses the simpler קֳדָמוֹהִי (*qŏḏāmôhî*) in the sense "before Him."

707. Lit., "a thousand thousands" (Qere אֶלֶף אַלְפִּי, *ʾelep ʾalpî*), which is exactly what both LXX traditions have (χίλιαι χιλιάδες, *chiliai chiliades*).

708. "Ministering to him" (יְשַׁמְּשׁוּנֵּהּ, *yᵉšammᵉšûnnēh*). *HALOT* (1998) suggests that the verb root *šᵉmaš* means "to serve." Although this is the only occurrence of this root in BAram. (and we have no parallels in BH), we do have Syr. *šammāšā*, "servant, deacon." LXX^{O} uses the Greek verb *therapeuō*, which in classical Greek can mean "do service to the gods" (LSJM, 792), and has the connotations of "serve, do reverence to, honor, wait upon, and even worship." LXX$^{\theta}$ uses the verb *leitourgeō*, which has the connotation of "performing religious service."

709. The translation "many tens of thousands" is an attempt to render MT's רִבּוֹ רִבְבָן (*ribbô riḇwān*). BDB (1112b) gives the meaning "myriad" for רִבּוֹ (*ribbô*), and *HALOT* (1977) has "many, ten thousand." Lit., this is "myriad, myriads" or "ten thousand, ten thousands." Most newer translations (except NASB) avoid the expression "myriad."

710. Taking the verb יְקוּמוּן (*yᵉqûmûn*) as a customary impf.

711. NET has "stood ready to serve him." The latter three words (not in the original) are implied from the context.

712. Lit., the Aram. is "judgment sat" (דִּינָא יְתִב, *dînāʾ yᵉṯiḇ*), or perhaps "in judgment He sat" (referring to the Ancient of Days). The latter is doubtful, however, in light of the use of the phrase in Dan 7:26. The noun *dîn* may be understood as a metonymy for the *court* that renders the judgment (so most translations). Both LXX traditions use *kritērion*, which can mean "a court of judgment, tribunal" (LSJM, 997).

the sound of the boastful words that the horn was speaking. I continued observing[713] until the beast was slain and its body was destroyed and given to *the* burning fire.[714] **12** As for the rest of the beasts, *though* their dominion[715] had been removed,[716] a prolonging of life was given to them for an appointed period of time.[717] **13** I continued observing in the night visions,

713. Regarding the second חָזֵה הֲוֵית (*ḥāzēh hăwêṯ*) in v. 11 (translated by the NET as "I was watching"), the NET adds this note: "The LXX and Theodotion lack the words 'I was watching' here. It is possible that these words in the MT are a dittography from the first part of the verse."

714. Lit., "to the burning of fire" (so LXX^{O} and LXX$^{\theta}$). The nouns are in construct, but most translations render the first noun adjectively (e.g., NIV, "into the blazing fire").

715. For Aram. שָׁלְטָנְהוֹן (*šāl^eṭān^ehôn* from the verb שָׁלְטָן, *šāl^eṭān*), the NET prefers the translation "their ruling authority" rather than "their dominion" (NASB, ESV). The corresponding Heb. verb *šālaṭ* means "to domineer, be master (of)," and the noun *šilṭôn* means "mastery." Similarly, Arab. *śulṭān* means "dominion, ruler, or a sultan."

716. The way this verse is handled by the translations reflects the difficulty in knowing how the judgment on the "rest of the beasts" relates *temporally* to the "little horn." The NET and NIV classify the first verb as a past perf. ("had already been removed" and "had been stripped"). The NIV, in fact, puts the whole verse in parenthesis, as though it were simply a parenthetical remark and not a subsequent action. Other translations (e.g., ESV, NASB, NRSV) classify the verb as a definite past ("was taken away"). Perhaps the solution is to make a distinction between how things are seen in the vision and the timing in reality, though the NIV's solution may be a good approach.

717. Lit., "a time and a season," but the expression is vague, combining two Aram. words for time, זְמַן (*z^eman*) and עִדָּן (*'iddān*). Archer (91) notes, "זְמַן (*z^eman*) points to time as an appointed moment for something to happen; עִדָּן (*'iddān*), on the other hand, refers to time as duration, or as the interval between a temporal *terminus a quo* and the *terminus ad quem*." Hartman (206) regards זְמַן וְעִדָּן (*z^eman w^e'iddān*) as a hendiadys, and translates this "for a limited time." Similarly, Feinberg (82), "for an appointed period of time." In general, this is an undesignated "period of time," though one appointed by God.

and behold, one like a son of man[718] was coming with[719] the clouds of heaven. He approached[720] the Ancient of Days and was presented[721] before Him. **14** Then to Him was given dominion, honor, and a kingdom,[722] that all the peo-

---

718. The one brought before the Ancient of Days is said to be "like a son of man" (כְּבַר אֱנָשׁ, *kᵊḇar ʾĕnāš*). The expression *bar ʾĕnāš* is functionally equivalent to Heb. *ben ʾāḏām*, and commonly means *a human being*. The Heb. form is found ninety-three times in Ezekiel and fourteen times elsewhere (also see *ben ʾĕnôš* in Ps 144:3). The sense of "human one" is evident in such passages as Num 23:19; Ps 8:4; Isa 51:12; and 56:2. Ezekiel is commonly addressed as "son of man," as is Daniel himself in Dan 8:17. Scholarly debate centers on whether to regard the referent as an individual (and specifically, in a messianic way) or in a corporate sense. Hartman (219) attempts to make a point of the preceding comparative *kᵊ* ("like"), insisting this figure must be *symbolic*, just as were the animal figures introduced earlier with *kᵊ* (note Dan 7:4, 6). Nevertheless, the particle *kᵊ* could just as well mean that he is *like* a human being (i.e., for the most part), while at the same time being significantly different than other humans. In any case, this phrase was Jesus' favorite self-designation for himself in the Gospels. Further discussion on interpretation can be found in the commentary.
719. Regarding the choice of "with" rather than "upon," see "Textual Note" above.
720. There is no warrant to argue on the basis of the verb מְטָא (*mᵊṭāʾ*) that the ascension of Christ is in view (so Calvin). According to *HALOT* (1914), *mᵊṭāʾ* means to "reach to" (with prep *lᵊ*), or "to attain to, come upon" when used with prep. *ʿaḏ* (as here). In the absolute use (without a prep.), it means "to occur, happen" (Dan 6:21 [Aram.], 25 [Aram.]). The NIV's "he approached" is appropriate. If the ascension of Christ is in view in this verse, it is not because of the lexical meaning of *mᵊṭāʾ* but on the basis of the broader theological import of the passage.
721. The translation "was presented" (though technically, active voice) reflects the Hapʿel perf. verb הַקְרְבוּהִי (*haqrᵊḇûhî*). Montgomery (304) notes, "The pass. 'he was presented' ... is the proper rendering of the Aram. idiom of the act. pl." *HALOT* (1972) indicates that the verb קְרֵב (*qᵊrēḇ*) in the Hapʿel means "to bring near, allow to enter." The corresponding Heb. verb *qāraḇ* means "to bring, bring near, present," and could be used in an official sense of *presenting tribute* (Judg 3:17) or *presenting sacrifices* (Mal 1:8). Montgomery (304) points out that the Aram. verb can be used in the sense of being "presented before" a king, i.e., given royal audience. See קרבתיך קדם סנחאריב, "I presented thee before Sennacherib" (Sachau, *Aramäische Papyrus*, 50, l. 2). Cf. NET "escorted before him."
722. The NET translates מַלְכוּ (*malḵû*) as "sovereignty" (cf. NIV "sovereign power"). The same word appears with the meaning "kingdom" in Dan 2:37, 39–42. These Gentile kingdoms are then replaced by a *kingdom* (same word) which will never be destroyed, a kingdom set up by the God of heaven (Dan 2:44). Significantly, it is "this kingdom" that is now given to "one like a son of man." Though "sovereignty" is a legitimate meaning for *malḵû*, the translation "kingdom" (so NASB) is preferable. Notice that the NET translates the second occurrence of *malḵû* in Dan 7:14 as "kingdom" ("His kingdom will not be destroyed"), which argues that the first occurrence should be as well.

ples, nations, and men of every language[723] might serve[724] Him. His dominion is an everlasting dominion that will not pass away, and His kingdom is one that will not be destroyed."

Commentary

7:9–10 *The seating of the Ancient of Days in the heavenly courtroom*. The opening scene consists of multiple thrones in a heavenly setting, with the focus of attention placed upon the Ancient of Days who sits as the supreme judge.[725] The verb translated "took His seat" (lit., "sat") is repeated at the end of v. 10. Though the latter (a singular verb) could be translated, "In judgment He sat," this is doubtful in light of Dan 7:26. A better translation, then, is "The court sat." The context makes clear that the imagery is designed to depict the Ancient of Days acting in judgment (not *ruling* in general), and there is a heavenly court that participates with him (i.e., is there to witness and affirm the judgment He renders). Most Christian commentators—but

723. Lit., "tongues" (but see note at Dan 3:4).

724. The translation "might serve" (יִפְלְחוּן, *yipl^əḥûn*) means more than "waiting upon" his needs. Of the ten times that פְּלַח (*pəlaḥ*) is used in Aram. Daniel, it is always used with the idea of service or worship of a deity. It is more than "to give honor" or "wait upon," because to render *pəlaḥ* (for Hebrews) to anyone other than Yahweh would be tantamount to idolatry (note the use in Dan 3:12). Thus, *TWOT* (1059) remarks, "The original meaning of the root was 'to cleave [open]' or 'divide in two.' From this meaning was derived the idea of cultivating a field and ultimately of cultivating (i.e., working hard at) the worship of a deity, hence the idea of service or worship of a deity." This may explain why LXX^{O} translates *pəlaḥ* with the Greek verb *latreuō*. When used in religious contexts, the latter has the meaning "to serve the gods with prayers and sacrifices," according to LSJM (1032). *HALOT* (1957) suggests the meaning "venerate" for *pəlaḥ* (cf. Akk. *palāḥu*, "to fear, respect, venerate").

725. Not all are convinced that the scene is a *heavenly* one. M. Smith, "Heaven or Earth? The Destination of the 'One Like a Son of Man' in Daniel 7.13–14" (paper presented at the annual national conference of the ETS, Atlanta, Nov. 19, 2015), argues that this represents a final theophany in which the Ancient of Days comes to earth for judgment and which leads in turn to the establishment of the divine throne-room on the earth. S. Beyerle, "'One Like a Son of Man': Innuendoes of a Heavenly Individual," in *Enoch and Qumran Origins: New Light on a Forgotten Connection*, ed. G. Boccaccini, 54–58 (Grand Rapids, Eerdmans, 2005), 58, on the other hand, after a comparative study with Qumranic literature and relevant concepts (e.g., glory) concludes, "A Comparison of motifs attested in the visionary scenes of Daniel 7:9–10 and 7:13–14 leads to the conclusion that the 'son of man' was part of an angel-like assembly in a heavenly sanctuary. He is characterized as an individual, subordinated to the enthroned God." Goldingay (167) argues, "The court is seated on earth (vv. 9–10), and 'among the clouds of the heavens' denotes the position of the figure about to be described as it moves toward that court."

not all—understand the Ancient of Days as a reference to God the Father.[726] (For similar descriptions of God in later intertestamental literature, see *1 En.* 46:1–2; 47:3; 98:2.) His white vesture and hair like wool probably stress his eternality (cf. Isa 43:13; 57:15a) or holiness. Certainly both are true of the Father. Since clothing in Scripture can reflect one's holiness (note Rev 16:15), it may even be that the white vesture reflects his holiness (which qualifies him to judge), whereas the hair like wool (normally associated with one's advanced age) reflects his eternality.[727] In any case, Daniel's seeing him makes for a significant visual shift after envisioning the "little horn." Miller (204) notes, "There is a startling contrast here. In vv. 7–8 the Antichrist is blaspheming the God of heaven, but in vv. 9–10 the sovereign Lord is shown sitting upon his throne, calmly preparing for the day of judgment."

The text does not say who is occupying the other "thrones" (plural). Goldingay's suggestion (165) that the plural number is used for emphasis (as though to amplify the throne of David as exalted and glorious) is doubtful. There are too many references in Scripture to multiple thrones to let it go at that. Young (151) is representative of those who see the thrones occupied by

---

726. The interpretation that the Ancient of Days must be God the Father has not always been embraced. Early church fathers debated the matter, and some held that this referred to Christ (e.g., St. Cyril of Alexandria and St. John of Damascus). For a helpful survey of the debate, see W. S. Royer, "The Ancient of Days: Patristic and Modern Views of Daniel 7:9–14," *SVTQ* 45 (2001): 137–62. He remarks (142), "The Church Fathers who identified the Ancient of Days with Christ generally did so from the exegetical standpoint that *all* Old Testament theophanies were, in fact, manifestations of the preincarnate Christ (or, at very least, prefigurations of Christ)." In a similar article surveying the treatment of Dan 7:9–10, 13–14 by early church fathers, G. K. McKay, "The Eastern Christian Exegetical Tradition of Daniel's Vision of the Ancient of Days," *JECS* 7 (1999): 139–61, points out how they were careful to assert that *what was seen* by Daniel was not the essence of God but what God wanted to reveal about himself (hence He does not really look like an old man). This is reflected, for instance, by Theodoret of Cyrus: "According to Theodoret, God forms visions of himself as he deems useful. Although God himself is 'bodiless, simple, and formless, not lending himself to description, but being descriptionless by nature,' at certain times God chooses to provide a vision of himself. ... For Theodoret, there is a great difference between viewing a likeness and actually seeing the divine. ... In no way can humanity view the true nature of God, for it remains wholly invisible and formless; however, physical forms recognizable to mortals can reflect specific aspects of God that cannot be directly revealed" (152). For a very thorough treatment of the historical identification of the "Ancient of Days" and "one like a son of man" in the early church and their relationship to one another, see Bucur, "The Son of Man and the Ancient of Days: Observations on the Early Christian Reception of Daniel 7," 1–27.

727. *1 En.* 41:1 is of interest here: "At that place, I saw the One to whom belongs the time before time. And his head was white like wool."

angelic beings. This interpretation is certainly possible, since Scripture does speak of angels who surround the heavenly throne of God (e.g., 1 Kgs 22:19; Ps 82:1). Some would understand the plural pronouns in Gen 1:26 as reference to an angelic court, but the interpretation of that verse is hotly debated and more likely refers to the plurality of the godhead within a unity.[728] An alternative view of Dan 7:9 is to see the thrones occupied by certain saints (so Miller, 204). Passages like Matt 19:28, Luke 22:30, 1 Cor 6:2, Rev 3:21, and Rev 20:4 do depict certain saints occupying thrones.[729] Unfortunately, the identity of twenty-four elders on thrones in Rev 4–5 is not easy to determine, though (in my opinion) the evidence leans in the direction of certain faithful human believers. The verse in Rev 20:4 is of particular interest in light of the fact that the return of Christ results in judgment upon the beast and the casting of him into the lake of fire (Rev 19:20), which many (including this author) would equate with Daniel's "little horn." In the final analysis, we must admit uncertainty as to the identity of those on the thrones. The main thing is that the Ancient of Days is the one pronouncing and enacting judgment; others are there to witness the event and glorify God who righteously judges.

The remainder of v. 9 describes the throne itself. It is aflame with fire, including the wheels on which it is positioned. Fire is often associated with God's presence in Scripture (note Exod 3:2; 19:16–18; Deut 33:2). There is a striking resemblance with the divine throne seen in Ezekiel's vision. It also had wheels (Ezek 1:15–20; 10:9–17) and had fire and lightning associated with it (Ezek 1:13, 27; 10:2, 6).

Verse 10 begins by describing a river of flowing fire associated with the Ancient of Days (imagery unique to Daniel in the OT), either coming from

---

728. Both B. K. Waltke, *Genesis, A Commentary* (Grand Rapids: Zondervan, 2001), 64, and G. J. Wenham, *Genesis*, 2 vols., Word Biblical Commentary (Waco, TX: Word, 1987, 1994), 1:28, understand the plural references in Gen 1:26 in regard to the angelic court. More recently, W. D. Barrick, "Divine Persons in Genesis: Theological Implications," DBTS 22 (2017): 8–10, has written a helpful article in which he outlines eight different interpretations of Gen 1:26. After a close examination of Gen 1:26 as well as the numerous theophanies found in Genesis, he rejects the angelic court interpretation and concludes that the book "provides significant information regarding a plurality of persons in the Godhead at work on earth" (20).

729. Y. Lee, "Judging or Ruling the Twelve Tribes of Israel? The Sense of Κρίνω in Matthew 19.28," *BT* 66 (2015): 138–50, explores the intertextual links of Matt 19:28 with Dan 7 and concludes (148): "The eschatological reward of Jesus' twelve disciples who have forsaken everything to follow him is to sit with the Son of Man on the throne of his glory and to judge the twelve tribes of Israel on twelve thrones. As we have observed, Matt 19.28 shows strong intertextual links with the heavenly vision of the enthronement of the Son of Man in Dan 7. Alluding to Dan 7.26–27, Jesus announces here that his twelve disciples, who have forsaken everything to follow him, would share the Son of Man's authority to judge nations, including the nation of Israel."

him or flowing before him (see translation note to v. 10). Its purpose is for bringing punishment on those whom He judges (cf. Pss 50:3; 97:3), especially the "little horn."[730] In light of the obvious parallels with Rev 19:20 and 20:10, this river of fire is the "lake of fire which burns with brimstone."

Regardless of how one interprets those upon the thrones in v. 9, the Ancient of Days is surrounded by thousands—even tens of thousands—who serve and wait upon him. In light of the very similar wording in Rev 5:11, these are presumably angels. This awesome army of holy angelic beings is there to serve the Lord who sits upon his throne. Furthermore, they witness the judgment he renders and the opening of "the books." More than once Scripture refers to divine records. In light of the context (esp. the dispensing of judgment against the "little horn"), these books are probably to be distinguished from "the book" mentioned in Dan 12:1 having the names of those to be delivered in the "end time," as well as from the "book of life" in Rev 20:12 having the names of the righteous saints who will not be hurt by the "second death" of the lake of fire (cf. Exod 32:32; Ps 69:28). From what is revealed in Rev 20:12–15, these "books" (plural!) are probably to be understood as the record of the works and ungodly acts of unbelievers, which they will be confronted with at the great white throne judgment.[731] They stand as something of a counterpart to the "book of remembrance" in Mal 3:16 that has the names of those who feared Yahweh and esteemed his name. The records in these books in Daniel present *the evidence* that they do not measure up to the righteousness of God. Those who reject the atoning sacrifice of the Lord Jesus Christ are essentially placing their hope in their own (deficient) righteousness. Jesus has indeed paid the price for the sins of all men, even of those who reject him (1 John 2:2). Yet the evidence of their unrighteousness remains on record.

7:11–12 *Judgment rendered the beasts and little horn*. With v. 11, we have a shift back to the fourth beast, marked by a return in the text to prose and a lengthy introduction formula. These two verses focus on the negative aspects of the court scene, namely judgment that is rendered. The outcome of the little horn is portrayed first, and then that of the other beasts of Daniel's vision.

Verse 11 once again calls attention to the arrogance and boastful words of the little horn (recall v. 8), one of the reasons for the condemnation of the beast by the heavenly court. This reminds the reader that *contemptuous pride* is at the root of this individual's character and actions. Just as Satan gives him his power (Rev 13:2), he also passes on to him that sin behind all sins, namely pride (cf. Ezek 28:17). The fact that his boastfulness and

---

730. Fire is used elsewhere as a symbol of God's judgment, as though destroying everything in its path (Isa 66:15–16; Jer 21:12; Ezek 21:31).

731. Extrabiblical literature makes reference to books that record the deeds of men during their time on earth as well as the good things and honor in store for those who died in righteousness. See *1 En.* 81; 93:1–3; 103:2; and *Jub.* 5:12–19; 16:9; 23:32.

self-aggrandizement is highlighted again in Dan 11:36 and Rev 13:5 reflects the seriousness of this trait. Yet he is not merely arrogant; Rev 13:5 indicates that he hurls "blasphemies" at God.

Such a wicked one as the antichrist will not succeed, however. Verse 11 reveals that he will be killed and his body given to the burning fire. The reference to his body substantiates that he is a real human. He may be indwelt or empowered by a demon(s), but he is not a demon or spirit-being. This verse must be correlated with Rev 19:17–21. In the latter passage, the "beast" (= little horn of Daniel) leads a number of the kings of the earth in war against the Lord Jesus at the second coming. The beast has no chance of success but is quickly seized and thrown alive into the lake of fire.

Also to be observed in v. 11 are the words "until the beast was killed." Since this beast is differentiated from the first three in v. 12, we must conclude that the "little horn" is the final manifestation of the fourth beast, the Roman Empire. This would imply that the fourth beast is not finished until the little horn is killed and destroyed at the second coming of Christ.

Having mentioned the demise of the fourth beast in v. 11, the fate of the first three beasts receives comment in v. 12 as something of a parenthetical remark. In each case, these kingdoms came to a point where they lost their dominion or authority (just as happened to Babylon in 539 BC when it was conquered by Cyrus the Great of Medo-Persia). Despite the loss of authority, however, each of these kingdoms was "permitted to go on living." Except for the fourth kingdom (which has an abrupt end when the antichrist is killed), the other three kingdoms experience an extension of life. Although their authority to rule is removed, the people and culture of each kingdom is absorbed into the next empire—at least for some duration of time, divinely determined.

7:13–14 *The kingdom and glory given to "one like a son of man."* Following the slaying of the little horn, the antichrist, the positive aspect of the judgment scene emerges as a certain individual termed "one like a son of man" is exalted to receive a kingdom.[732] Hill (139) observes the literary aspects that serve to underscore the importance of this couplet:

> The introductory formula ("in my vision at night I looked," v.13a) echoes the formula introducing the vision (v.2a) and forms an envelope for the literary unit (vv.2–14). The construction serves to underscore the importance of the final scene as the climax of Daniel's vision.

---

732. P. Owen, "Aramaic and Greek Representations of the 'Son of Man' and the Importance of the *Parables of Enoch*," in *Parables of Enoch: A Paradigm Shift*, ed. D. L. Bock and J. H. Charlesworth, 114–23 (London: Bloomsbury T&T Clark, 2013), traces the development of the messianic idea from Dan 7:13–14 to the *Parables of Enoch* and concludes than an *individual* is in view (not a corporate symbol).

The literature treating the subject "son of man" is so voluminous (and contentious) that space only allows for a cursory treatment here, and readers are referred to surveys found elsewhere for extended discussion.[733] Much debate has transpired concerning the possible pre-Christian sources behind the phrase, as well as Jesus' use of the phrase as his favorite self-designation.[734] Shepherd has observed, "The overwhelming consensus among critical scholars is that there is fundamental discontinuity between 'one like a son of man' of Dan 7:13 and 'the son of man' of the NT."[735] When it comes to "the Son of Man" in the Gospels, critical scholars engage in lively debate as to how Jesus used this phrase (including whether or not he even intended an allusion to Dan 7:13), which verses are truly "authentic sayings" of Jesus and which are not, and the extent to which the post-resurrection community of believers might have imposed an interpretation upon Jesus' words that he himself did not espouse. Evangelicals, however, reject such extreme conjectures, believing the NT does give us an accurate record of what Jesus said.

With that being said, any analysis and interpretation of "one like a son of man" in Daniel is complicated by several factors:

- The phrase "son of man" in Dan 7:13 is anarthrous, whereas Jesus spoke of himself as "*the* Son of Man" (and some have questioned whether Jesus even intended a connection between his use of the phrase and vv. 13–14).[736]

---

733. For a thorough survey of research identifying the "son of man" figure, see: P. M. Casey, *Son of Man: The Interpretation and Influence of Daniel 7* (London: SPCK, 1979); Day, *God's Conflict with the Dragon and the Sea*, 157–77; D. Burkett, *The Son of Man Debate: A History and Evaluation*, SNTSMS 107 (Cambridge: Cambridge University Press, 2004); and M. Müller, *The Expression 'Son of Man' and the Development of Christology: A History of Interpretation* (New York: Routledge, 2008). For an excellent survey of the research history (up through 1998) on the influences and traditions underlying Dan 7:2–14, see Eggler, *Influences and Traditions Underlying the Vision of Daniel 7:2–14*.

734. See esp., J. R. Donahue, "Recent Studies on the Origin of 'Son of Man' in the Gospels," *CBQ* 48 (1986): 484–98.

735. M. B. Shepherd, "Daniel 7:13 and the New Testament Son of Man," *WTJ* 68 (2006): 99.

736. J. D. G. Dunn, "The Danielic Son of Man in the New Testament," in *The Book of Daniel: Composition & Reception*, VTSup 83:2, ed. J. J. Collins and P. W. Flint, 528–49 (Leiden: Brill, 2001), 544, for example, remarks, "the presence of the phrase 'the Son of Man' is not itself proof of influence from Dan 7:13. There are indications that at least some of the Gospel 'Son of Man' sayings are derived rather from the typical Hebraic idiom, 'son of man' = man, human person, as in Ps 8:4 and Heb 2:6, in this case using the Aramaic form בַּר אֱנָשׁ." Dunn goes on to say (545), "Dan 7:13 was not used by Jesus himself, but was one of the scriptures drawn upon by the first Christians to help them make sense of what had happened to Jesus."

- Related to the first point is the fact that Dan 7:13–14 was penned in Aramaic, and although Jesus probably spoke in Aramaic in such passages as Mark 14:62 (his clearest allusion to the Daniel passage), the NT statements regarding "the Son of Man" were written in Greek.
- Outside of Daniel, "son of man" is a commonly used expression in the OT for a human being in general (e.g., Ps 8:4) or in reference to Ezekiel specifically (e.g., Ezek 2:1).
- There is a bit of tension between Dan 7:14 that indicates "one like a son of man" will be given a kingdom, and v. 18 where the saints of the highest one receive the kingdom.
- There is no conclusive evidence that "son of man" was a *commonly understood* expression in pre-Christian Judaism and much less a messianic title (though this is currently being reconsidered).[737]

In regard to this final bullet point, at the heart of this discussion is the question of whether or not there was a stable and generally accepted set of beliefs regarding messianism at the beginning of the Christian era. Horbury[738] concludes there was. The greater question is to what extent "the son of man" was associated with this hope. This is not to say, however, that there is no evidence of the expression "son of man" being used *messianically* prior to Jesus' ministry. We do find it, after all, in the fragmentary *Aramaic Apocalypse* (4Q246), in the *Parables of Enoch*, i.e., chaps. 37–71 of *1 Enoch* (also known as the *Similitudes*), and at least the concept in *4 Ezra* 13.[739] Regarding the latter, the vision begins with "something like the figure of a man" (13.3) arising from the sea. Later, God calls him "my son" (13.32), and in the latter days he takes his stand on Mt. Zion, destroying an army that attacks it, and regathering

737. N. Perrin, "The Son of Man in Ancient Judaism and Primitive Christianity: A Suggestion," *BR* 11 (1966): 17–28, has argued in this vein. F. F. Bruce, "The Background to the Son of Man Sayings," in *Christ the Lord*, FS D. Guthrie, ed. H. H. Rowdon, 50–70 (Leicester/Downers Grove, IL: IVP, 1982), 70, has concluded (as have many others) that "son of man" was not "a current title for the Messiah or any other eschatological figure" in first-century AD Judaism. For a study of messianic expectation in second temple Judaism in the light of the Dead Sea Scrolls, see J. J. Collins, *The Scepter and the Star: The Messiahs of the Dead Sea Scrolls and Other Ancient Literature*, ABRL (New York: Doubleday, 1995).

738. W. Horbury, "Messianic Associations of the 'Son of Man,'" *JTS* 36 (1985): 40.

739. One other pseudepigraphical work relevant to these studies is the *Testament of Abraham*, which shows obvious reliance on Dan 7, and in which Abel (the son of Adam) is given authority to judge creation. For a helpful study, see P. B. Munoa, "Chapter 3: The Exegesis of Daniel 7 in the *Testament of Abraham*," in *Four Powers in Heaven: The Interpretation of Daniel 7 in the Testament of Abraham*, JSPSup 28 (Sheffield: Sheffield Academic Press, 1998), 43–81.

the ten tribes of Israel. Though he is clearly a messiah figure, both Collins and Burkett point out differences with the "son of man" in *1 Enoch*.[740]

Aramaic Apocalypse (4Q246), published by É. Puech in 1992, has been dated to the first century BC.[741] There, a "son of man" figure has been given the title "Son of God" and becomes a great king over the whole earth. In Kuhn's opinion,

> ... the *Aramaic Apocalypse* not only borrows from Daniel 7 but also offers an interpretation of that text by designating the Danielic "one like a son of man" as the "Son of the Most High" and "Son of God." These titles, I claim, cast Daniel's eschatological redeemer against the royal background of the Davidic monarchy, and yet also mark a development in the transcendent character of this heavenly figure by attributing to him divine sonship.[742]

---

740. For a description and analysis of *4 Ezra* 13 (probably to be dated to the end of the first century AD), see J. J. Collins, "The Son of Man in First-Century Judaism," *NTS* 38 (1992): 459–66; and D. Burkett, "Son of Man in Apocalyptic and Rabbinic Texts," in *The Son of Man Debate; A History and Evaluation*, SNTSMS 107 (Cambridge: Cambridge University Press, 2004) 102–8. The latter contends that we must distinguish between the vision in 13.1–13 and the interpretation of the author in 13.25–52. Burkett also points out that although he is called God's "son," it appears that he is also a mortal human being that dies (107).

741. É. Puech, "Fragment d'une Apocalypse en Arameén (4Q246 = pseudo-Dan^{d}) et le 'Royaume de Dieu,'" *RB* 99 (1992): 98–131. K. A. Kuhn, "The 'One like a Son of Man' Becomes the 'Son of God,'" *CBQ* 69 (2007): 27, notes, "Puech, and Fitzmyer agree that on paleographic grounds the extant fragment of the *Apocalypse* is to be dated to the last third of the first century B.C.E."

742. Kuhn, "The 'One like a Son of Man' Becomes the 'Son of God,'" 24. Kuhn brings forth ample evidence demonstrating that the *Aramaic Apocalypse* is dependent upon Dan 7. He states (28), for instance, "The most striking verbal parallels between Daniel 7 and the *Apocalypse* consist of the two phrases שלטנה שלטן עלם ('whose dominion is an everlasting dominion' [Dan 7:14; cf. 4Q246 2:9]) and מלכותה מלכות עלם ('his/its kingdom will be an everlasting kingdom' [Dan 7:27; cf. 4Q246 2:5])." He goes on to conclude (30), "The nature and extent of the correspondences between these two texts indicate that the writer of the *Aramaic Apocalypse* intended to recast the Danielic 'one like a son of man' as a figure to be known by the titles 'Son of the Most High' and 'Son of God.' ... these titles present him in the royal tradition of the Davidic kingship." In a 2014 article, T. S. Ferda, "Naming the Messiah: A Contribution to the 4Q246 'Son of God' Debate," *DSD* 21 (2014): 175, has outlined six positions taken by scholars regarding "son of God" and "son of the Most High" in 4Q246. Observing the resemblance between 4Q246 and the positive naming form in the biblical text, he concluded that the messianic naming tradition best explains the naming of the "son" in i 9 and ii 1, and thus that the person identified in these lines is a "positive, messianic figure."

Of perhaps greater interest is the material found in the *Parables of Enoch*. According to Collins, "The earliest Jewish evidence for the interpretation and re-use of Dan 7.13–14 is found in the Similitudes of Enoch."[743] Although the phrase "son of man" occurs repeatedly in the *Parables of Enoch* as one who appears at the end of history to punish the wicked and vindicate the righteous, the dating of this portion of *1 Enoch* is greatly debated. (No fragment of the *Parables of Enoch*, i.e., chaps. 37–71, has been found at Qumran.) In general, scholars have taken the position that the *Parables of Enoch* were written after the time of Jesus' earthly ministry (though other portions of *1 Enoch* could have been pre-Christian). Collins, for example, has argued that they "should be dated to the early or mid first century C.E., prior to the Jewish revolt of 66–70 C.E., to which it makes no reference."[744] More recently, however, D. L. Bock—based on a lengthy and detailed survey of scholarly opinion about the *Parables of Enoch* from the time of R. H. Charles up through 2012—has argued for the "strong likelihood that the *Parables of Enoch* are Jewish and most likely were composed prior to the work of Jesus of Nazareth or contemporaneous with his Galilean ministry."[745] In the

743. Collins, "The Son of Man in First-Century Judaism," 451. Collins has concluded (449) that "Daniel 7 remains the source of Jewish expectation of an apocalyptic Son of Man," and that this figure refers to an individual (not a collective symbol), is identified as the messiah, and is pre-existent to creation (464–65).

744. J. J. Collins, *The Apocalyptic Imagination: An Introduction to Jewish Apocalyptic Literature*. 2nd ed. (Grand Rapids: Eerdmans, 1998), 178. Cf. M. A. Knibb, "The Date of the Parables of Enoch: A Critical Review," *NTS* 25 (1978–79): 359, who prefers a date in the period following AD 70; and C. L. Mearns, "Dating the Similitudes of Enoch," *NTS* 25 (1978–79): 369, who thinks of the late 40s AD. (Yet Knibb shows more *openness* to a pre-70 AD date in his 1995 work, "Messianism in the Pseudepigrapha in Light of the Scrolls," *DSD* 2 [1995]: 171.) G. Bampfylde, "The Similitudes of Enoch: Historical Allusions," *JSJ* 15 (1984): 9–31, more confident about the historical references of some allusions in the text, concluded that the original parables (less the interpolation in 67:4–13) were written before 50 BC.

745. D. L. Bock, "Dating the *Parables of Enoch*: A *Forschungsbericht*," in *Parables of Enoch: A Paradigm Shift*, ed. D. L. Bock and J. H. Charlesworth, 58–113 (London: Bloomsbury T&T Clark, 2013), 112. In summarizing scholarly research, Bock writes (106), "Nonetheless, the current state of research makes a turn of the era date for this material (from c. 40 BCE to the first half of the first century CE) the most likely setting with the period earlier in this range more likely than the later ... One factor that is not disputed is that there is no reference to the fall of Jerusalem in the *Parables of Enoch*. This is yet another key fact that favors an earlier date over one in the latter part of the first century CE. In summation, the likelihood is that the *Parables of Enoch* and ideas like them were in circulation at the time of the rise of the movement Jesus started."

same volume, J. H. Charlesworth came to similar conclusions.[746] If this more recent dating of the *Parables of Enoch* proves true, the relationship between the *Similitudes* and Jesus' use of "son of man" (as well as what this might have meant to first century hearers) will have to be carefully reconsidered.

There is no doubt that the *Parables* allude to Dan 7:9–10, 13–14, as the following excerpts show:[747]

> *1 En.* 46:1–4
>
> At that place, I saw the One to whom belongs the time before time. And his head was white like wool, and there was with him another individual, whose face was like that of a human being. His countenance was full of grace like that of one among the holy angels. And I asked the one—from among the angels—who was going with me, and who had revealed to me all the secrets regarding the One who was born of human beings, "Who is this, and from whence is he who is going as the prototype of the Before-Time?" And he answered me and said to me, "This is the Son of Man, to whom belongs righteousness, and with whom righteousness dwells. And he will open all the hidden storerooms; for the Lord of the Spirits has chosen him, and he is destined to be victorious before the Lord of the Spirits in eternal uprightness. This Son of Man whom you have seen is the One who would

---

746. J. H. Charlesworth, "The Date and Provenance of the *Parables of Enoch*," in *Parables of Enoch: A Paradigm Shift*, ed. D. L. Bock and J. H. Charlesworth, 37–57 (London: Bloomsbury T&T Clark, 2013), 56. In the "Preface" to the book (xiii), Charlesworth wrote that many leading scholars now "judge the *Parables of Enoch* to be Jewish. They concur that the work, most likely, was composed just before, or roughly contemporaneous with, Jesus from Nazareth. The author was probably an erudite Jew living in Galilee. His work represents the pinnacle of apocalyptic and messianic thought among devotees of Enoch."

747. The strongest links of *1 Enoch* to Dan 7 occur in chaps. 46–48 and 69–71 (see esp. 46:1, 2–4; 47:3; 48:2; 62:5, 7, 9, 14; 63:11; 69:27, 29; 70:1; 71:14, 17). For a helpful discussion and analysis of primary passages from *1 Enoch* evidencing a reliance upon Dan 7, see J. C. VanderKam, "Daniel 7 in the Similitudes of Enoch (*1 Enoch* 37–71)," in *Biblical Traditions in Transmission: Essays in Honour of Michael A. Knibb*, ed. C. Hempel and J. M. Lieu, 291–307 (Leiden: Brill, 2006), 292–302. Although VanderKam points out the objections of some scholars to *1 Enoch*'s reliance upon Dan 7 (e.g., Noth and Borsch), he nevertheless can affirm (304): "... the parallels are sufficiently close to have convinced almost all commentators that Daniel 7 is indeed a source for the similar passages in the Similitudes."

> remove the kings and the mighty ones from their comfortable seats and the strong ones from their thrones.[748]
>
> *1En.* 47:3
>
> In those days, I saw him—the Antecedent of Time, while he was sitting upon the throne of his glory, and the books of the living ones were open before him. And all his power in heaven above and his escorts stood before him.[749]

Although no mention is made in *1 Enoch* of "the Son of Man" coming with the clouds of heaven (Dan 7:13), Enoch's vision goes beyond that of Daniel by referring to the throne on which the Son of Man will sit (*1 En.* 51:3). Of further interest is the fact that *1 En.* 48:3 portrays the Son of Man's pre-existence, for he existed before the sun, stars, and heavens were made. Burkett summarizes how the "son of man" is presented in *1 Enoch*:

> The main part of the Similitudes of Enoch (1 Enoch 37–70) presents a pre-existent Messiah. This figure combines the attributes and functions of the one like a son of man in Daniel 7.13, the Davidic Messiah of Isaiah 11 and Psalm 2, the servant of the Lord in Second Isaiah, and Yahweh as eschatological judge. The Similitudes explicitly identify the figure as the Messiah (1 Enoch 48.10; 52.4). From a servant passage, his primary title is 'the Chosen One' (Isa. 42.1). God chose him and hid him in heaven before the world was created (1 Enoch 48.3, 6; 62.7). At the final judgment, he will sit on God's throne of glory and execute judgment for the righteous against the rebellious angels and sinners, especially the kings and rulers of earth.[750]

In Jewish rabbinical tradition (which, though later than NT documents, could preserve earlier traditions), there is evidence that "one like a son of man" in Dan 7:13 was regarded as the Messiah (though obviously not equated with Jesus). Casey has found ten references to Dan 7:13–14 in this literature, at

748. Charlesworth, *The Old Testament Pseudepigrapha*, 1:34. Although there might be some confusion as to whether the "son of man" in the *Parables* might be a reference to Enoch himself (see 71:14), it is clear on the basis of *1 En.* 70:1, where Enoch is raised to appear before the "Son of Man," that they are to be distinguished. Although this point has been debated, Collins, "The Son of Man in First-Century Judaism," 454, concludes, "*I Enoch* 70.1, then, makes a clear distinction between Enoch and the Son of Man, which cannot be avoided. This distinction, in fact, seems to be presupposed throughout the *Similitudes*, where Enoch sees the Son of Man without any suggestion that he is seeing himself."

749. Charlesworth, *The Old Testament Pseudepigrapha*, 1:35.

750. Burkett, "Son of Man in Apocalyptic and Rabbinic Texts," 98.

least four of which interpret this figure as Messiah: *b. Sanh.* 98a; *Num. Rab.* 13.14; *ʾAg. Ber.* 23.1; and *Midr. Haggadol Gen.* 49.10.[751]

We can safely say that although there might not have been a single Son of Man concept, there certainly had been speculation about an exalted figure whose roots lay in Dan 7. Bock points out,

> Even if a fixed portrait and title did not exist, the outlines of such a figure were emerging and the context for his activity was being appealed to regularly in the midst of expressions of eschatological hope. These ideas were 'in the air' and thus were available for reflection *and* development.[752]

Traditional Christian opinion has been to identify Daniel's "son of man" (*bar ʾĕnāš*) as a messianic reference, yet numerous alternative interpretations have been advanced (mainly from critical scholars). In general, interpretations can be classified in four broad categories:

(1) The "human being" view:

> According to this first view, the Aramaic phrase *bar ʾĕnāš* ("son of man") simply means a "human being" in general, without reference to any particular individual. In a similar vein, Driver suggests that this represents "a figure in human form."[753] The main defense for this view is the use elsewhere in the Old Testament for this phrase and its Hebrew equivalent (*ben ʾāḏām*). (See the translation note above regarding v. 13.)[754] Admittedly, this phrase is commonly used for a *human being*. This is reinforced by the parallelism in Ps 8:4, where "son of man" means *mankind* in that

751. Casey, *Son of Man*, 80–83. *Num. Rab.* 13.14, for instance, states: "How do we know that he [the Messiah] will hold sway on land? Because it is written ... Behold, there came with the clouds of heaven one like unto a son of man ... and there was given unto him dominion ... that all the peoples should serve him" (cited in D. Burkett, "Son of Man in Apocalyptic and Rabbinic Texts," 115). Secondary references include *Midr. Ps.* 21.5; *Tanchuma Toledoth* 20; *Midr. Ps.* 2.9; *ʾAg. Ber.* 14.3; and *Gen. Rab.* 13.11 and 13.12.

752. D. L. Bock, "The Use of Daniel 7 in Jesus' Trial, with Implications for His Self-Understanding," in '*Who Is This Son of Man?': The Latest Scholarship on a Puzzling Expression of the Historical Jesus*, ed. L. Hurtado and P. L. Owen, 78–100 (London: Bloomsbury T&T Clark, 2012), 90.

753. S. R. Driver, "Son of Man," in *Dictionary of the Bible*, 4 vols., ed. J. Hastings, 4:579–89 (Edinburgh: T&T Clark, 1902), 579. Yet Driver (579) did go on to acknowledge that in its context, this human figure *denoted* "the glorified and ideal people of Israel."

754. Collins (305) provides additional evidence from the DSS: "It is found in the indefinite sense ('which no man can number') in 1QapGen 21:13 and in the general sense, 'human being,' in 11QtgJob 9:9; 26:2–3."

passage. Furthermore, there is no definite article preceding "son of man" in Dan 7:13 that would demand the identification of a particular individual.

Somewhat related to this view is the suggestion that the promise is to a particular human being, namely Judas Maccabeus. This view is dependent on a dating of the book to the second century BC (common with critical scholars). Supposedly after Antiochus Epiphanes IV (the "little horn" of the fourth beast according to their view), Judas is given a rule. Although he is not a king, he is *like* one ("like a son of man" = like a king). This view was espoused very early by the anti-Christian philosopher Porphyry (ca. AD 232/4 – ca. AD 305) and has been affirmed more recently by Buchanan and Sahlin.[755] However, as demonstrated in the previous section (Dan 7:1–8), the fourth beast is most likely the Roman Empire, and thus Antiochus is not the "little horn."

(2) The collective or personification view:

A second major view interprets the reference to "one like a son of man" not as an individual at all, but rather as a collective representation or personification for a *group* of people.[756] The group is then understood as the Jewish people, the saints of the Most High, who stand to gain the kingdom. This view is also quite ancient, advocated in a modified form by Aphrem Syrus, a Christian author and theologian of Syriac Christianity (d. ca. AD 373). Although Aphrem Syrus held this view, he also saw an ultimate fulfillment in Jesus. Nevertheless, the collective interpretation came to be the standard view by the end of the nineteenth century (so Hitzig in his 1850 commentary). In a more particular form of this interpretation, the people are the "faithful Jews" of the second century BC (once again, a view held by critical scholars who accept the second-century BC dating of the book). This view has been defended in the noteworthy commentaries of Montgomery (317–24), Hartman (87), and more recently Newsom (235).

---

755. G. W. Buchanan, *The Book of Daniel*; and H. Sahlin, "Antiochus IV Epiphanes und Judas Mackabäus," *ST* 23 (1969): 41–68.

756. M. Casey, "The Corporate Interpretation of 'One Like a Son of Man' (Dan. Vii 13) at the Time of Jesus," *NovT* 18 (1976): 167–80, attempted to defend the corporate interpretation on the basis of midrashic interpretations found in *Midr. Ps.* 21,5 and *Tanch. Tol.* 20, which are hardly convincing in light of the internal problems found in the documents (not to mention the rabbinic gymnastics involved in their formulations). The exegesis of Dan 7:13–14 in its own context must be given primary weight.

Hartman's interpretation is also similar to the first view, for he uses the same arguments to defend the notion that the phrase properly applies to *human beings*. (Significantly, "son of man" is used in Ps 8 in a collective sense for *mankind*.) Yet he then applies it more specifically to those faithful Jews during the period of the Maccabees who were destined to be the recipients of the kingdom promise. Hartman (87) states, "... the 'one in human likeness' is not a real individual, celestial or terrestrial, but is only a symbol of 'the holy ones of the Most High,' a title given, as we shall see, to the faithful Jews—men, women, and children—who courageously withstood the persecution of Antiochus IV Epiphanes."[757]

Hartman seeks to justify a symbolic understanding of the "son of man" in light of the fact that the animal figures were not real animals but symbols. Furthermore, he defends the notion that a group of people are in view in light of Dan 7:27, which promises that the dominion of all the kingdoms will be taken and given to the *saints* of the Highest One.

Moloney develops the collective view further, so that "one like a son of man" (for him, the "saints of the Most High" based on a comparison of Dan 7:13–14 with Dan 7:27) *includes* a fulfillment in Jesus as the highest example of vindication of faithful yet suffering Israel. He writes,

> The expression "one like a son of man," used to describe the holy ones in Israel in Daniel 7, becomes "the Son of Man" in the person of Jesus. The nation of holy ones, prepared to obey the God of Israel in the conviction that in the end—despite all apparent human wisdom and appearances—God would have the last word, is assumed by Jesus as an individual, "the Son of Man."[758]

---

757. Hartman regards these faithful Jews as "the Israel of faith" which will replace the pagan empires (89). He also speaks of them as "faithful Israelites to be rewarded for their steadfastness in the face of persecution and martyrdom" (97–98).

758. F. J. Moloney, "*Constructing Jesus* and the Son of Man," *CBQ* 75 (2013): 736. T. Meadowcroft, "'One Like a Son of Man' in the Court of the Foreign King: Daniel 7 as Pointer to Wise Participation in the Divine Life," *JTI* 10 (2016): 245–63, has a similar view to that of Moloney. He writes (246), "The culmination of the vision in Dan 7 is the throne room scene in which the one like a son of man encounters the Ancient of Days. The subsequent interpretation of the vision appears to equate the one like a son of man with the people of God while also allowing for the distinctiveness of the one like a son of man within the people of God." The problem with such a formulation is that mutual participation in the kingdom of God (by both "one like a son of man" and by "the saints of the Highest One") does not logically mean they are to be equated. The kingdom can be given to both, though they remain distinct.

Despite all such arguments for a collective view, it still suffers from a fatal problem, namely the statement in Dan 7:14 that all the peoples, nations, and tongues will serve (i.e., worship) him. (See the translation note earlier regarding the word translated "serve" in v. 14.) Baldwin (150) also observes that the phrase is "son of man," not "son of Israel" (or Jacob), as one might expect had the Jewish people been in view. Finally, Collins (305) discounts Hartman's appeal to the symbolic animal figures to justify his symbolic understanding of "son of man": "the apparition of the 'one like a human being' is separated from the beasts in the text by the description of the Ancient of Days, which is generally accepted as a mythic-realistic symbol for God."

(3) The angelic view:

Other scholars have taken the collective view and modified it to interpret the *group* as angels (so J. Coppens). Defenders of this view have pointed out that it is customary in visions to have an angel(s) appearing in human semblance. Some proponents of the angelic interpretation hold that a *specific angel* is in view, such as Gabriel or Michael.[759]

Collins (304–10), for instance, views the "one like a son of man" as Michael and the "holy ones" as his angelic followers on whose behalf he receives the kingdom.[760] In support of this theory, it is noted that the "saints of the Most High" (*qadîšê ʿelyônîn*) in Dan 7:18 are said to receive the kingdom. The equivalent Hebrew term (*qᵊdôšîm*) commonly refers to *angels* in the MT and

---

759. Z. Zevit, "The Structure and Individual Elements of Daniel 7," *ZAW* 80 (1968): 396, views the "one in human likeness" as Gabriel, who represents "the holy ones of the Most High," i.e., the Jewish people in the Kingdom. U. B. Müller, *Messias und Menschensohn in jüdischen Apokalypsen und in der Offenbarung des Johannes*, SNT 6 (Gütersloh: Gütersloher Verlagshaus, 1972), 19–36, 217, sees him as Michael, the guardian angel of Israel. But since the guardian angel represents the nation, it comes to symbolize further eschatological Israel.

760. Regarding Collins' view, also see his *The Apocalyptic Vision of the Book of Daniel*, HSM 16 (Missoula, MT: Scholars Press, 1977), 141–46. Against Collins, see J. D. G. Dunn, "'Son of God' as 'Son of Man' in the Dead Sea Scrolls: A Response to John Collins on 4Q246," in *The Scrolls and the Scriptures: Qumran Fifty Years After*, ed. S. E. Porter and C. A. Evans, 198–210 (Sheffield: Sheffield University Press, 1997). The interpretation of the angel as Michael had been espoused earlier by N. Schmidt, "The Son of Man in the Book of Daniel," *JBL* 19 (1900): 22–28, and argued for more recently by Day, *God's Conflict with the Dragon and the Sea*, 172–77; Walton, "The Anzu Myth as Relevant Background for Daniel 7?" 80; and T. B. Slater, "One Like a Son of Man in First-Century Judaism," *NTS* 41 (1995): 189–90.

deuterocanonical books of the OT, but in some places are "men." Furthermore, similar phraseology in regard to angels is found elsewhere in the book of Daniel, though as Shepherd points out this is not conclusive:

> The strength of the angelic interpretation lies in the fact that angels or possible angelic figures are described as "like the appearance of a man" (Dan 8:15; 10:18), "man" (Dan 9:21; 10:5; 12:6–7), and "as the likeness of the sons of man" (Dan 10:16). But Daniel is also called a "son of man" (Dan 8:17), and the Aramaic phrase "like a son of man" (כבר אנש) is never used of anyone except the figure in Dan 7:13.[761]

In seeking to defend his angelic interpretation, Collins (309) argues against the messianic view on the basis that "nowhere in the book do we find either support for or interest in the Davidic monarchy," and the only ruler of Israel in the eschatological time frame of the book is Michael, the "prince" (10:21; 12:1). In response, one could point out that Collins is assuming a second-century BC date for the book and restricts the scope of fulfillment up to (but not beyond) this point. Otherwise, we clearly do have a Davidic Messiah in Dan 9.

The major weakness to this view, however, is that the suffering and defeat of the "holy ones" is implied in vv. 21 and 25.[762] Furthermore, the fact that all nations will *serve* (i.e., worship) "one like a son of man" is hardly fitting of an angelic figure.

(4) The messianic view:

The earliest interpretation among both Jews and Christians is the messianic one.[763] As previously demonstrated, there was already evidence of this in the intertestamental literature as attested by the repeated connection in *I Enoch* between the Son of Man and the Messiah (see *I En.* 37–71, esp. 46:1–6; 48:1–7). Even in the early centuries following the crucifixion, we find evidence in Jewish circles connecting the Danielic son of man with Messiah. Rabbi Akiba (early second century AD) took him to be the Messiah. In the Jewish Talmud he is said to be the Messiah, and

761. Shepherd, "Daniel 7:13 and the New Testament Son of Man," 103.

762. For further refutation of the angelic view, see V. S. Poythress, "The Holy Ones of the Most High in Daniel VII," *VT* 26 (1976): 208–13; and Hartman and Di Lella, 89–101.

763. The messianic interpretation is clearly affirmed in the following Jewish sources: *b. Sanh.* 98a; *Num. Rab.* 13:14; and *ʾAggadat Bĕrʾēšît* 14:3; 23:1.

this view was embraced by most rabbinical exegetes. Montgomery (321) writes,

> Joshua b. Levi, c. 250, taught that, if Israel deserved it, the Messiah would come with the clouds of heaven, after Dan. 7, or, if otherwise, riding upon an ass, after Zech. 9[9] (*Sanh.* 98*a*). This interpretation was followed by all the Jewish comm., with the exception of AEz., as noted above, including the Karaite Jepheth, *e.g.*, Rashi, 'This is King Messiah.'

Christian interpreters quite naturally saw the fulfillment in the Lord Jesus Christ, especially due to Jesus' frequent reference to himself as *the Son of Man* (e.g., Matt 16:28; 19:28; 24:27, 30, 39, 44; 25:31, 34; etc.).[764] Of particular importance is the reference in Mark 14:62. When asked at his trial by the Jewish high priest as to whether or not he was the Messiah, Jesus replied, "I am; and you shall see the Son of Man sitting at the right hand of Power, and coming with the clouds of heaven" (NASB). His response is a direct allusion to Dan 7:13–14, as his reference to the "clouds" makes clear (cf. Matt 24:30 and Luke 21:27–31 which associate this scene with the second coming).[765] Indeed, this response became the basis of the charge of blasphemy leveled against him. Yet Jesus' appeal to Dan 7:13–14 cannot be seen in isolation, as though this was a post-Easter maneuver by the early church to put words back into Jesus' mouth, portraying him as claiming something he never really believed about himself (as certain radical critical scholars have suggested). Jesus had consistently and frequently used the expression "the Son of Man" of himself throughout his public ministry. Now near the end of his ministry, he ramped up the significance of this self-identification by adding the words "coming with the clouds of heaven," which more clearly

764. The phrase "Son of Man" occurs about 84x in the gospels (cf. Acts 7:56).

765. For further discussion of the occurrences of "Son of Man" in the NT that include obvious reference or allusion to Dan 7:13–14, see Shepherd, "Daniel 7:13 and the New Testament Son of Man," 107–11. A. Y. Collins, "Daniel 7 and the Historical Jesus," in *Of Scribes and Scrolls: Studies on the Hebrew Bible, Intertestamental Judaism, and Christian Origins*, ed. H. W. Attridge, J. J. Collins, and T. H. Tobin (Lanham, MD: University Press of America, 1990) takes the unique view that Jesus did indeed have Dan 7:13 in mind in referring to himself as the Son of Man, but not in such a way as to identify himself with that figure. In light of the *heavenly character* of the Son of Man/Messiah in the Similitudes, she takes it that Jesus saw himself as an apocalyptic leader who would have an eschatological role in the near future. According to Collins (193), "After Jesus died and was vindicated in the eyes of his followers, they reinterpreted Dan 7:13 in such a way as to identify him with the 'son of man' mentioned there and interpreted this phrase messianically."

than before revealed that he saw himself as that kingly figure in Dan 7:13–14. (This connection had recently been revealed to his disciples in the Olivet Discourse—see Matt 24:30—but now he was stating it publicly with the religious leaders.) If in the context of Dan 7, "one like a son of man" was a bit ambiguous, Jesus was now removing all ambiguity and claiming to be that one. Furthermore, his use of the words "sitting at the right hand of Power" clarified that the question he had put to the religious leaders a few days earlier about Ps 110 ("David himself calls Him 'Lord'; so in what sense is He his son?"), was now one that He himself would answer: He is David's Lord who shall sit at God's right hand! By this, Jesus has neatly tied Ps 110:1 and Dan 7:13–14 together and in doing so has shown that the Davidic covenant promise of eternal kingship and the kingship promise of Dan 7 find their fulfillment in him.[766]

Shepherd has also pointed out a striking intertextual feature of Daniel that argues for the messianic interpretation, namely the Hebraism "at the end of the days" (בְּאַחֲרִית יוֹמַיָּא, *bᵊʾaḥărîṯ yômayyāʾ*) mentioned in Dan 2:28 (and also in the Hebrew text of 10:14). Since the nation's hope rides with a future king who appears at this time (Isa 2:2; Jer 23:20; 30:24; 48:47; 49:39; Ezek 38:16; Hos 3:5; Mic 4:1), Shepherd points out the connection,

> The use of "at the end of the days" in Daniel links the eschatology of the book to that of the rest of the canon. Therefore, the coming king from Judah is the most likely candidate for the head of the everlasting kingdom in Daniel (Dan 2:44; 3:33; 4:31; 6:27; 7:14, 18, 27). God is the ruler of the kingdom, and he gives it to whomever he pleases (Dan 4:14, 22, 29). His choice is the coming king from Judah—the one "like a son of man" in Dan 7:13.[767]

When all is considered, the messianic view has the most to commend it. After a lengthy discussion of the development of messianic theology in the OT, including such themes as dominion given to man (Gen 1:26), kingship (particularly in the Psalms), and even kingly suffering, Rowe posits three arguments that favor "one like a son of man" being a reference to Messiah rather than collectively the saints or some angelic figure:[768]

---

766. For an excellent discussion showing how Jesus' use of the question about David's *son* in Ps 110:1 paved the way for the declaration at his trial of being the Danielic "son of man" (Mark 14:62), see D. L. Bock, "The Use of Daniel 7 in Jesus' Trial," 78–84.
767. Ibid., 104.
768. R. D. Rowe, "Is Daniel's 'Son of Man' Messianic?" in *Christ the Lord*, ed. H. H. Rowdon, 71–96 (Leicester/Downers Grove, IL: Inter-Varsity Press, 1982), 94–96. Rowe's insights regarding the concept of "son of man" in relationship to messianic

1. The enthronement of God (v. 9) followed by the granting of kingship to 'one like a son of man' (v. 13) is reminiscent of the coronation of the Davidic king in Psalm 2. … the structure of the dream reflects the celebration of Yahweh's kingship, which we have seen in the Psalms is associated with the Davidic (messianic) king. …
2. It is difficult to conceive of the 'saints of the Most High' without a leader. … Having received the kingship, he shares it with the saints, by virtue of his close identification with them.
3. If, as we have seen, 'one like a son of man' who comes 'with the clouds of heaven' is a heavenly being, although he may represent the saints he cannot be merely a symbol for them. … it is the heavenly origin of the 'one like a son of man' which finally proves his individuality and thus (taken with other indications in the chapter) his messianic role.

In a 2005 article M. Albani argued for a synthesis of the various views. Nevertheless, Albani defended the aspect of individuality as over and against the collective interpretation (i.e., the "son of man" being the Jewish people). In doing so, he argued that the figure was in some way a royal messianic figure. As for him being given "dominion and glory and kingship," Albani asserted that he must be seen in light of Israelite royal ideology and concluded,

> This is the eschatological fulfillment of the promises still open for the Davidic dynasty (Pss 2:8f.; 89:27; 110). Although in the book of Daniel the "one like a son of man" is never *expressis verbis* identified with the Messiah, his function in the eschatological hope of Daniel 7 runs parallel to the role of the royal Messiah in messianic expectations.[769]

As pointed out earlier, some of the other views depend on a late dating of the book in the second century BC (a point refuted elsewhere). The angelic view is unlikely, because this would have the "little horn" fighting and defeating the angels. Furthermore, the term "saints" or "holy ones" (Aram. *qaddîšîn*; Heb. *qᵊdôšîm*) is not an exclusive term for "angels," and there is nothing in the context of Dan 7 to suggest the "holy ones" should be understood as angels. Why would "one like a son of man" refer to angels, when the angels had already been depicted in Dan 7:10 as those who stood before the Ancient

---

kingship are particularly insightful (82): "To summarize our consideration of messianic kingship in Israel, we have seen that in the context of worship the Davidic king was closely associated with the kingship of Yahweh, was sometimes represented as suffering and also played the role of 'representative man' (analogous to the first man) in relation to God; here he acted out, in his person and on behalf of his people Israel, on the one hand the frailty and humiliation of mankind and on the other the kingly authority and exaltation of mankind. In that role he was known as *ben ʾāḏām*."

769. M. Albani, "The 'One Like a Son of Man' (Dan 7:13) and the Royal Ideology," in *Enoch and Qumran Origins: New Light on a Forgotten Connection*, ed. G. Boccaccini (Grand Rapids: Eerdmans, 2005), 48.

of Days and attended him? Although "son of man" *can* refer to mankind in the OT, the "human being" view is insufficient for v. 13 in light of the *worship* that "one like a son of man" is given. The word used for "serving" him (NIV = worshiped) in v. 14 is the word פְּלַח (*pəlaḥ*), which in biblical Aramaic is always used with the idea of service or worship of a deity. It means more than "honor," because *pəlaḥ* clearly implies idolatry when not used of the true God. This same argument would militate against the angelic view.

Hence, "one like a son of man" refers to and finds its fulfillment in Jesus the Messiah. When properly understood, *son of man* does have reference to a *human being* (as it customarily does elsewhere in the OT). This one, however, who receives a kingdom is *like* a son of man, i.e., he does have a connection with humanity. If anything, Dan 7:13–14 should have prompted the reader to look for a Messiah who is both human on the one hand and yet able to receive *worship* on the other hand, i.e., he must be both human and divine. That is exactly what the virgin birth of Jesus of Nazareth provides: He was born of a woman (a virgin!) and yet conceived by the Holy Spirit. In the consciousness of Jesus, it was an easy transition from "one like a son of man" to "the Son of Man."[770] He, and he alone, is the representative of all mankind

---

770. Regarding Jesus' understanding and use of "son of man," see D. Bock, "The Son of Man in Luke 5:24," *BBR* 1 (1991): 109–21; and "The Use of Daniel 7 in Jesus' Trial." In both articles Bock clarifies how Jesus played upon the ambiguity of the phrase for his own purposes, first (in Luke 5:24) concerning his ability to forgive sins, and then late in his earthly ministry (in Mark 14:62—where He obviously draws upon Dan 7:13)—to signify his ultimate authority over the religious leaders. Bock's explanation of the shift from ambiguity in using the phrase (for most of his ministry) to intentional application with explicit connection to Dan 7 (near the end of his ministry) is insightful ("The Use of Daniel 7 in Jesus' Trial," 89):

> Numerous issues surround the discussion, including an intense debate over whether the expression is representative of a title (like the form of its consistent NT use) or is an idiom. If it is an idiom, then it has been argued that the meaning is either a circumlocution for "I" (Vermes) or an indirect expression with the force of 'some person' (Fitzmyer). It seems that, for most students of the problem today, a formal title, or at least a unified Son of Man concept, did not yet exist in the early first century and that Fitzmyer has more evidence available for his view on the idiom. It is the idiomatic element in the Aramaic expression and the lack of a fixed concept in Judaism that allow any 'son of man' remark to be ambiguous unless it is tied to a specific passage or context. This means the term could be an effective vehicle as a cipher for Jesus that he could fill with content, defining it as he used it. One can argue, looking at the flow of Jesus' ministry as it appears in the Synoptics, that Jesus used the term ambiguously initially and drew out its force as he continued to use it, eventually associating it with Daniel 7.

in that he has borne the punishment for the sins of each one. Grassmick explains the appropriateness of the phrase for the Lord Jesus:

> This title especially suited Jesus' total mission. It was free of political connotations, thus preventing false expectations. Yet it was sufficiently ambiguous (like a parable) to preserve the balance between concealment and disclosure in Jesus' life and mission (cf. [Mark] 4:11–12). It combined the elements of suffering and glory in a way no other designation could. It served to define His unique role as Messiah.[771]

Also to be noted in Dan 7:13 is that the "one like a son of man" comes with the *clouds* (עֲנָנֵי, *ʿănānê*) of heaven (or the sky). There is some evidence that the element of "clouds" (*ʿănānê*) was associated with the Messiah in rabbinic tradition.[772] In light of the *cloud motif* in the OT, it is not without significance that Messiah Jesus is said to appear this way. Clouds are frequently connected with theophanies in the OT (Exod 16:10; 19:9; Lev 16:2; Deut 1:33; 1 Kgs 8:10; Ps 104:3; Isa 19:1). The OT depicts the LORD (Yahweh) riding upon the clouds (as though his chariot), and this also hints at the deity of the Messiah in Dan 7:13. Yet there is no need, as some have suggested, to find an adequate background for vv. 13–14 in Canaanite mythology (such as the storm-god Baal as a "rider of the clouds"). That Canaanite myths would influence literature written so many centuries later is rather unlikely.

The NT takes up the imagery of a divine figure coming with clouds, envisioning a literal fulfillment at the time of Christ's second coming (Matt 24:30; Mark 13:26). The Matthaean passage reads, "Then the sign of the Son of Man will appear in heaven, and all the tribes of the earth will mourn. They will see *the Son of Man arriving on the clouds of heaven* with power and great

---

Bock goes on to conclude (99): "So Jesus' evocation of Son of Man before the Jewish leadership raises the issue of kingdom authority. Who speaks for God, Jesus or the leadership? The reaction of the Jewish leadership to Jesus in this scene shows that they got Jesus' point. What Jesus saw as vindication pointing to the support of his mission from God, they viewed as blasphemous, giving them a reason to take a political charge to Pilate."

771. J. Grassmick, "Mark," in *Bible Knowledge Commentary: New Testament*, ed. J. F. Walvoord and R. B. Zuck, 95–197 (Wheaton, IL: SP Publications, 1983), 140. F. F. Bruce came to similar conclusions in his 1982 article, "The Background to the Son of Man Sayings" (70):

> Jesus' special use of the expression (as distinct from its general Aramaic use in the sense of 'man', 'the man', or a possible use to replace the pronoun 'I') was derived from the 'one like a son of man' who is divinely vested with authority in Daniel 7:13f. Because it was a current title, it was not liable to be misunderstood, as current titles were, and Jesus was free to take up the expression and give it what meaning he chose.

772. *Tanḥuma Toledoth* 20 and Tg. 1 Chron 3:24.

glory" (NET). This is something of a counterpart to his ascension, when "he was lifted up and a cloud hid him from their sight" (Acts 1:9).

In that clouds are associated with both his ascension and the second coming, the question might rightly be asked as to when this event occurs that he is presented to the Ancient of Days and awarded dominion (or authority) and a kingdom. Given the general tenor of the passage, we would expect the *complete fulfillment* to occur at the general time of the second coming. First, if there is any chronological sequence to these events, we should observe that the authority and kingdom given to "one like a son of man" *follows* the destruction of the "little horn" of the fourth beast. Second, Dan 7 is parallel in many ways to Dan 2, and in the earlier chapter the kingdom that is never destroyed is established in the days of the ten toes and puts an end to the earlier kingdoms (2:44). As argued earlier, this has its fulfillment with the ten-king confederation of the tribulation. Granting these points, however, it may be that the *manner* and *timing* of fulfillment are more complex than we might at first expect. For a truly satisfactory answer, we would really need to consider all the revelation concerning the kingdom of God in Scripture. This would include those passages that also link Messiah's sitting at the right hand of God with his coming on the clouds (note Matt 26:64; Mark 14:62). Surely Christ is sitting at the right hand of the Father *now* and waiting for his enemies to be made a footstool for his feet (Heb 1:13). At the same time he can declare, "All authority has been given to Me in heaven and on earth" (Matt 28:18). Also needing to be considered is Ps 2. When has God the Father installed *his anointed one* as "My king" according to Ps 2:6? Verse 7 gives the answer: "today," i.e., the day when he has "begotten" the Son. In accordance with ancient Near Eastern custom, these are words of kingly coronation ("adoption imagery") utilized at a time that a new ruler enters in to his kingly role (cf. Ps 89:26–29).[773] In one very real sense, the coronation of Christ as king has been inaugurated with his resurrection and ascension to the Father's right hand. For this reason, Acts 13:33 associates the fulfillment of Ps 2:7 with the resurrection of Christ.[774] In light of broader theological considerations, then, it may be that Dan 7:13 does have a connection with Christ's resurrection and ascension. He has been given kingdom authority,

---

773. For substantiation, see M. Weinfeld, "The Covenant of Grant in the Old Testament and in the Ancient Near East," *JAOS* 90 (1970): 184–203. One piece of evidence that Weinfeld offers (191) comes from a treaty between Šupilluliumaš and Mattiwaza: "Mattiwaza, in describing how he established relations with Šupilluliumaš, says: '(The great king) grasped me with [his ha]nd ... and said: when I will conquer the land of Mittanni I shall not reject you, I shall make you my son, I will stand by (to help in war) and will make you sit on the throne of your father.'"

774. For a more complete discussion of the fulfillment of the Davidic promise to the Lord Jesus Christ and the connection to the resurrection and ascension of Jesus, see J. P. Tanner, "James's Quotation of Amos 9 to Settle the Jerusalem Council Debate in Acts 15," *JETS* 55 (2012): 65–85.

and yet he also waits for his enemies to be made a footstool for his feet, such that the *complete fulfillment* of vv. 13–14 is found in the second coming. Not until then will we find all peoples and nations *serving* him.

To be escorted into the presence of the Ancient of Days means that Messiah is given *royal audience* with God the Father. (See translation note to Dan 7:13 regarding the translation "presented before Him.") The NT is clear that before his incarnation, Jesus was with the Father and came forth from him to accomplish his will of dying for the sins of all. In John 17:5 Jesus declared, "And now, Father, glorify me in your own presence with the glory that I had with you before the world existed" (cf. John 7:29; 16:28). Since Jesus was with the Father in glory before his incarnation, Dan 7:13 seems to envision his reunion with the Father, having now accomplished his will on earth.

As a result of his successful completion of the Father's will, Jesus is appropriately given an inheritance fitting for an obedient son. As Heb 1:3 informs us, the Son has been "appointed heir of all things" (alluding to the promise in Ps 2:8 that his inheritance is "the nations"). The original divine intention for man to have dominion over all creation (Gen 1:26) is now entrusted to Jesus Christ. Daniel 7:14 clarifies that this inheritance for Christ consists of authority for ruling, glory appropriate to such an honor, and a kingdom over which to rule. Yet, unlike the powerful kingdoms of old depicted in Dan 7:1–8, this kingdom will be the most extensive of all; it will be universal. In this culminating kingdom of history all peoples, nations, and individuals of every language group will *serve* him. The word translated "serve" means far more than to render aid to, for in biblical Aramaic this term is always used in the sense of *service or worship given to what one believes to be deity*. (See translation note for Dan 7:14.) This argues strongly for the deity of Messiah (and why "one like a son of man" cannot merely be the Jewish people or any angel). There is also another clue from the OT regarding the doctrine of the Trinity. Messiah is distinct from the Ancient of Days (the Father) and yet is accorded worship as one who is divine. The full realization of Messiah's dominion and kingdom will not come about until the second coming. We could speak of this as the "consummative messianic kingdom." He will ask the Father to have the nations as his inheritance (in fulfillment of Ps 2:8), and then he will return in glory to forcefully lay hold of what is rightfully his. Or in the words of Ps 2:9 (ESV), "You shall break them with a rod of iron and dash them in pieces like a potter's vessel." (Rev 19:15 alludes to this verse in a context describing the second coming.) This will inaugurate his universal rule described in Ps 72:8–11. In the meantime, preparation is being made for this future kingdom as various peoples from all nations place their faith in Messiah Jesus, are redeemed, and are transferred "to the kingdom of His beloved Son" (Col 1:13). The latter looks at their being *made citizens* for this kingdom yet to come (not that the kingdom itself is fully operational). Finally, this kingdom as envisioned in Dan 7:14 is eternal. It will never deteriorate and pass into oblivion or be conquered (recall Dan 2:44).

Biblical Theology Comments

Dan 7:9–14 makes perhaps the richest contribution to biblical theology to come from the book of Daniel. Most of this theological *richness* has already been pointed out in the preceding commentary for this pericope. Though the phrase has perhaps a thinly veiled obscurity to it, nevertheless the "son of man" figure—one who himself participates in humanity—is ultimately confirmed in the progress of revelation of Scripture to be the Lord Jesus Christ. As for the divinely bestowed kingdom of God, first revealed in Daniel at 2:44–45, it is to him (the Lord Jesus) that this kingdom will be given, so that he might rule over all nations and ultimately bring Israel out of her spiritual blindness and oppression by beastly nations to the blessedness of his worldwide kingdom rule. This is exactly what we would expect in light of the Davidic covenant promise in 2 Sam 7:12–16 that God will raise up from David's descendants One who will have an eternal throne/kingdom.

In this light, it is hardly fitting that the promise in Dan 7:14 that "all the peoples, nations and men of every language might serve Him" would find fulfillment with any angel or any human group of saints. As pointed out in the commentary, the *cloud motif* at v. 13 associates vv. 13–14 with both Jesus' ascension to the Father's right hand as well as his return in glory to claim his victory and impose his kingly rule upon the world he created and went to the cross for. With his ascension to the Father's right hand, he has been proclaimed "Lord" (Acts 2:36) and possesses "all authority" (which he uses for building his church); with his second coming he will use his authority to bring the whole world into submission.

Application and Devotional Implications

The Bible presents the *certainties* of life—those matters that we can confidently believe, expect, and know will come to pass. One of these certainties is the kingdom that is going to be entrusted to "the Son of Man," the Lord Jesus Christ. There is not even a shadow of a doubt that He receives this kingdom and rules forever. Any attempt to oppose what God has purposed is certain to fail. Nevertheless, Satan is still bent on opposing this grand design of God—an attempt to prevent this kingdom from coming about with Jesus ruling righteously over all. Satan also has a plan, though it is a plan doomed to failure. He thinks he can thwart God's plan by introducing the antichrist ("the little horn") to deceive the earth and rule it. In Christ's first coming, Satan thought he could derail God's plan by offering Christ himself a tempting alternative. After showing Jesus all the kingdoms of the world and their grandeur, Satan said, "All these things I will give you, if you fall down and worship me" (Matt 4:9 NASB). Perhaps we fail to appreciate how tempting an offer that might have seemed to our Lord. He could have had all the "kingdoms of the world" without having to go to the cross. Yet having a kingdom just to have a kingdom (and the power thereof) was not his real goal. By going to the cross and dying for us, he now will have a kingdom made up of subjects who love, adore, and worship him forever. This is why Dan 7:14 says that all peoples, nations, and language groups will *serve* (i.e., worship) him. We don't do this because we are forced to. Rather, we know this is a king worthy of our love and worship. We gladly render our worship to him, because he gave so much for us to be a part of his kingdom. Just as the Lord Jesus had his sights set on the kingdom that he stood to gain from the Father, so our sights need to be set each day on how we can live for this kingdom and do what our king wants us to do in preparation for his return and reign. That is why we must not tire in our present labor. Because his kingdom is a *certainty*, we cannot afford to squander the time we are given to faithfully serve him as we await his return.

2. The interpretation of the visions given to Daniel (7:15–28)

Chapter 7 presents the first of a series of four visions given directly to Daniel. The details of what he saw in the first vision were described in vv. 1–14. Beginning with v. 15, Daniel is given the interpretation of his vision by an angelic being. Most of the details focus upon the fourth beast (kingdom) and the kings that emerge from it. First, however, we read of Daniel's personal distress over the experience of the vision and his need of an interpreter (vv. 15–16). Although many troubling times will accompany the days when these empires flourish, Daniel is given the consolation that ultimately God will bring in a kingdom—an eternal one—in which the saints of God will enter and possess along with the one "like a son of man."

a. Daniel's reaction to the visions and inquiry to understand (7:15–16)

Textual Notes

15.a-a. For the notoriously difficult expression בְּגוֹא נִדְנֶה, the editor of *BHS* proposes an emendation to בגו דנה or בְּגִין דְּנָה, meaning "on account of this." (דְּנָה means "which," and בְּגִין, from גִּין, means "for the sake of, account of"; *DTT*, 239.) But this is not convincing, since (1) the emendation does not account for the א, and (2) we have a very similar phrase in the *Genesis Apocryphon* (1QapGen 2:10), לגו נדנהא, meaning "within its sheath." See *DTT* (216) for גַּו as a prep. "within, among" (used in combination with either ב or ל), and *DTT* (879) for נִדְנָא, a noun, "sheath." Furthermore, LXX$^{\theta}$ translated ἐν τῇ ἕξει μου, "in my possession," which supports MT. Feinberg (82) concludes that בְּגוֹא נִדְנֶה simply means "within me" (so NASB). The idea would be that the body acts as a sheath for the human spirit within (so Rashi; Goldwurm, 207).

Translation

7:15 "As for me, Daniel, my spirit was distressed within me, and the visions of my mind kept alarming me. **16** I approached one of those standing *nearby*, and I was asking him for the exact meaning[775] of all this. So he spoke to me and informed me of the interpretation of the matter."[776]

---

775. The translation "the exact meaning" is lit., "the truth" (יַצִּיבָא, *yaṣṣîḇāʾ*, adj. meaning "certain, true"). Daniel desired to know the certain (or reliable) meaning of these things. Hartman (207) captures the point well in his translation: "I asked him what all this really meant."

776. "The matter" (from Aram. מִלָּה, *millâ*, "matter, affair"; *HALOT*, 1915). Contextually, the *matter* is the vision he had just seen. Hence, the NET translated as "vision."

Commentary

7:15–16 Daniel's distress and alarm is not due to the frightening imagery of the beasts he had seen, for he realizes its symbolic nature. In asking to know the exact meaning of the details of the vision, he wanted to know with certainty the proper interpretation. He would have sensed that much of the vision had ominous implications for his people, and the angelic interpretation would have confirmed this. Even after the explanations are given, v. 28 indicates that he was still alarmed.

One of those "standing nearby" is undoubtedly an angelic being (recall v. 10), though we are not told his exact identity. Gabriel provides this type of interpretative help later (8:16; 9:21) and thus could be the angelic interpreter here, though we cannot be sure of that. It is not unusual for an angel to have an interpreting role in response to a vision (cf. Zech 1:9, 14, 19). Even though such a feature is common to apocalyptic literature, this in and of itself is not a valid reason for dating the book late (as though it were from a later period when most apocalyptic literature flourished). One could just as easily argue that apocalyptic literature of the intertestamental period patterned itself after similar passages to this in earlier biblical literature.[777]

Daniel's reaction to the vision was not an uncommon experience. Elsewhere in the book we are told of similar reactions—physical, psychological, and emotional—upon receiving divine revelation (e.g., 8:17; 9:20; 10:7, 15–16; cf. Rev 1:17).

b. A summary explanation of the visions for Daniel (7:17–18)

Textual Notes

17.a. Although MT has "kings" (מַלְכִין, *malkîn*), both LXX^{O} and LXX$^{\theta}$ have βασιλεῖαι, "kingdoms." But this may be an attempt to harmonize with v. 23, where the fourth beast is a "fourth kingdom." Although MT is fine as is (so most translations), the NIV translated as "kingdoms."

18.a. We might have expected the sg. form עֶלְיוֹן (as is consistently the case in BH), or עִלָּאָה, "the Most High" (as in 4:14). The pl. form עֶלְיוֹנִין is also used in Dan 7:22, 25, 27.

777. R. Taylor, *Interpreting Apocalyptic Literature: An Exegetical Handbook* (Grand Rapids: Kregel, 2016), in his helpful analysis of apocalyptic literature points out that "certain passages in Old Testament prophetic literature point to an apocalyptic emphasis" (46). He went on to acknowledge that a number of the Old Testament prophets (some of whom clearly predate the era customarily assigned to apocalyptic literature) used language that moved beyond common prophetic rhetoric and stated (52), "The seeds of apocalyptic language can be seen here. In these writers an incipient apocalypticism is present in germ form, situated within contexts that employ other forms of prophetic speech. Many later writers followed in the train of these prophets, expanding such motifs considerably."

Translation

7:17 "These four great beasts are four kings[778] who will arise from the earth.
18 But the saints[779] of the Most High[780] will receive the kingdom and take

---

778. The translation "kings" is technically correct (see textual note above). The NIV, following LXX$^{\theta}$ and LXX^{O}, has "four kingdoms." Some (e.g., Rashi) have noted that even though "kings" is the proper translation, "the word is used here in its broader sense" (Goldwurm, 208). Hence, the kings stand for their kingdoms.

779. "Saints" is a translation of Aram. קַדִּישֵׁי, *qaddîšê* (here, construct form). The adj. *qaddîš* properly means "holy" and in its substantival use can be translated "saints" or "holy ones." No small debate has arisen as to whether this pertains to humans or angels. Those advocating the latter prefer the translation "holy ones." For a lengthy defense of the angelic view, see Collins (312–19). Yet both the NASB and NIV opt for the translation "saints" (which favors the human view). From a study of both Aram. *qaddîš* and its Heb. equivalent *qādôš*, it can easily be seen that these terms can be used for either *holy people* or angelic beings. The idea of God's *holy people* derives from the fact that Israel was called to be a "holy nation" (*gôy qādôš*) in Exod 19:6 and a "holy people" (*ʿam qādôš*) in Deut 7:6 and 26:19. Cf. Pss 16:3 and 34:10. Even within Daniel, both referents are found. The term is used of angels in such places as Dan 4:13 [Aram. 10]; 4:17 [Aram. 14]; 4:23 [Aram. 20]; and 2x in 8:13, and outside of Daniel in Deut 33:2; Ps 89:5 [6]; and Zech 14:5. In 8:24 the expression *ʿam qᵉdōšîm* could be debated but probably refers to "holy people." (If appositional, see Dan 11:15, 32 for examples of appositional plurals after "people"; other examples outside of Daniel include Exod 1:9; Ps 95:10; and Jer 31:2.) In coming to a conclusion, one must compare the similar phrase *ʿam qaddîšê ʿelyônîn* in Dan 7:27. In light of Deut 7:6, this should properly be translated "the holy people of the Most High" (taking into account the fact that the sg. *ʿam* can be followed by *qaddîš/qādôš* in the pl., as in Dan 8:24, and comparing the use of *ʿam* in Dan 11:15, 32). Collins is aware of the phrase in Dan 7:27 but attempts to defend the angelic view by taking *qaddîšê* as a *possessive* of *ʿam* (= the people under the protection of the holy ones of the Most High). The usage of *ʿam* in Daniel, however, stands against his argument (not failing to observe that Michael is a guardian angel for Israel). *qaddîšê ʿelyônîn* refers to the "holy (people) of the Most High," and thus the translation "saints" best suits the context.

780. The translation "the Most High" is a rendering of Aram. עֶלְיוֹנִין (*ʿelyônîn*), peculiar in that it is a pl. form. Goldingay (143) argues that "saints (or holy ones) of the Most High" should be *qaddîšê ʿelyôn*, and thus concludes that *ʿelyônîn* is a modifier of *qaddîšê* rather than a reference to God (as a pl. of majesty). He then translates the phrase in v. 18, "holy ones on high." When God is referred to as "the Most High" in Daniel, it is usually as *ʿillāyʾā*, a sg. form from the adj. *ʿillāy* (as in Dan 4:14, 21, 29, 31; 7:25). However, there is a form *ʿelyôn*, which can be pluralized with the *în* suffix. In Jewish Aram., this carried the meaning "uppermost, highest, or most high," and the pl. form could even be used for inanimate things (e.g., "highest of all sacrifices"). (See Jastrow, *DTT*, 1082–83 for details.) The singular form *ʿelyôn* in BH is used in Deut 26:19 meaning "high." A pluralized form of Aram. *ʿelyôn* with

possession of the kingdom forever—forever and ever."[781]

Commentary

7:17 The initial explanation by the angel is quite brief. Only one verse is given to explaining the four beasts, and then one verse commenting on the kingdom. Yet the verses form an important hinge within the structure of the chapter. Raabe (who regards this section slightly differently as vv. 16b–18) notes:

> In this structure the brief interpretation of vv. 16b–18 plays a significant role. It serves as a brief, all inclusive interpretation of the whole vision. In doing so, it quickly summarizes the preceding and dramatically anticipates what follows. V. 17 interprets the four beasts and v. 18 anticipates the saints' possession (*ḥsn*) of the kingdom (v. 22). It also serves as a *middle pivot* or *hinge* which connects with the beginning and end of the chapter.[782]

Although in v. 17 the "beasts" are equated with kings, we are told in v. 23 that the fourth beast represents a kingdom. There is no real discrepancy here, for each kingdom is headed by a king, and these go hand in hand. This was also true in the case of Nebuchadnezzar's dream in chap. 2. Each part of the statue represented a kingdom (note 2:39), and yet Nebuchadnezzar himself is said to be the head of gold (2:37). Hence, each beast represents a Gentile kingdom and a king who rules over it.

7:18 One additional detail about the kingdom is given in v. 18. The kingdom was previously said to be given to "one like a son of man." Now it is said that the "holy ones" (NASB "saints") *receive* this kingdom and possess it. There is no contradiction here, and this is clarified in v. 27. The Lord Jesus ("one like a son of man") is given the kingdom in which all will serve and obey him. As with any kingdom, however, he has subjects. In this case, the subjects are the "holy ones of the Most High," i.e., the people of God who are rightly related to him. They are given the privilege of entering and enjoying the

---

the meaning "Most High" is possible, perhaps parallel to the plural form *ʾelōhîm* in BH. Admittedly, this seems out of character, since the BH word *ʿelyôn*, when used of God, is always in the masc. sg. (see Num 24:16 and Deut 32:8). Nevertheless, if the LXX is a guide here, the meaning "Most High" (referring to God) seems the best option. Both LXX$^{\theta}$ and LXX^{O} translate the pl. *ʿelyônîn* by the singular Greek form *huphistou*. This observation is particularly interesting, since a pl. form of *huphistos* is expected when it is used in reference to the "heavens, (heavenly) heights" or in the expression "on high" (see Pss 70:19; 148:1; Job 31:2).

781. The translation "forever—forever and ever" for Aram. עַד־עָלְמָא וְעַד עָלַם עָלְמַיָּא (*ʿad̲-ʿālᵊmāʾ wᵊʿad̲ ʿālam ʿālᵊmayyāʾ*) is very emphatic. The word *ʿālam* in this context means "remote time, eternity" (*HALOT*, 1949), and thus the phrase together means something like "forever and ever and ever."

782. Raabe, "Daniel 7," 270–71.

blessedness of this ultimate kingdom established by God, which is a fitting inheritance for them.[783]

Although some have interpreted the "holy ones" as angels (see translation notes to v. 18), the more defensible position is that these are human beings in light of v. 27 which describes them as the "people (עַם, *ʿam*) of the holy ones of the Most High." Elsewhere in the Bible, *ʿam* does not refer to angels. Poythress argues in favor of the term "saints" (*qaddîšê*) referring to faithful Israelites in the last days in light of the kingdom promises of the OT: "Israel is promised a great kingdom elsewhere in the OT (Num. xxiv 7, Isa. lx 12, Mic. iv 8). ... On the other hand, an eschatological angelic kingdom is unknown to the OT and intertestamental literature."[784]

In the OT, Israel was called to be a "holy nation" to Yahweh (see Exod 19:5–6). In the progress of revelation, however, that privilege is extended to those Jews and Gentiles who place their faith in Jesus as Messiah (cf. 1 Pet 2:9–10). Given the eschatological setting for the fulfillment of this passage and the specific note in v. 27 that the "little horn" will wear down the holy ones (the saints), the focus seems to be on those saints living in the time of the antichrist, i.e., during the great tribulation. They could be Gentiles who are persecuted for their faith in the Lord Jesus at that time, or they could be those who suffer for being Jews but who in the final analysis turn in faith to Jesus as their Messiah. Their consolation is that they gain a place in Messiah's kingdom that follows. To be clear, they do not gain admission to the kingdom on the basis of their suffering. The NT specifies that one must first be born again (or "from above") and be declared "righteous," having received the righteousness of Christ by faith (John 3:3–6; Phil 3:8–9).

Once these persecuted saints of God enter into the kingdom, they possess it eternally. The Aramaic phrase is quite emphatic at this point. It is not merely forever, but forever and ever and ever. This is a natural corollary to Dan 7:14. Just as "one like a son of man" receives an everlasting dominion and a kingdom that will never be destroyed, so his people will assuredly possess this "secure kingdom" forever. This truth implies the doctrine of resurrection, for how could they possess the kingdom eternally if they were not capable of living eternally?

Biblical Theology Comments

The topic of apocalyptic literature is quite involved, and most scholars today would agree that the genre has multiple defining characteristics. One such

783. The Aram. word for "taking possession" of the kingdom is a Hapʿel form of חֲסַן (*ḥăsan*), used elsewhere in the OT only in Dan 7:22. Jastrow (*DTT*, 488–89), however, notes that this word was used in Jewish Aram. in the sense of *inheriting* something. Hence, we find it in *Tg. Onq.* Lev XXV, 46 in a verse discussing the bequeathing of slaves to one's sons (they are received as an inheritance). Cf. *b. Bat.* 148[b] and *Tg. Onq.* Deut XXXII, 8.

784. Poythress, "The Holy Ones of the Most High in Daniel VII," 209.

characteristic has to do with the role of mediating angels who explain the details of a visionary revelation to a receiving prophet. Although we have such a feature here in Dan 7, that does not necessarily lead to the conclusion that Daniel should be regarded as an example of apocalyptic literature that flourished in the latter part of the intertestamental period. Dating the book of Daniel late on the basis of mediating angels is faulty logic. Angelic intervention and explanation of visionary details is attested in biblical literature that predates the period generally assumed for apocalyptic literature. One such example is the book of Zechariah. Although critical scholars generally deny the unity of the book and its authorship, they typically affirm the unity of chaps. 1–8. These chapters contain numerous examples of an angel who explains the visionary details to God's prophet (e.g., Zech 1:9, 13, 19; 2:3; 4:1, 4–5; 5:5, 10; 6:4–5). Yet critical scholars generally date Zech 1–8 well before the intertestamental period. M. Coogan, for example, holds that these chapters were written in the sixth century BC.[785] In analyzing the angelic explanations within Zech 1–8, J. A. Soggin—another critical scholar—remarks, "Each time there is an explanation by an angel because the formulation of the visions is not clear; this element will later be typical of the apocalyptic genre."[786] By this statement, Soggin admits that angelic mediation for explanatory purposes is not unusual for biblical literature of the sixth century BC.

c. Further elaboration of the fourth beast in response to Daniel's inquiry (7:19–25)

Textual Notes

19.a. The Qere reading (כָּלְהֵין, 3fp suff.) would be expected, since the referent (הֵיוָן) is fem. The Kethib reading (כָּלְהוֹן) has a masc. pl. suffix.

19.b. Several MSS have ומ׳ (similarly, LXX$^{\theta}$ καὶ λεπτῦνον). Read וּמַדֱּקָה as in v. 7.

20.a. Although the Kethib and B19^{A} have וּנְפַלוּ (masc. pl.), we should read with the Qere, וּנְפַלָה (fem. pl.), since "horns" (קַרְנַיָּא) is fem. (so BDB, 1111d and *HALOT*, 1973).

22.a. There is a question whether יהב should be pointed יְהִב (Peʿil, *passive*) as the MT, or pointed יְהַב (Peʿal, *active*). (See Ezra 5:12 for an example of יְהַב.) The active form is supported by V^{S}, LXX, Syriac, and the Vg. Most Eng. VSS translate as passive, in which case "judgment" is the subject: "judgment was given for the saints." The NASB opts for the passive but adds the words "in

785. M. Coogan, *A Brief Introduction to the Old Testament: The Hebrew Bible in its Context* (Oxford: Oxford University Press, 2009), 346.

786. J. A. Soggin, *Introduction to the Old Testament*, rev. ed. (Philadelphia: Westminster, 1980), 331.

favor of" to clarify. That is, a favorable judgment was given for them. The NIV, however, goes with the active (and with "judgment" as the object): "the Ancient of Days came and pronounced judgment in favor of the holy people" (so Collins, 276). Note the passive form of יְהַב in Dan 7:27. As long as ל on קַדִּישֵׁי is translated "for, on behalf of" and not "to," there is little effective difference in how יהב is pointed. MT's pointing, יְהִב, is fine.

25.a. The *waw* on וְעִדָּנִין is lacking in 4QDan[a] and the Syr. Note לְמוֹעֵד מוֹעֲדִים וָחֵצִי in Dan 12:7.

Translation

7:19 "Then I wanted to know with greater certainty[787] about the fourth beast, which was different from all the others—exceedingly[788] dreadful, with teeth of iron and claws of bronze—*and which was* devouring, crushing, and trampling the rest with its feet. **20** And *I wanted to know more*[789] about the ten horns on its head, and the other one that came up and before which three *of the horns*[790] fell[791]—that horn that had eyes and a mouth uttering great *boasts*[792] and an appearance more formidable[793] than the others.[794] **21** As I continued

787. "To know with greater certainty" is an attempt to render the infinitive construct לְיַצָּבָא (*lᵊyaṣṣāḇāʾ*) into smooth English. Literally, this means "to gain certainty" (from the root יְצַב, *yᵊṣab*, "make certain, gain certainty").
788. יַתִּירָה (*yattîrâ*), from the adj. יַתִּיר (*yattîr*) meaning "preeminent, surpassing," is used here adverbially in the sense "exceedingly" (BDB, 1096). RJ (145) notes, "the ending –ā, mostly unstressed, the remnant of an ancient accusative ending, used adverbially."
789. The words "I wanted to know more" are not in the MT but added for clarification in the English translation.
790. The words "of the horns" are added for sake of clarity but understood on the basis of Dan 7:8.
791. Verse 20 says that these three horns "fell." BDB (1103a2) classifies this use of נְפַל (*nᵊpal*) as "to fall by violence" in contrast to category #1, "to fall down and do homage." In v. 8 it said that three horns were *uprooted* before it (אֶתְעֲקַרָו, *ʾeṯʿăqarāw*), probably implying militaristic conquest (see translation note at Dan 7:8).
792. For "great boasts" (lit., great things), see the translation note at Dan 7:8.
793. Lit., the MT says that its appearance was "greater" (adj. רַב, *raḇ*) than the others. Yet this raises the question: in what way is it greater? Size? Strength? More intimidating? The NASB translates "larger," while the ESV and NRSV simply have "greater." The NIV has "more imposing." Yet the NET's "more formidable" is probably the best option, as the word *formidable* has greater latitude and can refer to its size, strength, that it is imposing or causing fear.
794. It is worth observing that the word translated "the others" at the end of v. 20 is not the same word as that translated "the others" in 7:19a. In 7:19a we have the word שְׁאָרָא (*šᵊʾārāʾ*), which means "the rest, the remainder" (a general term). In v. 20, however, the "little horn" of the fourth beast has an appearance greater or more

observing, that horn was making war with the saints, and it prevailed[795] over them, **22** until the Ancient of Days came and a *favorable* judgment[796] was rendered for the saints of the Most High, and the time arrived for the saints to take possession of the kingdom. **23** So he explained,[797] 'The fourth beast will be a fourth kingdom on the earth that will be different from all the other kingdoms. It will devour all the earth, tread it down,[798] and crush it. **24** *As for* the ten horns, out of this kingdom, ten kings shall arise; then another shall arise after them. He will be different from the previous ones and will humble[799] three *of the* kings. **25** He will also speak words against the Most High, and he will oppress[800] the saints of the Host High. He will intend to

---

formidable than "the others." In the latter case, the word translated "the others" is חַבְרָתַהּ (*ḥaḇrāṯah*). The noun *ḥaḇrāh* implies some kind of relationship such as "fellow" or "comrade" (*HALOT*, 1869, gives the meaning "companion"). The insinuation is that the "little horn" collaborated with those represented by the "ten horns." This also implies that the "ten horns" must be contemporaneous with the "little horn," not successive rulers prior to him (his relationship is not merely with the final ruler of the ten horns).

795. Aram. יְכִל (*yᵉḵil*) means "to be able," but with ל of the person means "to prevail against" and thus to defeat (so *HALOT*, 1891).

796. Lit., "the judgment was given." The word "favorable" is added to the noun "judgment" (דִּינָא, *ḏînā'*) for sake of clarification. Cf. the textual note for v. 22 above.

797. Lit., "Thus he said" (although the adv. "thus," *kēn*, is lacking in LXX).

798. Regarding תְּדוּשִׁנַּהּ (*ṯᵉḏûšinnah*) from the root דוּשׁ (*dûš*), "to tread down, tread under," notice the switch in terms from רְפַס (*rᵉp̄as*) in v. 19 to דוּשׁ (*dûš*) in v. 23. The terms for "devour" and "crush" remain the same.

799. The verb שְׁפֵל (*šᵉp̄ēl*) basically means to "be low," and hence the causative stem (Hap'el) means to "be low, humiliate" (*HALOT*, 2001). (The NET translates "he will humiliate three kings.") The corresponding BH root שָׁפַל (*šāp̄al*) can have the additional meaning to "overthrow" in conquest (a stronger nuance), as in Isa 25:12 and 26:5. Hence, this verse leaves open the possibility that the "little horn" may either subdue three of the other horns (so Feinberg, 83), or he may conquer them. In either case, he will assert his power over them and (at least) bring them into submission.

800. The basic meaning of בְּלָא (*bᵉlā'*) is to "wear out" (*HALOT*, 1834). Although BDB (1084) suggests the fig. meaning "to harass continually," such a translation is probably too mild in this context (note the NET: "harass the holy ones ... continually"). The corresponding BH root בָּלָה (*bālâ*) can have the sense of "oppressing" people (so the Pi'el form in 1 Chr 17:9; cf. *Tg. Jes.* iii.15). Hence, he will "oppress" God's saints (so NIV), and in so doing will "wear them down" (NASB). Note Rev 13:7: "It was given to him to make war with the saints and to overcome them" (NASB).

change sacred seasons and law,[801] and they will be given into his hand for a time, *(two)* times,[802] and half a time.'"

Commentary

7:19–20. *Daniel's desire for further insight.* Having been given a cursory explanation of the vision in vv. 17–18, Daniel sought to know more about the fourth beast. In particular, he sought more precise information about the ten horns and the "little horn" that came up later. While the "teeth of iron" had been mentioned in v. 7, Daniel adds a previously unmentioned detail that this beast had "claws of bronze" (v. 7 did indicate that it trampled the remainder with its feet). This amplifies the destructiveness of this kingdom, just as bronze claws were powerful enough to tear a victim to shreds.

Regarding the eyes and the mouth uttering great boasts, see the commentary for v. 8. Although the horn that comes up last is called "little" in v. 8, it is now said in v. 20 that it had an "appearance more formidable than the others." The adjective "little" is not really indicative of his power, and clearly he emerges as stronger than the "ten horns." A more "formidable appearance" could pertain to its size, its strength, or its intimidation of others. (See translation note regarding "formidable.")

---

801. Lit., "to change times and law," לְהַשְׁנָיָה זִמְנִין וְדָת (*lᵊhašnāyâ zimnîn wᵊdāṯ*). Goldingay (143) takes the objects as a hendiadys, "times set by decree," as does the NET. The other possibility (other than a hendiadys) is that "times" (*zimnîn*) refers to "appointed times" such as the fixed dates for religious festivals (cf. BH *zᵊmān* in Esth 9:27). Note the NIV: "the set times and the laws." The NRSV emphasizes the religious aspect: "the sacred seasons and the law." Both LXX$^{\theta}$ and LXX^{O} translate quite literally, "times and law."

As for "law" (דָּת, *dāṯ*), this can refer to one of several things in BAram. This could be (1) a *decree* made by a king (Dan 2:13, 15; Ezra 78:26); (2) a *government law*, such as the law of the Medes and Persians (Dan 6:9, 13, 16); or (3) the *law of God* (Dan 6:6; Ezra 7:12, 14, 21, 26; *laws* of God, Ezra 7:25). We should note, however, in the case of #3 that in BAram, a modifying phrase like "of God" always accompanies *dāṯ* (which makes option #3 less likely). Yet, this could refer to governmental laws affecting religious matters.

802. The word "times" (עִדָּנִין, *ʿiddānîn*) is vocalized in the MT as a plural, yet there is good reason to regard this as a *dual form* (= "two times"). Montgomery (312) notes, "... the word is pointed as a pl., but the Aram. later having lost the dual, the tendency of M *[Masoretic punctuation]* is to ignore it in BAram." Rosenthal, *A Grammar of Biblical Aramaic*, 24, adds, "The dual is preserved only in remnants. ... All other forms of the dual of the masc. noun, including those with pronominal suffixes, are identical with the pl. forms and not distinguishable from them." This is confirmed by taking notice that the word "eyes" (*ʿayᵊnîn*) in Dan 7:8 *appears* to be in the plural, though it would naturally be understood as dual. (The word for "hands" can be found in Aram. as *yᵊḏayin*, Dan 2:34, 45.)

7:21–22 *Persecution followed by kingdom joy*. Daniel's cause for alarm may be primarily due to the fact that the "little horn" wages war with the saints (holy ones) of the Most High (vv. 21–22). In fact, the text says that he prevails against them, i.e., he overpowers them. He is not merely a political figure; he is also a persecuting tyrant whose aim is fixed on those who follow the one true God. Of course, he is not the first murderous tyrant in history who has sought to wipe out God's people, but he will probably be the most brutal. God obviously permits Satan to have such freedom for a limited time through his agent, the antichrist. According to Rev 13:7, "The beast was permitted to go to war against the saints and conquer them" (NET). Those who refuse to worship him (and/or his image) or who refuse the mark of his name are simply put to death (note Rev 13:8, 15; 14:9–12). Yet his persecution is not an ultimate defeat of the saints. They may lose their lives as martyrs for the sake of the Savior, but Jesus will return to defeat the antichrist, cast him into the lake of fire (Rev 19:20), and resurrect the martyred saints to reign with him in the millennial kingdom (the one thousand years mentioned in Rev 20:4–6). Not all believers of this period will die at the hands of the antichrist, for some will endure to the end and be delivered (Matt 24:13). For those who are martyred during the great tribulation, they will be resurrected to "take possession of the kingdom" (cf. Rev 20:4). All the suffering that these tribulation saints have to endure (even widespread martyrdom) will eventually be compensated by the joys of resurrection life in the kingdom of Messiah Jesus.

7:23–25 *The angel's explanation of the fourth beast*. The fourth beast is clearly said to represent a "kingdom on earth." On that, all agree. Yet all do not agree as to the identity of this fourth kingdom. I have sought to demonstrate elsewhere that this fourth kingdom must be the Roman Empire, rather than that of the Greek or Hellenistic kingdoms as argued by critical scholars (see commentary notes for Dan 2:31–45 and 7:1–8). If for no other reason, it is simply not true that the "kingdom of God" followed the Greek and Hellenistic kingdoms. Yet there is a way to make sense from this passage that the kingdom of God follows this fourth empire associated with Rome, as the following discussion will demonstrate.

I argued in the notes to Dan 7:1–8 that this fourth Roman kingdom is more complex than the previous ones and that the symbolism pictures it in terms of both a near and far fulfillment. That is, there is a historic fulfillment of the fourth kingdom with ancient Rome of the past, that vast empire that conquered Syria-Palestine in 64–63 BC under the famous Roman general Pompey and that lasted (in the west) until AD 476. Yet there is also a *second phase* of the Roman Empire to take place in the future during the time of the great tribulation. This is when the "ten horns" and the "little horn" will flourish.

Verse 24 says, "*As for* the ten horns, out of this kingdom, ten kings shall arise." Although some hold that these ten kings are *successive rulers*, the position taken in this commentary is that these are ten contemporaneous rulers.

That they are contemporaneous is true for several reasons: (1) This is the most natural understanding of Rev 17:12, where "ten horns" (clearly alluding to Dan 7) are said to have authority with the beast "for one hour." (2) Dan 7:24 indicates that the "little horn" humbles (NET "humiliates") three of the ten kings. If these were successive rulers, we would expect that he would subdue the last one in the series, i.e., the tenth one. The fact that he subdues three of them indicates that they must have been in power at the same time. (3) Rev 17:13 indicates that "they" (*plural!*, i.e., the ten horns) give their power and authority to the beast.

There is also the question as to whether or not to take the number ten literally. Young (159) discounts a literal interpretation, regarding the number ten as "merely indicative of completeness."[803] Collins (321), although espousing an interpretation in which the ten are literal, does not feel the number needs to be pressed literally.[804] Nevertheless, it seems best to take the number

---

803. Young (149), a conservative amillennialist, not only spiritualizes the number ten but does not even put the "ten horns" and the "little horn" in the same general time period. For him, the "little horn" is the antichrist (the traditional Christian interpretation), but the "ten horns" are an indefinite number of European kingdoms that trace their origin back to Rome and that span the entire time period between AD 476 and the time of antichrist. Such a view falters on the fact that Rev 17:12–13 places the "ten horns" in the future and in the same general period as the antichrist (just before the second coming). Also, he faces the same problems as any view that regards the "ten horns" as *successive* rulers. Even more significantly, which three rulers in church history does the antichrist humble/subdue?

804. Collins (321), following the trend of critical scholars who interpret the "little horn" as Antiochus IV Epiphanes of the second century BC, holds that the ten horns begin with Alexander the Great, followed by the first six Seleucid kings, and finally Seleucus IV and his two sons (Demetrius and a younger Antiochus). For him, the three subdued kings are Seleucus IV and his two sons; similarly, B. E. Scolnic, "Antiochus IV and the Three Horns in Daniel 7," *JHebScr* 14 (2014): 1–28. Others (e.g., Goldingay, 180) take the "ten kings" to be ten successive rulers from Alexander the Great to Seleucus IV. C. C. Caragounis, "The Interpretation of the Ten Kings of Daniel 7," *ETL* 63 (1987): 113, suggests that "the three uprooted horns may be Philip Arrhidaeus [*sic*] and Alexander Aegus, whose death opened the way to the emergence of the Seleucid empire and Seleucus IV, Philopator, whose removal brought Antiochus Epiphanes to the throne." Cf. Lucas (193), who discusses alternative suggestions concerning the identity of the "ten kings."

A. Blasius, "Antiochus IV Epiphanes and the Ptolemaic Triad: The Three Uprooted Horns in Dan 7:8, 20 and 24 Reconsidered," *JSJ* 37 (2006): 543, following a helpful historical survey of suggested interpretations for the three subdued kings, concludes that they are the Ptolemaic triumvirate (Ptolemy VI Philometor, his sister-wife Cleopatra II, and his younger brother, Ptolemy VIII Physcon) whose ambitions to reclaim Coele-Syria for Egypt were halted by Antiochus IV in his two campaigns of 170–169 and 168 BC.

ten literally. First, this would be the most natural way to understand it, in the absence of any remark to the contrary (why should it be taken symbolically if the literal meaning is perfectly acceptable in the context?). Second, the fact that the "little horn" subdues *three* of them argues that all ten are literal. If the number "three" is taken to be literal, why should the number ten—so close in range—be taken symbolically? (One cannot argue that *ten* is symbolic of "completeness," and at the same time argue that *three* is symbolic of "completeness.")

If, then, the ten kings and the literal horn are to come on the scene of history in the great tribulation, some people may refer to this as a revived Roman Empire, though there is no necessary reason why it will actually be called by the name "Rome" at that time. Whatever the future phase may be called, the main point is that it has sufficient continuity with the ancient Roman Empire that it is viewed in God's eyes as one empire.[805] That *continuity* could be either geographical or political, meaning that the future phase of this fourth beast/empire arises out of the territories or political sphere of what once constituted the Roman Empire. (See the commentary on Dan 9:26 for further confirmation of this view—a future ruler is linked to the Roman people that destroyed Jerusalem and the Jewish temple.) That continuity, of course, could potentially involve a vast area, encompassing much of present-day Europe as well as the countries of the Mediterranean. Speculation that the future phase might be fulfilled in the present-day European Union (formerly known as the European Community and European Economic Community) is simply that, speculation. This could just as well find its fulfillment in countries near the eastern Mediterranean (as Turkey, Syria, Jordan, Israel, and Egypt all once comprised part of the ancient Roman Empire). The point is that one should be careful in *over-speculating* and remain open to various possibilities of fulfillment. Furthermore, a political entity much like the European Union could serve as a precursor to a future entity that does not presently exist. What is of much interest in this discussion is that there seems to be a trend around the world to form political, military, and/or economic alignments for mutual benefit (e.g., NATO, ASEAN, and the League of Arab Nations). It is easy, given these modern-day alignments, to envision how a confederacy of nations represented by the "ten horns" of Dan 7 could easily develop.

In the early church, at the time the Roman Empire actually ruled the world, Christian scholars were prone to see a literal fulfillment in the not-so-distant future (and would not have thought in terms of a *revived* Roman Empire). Hence Jerome, an early church father (ca. AD 400), wrote, "We

---

805. Some have sought to build a case that the ancient Roman Empire never really ceased entirely but rather shifted in form, so that it continued through the ages among the Western nations of Europe and Europe's daughter, the United States. This is a debatable matter and the symbolism of Dan 7 is not dependent upon such a view.

should therefore concur with the traditional interpretation of all the commentators of the Christian Church, that at the end of the world, when the Roman Empire is to be destroyed, there shall be ten kings who will partition the Roman world amongst themselves."[806] Such a comment implies that the "ten kings" were viewed in his day (at least by many) as ten *contemporaneous* rulers to come forth from the Roman Empire. Other comments by Jerome also indicate that the common view of the early church was that the "little horn" was the antichrist to come.

According to Dan 7:24, the "little horn" (the antichrist) will "humble three kings." As explained in the translation notes to this verse, the word translated "humble" (יְהַשְׁפִּל, *yəhašpil*) can have the idea of *bringing low* or *overthrowing* militarily. This suggests that there is some type of action on his part to assert his military power and subdue them. The text does not tell us the circumstances that lead to this action, but it is not difficult to piece together the parts of the puzzle. What we can discern from a study of Daniel and Rev 13–17 is that at some future point, ten rulers come together by treaty to form a confederacy. This could be by force or for some mutually advantageous reason (such as economic gain or military defense). Whether this takes place before or after the start of Daniel's "seventieth week" (i.e., the seven years leading up to the second coming of Christ—see commentary on Dan 9:24–27), we simply do not know. What is clear is that these ten rulers will be united in a coalition during these final seven years. Since they also represent a phase of the fourth beast, we can presume that they also have tremendous military might (as ancient Rome once did).

Yet we learn from Rev 17:13 (NET), "These kings have a single intent, and they will give their power and authority to the beast" (cf. Rev 17:17—they give him their "kingdom"). The pertinent question is why the ten kings give their kingdom to the beast. We first need to see this in light of Rev 13. The antichrist is empowered by Satan himself, and it is Satan who gives him his throne and authority (Rev 13:2). (This may be part of the reason why Dan 7:24 says that "he will be different from the previous ones.") So, we must first realize that this is a satanic scheme, and Satan is the one behind these developments. Secondly, this satanic scheme aims at drawing the entire world to a point of worshiping both the antichrist and Satan himself, although true believers on earth at that time will not succumb to this (Rev 13:4, 8). Then, in light of Dan 7:24, we are told that the antichrist will *humble* three of the ten kings, a hostile action of a military nature. He apparently does not destroy these three, because Rev 17:16–17 indicates that the ten horns join league with the beast and unite with him in a "common purpose." Yet his action against the three probably has the effect of compelling the remaining seven kings to submit to his demands and sovereignty. They probably realize that they cannot match him militarily, so they join forces with him. As the

806. Jerome, *Commentary on Daniel*, trans. Archer, 77.

world looks on, people proclaim, "Who is like the beast? and Who is able to make war against him?" (Rev 13:4; cf. Dan 11:38).

While Dan 7:24 focuses upon antichrist's actions against the league of ten kings, v. 25 focuses upon his actions against God and those who follow him. The antichrist will be a fierce and outspoken critic of the God of heaven, even blaspheming his name (Rev 13:5). His rhetoric alone will prompt most people to turn away completely from the God of the Bible. Those who love God will pay a price, for he will oppress the saints of God, and in so doing "wear them out" (see the translation note to v. 25). Rev 13:7 adds, "The beast was permitted to go to war against the saints and conquer them." Although this will be a terrible time for all those who dwell on the earth, it will be especially bad for believers in Christ. Many of them will be martyred for their faith (cf. Rev 6:9–11).

A literal translation of Dan 7:25 is that he will "change times and law." This could mean that, like Hitler, he will attempt to radically restructure society and the laws governing nations. On the other hand, the context of v. 25 is primarily religious (his vehement hatred of the true God), which could suggest that the changes are primarily aimed against anything and anyone that interferes with his plan for the whole world to worship him. If the actions of Antiochus of old are any guide (and the book of Daniel does present him as a type of the antichrist), it may be insightful to recall what he did. Collins (322) summarizes,

> 2 Maccabees 6:6 says that a Jew 'could neither keep the Sabbath nor observe the feasts of his fathers' but had to participate in pagan sacrifices and celebrate the festival of Dionysus. The point of issue was apparently the suppression of the traditional Jewish observances and their replacement with pagan rites, rather than a change in the calendar of the traditional cult.

Miller (214) is probably correct then, when he writes, "'Set times' (*zimnîn*) are best understood to be religious holidays, which the antichrist will attempt to eliminate, and the 'laws' (*dāt*, sing. collective) are likely religious in nature as well." In an attempt to coerce the entire world into worshiping him, the antichrist will impose changes upon societies in order to strip away any vestige of worship, celebration, or pious act toward the true God. His efforts to do so, however, will ultimately fail. He may try to "change times and law" (לְהַשְׁנָיָה זִמְנִין וְדָת, *lᵉhašnāyâ zimnîn wᵉdāṯ*)—using similar terms that echo Dan 2:21—but he will be infinitely outmatched by the one who not only "changes the times and eras" (מְהַשְׁנֵא עִדָּנַיָּא וְזִמְנַיָּא, *mᵉhašnēʾ ʿiddānyyāʾ wᵉzimnayyāʾ*) but who also "deposes kings and sets up other kings." Indeed, the antichrist will be deposed and removed by the God of heaven who alone establishes world order.

A final note in v. 25 concerns the length of time that antichrist will be allowed to oppress the saints. They will be "delivered into his hand for time, *(two)* times, and half a time." The word translated "time" (Aram. *ʿiddān*) can mean time in general or a definite period of time, depending on the context.

As used in Dan 4:16, 23, 25, 32, it means a definite period of time consisting of a year. As explained in the translation note to Dan 7:25, the translation "times" should be understood as a *dual* form meaning "two times," i.e., two years. Consequently "half a time" would amount to one half of a year. (The expression "half a time" argues against any symbolic understanding of the whole phrase, as this would be inappropriate for a round number.) The best interpretation, then, of Dan 7:25 is that the expression "time, times, and half a time" means a period of three and one-half years.[807] Two further arguments support this conclusion. First, the same expression is used near the end of the book of Daniel (see 12:7), where it is compared to the slightly longer periods of 1290 days and 1335 days. Since a "prophetic year" in Scripture amounts to 360 days, a period of three and one-half years would be 1260 days.[808] To interpret "time, times and half a time" as three and one-half years is consistent with the temporal references given at the end of Daniel.

Second, this expression, "time, times, and half a time," is used interchangeably in the book of Revelation (Rev 12:14) with the phrase "1260 days" (12:6), both meaning three and one-half years. This is further confirmed in Rev 13:5, where the antichrist is said to have authority for forty-two months (another way of saying three and one-half years). Hence, God will allow Satan to manifest his diabolical plan through the antichrist, but he will only allow this for a period of three and one-half years. As will be seen later in discussion about the "abomination of desolation," this three and one-half year period of time is what the Bible refers to as the "great tribulation" (cf. Matt 24:15–22; Rev 7:14). This period will be climaxed by the second coming of Christ, who will return to put an end to the antichrist's evil reign of terror (2 Thess 2:8; Rev 19:19–21).

Biblical Theology Comments

The preceding commentary on Dan 7:19–25 is obviously significant for one's grasp of biblical eschatology, especially the events immediately preceding the second coming of Christ. In the view presented in this commentary the fourth kingdom is to be understood in a rather *elastic* way, i.e., partially

---

807. Critical scholars typically understand the "little horn" as a reference to Antiochus Epiphanes and would see the temporal reference being fulfilled during his time of rule (e.g., Montgomery, 313; Beasley-Murray, "The Interpretation of Daniel 7," 45). Hill (143) explains, "Some commentators relate the three-and-a-half years to the period between the desecration of the temple by Antiochus IV Epiphanes (15 Chislev in year 145 of the Seleucid era, or December 6, 167 BC) and its purification by Judas Maccabeus (25 Chislev in year 148 of the Seleucid era, or December 14, 164 BC)—a time span of three years and eight days (e.g., Hartman and Di Lella, 215–16). Yet Lucas, 194, prefers to understand the numbers symbolically, since three and one-half 'as half of the perfect number, seven ... denotes a short period of evil.'" Cf. *1 Macc.* 4:52.

808. For a defense of a "prophetic year" having 360 days, see the section on "*Calculating the sixty-nine 'weeks'*" under the commentary for Dan 9:25.

fulfilled in the Roman Empire of history past and partially fulfilled in the future great tribulation. Upon first consideration, this may seem to be a bit of an odd interpretation. However, it is the most defensible interpretation: (1) the book of Revelation takes up the elements of the beast and the ten horns and places their fulfillment in the Great Tribulation period; (2) Daniel 7 indicates that the judgment upon the little horn will be followed by the saints receiving the kingdom of God; and (3) the parallel revelation in the dream of Nebuchadnezzar (2:31–45)—also having four essential phases of Gentile power—concludes with the kingdom of God replacing them all. In fact, Dan 2:44 states, "In the days of those kings the God of heaven will set up a kingdom which will never be destroyed" (NASB). Since his kingdom puts an end to all these Gentile kingdoms, it simply cannot be fulfilled at the time of Jesus' first coming.

The following chart summarizes the prophetic outworking of the vision of Dan 7:

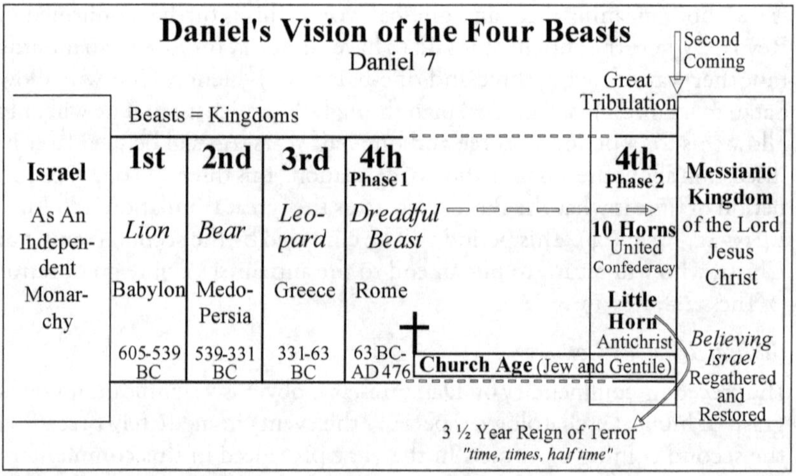

Application and Devotional Implications

Throughout this chapter we have seen various kingdoms in conflict, with each successive kingdom adding to the toll of human lives wasted by the ravages of war and lust for power. While there will be warfare in general as long as there are Gentile kingdoms, the chapter also emphasizes the suffering and persecution that the saints of God in particular will have to endure at the hands of the little horn. According to Dan 7:21 he overpowers them, and in v. 25 he "wears them down." His hatred for the saints and his persecution of them characterize his brutal use of power. Of course, we do not need to wait until the antichrist arises before we see the persecution of God's people. So many are already facing this, and indeed this has been true from the beginning of the church. Though it is unjustly received, it is nevertheless the price that many of God's precious people are called upon to pay in proclaiming the living Christ to a dying world.

Jesus, in his exhortation to those who sought to come after him, did not give any "soft sell" approach but dutifully warned those who wished to follow him to be prepared to pay the ultimate price of martyrdom (Mark 8:34–38). In this vein, I quote Penner at length:

> The demand of Jesus on his followers is to tread the path of martyrdom. As he prepared to send his disciples out as sheep among wolves, he told them that they would likely die in the process of carrying out their ministry. ... Just as Christ's cross was needed to establish his church, our crosses are needed to build his church (Matt 16:24). Both are needed. As Josef Ton observed, 'Christ's cross was for propitiation. Our cross is for propagation.' To be called to follow Christ is to receive a call to suffer (e.g., Acts 9:16; 14:22; 1 Thess 3:3; 1 Pet 2:21; 3:9, 17).
>
> It was this understanding that sacrifice, suffering, shame, and even death were the normal cost of discipleship that fueled the evangelistic efforts of the first-century church. They did not expect to experience all of the blessings of heaven in this world. They knew that by their faithfulness, even unto death, they were storing up rewards in heaven. Contrary to the Western belief that it is a blessing not to be persecuted, they knew that it was the persecuted who are blessed (Matt 10–12). Rather than following the common Western practice of thanking God for the privilege of living in a free country where we do not suffer for him, the early Christians thanked God for the honor of suffering for his sake (Acts 5:41). They knew that in order to bring life to others, they must die; to see others experience peace with God, they would have to suffer the violence of the world; to bring the love of God to a dying world, they would have to face the hatred of those whom they were seeking to reach.[809]

In reflecting on these ominous verses from Dan 7, we are led to reflect on the Apostle Paul's expression of ultimate faith and commitment: "I die daily" (1 Cor 15:31).

---

809. G. Penner, "A Biblical Theology of Persecution and Discipleship," in *Sorrow and Blood: Christian Mission in Contexts of Suffering, Persecution, and Martyrdom*, ed. W. D. Taylor et al., 71–76 (Pasadena, CA: William Carey Library, 2012), 73–74.

d. The eventual victory and establishment of Messiah's Kingdom (7:26–28)

Textual Notes

26.a. *BHS* editor proposes a 3fs suffix for שָׁלְטָנַהּ (comparing מִנַּהּ in 7:24) rather than MT's 3ms suffix form שָׁלְטָנֵהּ. Presumably, this proposal is due to the fact that the "little horn" is referred to and the word "horn" is fem. (as well as "beast" and "kingdom"). However, the 3ms suffix may still be appropriate, as the symbol looks ultimately to the human figure it stands for. Notice in v. 24 that the same individual is referred to by a 3ms independent personal pronoun (הוּא).

Translation

7:26 'But the court[810] will sit, and his dominion will be removed[811]—so as to annihilate and destroy it forever! **27** Then the kingdom and the dominion and the greatness of the kingdoms under all of heaven was given[812] to the people who are the saints[813] of the Most High. His kingdom is an eternal kingdom, and all the dominions will serve and obey him.'[814] **28** Here the

---

810. The translation "convene" (so NET) is appropriate, provided that *dîn* (normally meaning "judgment") is properly understood figuratively as "court" (the place where judgment is rendered)—and that seems to be the case here. For further discussion, see translation notes to Dan 7:10.

811. In regard to translating the 3mp Hap'el impf. verb יְהַעְדּוֹן (*yəha'dôn*) as passive (as most English versions have done), see GKC, 460 (§144g): "The 3rd plur. also is sometimes used to express an indefinite subject, ... In such a case the 3rd plur. comes to be equivalent to a passive, as very commonly in Aramaic."

812. The verb יְהִיבַת (*yəhîḇaṯ*)—translated "was given"—is a Pe'il perf., which marks a deliberate switch at this point from the preceding impf. verbs to the perf. Goldingay (146) regards this as a *future perfect*, "will have been given." Perhaps a better classification would be to regard this as a "prophetic perfect" that stresses the certainty of accomplishment of this important event: "the kingdom ... will be given to the people." Cf. *IBHS*, 490 (§30.5.1e) and observe the examples in Num 24:17; Isa 9:2 (Heb.), and Isa 9:5 (Heb.).

813. For a discussion about the translation and identity of the "saints," see translation note to Dan 7:18. There it was concluded that these are the human "saints" of God. The phrase *'am qaddîšê 'elyônîn* in v. 27 can be taken as appositional (= "the people, the saints of the Most High") rather than genitival, i.e., the people *who are* the saints of the Most High. Or *qaddîšê* could be understood as a *partitive genitive* (the "people" are part of the larger group of God's saints).

814. Rather oddly, the NRSV translates this phrase, "their kingdom shall be an everlasting kingdom." Most other Eng. translations have "his kingdom." NRSV assumes the antecedent is עַם (*'am*) in the previous clause. While it might be legitimate grammatically to view *'am* (a collective sg.) as the antecedent to the 3ms suffix on מַלְכוּתֵהּ (*malkûṯēh*), that is most unlikely contextually. Recall that Dan 7:14 depicted that one like "a son of man" was given dominion, glory, and a kingdom. The final

account ends.[815] As for me, Daniel, my thoughts were greatly alarming[816] me; even my countenance[817] began to change. Yet I kept the matter in my heart."[818]

Commentary

7:26–28 After three and a half years, the antichrist's reign of terror is brought to an end. The heavenly court (over which the Ancient of Days presides) acts in judgment to remove and destroy the dominion (or authority) of the antichrist. The wording of the Aramaic text for v. 26 is very emphatic. His authority is not only removed, but it is decisively destroyed. Furthermore, it is destroyed *forever*, meaning that he will never be allowed another opportunity.

With the antichrist out of the way and off the scene, the blessed kingdom predicted in both Dan 2:44 and 7:13–14 will finally be manifested. What is not said in Daniel, but which we know from Rev 20, is that Satan himself will be imprisoned in the abyss, so that he will not be able to deceive the nations for one thousand years. With both the antichrist and Satan removed, this kingdom of heaven will be the most righteous and blessed realm that history has ever known (cf. Isa 9:6–7; 11:1–9). This kingdom will be given to "one like a son of man" (just as Dan 7:13–14 promised), but in another sense it is "given to the people who are the saints of the Most High." That is, the kingdom is first and foremost entrusted to the Lord Jesus Christ. He is the king *par excellence*, the king over everything, or as Heb 1:2 puts it, he is

---

clause of v. 27 promises "all dominions will serve and obey Him" (observe the 3ms suffix indicating the object: לֵהּ, *lēh*). The dominions at that time do not serve (= worship) and obey the saints, but rather the one whom all the saints themselves worship and obey, the Lord Jesus Christ, the King of glory.

815. The opening words of v. 28 (עַד־כָּה סוֹפָא דִי־מִלְּתָא, *ʿad-kâ sôpāʾ dî-millᵉtāʾ*) are difficult to translate. Lit., "until here the end of the matter." Collins (276) suggests, "Here is the end of the account," and the NRSV simply translates, "Here the account ends," which captures the point quite well.

816. The first two verbs of the sentence are impf. in contrast to the final verb, נִטְרֵת (*niṭrēṯ*), which is a perf. Classify as past progressive imperfs. (action continually going on in past time). This emphasizes the ongoing experience of feeling alarmed.

817. Lit., "my splendor (זִיוַי, *zîway*, 'brightness of countenance') was changing upon me." Whether or not it was the color in his face that changed is not certain (note NET, "the color drained from my face"). It could simply be his facial expression. LXX^{O} translated *zîway* by the Greek ἕξις (*hexis*), "outward appearance." (Cf. translation notes to Dan 5:6, where the same expression is used.)

818. "In my heart" (בְּלִבִּי, *bᵉlibbî*). The point is not that he hid the matter from others. Rather, he cherished this matter *in his heart*, i.e., in his mind or innermost being. Cf. the expression "in my heart" in BH (e.g., Isa 63:4; Pss 4:8; 66:18; 119:11). Regarding נִטְרֵת (*niṭrēṯ*), commonly translated "kept" (so *HALOT*, 1930), compare the corresponding נָצַר (*nāṣar*) in BH. The latter not only means "keep," but also to guard with fidelity (so BDB, 665d3). Observe Prov 4:13, where the young man is counseled to guard מוּסָר, *mûsār* ("discipline" or "instruction").

"heir of all things." Then those who belong to him are allowed to enter the kingdom and participate in various capacities of its administration. Second Timothy 2:12 suggests that not all kingdom subjects will necessarily *reign* with Christ. Faithfulness and endurance are prerequisites for that honor (cf. Rev 2:25–28).

With the commencement of this kingdom, there will never be any *evil* Gentile rule again (like that of the beasts in Dan 7:1–8), though there will apparently be human nations that are subservient to the Lord Jesus ("dominions" in v. 27; cf. Ps 72:11; Zech 14:16). Furthermore, Messiah's kingdom will be eternal. Hence, the kingdom envisioned in this verse is not merely the "millennial kingdom" of one thousand years (mentioned in Rev 20). That is but the first phase of a kingdom that will know no end. As we are told in Rev 11:15, "The kingdom of the world has become the kingdom of our Lord and of his Christ, and he will reign for ever and ever" (NASB). In this kingdom there may be sub-rulers (having authority), but all will be in absolute submission and obedience to the Lord Jesus Christ.

In the final verse of the chapter, Daniel adds the comment concerning the impact that this vision made upon him personally. It alarmed him to the point that his physical countenance changed. Nevertheless, he cherished in his heart the insights he had gained from the vision.

Biblical Theology Comments

Daniel chaps. 2 and 7 are significant in terms of the contribution they make to biblical eschatology and kingdom theology in particular. Furthermore, they build upon previous kingdom revelation in Scripture such as God's determination that one from the line of Judah will ultimately rule over the people of the world (Gen 49:8–10); that one from the line of David will be God's "Son" and entrusted with an eternal throne-kingdom (2 Sam 7:12–16); that this "Son" will be God's "anointed one" having authority over the nations (Ps 2:7–9); that he will establish a kingdom of peace, righteousness, and justice (Ps 72; Isa 9:6–7; 11:1–9); and that his kingdom will be preceded by a time of great distress from which Israel as a nation will ultimately be rescued (Jer 30:5–11).

How the details of Dan 7 play out in regard to this kingdom theology is a matter where one's interpretation is affected by his view of the millennium. This is illustrated in the contrasting views of Young (amillennial) and Walvoord (dispensational premillennial), as the following charts clarify:

The interpretation of Dan 7 presented in this commentary is in line with that of the position of Walvoord above.

Application and Devotional Implications

In comparing the last half of Dan 7 with other biblical passages like 2 Thess 2:1–12 and Rev 13:1–10, it is clear that the "little horn" is a symbol for the antichrist, the most evil, murdering tyrant that the world will ever know. It is hard to comprehend men like Nero, Hitler, Stalin, Pol Pot, and Saddam Hussein. These are men who seem to have had almost no conscience, who

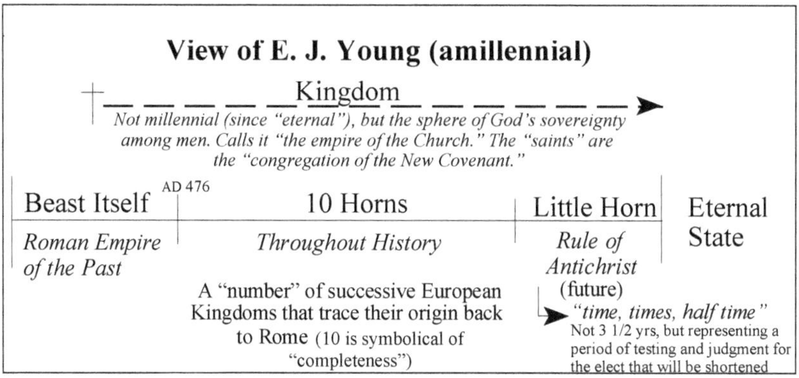

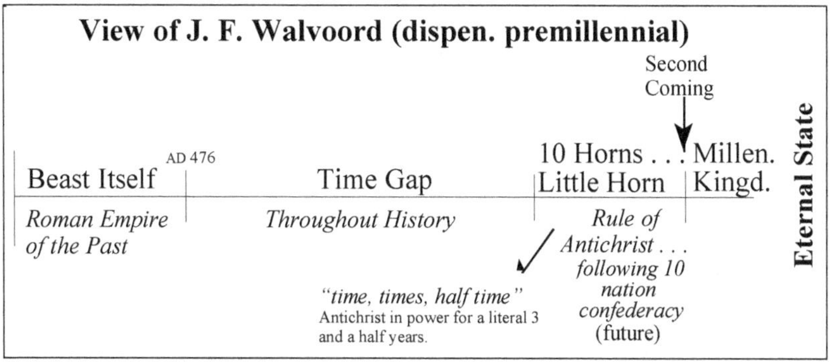

would sacrifice the lives of countless innocent people for the sake of their own selfish goals. Their basic tactic was similar: they would do whatever it took to strike terror and fear into the hearts of their subjects, so that no one would dare to question their actions or stand against them. Those who dared to do so paid for it with their own blood. Yet all such tyrants pale in comparison with the antichrist to come. He is the kingpin in Satan's war against the Lord God. What the antichrist will do to believers of that age is beyond comprehension. From what we know from Scripture, it will be a horrendous time. Sitting today in the comfort of one's home or in a nice relaxing coffee shop while reading about these times to come, it is virtually impossible to comprehend what it will be like to be a believer in that day.

One could easily console himself with thoughts that he or she will not likely be a part of the day and age in which the antichrist flourishes. Even if that were true, we should still ask ourselves what we can learn from this that would apply to our lives today. One thing that is obvious is the hatred with which Satan hates the children of God. Perhaps that is a thought worth pondering. Satan hates our lives and wants to destroy us, but God loves us with an everlasting love and wants the best for us (from an eternal perspective). Before we gravitate to Satan's turf or allow ourselves to drift into his ways, we should pause to consider what his attitude is toward us. It is one of utter contempt and hatred. Anything that might seem good that he attempts to offer us is only part of a trap to lure us into his destructive net. Oh, how we each need to cling so tightly to the One who gave his only Son for us! Let us trust in the Lord with all our heart. Let us realize that there is a kingdom that awaits us, a kingdom that will be better than any experience we have had or will have here on earth. Let us put our trust in the Lord and in the certainty of his Word.

Selected Bibliography (Daniel 7)

Albani, M. "The 'One Like a Son of Man' (Dan 7:13) and the Royal Ideology." In *Enoch and Qumran Origins: New Light on a Forgotten Connection*, ed. G. Boccaccini, 47–53. Grand Rapids: Eerdmans, 2005.

Angel, A. "Short Note: The Sea in 4Q541 7.3 and in Daniel 7:2." *VT* 60 (2010): 474–78.

Angel, J. L. "The Divine Courtroom Scenes of Daniel 7 and the Qumran *Book of Giants*: A Textual and Contextual Comparison." In *The Divine Courtroom in Comparative Perspective*, ed. A. Mermelstein and S. E. Holtz, 25–48. Leiden: Brill, 2015.

Aune, D. E. "Son of Man." In *ISBE*, 4 vols., ed. G. W. Bromiley, 4: 574–81. Grand Rapids: Eerdmans, 1988.

Barnes, C. "Lions and Bears and, Oh My! ... A Son of Man? Daniel's Use of Ancient Near Eastern Intertexts in Daniel 7." Paper submitted to New Orleans Baptist Theological Seminary in partial fulfillment of OTHB9420: Biblical Intertextuality. New Orleans, LA, March 12, 2015.

———. "The Surprising Ascension of the Son of Man." Paper presented at the annual national conference of the ETS. Atlanta, November 18, 2015.

Barrett, C. K. "The Background of Mark 10:45." In *New Testament Essays*, FS T. W. Manson, ed. A. J. B. Higgins, 1–18. Manchester: Manchester University Press, 1959.

Barrick, W. D. "Divine Persons in Genesis: Theological Implications." *DBSJ* 22 (2017): 3–20.

Beasley-Murray, G. R. "The Interpretation of Daniel 7." *CBQ* 45 (1983): 44–58.

Beyerle, S. "'One Like a Son of Man': Innuendoes of a Heavenly Individual." In *Enoch and Qumran Origins: New Light on a Forgotten Connection*, ed. G. Boccaccini, 54–58. Grand Rapids: Eerdmans, 2005.

Black, M. "The 'Parables' of Enoch (1 En 37–71) and the 'Son of Man.'" *ExpT* 88 (1976–77): 5–8.

———. "The 'Son of Man' in the Old Biblical Literature." *ExpT* 60 (1948–49): 11–15.

———. "The Throne-Theophany Prophetic Commission and the 'Son of Man.'" In *Jews, Greeks and Christians, Essays in Honour of W.D. Davies*, ed. R. Hamerton-Kelly and R. Scroggs, 57–73. Leiden: Brill, 1976.

Blasius, A. "Antiochus IV Epiphanes and the Ptolemaic Triad: The Three Uprooted Horns in Dan 7:8, 20 and 24 Reconsidered." *JSJ* 37 (2006): 521–47.

Boccaaccini, G., ed. *Enoch and the Messiah Son of Man: Revisiting the Book of Parables*. Grand Rapids: Eerdmans, 2007.

Bock, D. L. "Dating the *Parables of Enoch*: A *Forschungsbericht*." In *Parables of Enoch: A Paradigm Shift*, ed. D. L. Bock and J. H. Charlesworth, 58–113. London: Bloomsbury T&T Clark, 2013.

———. "Did Jesus Connect Son of Man to Daniel 7? A Short Reflection on the Position of Larry Hurtado." *BBR* 22 (2012): 399–402.

———. "The Son of Man in Daniel and the Messiah." Th.M. thesis, Dallas Theological Seminary, 1979.

———. "The Son of Man in Luke 5:24." *BBR* 1 (1991): 109–21.

———. "The Use of Daniel 7 in Jesus' Trial, with Implications for His Self-Understanding." In *Who Is This Son of Man?: The Latest Scholarship on a Puzzling Expression of the Historical Jesus*, ed. L. Hurtado and P. L. Owen, 78–100. London: Bloomsbury T&T Clark, 2011.

Borsch, F. H. *The Son of Man in Myth and History*. London: SCM, 1967.

Bowker, J. "The Son of Man." *JTS* 28 (1977): 19–48.

Bowman, J. "The Background of the Term 'Son of Man.'" *ExpT* 59 (1947–48): 283–88.

Brekelmans, C. H. W. "The Saints of the Most High and Their Kingdom." *OtSt* 14 (1965): 305–29.

Bruce, F. F. "The Background to the Son of Man Sayings." In *Christ the Lord*, FS D. Guthrie, ed. H. H. Rowdon, 50–70. Leicester/Downers Grove, IL: IVP, 1982.

Buchanan, G. W. "The Son of Man in Daniel and Enoch." In *To the Hebrews*, 42–48. AB 36. Garden City, NY: Doubleday, 1972.

Bucur, B. G. "The Son of Man and the Ancient of Days: Observations on the Early Christian Reception of Daniel 7." *Phronema* 32 (2017): 1–27.

Burkett, D. "Son of Man in Apocalyptic and Rabbinic Texts." In *The Son of Man Debate: A History and Evaluation*, ed. D. Burkett, 97–120. SNTSMS 107. Cambridge: Cambridge University Press, 2004.

Campbell, J. Y. "The Origin and Meaning of the Term 'Son of Man.'" *JTS* 48 (1947): 145–55.

Caragounis, C. C. "The Interpretation of the Ten Kings of Daniel 7." *ETL* 63 (1987): 106–13.

———. *The Son of Man*. WUNT 38. Tübingen: Mohr, 1986.

Casey, P. M. "The Corporate Interpretation of 'One Like a Son of Man' (Dan. VII 13) at the Time of Jesus." *NovT* 18 (1976): 167–80.

———. "General, Generic and Indefinite: The Use of the Term 'Son of Man' in Aramaic Sources and in the Teachings of Jesus." *JSNT* 29 (1987): 21–56.

———. *The Solution to the 'Son of Man' Problem*. LNTS 343. London: T&T Clark, 2007.

———. *Son of Man: The Interpretation and Influence of Daniel 7*. London: SPCK, 1979.

Charlesworth, J. H. "The Date and Provenance of the *Parables of Enoch*." In *Parables of Enoch: A Paradigm Shift*, ed. D. L. Bock and J. H. Charlesworth, 37–57. London: Bloomsbury T&T Clark, 2013.

———. "A Rare Consensus among Enoch Specialists: The Date of the Earliest Enoch Books." *Hen* 24 (2002): 225–34.

Chou, A. *I Saw the Lord: A Biblical Theology of Vision*. Eugene, OR: Wipf & Stock, 2013.

Collins, J. J. *The Apocalyptic Imagination: An Introduction to Jewish Apocalyptic Literature*. 2nd ed. Grand Rapids: Eerdmans, 1998. [See esp. 177–93 concerning the use of "son of man" in the Similitudes of *1 Enoch*.]

———. *The Apocalyptic Vision of the Book of Daniel*. HSM 16. Missoula, MT: Scholars Press, 1977.

———. "The Son of Man and the Saints of the Most High in the Book of Daniel." *JBL* 93 (1974): 50–66.

———. "The Son of Man in First-Century Judaism." *NTS* 38 (1992): 448–66.

———. "Stirring up the Great Sea: The Religio-historical Background of Daniel 7." In *The Book of Daniel in the Light of New Findings*, ed. A. S. Van der Woude, 121–36. BETL, 106. Louvain: Leuven Univ. Press, 1993.

Collins, A. Y. "Daniel 7 and the Historical Jesus." In *Of Scribes and Scrolls; Studies on the Hebrew Bible, Intertestamental Judaism, and Christian Origins*, ed. H. W. Attridge, J. J. Collins, and T. H. Tobin, 187–93. Lanham, MD: University Press of America, 1990.

Day, J. *God's Conflict with the Dragon and the Sea: Echoes of a Canaanite Myth in the Old Testament*. Cambridge: Cambridge University Press, 1985.

Dequeker, L. "'The Saints of the Most High' in Qumran and Daniel." *OtSt* 18 (1973): 133–62.

Di Lella, A. A. "The One in Human Likeness and the Holy Ones of the Most High in Daniel 7." *CBQ* 39 (1977): 1–19.

Donahue, J. R. "Recent Studies on the Origin of 'Son of Man' in the Gospels." *CBQ* 48 (1986): 484–98.

Driver, S. R. "Son of Man." In *Dictionary of the Bible*, 4 vols., ed. J. Hastings, 4:579–89. Edinburgh: T&T Clark, 1902.

Dumbrell, W. T. "Daniel 7." *Stimulus* 2 (1994): 26–31.

———. "Daniel 7 and the Function of Old Testament Apocalyptic." *RTR* 34 (1975): 16–23.

Dunn, J. D. G. "The Danielic Son of Man in the New Testament." In *The Book of Daniel: Composition & Reception*, ed. J. J. Collins and P. W. Flint, 528–49. VTSup 83:2. Leiden: Brill, 2001.

———. "'Son of God' as 'Son of Man' in the Dead Sea Scrolls: A Response to John Collins on 4Q246." In *The Scrolls and the Scriptures: Qumran Fifty Years After*, ed. S. E. Porter and C. A. Evans, 198–210. Sheffield: Sheffield University Press, 1997.

Eggler, J. *Influences and Traditions Underlying the Vision of Daniel 7:2–14: The Research History from the End of the 19th Century to the Present*. Fribourg: University Press; Göttingen: Vandenhoeck & Ruprecht, 2000.

Emerton, J. A. "The Origin of the Son of Man Imagery." *JTS* 9 (1958): 225–42.
Ferch, A. J. "Daniel 7 and Ugarit: A Reconsideration." *JBL* 99 (1980): 75–86.
———. *The Son of Man in Daniel 7*. Berrien Springs, MI: Andrews University Press, 1983.
Ferda, T. S. "Naming the Messiah: A Contribution to the 4Q246 'Son of God' Debate." *DSD* 21 (2014): 150–75.
Fitzmyer, J. "Another View of the 'Son of Man' Debate." *JSNT* 4 (1979): 58–68.
Fletcher-Louis, C. H. T. "The High Priest as Divine Mediator in the Hebrew Bible: Dan 7:13 as a Test Case." In *SBL Seminar Papers Series*, ed. E. H. Lovering, Jr, 161–93. Atlanta: Scholars Press, 1997.
Flusser, D. "The Four Empires in the Fourth Sibyl and in the Book of Daniel." *IOS* 2 (1972): 148–75.
Frank, R. M. "The Description of the 'Bear' in Dn 7,5." *CBQ* 21 (1959): 505–7.
Fröhlich, I. "Stars and Spirits: Heavenly Bodies in Ancient Jewish Aramaic Tradition." *AS* 13 (2105): 111–27.
———. *"Time and Times and Half a Time": Historical Consciousness in the Jewish Literature of the Persian and Hellenistic Eras*. JSPSup 19. Sheffield: Sheffield Academic Press, 1996.
Gardner, A. E. "Daniel 7,2–14: Another Look at its Mythic Pattern." *Bib* 82 (2001): 244–52.
———. "Decoding Daniel: The Case of Dan 7,5." *Bib* 88 (2007): 222–33.
———. "The Great Sea of Dan. VII 2." *VT* 49 (1999): 412–15.
———. "The 'Little Horn' of Dan 7,8: Malevolent or Benign?" *Bib* 93 (2012): 209–26.
Glasson, T. F. "The Son of Man Imagery: Enoch xiv and Daniel vii." *NTS* 23 (1976): 82–90.
Goldingay, J. "'Holy Ones on High' in Daniel 7:18." *JBL* 107 (1988): 495–97.
Gurney, R. "The Four Kingdoms of Daniel 2 and 7." *Them* 2 (1977): 39–45.
Hanhart, K. "The Four Beasts of Daniel's Vision in the Night in the Light of Rev. 13.2." *NTS* 27 (1980–1981): 576–83.
Hasel, G. F. "The First and Third Years of Belshazzar (Dan 7:1; 8:1)." *AUSS* 15 (1977): 153–68.
———. "The Four World Empires of Daniel Against Its Near Eastern Environment." *JSOT* 12 (1979): 17–30.
———. "The Identity of the 'Saints of the Most High' in Daniel 7." *Bib* 56 (1975): 173–92.
Hitchcock, M. L. "A Critique of the Preterist View of Revelation 17:9–11 and Nero." *BSac* 164 (2007): 472–85.
Horbury, W. "The Messianic Associations of 'The Son of Man.'" *JTS* 36 (1985): 34–55.
Joseph, S. J. "Was Daniel 7.13's 'Son of Man' Modeled after the 'New Adam' of the *Animal Apocalypse* (*1 Enoch* 90)? A Comparative Study." *JSP* 22 (2013): 1–27.
Kee, M. S. "The Heavenly Council and its Type-scene." *JSOT* 31 (2007): 259–73.

Knibb, M. A. "Messianism in the Pseudepigrapha in Light of the Scrolls." *DSD* 2 (1995): 165–84.

_______. "The Date of the Parables of Enoch: A Critical Review." *NTS* 25 (1979): 345–59.

Korner, R. J. "The 'Exilic' Prophecy of Daniel 7: Does It Reflect Late Pre-Maccabean or Early Hellenistic Historiography?" In *Prophets, Prophecy, and Ancient Israelite Historiography*, ed. M. J. Boda and L. M. W. Beal, 333–53. Winona Lake, IN: Eisenbrauns, 2013.

Kratz, R. G. "The Visions of Daniel." In *The Book of Daniel: Composition and Reception*, ed. J. J. Collins and P. W. Flint, 1:91–113. Leiden: Brill, 2001.

Kuhn, K. A. "The 'One Like a Son of Man' Becomes the 'Son of God.'" *CBQ* 69 (2007): 22–42.

Kvanvig, H. S. "An Akkadian Vision as Background for Daniel 7?" *ST* 35 (1981): 85–89.

———. *Roots of Apocalyptic: The Mesopotamian Background of the Enoch Figure and of the Son of Man*. Neukirchen-Vluyn, Germany: Neukirchener, 1988.

———. "Throne Visions and Monsters: The Encounter Between Danielic and Enochic Traditions." *ZAW* 117 (2005): 249–72.

Lacocque, A. "Allusions to Creation in Daniel 7." In *The Book of Daniel: Composition and Reception*, ed. J. J. Collins and P. W. Flint, 114–31. VTSup 83:2. Leiden: Brill, 2001.

———. "The Vision of the Eagle in 4 Esdras, a Rereading of Daniel 7 in the First Century C.E." *SBLSP* 20 (1981): 237–58.

Lee, Y. "Judging or Ruling the Twelve Tribes of Israel? The Sense of Κρίνω in Matthew 19.28." *BT* 66 (2015): 138–50.

Lenglet, A. "La structure littéraire de Daniel 2–7." *Bib* 53 (1972): 169–90.

Lester, G. B. *Daniel Evokes Isaiah: Allusive Characterization of Foreign Rule in the Hebrew-Aramaic Book of Daniel*. LHBOTS 606. London: Bloomsbury T&T Clark, 2015.

Lindars, B. *Jesus Son of Man*. Grand Rapids: Eerdmans, 1983.

Longenecker, R. N. "'Son of Man' as a Self-Designation of Jesus." *JETS* 12 (1969): 151–58.

Longman, T., III. "The Divine Warrior: The New Testament Use of an Old Testament Motif." *WTJ* 44 (1982): 290–307.

Lucas, E. C. "The Source of Daniel's Animal Imagery." *TynBul* 41 (1990): 161–85.

Lust, J. "Daniel VII and the Septuagint." *ETL* 54 (1978): 62–69.

Luter, A. B. "The 'Preaching Texts' of the Apocalypse (Dan 7:13 and Zech 12:10): Fulfillment and Theological Significance." *CTR* 12 (2014): 23–47.

Macumber, H. "A Monster Without a Name: Creating the Beast Known as Antiochus IV in Daniel 7." *JHebScr* 15 (2015): 1–26.

Marshall, I. H. "The Son of Man in Contemporary Debate." *EvQ* 42 (1970): 67–87.

McEntire, M. "The Graying of God in Daniel 1–7." *RevExp* 109 (2012): 569–79.

McKay, G. K. "The Eastern Christian Exegetical Tradition of Daniel's Vision of the Ancient of Days." *JECS* 7 (1999): 139–61.

Meadowcroft, T. "'One Like a Son of Man' in the Court of the Foreign King: Daniel 7 as Pointer to Wise Participation in the Divine Life." *JTI* 10 (2016): 245–63.
Mearns, C. L. "Dating the Similitudes of Enoch." *NTS* 25 (1978–79): 360–69.
Moloney, F. J. "Constructing Jesus and the Son of Man." *CBQ* 75 (2013): 719–38.
Mosca, P. G. "Ugarit and Daniel 7." *Bib* 67 (1986): 496–517.
Muilenburg, J. "The Son of Man in Daniel and the Ethiopic Apocalypse of Enoch." *JBL* 79 (1960): 197–209.
Müller, M. *The Expression 'Son of Man' and the Development of Christology: A History of Interpretation*. London and New York: Routledge, 2008.
Müller, U. B. *Messias und Menschensohn in jüdischen Apokalypsen und in der Offenbarung des Johannes*. SNT 6. Gütersloh: Gütersloher Verlagshaus, 1972.
Munoa, P. B. *Four Powers in Heaven: The Interpretation of Daniel 7 in the Testament of Abraham*. JSPSup 28. Sheffield: Sheffield Academic Press, 1998.
Noth, M. "The Holy Ones of the Most High." In *The Laws in the Pentateuch and Other Essays*, 215–28. Trans. D. R. Ap-Thomas. Philadelphia: Fortress, 1967.
Pae, C. H. "The Influence of Enoch 14 on the Composition of Daniel 7." In *Mapping and Engaging the Bible in Asian Cultures: Congress of the Society of Asian Biblical Studies 2008 Seoul Conference*, ed. Y. M. Lee and Y. J. Yoo, 265–84. Seoul, Korea: Christian Literature Society of Korea, 2009.
Patterson, R. D. "The Key Role of Daniel 7." *GTJ* 12 (1991): 245–61.
Perrin, N. "The Son of Man in Ancient Judaism and Primitive Christianity: A Suggestion." *BR* 11 (1966): 17–28.
Porter, P. A. *Metaphors and Monsters: A Literary-Critical Study of Daniel 7 and 8*. ConBOT Series 20. Uppsala: CWK Gleerup, 1983.
Poythress, V. S. "The Holy Ones of the Most High in Daniel VII." *VT* 26 (1976): 208–13.
Raabe, P. R. "Daniel 7: Its Structure and Role in the Book." *HAR* 9 (1985): 267–75.
Reynolds, B. E. "Another Suggestion for ὡς παλαιὸς ἡμερῶν in the Old Greek of Dan 7:13." *Hen* 30 (2008): 94–103.
———. "The 'One Like a Son of Man' According to the Old Greek of Daniel 7,13–14." *Bib* 89 (2008): 70–80.
Rowe, R. D. "Is Daniel's 'Son of Man' Messianic?" In *Christ the Lord*, ed. H. H. Rowdon, 71–96. Leicester/Downers Grove, IL: Inter-Varsity Press, 1982.
Royer, W. S. "The Ancient of Days: Patristic and Modern Views of Daniel 7:9–14." *SVTQ* 45 (2001): 137–62.
Sahlin, H. "Antiochus IV. Epiphanes und Judas Mackabäus." *ST* 23 (1969): 41–68.
Schaberg, J. "Daniel 7, 12 and the New Testament Passion-Resurrection Predictions." *NTS* 31 (1985): 208–22.
Schmidt, N. "The Son of Man in the Book of Daniel." *JBL* 19 (1900): 22–28.

Scolnic, B. E. "Antiochus IV and the Three Horns in Daniel 7." *JHebScr* 14 (2014): 1–28.

Segal, M. "Who is the 'Son of God' in 4Q246?: An Overlooked Example of Early Biblical Interpretation." *DSD* 21 (2014): 289–312.

Shea, W. H. "The Neo-Babylonian Historical Setting for Daniel 7." *AUSS* 24 (1986): 31–36.

Shepherd, M. B. "Daniel 7:13 and the New Testament Son of Man." *WTJ* 68 (2006): 99–111.

Slater, T. B. "One Like a Son of Man in First-Century Judaism." *NTS* 41 (1995): 183–98.

Smith, M. "Heaven or Earth? The Destination of the 'One Like a Son of Man' in Daniel 7.13–14." Paper presented at the annual national conference of the Evangelical Theological Society. Atlanta, November 19, 2015.

Snow, R. "Daniel's Son of Man in Mark: A Redefinition of the Earthly Temple and the Formation of a New Temple Community." *TynBul* 60 (2009): 305–8.

Sokoloff, M. "ʿămar nĕqē', 'Lamb's Wool' (Dan 7:9)." *JBL* 95 (1976): 277–79.

Staub, Urs. "Das Tier mit den Hörnen: Ein Beitrag zu Dan 7,7f." In *Hellenismus und Judentum: Vier Studien zu Daniel 7 und zur Religionsnot unter Antiochus IV*, ed. O. Keel and U. Staub. OBO 178. Freiburg: Universitätsverlag; Göttingen: Vandenhoeck & Ruprecht, 2000, 37–85.

Stokes, R. E. "The Throne Visions of Daniel 7, *1 Enoch* 14, and the Qumran *Book of Giants* (4Q530): An Analysis of Their Literary Relationship." *DSD* 15 (2008): 340–58.

Stuckenbruck, L. T. "'One like a Son of Man as the Ancient of Days' in the Old Greek Recension of Daniel 7,13: Scribal Error or Theological Translation?" *ZNW* 86 (1995): 268–76.

———. "The Throne-Theophany of the Book of Giants: Some New Light on the Background of Daniel 7." In *The Scrolls and the Scriptures: Qumran Fifty Years After*, ed. S. E. Porter and C. A. Evans, 211–20. Sheffield: Sheffield University Press, 1997.

Süring, M. L. "The Horn-motifs of the Bible and the Ancient Near East." *AUSS* 22 (1984): 327–40.

Thomas, R. L. "The Mission of Israel and of the Messiah in the Plan of God." *MSJ* 8 (1997): 191–210.

Trotter, J. R. "The Tradition of the Throne Vision in the Second Temple Period: Daniel 7:9–10, *1 Enoch* 14:18–23, and the *Book of Giants* (4Q530)." *RevQ* 25 (2012): 451–66.

Tuckett, C. M. "The Son of Man and Daniel 7: Inclusive Aspects of Early Christologies." In *Christian Origins: Worship, Belief and Society: The Milltown Institute and the Irish Biblical Association Millennium Conference*, ed. K. J. O'Mahony, 164–90. London, New York: Sheffield Academic Press, 2003.

———. "The Son of Man and Daniel 7: Q and Jesus." In *The Sayings Source Q and the Historical Jesus*, ed. A. Lindemann, 371–94. Leuven: Leuven University Press, 2001.

Van Henten, J. W. "Antiochus IV as a Typhonic Figure in Daniel 7." In *The Book of Daniel in the Light of New Findings*, ed. A. S. Van der Woude, 223–43. Louvain: Peeters, 1993.

Van Peursen, W. T. "Daniel's Four Kingdoms in the Syriac Tradition." In *Tradition and Innovation in Biblical Interpretation*, ed. W. T. Van Peursen and J. W. Dyk, 189–207. Leiden: Brill, 2011.

VanderKam, J. C. "Daniel 7 in the Similitudes of Enoch (*1 Enoch* 37–71)." In *Biblical Traditions in Transmission: Essays in Honour of Michael A. Knibb*, ed. C. Hempel and J. M. Lieu, 291–307. Leiden: Brill, 2006.

Vermes, G. "The Present State of the 'Son of Man' Debate." *JJS* 29 (1978): 123–34.

———. "The 'Son of Man' Debate." *JSNT* 1 (1978): 19–32.

———. "The Son of Man Debate Revisited (1960–2012)." In *Parables of Enoch: A Paradigm Shift*, ed. D. L. Bock and J. H. Charlesworth, 3–17. London: Bloomsbury T&T Clark, 2013.

———. "The Use of בר נשא/בר נש in Jewish Aramaic." In *An Aramaic Approach to the Gospels and Acts*, ed. M. Black, 310–30. 3rd ed. Oxford: Clarendon, 1967.

Viviano, B. T. "The Trinity in the Old Testament: From Daniel 7:13–14 to Matthew 28:19." *TZ* 54 (1998): 193–209.

Vlach, M. J. "The Trinity and Eschatology." *MSJ* 24 (2013): 199–215.

Walker, W. O. "Daniel 7:13–14." *Int* 39 (1985): 176–81.

Walton, J. H. "The Anzu Myth as Relevant Background for Daniel 7?" In *The Book of Daniel: Composition and Reception*, ed. J. J. Collins and P. W. Flint, 1:69–89. Leiden: Brill, 2000.

———. "Daniel's Four Kingdoms." *JETS* 29 (1986): 25–36.

Walvoord, J. F. "The Prophecy of The Ten-Nation Confederacy." *BSac* 124 (1967): 99–105.

———. "The Revival of Rome." *BSac* 126 (1969): 317–28.

Wilson, F. M. "The Son of Man in Jewish Apocalyptic Literature." *Studia biblica et theologica* 8 (1978): 28–52.

Wilson, R. R. "Creation and New Creation: The Role of Creation Imagery in the Book of Daniel." In *God Who Creates: Essays in Honor of W. Sibley Towner*, ed. W. P. Brown and S. D. McBride, Jr, 190–203. Grand Rapids: Eerdmans, 2000.

Wittstruck, T. "The Influence of Treaty Curse Imagery on the Beast Imagery of Daniel 7." *JBL* 97 (1978): 100–102.

Zacharias, H. D. "Old Greek Daniel 7:13–14 and Matthew's Son of Man." *BBR* 21 (2011): 453–61.

Zehnder, M., "Why the Danielic 'Son of Man' is a Divine Being." *BBR* 24 (2014): 331–47.

Zevit, Z. "The Structure and Individual Elements of Daniel 7." *ZAW* 80 (1968): 385–96.

Part II:
The Hebrew Section

The Revelation of God's Plan to Ultimately Rescue Israel, But Not Until She Has First Suffered at the Hands of Both Antiochus and the Antichrist (8:1–12:13)

Beginning with Dan 8:1, the language shifts back to Hebrew and remains so to the end of the book. Correspondingly, the theme of the book shifts from concern of God's dealings with the Gentile kingdoms that dominated Israel to the ultimate fate of the nation Israel itself. The vision of chap. 7 indicates that Israel will ultimately suffer at the hands of the antichrist before she will be rescued and Messiah's kingdom will be formally established. The remaining chapters focus on the nation's suffering in preparation for Messiah's rescue. This suffering comes not only at the hands of the antichrist but also at the hands of a figure who *typifies* him, namely Antiochus IV Epiphanes of the second century BC.

A. The Vision of the Ram and the Goat: Anticipated Persecution by Antiochus (8:1–27)

In contrast to the vision of four animals depicted in chap. 7, this chapter features only two animal figures symbolizing but two earthly kingdoms. The reason for this *narrowing* of kingdom concerns is due to the author's intention to focus on the rise of Antiochus IV Epiphanes from the second of these kingdoms. In the second century BC, Antiochus IV Epiphanes—a most despicable king—arose as ruler of the Seleucid dynasty (one of the remnants of the empire of Alexander the Great). During his reign, he harshly persecuted the Jewish people and sought to destroy every expression of worshiping the biblical God. Because of this, the Bible utilizes him as a *type* of the future antichrist to come. Chapter 8 reveals the rise of Antiochus and his hostility against Israel.

Structurally, the chapter divides into four basic sections, with the second and third sections each having three subdivisions in which the third subdivision of both highlights the "small horn" (Antiochus IV Epiphanes).[1]

1. For a slightly different understanding of the structure based on text linguistic analysis, see S. Nuñez, "Narrative Structure of Daniel 8: A Text Linguistic Approach," *JATS* 26 (2015): 88–110.

A Prologue with dating formula (8:1–2)
  B Daniel's account of the vision (8:3–14)
    1 The ram with two horns (8:3–4)
    2 The male goat and four horns (8:5–8)
    3 The small horn's hostility against Israel (8:9–14)
  B′ Gabriel's explanation of the vision (8:15–26)
    1 The encounter with Gabriel (8:15–19)
    2 The ram and goat explained (8:20–22)
    3 Elaboration of the small horn's hostility (8:23–26)
A′ Epilogue: Daniel's alarm (8:27)

1. The vision given to Daniel at Susa (8:1–14)

Long before Antiochus arose as a persecutor of Israel, God foretold his coming and hostility against Israel to Daniel in the sixth century BC by means of a vision from the Lord. The vision itself is recorded in verses 1–14.

This passage is very complicated, with numerous text-critical problems, and much variation between MT and the versions. Furthermore, there are a number of difficult translation problems (e.g., how best to translate צָבָא, *ṣāḇāʾ*, and how to render the repetitive occurrences of גָּדַל, *gāḏal*).

Textual Notes – Dan 8:1–14

1.a. The spelling בֵּלְאשַׁצַּר is found here and in Dan 5:30 and 7:1. In all other places, the spelling is בֵּלְשַׁאצַּר (5:1, 2, 9, 22, 29).

2.a-a. The first four words are lacking in LXX$^{\theta}$, but LXX^{O} has something comparable to MT. 4QDan[b] has at least part ("when I looked").

2.b-b. וָאֶרְאֶה בֶּחָזוֹן is lacking in both LXX^{O} and LXX$^{\theta}$ but present in 4QDan[a].

3.a. 4QDan[a], 4QDan[b], and LXX^{O} add the word "great," i.e., "a great ram." The addition was probably in anticipation of what is said of the ram in v. 4.

4.a. Some MSS have a word for "eastward" (so Pap. 967, MS 88, S, and 4QDan[a]), although this is lacking in MT and LXX$^{\theta}$. Collins (325) includes it, but Goldingay (196) does not.

5.a. The negative particle וְאֵין is unusual here. Normally this has the meaning "but no one," "there is not," or "there is none." *BHS* editor proposes ואֵינֶנּוּ. However, the use of אֵין again in v. 27 argues for it here, albeit in a rarer sense "was not."

5.b. For חָזוּת, LXX^{O} translated as ἓν ("one"), which might suggest an original reading אַחַת, and hence *BHS* editor proposes קֶרֶן אַחַת ("a horn"). Yet the originality of חָזוּת finds support with LXX$^{\theta}$'s θεωρητὸν (LSJM, 797, "that which may be seen," i.e., that which is noticeable).

8.a. Cairo Geniza and a few Hebrew MSS have ובע' in place of MT's וּכְעָצְמוֹ. However, וּכְעָצְמוֹ is the more difficult reading. Furthermore, the prep. כְּ can be used temporally in the sense "as soon as" (Dan 10:9, 19; 11:4).

8.b. The noun חָזוּת is lacking in the Vg. and LXX$^{\theta}$ (κέρατα τέσσαρα, "four horns"). LXX^{O} translated this as ἕτερα ("others"), i.e., four others came up, implying that LXX^{O} read this as אֲחֵרוֹת ("others") rather than חָזוּת. Goldingay (194) omits it as an intrusion from v. 5, and Collins (325) holds that חָזוּת "is either a misplaced gloss (Montgomery, 332) or a corruption of אחרות (G: ἕτερα under the influence of v. 5)." However, even though the horn of v. 5 was described as חָזוּת does not demand that the four horns (Alexander's successors in the symbolism) cannot also be described as חָזוּת. Like the horn of Alexander, they are also conspicuous or noticeable; they were *prominent*.

9.a. Some MSS have מהן (fem.) rather than MT's מהם (masc.), which is understandable in light of the fact that "horns" (to which it refers) is fem. As for the possibility of the masc. form being original, see GKC 440 (§135o) and 465 (§145o) regarding gender confusion.

9.b. Similarly to the preceding, the margin of some Editions has the fem. verb form יָצְאָה.

9.c. *BHS* editor proposes reading this as אַחֶרֶת, "another" (cf. BDB, 859). This explains why the NIV and NRSV translate as "another horn," rather than "a horn" or "a small horn."

9.d. The prep. מ on מִצְּעִירָה is perplexing. Collins (325) simply omits the מ and reads "a small horn." Both LXX^{O} and LXX$^{\theta}$ translate as ἰσχυρὸν, "strong, mighty, powerful" (possibly reading MT as צְעִירָה, fem. noun, "youth, young"). The NET and NASB translate מִצְּעִירָה adjectively, "small horn" (contrast NIV, "another horn, which started small").

9.e. Instead of הַצֶּבִי ("the beautiful"), LXX^{O} translates "the north," assuming *haṣṣāpôn*. LXX$^{\theta}$, on the other hand, translates "the host," assuming *haṣṣābāʾ*. Yet the use of הַצֶּבִי elsewhere in Daniel as a reference to Israel and the focus on Israel in the following verses supports the reading in MT.

11.a. Rather than the Hipʿil verb הֻרַים, several MSS as well as Qere read הוּרַם, Hopʿal (passive) of רום. The passive form is supported by both LXX^{O} and LXX$^{\theta}$, which translate by the passive verb ἐρράχθη, "was thrown down, overthrown."

12.a-a. Rather than וְצָבָא תִּנָּתֵן (with Nipʿal impf. verb), *BHS* editor proposes וּצְבָאָה נִתַּן (with Nipʿal perf.). Both LXX^{O} and LXX$^{\theta}$ translate with aorist passive verbs (though different words). The NET accepts *BHS'* proposal and translates "was given over" (similarly, NIV and NRSV). The NASB and ESV, however, retain the imperfect and translate as future tense.

12.b. Rather than the Hip'il verb וְתַשְׁלֵךְ, a couple of medieval MSS and LXX read as a Hop'al (passive), וְתֻשְׁלַךְ. Most Eng. VSS go with the Hip'il, but the NIV translates as a passive, "was thrown to the ground." Since the difference is only a matter of pointing, this could go either way.

14.a. Most Eng. VSS accept MT's reading אֵלַי ("to me"), which presumes that an angelic being spoke to Daniel. One MS (plus LXX and S) read אֵלָיו ("to him"), which presumes that Daniel overheard one angel speaking to another angel. The NRSV follows the alternative reading, "to him."

Translation

8:1 In the third year of the reign of Belshazzar the king, a vision appeared to me, Daniel, subsequent to the one which had appeared to me previously.[2] **2** I looked in the vision, and while I was looking, I was in the fortified[3] city of Susa in the province Elam. As I *continued* looking[4] in the vision, I was by[5] the

2. בַּתְּחִלָּה (*battᵉḥillâ*) normally means "in the beginning, at the first." For the idea "previously," we might expect בָּרִאשֹׁנָה (*bāri'šōnâ*), as in Gen 13:3–4. However, in usage *batᵉḥillâ* can mean "previously" (e.g., Dan 9:21).

3. Lit., this reads "in Susa the '*bîrâ*'" (בְּשׁוּשַׁן הַבִּירָה, *bᵉšûšan habbîrâ*), in which case *bîrâ* is in apposition to "Susa" (σουσα in the LXX). Yet the meaning of *bîrâ* was not entirely clear to the LXX translators. LXX^{θ} simply left it ambiguous and transliterated, βάρει (*barei*), whereas LXX^{O} translated as "city" (πολις, *polis*). According to *HALOT* (123), this is "from Akk. *birtu*, pl. *birānātu* fortified town, citadel." The sense of "fortress city" is evident in Neh 1:1, where the same expression is used (cf. Esth 1:2). NET translated "in Susa the citadel," and Collins (325) rendered this "fortified city." The latter better reflects the idea that the whole city was a fortified one. Elsewhere, Collins (329) points out "the ubiquitous references to יב בירתא, 'Elephantine the fortress,' in the Elephantine papyri. The terms בירתא and קריתא are used interchangeably for Samaria in the Samaria papyri."

4. Lit., "Then I looked in the vision" (exactly as the beginning of v. 2). These words are lacking in both LXX^{O} and LXX^{θ} (probably considered an unnecessary duplication) but are found in 4QDan[a].

5. For the prep עַל (*'al*) designating proximity ("by"), see BDB, 755d6.

canal Ulai.[6] **3** Then I lifted up my eyes and looked, and behold, a[7] ram was
standing in front of the canal, and it had two horns.[8] Now the two horns were
long, but one was longer than the other, and the longer one came up after
the other.[9] **4** I saw the ram butting[10] westward, northward, and southward.
No animal was able to stand before it, and there was no one to rescue from
his power.[11] He did as he pleased and magnified himself.[12] **5** While I was

---

6. The final two words of the sentence (אוּבַל אוּלָי, *ʾûḇal ʾûlāy*) were handled differently by the LXX translators. LXX$^{\theta}$ has ἐπὶ τοῦ Ουβαλ (*epi tou Oubal*), omitting אוּלָי (*ʾûlāy*), "*I was* by the Oubal." LXX^{O}, on the other hand, has πρὸς τῇ πύλῃ Αιλαμ (*pros tēi pulēi Ailam*), "*I was* by the gate of Olam." The latter translated *ʾûḇal* as πυλη ("gate, door"). Goldingay (194, 196), after much discussion, suggests this derives from Akk. *abullu*, "city gate." BDB (385), however, indicates that אוּבַל (*ʾûḇal*) means "stream, river," and *HALOT* (7) "watercourse, canal." Although the NRSV translates as "river," most Eng. VSS translate this as "canal," i.e., a large artificial waterway. L. Waterman, "A Note on Daniel 8 2," *JBL* 66 (1947): 319, reveals the proper derivation and meaning of *ʾûḇal*: "It can be referred to the common Semitic root *wabālu*, written *yābal* in Hebrew, which means 'to bring, to carry.' As a word applied to water, it reflects the practice of irrigation, as was familiar in Babylonia; hence *ubal* is strictly 'a conduit,' that is, an artificial channel or stream-bed, and is comparable to Akkadian *palgu*, which applies more especially to the irrigation laterals taken off a main channel. … A further Hebraized form *yibal* occurs in Isa 50 35 and 44 4, in the same meaning." (Note: the reference given by Waterman should be Isa 30 25, not 50 35).

7. For אֶחָד (*ʾeḥāḏ*) sometimes functioning as an English indefinite article, see GKC, 401 (§125b).

8. Here, קֶרֶן (*qeren*) occurs in the *dual* (קְרָנַיִם, *qerānāyim*), hence "two horns."

9. When בָּאַחֲרוֹנָה (*bā ʾaḥărônâ*) is used in regard to time, it typically means "afterward(s)";" hence, "after the other." See Deut 13:10; 17:7; 1 Kgs 17:13.

10. The Piʿel ptc. מְנַגֵּחַ (*m^ənagēaḥ*) is from a root נָגַח (*nāgaḥ*), meaning to "push, thrust, gore" (BDB, 618), but "butting" would be the most appropriate translation in this context (i.e., for a ram). Although נָגַח (*nāgaḥ*) can mean "gore" (Exod 21:28), it does not have to have this meaning. The nuance "push, thrust at" is evident in such places as Ps 44:6 (Eng. 5) and Ezek 34:21.

11. Lit., "from his hand." Here "hand" is a metonymy of cause for effect, i.e., the power or authority of the person (cf. BDB, 390 2).

12. There is a noticeable repetition of the word גָּדַל (*gāḏal*) in Dan 8, sometimes in the Qal (vv. 9, 10) and sometimes in the Hipʿil (here and in vv. 8, 11, 25). In the Qal, *gāḏal* means to "become great" or "be magnified, exalted." In the Hipʿil, *gāḏal* can mean to "magnify or exalt oneself" or to "do great things" (the latter nuance seems to be lacking in the Qal). When used of God, the nuance of the Hipʿil is clearly that of doing great things (Joel 2:20, 21; Ps 126:2, 3). Elsewhere, the Hipʿil typically means to exalt oneself or act arrogantly (see Jer 48:26, 42; Ps 53:13 [H]; Lam 1:9; and Zeph 2:10). Yet Goldingay (194, and comments at 196–97) translates v. 4, "Acting as it pleased, it did great things." Similarly, Collins (325) has "and grew great" (i.e., with reference to the Persian Empire). Likewise, the NIV has "and became great."

contemplating,[13] then behold, a male goat[14] was coming from the west across the surface of the whole earth,[15] but without touching the earth. Now this goat had a noticeable[16] horn between its eyes. **6** And he came up to the ram having two horns that I had seen standing before the canal, and he rushed at him in the fury of his strength.[17] **7** Then I saw him coming near the ram, and he was enraged at him. He struck the ram, and shattered his two horns, so that the ram had no strength to stand before him. Then he hurled him to the ground and trampled on him, and there was no one to deliver the ram from his power.[18] **8** Then the male goat magnified himself beyond measure.[19] Yet as soon as he had become mighty, the large horn was broken. Then in its place arose four *other* noticeable horns toward the four winds of heaven.

9 Then out of one of them came forth a small horn, and he grew exceedingly great[20] toward the south, toward the east, and toward the beautiful

---

In contrast, the NET has "acted arrogantly," while the NASB has "magnified himself." These are very different ideas, one being that he accomplished great things, and the other that he acted arrogantly. The use of *gāḏal* in the Hipʿil in Dan 8:25, however, is insightful. The phrase includes the words "in his heart" (וּבִלְבָבוֹ, *ûḇilḇāḇô*), which every translation takes in a pejorative sense. The point is that he magnified himself in his heart, i.e., acted arrogantly, and this is the sense that the Hipʿil use of *gāḏal* seems to have throughout Dan 8 (cf. 11:36).

13. In the previous verses, the text emphasizes that Daniel "saw" (or "observed"), using a form of the verb רָאָה (*rāʾâ*), "to see." Verse 5, however, uses the ptc. מֵבִין (*mēḇîn*), from בִּין (*bîn*) "to discern." NET's "contemplating all this" captures the idea quite well.

14. Lit., "the he-goat of the goats" (צְפִיר־הָעִזִּים, *ṣᵉpîr-hāʿizzîm*). Interestingly, S adds an interpretative gloss: "The he-goat, Alexander, son of Philip."

15. Or "land" (so NET). The NIV has "earth." Collins (325) translates the first occurrence of אֶרֶץ (*ʾereṣ*) as "earth" but the second as "ground."

16. The noun חָזוּת (*ḥāzûṯ*) means "vision, conspicuousness" (BDB, 303). The LXX$^{\theta}$ translated as θεωρητὸν (*theōrēton*), "that which may be seen" (LSJM, 797). The horn was quite *noticeable*.

17. The final two words (בַּחֲמַת כֹּחוֹ, *baḥămaṯ kōḥô*) are taken by the NIV as a hendiadys, "in great rage." Lit., "in the burning anger of his strength." Collins (323) suggests "in the fury of his strength."

18. Lit., "and there was not a deliverer for the ram from his hand."

19. The phrase עַד־מְאֹד (*ʿaḏ–mᵊʾōḏ*) is used some 17x in the OT and functions to amplify the action implied by the verb. It means to do something *excessively*. This could be translated "exceedingly" (see Gen 27:34) or even "beyond measure" (Isa 64:11).

20. According to BDB (452), וַתִּגְדַּל־יֶתֶר (*wattigdal-yeṯer*) means to "grow great in excess, exceedingly" (the noun *yeṯer* meaning "excess"). Note the use in this case of *gāḏal* in the Qal (contrast vv. 4, 8). Here, the idea is that of growing great in political strength and the expansion of his realm.

land.[21] **10** He even grew as far as the host[22] of heaven and caused some[23] of the host and some of the stars to fall to the earth and trampled them. **11** He even magnified himself as far as the Commander[24] of the host. On account of him, the regular sacrifice[25] was abolished, and the place of His sanctuary[26] was cast down. **12** Then the host, together with[27] the regular

---

21. Although the word "land" is not in the Hebrew text, most Eng. VSS add the word. הַצֶּבִי (*haṣṣeḇî*), a noun meaning "beauty," is commonly understood to be a cryptic reference to Israel, "the Beautiful Land," in light of Dan 11:16, 41. In 11:16, the word "land" is explicit: אֶרֶץ־הַצְּבִי (*ʾereṣ-haṣṣᵉḇî*). In Ezek 20:6, Israel is called "the glory of all lands" (צְבִי הִיא לְכָל־הָאֲרָצוֹת, *ṣᵉḇî hîʾ lᵉḵol-hāʾărāṣôṯ*).
22. The word "host" (צָבָא, *ṣāḇāʾ*) is used repeatedly in vv. 10, 11, 12, and 13 (though some VSS translate as "army"). Fundamentally, the word means a collection of persons or things whose purpose is to render service to Yahweh. Frequently this is for the purpose of warfare, but the term can easily apply to those who render service at the tabernacle (Num 4:23; 8:24). The cognate verb means to fight (Num 31:7), and the noun easily takes the meaning "army" (Judg 4:2) or "war" (Num 1:3). The idea of a collective entity that stands ready to serve helps us understand other nuances of meaning. Hence, *ṣāḇāʾ* can refer to the heavenly angelic host (1 Kgs 22:19) as well as the celestial bodies in the heavens, i.e., the sun, moon and stars (Gen 2:1; Deut 4:19). Yet it can also refer to the *people* of God, i.e., the Hebrew people (Exod 12:41). Context, of course, determines the precise meaning.
23. See BDB, 580d 3b(a) for the partitive use of the prep. מִין (*mîn*) and see Exod 16:27 for an example.
24. The word שַׂר (*śar*) is typically translated "commander" or "prince," though it has a wide range of usage. It can refer to military commanders, nobles, chieftains, rulers, and various government officials. In Dan 12:1 it refers to the archangel Michael. The fundamental idea seems to be that of *ruling over others*, whether as the highest official (king) or as a lesser official with delegated authority. Yet, it can even refer to Yahweh himself as the ultimate ruler of the universe (cf. Josh 5:14), and BDB (979) suggests that God is in view in Dan 8:11.
25. "Regular sacrifice" translates the single Heb. word הַתָּמִיד (*hattāmîḏ*), a noun meaning "continuity" or something done continuously. W. C. Kaiser, "תָּמִיד," in *TWOT*, 1:493, notes the technical meaning that *tāmîḏ* had in the sacrificial system: "Most frequently this word is used in an adjectival genitive construction with *ʿōlâ* for the continual whole burnt offering made to God every morning and evening (Ex 29:42; Num 28:6, 10, 15, 23; Ezr 3:5; Neh 10:34; cf. Ezk 46:15, every morning; and the continual *minḥâ*, Num 4:16; Neh 10:34; Lev 6:13. The word is used alone to designate the daily burnt offering in Dan 8:11–13; 11:31; 12:11."
26. The term מִקְדָּשׁ (*miqdāš*) can mean a "sacred thing" in general, but it is a specific term for God's earthly sanctuary at Jerusalem (Exod 25:8). It is used two other times in Daniel with the temple in view (9:17; 11:31).
27. See BDB (755c II4c) for the case of the prep. עַל (*ʿal*) denoting "with, together with."

sacrifice, was given over on account of a defiant transgression.[28] He flung truth to the ground and succeeded *in what* he did.[29] **13** Then I heard a certain holy one speaking, and another holy one replied to that certain one who was speaking, "This vision about[30] the regular sacrifice and the desolating[31] defiant transgression (*involving* a trampling of both the holy place[32] and the host), how long[33] is this allowed *to go on*?" **14** He said to me, "Until 2300 evenings and mornings,[34] and then the holy place will be set right."[35]

---

28. "On account of rebellion" is actually one word in Hebrew, בְּפָשַׁע (*bᵊp̄āšaʿ*). The prep בְּ (*bᵊ*) is used here with a causal force (see BDB, 90 III 5). The noun פֶּשַׁע (*pešaʿ*) basically means "transgression" (BDB, 833) but is translated "rebellion" or "wickedness" in some Eng. VSS. Regarding the verb פָּשַׁע (*pāšaʿ*), Luc states, "As part of the terminology for sin, *pšʿ*, transgression, has a narrower meaning than *ḥṭʾ* and *ʿwn*. Originated from the political sphere to mean 'rebellion' (e.g., 2 Kgs 1:1) and used 136x in OT, it normally implies willful violations by an inferior against a superior (e.g., Prov 28:24). In biblical theology, the term refers to an open and brazen defiance of God by humans. In Ezek 2:3, its use in parallel with *mrd*, rebel, reinforces its primary connotation: 'Son of man, I am sending you to ... a rebellious nation that has rebelled against me; they and their fathers have been in revolt (*pšʿ*) against me'" (*NIDOTTE*, 3:706). The word is appropriate for describing Israel's rebellion against the Mosaic covenant (Isa 1:28; 48:8; Ezek 2:3; Hos 8:1). Yet the "rebellion" in the case of Dan 8:12 need not be that of Israel against Yahweh. In light of v. 13, this appears to be a defiant rebellious assault of Antiochus IV.

29. The final phrase is lit., "he took action and succeeded" (וְעָשְׂתָה וְהִצְלִיחָה, *wᵊʿāśᵊṯâ wᵊhiṣlîḥâ*).

30. The word "about" is not in the text but has been added. The words הַתָּמִיד וְהַפֶּשַׁע (*hattāmîḏ wᵊhappešaʿ*) are technically not in construct with הֶחָזוֹן (*heḥāzôn*), though they represent the content of the vision.

31. The ptc. שֹׁמֵם (*šāmēm*) can mean either "be desolated" or "be appalled." Of the eight times this occurs in Daniel, it normally has the nuance of "desolating."

32. Normally when the word קֹדֶשׁ (*qōḏeš*) is used for the temple, it has the definite article (as in 9:26). However, there are a few instances when the indefinite form is used for the temple (Exod 29:31; Lev 6:9, 19, 20; 10:13; Isa 43:28; Mal 2:11; Ps 134:2; 1 Chr 24:5).

33. עַד־מָתַי (*ʿaḏ-māṯay*) occurs some 28x in the OT in the sense "how long?" (e.g., Exod 10:3).

34. Rather strangely there is no conjunction joining עֶרֶב (*ʿereḇ*) and בֹּקֶר (*bōqer*). However, the conjunction is found in v. 26: הָעֶרֶב וְהַבֹּקֶר (*hāʿereḇ wᵊhabbōqer*).

35. The verb צָדֵק (*ṣāḏēq*) basically means "be righteous, just." In the case of the Nipʿal use in Dan 8:14, BDB (842d) suggests "be put right." NASB and ESV use the translation "restored," which is appropriate, since the context concerns the restoration of the temple that had been desolated. Both LXX^{O} and LXX$^{\theta}$ translated as καθαρισθήσεται (*katharisthēsetai*), "will be purified/cleansed." Based on a study of the semantic range of *ṣāḏēq*, R. M. Davidson, "The Meaning of *Niṣdaq*, 112," *JATS* 7 (1996): 107–19, explains the basis for the LXX translation: "The close synonymous

Commentary

a. Introduction to the vision (8:1–2)

8:1 The chapter begins by telling us the date of the vision, namely in the third year of King Belshazzar's reign. This would be approximately 551–50 BC, two years after the vision that Daniel received in chap. 7 (note 7:1). This indicates that Daniel would have had two years to reflect on what had been revealed to him in chap. 7. Thus, the vision in chap. 8 would build upon what he already knew, although the focus in chap. 8 would center on the second and third kingdoms rather than the fourth. The date of this new vision was significant for another reason. It came about the time that Cyrus was rising up as a military leader for the Medes and Persians. The details of this period are difficult to determine with certainty, given the discrepancy in the historical accounts recorded by Herodotus and Xenophon. (See the section "Historical Context for the Book of Daniel" in the "Introduction" for discussion.) According to Herodotus, Cyrus had defeated the Median king Astyages and subjugated the Medes to the Persians prior to 539 BC. More likely, however, is Xenophon's account that Cyrus led the combined armies of the Medes and Persians against their common foes, though remaining subordinate to the Median kings Astyages and his son Cyaxares II. In either case, it does seem that Cyrus had begun to play a leading role in the military excursions of the Medes and Persians prior to Babylon's downfall in 539 BC. For example, it appears that Cyrus led a successful attack by the Medes and Persians against the Lydians about 546 BC, defeating their king, Croesus of Lydia (a powerful and strategic kingdom in west-central Turkey). This was a blow to Nabonidus, as he had vainly attempted to forge an alliance with Egypt and Lydia in an effort to resist his powerful neighbors to the east, Media and Persia. As Daniel received this vision in chap. 8, God was about to set in motion the events that would lead to Babylon's conquest and eventually to Israel's suffering at the hands of Antiochus IV Epiphanes.

8:2 The first thing that Daniel saw in the vision was himself in Susa.[36] This was a historic city (and capital) of the ancient Elamite Empire, located about 350 km. to the east of Babylon (in present-day southwest Iran). In v. 2 Susa

---

association of *ṣdq* with *zākāh*, *bôr*, and especially with *ṭahēr*, strongly suggests that a second extended meaning of *ṣdq* moves into the cultic realm with the semantic nuance of 'cleansing' or 'purification.' Thus the LXX (Greek Septuagint) translation of *niṣdaq* with the verb *katharízo* need not be based upon the misreading of a hypothetical Aramaic manuscript source of Daniel 8 (as has been suggested) but rather the LXX translators may have recognized this pronounced nuance embedded within the semantic range of *ṣdq*, particularly in a cultic setting, as in Dan 8:14 and Job 4:17."

36. Scholars debate whether Daniel was literally transported to Susa or whether he simply saw himself there in the vision. We cannot be certain about this, and an answer to this is not essential to the interpretation of the chapter. Josephus (*Ant.* 10.11.7) thought Daniel was physically there, though the Syriac version states that

is described by the Hebrew word *bîrâ*. Sometimes translated "citadel" or "fortress," *bîrâ* can refer to a palace or temple (1 Chr 29:19), a fortress within a city (Neh 2:8), or more commonly to the city itself as a fortress (Neh 1:1; Esth 1:2). The latter is probably the idea, especially since the word *bîrâ* is placed here in apposition to the word Susa. The idea, then, is that Susa was a *fortified city*. Susa had been a very powerful city during the latter part of the second millennium BC, often domineering over Babylonia and Assyria. About the year 640 BC, however, the Assyrian king Ashurbanipal conquered Elam and destroyed Susa. Yamauchi reports that Nabopolassar (r. 626–605 BC) restored the Elamite gods from Uruk to Susa.[37] Why then did Daniel see himself here in Susa, since it was probably only in a weakened state in Daniel's day? The significance probably has to do with what Susa was about to become in the near future. When the Persian King Darius I came to the throne (r. 522–486 BC), he made Susa one of the capitals of the Persian Empire, along with Persepolis and Ecbatana. Susa then functioned as the diplomatic and administrative capital of the empire and served as the residence of the royal family during the winter months (it was too hot to live there in the summer).

Daniel also took note that he was beside the Ulai Canal. This was known classically as the Eulaeus river, which passed close to Susa on the northeast.[38] Baldwin (173–74) notes, "The river *Ulai* (Gk. *'Eulaios*) was originally the name of a canal on which Susa was built, though in the time of Alexander it was the name of the Abi-diz waterway to the east of Susa, down which he sailed his fleet."[39] From this position, he had a panoramic view of the fortified city of Susa—soon to be a major stronghold of the Persians. This

---

Daniel saw in his dream that he was in Susa. The idea of being transported in vision to another location is found elsewhere in Ezek 8:3; 11:24; 40:2.

37. Yamauchi, *Persia and the Bible*, 293.

38. Pliny, *Nat Hist*, 6.27. Waterman, "A Note on Daniel 8 2," 319, describes this waterway: "The Ulai, Akk. *U-la-a-a*, has been recognized not to be a river, but an artificial stream–bed or canal, starting from the Kerkha (Choaspes) at a point about twenty miles N. W. of ancient Susa and extending in a southeasterly direction, so that it passed fairly close to the northern part of Susa and farther on joined the Abdizful (Coprates), which in turn empties into the Karun to the southeast of Susa."

39. Baldwin references the article of J. J. Finkelstein, "Mesopotamia," *JNES* 21 (1962): 89. G. Rawlinson, *Biblical Topography* (London: James Nisbet & Co., 1887), 78–79, elaborates, "The special river of Susa is called by Herodotus the Choaspes but by Daniel and in the Assyrian records, the Ulai. The Ulai can scarcely be other than the Greek Eulseus which the Greek geographers describe as a large stream east of the Choaspes, and which has been generally identified with the Kuran. All accounts agree that Susa was on a large river—one that was navigable. But at present the only stream that washes the ruins is the Shapur, which is little more than a rivulet. The difficulties seemed insuperable until it was found that the Kerkhah, which all agree to be the Choaspes, once bifurcated at Pai Pal flowing from that point in two channels, one (the western) that in which it flows at present, and the other (the eastern) passing

was a fitting place for Daniel to behold this vision, since Medo-Persia was about to conquer Babylon, an event that would in turn lead to the rise of the Hellenistic empires.

b. The ram with the two horns: Medo-Persia (8:3–4)

8:3 In his vision Daniel once again sees Gentile kingdoms depicted as animals, a similar technique to that found in chap. 7, except that different animals are utilized in the new imagery. The first animal that Daniel sees is a ram with two horns beside the Ulai Canal. This is interpreted for the reader in 8:20 as representing Medo-Persia. (Recall that Medo-Persia was represented in Dan 7:5 as a bear.) The choice of the ram in this context for Medo-Persia may simply provide a convenient means of illustration, since the horns of the animal represent the two major parts of the empire. On the other hand, there is evidence that the ram may have been of some significance to the Persian realm. Ammianus Marcellinus (a Roman historian of the fourth century AD) indicated that the Persian ruler carried the gold head of a ram when he marched before his army.

The two horns, however, are not of equal length. One was longer than the other, and this longer one came up last, the significance of which is not hard to understand. Early on, the Medes were a stronger power than the Persians, as evidenced by the fact that they joined forces with Babylonia in 612 BC to defeat Assyria and destroy the famous city of Nineveh. Later, however, the two empires merged and eventually came to be ruled by a long line of Persian kings. Hence the longer horn that came up later signifies the dominant role that Persia had in the course of their history. In fact, not long after Cyrus' day, this empire simply became known as the Persian Empire. That the ram represents one kingdom (Medo-Persia) supports the interpretation given earlier that the four kingdoms of chap. 7 must include Rome. Even Collins (330), who opposes the inclusion of Rome, is forced to admit this: "The representation of Media and Persia as two horns of the same kingdom departs from the view of the four kingdoms standard throughout the book, which treats Media separately."

8:4 In v. 4, the ram is seen butting in each direction except *eastward*. Since this verse goes on to indicate that no animal was able to stand before it, the "butting" of the ram probably indicates its primary military achievements. In 546 BC Medo-Persia conquered the small but significant kingdom of Lydia (in present-day west-central Turkey)—ruled by the legendary Croesus, famous for his gold—a northward conquest. In 539 the Medes and Persians conquered Babylon to the west. Finally, in 525 BC (during the rule of Cambyses, the son of Cyrus) they overpowered Egypt, a southward conquest. There were no major military conquests to the east. With these

---

close to Susa, absorbing the Shapur, and joining the Kuran a little above Ahwaz. It was this stream which the Assyrians called 'Ulai,' and the Greeks 'Eulaeus.'"

conquests, the Persian Empire did as it pleased, i.e., it came to control more territory than any empire before it in history and thus held unrivaled power.

c. The male goat: Greece and its division into four parts (8:5–8)

8:5 The second animal that Daniel sees in this vision is a male goat, interpreted in v. 21 as Greece. The goat had a noticeable (or conspicuous) horn between its eyes, which v. 21 interprets as the first king. This is a clear reference to Greece's most famous king, Alexander the Great of Macedon (356–323 BC).[40] His father, Philip, had united the Grecian city-states and territories, and upon his death Alexander took up his father's mantle with the aim of exacting revenge upon Persia. Thus, the remark that the male goat was coming from the west reflects Alexander's advance from Greece (in the west) toward Persia. He also moved over the surface of the earth without touching it. This reflects the incredible speed at which Alexander moved his forces and conquered the Persian Empire (recall Alexander's description in Dan 7:3 as a leopard with wings). Whereas Medo-Persia took decades to establish her power through conquest, Alexander conquered the known world in three short years (334–331 BC).

8:6–7 These verses depict Alexander's clash with the Persian armies. Verse 7 notes that, being infuriated at Persia, he went against her in the fury of his strength. The Greeks had long been embittered against Persia since the early fifth century BC. Both Darius I (522–486 BC) and his son Xerxes I (486–465 BC) had made military assaults on Greece. Yet the Persians suffered severe defeats at the hands of the Greeks at the Battle of Marathon (490 BC) and the Battle of Salamis (480 BC). Even though the far-outnumbered Greeks had been able to repulse the Persian army and navy, Persia managed to loot and destroy Athens, a "bitter pill," as it were, that the Greeks had never forgotten. Alexander's father, Philip II, had stirred up his generation to overthrow the Persian Empire, and upon his unexpected death Alexander readily stepped in to lead the charge. He left Greece in the spring of 334 BC at the mere age of twenty-three with a relatively small army, vastly inferior in size to the Persians. In some of the most surprising—but yet incredibly brilliant—military maneuvers, he managed to pull off a series of "upsets" against the Persian forces that vastly outnumbered him.

1) May 334 BC: Alexander pushed into Asia Minor and defeated the Persian forces at the Granicus River (near modern-day Ergili in northwest Turkey).
2) Oct 333 BC: Alexander defeated a great Persian army of 600,000 footmen at the battle of Issus near the northeastern tip of the Mediterranean Sea. This time, the Persian army was led by King

40. Of the many accounts of Alexander's life, that by I. Worthington, *Alexander the Great: Man and God* (Harlow, UK: Pearson, 2004), has proven to be one of the best-researched and most helpful.

Darius III himself, though he managed to escape and face Alexander later at Gaugamela.

3) 332 BC: Alexander invaded Egypt after a costly victory at Tyre and was readily welcomed as a liberator (the Egyptians hated the Persians). With his rear position protected, he was now free to attack Darius directly.
4) Oct 331 BC: In a final showdown, Alexander decisively defeated the Persians at Gaugamela (near Arbela) in Assyria (just east of the ancient site of Nineveh). Darius III fled in retreat but was soon killed. Alexander was then free to march into Babylon and subsequently into Susa and Persepolis.

Alexander's final defeat of Persia at Gaugamela is probably what the latter part of Dan 8:7 depicts: "Then he hurled him to the ground and trampled on him, and there was no one to deliver the ram from his power."

8:8 Alexander's victory over Persia was not the last of his military exploits, but it firmly established him as undisputed ruler of the largest empire yet known to man, an empire that included Greece, Asia Minor, Syria, Egypt, Assyria, Babylonia, and Persia. At this point, Alexander was a mere twenty-five years of age. Unfortunately, he did not have the humility to go with his military genius. Rather, he came to think of himself as divine and sought to be worshiped as a god while still alive. According to v. 8a, "Then the male goat magnified himself beyond measure," which probably reflects his vain aspirations of divinity. Verse 8 goes on to say, "Yet as soon as he had become mighty, the large horn was broken." While he was still in the prime of his power (less than thirty-three years of age), he died quite unexpectedly at Babylon. The exact cause of his death is still unknown, though it seems that he may have died as a result of a fever and severe alcohol poisoning (he and a number of his men had been drinking wine in great excess).

Being still quite young, there was no heir in position to take over Alexander's vast empire. His wife Roxane (despised by many because she was not Macedonian) was pregnant with a son, but both of them were assassinated shortly after Alexander's death. It was now left to his generals (known as the Diadochi or "successors") to settle the matter by war and intrigue. From Alexander's death in 323 BC until the defeat of Antigonus in 301 BC, countless wars and assassinations raged on.[41] In the final analysis, the empire was carved up into four primary parts, each headed by one of Alexander's generals. This fulfilled the words in v. 8, "Then in its place arose four other noticeable horns" (equivalent to the four heads on the leopard in 7:6). This

---

41. For a helpful account of this period of struggle, see E. Will, "The Succession to Alexander," in *The Cambridge Ancient History, VII Part 1: The Hellenistic World*, ed. F. W. Walbank et al., 23–61 (Cambridge: Cambridge University Press, 1984).

interpretation is confirmed by 8:22. These "four horns" (commanders) and their respective territories were:[42]

(1) Lysimachus: Thrace and Bithynia (much of Asia Minor)
(2) Cassander: Macedonia and Greece
(3) Seleucus: Syria, Babylonia, and the lands to the east
(4) Ptolemy: Egypt, the land of Judah, and Arabia Petrea

d. The "Small Horn" and his hostility against Israel (8:9–14)

8:9 Once again we are introduced to a small horn. Although this designation sounds similar to the "little horn" of chap. 7, these clearly do not have the same individuals in view. In the earlier case, the little horn of chap. 7 symbolized the future antichrist who arises out of what had once been the Roman Empire. The "small horn" of Dan 8, however, is said to come forth from one of the "four noticeable (or conspicuous) horns" that emerged from the empire founded by Alexander the Great. The "little horn" of chap. 7 is followed by God's kingdom, but the "small horn" of chap. 8 is not. Most commentators are in agreement of identifying this small horn in 8:9 as being Antiochus IV Epiphanes.[43] The "noticeable horn" from whom he is said to come forth is Seleucus I Nicator, one of Alexander's generals who took control of Syria and Babylonia following Alexander's death. This Seleucus (r. 312–280 BC) was the founder of the Seleucid dynasty (which came to be centered in Syria). The year 312 BC is used for the beginning of the Seleucid Empire, because that is the year that Seleucus regained control of Babylonia. Antiochus IV Epiphanes (r. 175–164 BC) was a descendant of Seleucus I. He is given considerable attention in Dan 8 and 11 because of the horrible atrocities he committed against the Jewish people and their religion. In this role as a persecutor, he prefigures the eventual antichrist.

Daniel 8:9 goes on to say that this "small horn" (Antiochus IV) grew exceedingly great "toward the south, toward the east, and toward the beautiful *land*." Antiochus became a powerful ruler in his day, and one of his achievements was his victories over the Ptolemaic dynasty in Egypt (to the south). He also made successful expeditions against rebellious elements in Armenia and Parthia (to the east). The "beautiful *land*" (הַצֶּבִי, *haṣṣeḇî*) comes

42. Newsom (262), following Collins (331), acknowledges that there were more than four who contested for power, but the most important of them would have been Ptolemy Lagus (Egypt), Philip Aridaeus (Macedonia), Antigonus Monophthalmus (Asia Minor), and Seleucus Nicator (Mesopotamia/Syria). Although Arrhidaeus (the more common spelling) did rule Macedonia initially, he was killed by 317 BC and was not actually one of the key rulers at the time when the Fourth War of the Diadochi ended in 301 BC, when Antigonus was defeated and killed. It is better to understand the four horns as the ones that emerged victorious after 301 BC.

43. There are exceptions to the interpretation that the small horn represents Antiochus IV. For an example, see M. A. Hassler, "The Identity of the Little Horn in Daniel 8: Antiochus IV Epiphanes, Rome, or the Antichrist?" *MSJ* 27 (2016): 33–44.

from a word meaning "beauty, honor." This is a reference to the land of Judah (later known as Palestine), as is clear from the use of this expression in Dan 11:41 (cf. Ezek 20:6).[44] Antiochus was notorious for his interference in the affairs of Judah and the exertion of his military muscle against the Jews.

8:10 Having mentioned Antiochus' military aggression against the land of Judah in v. 9, his actions are then depicted symbolically in v. 10. The land of Judah, being the homeland of God's covenant people, was special. Hence, his aggression against the land of Judah was as though he made an assault upon "the host of heaven." The Hebrew word translated "host" (צָבָא, *ṣᵊḇāʾ*) is often used of angels in the service of God, sometimes of an army, and at other times of literal stars (Jer 33:22). However, of the seventeen times that the phrase "host of heaven" is used in the OT, it means the celestial bodies in the heavens (an exception is 1 Kgs 22:19 = 2 Chr 18:18 where it refers to the angelic court). See, for example, Deut 17:3. Obviously Antiochus did not literally ascend to heaven. Yet in becoming greater militarily, his attempt to subjugate the land of Judah was likened in Daniel's vision to an assault on heaven itself. The reference to "host" (NET, army) and "stars" is best understood as the celestial bodies in the sky, not angels.[45] Antiochus' hurling them down to earth and trampling them is *symbolic* of what he did to the Jewish people. Although some scholars have understood v. 10 as depicting an assault on the angelic court, this interpretation has problems: (1) the following verses (11–12) clarify that what is in view are his atrocities on the Jewish people and the Jerusalem temple, not angels; and (2) the word for "trampling" in v. 10 (Heb. רָמַס, *rāmas*) was used earlier in v. 7 of Alexander's brutality in slaughtering Persian soldiers. When used figuratively, this word means to dominate, prevail over, and decisively defeat or persecute severely. Antiochus did that to the Jewish people, but he did not do that to angels. So, it is better to understand this in regard to the stars and other celestial objects, with that in turn symbolizing his harsh persecution of the Jewish people (so Miller, 226). This is well documented in the books of I and II Maccabees (see esp. 1 Macc 1:29–32; 1:52–61). Perhaps the idea of "stars" was appropriate imagery, because God had promised to Abram that his descendants would become as the stars in number (Gen 15:5; cf. Dan 12:3). Also, in Exod 12:41 the term "host" was used of "the hosts of Yahweh" (i.e., the Hebrews) who went out of the land of Egypt (cf. Exod 7:4; 12:17).

44. The land of Judah was considered the Beautiful Land precisely because God had set this land apart for Abraham and his descendants, and it was there that the temple was built in which his shekinah glory dwelt.

45. Baldwin's suggestion (173) that the stars refer to earthly monarchs (Isa 24:21), namely "rival kings who suffered a cruel fate at the march of this upstart (cf. Rev. 12:4)," fails to take into account that the stars in this context pertain to the "Beautiful Land," i.e., Israel. Collins (332) takes the "host" to be "the good angels."

8:11–12 These verses look at some of the more specific acts of Antiochus. We see, for instance, his arrogance against "the Commander of the host" (שַׂר־הַצָּבָא, *śar-haṣṣāḇāʾ*). Some have suggested this might be the high priest, Onias III, who was assassinated under Antiochus' rule about 171–170 BC, or perhaps even the angel Michael (see Dan 12:1 where the term *śar* is used of him).[46] More likely, however, this refers to Yahweh himself in light of the way the term *śar* is used in Dan 8:25 for "the Prince of princes," שַׂר־שָׂרִים, *śar-śārîm* (cf. Josh 5:14, where Joshua meets the "captain/commander of the host of Yahweh," שַׂר־צְבָא־יְהוָה, *śar ṣᵊḇāʾ yhwh*).[47] Not only did Antiochus exalt himself by having coins minted with the inscription "Theos Epiphanēs" (i.e., god manifest), but he sought to eradicate the biblical faith in Jerusalem and replace it with Hellenistic worship of the Greek gods. Waltke summarizes his actions:

> Further, the sanctuary in Jerusalem was to be polluted and called 'Jupiter Olympius' (2 Macc. 6:1f.), probably a Syrian deity in Hellenistic garb ... On Chislev 15 Antiochus instituted the pagan festival of 'light,' which celebrated the rebirth of the sun, and had a Greek altar erected upon the old altar in the temple court (Dnl. 11:31; cf. Josephus *Ant.* xii.5.4); the first victim was sacrificed to Jupiter Olympius on the twenty-fifth (Dec 16, 167 BC) of the same month. Such an offering to Antiochus was to be made on the twenty-fifth of every month, since that date was celebrated as his birthday.[48]

Furthermore, by his order "the daily sacrifice was abolished." The "daily sacrifice" is just one word in the Hebrew text, הַתָּמִיד (*hattāmîḏ*, meaning "continuously"). This is a technical expression for the daily sacrifices that were offered at the Jewish temple according to Exod 29:38–42 and Num 28:2–8. These sacrifices were to be done "each day regularly" (*lāyyôm tāmîḏ*). The daily sacrifice consisted of the offering of a lamb along with a grain offering and a

---

46. Cf. G. Bampfylde, "The Prince of the Host in the Book of Daniel and the Dead Sea Scrolls," 131, who attempts to argue (unconvincingly in my opinion) that the Prince of the host in Dan 8:11 (= Prince of princes in 8:25) is "the supreme arch-angel, the chief of the patron princes and warrior for heaven. He alone can reveal the future of kingdoms on earth and the wars that are to be fought." He also argues that this Prince is "related in some way to the 'Prince of Light(s)' and 'the Angel of Truth' of the Zadokite Documents (CD 5, 18), the Manual of Discipline (1QS 3, 20.24), and the War Scroll (1QM 13, 10–11; 17, 6)." Yet the mere use of the term "prince" in the DSS documents is not sufficient evidence to equate this one with "the Prince of the host" of Dan 8:11.

47. This position (the captain/commander = Yahweh) is also taken by Montgomery (335), Wood (214), and Miller (226).

48. B. K. Waltke, "Antiochus IV Epiphanes," in *ISBE*, 4 vols., ed. G. W. Bromiley, 1:145–46 (Grand Rapids: Eerdmans, 1979), 146.

drink offering, both in the morning and at twilight, as a soothing aroma to Yahweh. In addition to halting the important daily sacrifices, by Antiochus' orders "the place of His sanctuary was cast down." The "sanctuary" (מִקְדָּשׁ, *miqdāš*) is a reference to the earthly temple in Jerusalem (Exod 25:8; Dan 9:17). Antiochus did not *destroy* the Jewish temple, but he profaned it and thereby rendered it unfit for use. The first stage of this atrocity took place in 169 BC when he himself entered the holy of holies and plundered the temple, as recorded in 1 Macc 1:20–24:

> While returning from his conquest of Egypt in the year 143, Antiochus marched against (Israel and) Jerusalem with a strong army. ... Arrogantly entering the temple, he took the golden altar and the candelabrum with all its furnishings and the table for the showbread and the libation jars and the bowls and the golden ladles and the curtain. He stripped off all the cornices and the ornamentation of gold from the front of the temple and took the silver and the gold coin and the precious articles, whatever he found of the treasures on deposit. With all this loot he returned to his own country, having polluted himself with massacres and uttered words of great arrogance.[49]

Two years later (in Dec 167 BC), he went even further when he committed a most abominable sacrilege and attempted to destroy the biblical faith altogether. This is recorded in 1 Macc 1:54–61:

> On the fifteenth day of Kislev ... the king had an abomination of desolation built upon the altar, and in the outlying towns of Judah they built illicit altars, and at the doors of the houses and in the squares they offered illicit sacrifices. Whatever scrolls of the Torah they found, they tore up and burned; and whoever was found with a scroll of the Covenant in his possession or showed his love for the Torah, the king's decree put him to death. Through their strength they acted against the Israelites who were found in the towns each month, as on the twenty-fifth day of the month they would offer sacrifices on the illicit altar which was upon the temple altar. The women who had had their sons circumcised they put to death according to the decree, hanging the babes from their mother's necks and executing also their husbands and the men who had performed the circumcisions.[50]

The sacrilege on Chislev 15 of 167 BC took place when Antiochus' men erected a pagan altar on top of the altar of burnt offering, followed by the offering of a pagan sacrifice on this foreign altar on Chislev 25. Daniel 8:12

---

49. J. A. Goldstein, *I Maccabees: A New Translation with Introduction and Commentary*, AYB 41 (New Haven, CT: Yale University Press, 2008), 205.
50. Ibid., 206.

explains that it was on account of transgression that the host (the Jewish people) and the regular sacrifice were given over to Antiochus. The word for "transgression" (rendered "rebellion" in some translations) is the Hebrew word פֶּשַׁע (*peša*ʿ), which normally signifies sin in the sense of *revolting* against the authority of God. This "transgression" could be that of the Jewish people, which brought about divine judgment (so Baldwin, 176), or it could be the atrocities of Antiochus himself. If the transgression is that of the Jewish people, this could refer specifically to the abomination of the priesthood, a treachery that certain Jews carried out. The legitimate high priest of this time was Onias III, but his Egyptian sympathies aroused the disfavor of those Jews who were pro-Seleucid. Soon a power struggle arose over the position of high priest. One Jew named Menelaus arranged for Onias to be assassinated and bribed Antiochus for the position of high priest (though he had no legitimate claim to the priesthood). Funds from the temple treasury were used for paying off Antiochus.

Nevertheless, the "transgression" is more likely that of Antiochus, seeing that the same word *peša*ʿ is used in the very next verse, apparently of the desolation that he brought about. Antiochus also "flung truth to the ground" when he ordered copies of Scripture to be burned. At least for a season, Antiochus "succeeded in what he did," i.e., he was able to do what he wanted and accomplish his goals—but only as long as God in his sovereignty permitted him to do so.

8:13–14 By God's grace, Antiochus' reign of terror was limited. A courageous Jewish family known as the Maccabees rose up and inspired a successful revolt against Antiochus, though it took a few years to achieve the victory. Finally, in December of 164 BC, the temple precinct was secured and the temple itself was cleansed and rededicated to Yahweh, thus enabling the sacrificial system to be reinstituted. Daniel, writing in the sixth century BC, could only see these events, however dimly, from afar. Yet in the vision he did hear two holy ones (angels) discussing the length of time that this "desolating defiant transgression" of Antiochus would be allowed to go on in which the "holy place" (the temple) and the host (Jewish people) would be trampled. The question "how long?" is a characteristic feature of lament psalms but also found at times in the OT prophets (e.g., Isa 6:11; Jer 12:4; Zech 1:12).

The answer was given in v. 14: it would be for a period of 2300 evenings and mornings (cf. v. 26). Since the final part of v. 14 indicates that "the holy place will be put right again"—which seems to look at the cleansing and rededication of the Jerusalem temple—the concluding time (the *terminus ad quem*) must be in December of 164 BC according to the testimony recorded in 1 Macc 4:52–59:[51]

51. Cf. J. Finegan, *Handbook of Biblical Chronology*, rev. ed. (Peabody, MA: Hendrickson, 1998), 103. He defends the December 164 BC date and explains the calendar systems of that period.

> They rose early on the morning of the twenty-fifth day of the ninth month (that is, the month of Kislev *[November-December]*), in the year 148 *[of the Seleucid era, i.e., 164 BC]*, and they brought a sacrifice according to the Torah upon the new altar of burnt offerings which they had built. At the very time of year and on the very day on which the gentiles had profaned the altar, it was dedicated to the sound of singing and harps and lyres and cymbals. The entire people prostrated themselves and bowed and gave thanks to Heaven Who had brought them victory. They celebrated the dedication of the altar for eight days, joyfully bringing burnt offerings and sacrificing peace offerings and thank offerings. They decorated the front of the nave with golden cornices and bosses and restored the gates and the chambers and fitted them with doors. The people were overjoyed as the shame inflicted by the gentiles was removed. Judas and his brothers and the entire assembly of Israel decreed that the days of the dedication of the altar should be observed at their time of year annually for eight days, beginning with the twenty-fifth of the month of Kislev, with joy and gladness.[52]

This occasion has been commemorated ever since as the feast of Hanukkah, which means "dedication" (cf. John 10:22).[53] Thus, the number 2300 apparently refers to a period of time prior to December of 164 BC. How this is to be calculated, however, is unclear, and evangelical scholars differ on this. The text of Dan 8:14 literally says that this period of time would be 2300 "evening morning" (without the conjunction "and," but v. 26 has the same expression with the conjunction). Some would understand this to be 2300 days, which would mean a period of roughly six years and four months.[54] Others, however, would understand this to be 1150 days (1/2 of 2300), based on the idea that the "regular (or daily) sacrifice" was offered *twice daily* and that the text has in view the number of daily sacrifices that were missed.[55] Further complicating a solution is whether time should be reckoned according to a lunar calendar with months of thirty days (as the

52. Goldstein, *I Maccabees*, 272–73.

53. For a helpful study of Hanukkah and its background, see J. R. Lancaster and R. L. Overstreet, "Jesus' Celebration of Hanukkah in John 10," *BSac* 152 (1995): 318–33.

54. Some who favor the interpretation of 2300 days point out that the idea of "evening morning" is reminiscent of Gen 1:5: "and there was evening and there was morning, one day." Those who favor the 1150-day theory would respond, however, that the intention of the author is not to allude to Gen 1:5 but to underscore the evening and morning daily sacrifices, especially since the text makes a point about the "regular sacrifice" at least three times (in Dan 8:11, 12, and 13).

55. According to Bentzen (71), the 1150-day theory dates back to Ephraem Syrus (d. AD 373).

Jews were known to have used), or whether a year of 365 ¼ days should be used. The first view (2300 days) would result in a period from roughly July/August of 170 BC to December 164 BC.[56] The second view (1150 days) would result in a period from roughly September-October 167 BC to December 164 BC. The latter view would correspond more closely to the time frame that Antiochus actually halted the "regular sacrifice." According to 1 Macc 1:41–55, Antiochus wrote a letter in which he "forbid burnt offerings and sacrifices and drink offerings in the sanctuary" *prior to* the sacrilege (the abomination of desolation) of December 167 BC.

> **The king wrote** to all his kingdom, for all to become one people and for each to abandon his own customs. All the gentiles agreed to the terms of the king's proclamation. Many Israelites, too, accepted his religion and sacrificed to idols and violated the Sabbath. The king sent letters by messengers to Jerusalem and the towns of Judah containing orders to follow customs foreign to the land, to put a stop to burnt offerings and meal offering and libation in the temple, to violate Sabbaths and festivals, to defile temple and holy things, to build illicit altars and illicit temples and idolatrous shrines, to sacrifice swine and ritually unfit animals, to leave their sons uncircumcised, and to draw abomination upon themselves by means of all kinds of uncleanness and profanation, so as to forget the Torah and violate all the commandments. Whoever disobeyed the word of the king was to be put to death. **Letters to the same effect he wrote to all his kingdom**, and he appointed officers to watch over all the people and sent orders to the towns of Judah to offer sacrifices in every town. Many from among the people gathered around the officers, every forsaker of the Torah, and they committed wicked acts in the land and drove Israel into hiding places in all their places of refuge. On the fifteenth day of Kislev in the year 145 *[of the Seleucid era, i.e., 167 BC]* the king had an abomination of desolation built upon the altar, and in the outlying towns of Judah they built illicit altars, and at the doors of the houses and in the squares they offered illicit sacrifices.[57]

An exact date for the letters mentioned in the above passage from *I Maccabees* is not stated, but this is clearly *before* the atrocities that took place in the month Chislev (November-December) of 167 BC. If the 1150-day theory is correct, this theoretically could correspond to the period from the issuance or enforcement of the letter (in which sacrifices were forbidden) until the temple was finally cleansed and rededicated in December of

---

56. Those who favor the 2300-day theory often attempt to link the *terminus a quo* of 170 BC with the assassination of the legitimate high priest, Onias III.
57. Goldstein, *I Maccabees*, 206 (emphasis mine).

164 BC. This suggestion is very much in line with Goldstein's own chronological reconstruction of this period. He states, "Antiochus IV decrees that on penalty of death the turbulent Jews, including all those in Judaea, must cease observing the Torah and follow an imposed polytheistic cult, said to be a 'purified Judaism,' free of the tendencies which had turned the Jews into 'rebels.'"[58] In Goldstein's own rough estimate, he concludes that this took place between Nisan (April) and Kislev (December) of 167 BC. If the actual date were closer to September/October of 167 BC, then we would have an exact match for the 1150 days in which the daily sacrifices had been skipped.

Admittedly a final solution for the dates of this period is not possible based on the limited data that we have at this time. Nevertheless, the termination of the period of "2300 evenings and mornings" is certainly in December of 164 BC when the temple in Jerusalem was cleansed and rededicated for use (and the daily sacrifices resumed).[59] Interpreting the 2300 as "years" instead of daily sacrifices led William Miller, founder of the Seventh Day Adventists, to mistakenly calculate the return of Christ in AD 1843–1844.[60] Yet there is no hint from the text that the number should be understood non-literally as years instead of days.[61] The time period most certainly pertains to Antiochus IV in the second century BC. Since the book of Daniel uses Antiochus as a type of the latter-day antichrist, a study of Antiochus and his persecution of God's people offers insight as to what might be expected of the antichrist himself.

---

58. Ibid., 163.

59. C. Schedl, "Mystische Arithmetik oder geschichtliche Zahlen?" *BZ* 8 (1964): 101–5, attempts to argue that the 2300 mornings/evenings of Dan 8:14 extended from December 6, 167 BC, when Antiochus IV Epiphanes defiled the Jerusalem Temple, to January 31, 163 BC. The latter date was supposedly the completion of a fortification around Jerusalem designed to prevent future desecrations. S. Allen, "On Schedl's Attempt to Count the Days of Daniel," *AUSS* 4 (1966): 105, however, took issue with Schedl's thesis, arguing that he did not "produce any evidence for the completion of the fortification on this precise date," and hence this terminal point was merely speculative.

60. D. L. Rowe, *God's Strange Work: William Miller and the End of the World*, Library of Religious Biography (Grand Rapids: Eerdmans, 2008), provides an analysis of Miller's life, views and influence.

61. For a more recent attempt to argue that days represent years, see J. B. Doukhan, *Daniel: The Vision of the End*, rev. ed. (Berrien Springs, MI: Andrews Univ. Press, 1989); and W. H. Shea, "Supplementary Evidence in Support of 457 BC as the Starting Date for the 2300 Day—Years of Daniel 8:14," *JATS* 12 (2001): 89–96. Shea's thesis rests on understanding "the word to restore and rebuild Jerusalem" in Dan 9:25 as a *word from Ezra* in the fall of 457 BC. To this he adds 2300 years to arrive at a time between the fall of AD 1843 and the fall of 1844 (as though the 2300 evenings and mornings of Dan 8:14 were meant to be understood as years rather than days).

Evaluation of Arguments. The following chart reflects the diversity of opinion as to whether the "2300 evenings and mornings" should be viewed as 2300 days or 1150 days, though some prefer to view the number for its symbolic significance or simply not take any position at all.

Interpretation of the 2300 Evenings and Mornings (Dan 8:14)

2300 Days *Literal*	2300 Days *But stresses the Symbolic Significance*	1150 Days *Literal (2 Sacrifices Each Day)*	Non-Committal *(Takes no position)*
LXX^{O}, LXX$^{\theta}$, Vulgate Theodoret of Cyrus (215) Jerome (86–87 in Archer ed) Calvin (2:109) J. Walvoord (190; 1971 ed) L. Wood (218–19) C. Feinberg (107) D. Campbell (125) S. Miller (229–30) T. Constable (104)	Keil (302–7) Young (174) Goldingay (213, 220)	Zöckler (178; in Lange's) J. Montgomery (343) L. Hartman (227, 237) J. Baldwin (176) G. Archer (103) D. Pentecost (1358–59) J. Collins (336) A. Hill (150–51) C. Newsome (267) (also spiritual sign.) NIV Study Bible	R.Wallace (140) E. Carpenter (414) Note: Although Walvoord took the 2300-day position in his 1971 commentary, he takes a non-committal position in his shorter 2012 work (235).

Those who take the position that 2300 literal days are in view assert that the *terminus a quo* is the murder of the high priest Onias III in the earlier part of Antiochus' reign (so Miller, 230). Yet there was no abridgement of temple services at that time. A further weakness of this view is that the text gives no hint that the *terminus a quo* should even be linked with the murder of Onias III. The passage in 2 Macc 4:30–34 that describes the murder of Onias III does not provide any exact date. Though Waltke gives a general date for Onias' death as 170/69 BC,[62] more recently, Goldingay (210) has given a date for Onias' murder as 171 BC, too early to mark the *terminus a quo* of the 2300 days. Rappaport, having pointed out that the period leading up to the death of Onias is one of conflicting accounts, goes

62. Waltke, "Antiochus IV Epiphanes," 145.

on to say, "Jason was dethroned by Menelaus, brother of Simon, in the year 172 b.c.e. Menelaus wished to dispose of Onias, the legitimate high priest. To achieve his aim he bribed Andronicus, a regent for Antiochus IV at that time, to murder Onias."[63] Attempting to link the *terminus a quo* to the death of Onias III, therefore, is far from convincing. Without a firm date in the fall of 170 BC of an event of great significance regarding the temple, the sacrificial system, or the Jewish religion, the position of 2300 days remains quite questionable.

Walvoord (189) attempted to argue for 2300 days based on Hebrew parallels (e.g., forty days and forty nights). Yet this is not convincing. For his position to be valid, we would have expected the text to say "2300 evenings and 2300 mornings," which it does not. Furthermore, an imagined parallel does not really apply here, because the point is not about "days and nights" but about daily sacrifices.

The position of 1150 days is not, however, without its own weaknesses. In OT usage, an evening and morning specified a day, as Keil (303) pointed out. The fact that the text says evening and then morning may also be of significance. This would call to mind the account in Gen 1, which named evening first and then morning. In the description of the daily sacrifice in Exod 29:38–42, on the other hand, the morning sacrifice is first described and then the evening sacrifice.[64] One could reply that if 2300 days was the time of concern, there would be no need to even mention evenings and mornings. The fact that they are mentioned suggests the concern is over the sacrifices at this time, a point directly related to the context, since v. 14 is the answer to the question posed in the previous verse about how long the vision of the *regular sacrifice* (הַתָּמִיד, *hattāmîḏ*) would apply. All things considered then—and admitting that either position is possible—the position of 1150 days has more to commend it than that of 2300 days, and the period of concern (the length of time regarding the vision of the regular or daily sacrifices) seems to extend from a time in the early fall of 167 BC until the temple cleansing and restoration in December of 164 BC.

Biblical Theology Comments

Daniel 8:1–8 depicts a chain of events that culminate in the victorious conquest of the Persian Empire by Alexander the Great in 331 BC. Alexander's

---

63. U. Rappaport, "Onias," in *AYBD*, 5:24.

64. Cf. S. J. Schwantes, "*ʿEREḆ BŌQER* of Dan 8:14 Re-examined," *AUSS* 16 (1978): 375–85. In addition to the argument that *ʿereḇ bōqer* represents phraseology borrowed from Gen 1 (thus indicating a full day), Schwantes (385) also appeals to the "fact that the expression *ʿereḇ bōqer* stands exceptionally in the singular in contrast to all other enumerations in the book," thus favoring the view that it represents a unit of time.

conquest of Persia had several significant results for civilization and later history, all of which affects biblical theology. First, the Greek language (*Koine* Greek) was spread throughout the civilized world, which paved the way for Christian evangelism and the distribution of the Scriptures in Greek. Second, Alexander's exploits led to even further dispersion of Jews throughout the civilized world in the following centuries, which in turn led to a distribution of the OT in Gentile areas (as well as the propagation of fundamental doctrines such as monotheism, the Creator God, resurrection, and a Messiah who would bring in an era of righteousness). Third, there was a power shift in the world from the east to the west that Christianity eventually benefitted from as it eventually gained legitimacy under the Roman Empire and expanded throughout Europe.

Daniel 8:9–14 introduces us to the despicable Antiochus IV Epiphanes. In chaps. 1–6 of Daniel, we see the sovereignty of God at work in humbling pagan kings whose pride had caused them to usurp God's glory or whose hostility against God's servants needed to be countered. Yet despite the mockery of the God of heaven in the case of Belshazzar in Dan 5, we do not really see these Babylonian kings *declaring war*, as it were, against Yahweh. In the case of Antiochus IV Epiphanes, however, we see an intensified assault by a pagan king against the sovereign God, his people, the promised land, and the biblical worship system. In Antiochus, rebellion of man against God ascends to a higher level. Merrill writes,

> The rebellion of the creation against its Creator, epitomized perhaps in the self–sufficient posture of mortal kings, finds expression also in the political structures and national entities over which these monarchs reign. Thus rulers and their subjects alike stand condemned as lawless anarchists who refuse to acknowledge and capitulate to the sovereignty of God.[65]

What Merrill describes is most profoundly illustrated in the case of Antiochus IV, indeed a "lawless anarchist" whose every action serves to exemplify the eventual antichrist.

Application and Devotional Implications

History is replete with examples of ungodly tyrants who have persecuted God's people. Daniel 8 focuses on one of the more notorious of these, namely Antiochus IV Epiphanes. In his arrogance and puffed–up ego, he "magnified himself as far as the Commander of the host." That is, he sought to defy Yahweh God by attacking the very heart of God's earthly work at that time, Jerusalem of the "Beautiful Land" and the home of the temple dedicated to God's glory. In his arrogant defiance, he went so far as to desecrate the temple site, abolish the sacrificial system God had instituted

65. E. Merrill, "A Theology of Ezekiel and Daniel," in *A Biblical Theology of the Old Testament*, ed. R. B. Zuck (Chicago: Moody, 1991), 392–93.

(and which pointed to the atoning work of the Lord Jesus Christ), ban the practice of Judaism, and burn copies of the Word of God. For a season, he succeeded in his diabolical plans. Many faithful believers at that time suffered as a result. Yet v. 14 reminds of something very important. How long would this go on? God determined that it would be 2300 evenings and mornings. However one wishes to understand this length of time, the important fact is that God limited it to a precise period. Antiochus, the madman who hated God and God's people, could do no more than what God had determined he could do. Yahweh God is ever sovereign, and in his sovereignty he had set a limit on just how far Antiochus would be allowed to pursue his agenda of evil.

So it is today. Evil still flourishes, and new agents of evil have risen up to terrorize the earth and especially those who would seek to follow Yahweh. Yet we would do well to remember that they have limited time in which to act, whether it be more or less than "2300 evenings and mornings." In fact, they can do nothing unless it has been authorized by the sovereign God of heaven. And they cannot do so even one day more than what they have been authorized. Certainly we will struggle to see the purpose in their being allowed to carry out their atrocities, but evil is not out of control or beyond the power of our God. Suffering will always characterize life until the fullness of God's kingdom has been established and Messiah Jesus reigns in righteousness. Yet in the meantime, evil men are under his sovereign control, and their allotted time is limited. They will not succeed, but God's people will ultimately triumph!

2. Gabriel gives Daniel insight about the vision (8:15–27)

Daniel 8:1–14 gives the content of what Daniel had seen in his vision. Now an angel named Gabriel comes to Daniel and offers additional insight about this vision. Newsom (268) insightfully points out, "That a new section of the vision report opens with v. 15 is indicated by the similarity between v. 15 and v. 1. In both a form of the verb 'to see' (*rāʾâ*) occurs, along with a reference to the vision (*ḥāzôn*) and the emphatic self-identification 'I, Daniel' (*ʾănî dānîyēʾl*)." Conservative scholars, including the present author, understand this passage (with its focus on Antiochus IV Epiphanes) to be a genuine prophecy given to Daniel in the sixth century BC. Critical scholars, however, view this as a quasi-prophecy (or *ex eventu* prophecy) written during the years 167–165 BC. Representing the latter, Goldingay (218) states, "the real date of the seer's vision is in the 160's BC and it concerns events that are present and imminent, not distant, for seer and audience." Such a stance undermines the authority and reliability of God's Word. (See the "Introductory Matters" for a refutation of the late dating of the book of Daniel.)

Textual Notes

19.a. LXX$^{\theta}$ adds the words ἡ ὅρασις ("the vision") at the end of the sentence, and *BHS* editor suggests inserting הֶחָזוֹן. However, it is more likely that LXX$^{\theta}$

made the insertion to conform with the ending of v. 17, as the final words in the Greek are the same in both verses.

20.a. LXX, S, and Vg. all have a singular form, "king," suggesting מֶלֶךְ should be read. However, the plural construct מַלְכֵי is reasonable, if the kings are viewed collectively. That is, Medo-Persia had one king after another until Alexander put an end to their line.

21.a. The MT reading, וְהַצָּפִיר הַשָּׂעִיר, is admittedly awkward (הַשָּׂעִיר does not occur elsewhere in Daniel). The LXX translated the second word (הַשָּׂעִיר) as τῶν αἰγῶν, which might suggest they were reading הָעִזִּים. But this is probably an attempt to conform to the two-word description צְפִיר־הָעִזִּים (LXX: τράγος αἰγῶν) in Dan 8:5. If the Heb. is understood as being in apposition, there is no need to delete the second word (as *BHS* suggests).

22.a. LXX (similarly Vg) has τοῦ ἔθνους αὐτοῦ, suggesting מִגּוֹיוֹ ("from his nation") rather than MT מִגּוֹי ("from a nation"). This is very possible if the final *waw* was accidentally omitted.[66] Goldingay (199), following Ginsberg (56), proposes a different reading altogether. Rather than a root גּוֹי, he proposes גֵּו, a noun meaning "midst," as in Job 30:5 (and note the corresponding Aram. word in Dan 3:21). Against this is the fact that neither LXX tradition understood it this way, and this also fails to account for the final *yôd* on מִגּוֹי.

23.a. Pointed as a participle, הַפֹּשְׁעִים is translated "transgressors" or "rebels." LXX (similarly Vg. and S), however, rendered this τῶν ἁμαρτιῶν αὐτῶν ("their transgressions/sins"), suggesting the Heb. be pointed הַפְּשָׁעִים ("transgressions") rather than הַפֹּשְׁעִים ("transgressors"). Goldingay (195), NIV, NASB, and ESV go with the latter, but Collins (327), Newsom (253), NRSV, and the NET side with the former reading, הַפְּשָׁעִים ("transgressions").

24.a-a. These words are lacking in LXX^{θ} and Pap. 967 but are found in MS 88 and Syh. Newsom (255) regards them as an intrusion from v. 22, where the same words appear (so *BHS* ed.). Most Eng. VSS, however, retain them (except NRSV).

24.b. *BHS* suggests reading יָשִׂיחַ (Qal impf. of שִׂיחַ = "he will utter, speak about") or יְשׂוֹחֵחַ (Po'lel impf. of שִׂיחַ = "he will consider, devise"), rather than MT יַשְׁחִית ("he will destroy/devastate"). The suggested emendation stems from the use of נִפְלָאוֹת in Dan 11:36 (יְדַבֵּר נִפְלָאוֹת = "he will utter

---

66. R. A. Taylor, *Interpreting Apocalyptic Literature: An Exegetical Handbook* (Grand Rapids: Kregel Academic, 2016), 159, favors emending to מגויו. He reasons, "It seems likely that the Masoretic text has suffered here from haplography, whereby the *yod-waw* sequence of letters was written simply as *yod*. Due to the similarity of these two letters in the ancient script, confusion of *waw* and *yod* is in fact one of the most common of all scribal mistakes."

presumptuous things" NET). Hence, Collins (327) translates 8:24, "and he will devise wondrous things";" and Newsom (255) "he will plan marvelous things." Yet all the Eng. VSS go with MT. NIV's "he will cause astounding devastation" captures the point quite well.

24.c-c. *BHS* suggests transposing the final two words (וְעַם־קְדֹשִׁים)—but without the *waw*—after וְעַל at the beginning of v. 25, as though these words had been misplaced from there. Hence, Collins (327) adds them to v. 25 ("and his plotting will be directed against the holy ones"). Yet this goes against most all manuscript evidence (including LXX).

Translation

8:15 When I, Daniel, had seen the vision, I sought for understanding, and behold, standing before[67] me was one having an appearance of a man. **16** And I heard a human voice[68] *from* the midst[69] of the Ulai, and he called out saying,[70] "Gabriel, give understanding of the vision to this man."[71] **17** So he came near to where I was standing,[72] and when he approached I was suddenly gripped with fear[73] and fell prostrate.[74] But he said to me, "Understand, son of man, that the vision pertains to *the* time of the end."[75] **18** While he was speaking with me, I fell into a deep sleep, prostrate on the ground, but he touched

67. The form לְנֶגְדִּי (*lᵉnegdî*) occurs some 10x in the OT. For the meaning "before me," see 2 Sam 22:23; Hab 1:3; and Ps 16:8.

68. Lit., "a voice of a man" (קוֹל־אָדָם, *qôl-ʾādām*). The translation "human voice" is favored by Collins (327), Goldingay (195), NRSV, and the NET.

69. The Heb. Prep. בֵּין (*bên*) normally means "between," and BDB (107) suggests בֵּין אוּלָי (*bên ʾûlāy*) means "between its banks" (so NET; cf. Dan 12:6–7). Both LXX^{O} and LXX$^{\theta}$, however, translated as ἀνὰ μέσον (*ana meson*), meaning "in the midst of" (see LSJM, 57).

70. Lit., "he called (out) and said" (*waw* consecutive verbs).

71. הַלָּז (*hallāz*) is a rare synonym of זֶה(*zeh*), meaning "this one," i.e., "this man" (being masc. sg.).

72. Lit., "*to* my standing place," a noun (עָמְדִי, *ʿomdî*).

73. "Suddenly gripped with fear" renders the Nipʿal verb נִבְעַתִּי (*nibʿattî*). BDB (130) gives the meaning "be terrified," for the Nipʿal of בָּעַת (*bāʿat*), but *HALOT* (147) suggests, "gripped by a sudden fear." Goldingay (199) downplays the fear aspect and argues for the idea of being "overwhelmed." Yet most Eng. VSS have a translation that reflects the element of fear.

74. Lit., "on my face" (עַל־פָּנָי, *ʿal-pānāy*).

75. The expression עֶת־קֵץ (*ʿet-qēṣ*), "time of end," only occurs in the book of Daniel. See Dan 11:35, 40; 12:4, 9 for the same or similar combination (without the *maqqeph*), usually proceeded by עַד (*ʿad*), "until."

me and made me stand upright.[76] **19** Then he said, "Behold! I will explain to you what will happen in the latter *period*[77] of wrath, for it pertains to the appointed time of the end. **20** The ram that you saw that had two horns *represents* the kings of Media and Persia. **21** The male goat[78] *represents* the king of Greece, and the large horn between its eyes represents the first king. **22** As for the broken *horn* in whose place there arose four *horns*, from *his*[79] nation four kingdoms shall arise, but not with his power. **23** In the latter

---

76. The final clause involves a cognate accusative: וַיַּעֲמִידֵנִי עַל־עָמְדִי (*wayya'ămîḏēnî 'al-'omḏî*). Lit., "he caused me to stand at my standing place." The idea is that he was made to stand upright. Collins (327): "set me on my feet" (so NRSV).

77. "In the latter *period*," Heb בְּאַחֲרִית (*bə'aḥărîṯ*). For discussion of *bə'aḥărîṯ*, see commentary at Dan 2:38. This prepositional phrase occurs some 17x in the OT in the sense "in the latter," "in the last," or "in the coming." When used of time (e.g., "days"), it often refers eschatologically to the time just preceding and including the messianic era (e.g., Deut 4:30; Isa 2:2; Jer 23:20; Ezek 38:8, 16; Hos 3:5; Mic 4:1). In other instances, it may simply refer to a less specific time in the distant future.

78. The MT has הַצָּפִיר הַשָּׂעִיר (*haṣṣāp̄îr haśśā'îr*), lit., "the he-goat, a buck." Though a slightly different expression, this refers to the same goat in Dan 8:5 (צְפִיר־הָעִזִּים, *ṣəp̄îr-hā'izzîm*), which was translated "male goat." Because the adjective שָׂעִיר (*śā'îr*) means "hairy" (see Gen 27:11, 23), the NASB and NIV have translated הַצָּפִיר הַשָּׂעִיר (*haṣṣāp̄îr haśśā'îr*) in v. 21 as "shaggy goat." Other translations simply have "male goat." Both LXX^{O} and LXX$^{\theta}$ translated v. 21 the same as v. 5, ὁ τράγος τῶν αἰγῶν (*ho tragos tōn aigōn*), without any reference to "shaggy."

79. MT does not have the pronominal suffix "his," although most Eng. VSS add the word in light of its presence in the LXX (τοῦ ἔθνους αὐτοῦ, *tou ethnous autou*) and Vg. See textual note above.

period of their rule, when the transgressors[80] finish,[81] a king will arise, who is merciless[82] and a deceptive dealer.[83] **24** His power will be mighty, yet not by his power. He will be incredibly destructive,[84] and he will be successful in

80. The phrase כְּהָתֵם הַפֹּשְׁעִים (*kᵊhāṯēm happōšᵊ ʿîm*) is very difficult to translate and to understand. First, how is the presumed original הפשעים to be pointed? MT pointed it as a ptc., הַפֹּשְׁעִים (*happōšᵊ ʿîm*), "transgressors" (or perhaps "rebels"). *BHS*, however, suggests this be read as a noun, הַפְּשָׁעִים (*happᵊšā ʿîm*), "transgressions." Either vowel pointing is legitimate. LXX (τῶν ἁμαρτιῶν αὐτῶν, *tōn hamartiōn autōn*) seems to have read this as a noun, "transgressions" or "sins." Some Eng. VSS opt for "transgressors" (NASB, NIV, ESV, NKJV), but others for "transgressions" (NRSV, NET "rebellious acts"). Goldingay (195) has "when the rebels reach full measure," though Collins (327) has "when their sins are complete" (similarly Newsom, 253). Some appeal to a similar concept of "sins" in Gen 15:16, but the terminology is quite different. Either option is possible and makes sense in the context (recall the earlier use of פֶּשַׁע, *peša ʿ*, in Dan 8:12, 13 in regard to Antiochus' "transgression"). In view of the mention of the four kingdoms in v. 22 and the pronominal suffix "their" (their rule) in the preceding phrase, it is easy to understand why the Masoretes would have pointed this as a participle (meaning that "transgressors" are in view). Also, the LXX reading ("transgressions") may necessitate an emending of the preceding inf. constr. from כְּהָתֵם (*kᵊhāṯēm*, Hip ʿil) to כְּתֹם (*kᵊṯōm*, Qal), as *BHS* mentions. (See following footnote.) Hence, there is a slight preference for הַפֹּשְׁעִים (*happōšᵊ ʿîm*), "transgressors."

81. The MT has כְּהָתֵם (*kᵊhāṯēm*), a Hip ʿil inf. Some (e.g., Collins, 327) read this as a Qal inf., כְּתֹם (*kᵊṯōm*). As a Hip ʿil inf. constr. (3x in OT), this would mean to "finish, complete, cease doing" something. The Qal inf. constr. (20x in OT) means to "be finished, completed, destroyed."

82. Lit., "strong or fierce of face" (עַז־פָּנִים, *ʿaz-pānîm*). Collins (327) suggests "boldfaced." In Deut 28:50 we have a similar phrase, גּוֹי עַז פָּנִים (*gôy ʿaz pānîm*). In that context, the following relative clause states, "who will have no respect for the old, nor show favor to the young." That is, they will show no mercy. The translation "merciless" fits the context of Dan 8:23 perfectly.

83. The final trait mentioned about this king is מֵבִין חִידוֹת (*mēḇîn ḥîḏôṯ*), lit., "understanding enigmas or riddles," but here an idiom. BDB (295 #4) suggests "skilled in double-dealing;" *HALOT* (309), "with a good knowledge of intrigue"; Collins (339), "adept in duplicity"; and Miller (234), "a master of political intrigue." Recall the use of Aram. אֲחִידָה (*ʾăḥîḏâ*) in Dan 5:12, where it was used positively of Daniel declaring/solving riddles. In 8:23 it seems to relate to Antiochus as perceptive and shrewd, which contributes to his *deceptiveness* (note the deceptiveness of Antiochus brought out in 11:21, 23, 27, 32).

84. Lit., "and in extraordinary ways (or to an extraordinary extent) he will destroy" (וְנִפְלָאוֹת יַשְׁחִית, *wᵊniplā ʾōṯ yašḥîṯ*). Regarding the proper verb to read (יַשְׁחִית, *yašḥîṯ*), see the textual note for this verse.

what he attempts.[85] He will destroy mighty men, even[86] a holy people.[87] **25** And by treachery[88] he will cause deceit to succeed by his power.[89] In his heart he will magnify himself, and he will destroy many who will be unsuspecting *of his schemes*.[90] He will even take a stand against the Prince of princes.[91] Yet he will be crushed[92] apart from human agency.[93] **26** So the vision that has been

85. Lit., "he will succeed and take action" (הִצְלִיחַ וְעָשָׂה, *hiṣlîaḥ wᵊʿāśâ*). This is a verbal hendiadys in which the first verb modifies the action of the following verb. The idea is that he "acts successfully."

86. For the case of *emphatic waw* translated "even," see *IBHS*, 648 (§39.2.1b); cf. GKC, 484–85 (§154a).

87. Though plural in this instance (עַם־קְדֹשִׁים, *ʿam–qᵊḏōšîm*), the Hebrew people are referred to elsewhere in similar terms, עַם קָדוֹשׁ (*ʿam qāḏôš*). See Deut 7:6; 14:2, 21; 26:19; 28:9. In Daniel, the singular noun עַם (*ʿam*) is typically followed by a plural form (see Dan 11:15, 32). Regarding the placement of this phrase in relation to v. 25, see textual note above.

88. The noun שֵׂכֶל (*śēḵel*) is normally a *wisdom* term (often found in Proverbs), meaning "skill, insight, prudence." Yet it can be used in a negative sense as "cunning, craft" (BDB, 968 #3). The term מִרְמָה (*mirmâ*), translated here "deceit," is used of Antiochus in Dan 11:23.

89. Lit., "by his hand," used here as a metonymy for power.

90. There is a question as to how best to translate בְשַׁלְוָה (*ḇᵊšalwâ*), a noun meaning "quietness, ease, prosperity." Goldingay (195) suggests "with ease," and the NASB has "while they are at ease." Yet the use of this term in Dan 11:21, 24 suggests that it has more to do with the *actions* of the aggressor than with the state of the victims. He catches them "unawares" (Montgomery, 351; so BDB, 1017). Both LXX^{O} and LXX$^{\theta}$ translated *ḇᵊšalwâ* in 8:25 as δόλῳ (*dolōi*), "by deceit." Furthermore, in 11:24 (describing Antiochus' greedy tactics), LXX^{O} used the word ἐξάπινα (*exapina*), a word meaning "suddenly, unexpectedly," to translate *ḇᵊšalwâ*. The point is that by his deceptive approach, he catches them unsuspecting. NET's "he will destroy many who are unaware of his schemes" captures the idea quite well (cf. ESV, "Without warning he shall destroy many").

91. This is the only occurrence of שַׂר־שָׂרִים (*śar-śārîm*), commonly translated "Prince of princes." A related title "Commander of the host" (שַׂר־הַצָּבָא, *śar haṣṣāḇāʾ*) appeared in Dan 8:11. See translation note for v. 11 for general comments about שַׂר (*śar*), and then the commentary for discussion of the phrase.

92. In the Nipʿal stem, שָׁבַר (*šāḇar*) generally means to be "broken." BDB (990d) indicates a figurative meaning for the Nipʿal, "to be crushed, destroyed."

93. וּבְאֶפֶס יָד (*ûḇᵊʾepes yāḏ*) is lit., "but without a hand." The word בְּאֶפֶס (*bᵊʾepes*), from a verb meaning "to cease," is used three other times in the OT in the sense of "without, for lack of" (Isa 52:4; Job 7:6; Prov 26:20). A similar concept occurs in Dan 2:34 (דִּי־לָא בִידַיִן, *dî-lāʾ ḇîḏayin*) where "a stone was cut out without hands," i.e., apart from human agency. LXX$^{\theta}$, at this point, is puzzling: ὡς ᾠὰ χειρὶ συντρίψει (*hōs ōia cheiri suntripsei*), "he will crush like eggs by hand." B. A. Zuiddam, "The Shock Factor of Divine Revelation: A Philological Approach to Daniel 8 and 9," *SJOT* 27

told of the evenings and mornings is true. But as for you, seal up the vision, for it pertains to the distant future."[94] **27** Then I, Daniel, was overcome and lay sick[95] for *several* days. *At last* I arose and performed the king's business, but I was astonished at the vision and without[96] understanding.

Commentary

a. The encounter with Gabriel (8:15–19)

8:15–17 Daniel did not fully grasp the meaning of the vision that he had seen, and thus God sent an angel to give him further insight.[97] Upon first seeing this angel, Daniel's impression was that he had "an appearance of a man." The word translated "man" is the Hebrew word *geḇer*, which normally emphasizes a male at the height of his powers. This is also the root word of the angel's name, Gabriel (*geḇer* plus the word for God, *ʾēl*), which literally means "man of God"—perhaps with emphasis upon his strength—or (if meant to glorify God) "mighty one of God" or even possibly "God is a mighty one."[98] Though

---

(2013): 257, attempts to unravel the anomaly, suggesting that LXX$^{\theta}$ took אֶפֶס (*ʾep̱es*) as "non-existence" and understanding יִשָּׁבֵר (*yiššāḇēr*) as an active impf. verb. He explains, "For all practical intents and purposes the Hebrew consonant text allows a translation like: 'And to non-existence shall his hand crush.' If this expression led the ancient mind to fill in the ellipse of the object, the translation could easily end up as: 'And <like eggs his> hand shall crush.'"

94. Lit., "it pertains to many days" (לְיָמִים רַבִּים, *ləyāmîm rabbîm*). The same phrase occurs in Ezek 12:27, where it has the idea of "many years in the future."

95. Commentators struggle with how best to understand נִהְיֵיתִי וְנֶחֱלֵיתִי (*nihyêṯî wəneḥĕlêṯî*). Rather than taking נִהְיֵיתִי (*nihyêṯî*) as a Nipʿal perf. of הָיָה (*hāyâ*), "was done, finished, gone" (and translated "exhausted" or "overcome" as with most Eng. VSS), it may be possible to regard this as a Nipʿal perf. of הָוָה (*hāwâ*). Montgomery (355) pointed out that the classic Jewish exegetes, Rashi and Ḳimḥi, "boldly etymologize from הַוָּה "ruin,' Job 6². " Montgomery himself (356) translated "I was befallen (stricken) and I was sick." *HALOT* (241) indicates a second root הוה meaning (1) to become or (2) to lie (down), and cites Eccl 11:3 as an example of the latter: "wherever the tree falls, there it lies (שָׁם יְהוּא, *šām yəhûʾ*). This may shed light on why LXX$^{\theta}$ translated *nihyêṯî* as ἐκοιμήθην (*ekoimēthēn*), aor. pass. of κοιμαω (*koimaō*), meaning "to lull, put to sleep" and in the pass., "to fall asleep, go to bed" (LSJM, 967). Goldingay (195, 200) renders the Heb. construction idiomatically, "fell ill." NRSV's "overcome and lay sick" is perhaps as plausible a translation as any.

96. For the sense of אֵין (*ʾên*) meaning "without," see BDB, 34d 4 (e.g., Exod 21:11; Deut 32:4).

97. Miller (231) claims the one sent to him is not an angel but rather God himself.

98. Baldwin (176) indicates that Gabriel means "God has shown himself strong." She also points out that for the OT, only in the book of Daniel do we have angels named (also Michael in 10:13). In *1 Enoch* 9:1; 20:1–8, we are told of several archangels with names (Raphael, Uriel, Raguel, Saraqqel, and Remiel). Newsom (268) adds, "In the

only mentioned by name four times in Scripture, Gabriel is obviously an important angel, being chosen to announce to Mary that she would bear the virgin-born Son of God (cf. Dan 9:21; Luke 1:19, 26). In any case, an *unknown person* called to Gabriel to give Daniel understanding. Who is he? Though he spoke with a human voice, he commanded such an angel as Gabriel. This raises the possibility that he may be the preincarnate Lord Jesus Christ.[99] The fact that he spoke from the midst of the Ulai (between the banks?) is apparently in the pattern later seen in the fourth vision (Dan 12:7). As Gabriel approached Daniel, he "was suddenly gripped with fear" and fell prostrate to the ground, a rather standard response to an angelic appearance (compare Dan 10:9; Josh 5:14; Ezek 1:28; 3:23; 44:4; Rev 1:17; and outside Scripture at *1 En.* 14:14, 24; 4 Ezra 10:29–30; *Apoc. Ab.* 10:2).[100] Gabriel then addressed him as "son of man" (similar to the way Ezekiel was frequently addressed). Wood (221) adds, "The form of address, 'son of man,' emphasizes Daniel's own inability, being merely man, to know the nature of such a vision himself."

Gabriel's first insight was to reveal that this vision "pertains to the time of the end." This expression "the time of the end" (Heb. *ʿeṯ-qēṣ*) appears four other times in the OT, all in Daniel (note 11:35, 40; 12:4, 9).[101] It would be hard not to associate the occurrence of this rare expression in Dan 8 with those in chaps. 11 and 12. Yet when we examine these latter occurrences, they are clearly to be associated with the great time of distress that takes place in the days of the antichrist of the "end times" (called "the king" in 11:36). This opens the possibility that though the vision describes the atrocities of Antiochus IV in the second century BC, it goes beyond that to convey truths related to the days of the antichrist in the far distant future. (See "Biblical Theology Comments" at the end of the chapter for further discussion.)

Dead Sea Scrolls, Gabriel is also mentioned along with other archangels in the *Book of Noah* (1Q19 frg. 2 4) and in the *War Scroll* (1QM 9.16; 4Q285 frg. 1 3)."

99. Jerome (trans. Archer, 88) mentioned the Jewish tradition that the one speaking to Gabriel was actually the angel Michael: "The Jews claim that this man who directed Gabriel to explain the vision to Daniel was Michael [himself]." Yet according to *Gen. Rab.* 27:1, the voice in v. 16 is attributed to God.

100. Apart from a response to an angelic appearance, bowing was also a typical social gesture for communicating respect for someone of higher standing (Gen 33:7; 1 Sam 20:41; 2 Sam 9:6).

101. Of course a shorter reference to "the end" is found elsewhere (e.g., Ezek 7:2, 3; 21:25, 29; 35:5). Baldwin (177) focuses on these references outside Daniel rather than the specific phrase in Daniel to conclude that only a general "end" is in view. She states, "In each case the end meant the end of rebellion against God, because he intervened in judgment." Yet the usage in Daniel of the full phrase weighs heavier than the mere reference to "end" outside Daniel.

8:18–19 So powerful was Daniel's encounter with the angel Gabriel that it caused him to fall into a deep sleep (similar to what Abram experienced in Gen 15:12). Regarding the verb "fell into a deep sleep" (נִרְדַּמְתִּי, *nirdamtî*), Goldingay (214–15) states, "it denotes a coma-like state of deep sleep brought about by supernatural agency, especially in connection with visionary experiences (Gen 2:21; 15:12; 1 Sam 26:12; Job 4:13; 33:15; cf. *T. Levi* 2.5)." Yet Gabriel touched him and made him stand upright, because Daniel needed to hear important truths. The idea of a supernatural, strengthening touch appears elsewhere in Dan 10:10, 16, 18; Rev 1:17; and *1 En* 60:4; *4 Ezra* 5:15. Yet being asleep and being restored was a part of what Daniel saw in the vision, for he himself was actually in Babylon. Gabriel was there to inform Daniel what would occur at "the latter period of wrath" (בְּאַחֲרִית הַזָּעַם, *bᵊʾaḥărîṯ hazzāʿam*). This exact expression does not occur elsewhere in the OT, but the word for "wrath" does occur one other time in Daniel, namely Dan 11:36.[102] In that context the antichrist is in view, and the text says that "he will succeed until the time of wrath is completed." This tends to confirm what was said in the previous paragraph about the "time of the end." The wrath exercised by Antiochus IV is *anticipatory* of the latter-day wrath that will come at the hands of the antichrist. Young (177), however, insists that the wrath (or *indignation*) is a technical term for designating the wrath of God and his displeasure. For him, the period of indignation has its early portion in the Babylonian captivity and its latter portion in the abominations of Antiochus. Young's position (limiting this to its conclusion in Antiochus) fails to take into account the usage of this terminology in Dan 11. Furthermore, the period of Antiochus' oppression certainly brought no end to Jewish suffering. Hence, Wood (223) argues, "Antiochus' oppression is seen to provide a partial fulfillment of the prophetic vision, but that of the antichrist the complete fulfillment." (In my view there is a more accurate way to describe this than *partial fulfillment*. See discussion at v. 23.) Wood goes on to say (223), "Since truth concerning the antichrist has already been presented in Nebuchadnezzar's dream and Daniel's first vision, and since it will be again in both Daniel's third and fourth times of revelation, it is no way strange to find it here." Since the similarity of language describing Antiochus in Dan 8:23–25 is so akin to that describing antichrist in Dan 7:24–26, we can say that the character of the one is simply mirrored by the other.

---

102. Quite often, "wrath" (*zāʿam*) refers to God's wrath (e.g., Isa 26:20; Ezek 22:24), but in view of the context of Daniel, the reference in v. 19 appears to be wrath brought on by Antiochus IV. Goldingay agrees. He sees the "latter period of wrath" as the culmination in Antiochus IV of a lengthy period of oppression against Israel. He argues (215) that "the ongoing period of wrath is one in which they are continuing to be treated harshly rather than because of their own sin. … [T]he fact that the vision begins with the Persian era suggest that the whole period from the exile to Antiochus is the period of wrath denoted here."

Gabriel ends v. 19 by saying that the vision pertains to "the appointed time of the end" (מוֹעֵד קֵץ, *mô ʿēḏ qēṣ*). This expression occurs elsewhere only in 11:27, 35. The latter verse makes clear that the "time of the end" was not fulfilled with Antiochus but must wait for the "appointed time" when it will be fulfilled, i.e., with "the king" introduced in 11:36, namely the antichrist (contra Goldingay, 216, who argues that "the 'end' must still be the punctiliar moment of the termination of the Antiochene persecution and the vindication of the sanctuary"). Hill (153) correctly points out, "The fact that this is 'the *appointed time* of the end' emphasizes that 'the "time" has been set ... by the Lord of history' (Miller, 233), underscoring God's sovereignty over the historical process."

b. Gabriel's explanation of the vision (8:20–26)

8:20–22 The main symbols of Daniel's vision are now clearly interpreted for the reader, and these have already been previously discussed. Worth pointing out is that the kings of Media and Persia are symbolized by one animal, indicating that they are one entity (one kingdom). This is consistent with our interpretation of the bear in Dan 7:4 as Medo-Persia and suggests that critical scholars are wrong who claim the second beast of Dan 7 is Media and the third beast is Persia. The main point is that the Medo-Persian Empire would be conquered by Greece.[103]

In 8:22 the four horns that arise in the place of the "large horn" of the male goat represent the four kingdoms that arose from Alexander's massive empire (see comments on 8:8). Verse 22 goes on to say, "but not with his power." This should not be taken to mean that the four generals who divided up Alexander's empire came to rule over kingdoms that were small or insignificant. Quite the contrary, each of them held enormous power. Yet they did not have the incredible power that Alexander wielded.

8:23–25 In light of v. 22, the expression "their rule" must refer to the four Hellenistic kingdoms that arose from Alexander's empire. Hill (154) agrees: "The 'latter part of their reign' (v. 23a) refers to a period near the end of the era of the four kings who succeed Alexander the Great and carve up his empire into quadrants." Following Alexander's death, Judah (later known as Palestine under Roman rule) was at times under the power of the Ptolemaic kingdom of Egypt and at other times under the Seleucid empire of Syria.

---

103. The word for "Greece" in v. 21 is יָוָן (*yāwān*), the name by which the Hebrews knew the Greeks (cf. Gen 10:2, 4; Isa 66:19; Ezek 27:13). Even though certain Macedonian rulers (e.g., Seleucus and Ptolemy) would later come to rule over other areas beyond historic Greece, there really is no justification for trying to make *yāwān* in this chapter mean "Turkey," and from this to postulate a purely futuristic interpretation of the details, so as to predict a yet future battle between Turkey and Iran (so J. Richardson, "What Comes Next in the Middle East," posted 27 Feb. 2015, online: http://www.joelstrumpet.com/?p=7364).

By the time of the second century BC, however, Judah was primarily under Seleucid rule. The harsh tactics of Antiochus IV (r. 175–164 BC) spawned the Maccabean revolt against Syria, and by 142 BC Simon (the last surviving son of Mattathias Maccabee) gained independence from Syrian control.[104] Thus the merciless and deceitful king of v. 23 must be a reference to Antiochus IV Epiphanes, who indeed ruled over Judah "toward the end" of the rule by the Hellenistic powers. By this time the Hellenistic "transgressors" were about to finish their course, i.e., their atrocities and harsh dealings against the Jewish people. The NET Bible, on the other hand ("when rebellious acts are complete"), has in view transgressions or sinful acts committed. (For discussion of the difficult phrase, כְּהָתֵם הַפֹּשְׁעִים [*kᵊhāṯēm happōšᵊʿîm*], and whether this should be translated "transgressors" or "transgressions," see the translation note at v. 23.) Miller (234), though preferring the translation "rebels," argues that what is in view is the rebellion by unfaithful Jews who have forsaken God and his law. The idea would be that God patiently put up with their rebellious acts for many years, but finally judgment was due, and he used Antiochus to afflict them.[105] (For this concept in Scripture, see Gen 15:16; Matt 23:32; and 1 Thess 2:16.) The NASB, however, renders this "when the transgressors have run their course" (which could be interpreted to mean the Hellenistic rulers). Both translations are possible, depending on how the Hebrew word הפשעים (*hpšʿim*) is pointed. However, the context tends to favor that the Hellenistic rulers are in view: (1) the word *pešaʿ* was used in 8:12–13 of Antiochus' transgression against the people of God; and (2) vv. 22–23 are primarily describing the Gentile kings (and their kingdoms) that Israel became subject to, not the Jewish people themselves. Hence, with the ascent of Antiochus IV to the throne of the Seleucid empire, the long period of Israel being ruled by one of the Hellenistic kingdoms (either under the Ptolemies of Egypt or the Seleucids of Syria) was finally drawing to a close.[106]

---

104. H. W. Hoehner, "Hasmoneans," in *ISBE*, 2:621. Cf. W. C. Kaiser, *A History of Israel* (Nashville: Broadman & Holman, 1998), 477–86, for a brief introduction on "The Hasmonean Kingdom." Under Simon, the son of Mattathias Maccabee, Judea gained her independence from Syria in 142 BC. Because of his achievements, the Jews in 140 BC conferred upon him the position of leader and high priest (see 1 Macc 14:25–40), and properly speaking this is the beginning of Hasmonean rule. Simon was succeeded by his son named John as high priest and ruler of the people. John took the ruling name of John Hyrcanus I and ruled 135–104 BC.

105. Wood (225) also advocates this view: "these transgressors are not the heathen oppressors, but the Jews themselves, who, following their return from captivity, will have continued in sin to an extent causing God to permit their experiencing a punishing oppression." Yet he offers no real support for why v. 23 should be understood this way.

106. Goldingay (217) agrees: "Likely here, then, the rebels are Gentiles. Further, the notion of rebels or rebellions reaching full measure applies better to Gentiles:

As pointed out above, the "deceitful king" in v. 23 must be Antiochus IV. On the other hand, this passage need not be limited to Antiochus. In light of 8:17–19, the vision also looks beyond Antiochus to "the appointed time of the end." It seems that Antiochus is used in Daniel as a *type* of the future antichrist, and therefore the description of the king in vv. 23–25 refers first to Antiochus but ultimately to the antichrist himself. (Regarding a typological interpretation and the hermeneutics of fulfillment, see the "Biblical Theology Comments" at the end of the chapter for further discussion.) Seen in this light, these verses do give us insight into the ways and character of the antichrist who will arise in the future period of great tribulation.

Verse 23 points out that the king will be merciless and a deceitful dealer. Regarding the translation "merciless" (עַז־פָּנִים, *ʿaz-pānîm*), the Hebrew text literally means "fierce of face." In light of the use of this expression in Deut 28:50, it signifies that he will be *without mercy* toward everyone. The translation "deceitful dealer" literally means "understanding riddles/enigmas" (מֵבִין חִידוֹת, *mēḇîn ḥîḏôṯ*). BDB (295) suggests the idea "skilled in double-dealing," i.e., he will be a master of political intrigue.[107]

According to v. 24, he will be a mighty ruler, "yet not by his power." Whether Antiochus or the antichrist, both will wield great might, but there is another source of power behind them. The real power behind the throne is Satan who relishes the chance to persecute God's people and uses both these individuals as his puppet. Regarding the antichrist, we are told that "the dragon gave the beast his power, his throne, and great authority to rule" (Rev 13:2). As the remainder of v. 24 points out, he will use this satanic power to bring horrible destruction upon others, and specifically upon God's people.[108] The book of Revelation confirms that the antichrist will persecute both the

---

see Gen 15:16; Wis 19:1–4; but especially, with reference to the Antiochene period, 2 Macc 6:13–16."

107. Wood (226) appeals to the positive reference to "riddles" in Dan 5:12 to argue that the point of *mēḇîn ḥîḏôṯ* is not to bring out Antiochus' deceptiveness but rather has ability (like Daniel) to solve difficult problems. Against this, however, is the fact that the context (8:23–25) is aimed at describing the wickedness of Antiochus, not his commendable features.

108. Goldingay (218) regards the "mighty men" (*ʿăṣûmîm*) and the "holy people" (*qᵉḏōšîm*) that Antiochus destroys (v. 24) as one and the same, though this is not evident from the text itself. *ʿāṣûm* only occurs one other time in Daniel (see 11:25), and that in regard to an Egyptian army. Archer (104) takes them to be the "nobles and regional commanders of his [Antiochus'] own realm who supported rival claimants to the throne." Similarly, Hill (155) argues that the "mighty men" are "probably other rivals to the Seleucid throne whom Antiochus 'liquidated' along the way on his rise to power." Finally, Miller (235) takes them to be "the many important persons throughout the world, military and otherwise, who were killed by Antiochus and his armies."

Jews and the believers in Jesus, and many will be martyred for their faith (cf. Rev 12:13–17; 13:7; 20:4).

In v. 25 the deceitfulness of the king is emphasized again, as well as his arrogant attitude (lit., "he will magnify himself in his heart"). Like many other cruel despots of history, this king will be a proud self-exalting ruler who has no concern for anyone other than himself. Antiochus had the words *theos epiphanēs* inscribed on the coins he minted, meaning "God manifest." This need not be taken to mean that he thought himself to be a god, but that he saw himself as the earthly representative of the Greek gods. According to 2 Thess 2:4, the antichrist will take his arrogance to the highest level, for "he takes his seat in the temple of God, declaring himself to be God" (NET). The fact that many will be "unsuspecting of his schemes" is illustrated by the surprise attack on Jerusalem reported in 1 Macc 1:29–30. The chief collector of tribute at first spoke deceitfully of peace, only to later fall upon the city.

Antiochus' campaigns of destruction and godless arrogance will know no bounds, for he will take a stand against "the Prince of princes" (Heb. *śar-śārîm*, the only occurrence of this phrase in the OT). The term "prince" in this context should not be thought of as a secondary official, as the English word implies (a prince being beneath a king).[109] In Dan 8:25 the term is undoubtedly a reference to the God of heaven, the One who stands as prince (i.e., having ruling authority) over the rulers of the earth (cf. 4:26, 34–35) and over angelic authorities (note 10:20; 12:1). Whereas Antiochus defied God and attacked his temple, set up a statue of Zeus on the temple altar and offered profane sacrifices there, burned the Word of God, and massacred many Jewish people, the antichrist will personally attack Jesus Christ and all those aligned with him. In both cases, however, it is to no avail. Verse 25 indicates he will be "crushed apart from human agency" (and this is presumably the finale of the "2300 evenings and mornings"). With this comes the restoration of the earthly sanctuary and thus the vindication of God's sovereignty. Neither Antiochus nor the antichrist will be stopped by human armies, but rather by divine act. Antiochus did not die in battle, but following a failed attempt to plunder the riches stored in the temple of Nanaea in Elymais (southwest Iran), he received word that his forces had been routed by the Jews back in Judah. He then died insane in Persia, full of grief and remorse. The antichrist will be personally defeated—not by human agency—but by Jesus Christ Himself at our Lord's return in glory (Rev 19:19–21). An account of Antiochus' demise is given in 1 Macc 6:5–16:

> A messenger reached him in Persia with the news that his armies which had marched into the land of Judah had been routed; that Lysias had set out at the head of a strong force and had been repulsed by the Jews, who had gained in arms and in wealth and

109. See the translation note at Dan 8:11 for a discussion of the word שַׂר (*śar*) as one who rules or exercises authority over others.

> especially through the abundant plunder which they had taken from the armies they had defeated; that the Jews had destroyed the abomination which he had built upon the altar in Jerusalem, and they had surrounded the temple as it was before with high walls, and also their town of Beth-Zur. When the king heard this news, he was thunderstruck and so deeply dismayed that he took to his bed and sank into melancholia because his plots had been foiled. There he lay for many days as his great distress grew worse. Finally, he realized that he was dying. He summoned all his friends and said to them, "Sleep has fled from my eyes and the weight of anxiety has broken my heart. I have said to myself, 'How deep I have sunk in distress! How great is the tempest which has now come upon me, kind though I was and popular in my realm.' Now, however, I remember the wicked deeds which I perpetrated in Jerusalem which I took all the silver and gold vessels there and for no cause sent orders to exterminate the inhabitants of Judah. I have come to understand that because of these deeds these evils have come upon me as I die in great agony on foreign soil." He summoned Philip, one of his friends, and gave him power over all his kingdom, handing over to him his diadem, his robe, and his ring, for Philip to bring to his son Antiochus, of whom Philip was to be the guardian until the boy was ready to rule. Thereupon King Antiochus died in the year 149 *[of the Seleucid era]*.[110]

8:26 Reference to the vision of "the evenings and mornings" clearly connects the angel's explanation in 8:20–25 with what had been foretold earlier about Antiochus in vv. 9–14. The fulfillment, however, is for "the distant future" (i.e., some unspecified time far beyond the days of Daniel). Thus Daniel was instructed to "seal up the vision." The Hebrew word for "seal up" (סְתֹם, *sᵊṯōm*) means to "stop up, keep closed" (most often used of closing up a water well to prevent its use). Some translations (e.g., NASB) favor the idea that Daniel is to keep the meaning hidden ("keep the vision secret"). However, the word *sᵊṯōm* is used again in 12:4, 9 in parallel with the word חֲתֹם (*ḥăṯōm*), also meaning to "seal, seal up," as of a document that is rendered *official* and preserved for the intended recipient (cf. 1 Kgs 21:8; Isa 8:16; Jer 32:10). The usage in Dan 12:4 possibly sheds light on the intended nuance of meaning here. Daniel did not personally understand all the vision or its significance, but he was responsible for recording and preserving it, that it might one day benefit those who would experience its reality (so Wood, 229). Hill (155–56) sees both nuances in view: "Daniel is instructed to 'close up and seal' the scroll or book of his visions both for the purposes of safeguarding them

110. Goldstein, *I Maccabees*, 306–7. Goldstein regards this account of Antiochus' demise to be fictitious, but there is probably some degree of truth to it.

for the future and keeping them secret until the time of the generation for whom there were intended."

c. Daniel's alarm over the vision (8:27)

Receiving such a frightening vision and encountering Gabriel had a profound impact upon Daniel, even to the point of being physically sick. The vision was alarming to Daniel, even though he lacked a full understanding of its meaning. After some amount of time, however, he was able to return to "the king's business." We are not told in this verse just what position Daniel now held in Babylonia or what his relationship was with Belshazzar (clearly the vision takes place in his reign). Daniel 5:10–16 seems to imply that Daniel was virtually unknown to Belshazzar by 539 BC. Perhaps Daniel held his current position as a result of appointment by Nabonidus, the father of Belshazzar (the latter was made a co-ruler). We simply do not know.

Biblical Theology Comments

The vast majority of commentators on the book of Daniel agree that the primary fulfillment of this chapter, particularly Dan 8:23–25, is with Antiochus IV Epiphanes, the ruler of the Seleucid Empire from 175 BC to 164 BC. Some, however, would argue that the passage goes *beyond* Antiochus to find a fulfillment in some way with the latter-day antichrist. This raises the hermeneutical question of not only *what* fulfillment there is, but also *how* it comes about.

Walvoord (1971 ed., 192–96) describes and analyzes four distinct views regarding the fulfillment of Dan 8.[111] He lists these (192) as:

> (1) the historical view that all of Daniel 8 has been fulfilled; (2) the futuristic view, the idea that it is entirely future; (3) the view based upon the principle of dual fulfillment of prophecy, that Daniel 8 is intentionally a prophetic reference both to

---

111. Critical scholars and many amillennialists take the historical view (that fulfillment is limited to Antiochus). For an exception, see Leupold (361). Those holding the futuristic view are rare, but see G. H. Pember, *The Great Prophecies Concerning the Gentiles, the Jews, and the Church of God*, 2nd ed. (London: Hodder and Stoughton, 1885), 104; and S. P. Tregelles, *Remarks on the Prophetic Visions in the Book of Daniel*, 5th ed. (London: Samuel Bagster and Sons, 1864), 81–82. For Tregelles, the horn of chap. 7 and the horn of chap. 8 are one and the same. For a modern futuristic treatment, see M. Hassler, "The Identity of the Little Horn in Daniel 8: Antiochus IV Epiphanes, Rome, or the Antichrist?" *MSJ* 27 (2016): 33–44. He concludes (44), "The Little horn of Daniel 8:9–14 constitutes the same individual as the king of verses 23–26. He emerges as a distant eschatological dictator known also as the little horn of chapter 7, the coming prince of 9:26–27, and the despicable person of chapters 11–12. The NT calls him the antichrist."

For the dual fulfillment view, see Wood (222–24), Feinberg (109–11), and Campbell (126–28). Those taking the typical interpretation are mentioned in the discussion.

> Antiochus Epiphanes, now fulfilled, and to the end of the age and the final world ruler who persecutes Israel before the second advent; (4) the view that the passage is prophecy, historically fulfilled but intentionally typical of similar events and personages at the end of the age.

He concludes his discussion (196) by stating his preference for the *typical view*:

> A variation of the view that the last part of the chapter is specifically futuristic is found in the interpretation which has much to commend itself. This variation regards the entire chapter as historically fulfilled in Antiochus, but to varying degrees foreshadowing typically the future world ruler who would dominate the situation at the end of the times of the Gentiles. In any case, the passage intentionally goes beyond Antiochus to provide prophetic foreshadowing of the final Gentile ruler.

Identifying this as "double fulfillment"—with a partial fulfillment in Antiochus and a more complete fulfillment in antichrist—is not as accurate hermeneutically. The description of the wicked ruler, the main character of the chapter, does indeed find fulfillment in Antiochus IV. There are really no details unaccounted for in vv. 23–26, such that we need to find another personage to account for any of the descriptive details.

The point, rather, is that though the passage accurately and completely describes Antiochus IV, it *hints at* a deeper level of fulfillment, as suggested by the temporal notices that are picked up again in chaps. 11 and 12 where more overtly both Antiochus IV and antichrist are in view. There is a shift from Antiochus IV in 11:20–35 to the one of whom he is a type in 11:36–45, namely the antichrist. Miller (232), on the other hand, though following the *typical interpretation*, does so not because of the temporal notices but rather on account of the parallels between their characters and careers. He provides a helpful list of these (237–38). In either case, that the passage does have a typical fulfillment (Antiochus IV *foreshadows* the future antichrist) is the best way to understand the connection hermeneutically.[112] A number of key evangelical scholars have taken this position: Walvoord (196), Miller (232), Pentecost (1359), and Archer (106). Those taking the *dual fulfillment view* (Wood, Feinberg, and Campbell), though following a slightly different hermeneutic, agree that ultimately this passage has the antichrist in view.

Finally, just as Antiochus IV was defeated, so will the antichrist himself. Merrill writes,

> The anti-God forces of human government will one day be led, or at least epitomized, by a dictatorial figure who will make a last

112. Merrill, "A Theology of Ezekiel and Daniel," 393, refers to Antiochus IV as "a prototype of the Antichrist."

> stand attempt to dethrone the Lord of heaven but who will fail miserably to do so. His defeat and the defeat of godless human institutions that he represents will usher in the glorious Kingdom of God.[113]

Application and Devotional Implications

The portrait given of Antiochus IV Epiphanes in Dan 8:23–25 is that of a maniacal tyrant. He is arrogant, deceitful, merciless, power hungry, and destructive. Of course, he is not the first or only such ruler like this whom history has witnessed. In contrast, God is holy, good, merciful, kind, gracious, and loving. The challenging question for us is why God—who as the creator of the universe is absolutely sovereign and all-powerful—would allow such men as Antiochus to rise up to rule over mankind and assert their selfish, evil, and ungodly agendas on others. If God really has the ability to control who comes to the throne—whether they be tyrants who impose their will on others or who are elected to the position they hold—why does he not simply orchestrate things in such a way that only good men are allowed to be kings, presidents, or rulers?

The question is tied in, of course, to why God allows evil at all to enter his creation. Yet that we can more easily understand. Satan has been allowed to propagate evil on earth in his opposition to God. But why allow his ungodly agents to become the ones who dominate nations and kingdoms, especially those who are not only wicked but dishonoring and directly opposing the Lord God? We will probably not know this side of heaven why and how God makes such decisions about earthly rulers. What we do know is that we, as Christians, are called to subject ourselves to them:

> Let every person be subject to the governing authorities. For there is no authority except from God, and those that exist have been instituted by God. Therefore whoever resists the authorities resists what God has appointed, and those who resist will incur judgment. Rom 13:1–2 (ESV).

Many times this will mean submitting to evil and corrupt rulers (though submission does not mean doing evil ourselves, as we must obey the will of God above the will of man). The presence of evil and corrupt rulers serves to remind us that the kingdom we are looking for is not here on earth (though as good citizens we should want to be good stewards of God's creation). Jesus points us in the right direction by His response to Pilate: "My kingdom is not of this world. If my kingdom were of this world, my servants would have been fighting, that I might not be delivered over to the Jews. But my kingdom is not from the world" (John 18:36, ESV). From this we learn not to put all our hopes and dreams in the political powers that operate in this world. Where God allows, we should certainly exercise our right to influence

113. E. Merrill, "The Theology of the Postexilic Prophets," 552–53.

our nation for good. Yet many Christians will live under regimes that are not only corrupt but hostile to Christianity itself. Suffering and persecution may be the result. When this happens, we must remind ourselves of what is worth suffering for and be willing to pay a price for the faith we have embraced.

Selected Bibliography (Daniel 8)

Allen, S. "On Schedl's Attempt to Count the Days of Daniel." *AUSS* 4 (1966): 105–6.

Bampfylde, G. "The Prince of the Host in the Book of Daniel and the Dead Sea Scrolls." *JSJ* 14 (1983): 129–34.

Butt, K. "The Prophecy of Daniel 8." *Bible and Spade* 25 (2012): 60–66.

Davidson, R. M. "The Meaning of Niṣdaq in Daniel 8:14." *JATS* 7 (1996): 107–19.

Doukhan, J. B. *Daniel: The Vision of the End*, rev. ed. Berrien Springs, MI: Andrews University Press, 1989.

Finkelstein, J. J. "Mesopotamia." *JNES* 21 (1962): 73–92.

Gane, R. "The Syntax of Tēt Vᵉ … in Daniel 8:13." In *Creation, Life and Hope: Essays in Honor of Jacques B. Doukhan*, ed. J. Moskala, 367–82. Berrien Springs, MI: Andrews University Press, 2000.

Gardner, A. "Dan 8,1–2: Keynote to the Following Vision and Advice to the Righteous." *CNS* 35 (2014): 429–50.

Goldstein, J. *I Maccabees: A New Translation with Introduction and Commentary*. AYB 41. New Haven. CT: Yale University Press, 2008.

Graves, R. H. *Daniel's Great Period of "Two Thousand and Three Hundred Days."* London: Nisbet, 1854.

Gross, W. "The 'Little Horn' of Daniel 8." Th.M. thesis, Dallas Theological Seminary, 1966.

Hasel, G. F. "The First and Third Years of Belshazzar (Dan 7:1; 8:1)." *AUSS* 15 (1977): 153–68.

Hassler, M. A. "The Identity of the Little Horn in Daniel 8: Antiochus IV Epiphanes, Rome, or the Antichrist?" *MSJ* 27 (2016): 33–44.

Hauhnar, L. "Resistance to the Atrocious Powers: An Exegetical Analysis on Daniel 8:1–14." *Bangalore Theological Forum* 47 (2015): 24–39.

Hoehner, H. W. "Hasmoneans." In *ISBE*, ed. G. W. Bromiley, 2:621. 4 vols. Grand Rapids: Eerdmans, 1982.

Kaiser, W. C. *A History of Israel*. Nashville: Broadman & Holman, 1998.

Kosmala, H. "The Term *geber* in the OT and in the Scrolls." In *Congress Volume: Rome, 1968*, 159–69. VTSup 17. Leiden: Brill, 1969.

Krauss, S. "Some Remarks on Daniel 8. 5ff." *HUCA* 15 (1940): 305–11.

Lancaster, J. R., and R. L. Overstreet. "Jesus' Celebration of Hanukkah in John 10." *BSac* 152 (1995): 318–33.

Leatherman, D. W. "Structural Considerations regarding the Relation of Daniel 8 & Daniel 9." In *The Cosmic Battle for Planet Earth*, ed. R. du Preez and J. Moskala, 293–305. Berrien Springs, MI: Andrews University Press, 2003.

Matheny, J. F., and M. B. Matheny. *Collision Course: The Ram and the Goat of Daniel 8*. Brevard, NC: Jay and Associates, 1993.

Miller, P. D. "Animal Names as Designations in Ugaritic and Hebrew." *UF* 2 (1970): 177–86.

Moore, G. F. "Daniel viii 9–14." *JBL* 15 (1896): 194.

Nuñez, S. "Narrative Structure of Daniel 8: A Text Linguistic Approach." *JATS* 26 (2015): 88–110.

———. "The Vision of Daniel 8: Interpretations from 1700 to 1900." Andrews University Seminary Doctoral Dissertation Series 14. Berrien Springs, MI: Andrews University Press., 1987.

Porter, P. A. *Metaphors and Monsters: A Literary-Critical Study of Daniel 7 and 8*. ConBOT Series 20. Uppsala: CWK Gleerup, 1983.

Pröbstle, M. "A Linguistic Analysis of Daniel 8:11, 12." *JATS* 7 (1996): 81–106.

Rappaport, U. "Onias (Person)." In *AYBD*, ed. D. N. Freedman, 6 vols., 5:23–24. New York: Doubleday, 1992.

Rawlinson, G. *Biblical Topography*. London: James Nisbet & Co., 1887.

Rowe, D. L. *God's Strange Work: William Miller and the End of the World*. Library of Religious Biography. Grand Rapids: Eerdmans, 2008.

Schedl, C. "Mystische Arithmetik oder geschichtliche Zahlen?" *BZ* 8 (1964): 101–5.

Schwantes, S. J. "*ʿEREB* BŌQER of Dan 8:14 Re-examined." *AUSS* 16 (1978): 375–85.

Shea, W. H. "Supplementary Evidence in Support of 457 B.C. as the Starting Date for the 2300 Day—Years of Daniel 8:14." *JATS* 12 (2001): 89–96.

Tabola, L. "'In the Citadel of Susa, in the Province of Elam': The Chronological Significance of the Topographical Annotation in Daniel 8:2." *PJBR* 12 (2013): 71–81.

Waltke, B. K. "Antiochus IV Epiphanes." In *ISBE*, 4 vols., ed. G. W. Bromiley, 1:145–46. Grand Rapids: Eerdmans, 1979.

Waterman, L. "A Note on Daniel 8.2." *JBL* 66 (1947): 319–20.

Will, E. "The Succession to Alexander." In *The Cambridge Ancient History, VII Part 1: The Hellenistic World*, ed. F. W. Walbank et al., 23–61. Cambridge: Cambridge University Press, 1984.

Willis, A. C. M. "Myth and History in Daniel 8: The Apocalyptic Negotiation of Power." In *Myth and Scripture*, ed. D. E. Callender, Jr, 149–75. Atlanta: SBL Press, 2014.

Worthington, I. *Alexander the Great: Man and God*. Harlow, UK: Pearson Education, 2004.

Zuiddam, B. A. "The Shock Factor of Divine Revelation: A Philological Approach to Daniel 8 and 9." *SJOT* 27 (2013): 247–67.

B. The Vision of the 70 "Weeks" Prophecy: God's Timetable for Israel (9:1–27)

This is the third in a series of four visions given to Daniel. Unlike the previous visions Daniel does not "see" strange beastly creatures, but he does encounter the angel Gabriel, who reveals to Daniel details of Israel's prophetic future. This angelic encounter comes in response to a mighty prayer offered by Daniel. In the previous two chapters, Daniel learned that Israel's future was clouded by "dark days." The nation would continue to be dominated by Gentile powers. Then a ruthless ruler would arise from the Hellenistic kingdoms (namely Antiochus IV Epiphanes in the second century BC) who would severely persecute the Jews. Yet he was but a type of an even more oppressive ruler to arise in the far distant future, revealed to Daniel as the "little horn" of the fourth beast but known elsewhere in the Bible as the antichrist. Yet even in Daniel's own day the nation remained in exile in Babylon. Daniel's prayer in this chapter focuses upon God's deliverance of the nation from exile. In response, God reveals amazing details of the nation's future, looking beyond the near-term deliverance from exile to the arrival of Messiah and finally to the completion of the nation's desolations by the antichrist.

The chapter opens with a scene shortly after Babylon's defeat in which Daniel learned through a reading of Jeremiah's writings that God predestined the Babylonian exile to last seventy years (vv. 1–2). The central part of the chapter (vv. 3–19) is a record of the prayer that Daniel made as he interceded on behalf of the nation. Most of the prayer is a confession of the nation's wrongdoing and covenant unfaithfulness (vv. 4–14), but then it turns to a plea for mercy and Jerusalem's restoration (vv. 15–19). The final portion of the chapter (vv. 20–27) concerns the appearance of Gabriel, who provides a new revelation of God's plan for the nation in three stages. Though the temple and the city will be rebuilt in the near future, many more years will pass before her desolations are finally brought to a close.

Critical scholars (including Goldingay, 237) pass this chapter off as "quasi-prophecy" (written not by Daniel in the sixth century BC but by a pseudonymous author in the second century BC) concerned with the desolations suffered at the hands of Antiochus IV Epiphanes during the years 167–164 BC. They are greatly mistaken, for Jerusalem was not destroyed at that time (note 9:26). Furthermore, they deny that either of the references to *māšîaḥ* in vv. 25 and 26 refer to the Lord Jesus Christ, which has been the historic position of the Christian church. Although there is no universally accepted interpretation of the final prophecy (vv. 24–27) among evangelicals, there is general agreement that this passage finds at least part of its fulfillment with Christ in the first century followed by Jerusalem's destruction in AD 70 (while some would see v. 27 extending to the period just preceding the second coming).

1. Daniel's Observation from Jeremiah's Prophecy (9:1–2)

Textual Notes

1.a. If the Masoretic pointing is retained, this would be the only instance of מלך in the Hop'al stem. Both LXX^{O} and LXX$^{\theta}$ have εβασίλευσιν ἐπὶ (aorist active of βασιλεύω), which presupposes a Hip'il verb form, perhaps הִמְלִךְ (similarly Vg. and S). (Note the NRSV, "who became king.") However, elsewhere the Hip'il 3ms always has a *yod* infix, e.g., הִמְלִיךְ (so 1 Sam 15:35; 1 Kgs 1:43; Jer 37:1). Hence, it is best to retain the Masoretic pointing of the Hop'al, despite its rarity. This need not imply that someone with greater authority than Darius appointed him to this position (e.g., Cyrus). Often in the OT, when the subjects of the kingdom wanted a man for their king, they "made him king" (e.g., 1 Kgs 11:12; 12:20). His subjects "made him king," and hence he was "made king." Goldingay (239) adds, "His 'being made king' of Babylon here may reflect his 'acquiring/receiving' the kingship of Babylon there."

2.a. LXX^{O}'s translation ὀνειδισμου ("reproach," sg.) reflects a misreading as לחרפת (Heb. חֶרְפָּה = "reproach").

Translation

9:1 In the first year of Darius, son of Ahasuerus,[114] a descendant of the Medes, who was made[115] king over the kingdom of the Chaldeans— **2** in the first year

114. There is no need to translate אֲחַשְׁוֵרוֹשׁ (*'ăḥašwērôš*) as Xerxes, as the NIV has done, in following LXX^{O}'s Ξέρξου (*Xerxou*), though it is true that Xerxes is a Greek name for Ahasuerus. The problem is that this tends to confuse Ahasuerus, the father of Darius the Mede, with Ahasuerus of the book of Esther (who is commonly believed to be Xerxes I). Newsom (289) is representative of those guilty of falsely charging the author with confusion of Persian kings: "In the succession of *Persian* kings, Darius I was the father of Xerxes I, so the author may have borrowed the names and reversed the sequence to create the genealogy of Darius the Mede." But the author of Daniel was not mistaken, and Darius the Mede is not his confusion with the famous Persian king Darius I. If the theory advocated in the commentary at Dan 5:31 is correct, this Darius the Mede is the king mentioned by Xenophon, known historically as Cyaxares II. His father was Astyages, which is thus another name for Ahasuerus mentioned in Dan 9:1. It was not unusual in ancient times for a king, at his coronation, to take a throne name in addition to his birth name (so Baldwin, 182). Goldingay (239), citing Frye, adds, "אחשורוש (Ahashweros) is the regular BH equivalent of OP Khshayarsha. ... Khshayarsha, like Dārayavaush itself, is probably a throne name, meaning 'hero among rulers' (Frye, *Heritage*, 97)." Most English translations render אֲחַשְׁוֵרוֹשׁ (*'ăḥašwērôš*) in Dan 9:1 as Ahasuerus.

115. Observe the Textual Note for the verb form הָמְלַךְ (*homlak̠*), "was made king." Though a Hop'al form, this need not imply that he was a subservient ruler to a higher authority (such as Cyrus). The fact that Darius was "made king" (rather than

of his reign, I, Daniel, observed[116] in the books,[117] *according to* the word of Yahweh[118] to Jeremiah the prophet, the number of years to be fulfilled[119] for the desolations of Jerusalem, *namely* seventy years.

Commentary

9:1 Chapter 9 is dated to the first year of Darius son of Ahasuerus. This is no doubt the same ruler first mentioned in Dan 5:31 and subsequently in chap. 6, namely Darius the Mede. For discussion of his identity, see the commentary at 5:31 as well as "Section 5" of "Alleged Historical Inaccuracies" under "Objections to the Traditional Date and Authorship" in the "Introduction" to the book. As suggested by Steven Anderson and others (incl. Calvin and C. F. Keil), this Darius the Mede may very well be Cyaxares II, the last Median king and son of Astyages, according to the account of the Greek historian Xenophon.[120]

Darius presumably took up the role of king over Babylon not long after the defeat of the city in Oct 539 BC at the hands of Cyrus. In keeping with the Persian and Babylonian custom of "accession year" dating, "the first full year of his reign was reckoned as beginning with the next New Year's day, i.e., with the next Nisanu 1 in the Babylonian calendar."[121] Hence, the time from the beginning of his reign until the following spring was considered his "accession year," and his first *regnal* year would be from Nisan 1, 538 BC until Nisan of 537. The reference in 9:1 to "the first year" could conceivably

---

"became king") only means that this realm had not been under the authority of the Median king up until this point. Now that the authority of the Median king was being extended over the realm of the Babylonians, Darius is said to be "made king" over this additional territory.

116. For the meaning "observe" for the Qal form בִּינֹתִי (*bînōṯî*), see BDB, 106d 3. Hill (161) points out, "The word בִּינֹתִי, *bînōtî*, is an anomalous form for the Qal stem of the verbal root בין, *byn*, prompting some commentators to regard the term as a shortened form of the Hipʿil stem (e.g., Hartman and Di Lella, 241; Goldingay, 226) and translate it 'considered' rather than 'understood' (so NIV). The Qal form of the MT is preferred, and the word expresses the idea of observing." So NASB.

117. There is no reason to think that because the word "books" is pointed as definite (בַּסְּפָרִים, *bassᵊp̄ārîm*) that this would indicate a *fixed canon* had been established at this time (as though this would imply a late dating for Daniel). Wood (233) correctly notes, "It is only to be expected that the Judeans, exiled for many years by this time in Babylonia, would have had with them a number of Old Testament writings which were generally recognized as sacred."

118. This is the first instance of the Tetragrammaton, Yahweh (יהוה), in the book of Daniel. Indeed, all eight occurrences of the divine name in Daniel occur in this chapter alone.

119. Lit., "for fulfilling (Piʿel inf. constr.) the desolations of Jerusalem."

120. Anderson, *Darius the Mede*.

121. Finegan, *Handbook of Biblical Chronology*, 75.

be referring to either his first accession year or to his first regnal year. This would have been approximately twelve to thirteen years since the vision recorded in chap. 8.

9:2 At that time, either the latter part of 539 or perhaps in 538 BC, while in Babylon, Daniel was studying the writings of the prophet Jeremiah. The latter never went into the Babylonian exile but rather remained in Jerusalem until after the fall of the city in 586 BC, after which he was taken to Egypt. That copies of his writings were made and distributed so soon to those in exile in Babylon evidences their quick recognition as Scripture. Daniel (as did others) certainly regarded them as the inspired Word of God, since he referred to them as "the word of Yahweh to Jeremiah the prophet." An alternative view is that the portions of Jeremiah that Daniel had access to were the letters sent from Jerusalem mentioned in Jer 29:1, 10, 25 (see Hill, 160).[122]

In studying Jeremiah's writings, Daniel took special notice of Jer 25:8–12 and 29:10.[123] This first passage is particularly significant, for it specified that Nebuchadnezzar (specifically naming him) would attack the land and the Jews would serve him for seventy years. Daniel indicates that this seventy-year period was the time for the fulfilling of the desolations of Jerusalem.[124] The word "desolation" (חָרְבָּה, *ḥorbâ*) was used three times in Jer 25 (vv. 9, 11, 18), and indicates a laying waste of something or bringing it to ruin. The beginning of this seventy-year period was not 586 BC when Jerusalem was destroyed, but an earlier date (perhaps 609 BC and certainly no later than 605 BC), since Jer 25:12 indicated that God would punish the king of Babylon

122. Cf. G. H. Wilson, "The Prayer in Daniel 9: Reflection on Jeremiah 29," *JSOT* 48 (1990): 93.

123. 2 Chr 36:21 is also associated with Jeremiah's prophecies, yet with emphasis upon the land being able to enjoy its sabbaths. For this, the Chronicler has apparently drawn upon Lev 26:34. A. E. Gardner, "The Way to Eternal Life in Dan 12:1e–2 or How to Reverse the Death Curse of Genesis 3," *ABR* 40 (1992), 5 adds, "A further allusion which applies to both Dan 9:2 and 9:24 is Lev 25:8 where 'seven sabbaths of years' appear. 'Desolations of Jerusalem' in Dan 9:2 has been culled from Isa 52:9, a passage which, like 2 Chr 36:21, deals with the end of the exile."

124. There seems to have been a reason why the Lord chose seventy years for the length of the exile. According to 2 Chr 36:19–21, the land was to "enjoy its sabbaths." Lev 25:2–5 stipulated that the land was to rest every seventh year (not used for agriculture), but the people had neglected to keep this command. Also, according to Lev 26:43, the land was to be abandoned in order to "make up for its sabbaths while it is made desolate without them." Apparently the people had failed to observe the sabbath land rest seventy times, and so the Lord made the exile seventy years to allow the land to make up for the *sabbath years* that had been missed.

when the seventy years were completed.[125] In reading Jeremiah's prophecies, Daniel would have realized that the defeat of Babylon also meant the completion of the seventy years of desolation. This encouraged him that God's restoration of Judah was possible, which led in turn to his praying for his homeland and Jerusalem in particular.

Biblical Theology Comments

Numbers play an interesting role throughout the Bible. From Jeremiah's prophecies in Jer 25:12 and 29:10, exactly seventy years—not 68 or 73—were determined for the desolation of the land of Judah. God obviously works by a carefully construed timetable, and history progresses according to his meticulous calculations. Other examples could easily be summoned for consideration. According to Exod 12:41, "at the end of four hundred and thirty years, to the very day, all the hosts of the LORD went out from the land of Egypt" (NASB). In 1 Kgs 6:1 we read, "Now it came about in the four hundred and eightieth year after the sons of Israel came out of the land of Egypt, ... that he began to build the house of the LORD" (NASB). Though some might regard these as merely *round numbers*, the example from Exod 12:41 cautions us to treat them literally. They underscore that history is not randomly progressing but is under the careful watch and control of Yahweh God of heaven. He makes decisions regarding nations and ensures that everything operates according to his timetable.

---

125. If seventy years are reckoned from 586 BC, the *terminus ad quem* would be about 516 BC (approximately the year that the temple reconstruction was completed). However, the Babylonians had been removed from power some twenty-three years earlier (539 BC). Jer 25:12 indicates that the king of Babylon would be punished when the seventy years were *completed*. So the "completion" of the seventy years must be significantly earlier than 516 BC. The same logic would apply to using 597 BC, Nebuchadnezzar's second invasion, as the beginning date (as Collins, 349, has asserted). Those who try to identify the *terminus a quo* with 605 BC are forced to admit that "the seventy years" is nothing more than a round number (so Hill, 160). An alternative to using the year 605 BC as the *terminus a quo* would be to use the date 609 BC, as R. Winkle, "Jeremiah's Seventy Weeks for Babylon: A Re-Assessment. Part II: The Historical Data," *AUSS* 25 (1987): 289–99, has suggested. This would be the year that Nebuchadnezzar made a final and conclusive defeat of the last remnant of the Assyrian armies led by Aššur-uballiṭ II at Harran. This marked the end of the Assyrian Empire and the rise to power of Babylon under Nebuchadnezzar. In conjunction with this event, Pharaoh Neco II of Egypt killed King Josiah (July 609 BC), and Judah lost her independence and became a vassal state of Egypt and four years later of Babylon itself. Jer 25:11 mentions multiple nations serving the king of Babylon during these seventy years (and these are described in Jer 25:17–26), so that the seventy years represented not just an affliction upon Judah. This began to take place in the aftermath of Nebuchadnezzar's victory at Harran in 609 BC. Seventy years after 609 BC would be 539 BC, the year Babylon was overthrown.

As for the seventy years allocated for the Babylonian exile and the desolation of the land of Judah, this number was not chosen without reason. Second Chronicles 36:21 reveals that the choice of seventy years was "to fulfill the word of the LORD by the mouth of Jeremiah, until the land had enjoyed its sabbaths. All the days of its desolation it kept sabbath until seventy years were complete" (NASB).

Application and Devotional Implications

Daniel would have learned from his studies in God's Word (in this case, the book of Jeremiah) not only that the nation would be afflicted by Babylon for seventy years but also that God was exact in his determination of the nation's discipline. God had a carefully devised plan—it was under his control, it had a fixed beginning, and it had a fixed terminus. Certainly this reflects God's sovereignty and his control of the nations of the world, but it also reflects his careful planning and setting of boundaries upon the discipline he has purposed. Those of Judah (including Daniel and Jeremiah) no doubt felt the pain of God's hand of discipline, and yet there was comfort in knowing that he was in full control and that the discipline would not go beyond what he had called for. We also see that, in spite of Judah's sin, God remained faithful to his promises and never disowned his people.

The Lord is still a God who disciplines his people for their own good and so they may share in his holiness (Heb 12). Yet he does so out of love for his own. Fortunately for those of us who are his children, we have the assurance that such discipline is not in danger of spinning out of control. God's plans for us (including his discipline) are carefully planned out, perfectly timed, and administered with precision and purpose.

2a. Daniel's Prayer, Part 1: Humility and Confession (9:3–14)

Several critical scholars have questioned whether the prayer of chap. 9 was composed by the person who wrote the rest of the chapter or whether it was original to the composition (see Newsom, 288–89, for discussion).[126] Goldingay, however, has affirmed its originality. He concludes (237), "The difficulty of the hypothesis that the prayer is a later addition to the chapter lies in the close links between prayer and context." Contextually, the prayer is quite appropriate, for restoration to the land demanded first and foremost

126. L. Dequeker, "King Darius and the Prophecy of Seventy Weeks, Daniel 9," in *The Book of Daniel in the Light of New Findings*, ed. A. S. van der Woude (Leuven: Leuven University Press, 1993), 195, for instance, writes, "It is generally agreed that the prayer was not composed by the author of Daniel 9, in particular because the deuteronomistic theology (exile as a punishment for sin) is too different from the apocalyptic doctrine of Daniel." In response, such theology is not out of place in light of the opening scene of the book as Jerusalem is laid under siege and the Babylonian exile commences. Exile and the hope of restoration is very germane to the book.

the repentance of the people (discussion to follow). Some scholars assert that the writing style of the prayer differs from the surrounding material, as though this might indicate a different author. However, the nature of the material itself (recorded prayer) could account for this, just as any author might write poetry in a different style than a historical treatise.

Why after reading the prophecy of the seventy years for the Babylonian exile did Daniel launch into a prayer of humility and confession on behalf of the nation? The subject of Judah's restoration must be understood to fully appreciate Daniel's prayer in chap. 9. The whole experience of going into exile in Babylon was a fulfillment of the discipline that God had forewarned the nation of years earlier under Moses (see Deut 28–29). He promised to shower them with blessings if they obeyed his covenant (see Deut 28:1–14), but he also warned them that He would discipline them for covenant disobedience (Deut 28:15–68; cf. Lev 26:14–39). The discipline would be progressive, and ultimately (if Israel continued in disobedience) it would culminate in their exile from the land of promise (Deut 28:64–68). Yet God also revealed his plan for the nation's restoration to blessing in Deut 30:1–10. Essentially, this meant that the nation would have to repent and turn back to the Lord wholeheartedly, and then God would regather the nation back to their land and bless them. According to Lev 26:40–41, this had to include the confession of their iniquity and covenant unfaithfulness, as well as that of their forefathers. Hence, Daniel's prayer in chap. 9 is a prayer of national repentance and confession as a precondition for God regathering his people to the land and restoring them to blessing.[127] What comes as something of a surprise at the end of the chapter (vv. 24–27) is that God reveals to Daniel that his plans for national discipline extend far beyond the current seventy years, even though Israel would be allowed to return to the land in Daniel's lifetime.

Textual Notes

10.a. Although LXX^{O} (and similarly Vg) has a singular form, τῷ νομῷ σου, MT's plural form ("laws") is reasonable and has the support of LXX$^{\theta}$.

11.a. Some MSS have the 2ms suffix לְךָ to conform to the previous divine references in the verse (NIV, NRSV, and NET translate "you"), yet MT's לוֹ (3ms)

127. Collins (349–50) observes, "Daniel's prayer is of a type familiar in post-exilic Jewish literature: compare Ezra 9:6–15; Neh 1:5–11; 9:5–37; Psalm 79; Bar 1:15–3:8; and the *Prayer of Azariah* and the *Words of the Heavenly Luminaries* from Qumran. All these prayers are characterized by a strongly Deuteronomic theology. They all involve a confession of Israel's sin and affirmation of God's justice and appeal for mercy, not because of Israel's merit but for God's own sake." For further help in comparing the prayer of Dan 9 to prayers from Second Temple literature, including texts from the Apocrypha and Pseudepigrapha, the writings of Philo and Josephus, and texts from Qumran, see M. D. Matlock, *Discovering the Traditions of Prose Prayers in Early Jewish Literature* (London: T&T Clark, 2012).

is probably original (the more difficult reading). Goldingay (227) points out that within the context of the prayer, there is a tendency to easily shift back and forth between 2nd and 3rd person.

12.a. This should be read דְּבָרָיו, not as L's דְּבָרִיו. Both LXX traditions translated as a plural, and the correct plural form is דְּבָרָיו (see, for example, Gen 37:8).

13.a. The sign of the accusative at this position is difficult to explain, and *BHS* suggests deleting. Goldingay (227) mentions several possible explanations but assumes that this marks a resumption in thought from רָעָה גְדֹלָה in v.12. Some MSS repoint the following verb בָּאָה as הֵב– (Hiphil), so as to make the subject "He" rather than כָּל־הָרָעָה הַזֹּאת, i.e., "He has brought on us all this calamity." Most Eng. VSS ignore the particle אֵת and regard כָּל־הָרָעָה הַזֹּאת as the subject, "all this calamity has come upon us."

Translation

9:3 So I turned[128] to the Lord God to seek *Him* by prayer and supplication,[129] with fasting and sackcloth and ashes. **4** And I prayed to Yahweh God and confessed, saying,[130] "O Lord God—the great and awesome God who faithfully[131] keeps *His* covenant *promises*[132] to those who love Him and keep His commandments—**5** we have sinned, committed iniquity, acted wickedly, rebelled, and turned aside from Your commandments and

128. Lit., "gave my face to the Lord." The idea is that he gave his full attention to seeking the Lord in prayer. Miller (242) suggests the idiom may also imply that Daniel was "determined to look to God in prayer until the Lord gave him an answer." Hill (162) goes so far as to suggest that the "idiom alludes to the practice of facing Jerusalem when a Hebrew prays." Cf. 1 Kgs 8:35.

129. Grammatically the noun is plural, but BDB (337) calls it an abstract plural, i.e., it expresses a singular concept. It sums up the whole experience of supplicating God. Compare the use in Zech 12:10.

130. Technically וָאֹמְרָה (*wāʾōmᵊrâ*) is a *waw*-consecutive form ("and I said") but is expressed here as a participle in an effort to render the verb chain into smooth English.

131. Lit., the Hebrew has "who keeps (the) covenant and (the) *ḥeseḏ*." The term *ḥeseḏ* has no exact English equivalent but is probably best rendered as "loving loyalty," as the nuance of *faithfulness* is fundamental to the meaning of the word. When used of God, it speaks of his loving devotion and faithfulness to those with whom he is in covenant relation. In this sentence, the idea is best expressed adverbially, "faithfully keeps."

132. The word "promises" is supplied in the translation to clarify the point. To say that God "keeps covenant" means that he is faithful to the *promises* of the covenants he made with Israel.

ordinances.[133] **6** Nor have we given heed to Your servants, the prophets, who spoke by Your authority[134] to our kings, our high officials,[135] and our fathers,[136] even to all the people of the land. **7** You, O Lord, have acted righteously,[137] while open shame[138] *has befallen* us, as this day—for the men of Judah, for the inhabitants of Jerusalem, and for all Israel both near and far away in all the lands where You have driven them on account of their unfaithful deeds against You. **8** O Yahweh, open shame *is now* ours—our kings, our high officials, and our fathers—because we have sinned against You. **9** To the Lord our God belongs compassion and forgiveness, though[139] we have rebelled against Him. **10** Nor have we given heed to the voice of Yahweh our God so as[140] to walk in His laws which He placed before us through[141] His servants, the prophets. **11** All Israel has transgressed Your Law and turned aside, so

133. Usually מִשְׁפָּטִים (*mišpāṭîm*) is rendered "judgments." Yet to clarify, these are not court judgments for offenses but rather those ordinances for man to live by that God has judged to be right and in keeping with his holiness.

134. Lit., "in Your name," but this implies the authority that would be signified by God's name. Compare Goldingay (225), "as your representatives."

135. Elsewhere in Daniel, שַׂר (*śar*) is translated "leaders, princes." But BDB (978) indicates a broad usage: "chieftan, chief, ruler, official, captain, prince." The word "high" is added to clarify that these were not minor officials.

136. Oftentimes, וַאֲבֹתֵינוּ (*wa'ăḇōṯênû*) would indicate the ancestors of the nation (e.g., Num 20:15; Deut 5:3; 26:3, 7, 15). Goldingay (227), however, tries to make a point that in this context (a list of more current national leaders) they more likely represent heads of local social/kinship groups. The use in v. 8 would tend to support this suggestion (though, more remotely, v. 16 seems to have the national ancestors in view). Collins (350) concurs, "The fathers are probably the heads of the 'fathers' houses' or family elders" (cf. Montgomery, 364); similarly, Newsom (293). Cf. Ezra 2:68 where the expression "the heads of fathers' households" is expressed in Heb. as רָאשֵׁי הָאָבוֹת (*rā'šê hā'āḇôṯ*).

137. Lit., "belonging to You, O Lord, is righteousness." Yet the noun צְדָקָה (*ṣᵉḏāqâ*) has in view not God's general attribute of being righteous, but specifically the fact that he has been righteous in the way he has dealt with the nation in disciplining them with exile, i.e., he has acted righteously in punishing his people. There is no fault found in him regarding the destruction and calamity the nation has suffered.

138. Lit., "shame of face" (בֹּשֶׁת הַפָּנִים, *bōšeṯ happānîm*).

139. The particle כִּי (*kî*) is not causal in this case (despite the fact several Eng. VSS translate as "for"). The NET translates as concessive, which makes good sense. Goldingay (225), on the other hand, takes the כִּי (*kî*) clause as initiating a new sentence

140. "So as," taking the infinitive with prefixed *lamed* preposition (לָלֶכֶת, *lāleḵeṯ*) as a result clause; see *IBHS*, 606 (§36.2.3d).

141. Lit., "by the hand." But the "hand" is a metonymy for the means by which God accomplished this; see E. W. Bullinger, *Figures of Speech Used in the Bible* (Grand Rapids: Baker, 1968), 546. He did this *by means of* or *through* his prophets.

as not to heed Your voice. So the curse[142]—the sworn promise[143] written in the law of Moses the servant of God[144]—has been poured out[145] upon us, for we have sinned against Him. **12** He has confirmed His words that He spoke against us and against our rulers[146] who governed us by bringing[147] on us *such* a great calamity—that which has not been done under all of heaven like what has been done with Jerusalem. **13** Just as has been written in the Law of Moses,[148] all this calamity[149] has come on us; yet we have not sought the favor[150] of Yahweh our God by turning[151] from our iniquities and paying

---

142. The word for "curse" in Deut 28:15 is not אָלָה (*ʾālâ*) but קְלָלָה (*qᵊlālâ*), though the terms are basically synonymous. The word אָלָה (*ʾālâ*) was used in Deut 29:19 (Heb. 29:18): "It shall be when he hears the words of this curse (הָאָלָה, *hāʾālâ*) ..." Hence the word הָאָלָה (*hāʾālâ*) in Dan 9:11 no doubt has reference to the "curse" forewarned of in Deut 28–29.
143. שְׁבוּעָה (*šᵊḇûʿâ*) normally means "an oath," but it comes from the verb שָׁבַע (*šāḇaʿ*), meaning "to swear" (i.e., to promise something). The NET takes הָאָלָה וְהַשְּׁבֻעָה (*hāʾālâ wᵊhaššᵊḇuʿâ*) as a hendiadys, "the judgment solemnly threatened." Similarly, Goldingay (225), "the solemn curse." An alternative is to take the phrase beginning with *wᵊhaššᵊḇuʿâ* as an amplification of the Deuteronomic "curse." Although שְׁבוּעָה (*šᵊḇûʿâ*) is primarily used positively of God's oath to give Abram's seed the land of promise (e.g., Deut 7:8; Jer 11:5), it is used here to speak of what Yahweh had sworn would happen to the nation for continued covenant unfaithfulness (cf. Lev 26:27–45; Deut 28:15–68; 29:20). Wood (239) adds, "the oath (*shᵊḇuʿah*, from *shabaʿ*, 'to swear'), used in various forms, was added to statements, usually either promises or warnings, to lend a sense of authority or solemnity. The thought here is that God's punishing curse, backed by His solemn oath, had been poured out upon Israel."
144. Regarding Moses as "the servant of God," see Deut 34:5; Josh 1:1; 8:31; Neh 10:29.
145. Collins (350) notes, "The motif of 'pouring out' is often used for the divine anger: Jer 7:20; 42:18; 44:6; 2 Chron 12:7; 34:25; Ps 79:6."
146. Lit., "our judges who judged us," but the translation "rulers" is more appropriate (to avoid confusion with those specific rulers before the monarchy known as "judges").
147. "By bringing," taking the infinitive with prefixed *lamed* preposition (לְהָבִיא, *lᵊhāḇîʾ*) as epexegetical to the main verb; see *IBHS*, 608 (§36.2.3e).
148. Regarding the expression, "as has been written in the Law of Moses," see Josh 8:31; 1 Kgs 2:3. Collins (350) points out that "כאשר כתוב becomes a conventional formula for citing Scripture at Qumran (1QS 5:17; 8:14; 4QFlor *174*, 2:3)."
149. See the Textual Note to this verse above. Most Eng. VSS ignore the particle אֵת (*ʾēṯ*) and translate "all this calamity" (כָּל־הָרָעָה הַזֹּאת, *kol-hārāʿâ hazzōʾṯ*) as the subject of the verb בָּאָה (*bāʾâ*).
150. Lit., "the face of Yahweh." Here "face" is a metonymy for the Lord's presence where one finds *favor* before him (Bullinger, *Figures of Speech*, 647; cf. Job 11:19). The verb itself (חָלָה, *ḥālâ*) means to "mollify, appease, entreat the favor of" (BDB, 318).
151. "By turning," taking the infinitive with prefixed *lamed* preposition (לָשׁוּב, *lāšûḇ*) as epexegetical to the main verb; see *IBHS*, 608 (§36.2.3e).

attention[152] to Your truth.[153] **14** Thus Yahweh kept in mind[154] the calamity and brought it upon us. Indeed,[155] Yahweh our God has been righteous in all[156] He has done, but we have not given heed to His voice.

Commentary

a. Daniel's humility before God (9:3–4)

9:3 Following his reflection on the passages from Jeremiah, Daniel "sought" the Lord in prayer, not for enlightenment (as Hartman and Di Lella have wrongly assumed, 245–46) but by way of penitential prayer. The whole prayer (vv. 3–19) has distinctive allusions to earlier passages (possibly as much as 85 percent), which has prompted Towner (129) to describe Daniel's prayer as "a meditation of Scripture upon earlier Scripture."[157] Newsom (292), having

---

152. In the Hip'il stem, the verb שָׂכַל (*śāḵal*) often means to "prosper, have success." Yet an alternative nuance for the Hip'il is "to consider, give attention to" (BDB, 968 #2), which is appropriate here. Giving attention to God's truth should lead in turn to insight or comprehension (which is meaning #3 that BDB gives for the Hip'il of *śāḵal*). Newsom (296) notes the significance of this in the larger context of Daniel: "The mention of 'gaining insight' (*lĕhaśkîl*) ... is unusual. The root *śkl* is something of a leitmotif in Daniel (1:4, 17; 9:13, 22, 25; 11:33, 35; 12:3, 10), and ... the word stands out because of the role it plays more generally in the book. Appropriate religious dispositions are achieved through discernment, and the object of discernment in this case is God's *'ĕmet*."

153. In this context, אֱמֶת (*'ĕmeṯ*) does not have in view abstract truth, but more specifically the truth that had been revealed to God's people through his Word (cf. John 17:17). Goldingay (225), on the other hand, suggests "your faithfulness" (i.e., God being true to His Word), but this seems to ignore the juxtaposition with "iniquities" (one turns from his iniquities to embrace God's Word—his truth—and live by it). The NET's "your reliable moral standards" comes closer to the right idea.

154. The verb שָׁקַד (*šāqaḏ*)—translated here "kept in mind"—has a basic meaning of "to watch, remain awake" (BDB, 1052). NET: "was mindful of." The idea is that Yahweh has watched over the promise of calamity foretold in Deut 28–29 and never lost sight of it. He did not forget about it for a second and has thus fulfilled his Word.

155. I take the particle כִּי (*kî*) as "emphatic (inded, surely, certainly) rather than causal. So NRSV. See *IBHS*, 662–68 (§39.3.4).

156. Lit., "concerning all His deeds that He has done." This has been simplified in the translation to avoid what in English would sound redundant.

157. The prayer of Dan 9 is certainly rich in intertextual links. Demonstrable parallels include Deut 28, 1 Kgs 8, Ezra 9, Neh 1 and 9, Isa 10, Jer 25–29, and Ezek 28. In addition to these, the links with Leviticus are particularly strong, as G. G. Harper, "The Theological and Exegetical Significance of Leviticus as Intertext in Daniel 9," *JESOT* 4 (2015): 39–61, has ably demonstrated. He concludes (61), "it is evident that Lev 16, 25 and 26 exert a significant influence on the vocabulary and theology of Dan 9. The text is, as Kline says, 'saturated' with Mosaic expressions."

pointed out the similarity of Daniel's prayer to other penitential prayers, has noted:

> The vocabulary and style of the various penitential prayers show a great deal of similarity, drawing extensively on words and phrases characteristic of Deuteronomistic theology. The vocabulary and set phrases form a dense intertextual web of allusions to other passages, particularly from Deuteronomy and Jeremiah (for a list of parallels, see Montgomery 363–68).

In reading Jer 29, Daniel would have noticed the call to prayer and repentance expressed in vv. 12–13: "Then you will call upon Me and come and pray to Me, and I will listen to you. You will seek Me and find *Me* when you search for Me with all your heart." Regarding the word בָּקַשׁ (*bāqaš*), translated "seek" in both Dan 9:3 and Jer 29:13, Hill (162) notes, "More generally, this word in the OT prophets means to turn to God in humility and repentance as a demonstration of dependence and covenantal loyalty (cf. C. Chhetri, "בָּקַשׁ," *NIDOTTE*, 1:724–25)." "Fasting, sackcloth, and ashes" were the outward indications of one who wished to "lament" in ancient Israel (cf. Jonah 3:6; Esth 4:1–4; Ezra 9:3–4; Neh 9:1).[158] They also reflect the obvious sincerity and humility behind Daniel's prayer of confession. Hill regards the whole prayer as a communal confession. He states (163), "The literary form of the prayer is usually identified as that of communal confession (note the use of the first-person plural pronouns; vv. 5–7, etc.), perhaps an adaptation of the community lament (cf. Goldingay, 234–35)." Thus, Daniel's prayer functioned canonically as the fulfillment of the injunction laid out in Lev 26:40–42, "If they confess their iniquity and the iniquity of their forefathers, in their unfaithfulness which they committed against Me ... then I will remember My covenant ... and I will remember the land" (NASB).

Daniel wished to supplicate God for something, namely Israel's restoration to the land, and a humble spirit on his part was essential. This is not to say that Daniel's prayer alone would have been sufficient for Israel's national confession and repentance, but Daniel was certainly being faithful to do his part and is representative of what was really the obligation of the entire nation. Knowing that Daniel had a habit of praying three times a day (Dan 6:10), we should not be surprised at his diligence in prayer as recorded in this chapter.

Daniel directed his prayer (v. 3) to "the Lord God" (אֲדֹנָי הָאֱלֹהִים, *ʾădōnāy hāʾĕlōhîm*). Miller (242) points out, "The name *ʾădōnāy* means 'owner, ruler, or sovereign' and identifies Yahweh as the owner and ruler of the universe. Not only was he able to hear Daniel's prayer, but he had the power to direct the affairs of world history in order to answer his prayer." Yet we read in v. 4 that Daniel "prayed to Yahweh (יְהוָה, *yhwh*) God, and in this case he uses the personal name for God, Yahweh. Miller (242) adds, "Specifying Yahweh

158. Cf. K. D. Berghuis, "A Biblical Perspective on Fasting," *BSac* 158 (2001): 93–94.

as 'my God' also emphasizes that Daniel rejected the false idols of Babylon; his God was Yahweh."

9:4. Even though this is a prayer of confession about Israel's failure, it was very appropriate to begin with an acknowledgment of God's greatness and faithfulness. Israel's God alone was the "great and awesome God" (on this phrase, see Deut 7:21; Neh 1:5), a reminder of how privileged this nation had been and therefore how responsible they were to him (cf. Deut 4:7–8). Furthermore, Israel's misfortune and exile were not the result of any failure on His part. Quite the contrary, he "faithfully keeps His covenant promises." If Israel had loved him and kept his commandments, they would have discovered just how true this was and how much more he could have blessed them. As to which covenant is in view, Hill (164) is probably correct in recognizing that "the word 'covenant' in the context of Daniel's situation may be used as an umbrella term for Yahweh's covenantal tradition with Israel (i.e., the covenants with Abraham, Israel at Mount Sinai, and David)."

b. Confession of the nation's sin and God's righteous judgment (9:5–14)

9:5–6 These verses initiate a lengthy confession section, summarizing the basic problem of the nation. Verse 5 is a clear admission that the nation had been disobedient to her God. To underscore the point, Daniel used five different words or concepts to emphasize this: sinned, committed iniquity, acted wickedly, rebelled, and turned aside from God's commandments. He did not try to minimize their failure by calling it a mere mistake. The nation was as guilty of sin as it possibly could be, and this had to be owned up to.

In spite of their guilt, God had made efforts to help the nation back to the pathway of blessing. He did this by raising up prophets (tokens of his grace) who confronted the disobedient nation and pointed the people back to the Law.[159] From kings to the common inhabitants of the land, all had heard from God's prophets and therefore had been given sufficient opportunity to repent and turn back before God's judgment fell.

9:7–8 Sin always exacts a price, and in Israel's case the outcome was in their being thoroughly humiliated before the other nations of the world. Her shame was in the destruction of the city and temple, followed by having to go into captivity. How could it be that the one nation that knew and served the only true God and had his laws could end up like this? Being chosen and privileged was not to be taken lightly; they were responsible to love him and be faithful to his covenant. As it were, they reaped what they had sown, and their humiliation and open shame were a direct fulfillment of Deut 29:22–28. On being scattered to other lands, see Jer 16:15; 23:3; 32:37.

159. Regarding the expression "My servants the prophets," compare Jer 25:3–4; 26:5; 29:19; 35:15; 44:4–5; Ezra 9:11.

9:9–10 Was this God of heaven too exacting? Too strict? No, he is a God who is compassionate and forgiving (cf. Exod 34:6; Neh 9:17). Goldingay (243) calls "compassion" (הָרַחֲמִים, *hāraḥămîm*) a feelings word, as it denotes strong emotion. He goes on to say (244), "רחם itself refers to the womb, and a sense that רחמים denotes the strong feelings of love and concern that might be expected within the family on the part of a mother, a father, a husband, or a brother underlies a number of occurrences of this and the related verb." Yet he is careful to add that it does not denote *mere* feelings but suggests a compassion that instinctively issues in action. Daniel's people could have availed themselves of God's gracious and forgiving character at any time. Instead, they "rebelled against Him" and neglected to heed "His servants, the prophets."

9:11–14 The common idea of these verses is that God's Word proves true. The "sworn promise written in the law of Moses" is a reference to the Deuteronomic principle of curses for disobedience, the ultimate form being the devastation of their cities and fields followed by exile from the land.[160] What God had forewarned the people of by his Word indeed came true. This underscores how important it is to obey the Word of God, because the Lord is watching over his Word to confirm it. Verse 13 is an acknowledgment that they had the written Word of God, in the form of what had been "written in the law of Moses," and this—God's Word—was pure truth they could rely on. Having failed to heed the Word (having disobeyed), the nation received the calamity they rightly deserved, namely the devastation that Nebuchadnezzar and the Babylonians inflicted upon them from 605 BC until Jerusalem and the temple were destroyed in 586 BC. Israel alone bore the responsibility, for God is "righteous in all He has done." No blame or fault could be attributed to Him.

Biblical Theology Comments

Two important theological truths emerge from this section: (1) for those who have sinned, Yahweh is a God of restoration (though not necessarily eliminating the consequences of one's wrong choices); and (2) prayer is the proper pathway to unlocking his compassion and forgiveness. Daniel's sincere contrition before God in prayer not only fulfilled a need historically (Israel's regathering from exile), but it stands as a model to believers of all times of what it means to seek God in the midst of divine discipline.

---

160. The words "the curse—the sworn promise" (lit., "the curse and the oath," הָאָלָה וְהַשְּׁבֻעָה, *hā ʾālâ wᵊhaššᵊḇuʿâ*) form a unique combination. Newsom (295) points out, "Although that phraseology is not used in the pentateuchal covenant traditions, the solemn and ceremonial making of the covenant (Exod 24:6–8; Deut 29:1 [28:69]) was understood to bind the people to obedience and to require them to accept as legitimate the enforcement of the covenant curses in case of persistent disobedience."

Application and Devotional Implications

Although Daniel's prayer in Dan 9:3–19 is specifically a prayer of national confession in keeping with the principles of blessing, curse, and restoration found in the Pentateuch (Deut 28–30), nevertheless there are principles we can all learn from his prayer that are applicable to personal sin and confession. These principles could be outlined as:

1. One should approach God in humility and sincerity, being careful to revere him as "the great and awesome God," a God to be taken seriously (9:3–4).
2. There must be an acknowledgment on our part that we are wrong—we have not merely made a mistake, but we have sinned in disobeying the will of God (9:5).
3. There should be an acknowledgment that though God had revealed his will to us, we are guilty of rejecting his counsel (9:6).
4. We should accept the fact and take responsibility for our sin by acknowledging that sin always has a price, and whatever consequences we suffer are simply what we deserve (9:7–11a).
5. We should admit that God's Word is right, and divine discipline is what we should expect from a God who is true to his Word—rather than using confession as a tool by which we hope to escape the consequences of our infidelity (9:11b–13).
6. Never should we blame God for any suffering we incur when under discipline or allow ourselves to be embittered against him (9:14). Only out of immaturity would we ever say, "O God, how could you allow this to happen to me?"

2b. Daniel's Prayer, Part 2: Petition for God's mercies and the restoration of Jerusalem (9:15–19)

Verses 15–19 of Dan 9 constitute the petition section of Daniel's prayer. Although elements of confession still surface in this section, the primary emphasis is upon petitioning God for what he wants him to do, namely to mercifully forgive the nation of its sin and to restore Jerusalem and the temple. The key motif of this petition, however, is the concern for God's *name*, i.e., his reputation in the eyes of the entire world. Reference to God's "name" is made at least three times in the paragraph (vv. 15, 18, 19), "for your own sake" is mentioned twice (vv. 17, 19), and several times Daniel states that the temple and city of Jerusalem are associated with God's name. Thus, the concern for God's "name" is the driving motivation for him to act. Newsom (296) points out that this is "developed through the frequent repetition of the second-person-singular possessive pronoun 'your.' The appeal refers to 'your people' (3x: vv. 15, 16, 19), 'your city Jerusalem,' 'your holy mountain,' 'your servant,' 'your desolate sanctuary,' and 'your city.'"

Textual Notes

17.a. The ending to the verse, לְמַ֖עַן אֲדֹנָֽי (*ləmaʿan ʾădōnāy*), is questionable.

LXX^{O}, LXX$^{\theta}$, S, and Vg. all have different translations. LXX$^{\theta}$, for instance, has ἕνεκέν σου, κύριε, "for your sake, O Lord," which would suggest a Heb. original, לְמַעַנְךָ אֲדֹנָי (*l^{ə}ma ʿăn^{ə}kā ʾăḏōnāy*). We have the very form לְמַעַנְךָ (*l^{ə}ma ʿăn^{ə}kā*) in v. 19. Goldingay (225) translates, "for my Lord's sake," assuming that the variant translations argue for the originality of MT. Most Eng. VSS, however, side with LXX$^{\theta}$.

18.a. The Kethib reading is פְּקֻחָה (Qal impv. masc. sg. with paragogic ה). Of the five other occurrences of the Qal impv. masc. sg. form in the OT, it is always without a paragogic ה. However, this seems to be a stylistic preference of the author in light of several imperatives with paragogic ה in v. 19. The Qere reading is פְּקַח.

Translation

9:15 And now, O Lord our God, who brought Your people out from the land of Egypt by a mighty hand[161] and made a name[162] for Yourself as *it is* this day. We have sinned and acted wickedly. **16** O Lord, according to all Your righteous acts,[163] let Your anger and wrath[164] turn back from Your city Jerusalem, Your holy[165] mountain. For on account[166] of our sins and the iniquities of our fathers, Jerusalem and Your people *have become* a reproach[167] to all those surrounding us. **17** And now, give heed, our God, to the prayer of Your servant and to his supplications, and restore Your favor[168] upon Your

---

161. The NET interprets the figure: "with great power." This is a commonly used expression to speak of God's bold intervention in human affairs (e.g., Deut 6:21; 9:26).
162. "Made a name for Yourself" is a literal translation of the Heb., but Goldingay's (225) "earned renown for Yourself" is an excellent rendition of this. The word "name" is a metonymy for one's reputation (or fame) and how one is known by others.
163. The pl. צִדְקֹתֶךָ (*ṣiḏqōṯekā*) looks at the mighty righteous acts of God, not his attribute of righteousness (though the former proceeds from the latter). Cf. Judg 5:11; 1 Sam 12:7; Mic 6:5; Ps 103:6.
164. Most Eng. VSS translate "anger and wrath" separately, but the NET has "raging anger," as the second term makes the first more emphatic.
165. In the expression הַר־קָדְשֶׁךָ (*har-qoḏšekā*), lit., "mountain of your holiness," the word קֹדֶשׁ (*qōḏeš*) is a genitive of attribute. Translate "Your holy mountain" (compare Pss 2:6; 15:1).
166. The prep בְּ (*b^{ə}*) on בַחֲטָאֵינוּ (*ḇaḥăṭāʾênû*) has a causal force. See BDB, 90 III 5.
167. חֶרְפָּה (*ḥerpâ*) means "reproach," but Goldingay's "objects of scorn" (225) captures the point very well. NET has "mocked by all our neighbors." Cf. Ps 44:14 (Heb.).
168. "Restore Your favor" is lit., "make Your face shine" (הָאֵר פָּנֶיךָ, *hāʾēr pānêkā*). This is an idiomatic expression that speaks of God extending his favor. This appears in Num 6:25 as a priestly blessing. In Ps 67:1 [Heb. 67:2] it is used in parallel with "being gracious and blessing," while in Ps 80:3 it is used in parallel with "restoring."

desolated[169] sanctuary for Your sake,[170] O Lord. **18** Incline Your ear, my God, and hear! Open Your eyes and look upon our desolations and the city that bears Your name![171] For not on account of our righteous deeds[172] are we presenting[173] our supplications before You, but on account of Your great[174] compassion. **19** O Lord, hear! O Lord, forgive! O Lord, give attention and take action! For Your sake, my God, do not delay, for Your city and Your people bear Your name!

Commentary

9:15–16 The words "and now" (וְעַתָּה, *wᵊʿattâ*) mark the transition from a confession of sin to an appeal for mercy. These two verses introduce the topic of God's "name." In days past, God "made a name for Himself" (i.e., glorified his name/reputation in the eyes of the nations) when he brought the Hebrew people out of the bondage of Egypt with a mighty display of power. The mention of the exodus event was significant, as Miller (248) has observed: "The reference to the exodus apparently was intended to call attention to Yahweh's role as the covenant-keeping God who delivered Israel from Egypt in order to fulfill his covenant promises to Abraham and to establish his reputation ('name') among the nations." Just as God made a name for himself in the past by his deliverance of his people from Egypt, Daniel's mention of it in his prayer was a subtle suggestion that God might once again show his power in delivering his people and restoring them to the land of promise. With the words "we have sinned and acted wickedly," Daniel is quick to add that any *stain* on God's reputation at the present time was not due to any fault of his or lack of power. Yes, Israel is seemingly disgraced before the nations and many will no doubt discount the validity or power of her God, but Israel bears the blame for that.

---

169. Collins (351) observes, "The word שמם is used in Dan 8:13; 9:26; 11:31; 12:11 with reference to the profanation of the temple. It is not peculiar to Daniel, however, as it is used with reference to Zion already in Lam 5:18."

170. See Textual Note above. LXX$^{\theta}$'s ἕνεκέν σου, κύριε (*heneken sou kurie*), "for Your sake, O Lord," suggests a Heb. original of לְמַעַנְךָ אֲדֹנָי (*lᵊmaʿănᵊkā ʾăḏōnāy*). Most Eng. VSS translate it this way (see Goldingay, 225, 228 to the contrary).

171. Lit., "the city over which Your name is called." The idiom implies ownership and identification with (cf. 2 Sam 12:28; Isa 4:1; Amos 9:12). Goldingay (225) suggests, "which bears your name." The reference is to the place specified in Deut 12:5 where Yahweh indicated he would put his name.

172. For the plural of צְדָקָה (*ṣiḏāqâ*) meaning "righteous acts/deeds," see BDB, 842 #7.

173. In this case, the Heb. verb נָפַל (*nāpal*) should be translated "present," as it occurs in a Heb. idiom (מַפִּילִים תַּחֲנוּנֵינוּ לְפָנֶיךָ, *mappîlîm taḥănûnênû lᵊpānêkā*) meaning "presenting our supplications before You." See BDB, 658 #6, and compare similar usage of the idiom in Jer 28:26; 42:9.

174. The Heb. adj. רַב (*raḇ*) means "much, many, great." In some cases it can have the idea of "abundant."

God's *name* was indelibly linked with the city of Jerusalem, because with the construction of the temple by Solomon God had caused his name to dwell there (cf. 1 Kgs 8:28–29, 43). Thus, restoration of the city and temple would bring honor to God's name once again. Newsom (296) adds, "The centrality of Jerusalem and the sanctuary in the appeal is striking, mentioned six separate times in these five verses." Daniel, of course, did not expect God to do this in some unjust way—the discipline of the exile was "according to all Your righteous acts" (and the exercise of his anger and wrath had been appropriate). Yet with the nation still in exile, Jerusalem and God's people had become a reproach—objects of scorn—to all the surrounding nations. Since God's name was linked with Jerusalem and the Hebrew people, then he, too, was mocked.

9:17–19 Having introduced the concern for God's name in vv. 15–16 and having appealed for God to turn away his anger and wrath, Daniel then asked God to restore his favor upon his city and people (positive emphasis). The words "our God" from the lips of Daniel are significant. Israel had gone into exile primarily because of her history of idolatry—she had turned to other gods. If there was to be a restoration for the nation, then she must once again return to the first commandment: "you shall have no other gods before Me." Yet reversal of the nation's discipline was not for her comfort or ease (much less what she deserved), but for the Lord's sake. God's interests and God's glory were the main motivation for him to act. As the psalmist cried out, "Why should the nations say, 'Where is their God?'" (Ps 79:10 NASB). The words "restore Your favor" are literally "cause Your face to shine on," an idiom for God to graciously act in a favorable way. Goldingay (254) explains:

> The metaphor presupposes first that a person's happiness shows in the brightness of his or her face (cf. 1 Sam 14:27, 29); then that this same brightness directed toward other people is an indication of regard and favor (cf. Job 29:24; Prov 16:15). In such passages, the expression is regularly used in association with words such as 'save,' 'bless,' and 'redeem,' the verbs characteristic of a lament's plea for God to act.

The main object in need of God's restoring favor is the desolated sanctuary, implying Daniel's hope that God will make possible the rebuilding of the temple that had been destroyed by the Babylonians in 586 BC.

Using vivid anthropomorphisms—"Incline Your ear" (i.e., listen attentively) and "open Your eyes"—Daniel acknowledged again the proper basis for God to act.[175] If God chooses to answer this prayer, it is "not on account of our righteous deeds" but rather because of his "great compassion." Whatever favor God might choose to render, it would be grace, for the nation was not

175. Regarding the expressions "incline Your ears ... open Your eyes," see 2 Kgs 19:16; Isa 37:17.

deserving of his kindness. Their only hope could be in his compassion (and fortunately for all, his compassion is abundant). Likewise, we today have no right to ask for anything until we see that we deserve nothing!

In the conclusion to the petition (9:19), Daniel utilized five successive imperatives to underscore the sincerity and urgency of his appeal to God. Notice that Daniel did not expect God to answer favorably apart from extending forgiveness. Then he repeated the main theme of the petition: God's city and people were linked with his name, and therefore he should act for the sake of his own reputation and glory. In his final appeal, Daniel pleads that God act quickly and without delaying (וַעֲשֵׂה אַל־תְּאַחַר, *wa ʿăśēh ʾal-tᵊʾaḥar*), a motif common to the psalms.[176]

Biblical Theology Comments

Under the entry for "Name" in *ISBE*, Hawthorne writes,

> In the Bible "name" is that title, label, designation by which a person, place, or thing can be known or marked out as distinguishable from another. More fundamentally, however, "name" is that which (1) reveals the true nature of its bearer (1 S. 25:25), so that to know the name is to know the person (Ps. 9:10 [MT 11]), or (2) designates the relationship that exists between entities, especially between God and His people (2 Ch. 7:14; Isa. 43:6f.).[177]

God's "name" is that which he is known for. This might refer to his character, his actions, or simply his reputation. In Isa 63:16, for example, the prophet declares, "You, O Lord, are our Father, our Redeemer from of old is Your name" (NASB). Of course, God was known for other things besides being the nation's Redeemer, but in this instance the prophet chose to highlight that aspect of *redeeming*. In the Psalms, Israel's hymnbook, the words "Your name" are mentioned forty-six times, underscoring the correlation between what God was known for and the praise he should thereby receive.

Above all else, God's name was to receive glory. In Ps 79:9 the psalmist cried out, "Help us, O God of our salvation, for the glory of Your name; and deliver us and forgive our sins for Your name's sake" (NASB). The psalmist understood that God's deliverance and forgiveness brought glory to his reputation. As God acted in loving loyalty and faithfulness to his covenant people, all the honor and glory went to him. Ps 115:1 (NET): "Not to us, O Lord, not to us! But to your name bring honor, for the sake of your loyal

---

176. Goldingay (254–55) points out, "Such an appeal to God not to delay acting closes off the pleas in Pss 40:18 [17]; 70:6 [5]. It recalls the 'how long ... ?' that features in the lament itself (Pss 6:4 [3]; 13:2–3 [1–2]; 74:10; 79:5; 80:4; 89:46; 90:13) and the positive plea not to delay, 'hurry' to help us (e.g., 22:20 [19]; 38:23 [22]; 40:14 [13]; 70:2, 6 [1, 5]; 71:12)."

177. G. F. Hawthorne, "Name," in *ISBE*, 3:480.

love and faithfulness." This was the spirit in which Daniel prayed and, in so doing, sought to move God to action.

Application and Devotional Implications

As pointed out in the commentary, the concern for God's "name" (his reputation, what he is known for) is the driving force behind the petition section recorded in Dan 9:15–19. One important aspect of God's "name" is his "great compassion" (v. 18). Although he is a righteous and holy God who acts against sin, he is also a God of incredible compassion. This means he feels for us and longs to be merciful to us. This is what leads him to deal with us according to *grace*, by which we are given what we do not deserve. Believers who humble themselves before God and properly confesses their sin will always find that God deals with them better than they deserve (even though consequences for sin may have to be faced). Knowing of God's grace, however, does not mean we have a right to demand *better treatment* by him. In fact, we have no right to ask for anything until we first see that we deserve nothing! Yet the grace and compassion of God can prompt us to petition God for outcomes that will bring glory to him.

3. God's response to Daniel's prayer (9:20–27)

The remainder of the chapter records God's answer to Daniel's prayer. God's response brings both good news and bad news. Yes, the present period of exile in Babylon is over. God will soon use Cyrus to issue a decree permitting the return of the Jews to Judah. By the year 516–515 BC, the temple will be rebuilt under the leadership of Zerubbabel (although it is doubtful that Daniel lived to see this). The bad news is that the present seventy-year exile has not been deemed sufficient to complete the desolations upon Jerusalem. A much longer time—seventy times seven years—will be needed for that. The Babylonian exile served to put an end to the nation's besetting sin of idolatry, but a much longer time period will be necessary for a complete cleansing of the nation's sins.

a. Gabriel's appearance to give Daniel insight (9:20–23)

Textual Notes

21.a. LXX has καὶ ἰδοὺ (ὁ) ἀνήρ (similarly Vg), which might suggest reading וְהִנֵּה ה', "then behold the man." Yet the MT makes sense as is, and the Greek translation may have simply been a way of emphasizing Gabriel's sudden intrusion.

21.b-b. Regarding מֻעָף בִּיעָף, although the Cairo Geniza and several MSS read instead מוּעָף, the greater question is whether the lemma of מֻעָף is יָעֵף ("to be weary") or עוּף ("to fly"). If the first option, then it applies to Daniel, but if the second, then it applies to the angel. Supporting the option of עוּף ("to fly") are the LXX, S, and Vg. LXX^{O} has τάχει φερόμενος, "being carried swiftly" (similarly S and Vg), while LXX$^{\theta}$ has only πετόμενος ("flying"). However, if the Hebrew root was עוּף, we would only find a מ prefix in the Poʿlel stem, along with duplication, i.e., מְעוֹפֵף (attested in Isa 14:29; 30:6). It is better, then, to understand מֻעָף as a Hopʿal passive participle meaning "wearied" (in regard to Daniel). So NET, NASB, and Goldingay (228). Compare Dan 7:28; 8:27; 10:8–9, 16–17 for similarity of experience by Daniel. Observe, however, that the NIV, ESV, and NRSV take the other option: "Gabriel ... came in swift flight" (similarly, Collins, "in flight," 345).

22.a. In contrast to MT's וַיָּבֶן ("and he gave instruction"), LXX$^{\theta}$ has καὶ συνέτισέ με ("and he caused me to understand"), which presumes a pronominal suffix form וַיְבִינֵנִי. LXX^{O}, on the other hand, presumes a different verb altogether: καὶ προσῆλθε ("and he came"), hence וַיָּבֹא, from בּוֹא. Yet MT's וַיָּבֶן is acceptable: "and he gave instruction and spoke with me."

23.a. The present text is quite abrupt: "and I have come to make known." Two MS versions have a prepositional phrase added: לְךָ ("to you"). LXX adds the pronoun σοι. The insertion of לְךָ is reasonable. Although the NRSV has "to declare it," most Eng. VSS add the word "you."

23.b. Although *BHS* editor proposes adding אִישׁ before חֲמוּדוֹת (hence "a man highly esteemed") in conformity with אִישׁ־חֲמֻדוֹת in 10:11 and 10:19, the shorter reading here is reasonable. "For you are highly esteemed." LXX^{O} (ὅτι ἐλεεινὸς εἶ, "for you are one shown mercy") appears to have misread the root חמד as חמל (the noun חֶמְלָה means "compassion, mercy").

Translation

9:20 Now while I was still speaking and praying and confessing my sin and the sin of my people, Israel, and presenting my supplication before Yahweh my God concerning[178] the holy mountain of my God— **21** while I was still speaking in prayer, the man Gabriel, whom I had seen in a vision previously in my extreme weariness,[179] came[180] to me at[181] the time of the evening offer-

178. The preposition עַל (*ʿal*) can be translated "concerning" (so NET, Collins, 345), "for" (NIV, ESV), or "on behalf of; for the sake of" (NASB, NRSV). For the latter, see BDB, 754 II f(c).

179. Regarding the translation of מֻעָף בִּיעָף (*muʿāp̱ bîʿāp̱*), see the textual note above. The evidence favors understanding מֻעָף (*muʿāp̱*) as a Hopʿal pass. ptc. (from יָעֵף, *yāʿēp̱*) meaning "wearied" (in regard to Daniel). Together, מֻעָף בִּיעָף (*muʿāp̱ bîʿāp̱*) is an intensification: "in my extreme weariness."

180. Lit., "touched, reached." Focus is on his arrival, though the ptc. in biblical Hebrew is timeless (tense is determined by context). Here it is punctiliar (so Goldingay, 228). English "came to him" best captures the idea.

181. Some Eng. VSS render כְּעֵת (*kᵊʿēṯ*) as "about that time" (so NASB, NET, NIV), but Goldingay (228) argues that it should properly be rendered "at the time" (so ESV, NRSV). The phrase כְּעֵת (*kᵊʿēṯ*) occurs 18x in the OT, and a survey of usage indicates

ing. **22** And he gave instruction[182] and spoke with me, saying,[183] "Daniel, I have now come forth to give you insight with understanding. **23** At the beginning of your supplication a message[184] went forth, and I have come to declare *it* to you,[185] for you are highly esteemed.[186] So consider the message and understand the vision."

Commentary

Once again Gabriel is used to help communicate and bring understanding to Daniel (recall Dan 8:16). It is possible, though not certain, that Gabriel appeared directly to Daniel rather than in a vision itself.[187] He is called "the man Gabriel" only to indicate that he appeared to Daniel in human form, for certainly he is an angelic being (cf. Luke 1:19, 30). If the translation "in my extreme weariness" is correct (some translations have "caused to fly swiftly," referring to the angel's speed), this might indicate that Daniel had been praying and fasting (cf. v. 3) for quite some time. Daniel acknowledged that in his prayer he had been confessing his sin and the sin of his people, Israel. This reflects that he considered himself a guilty party before Yahweh as well as a representative for the people. His prayer also was focused on "the holy mountain of God," the same phrase encountered earlier in v. 16 as a reference

---

that both "about" and "at" are acceptable translations (so BDB, 454d 3b). See Isa 8:23 for a good case of translating more precisely, the time *at which*).

182. Some commentators (e.g., Collins, 345) prefer to translate "and he came" (reading וַיָּבֹא, *wayyāḇō'*, with LXX^{O}) rather than "and he gave instruction" or "and he taught." See textual note above for discussion.

183. Lit., "and he said," but translated here as a ptc. introducing reported speech ("saying") for smoother Eng.

184. Heb. דָּבָר (*dāḇār*). Although commonly translated "a word," this can be translated in other ways depending on the context, e.g., "matter, thing, affair, command, report, utterance, decision, sentence (judicial)" (see BDB, 182–83 for discussion, although BDB itself opts for "word of command" (182b I 1b). Most Eng. VSS go with "word" (NIV, ESV, NRSV, and Collins, 345), while some go with "command" (NASB, NKJV), and the NET with "message." The latter is quite appropriate in view of the following context, though "decision" (BDB, 182c I 1h) is another possible choice. In reading vv. 24–27, it is partly a "decision" (Yahweh has determined *seventy years*) and partly a message (what will take place during that time frame).

185. For the addition of the words "to you" (לְךָ, *lᵉkā*), see textual note above.

186. "Highly esteemed" is a translation of the noun חֲמוּדָה (*ḥămûḏâ*), "desirableness, preciousness," from the verb חָמַד (*ḥāmaḏ*), "to desire, take pleasure in." NET: "of great value in God's sight." A fuller expression אִישׁ־חֲמֻדוֹת (*'îš-ḥămuḏôṯ*), "man of high esteem," occurs in 10:11 and 19, and in light of that, Collins (345) translates v. 23 "a beloved man."

187. Hartman (249) denies that a literal visitation by Gabriel occurred. He states, "The presentation of a revelation by an angel was a literary device used by apocalyptic writers."

to the city of Jerusalem. The repetition in Dan 9:20 suggests that Daniel's primary concern was with Jerusalem and its "desolate sanctuary."

Although Daniel still dwelt in Babylon and the temple sacrifices were not conducted at this time, v. 21 makes a point that Gabriel came "at the time of the evening offering" (probably meaning "at twilight"—lit., between the two evenings—according to Exod 29:39).[188] During the period of exile, some of the Jews used this as a time of prayer (cf. Ezra 9:5; Ps 141:2), and this was probably the appointed time of Daniel's evening prayer. Daniel's prayer was probably much longer than what is recorded in chap. 9, but in any case, Gabriel was dispatched to bring insight to Daniel, not *after* Daniel had finished praying but at the very beginning of his supplication. He learned from this that God's answer to his prayer was granted as soon as he began to pray, which is a reminder to everyone how eager God is to respond to the prayers of his people who come before him in faith, in humility, and with a contrite heart (cf. Ps 51:17 [Heb. 19]; Isa 57:15). As a result of Daniel's prayer, God responded by sending a "word" (דָּבָר, *dāḇār*) by way of Gabriel to Daniel. This is a very flexible term (see translation note above for discussion) that is probably best translated "word of command," or better yet "message" in this instance. This refers to all that is revealed in the following paragraph (Dan 9:24–27), since the final statement in v. 23 instructs Daniel to "consider the message (*dāḇār*)." As will be seen from a study of vv. 24–27, this message brought not only an assurance that the city would be restored and rebuilt but further revelation of what awaited the Jewish people and the city of Jerusalem in the distant future.

The words "to give you insight" (לְהַשְׂכִּילְךָ, *lᵉhaśkîlᵉkā*, from the verb שָׂכַל, *śāḵal*) reflect that Daniel would be like those mentioned in 11:33 who had insight among the people and could give understanding to those suffering persecution. As a personal encouragement to Daniel, Gabriel informed him that he was "highly esteemed." This translates a single word, חֲמוּדוֹת (*ḥămûḏôṯ*), meaning something very precious, treasured, or highly esteemed. To be thought of this highly would have been a great encouragement to Daniel.

Biblical Theology Comments

The name "Gabriel" is only mentioned four times in the Bible (Dan 8:16; 9:21; Luke 1:19, 26). That this is an angel of high position is confirmed in how he introduced himself to Zacharias, the father of John the Baptist: "I am Gabriel, who stands in the presence of God" (Luke 1:19). In Luke's Gospel Gabriel is sent to Zacharias to give him the joyful news that his wife will bear a son that will be the forerunner of Israel's Messiah, and then to Mary

---

188. A lot of discussion has gone into the interpretation of this expression, "between the two evenings." In general, this would be the late afternoon or early evening. *Tg. Onq.* said "between the two suns," which the Talmud explained as the time between the sunset and the time the stars became visible.

announcing that she (a virgin) will bear the Lord Jesus, the one destined to kingdom rule in fulfillment of the Davidic covenant promise. If these two appearances in Luke's Gospel are any indication, for Gabriel to be sent on a divine mission is of extreme importance. This reinforces the importance of Gabriel's appearance to Daniel to give him insight with understanding. The message Gabriel had for Daniel was of great importance and had enormous implications for the welfare and history of the nation.

Application and Devotional Implications

In the realm of mankind, those who are typically admired—society's heroes—are those who have made some great achievement or who possessed some great skill. For example, they might be some phenomenal sports legend like Michael Jordan or Babe Ruth. Or they might be some notable politician, famous actor, wealthy philanthropist, brilliant scientist, or courageous explorer. What draws the admiration of people is what they have done or achieved. While it is not wrong to applaud such achievements (especially record-setting ones), God has a different value system. Daniel was a man whom God considered "highly esteemed," yet he was not what the world might consider a hero. Rather, he was a man of faith, integrity, and prayer, values the world would hardly consider as praiseworthy. From an eternal perspective, however, those who receive the praise of God will be far better off than those who receive the greatest applause on earth. Why? Because God gives eternal rewards, and they don't necessarily go to great athletes, actors, and scientists. Rather, they go to men and women who lived lives of faith, persevered in prayer, remained faithful through trials, and glorified Jesus Christ while on earth. God's praise—"you are highly esteemed"—should be what every Christian longs to hear from the Master who will one day come again!

b. Revelation of the Seventy-"Weeks" Prophecy (9:24–27)

The seventy-"weeks" prophecy of Daniel 9:24–27 represents not only the greatest interpretative challenge to the book of Daniel but may possibly be the most difficult passage to interpret in all the Old Testament. J. A. Montgomery (400–401) went so far as to say, "The history of the exegesis of the 70 Weeks is the Dismal Swamp of O.T. criticism." There are so many books and articles treating this one passage that it is practically impossible for any one person to read, evaluate, and interact with everything that has been written. The challenges are immense, beginning with one's view of the dating of the book (which has led critical scholars to understand this as quasi-prophecy written after-the-fact (*vaticinium ex eventu*), namely with the evil rule of Antiochus IV Epiphanes in view. There are also the challenges of textual criticism, translation, understanding unique terms and concepts, and ancient chronological reckoning essential for a correct interpretation.

The most fundamental issue to this passage is the question of whether or not this is a messianic prophecy fulfilled in Jesus Christ. Critical scholars have argued that it is not, but rather that it describes events related to the rule of Antiochus IV Epiphanes (r. 175–164 BC). This issue will be discussed separately at point iii below. The position of critical scholarship is rejected, however, on two major counts: (1) a careful study of the date and authorship of the book (see "Introductory Matters") leads to the conclusion that the book was written by the historical person of Daniel in the sixth century BC; and (2) the mention of the *destruction* of the city and sanctuary in Dan 9:26 argues against a fulfillment in the second century BC, since no such event happened in that time period.[189] Early church fathers were virtually unanimous in seeing this as a messianic passage (discussed at point ii below), and most evangelical scholars today agree with this conclusion. Naturally, they do not agree on all interpretative details of the passage, but in general they view it messianically.

The other major interpretative challenge is in how to understand the chronological outworking of the "seventy weeks." Almost all scholars (both critical and conservative) understand that the word "week" (שָׁבוּעַ, *šāḇûaʿ*) is a unique Hebrew term meaning in this context a period of seven years (see point i below). Yet questions remain. Are these to be taken literally or symbolically? If literally, what is the *terminus a quo* and the *terminus ad quem*? Furthermore, are these seven-year segments of time continuous and uninterrupted, or can there be a hiatus (a gap of time) at some juncture? There are representatives from early church history as well as among modern evangelicals who believe there is a gap of time before the commencement of the final "week."

Because the treatment of Dan 9:24–27 is so lengthy, the following outline is provided:

Introductory Issues Regarding Dan 9:24–27
- i. The Meaning of "Week" (שָׁבוּעַ, *šāḇûaʿ*)
- ii. The Early Church Fathers on Dan 9:24–27
- iii. The View of Modern Critical Scholars on Dan 9:24–27
- iv. A Defense of the Messianic Interpretation of *māšîaḥ* (מָשִׁיחַ)
- v. Chronological Details Pertaining to Christ's First Coming
- vi. Survey of Views Regarding the Seventy "Weeks"
- vii. A Defense of Artaxerxes' Authorization to Nehemiah Original

Text
Textual Notes
Translation
Commentary
Biblical Theology Comments

---

189. Critical scholars try to escape the difficulty of this verse by arguing that the verb שָׁחַת, *šāḥaṯ* (normally translated "destroy") should be translated "corrupted" in this case (i.e., they corrupted—not destroyed—the city and sanctuary). For a refutation of this point, see the discussion under "Additional Exegetical Comments."

Introductory Issues Regarding Dan 9:24–27

i. The Meaning of "Week" (שָׁבוּעַ – *šāḇûaʿ*)

Israel's time of exile under Babylon had been seventy years (שִׁבְעִים שָׁנָה, *šiḇʿîm šānâ*), but this did not satisfy God's righteous anger against his people, nor did Israel yet have a "heart" for God (Deut 5:29). More time was needed before Israel's final restoration would be complete. This would take not seventy years, but seventy "weeks" of years, i.e., seventy times seven (cf. Lev 26:18 where God threatened to punish his disobedient people "sevenfold" for their sins). The term "week" (שָׁבוּעַ, *šāḇûaʿ*) as used in this context is a term unique to Hebrew for which English has no true equivalent. The term *šāḇûaʿ* basically means "a unit of seven," and when applied to *time* means seven periods of time, with the extent of each period being either clearly stated or implied from the context. In Dan 10:3 (Eng. v. 2) for example, we find the word used again but as "weeks of days" (שְׁלֹשָׁה שָׁבֻעִים יָמִים, *šᵉlōšeṯ šāḇuʿîm yomîm*), i.e., three seven-day weeks are in view. Most scholars (critical as well as conservative) agree that in the context of Dan 9, "weeks of years" are in view.[190] The timeframe, then, for the outworking of God's purposes as stated in Dan 9:24 must be seventy "seven-year periods" or seventy *heptads*. In its totality, this would be 490 years. As mentioned previously, though, not all would take these years literally.

There are a number of reasons that can be given in defense of the assertion that a "week" (שָׁבוּעַ, *šāḇûaʿ*) in this context means a period of seven years:

---

190. For discussion of "weeks" (שָׁבוּעַ, *šāḇûaʿ*) as seven years, see J. C. Whitcomb, "Daniel's Great Seventy-Weeks Prophecy: An Exegetical Insight," *GTJ* 2 (1981): 259–63; H. Hoehner, "Chronological Aspects of the Life of Christ: Part VI: Daniel's Seventy Weeks and New Testament Chronology," *BSac* 132 (1975): 47–65; and P. D. Feinberg, "An Exegetical and Theological Study of Daniel 9:24–27," in *Tradition and Testament*, ed. J. S. Feinberg and P. D. Feinberg, 189–220 (Chicago: Moody, 1981). Arguing that *šāḇuʿîm* means literal "weeks" rather than "units of seven," see G. F. Hasel, "The Hebrew Masculine Plural for Weeks in the Expression 'Seventy Weeks' in Daniel 9:24," *AUSS* 31 (1993): 105–18; and F. W. Hardy, "The Hebrew Singular for 'Week' in the Expression 'One Week' in Daniel 9:27," *AUSS* 32 (1994): 197–202. L. McFall, "Do the Sixty-Nine Weeks of Daniel Date the Messianic Mission of Nehemiah or Jesus?" *JETS* 52 (2009): 686–88, quite uniquely, has argued that each "week" is equivalent to a single year.

- The word *šāḇûaʿ* has been used in earlier biblical literature in the sense of "seven years." For example, in Gen 29:27–28 there is the case of Jacob who was willing to serve Laban for a *šāḇûaʿ* (seven years) in exchange for his daughter's hand in marriage.
- The term *šāḇûaʿ* is attested in other Jewish literature with the meaning "seven years." In the Mishnah, for example, we find this statement: "The Sanhedrin that puts to death one person in seven years (בְּשָׁבוּעַ, *bᵊšāḇûaʿ*) is termed tyrannical."[191]
- Daniel had been thinking in terms of years (Dan 9:1–2), so contextually this would be the most natural way to understand *šāḇûaʿ* at the end of the chapter.
- It simply is not possible for all the purposes of God mentioned in Dan 9:24 to have been fulfilled in 490 days or even 490 months. Furthermore, if "week" meant a period of seven days, then Dan 9:27 calls for a covenant being made for seven days (which is doubtful).
- The final "week" in 9:27 most likely means seven years. The covenant is broken in the middle, and the final period of three and one-half parallels the three and one-half years of Dan 7:25 (cf. Rev 11–13). (Admittedly, this argument assumes the same persons are in view in Dan 7:25 and 9:27, but see the commentary at 9:27 in defense of this.)
- The seventy years of captivity was a judgment for 490 years of failure to keep the sabbatical years. So, 490 years are assigned for the completion of Israel's desolations.

> The most convincing reason is that Daniel had been thinking about seventy years of captivity (Jer. 25:11; 29:10). Every year of exile represented a cycle of seven years in which the seventh year, the sabbatical year, had not been observed. Thus, the 70 years of captivity were the result of having violated seventy sabbatical years. This would have been done over a period of 490 years. Daniel now is given a prophecy of units of seven concerning 490 years (2 Chron. 36:21; cf. Lev. 26:33–35; Jer. 34:12–22).[192]

---

191. Mishnah 4 (נזיקין), *Makkot* (מַכּוֹת) 1:10. Cf. Babylonian Talmud (*Sanhedrin* 97a). For Jewish calculations of Dan 9:24–27 (both messianic and non-messianic) that assumed *šāḇûaʿ* meant "seven years," see R. T. Beckwith, "Daniel 9 and the Date of Messiah's Coming in Essene, Hellenistic, Pharisaic, Zealot and Early Christian Computation," *RevQ* 10 (1979–1981): 521–42. Montgomery (373) points out that *šāḇûaʿ* has the meaning "seven years" throughout Jubilees. At Qumran the concept appears in the "Rule of the Community," 1QS 10:7–8 (cf. *Dam* 16:4).

192. Feinberg, "An Exegetical and Theological Study of Daniel 9:24–27," 209.

- The Argument of Analogous Hebrew Usage

  The word *šāḇûaʿ* has an interesting parallel with עָשׂוֹר (*ʿāśôr*), which although normally meaning "ten days" can also mean "ten strings" or "an instrument of ten strings." Hence, the word עָשׂוֹר (*ʿāśôr*) must mean a "unit of ten" and only context determines whether it means "ten days" or "ten strings."

- The word *šāḇûaʿ* appears three times in the OT with the word "days" (יָמִים, *yomîm*) added, suggesting that *šāḇûaʿ* alone was not sufficient to indicate seven days. Hence, in Dan 10:3 [Eng. v. 2] we find שְׁלֹשֶׁת שָׁבֻעִים יָמִים (*šᵊlōšeṯ šāḇuʿîm yomîm*), which means three periods of seven days (= 21 days). Apparently, by adding "days" to the end, the author did not want his readers to think of the unit of seven the same way as in chap. 9.

ii. The Early Church Fathers on Dan 9:24–27

In a previous survey of the first five hundred years of church history, I identified eleven church fathers who commented, to one degree or another, on Dan 9:24–27.[193] Those who did so were Irenaeus (writing ca. AD 180), Clement of Alexandria (AD 200), Tertullian (ca. AD 203), Hippolytus (ca. AD 202–230), Julius Africanus (after AD 232), Origen (after AD 215), Eusebius (ca. AD 314–318), Apollinaris of Laodicea (ca. AD 360), Julius Hilarianus (ca. AD 397), Jerome (AD 407), Augustine (ca. AD 407–430), and Theodoret of Cyrus (ca. AD 433). I repeat here the conclusion to that study:[194]

> Not until rather late—with Irenaeus about A.D. 180—is the first substantial discussion of Daniel's seventy-weeks prophecy recorded. Surprisingly Justin Martyr in his *Dialogue with Trypho the Jew* (mid-second century A.D.) made no mention of it, whereas for many of the early church fathers this was regarded as a primary apologetic argument against Jewish unbelief. Also one must keep in mind that the early church fathers had limited access to accurate chronological information and understandably could not always correctly calculate the time periods. And sometimes they confused certain historical figures (e.g., Darius the Persian king for Darius the Mede).

193. J. P. Tanner, "Is Daniel's Seventy-Weeks Prophecy Messianic? Part 1," *BSac* 166 (2009) 181–200. To this can be added Theodoret of Cyrus, whose view was not included in this article. See *Theodoret of Cyrus: Commentary on Daniel*, trans. R. C. Hill (Atlanta: SBL, 2006), 239–61. R. J. Endresz, "Daniel: A Survey of Patristic Exegesis," *Phronema* 31 (2016): 123–52, came to very similar conclusions as my own in regard to the early church fathers, i.e., that Daniel was both prophetic and messianic (though they differed in the interpretation of certain eschatological details).

194. Tanner, "Is Daniel's Seventy-Weeks Prophecy Messianic? Part 1," 198–200; used by permission.

Yet from the literature that is available, some vital conclusions can be drawn. All the early church fathers, along with Jewish scholars, interpreted each "week" as a period of seven years and applied this quite literally (though Origen took the final week as seventy years, i.e., a week of decades rather than years). Significantly, of the eleven early church fathers surveyed in this study all but one of them held to some form of messianic interpretation of Daniel's prophecy (the lone exception being Hilarianus who held to a fulfillment in the time of Antiochus IV Epiphanes in the second century B.C.). Virtually all these saw the first sixty-nine weeks, if not the entire seventy weeks, as fulfilled at Christ's first advent (the exceptions being Hilarianus and Apollinaris, the latter viewing the seventy weeks as the time between the two advents of Christ). One of the other common points of agreement is that the 'most holy' in Daniel 9:24 refers to Jesus Christ.

Though most early church fathers took a messianic view of the seventy-weeks prophecy, they tended to favor a messianic-historical position, meaning that the entire seventy weeks was fulfilled at some point in the first century A.D. Only a few opted for a messianic/eschatological position in which the seventy weeks would not be completed until some future point beyond the first century, such as the reign of antichrist or the second advent of Christ. This latter position is found in Irenaeus, Hippolytus, and Apollinaris (all of whom were chiliasts). Related to this, Irenaeus and Hippolytus (along with Julius and Hilarianus) held to the six-thousand–year theory and expected the end of the age and the return of Christ about A.D. 500.

Despite their agreement about the messianic interpretation in general, they differed greatly in their interpretations of the details. Most of them saw the terminus a quo of the seventy weeks at some point in the sixth century B.C., either with Darius or Cyrus (some calculating on the basis of Cyrus' advent as king in 559 B.C. and others calculating from his conquest of Babylon in 539). As far as can be determined, the earliest church father to adopt a date in the fifth century B.C. was Julius Africanus, who opted for the twentieth year of Artaxerxes in 444 B.C. ... Others who followed him in this were Polychronius and Theodoret of Cyrus in the fifth century A.D. Julius' treatment of the seventy-weeks prophecy must have been held in high regard in the early church, as his view is the only one that is repeated by both Eusebius and Jerome.[195]

195. Zöckler remarks that the Venerable Bede (*De temporum ratione*) and Thomas Aquinas (in his commentary on Daniel) take substantially the view of Julius Africanus ("Daniel," 207).

Regarding the two references to מָשִׁיחַ (*māšîaḥ*) in Daniel 9:25 and 26, only rarely are these both understood as references to Jesus Christ. Eusebius in fact held that both refer to the line of high priests extending from the sixth to the first century B.C. Hippolytus said the one in verse 25 refers to Joshua the high priest at the time of the return from the Exile and the second one refers to Jesus. Origen, on the other hand, said the first one is Jesus and the second one is the high priesthood.

In their mathematical calculations very few church fathers identified the termination of the sixty-nine weeks with the death of Christ, ... Several church fathers (Clement, Julius, and apparently Hippolytus) said the sixty-nine weeks terminated with the birth of Christ or at the commencement of His public ministry. Only one, Julius, attempted to base his calculations on nonsolar years in light of Hebrew numeration and to adjust the total number of years accordingly (from 490 to 475).[196]

Regarding the final week in Daniel 9:27, not all discussed the matter of the sacrifices. Of those who did, some took the sacrifices literally but others (e.g., Hippolytus) took them spiritually, that is, as spiritual sacrifices by believers. Of greater interest was how they saw the relationship of the seventieth week to the sixty-nine weeks. Hippolytus, one of the few who did, viewed the final week eschatologically at the time when the antichrist will reign. For Clement, the hiatus was in A.D. 70 when Jerusalem and the temple were destroyed. Some church fathers understood that the one making the covenant in verse 27 is Christ (with the new covenant for the church), but many (e.g., Irenaeus) associated verse 27 with the antichrist (a dominant theme for many early church fathers) and related this verse to Daniel 7, Daniel 8, 2 Thessalonians 2, and Revelation 13.

Thus there was a strong consensus among the early church fathers (a near unanimous position, in fact) that Daniel's seventy-weeks prophecy was fulfilled in Christ, that is, they held a generally messianic interpretation of the passage. On the other hand they varied greatly in how they understood the details and how they based their calculations.

iii. The View of Modern Critical Scholars on Dan 9:24–27

In keeping with their general view of the book, critical scholars deny that the historical person Daniel of the sixth century BC wrote Dan 9:24–27. Furthermore, rather than seeing this as predictive prophecy of the coming Messiah, they see this as a description of various events during the Maccabean

---

196. To this can be added Theodoret of Cyrus, who in his *Commentary on Daniel* (249) also calculates the 490 years according to the Hebrew lunar calendar.

period when the Syrian ruler Antiochus IV Epiphanes sought to impose Hellenism on Judah and suppress Jewish observance of the Mosaic law.[197] Hartman (253–54) concluded that this passage was written during the days of Antiochus IV after he had desecrated the temple in 167 BC, but before the reconsecration of the temple in December of 164 (so Goldingay, 237).

Regarding the issuing of a "word" to restore and rebuild Jerusalem, Montgomery (379) takes this as the word to Jeremiah mentioned in Dan 9:2. He then interprets the second *māšîaḥ* (מָשִׁיחַ) in Dan 9:26 as the high priest Onias III who was killed about 171 BC, which leads him to understand the first *māšîaḥ* (v. 25) also as a priest, and hence, Joshua ben Jehozadak (though others have taken *māšîaḥ* as Cyrus the Great or Zerubbabel).[198] Montgomery reasons (379), "The interest of the writer lies, not in the legitimate royal line, still less in an accidental figure like Cyrus, but in the maintenance of the cult." Hartman is more specific about the "word" (Jer 29:10), which he says (247) "occurs in a letter written by the prophet in the reign of King Zedekiah of Judah (cf. 28:1), i.e. in the year 594 BC, to the Jews who had been taken as exiles to Babylonia in 597 B.C." For Hartman, then, the first segment (seven weeks) can begin in 594 or 586, as either would be "sufficiently close to the quasi-artificial figure of 'seven weeks' of years" (251).

There is a difference of opinion as to how to regard the numbers themselves (7 + 62 + 1).[199] Montgomery (391), for example, took all the numbers literally: "And that the present number is to be taken literally appears from its division, not into symbolical aliquot parts, e.g., 7 x 10, but into an irregular series, 7 + 62 + 1, a half-year within the last year also being specified." He viewed the "sixty-two weeks" as "the age between the Return and the epoch of the Maccabees" (380). He was very aware that this interval does not work out mathematically. Rather than 434 years (62 x 7), it is more like 367 years. Having argued for a literal interpretation of the numbers, Montgomery (393) chose to resolve the chronological difficulty by simply charging the author with an error in his historical understanding: "We can meet this objection only by surmising a chronological miscalculation on the part of the writer."

---

197. Notable critical scholars embracing this view include O. Zöckler (Lange's, 1870), S. R. Driver (Cambridge, 1922), J. A. Montgomery (ICC, 1927), R. H. Charles (1929), Hartman (AB, 1978), J. E. Goldingay (WBC, 1989), J. J. Collins (Hermeneia, 1993), and C. A. Newsom (WOTL, 2014).

198. Rather uniquely, M. Segal, "The Chronological Conception of the Persian Period in Daniel 9," *JAJ* 2 (2011): 300, takes the *māšîaḥ* of Dan 9:25 to be Nehemiah based on the chronological notices in *Seder Olam*.

199. For an attempt to understand Dan 9:24–27 in light of various Qumran documents concerned with chronological periods (namely the *Book of Jubilees*, the *Apocalypse of Weeks*, and 4Q390), see D. Dimant, "The Seventy Weeks Chronology (Dan 9,24–27) in the Light of New Qumranic Texts," in *The Book of Daniel in the Light of New Findings, Papers from a Conference at Louvain, August 20–22, 1991*, ed. A. S. van der Woude, 57–76 (Louvain: Leuven University Press, 1993).

Hartman, however, offers a different explanation. He thinks the author only intended the first segment (forty-nine years) and the last part (seven years) to be accurate and literal, but not the middle segment. Hartman (250) explains the author's approach: "He balances this by making the first section of the 490-year period 'seven weeks' or forty-nine years. The long middle section of 'sixty-two weeks' of years, or 434 years, is an artificial number, created for the purpose of bringing all three periods to a total of 'seventy weeks' of years."

In general, then, the first seven weeks cover the period 586–538 BC. Montgomery (379) explains, "The rites were suspended in 586, at the destruction of the temple, and were resumed 538 upon the Return, *i.e., circa* 49 years."

Critical scholars observe the *ʾatnāḥ* (Masoretic punctuation marker) in v. 25 and consequently put a break after the first seven "weeks," thereby beginning a new sentence with the sixty-two weeks. Yet this results in an assertion that the *rebuilding* takes sixty-two weeks (434 years). Observe, for instance, Goldingay's translation of Dan 9:25: "From the coming forth of a word to build a restored Jerusalem to an anointed, a leader, there will be seven sevens. For sixty-two sevens it will be restored and rebuilt, square and moat" (similarly Collins, 346, "For sixty-two weeks it will be built again with square and moat"). Montgomery (380) tries to escape the dilemma of this conclusion by arguing for an implied insertion, "Jerusalem shall be rebuilt *and remain so* for 62 weeks but in distressful conditions" (emphasis mine). In any case, Hartman (251) thinks the second segment (sixty-two weeks) refers primarily to the rebuilding of Jerusalem's walls under Nehemiah.

As mentioned above, critical scholars typically take the second *māšîaḥ* as the martyred high priest Onias III, assassinated by his Jewish rival at Antioch (cf. 2 Macc 4:23–28).[200] As for the "prince to come" in Dan 9:26, Goldingay offers this suggestion: "Presumably the 'leader to come' (נגיד הבא) is also a representative of the high-priestly line, one who follows Onias. The reference will then be to Onias' successor Jason (Bevan), who both corrupted and devastated ... the people of Jerusalem (see 2 Macc 4–5)." Montgomery (383), on the other hand, identified the "prince to come" as Antiochus. In either case, the "prince to come" is someone in the Antiochene age. As for "the people" with him, Montgomery (383) suggested that they were either Antiochus' army or the Hellenistic group; cf. 1 Macc 1:34, "and he [Ant.] put there [in Jerusalem] a sinful folk (ἔθνος)."

Identifying "the people of the prince who is to come" as an army or armed group in the Antiochene age, however, entails a grave problem for the entire theory held by critical scholars. Dan 9:26 says that they will "destroy the city and the sanctuary," which obviously never happened *literally* in the second century BC. Critical scholars attempt to escape this dilemma by arguing that the word translated "destroy" should be understood as meaning "corrupt" or "ruin." But this argument does not hold water (for a refutation,

200. So Montgomery (381), Hartman (251), and Goldingay (262).

see "The Meaning and Implications of *šāḥaṯ* in 9:26" under "Additional Exegetical Comments" at end of section).

Regarding the mention of "flood" at the end of Dan 9:26, Montgomery (383) explains this in regard to the end of Antiochus' life: "'His end in an overwhelming' refers then to the final catastrophe of Ant.'s life, the rt. שׁטף, of an overwhelming flood, being frequently used of the divine wrath, *e.g.*, Nah. 1[8], *cf.* Is. 10[22]."

The covenant mentioned in 9:27 consists then of a secular covenant initiated by Antiochus. Montgomery (385) understands the vague pronoun "he" as Antiochus, who makes a secular covenant with the renegade Jews: "The historical background of the sentence so interpreted is clear: the clever diplomacy whereby Ant. made his bargain with the worldly majority, at least of the aristocracy, in Jerusalem" (similarly, Hartman, 240, "he will make a strong alliance"). Elsewhere Hartman (252) elaborates, "The reference here is to the pact made between Antiochus and the renegade Jews who favored Hellenistic culture, as described in 1 Macc 1:11–14."

The reference to causing sacrifices to cease would then refer to Antiochus' defilement of the temple and halting of sacrifices for the final period (approximately three and one-half years) of his rule. As for the "abomination of desolation," Montgomery (388) concludes, "The phrase then refers to the installation by Ant. of rites to the Olympian Heavenly Zeus in the temple sanctuary, acc. to I Mac. I[54 59]."

iv. A Defense of the Messianic Interpretation of māšîaḥ (מָשִׁיחַ)[201]

Despite the overwhelming consensus of opinion throughout church history favoring the messianic interpretation of Dan 9:24–27, this interpretation has not only been challenged by critical scholars, but even more recently by some who claim to be evangelicals.[202] English Bible translations are mixed in how they render the term *māšîaḥ* (מָשִׁיחַ). Some translations (e.g., the KJV, NKJV, and NASB) use the word "Messiah" (capitalized) in vv. 25 and 26, clearly suggesting the promised Messiah of the Old Testament is in view. The NIV

---

201. Most of the material in this section is extracted from my article, "Is Daniel's Seventy-Weeks Prophecy Messianic? Part 2," *BSac* 166 (2009): 320–24, and used by permission. Slight modifications have been made to adapt to the formatting style of this commentary.

202. Examples of evangelicals rejecting the messianic interpretation of Dan 9:24–27 include J. Goldingay (WBC), T. McComiskey, "The Seventy Weeks of Daniel against the Background of Ancient Near Eastern Literature," *WTJ* 47 (1985): 18–45, and R. B. Chisholm, *Handbook on the Prophets* (Grand Rapids: Baker, 2002), 312–17. Goldingay is listed because the preface to the book claims that the commentary is *evangelical* (though he embraces the critical viewpoint).

translates both references as "the Anointed One," which, although a different translation, amounts to the same identification by the use of capital letters.[203]

In v. 25 the figure is referred to as מָשִׁיחַ נָגִיד (*māšîaḥ nāgîḏ*) and in v. 26 as simply מָשִׁיחַ (*māšîaḥ*). Theoretically it is possible that these expressions could be translated as something other than "Messiah," and it is also possible that two different individuals (at different points in history) might be intended. The question, however, is not what these terms might theoretically mean but what the author (both human and divine) *intended* by them.

The noun מָשִׁיחַ (*māšîaḥ*) is derived from the verb מָשַׁח (*māšaḥ*), meaning "to anoint." Anointing was a practice in the Old Testament for someone entering an office or important service for the Lord or for marking inanimate objects to consecrate them before the Lord.[204] For example, the first use of the verb מָשַׁח (*māšaḥ*) in the Old Testament occurs in Gen 31:13 in reference to the stone pillar at Bethel that Jacob anointed with oil to commemorate the place where God visited him in a dream and confirmed to him the Abrahamic promises. The stone pillar was no longer a mere rock; it now served as a witness to the vows the patriarch had made. Once anointed, these persons or objects were no longer *ordinary,* for they were now marked out for God's use and his purposes.

People who were anointed included the high priest, kings, and even (at times) prophets. The first anointing of a person occurred when Moses anointed Aaron as the first high priest (Lev 8:12). Subsequently, other high priests were anointed (16:32). Kings were anointed as rulers, as were Saul (1 Sam 10:1) and David (16:1, 13). Although anointing of prophets is rarely mentioned, Elisha was anointed by Elijah (1 Kgs 19:16).[205]

The noun מָשִׁיחַ (*māšîaḥ*), used of a person who is anointed, occurs thirty-eight times in the Old Testament. Although מָשִׁיחַ (*māšîaḥ*) was used of the anointed high priest, two observations are in order. First, *māšîaḥ* was only rarely used as a term to designate a high priest and was not used of a priest after Moses' day (confined to Lev 4:3–5, 16; 6:15 [Heb. 22]).[206] Second, in the

---

203. The NRSV, on the other hand, has "an anointed ruler" in v. 25 and "an anointed one" in v. 26 (both lower case). That a non-messianic interpretation is intended by the NRSV is made clear by the punctuation it uses in Dan 9:25, separating the seven weeks from the sixty-two weeks. The "anointed one" comes after seven weeks, which would suggest an individual in the sixth or fifth century BC. The NET and ESV are more ambiguous, using "anointed one" in lower case, which, while not necessarily rejecting the messianic interpretation, does not intentionally affirm it.

204. For detailed studies of מָשַׁח (*māšaḥ*) and its derivatives see John N. Oswalt, "משׁח," in *NIDOTTE*, 2:1123–27; and K. Seybold, "מָשַׁח," in *TDOT*, 43–54.

205. Other possible references to prophets as anointed ones include 1 Chr 16:22 and Ps 105:15, but these are subject to debate.

206. Although the noun form מָשִׁיחַ (*māšîaḥ*) *as a title* was restricted to occurrences in the Pentateuch, the verb מָשַׁח (*māšaḥ*) was used of Zadok, anointed as priest in Solomon's day (1 Chr 29:22), and the Pentateuch looks forward to anointing priests

few cases where it was used of a high priest, it always occurred in the format הַכֹּהֵן הַמָּשִׁיחַ (*hakkōhēn hammāšîaḥ*), "the anointed priest." Twice *māšîaḥ* (in the plural) was used of the patriarchs as recipients of the Abrahamic covenant (1 Chr 16:22; Ps 105:15). Only once was it ever used of a foreign king, namely Cyrus in Isa 45:1.[207] In most cases the word was used of the king who ruled over the theocratic nation, primarily of Saul and David. It would not be accurate to say that מָשִׁיחַ (*māšîaḥ*) in the OT never referred to "the Messiah." Because of the promises given to David that one from his line would ultimately have an eternal throne and kingdom (2 Sam 7:12–16), high expectation was placed on the Davidic kings as God's "anointed," with the anticipation that in one of them these promises would find their ultimate fulfillment. For example, in Ps 132:17–18 God proclaimed, "There I will cause the horn of David to spring forth; I have prepared a lamp for Mine anointed [לִמְשִׁיחִי, *limšîḥî*]. His enemies I will clothe with shame, but upon himself his crown shall shine." The clear reference to the Davidic covenant in v. 11 supports this interpretation.

Some verses that refer to David may also find their ultimate fulfillment in the Messiah. A case in point is Ps 2:2, "The kings of the earth take their stand and the rulers take counsel together against the Lord and against His Anointed (מְשִׁיחוֹ, *mᵉšîḥô*)," which Acts 4:25–28 clearly indicates has been fulfilled in Jesus. Indeed, he is the "anointed one" par excellence, being anointed by God the Father "with the Holy Spirit and with power" (Acts 10:38). Oswalt adds, "Even during intertestamental times rabbis were already understanding the unqualified references in the Ps to find their ultimate significance in this eschatological figure. ... Once the NT identified Jesus as the Anointed One, the Messiah, all the unqualified references to the 'anointed one' in the OT could be seen to have even more relevance."[208]

Still other verses include promises for the Davidic king that have their ultimate realization in David's greater Son (e.g., Pss 18:50 [Heb. 51]; 20:6 [Heb. 7]). Also, Isaiah anticipated the anointing of the servant of Yahweh in Isa 61:1, undoubtedly a messianic text. In light of the universal scope of the king's reign, Hannah's prayer finds its fulfillment in the Messiah. "The Lord will judge the ends of the earth; and He will give strength to His king, and will exalt the horn of His anointed [מְשִׁיחוֹ, *mᵉšîḥô*]" (1 Sam 2:10 NASB).

---

in generations after Aaron (Exod 30:30–31; Lev 16:32; Num 35:25). Cf. the expression בְנֵי־הַיִּצְהָר (*bᵉnê-hayyiṣhār*, "sons of [olive] oil") used of Zerubbabel and Joshua in the postexilic period (Zech 4:14).

207. Elsewhere the verb מָשַׁח (*māšaḥ*) was used of Hazael of Aram. in 1 Kgs 19:15. Elijah was to anoint Hazael as king, so that he might become a divine scourge on Israel. Yet he is not *titled* "My anointed."

208. Oswalt, "משח," 2:1126. A case in point is Ps 45:6–7 [Heb. vv. 7–8] ("God, Your God, has anointed You"), which the author of Hebrews understands as fulfilled in the Lord Jesus (Heb 1:8–9).

Thus, there is good evidence that the meaning "the ultimate Son of David" is within the semantic range of meaning for מָשִׁיחַ (*māšîaḥ*).

As already noted, this noun in Dan 9:25–26 does not refer to a high priest because the designation מָשִׁיחַ (*māšîaḥ*) for a high priest was not used beyond the Mosaic period, and whenever it was used it was always *clarified* by juxtaposition with the word "priest" in the articular expression הַכֹּהֵן הַמָּשִׁיחַ (*hakkōhēn hammāšîaḥ*).

Some appeal to Isa 45:1 to support their contention that the Persian king Cyrus is the מָשִׁיחַ (*māšîaḥ*) of Dan 9:25. But this seems improbable because the term *māšîaḥ* in Isa 45:1 is *clarified* by the juxtaposition of Cyrus' name with the term *māšîaḥ* (לִמְשִׁיחוֹ לְכוֹרֶשׁ, *limšîḥô lᵉḵōreš*). This shows that this foreign king is described by God as His anointed one. However, such clarification is noticeably absent in Dan 9:25.

In Dan 9:25–26 מָשִׁיחַ (*māšîaḥ*) is used in a unique way. Only here does *māšîaḥ* occur without the article and without any qualifying noun or pronoun. The more formal designation for the king of Israel was "Yahweh's anointed" or sometimes "My anointed" (1 Sam 2:35), "Your anointed" (Ps 132:10), or "His anointed" (1 Sam 12:3). In Dan 9:25, however, the one in view is designated מָשִׁיחַ נָגִיד (*māšîaḥ nāḡîḏ*), an expression that occurs nowhere else in the Old Testament. The expression is doubly unique. The noun נָגִיד (*nāḡîḏ*), which occurs forty-three times in the Old Testament, has a wide semantic range. It basically means "leader, ruler, prince" and is used most frequently for various kings of Israel (for Saul in 1 Sam 9:16 and David in 2 Sam 5:2). Several times נָגִיד (*nāḡîḏ*) is used of a priest (e.g., 1 Chr 9:20), twice of foreign rulers (Ps 76:12; Ezek 28:2), once of nobles (Job 29:10, in the plural), and a few times of military commanders (1 Chr 13:1) and tribal heads (27:16). Yet only rarely does the term occur in the prophets.[209] However, in Isa 55:4 the term נָגִיד (*nāḡîḏ*) is used in a prophetic reference to the Messiah. "Behold, I have made him a witness to the peoples, a leader (נָגִיד, *nāḡîḏ*) and commander for the peoples." Hence, both נָגִיד (*nāḡîḏ*) and מָשִׁיחַ (*māšîaḥ*) can refer to the Messiah, the promised Son of David.

The question, however, is how מָשִׁיחַ נָגִיד (*māšîaḥ nāḡîḏ*) should be understood in Dan 9:25. Is there anything in the preceding context that would qualify as a suitable reference to the Messiah? Of course, Dan 8 refers to Antiochus IV Epiphanes, and by way of typology to the antichrist himself. And the "little horn" is referred to in Dan 7. However, these are unsuitable candidates for *māšîaḥ*, because in biblical literature a *māšîaḥ* is always someone (as king or priest) who represents God or who acts as an agent to advance his covenant purposes. A suitable candidate in a previous chapter in Daniel makes perfect sense, namely "One like a Son of Man" to whom is "given dominion, glory and a kingdom, that all the peoples, nations, and men of every language might serve Him" (7:13–14).

---

209. In the prophets נָגִיד (*nāḡîḏ*) is found only in Isa 55:4; Jer 20:1; Ezek 28:2; Dan 9:25–26; and 11:22.

Daniel 9 is also linked to chap. 7 by similar temporal notices and by reference to the antichrist. Daniel 9:27 speaks of an individual who makes a covenant with Israel for a week but breaks it in the middle of the week. Since a "week" (שָׁבוּעַ, *šābûaʿ*) is a period of seven years—as virtually all scholars maintain, whether conservative or critical, and regardless of their eschatological persuasion, though some would treat it symbolically—then half a week represents a period of three and a half years. This corresponds precisely to the "time, times, and half a time" in 7:25 (i.e., three and a half years) in which the "little horn" of 7:8 is allowed to exercise his evil rule.[210] This is not mere coincidence; the same figure (the antichrist) is in view in both passages. This link, then, serves to support contextually the argument that the מָשִׁיחַ (*māšîaḥ*) of 9:25 is the "Son of Man" of 7:13, namely *the* Messiah.

v. Chronological Details Pertaining to Christ's First Coming

Having established that the term מָשִׁיחַ (*māšîaḥ*) in Dan 9:25 and 9:26 refers to *the* Messiah, the Lord Jesus Christ, and hence that the first sixty-nine weeks pertain to him, there is a need to establish firm dates for Christ's ministry and crucifixion as a prelude to calculating the timespan. Scholars have proposed dates for the crucifixion ranging anywhere from AD 26 to AD 36. The great diversity of opinion on this subject should caution us about being overly dogmatic, yet we can draw some reasonable conclusions from Scripture.[211]

The first factor to consider is that Jesus died in a year in which Passover (fourteenth of Nisan) fell on a Friday. Even though some have argued for the crucifixion on a Thursday (and some even on a Wednesday), most scholars agree that Jesus died on a Friday. Mark 15:42 states, "When evening had already come, because it was the preparation day, that is, the day before the

---

210. The word translated "time" (Aram., עִדָּן, *ʿiddān*) can mean time in general or a definite period of time, depending on the context. In Dan 4:16, 23, 25, 32 it means a definite period of a year. The word "times" in 7:25 is vocalized in the Masoretic text as a plural (עִדָּנִין, *ʿiddānîn*), yet there is good reason to regard this as a *dual form* ("two times"). As Montgomery notes (312), "The word is pointed as a pl., but the Aram. later having lost the dual, the tendency of M is to ignore it in BAram." Rosenthal, *A Grammar of Biblical Aramaic*, 24 adds, "The dual is preserved only in remnants. ... All other forms of the dual of the masc. noun, including those with pronominal suffixes, are identical with the pl. forms and not distinguishable from them." This is confirmed by the fact that the word "eyes" (עַיְנִין, *ʿaynîn*) in Dan 7:8 seems to be in the plural, though it would naturally be understood as dual. (The word for "hands" in Aramaic is יְדַיִן, *yᵉdayin*.) The best interpretation, then, of Dan 7:25 is that the expression "time, times, and half a time" means a period of three and a half years.

211. R. T. Beckwith, "Cautionary Notes on the Use of Calendars and Astronomy to Determine the Chronology of the Passion," in *Chronos, Kairos, Christos*, ed. J. Vardaman and E. M. Yamauchi, 183–208 (Winona Lake, IN: Eisenbrauns, 1989).

Sabbath" (NASB; cf. Matt 28:1; Luke 23:56; John 19:31). Furthermore, that the Friday of Jesus' crucifixion would have been the fourteenth of Nisan (the day of Passover) is clear from John 19:14, "Now it was the day of preparation for the Passover; it was about the sixth hour. And he said to the Jews, 'Behold, your King!'" (NASB).[212] Matthew tells us that darkness fell upon all the land from the sixth hour until the ninth hour, i.e., from twelve noon until three pm, and that Jesus cried out with the words of Ps 22:1 "about the ninth hour."

The ninth hour would have corresponded to the time the Jews were instructed to kill the Passover lamb. Yahweh instructed the people in Exod 12:6, "You shall keep it until the fourteenth day of the same month, then the whole assembly of the congregation of Israel is to kill it at twilight" (NASB). The word translated "twilight" is בֵּין הָעַרְבָּיִם (*bên hāʿarbāyim*), lit., "between the two evenings," a phrase that has given rise to much discussion. Deuteronomy 16:6 expresses this as "in the evening, when the sun goes down" (בָּעֶרֶב כְּבוֹא הַשֶּׁמֶשׁ, *bāʿāreḇ kᵉḇôʾ haššemeš*). Kaiser summarizes the primary explanations:

> ... "between the two evenings" ... is explained in two ways: (1) between sunset and dark (Aben–Ezra, Qaraites, Samaritans, KD) or (2) between the decline of the sun (three to five o'clock) and sunset (Josephus, Mishna, and modern practice). Deuteronomy 16:6 fixes the time at "when the sun goes down," the same time set for the lighting of the lamps in the tabernacle (30:8) and the offering of the daily evening sacrifice (29:39).[213]

More specifically, Josephus noted that it was the custom in his day to offer the lamb about three o'clock in the afternoon (*Ant.*, XIV, 4:3).

---

212. Some scholars hold the minority position that Jesus died on Nisan 15, since Jesus ate a Passover meal with his disciples on the evening before his crucifixion (see Mark 14:12). John, however, implies that the Passover meal had not yet been eaten at the time of Jesus' trial (18:28), which suggests that the day of Jesus' death was Nisan 14. D. A. Carson and D. J. Moo, *An Introduction to the New Testament* (Grand Rapids: Zondervan, 2005), 127, indicate a preference for Nisan 15; cf. C. J. Humphreys and W. G. Waddington, "The Date of the Crucifixion," *JASA* 37 (1985): 2–10.

213. W. Kaiser, "Exodus," in *EBC*, 2:373. D. Stuart (*Exodus*, 275) adds, "This was to take place 'at twilight' so that there would be enough light for the process of slaughter, which also involved skinning, removing entrails, tying up for spit roasting, laying the proper fire. The eating itself took place later, after nightfall (v. 8), when the moon was full (the fourteenth day being the middle of the twenty-eight day lunar cycle, thus the exact time of the full moon). So there was maximal nighttime light for gathering together and eating, and, as well, the timing would function in commemoration of the coming full moon nighttime flight from Egypt that characterized the exodus (vv. 11–13)."

In light of the above, the year of Christ's crucifixion must have been a year in which Passover (Nisan 14) fell on a Friday.[214] Based on several studies involving astronomy, Hoehner concluded that "the calculations of astronomers would limit the probable years of Christ's crucifixion on Friday, Nisan 14, to the years 30, 33, and 36, with A.D. 27 as an unlikely possibility."[215]

The year AD 27 can be ruled out, however, in light of Luke 3:1–2, which indicates that John the Baptist's ministry started in Tiberius' fifteenth year. Following a detailed study, Finegan concludes, "For Luke and his intended readers, therefore, it is most likely that the 'reign' of Tiberius meant Tiberius' own sole rule (from the death of Augustus, Aug 19, A.D. 14) and that this rule is to be reckoned in terms of the Julian calendar."[216] He goes on to explain that the fifteenth year of Tiberius would be equivalent to the full year January 1 to December 31, AD 29.[217] Hence, John's ministry began sometime during this year (AD 29), and Finegan reasons even further (taking into account a statement of Eusebius in regard to Tiberius' fifteenth year) that "Jesus was baptized and began his public ministry in the fall of A.D. 29."[218]

The next relevant issue is the duration of Jesus' ministry. Three Passovers are explicitly mentioned in the Gospel of John (2:13; 6:4; 11:55). After a lengthy discussion examining various theories for the duration of Jesus' ministry, Hoehner concludes:

> Therefore the three-year ministry of Jesus from the first Passover to the passion Passover is the most viable option. Of course, since Jesus' baptism and public ministry preceded the first Passover,

---

214. So Finegan, *Handbook of Biblical Chronology*, 353–58.

215. H. W. Hoehner, *Chronological Aspects of the Life of Christ* (Grand Rapids: Zondervan, 1977), 100. Cf. J. K. Fotheringham, "The Evidence of Astronomy and Technical Chronology for the Date of the Crucifixion," *JTS* 35 (1934): 160–61.

216. Finegan, *Handbook of Biblical Chronology*, 338. This date of August 19, AD 14 is affirmed by most modern scholars; cf. Chris Scarre, *Chronicle of the Roman Emperors* (London: Thames and Hudson, 1995), 27; and B. Messner, "'In the Fifteenth Year' Reconsidered: A Study of Luke 3:1," *Stone-Campbell Journal* 1 (1998): 202–5. E. L. Martin, "The Nativity and Herod's Death," in *Chronos, Kairos, Christos*, ed. J. Vardaman and E. M. Yamauchi, 85–92 (Winona Lake, IN: Eisenbrauns, 1989), 89, notes that surviving coins and inscriptions reckon Tiberius' reign from either January 1 or August 19, AD 14.

217. Finegan, *Handbook of Biblical Chronology*, 339.

218. Ibid., 342. Hoehner, *Chronological Aspects of the Life of Christ*, 43–44, concurs with Finegan on the beginning date for Jesus' ministry, as does D. Bock, *Luke 1:1–9:50*, BECNT, 284. Marshall, *Commentary on Luke*, 133, states, "Nearly all modern writers reckon from the death of Augustus on 19th August, A.D. 14. If the regnal years are counted inclusively from this date we arrive at AD 28/29, there being various minor differences among scholars regarding exactly when the fifteenth year would commence."

the total length of His ministry would be about three and a half years.[219]

Since there is no indication in the Gospels that Jesus' ministry lasted six years, the year AD 36 for Christ's crucifixion is most improbable. Furthermore, a three-and-a-half-year public ministry beginning in the fall of AD 29 essentially rules out the possibility of Christ's crucifixion in the year AD 30.[220] Hence, the crucifixion of Jesus can be reasonably dated to the month Nisan in the year AD 33. Fotheringham, Hoehner, Maier, Finegan, Steinmann, and Köstenberger are all in agreement with this conclusion.[221] Since the day of

---

219. Hoehner, *Chronological Aspects of the Life of Christ*, 60.

220. Not all scholars rule out the AD 30 date. Carson and Moo, *An Introduction to the New Testament*, 126–27, for instance, admit that the two most viable dates for the crucifixion are AD 30 and AD 33. Although they date Jesus' baptism to AD 28 or 29 (based on Luke 3:1), they hold to a shorter duration of Christ's ministry and prefer the view that Jesus died on Nisan 15 rather than the 14th, and therefore conclude that "the A.D. 30 date is slightly preferable" (127). Archer (114) also holds to the AD 30 date for the crucifixion; cf. L. A. Foster, "The Chronology of the New Testament," in *EBC*, 1:598–99, 607; and J. P. Meier, "A Chronology of Jesus' Life," in *A Marginal Jew: Rethinking the Historical Jesus*, vol. 1, *The Roots of the Problem and the Person*, ABRL (New York: Doubleday, 1991), 372–433.

Yet the statement in John 2:20 at the time of Christ's cleansing of the temple during the first Passover of his public ministry argues against the AD 30 date. In this verse the Jews state that "it took forty-six years to build this temple" (ναὸς, *naos*), or it could be translated differently to indicate it had been built forty-six years ago. Hoehner, *Chronological Aspects of the Life of Christ*, 42, argues that the aorist passive verb in John 2:20 (οἰκοδομήθη, *oikodomēthē*) should be understood as an effective or perfective aorist looking at the results of the action, namely the temple has stood as a completed building for forty-six years. Finegan, *Handbook of Biblical Chronology*, 348, argues that this refers to the temple *edifice* (not the entire temple precinct), which had been completed under Herod the Great in 18/17 BC (cf. Josephus, *Ant.* 15:354; 15:380; and 15:421). According to Finegan and Hoehner, this would bring the date to AD 29/30, and would mean that Jesus' first Passover was the spring of AD 30. Yet he was obviously not crucified at that occasion. Köstenberger, *John*, 109, comes to the same conclusion: "Forty-six years later is A.D. 29/30 ... , which places Jesus' first Passover in the spring of A.D. 30," and he adds in a footnote (29), "Assuming a three-year ministry, we see that this puts the crucifixion at A.D. 33."

221. Fotheringham, "The Evidence of Astronomy," 161; Hoehner, *Chronological Aspects of the Life of Christ*, 111; P. L. Maier, "The Date of the Nativity and the Chronology of Jesus' Life," in *Chronos, Kairos, Christos: Nativity and Chronological Studies Presented to Jack Finegan*, ed. J. Vardaman and E. M. Yamauchi, 113–30 (Winona Lake, IN: Eisenbrauns, 1989), 125; J. Finegan, *Handbook of Biblical Chronology*, 368; A. Steinmann, *From Abraham to Paul* (St. Louis, MO: Concordia, 2011), 281; and A. J. Köstenberger, "The Date of Jesus' Crucifixion," in *ESV Study*

Passover occurs at the time of the full moon (which can be astronomically calculated), we can reasonably conclude that Jesus' crucifixion took place on April 3 of the year AD 33.[222]

In conclusion, Jesus was baptized by John the Baptist and began his public ministry in the fall of AD 29, his first Passover appearance mentioned in John 2:13 took place in the spring of AD 30, and his crucifixion occurred on April 3, AD 33.

vi. Survey of Views Regarding the Seventy "Weeks"[223]

Although there is a consensus that the seventy "weeks" are to be understood as *weeks of years* (and hence a total of 490 years), there is great diversity on the interpretation of the details and what timespans the segments (7 + 62 + 1) represent. In general, the interpretations can be divided into two major categories, messianic and non-messianic, the latter including the general Jewish view. The three non-messianic views will be surveyed first.

(a) Roman Destruction View (AD 70)

Adherents. This is generally a Jewish view. Representatives include Saadia, Rashi, Ibn Ezra, and Nahmanides, as well as the Seder Olam Rabbah.[224]

Description. This view sees the prophecy culminating with the destruction of the second temple in AD 70 (or possibly as late as AD 135 when the Bar Kokhba revolt was quashed). The "word/decree" in Dan 9:25 is that of Cyrus. The first seven weeks

---

Bible, ed. W. Grudem, 1809–10 (Wheaton: Crossway, 2008), 1809–10. Cf. C. J. Humphreys and W. G. Waddington, "The Jewish Calendar," *TynBul* 43 (1992): 339–40, 350. Also taking the AD 33 date is P. Keresztes, *Imperial Rome and the Christians*, vol. 1, *From Herod the Great to about 200 A.D.* (Lanham, MD: University Press of America, 1989) 36–38.

222. H. H. Goldstine, *New and Full Moons 1001 B.C. to A.D. 1651*, 87. So Fotheringham, "The Evidence of Astronomy," 161.

223. This commentary will only be concerned with the major views of Daniel's seventy weeks prophecy, not minor views held by only a very few. For example, P. Mauro (*The Seventy Weeks and the Great Tribulation*) held a first century messianic literal view, but understood the "decree" of Dan 9:25 to refer to Cyrus' decree. He claimed that there are sixty-nine "weeks" of years (483 years) from Cyrus' decree (normally dated ca. 539/38 BC) until Jesus Christ, in defiance of all known chronology.

224. For some elaboration of Jewish interpretations, see Rabbi H. Goldwurm, *Daniel*, 259–66; also G. Sigal, *The 70 Weeks of Daniel (9:24–27)*. R. Chazan, "Daniel 9:24–27: Exegesis and Polemics," in *Contra Judaeos: Ancient and Medieval Polemics Between Christians and Jews*, ed. O. Limor and G. G. Stroumsa (Tübingen: Mohr, 1996), 143–59, provides a very helpful survey comparing and contrasting the treatment of Dan 9:24–27 by Saadia and Nahmanides. Chazan's article focuses on the arguments that both Saadia and Nahmanides utilized in their efforts to refute the Christian messianic interpretation of Dan 9:24–27.

are equated with the time from Jerusalem's destruction until 538 BC, while the next sixty-two weeks are the time in the land until the first Jewish revolt in the AD 60s. The final week represents the years leading up to Jerusalem's destruction in AD 70. The "anointed one" in v. 25 is usually understood as Cyrus, while the "anointed one" in v. 26 is thought to be King Agrippa at the time of the AD 70 event (so Rashi). The one making the covenant in v. 27 represents the Romans in the first century AD.

Evaluation. As with any of the non-messianic views, this view faces a problem in properly understanding the term *māšîaḥ* (מָשִׁיחַ). See section iv above. Furthermore, the period from 538 BC until the AD 60s is far too long to be "sixty-two weeks" (434 years), unless one resorts to "symbolic numbers" (yet notice that the first and final segments are understood literally).

(b) The Maccabean View

This is the view (non-messianic) held by most critical scholars today (including Goldingay). This view is described at length in section iii above. In general, most details of the passage are said to be fulfilled in the Maccabean era during the reign of Antiochus IV Epiphanes (i.e., during the years 171–164 BC).

Evaluation. (1) This view fails to do justice to the term *māšîaḥ* (מָשִׁיחַ). See section iv above. (2) Though the first and third segments (weeks of years) are taken literally, the second segment of sixty-two weeks has to be spiritualized, since the period from 538/536 BC to 171/70 BC is not 434 years, but approximately 367 years. (3) This view does not do adequate justice to the goals of the seventy "weeks" as laid out in Dan 9:24. (4) The argument that *šāḥaṯ* in 9:26 (normally translated "destroy") means "corrupt" or "ruin" is not convincing (for a refutation, see "The Meaning and Implications of *šāḥaṯ* in 9:26" under "Additional Exegetical Comments" at end of this section). Simply put, Antiochus did not *destroy* the city of Jerusalem and the sanctuary.

(c) The Maccabean Double Fulfillment View

Adherent. R. B. Chisholm (though his view has similarities to that of T. E. McComiskey).[225]

Description. This is another non-messianic view. Chisholm understands the "word/decree" in Dan 9:25 to refer to the *announcement* made to Jeremiah in Jer 30:18 (ca. 597–586 BC). He appeals to Isa 45:1, where Cyrus is called "anointed one," to establish that the word *māšîaḥ* does not always have to refer to

225. See Chisholm, *Handbook on the Prophets*, 313–17; and McComiskey, "The Seventy 'Weeks' of Daniel," 18–45.

the Messiah. He claims (following McComiskey) that the Hebrew grammar demands that the seven weeks be separated from the sixty weeks. Thus it is not sixty-nine (7 + 62) weeks until "Messiah the prince," but seven weeks (ca. 49 years) until "*māšîaḥ* the prince/ruler" (i.e., Cyrus). He would see the first seven weeks as the period from the announcement to Jeremiah (ca. 597–586 BC) until Cyrus' conquest of Babylon in 539 BC. For him, the next sixty-two weeks are not literal, but extend from 539 BC until Antiochus (r. 175–164 BC). The final week is the period of approximately seven years that Antiochus persecutes Israel, beginning with the murder of the high priest, Onias III, ca. 171 BC. Although the prophecy finds fulfillment with Antiochus, Chisholm claims that this has double fulfillment with the antichrist. Hence, although the prophecy is not messianic, it is ultimately eschatological.

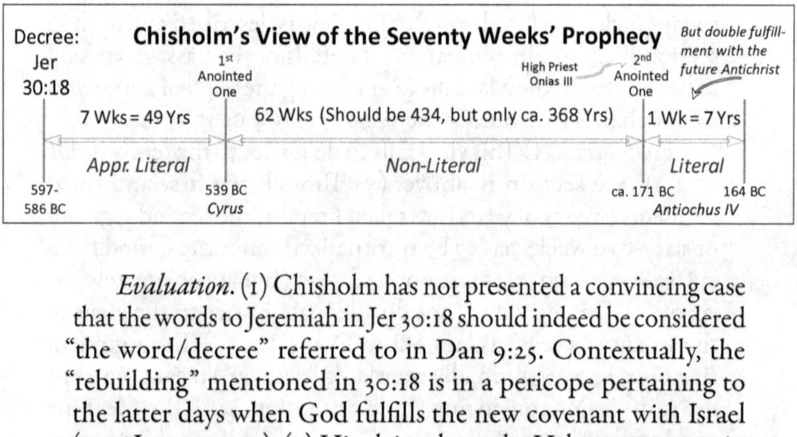

Evaluation. (1) Chisholm has not presented a convincing case that the words to Jeremiah in Jer 30:18 should indeed be considered "the word/decree" referred to in Dan 9:25. Contextually, the "rebuilding" mentioned in 30:18 is in a pericope pertaining to the latter days when God fulfills the new covenant with Israel (note Jer 30:22, 24). (2) His claim about the Hebrew grammar in Dan 9:25 pertains to a punctuation device, not the actual words of the text. This punctuation device (*'aṯnāḥ*) was not part of the original inspired text but was added centuries after Christ by some Jewish scribes known as the Masoretes. (See the section under "Additional Exegetical Comments," "The Placement of the *Athnach* in 9:25.") (3) In Chisholm's view, some of the numbers are literal while others are not. The first seven weeks (49 years) are approximately literal, the sixty-two are clearly not, and the final week (seven years) is literal.[226] Not only has he failed to establish

226. In defense of a symbolic view of the numbers, Chisholm (317) states, "The image of seventy units of seven (or 'weeks') is probably calendrical, with the symbolism of seven and seventy suggesting completeness. The symbolic use of the number seven and of multiples of seven in the ancient Near East is well-attested."

that all the numbers should not be taken literally, but he has not even been consistent in how he has regarded them.

(d) First-Century Messianic Symbolic View

Adherents. Most of those taking this view hold to an amillennial eschatology: E. J. Young, M. Kline, and A. Hoekema.

Description. This is a messianic view which sees all the details of the prophecy fulfilled in the first coming of Christ (admittedly the more dominant view in the early church), though not taking all the numbers literally. The reference to *māšîaḥ* in both Dan 9:25 and 26 is understood as a reference to Jesus Christ. Yet he is also said to be the one making a covenant with God's people in v. 27. The initial "word/decree" is thought to be that of Cyrus about 538 BC (Ezra 1:1–4; 6:3–5). Key to this view is a spiritualizing of the numbers (7 + 62 + 1). Hence, the first seven weeks represent the time from the decree in 538/37 BC until the completion of the work by Ezra and Nehemiah (obviously more than seven literal "weeks"). The next sixty-two weeks extend further to the first advent of Christ. The "prince/leader to come" refers to Titus according to Young, but to Jesus Christ according to Kline. The final week occurs in the first century AD, with the crucifixion taking place in the middle of the week, whereby Jesus Christ makes a covenant with the church ("ratified" at the time of the crucifixion). In doing so, Jesus de-legitimizes the sacrificial system. The latter half of the final week comes "later." Young and Hoekema see this fulfilled with Titus in AD 70, while Kline takes it as an eschatological judgment.

Evaluation. Although this is (correctly) a messianic view, there are problems. (1) This view fails to do justice to the six purposes mentioned in Dan 9:24 (they simply are not all fulfilled by the time of the first century). (2) This view fails to substantiate that the time segments should be treated non-literally, especially since the seventy years of exile were literal. (3) The claim that Christ is the one making the covenant in v. 27 fails on the basis that he did not put an end to sacrifice and offering (to say that he de-legitimizes the sacrificial system is to spiritualize the meaning of these words).

(e) First-Century Messianic Literal View

Adherents.[227] G. Hasel, J. B. Payne, R. J. M. Gurney, P. J. Gentry, and J. T. Parry.

---

227. See G. Hasel, "The Seventy Weeks of Daniel 9:24–27," *Ministry* 49 (1976): 5D–23D; J. B. Payne, "The Goal of Daniel's Seventy Weeks," *JETS* 21 (1978): 97–115; R. J. M. Gurney, "The Seventy Weeks of Daniel 9:24–27," *EvQ* 53 (1981): 29–36; P. J.

Description. This messianic view also understands the prophecy to be completely fulfilled in the first century, but unlike the previous view, this one takes the numbers literally. The *terminus a quo* of the "word/decree" in Dan 9:25 is said to commence with the decree to Ezra in 458 BC (so Gurney and Payne) or 457 BC (Hasel, Gentry, and Parry). The first sixty-nine "weeks" (483 years) then run to the time of the baptism of Jesus (AD 26 according to Gurney and Payne, but AD 27 according to Hasel, Gentry, and Parry).

The final "week" or seven years begins with Jesus' baptism and is marked by the crucifixion of Christ in the middle of the week (AD 30 according to Gurney, but AD 31 for Hasel, Gentry, and Parry). The last half of the final "week" extends into the first few years of the early church, culminating in AD 33, when the early church was driven from Jerusalem (Payne, 109, 114) and Paul was commissioned as the apostle to the Gentiles (Gurney, 34). The latter supposedly represents the culmination of Christ's work of establishing the new covenant. For Gurney, by the end of the final week "the Jews themselves were rejected from being God's special, chosen people." Hasel (14–16) counts from 457 BC to AD 27 for the first sixty-nine "weeks." Yet he places Christ's crucifixion at AD 31 (a year in which Nisan 14 did not fall on a Friday!), and understands AD 34 as the time when the "last half of the week comes to an end with (1) the death of Stephen (Acts 9:1), (2) the scattering of the Christians from Jerusalem, (3) the carrying of the gospel to the Gentiles and possibly (4) the conversion of Paul."[228] Gentry, however, understands the latter portion of Dan 9:27—which for him is parallel to 9:26b—not as the immediate three and one-half years following the crucifixion but rather as the period leading up to AD 70 and the Jews themselves being the ones committing the abomination of desolation, i.e., certain Jewish zealots were responsible for the destruction of the city and sanctuary.[229]

Evaluation. Commendably, this view does take *māšîaḥ* in both Dan 9:25 and 26 as a reference to Jesus Christ and does attempt to treat the "weeks" literally. Yet to claim that Christ is the one who makes the covenant with Daniel's people in v. 27, following which he puts an end to sacrifice and offering, is not convincing. If the covenant of v. 27 is supposedly the "new

---

Gentry, "Daniel's Seventy Weeks and the New Exodus," *SBJT* 14 (2010): 26–44; and, J. T. Parry, "Desolation of the Temple and Messianic Enthronement in Daniel 11:36–12:3," *JETS* 54 (2011): 485–526.

228. Hasel, "The Seventy Weeks of Daniel 9:24–27," 16.

229. Gentry, "Daniel's Seventy Weeks and the New Exodus," 38–40.

covenant," why would the text say that Christ makes this covenant for "one week"? The latter part of v. 27 concerning the "wing of detestable idols" (or "wing of abominations," NASB) and one who desolates seems nonsensical to this view. What would this have to do with the three and a half years following the crucifixion? Finally, to argue that the "word/decree" to restore and rebuild Jerusalem is the decree to Ezra in 458/57 BC and that the year of crucifixion is AD 30 or 31 is very problematic—see evaluation below for "Messianic Postponement View" (solar-year calculation).

(f) Messianic Symbolic-Eschatological View

Adherents. T. Kliefoth,[230] C. F. Keil, H. C. Leupold.

Description. Like the preceding, this also is a messianic view. The reference to *māšîaḥ* in both Dan 9:25 and 26 is understood as a reference to Christ. However, in this view only part of the details are fulfilled in the first coming of Christ, whereas other details await His second coming. The seventy "weeks" are *symbolic* of three periods, and the "word/decree" is that of Cyrus about 538 BC. Then the first seven "weeks" symbolize the period from Cyrus until Christ's first coming, the next sixty-two "weeks" symbolize the present age as the "spiritual Jerusalem" now being built, and the final "week" pertains to the antichrist in the future. Leupold takes the covenant of Dan 9:27 as one made in imitation of Christ and imposed upon the masses. Keil understands that the covenant is made to deceive people to follow him (the antichrist) as God.

Evaluation. By taking a consistently symbolic approach, this allows the interpreter to make the numbers mean whatever he wants them to mean. However, this is not in keeping with a historical-grammatical-literal hermeneutic, where words should be understood to mean what the author meant them to mean. Those taking this view not only symbolize the numbers, but they also symbolize Jerusalem (which for Daniel was clearly the literal physical city that he had prayed for) to mean a spiritual Jerusalem, namely the church. Then the antichrist is said to hate and persecute this latter city and temple. Finally, this view takes as its *terminus a quo* the decree of Cyrus in 538 BC (see Ezra 1:1–4; 6:3–5). However, a close examination of these passages reveals that the decree of Cyrus concerned the temple, not the rebuilding of the city. Furthermore, within forty-nine years (seven "weeks" of

---

230. T. Kliefoth, *Das Buch Daniels* (Schwerin: Sandmeyer, 1868), is said to be the first to establish exegetically the symbolic interpretation, and he is followed in this by both Keil and Leupold (all Lutheran exegetes).

years) of this decree, i.e., by about 489 BC, the city of Jerusalem was obviously not rebuilt and restored.

(g) Messianic Postponement View (Solar-Year Calculation)

The final two views are both messianic and take the final "week" to refer to a seven-year period of time preceding Christ's return when the antichrist reigns. They take the time segments literally, but differ in how they calculate the time involved and in what they regard the "word/decree" of Dan 9:25 to refer to.

Adherents. L. Wood, G. L. Archer, and S. R. Miller.

Description. This is a literal approach that understands the "word/decree" of Dan 9:25 as referring to a decree of Artaxerxes to Ezra about the year 458–457 BC. The first seven "weeks" are understood as the period 458/457–409/408 BC when presumably the city of Jerusalem and its walls were being rebuilt (under Ezra and Nehemiah). Assuming the "years" are meant to be understood as *solar years*, sixty-nine weeks of years (7 + 62 = 483 years) from 458/457 BC would extend to AD 27/26, which they would view as the beginning of Jesus' public ministry.[231] Miller (265) defends the notion that the coming of the Messiah refers to Jesus' baptism, stating that this "is the most likely choice since it was at that time that Jesus officially took upon himself the role of the Messiah and began his public ministry." The final "week" does not immediately follow the first sixty-nine weeks, but is postponed. It is fulfilled when the antichrist makes a covenant with the Jewish people (v. 27) that initiates the final seven years leading up to Christ's return. The "desolation" mentioned in v. 27 refers to antichrist halting the literal sacrificial system in a rebuilt Jewish temple during the tribulation period, followed by his three and one-half year reign of terror described in the book of Revelation and elsewhere.

Evaluation. While there are several commendable things about this view (being literal, messianic, and yet eschatological), it nevertheless has considerable problems. First, there is no mention in the Ezra passage of Artaxerxes authorizing the rebuilding of the city (Ezra 7:12–26), but rather the decree permits a return of the Jews "to adorn the house of the LORD which is in Jerusalem" (Ezra 7:27). Second, and of greater weight, this view relies entirely on the dates for Christ's ministry of AD 26/27 for his baptism and AD 30 for his crucifixion. Although these dates have been advocated by some New Testament scholars in the past, they are generally rejected today and cannot be reconciled with the chronological

231. Wood (253) and Miller (266) understand the sixty-nine "weeks" of years to run from 458 BC to AD 26, whereas Archer (114) suggests the dates 457 BC to AD 27.

notices in the New Testament (noticeably Luke 3:1–2 and John 2:20). As argued in section v above ("Chronological Details Pertaining to Christ's First Coming"), the crucifixion most likely took place in the month Nisan of AD 33.

(h) Messianic Postponement View (Prophetic-Year Calculation)

This view is similar to the preceding but takes as its *terminus a quo* the authorization to Nehemiah in 444 BC and bases its calculations on "prophetic years" (having 360 days) rather than solar years. As with the preceding view, the final "week" is taken to be the seven years prior to Christ's return when the antichrist makes a covenant with Israel.

Adherents. R. Anderson, A. J. McClain, J. Walvoord, C. L. Feinberg, P. Feinberg, H. W. Hoehner, J. D. Pentecost, and J. P. Tanner.

Description. This is a literal approach that understands the "word/decree" of Dan 9:25 as referring to a word from Artaxerxes in the year 445/444 BC, authorizing Nehemiah to return to Jerusalem to rebuild it and its walls. The first seven "weeks" are understood as the next forty-nine years when presumably the city of Jerusalem and its walls were being rebuilt. The "years," however, are meant to be understood as *prophetic years* of 360 days each. The sixty-nine "weeks" of years (7 + 62 = 483 years) would then extend from 444 BC to AD 33, the more commonly recognized year of Christ's crucifixion (as demonstrated in section v above).

Like the previous view, the final "week" does not immediately follow the first sixty-nine weeks, but is postponed. It is fulfilled when the antichrist makes a covenant with the Jewish people (v. 27) that initiates the final seven years leading up to Christ's return.

Evaluation. The primary concern over this proposal is that the mathematical calculations can only be made to work by assuming years of 360 days (a *prophetic year*) rather than solar years of approximately 365 ¼ days. Nevertheless, this is the view adopted in this commentary, a defense of which is given in the following section.

vii. A Defense of Artaxerxes' Authorization to Nehemiah

The Background with Julius Africanus. Sometimes the accusation is made that the view of Artaxerxes' authorization to Nehemiah in 444 BC is *the dispensationalist* view. While it is true that many dispensationalists take this position, it is not necessarily limited to this eschatological persuasion. In fact, Julius Africanus in the early third century AD championed the "word" of Artaxerxes in the twentieth year of his reign as the proper *terminus a quo*. He wrote, "And the beginning of the numbers, that is, of the seventy weeks which make up 490 years, the angel instructs us to take from the going forth of the commandment to answer and to build Jerusalem. And this happened in the twentieth year of the reign of Artaxerxes king of Persia."[232] It is true that most church fathers who wrote on Dan 9:24–27 in the first five hundred years of church history did not take this position (a *terminus a quo* in Artaxerxes' twentieth year).[233] However, Julius Africanus was considered the most notable chronographer in the early church, famous for his *Chronographia*. In this, he devoted an entire treatise to the seventy-weeks passage entitled "On the Weeks and This Prophecy," though only portions of his work are extant today.[234] Julius Africanus further indicated that the twentieth year of Artaxerxes was in the fourth year of the eighty-third Olympiad, and Finegan has shown that Nisan occurred in that year in the spring of 444 BC.[235]

Julius Africanus is also noteworthy for his attempt to calculate the seventy "weeks" of years using lunar rather than solar years. I have summarized his view elsewhere:

> According to Julius this results in a span of 475 years. He argued, however, that 490 years (seventy weeks) is equivalent to 475 years when viewed according to Hebrew numeration. The Jews, he said, reckoned a year as 354 days rather than 365 ¼ days. The former represents twelve months according to the moon's course, while the latter is based on the solar year. This amounts to a difference of 11 ¼ days per year but is eventually made up by the insertion of extra months at eight-year intervals. "Hence the Greeks and the Jews insert three intercalary months every eight years. For eight times 11 ¼ days makes up 3 months." Thus, over a 475-year period, there would be over fifty-nine eight-year periods in which three months would be added, or close to fifteen years in all, and by

232. Julius Africanus, *The Extant Fragments of the Five Books of the Chronography of Julius Africanus*, in *The Ante-Nicene Fathers*, vol. 6, ed. A. Roberts and J. Donaldson, 130–38 (Edinburgh, 1867; reprint, Grand Rapids: Eerdmans, 1989), 16.1.

233. Although a minority position, perhaps, there were other early church fathers who took the *terminus a quo* as Artaxerxes' twentieth year, as did *Theodoret of Cyrus* (247), writing ca. AD 433.

234. See A. A. Mosshammer, ed., *Georgii Syncelli Ecloga Chronographica* (Leipzig: Tübner, 1984), 393.23–24. Portions of Africanus' views are also preserved in Eusebius, *Demonstratio Evangelica*, trans. W. J. Ferar (London: SPCK, 1920), book 8, chap. 2; and Jerome's *Commentary on Daniel.*

235. Finegan, *Handbook of Biblical Chronology*, 92–98. The eighty-third Olympiad was July 1, 445 BC to June 30, 444 BC. Following Xerxes' death in 465 BC, the accession year of Artaxerxes consisted of the remainder of 465 until Nisan of 464 BC. His first regnal year as king (according to the Persian system) would be Nisan 464 to Nisan 463, making his twentieth regnal year according to this system begin in Nisan 444 BC.

this means Julius explains how 490 years by Hebrew numeration would be equivalent to nearly 475 solar years.[236]

A Rationale for Artaxerxes' Authorization to Nehemiah. In section vi above, eight different views of Daniel's seventy "weeks" prophecy were surveyed, and only one of these takes as its *terminus a quo* the authorization of King Artaxerxes to Nehemiah. There are several reasons, however, why this should be regarded as the correct starting point:

(a) According to Dan 9:25, the rebuilding of Jerusalem was to be a major component of the prophecy: Jerusalem "will be built again with a public square and town-moat, even in distressful times." Yet, although the temple had been rebuilt by 516/515 BC, it is obvious from the report given in Neh 1 that the city itself (including its walls and gates) was still quite dilapidated and in need of being rebuilt. If the "word/decree" of Cyrus in 538 BC or of Artaxerxes earlier in 458/457 BC had been for the purpose of rebuilding the city, we would have to conclude that it failed to happen within the first seven "weeks" of years (i.e., forty-nine years).

(b) Nehemiah's request before King Artaxerxes was specifically to rebuild the city (2:5), and the king's royal authorization to Nehemiah (2:7–8) was specifically for that purpose.

(c) Also in fulfillment of Dan 9:25, the book of Nehemiah (as well as Ezra 4:7–23) indicates that the restoration of Jerusalem was done "in distressful times."

The Date of Artaxerxes' Authorization to Nehemiah. According to Neh 2:1, Nehemiah appeared before Artaxerxes in the month Nisan (March-April) of the king's twentieth year. However, there are several problems to be solved in order to establish the exact date. First, the previous report that Nehemiah received was in the month Chislev (November-December) of "the twentieth year," which would presumably make the following Nisan the "twenty-first year," yet Neh 2:1 says twentieth year. Commentators have proposed various solutions to the problem, such as (1) the author made a mistake; (2) the reference in Neh 1:1 pertained not to Artaxerxes, but to Nehemiah's twentieth year of service in the Persian court;[237] (3) the date in Neh 1:1 was added by a later editor (so Williamson, 166); or (4) Nehemiah was reckoning the dates according to a Tishri-to-Tishri calendar rather than the Nisan-to-Nisan calendar more commonly used by the Persians (so Thiele, 68, et al.).[238]

---

236. Tanner, "Is Daniel's Seventy-Weeks Prophecy Messianic? Part 1," 191–92. The quotation is from *The Extant Fragments of the Five Books of the Chronology of Julius Africanus*, 6:135.

237. So Steinmann, *From Abraham to Paul*, 213.

238. For discussion, see E. R. Thiele, *A Chronology of the Hebrew Kings* (Grand Rapids: Zondervan, 1977), 68, fn 3; F. C. Fensham, *The Books of Ezra and Nehemiah*, NICOT (Grand Rapids: Eerdmans, 1982), 149–50; H. G. M. Williamson, *Ezra,*

However the relationship between Neh 1:1 and 2:1 is to be understood, the latter verse is clear that Artaxerxes' permission/authorization to Nehemiah took place in Nisan of the king's twentieth year. A further difficulty, however, is whether Nisan of Artaxerxes' twentieth year occurred in 445 or 444 BC.[239] What is commonly acknowledged is that Xerxes (the father of Artaxerxes) was assassinated in the latter half of 465 BC.[240] According to Yamauchi, there was a brief interlude in which several men contested for the throne, but before the end of the year Artaxerxes, his son, had established himself as the next king.[241] Yamauchi indicates that following Artaxerxes' accession year, "his first regnal year is reckoned from April 13, 464."[242] Yet that date would be according to a Nisan-to-Nisan system, which the Persians are known to have employed.[243] The question, however, is whether Nehemiah meant twentieth year according to a Nisan system or according to a Tishri system, and if he meant a Tishri system, was he counting from 465 BC or 464 BC?[244] There are three possibilities leading to different results:

(1) Nisan-to-Nisan, with his first year starting Nisan of 464 BC, → 20th = Nisan 445 BC

Nehemiah, WBC (Waco, TX: Word, 1985), 166–70; E. M. Yamauchi, "Ezra, Nehemiah," in *EBC*, 4:572; M. Breneman, *Ezra, Nehemiah, Esther*, NAC (Nashville: Broadman & Holman, 1993), 167–69; Steinmann, *Ezra and Nehemiah*, 195–214; and Loken, *Ezra, Nehemiah*, EEC, (Bellingham, WA: Lexham, 2011), see Neh 1:1.

239. Yamauchi, *Persia and the Bible*, 253; Finegan, *Handbook of Biblical Chronology*, 268; Briant, *From Cyrus to Alexander*, 583; and Steinmann, *From Abraham to Paul*, 214, assert that Nisan of Artaxerxes' twentieth year was 445 BC, but Hoehner, *Chronological Aspects*, 138, that it was 444 BC.

240. Yamauchi, *Persia and the Bible*, 239 and Briant, *From Cyrus to Alexander*, 566, claim that this took place in August 465 BC at the hands of the captain of the bodyguard, Artabanus. Olmstead, *History of the Persian Empire*, 289, however, asserted that Xerxes was assassinated "near the end of 465." Hoehner, *Chronological Aspects*, 127, claims that "Xerxes died shortly after December 17, 465 BC and Artaxerxes immediately succeeded him."

241. For a detailed discussion of the assassination and transition to Artaxerxes (including interaction with historical sources), see Briant, *From Cyrus to Alexander*, 563–67.

242. Yamauchi, *Persia and the Bible*, 248.

243. Finegan, *Handbook of Biblical Chronology*, 75.

244. In defense of the idea that Nehemiah was employing a Tishri-to-Tishri system in Neh 1–2, see Thiele, *A Chronology of the Hebrew Kings*, 68, fn 3; and Hoehner, *Chronological Aspects*, 127. S. H. Horn and L. H. Wood, "The Fifth-Century Jewish Calendar at Elephantine," 14, 20, have demonstrated that this method was used by the Jews in Elephantine (Egypt under Persian rule) during the same time period as Nehemiah.

(2) Tishri-to-Tishri, with his first year starting Tishri of 465 BC, → 20th = Nisan 445 BC
(3) Tishri-to-Tishri, with his first year starting Tishri of 464 BC, → 20th = Nisan 444 BC

Unfortunately, we cannot be certain as to which is intended. One might argue that the first is the most logical, as this would be in keeping with Persian reckoning. The second might be correct if Artaxerxes took the throne before Tishri of 465 BC (which is not certain). The third could be correct if Nehemiah was using a Tishri-to-Tishri system and the count began with Tishri of 464 (implying that his rule from late 465 to Tishri of 464 was his accession year).[245] Despite some degree of uncertainty, the third option seems best for two reasons: (1) this would resolve the tension between Neh 1:1 and 2:1; and (2) the third option is the only one that harmonizes with the statement of Julius Africanus that the twentieth year of Artaxerxes was in the fourth year of the eighty-third Olympiad (see above, July 1, 445 BC to June 30, 444 BC). In conclusion, Nisan of 444 BC is the best option for the authorization of Artaxerxes to Nehemiah to return and rebuild Jerusalem, though admittedly not beyond question.

Textual Notes

24.a. MT has לְכַלֵּא, yet this raises the question as to whether the root is כָּלָה ("to finish, be complete, at an end, accomplished") or כָּלָא ("to shut up, restrain, withhold"). Seeing that כָּלָה is extremely well attested in the Piʿel whereas כָּלָא only occurs in the Qal and Nipʿal in BH, the root is surely כָּלָה (so Goldingay, 229; BDB, 478a 1a); cf. GKC, 213, 216–17 (§75aa, rr). Also note the aorist inf. συντελεσθῆναι ("to complete") in both LXX^{O} and LXX$^{\theta}$. NET explains לְכַלֵּא as an "alternative (metaplastic) spelling of the root כָּלָה."

24.b. LXX^{O} has τὴν ἁμαρτίαν (with article), whereas LXX$^{\theta}$ simply has ἁμαρτίαν. The latter could raise the question whether the Heb. should be פֶּשַׁע rather than הַפֶּשַׁע. In light of Heb. MSS to the contrary, it is best to respect MT's הַפֶּשַׁע.

24.c. The Kethib reading is וּלַחְתֹּם (from חָתַם, "to seal, seal up") in contrast to Qere וּלְהָתֵם (from תָּמַם, "to complete, finish"). LXX$^{\theta}$ (τοῦ σφραγίσαι, "to seal") supports the Kethib, yet LXX^{O} (σπανίσαι, "to lack" or trans., "to exhaust, use up") supports the Qere (so S, Vg., and L). Collins (345) suggests Kethib's וּלַחְתֹּם can be explained as an assimilation to ולחתם that occurs later in 24b, and therefore opts for Qere's וּלְהָתֵם (so NET; Goldingay, 229; and Newsom, 286).

245. Finegan, *Handbook of Biblical Chronology*, 253, asserts, "... Ezra-Nehemiah use Tishri years even for the kings of Persia."

24.d. Kethib has חַטָּאוֹת (pl., supported by LXX^{O} ἀδικίας), but Qere has חַטָּאת (sg., supported by LXX$^{\theta}$ ἁμαρτίας, Cairo Geniza and many MSS). Goldingay (226, 229) sides with the plural reading, as does Collins (345) and the NKJV, though most other Eng. VSS opt for Qere's singular (so NASB, NET, NIV, ESV, NRSV). Perhaps the latter are persuaded by the singular forms הַפֶּשַׁע and עָוֺן that bracket it. Yet Goldingay (229) sees the singular as a deliberate assimilation to הַפֶּשַׁע, and concludes, "Perhaps the three expressions for sin ('the rebellion,' 'failures,' 'waywardness') deliberately vary (article with s, anarthrous pl, anarthrous s)." Admittedly, a decision is difficult, but the consistency of singular forms argues in favor of the Qere.

25.a. The MT has וְחָרוּץ, which BDB (358d) lists as a masc. noun meaning "trench, moat" (similarly, *DCH*, 3:315, "channel, moat"). *HALOT* (352) defines חָרוּץ as a "town-moat." The problem is that this is a hapax (though attested in an Aram. inscription as חֲרִיצָה and Akk. *ḫariṣu*), and *BHS* editor proposes (on the basis of S, "street") a root חוץ, which generally means "outside" but can have a more specific meaning of a "street" (BDB, 300 2a). Cf. בְּחוּצוֹת, "in the streets" (Jer 5:1), and מִחוּץ, "from the street" (Jer 9:20). LXX^{O} is missing the latter half of v. 25, but LXX$^{\theta}$ (similarly Vg) translated as τεῖχος, meaning a "wall," and especially a "city-wall" or "embankment" (LSJM, 1767). Apart from the KJV and NKJV ("wall," following LXX$^{\theta}$), most other Eng. VSS accept MT and translate "moat" or "trench" (so Goldingay, 226; Collins, 346). Montgomery (380) supports the latter: "The word is now known also from the ZKR Inscr., i, 11. 9 *f.*: 'they made a wall higher than Hazrak and dug a trench (חרץ = *ḥarûṣ* or *ḥarîṣ*) deeper than its trench.'"

25.b. MT's וּבְצוֹק הָעִתִּים ("even in the distress of times") is a bit awkward. In light of S (*lšwlm zbn'*, "to complete the time"), *BHS* editor proposes 'וּבקֵץ ה (reversal of צ and ק), "at the completion of times," and connects with v. 26 (so Goldingay, 230). As Collins (346) notes, however, "a reference to the end of times seems premature in the context of the sixty-two weeks." LXX$^{\theta}$ has καὶ ἐκκενωθήσονται οἱ καιροί, "the times will be left desolate." (The passive of ἐκκενόω means "be left desolate"; LSJM, 508.) Most Eng. VSS side with MT and offer a translation similar to NET's "in distressful times."

26.a-a. *BHS* editor proposes that a word has dropped out from this clause, perhaps דִּין ("judgment") or אָוֶן ("iniquity"). In support of דִּין is LXX$^{\theta}$: καὶ κρίμα οὐκ ἔστιν ἐν αὐτῷ, "and there is no judgment in him" (grounds for condemnation?). However, MT's וְאֵין לוֹ is sensible as is ("he will have nothing"); note LXX^{O}'s very literal καὶ οὐκ ἔσται. More discussion in translation notes and commentary.

26.b. *BHS* editor suggests that in place of יַשְׁחִית (Hipʿil impf.), we should probably read יִשָּׁחֵת (Nipʿal impf.), even though the latter only has the support of one MS and S. Furthermore, the Nipʿal of שָׁחַת is rare (only 6x out of 142 occurrences of שָׁחַת in OT). Finally, both LXX^{O} and LXX$^{\theta}$ translated שחת with active verbs (LXX^{O} by φθερεῖ, and LXX$^{\theta}$ by διαφθερεῖ).

26.c. Rather than MT's עַם ("people"), *BHS* editor suggests reading as עִם ("with") instead. This would change the sense from "the people of the prince who is to come will destroy the city and the sanctuary" to "he will destroy the city and the sanctuary together with the prince who is to come." The alternative reading עִם ("with") does have the support of LXX$^{\theta}$ (σὺν τῷ ἡγουμένῳ τῷ ἐρχομένῳ). However, only one other Heb. MS supports this reading. Goldingay (230) readily dismisses the suggestion: "this looks like an attempt to make easier sense of an apparently difficult MT, and/or a reinterpretation of it based on the conviction that 'a prince to come' is the same as the 'prince' of v. 25." All major Eng. VSS side with MT's עַם ("people").

26.d-d. Newsom (286), who mistakenly takes the "ruler" in v. 26 to be Antiochus IV, finds MT's נָגִיד הַבָּא to be an odd way of referring to him, as well as the remark "and his end" (וְקִצּוֹ), "since v. 27 devotes several clauses to the activity of Antiochus, only describing his fate in the very last words of the verse." Therefore, she attempts to solve the difficulty by redividing the phrases (to put the ptc. בָּא with קִצּוֹ rather than with נָגִיד), and emending the text to *ûbāʾ haqqēṣ*, "and the end will come." Yet the proposed emendation is unnecessary, since Antiochus IV is not the נָגִיד in view (not to mention that the emendation involves dropping the ה on הַבָּא, and moving the *waw* from וְקִצּוֹ to בָּא).

27.a. Rather than MT's יַשְׁבִּית (Hipʿil impf. = "cause to cease; put an end to"), *BHS* editor proposes יִשְׁבֹּת (Qal impf. = "shall cease"), based on Symmachus' (σ′) παύσεται and Vg. *deficiet*. Against this, however, is LXX$^{\theta}$'s ἀρθήσεταί (fut. pass. of αἴρω) meaning "will be removed" or "will be taken away". Regarding the form ἀρθήσεταί, see Isa 16:10; 17:1.

27.b-b. For plural שִׁקּוּצִים, both LXX^{O} and LXX$^{\theta}$ have a singular form, βδέλυγμα ("abomination"). Moreover, for the following participle מְשֹׁמֵם (masc. sg.), LXX^{O} and LXX$^{\theta}$ both have a plural form τῶν ἐρημώσεων. So LXX treats these as a genitive construct, βδέλυγμα τῶν ἐρημώσεων ("an abomination of desolations"), but MT does not: שִׁקּוּצִים מְשֹׁמֵם ("abominable idols, one who desolates"). *BHS* editor proposes MT be read as singular שִׁקּוּץ (observe הַשִּׁקּוּץ מְשׁוֹמֵם in 11:31 and שִׁקּוּץ שֹׁמֵם in 12:11). However, one could also argue that LXX deliberately emended the text to singular (βδέλυγμα) in an effort to conform 9:27 to 11:31 and 12:11.

Translation

9:24 "Seventy 'weeks' [*heptads*][246] have been determined[247] for[248] your people

---

246. The meaning of "week" is discussed above in section i of the introductory comments, "The Meaning of 'Week' (שָׁבוּעַ, *šābûaʿ*)." A "week" (*šābûaʿ*) means a period of seven years.

247. The vb. חָתַךְ (*ḥātak*) is a hapax, lit. to "cut, divide," from which derives the nuance "to determine" (BDB, 367b) or "be decreed" (Montgomery, 373), or "to decide" (amply attested in JArm; *DTT*, 513).

248. Taking עַל (ʿ*al*) in the sense of "concerning" (BDB, 754d II 1f[*g*]).

and your holy city,[249] to finish the transgression, to bring about an end to sin,[250] to atone for iniquity, to bring in everlasting righteousness, to seal up vision and prophecy,[251] and to anoint[252] the most holy place.[253] **25** So you are to know and comprehend *that* from the going forth of a word[254] to restore and rebuild Jerusalem until[255] Messiah the Ruler[256] *there will be* seven 'weeks'[257]

---

249. See v. 16; this is clearly Jerusalem. LXX^O explicates, τὴν πόλιν Σιων (*tēn polin Siōn*), "the city Zion."

250. Reading singular חַטָּאת (*ḥaṭṭā'ṯ*) with the Qere (so Montgomery, 373). See Textual Note above.

251. NET takes חָזוֹן וְנָבִיא (*ḥāzôn wᵉnāḇî'*) as a hendiadys, "prophetic vision" (so Hartman, 244; Chisholm, *Handbook on the Prophets*, 313). Most other Eng. VSS do not.

252. In contrast to MT's לִמְשֹׁחַ (*limšōaḥ*, "to anoint"), LXX^O has εὐφρᾶναι (*euphranai*), "to rejoice in or celebrate" the most holy place. S has "the messiah."

253. S and Vg. read קֹדֶשׁ קָדָשִׁים (*qōḏeš qāḏāšîm*) as masculine, i.e., "a most holy one" (namely Messiah). Many early church fathers took *qōḏeš qāḏāšîm* as a reference to Messiah Jesus. Yet this is more likely a reference to the temple (see discussion in commentary).

254. The noun דָּבָר (*dāḇār*) is very flexible in meaning. The most common nuance is "word," but—depending on the context—it can mean "thing, act, matter, message, command or decree" (see BDB, 182–84 for full discussion). Most Eng. VSS render this as either "word," "command," or "decree." Yet this does not have to be a *formal decree* (a royal decree?), and therefore a more flexible term is preferred. The translation "directive" avoids the problem of "decree," and yet is not quite as stern or formal as "command" (*dāḇār* can even mean "advice," "counsel," "promise," or "decision"). Although "directive" would be a suitable term for a king's *authorization* (if that is what is in view), it would not be appropriate if this refers to a "word" from God. Hence, a more neutral term is preferred, and the simple translation "word" gives the most flexibility.

255. LXX^O reads "you will build Jerusalem 'a city for the Lord'" (πόλιν κυρίῳ, *polin kuriōi*), taking the prep. עַד (*'aḏ*) as עִיר (*'îr*, "city"), and taking מָשִׁיחַ נָגִיד (*māšîaḥ nāgîḏ*) as "the Lord" (κυριος, *kurios*).

256. The interpretation of מָשִׁיחַ נָגִיד (*māšîaḥ nāgîḏ*) is crucial to the interpretation of the passage. See section iv above for discussion and defense of this as a designation for the Messiah. Note how the early VSS understood this. Vg. has *Christum ducem*, and S has "king messiah." Also see LXX^O's "a city for the Lord" in the preceding footnote.

257. In the MT there is a punctuation marker (*'aṯnāḥ*) immediately following "seven weeks." Some scholars see a major break at this point, which would imply that מָשִׁיחַ נָגִיד (*māšîaḥ nāgîḏ*) comes after seven "weeks" of years (not 7 + 62). If valid, this would rule out a messianic interpretation. However, the *'aṯnāḥ* was not part of the original text and should not be understood this way. See section 2 under "Additional Exegetical Comments" ("The Placement of the *'aṯnāḥ* in 9:25") for discussion and defense of this position.

and sixty-two 'weeks.' It will be built again[258] with a public square[259] and town-moat,[260] even in distressful times.[261] **26** Then after the sixty-two 'weeks,' Messiah[262] will be cut off and have nothing,[263] and the people[264] of the ruler who is to come will destroy both[265] the city[266] and the sanctuary. Its end *will come* with a flood, and until *its* end, war *that brings* desolations[267] has been determined. **27** Then he will enforce a covenant for the many for one 'week,' but in the middle of the 'week' he will put an end to sacrifice and offering.

---

258. תָּשׁוּב וְנִבְנְתָה (*tāšûḇ wᵊnibnᵊṯâ*) is a verbal hendiadys, "will be built again." So Collins (346) and most Eng. VSS. See 2 Kgs 21:3 and 2 Chr 33:3.

259. Regarding רְחוֹב (*rᵊḥôḇ*), Hartman (244) notes, "Literally, the 'plaza' (Hebrew *rᵊḥôb*) or wide open space in a city just inside the city gate, used as a market place, forum, place for judicial cases, etc.; here understood for the 'streets' of the city in general, as *pars pro toto*." Goldingay (229), however, argues for "a broad open place," but not a "street." In Neh 8:1 this was an open square where all the public could gather; hence, a public square.

260. The word חָרוּץ (*ḥārûṣ*) is a hapax. See textual note above for discussion. Newsom (286), who translates *ḥārûṣ* as "fosse" explains this as a "ditch at the bottom of a rampart. Thus the phrase would refer to Jerusalem as a fortified city." Hartman (244), however, understands this "in the sense of a trench cut into the rock outside the city walls in order to increase the exterior height of the walls."

261. Understanding הָעִתִּים (*hāʿittîm*) as a *genitive of specification*, "distress in regard to the times"; cf. *IBHS*, 151 (§9.5.3c).

262. Vg., "Christ."

263. Collins (346) wants to emend וְאֵין לוֹ (*wᵊʾên lô*) to וְאֵין עוֹזֵר לוֹ (*wᵊʾên ʿôzēr lô*), "and there is none to help him," in light of Dan 11:45. However, there is no MS support for this, and neither LXX^{O} nor LXX$^{\theta}$ reflect this in their translations. See textual note above. Newsom (286), on the other hand, suggests emending to *wĕʾênennû*, "and he will be no more," following LXX^{O}. Hartman (240) reads (with a few MSS) *hāʿîr* for *wᵊhāʿîr*, and joins with וְאֵין לוֹ (*wᵊʾên lô*), resulting in "the city is no longer his." Goldingay (226, 230) adds "city and sanctuary" to וְאֵין לוֹ (*wᵊʾên lô*)—ignoring the *ʾaṯnāḥ* that he argued for in v. 25—so as to read, "and will have neither the city nor the sanctuary." Yet MT's "and will have nothing" makes sense without having to resort to emendation and can be explained theologically (see commentary).

264. Newsom (286) has pointed out that the word "people" (עַם, *ʿam*) in Dan 9:26 "can refer to a military body, as in 1 Sam 14:17; 2 Sam 2:26; 10:10; 2 Kgs 13:7; etc." Rather than "people" (עַם, *ʿam*), the LXX$^{\theta}$ understood עם to be pointed עִם (*ʿim*), a preposition meaning "with." For discussion and refutation, see the textual note 9:26c above.

265. For וְ – וְ in the sense of "both ... and," see GKC, 484–85 (§154*a* 1(*b*)).

266. Normally a direct object that is definite will be preceded by the sign of the accusative (אֵת or אֶת־), but this is not always the case with the verb שָׁחַת (*šāḥaṯ*). Note Deut 9:26 and Jer 11:19.

267. Understanding שֹׁמֵמוֹת (*šōmēmôṯ*) as a genitive of specification (so Montgomery, 385).

Then on the wing[268] *(the temple) will be* an *utter* abomination[269] *by* one who makes desolate, even until a predetermined destruction[270] is poured out on the one who desolates."

---

268. Understanding כְּנַף (*kᵊnap̱*) is difficult. In general, the noun *kānāp̱* means a "wing" (e.g., of a bird or insect) or "extremity" (BDB, 489). Yet וְעַל כְּנַף שִׁקּוּצִים מְשֹׁמֵם (*wᵊʿal kᵊnap̱ šiqqûṣîm mᵊšōmēm*) is very obscure. Lit., "and on the wing of abominations (or detestable idols), one who desolates." Collins (346–47) attempts to solve the difficulty by emending the text, from כְּנַף (*kᵊnap̱*) to כנם, "their place," the result being "and the desolating abomination will be in <u>their</u> <u>place</u>" (i.e., in the place of the sacrifice and grain offering). Compare עַל־כַּנּוֹ (*ʿal-kannô*) at Dan 11:20, 21, 38. So Montgomery (387), Hartman (240), and Newsom (286). Not only is this an unwarranted emendation, but it lacks support in the VSS. Both LXX^{O} and LXX$^{\theta}$ understand this as a reference to the temple, translating *wᵊʿal kᵊnap̱* as ἐπὶ τὸ ἱερὸν (*epi to hieron*). Cf. Vg., *in templo*. The word ἱερὸς (*hieros*) is used 72x in the NT of the temple. The peculiar phrase in Matt 4:5, ἐπὶ τὸ πτερύγιον τοῦ ἱεροῦ (*epi to pterugion tou hierou*), normally translated "on the pinnacle of the temple," is a possible clue that כְּנַף (*kᵊnap̱*) has an association with the temple. The noun πτερύγιον (*pterugion*) means anything like a wing (LSJM, 1547), e.g., fins, rudder of a ship, a peak, or pointed roof. While "wing" (*kᵊnap̱*) would have little meaning to modern readers, perhaps it was a word that implied the "temple" in ancient times (which explains why the LXX translators took it that way).

269. "Utter abomination" is a translation of the single Heb. word שִׁקּוּצִים (*šiqqûṣîm*). The basic meaning of *šiqqûṣ* is "detested thing" (BDB, 848a). *HALOT* (1640) gives the meaning "abhorrence, an object to abhor, horror, monster." Of the 28x the word occurs in the OT, it almost always refers to abominations in the sense of pagan idolatry. NASB translates "abominable idols" in 2 Chr 15:18 and "detestable idol" in 1 Kgs 11:5 (cf. Ezek 5:11). Although שִׁקּוּצִים (*šiqqûṣîm*) in Dan 9:27 is plural by form, it is possible to view this as a *plural of amplification* (in which the pl. serves to intensify the idea of the stem). See GKC, 397–98 (§124e-f) for full discussion. GKC offers numerous illustrations, e.g., כִּפֻּרִים (*kippurîm*, atonement), אֲהָמִים (*ʾŏhāmîm*, fornication), נִאֻפִים (*niʾup̱îm*, adultery), and שַׁלְמֹנִים (*šalmōnîm*, bribery). The fact that we have this same combination of words (i.e., *šiqqûṣ* and *šāmēm*) twice elsewhere in Daniel (11:31 and 12:11) in similar usage—but in those cases *šiqqûṣ* is in the singular—argues for the plural of amplification here, hence, "utter abomination." הַשִּׁקּוּץ מְשׁוֹמֵם (*haššiqqûṣ mᵊšômēm*, "the abomination that causes desolation") in 11:31 clearly refers to Antiochus' atrocity at the Jerusalem temple, but שִׁקּוּץ שֹׁמֵם (*šiqqûṣ šōmēm*, "abomination causing desolation") in 12:11 refers to the eschatological future and must refer to the same atrocity as that in 9:27 (cf. Matt 24:15, Jesus' prediction of the "abomination of desolation" that takes place in the tribulation era).

270. Collins (347) takes כָּלָה וְנֶחֱרָצָה (*kālâ wᵊneḥĕrāṣâ*) as a hendiadys, "predetermined destruction" (lit., "a destruction, even one determined"). Similarly, Montgomery (389), "a determined end."

Commentary

9:24. Gabriel begins relating the divine message by stating, "Seventy 'weeks' have been determined for your people and your holy city." Scholars almost unanimously agree that the term translated "week" (שָׁבוּעַ, *šāḇûaʿ*) means in this context a period of seven years (see section i above, "The Meaning of 'Week'"). Just as today we speak of a decade as a span of ten years, the Jews had the term *šāḇûaʿ*, meaning "seven years" (i.e., a heptad). Seventy "weeks," then, would be a total of 490 years. Seeing that this is divided into three uneven segments (7 + 62 + 1), we should not regard the seventy as a round number but should understand it literally. Hence, the three phases to the prophecy take place in seven "weeks" (49 years), sixty-two "weeks" (434 years), and one "week" (7 years).

In response to Daniel's prayer (9:3–19), God now revealed to Daniel the divine program for the restoration of Jerusalem and the temple. In light of Daniel's petition (9:15–19), "your people and your holy city" most certainly mean the Jewish people and Jerusalem and must not be spiritualized to mean "the church" or a "heavenly Jerusalem." Not only does consistency of interpretation demand this, but the Jerusalem of this passage is one that is rebuilt and then destroyed again. Daniel had been thinking about the seventy years of captivity (Jer 25:11; 29:10), but God revealed to him that seventy more *periods of seven years* (i.e., a total of 490 years) would still be needed to complete the desolations of Jerusalem that so concerned him.

The remainder of v. 24 points out six major goals that will be accomplished by the completion of the seventy "weeks." In addition to these, a careful reading of vv. 25–27 reveals other significant events that will take place along with these six goals, e.g., the rebuilding of Jerusalem, the coming of Messiah, the destruction of the city and sanctuary (again), and the coming of one who "desolates." The six goals described in v. 24 fall into two groups. The first three are concerned with God's dealing with that which is negative (transgression, sin, and iniquity), while the final three are positive in nature (the fulfillment of God's righteous purposes in history, including an era of righteousness and temple restoration).

The first goal is "to finish the transgression" (לְכַלֵּא הַפֶּשַׁע, *lᵉḵallēʾ happešaʿ*). The same word *pešaʿ* was used previously in Dan 8:12–13 to speak of Antiochus' transgression against the biblical faith and his atrocities against the Jewish people. However, in this context it is the transgression of Israel that is in view (the following infinitives link this to sin and iniquity). The word fundamentally means "rebellion,"[271] and hence this looks at Israel's long history of rebellion against Yahweh God. Indeed, Israel's apostasy and rebellion against Yahweh was the primary cause of the Babylonian exile, and even though the present exile was now ending, her rebellion against him was continuing (eventually climaxing with her rejection of Messiah Jesus). Her rebellion was described poetically in Deut 32:15–43, where Israel is said to

---

271. G. H. Livingston, "פֶּשַׁע," in *TWOT*, 2:741.

have provoked Yahweh to jealousy by her continual turning from the Rock of her salvation. God not only promised to bring calamity on the nation, but he promised, "I will make them jealous with those who are not a people; I will provoke them to anger with a foolish nation" (Deut 32:21, NASB). This bears witness to God's salvific work among the Gentiles in the present age (Rom 10:19). Nevertheless, Israel's rebellion did not result in her being permanently cast off nor her being replaced by the church. Rom 11:11 declares, "I say then, they did not stumble so as to fall, did they? May it never be! But by their transgression salvation has come to the Gentiles, to make them jealous" (NASB). One day—at the close of the tribulation period—Israel's rebellion against the Lord will come to an end. Romans 11:25–27 goes on to depict the conclusion of her transgression and her full restoration that will be implemented at Christ's return.

The second goal listed in Dan 9:24 is "to bring about an end to sin" (לְהָתֵם חַטָּאת, *lᵊhāṯēm ḥaṭṭāʾṯ*).[272] This is similar to the first goal, but perhaps with the *means* in view. For this to happen, Messiah Jesus will have to be punished for the sins of the nation (Isa 53), though his death will ultimately pay the price of sin for everyone, not just those of Israel. At the time of his second advent, he will cleanse the nation and remove her sin—a blessing that will only benefit those who humble themselves and turn to him in faith (Ezek 36:24–25; 37:23; Zech 5; 13:1). Archer (112) suggests that this goal has in view not only the payment for sin but ridding the world of sin: "the bringing in of a new society in which righteousness will prevail in complete contrast to the present condition of mankind." If the latter is in view, this will come about in the promised kingdom when Christ will rule as king over the world.

The third goal is "to atone for iniquity" (לְכַפֵּר עָוֹן, *lᵊḵappēr ʿāwōn*). Regarding the verb *kipper* (כִּפֶּר), Goldingay (229) notes, "in Arabic *kpr* can mean 'to cover,' but the Heb. meaning links rather with Akk. *kaparu/kuppuru* 'cleanse': *CAD*." Hence, to "atone" means to *purge* iniquity (i.e., wipe it clean) on the basis of sacrifice, and thus to grant forgiveness. The ground for this is the crucifixion of Christ at Calvary. There is an application of this to Israel as a nation at her eschatological national day of atonement in conjunction with the return of Christ (Zech 3:8–9; 13:1).

The final three goals (three positive blessings) also find their fulfillment at the second coming of Christ. The fourth goal is "to bring in everlasting righteousness" (לְהָבִיא צֶדֶק עֹלָמִים, *lᵊhāḇîʾ ṣeḏeq ʿōlāmîm*). This should not be confused with the idea of "forensic righteousness" that is taught in the New Testament (e.g., Romans). The idea of Messiah Jesus establishing a kingdom of righteousness is a recurrent theme in the Old Testament prophets (Isa 11:2–5; 60:21; Jer 23:5–6), and that is what this verse has in view (recall the

272. See textual notes for this verse regarding the Kethib-Qere readings.

kingdom promise to a "Son of Man" in Dan 7:13–14).[273] When he reigns as king over a kingdom of regenerated subjects and with Satan bound in the abyss (Rev 20:1–3), righteousness will flourish on the earth. In fact, he will be called "Yahweh our righteousness" (Jer 23:6). Psalm 72:2–3 (a messianic psalm) eloquently describes this time when he will rule from sea to sea with all nations serving him:

> "Then he will judge Your people with righteousness
> (בְצֶדֶק, *bᵊṣeḏeq*)
> And Your afflicted with justice
> The mountains will bring peace to the people,
> And the hills, in righteousness" (author's translation)

The fifth goal to be accomplished is "to seal up vision and prophecy" (לַחְתֹּם חָזוֹן וְנָבִיא, *laḥtōm ḥāzôn wᵊnāḇî'*). To "seal" (Heb. *ḥāṯam*) can mean (1) to authenticate by sealing (1 Kgs 21:8; Jer 32:10–11, 44); (2) to conceal something or make it inaccessible (Isa 29:11; possibly Dan 12:4, 9); or (3) to secure something or preserve it securely (possibly Dan 12:4, 9; Deut 32:34). If the latter idea is intended, the prophetic vision is sealed up now (for preservation) but will be ultimately realized in the "end of time" (cf. Dan 8:25; 12:4, 9). This looks at the full realization of what God said he would do in fulfilling his program with Israel, especially her restoration in preparation for Messiah's kingdom (keeping in mind that the vision pertains to Daniel's people and their holy city, i.e., Jerusalem).

The sixth and final goal is "to anoint the most holy place" (לִמְשֹׁחַ קֹדֶשׁ קָדָשִׁים, *limšōaḥ qōḏeš qāḏāšîm*). Although the word "place" is not technically in the Hebrew text, this is the correct understanding. Whenever the "holy of holies" is referred to, this is rendered in a slightly different way: קֹדֶשׁ הַקֳּדָשִׁים, *qōḏeš haqqŏḏāšîm* (e.g., Exod 26:33, 34). The words "most holy" (*qōḏeš qāḏāšîm*) usually do not refer to a person—though possibly in one case they do (see 1 Chr 23:13 regarding Aaron). A number of early church fathers (e.g., Hippolytus, iv. 32.4) understood this—mistakenly in my opinion—as a reference to Jesus, the Most Holy One.[274] This view was even generally adopted

273. Goldingay's suggested translation "lasting vindication" (229) misses the point. The translation "vindication" is possible for *ṣeḏeq* only in some very rare cases (e.g., Ps 35:27). In contrast, the common meaning of *ṣeḏeq* is "righteousness," with secondary meanings of "justice, right, just, justness" (see BDB, 841).

274. See translation notes above for this phrase and how it was rendered in certain versions to reflect a messianic understanding. Theodoret of Cyrus, a Syrian bishop who wrote a commentary on Daniel ca. AD 433, would be an example of one taking the messianic interpretation: "Now, what is this *holy of holies*? … it is Christ the Lord, who foretells in Isaiah, 'The Spirit of the Lord is upon me, hence the Lord anointed me.' Testimony is given to him by David to the effect that 'he loved righteousness and hated iniquity, and hence he was anointed with the oil of gladness above his fellows. … the Savior, who is known as holy of holies for his being the fount of

by the reformers (so Luther, Calvin) and more recently by Pusey (182), and is even found among Jewish exegetes (so Ibn Ezra and Nachmanides). Yet Montgomery (375) is more correct when he writes,

> The term is used always of sacrosanct things or places: of the tent of meeting, the temple, its *debîr* or *adyton*, of the territory belonging to the temple, the altars, holy vessels, incense, sacrificial flesh, etc. ... Only once is it possibly used of a person, I Ch. 23^{13}, 'And Aaron was separated to sanctify him as most holy,' which latter clause, however, may mean 'that he should consecrate the most holy.' This well-nigh universal use of 'the holiest' compels us to interpret the term as of either the temple or especially the altar of burnt offerings.

Likewise, Goldingay (229) understands it to refer to the temple or objects related to it. Often these words describe the altar or furnishings of the tabernacle as being "most holy" (Exod 29:37; 30:29). Significantly, the "sanctuary" (*hammiqdāš*) in Ezekiel's eschatological vision is called "most holy" (*qōḏeš qāḏāšîm*) in Ezek 45:3, as is the entire top of the mountain for the sanctuary (Ezek 43:10–12; note esp. v. 12). Hence, the anointing of a most holy place, though it may have some partial fulfillment with Zerubbabel's rebuilt temple in 516 BC, most likely looks to the proper inauguration of a millennial temple following Jesus' return (so Archer, 113).[275] Cf. Isa 2:1–4. This interpretation is in keeping with the general eschatological overtones seen in the other five goals.

An understanding of these six goals is crucial for the proper interpretation of the remaining three verses. For example, the common viewpoint of critical scholars is that Dan 9:24–27 finds its complete fulfillment in the days of Antiochus Epiphanes and the Maccabean revolt during the years 171–164 BC. However, the above six goals were certainly not fulfilled (and could not be) by this stage of history. Furthermore, they could not even be fulfilled completely in the first advent of Christ (which eliminates the first century messianic views), suggesting that the seventy "weeks" must extend until Christ's return.

9:25. Several interpretative problems immediately arise at v. 25. Who is the "anointed one" (some translations, as does this commentary, have "Messiah")? Is this figure the same as the "anointed one" in v. 26? What "word" (command? decree?) is in view, and what date was it issued? Does the "anointed one" come after the first seven "weeks" or after sixty-nine "weeks" (with

---

holiness, and who is anointed in his humanity by the Holy Spirit ...'" (*Theodoret of Cyrus*, 243–44).

275. A. Hill (170) sees the fulfillment in the near future: "The immediate reference of the final clause is most likely the rededication of the Jerusalem temple, the 'Most Holy Place' (Heb. *qōḏeš qāḏāšîm*) for the Hebrews of Daniel's day (so Lucas, 242)."

seven and sixty-two combined)? Scholars differ greatly on their answers to these questions.

The first crucial interpretation is the matter of "a word to restore and rebuild Jerusalem." As pointed out in the translation note, "word" (Heb. דָּבָר, *dāḇār*) is a flexible term. It can mean something as simple as an utterance or more formally "a decree" (either by God or by man). Coming from a superior (such as God or a king), it can also mean "a command." Yet it does not have to mean a formal decree, and hence even a *word of permission* is an acceptable nuance.

Critical scholars are virtually unanimous in seeing this as a decree or pronouncement in the sixth century BC.[276] Conservative commentators, on the other hand, usually opt for one of three possibilities:[277] (1) the decree of Cyrus about 538 BC—see Ezra 1:1–4; 6:3–5 (so Calvin, E. J. Young, M. Kline, A. Hoekema, T. Kliefoth, C. F. Keil, H. C. Leupold, and D. L. Cooper); (2) the decree of Artaxerxes to Ezra about 458/457 BC—see Ezra 7:11–26, note esp. v. 21 (so G. Hasel, J. B. Payne, R. G. M. Gurney, G. L. Archer, S. Miller, and L. Wood); or (3) the authorization of Artaxerxes to Nehemiah about 445/444 BC—see Neh 1–2 (so R. Anderson, A. J. McClain, J. F. Walvoord, J. D. Pentecost, C. L. Feinberg, P. Feinberg, and H. W. Hoehner).

The first suggestion (Cyrus' decree in 538 BC) is the least likely. First, his decree was primarily to allow the Jews to return and rebuild the temple, and the rebuilding of the city did not come until much later. If the "seven weeks" (i.e., 49 years) refers to the time for the rebuilding of the city, this simply did not happen within forty-nine years of the return in 538 BC, as is clear from a fair reading of Neh 1. Second, a total of sixty-nine "weeks" (i.e., 483 years) from 538 BC would result in 55–54 BC, a date irrelevant for any

---

276. Critical scholars typically date this "command" (or decree) early (in the sixth century BC). Montgomery (378) argued that it must have something to do with God's word to Jeremiah in light of Dan 9:2, i.e., with Jer 25. Collins (354) thinks this must be a divine decree, not that of a Persian king, in light of the use of the same word (Heb. *dāḇār*) in Dan 9:23. He thus sees this as part of the revelation given to Daniel about the time of the first year of Darius the Mede (note Dan 9:1). Similarly, Segal, "The Chronological Conception of the Persian Period in Daniel 9," 296. Hartman (250), on the other hand, relates it to the announcement given to Jeremiah in Jer 29:10, which he would date at 594 BC based on Jer 28:1. The end result for these is the same, as they see the first seven "weeks" depicting the time until the arrival of the "anointed one" in 538 BC, namely Cyrus the Great (or for Collins, 355, the high priest Joshua). (For them the seven "weeks" is only approximate or simply a literary device of little consequence.)

277. Lucas (242–43) lists seven possibilities for the "word/decree," though conservatives generally prefer one of three main options. One exception among conservative commentators is Chisholm who takes this as God's announcement through Jeremiah (see Jer 30:18), which he would date between 597 and 586 BC. See section vi above, "Survey of Views" for elaboration and evaluation.

candidate as "the anointed one." The second suggestion, the decree to Ezra in 458–457 BC, is more plausible, yet not without problems. Sixty-nine "weeks" (i.e., 483 years—assuming solar years of approx. 365 ¼ days) from this date would be AD 26/27, which some believe to be the commencement of Jesus' public ministry following his baptism (assuming the death of Christ occurred in AD 30). Against this view is that (1) there in no mention in the Ezra passage about the rebuilding of the city, but only a return of more Jews to the land and an "adorning" of the temple; and (2) there is a growing consensus among conservative scholars engaged in chronological studies that Christ's public ministry began in AD 29 and his crucifixion took place in AD 33.[278] The third suggestion, namely the authorization of Artaxerxes to Nehemiah about 445/444 BC is probably the best.[279] The idea of "authorization" or "word of permission" is certainly in keeping with the lexical meaning of *dāḇār*.

The main strengths of this third view are (1) Nehemiah's request to Artaxerxes was specifically to rebuild the city (Neh 2:5–8); (2) the book of Nehemiah (and Ezra 4:7–23) indicates that the restoration was done in the most distressing circumstances (note the ending to Dan 9:25!); and (3) this is the only view, if the numbers are to be taken literally, that harmonizes with an AD 33 date for Christ's crucifixion (proof to follow).

Regarding the identity of the "anointed one" (מָשִׁיחַ, *māšîaḥ*) in Dan 9:25, this is surely the Lord Jesus Christ (contrary to claims of critical scholars). For discussion, see translation notes and section iv above ("A Defense of the Messianic Interpretation of *māšîaḥ*"). This was virtually the unanimous position in the first five hundred years of church history (see section ii above for elaboration). As a result, this author uses the translation "Messiah" (as do the NKJV and NASB), which is simply a transliteration of the Hebrew word מָשִׁיחַ (*māšîaḥ*). In the Old Testament, both priests and kings were anointed at the time of their commencement to office, but the title "Messiah" (Gk. *Christos*) came to signify above all else the one who was expected to come in fulfillment of the promise to David, a son who would inherit an eternal throne and kingdom. Furthermore, in Dan 9:25 he is called מָשִׁיחַ נָגִיד (*māšîaḥ nāgîḏ*), the latter term *nāgîḏ* designating him as "ruler." (Although "prince" is a legitimate translation of *nāgîḏ*, this carries a different connotation in English, and thus "ruler" is more suitable.) Even kings in the Old Testament are sometimes designated as a *nāgîḏ* (e.g., Saul in 1 Sam 9:16), and thus there is no reason to think of him as anything less than a *ruling king*. This was the promise to him according to the Davidic Covenant (2 Sam 7; Ps 2:7–9) and affirmed to him as "Son of Man" in Dan 7:13–14.

A common objection to the messianic interpretation of *māšîaḥ nāgîḏ* is that there is a punctuation mark known as an *ʾaṯnāḥ* in Dan 9:25 placed

278. For a defense of the AD 33 date for Christ's crucifixion, see section v above ("Chronological Details Pertaining to Christ's First Coming").

279. I have argued specifically for 444 BC in section vii above ("A Defense of Artaxerxes' Authorization to Nehemiah").

between "seven weeks" and "sixty-two weeks."[280] This supposedly disjoins the two temporal references, resulting in the statement that there are only "seven weeks" (of years, i.e., 49 years) from the word to restore Jerusalem until the "anointed one," which would effectively eliminate the messianic interpretation. However, one should be aware that this punctuation mark was *not* part of the original text but only added centuries later. Furthermore, there are other explanations for this apart from serving as a major disjunctive indicator in the sentence. For those wishing a more technical explanation refuting the claim based on the *ʾaṯnāḥ* of Dan 9:25, see "The Placement of the *Athnach* in 9:25" under "Additional Exegetical Comments" (below). Hence, Dan 9:25 affirms that there will be seven "weeks" and sixty-two "weeks" from this word to restore and rebuild Jerusalem until Messiah the Ruler.

The question may be asked, why then does the verse not simply say that there will be sixty-nine "weeks" from the word to rebuild until Messiah, rather than seven and sixty-two? The emphasis of this verse is not so much on Messiah as it is on the *rebuilding* of Jerusalem (notice the expressions "restore and rebuild" and "build again"). We can assume from this that the seven "weeks" (49 years) are for the completion of the rebuilding project, after which there will be another sixty-two "weeks" until Messiah. As argued above, the "word" to restore and rebuild Jerusalem speaks of the authorization of King Artaxerxes to Nehemiah as recorded in Neh 2:1–8. Although the initial rebuilding of the wall was accomplished in an amazing fifty-two days (Neh 6:15), that certainly was not the full extent of Jerusalem's restoration. Rather, that seems to have been a quick project to rough in the wall and close up the breaches in order to provide minimal protection to the inhabitants from outside attack. A full restoration would take many more years. Even after the wall had been rebuilt, we read in Neh 7:4, "Now the city was large and spacious, but the people in it were few and the houses were not built" (NASB). That it might take another forty-nine years for the city to be fully restored and rebuilt is quite reasonable. The final part of Dan 9:25 indicates, "It will be built again with a public square and town-moat, even in distressful times." Regarding the translation and meaning of "public square" and "town-moat," see the translation notes above to this verse. The first looks at an open public forum area within the city, while the other term (a hapax and hence more obscure) is generally thought to have something to do with the outside of the city walls, perhaps a cutting into the stone or a rampart that would make the city walls more difficult to assault. This would certainly go beyond what Nehemiah accomplished in his initial (and brief!) rebuilding effort (Neh 3–6).

Apart from the seven "weeks" allocated to the full restoration of Jerusalem, Dan 9:25 indicates that it would be a total of sixty-nine "weeks"

---

280. This is the typical position of critical scholars but has even been defended more recently by some evangelicals (e.g., McComiskey, "The Seventy Weeks of Daniel," 19–25; and Chisholm, *Handbook on the Prophets*, 313, fn 67).

from the going forth of the word to rebuild Jerusalem until Messiah the Ruler. Exactly how one is to calculate this time span has been the great enigma for commentators throughout the centuries. At least eight primary views for interpreting these verses and calculating the time segments have been proposed (see section vi above, "Survey of Views Regarding the Seventy 'Weeks'"). The proposal presented in this commentary is based on three critical presuppositions:

(1) The seventy "weeks" (i.e., the time spans of seven-year periods, 7 + 62 + 1) must be taken literally. This is not only consistent with a literal-historical-grammatical hermeneutic, but is also consistent with the fact that Daniel had been thinking about seventy literal years of captivity (Dan 9:2; Jer 25:11; 29:10) and the fact that the seventy years were the result of having violated seventy sabbatical years—a period of 490 literal years (2 Chr 36:20–21).

(2) The reference to *māšîaḥ* should be understood as the Lord Jesus Christ (as argued in section iv above, "A Defense of the Messianic Interpretation of *māšîaḥ*").

(3) Any proposed interpretation for the time span "until Messiah the Ruler" must be in harmony with the fact that Jesus was crucified in AD 33 (as argued in section v above, "Chronological Details Pertaining to Christ's First Coming").

If these three presuppositions are correct, then the only view that can satisfy all three requirements is the one based on the authorization to Nehemiah as recorded in Neh 2:1–8. This is the one I have labeled the "messianic postponement view (prophetic-year calculation)." According to this view, it would be sixty-nine (7 + 62) "weeks" (i.e., 483 years) from the word to restore and rebuild Jerusalem—given by Artaxerxes, the Persian king, to Nehemiah—until Messiah the Ruler. What, then, is the *terminus a quo* and the *terminus ad quem* of this time span?

According to Neh 2:1, the *terminus a quo* was the month Nisan of the twentieth year of Artaxerxes. No specific day of the month was indicated, only that it was the month Nisan (generally in March-April). A very important question, however, is the matter of the exact year this took place. The Julian calendar, introduced by Julius Caesar, did not go into effect until 45 BC (and was eventually refined and replaced by the Gregorian calendar in AD 1582). Before this time, nations had other ways of tracking time, such as by the reigns of kings or by the four-year Olympiads. For this reason, trying to establish firm dates for events in antiquity is difficult and sometimes imprecise. Nevertheless, I have tried to reason in a previous section that Artaxerxes' authorization permitting Nehemiah to return and rebuild the city probably took place in Nisan of 444 BC (see section vii above, "A Defense of Artaxerxes' Authorization to Nehemiah").

Calculating the sixty-nine "weeks." The more challenging aspect of this verse is how to calculate the sixty-nine "weeks" from Artaxerxes' authorization to Nehemiah "until Messiah the Ruler." Given that each "week" (*šāḇûaʿ*)

amounts to seven years, sixty-nine "weeks" would total 483 years. If by "year" we mean a solar year of approximately 365 ¼ days, then the time until Messiah from Nisan of 444 BC would be AD 40 (keeping in mind that there is no year zero). Yet this date would be well past the time of Messiah by anyone's reckoning. An alternative method would be to assume that the years are "prophetic years" of 360 days.

In defense of using "prophetic years" of 360 days (12 months of 30 days each), several lines of reasoning can be offered: (1) several ancient countries had calendar systems based on a lunar year of 12 months that totaled less than 365 1/4 days but with some method of correcting to the solar year (intercalation);[281] (2) in recounting the story of the flood in Noah's day, we are told that the water prevailed on the earth 150 days (Gen 7:24; 8:3), and yet this was from the "second month, seventeenth day" (Gen 7:11) until the "seventh month, seventeenth day" (8:4), i.e., five months of thirty days each;[282] and (3) the connection between Dan 9:27 and the book of Revelation suggests that thirty-day months are in view. If the antichrist is the main subject of Dan 9:27 (as argued in the commentary to follow), his "making desolate" for the second half of the seventieth week would correspond to the "time, times and half a time" (three and a half years) of Dan 7:25, which in turn is clarified in Revelation (11:2–3; 12:6, 14; and 13:5) as being 1260 days or forty-two months, i.e., a three-and-a-half-year period based on months of thirty days.

Based on prophetic years of 360 days, then, the 483 years specified in Dan 9:25 would result in 173,880 actual days (360 x 483). To express this in terms of a solar year calendar, the 173,880 days would need to be divided by 365.2421897 (a "mean tropical year"). The result would be just over 476 solar years (476.068). Hence, sixty-nine "weeks" of years (476.068 solar years) from Artaxerxes' authorization to Nehemiah in the month Nisan of 444 BC would bring us to the spring of AD 33, the very season in which Jesus entered Jerusalem for the final time and was subsequently crucified.

A word of caution. While others have tried to calculate the sixty-nine "weeks" *to the very day*, it is better to exercise caution and not be overly speculative about this calculation for several reasons.[283] First, though the

---

281. Cf. P. Van Der Meer, *The Ancient Chronology of Western Asia and Egypt* (Leiden: Brill, 1947), 1–2.

282. For discussion, see Finegan, *Handbook of Biblical Chronology*, 15–16.

283. Robert Anderson, *The Coming Prince: The Marvelous Prophecy of Daniel's Seventy Weeks concerning the Antichrist*, 5th ed. (London: Hodder & Stoughton, 1895; repr., 15th ed., Grand Rapids: Kregel, 1963), attempted to argue that the sixty-nine weeks could be calculated exactly from Nisan 1 (March 14), 445 BC until April 6, AD 32, the day (according to him) of Christ's triumphal entry in fulfillment of Zech 9:9; so A. J. McClain, *Daniel's Prophecy of the Seventy Weeks* (Grand Rapids: Zondervan, 1940, 1969), 19. Hoehner, *Chronological Aspects*, 135–39, followed the same procedure but updated Anderson's dates from Nisan 1 (March 5), 444 BC until March 30, AD 33. J. D. Pentecost, "Daniel," in *Bible Knowledge Commentary: OT*, ed.

444 BC date has more to commend it, we cannot be absolutely positive that Artaxerxes' authorization to Nehemiah in the twentieth year of his reign occurred in 444 BC rather than 445 BC (see discussion in section vii, "A Defense of Artaxerxes' Authorization to Nehemiah"). Second, Neh 2 only indicates that it took place in the month Nisan without specifying the exact day. Third, in Jewish chronology, an intercalary month could be added from time to time to realign their calendar system with the solar year, but there is debate as to whether or not an additional intercalary month might have been inserted prior to Nisan 1 of 444 BC as well as to AD 33.[284] The Jews are known to have used a lunisolar calendar, basically lunar but with ways to correct the calendar so as to synchronize with the solar calendar.[285] This kept their calendar (which corresponded to agricultural seasons) from drifting far out of alignment from a true solar year. Fourth, even though we know that Jews added in an extra month (an intercalary month) from time to time to correct their calendar, there is some evidence indicating they may not have used the same system throughout this period.[286] Fifth, there is no firm consensus as to what day Nisan 1 of 444 BC might have been according to

---

J. F. Walvoord and R. B. Zuck (Wheaton, IL: Victor, 1985), 1363, and J. F. Walvoord, *The Prophecy Knowledge Handbook* (Wheaton, IL: Victor, 1990), 254, use a similar method (and dates) as Hoehner. Rather than using the decimal equivalent for days (365.242) as Hoehner did, Pentecost and Walvoord simply used 365. But then they added in 116 days for leap years, and 24 days for March 5–March 30 (Hoehner had used 25!).

284. The Jews debated among themselves as to when it was proper to add in an intercalary month. See Babylonian Talmud, *Sanh.* 10b–13b.

285. The Hebrew lunar year—appr. 354.37 days, with some months having 30 days and others 29—was about eleven days shorter than the solar cycle. To compensate, the nineteen-year Metonic cycle was used to bring it into line with the solar cycle, with the addition of an intercalary month every two or three years, for a total of seven times per nineteen years. Even with this intercalation, the average Hebrew calendar year is almost seven minutes longer than the current mean solar year, so that every 217 years the Hebrew calendar will fall a day behind the current mean solar year.

286. Julius Africanus referred to a different system. "The Jews, he said, reckoned a year as 354 days rather than 365 ¼ days. The former represents twelve months according to the moon's course, while the latter is based on the solar year. This amounts to a difference of 11 ¼ days per year but is eventually made up by the insertion of extra months at eight-year intervals. 'Hence the Greeks and the Jews insert three intercalary months every eight years. For eight times 11 ¼ days makes up 3 months'" (Tanner, "Is Daniel's Seventy-Weeks Prophecy Messianic? Part 1," 191–92). Cf. *Theodoret of Cyrus* (249) who also mentions a different methodology than the one based on a nineteen-year Metonic cycle, in order to synchronize the Jewish 354-day calendar with the solar year.

a Julian calendar. Hoehner argued that it was March 5, 444 BC, yet others have suggested different dates.[287]

In light of the points above, it may be best to simply conclude that sixty-nine "weeks" is roughly equivalent to approximately 476 solar years, and that the sixty-nine "weeks" have a *terminus a quo* at Nisan 444 BC and a *terminus ad quem* in the spring of AD 33. Furthermore, there is no real need to calculate to the very day (as though it might fall exactly on the day of the triumphal entry or the day of Christ's crucifixion).[288] The prophecy in Dan 9:25 only indicates that it would be sixty-nine "weeks" until Messiah the Ruler, without specifying any certain event in his life. More important is what takes places following the completion of the sixty-nine "weeks," which brings us to v. 26.

9:26 Verse 26 describes several important events that will take place after the first sixty-nine "weeks." As seen from a study of v. 25 (above), the sixty-ninth "week" concluded in the spring of AD 33. In light of what was revealed earlier in the Old Testament about Messiah (including Dan 2:44 and 7:13–14), one might think that His coming would be accompanied by the establishment of His glorious kingdom on earth in which He would reign as king over all. Yet Yahweh had a different plan and timing of events. The kingdom would eventually come, but first Messiah would be "cut off" after the second stipulated period, the sixty-two weeks. We observed in v. 25 that he was called "Messiah the Ruler" (מָשִׁיחַ נָגִיד, *māšîaḥ nāgîḏ*), but in v. 26 simply "Messiah" (מָשִׁיחַ, *māšîaḥ*). Yet this is no reason to conclude that two different individuals are in view (as critical scholars attempt to argue). The first introduces him as the Messiah who will become the "Ruler" in fulfillment of the promises

287. Anderson, *The Coming Prince* argued that Artaxerxes' authorization occurred on March 14, 445 BC. R. A. Parker and W. H. Dubberstein, *Babylonian Chronology 626 B.C.–A.D. 75* (Providence, RI: Brown Univesity Press, 1956), 32, stipulate that it was April 3, 444 BC. Goldstine, *New and Full Moons*, 47, indicates there was a full moon on March 27 and again on April 26 of 444 BC. S. A. Smith, "Two Significant Problems with Harold Hoehner's Chronology of the Life of Christ" (accessed 3 July 2015, http://www.biblicalreader.com/reader/Harold_Hoehners_Chronology.htm), claims, "The start-date of March 5 (444 BC) that Hoehner gives for Nisan 1 (the presumed start-date of the Seventy-Weeks Prophecy) is incorrect; March 5, 444 BC fell on II Adar 2, while Nisan 1 fell on April 2. Likely the reason for this error was a failure to recognize that 445/444 BC (year 3317 in the Hebrew Calendar) was a year with an intercalary month. The difference between II Adar 2 and Nisan 1 is 28 days. Thus, at the outset, Hoehner's calculation was thrown off by 28 days."

288. This is not to say that the prophecy *cannot* work out to the very day, but only that there are too many unknowns to us today to be able to substantiate this. Hoehner sought to work out the calculations to the very day, which resulted (for him) in having the triumphal entry fall on a Monday, rather than a Sunday, in the year AD 33.

to David (2 Sam 7) and reiterated elsewhere (Ps 2:7–9; Mic 5:2). In v. 26, however, there is no need to specify again his role as "Ruler" in the second mention of him in this passage. Furthermore, had two different individuals been intended, we would have expected more differentiation to have been made by the author to clarify this point, especially given the fact that the term *māšîaḥ* occurs in the very next verse.

This "cutting off" of Messiah suggests a violent death.[289] The fulfillment of this "cutting off," then, is the crucifixion of the Lord Jesus on Nisan 14, AD 33, thereby fulfilling the prophecy of Isa 52:13–53:12. As a result, he is said to "have nothing." The text is not clear to what this refers (commentators have made numerous suggestions), but the most logical explanation has to do with what was promised the "Son of Man" in Dan 7:13–14, namely his everlasting dominion and a kingdom that would not be destroyed.[290] From the broader context of the book of Daniel, that is what we would have expected for Messiah. Ultimately, of course, this kingdom promise will be fully realized, but not immediately after the sixty-two "weeks" when he is "cut off." Apart from the kingdom promise, however, he does gain some important things. For instance, he would ascend to the Father's right hand and be glorified, and he would become Head over the church.

Verse 26 goes on to describe the sad fate that would befall the Jewish people who crucified Messiah: "the people of the ruler who is to come will destroy the city and the sanctuary." In light of the context of Dan 9, this can only refer to Jerusalem and her temple. Yet if this follows the sixty-two "weeks" and Messiah's death, then this must refer to Jerusalem of the first century AD. This is indeed in keeping with known history. In the year AD 66 during the troubled reign of Emperor Nero, the Jews of Palestine revolted against the Roman Empire. Nero sent one of his commanders named Vespasian to put down the revolt. Before the victory could be clinched, however, Nero committed suicide (AD 68), prompting Vespasian to return to Rome as the new Roman emperor. As a result, Vespasian's son Titus took over the campaign in Judea. On September 26, AD 70, Jerusalem fell, and Herod's temple was leveled in fulfillment of Christ's prediction (Matt 24:2; Luke 21:20–24).

We do well to observe that v. 25 anticipated the "word" calling for the rebuilding and restoration of Jerusalem, whereas v. 26 brings us to the final period of Jerusalem and the temple after it had stood for several centuries. With the formal rejection of Jesus as Messiah, God's judgment on that first century AD generation of Jews was inescapable. The Roman army under Titus was merely the Lord's agent to carry out this judgment. Appropriately then,

289. The Hebrew word for "cut off" (כָּרַת, *kāraṯ*) is used elsewhere of making a covenant based on the death of a sacrificial animal (Gen 15:10, 18). The same word is also used of the death penalty (Lev 8:20) and always of an unnatural violent death (cf. Isa 53:8).

290. Archer (113), for example, suggests that "he will be bereft of followers; all of them will flee from him at the time of his arrest, trial, and death."

Jesus could indict the national leadership for not "recognizing the time of your [messianic] visitation" (Luke 19:44). For this, they suffered the gravest of consequences: the destruction of Jerusalem, the destruction of the temple, and in the aftermath of these events the dispersion of the Jewish people from the land itself.

Because this statement in v. 26 refers so explicitly to the destruction of Jerusalem and the temple in AD 70—therefore ruling out a possibility of the passage being fulfilled in the second century BC during the reign of Antiochus IV—critical scholars have sought to find other ways to avoid a straightforward reading of the text. They have done this in two ways. The first is by trying to give the word translated "destroy" (שָׁחַת, *šāḥaṯ*) a different meaning. Rather than translate *šāḥaṯ* as "destroy," they attempt to translate it as "corrupt."[291] With this translation, they can claim that the verse refers to Antiochus who *corrupted* Jerusalem and the temple operation. Yet a thorough lexical study of *šāḥaṯ* supports the translation "destroy." For substantiation, see "The Meaning and Implications of *šāḥaṯ* in 9:26" in the "Additional Exegetical Comments" at the end of this section.

A second way of averting the implications of v. 26 (i.e., Jerusalem's AD 70 destruction) is by altering the punctuation and flow of the sentence. Notice Goldingay's (226) translation:

> ... an anointed will be cut off
> and will have neither the city nor the sanctuary.
> A leader to come will devastate a people ...

He takes the words "the city and the sanctuary" and removes them from being the object of the verb "destroy" (*šāḥaṯ*, which he translates as "devastate") and joins them to the preceding clause. Rather than "having nothing," the "anointed" has neither the city nor the sanctuary.[292] Also, the word "people," rather than being the subject of the sentence is now made the object. This, however, would not be the most natural translation. First, Goldingay ignores the *ʾaṯnāḥ* punctuation marker (which he insisted on for v. 25) that comes after "and will have nothing" (וְאֵ֣ין ל֑וֹ, *wᵊʾên lô*) and that separates "the city and the sanctuary" from the next clause.[293] Second, to make "people" the object of the verb "destroy" (*šāḥaṯ*) is awkward at best, seeing that it forces him to make the more remote words "a leader to come" as the subject. Normally, Hebrew word order would expect the reverse. Third, if "people" meant "the Jewish people" (as he so interprets), we would expect "the people" or "your

291. Collins (357) remarks, "The Syrians did not demolish Jerusalem, but they made it desolate by the corruption of the cult."

292. Goldingay rejects the translation of *māšîaḥ* as Messiah, preferring "anointed" instead, whom he assumes to be the high priest Onias III.

293. I am not claiming that the *ʾaṯnāḥ* punctuation marker cannot be questioned or challenged, only that Goldingay is inconsistent at this point.

people" as in v. 24, not "a people."[294] It is worth pointing out that nearly every major English version (including NIV, NET, NRSV, NKJV, and ESV) supports the translation "destroy" and has something similar to NASB's "and the people of the prince who is to come will destroy the city and the sanctuary."

A careful study of this period of the Jewish revolt reveals that Jerusalem's end came like a flood. Goldingay (230) has pointed out that the word "flood" (שֶׁטֶף, *šeṭep̄*) "more often denotes the flood of calamity brought by an oppressor (11:10, 22, 26, 40)." This "flood," then, involved a desolating war in the land for about seven years, beginning at Caesarea in AD 66 and lasting until the final assault at Masada in AD 73.[295]

Finally, we should observe more carefully who is said to destroy Jerusalem and the temple in AD 70: "the people of the ruler who is to come." Obviously "the people" must refer to the Roman soldiers under Titus. The word translated "people" (עַם, *ʿam*) can have in view a military unit as it does in 1 Sam 17:14. The Hebrew term for "ruler" (נָגִיד, *nāgîḏ*)—sometimes translated "prince"—is the same word that was used for Messiah in v. 25. This is a general term, and in this context simply means a *ruler* (so the NIV). Yet this ruler is not the Roman commander at the time of the Jewish revolt but rather one who is still to come. Verse 26 is making the point that this "people"—part of the first-century AD Roman army—destroyed Jerusalem and its temple and that there is a future coming ruler who is connected to them in some way. Chapter 7 of Daniel has already revealed that the antichrist would come to possess a kingdom that emerges out of the fourth beast, the Roman Empire. Dan 9:26 builds upon what had been revealed earlier in chap. 7. This ruler of 9:26, then, is the future antichrist. Verse 27 makes this clear.

9:27 The final verse of the chapter addresses the seventieth and final "week," i.e., the final seven years of the prophecy. Three crucial questions must be addressed: (1) Who is the one making the covenant? (2) What is the nature of the covenant? and, (3) Does the seventieth "week" immediately follow the first sixty-nine "weeks"? Critical scholars assume that the one making this covenant is Antiochus IV Epiphanes about 171/70 BC. This theory, however, is wrong, because the destruction of Jerusalem and the temple (mentioned in v. 26) did not take place at that time. Some conservative scholars, on the other hand, have suggested that the one making the covenant is Messiah Jesus. But this interpretation cannot be correct either. The text says, "he will confirm

---

294. By separating "people" from "leader to come," Goldingay is disrupting the genitive construct chain (עַם נָגִיד הַבָּא, *ʿam nāgîḏ habbāʾ*). This would make "people" (עַם, *ʿam*) anarthrous. Otherwise, it would be articular in light of the ptc. הַבָּא (*habbāʾ*) at the end of the chain having the definite article.

295. Miller (268) adds, "'Flood' is a figure emphasizing the magnitude of the devastation (cf. Isa 8:7–8; 28:2; ...). The Roman destruction of Jerusalem in AD 70 did indeed come like a great 'flood' that swept over the city and destroyed it."

(or enforce) a covenant with the many for one week."[296] The pronoun "he" of this sentence is best understood in light of its nearest antecedent, namely "the ruler who is to come" in v. 26—the one that is related in some way to the ancient Roman Empire. This suggests that the one confirming the covenant is the antichrist, the one said to arise from the Roman Empire in Dan 7.[297] The temporal comparison between 9:27 and 7:25 tends to confirm this interpretation. The final "week" is divided into two halves by the suspension of the sacrificial system. As a result, the "covenant enforcer" turns to "causing desolation" during the second half, i.e., three and a half years—the same time span as the one who assaults the Most High and his saints in 7:25.

If, then, Dan 9:27 pertains to the time of the antichrist, the seventieth and final "week" obviously does not immediately follow the first sixty-nine. Not surprisingly, some have objected to a hiatus in the seventy "weeks," whereby the final week is suspended unto the eschatological future.[298] Yet the seventieth "week" cannot immediately follow the first sixty-nine.[299] If

---

296. Goldingay (230) argues for taking "covenant" as the subject of the sentence rather than the object: "A covenant will prevail for the multitude." This is highly unlikely since it involves a fem. subject with a masc. verb. Goldingay tries to defend this by appeal to GKC, 462–63 (§145c).

297. It is worth noting that the antichrist interpretation of Dan 9:27 is embraced not only by most premillennial scholars but also by some amillennial ones (e.g., T. Kliefoth, C. F. Keil and H. C. Leupold). This position was also held by several early church fathers, such as Irenaeus (*Against Heresies*, in *The Ante-Nicene Fathers*, 1:554), Hippolytus (*Commentary on the Prophet Daniel*, 2.22), and Origen (*Contra Celsum*, book 2, chap. 49 in *The Ante-Nicene Fathers*, 4:450–51; and book 6, chap. 46, 4:594–95). Note, however, that Origen may have voiced a different interpretation in his commentary on Matthew; cf. L. E. Knowles, "The Interpretations of the Seventy Weeks of Daniel in the Early Fathers," *WTJ* 7 (1945): 149–50. Finally, there is the opinion of Apollinaris of Laodicea (preserved in Archer, *Jerome's Commentary on Daniel*, 104–5). He took Dan 9:27 to refer to the antichrist, though he held the unorthodox view that the entire seventy weeks spanned the time between the first and second coming of Christ, and thus he expected Dan 9:27 to be fulfilled before the year AD 500.

298. Although Clement of Alexandria (writing ca. AD 200) did not follow the antichrist interpretation of Dan 9:27, he nevertheless posited a gap between the first sixty-nine weeks and the seventieth week. For him, the final week encompassed both Nero's erection of an "abomination" in Jerusalem as well as the destruction of the city and temple in Vespasian's reign. Cf. W. Adler, "The Apocalyptic Survey of History Adapted by Christians: Daniel's Prophecy of 70 Weeks," in *The Jewish Apocalyptic Heritage in Early Christianity*, ed. J. C. VanderKam and W. Adler, 201–38 (Minneapolis, MN: Fortress, 1996), 225.

299. For a defense of the postponement view of Dan 9:27, see J. R. Price, "Prophetic Postponement in Daniel 9:24–27," in *Progressive Dispensationalism: An Analysis of the Movement and Defense of Traditional Dispensationalism*, ed. R. J. Bigalke, 215–56

the events of v. 27 follow all the details of v. 26 (as a natural reading of these verses would imply), then the covenant mentioned in v. 27 is carried out *after* Jerusalem's destruction in AD 70. If the first sixty-nine "weeks" cover the time leading up to Messiah's crucifixion in AD 33, and the making of the covenant that begins the seventieth "week" follows the events of AD 70, then there must be a *gap in time* before the seventieth "week." That this gap extends all the way to the second coming of Messiah Jesus makes sense in light of the six goals that were laid out in v. 24, some of which could not have been accomplished in Christ's first coming (e.g., sealing up vision and prophecy). Furthermore, the "abomination of desolation" to which this verse apparently alludes (cf. Dan 12:11) is regarded by Christ as a *future event* connected with his second coming (Matt 24:15).

What, then, is the nature of this covenant? The word translated "covenant" (Heb. בְּרִית, *bᵊrîṯ*) can mean a biblical covenant or (in a more general sense) an alliance, treaty, agreement, or pact (BDB, 136). The text does not tell us the exact nature of this *bᵊrîṯ*, but apparently the antichrist either coerces or forces Israel (the "many" in v. 27) to agree to the terms of this *bᵊrîṯ*.

Some (e.g., Miller, 271) have supposed this to be a peace covenant that Israel will make with the latter-days antichrist, in which he will guarantee their protection and security in exchange for their allegiance (though he eventually betrays them).[300] The problem with this view is that there is nothing in the context to support the idea that a peace treaty or *covenant of protection* is in view, nor is this thesis taught elsewhere in Scripture. Yet the *context* of Dan 9:27 does support an alternative view. The fact that he eventually "puts an end to sacrifice and offering" suggests that this covenant has something to do with the ancient Mosaic law. If the antichrist's purpose is to masquerade and deceive the Jewish people into thinking he is the real Messiah, then it makes sense that this *bᵊrîṯ* in Dan 9:27 is related to the Mosaic law. (See commentary at Dan 11:37 for a discussion and defense of the idea that the antichrist will be ethnically Jewish, i.e., he will be a Jewish false messiah.)

Daniel 9:27 is often translated to say that "he will make a firm/strong covenant," or "he will confirm a covenant." The actual Hebrew text is הִגְבִּיר בְּרִית (*higbîr bᵊrîṯ*). This is the only time in all the Old Testament that the verb גָּבַר (*gāḇar*) occurs with the noun בְּרִית (*bᵊrîṯ*). Furthermore, the verb *gāḇar* in this verse is in the Hipʿil stem, making this construction all the more unique, since the Hipʿil of *gāḇar* only occurs one other time, namely Ps 12:5 (Eng. 12:4). In that instance, most translations have something like "with our tongue we will prevail," though this provides little insight for Dan 9:27.

(Lanham, MD: University Press of America, 2005). He argues for a *postponement of fulfillment* in light of contingency passages like Acts 3:19–21, whereby the return of Christ is conditioned on Israel's national repentance.

300. Wood (259) considers this to be "some type of nonaggression treaty, recognizing Israel's rights."

In general, the Hip'il stem is a *causative* of the Qal stem. In the Qal stem, *gāḇar* means "to be strong, be mighty, or prevail" (BDB, 149d). A search of all the occurrences of *gāḇar* in the Qal stem (17x in the Old Testament) reveals that it can also mean "to surpass" (once, Gen 49:26) or "to be great" (4x). The Hip'il of *gāḇar* in Dan 9:27, then, might mean something like "he will cause a covenant to be strong or great for the many." This does not seem to lend support to the idea that the covenant itself is "strong," much less that he "confirms" the covenant. Rather, the idea seems to be that he *strongly establishes* a covenant with the many, or perhaps that he *enforces a covenant* (he causes it to prevail or be binding).[301] This receives some support from LXX$^{\theta}$, δυναμώσει διαθήκην (*dunamōsei diathēkēn*), "he will strengthen a covenant."

In light of the contextual clue about "sacrifice and offering," the words הִגְבִּיר בְּרִית (*higbîr bᵊrîṯ*) are best understood to mean that the antichrist will pose as a false messiah who dupes Israel (at least initially) and *causes* the Mosaic covenant *to prevail* in the land (i.e., he *enforces* it). Actually, the expectation in orthodox Jewish eschatology is that Messiah will uphold the Mosaic law and usher in an age of righteousness.[302] Verses like Isa 2:3, "for

---

301. Baldwin (191) comes very close to this same conclusion when she states that the verb "has the implication of forcing an agreement by means of superior strength." Lacocque (187, 198), though interpreting this passage in light of Antiochus IV, offers a similar translation: "He will impose a covenant on many for one week." In a more technical study of the verb *gāḇar*, S. Paul, "Mesopotamian Background of Daniel 1–6," in *The Book of Daniel: Volume 1, Composition and Reception*, ed. J. J. Collins and P. W. Flint, 55–68 (Leiden: Brill, 2001), 59 writes, "The Hebrew verb, whose root גבר in the *qal* means 'to be strong' and in the *hip'il*, as here, means 'to make strong,' is none other than the semantic equivalent of the Akkadian *dunnunu* and Aramaic תקף, and shares with its cognates the legal meaning 'to make valid and binding.'"

302. The following is taken from the entry on "Eschatology" in the 1906 edition of *The Jewish Encyclopedia* (online: <http://www.jewishencyclopedia.com/articles/5849-eschatology#anchor10>): "Whereas the Babylonian schools took it for granted that the Mosaic law, and particularly the sacrificial and priestly laws, will be fully observed in the Messianic time (Yoma 5b *et al.*), the view that a new Law of God will be proclaimed by the Messiah is occasionally expressed (Eccl. R. ii. 1; Lev. R. xiii., according to Jer. xxxi. 32)—'the thirty commandments' which comprise the Law of humanity (Gen. R. xcviii.). 'Ye will receive a new Law from the Elect One of the righteous' (Targ. to Isa. xii. 3). The Holy One will expound the new Law to be given by the Messiah (Yalḳ. ii. 296, to Isa. xxvi.); according to Pes. xii. 107a, He will only infuse new ideas ('ḥiddush debarim'); or the Messiah will take upon himself the kingdom of the Law and make many zealous followers thereof (Targ. to Isa. ix. 5 *et seq.*, and liii. 11–12)."

the law will go forth from Zion," could certainly be taken to support such a view (though my personal view on this verse differs).[303]

According to Dan 9:27, the antichrist goes to the extreme of putting "an end to sacrifice and offering" in the middle of the final seven years, i.e., three and a half years following his enforcement of the covenant. Notice that the text does not go so far as to say he breaks his alliance with the Jews at this point, only that he makes an important change in regard to the offering of sacrifices. This verse implies, then, that some sort of Jewish temple will be standing and operational at that time. The operation of a sacrificial system implies this, and other New Testament verses confirm it (e.g., Matt 24:15; 2 Thess 2:4; Rev 11:1–3).

The remainder of Dan 9:27 is difficult to translate, as well as to understand. We are told that "on the wing of an *utter* abomination will come one who makes desolate." The one who "makes desolate" is the antichrist himself, the same one who put a halt to the offering of sacrifices. The verb translated "to desolate" is a Poʿlel participle of שָׁמֵם (*šāmēm*), meaning "appalling, causing horror" (BDB, 1031a), although *HALOT* (1565) suggests the meaning "the one who devastates" for Dan 9:27.[304] Although both meanings—"to desolate" and "to devastate" (or destroy)—are acceptable nuances for שָׁמֵם (*šāmēm*), the former seems to be more suitable in the case of Dan 9:27.[305] By a most despicable act, the antichrist will commit a desolating sacrilege.

The words "on the wing of an *utter* abomination" hint at what the antichrist does that is so desolating. Regarding "wing," the LXX translators

---

303. My understanding of Isa 2:3 is that the Lord's *teaching* will go forth from Jerusalem, not necessarily the Mosaic law. The word "law" (תּוֹרָה, *tôrâ*) can have a more general meaning of "teaching, instruction" (BDB, 435).

304. I. Meyer ("שָׁמֵם," *TDOT*, 15:243) understands מְשֹׁמֵם (*mᵉšōmēm*) in Dan 9:27 to refer not to the person behind the atrocity but to the act itself (though he interprets 9:27 in light of Antiochus IV). He concludes, "On the 'wing of abominations' (*ʿal-kᵉnap̱*) ... will come something that brings desolation (*mᵉšōmēm*)—putting an end to the legitimate cult."

305. H. J. Austel, "שָׁמֵם (*šāmēm*)," in *TWOT*, 936–37, points out, "The book of Daniel has four passages employing the Polel form of the verb (*mĕšōmēm* and *šōmēm*). There is a causative (or, better, factitive) force here similar to the use of the Hiphil, except that the Hiphil generally involves a physical devastation, while the Polel seems to put more stress on the fact that someone has caused the sanctuary or altar to be polluted, thus rendering it unfit for the worship and service of God. These passages are Dan 8:13; 11:31; 9:27; and 12:11. In the first two, Antiochus Epiphanes is depicted as doing away with proper sacrifices and in 11:31 as setting up an 'abomination' (*šiqqûṣ*), generally understood to be an idol or pagan altar. In this activity he foreshadows the Antichrist as described in 9:27 and 12:11. ... The presence of this abomination in the sanctuary makes it desolate, unfit for proper worship."

understood it to imply the temple or a part of the temple.[306] The connection of the word "wing" (כְּנַף, *kᵊnap̱*) with the temple is not readily apparent, yet the LXX translated "on a wing" (עַל כְּנַף, *ʿal kᵊnap̱*) as ἐπὶ τὸ ἱερὸν (*epi to hieron*), "on/in the temple." (See the translation note to Dan 9:27 above for discussion.) Perhaps there is a connection with the cherubim that were stationed in the holy of holies and whose *wings* (כְּנָפַיִם, *kᵊnāp̱ayim*) overshadowed the mercy seat (1 Kgs 6:24, 27; 8:6–7), but admittedly there is no confirmation for this suggestion. In any case, the LXX translation helps explain the NIV's rendering of this verse: "And at the temple he will set up an abomination that causes desolation." Assuming the LXX translators understood *kᵊnap̱* correctly (that it was a word implying the temple), the NIV translation seems to reflect the correct idea.

"Utter abomination" translates the participle מְשֹׁמֵם, *mĕšōmēm* (see translation note above for an explanation of this rendering as a plural of amplification). This is not merely an abomination but a most despicable abomination. If "wing" is a cryptic reference to the temple, then the verse is suggesting that the antichrist commits an act at the temple site that can only be described as an "utter abomination."[307] What the antichrist will do goes beyond what Antiochus IV did in defiling the temple site in 167 BC.

Taking Dan 9:27 as a whole, the antichrist will commit a twofold atrocity. First, he will halt the sacrifices at the temple that had been observed up until this point. Second, he will commit the "utter abomination," which is most likely that described in 2 Thess 2:4: he [the man of lawlessness] "opposes and exalts himself against every so-called god or object of worship, so that he takes his seat in the temple of God, proclaiming himself to be God" (ESV). Also, this is most likely connected with the "abomination of desolation" that Jesus prophesied of in Matt 24:15 (the words "standing in the holy place" undoubtedly relate this blasphemous act to the temple).[308] Jesus went on to

---

306. T. F. Williams, "שׁמם," in *NIDOTTE*, 4:169, notes, "In Dan 9:27 the desolating abomination is said to be lit. 'on a wing,' *ʿal-kᵊnap*. This is likely an allusion to the winglike horns on the corners of the altar, cf. NJPSV: 'at the corner [of the altar]' (but cf. NRSV 'in their place,' i.e., the place of sacrifice [emending to read *ʿal kannām*]; or NIV: 'on a wing [of the temple],' i.e., the pinnacle of the temple [cf. LXX; Vg.; Matt 4:5])." In response, however, the word "desolating" (*mᵊšōmēm*) is a masc. sg. ptc., whereas "abomination" (*šiqqûṣîm*) is masc. pl. Hence *mᵊšōmēm* does not modify *šiqqûṣîm*.

307. For further study, see J. R. Price, "The Desecration and Restoration of the Temple in the Tanach, Jewish Apocalyptic Literature, and the New Testament" (Ann Arbor, MI: UMI, 1993). Several early church fathers understood that the "abomination of desolation" (also 12:11) would be committed by the antichrist. So Irenaeus, *Against Heresies*, 2.25.2; Hippolytus, *Scholia on Daniel*, 1342; and Cyril of Jerusalem, *Catechetical Lectures*, 4.15.

308. Regarding the historical development of the expression "abomination of desolation," see Hartman (253).

warn that this event marked the onset of the "great tribulation" (Matt 24:21) and that those who heed his words should flee Judea at this point. Following this "abomination of desolation," the antichrist then has three and a half years during which he will be allowed to terrorize the earth and cause the unbelieving world to worship him (Rev 13:5; Dan 7:25), which corresponds to the second half of the final "week" in Dan 9:27.

Nevertheless, the antichrist—the one who desolates—will only be allowed to rule and wage war "until a predetermined destruction is poured out on" him. In light of such passages as 2 Thess 2:8–12 and Rev 19:19–21, the antichrist will be personally stopped by Christ himself at his second coming and cast into the "lake of fire." That's his "predetermined" end (cf. Dan 7:26).

Biblical Theology Comments

Dan 9:24–27 is perhaps one of the most theologically significant passages in all the Old Testament. In these four verses, we are given powerful insight about Messiah Jesus, the timing of his first coming, the expectation that he will be put to death, information about the rebuilding of Jerusalem and its subsequent destruction in AD 70 following Messiah's death, and finally the antichrist's arrival to deceptively enforce the Mosaic covenant only to betray the Jewish people when he halts the sacrificial system and desolates the temple operation. The period in which antichrist carries out his diabolical mission lasts seven years, though the time from halting the sacrificial system (in the middle of the final *šāḇûa'*) until his ultimate defeat will be three and a half years. The passage is not only significant christologically for what it teaches about Messiah Jesus but also for the foundation it lays for New Testament eschatology. The idea of a final seven-year period of tribulation preceding the second coming is not found in the New Testament, but only here in Dan 9:24–27 (though the book of Revelation does disclose the length of the second half of this period, namely the three and a half years—or 1260 days or 42 months—during which antichrist turns against the Jewish people). To fail to see the term מָשִׁיחַ (*māšîaḥ*) as Messiah Jesus or to attempt to interpret the passage in terms of Antiochus IV Epiphanes in the second century BC is to utterly undermine the passage of its rich theological contribution to biblical Christology and eschatology.

Application and Devotional Implications

One of the important truths coming out of Dan 9:24–27 is that even though Jerusalem and the temple would be rebuilt (v. 25), they would eventually be destroyed again (v. 26). And if the interpretation of Dan 9:27 and the book of Revelation as presented in this commentary is correct, they will probably be rebuilt and destroyed yet again. In Daniel's mind, Jerusalem was God's city—called by his name (vv. 16, 18). He also spoke of the temple as "Your desolated sanctuary" (v. 17). Yet God was quite willing to let his city, his temple, and his people be decimated by the hands of men. To God these were important, but he did not put all his stock in their temporal value. Eternal accomplishments were of far greater importance.

More significantly still, God even allowed his precious Son ("Messiah the Ruler") to be "cut off and have nothing"—put to death as an innocent lamb. God did so, because the eternal accomplishment of our Lord's supreme act in shamefully being crucified to a cross would be of far greater importance than the momentary ignominy he had to endure. By his sacrificial act, eternal redemption would be made possible for sinful mankind who otherwise would have no hope of standing in God's presence and enjoying eternity with him.

We, too, need to think in terms of living for that which is of eternal value rather than that which merely gives us temporal satisfaction and pleasure. Though it is not wrong to enjoy things of this world, if we are not careful we can easily settle for that which is most comfortable and challenges us less rather than that which has greater value in light of eternity. Those of us in Western societies live in an age of unrivaled materialism, and this can all too easily become the determinative factor in our life—as to what we do and what we live for. If God calls upon us to relinquish those things or to leave our comfort zones, are we willing to do that? Many a missionary has learned the blessing of giving up much in this life in order that God might bring forth fruit for eternity from the sacrifice of his or her earthly comforts, health, and wealth. The missionary martyr, Jim Elliott, once said, "He is no fool who gives up what he cannot keep to gain what he cannot lose!"

Additional Exegetical Comments

1. A Case for Taking the Seventy Weeks Literally Rather Than Symbolically[309]

Those who follow the Maccabean theory of a second-century BC fulfillment (as well as those who interpret the מָשִׁיחַ [*māšîaḥ*] of Dan 9:26 as the antichrist) are forced to argue that the period of seventy weeks should be understood symbolically. Ample research has been done on the Hebrew term "weeks" (שָׁבֻעִים, *šābuʿîm*) to establish that this means a *period of seven* and that in this context it implies a period of seven years.[310] Hence the seventy weeks represent a total of 490 years, and even most critical scholars acknowledge this.[311]

---

309. Most of the material in this section is extracted from my article in *BSac,* "Is Daniel's Seventy-Weeks Prophecy Messianic? Part 2" (see pp. 331–34) and used by permission. Slight modifications have been made to adapt to the formatting style of this commentary.

310. For discussions of "weeks" as seven-year periods see John C. Whitcomb, "Daniel's Great Seventy-Weeks Prophecy: An Exegetical Insight," 259–63; Harold W. Hoehner, "Chronological Aspects of the Life of Christ; Part VI: Daniel's Seventy Weeks and New Testament Chronology," 47–65; and Paul D. Feinberg, "An Exegetical and Theological Study of Daniel 9:24–27," 189–220.

311. See, for example, Collins, *A Commentary in the Book of Daniel*, 352.

In seeking to build his case that these seventy "sevens of years" (490 years) should be understood symbolically, McComiskey appeals to the idea that in ancient Near Eastern literature the numbers seven and seventy had a symbolic significance.[312] He writes,

> According to the view presented here the structure of Dan 9:24–27 is based on seventy *šābu ʿîm* which span the period of time from Jeremiah's prophecy to the antichrist. There is no apparent interruption in the sequence. The numerical concepts of seven and seventy are understood to have a symbolic significance. That significance, we have learned, is the concept of totality or fullness.[313]

Yet those who argue for a symbolic understanding of the seventy weeks of years are overlooking the obvious. Daniel's prayerful confession and plea on behalf of the nation in Dan 9 began with his reading Jer 25:11–12 and 29:10 that the nation's exile in and servitude to Babylon would end after seventy years (not after 490 years) and the Babylonian king would be punished. Judah lost her independence in 609 BC when Pharaoh Neco II of Egypt killed King Josiah and Judah became a vassal state of Egypt, only to be made a vassal state of Babylon four years later. In 539 BC—seventy years later—Babylon was overthrown, and the prophecy of Jeremiah was literally fulfilled. Daniel hoped that Jerusalem's desolations would be complete with Babylon's downfall, but the Lord showed him that seventy *sevens of years* would still be needed for her desolations to be fulfilled. Since the latter was established on a foundation of seventy literal years, logically the extended period should be viewed literally as well.

A second critical weakness of the symbolic view of the seventy weeks has to do with the Jewish interpretations of Daniel's seventy-weeks prophecy—some messianic and some non-messianic—that preceded the destruction

---

312. McComiskey, "The Seventy 'Weeks' of Daniel," 35–44. Collins (352) adds, "Periodization of history is a standard feature of the 'historical' apocalypses and often uses ten as the schematic number." Cf. A. Y. Collins, "Numerical Symbolism in Jewish and Early Christian Apocalyptic Literature," *ANRW* 21 (1984): 1224–49; and S. Tzoref, "*Pesher* and Periodization," *DSD* 18 (2011): 129–54. Based on a study of several Qumran documents exhibiting heptadic structures, R. Haydon, "The 'Seventy Sevens' (Daniel 9:24) in Light of Heptadic Themes in Qumran," *JESOT* 3 (2014): 212, concludes that "the heptadic structure 'seventy sevens' is not primarily a sum of years, but a timespan that traces the journey of the faithful saints (Dan 7:22–27) from Exile (Eden, Egypt, Assyria, etc.) to restoration in *its fullest iteration* ('to end sin ... bring in everlasting righteousness')." Similarly, R. S. Hess, "The Seventy Sevens of Daniel 9: A Timetable for the Future," *BBR* 21 (2011): 329, rejects a literal understanding of the 490 years in light of what he believes is "the Bible's tendency to approximate large epochs and to fit them within schemes of 'ideal' numbers such as 7,12, 40, or multiples thereof."

313. McComiskey, "The Seventy Weeks of Daniel," 41.

of the temple in AD 70. Beckwith has demonstrated that three types of chronological schemes were used in Jewish literature: (a) the Hellenistic scheme (which existed in two forms: one from the Old Greek Septuagint translation and a second from the Hellenistic Jewish historian Demetrius); (b) the Essene scheme embodied in the Book of Jubilees and other works from the mid-second century BC; and (c) the Pharisaic scheme, first attested in the *Assumption of Moses*.[314] Some of these Jewish chronological schemes were messianic (but not related to Jesus) and some non-messianic, and yet they were *all* based on a computation of a literal 490 years stemming from Daniel's prophecy. Significantly, these reckonings derive from the very period of time (the intertestamental period in which apocalyptic literature flourished) when McComiskey has said symbolic figures were used in Jewish and non-Jewish literature. While apocalyptic literature did utilize symbolic figures at times, the evidence regarding Dan 9:24–27 is strongly to the contrary. This is a particularly important point, since those advocating these various Jewish schemes relied primarily on the Hebrew text (predating the Christian era) and not the later Theodotionic Greek text. Furthermore, in the early centuries following the crucifixion of Jesus Christ, two primary Jewish interpretations of this passage—that of Josephus and that of the second-century AD Jewish chronological work, *Seder Olam Rabbah*—viewed the 490 years literally and viewed the *terminus ad quem* as in the events of AD 70.[315]

Thus the מָשִׁיחַ נָגִיד (*māšîaḥ nāgîḏ*) of Dan 9:25 would be expected after seven and sixty-two "weeks," that is, 483 years from the time that the decree (דָּבָר, *dāḇār*) was made to restore and rebuild Jerusalem. Since it can be easily demonstrated that such a period of time existed until the Lord Jesus Christ in his first advent, and since the Messiah, Son of David, is the most probable understanding of מָשִׁיחַ (*māšîaḥ*) in this context, this interpretation best

314. Beckwith, "Daniel 9 and the Date of Messiah's Coming," 522–32. One of the factors contributing to the differences between the various Jewish interpretations is that they used different dates for the time of the Babylonian exile. In fact, except for Demetrius they all tended to date the exile later than historians do today, primarily because their records for the Persian period were inaccurate and too short.

315. See Beckwith, "Daniel 9 and the Date of Messiah's Coming," 533–37; and H. W. Guggenheimer, *Seder Olam: The Rabbinic View of Biblical Chronology*, 240–46. Beckwith presents the case that Josephus interpreted the "anointed one" (who was cut off, Dan 9:26) as the high priest Ananus, who was murdered by the Idumaeans in the temple in AD 66 (see Beckwith, "Daniel 9 and the Date of Messiah's Coming," 535–36). An alternative Jewish view was to see the *terminus ad quem* of the 490 years in the Bar Kokba revolt of the second century AD, based on a reckoning of Daniel's prophecy from the end of the exile rather than its beginning. Based on this outlook, the Messiah could be expected between AD 133 and 140, the very time when Bar Kokba (regarded by his followers as "Son of a Star," i.e., the Messiah, based on Num 24:17–19) inspired the third and final Jewish rebellion. For Josephus' view that the 490 years culminate in the AD 70 destruction, see *Ant.* 10.11.7 §276.

accounts for the many variables.[316] Another point to note is that the מָשִׁיחַ (*māšîaḥ*) in v. 26 is the same figure as the מָשִׁיחַ נָגִיד (*māšîaḥ nāg̱îḏ*) in v. 25. These are the only two anarthrous constructions of מָשִׁיחַ (*māšîaḥ*) in the OT, and the difference between them can be easily explained by noting that once the author introduced him as מָשִׁיחַ נָגִיד (*māšîaḥ nāg̱îḏ*) in v. 25, he simply needed to refer to him by the more abbreviated designation מָשִׁיחַ (*māšîaḥ*) in the following verse. With such close proximity of the references one would not expect two different individuals. As Feinberg has ably demonstrated, the Hebrew term for "cut off" (כָּרַת, *kāraṯ*) in v. 26 is an appropriate reference to Christ's sacrificial death on the cross.

> The "cutting off" of Messiah indicates a violent death. The Hebrew word is used of making a covenant, involving the death of a sacrificial animal (Gen 15:10, 18). The word is used of the death penalty (Lev 7:20) and always of an unnatural violent death (cf. Isa 53:8).[317]

McComiskey, however, argues that the second מָשִׁיחַ (*māšîaḥ*) in verse 26 cannot refer to Jesus Christ because, he says, the words "and have nothing" would be contrary to what had been predicted in 7:13–14 that the Son of Man will receive universal dominion. Yet this objection is not convincing. The implication of the words "and have nothing" is that following Christ's death (after the first sixty-nine weeks) he did not receive the full realization of these promises *at that time*. These promises regarding his kingdom await his second coming (Luke 21:27–31).

2. The Placement of the Athnach *in 9:25*[318]

Although the "Son of Man" in Dan 7:13–14 is the most logical referent for מָשִׁיחַ נָגִיד (*māšîaḥ nāg̱îḏ*) in 9:25, McComiskey (following the argument

---

316. Those who take the messianic view of this prophecy and who understand the time periods literally do not all hold to the same method of calculation. Archer and Miller believe that the sixty-nine sevens extended from the decree of Artaxerxes with Ezra about 457 BC to the commencement of Christ's public ministry in AD 26/27, based on solar year calculations (Archer, 114–16; and Miller, 263–65). But Hoehner and P. Feinberg believe that the sixty-nine sevens extend from the decree of Artaxerxes with Nehemiah in 444 BC to the passion week of Christ in AD 33, based on prophetic or lunar years of 360 days. With either view the effect is the same: the calculations are literally true of Christ (Hoehner, "Chronological Aspects of the Life of Christ; Part VI: Daniel's Seventy Weeks and New Testament Chronology," 47–65; and Feinberg, "An Exegetical and Theological Study of Daniel 9:24–27," 189–220).

317. Feinberg, "An Exegetical and Theological Study of Daniel 9:24–27," 202.

318. The material in this section is extracted from my article in *BSac*, "Is Daniel's Seventy-Weeks Prophecy Messianic? Part 2" (see 325–28) and used by permission. Slight modifications have been made to adapt to the formatting style of this commentary.

commonly used by critical scholars) objects to this identification because of a punctuation marker known as an *ʾatnāḥ* in the Masoretic text.[319] That mark (֑) is placed between the words "seven weeks" (שָׁבֻעִים שִׁבְעָה, *šābu ʿîm šib ʿâ*) and "sixty-two weeks" (וְשָׁבֻעִים שִׁשִּׁים וּשְׁנַיִם, *wᵉšābu ʿîm šiššîm ûšᵉnayim*). McComiskey says this means that the מָשִׁיחַ נָגִיד (*māšîaḥ nāgîd*) appears after seven weeks (of years) from the issuing of the "decree [דָּבָר, *dābār*] to restore and rebuild Jerusalem," not after sixty-nine weeks (seven and sixty-two weeks). If McComiskey is correct, then the מָשִׁיחַ נָגִיד (*māšîaḥ nāgîd*) in v. 25 cannot be the Messiah, Jesus Christ. Instead, he would be someone who appeared seven weeks (i.e., forty-nine years) following the decree—though McComiskey takes the seven weeks symbolically, not literally.[320] The NRSV reflects this understanding of the *ʾatnāḥ* in its translation. "Know therefore and understand: from the time that the word went out to restore and rebuild Jerusalem until the time of an anointed prince, there shall be seven weeks; and for sixty-two weeks it shall be built again with streets and moat, but in a troubled time."

This translation, however, is not convincing. First, in their original form the Hebrew manuscripts did not have vowel points or accentuation markers. These were added by Jewish scribes known as Masoretes many centuries after the time of Jesus' crucifixion. The primary Hebrew manuscripts—the Aleppo Codex and Codex Leningradensis—are from the Ben Asher family of Masoretes of the tenth century AD. Various systems of vowel pointing and accentuation were developed gradually, but this one goes back to about AD 600–700, and it was standardized by the Western Masoretes of Palestine in the ninth and tenth centuries.[321] Thus there is nothing inspired about the

---

319. T. McComiskey, "The Seventy Weeks of Daniel against the Background of Ancient Near Eastern Literature," *WTJ* 47 (1985): 18–45.

320. Several suggestions have been made as to which decree is referred to in Dan 9:25. The more common suggestions are (a) the decree of Cyrus about 539–538 BC permitting the return from exile and rebuilding of the temple (Ezra 1:1–4; 6:3–5); (b) the decree of Artaxerxes to Ezra about 457 BC (Ezra 7:11–26); and (c) the authorization of Artaxerxes permitting Nehemiah to return to Jerusalem in 444 BC (Neh 1–2). McComiskey rejects the idea that a royal decree is meant, choosing to take דָּבָר (*dābār*) in 9:25 as a "prophetic word," namely the prophecy of Jer 29:10 ("The Seventy 'Weeks' of Daniel," 26). While McComiskey's suggestion is certainly possible (granting that *dābār* is not a specific term for "decree"), דָּבָר (*dābār*) can certainly be used of a king's *command* (e.g., 1 Chr 21:4), thus making possible any of the first three suggestions. More recently Chisholm, *Handbook on the Prophets*, 315, has argued that דָּבָר (*dābār*) in Daniel 9:25 refers to the prophetic decree in Jer 30:18, a passage that he dates to 597–586 BC.

321. The history of vowel pointing and accentuation is carefully explained by E. Würthwein, *The Text of the Old Testament*, 2nd ed., trans. E. F. Rhodes (Grand Rapids: Eerdmans, 1995), 21, who writes, "It is not known when pointing originated. ... Bruno Chiesa's study of indirect sources suggests a time between AD 650

accentuation markers, and they are certainly subject to debate. The primary Greek version of Daniel (which was accepted by the early church fathers) was the text of Theodotion. Although there is some dispute as to the identity of Theodotion and when this text originated, the point is that this Greek text reflects no bifurcation of the verse between the two temporal references.[322] Beckwith highlights the significance of these early translations that preceded the imposition of Masoretic punctuation: "In the Septuagint, in THEODOTION, in SYMMACHUS and in the Peshitta the 7 and 62 weeks are treated as a single period, at the end of which the anointed one comes. The same is true even of AQUILA'S translation, though AQUILA'S rabbinical education was unimpeachable."[323] Even Jerome, who knew Hebrew and lived in Palestine in the latter part of the fourth century AD, where he certainly would have known of the best manuscripts of that day, made no indication in his Latin Vulgate translation of separating the seven and sixty-two weeks. He translated מָשִׁיחַ נָגִיד (*māšîaḥ nāgîḏ*) quite literally as *christum ducem* ("Christ, a leader"). It is therefore surprising that Goldingay (229) would remark, "MT's division of the verse ... seems more natural." The versions that were made prior to the time the Masoretes added the punctuation obviously did not think that separating the seven and sixty-two "seemed more natural."

Because of the heated verbal polemics between Christians and Jews over the centuries, some might even claim that Jewish scribes purposely inserted the *ʾaṯnāḥ* in v. 25 in order to refute the Christian claim that Jesus

---

and 750 as more probable, because the Babylonian Talmud which was completed about AD 600 makes no reference to pointing. Moshe Goshen-Gottstein also assumes a time around AD 700 as "probable."

322. Granted, not all scholars are persuaded by Theodotion's translation of Dan 9:25 (some would see it as a *divergence* from the Hebrew text rather than a faithful rendition of it). Yet it should be admitted that Theodotion *may* be an accurate and unbiased translation, barring any evidence to the contrary. In any case, Theodotion's translation was significant, as Adler, "The Apocalyptic Survey of History Adapted by Christians," 223, acknowledges: "The impact of this rendering on Christian exegesis was profound. It offered chronographers an additional 49 years to fill up the interim period between the 'going forth of the word' and Christ's advent. At the same time, it allowed interpreters to impose a single messianic interpretation on the χριστὸς ἡγούμενος of verse 25 and the events of verse 26. Neither the Vulgate, nor the Syriac text, nor the other Greek versions did much to dispel the impression. To the contrary, their renderings, even more than Theodotion, encouraged interpreters to assume that the 69 weeks formed a single block of time and that verses 25 and 26 referred to the same 'anointed one.'"

323. Beckwith, "Daniel 9 and the Date of Messiah's Coming in Essene, Hellenistic, Pharisaic, Zealot and Early Christian Computation," 522.

is the predicted Messiah. Yet this theory can neither be proved or disproved.[324] Beyond these points, however, some clarification is needed about the purpose and accuracy of the Masoretic use of the *ʾatnāḥ*. It is sometimes mistakenly assumed that the *ʾatnāḥ* served always as a disjunctive accent, marking a major break between clauses. Although it certainly had this use, that was not its only function. Genesis 1:1 contains an example of the nondisjunctive use of the *ʾatnāḥ*, where the punctuation marker is placed beneath אֱלֹהִים (*ʾĕlōhîm*), thereby separating "In the beginning God created" from "the heavens and the earth." Here the *ʾatnāḥ* has more of an *emphatic* function, causing the reader to pause in thought after reading of Elohim the Creator God before reading what he created. In an excellent analysis of the Hebrew *ʾatnāḥ*, Owusu-Antwi remarks, "It is a distinguishing feature that the Hebrew verse is divided into two parts termed 'dichotomy,' for the purposes of chanting. The *ʾatnāḥ* is generally employed to mark the caesura of the dichotomy. Although *ʾatnāḥ* is the principal divider within the verse, the accentuators did not hesitate to make strict rules for logical (or syntactical) division give way, when they wished to express *emphasis*, or otherwise give effect to the reading."[325]

Owusu-Antwi suggests several more ways in which the *ʾatnāḥ* is used. A second case is seen in Gen 35:9, where the *ʾatnāḥ* indicates a pause other than a full disjunctive, where an English comma would be appropriate. A third case is the use of the *ʾatnāḥ* as a pause, somewhat like a colon or semicolon, as in Gen 6:15. A fourth case is in 1 Kgs 8:42, where the *ʾatnāḥ* has a parenthetical purpose. Owusu-Antwi then surveys the possible ways the *ʾatnāḥ* was used with numbers. In Num 1:46, which has the number 603,550, an *ʾatnāḥ* occurs between six hundred and three thousand, and five hundred and fifty, as though to mark thousands from hundreds. There is certainly no full disjuncture in this case; rather, the *ʾatnāḥ* aids in clarification.

---

324. Though no evidence exists that the Masoretes had any bias in inserting the *ʾatnāḥ*, some church fathers were aware of Jewish anti-Christian interpretations of Dan 9. "Indeed, much of the commentary on Dan 9:24–27 is marked by its polemic anti-Jewish flavor. Jerome, on uncertain authority, goes so far as to suggest that the interpretation of Dan 9:26 by the Jews of his time was guided by anti-Christian animus. While allowing that the death of the 'anointed one' predicted in v. 26 may have referred to Christ, the 'Hebrews,' he says, took the words ואין לו to mean that 'the kingdom of the Jews will not be his.' In opposing the manifest messianic meaning of Daniel 9, Eusebius states the Jews willfully misrepresented these verses by insisting that the events forecast in the prophecy had not yet been realized" (Adler, "The Apocalyptic Survey of History Adapted by Christians," 220–21).

325. B. Owusu-Antwi, *The Chronology of Dan 9:24–27*, Adventist Theological Society Dissertation Series 2 (Berrien Springs, MI: Adventist Theological Society, 1995), 186 (emphasis his).

In some cases the *ʾatnāḥ* has been wrongly placed. These have been identified by Wickes in his detailed analysis of Hebrew accentuation.[326] Even in Dan 9:24 the *ʾatnāḥ* may be inappropriately placed. One might expect that the *ʾatnāḥ* would be placed after the first clause stating the time involved (i.e., after the words "your holy city") or after the word "iniquity" (עָוֹן, *ʿāwōn*). The latter would divide the first three infinitives (each involving a word for sin) from the final three infinitives (each of which is positive in nature). Yet this is not the case. Instead the *ʾatnāḥ* is placed after the fourth infinitive ("to bring in everlasting righteousness").

In v. 25 the presence of the *ʾatnāḥ* between the "seven weeks" and "sixty-two weeks" should not be the governing factor for understanding this verse. As already noted, the *ʾatnāḥ* was not in the original Hebrew text but was added by Jewish Masoretic scribes who lived centuries after the crucifixion. Furthermore, an *ʾatnāḥ* does not always indicate a full disjunctive accent but can have other functions (e.g., giving emphasis or clarification). Some may object that the verse should have said "sixty-nine" weeks rather than "seven and sixty-two" (if that was indeed the intended time until Messiah). However, there is good reason for expressing *two stages* of time. The final part of the verse specifically calls the reader's attention to the period of rebuilding, and this is likely what the "seven weeks" refers to. Besides, it is illogical to separate the sixty-two weeks from the seven weeks and have a separate sentence begin in v. 26, for this implies that the rebuilding efforts took sixty-two weeks of years (i.e., 434 years).[327]

3. The Meaning and Implications of šāḥaṯ *(שָׁחַת), "Destroy," in 9:26*

The meaning and translation of the verb *šāḥaṯ* (שָׁחַת) in Dan 9:26 have significant implications for the interpretation of vv. 24–27 as a whole. If *šāḥaṯ* means "destroy," as most English versions render it, then this passage was not fulfilled in the second century BC as critical scholars maintain.[328] Yet critical scholars will often attempt to avert this dilemma by arguing that *šāḥaṯ* means "moral corruption" in this case (i.e., Antiochus *corrupted* Jerusalem and the temple cult). The evidence, however, does not support this assertion. Several lines of evidence confirm this.

---

326. W. Wickes, *Two Treatises on the Accentuation of the Old Testament* (Oxford: Clarendon, 1881; repr., New York: KTAV, 1970), 74.

327. McComiskey, "The Seventy 'Weeks' of Daniel," 25, suggests that "sixty-two weeks" is the time Jerusalem "continues to exist" following the rebuilding. Yet the text makes no point about Jerusalem's continuation of existence; only its rebuilding is referred to. Montgomery (380) argued for an implied insertion: "Jerusalem shall be rebuilt *and remain so* for 62 weeks but in distressful conditions" (emphasis mine).

328. The following English versions all translate *šāḥaṯ* as "destroy," not "corrupt": KJV, NKJV, NASB, NIV, NRSV, NET, and ESV.

A. Greek Septuagint Translations. Though neither of the two Greek traditions we now have for Daniel follow the Hebrew text perfectly, they do not translate Dan 9:26 in the sense of "moral corruption." These translations show that the Greek translators understood *šāḥaṯ* (שָׁחַת) in the sense of *physical destruction*.[329]

(1) Old Greek: "And after seven and seventy and sixty-two weeks, an anointing will be removed and will not be. And a king of nations will demolish (φθερεῖ, *phtherei*) the city and the sanctuary along with the anointed one."

(2) Theodotion: "And after the sixty-two weeks, an anointing will be destroyed, and there is no judgment in it. And it will destroy (διαφθερεῖ, *diaphtherei*) the city and the sanctuary along with the leader who is to come."

B. Lexical Usage. In Dan 9:26 the verb *šāḥaṯ* (שָׁחַת) appears in the Hipʿil stem as *yašḥîṯ* (יַשְׁחִית).

(1) BDB (1007): BDB suggests that the general lexical meaning is "to go to ruin." The verb is quite common, appearing about 142x in the Old Testament. It is not found in the Qal stem, but does appear in the Nipʿal and Piʿel stems, and most frequently in the causative stems of the Hipʿil (96x) and Hopʿal. In the Hipʿil stem (the most frequent), it can mean (1) spoil, ruin, destroy; or (2) pervert, corrupt. BDB gives evidence of both meanings in the Hipʿil, though the first meaning is far more dominant. Note should be made of *šāḥaṯ* (שָׁחַת) in Gen 18:28, 31, and 32, where it is used specifically of *physically* destroying a city (Sodom in view).

Regarding Hipʿil meaning #2 ("pervert, corrupt"), BDB suggests only a few verses with this nuance. In four cases, it is simply part of the title of a psalm (57:1; 58:1; 59:1; 75:1). Some of the examples given by BDB are probably better categorized under meaning #1 (e.g., Prov 6:32—a man committing adultery *destroys* himself; cf. Prov 18:9; 28:24). In most other cases, the idea is either "acting corruptly in a moral sense" (e.g., Gen 6:12; Ps 14:1=53:2) or of the Hebrew people *by their own choice* acting corruptly by disobedience to the Mosaic law (Deut 31:29; 2 Chr 27:2; Isa 1:4; Jer 6:28; Zeph 3:7) and especially by turning to idols (Deut 4:16, 25; Judg 2:19). Twice it is used in Ezekiel of moral corruption but in a figurative way of covenant disobedience (Ezek 16:47; 23:11). BDB does not assign the case of Dan 9:26 to meaning #2 ("pervert, corrupt") and, more significantly, there are no cases where the Hipʿil means to cause others to be corrupt or act corruptly, or to cause the corruption of a city or temple operation.

(2) *HALOT* (1469–72): *HALOT* has a longer and more detailed discussion. For the Hipʿil stem, the main categories are (1) to ruin, destroy; (2) to annihilate, exterminate; (3) of "particular instances" (including corrupt action); (4) as a title of several psalms; and (5) substantival use of

329. The Greek translations given here are those provided by the CCAT program at the University of Pennsylvania. Available at <http://ccat.sas.upenn.edu/nets/edition/40-daniel-nets.pdf>.

the participle as a "destroyer." Yet *HALOT* makes no specific reference to Dan 9:26.

(3) *TDOT* (J. Conrad, 14:583–99): Conrad provides a rather long discussion, but here are a few comments to be gleaned from a reading of the entry for *šāḥaṯ* (שָׁחַת). Since the word does not occur in the Qal, pinpointing the basic meaning is difficult. Yet, "In light of Arabic evidence as well as syntactical and semasiological considerations regarding the Hebrew piel and hiphil, however, one can also deduce a basic transitive meaning of 'destroy, ruin suddenly, unexpectedly'" (584). Conrad notes (584) that the Piʿel and Hipʿil stems are dominant: "Evidence associated with the piel and hiphil as the predominant conjugation stems suggests that the verb signifies an act of ruthless destruction subjecting the object to complete annihilation or decimating and corrupting it so thoroughly that its demise is certain. ... the hiphil emphasizes the subject's intent to carry out such destruction, being used when the reference is to current or durative acts of this sort." He gives considerable discussion to the Piʿel and Hipʿil usage in regard to war and power politics, as the word most often occurs in this context: "Destructive and extirpative action occurs above all in war and the verb is associated with this theme with particular frequency. One adversary advances ruthlessly against the other with the goal of completely overcoming and beating him, of annihilating him as an independent entity" (585). Under this same discussion (war and power politics), Conrad makes brief mention of Dan 9:26: "The figure of the *nāgîḏ* in 9:26 whose (military) 'people' will destroy, i.e., proceed with military force against Jerusalem and its sanctuary, is probably also to be identified with Antiochus IV" (587). Although Conrad accepts the critical position that the *nāgîḏ* is Antiochus IV (a conclusion he bases on other considerations), he understands that *šāḥaṯ* (שָׁחַת) in Dan 9:26 means to destroy by use of military force—not to corrupt/pervert (e.g., corrupting the temple worship). His attempt, however to limit the action (merely "<u>proceed</u> with military force") fails to do justice to *šāḥaṯ* when used in the sense of "destroy." They did more than march against the city and sanctuary.

c. A Survey of Critical Commentaries. (1) Collins, Hermeneia (346): Collins translates Dan 9:26, "The host of a ruler who is to come <u>will destroy</u> the city and the sanctuary." Naturally, Collins takes the critical interpretation that this passage is fulfilled in the days of Antiochus IV. He concludes (357): "*will destroy the city:* The Syrians did not demolish Jerusalem, but they made it desolate by the corruption of the cult." Despite translating *šāḥaṯ* (שָׁחַת) as "destroy," his interpretation (rather inconsistently) is that of corruption of the cult. Furthermore, if we pay close attention to the text, while there might be some legitimacy to the idea that Antiochus *corrupted* the sanctuary, that idea is not natural in regard to the city. The text says that a certain people connected with a *nāgîḏ* (ruler) carried out *šāḥaṯ* (שָׁחַת) of the city. The most natural way to understand this would be that they destroyed the city—not that they corrupted the city. (See further comments on this point below with Montgomery.) The point here is that *šāḥaṯ* (שָׁחַת) needs to be understood in the same way regarding the city as it does in regard to the sanctuary, and since destruction of the city is the most natural understanding (barring any evidence to the contrary), then *šāḥaṯ* (שָׁחַת) of the sanctuary should be understood the same way.

(2) Goldingay, WBC (226, 230, 262): Goldingay translates (226): "an anointed will be cut off and will have neither the city nor the sanctuary. A leader to come will devastate a people." Notice that in his translation he does not use either "destroy" or "corrupt/pervert." And yet his following comments and commentary do not seem consistent at all with his translation. He notes (230) that *šāḥaṯ* (שָׁחַת) is used elsewhere in Daniel at 8:24–25 and 11:17. Regarding the latter, he asserts, "there it could refer to moral/religious rather than to physical damage." Yet this is very doubtful. Looking closely at 11:17, the verse is teaching that Antiochus III is going to give his daughter Cleopatra to be the wife of Ptolemy V (about 194/93 BC). His motive is that by doing so, this will "ruin it." The pronominal suffix with לְהַשְׁחִיתָהּ (*lᵊhašḥîṯāh*) is feminine, referring back to its antecedent "kingdom" (fem. noun). Antiochus III was hoping to ruin or devastate Ptolemy's kingdom rule, so that he would not be in position to field an army against him again. Goldingay's suggestion of "moral/religious" damage does not fit the context.

Goldingay (262) follows the typical critical interpretation that the "anointed" one is Onias III and that the *nāḡîḏ* (he translates "leader to come") is a representative of the high priestly line, namely Jason, "who both corrupted and devastated—the two possible senses of ישחית—the people of Jerusalem (see 2 Macc 4–5)." Notice that Goldingay, although he tries to capture both senses "corrupt" *and* "devastate" for the Hipʿil of *šāḥaṯ* (שָׁחַת), does *not* apply this to the city but only to the people (as a result of his own faulty translation that removes "city and sanctuary" to the preceding clause).[330]

(3) Montgomery, ICC (383): Montgomery translates: "And the city and the sanctuary shall destroy [=be destroyed by] the folk of a prince that is to come." Like Goldingay, Montgomery (381) understands the "anointed one" in 9:26 as a reference to Onias III. Yet Montgomery takes the *nāḡîḏ* (prince) to be Antiochus IV. His comments on *šāḥaṯ* (שָׁחַת) are interesting: "The word translated 'destroy' ישחית, is generally taken in the physical sense, so 8[24], 11[17], but there was little destruction effected by the Greeks in the Holy City; it may then be understood in its moral sense, 'corrupt'" (383). My first comment in response: notice that Montgomery acknowledges that *šāḥaṯ* (שָׁחַת) in the other places used by Daniel (namely 8:24 and 11:17) has the meaning "destroy." This is in contrast to Goldingay, who vainly attempted to argue a moral corruption for 11:17. Second, notice the *reasoning* for Montgomery's

330. For an evaluation and refutation of Goldingay's translation, see the commentary above at Dan 9:26. Hartman (240)—who also emends the text and redivides the clauses, though differently from Goldingay—translates, "and the soldiers of a prince will <u>ruin</u> the sanctuary." He moves "city" to the preceding clause (when the city is no longer his), but he had to emend the *waw* on *wᵊhāʿîr* (וְהָעִיר) to do that and move *habbāʾ* (הַבָּא) to the next clause ("Then the end <u>will come</u> like a flood").

preference for *šāḥaṯ* (שָׁחַת) meaning "in a moral sense, 'corrupt'" in 9:26. It is because (presuming that predictive prophecy is not possible) 9:26 must have Antiochus IV in view. Since Antiochus did *not* physically destroy Jerusalem and its temple, another lexical meaning must be true for *šāḥaṯ* (שָׁחַת). He does this despite the fact that the overwhelming normative usage of the Hipʿil of *šāḥaṯ* (שָׁחַת) means "destruction," that it has this meaning (as he himself acknowledges in 8:24 and 11:17), and that the nuance of "physical destruction" makes perfect sense in 9:26 *unless* one has already made up his mind that the verse *must* be fulfilled in the days of Antiochus IV. Finally, I would point out that the text says that a "people" will destroy the *city*, not that a "people" will morally corrupt the Hebrew people. For Montgomery's point to be valid, "city" would have to be metaphorically understood as "the people of that city." While this is possible, it would need to be substantiated. But since the physical meaning (destruction of the city itself) makes perfect sense, there is no need to opt for a metaphorical understanding.

D. CONCLUSIONS REGARDING ŠĀḤAṮ IN DAN 9:26. Dan 9:26 indicates that a "people (of the prince that will come) will destroy the city and the sanctuary." The word translated "destroy" is the Hebrew verb *šāḥaṯ* (שָׁחַת) in the Hipʿil stem. The translation "destroy" is the normative (most frequent) meaning of the word, i.e., the translation that one would normally expect. For this reason, both LXX^{O} and LXX^{θ} translated *šāḥaṯ* with a Greek word meaning "destroy" (not "corrupt"). Almost all English versions today have likewise used the translation "destroy."

It is true that *šāḥaṯ* in the Hipʿil stem can have the meaning "corrupt" in a few cases. However, in these rarer cases, the idea is that someone (or group) *acts corruptly* (i.e., they make the choice to act corruptly, usually by disobeying the Mosaic law). The verb *šāḥaṯ* (שָׁחַת) in the Hipʿil stem does not carry the meaning *to corrupt* someone else or something else, such as a city or religious system. Whenever *šāḥaṯ* (שָׁחַת) in the Hipʿil has a tangible object in view, the meaning is not "corrupt" but "destroy."[331] Obviously, the verb has such a tangible object in this sentence, namely the city and sanctuary. This is consistent with the fact that in all cases where a city or stronghold appears as the object of the verb acting transitively (Gen 18:28, 31, 32; 19:13, 14; 2 Sam 20:15, 20; Jer 6:5; Lam 2:8), the meaning is always that of physical destruction, not moral corruption. Hence, "destroy" is the proper translation in the case of Dan 9:26.

---

331. In addition to surveying the biblical data, I have also researched the thirty-five cases of *šāḥaṯ* (שׁחת) occuring in M. G. Abegg Jr., *Qumran Sectarian Manuscripts* (Bellingham, WA: Logos Bible Software, 2003), and have found the same principle to be true. One may corrupt his ways (e.g., 4Q222 f1:3), but when tangible objects are in view, *šāḥaṯ* (שׁחת) carries the nuance "to destroy, raze" (e.g., "the earth," 1QpHab 4:13 and 4Q422 2:11; or "peoples," 4Q434 f2:2).

Since Antiochus IV in the second century BC did *not* destroy the city and the sanctuary, the Maccabean theory for Dan 9:24–27 is invalid.[332] The correct interpretation is that the Romans destroyed the city of Jerusalem and the Jewish temple in AD 70. Critical scholars err in their attempt to link Dan 9:26 to Antiochus IV in the second century BC.

4. Chart: Summary of Various Views on the "Seventy Weeks" Prophecy

See the charts in the appendix on pages 774–79.

Selected Bibliography (Chapter 9)

Abegg, M. G., Jr. *Qumran Sectarian Manuscripts*. Bellingham, WA: Logos Bible Software, 2003.

Adler, W. "The Apocalyptic Survey of History Adapted by Christians: Daniel's Prophecy of 70 Weeks." In *The Jewish Apocalyptic Heritage in Early Christianity*, ed. J. C. VanderKam and W. Adler, 201–38. Minneapolis, MN: Fortress, 1996.

Anderson, R. *The Coming Prince*. 5th ed. London: Hodder & Stoughton, 1895. Repr., 15th ed., Grand Rapids: Kregel, 1963.

Applegate, J. "Jeremiah and the Seventy Years in the Hebrew Bible: Inner-biblical Reflections on the Prophet and his Prophecy." In *The Book of Jeremiah and its Reception*, 91–110. Louvain: Leuven University Press, 1997.

Athas, G. "In Search of the Seventy Weeks of Daniel 9." *JHS* 9 (2009): 1–20.

Auchincloss, W. S. "Darius the Median." *BSac* 66 (1909): 536–38.

Avalos, H. "Daniel 9:24–25 and Mesopotamian Temple Rededications." *JBL* 117 (1998): 507–11.

Baumgarten, J. M. "The Heavenly Tribunal and the Personification of Ṣedeq in Jewish Apocalyptic." *ANRW* ii 10, 1 (1979): 219–39.

Beckwith, R. T. "Cautionary Notes on the Use of Calendars and Astronomy to Determine the Chronology of the Passion," in *Chronos, Kairos, Christos; Nativity and Chronological Studies Presented to Jack Finegan*, ed. J. Vardaman and E. M. Yamauchi, 183–205. Winona Lake, IN: Eisenbrauns, 1989.

———. "Daniel 9 and the Date of Messiah's Coming in Essene, Hellenistic, Pharisaic, Zealot, and Early Christian Computation." *RevQ* 10 (1979–1981): 521–42.

———. "The Significance of the Calendar for Interpreting Essene Chronology and Eschatology." *RevQ* 10 (1979–81): 167–202.

Berghuis, K. D. "A Biblical Perspective on Fasting." *BSac* 158 (2001): 86–103.

Bergsma, J. S. "The Persian Period as Penitential Era: The 'Exegetical Logic' of Daniel 9.1–27." In *Exile and Restoration Revisited; Essays on the*

332. Baldwin (190) concurs, "Commentators who argue that Antiochus Epiphanes fulfilled this prophecy are at a loss to account for the fact that he destroyed neither the temple nor the city of Jerusalem, though undoubtedly much damage was done (1 Macc. 1:31, 38)."

Babylonian and Persian Periods in Memory of Peter R. Ackroyd, ed. G. N. Knoppers and L. L. Grabbe, 50–64. T&T Clark, 2011.
Blaising, C. A. "The Day of the Lord and the Seventieth Week of Daniel." *BSac* 169 (2012): 131–42.
Boccaccini, G. "The Solar Calendars of Daniel and Enoch." In *The Book of Daniel: Composition and Reception*, vol. 2, ed. J. J. Collins and P. W. Flint, 311–28. Leiden: Brill, 2001.
Bowker, J. W. "Intercession in the Qur'an and the Jewish Tradition." *JSS* 11 (1966): 69–82.
Chazan, R. "Daniel 9:24–27: Exegesis and Polemics." In *Contra Judaeos: Ancient and Medieval Polemics Between Christians and Jews*, ed. O. Limor and G. G. Stroumsa, 143–59. Tübingen: Mohr, 1996.
———. "The Messianic Calculations of Nahmanides." In *Rashi (1040–1990). Hommage à Ephraïm E. Urbach*, ed. G. Sed-Rajna, 631–36. Paris: Editions du Cerf, 1993.
Chisholm, R. B. *Handbook on the Prophets*. Grand Rapids: Baker, 2002.
Christie-Miller, I. "Matfre Ermengaud's *Breviari D'Amor* and Daniel 9.26." *JSOT* 66 (1995): 113–17.
Collins, A. Y. "Numerical Symbolism in Jewish and Early Christian Apocalyptic Literature." *ANRW* 21 (1984): 1224–49.
Cooper, D. L. *The 70 Weeks of Daniel*. Los Angeles, CA: Biblical Research Society, 1941.
Dequeker, L. "King Darius and the Prophecy of Seventy Weeks, Daniel 9." In *The Book of Daniel in the Light of New Findings*, ed. A. S. van der Woude, 187–210. Louvain: Leuven University Press, 1993.
Dimant, D. "Dan 9,24–27 in the Light of New Qumranic Texts." In *The Book of Daniel in the Light of New Findings*, ed. A. S. van der Woude, 57–76. Leuven: Leuven University Press, 1993.
Doukhan, J. "The Seventy Weeks of Daniel 9: An Exegetical Study." *AUSS* 17 (1979): 1–22.
Dunn, G. D. "Tertullian and Daniel 9:24–27: A Patristic Interpretation of a Prophetic Time-Frame." *ZAC* 6 (2002): 352–67.
Endresz, R. J. "Daniel: A Survey of Patristic Exegesis." *Phronema* 31 (2016): 123–52.
Feinberg, P. D. "An Exegetical and Theological Study of Daniel 9:24–27." In *Tradition and Testament*, ed. J. S. Feinberg and P. D. Feinberg, 189–220. Chicago: Moody, 1981.
Flesher, L. S. "Daniel 9:24–27 and the Tribulation." *RevExp* 109 (2012): 583–91.
———. "Tricksters and Martyrs: Rereading Daniel 9 as Lament with the Context of the Entire Book." In *Why? ... How Long? Studies on Voice(s) of Lamentation Rooted in Biblical Hebrew Poetry*, ed. L. S Flesher, C. J. Dempsey, and M. J. Boda, 132–56. London and New York: Bloomsbury T&T Clark, 2014.
Ford, D. *In the Heart of Daniel: An Exposition of Daniel 9:24–27*. New York: iUniverse, 2007.

Fotheringham, J. K. "The Evidence of Astronomy and Technical Chronology for the Date of the Crucifixion." *JTS* 35 (1934): 146–62.
Francisco, C. T. "The Seventy Weeks of Daniel." *RevExp* 57 (1960): 126–37.
Frerichs, W. W. "How Many Weeks Until the End?" *WW* 15 (1995): 166–74.
Frölich, Isa. *"Time and Times and Half a Time": Historical Consciousness in the Jewish Literature of the Persian and Hellenistic Eras.* JSPSup 19. Sheffield: Sheffield Academic Press, 1996.
Fruchtenbaum, A. "The Seventy Sevens of Daniel." Study 6: Ariel Ministries' Messianic Bible Study #067. 2005. Cited 20 May 2015. Online: http:// www. messianicassociation.org/ezine37-af.christology-messianic.htm.
Frye, R. N. *The Heritage of Persia.* London: Weidenfeld, 1962.
Gardner, A. E. "The Way to Eternal Life in Dan 12:1e–2 or How to Reverse the Death Curse of Genesis 3." *ABR* 40 (1992) 1-19.
Gentry, P. J. "Daniel's Seventy Weeks and the New Exodus." *SBJT* 14 (2010): 26–44.
Grabbe, L. L. "Chronography in Hellenistic Jewish Historiography." *SBLSP* 17 (1979): 43–68.
———. "The Seventy-Weeks Prophecy (Daniel 9:24–27) in Early Jewish Interpretation." In *The Quest for Context and Meaning: Studies in Biblical Intertextuality in Honor of James A. Sanders*, ed. C. A. Evans and S. Talmon, 595–611. Leiden: Brill, 1997.
———. "'The End of the Desolations of Jerusalem': From Jeremiah's 70 Years to Daniel's 70 Weeks of Years." In *Early Jewish and Christian Exegesis: Studies in Memory of William Hugh Brownlee*, ed. C. A. Evans and W. F. Stinespring, 67–72. Atlanta: Scholars Press, 1987.
Gruenthaner, M. J. "The Seventy Weeks." *CBQ* 1 (1939): 44–54.
Gurney, R. J. M. "The Seventy Weeks of Daniel 9:24–27." *EvQ* 53 (1981): 29–36.
Hardy, F. W. "The Hebrew Singular for 'Week' in the Expression 'One Week' in Daniel 9:27." *AUSS* 32 (1994): 197–202.
Harper, G. G. "The Theological and Exegetical Significance of Leviticus as Intertext in Daniel 9." *JESOT* 4 (2015): 39–61.
Hasel, G. F. "The Hebrew Masculine Plural for Weeks in the Expression 'Seventy Weeks' in Daniel 9:24." *AUSS* 31 (1993): 105–18.
———. "The Seventy Weeks of Daniel 9:24–27." *Ministry* 49 (1976): 5D–23D.
Haydon, R. "'The Law and the Prophets' in MT Daniel 9:3–19." *BBR* 24 (2014): 15–26.
———. "The 'Seventy Sevens' (Daniel 9:24) in Light of Heptadic Themes in Qumran." *JESOT* 3 (2014): 203–14.
Heard, W. J. "The Maccabean Martyrs' Contribution to Holy War." *EvQ* 58 (1986): 291–318.
Hess, R. S. "The Seventy Sevens of Daniel 9: A Timetable for the Future." *BBR* 21 (2011): 315–30.
Hoehner, H. W. *Chronological Aspects of the Life of Christ.* Grand Rapids: Zondervan, 1977.

———. "Chronological Aspects of the Life of Christ Part VI: Daniel's Seventy Weeks and New Testament Chronology." *BSac* 132 (1975): 47–65.

Hoekema, A. A. "Seventy Weeks." In *ISBE*, ed. G. W. Bromiley, 4:427–28. 4 vols. Grand Rapids: Eerdmans, 1988.

Holtzman, F. "A Re-examination of the Seventy Weeks of Daniel." Th.M. thesis, Dallas Theological Seminary, 1974.

Jones, B. W. "The Prayer in Daniel IX." *VT* 18 (1968): 488–93.

Kalafian, M. *The Prophecy of the Seventy Weeks of the Book of Daniel: A Critical Review of the Prophecy as Viewed by Three Major Theological Interpretations and the Impact of the Book of Daniel on Christology*. Lanham, MD: University Press of America, 1991.

Kline, M. G. "The Covenant of the Seventieth Week." In *The Law and the Prophets: Old Testament Studies Prepared in Honor of Oswald Thompson Allis*, ed. J. H. Skilton, 452–69. Nutley, NJ: Presbyterian & Reformed, 1974.

Knibb, M. A. "The Exile in the Literature of the Intertestamental Period." *HeyJ* 17 (1976): 253–72.

Knowles, L. E. "The Interpretations of the Seventy Weeks of Daniel in the Early Fathers." *WTJ* 7 (1945): 136–60.

Krauss, S. "The Jews in the Works of the Church Fathers." *JQR* 5 (1892): 122–57.

Laato, A. "The Seventy Yearweeks in the Book of Daniel." *ZAW* 102 (1990): 212–25.

Lacocque, A. "The Liturgical Prayer in Daniel 9." *HUCA* 47 (1976): 119–42.

Larson, D. "A Comparison of the Decrees of Artaxerxes' 20th Year and Cyrus' First Year as the Beginning Point of Daniel's Seventy Weeks." M.Div. thesis, Grace Theological Seminary, 1987.

Larssen, G. "When Did the Babylonian Captivity Begin?" *JTS* 18 (1967): 417–23.

Leatherman, D. W. "Structural Considerations regarding the Relation of Daniel 8 & Daniel 9." In *The Cosmic Battle for Planet Earth*, ed. R. du Preez and J. Moskala, 293–305. Berrien Springs, MI: Andrews Univ., 2003.

Lurie, D. H. "A New Interpretation of Daniel's 'Sevens' and the Chronology of the Seventy 'Sevens.'" *JETS* 33 (1990): 303–9.

Lust, J. "Cult and Sacrifice in Daniel: The Tamid and the Abomination of Desolation." In *Ritual and Sacrifice in the Ancient Near East*, ed. J. Quaegebeur, 283–99. Leuven: Uitgeverij, 1993.

MacRae, A. A. "The Seventy Weeks of Daniel." Paper presented at the annual meeting of the Evangelical Theological Society, Deerfield, IL, 1978.

Matheny, J. F. and M. B. *The Seventy Weeks of Daniel: An Exposition of Daniel 9:24–27*. Brevard, NC: Jay and Associates, 1990.

Matlock, M. D. *Discovering the Traditions of Prose Prayers in Early Jewish Literature*. London: T&T Clark, 2012.

Mauro, P. *The Seventy Weeks and the Great Tribulation*. Boston: Hamilton, 1923; reprint, Swengel, PA: Herendeen, 1944.

McCall, T. "How Soon the Tribulation Temple? Part 1." *BSac* 128 (1971): 341–51.

McClain, A. J. *Daniel's Prophecy of the Seventy Weeks.* Grand Rapids: Zondervan, 1940, 1969.
McComiskey, T. "The Seventy Weeks of Daniel against the Background of Ancient Near Eastern Literature." *WTJ* 47 (1985): 18–45.
McFall, L. "Do the Sixty-Nine Weeks of Daniel Date the Messianic Mission of Nehemiah or Jesus?" *JETS* 52 (2009): 673–718.
———. "Was Nehemiah Contemporary with Ezra in 458?" *WTJ* 53 (1991): 263–93.
McLean, J. A. *The Seventieth Week of Daniel 9:27 as a Literary Key for Understanding the Structure of the Apocalypse of John*. Lewiston, NY: Mellen Biblical Press, 1996.
McNamara, M. "Seventy Weeks of Years." In *The New Catholic Encyclopedia*, 13:39–40. 2nd ed. Farmington Hills, MI: Gale Group Inc., in Cooperation with Catholic University of America, 2003.
Meadowcroft, T. "Exploring the Dismal Swamp: The Identity of the Anointed One in Daniel 9:24–27." *JBL* 120 (2001): 429–49.
Montgomery, J. A. "A Survival of the Tetragrammaton in Daniel." *JBL* 40 (1921): 86.
Newman, R. C. "Daniel's Seventy Weeks and the Old Testament Sabbath-Year Cycle." *JETS* 16 (1973): 229–34.
Owusu-Antwi, B. *The Chronology of Dan 9:24–27*. Adventist Theological Society Dissertation Series 2. Berrien Springs, MI: Adventist Theological Society Publications, 1995.
Park, J. H. "Overtones of the Jubilee in the Seventy Weeks of Daniel 9:24–27." *JAAS* 14 (2011): 41–64.
Parry, J. T. "Desolation of the Temple and Messianic Enthronement in Daniel 11:36–12:3." *JETS* 54 (2011): 485–526.
Paul, S. "The Mesopotamian Background of Daniel 1–6." In *The Book of Daniel: Volume 1, Composition and Reception*, ed. J. J. Collins and P. W. Flint, 55–68. Leiden: Brill, 2001.
Payne, J. B. "The Goal of Daniel's Seventy Weeks." *JETS* 21 (1978): 97–115.
———. "The Goal of Daniel's Seventy Weeks: Interpretation by Context." *Presbyterion* 4 (1978): 33–38.
Pierce, R. W. "Spiritual Failure, Postponement, and Daniel 9." *TJ* 10 (1989): 211–22.
Poythress, V. S. "Hermeneutical Factors in Determining the Beginning of the Seventy Weeks (Daniel 9:25)." *TJ* 6 (1985): 131–49.
Price, J. R. "The Desecration and Restoration of the Temple in the Tanach, Jewish Apocalyptic Literature, and the New Testament." Ann Arbor, MI: UMI, 1993.
———. "Prophetic Postponement in Daniel 9 and Other Texts." In *Issues in Dispensationalism*, ed. W. R. Willis and J. R. Master, 132–65. Chicago: Moody, 1994.
———. "Prophetic Postponement in Daniel 9:24–27." In *Progressive Dispensationalism: An Analysis of the Movement and Defense of*

Traditional Dispensationalism, ed. R. J. Bigalke, 215–56. Lanham, MD: University Press of America, 2005.

Ray, C. H. "A Study of Daniel 9:24–27 Part I." *CTJ* 5 (2001): 166–85; Part 2: *CTJ* 5 (2001): 303–23; Part 3: *CTJ* 6 (2002): 71–89; Part 4: *CTJ* 6 (2002): 202–19.

Redditt, P. L. "Daniel 9: Its Structure and Meaning." *CBQ* 62 (2000): 236–49.

Rosscup, J. E. "Prayer Relating to Prophecy in Daniel 9." *MSJ* 3 (1992): 47–71.

Sawyer, J. F. A. "Types of Prayer in the Old Testament." *Semitics* 7 (1980): 131–43.

Segal, M. "The Chronological Conception of the Persian Period in Daniel 9." *JAJ* 2 (2011): 283–303.

Shea, W. H. "Poetic Relations of the Time Periods in Dan 9:25." *AUSS* 18 (1980): 59–63.

Shin, Young-Sun. "An Analysis of Daniel 9:24–27." Th.M. thesis, Dallas Theological Seminary, 2000.

Showers, R. E. "New Testament Chronology and the Decree of Daniel 9." *GJ* 11 (1970): 30–40.

Sigal, G. "Daniel's Seventy Weeks (Daniel 9:24–27)." In *The Jew and the Christian Missionary: A Jewish Response to Missionary Christianity*, 109–22. New York: KTAV, 1981.

———. *The 70 Weeks of Daniel (9:24–27)*. Bloomington, IN: XLIBRIS, 2013.

Smith, S. A. "Two Significant Problems with Harold Hoehner's Chronology of the Life of Christ." Accessed 3 July 2015. Online: http://www.biblicalreader.com/reader/Harold_Hoehners_Chronology.htm.

Spangenberg, I. J. J. "The Septuagint Translation of Daniel 9: Does it Reflect a Messianic Interpretation?" In *The Septuagint and Messianism*. Leuven: Leuven University Press, 2006. 430–42.

Tanner, J. P. "Is Daniel's Seventy-Weeks Prophecy Messianic? Part 1." *BSac* 166 (2009): 181–200.

———. "Is Daniel's Seventy-Weeks Prophecy Messianic? Part 2." *BSac* 166 (2009): 319–35.

Tomasino, A. J. "Oracles of Insurrection: The Prophetic Catalyst of the Great Revolt." *JJS* 59 (2008): 86–111.

Tzoref, S. "*Pesher* and Periodization." *DSD* 18 (2011): 129–54.

Ulrich, D. R. *The Antiochene Crisis and Jubilee Theology in Daniel's Seventy Sevens*. *OtSt* 66. Leiden/Boston: Brill, 2015.

———. "How Early Judaism Read Daniel 9:24–27." *OTE* 27 (2014): 1062–83.

———. "The Need for More Attention to Jubilee in Daniel 9:24–27." *BBR* 26 (2016): 481–500.

van Deventer, H. J. M. "The End of the End: Or, What Is the Deuteronomist (Still) Doing in Daniel?" In *Past, Present, Future: The Deuteronomistic History and the Prophets*, ed. J. C. de Moor and H. F. van Rooy, 62–75. Leiden: Brill, 2000.

———. "Suffering, Psalms and Allusion in Daniel 9." *OTE* 25 (2012): 207–26.

Van Kooten, G. H. "The Desecration of 'the Most Holy Temple of All the World' in the 'Holy Land'; Early Jewish and Early Christian Recollections of Antiochus' 'Abomination of Desolation.'" In *The Land of Israel in Bible, History, and Theology; Studies in Honour of Ed Noort*, ed. J. T. van Ruiten and J. C. de Vos, 291–316. Leiden/Boston: Martinus Nijhoff/Brill, 2009.

Venter, P. M. "Constitualised Space in Daniel 9." *HvTSt* 60 (2004): 607–24.

———. "Daniel 9: A Penitential Prayer in Apocalyptic Garb." In *The Development of Penitential Prayer in Second Temple Judaism*, vol. 2 of *Seeking the Favor of God*, ed. M. J. Boda, D. K. Falk, and R. A. Werline, 33–49. SBL Early Judaism and Its Literature 22. Atlanta: SBL, 2007.

Wacholder, B. Z. "Chronomessianism: The Timing of Messianic Movements and the Calendar of Sabbatical Cycles." *HUCA* 46 (1975): 201–18.

Walvoord, J. F. "Is the Seventieth Week of Daniel Future?" *BSac* 101 (1944): 30–49.

———. "Will Israel Build A Temple in Jerusalem?" *BSac* 125 (1968): 99–106.

Werline, R. A. *Penitential Prayer in Second Temple Judaism: The Development of a Religious Institution*. SBLEJL 3. Atlanta: Scholars Press, 1998.

Werman, C. "Epochs and End-Time: The 490-Year Scheme in Second Temple Literature." *DSD* 13 (2006): 229–55.

Whitcomb, J. C. "Daniel's Great Seventy-Weeks Prophecy: An Exegetical Insight." *GTJ* 2 (1981): 259–63.

Wilson, G. H. "The Prayer of Daniel 9: Reflection on Jeremiah 29." *JSOT* 48 (1990): 91–99.

Winkle, R. E. "Jeremiah's Seventy Weeks for Babylon: A Re-Assessment. Part II: The Historical Data." *AUSS* 25 (1987): 289–99.

C. The Final Vision: Sufferings from Antiochus and Antichrist, but Then Rescue (10:1–12:13)

Chapters 10–12 comprise the fourth and final vision given to Daniel. Being the last vision given to Daniel, it is (not surprisingly) the longest. The scope of events covers the atrocities suffered by the Jews from Daniel's day through the period of Seleucid rule (especially under Antiochus IV Epiphanes in the second century BC) and finally those at the hands of the antichrist himself in the latter days (Antiochus being a type of the antichrist). In the final analysis, however, God rescues his covenant people and resurrects the righteous to enjoy Messiah's kingdom.

The detailed references to known historical events (especially in Dan 11:2–35) have prompted critical scholars to regard this material as *vaticinium ex eventu* (i.e., prophecy after the fact). Hill (184) points out that these scholars (who conclude the material was written in the second century BC) "typically understand the purpose of this last section of the book as an exhortation to Jews to adopt 'a certain form of behavior, namely resistance to Seleucid/reformist pressures' (Goldingay, 285)." This theory, however, is seriously flawed. In addition to the defense of a sixth-century BC date as argued in the introduction of this commentary, there are several points detrimental to the critical viewpoint. First is the illogic of assuming the author erroneously recorded the death of Antiochus in 11:40–45, which (they say) is an indication the book was written shortly before his death about 164 BC (as otherwise he would have recorded Antiochus' death correctly). Baldwin (204) wisely remarks: "If the author proved to be wrong in his prediction of the way Antiochus would meet his end, there was no reason to suppose he would be any more reliable in his understanding of spiritual issues." To this, I would add how unlikely the Jewish scribes would have been to have accepted Daniel as canonical if they had known this to be the case. Second, to assume this material was "prophecy after the fact" is hardly convincing in light of Rome's rise to power. A second-century BC author (as they assume) certainly would not have thought of "the end" coming in the time of Antiochus in light of the rise of Rome. Again, Baldwin (205) refutes this line of reasoning:

> Already before the end of the third century the shadow of Rome was falling over the eastern Mediterranean, and no supernatural prophet was needed in the middle of the second century to forecast the rise of a new world empire. It is therefore naïve to suggest that the writer thought the end of all things was imminent in the time of Antiochus Epiphanes.

Third, had the author erroneously recorded the death of Antiochus in 11:40–45, this "defect" would have been apparent to the Jewish priests and scribes, who would have certainly excluded the book of Daniel from the canon of Scripture on that basis. As amazing as it is that a prophet living in the sixth century BC could have written in such precise detail of historical events as recorded in 11:2–35, this is not only true but a testimony to the wisdom and greatness of the God to whom Daniel bowed the knee.

1. Preparation of Daniel for the vision (10:1–11:1)

Daniel had humbled himself for three weeks while seeking understanding (10:12). In response, God gave him a new vision. First, however, he needed to be prepared for receiving the vision. This preparation included his encounter with "a certain man dressed in linen" (vv. 4–9) and subsequently with an angel (10:10–11:1).

a. The occasion of the vision (10:1–3)

Textual Notes

1.a. LXX^{O} has τῷ πρώτῳ, "the first," rather than "the third." LXX$^{\theta}$, however, has τρίτῳ ("the third"), agreeing with MT. Possibly LXX^{O} was assimilating to Dan 1:21.

1.b. Both LXX^{O} and α'(Aquila) have future tense verb forms (διανοηθήσεται and συνήσει, respectively), which suggests a reading יָבִין. Yet the parallel final clause supports a Qal perfect form.

Translation

10:1 In the third year of Cyrus, king of Persia,[333] a message was revealed to Daniel whose name was called Belteshazzar.[334] The message was true and *involved* great warfare.[335] Yet he understood the message and had an understanding of the vision. **2** In those days, I Daniel had been mourning[336] for three entire[337] weeks. **3** I neither ate delicacies[338] nor did meat and wine enter

---

333. Although the title מֶ֣לֶךְ פָּרַ֔ס (*melek̲ pāras*) was commonly used in the Greek period, R. D. Wilson, "The Title 'King of Persia' in the Scriptures," *PTR* 15 (1917): 90–145, has pointed out that this was a regular title for Persian kings in Ezra. Collins (372) also adds that this title was used for Cyrus by the Chronicler (e.g., 2 Chr 36:22; Ezra 1:1), and Cyrus was referred to by this title in the *Nabonidus Chronicle* 2:15 (see *ANET*, 306).

334. This name בֵּלְטְשַׁאצַּ֑ר (*bēlᵉṭᵉša ʾṣṣar*) was first used in Dan 1:7. Yet it was last used in 5:12, as Darius the Mede did not call him by that name, as far as we know.

335. There is debate as to how best to translate צָבָ֣א (*ṣāb̲ā ʾ*), as the most common meaning is "army," or metaphorically "hard service" (Isa 40:2; Job 7:1; 14:14). Driver (152) understood it as applying to the coming time of severe hardship. Baldwin (199) thinks "this cryptic expression refers to the struggle involved in understanding it." Yet, this verse is introductory to the final vision, encompassing the remainder of the book outlining warfare or armed conflict that lies ahead. Hence Goldingay (275) acknowledges, "But it can also mean 'war,' and a reference to the heavenly and earthly conflicts of 10:12–12:4 ... best fits the context."

336. For the construction הָיִ֥יתִי מִתְאַבֵּ֖ל, *hāyît̲î mit̲ ʾabbēl* (verb הָיָה, *hāyâ*, plus ptc.), Waltke and O'Connor note, "By connecting a finite form of היה with a following predicate participle, an aspectual and/or modal index is assigned to the participle, yielding forms that are past progressive"; *IBHS*, 628 (§37.7.1b). Hence, "had been mourning."

337. The word יָמִֽים (*yāmîm*) is not in construct with שָׁבֻעִ֖ים (*šāb̲u ʿîm*) but in apposition to it. See GKC, 424 (§131d). When a period of time and its contents are placed in apposition, the latter indicates the fullness of the time (hence, "whole" or "entire" weeks).

338. Lit., "food of desireableness" (לֶ֣חֶם חֲמֻד֜וֹת, *leḥem ḥămud̲ôt̲*). In this case, the noun in the construct state (*ḥămud̲ôt̲*) is a genitive of attribute, functioning as an adjective (= desirable food). At the same time, *ḥămud̲ôt̲* is in the plural, but here as an abstract noun. Waltke and O'Connor, *IBHS*, 120 (§7.4.2a), note, "An *abstract noun* is frequently expressed by a plural, which may have originally signified the diverse concrete manifestation of a quality or state." So, this is not a *plural of number* but of quality. Hence, "desirable food," i.e., delicacies.

my mouth, nor did I even[339] anoint myself with oil, until the entire three weeks were completed.[340]

Commentary

10:1 According to v. 1, this final vision came "in the third year of Cyrus king of Persia," i.e., the third year in reference to his conquest of Babylon.[341] Cyrus had conquered Babylon in October of 539 BC. If his first regnal year began the following Nisan (March/April of 538 BC), then his third year would have been from March/April of 536 to March/April of 535 BC.[342] The vision is also

339. The word "even" is supplied on account of the genitive absolute וְסוֹךְ (*wəsôḵ*) that intensifies the main verb.

340. Regarding the verb מְלֹּאת (*məlōʾṯ*), see BDB, 570b 1b, "especially of days, years, *be full, accomplished, ended.*"

341. The fact that Dan 10 is dated by Cyrus king of Persia whereas Dan 9 was dated by Darius the Mede may imply that this Darius had died by the time of Dan 10 and a new "king of Babylon" had not yet been appointed. According to P. Briant, *From Cyrus to Alexander: A History of the Persian Empire*, trans. P. T. Daniels (Winona Lake, IN: Eisenbrauns, 2002), 64, sometime in Cyrus' fourth regnal year a certain Gubāru was given the title "governor (*pihatu*) of Babylonia and Trans-Euphrates." S. Anderson, *Darius the Mede*, on the other hand, takes the position that Darius the Mede (i.e., Cyaxares II) was already advanced in age at the time of Babylon's conquest and lived for only a couple more years, at which time Babylon came under the direct rule of Cyrus himself. He explains (iii),

> Cyrus shared power with a Median king until about two years after the fall of Babylon. This king is called Cyaxares (II) by the Greek historian Xenophon, but is known by his throne name Darius in the book of Daniel. Cyrus did not make a hostile conquest of Media, did not dethrone the last Median king, and did not become the highest regent in the Medo-Persian Empire until after the fall of Babylon. Cyrus was Darius' co-regent, the hereditary king of the realm of Persia, the crown prince of Media, and the commander of the Medo-Persian army—yet it was still Darius who was officially recognized as the highest power in the realm. Darius died naturally within two years after the fall of Babylon, and as he had no male heir and Cyrus had married his daughter, Cyrus inherited his position upon his death and united the Median and Persian kingdoms in a single throne.

342. According to Finegan, *Handbook of Biblical Chronology*, rev. ed., 75, the Babylonians used what is called the "accession-year" method of reckoning a king's reign. According to this system, the time from the point that a new king begins to rule until the next New Year (in the month Nisan of the spring, i.e., March/April) is called his "accession year." Then the first year following Nisan 1 is called his first "regnal year." For Cyrus, then, his "accession year" was from October of 539 BC until Nisan 1 of 538 BC, and the first "regnal year" of his reign was from Nisan of 538 to Nisan 537 BC. However, Finegan's calculation would be true only if a new accession year began in Nisan rather than in Tishri. Contrast Shea's reckoning two notes

said to have taken place in the "first month" according to Dan 10:4. The "first month" would be the month Nisan (March/April).[343] Therefore, the time of this final vision is during the month Nisan of 536 BC (unless counting is done based on a Tishri system, as Shea has argued, in which case the final vision would be in Nisan of 535 BC).[344]

This date was extremely important, coming at a time when it gave Daniel a much clearer perspective on current events of his day. The vision to Daniel in chap. 9 had been given two years earlier. Following that vision, Yahweh had moved Cyrus in 538 BC to issue a proclamation permitting the return of the Jewish exiles to their land (Ezra 1:1–4), and Daniel's prayer was thus answered. By September/October of 538 BC, the returning Jews had rebuilt the altar in Jerusalem (Ezra 3:1–6), and by the late spring of 537 BC they had begun work on the foundation of the temple (Ezra 3:7–13).[345] The work quickly stopped, however, on account of hostilities from their enemies living in the land (Ezra 4:1–5). By the following spring of 536 BC, Daniel would have heard of the difficulties facing his people back in Judah. As the "first month" approached (Nisan 536 BC), when Passover was due to be celebrated, Daniel's heart was probably heavy on account of the suspension of the temple-rebuilding efforts.

Verse 1 of Dan 10 is an introduction to the whole final vision, and therefore the "message" is actually that which is revealed later in 11:2–12:4. The remainder of Dan 10 informs us of the circumstances that led up to the communication of this message from God. That is, 10:2–11:1 informs us of the occasion at which time Daniel received the "message." Although

---

below; W. H. Shea, "Wrestling with the Prince of Persia: A Study on Daniel 10," *AUSS* 21 (1983): 226–28.

343. Note that Ezekiel who also lived in Babylonia during the exilic period regarded Nisan as the "first month," as did others in the post-exilic period (Ezek 45:21; cf. 2 Chr 35:1; Esth 3:7).

344. Shea, "Wrestling with the Prince of Persia," 226–28, argues—in contrast to Finegan—that the date should be based on a Judahite calendar rather than a Babylonian one (counting a new accession year from Tishri rather than Nisan), such that the first month of the third year would be Nisan of 535 BC. This, Shea argues, would be more consistent with the dating notice in Dan 1:1.

345. We cannot be absolutely certain about these dates. Ezra 1:1 informs us that Cyrus' decree was issued in his first year, and I am assuming here that this means his first regnal year (starting Nisan 1 of 538 BC), following the conquest of Babylon in Oct 539 BC. According to Ezra 3:1, we are told that the people built the altar in the seventh month (September/October), but we do not know if this was September/October of 538 or 537. If the decree came early enough in 538, then they could have been back in the land before the seventh month of 538 BC (which I have assumed). According to Ezra 3:8, the foundation for the temple was laid in "the second year of their coming to the house of God at Jerusalem in the second month." The second month is the month Iyyar (April/May), but the actual date for the "second year" is not clear. The earliest that this could have been would be late spring of 537 BC.

this message is said to be concerned about "great warfare," this should not be taken to mean that only one single conflict is in view. The word translated "warfare" (צָבָא, *ṣāḇāʾ*) most often has a military connotation, such as "army," "war," or "hosts" (organized for war). In some cases it can refer to "hardship" or "struggles" in general (e.g., Job 10:17; 14:14; Isa 40:2). Here, however, it probably refers to a more protracted state of "warfare," namely the warfare and conflicts that bear on Israel as described in Dan 11–12. In light of 10:14, these were the conflicts of war that awaited the nation "in the latter days." Although v. 1 states that Daniel "understood the message," this probably only means that he understood the general gist of the message. Daniel 12:8 reflects that he did not understand everything fully (certain details still puzzled him).

10:2–3 Prior to the angel revealing the message to Daniel, he had been "mourning for three entire weeks." During this time he fasted—at least from "delicacies" and certain other foods and drink, including meat and wine (possibly a reference to the royal fare Daniel was customarily served in his position at the royal court). (This indicates that his diet of vegetables and water in chap. 1 was probably discontinued after his period of training, though his discretion in obeying God in his diet no doubt continued.) Furthermore, he did not "anoint himself with oil." The latter was a practice of anointing one's face with oil to refresh and preserve it from the hot sun (cf. Pss 104:15; 121:6). This was also associated with rejoicing and therefore inappropriate for a time of mourning (Ps 45:7; Prov 27:9). According to 2 Sam 12:20, anointing oneself was part of a procedure whereby one bathed, anointed himself with oil, and then adorned himself with clean clothes (cf. Ruth 3:3).

In light of Dan 10:4, Daniel's mourning was during the general season of Passover and the Feast of Unleavened Bread. Such abstentions, though appropriate for the festivals in the seventh month, were generally not done at the season of Passover and Unleavened Bread. In fact, to properly observe these festivals, one would normally eat the Passover meal, and then eat unleavened bread for seven days. The fact that Daniel chose to fast at the time of these festivals suggests that something was strongly motivating him to do so. The word translated "mourning" in v. 2 often has a sense of deep sorrow and grief (compare the use of this form of the verb *ʾāḇal* in Gen 37:34 and 1 Sam 15:35). In light of the historical context, it is reasonable to assume that Daniel was *deeply troubled* over the sad turn of events incurred by the Jews who had returned to the land of Judah and that had brought the rebuilding of the temple to a halt (note Ezra 4:4–5). What had been for a moment a cause of rejoicing (Cyrus' decree in his first year to permit their return) had now turned to disappointment. A closer look at Ezra 4:5 reveals that their enemies in the land "were hiring advisors to oppose them." This may indicate that the non-Jewish people in the land were paying bribes to the king's counselors at the Persian court to turn the heart of the king against the temple rebuilding program.[346] This may have confused Daniel, prompting him to seek Yahweh to gain a proper understanding (note Dan 10:12). Daniel was not the type of man who would *only* mourn. Surely he must have also prayed, and this is confirmed in 10:12 where the angel says to him, "Your words were heard, and I have come in response to your words."

Biblical Theology Comments

In light of the chronological notice at Dan 10:1 (the third year of Cyrus), the reason for Daniel's mourning (vv. 2–3) is very likely the troubling situation in Judah that Daniel would have heard about (as argued in the commentary above). Though the altar had been built and the foundation of the temple had been laid within two years of the return from exile (Ezra 3:1–11), the returning exiles had ceased work on rebuilding the temple shortly thereafter on account of the hostile actions of the surrounding peoples. At the heart of this dilemma, however, was a spiritual battle taking place. Just as the angel explained to Daniel that he was delayed due to the opposition of an evil spirit (Dan 10:13), so it is likely that behind the conflict back in Judah was a spiritual battle involving angelic beings. Satan would no doubt be opposed to the rebuilding of the temple in Jerusalem where God could be worshiped and praised by his people. We can extrapolate from the general tenor of Dan 10 that the troubles in Judah were ultimately rooted in Satan's hatred for the Jewish people and for God's temple program. Daniel may have been too old to have returned to Judah at this time to personally do something about this, but he did something that was even more crucial: he resorted to fasting and praying, and in so doing he was fighting on his knees.

Application and Devotional Implications

Daniel's actions in vv. 2–3 reflect that he was a man who cared more about spiritual matters than he did about earthly comforts. As this man of God (now well along in his eighties) thought back to his childhood days in Jerusalem and remembered the former temple, he could not help but yearn for the temple to be rebuilt and for God's people to be gathered there again in worship of the one and only true God. That this was being hindered and delayed grieved him. Nevertheless, grieved though he might have been, he used this as a stimulus to prayer rather than as an excuse to remain dejected

346. F. C. Fensham, *The Books of Ezra and Nehemiah*, NICOT (Grand Rapids: Eerdmans, 1982), 68, suggests that the "advisors/counselors" were actually the Persian governors who were taking bribes to act against the Jewish returnees. However, the word translated "advisors" (יוֹעֲצִים, *yô ʿăṣîm*) is commonly used of those who acted as counselors or advisors to a king, not those who served as governors (e.g., Isa 19:11; 1 Chr 27:33). They served at the king's court and had direct access to him. The word translated "hiring" (Heb. verb root *sāḵar*)—often meaning to pay someone legitimate wages—can mean to pay someone for evil purposes, and thus the idea of "bribing" is valid (see Deut 23:5; Neh 6:12–13).

and disillusioned. His "words that were heard" (10:12) were his words uttered in prayer—in private communion with God. There is a principle here we would do well to remember: when discouragements come our way, we can let such things defeat us, or we can let them goad us on to kneeling at the throne of grace where we bow before the Living God who is mighty to act and who has the power to turn things around. And indeed, not long after Daniel's death, the temple in Jerusalem was rebuilt.

b. The vision of the "man dressed in linen" (10:4–9)

A question immediately arises as to the identity of this "man" whom Daniel encounters in v. 5. Related to this is whether or not this is the same figure as described in v. 10 and following. The conclusion presented here is that these are not the same individuals. (See explanation at Dan 10:10.) Several evangelical scholars have rightfully concluded that the figure in vv. 4–9 is the preincarnate Jesus Christ.[347] The description of this "man" in Daniel is strikingly similar to the apostle John's encounter with the glorified Christ in Rev 1, and we can also observe certain parallels with the apostle Paul's encounter with Christ on the Damascus road. The following chart summarizes these parallels.

Textual Notes

5.a. Scholars debate MT's אוּפָז. Is this a place name or a descriptive term modifying כֶּתֶם? 4QDan^c unfortunately is cut off at that point and so provides no help. The only other use of אוּפָז occurs in Jer 10:9 in the form מֵאוּפָז ("from Uphaz"). The prep. מ would lend support to the idea of a place name, as would the previous line of that verse with a paralleling expression "silver from Tarshish" (מִתַּרְשִׁישׁ). Further support is found in LXX^θ's transliteration Ωφαζ. However, such a location (Uphaz) is unknown. Collins (361), following Tg. and S, reads a slightly emended אוֹפִיר and translates as a place name "Ophir." Ophir occurs 13x in the OT (see "gold from Ophir" in Ps 45:9[H 10], בְּכֶתֶם אוֹפִיר, which is strikingly similar to Dan 10:5). Ophir was famous for its high quality of gold (Job 28:16), which many would locate as a site in South Arabia (cf. 1 Kgs 9:28; 22:48 [H 49]). Goldingay (271) translates בְּכֶתֶם אוּפָז in Dan 10:5 as "pure gold," based on a verb פָּזַז meaning "refined" (BDB, 808), and the noun פַּז "refined or pure gold." Cf. 1 Kgs 10:18, זָהָב מוּפָז, "refined gold." From this root, we find רֹאשׁוֹ כֶּתֶם פָּז ("his head *is* like gold, pure gold") in Song 5:11. Most Eng. VSS side with MT and translate "Uphaz."

347. Evangelicals holding to the view that the "certain man" of Dan 10:4–9 is a theophany of the Lord Jesus Christ include Keil (410), Young (225), Walvoord (1971 ed., 243; 2012 ed., 306–7), C. Feinberg (141), Campbell (153–54), and Miller (281–82). On the other hand, Pentecost (1365) interprets this as Gabriel, while Leupold (447–48), Archer (123), Wood (268), and Hill (180) view him as an unknown angel. Keil (411) reported that Hengstenberg and some rabbis understood this one to be the angel Michael.

Dan 10:4–9	**Rev 1:12–17 and Acts 9:4, 7; 22:9; 26:14**
5 I lifted up my eyes and looked, and behold,	Rev 1:12 I turned to see whose voice was speaking to me, and when I did so, I saw seven golden lampstands,
a certain man clothed with a linen garment	Rev 1:13 and in the midst of the lampstands was one *like a son of man*. He was dressed in a robe extending down to his feet
and *having* his loins girded with gold from Uphaz.	and he wore a wide golden belt around his chest.
	Rev 1:14 His head and hair were as white as wool, even as white as snow,
6 His body *was* as topaz,	
and his face *had* the appearance of lightning.	Rev 1:16b His face shone like the sun shining at full strength.
His eyes *were* as flaming torches,	Rev 1:14 and his eyes were like a fiery flame.
his arms and feet like the gleam of burnished bronze,	Rev 1:15 His feet were like polished bronze refined in a furnace,
and the sound of his words *was* like a roaring crowd.	and his voice was like the roar of many waters.
7 Now I, Daniel, alone saw the vision, but the men who were with me did not see the vision. Yet great terror fell upon them, and they fled *where they could* hide themselves.	Acts 9:7 Now the men who were traveling with him stood there speechless, because they heard the voice but saw no one. Acts 22:9 Those who were with me saw the light, but did not understand the voice of the one who was speaking to me.
8 Then I alone was left and saw this great vision. Now no strength remained in me. Even my complexion turned a deathly pale, and I retained no strength. 9 But I heard the sound of his words, and when I heard the sound of his words, then I began to fall into a heavy sleep on my face, with my face to the ground.	Rev 1:17 When I saw him I fell down at his feet as though I were dead, but he placed his right hand on me and said: "Do not be afraid! I am the first and the last." Acts 9:4 He fell to the ground and heard a voice saying to him, "Saul, Saul, why are you persecuting me?" Acts 26:14 When we had all fallen to the ground, I heard a voice saying to me in Aramaic, "Saul, Saul, why are you persecuting me? You are hurting yourself by kicking against the goads."

7.a. In contrast to the more common masc. form מַרְאֶה, MT has מַרְאָה. Dan 10:7 is pointed מַרְאֶה in the Cairo Geniza MS. However, there is a fem. form of this noun, מַרְאָה (cf. Num 12:6; 1 Sam 3:15; plus, a pl. form in Gen 46:2). Observing הַמַּרְאָה הַגְּדֹלָה in Dan 10:8 (with a fem. Adj.), however, supports MT's מַרְאָה in Dan 10:7.

7.b. The inf. construct בְּהֵחָבֵא ("while hiding themselves") is translated ἐν σπουδῇ ("in haste") by LXX^{O}, and ἐν φόβῳ ("in fear") by LXX$^{\theta}$. Yet 4QDan^{c} has the same reading as MT.

Translation

10:4 On the twenty-fourth day of the first month, while I was beside[348] the great river, the Tigris,[349] **5** I lifted up my eyes and looked, and behold, a certain man clothed with a linen garment[350] and *having* his loins girded with gold from Uphaz.[351] **6** His body *was* as topaz,[352] and his face *had* the appearance of lightning. His eyes *were* as flaming[353] torches, his arms and feet

---

348. The combination עַל יַד (*ʿal yad̲*) is a special use of *yad̲* meaning "beside" (see BDB, 391c 5h[3]; and note Jer 46:6).

349. Goldingay (275) acknowledges that הוּא חִדָּקֶל (*hûʾ ḥiddāqel*) is not a gloss. Normally the words "the great river" (הַנָּהָר הַגָּדוֹל, *hannāhār haggād̲ôl*) are applied to the Euphrates River (Gen 15:18; Deut 1:7; Josh 1:4; cf. Rev 9:14; 16:12), and perhaps for this reason S translated as *perat* (the Euphrates). Yet חִדָּקֶל (*ḥiddāqel*) is rightly understood to be the Tigris River (also used in Gen 2:14). LXX^{O} translated as Τιγρης (*Tigrēs*), and LXX$^{\theta}$ simply transliterated as Εδδεκελ (*Eddekel*).

350. Although בַּדִּים (*baddîm*) is technically plural, Joüon, 500 (§136b), regards this as a pl. of composition.

351. See textual note to v. 5 for discussion and translation of אוּפָז (*ʾûpāz*). The term is found in Jer 10:9 as a place name, and this is supported by LXX$^{\theta}$'s transliteration Ωφαζ (*Ophaz*). However, the location is unknown.

352. The Heb. term is תַּרְשִׁישׁ (*taršîš*), occurring elsewhere in Exod (2x), Ezek (3x), and Song (1x). BDB (1076d) defines this as "a precious stone, perhaps *yellow jasper*, or other gold-coloured stone." Both LXX^{O} and LXX$^{\theta}$ transliterated as θαρσις (*tharsis*). *HALOT* (1798) defines it as "a precious stone, probably topaz," and Goldingay (271) translates as "topaz." Yet Goldingay indicated in his notes that it was known in Greek as chrysolite (275). In Exod 28:20, the LXX translated תַּרְשִׁישׁ (*taršîš*) as χρυσόλιθος (*chrusolithos*), i.e., chrysolite. Josephus (*Ant.* 3:168) understood this to be chrysolite. Collins (361) translates this "chrysolite," as does the NIV-1984. Yet the NIV-2011 changed to "topaz." Possibly these are the same (BDAG, 1093, indicates for χρυσόλιθος [*chrusolithos*] that "the ancients [Pliny, *NH* 37, 42] applied the term to yellow quartz or yellow topaz"). The NASB and ESV translated as "beryl," though the NET has "yellow jasper." Obviously there is uncertainty and no consensus. If indeed this is "topaz," pure topaz is colorless and transparent, though it is typically tinted on account of impurities.

353. Taking אֵשׁ (*ʾēš*), "fire," as a genitive of attribute, hence, "fiery" or "flaming."

like the gleam of burnished bronze, and the sound of his words *was* like a roaring crowd.[354] **7** Now I, Daniel, alone saw the vision, but the men who were with me did not see the vision. Yet great terror fell upon them, and they fled *where they could* hide themselves.[355] **8** Then I alone was left and saw this great vision. Now no strength remained in me. Even my complexion[356] turned a deathly pale,[357] and I retained no strength. **9** But I heard the sound of his words, and when I heard the sound of his words,[358] then I began[359] to fall into a heavy sleep on my face, with my face to the ground.

Commentary

10:4 Daniel's three weeks of mourning during the Passover season came to a halt on the twenty-fourth day of the first month (Nisan). Passover itself would have been on the fourteenth of Nisan, and the Feast of Unleavened Bread would have run through the twenty-first of Nisan (Exod 12:18; Lev 23:5–6). The twenty-fourth of Nisan, then, would have been three days after Unleavened Bread had ended. There is no known reason why Yahweh chose this particular day to bring the "message" to Daniel. Verse 3 stresses the fact that Daniel's abstinence continued until the entire three weeks were completed. Perhaps Daniel had purposed in his heart to fast and mourn for three weeks, and thus the final day (the twenty-fourth of the month) was an

---

354. "Roaring crowd" for Heb. הָמוֹן (*hāmôn*). *HALOT* (250) suggests six nuances of meaning, including #3 "noise, roar, din," and #5 "multitude, crowd." Goldingay (271) has "thundering," and Collins (361) "multitude." The NET has "a large crowd." The point is that when he spoke, he did so with much force and authority.

355. Lit., "while hiding themselves" (prep. בְּ [*bᵊ*] on an inf. construct commonly forms a temporal clause).

356. The proper translation of הוֹדִי (*hôḏî*) is difficult. BDB (217b 3c) gives the basic def. of "splendor, majesty, vigor." *HALOT* (241) suggests "complexion" for this verse. Goldingay (271) and NET go with "vigor" ("my vigor disappeared"), though Collins (361) prefers "dignity" ("my dignity was undone"). LXX^{O} used the translation πνευμα (*pneuma*), "spirit," while LXX$^{\theta}$ has ἡ δόξα μου (*hē doxa mou*), "my glory." The latter suggests that his complexion or countenance is in view, as *HALOT* prefers. In general, this idea is reflected in the NIV, ESV, and NRSV.

357. Lit., "was turned/changed on me to destruction/ruin" (נֶהְפַּךְ עָלַי לְמַשְׁחִית, *nehpaḵ ʿālay lᵊmašḥîṯ*). The idea seems to be that his complexion (or countenance) was ruined (i.e., undone). The NIV's "deathly pale" is perhaps a good way to express the intended idea in Eng. (so NRSV).

358. R. Taylor, "The Book of Daniel in the Bible of Edessa," *Aramaic Studies* 5 (2007): 244, prefers the Peshitta (which lacks the repetition) over the MT at this point. He writes, "The repetition is probably due to dittography. P lacks the first clause and reads only the second, in agreement with the Septuagint."

359. Regarding הָיִיתִי נִרְדָּם (*hāyîṯî nirdām*), see Waltke and O'Connor, *IBHS*, 629 (§37.7.1b #15). When a final form of הָיָה (*hāyâ*) is followed by a predicate participle, the aspectual notion may be inchoative ("began to …").

appropriate day for God to grant him understanding. At this time Daniel was not in Babylon (along the Euphrates) but rather at some location along the bank of the great river, the Tigris.[360] This also bears witness to the fact that Daniel did not accompany the returnees to Jerusalem.

10:5–6 Some have thought the "man dressed in linen" to be an angel, and specifically the angel Gabriel (so Montgomery, 420).[361] Although Gabriel had appeared previously in the book as a divinely sent messenger to Daniel, it is doubtful that Gabriel is in view here. First, in Daniel's encounter with Gabriel in 8:15–18, Gabriel's appearance was not described in detail as was the "man dressed in linen" of chap. 10. Had they been the same individual, we would have expected the detailed description to have been given in the first encounter. Second, although there are some similarities of Daniel's fearful reaction in both 8:15–18 and 10:8–9, we observe that Daniel did not have a reaction of fear upon encountering Gabriel in 9:21–23. This suggests that once he had met and heard from Gabriel in chap. 8 (where he was initially afraid), he did not have such a fearful reaction on subsequent encounters. Yet when Daniel does react in fear in 10:8–9, his fear seems to exceed that experienced in 8:15–18 (in chap. 10 there is a loss of strength and change in his countenance).[362] These observations would suggest that Daniel encountered a new individual in chap. 10, one even more awesome and imposing than his encounter with Gabriel in chap. 8.

---

360. If Daniel had been at this location along the Tigris River for the entire month of Nisan, he would have missed the huge Babylonian festivities associated with the Babylonian New Year during this same month (the *akītu* festival). During this festival the Babylonian version of the creation epic (*Enuma Elish*) was recited before Marduk. Block further describes this important time in Babylon: "The Babylonian New Year Festival was an elaborate affair, apparently incorporating aspects of several originally separate rituals. The event seems to have had several objectives: (1) to celebrate the supremacy and enthronement of Marduk; (2) to ensure the success of the enterprises of the coming year; (3) to affirm the king's status as high priest of Marduk; (4) to celebrate the enthronement of Nabû; (5) to mark the New Year on the calendar" (D. I. Block, "New Year," in *ISBE*, 3:529).

361. G. Bampfylde, "The Prince of the Host in the Book of Daniel and the Dead Sea Scrolls," *JSJ* 14 (1983): 131, has attempted to argue that not only is the figure in Dan 10:4–9 the same as in 10:10–21, but that he is to be equated with the Prince of the host in 8:11, the supreme archangel over the warrior angels and "related in some way to the 'Prince of Light(s)' and 'the Angel of Truth' of the Zadokite Documents (CD 5, 18,1), the *Manual of Discipline* (IQS 3, 20.24), and the *War Scroll* (1QM 13, 10–11; 17,6)."

362. Charles (258)—though taking the "man dressed in linen" as an angel—rejected the notion that he was Gabriel but rather an angel of higher rank, seeing that he had a more powerful effect on Daniel and that his name was not mentioned.

Rather than Gabriel, what we have in Dan 10:5–6 is a succinct description using symbolic imagery of the preincarnate Christ.[363] Although he is introduced here as a "certain man," the exalted portrayal of him in these verses is too majestic for him to be merely a man, or even an angel for that matter. Recall that the one promised an eternal kingdom in 7:13–14 was called "one like a son of man" (thereby linking him with humanity). Scripture never hesitates to call Jesus a man, because he fully partook of our humanity (though without a sin nature by virtue of his virgin birth), while at the same time presenting him as "Lord" (cf. 1 Tim 2:5).

Although the individual's description has certain affinities to Ezekiel (especially Ezek 1; cf. 9:2), the correspondences with Rev 1 are even stronger.[364] His apparel in v. 5 is like that of an OT priest, anticipating his priestly ministry. The word for "linen garment" (בַּדִּים, *baddîm*) is used elsewhere of the material for priestly garments (Exod 23:42; 1 Sam 2:18).[365] That "his loins were girded with gold from Uphaz" describes a golden sash about his waist—the word "loins" (מָתְנָיו, *moṯnāyw*) can sometimes refer to one's waist, e.g., 2 Sam 20:8; Isa 11:5; Jer 13:1.[366] Since a typical priest's sash was made of linen (Lev 16:4), this golden sash would have been distinctive.[367] Archer (123) adds, "the belt or sash (*ḥ*ᵃ*gurîm*, lit., 'girded,' 'belted') around his waist was

---

363. Pentecost (1366) objects to the identification of the "certain man" being Christ. He states, "… in favor of this messenger being an angel is the improbability of Christ being hindered by a prince (demon) of Persia (10:13) and needing the help of the angel Michael, and the fact that the person is giving a message from heaven." The problem with this argument, however, is that it wrongly assumes that the "certain man" of Dan 10:4–9 is one and the same as the angel in 10:10–11:1. E. Merrill, "A Theology of Ezekiel and Daniel," in *A Biblical Theology of the Old Testament*, ed. R. B. Zuck, 365–95 (Chicago: Moody, 1991), 388, on the other hand, argues against an angelic interpretation: "Though many scholars identify this 'man' clothed in linen as an angel, perhaps Gabriel or Michael, the extravagance of the description and the comparison with other texts, particularly in the New Testament (cf. Rev. 1:13–16; 2:18), make certain that this Being is none other than divine."

364. Not only does Dan 10:4–6 have certain affinities with Ezek 1 and Rev 1, but C. Rowland, "A Man Clothed in Linen; Dan 10:6ff. and Jewish Angelology," *JSNT* 24 (1985): 99–110, has demonstrated connections of Dan 10:4–6 to two pseudepigraphic works, namely *Joseph and Aseneth* 14 and the *Apocalypse of Abraham* 11.

365. For further insight into the priestly garments, see Josephus (*Ant.*, iii.7.1–2 [151–56]).

366. Both Exod 28:39–40 and Lev 8:7 mention the "sash" (אַבְנֵט, *ʾaḇnēṭ*) that was worn by the high priest. In Lev 8:7 we are told that when Moses consecrated Aaron, he "girded him with the sash" (וַיַּחְגֹּר אֹתוֹ בָּאַבְנֵט, *wayyaḥgōr ʾōṯô bāʾaḇnēṭ*), using the same word for "gird" (חָגַר, *ḥāgar*) as in Dan 10:5.

367. The NET adds the following note to Song 5:11, "In the OT gold is frequently used in comparisons to emphasize the idea of beauty, value, or rarity (Job 28:12–19; Pss 19:11; 119:127; Prov 8:19; Isa 13:12; Lam 4:2). Palestine had no known sources of

made of the 'finest gold' (*keṯem*), in the form of chain-links, hinged panels, or gold thread embroidery."

Daniel, in an attempt to convey the preincarnate Son's incredible beauty and majesty, described his whole body as resembling "topaz."[368] The glory radiating from his face was as intense as lightning. In a similar manner, three of the apostles saw Jesus on the Mount of Transfiguration in radiant glory: "His face shone like the sun" (Matt 17:2). This is how all God's children will one day see him in the future kingdom. Having "eyes as flaming torches" reflects the incredible piercing vision he has to see the hearts of all, and thus to know and evaluate his church (cf. Rev 2:18). His "arms and feet like the gleam of burnished bronze" (cf. Rev 1:15; 2:18) reflect that his life and works have been *tested by fire* and proven true and faithful. At the same time, bronze often is used to describe the virtue of strength (cf. Mic 4:13). The final thing highlighted is the words he uttered. The fact that "the sound of his words *was* like a roaring crowd" is indicative of the authority and power with which He speaks (and acts!). His voice called forth all creation (John 1:3), and He upholds all things by the word of his power (Heb 1:3). No wonder the Roman centurion could say to Him, "Lord ... just say the word, and my servant will be healed" (Matt 8:8).

The crucial question that should be asked is why Daniel suddenly saw this "man," the Lord Jesus, on the twenty-fourth of Nisan in 536 BC. The angel reveals God's "message" for Daniel later, but the preliminary encounter with Christ does serve an important purpose. If Daniel had been mourning due to the halting of the temple construction and was perplexed that God's people seemed to be suppressed, his discouragement would be immediately overcome by the glorious spectacle of seeing Messiah Jesus. One sight of the future king of the nations would have boosted Daniel's morale and given him the confidence that his God was in control of the nations, and his program would ultimately succeed.

10:7–9 The encounter with Messiah Jesus had a powerful effect upon Daniel and those with him. The men with him were divinely prevented from seeing the vision, but yet they could sense the divine presence.[369] As they did, they were frightened and ran away to hide. Daniel, however, remained there to behold the vision of Christ. In doing so, he was completely depleted of strength (compare the apostle John's reaction to the vision of Christ on

---

gold, but had to import it, making it a rare and precious commodity (R. V. Wright and R. L. Chadbourne, *The Gems and Minerals of the Bible*, 65)."

368. The translation "topaz" for Heb. תַּרְשִׁישׁ (*taršîš*) is not at all certain. See translation note for discussion. Others render this "chrysolite," "beryl," or "yellow jasper."

369. Cf. 2 Kgs 6:15–17, where only Elisha at first saw the angelic host encircling Dothan, but after intercessory prayer, his young assistant was enabled to see them too. Also, see Acts 9:7 where the companions of Saul could not see the vision of the risen Christ, but only heard his voice.

Patmos—"I fell down at his feet as though I were dead"). Yet Daniel does record that he "heard the sound of his words," though unfortunately we are not told what he heard. Having heard Messiah's voice, however, Daniel "fell into a heavy sleep" (cf. Dan 8:18). These five words translated "fell into a heavy sleep" are only one word in Hebrew, the participle נִרְדָּם (*nirdām*). This word can be used of heavy sleep in general, but it can also be used of a deep sleep induced by God himself, as God did in the cases of Adam (Gen 2:21) and Abraham (Gen 15:12).

Biblical Theology Comments

If Daniel 10:4–9 represents a vision in which Daniel sees the preincarnate Christ (as argued in this commentary), then this passage is obviously rich in its contribution to Christology. It is also the culmination or crescendo of messianic revelation in the book of Daniel. In 2:34 Christ was represented symbolically as a stone cut out of the mountain. In 7:13–14 he is referred to as "One like a Son of Man" destined to receive glory and a kingdom. In 9:25–26 he is the Messiah (*māšîaḥ*) who will be ruler, yet also "cut off" (put to death). Now in 10:4–9 he is seen as a priestly figure so dazzling that he can only be described with figurative expressions. Obviously human words are inadequate to depict his beauty and attributes. If the sight of the Lord Jesus Christ in vision caused Daniel to fall into a deep sleep with his face to the ground (10:9), one can only imagine what it will be like to see him face to face in all his glory. In contrast, however, is the visible appearance of Christ in his incarnation, for people were shielded from seeing his glory. In Isa 53:2 it is written, "He had no beauty or majesty to attract us to him, nothing in his appearance that we should desire him" (NIV). He came forth from the Father, and in so doing "did not regard equality with God a thing to be grasped, but emptied Himself, taking the form of a bond-servant and being made in the likeness of men" (Phil 2:6–7, NASB). Yet he ascended again to the Father, and in so doing returned to his glory, a glory that will eventually be revealed to his own at his appearing (Titus 2:13).

Application and Devotional Implications

In Dan 10:8 Daniel records that he "saw this great vision." The vision of the man dressed in linen was indeed a "great vision." In fact, this is the only place in the entire Bible that uses this expression "great vision." To encounter the Lord Jesus Christ would have made an incredible impact on this great Old Testament saint. Daniel had been told in chap. 7 that "one like a Son of Man" would eventually rule over God's kingdom, and then in chap. 9 that Messiah would be "cut off." Now Daniel is allowed to see him in a vision, which was such a powerful experience that it totally unnerved him and left him lying on the ground in a deep sleep. The apostle John (who had seen and known Jesus in his earthly incarnate form) went on to write, "Beloved, now we are children of God, and it has not appeared as yet what we will be. We know that when He appears, we will be like Him, because we will see Him just as He is" (1 John 3:2, NASB). Daniel saw the Lord Jesus in a vision, but we will see him face to face. Our experience upon that occasion will also be incredible, so much so that we will be transformed into his likeness. This is the great hope of every born-again believer—to see our glorious Savior in all his splendor and majesty. We really have something to look forward to!

c. The visitation of the angel to give Daniel understanding regarding the "latter days" (10:10–11:1)

Beginning in v. 10, we are introduced to a different figure. That he is not the Lord Jesus Christ is evident, seeing that he has to receive angelic help when fighting according to v. 13. The Lord Jesus would never need angelic help to overcome his opponents (compare the Lamb's triumph at his return in Rev 19:11–21). This is apparently an angel, because he is in league with Michael (whom Jude 9 calls "the archangel"). He might be Gabriel, since Gabriel had been used to convey the understanding of a vision to Daniel on a previous occasion (see Dan 8:15–19). Whether Gabriel or another angel, his mission was to convey God's "message" to Daniel.

Textual Notes

10.a-a. The phrase וְכַפּ֥וֹת יָדָֽי is lacking in LXX$^{\theta}$. The phrase is present in LXX^{O}, though with רַגְלַ֫י ("my feet") rather than יָדָֽי ("my hands"), supported by one Heb. MS.

13.a-a. Rather than MT's וַאֲנִ֗י נוֹתַ֣רְתִּי ("and I had been left there"), both LXX traditions have *καὶ αὐτὸν … κατέλιπον* ("and I left him [there]"). MT (as well as Vg. and S) has the passive (Nipʿal), meaning the angel speaking to Daniel was left there. LXX has the active (aorist), suggesting that the angel had left Michael there. Most Eng. VSS side with MT, but NRSV and NLT reflect the latter. Yet this would necessitate emending the text to וְאֹתוֹ הוֹתַרְתִּי.

13.b. LXX has an additional term following אֵ֫צֶל. LXX^{O} inserts *στρατηγοῦ* ("strategos, general"), and LXX$^{\theta}$ *ἄρχοντος* ("ruler"). Vg: "king of the Persians." 6QDan has מלוכת or שׂר מלכות. If the text is emended to שׂר מלכות ("the prince of the kingdom of Persia") on the basis of 6QDan and the singular titles found in the version (so Collins, 362), then the angel is saying that he had been left with the *king* (sg.), not *kings* (pl.) of Persia. Yet Goldingay (276) is probably correct when he points out that LXX and 6QDan appear to be an assimilation to וְשַׂ֣ר מַלְכ֣וּת פָּרַ֔ס at the beginning of Dan 10:13.

16.a. LXX^{O} has the addition of *χειρὸς* following כִּדְמוּת, hence "in the likeness of a human hand." Flint points out that "the reconstructed form of pap6QDan shows that it most likely read *something in the form of a human hand* (as does the Septuagint)."[370] Collins (362) adds, "The editors of 6QDan

---

370. P. Flint, "The Biblical Scrolls and the Text of the Hebrew Bible/Old Testament," in *The Meaning of the Dead Sea Scrolls*, ed. J. VanderKam and P. Flint, 103–53 (San Francisco: HarperSanFrancisco, 2004), 138.

(in *DJD*, 3.115) restore יד on the basis of the Greek, since the verb appears as feminine: נגעה." Yet "hand" is lacking in other known Heb. MSS, in LXX$^{\theta}$, and is not reflected in the similar statement in Dan 10:18.

19.a. Rather than MT's חֲזַק וַחֲזָק, LXX has two different words: *ἀνδρίζου καὶ ἴσχυε*. Hence, *BHS* editor proposes either וֶאֱמָץ or וְהִתְחַזֵּק for the second חֲזָק, so as to avoid the duplication. However, LXX's choice to use two different terms may simply be a stylistic choice, rather than a reflection of a different Heb. Vorlage.

1.a. Rather than MT's "Darius" (דָּרְיָוֶשׁ), LXX (and similarly Arabic) has Κύρου ("Cyrus"). However, the following הַמָּדִי ("the Mede") strengthens the case for MT. דָּרְיָוֶשׁ is the harder reading, as it is easy to understand why a LXX translator would try to conform the text to Dan 10:1. The reading "Darius" is also supported by 4QDan^{c}.

1.b. In contrast to עָמְדִי (Qal inf. Const.), 4QDan^{c} has עמדתי (Qal perf.), which Collins (362) favors. This is supported by LXX$^{\theta}$'s ἔστην (aorist indicative).

Translation

10:10 Then behold, a hand touched me, so that[371] I tottered,[372] *falling* on my knees and hands.[373] **11** Then he said to me, "Daniel, man of high esteem,[374] understand the words that I am about[375] to say to you and stand upright,[376] for I have now been sent to you." When he said this[377] to me, I stood up trembling. **12** Then he said to me, "Do not fear, Daniel, for from the first day that you set your heart to understand and to humble yourself before your God, your words were heard, and I have come on account of your words. **13** But the prince of the kingdom of Persia was withstanding[378] me twenty-one days. And behold, Michael, one of the chief princes, came to help me, for I had been left

371. For an example of a *waw*-consecutive clause expressing result, see Gen 26:14.

372. The verb וַתְּנִיעֵנִי (*wattᵊnîʿēnî*) is a Hipʿil form of נוּעַ (*nûaʿ*). According to BDB (631b), *nûaʿ* means "to wave or totter" in the Qal, and in the Hipʿil "to toss about, shake, cause to totter, disturb, or cause to wander." For Dan 10:10, BDB suggests "set me tottering on my knees and hands." *HALOT* (681–82) classifies Dan 10:10 under "to shake up, disturb." Goldingay (272) argues that "set me trembling" is too gentle and opts for "shook me." Given that a more specific word for "tremble" (רָעַד, *rāʿaḏ*) is used in the following verse, the idea of being shaken or made to totter seems to be the right idea in v. 10. Cf. NRSV, "roused me to my hands and knees."

373. Lit. "on my knees and the palms of my hands."

374. For אִישׁ־חֲמֻדוֹת (*ʾîš-ḥămuḏôṯ*), see translation note at Dan 9:23.

375. The ptc. דֹּבֵר (*dōḇēr*) is a case of *futurum instans* (see *IBHS*, 627 [§37.6f.]), which has the sense of action about to be commenced.

376. Lit., "and stand at your place" (וַעֲמֹד עַל־עָמְדֶךָ, *waʿămōḏ ʿal-ʿomḏekā*).

377. Lit., "this word" (הַדָּבָר הַזֶּה, *haddāḇār hazzeh*).

378. Lit., "was standing before me." Cf. Josh 5:13 where it has the sense of "confronting."

there with the kings of Persia. **14** Now I have come to give you understanding *about* what will happen to your people in the latter days,[379] for *there is* still a vision for *those future* days." **15** When he had spoken these words with me, I turned[380] my face to the ground and was speechless. **16** And behold, one in human likeness[381] touched my lips, and I opened my mouth and spoke. Then I said to the one who stood before me, "My lord,[382] on account of the vision, I am overcome with anguish[383] and have retained no strength. **17** How can my lord's servant speak with *such a one as*[384] my lord? As for me, no longer does *any* strength abide in me, nor does any breath remain in me." **18** Then the one having a human[385] appearance touched me again[386] and strengthened me. **19** And he said, "Do not fear, o man of high esteem; peace to you. Be very courageous!"[387] And when he had spoken with me, I gained strength and said, "May my lord speak, for you have strengthened me." **20** Then he said, "Do you know why I have come to you? Yet now I must return[388] to fight with the prince of Persia. So I am departing, and behold, the prince of

---

379. Regarding the expression "the latter days" (בְּאַחֲרִית הַיָּמִים, *bᵊʾaḥărîṯ hayyāmîm*), see commentary at Dan 2:28.

380. Lit., "gave" (נָתַתִּי, *nāṯattî*) or "put, set" (see BDB, 680 #2). Hence, "I set my face to the ground."

381. Lit., "as the likeness of sons of man" (כִּדְמוּת בְּנֵי אָדָם, *kiḏmûṯ bᵊnê ʾāḏām*). See Ezek 8:2 for a similar construction.

382. The personal address "my lord" (אֲדֹנִי, *ʾăḏōnî*) is used here as a title of respect, not of divinity.

383. Lit., "my pains have turned on me" (נֶהֶפְכוּ צִירַי עָלַי, *nehep̱kû ṣîray ʿālay*). The word "pain" (צִיר, *ṣîr*) is used of the pains of a woman in childbirth (e.g., 1 Sam 4:19). Yet the pain can also be emotional (cf. Isa 13:8). The word is used metaphorically in Isa 21:3 to describe the reaction to a "hard" or "intense" vision. The NIV's "overcome with anguish" captures the sense well, as does the NET's "anxiety has gripped me."

384. The construction זֶה ... זֶה (*zeh ... zeh*) has the idea of one to the other (cf. BDB, 260d 1b).

385. Lit., "as an appearance of a man." The noun "man" is a genitive of attribute modifying "appearance."

386. וַיֹּסֶף (*wayyōsep̱*) serves together with וַיִּגַּע (*wayyiggaʿ*) as a verbal hendiadys to express doing something *again* (in this case, "touched again").

387. The imperative חֲזַק (*ḥăzaq*) means "be strong" and the repetition serves to give emphasis (cf. Josh 1:9). *ḥăzaq* can also mean to be "firm" or "have courage" (so BDB, 304b 2c). Hence, "be very courageous!"

388. The translation "must return" is based on an understanding of the imperfect verb אָשׁוּב (*ʾāšûḇ*) as an obligatory imperfect, or what Waltke and O'Connor call "the non-perfective of obligation"; *IBHS*, 509 (§31.4.g).

Greece is about[389] to come. **21** However,[390] I will tell you what is inscribed in the reliable writing.[391] Yet there is no one strongly supporting[392] me against these, except Michael, your prince. **11:1** Now in the first year of Darius the Mede,[393] I myself arose[394] to strengthen and *be*[395] a protection for him."

Commentary

10:10–11 These two verses depict Daniel's encounter with the angel. Initially, Daniel had great difficulty in getting up from the ground where he had fallen face down (v. 9). A touch from the angel enabled Daniel to get to his hands and knees. The angel, wanting Daniel to stand back upright, encouraged him by addressing him as "a man of high esteem" (אִישׁ־חֲמֻדוֹת, *ʾîš-ḥămuḏôṯ*). This is similar to the way Gabriel addressed Daniel in 9:23, and this certainly reflects the high esteem that Daniel had in God's eyes. Archer (124) writes, "But observe that Daniel's privileged status as one especially precious to God resulted from his complete absorption in the will and glory of the Lord to whom he had yielded his heart." The angel also exhorted Daniel to understand the words he was about to tell him. With this, Daniel stood up, though even then he did so trembling.

10:12–14 Before the angel revealed the "message" itself to Daniel, he first admonished Daniel not to be afraid (a standard reassurance given by heavenly

---

389. The ptc. בָּא (*bāʾ*) is a case of *futurum instans* (see *IBHS*, 627 [§37.6.f]), which has the sense of action about to be commenced.

390. The adv. אֲבָל (*ʾăḇāl*) could be translated "indeed," having an asseverative rather than adversative force. In support of this, see M. Segal, "Monotheism and Angelology in Daniel," in *One God—One Cult—One Nation: Archaeological and Biblical Perspectives*, ed. R. G. Kratz and H. Spieckermann, 405–20, BZAW 405 (Berlin: de Gruyter, 2010), 410, fn 8.

391. The word כְּתָב (*kᵉṯāḇ*) means a "writing, edict, or document" (*TWOT*, 458). The genitive noun אֱמֶת (*ʾĕmeṯ*) is a genitive of attribute. This is neither a title ("The Book of Truth") nor a document about truth. Rather, this is a *reliable* writing or "dependable book" (so NET).

392. For a similar construction as מִתְחַזֵּק עִמִּי (*miṯḥazzēq ʿimmî*), see 1 Chr 11:10.

393. A number of critical scholars consider 11:1 (or at least 11:1a) to be a late gloss and also propose a reordering of the text in 10:20–11:2. See, for example, Di Lella (285) and Montgomery (416). Against the notion of a gloss, see P. David, "Daniel 11,1: A Late Gloss?" in *The Book of Daniel in the Light of New Findings*, ed. A. S. van der Woude, 505–14 (Leuven: Leuven University Press, 1993), 505–6. Segal, "Monotheism and Angelology in Daniel," 411, argues that the "problematic order" is the result of *textual growth*.

394. While it is possible to accept MT's infinitive construct reading, עָמְדִי (*ʿomḏî*), functioning as a finite verb (see *IBHS*, 611 [§36.3.2]), it seems preferable to read with 4QDan^c, עמדתי (*ʿmdtî*), a Qal perf. form. See textual note above for discussion.

395. Technically this is a prepositional phrase. Lit., "for a protection to him."

visitors: Gen 15:1; 26:24; Judg 6:23; and cf. Luke 1:13, 30) and then explained why there was a delay in the divine response. The delay had nothing to do with Daniel or his prayer (as if he had not prayed correctly or fervently enough). When the angel proclaimed, "your words were heard," we realize that Daniel had not only mourned (recall v. 2) but had also prayed. Although he prayed and fasted for three entire weeks, his prayer was heard from the very first day.

The real reason why it had taken three weeks for the angel to come is that he had been extremely occupied in spiritual warfare at the highest levels. He explained, "the prince of the kingdom of Persia was withstanding me twenty-one days." The word translated "prince" (שַׂר, *śar*) can mean a "ruler," "leader," or "high official." Since this same word is used of Michael in v. 21, this "prince of the kingdom of Persia" is most likely an angelic being.[396] Because he was "opposing" an angel sent by God (note that v. 20 says they were fighting), this "prince" must not only be an angel but more precisely a demonic angel. For this reason, "Michael, one of the chief princes,"—whose name means "Who is like God?"—came to help this holy angel in his fight with the demonic angel. This obviously reveals a great deal about the unseen spiritual world. Angelic beings are involved in fierce fighting. Although they may oppose and hinder a believer's prayers and God's responses, they only do so to the extent that the sovereignty of God permits them. Archer (125) explains,

> While God can, of course, override the united resistance of all the forces of hell if he chooses to do so, he accords to demons certain limited powers of obstruction and rebellion somewhat like those he allows humans. In both cases the exercise of free will in opposition to the Lord of heaven is permitted by him when he sees fit. But as Job 1:12 and 2:6 indicate, the malignity of Satan is never allowed to go beyond the due limit set by God, who will not allow the believer to be tested beyond his limit (1 Cor 10:13).

The fact that Michael would be brought in to assist the holy angel is telling. Jude 9 describes Michael as "the archangel," and Dan 12:1 refers to

396. Shea, "Wrestling with the Prince of Persia," 234, takes the position that the "princes" in chap. 10 are not demonic angels but human leaders standing in opposition to God's work. For him, the "prince of the kingdom of Persia" was Cambyses, the son of Cyrus (so Calvin, 2:252). Shea's thesis, however, is analyzed and refuted by D. E. Stevens, "Daniel 10 and the Notion of Territorial Spirits," *BSac* 157 (2000): 410–31. For example, for Shea's thesis to work, Cambyses would need to be referred to as both "the prince" and a king of Persia within the same verse (Dan 10:13). T. Meadowcroft, "Who are the Princes of Persia and Greece (Daniel 10)? Pointers Towards the Danielic Vision of Earth and Heaven," *JSOT* 29 (2004): 99–113, also holds that the "princes" are human leaders.

him as "the great prince who watches over your (i.e., Daniel's) people."[397] This high-ranking angel (perhaps the highest!) is given the responsibility of protecting God's covenant people, the Jews. Obviously something important was at stake in this angelic battle. According to Dan 10:13, the holy angel had been "left there with the kings of Persia." The term "kings" (Heb. מַלְכֵי *malḵê*) indicates that these are different from the "princes." Care should be taken to observe that the word for "king" is in the plural.[398] This, then, would most likely refer to Cyrus and his son, Cambyses. Although Cambyses' accession year was not until 530 BC (when Cyrus was killed in battle), there is a strong possibility that he had a co-regency with his father prior to that.[399] We do know that Cambyses was with Cyrus at the conquest of Babylon in 539 BC and was obviously held in high esteem at that time.[400]

If this holy angel had been left with the kings of Persia and was opposed by a demon identified as "the prince of the kingdom of Persia," then it stands to reason that the angelic struggle focused on their access to and influence with these human kings. Scripture elsewhere reveals Satan as the "prince of this world" (John 12:31; 14:30; 16:11), and he has a large contingent of demonic angels who are organized in different ranks for the purpose of opposing the Lord God (Eph 1:21; 6:12; Rev 9:1–2, 11). Hence this "prince of Persia" was a demonic angel assigned to Persia. Care should be taken here, however, not to label this a "territorial spirit," as though a *geographical assignment* is the issue. More accurately, the stress is on *sociopolitical structure*,

---

397. According to *1 Enoch*, both Michael and Gabriel are among the seven archangels of God (*1 En.* 20:5). Collins (375) notes, "In the Qumran *War Scroll* he is listed as one of the four archangels in 1QM 9:15–16, and, most significantly, he is given authority among the אלים in 1QM 17:6–7."

398. See textual note to v. 13 defending MT's reading of the plural form, מַלְכֵי (*malḵê*), as opposed to the singular in 6QDan and the versions.

399. Briant, *From Cyrus to Alexander*, 49, writes of Cyrus, "The last ten years of his reign are poorly known. All we know is that in 530 the king launched an expedition against the Massagetae of Central Asia. ... Before departing, Cyrus took steps to ensure the succession. He sent back to Persia his oldest son Cambyses, 'whom he had named as his successor.' This note from Herodotus (I.208) is confirmed by a passage in Ctesias (*Persica*, §8)." Shea, "An Unrecognized Vassal King of Babylon in the Early Achaemenid Period II," *AUSS* 9 (1971): 101–3, and "Wrestling with the Prince of Persia," 239–44, argues rather convincingly that Cambyses was co-regent as early as 535 BC.

400. According to the Nabonidus Chronicle (see *ANET*, 306), Cambyses entered Babylon with his father Cyrus, and he made an important appearance at the temple of Marduk. On the famous Cyrus Cylinder (*ANET*, 316), Cyrus urges prayer for both himself and his son, Cambyses: "May all the gods whom I have resettled in their sacred cities ask daily Bel and Nebo for a long life for me and may they recommend me (to him); to Marduk, my lord, they may say this: 'Cyrus, the king who worships you, and Cambyses, his son.'"

meaning that this demon was targeting the empire and the human authorities behind that empire.[401] This demon's purpose was to manipulate and control decisions coming out of the Persian court that affected the whole empire. This was relevant to Daniel because the Jewish people at this time were under the authority of Persia. If the demon could turn the hearts of the Persian rulers against Judah and/or influence them to pass laws and commands detrimental to the Jews, then this would thwart God's program. Appropriately, Michael himself (as guardian of the Jewish people) came to assist in this battle.

Having explained the reason for his delay, the angel goes on in v. 14 to explain his purpose in coming to Daniel. This vision pertained to a time still in the future, and the angel's mission was to help Daniel understand what would happen to his people "in the latter days." This expression, "the latter days," occurs ten times in the Old Testament.[402] It more often has in view the far distant future involving the events just prior to the messianic era, as well as the days when Messiah rules in his kingdom (see esp. Deut 4:30; Isa 2:2; and commentary at Dan 2:28). The message about to be revealed to Daniel was to help provide understanding for him about the future of his people, some of which would unfold in the upcoming centuries and some of which would be in the far distant future at the climax of history when Messiah Jesus returns.

10:15–17 These three verses record Daniel's astonished reaction and his loss of strength. At first Daniel appeared speechless, but he was aided by "one in human likeness" (apparently the same holy angel). This one touched his lips, thus enabling him to speak (cf. Isa 6:6–7, though Hill, 183, points out, "Unlike Isaiah's situation, the need here is strength, not cleansing"). Yet Daniel could only confess how weak he felt and how overwhelmed he was that an angel would be conversing with him. Daniel's use of the title "my lord" (אֲדֹנִי, *ʾăḏōnî*) in v. 16 is not an indication of deity but an address of respect (somewhat equivalent to English "sir," but an acknowledgment of the angel's superior role).

---

401. So Stevens, "Daniel 10 and the Notion of Territorial Spirits," 427–29. The angels (along with Michael) were fighting demonic spirits, which Stevens regards as "empire spirits" (not territorial). He concludes with sound advice related to a theology for spiritual warfare. He notes that Daniel did not engage in prayer for the purpose of "binding" or "evicting" them. Regarding the theological and terminological influence of Daniel upon Paul's comments in Eph 6:10–20, see G. R. Smillie, "Ephesians 6:19–20: A Mystery for the Sake of Which the Apostle is an Ambassador in Chains," *TJ* 18 (1997): 199–222.

402. Deut 4:30; 31:29; Isa 2:2 (= Mic 4:1); Jer 23:20; 30:24; 48:47; 49:39; Ezek 38:16; Dan 10:14.

10:18–11:1 The angel then made a second touch, this time not to enable Daniel to speak but to be strengthened and take courage. Once Daniel felt the supernatural strengthening, he was ready to listen to the message brought by the angel. The angel's greeting, "peace to you" (שָׁל֣וֹם לָ֔ךְ, *šālôm lāḵ*), was not so much a salutation. Di Lella (265) notes, "But if this were the meaning here, one would expect the phrase to be the first words addressed to Daniel; hence, it seems more probable that the phrase should here be understood as a statement of fact: 'You have *šālôm,*' i.e. 'You are safe.'" Collins (375) indicates that it "has probably a fuller sense here, in restoring the well-being of the visionary."

The question at the beginning of v. 20 ("Do you know why I have come to you?") is no doubt rhetorical, prompting Daniel to reflect further on these angelic conflicts and the revelation of warfare, suffering, and persecution that lay in store for Daniel's people.

In v. 20 the angel informs Daniel that he must return "to fight with the prince of Persia." Spiritual warfare among these angels was not over but would continue. Satan would continue to assault the Persian courts, seeking to influence the earthly rulers of the empire in ways hostile to God's plans and people (e.g., Haman's attempt to persuade King Ahasuerus [= Xerxes I, r. 486–465 BC] to have the Jews exterminated). The angel also instructed Daniel that the prince of Greece was coming. This was not a reference to Alexander the Great personally, although this statement does anticipate that the Persian Empire would be followed by the Greek rulers, beginning with Alexander in 331 BC. Once Greece and her rulers rose to overthrow Persia, Satan would appoint another demonic angel (the prince of Greece) to try to control or adversely influence this new political empire.

In v. 21 the angel referred to what had been "inscribed in the reliable writing" (not a title, "The Book of Truth") which he would now make known to Daniel.[403] This is the "message" that he was sent to convey in response to Daniel's prayers (recall 10:1), and which is recorded in 11:2–12:4. Hill (186) asserts, "Presumably this ... contains the course of history for the nations and the Hebrews as God's people, a portion of which is about to be revealed to Daniel."

In the latter part of v. 21, the angel affirmed that he had no one strongly supporting him against these other demonic angels (the "princes") except Michael. In calling Michael "your prince," he used the plural form of the word "your." Michael was not Daniel's personal protective angel but that of Daniel's people, the Jews (cf. 12:1). Seow (168) points out the encouragement it would have been for Daniel in knowing that "even though the enemies of Israel seem to have supernatural powers on their side, the people of Israel, too, have their supernatural protectors, most notably Michael."

---

403. See translation note for Dan 10:21 on "a reliable writing" (taking אֱמֶת, *ʾĕmeṯ*, as a genitive of attribute).

As a number of scholars have pointed out, Dan 11:1 is actually the last verse of the final paragraph in chap. 10 (a better chapter break is *after* 11:1). The angel that had been speaking to Daniel (the "I" of this verse) indicates that he "arose to strengthen and be a protection for him" in the first year of Darius the Mede. Since the word "to strengthen" is the same word used in 10:21 of the angel Michael's help to his fellow angel, the subject of this verse is the holy angel, not Daniel. That is, from Darius' first year (539 BC)—when Babylonian rule collapsed and the Jews came under Persian rule—this holy angel had arisen to encourage and strengthen Michael.[404] Hence, these two angels were a mutual help and strength to one another. At crucial times they came to one another's aid in an effort to influence what was taking place at the Persian courts and counter the evil plotting of the demonic angels.

Biblical Theology Comments

Dan 10:10–11:1 is highly significant for the theological contribution it makes to our understanding of angelology and demonology. The "princes" of this text unit are not human rulers but angelic beings. The fact that they have been given assignments pertaining to certain kingdoms reveals the strategic nature by which the demonic angels are organized. Recognizing this helps our understanding of true spiritual warfare. As pointed out in the commentary, however, rather than identifying these demonic angels as territorial spirits, it is more accurate to understand their role as that of targeting *sociopolitical realms*. That is, they are assigned the task of influencing empires and the political leaders who hold positions of power in these empires. To understand the spiritual warfare that goes on behind the scenes, as it were, serves to properly introduce the following chapter with its detailed analysis of conflict that raged among the successors of Alexander the Great. W. J. Heard explains:

> What follows is an account of the Hellenistic war between nations and kings on the earth. The introductory verses have served to inform the reader that the earthly battles are but one level of reality in a two-storey universe where the earthly and heavenly confrontations were merely two dimensions of the same battle. The pre-eminence of the celestial struggle is transparent because the earthly king does as he pleases and sets himself against the heavenly host and even against the 'God of gods' (11:36) and is only defeated when Israel's archangel, Michael, intervenes (12:1). Thus the battle in the heavenlies is clearly the decisive one.[405]

---

404. Understanding Dan 11:1 in the durative sense that the angel had been standing with Michael to strengthen and support him "since the first year of Darius the Mede."

405. W. J. Heard, "The Maccabean Martyr's Contribution to Holy War," *EvQ* 58 (1986): 311.

Application and Devotional Implications

Daniel 10 has significant implications for the prayer life of a believer. Notice, first, how Daniel's prayer set off a great deal of angelic warfare. Archer (124) writes, "These verses give us a fascinating insight into the supernatural forces involved when a believer engages in protracted and earnest prayer. Though James 5:16 tells us that 'prayer of a righteous man is powerful and effective,' we may not realize the mighty forces that are unleashed when we really devote ourselves to intercession before the throne of grace." Second, we learn that answered prayer is not always straight from God to the praying believer, for the process includes the angelic realm. Third, we must practice the principle of "indiscourageable persistence"! Though there may be hindering factors of which a praying Christian knows nothing, one must keep in mind that prayer itself is immediately heard. Jesus' teaching in Luke 18:1 on persistence in prayer is introduced this way: "Now He was telling them a parable to show that at all times they ought to pray and not to lose heart" (NASB). Fourth, Daniel was old but still a praying saint. Even a feeble old man on his knees in prayer is a threat to the demonic realm! Finally, recall the angel's address to Daniel, "O man of high esteem." The reason for such an affirmation was not because the angel was so impressed with Daniel's resumé but because Daniel was a man given to prayer (as Dan 10:2–3 bears witness to).

Selected Bibliography (Daniel 10)

Bampfylde, G. "The Prince of the Host in the Book of Daniel and the Dead Sea Scrolls." *JSJ* 14 (1983): 129–34.

Block, D. I. "New Year." In *ISBE*, 4 vols., ed. G. W. Bromiley, 3:529–32. Grand Rapids: Eerdmans, 1986.

Custer, J. S. "Man of Desires: Eros in the Book of Daniel." *The Downside Review* 119 (2001): 217–30.

David, P. "Daniel 11,1: A Late Gloss?" In *The Book of Daniel in the Light of New Findings*, ed. A. S. van der Woude, 505–14. Leuven: Leuven University Press, 1993.

Flint, P. "The Biblical Scrolls and the Text of the Hebrew Bible/Old Testament." In *The Meaning of the Dead Sea Scrolls*, ed. J. VanderKam and P. Flint, 103–53. San Francisco: HarperSanFrancisco, 2004.

Heard, W. J. "The Maccabean Martyr's Contribution to Holy War." *EvQ* 58 (1986): 291–318.

Meadowcroft, T. "Who are the Princes of Persia and Greece (Daniel 10)? Pointers Towards the Danielic Vision of Earth and Heaven." *JSOT* 29 (2004): 99–113.

Otzen, B. "Michael and Gabriel. Angelological Problems in the Book of Daniel." In *The Scriptures and the Scrolls: Studies in Honour of A. S. van der Woude on the Occasion of his 65th Birthday*, ed. F. G. Martínez, A. Hilhorst, and C. J. Labuschagne, 114–24. VTSup 49. Leiden: Brill, 1992.

Rowland, C. "A Man Clothed in Linen: Daniel 10.6ff. and Jewish Angelology." *JSNT* 24 (1985): 99–110.

Segal, M. "Monotheism and Angelology in Daniel." In *One God—One Cult—One Nation: Archaeological and Biblical Perspectives*, ed. R. G. Kratz and H. Spieckermann, 405–20. BZAW 405. Berlin: de Gruyter, 2010.
Shea, W. H. "An Unrecognized Vassal King of Babylon in the Early Achaemenid Period II." *AUSS* 9 (1971): 101–3.
———. "Wrestling with the Prince of Persia: A Study on Daniel 10." *AUSS* 21 (1983): 225–50.
Smillie, G. R. "Ephesians 6:19–20; A Mystery for the Sake of Which the Apostle is an Ambassador in Chains." *TJ* 18 (1997): 199–222.
Stevens, D. E. "Daniel 10 and the Notion of Territorial Spirits." *BSac* 157 (2000): 410–31.
Taylor, R. "The Book of Daniel in the Bible of Edessa" *Aramaic Studies* 5 (2007): 239–53.
Wilson, R. D. "The Title 'King of Persia' in the Scriptures." *PTR* 15 (1917): 90–145.
Wright, R. V., and R. L. Chadbourne. *The Gems and Minerals of the Bible*. New Canaan, CT: Keats, 1977.

2. *Predictions of the Near Future—Now Historically Fulfilled (11:2–35)*

Dan 11:2–12:4 forms the heart of God's "message" to Daniel in response to his fasting and prayers. In this message God reveals to Daniel a glimpse of the nation's future history in two parts, both of which will be full of warfare and conflicts. The first part (11:2–35) traces the history of the nation from the time of Daniel (under Cyrus' reign) until the early second century BC. For most of this period Judah is caught up in a struggle between two larger powers: the Seleucid Empire to the north and the Ptolemaic Empire of Egypt to the south. This struggle culminates with Antiochus IV Epiphanes coming to the Seleucid throne, under whose reign the Jews are severely persecuted (vv. 21–35).

a. From the time of the Persian Empire to Antiochus IV (11:2–20)

The angel is careful to trace the historical background to Antiochus IV so as to show the developments that brought him to the throne. There is an emphasis during this period on treachery, strife, warfare, greed, hatred, destructiveness, assassinations, vengeance, and vindictiveness. All these evil traits come to characterize Antiochus himself.

Textual Notes

2.a-a. The text at this point is difficult. *BHS* notes that two MSS omit את, while a couple of MSS have אֶל ("against"). Also, LXX varies from MT (e.g., LXX has ἐπαναστήσεται, "they will rise up against" rather than MT's יָעִיר, "he will arouse"). Although MT is supported by 4QDan[c], most Eng. VSS accept MT's יָעִיר and supply the word "against" (siding with אֶל). הַכֹּל can serve as the object of a verb without the direct object marker אֶת (for examples, see Ezra 1:11; 2 Chr 36:17,18).

6.a. Two MSS omit the initial *waw* on וּזְרֹעוֹ.

6.b. Most Eng. VSS accept MT's plural form, וּמְבִיאֶיהָ, "those who brought her." A number of manuscript Edd. have the singular –אָהּ ("the one who brought her"), which explains why the NET takes the singular. Yet both LXX^{O} and LXX$^{\theta}$ support the plural reading.

6.c. MT has the ptc. וְהַיֹּלְדָהּ, "he who fathered her," which is favored by Goldingay (272) and reflected in the NIV, ESV, and NLT (similarly, NASB, "the one who sired her"). LXX$^{\theta}$ (ἡ νεᾶνις) assumes the pointing וְהַיַּלְדָּה, "the young woman." *BHS* suggests reading וְיַלְדָּהּ, "her child" (so Montgomery, 430, and Collins, 364, followed by NET and NRSV), though that involves an emendation (omission of ה). Goldingay (277) argues for the MT reading: "MT seems to assume that throughout v 6 the reference is to those involved in establishing the marriage—and thus to father rather than to child" (similarly Keil, 435). A solution is difficult, but the reading וְיַלְדָּהּ, "her child," makes more sense historically (Berenice did have a son by Antiochus II). Wood (285) notes, "... it is known that her child did die at this time. Her father, as noted, also had died, but apparently not as a result of Laodice's wrath." Miller (293) and Di Lella (289) also favor the translation "her child."

10.a. Read with Qere the plural וּבָנָיו rather than Kethib's singular וּבְנוֹ. Although LXX^{O} supports the Kethib reading, the plural is supported by LXX$^{\theta}$, S, and Vg. In addition, to read the singular וּבְנוֹ would necessitate emending the following plural verb forms. Scholars are divided on this decision: Ginsburg (47) and Di Lella (258) prefer the Kethib reading (sg.), whereas Driver (169), Montgomery (436), and Collins (378) prefer Qere's plural (Goldingay [277] is cautious but gives the Qere a slight preference). B. Scolnic, "The Sons of Seleucus II and the Historicity of Dan 11:10," *VT* 66 (2016): 304–15, defends the plural reading on the basis of the historical background involving the two sons of Seleucus II.

10.b. Rather than the plural form וְיִתְגָּרוּ, read Qere's singular וְיִתְגָּרֶה (as many MSS, as well as LXX and Vg).

12.a. Rather than יָרוּם (Kethib), several MSS (including Cairo Geniza) as well as Qere read וְרָם.

12.b. Although the expected plural form is רִבּוֹת (so Neh 7:70), the form רִבֹּאוֹת is found in Ezra 2:69.

14.a. Rather than the Hitpaʿel form יִנַּשְּׂאוּ, a few MSS have the Nipʿal form יִנָּשְׂאוּ.

17.a. Rather than MT's וִישָׁרִים ("and the upright"), most Eng. VSS understand מֵישָׁרִים ("equitable agreement" or "alliance"), as seen already in v. 6. Note that

LXX^{O} translated as συνθήκας, a "treaty" (though XXL$^{\theta}$ has εὐθεῖα, "straight" or "straightforward").

17.b. Rather than MT's וְעָשָׂה, read יַעֲשֶׂה as appears to be the case in 4QDan^{c} (though admittedly י and ו are difficult to distinguish in 4QDan^{c}). The imperfect form יַעֲשֶׂה makes better sense if the reading מֵישָׁרִים is adopted for 11:17a above.

17.c. Although MT reads וּבַת הַנָּשִׁים ("daughter of women")—which is followed by XXL$^{\theta}$, 4QDan^{c} has "men" rather than "women" (observe θυγατέρα ἀνθρώπου in LXX^{O}). Cf. "daughters of men" (בְּנוֹת הָאָדָם) in Gen 6:2. *BHS* proposes וּבַת אֲנָשִׁים. Although the expression וּבַת הַנָּשִׁים does not occur elsewhere in the OT, מִבְּנוֹתֵינוּ לְנָשִׁים ("any of our daughters in marriage") in Judg 21:7 has some similarity. The NIV translates Dan 11:17 as "a daughter in marriage" (similarly NET, NRSV, and NLT), while the NASB and ESV retain MT's "daughter of women." In any case, the reference is to Cleopatra I.

18.a. MT begins the verse with וְיָשֵׁב ("and he will turn"), which is supported by ἐπιστρέψει in LXX$^{\theta}$ (and similarly S and Vg). The Qere reading, however, is וְיָשֵׂם ("and he will set"), and this is supported by Cairo Geniza (וישים) as well as καὶ δώσει ("he will give") in LXX^{O}. However, the reading וְיָשֵׁב is to be preferred for two reasons: (1) we have a similar situation at the beginning of v. 19, and it is unlikely that a scribe would have mistakenly written וְיָשֵׁב twice, if the correct reading had been וְיָשֵׂם; and (2) a form of the verb שׁוּב occurs eleven times in Dan 11 to describe military movements from one location to another (hence, a common technique).

18.b. Read with a few MSS לָאִיִּים (definite), and in agreement with LXX^{O} and LXX$^{\theta}$.

20.a. The Cairo Geniza correctly points as a construct form הֲדַר (contrast MT's הֶדֶר).

Translation

11:2 "Now I will tell you *the* truth. Behold three more kings will arise for Persia. Then a fourth will amass greater riches[406] than all *of them*, and when he has gained[407] power through his riches, he will arouse everyone against[408] the kingdom of Greece. **3** Then a mighty king will arise and rule over a great

406. יַעֲשִׁיר עֹשֶׁר (*ya ʿăšîr ʿōšer*) involves a cognate accusative, intensifying the action of the verb.

407. The verb "gained" is supplied in the Eng. translation, although there is no verb in the Heb. Lit., "and when his power by his riches."

408. See the textual note regarding אֵת (*ʾēṯ*). Most Eng. VSS understand a preposition אֶל (*ʾel*, "against") rather than the sign of the accusative (as is true in a couple of Heb. MSS).

dominion, and he will do as he pleases.[409] **4** But as soon as he has arisen, his kingdom will be broken and divided to the four winds of heaven, yet not to his posterity[410] nor according to his dominion over which he ruled, for his kingdom will be uprooted and *given* to others besides[411] these. **5** Then the king of the South[412] will become strong along with one of his commanders[413] who will grow stronger than he[414] and *even* rule with a greater dominion than his dominion. **6** Some years later[415] they will form an alliance when the daughter of the king of the South shall come to the king of the North to ratify[416] an equitable agreement.[417] Yet she will not retain her *position of* strength[418] nor will he be able to stand by[419] his strength, but she will be given over along with her entourage,[420] including her child[421] and the one who

---

409. Lit., "according to his pleasure" (כִּרְצוֹנוֹ, *kirṣônô*).
410. The translation "to his posterity" is lit. "to *that* after him" (לְאַחֲרִיתוֹ, *lᵊʾaḥărîṯô*).
411. For מִלְּבַד (*millᵊḇaḏ*) with the meaning "besides," see BDB, 94d e.
412. This is the first of many references in chap. 11 to the king of the South and king of the North. The kings of the South always refer to the rulers of Egypt, whereas the kings of the North represent the rulers associated with the Seleucid Empire. Some English translations (e.g., NASB, NIV) choose to capitalize South and North, since these terms refer primarily to specific empires. This practice will be followed here.
413. The noun שַׂר (*śar*) can be translated "commander, chief, ruler, official, captain, or prince," though the main point is that he was subordinate to the other. Historically, Seleucus I was *subordinate* to Ptolemy I, having served as one of Ptolemy's generals for a time during the wars of the Diadochi.
414. The verb חָזַק (*ḥāzaq*) means to be or grow strong, or to strengthen. The Qal form followed by the preposition עַל (*ʿal*) can mean to be strong upon/against (Gen 47:20; Ezek 3:14), to prevail over (1 Chr 21:4; 2 Chr 27:5), or to act arrogantly against (Mal 3:13). During most of the wars of the Diadochi, Ptolemy I and Seleucus I were allies, and although they eventually turned against one another, it is not accurate to say that Seleucus defeated or prevailed over Ptolemy. Seleucus did grow continually stronger, became independent of Ptolemy, and went on to establish an empire of his own (even larger and stronger than that of Ptolemy's).
415. For the translation of וּלְקֵץ שָׁנִים (*ûlᵊqēṣ šānîm*) as "some years later" (lit., "and at an end of years"), see 2 Chr 18:2.
416. Lit., "make."
417. מֵישָׁרִים (*mêšārîm*) refers to something that is even or equitable, in this case "an equitable agreement."
418. Lit., "the power of the arm" (כּוֹחַ הַזְּרוֹעַ, *kôaḥ hazzᵊrôaʿ*).
419. See textual note above. Not all Heb. MSS have the initial *waw* on וּזְרֹעוֹ (*ûzᵊrōʿô*). The noun is thus treated as a prepositional phrase modifying the verb יַעֲמֹד (*yaʿămōḏ*).
420. The translation "entourage" is literally, "those who brought her" (וּמְבִיאֶיהָ, *ûmᵊḇîʾeyhā*). See textual note above for defense of the plural form.
421. For the translation "her child" (rather than "he who fathered her"), see the textual note above. The NET and NRSV favor the translation "her child," along with several conservative commentators.

supported her in *those* times. **7** Then one from her family line[422] will rise up
in his place[423] and come against *their* army, enter the fortress of the king of
the North, take action against them, and prevail.[424] **8** Also their gods along
with their molten images *and* precious[425] vessels of silver and gold, he will
take captive into Egypt. Then for some years he will desist[426] from *attacking*
the king of the North. **9** Yet *the latter*[427] will enter the realm of the king of
the South, and then return to his *own* land. **10** Then his sons[428] will become
stirred up for war[429] and gather a multitude *into* a large army, and he will
keep[430] advancing,[431] overflow *like a river* and pass through, so as to again[432]
extend the war right up to *his* fortress. **11** The king of the South will then
be enraged and go forth and fight with[433] the king of the North. The *latter*
will raise a large multitude, but that multitude will be given into his hand.
12 When the multitude is swept away, his heart will be lifted up.[434] Though
he will cause tens of thousands to fall, he will not *continue to* prevail,[435] **13** for

---

422. Lit., "from a shoot of her stock" (i.e., from her family line).
423. כֵּן (*kēn*) means "base, pedestal, office," but see BDB (487d 2) for the meaning "place."
424. See BDB (305a 5) for the meaning "prevail" for the Hip'il of חָזַק (*ḥāzaq*).
425. Lit., "vessels of their delight," taking חֶמְדָּתָם (*ḥemdāṯām*) as a genitive of attribute (= precious vessels).
426. The verb עָמַד (*'āmaḏ*), "to stand," can have the idea "to stop, cease moving" (see BDB, 764a 2). Also compare Ps 38:12, where עָמַד (*'āmaḏ*) followed by the prep. מִן (*min*) means to "stand aloof from."
427. The words "the latter" (i.e., the king of the North) are added for sake of clarity.
428. On the plural "sons," see textual note above.
429. The Hitpa'el of גָּרָה (*gārâ*) can mean to "excite oneself (against a foe), wage war" (BDB, 173c2). *HALOT* (202) suggests for Dan 11:10 "to get ready (for battle)." The NIV has "will prepare for war." Collins (364) suggests "will be stirred up," which is the main aspect. The idea seems to be in this context that their emotions were worked up, prompting themselves to launch a new invasion against Egypt. They were "stirred up for war."
430. The infinitive absolute בוֹא (*ḇô'*) intensifies the action of the main verb בָּא (*ḇā'*).
431. R. Taylor, "The Book of Daniel in the Bible of Edessa," argues that although MT lacks a prepositional phrase בּוֹ (*bô*, "against it") following וּבָא בוֹא (*ûḇā' ḇô'*), it should probably be included, as it is attested in the Peshitta, LXX^{O}, and some medieval Heb. manuscripts. He reasons, "The prepositional phrase may have been lost in the MT due to haplography caused by similarity to the immediately preceding words ובא בוא" (244).
432. The words וְיָשֹׁב וְיִתְגָּרוּ (*wᵉyāšōḇ wᵉyiṯgārû*) function here as a verbal hendiadys, meaning to do something *again* (in this case, to wage war again).
433. Lit., "with him."
434. The NET clarifies the figure, "he will become arrogant."
435. This is similar to an "imperfect of capability"; *IBHS*, 507 (§31.4c). He could not go on prevailing.

the king of the North will again[436] raise a larger multitude than before. After an interval of time, he will keep on advancing[437] with a great army and much equipment.[438] **14** In those times many will rise up[439] against the king of the South. Even the violent ones among your people will rise up[440] in order to fulfill[441] the vision, but they will stumble. **15** Then the king of the North will come and build up[442] a siege mound and capture a well-fortified city,[443] but the forces[444] of the South—even his finest troops[445]—will not be able to withstand[446] *them*, for they will have no strength to withstand. **16** So the one who comes against him will do as he pleases, and no one will be able to withstand him. He will even stay[447] in the Beautiful Land,[448] with all of

436. וְשָׁב ... וְהֶעֱמִיד (*wəšāḇ ... wəheʿĕmîḏ*) forms a verbal hendiadys, "to raise again."
437. Regarding יָבוֹא בוֹא (*yāḇôʾ ḇôʾ*), see comments at Dan 11:10 pertaining to the supplementary infinitive absolute.
438. רְכוּשׁ (*rəḵûš*) basically means "property, goods," though BDB (940d 3) mentions "camp baggage" in regard to this verse. *HALOT* (1236) indicates that it can mean the "equipment of warriors" or even the "baggage-train of an army." Basically, then, this refers to all the equipment and supplies they would need for their invasion.
439. Lit., "take a stand."
440. As mentioned in the textual note for this verse, the verb could be a Hitpaʿel form יִנַּשְּׂאוּ (*yinnaśśəʾû*), though a few MSS point as a Nipʿal form יִנָּשְׂאוּ (*yinnāśəʾû*). As a Hitpaʿel, this could mean "to lift oneself up, exalt oneself" (*BDB* 672a). As a Nipʿal, it would mean "be lifted up, be exalted, or rise up" (BDB, 671d). Since the original text had no vowel pointing, this could be taken either way. Though there is very little difference in meaning between the two options (especially since *HALOT*, 727 indicates the Hitpaʿel can mean "arise"), the translation "rise up" is suitable for Eng. translation.
441. For the meaning "fulfill" for the Hipʿil of עָמַד (*ʿāmaḏ*), see BDB, 764d 5.
442. Lit., "pour out," but the imagery is that of pouring out baskets of dirt in order to build up a siege mound.
443. Lit., "city of fortifications" (עִיר מִבְצָרוֹת, *ʿîr miḇṣārôṯ*), taking *miḇṣārôṯ* as a genitive of attribute.
444. זְרוֹעַ (*zərôaʿ*) is normally "arm, shoulder," but see BDB, 284b 3 for the special nuance of "*forces*, political and military."
445. Heb. וְעַם מִבְחָרָיו (*wəʿam miḇḥārāyw*), "people of his choicest ones," taking *miḇḥārāyw* as a genitive of attribute (choicest, best, finest). His "people" in this context are obviously his fighting troops.
446. Taking יַעֲמֹדוּ (*yaʿămōḏû*) as an imperfect of capability (negated).
447. Eng. VSS vary on their translation of וְיַעֲמֹד (*wəyaʿămōḏ*), but the verb עָמַד (*ʿāmaḏ*) followed by prep. בְּ (*bə*) can have the nuance "to remain, stay" as in Gen 19:17 (cf. BDB, 764b 3b).
448. בְּאֶרֶץ־הַצְּבִי (*bəʾereṣ-haṣṣəḇî*), "in the land of beauty," taking *haṣṣəḇî* as a genitive of attribute. Cf. Dan 8:9 and 11:41 for a similar reference to the land of Israel.

it[449] in his power. **17** And he will set his face on coming in the strength of his whole kingdom and will make[450] an alliance[451] with him. He will give to him *his* daughter in marriage[452] in order to ruin *his kingdom*,[453] but *this plan* will not succeed, nor will she support[454] him. **18** Then he will turn his face to coastal regions and capture many, but a commander will put a halt to his scorn.[455] In addition,[456] he will return his scorn to him. **19** So he will turn his face to the fortresses of his land, but he will stumble and fall, to be seen no more.[457] **20** Then one will arise in his place who will send out[458] a tribute

---

449. Most Eng. translations assume a noun כָּלָה (*kālâ*) meaning "complete destruction, annihilation" (BDB, 478d 2b). The NRSV, however, takes this as the noun כל (*kōl*) meaning "all" with a 3fs suffix (see, for example, כֻּלָּהּ, *kullāh*, in Gen 13:10). Likewise, Collins (365) translates "and it will be all," though Goldingay (273) has "with destruction in his power." Either option fits. If read as "all of it will be in his power," the idea would be that with Antiochus III's conquest of Sidon, all of Coele-Syria (including Phoenicia and Israel) came under Seleucid rule and never fell again to Egyptian rule. This was the case and remained so until Judean independence under the Maccabees.

450. Read יַעֲשֶׂה (*ya'ăśeh*) with *yod* prefix rather than *waw*. See textual note for further discussion.

451. See textual note for this verse and compare מֵישָׁרִים (*mêšārîm*) in Dan 11:6.

452. Some read as "daughter of women," but see discussion in textual note at this point.

453. The words "his kingdom" are not in the Heb. Instead there is a 3fs pronominal suffix (though 4QDan[c] has a masc. suffix). Several Eng. VSS understand the fem. pronominal suffix to refer to the "kingdom" of Ptolemy V (so NET, NIV, ESV, NRSV, and NLT). The NLT translation of the final sentence accurately captures the point: "He will give him a daughter in marriage in order to overthrow the kingdom from within, but his plan will fail."

454. Lit., "and she will not be for him."

455. Understanding חֶרְפָּה (*ḥerpâ*) as the reproach cast upon another (= scorn). NET translates as "shameful conduct" and NIV as "insolence."

456. MT's לוֹ בִּלְתִּי (*lô biltî*) is admittedly difficult, and perhaps the text is even corrupt at this point. The particle בִּלְתִּי (*biltî*) is normally used as a negation (= not, except). Some Eng. VSS simply omit the phrase; the NET translates "in addition" as a way of bridging to the next clause. The NLT captures the sense of the last clause well: "and cause him to retreat in shame."

457. The final clause is lit., "and will not be found" (וְלֹא יִמָּצֵא, *wəlō' yimmāṣē'*).

458. Lit., "cause to pass through" (מַעֲבִיר, *ma'ăbîr*).

collector[459] to maintain the royal splendor.[460] Yet in a very short time[461] he will be broken (though not in anger or in battle)."

Commentary

This section of the book of Daniel is particularly difficult to understand, as it presupposes that the reader has a good knowledge of historical events that took place from the Persian period (when Daniel lived) until the rise of the Seleucid ruler known as Antiochus IV Epiphanes (r. 175–164 BC). These verses (as well as 11:21–35) describe the hostilities that transpired between two rival kingdoms, namely the Ptolemaic kingdom of Egypt (the South) and the Seleucid kingdom with its chief city at Antioch of Syria (the North). Daniel 11:2–35 is significant for at least two reasons: (1) it traces the 150-year conflict between the rulers of Egypt and Seleucia in which Judah was caught in the middle and (2) it reveals how Antiochus IV Epiphanes (the historic persecutor of ancient Judah) came to power and carried out his atrocities.

Note: Because the references to historical figures in these verses are rather obscure to most readers, I will start the commentary on each verse by restating the translation and using brackets to specify the identity of each person referred to.

i. Origins of the conflict between the Ptolemies and Seleucids during the Persian period (11:2–4)

These three verses show how certain events during the Persian period set the stage for the long period of struggle between the Ptolemaic and Seleucid rulers.

11:2 "Now I will tell you *the* truth. Behold three more kings will arise for Persia. Then a fourth *[Xerxes I]* will amass greater riches than all *of them*, and when he has gained power through his riches, he will arouse everyone against the kingdom of Greece."

Cyrus was the first of the Persian kings to rule following Israel's deliverance from the Babylonian captivity. The three kings mentioned in v. 2 refer

---

459. For the Qal ptc. נֹוגֵשׂ (*nôgēś*), Collins (366) has "tribute collector." See Deut 15:2–3 where נָגַשׂ (*nāgaś*) is used of *exacting* wealth from another. LXX$^{\theta}$ translated as a "transgressor" (παραβιβάζων, *parabibazōn*), which perhaps has influenced Goldingay (273): "an oppressor of imperial splendor."

460. Translation of הֶדֶר מַלְכוּת (*heḏer malḵûṯ*) is difficult. The Cairo Geniza points הדר as a construct form (הֲדַר, *hăḏar*). Though the NASB translates as a geographical reference to Jerusalem and its environs ("the Jewel of *his* kingdom"), most Eng. VSS have something similar to NIV's "to maintain the royal splendor" (taking *malḵûṯ* as a genitive of attribute). Although the word "maintain" is not in the text, this could be understood, if *heḏer* is regarded as a genitive of purpose (i.e., a tribute collector *for* the splendor of the kingdom).

461. Lit., "yet in days few" (וּבְיָמִים אֲחָדִים, *ûḇᵊyāmîm ʾăḥāḏîm*).

to his successors: Cambyses (ca. 530–522 BC), Pseudo-Smerdis (ca. 522 BC), and Darius I Hystaspes (ca. 522–486 BC). Although Cyrus himself served relatively wisely as the first of the Persian kings, the fourth king, Xerxes I (485–465 BC), launched a major invasion against the kingdom of Greece. This Xerxes I is the same as King Ahasuerus of the book of Esther. Soon after his accession in 485 BC, Xerxes brutally crushed revolts in Egypt and Babylonia, which contributed to his riches and power. He was now ready to use this acquired wealth and power against Greece in revenge for their earlier embarrassment of the Persians.[462] The banquet scene depicted in Esth 1 was not merely a drinking feast but more so an occasion for Xerxes to bring together the noble officials of the Persian Empire to stir up everyone against the kingdom of Greece and lay plans for a large-scale invasion. This great expedition against Greece began in the spring of 481 BC, yet it resulted in the humiliating loss of the Persian navy at Salamis to the west of Athens in 480 BC. Furthermore, Xerxes' army was eventually defeated at Plataea (northwest of Athens) in 479 BC. The only consolation for the Persians was a brief conquest of Athens itself, in which they destroyed the old Parthenon, an act that left a bitter taste with the Greeks for centuries.

11:3 "Then a mighty king *[Alexander the Great]* will arise and rule over a great dominion, and he will do as he pleases."

For the next nearly 150 years, ill feelings between Persia and Greece continued to simmer. At last a mighty king arose, Alexander the Great, who roused the Greeks to invade the Persian Empire, partly on the premise of seeking revenge for Athens but more so for the lust of conquest itself. Alexander succeeded his father, Phillip II of Macedon, to the throne in 336 BC, and in 334 BC launched an attack against the Persian Empire (which at that time was under the rule of Darius III, r. 336–330 BC). In just three and a half years Alexander exercised his great authority to conquer the mighty Persian Empire, striking a final victory at Gaugamela in October 331 BC.

11:4 "But as soon as he has arisen, his kingdom will be broken and divided to the four winds of heaven, yet not to his posterity nor according to his dominion over which he ruled, for his kingdom will be uprooted and *given* to others besides these."

Because of his untimely death in 323 BC at age thirty-two, Alexander's rise to power was short-lived. Without a son old enough to inherit his throne,

---

462. The roots of this conflict go back to the reign of Cyrus. When Cyrus conquered Lydia in 547 BC, the Greek cities of Ionia in western Turkey were subjected to the Persians. Later participation by the Athenians in an Ionian revolt during the reign of Darius I led the latter to send Persian forces against Greece in 492 BC. A second Persian expedition in 490 BC resulted in the famous Battle of Marathon in which the much larger Persian force was routed by the Greeks.

his kingdom fell not to his posterity but rather was broken up as his military commanders scrambled to grab what power they could for themselves.[463] In the final analysis, Alexander's kingdom was distributed toward the four winds of the sky, i.e., four of his generals managed to carve up his empire into four primary parts (see notes on Dan 8:5–8). Yet none of his successors came close to having the authority he exercised.

(1) Lysimachus:	Thrace and Bithynia (and much of Asia Minor)
(2) Cassander:	Macedonia and Greece
(3) Seleucus I:	Syria, Babylonia, and the lands to the east
(4) Ptolemy I:	Egypt, Israel, and Arabia Petrea

ii. Conflict between the Ptolemies and Seleucids prior to Antiochus III (11:5–9)

Introduction to the conflicts. Two of the successors of Alexander were Ptolemy I Soter (r. 323–282 BC) and Seleucus I Nicator (r. 312–280 BC). Ptolemy became head of Egypt, and he and his descendants are referred to as the "kings of the South" throughout Dan 11. Seleucus and his descendants ruled over northern Syria and various other countries; they are referred to as the "kings of the North" in Dan 11. Knowing the background of their rise to power helps one understand the political tension that ensued. When Alexander arrived in Egypt in 332 BC, the country quickly surrendered to him (thus bringing an end to Persian rule over Egypt). Before marching on to conquer Persia, Alexander left an occupation force of 20,000 men in place (mostly Macedonians and Greeks). Upon Alexander's death in 323 BC, Ptolemy (who had been one of Alexander's most trusted generals) obtained from Perdiccas, the holder of Alexander's seal, the right to administer Egypt. Yet for the next twenty-two years, until 301 BC, numerous battles (the Wars of the Diadochi, i.e., successors) were fought for control of Alexander's empire. Ptolemy had no problem in holding on to Egypt, but there was dispute over the territories of Judah, Phoenicia, and lower Syria. Initially, Ptolemy laid claim to these territories known as "Syria and Phoenicia" (or Coele-Syria) as early as 318

463. Alexander did have a son by Princess Roxana of Bactria, whom they named Alexander IV. However, during the Wars of the Diadochi, the young son was murdered ca. 309 BC. For the dating of Alexander IV's murder to the year 309 BC, see N. G. L. Hammond and F. W. Walbank, *A History of Macedonia: 336–167 B.C.* (Oxford: Oxford University Press, 1988), 3:165–68. B. Z. Wacholder, "The Beginning of the Seleucid Era and the Chronology of the Diadochoi," in *Nourished with Peace, S. Sandmel Memorial*, ed. F. E. Greenspahn et al., 183–211 (Chico, CA: Scholar's Press, 1984), however, dates the murder to 305 BC.

BC.[464] This area became highly prized for several reasons: (1) it served as an important buffer zone between Egypt and Northern Syria; (2) the choice timbers of the Phoenician forests were essential for shipbuilding and a strong naval presence in the Mediterranean; and (3) the numerous caravan trails through the Middle East had important outlets at the eastern Mediterranean and particularly with Phoenicia.

One of the other rival successors named Antigonus, a Macedonian general and satrap under Alexander, claimed authority over most of Asia, seized the treasures at Susa, and also entered Babylon, where Seleucus was governor. Forced to flee Babylon about 316 BC on account of the aggressions of Antigonus, Seleucus sought refuge with Ptolemy, and the two entered into league with one another (along with Lysimachus and Cassander) against Antigonus. By 314 BC, Antigonus invaded Syria and besieged Tyre, and several years of war followed, during which Ptolemy was forced to withdraw from Coele-Syria. A victory at the battle of Gaza in 312 BC by Seleucus over Demetrius, the son of Antigonus, allowed Ptolemy to once again occupy Coele-Syria, only to have to pull out again shortly afterwards. By the time peace was established in 311 BC, the government of Asia Minor and Syria was provisionally secured by Antigonus. Yet this was not to last.

In 301 BC the division of Alexander's empire was finally settled with the battle of Ipsus (in Phrygia of Asia Minor). In this famous battle, the armies of Antigonus and his son Demetrius were pitted against the coalition of Cassander, Lysimachus, and Seleucus. (Ptolemy supported the latter coalition but did not appear at the battle.) Antigonus was soundly defeated, and in the aftermath Seleucus received the bulk of Antigonus' lands in the east (including Babylonia and northern Syria) as well as eastern Asia Minor. Seleucus I moved his capital from a location in Babylonia (Seleucia-on-the-Tigris) to Antioch in northern Syria. Seleucus also claimed parts of Coele-Syria, which created a conflict with Ptolemy (with whom he had previously been allied). Ptolemy challenged him on this by occupying the lower parts of Syria up to the river Eleutherus in Phoenicia. The issue failed to be completely resolved:

> The conquerors of Antigonus, suspicious, ordered Ptolemy to surrender this territory to Seleucus, but he refused. Seleucus, invoking the old friendship between himself and Ptolemy, agreed

---

464. The term Coele-Syria means the "hollow" of Syria. Strictly speaking, this refers to the Beqaa Valley of present-day Lebanon and the surrounding areas, including both Damascus and the entire area south of the river Eleutherus of Lebanon, and even the land of Judah. The river Eleutherus is also known as An Nahr al Kabir (the Great River), and once formed the northern part of the border between Lebanon and Syria (flowing into the Mediterranean Sea).

provisionally to let the territory go, but not without making it clear that he was not renouncing his rights over Coele-Syria.[465]

This failure to come to a firm agreement on the rightful ownership of Coele-Syria (including the biblical lands of Judah) became the origin of the Syrian Wars between the Ptolemaic and Seleucid kings. Judah was continually caught in the middle of their conflicts. The following chart shows the two kingly lines:

Alexander the Great (336–323 BC)	
The Ptolemies	The Seleucids
Ptolemy I Soter, son of Lagi (323–282)	Seleucus I Nicator (312/11–280)
Ptolemy II Philadelphus (282–246)	Antiochus I (280–261)
Ptolemy III Euergetes (246–221)	Antiochus II (261–246)
Ptolemy IV Philopator (221–203)	Seleucus II (246–226)
Ptolemy V Epiphanes (203–181)	Seleucus III (226–222)
Ptolemy VI Philometor (181–146)	Antiochus III the Great (222–187)
	Seleucus IV (187–175)
	Antiochus IV Epiphanes (175–164)

11:5 "Then the king of the South *[Ptolemy I]* will become strong along with one of his commanders *[Seleucus I]* who will grow stronger than he and *even* rule with a greater dominion than his dominion."

Verse 5 introduces the two initial antagonists. Both the king of the South (Ptolemy I) and one of his commanders (Seleucus I) would grow strong.[466] Both "grew strong" in the sense that they survived the struggle for a piece of Alexander's empire (the Wars of the Diadochi) and became two of the chief inheritors. Although these two were initially friends and allies (they stood together against Antigonus), their dispute over the territory of Coele-Syria caused Seleucus to resist Ptolemy. In fact, Seleucus would go on to rule a kingdom greater than Ptolemy's. Following the battle of Ipsus, Seleucus' kingdom included all of northern Syria, Babylonia, and many lands that once comprised the eastern provinces of Alexander's empire (including parts of Asia Minor). Appian in his *History of Rome* reported that "he [Seleucus] acquired Mesopotamia, Armenia, 'Seleucid' Cappadocia, Persis, Parthia,

465. E. Will, "The Succession to Alexander," in *Cambridge Ancient History*, vol. 7, part 1 (Cambridge: Cambridge University Press, 1984), 60. Seleucus probably felt some sense of obligation to Ptolemy, since it was because of Ptolemy's help that Seleucus had been able to reestablish himself as ruler over Babylonia. Later Seleucid kings, however, were not so sympathetic and understanding toward the Ptolemaic rulers.

466. At one point Seleucus had the opportunity to directly support Ptolemy, as he commanded Egyptian squadrons in the Aegean Sea against Antigonus.

Bactria, Arabia, Tapouria, Sogdia, Arachosia, Hyrcania, and other adjacent peoples that had been subdued by Alexander, as far as the river Indus, so that the boundaries of his empire were the most extensive in Asia after that of Alexander."[467] At the end of his life, he was attempting to take Macedonia and Thrace but was assassinated by Ptolemy I's elder son (i.e., Ptolemy Keraunos) about 281 BC.[468]

11:6 "Some years later they will form an alliance when the daughter of the king of the South *[Berenice]* shall come to the king of the North *[Antiochus II]* to ratify an equitable agreement. Yet she *[Berenice]* will not retain her *position of* strength nor will he *[Antiochus II]* be able to stand by his strength, but she will be given over along with her entourage, including her child and the one who supported her in *those* times."

Following the death of Ptolemy I (282 BC) and Seleucus I just one year later (281 BC), their sons soon found themselves (by 275 BC) in conflict over the issue of Coele-Syria. This led to the First Syrian War (274–271 BC), initiated by Ptolemy II Philadelphus against the son and successor of Seleucus I, namely Antiochus I Soter (r. 281–261 BC). Initially Ptolemy II launched a military campaign against Seleucid Syria but had to retreat "in the face of an advance by Antiochus I who mobilized new units in Babylon."[469] Yet Antiochus I had to call off his plans, and Damascus remained a Ptolemaic stronghold.

By the time that a new Seleucid king came to the throne in 261 BC (Antiochus II), hostilities flared up again that led to the Second Syrian War (260–253 BC). When peace was finally concluded in 253 BC, this was strengthened by a marriage alliance ("an equitable agreement") between the two kingdoms. The daughter of the king of the South is a reference to Berenice (the daughter of Ptolemy II and his first wife Arsinoe I of Egypt), who was brought to the king of the North (Antiochus II) to become his wife in the spring of 252 BC.[470] Supposedly her son would become the next king upon Antiochus's death. Ptolemy II Philadelphus accompanied his daughter to the border-fortress city of Pelusion in the eastern Delta area of Egypt, along with vast quantities of silver and gold. Then the bride was brought to Antiochus

---

467. Appian, "The Syrian Wars," in *History of Rome*, §55, n.p. (accessed 17 Aug. 2015), online: http://www.livius.org/ap-ark/appian/appian_syriaca_11.html.

468. Upon regaining control of Babylonia, Seleucus established his capital there at Seleucia-on-the-Tigris (near modern Baghdad) in 305 BC. Later he moved his main capital to Antioch in northern Syria, but in 293 BC he placed his son Antiochus as viceroy at Seleucia-on-the-Tigris to rule over the eastern provinces.

469. G. Hölbl, *A History of the Ptolemaic Empire* (London: Routledge, 2001), 40.

470. This is the date given in Hölbl (ibid., 44). Some historians, however, date this marriage at 250 BC.

as far away as the border of the empire, just north of Sidon. (It seems that the boundary between the two empires remained at the Eleutherus River.)

This attempt to resolve the international dispute between Ptolemaic Egypt and the Seleucid Empire, however, did not succeed. Antiochus II already had another wife, Laodice—whom he divorced—and children by her. He had exiled her to Ephesus (following an agreement with Ptolemy II), and the right of succession was to pass to Berenice's children. Antiochus died rather unexpectedly in early 246 BC (many suspect by poisoning in the home of Laodice at Ephesus), and thus did not continue in his strength. Furthermore, Berenice did not retain her position of power. Laodice, the former queen, asserted that Antiochus on his deathbed had proclaimed that one of her sons, Seleucus II, would be the new king. Berenice, who was living in the palace at Antioch, tried to protest and appealed to Ptolemy III of Egypt for help.[471] Laodice's partisans at Antioch quickly murdered Berenice and her son. Hence she (Berenice), together with those who brought her (her Egyptian entourage), and her child were all "given over" at that time.[472] The words "given over" probably imply they were betrayed and put to death (cf. 2 Sam 20:21).[473]

11:7 "Then one from her family line *[Ptolemy III]* will rise up in his place and come against their army, enter the fortress of the king of the North *[Seleucus II]*, take action against them, and prevail."

These atrocities against Berenice (and thus against Ptolemaic Egypt) inaugurated the Third Syrian War (246–241 BC). "One from her family

---

471. One of the strange facts in the case is that both Ptolemy II Philadelphus and Antiochus II died in the same year, 246 BC. Thereupon, Ptolemy III Euergetes, the brother of Berenice, became the new ruler of Egypt.

472. Regarding the translation "her child" rather than "he who fathered her," see the textual note for Dan 11:6 above. MT has the ptc. וְהַיֹּלְדָהּ (*wəhayyōləḏāh*), "and he who fathered her," but the reading וְיַלְדָּהּ (*wəyaldāh*), "and her child," is thought by some to make more sense historically. The latter, however, involves an emendation (omission of the definite article ה). Montgomery (430) and Collins (364), followed by NET and NRSV, favor the translation "her child."

473. It is not altogether clear whom the text refers to in the final part of Dan 11:6. If the word translated "the one who brought her" is indeed singular in the original Heb. text, then this could refer to Antiochus II. Some MSS, however, have a plural form ("those who brought her")—the reading preferred in this commentary—which would then be a reference to her Egyptian attendants or entourage. The identity of "the one who supported her" is likewise unclear. Details of the death of Berenice's father, Ptolemy II, are sketchy, and it does not seem that he died as a result of Laodice's actions. According to Hölbl (*A History of the Ptolemaic Empire*, 46), Ptolemy II died early in 246 BC, and Ptolemy took over the office of king from his father on January 28.

line" (namely Berenice's brother and the new Egyptian Pharaoh Ptolemy III) traveled to Syria and came against their (the Seleucid) army, only to discover that Berenice and her son had been murdered. Ptolemy III had Laodice killed and entered the fortress of the king of the North, i.e., the Seleucid fortified palace at Antioch, which was still controlled by those loyal to Berenice.[474] Having been favorably received at Antioch, Ptolemy III went on to lead a campaign through Syria. He met little resistance and was thus able to "take action against them and prevail." Sources claim that this was one of the most successful campaigns in Ptolemaic history, as Ptolemy III marched all the way to Mesopotamia.

11:8 "Also their gods along with their molten images and precious vessels of silver and gold, he *[Ptolemy III]* will take captive into Egypt. Then for some years he will desist from attacking the king of the North *[Seleucus II]*."

Ptolemy's triumphant campaign through the Seleucid Empire as far as Mesopotamia was not so much one of warfare as it was of plundering and pillaging. He confiscated numerous objects of value, even taking their gods (idols) into captivity to Egypt, along with their molten images and prized vessels of silver and gold. (The capture of a nation's gods was regarded as a sign of their subjugation.) Then in early 245 BC, Ptolemy III made a sudden return to Egypt on account of an uprising of local Egyptians. His relocation to Egypt finally allowed Seleucus II (r. 246–226 BC) to assert himself and gain control over the Seleucid Empire. Though minor skirmishes continued between the two, Ptolemy apparently did not muster another large invasion against Seleucus but rather withdrew for some years from the king of the North.

11:9 "Yet the latter *[Seleucus II]* will enter the realm of the king of the South *[Ptolemy III]*, and then return to his own land."

Toward the end of the Third Syrian War (242/241 BC), there was fighting that took place near Damascus. The Roman historian Justinus even records that Seleucus II attempted an attack on Egypt about this time (though we have very little historical data about this). This may be the invasion by the king of the North referred to in v. 9, though it must have been brief. In any case, the Seleucid king had to soon return to his own land. By 241 BC peace was agreed upon, one that was quite favorable to the Ptolemies. One of the more important agreements was the acquisition by Egypt of Seleucia Pieria, the port city on the Orontes River of the western Seleucid capital of Antioch. This must attest to the strength of the Ptolemaic navy in the eastern Mediterranean. As for Seleucus II, he was beset with political and military

474. Laodice's son and rival claimant to the throne, Seleucus II Callinicus (r. 246–226 BC), was recognized in large parts of Seleucid Asia Minor, but not elsewhere at this time.

troubles in various parts of his realm that prevented him from being able to wage war with Egypt during the remainder of his reign.

iii. Seleucia's eventual domination under Antiochus III (11:10–20)

(A) ANTIOCHUS III'S INITIAL LOSES TO THE EGYPTIANS (11:10–12).

11:10 "Then his sons *[Seleucus III and Antiochus III]* will become stirred up for war and gather a multitude *into* a large army, and he *[Antiochus III]* will keep advancing, overflow *like a river* and pass through, so as to again extend the war right up to *his* fortress."

The Seleucid Empire under Seleucus II and Seleucus III was a time of weakening and loss of territorial control as a result of war on two fronts, in the east against the Parthians and in Anatolia against the Galatians and Pergamum (which had the support of Ptolemy III). When Seleucus II died in 226/225 BC, his son Seleucus III Soter (also called Seleucus Ceraunus) reigned in his place (226/225–223/222 BC).[475] Scolnic defends the plural reading "sons" at the beginning of Dan 11:10, suggesting that Seleucus III and his brother, Antiochus III, were working together to build up their troop numbers in preparation for expanding the Seleucid kingdom:

> Dan 11:10 is historically accurate when it states that Seleucus II had two sons who went in different directions (Seleucus III to the west, Antiochus III to the east) and hoped to restore the greatness and breadth of the kingdom. Two sons, equal in this view, set out, but one of them succeeds and the other drops from view.[476]

Seleucus III was assassinated in Anatolia by members of his army while on campaign against Attalus I of Pergamon. Antiochus III—being then only eighteen years of age—succeeded his brother to the throne in 222 BC.[477] Eusebius adds that Antiochus III was in Babylon at the time of the assassination: "He was succeeded by his brother Antiochus, whom the army summoned from Babylon."[478] Antiochus III's aim—like his brother's—was to restore the empire to its original size that it had been under Seleucus I, and he sought to reclaim the disputed territories of Coele-Syria. This is the one that (according to Dan 11:10b) mustered a large army and advanced like an overflowing river.

The rule of Ptolemaic Egypt changed in 221 BC. Ptolemy III died and was replaced by his son, Ptolemy IV Philopator (r. 221–204 BC). Ptolemy IV was a weak ruler, and under him the Ptolemaic kingdom began to decline.

---

475. Some scholars put the date of Seleucus III's reign as 225–223 BC. Hölbl, *A History of the Ptolemaic Empire*, 128, puts his death as 222 BC, while being more open about the beginning of his reign (226/225 BC).

476. B. Scolnic, "The Sons of Seleucus II and the Historicity of Dan 11:10," *VT* 66 (2016): 314.

477. Polybius 4.2.5.

478. Eusebius, *Chron.*, 1.40.12.

Antiochus III saw in this an opportunity to expand his own kingdom. Hence, he wasted no time in attempting an assault upon the Ptolemaic forces occupying strongholds in the Beqaa Valley of Phoenicia (present-day Lebanon). Yet he was unsuccessful and had to withdraw. At the same time, Antiochus was side-tracked in putting down a usurper named Molon in the eastern satrapies of Media and Persis (present-day Iran), which he managed to do in 220 BC.[479] Antiochus' next step was to resume his attack upon the northern Ptolemaic frontier by seizing the naval stronghold of Seleucia Pieria (the port city for Antioch), which was still under Egyptian control. This he did in 219 BC, thereby initiating the Fourth Syrian War (219–217 BC). He was aided in this by the Ptolemaic strategos, Theodotos of Aetolia, who betrayed the Egyptians and delivered the province of Coele-Syria to Antiochus. By this Antiochus quickly took control of Tyre and Ptolemais, gaining forty naval ships in the process. It seems the Egyptian strategy was to allow Antiochus to make small gains while secretly mobilizing a large army in preparation for war.

11:11 "The king of the South *[Ptolemy IV]* will then be enraged and go forth and fight with the king of the North *[Antiochus III]*. The *latter* will raise a large multitude, but that multitude will be given into his hand."

By 217 BC the Egyptians were ready to counter Antiochus' assault. The king of the South (Ptolemy IV) was enraged and marched out to fight Antiochus at the battle of Raphia (southwest of present-day Gaza).[480] This took place on June 22, 217 BC. In this huge battle, Ptolemy had 70,000 infantry, 6,000 cavalry, and 73 African war elephants. Antiochus had 62,000 infantry, 6,000 cavalry, and 103 elephants (but the larger Asian type). Antiochus was also joined by 10,000 Nabataeans and other Arab tribes. In the end, the army of Antiochus was delivered into the hand of Ptolemy, and as a result Ptolemy regained the important territory of Coele-Syria while Antiochus retreated to Antioch.

11:12 "When the multitude is swept away, his *[Ptolemy IV's]* heart will be lifted up. Though he will cause tens of thousands to fall, he will not *continue* to prevail, ..."

The great Egyptian victory at Raphia in 217 BC secured the northern borders of the Ptolemaic kingdom for the remainder of the reign of Ptolemy

---

479. Collins (378) notes, "Initially he had to put down a revolt by Molon, satrap of Media and then deal with the secession of Achaeus in Asia Minor." Cf. E. R. Bevan, *The House of Seleucus*, 2 vols. (London: Arnold, 1902), 1:300–320. Prior to being defeated by Antiochus, Molon had managed to defeat the generals that Antiochus had sent against him. He also occupied the important city of Seleucia-on-the-Tigris, and he had coins minted depicting him as king.

480. Regarding details of the battle, see Polybius, 5.79; and Bevan, *The House of Seleucus*, 1:318–20.

IV. History records that Ptolemy, the king of the South, became quite arrogant as a result of his victory. Though he was responsible for the death of thousands, he did not continue to prevail.[481] That is, though he recovered Coele-Syria and Phoenicia, he failed to press his advantage and his supremacy did not continue. He seemed to lack his father's instinct for war-making. The remainder of his reign was characterized by licentious living and an insatiable appetite for festivities and neglect of duties. Although Antiochus was unable to mount another war against him, by the end of Ptolemy's reign in 204 BC his kingdom was in decline and revolt had broken out among his Egyptian subjects.[482] As for Antiochus III, he spent the next thirteen years of his rule putting down revolts in his own kingdom, though in this he was quite successful.[483]

(B) ANTIOCHUS III'S DEFEAT OF THE EGYPTIANS (11:13–16).

11:13–14 "for the king of the North *[Antiochus III]* will again raise a larger multitude than before. After an interval of time, he will keep on advancing with a great army and much equipment. [14] In those times many will rise up against the king of the South *[Ptolemy V]*. Even the violent ones among your people *[Jewish revolutionaries]* will rise up in order to fulfill the vision, but they will stumble."

In the years following the battle of Raphia, Antiochus not only recovered from defeat but actually gained power in the outer portions of his empire. During the years 216 to 213 BC, he successfully put down a certain Achaios in Asia Minor (who was backed by the Ptolemaic government). Turning his attention to the eastern satrapies, he had spectacular success from 212 to 205 BC, as a result of which he assumed the title of "Basileus Megas" (Great King)—the traditional title of Persian kings—and was referred to as "Antiochus the Great" (reminiscent of Alexander). Following the death of Ptolemy IV in 204 BC, Antiochus III (the Great) saw his opportunity to finally strike back at Egypt. The new Egyptian king, Ptolemy V Epiphanes, was but six years of age, and there was much turmoil in Alexandria due to fighting over the regency. Early in 202 BC Antiochus began what has become known as the Fifth Syrian War (202–195 BC), when he raised "a larger multitude than before" (11:13). In this he was aided by his alliance with Philip V of

---

481. Antiochus lost over 14,000 men in defeat (Montgomery, 433, reports he lost 17,000).

482. Although the Ptolemaic dynasty was never seriously endangered by opposition from the native population, it is a fact that Upper Egypt rose against Alexandria (the heart of Ptolemaic rule) in 207/206 BC and was ruled by a rebel-king from 205/204 onwards.

483. Antiochus' success in putting down internal revolts included the eastern parts of his empire, during which he looted a temple in Ecbatana. Cf. Polybius 10.27; and Bevan, *The House of Seleucus*, 2.17–18.

Macedonia ("in those times many will rise up against the king of the South"), as the two leaders agreed to conquer and share the Ptolemies' non-Egyptian territories.[484] Joining with them were some pro-Seleucid Jewish revolutionaries, discontented with Egypt's rule over Judah, termed "the violent ones among your people" (11:14).[485] The intent of the statement in v. 14 that they rose up "in order to fulfill the vision" is not clear.[486] Collins (380) suggests that they had claimed "visionary support."[487] In any case, they did not succeed in their efforts (they stumbled). This may refer to an initial (though brief) success of an Aetolian (Greek) general named Skopas, whom Ptolemy V had placed in command of Coele-Syria. Miller (295) notes that he squelched a Jewish uprising against Egypt and, in so doing, punished the leaders of Jerusalem and Judah who had rebelled against the Ptolemaic government.

Nevertheless, Antiochus' uprising against Egypt was underway and headed for success. He first conquered Damascus (202 BC) and then proceeded to occupy large parts of the land of Judah throughout the course of 201 BC (including the fortress in Gaza), while the coastal cities of Phoenicia remained in the hands of the Ptolemaic kingdom. Fortunately for Antiochus, the Ptolemaic governor (named Ptolemaios) defected to Antiochus, for

---

484. In the winter of 203/202 BC, Antiochus and Philip V of Macedonia came to a secret agreement to divide up the Ptolemaic Empire and to eliminate the Ptolemaic hegemony in the eastern Mediterranean. Jerome adds, "those provinces which had previously been subjected to Egypt rose up in rebellion, and even Egypt itself was troubled with seditions. Moreover Philip, King of Macedon, and Antiochus the Great made peace with each other and engaged in a common struggle against Agathocles and Ptolemy Epiphanes, on the understanding that each of them should annex to his own dominion those cities of Ptolemy which lay nearest to them" (*Commentary on Daniel*, 125). (Agathocles was an Egyptian Greek nobleman who served as guardian and regent of the young boy-king of Egypt, Ptolemy V Epiphanes.)

485. Not all Judeans, however, supported Antiochus III. There were others who favored Ptolemaic rule.

486. Miller (295) assumes that fulfilling the vision refers to the prophecy recorded here in Dan 11. Jerome (*Commentary on Daniel*, 125) offers a very different interpretation. He claims that the high priest, Onias, fled to Egypt at this time along with a large number of the pro-Ptolemaic Jews and that he even built a Jewish temple in Egypt. Supposedly, "Onias affirmed that he was fulfilling the prophecy written by Isaiah: 'There shall be an altar of the Lord in Egypt, and the name of the Lord shall be found in their territories' (Isa. 19:19)." Thus, in Jerome's opinion, these Jews who had fled to Egypt were the renegades referred to in Dan 11:14.

487. Some have thought Dan 11:14–15 pertains to messianic circles that tried to take advantage of the political upheavals to establish some sort of political alternative. Cf. E. Täubler, "Jerusalem 201 to 199 B.C.E.: On the History of a Messianic Movement," *JQR* 37 (1946–1947): 1–30, 125–37, 249–63.

which he was rewarded with the title of strategos of the Seleucid province of "Coele Syria and Phoenicia."

11:15 "Then the king of the North *[Antiochus III]* will come and build up a siege mound and capture a well-fortified city, but the forces of the South *[Egyptians]*—even his finest troops —will not be able to withstand *them*, for they will have no strength to withstand."

In 200 BC Antiochus launched his second offensive, defeating the Ptolemaic general Skopas at Panion (later known as Caesarea Philippi). Significantly, this battle marked the end of Ptolemaic rule in Judah. Skopas was forced to retreat with 10,000 men to Sidon, only to be besieged there by Antiochus, thereby fulfilling the words of Dan 11:15, "the king of the North will come and build up a siege mound and capture a well-fortified city." The Ptolemaic government, however, was not able to send relief troops to his assistance. Shutting himself up within the walls of Sidon, after an ineffectual attempt by Ptolemy to relieve him, Skopas was ultimately compelled by famine to surrender in 199 BC to Antiochus III.[488] The important port-city of Sidon then fell to Seleucid control, as "the forces of the South" were simply not able to withstand the assault of Antiochus III. This event also enabled the Seleucids to maintain control over the interior lands.

11:16 "So the one who comes against him will do as he pleases *[i.e., Antiochus III]*, and no one will be able to withstand him. He will even stay in the Beautiful Land *[Judah]*, with all of it in his power."

With Egypt too weak to mount another offensive, Antiochus could "do as he pleased," with "no one able to withstand him" (11:16a).[489] Rather than making a direct attack upon Egypt proper, Antiochus spent the first half of 198 BC extending his control over the rest of the former province of Coele-Syria, gaining control over Judah and Jerusalem.[490] Hence, he could "stay in the Beautiful Land," i.e., Judah. All of Coele-Syria, Phoenicia, and Judah were now "in his power" (11:16b), and he had complete domination, the prize that the Seleucid kings had long sought (and felt was their rightful possession) since the battle of Ipsus in 301 BC.

(c) The Dismal End to Antiochus III's Reign (11:17–20)

11:17 "And he *[Antiochus III]* will set his face on coming in the strength of his whole kingdom and will make an alliance with him. He *[Antiochus III]* will give to him *[Ptolemy V] his* daughter in marriage in order to ruin *his kingdom*, but *this plan* will not succeed nor will she support him *[Antiochus III]*."

---

488. See Polybius XIII.1–2, XVI.18–19; and Josephus, *Ant.*, XII.3.3.

489. The remark "he could do as he pleased," was also said of Alexander the Great (Dan 11:3) as well as "the king" of v. 36 (the antichrist).

490. Regarding Antiochus' reception at Jerusalem, see Josephus, *Ant.* XII.3.3 §138.

Theoretically, Antiochus could have attempted a direct assault on Egypt, though he did not. Instead, Antiochus used this time to extend his power in Asia Minor, initiating a great campaign there in 197 BC in which a number of previously Ptolemaic cities came under Seleucid control. The capstone to this was Antiochus' conquest of Ephesus in the autumn of 197 BC, which had been a powerful and well-garrisoned Ptolemaic base. By the close of 197 BC, the Alexandrian government had lodged its complaints in Rome against Antiochus' conquests (especially in Asia Minor), and the Roman senate sent a man of consular rank, L. Cornelius Lentulus, to help resolve the tensions. With this, Rome was clearly extending its influence into the eastern Mediterranean (which would lead in the course of time to her conquest of all these territories).

In 196 BC Rome attempted to exert pressure on Antiochus to come to peace with Ptolemaic Egypt and return the captured territories. This prompted Antiochus to make a diplomatic maneuver at peace by means of a political marriage.[491] In the winter of 194/193 BC Antiochus' daughter Cleopatra I (though only about ten years old) was wed to the sixteen year-old Egyptian king, Ptolemy V Epiphanes (r. 204–180 BC), at Raphia.[492] Yet, Antiochus did this with treachery in mind: "He will give to him *[Ptolemy V]* his daughter in marriage in order to ruin his kingdom" (11:17). In the ensuing years, however, this tactic did not turn out to his advantage. Hölbl explains,

> In spite of the dynastic union, Antiochus III did not succeed in persuading the Ptolemaic court to maintain a neutral position regarding events in Asia Minor. The Ptolemies, for their part, had failed for a second time in their efforts to preserve their own interests in Asia by associating themselves with Rome in the war against Antiochus.[493]

11:18 "Then he *[Antiochus III]* will turn his face to coastal regions and capture many, but a commander *[a Roman general]* will put a halt to his scorn. In addition he will return his scorn to him."

---

491. This political marriage involved an interesting dowry. Collins (381) reports, "According to Josephus, Cleopatra's dowry was supposed to include Coele-Syria, Samaria, Judea, and Phoenicia (*Ant.* 12.4.1 §154). Polybius (28.20.9) reports that Antiochus Epiphanes later denied the existence of this agreement and convinced envoys from Greece that he was right."

492. Cleopatra I later became the sole ruler of Egypt upon the death of Ptolemy V, until their infant son (Ptolemy VI Philometor) was old enough to assume rule of the empire.

493. Hölbl, *A History of the Ptolemaic Empire*, 141.

Despite his success in confiscating Coele-Syria for the Seleucids, Antiochus the Great's career had a rather dismal end. Following the marriage alliance, Antiochus turned his attention to the coastal regions of Asia Minor where he captured many of them, which eventually brought him into conflict with Rome, the emerging new power in the eastern Mediterranean region.[494] Antiochus invaded Greece in 192 BC with a 10,000-man army and was even elected the commander in chief of the Aetolians (in their opposition to Rome). Yet the Romans prevailed against Antiochus. In 191 BC the Romans under the command of Manius Acilius Glabrio routed Antiochus at Thermopylae, forcing him to withdraw to Asia. Then in 190 BC a decisive Roman victory was achieved by Lucius Cornelius Scipio Asiaticus at the battle of Magnesia (eastern province of central Greece), thereby driving Antiochus out of Asia Minor and giving these territories into Roman hands. This is the Roman commander who would "put a halt to his scorn" (v. 18). Antiochus was made to pay for his conduct by signing the Treaty of Apamea in 188 BC, thereby abandoning all the country north of the Taurus Mountains, which Rome distributed amongst her friends.[495]

11:19 "So he *[Antiochus III]* will turn his face to the fortresses of his land, but he will stumble and fall, to be seen no more."

The Treaty of Apamea had two important results for Seleucid history (one of which significantly affected Judah). First, it called for the taking of twenty hostages to Rome, one of whom happened to be the son of Antiochus III, Mithridates, who would later be renamed Antiochus IV Epiphanes. A second result of this treaty was a growing assertion of independence by the outlying provinces of the empire. This prompted Antiochus III to make yet another expedition to the eastern provinces, or as v. 19 states, "he will turn his face to the fortresses of his land." In doing so, he came to Elymaïs, close to the ancient Persian capital of Susa, but more recently having come under Parthian control. There in the middle of 187 BC, Antiochus and his soldiers were killed while plundering the temple of Bel by the outraged inhabitants of the area (as they sought to secure money to pay the tribute owed to Rome).[496] Dan 11:19b summarizes the death of Antiochus the Great: "he will stumble and fall, to be seen no more."

494. Antiochus succeeded in taking Thrace by 196 BC (which comprised modern-day northeast Greece, Bulgaria, and the European part of northwest Turkey).

495. Apameia (present-day Dinar located in west-central Turkey) was an ancient city of Phrygia that had been founded by Antiochus I and came to be a seat of Seleucid power. At this city Antiochus the Great collected his army and then encountered the Romans at Magnesia.

496. Cf. Diodorus 28.3; 29:15; Strabo 16.1.8; and Justin 32.2.1–2.

11:20 "Then one will arise *[Seleucus IV]* in his place who will send out a tribute collector to maintain the royal splendor. Yet in a very short time he *[Seleucus IV]* will be broken (though not in anger or in battle)."

The next in line to Antiochus III (the Great) was Seleucus IV Philopator (r. 187–175 BC). He is the one who v. 20 says will arise after Antiochus III and "send out a tribute collector to maintain the royal splendor." Although Seleucus IV had the advantage of a large kingdom (which included Syria, Cilicia, Judah, Mesopotamia, Babylonia, and Nearer Iran—the last being Media and Persia), unfortunately he was strapped with a heavy war indemnity exacted by Rome and was forced to secure more financial resources by heavy taxation. The commonly held view is that it was for this reason, around 178 BC, that Seleucus sent out a "tribute collector" (נוֹגֵשׂ, *nôgēś*) named Heliodorus to go throughout his empire to collect tribute and taxes for paying Rome. Scolnic, however, has challenged this view, claiming that the annual tribute of one thousand talents due to Rome (as mandated by the Treaty of Apamea and signed by his father Antiochus III in 188 BC) was not so exorbitant as to pressure Seleucus into taking extreme measures of taxation. Instead he postulates (based on a study of Dan 11:20, 2 Macc 3, and various extrabiblical documents and inscriptions) that heavier taxation was sought to support the king's own aggrandizing purposes:

> ... Seleucus IV sent a tax collector to raise extraordinary revenues from his kingdom not for the sake of war and conquest but only for his royal splendor, and that he died not in war but because of a cold-blooded assassination that was a direct result of his policies. It is thus fair to speculate that something happened in the process of collection that then led Heliodorus to assassinate the king.[497]

In either case, his ambitious policies were, not surprisingly, unpopular with his people.

As Dan 11:20 indicates, Seleucus IV did not die in battle. Rather, he was assassinated ("broken though not in anger or in battle") by his own official, Heliodorus, upon the latter's return from a trip to collect revenue at Jerusalem (cf. 2 Macc 3:1–40). According to Scolnic, the assassination took place on September 5, 175 BC.[498] Heliodorus then attempted to seize the throne for himself (or to rule as regent for a younger son of Seleucus named Antiochus—not to be confused with Antiochus IV). Yet this attempt

497. B. Scolnic, "Heliodorus and the Assassination of Seleucus IV according to Dan 11:20 and 2 Macc 3," *JAJ* 7 (2017): 384.

498. B. Scolnic, "Seleucid Coinage in 175–166 BCE and the Historicity of Daniel 11:21–24," *JAH* 2 (2014): 28.

by Heliodorus proved unsuccessful, as he was out-maneuvered by Antiochus IV.[499]

Biblical Theology Comments

In Dan 8:8 the large horn of the male goat symbolized Alexander the Great, and with his passing "there came up four conspicuous horns." These have been identified as four of Alexander's generals who carved up his vast empire. According to v. 9, a "small horn" would come out of one of these four. The fulfillment of this, as has been noted, came about with Antiochus IV Epiphanes (the small horn), who eventually arose from the empire of Seleucus I, one of the four generals of Alexander. This represents a chronological leap of more than a hundred years from Seleucus' reign (312/311–280 BC) to that of Antiochus IV (175–164 BC). The historical material in 11:5–20 provides the detailed information that fills in this gap.

The primary purpose of the material in 11:2–20, though, is to show how Antiochus IV's reign was a product of the struggle between Egypt (the southern empire ruled by the Ptolemies) and Syria (the northern empire ruled by the Seleucid kings). Not only did the struggles between these two great empires set the stage for Antiochus IV's reign, but as the enmity between them played itself out, tiny Judah was significantly affected. In fact, at the heart of the struggle was the quest for control of the *land between* them. Though tiny and insignificant in some ways, Judah was the prize that each desperately sought. Theologically, this underscores the crucial role that "the promised land" plays in the drama of world history.

Application and Devotional Implications

The mood of Dan 11:2–20 is indeed grim. Notice the emphasis on treachery, betrayal, strife, broken treaties, warfare, greed, hatred, the use of marriage for political ends, assassinations, vengeance, destructiveness, and vindictiveness. All this represents the abuse of political and military power, reflecting kingdoms built upon the sinful and self-centered impulses of man living contrary to God's will and ways. What is noticeably absent from the lives of

499. According to J. W. Swain, "Antiochus Epiphanes and Egypt," *CP* 39 (1944): 73–94, Antiochus IV formed a strong relationship with Eumenes II, king of Pergamon, and the latter assisted Antiochus IV in ousting Heliodorus. Swain writes (79), "... when news came that Heliodorus had murdered Seleucus and was ruling Syria, Antiochus was Eumenes' choice as the man who, by becoming king of Syria, could best crush Heliodorus and continue Greek rule there. Eumenes and Antiochus then formed an alliance which lasted throughout the latter's life. A Pergamene army under Attalus, the king's brother, escorted him to the frontier; but in order that Antiochus might seem to come freely, the troops went no farther, and he proceeded to the capital. Heliodorus fled and Antiochus took over the government without meeting armed resistance."

those portrayed in these verses is true inner peace and the love of God. Yet multitudes of people on earth had to experience suffering, war, and death as a result of such ungodly leaders.

As believers in Christ, we know that the abuse of political leadership has been a part of human existence from the beginning and will continue to be so. We also know that such leaders as Hitler and Stalin are not the worst the world will ever see. The Bible reveals that antichrist is yet to come, a Satan-empowered ruler who will have a special hatred for God's people. We must be prepared to suffer at the hands of ungodly leaders, even as many of our brothers and sisters already have, and as many more will suffer in the great tribulation to come. At the same time, we are called to live out a way of life that is radically different than the world's quest for power. As Jesus said in John 13:35, "By this all men will know that you are My disciples, if you have love for one another" (NASB). Hence, we must always remember that we are not to emulate the ways of such ungodly leaders as described in Dan 11. Rather, we are called to follow our Lord Jesus Christ: "love one another, even as I have loved you." We do this by (1) not living self-centeredly or for selfish gain, (2) being a servant to others, and (3) laying down our lives for the brethren (1 John 3:16). If in the process of pursuing love we do not attain to positions of power and influence in this life, we do well to remember that it is better to rule with Christ in the kingdom to come.

b. During the reign of Antiochus IV (11:21–35)

Throughout this chapter, the author has sought to trace the political and military history that evidences the strife between the rulers of Egypt (the kings of the South) and those of the Seleucid Empire (the kings of the North). This background information has helped set the stage for the appearance of Antiochus IV Epiphanes (r. 175–164 BC).[500] Already in the book of Daniel, Antiochus IV has received much attention, particularly in Dan 8. In that chapter the hostile persecution of Antiochus IV against the Jewish people

500. According to J. Morgenstern, "The King-God among the Western Semites and the Meaning of Epiphanes," *VT* 10 (1960): 138–97, Antiochus IV obtained the title "Epiphanes" while attending a festival at Tyre, when the assembled multitude hailed him with the salute, "You are a god!" He notes (164), "But certainly it was at this Festival of the Awakening of Melcarth, celebrated in Tyre in 172 BC, that he, the Syrian king, enacted the role of the resurrected, youthful, radiant god, returning to his people, and thus acquired for himself the title Epiphanes. Henceforth not only did he regard himself as a god and so represent himself, but also he insisted that his subjects likewise so regard him. Accordingly his coins entitle him *Theos*, 'God', and the communication sent to him by the Samaritans begins, 'To King Antiochus, the God, Epiphanes.'"

and the biblical faith was highlighted. Now again in chap. 11, Antiochus IV receives major attention. The reason for such emphasis upon him is that in his character and brutal actions against the Jewish people, Antiochus IV is a *type* of the antichrist to come. This is why the author, after surveying the evil reign of Antiochus IV in 11:21–35, stops his historical survey at that point and jumps ahead to "the end time" (note vv. 35, 40). Just as the historical Antiochus IV of the second century BC committed an "abomination of desolation" (Dan 11:31), so a future evil ruler (the antichrist) will commit an even more offensive "abomination of desolation" (note Dan 12:11 and compare Matt 24:15).

Textual Notes

22.a. As the MT stands, וּזְרֹעוֹת הַשֶּׁטֶף appears to be a construct, lit., "and the forces of the flood." The NIV takes it this way, translating הַשֶּׁטֶף as a genitive of attribute, "an overwhelming army" (similarly NASB, "overflowing forces"; and Goldingay [273], "overwhelming forces"). Yet without emending the text, *BHS* proposes pointing this as a Nipʿal inf. abs., הִשָּׁטוֹף, intensifying the action of the main verb, יִשָּׁטְפוּ. The result (יִשָּׁטְפוּ הִשָּׁטוֹף) would be something like "suddenly swept away" or "utterly swept away." Favoring the Nipʿal inf. abs. reading are the NET, ESV, NRSV, and Collins (366). To have the cognate forms השטף ישטפו juxtaposed as they are would commonly be understood as the first being an inf. abs.

24.a. LXX$^{\theta}$ reads (probably mistakenly) מצרים ("Egypt") rather than מבצרים ("fortresses").

26.a. Several MSS as well as 4QDan^{c} have ישטף, which would allow for vocalizing as a Nipʿal impf. (יִשָּׁטֵף). (The Vg. and S also support the passive.) This would change the meaning from "his army will overflow" (active) to "his army will be overwhelmed [or swept away]" (passive). Though the NASB translates as an active verb, the Nipʿal reading is followed by most other Eng. VSS (NET, NIV, ESV, NRSV, NKJV). Collins (366) also argues for the Nipʿal, though Goldingay (279) argues against it (preferring "will pour away").

27.a. MS 88 and Syh mistake לבבם ("their heart") for לבדם ("alone"): "the two kings will eat *alone* together."

30.a. Neither LXX^{O} nor LXX$^{\theta}$ take צִיִּים as "ships." LXX$^{\theta}$ takes this as a verb יצאים ("those who go forth"), translating "and the Kittians who go forth will come against him." LXX^{O} has "and the Romans will come and drive him out." Yet Heb. MSS clearly read צִיִּים.

33.a. 6QDan has an initial *waw* ("and"), and similarly LXX^{O}.

Translation

11:21 Then in his place a despicable[501] person will arise upon whom royal[502]

501. בָּזָה (*bāzah*)—here as a Nip'al ptc.—means "despised, worthless, vile, contemptible, or despicable" (BDB, 102c). As the first statement about Antiochus IV in this text unit, this descriptive most likely represents the Bible's estimation of him in light of his persecution of the Jews and the biblical religion. Scolnic, however ("Antiochus IV as the Scorned Prince in Dan 11:21," 572), contends that the meaning is not that of being despised/contemptible but rather of being "scorned" in the sense that he had not been given appropriate royal honors. He sees this as the first step in a process that eventually led to Antiochus IV becoming the Seleucid king and that supposedly, "before his rise to power, Antiochus IV, son of the late king Antiochus III and brother of the current king Seleucus IV, had been scorned and had not been given appropriate royal honors and that this rejection may have motivated him to avenge himself and rise to power by killing those who had scorned him." Yet Scolnic's attempt to defend the meaning "scorned, rejected" for the Nip'al ptc. *nibzeh* should be rejected. Not only does this run counter to all Eng. VSS, but it receives no support from primary lexical resources (e.g., *HALOT*, "despised, despicable," 1:117; *TDOT*, "disapproval as contempt," 2:63–64; and *NIDOTTE*, "a man worthy of contempt," 1:629). While Scolnic insists (576) that LXX$^{\theta}$'s ἐξουδενώθη (*exoudenōthē*, aor. pass. of ἐξουδενέω, *exoudeneō*) does not mean "contemptible/vile" but "spurned and deprived of all status and the royal prerogatives," he is incorrect. Use of the same Greek verb in the LXX of Judg 9:38 ("Is this not the people whom you despised?") reveals that *exoudeneō* does mean being "despised."

Scolnic (574) tries to appeal to Gen 25:34 to argue that Esau *spurned* his birthright, but this is unconvincing. While it could be argued that he rejected the birthright, the normal meaning "despise" fits perfectly: Esau despised his birthright in the sense that he saw no value in it. That is, Gen 25:34 is no proof of Scolnic's thesis. Scolnic also attempts to argue that the statement about Antiochus IV in Dan 11:21 is parallel to the second half of the verse ("upon whom royal honor has not been conferred"). Here, however, Scolnic misses the point of the second half, namely that royal honor was not rightfully his to begin with (not that the people took action to keep it from him). Finally, his appeal to *nibzeh* in Isa 53:3 fails. He argues (575) for "scorned of men" rather than "contemptible." Yet the final line of Isa 53:3 suggests that it is their *attitude* toward the Suffering Servant—not their rejection of him—that is the point in this verse: "he was despised and we considered him insignificant." Hence, Dan 11:21 does not refer to *scorning actions* of the Seleucid people against Antiochus IV (keeping him from having royal honors) as a first step in a chain of events that resulted in him retaliating and eventually becoming king.

502. Understanding מַלְכוּת (*malkût*) as a genitive of attribute ("royal honor"). So NET, ESV, NRSV, Collins (366), and Goldingay (273). The NASB, in contrast, has "the honor of kingship."

honor has not been conferred.[503] He will come unexpectedly[504] and seize the kingdom through intrigue.[505] **22** And forces will be utterly[506] swept away[507] before him and devastated, and also a prince[508] of *the* covenant. **23** After forming an alliance with him, he will deal deceitfully, go up and become

---

503. Lit., "they have not given on him honor of royalty" (active verb).

504. The proper translation of בְּשַׁלְוָה (*b*ᵊ*šalwâ*) is not easy. Basically שַׁלְוָה (*šalwâ*) means "quietness, ease" and emphasizes *security* and sometimes *prosperity*. Yet *b*ᵊ*šalwâ* has received varying translations: NASB "in a time of tranquility"; NIV "when its people feel secure"; NRSV and ESV "without warning"; NET "in a time of prosperity"; NLT "when least expected"; Collins (366) "in stealth"; and Goldingay (273) "with ease." Though LXX^θ's εὐθηνία (*euthēnia*), "prosperity" supports the NET, LXX^O's ἐξάπινα (*exapina*), "suddenly, unexpectedly," would support the NRSV, ESV, and NLT. Cf. the translation notes for *b*ᵊ*šalwâ* at Dan 8:25 where the *unexpectedness* of his actions appears to be the main idea (there the NET translated Dan 8:25 as "unaware of his schemes").

505. חֲלַקְלַקּוֹת (*ḥălaqlaqôṯ*) means "smoothness, slipperiness, flattery, or fine promises" (BDB, 325c 2). LXX^O (ἐν κληροδοσίᾳ, *en klērodosia*) mistakenly thought this was from חֵלֶק (*ḥēleq*), "lot," as though he prevailed *by lots* (i.e., the distribution of land to gain favor and power). LXX^θ, however, had ἐν ὀλισθρήμασιν (*en olisthrēmasin*), "by slip" (or "slipperiness"). *ḥălaqlaqôṯ* reflects the *underhanded way* (deceitfulness) by which he operated. "Flatteries" (so ESV) may be too limiting. The NASB, NIV, and NRSV have "by intrigue" which captures the point well, though NET's "through deceit" is certainly valid.

506. Pointing as הִשָּׁטֹף (*hiššāṭōp*), a Nipʿal inf. abs., rather than MT's הַשֶּׁטֶף (*haššeṭep*). See textual note above for discussion. B. Scolnic, "Antiochus IV as the Man Who Will Overflow the Flood and Break its Arms [Daniel 11.22]," *BT* 65 (2014): 24–33, on the other hand, attempts to defend MT's pointing. He identifies the "forces" (pl.) as various opponents within the Seleucid Empire that Antiochus IV had to overcome to gain ultimate power, along with Pergamum and Rome that he had to contend with prior to his conflicts with Egypt. He concludes (31), "In the context of Dan 11.20–24, ... the verse uses mythic metaphors to paint the picture of a single man, a usurper who does not have a legal right to the throne, who overcomes the greatest forces of his time through tricky strategy, clever alliances, bribery, and intrigue. Verse 22, in which Antiochus breaks the arms of the flood with overwhelming force, is enclosed by vv. 21 and 23–24, which make it clear that he ascends to the kingship by sly, gradual treachery in the years 175–170."

507. On the idea of an advancing army sweeping across territory like a flood, compare Dan 11:10, 26, 40.

508. נָגִיד (*nāḡîḏ*) can be translated "prince, ruler, or leader," though most Eng. VSS go with "prince" in Dan 11:22. The combination of נָגִיד (*nāḡîḏ*) and בְּרִית (*b*ᵊ*rîṯ*) only occurs here, and the expression is anarthrous: "a prince of a covenant."

mighty with *only* a few people.[509] **24** Without warning[510] he will come with stout *warriors*[511] of *the* province and do what his fathers never did, nor even the fathers of his fathers. He will distribute[512] booty and spoil and *valuable* goods to them, and he will devise plans against fortified *cities*[513] (but only for a time). **25** Then he will arouse his strength and courage[514] against the king of the South with a great army. So the king of the South will wage war[515] with a great and exceedingly mighty army. Yet he will not prevail, for plots[516]

---

509. B. Scolnic, "The Milesian Connection: Dan 11:23 and Antiochus IV's Rise to Power," *VT* 63 (2013): 89, translates בִּמְעַט־גּוֹי (*bimʿaṭ-gôy*) as "with a few of a nation" and attempts to identify them as certain Milesians who helped bring Antiochus IV to power. He suggests that "the Milesians Apollonius, governor of Coele Syria and Phoenicia, and Timarchus, later satrap of Babylonia and his brother Heraclides, later treasurer of the kingdom, formed a web that helped to bring Antiochus IV to the Seleucid throne with the essential help of Eirenias, the Milesian statesman who was an ambassador to both Eumenes II, king of Pergamon, and the Seleucid court." His thesis, however, rests on a great deal of uncertainties and conjecture.

510. The introductory word בְּשַׁלְוָה (*bᵉšalwâ*) is the same word that appeared in v. 21 (see translation note above), where the translation "unexpectedly" was selected. The translation "without warning" here expresses the same idea but reads better in this particular sentence (so NRSV, ESV, and NLT).

511. וּבְמִשְׁמַנֵּי מְדִינָה (*ûḇᵉmišmannê mᵉḏînâ*) can be understood in two different ways. The noun מִשְׁמָן (*mišmān*), used 4x in the OT, basically means "fatness" (related to שֶׁמֶן, *šemen*, "fat, oil"). Aside from Dan 11:24, it means "fatness" in Ps 78:31, but something like "stout ones (warriors)" in Isa 10:16 and Ps 78:31. LXX$^{\theta}$, however, seems to have understood the phrase in terms of "fertile regions" (ἐν πίοσιν χώραις, *en piosin chōrais*), and this has influenced how most modern Eng. VSS translate the phrase. NRSV, NKJV, and ESV go with "the richest parts," NIV "the richest provinces," and Collins (366) has "the most prosperous regions." Goldingay (273), however, has "with the powerful ones of a province." The translation "stout ones (*warriors*)" is a bit more preferable: (1) this is how מַשְׁמַנִּים (*mašmannîm*) was understood in Isa 10:16 and Ps 78:31; and (2) this provides a suitable identity for the pronoun "to them" (לָהֶם, *lāhem*) in the second half of the verse. The other translation option "the richest parts" leaves the pronoun "them" dangling without any suitable identity.

512. Lit., "scatter" (Heb. בָּזַר, *bāzar*).

513. Cf. עִיר מִבְצָרוֹת (*ʿîr miḇṣārôṯ*) in Dan 11:15.

514. Lit., "heart" (לֵבָב, *lēḇāḇ*). See BDB (524b II 10) for the idea of *lēḇāḇ* as the "seat of courage." The NKJV, NIV, and NASB translate as "courage." Some others (NRSV, Goldingay, 273) translate as "determination."

515. The Hitpaʿel of גָּרָה (*gārâ*) can have the meaning of "excite oneself against, wage war" (see BDB, 173c 2).

516. מַחֲשָׁבוֹת (*maḥăšāḇôṯ*) means "plans" (see use in v. 24 above), though Collins (366) suggests in this case "plots" because of the negative implications of the context.

will be devised[517] against him. **26** Those who eat his choice food[518] will intend to crush[519] him. His army will be swept away,[520] and many will fall slain *in battle*.[521] **27** As for the two kings, their heart *will be intent* on evil;[522] they will speak lies *while sitting together* at the same table. But this[523] will not succeed, for the end is still *to come* at the appointed time. **28** Now he will return to his *own* land with many *valuable* goods, but his heart *will be set* against the holy covenant. So he will act *accordingly* and then return to his *own* land. **29** At the appointed time, he will return and come into the South, but this latter *visit*[524] will not turn out[525] as before.[526] **30** Ships of Kittim[527] will come against him, and he will be disheartened. So he will return and be outraged[528]

---

517. The active verb יַחְשְׁבוּ (*yaḥšᵊḇû*) is translated as a passive on account of the indefinite subject; cf. GKC, 460 (§144g).

518. Concerning פַּת־בַּג (*pat̠-bāg*) as the king's royal food, see Dan 1:5. Collins (366) suggests "royal provisions" for Dan 11:26.

519. The verb שָׁבַר (*šāḇar*) means "to break, shatter," though BDB (990c) suggests the figurative idea of "crush" for this verse. Some translations want to translate as "destroy," but because neither king was literally destroyed, they will modify this to "attempt to destroy" (see NET, NIV). Perhaps it is better to classify the verb as a "desiderative imperfect." Waltke and O'Connor identify this use as a "*non-perfective of desire*" to denote a wish or desire; *IBHS*, 509 (§31.4.h). Then translate, "they will intend to crush him."

520. See textual note for Dan 11:26, defending the vocalization of the verb as a Nipʿal impf. (יִשָּׁטֵף, *yiššāṭēp̱*).

521. The words "in battle" are added to clarify the manner in which they "fall."

522. Lit., "their heart to evil intentions." A verb needs to be added for smooth English and slightly reworded.

523. Lit., "it" (implied subject in the verb). The intended subject is unclear. This could refer to their evil intentions or to their alliance (that was fraught with deception). The fact that it must wait for the appointed time implies that what is in view is their evil intentions to do each other in (i.e., defeat the other).

524. See BDB (30d b), where אַחֲרוֹן (*ʾaḥărôn*) can refer to time (= latter or last). The idea in view is his "latter visit," and so the word *visit* is added for clarification.

525. Lit., "will not be."

526. See BDB (911d 3a[1]), where רִאשׁוֹן (*riʾšôn*) can have the nuance "before, formerly."

527. Kittim (כִּתִּים, *kittîm*) is translated as "the west" by Goldingay (273). He explains that this was "originally a town in Cyprus, then the island as a whole, hence a form for Cyprus and beyond." *HALOT* (504–5) understands this in its broader sense as the "Mediterranean coast-lands." LXX^{O} gave an interpretative translation, Ῥωμαῖοι (*Rhōmaioi*), "the Romans." Cf. Vg., *et Romani*. Most commentators have understood the reference to Kittim as being the Romans (cf. Num 24:24). See commentary for more discussion.

528. Most translations assume that it is Antiochus' *attitude* that is in view, and hence the translation "be outraged" (cf. Collins, 367, "rage against"). Goldingay (279),

against the holy covenant and act *accordingly*. He will return and show favor[529] to those who forsake the holy covenant. **31** Then forces[530] from him will arise, profane the sanctuary fortress,[531] abolish the daily sacrifice, and set up the abomination[532] of desolation.[533] **32** Also by smooth *words*[534] he will turn to godlessness[535] those who act wickedly *toward* the covenant. But the people who know their God will stand firm[536] and take action. **33** Those of the people with insight will give understanding[537] to the many. Yet they will stumble by

---

however, thinks the point is the harshness of his *actions*, and translates "he will take harsh actions."

529. The verb בִּין (*bîn*) basically means "to discern." However, see BDB (106d 3e) for the specialized use "to observe, mark, give heed to, distinguish, consider." The idea "to distinguish" could be captured by the translation "show favor" (so NIV) or "pay respect to." Cf. the NET "to honor," and NRSV "pay heed to."

530. For זְרֹעִים (*zᵉrōʿîm*, literally "arms") as *military forces*, see BDB (284b 3) and compare Dan 11:15.

531. Technically, הַמִּקְדָּשׁ הַמָּעוֹז (*hammiqdāš hammāʿôz*) are not in construct. Lit., the Heb. reads "the sanctuary, the fortress." Proposed translations include "fortified sanctuary" (NET); "the temple fortress" (NIV); "the sanctuary fortress" (NASB); and "the temple and fortress" (NRSV).

532. שִׁקּוּץ (*šiqqûṣ*) occurs 3x in Daniel (9:27; 11:31; 12:11). The basic meaning is "detested thing," often with idols in view. Both LXX^{O} and LXX$^{\theta}$ translated as βδέλυγμα (*bdelugma*), "abomination."

533. שָׁמֵם (*šāmēm*) occurs 8x in Daniel (8:13, 27; 9:18, 26, 27; 11:31; 12:11). The word can mean either "to destroy" or "to devastate." LXX$^{\theta}$ translated the phrase βδέλυγμα ἠφανισμένον (*bdelugma ēphanismenon*), "a destroyed abomination" (the verb ἠφανισμένον, *ēphanismenon*, is a perf. pass. ptc. of ἀφανιξω [*aphanixō*], "to destroy"). LXX^{O}, on the other hand, translated the phrase βδέλυγμα ἐρημώσεως (*bdelugma erēmōseōs*), "abomination of desolation." Since there is no evidence from this historical context that what Antiochus constructed actually destroyed anything, the translation "devastate" is preferred, hence "an abomination of desolation" (so most Eng. VSS).

534. The adjective "smooth" (חָלָק, *ḥālāq*) is in the plural and apparently refers to his words. Cf. BDB (325c 3), as substantival = "flattery" (so NIV and Collins, 367). Yet the way he uses his words could go beyond flattery (e.g., Eng. "smooth talker").

535. The verb חָנֵף (*ḥānēp̱*) means "be polluted, profane." See BDB (338a 2) for the Hipʿil meaning "be profane, godless." *HALOT* (335) suggests for the Hipʿil "to defile, ruin" (cf. NET, "defile"). By turning them away from the Mosaic covenant, Antiochus was turning them to godlessness. Goldingay's translation (273) is quite suggestive in light of the historical context: "turn into apostates."

536. The translation "stand firm" is an attempt to render the single Heb. word יַחֲזִקוּ (*yaḥăziqû*), Hipʿil of חָזַק (*ḥāzaq*). The fundamental idea behind *ḥāzaq* is "to be strong, firm." For Dan 11:32, BDB (305a 1c) suggests "display strength," though Collins (367) has "stand firm" (so NRSV). Cf. NIV, "will firmly resist him."

537. The verb בִּין (*bîn*) basically means "to discern." See BDB (107a 3c) for the Hipʿil meaning, "give understanding, teach."

sword and by flame, by captivity and by plunder, *many* days. **34** Now when they stumble, they will be granted a little help.[538] Many will join with them, *though* insincerely.[539] **35** Some[540] of those having insight will stumble[541] in order to refine, purify, and cleanse[542] them until *the* end[543] time, for *it is* still *to come* at the appointed time.

Commentary

This section describing Antiochus IV Epiphanes will cover his rise to power (vv. 21–24), his rivalry with Egypt (vv. 25–28), his persecution of the Jews after the second Egyptian Campaign (vv. 29–31), and the Jewish uprising against him known as the Maccabean revolt (vv. 32–35).

i. Antiochus's Rise in Power (11:21–24)

11:21 Succeeding Seleucus IV on the Seleucid throne was one simply described as a "despicable person." This was Antiochus IV Epiphanes, who came to rule in the autumn of 175 BC. Among the ancient tyrants, he was the most brutal oppressor of the Jewish people. Although he was a son of Antiochus III (brother to Seleucus IV), he was not next in line to the throne. The true heir was Seleucus' son, Demetrius I Soter, but he was being retained as a hostage in Rome.[544] Taking advantage of Demetrius' absence, Antiochus seized the throne for himself. Hence, the royal honor—the right to rule as

---

538. יֵעָזְרוּ עֵזֶר (*yēʿāzᵊrû ʿēzer*) involves a cognate accusative: "They will be helped a little help" = "they will be given a little help."

539. For חֲלַקְלַקּוֹת (*ḥălaqlaqôṯ*), see the previous use in Dan 11:21 and consult the translation note there. The idea of deceitfulness is at the heart of this word. For v. 34, NET translates "deceitfully," NASB "in hypocrisy," while NRSV and Collins (367) "insincerely" (similarly, NIV "who are not sincere").

540. See BDB (580d 3b[a]) for the partitive use of the preposition מִן (*min*).

541. Notice the wordplay between "those having insight" (הַמַּשְׂכִּילִים, *hammaśkîlîm*) and those who "stumble" (יִכָּשְׁלוּ, *yikkāšlû*), the first from שָׂכַל (*śāḵal*) and the second from כָּשַׁל (*kāšal*).

542. לָבֵן (*lāḇēn*) can mean to "be white" in the Qal stem, but in the Piʿel it means "to whiten, cleanse" (see *HALOT*, 517).

543. Taking קֵץ (*qēṣ*) as a genitive of attribute = "an end time."

544. Antiochus himself had been sent as a hostage to Rome in 189 BC as one of the terms of agreement with Rome following the battle of Magnesia. About 176 or early 175 BC, Rome released him in exchange for his nephew Demetrius I (the eldest son of his brother, Seleucus IV). Antiochus IV proceeded to raise an army and secure the throne for himself. Later in history, after Demetrius I reached the age of twenty-four, he did finally come to rule over the Seleucid Empire (r. 161–150 BC). He is infamous in Jewish history for his victory over the Maccabees, killing Judas Maccabeus in Nisan, 160 BC.

king—had not been rightfully conferred upon him. Rather, he had seized the kingdom, not by warfare but through intrigue (or deceit).[545]

Antiochus' relationship with Egypt was complicated by the fact that he was the uncle to Egypt's ruler, Ptolemy VI Philometor. (Antiochus IV's sister, Cleopatra I, had been given in marriage to Ptolemy V, and Ptolemy VI was the resulting son.) When Ptolemy V died in 180 BC, however, Ptolemy VI was only six years old and too young to rule. Hence Cleopatra I (Antiochus' sister) ruled on his behalf during the years 180–176 BC, and she had pro-Seleucid sympathies. Her death in 176 BC, however, set the empire on a different course. Two court members (Lenaios and Eulaios) became the effective guardians and leaders for Ptolemy VI (now age ten). One of their top foreign policies was the reconquest of Coele-Syria, and thus they set out to achieve this goal. Shortly thereafter, in 175 BC, Antiochus IV came to rule the Seleucid Empire.[546] Sometime between 174 and 172 BC, a great festival was held in Alexandria, and Antiochus sent an envoy to represent him. While there, this envoy observed the new hostile attitude toward the Seleucids. Antiochus IV then began taking precautionary measures for what became known as the Sixth Syrian War (170/169 –168 BC).

11:22–24 Due to the lack of information about precise dates and events leading up to the Sixth Syrian War, it is difficult to ascertain the exact meaning of these verses.[547] What we do know is that at the time of the buildup to

---

545. In addition to Demetrius, Seleucus IV had an infant son, also named Antiochus.

546. There is some uncertainty as to whether or not Antiochus IV actually became the sole king in 175 BC or at a later date. An alternative theory (so Scolnic, "Seleucid Coinage in 175–166 BCE and the Historicity of Daniel 11:21–24") is that he ruled for a time as co-regent with the younger son of Seleucus IV (also named Antiochus) until finally having the boy Antiochus murdered. Unfortunately, historical details for the period 175–170 BC are sketchy.

547. Collins (382) understands v. 22 to be "a general introductory statement that anticipates the effect of Antiochus's reign." Scolnic ("Seleucid Coinage in 175–166 BCE and the Historicity of Daniel 11:21–24"), however, has sought to demonstrate that Dan 11:21–24 is intended to show the slow determined plotting of Antiochus IV to gain the sole right of kingship, a process that was not completed until his nephew, Antiochus son of Seleucus IV, was finally murdered in 170 BC. Scolnic (28) suggests the following sequence of events:

1. Seleucus IV is assassinated by Heliodorus on September 5, 175, and is succeeded by his son, the boy Antiochus. 2. The future Antiochus IV (younger brother of Seleucus IV) who has been a hostage in Rome is accompanied by the Pergamene army to the borders of the Seleucid kingdom. 3. A short time later in 175, Heliodorus flees (or is killed) and Antiochus IV becomes regent and perhaps co–king with Antiochus, son of Seleucus IV. 4. Antiochus IV replaces Onias III, high priest of Judaea, with the priest's brother Jason; he also makes his friends, the Milesian brothers Timarchus and Herakleides, satrap of Babylon and Treasurer of

war between the Seleucid Empire and Egypt, there were also complicating developments occurring in Judah. Prior to Antiochus IV coming to rule, the primary leader in Judah was the high priest, Onias III. Onias, however, held Egyptian sympathies and took a pro-Ptolemaic stance. At the same time, there was a movement taking place among some of the Jewish population in favor of Hellenization (promoting Greek culture and thinking—often at odds with Torah), and this had the backing of the powerful Tobiad family of Jerusalem. Hence, upon Antiochus' ascension, the aristocratic Tobiad family helped to replace Onias III by his brother, Jason, who was both pro-Seleucid and pro-Hellenistic. This was accomplished by the payment of more tribute money to Antiochus. Sometime about 172 BC, however, the Tobiads sought to oust Jason for a man even more loyal to themselves, namely Menelaus, who was not in the priestly line and had no legitimate claim to the high priesthood. Menelaus arranged for the murder of Onias III and paid even higher tribute money to Antiochus, by which he became the new high priest. This, however, sparked a civil war within Judah, a troublesome matter for Antiochus at a time when he needed stability within his kingdom. The mention of a "prince of *the* covenant" in v. 22 is often thought to be a reference to the Jewish high priest, Onias III.[548] According to vv. 23–24, Antiochus IV used deception and bribery to accomplish his schemes for rallying the empire around him.

---

the kingdom, respectively (App. *Syr.* 234). 5. In 170, after the birth of his own son, the future Antiochus V, Antiochus IV has Seleucus IV's son Antiochus (and Onias III) killed, becoming sole king (BKL).

548. The expression "a prince of *the* covenant" (נְגִיד בְּרִית, *nāgîḏ bᵊrîṯ*) only occurs here, and the interpretation is admittedly difficult. The dominant view is that the "prince" is Onias III (so Walvoord [1971], 265; Baldwin, 213; Wood, 295; and Goldingay, 299), though Miller (299)—following a view held by Calvin and Feinberg (166)—asserts that it is Ptolemy VI Philometor, "because he agreed (made a covenant) to become an ally of Antiochus if the Syrians would help him regain his throne in Egypt, which had been taken by his younger brother, Ptolemy VII Euergetes II (Physcon)." The problem with Miller's suggestion is that the reference to "covenant" is clearly used in other verses of this pericope in reference to Judah, e.g., Antiochus being enraged at the "holy covenant" in v. 30 (cf. v. 32). Collins (382), on the other hand, thinks the reference to making alliances pertains to an alliance made with Pergamum (which enabled Antiochus to gain power with a small force). H. H. Rowley ("The 'Prince of the Covenant' in Daniel xi. 22") attempted to argue that the correct personage was a younger son of Seleucus Philopator, also named Antiochus (whom Antiochus IV had murdered). Rowley writes (26), "*V.*[22] then refers to the complete overthrow of all who opposed his assumption of the power, and it would be fitting to append to this a reference to the elimination of his nephew, which quickly followed, and which preceded the events dealt with in *vv.*[23–25]." Rowley's argument, however, has not been well-received, as he was forced to argue for the translation "rightful prince" for *nāgîḏ bᵊrîṯ* based on what he claimed was the author's *mistranslation* in Dan 11:22. However, Scolnic, "Seleucid Coinage in 175–166 BCE and the Historicity of

Polybius (26.10) informs us that "in the sacrifices he furnished to cities and in the honors he paid to the gods he far surpassed all his predecessors."[549]

ii. Antiochus's rivalry with Egypt (11:25–28)

11:25 Scholars debate the exact course of events by which Antiochus IV engaged Egypt, but there is a consensus that Antiochus carried out two primary campaigns against Egypt. The first of these took place in 169 BC when Antiochus mobilized his forces "against the king of the South with a great army." Prior to the invasion, the guardians of the young king stirred up the hearts of the people for a swift acquisition of Coele-Syria, and in the late fall of 170 BC they rearranged the rule of Egypt. In place of the sole reign of Ptolemy VI, they established a triumvirate joint rule of the three Ptolemaic siblings, i.e., Ptolemy VI, his sister-wife Cleopatra II, and their younger brother Ptolemy VIII Physcon. Antiochus was quite successful against the Ptolemaic forces, defeating them first between Pelusion and Mount Casius (near Gaza), then seizing the fortress-city of Pelusion on the Egyptian border, occupying a large part of Lower Egypt, and finally moving against the capital area at Alexandria. Hence the king of the South (Ptolemy VI) was not able to prevail. In Antiochus' favor was that Rome was engaged in the third Macedonian war (171–168 BC) against King Perseus of Macedonia and therefore could not interfere with his invasion of Egypt.[550] The reference to "plots devised against him" may refer to the treachery of Ptolemy's guardians in undermining his rule, or it may refer to Antiochus' plans against Ptolemy. Verse 26 seems to support the former.

11:26 "Those who eat his choice food" appear to be the leading figures at the Egyptian court of Alexandria, the real power-wielders behind the throne. (By 170 BC, Ptolemy VI was still only about sixteen years of age.) As a result of their counsel and leadership, the Egyptian army was thrust into war against Antiochus, in which Ptolemy's army was swept away and many fell slain in battle.

11:27 Before Antiochus stormed Alexandria, a meeting was arranged between him and his nephew, Ptolemy VI. This meeting was held in Antiochus' camp, at which these two kings, their hearts intent on evil, traded "lies while sitting at the same table." The two managed to reach some kind of agreement,

---

Daniel 11:21–24," 27–28, has more recently revived and supported Rowley's thesis that Antiochus, son of Seleucus IV, is the prince in view.

549. Quotation cited in Collins (382). Cf. 1 Macc 3:30 and Josephus, *Ant.*, 12.7.2 §294.

550. Regardless of who might be the victor (whether Ptolemaic Egypt or the Seleucid king), it would not have been in Rome's best interest for Egypt and the Seleucid Empire to merge and unite. Rome was not powerful enough at this time in history to counter their combined forces. Rome's tactic, then, was to remain neutral but to try and keep Egypt and the Seleucid Empire separate.

although the exact details are not known. It seems that Antiochus deceptively posed as the protector of young Ptolemy VI, whereby all Egypt would be subjugated to Antiochus in order for him to preserve it for Ptolemy.[551] Yet the latter seems to have acted just as treacherously. Whatever scheme they each sought to achieve, it did not succeed, for the end was still to come at the appointed time. Their conflict was not meant to be resolved so soon, and it had to run its predetermined course.

11:28 The powers in Alexandria rejected the agreements of the two kings and acclaimed Ptolemy's younger brother as king (i.e., Ptolemy VIII Euergetes). At that Antiochus attacked Alexandria, but failed to take it. The Alexandrians were able to mount a good defense of the city, and domestic troubles back in Syria or Judah caused Antiochus to return to Syria in the autumn of 169 BC (cf. 1 Macc 1:20). The king of the North (Antiochus IV) returned "to his own land with many valuable goods." Before leaving, however, Antiochus left Ptolemy VI in Memphis for his protection, and Pelusion was kept under siege.

On his return trip to Syria, Antiochus passed through Jerusalem. For an undisclosed reason, Antiochus' heart was set "against the holy covenant."[552] The "holy covenant" refers to that special covenant relationship that the Jews had with God (hence the biblical faith), and Antiochus acted hostilely by plundering the Jewish temple. Having taken such action, he then returned to his own land of Syria. The following report is given in 1 Macc 1:20–24:

> After subduing Egypt, Antiochus returned in the one hundred forty-third year *[i.e., 169 BC]*.[553] He went up against Israel and came to Jerusalem with a strong force. He arrogantly entered

551. Collins (383) reports, "Philometor went with Antiochus to Memphis. According to Porphyry, Antiochus deceived his nephew with a show of friendship and subjugated all Egypt to himself." For this, see Jerome at Dan 11:21.

552. It is certainly very possible that the heavy financial demands of this first Egyptian campaign prompted Antiochus IV to plunder the Jerusalem temple. One must also remember that Antiochus was still paying tribute to Rome as part of the agreement of the Treaty of Apamea in 188 BC.

553. The dates given by the author of 1 Maccabees are in accord with the Seleucid system of dating, which began with the commencement of Seleucus I's rule in 312 BC. Hence, the 143rd year would be 169 BC. Goldstein, *1 Maccabees: A New Translation with Introduction and Commentary*, 207, fn 20, reports, "The year 144 Sel. Mac. began October 16, 169 b.c.e. A cuneiform tablet from Babylon dated between August 18 and September 16, 169, still reports Antiochus' victories in Egypt as the news of the day; see Introduction, Part VI, n. 71. Hence, the sack of Jerusalem probably occurred in September or early October." In note 71 he mentions: "Partially published in Theophilus G. Pinches, *The Old Testament in the Light of the Historical Records of Assyria and Babylonia*, 2d ed. (London: Society for Promoting Christian Knowledge, 1903), pp. 480–81, 553; see also A. T. Olmstead, 'Intertestamental Studies,' *JAOS* 56 (1936), 247."

> the sanctuary and took the golden altar, the lampstand for the light, and all its utensils. He took also the table for the bread of the Presence, the cups for drink offerings, the bowls, the golden censers, the curtain, the crowns, and the gold decoration on the front of the temple; he stripped it all off. He took the silver and the gold, and the costly vessels; he took also the hidden treasures that he found. Taking them all, he went into his own land.

iii. Antiochus' Persecution of the Jews after the Second Egyptian Campaign (11:29–31)

11:29 During Antiochus' absence from Egypt, the two Ptolemaic brothers reconciled, and joint rule was re-established. Antiochus interpreted this as a breach of the agreement that he had with Ptolemy VI and therefore quickly mounted a new invasion of Egypt in the spring of 168 BC ("the appointed time" at which he again invaded the South). He moved into Memphis without a battle and was prepared to assault Alexandria again. According to v. 29, however, "this latter visit will not turn out as before." That is, Antiochus was not to be so successful this time as he had been in the invasion of 169 BC.

11:30 The problem for Antiochus was that "the ships of Kittim" came against him.[554] "Kittim"—though often meaning "Cyprus" specifically—was sometimes used in Jewish literature as a designation for the Mediterranean coastlands in general and at times even for Rome specifically.[555] Rome had

---

554. Grammatically, Dan 11:30a can be translated, "And the ships of Kittim will come with him." (The preposition בְּ (*bᵊ*) can be translated "with" or "against.") This is the view of B. Scolnic and T. Davis, "How *Kittim* Became 'Rome': Dan 11,30 and the Importance of Cyprus in the Sixth Syrian War," *ZAW* 127 (2015): 304–19, who understand the statement in a positive sense. They argue that *Kittim* in Dan 11:30 means Cyprus and not Rome (or Romans) as some ancient interpretations and many modern commentators have understood it. Instead they believe that Dan 11:30 is a valuable historical witness to the important role of Cyprus in the sixth Syrian war. Their argument depends, in part, on a dating of the book to 165 BC and retranslating the Nip'al form of the verb כָּאָה (*kāʾâ*) to mean "drive out" rather than "be disheartened." (*kāʾâ* has the meaning "be disheartened" in the only other two instances in BH, namely Ps 109:16 and Ezek 13:22.) Scolnic and Davis translated 11:30: "And the ships of Cyprus will come back with him, but he will be driven out." The authors point out that Antiochus IV had conquered Cyprus in 168 BC and thereby came to Egypt with ships acquired from this recent conquest of Cyprus.

555. Josephus (*Ant.* 1.6.1 §128) wrote, "Cethimus possessed the island Cethima; it is now called Cyprus: and from that it is that all islands, and the greatest part of the seacoasts, are named Cethim by the Hebrews; and one city there is in Cyprus that has been able to preserve its denomination; it is called Citius by those who use the language of the Greeks, and has not, by the use of that dialect, escaped the name of Cethim." 1 Macc 1:1 indicated that Alexander the Great came from Chetiim, and

concluded its war with Macedonia with a victory over King Perseus of Macedonia in June of 168 BC, and hearing of Antiochus' march on Alexandria, quickly sent a Roman fleet to intervene. The Roman consul, Gaius Popillius Laenas swiftly confronted Antiochus, handing him a letter (a *senatus-consultum*) from the Roman Senate ordering him not to fight and instead to withdraw from Egypt. Hölbl records their confrontation,

> Popillius refused to acknowledge Antiochus's greeting and presented him with the Roman ultimatum which was very straightforward in its demand: the immediate cessation of the war and complete withdrawal from Egypt in the shortest time possible. When Antiochus asked for time to consider, Popillius drew a circle with a stick around the king and 'bade him to give his answer to the note within the circle' (Plb. XXIX.27.5). The humiliated Seleucid king agreed to the ultimatum and acted accordingly.[556]

Antiochus departed from Egypt in late July of 168 BC for Syria, but—disheartened by Rome's intervention—he was not in a pleasant mood at all. Returning through Jerusalem once again, he vented his rage "against the holy covenant." During the time of Antiochus' second Egyptian campaign, there

---

in 8:5 that Perseus, king of Macedonia, was called "king of Kittim," reflecting an understanding of *Kittim* as the Mediterranean coastlands (sometimes Greece specifically). In Gen 10:4, the sons of Javan are identified as Elishah, Tarshish, Kittim, and Dodanim; and the Rabbinic midrashic compilation *Gen. Rab.* 37,1 identifies the third in the list (Kittim) as "Italy." LXX^{O} translated Dan 11:30, "and the Romans will come and drive him out." *Tg. Onq.* took Kittim in Num 24:24 as Rome. Among the DSS, there are some 57 references to Kittim in the sectarian documents and five references among the biblical documents (examples include 1QpHab 2:12, 14; 3:4, 9; 4:10; 4QpIsa^{a} 3:7, 9, 12; 4QpNahum 1:3 [= 4Q169 *Frag. 3+4*, col. 1:3]; and 1QM 1:2, 4, 6). Although the intended reference is vague in many examples, the most conclusive proof for a Roman identification appears in 4Q169 *Frag. 3+4*, col. 1:2–3 (pesher MS of Nahum):

> Its interpretation concerns Deme]trius, king of Yavan, who wanted to enter Jerusalem on the advice of the those looking for easy interpretations, [but he did not enter, for God had not given Jerusalem] into the hand of the kings of Yavan from Antiochus up to the appearance of the chiefs of the Kittim.

Finally, D. W. Baker argues that Kittim in the *Midrash Pesher of Habakkuk* refers to the Romans: "Their distant maritime homeland and their apparent domination of Israel at the time of the Pesher itself support the interpretation of the Kittim as the Romans" ("Kittim," in *AYBD*, 4:93).

Arguing that Kittim means the island of Cyprus rather than Rome, see Scolnic and Davis, "How *Kittim* Became 'Rome': Dan 11,30 and the Importance of Cyprus in the Sixth Syrian War," and consult the preceding footnote.

556. Hölbl, *A History of the Ptolemaic Empire*, 147–48.

had been a rebellion in Jerusalem, as Jason (the former high priest) made an attempt to overthrow Menelaus and retake Jerusalem.[557] In light of recent events, perhaps Antiochus felt compelled to communicate a message that insurrection would not be tolerated. Such opposition to Hellenization and Seleucid authority could only be interpreted as sympathy for Egypt, for only from Egypt could the rebels hope to receive support for the liberation movement. Therefore, upon reaching Jerusalem, he had the walls of the city torn down, slaughtered thousands of Jews, and sold many more into slavery (cf. 2 Macc 5:11–14). In addition, he himself entered the holy of holies with Menelaus as his guide (cf. 2 Macc 5:15–16). Antiochus' policy was to show favor to (or honor) "those who forsake the holy covenant," i.e., he would act favorably to those Jews willing to turn from the biblical faith and embrace his plans of Hellenization for Judah (cf. 1 Macc 1:1–15 and 2 Macc 4–5).[558]

11:31 To make sure that the rebellious Jews (i.e., those who opposed him) presented no threat to his kingdom, Antiochus left one of his soldiers, named Apollonius, behind in Jerusalem with the task of putting down any and all attempts at insurrection. In the aftermath, Apollonius' stay in Jerusalem only made things worse. For instance, there was the pollution of the temple by Gentiles worshipping other deities, as well as sacred prostitution. Eventually Antiochus began to see the Jewish faith as detrimental to the unification of his realm. Hence, B. W. Jones, in seeking a satisfying explanation for Antiochus' hostility, concluded: "To the king, Jewish particularism was subversive and represented a threat to his political security."[559]

Hence Antiochus issued orders for a further religious persecution to take place in December of 167 BC. Antiochus' forces rose up to profane the sanctuary fortress, stopping the daily sacrifice. The two daily sacrifices

---

557. This may have been spurred by a false report that Antiochus had been killed in Egypt. Cf. 2 Macc 5:5.

558. A. van der Kooij, "The Concept of Covenant (*BERÎT*) in the Book of Daniel," in *Book of Daniel in the Light of New Findings*, ed. A. S. van der Woude, 495–501 (Louvain: Leuven University Press, 1993), attempts to argue that קֹדֶשׁ (*qōḏeš*) is not modifying בְּרִית (*bərîṯ*), hence "holy covenant," but rather is specifically a reference to the "sanctuary." Hence, this is the covenant concerning the holy place, i.e., the sanctuary. He concludes (500), "The covenant of priesthood is about the priestly duties (see also Neh 13,29), but in a sense derived from that 'the covenant concerning the sanctuary' refers to the temple cult." For him, Dan 11:28, 30 refers specifically to the actions taken by Antiochus against the temple cult and the resulting complicity by those priests who despised the sacrifices and neglected their duties. The problem with his thesis is that when "the sanctuary" is in view, the Hebrew is either הַקֹּדֶשׁ (*haqqōḏeš*) or מִקְדָּשׁ (*miqdaš*).

559. B. W. Jones, "Antiochus Epiphanes and the Persecution of the Jews," in *Scripture in Context*, ed. C. D. Evans et al., 263–90, PTMS 34 (Pittsburgh: Pickwick, 1980), 282.

(morning and evening) were halted, the whole temple sanctuary was polluted, and Jews attempting to follow the biblical faith were severely persecuted.[560] Some of Antiochus' policies included:

(a) A special emissary was sent to Judah to force the Jews to transgress the laws of their religion.
(b) Jewish ritual was prohibited (1 Macc 1:45–6).
(c) The sacred precincts were formally given over to the worship of Zeus Olympias (1 Macc 1:54; 2 Macc 6:2).
(d) Copies of the Torah were burned.
(e) Sabbath keeping and circumcision were forbidden.
(f) Jews were forced to celebrate the king's birthday every month and to participate in the festal procession of Dionysus.
(g) High places and altars on which swine and other animals were to be sacrificed were erected throughout Judah. Inspectors were appointed to enforce this.

Regarding the profaning of the sanctuary fortress, Collins (385) reports:

> The temple was fortified in this period, as can be seen from 1 Macc 4:60; 6:7, where the fortifications are rebuilt. It is called a fortress (בירה) in 1 Chr 29:1, 19. Apollonius tore down the walls of Jerusalem but built a new citadel, the Akra, in the City of David.[561]

Perhaps the most grievous offense was the setting up of "the abomination of desolation" (הַשִּׁקּוּץ מְשׁוֹמֵם, *haššiqqûṣ məšômēm*). There is some debate as to what is meant by this, whether an altar or a sacrifice (perhaps a swine). First Maccabees understood this as a small pagan altar erected on top of the altar of burnt offering (1 Macc 1:59; 4:44), an abomination to the worship of Yahweh God.[562]

560. For further explanation of the two "daily sacrifices," see this commentary at Dan 8:11–12.

561. Cf. 1 Macc 1:31–35.

562. The following report is given in 1 Macc 1:54 and 59: "Now on the fifteenth day of Chislev, in the one hundred forty-fifty year [i.e., Dec 167 BC], they erected a desolating sacrilege on the altar of burnt offering. ... On the twenty-fifty day of the month they offered sacrifice on the altar that was on top of the altar of burnt offering."

However, J. Lust, "Cult and Sacrifice in Daniel: The Tamid and the Abomination of Desolation," in *The Book of Daniel; Composition and Reception*, vol. 2, ed. J. J. Collins and P. W. Flint, 671–88 (Leiden: Brill, 2001), 682, points out that although 1 Maccabees takes the *haššiqqûṣ məšômēm* as an altar, the text of Daniel leans more to the idea that a sacrifice itself is in view. Furthermore, though Josephus refers to this matter in two separate works, he appears to be inconsistent (see *Ant.* 12 §251–53 and *Wars* 1.1 §32). Lust concludes (684): "In summary we may say that 1 Maccabees, followed by Josephus in his *Antiquities*, suggests that the 'abomination' is to be understood as a pagan altar set up upon the altar of the Lord. In his *Jewish War*,

iv. The Jewish uprising against Antiochus: The Maccabean revolt (11:32–35)

11:32 To those Jews who sought to be faithful to Yahweh God, Antiochus' assault on their faith (and the killing of many of their people) was an unimaginable horror. Yet there were some unfaithful Jews ("those who act wickedly *toward* the covenant," מַרְשִׁיעֵי בְרִית, *maršîʿê ḇᵊrîṯ*) who followed Antiochus' smooth words, forsook Yahweh and his Word, and fully embraced the program of imposing Hellenism.[563] By their wicked actions against the Lord's covenant, Antiochus succeeded in turning them to godliness. In contrast

---

however, Josephus is less explicit and seems rather to agree with the presentation in the book of Daniel." LXX^{O} and LXX$^{\theta}$ translated *haššiqqûṣ mᵊšômēm* differently (see translation note at v. 31), though both Greek traditions indicate that the Hellenists *give* the abomination (using a future tense of δίδωμι, *didōmi*), which leads Lust (682) to conclude that it is a sacrifice that is given to replace the Tamid.

G. H. Van Kooten, "The Desecration of 'The Most Holy Temple of all the World' in the 'Holy Land': Early Jewish and Early Christian Recollections of Antiochus' 'Abomination of Desolation,'" in *The Land of Israel in Bible, History, and Theology: Studies in Honour of Ed Noort*, 291–316 (Leiden: Brill, 2009), discusses the views of Josephus, Porphyry, and Jerome in comparison with 1 and 2 Maccabees. He notes (310) that the "opinion of Porphyry includes a detail not found in 1 and 2 Maccabees and Josephus that in addition to an image of Zeus, statues of Antiochus were also set up in the Jerusalem temple. 1 Maccabees speaks simply of the erection of 'a desolating sacrilege on the altar of burnt offering' (1:54; cf. 4:36–61); it is the author of 2 Maccabees who implies that an image of Zeus was erected, because he talks of the pollution of the temple in Jerusalem which is transformed into a temple of the Olympian Zeus (6:2). ... It is only in 2 Macc 6:2, thus, that the abomination of desolation is linked to Zeus, but statues of Antiochus are not mentioned anywhere. Porphyry's mention of them seems to be a conflation with the events under Caligula, when an image of this emperor was due to be set up in the Jerusalem temple (see Philo, *Legatio ad Gaium*)."

563. The "wicked" who appear at the time of the Maccabean revolt in Dan 11:32 (or more specifically, "those who act wickedly *toward* the covenant"—the *maršîʿê ḇᵊrîṯ*) probably function as something of forerunners to the eschatological "wicked" (רְשָׁעִים, *rᵊšāʿîm*) mentioned in Dan 12:10. The term for both derives from the root רשע (*rāšaʿ*). S. Thompson, "Those Who Are Wise: The *maskilim* in Daniel and the New Testament," in *To Understand the Scriptures: Essays in Honor of W. H. Shea*, ed. D. Merling, 215–20 (Berrien Springs, MI: Institute of Archaeology, 1997), distinguishes three specific groups in Dan 11:21–12:13: the "maskilim" (*maśkîlîm*), "the many" (*rabbîm*), and the "wicked" (*rᵊšāʿîm*). He states (217), "The evidence suggests they [the *rᵊšāʿîm*] are Israelites who have ceased to respond to Yahweh's offer of righteousness and who no longer heed his wisdom, as communicated via the *maskilim*, thus creating tension between the wicked and the rest of Israel. ... the *maskilim* in Daniel seem to be discerners of the will of Yahweh, especially as it comes in apocalyptic format. They are also instructors to the covenant community, *harabbim*, during the time of the end. Partly by their response to the spiritual guidance from the

to the unfaithful Jews were "the people who know their God." They were determined to stand firm against Antiochus and take action.[564] That is, they resisted all the efforts of Antiochus to snuff out the biblical faith and rose up against him (1 Macc 1:62–63).[565] Leading this effort to stand firm was a certain priest named Mattathias (father of Judas Maccabeus), who had moved to the village of Modein. When Antiochus' officials came to Modein to force the villagers to commit apostasy and sacrifice on the pagan altar, Mattathias resisted. The following account from 1 Macc 2:22–28 describes the scene:

> "We will not obey the king's words by turning aside from our religion to the right hand or to the left." When he had finished speaking these words, a Jew came forward in the sight of all to offer sacrifice on the altar in Modein, according to the king's command. When Mattathias saw it, he burned with zeal and his heart was stirred. He gave vent to righteous anger; he ran and killed him on the altar. At the same time he killed the king's officer who was forcing them to sacrifice, and he tore down the altar. Thus he burned with zeal for the law, just as Phinehas did against Zimri son of Salu.

With this bold step, the rebellion against Antiochus IV Epiphanes was launched, which came to be known as the Maccabean revolt.[566] (The initial commander of the Jewish rebels was Judas Maccabeus.)

---

maskilim the *rabbim* are polarized into two groups, the faithful and righteous ones, versus the *resha'im*, who having rejected wisdom are denied Yahweh's righteousness."

564. D. S. Barrett, "Patterns of Jewish Submission and Rebellion in the Hellenistic-Roman World," *Prud* 5 (1973): 99–115, has analyzed four major revolutions of the Jews in antiquity (including the Maccabean revolt as well as three uprisings against Rome) for help in understanding reasons of causation.

565. Heard, "The Maccabean Martyr's Contribution to Holy War," 294, makes a case that Judas' victory is portrayed differently in 1 Maccabees than in 2 Maccabees. He writes:

> While in 1 Maccabees the successes of the army were dependent upon military strategy, weapons and the courage of the soldier, 2 Maccabees de-emphasises these factors and stresses the role of the martyrs. The writer of 2 Maccabees admits that the victories of Judas did bring salvation to Israel, but he prefaces the account of the military triumph with two martyrological pericopae to demonstrate that it was *the martyrdoms* that effected the turning point in the historical drama. Judas' successes were directly dependent upon the sacrifice of the martyrs.

566. For an in-depth treatment of the Maccabean revolt, see B. Bar-Kochva, *Judas Maccabaeus: The Jewish Struggle Against the Seleucids* (Cambridge: Cambridge University Press, 1989).

11:33–35 The Maccabean revolt against Antiochus was a long and bloody feud that extended over several years. During this difficult period, certain Jews with insight (מַשְׂכִּילִים, the *maśkîlîm*) among the people were able to give understanding to others.[567] These would have been the ones wise in the knowledge of the Scriptures who could exhort the masses of common people ("the many," *rabbîm*) to remain faithful to God and obey him. Yet there would be a price to pay in remaining faithful to God. Some would stumble "by the sword," meaning they would be killed in battle. Others would be tortured "by flame," while still others would be caught and taken captive or have their homes plundered. They would experience victories at times but also stumble in death and defeat on other occasions.

Heard correctly notes that the resistance of the *maśkîlîm* was not based on the expectation of future exaltation alone but also the present experience of wisdom. He explains:

> The nature of the resistance is twofold: suffering and teaching. Through their efforts the maskilim 'makes many understand' thus initiating them into the eschatological mysteries thereby turning

567. A number of studies have been conducted exploring the relationship between the *Maskilim* in Dan 11–12 and the Qumran community. C. Hempel, "*Maskil(im)* and *Rabbim*: From Daniel to Qumran," in *Biblical Traditions in Transmission: Essays in Honour of Michael A. Knibb*, 133–56 (Leiden: Brill, 2006), 143, points out that in the common view "the *Maskil* appears as a key community functionary in the sectarian scrolls and the community itself which he leads has adopted the designation *ha-rabbim*." While it is true that both terms (*Maskilim* and *ha-rabbim*) are found in abundance in the Community Rule (her focus of study), there is a need for caution in drawing conclusions. She points out, "It is true that we have both the *Maskil* and the designation *ha-rabbim* as important terms in the Community Rule, but the two terms are never closely linked to one another with one possible partial exception" (143). Furthermore, one must keep in mind that most studies comparing Dan 11–12 with Qumran documents are based on the (faulty) presumption that the book of Daniel dates to the second century BC. Almost all English translations understand *maśkîlîm* in Dan 11:33 and 12:3 as a *general reference* to those who are wise (or have insight), not a specific class of instructors. Yet M. Leuchter, "From Levite to *Maśkîl* in the Persian and Hellenistic Eras," in *Levites and Priests in Biblical History and Tradition*, ed. M. A. Leuchter and J. M. Hutton, 215–32 (Atlanta: SBL, 2011), while offering no sufficient evidence, asserts that the *maśkîlîm* were not only a special class of instructors functioning in the Hellenistic period but that they came to replace the Levites in terms of their responsibility and authority for composing and transmitting sacred revelation. He writes (230), "... the wisdom of the משׂכלים demands a new understanding of who holds exegetical authority over sacred texts. It is not priests and Levites associated with the Jerusalem temple who secure divine blessing, but scribes who liberate Levitical modes of exegesis from cultic moorings and extend them to the masses."

> them to righteousness and emboldening them to stand for the Law. The maskilim impart wisdom and this wisdom enables the maskil to make prudent decisions in the time of crisis. He can discern the true nature of the conflict and thereby remain true to God and his word. This wisdom also imparts strength to undergo suffering because he is assured glory in the inbreaking eschatological kingdom. The emphasis of this wisdom is always soteriological and eschatological.[568]

Nevertheless, not all would join in with the Maccabees out of pure motives. According to v. 34, some would even unite with them "insincerely," probably meaning that their motivation was not for purely spiritual reasons but more so for their hatred of the Seleucid intruders. Yet even those who did have pure motives and spiritual insight would "stumble," meaning that they would die in the course of the revolt (recall v. 33—"they will stumble by sword and by flame"). Yet from God's perspective, this would serve a good purpose, for the result would be refinement, purification, and cleansing of the nation (v. 35).

As difficult as this period of persecution under Antiochus was, however, this would not be the greatest trial and testing that the Jewish people would have to go through. That would be reserved for "the end time," which would come in God's "appointed time" (v. 35).

Summary of the Outcome of the Maccabean Revolt. Mattathias encouraged all the Jews to join in the struggle against Seleucid rule and the Seleucid attempt to impose the numerous ungodly aspects of Hellenism upon Judah (e.g., pagan altars and sacrifice). Joining Mattathias and his sons in the revolt were the Hasidim, those faithful to Torah. Following Mattathias' death in 166 BC, his son Judas took up the leadership and was able to defeat the Syrian governors Apollonius and Seron in his first year (1 Macc 3:10–26; Josephus *Ant.* xii.7.1). One thing in Judas' favor was the fact that Antiochus had to give much of his attention to troubles in the eastern part of the empire. Leaving behind a trusted commander named Lysias in charge of the Judean campaign, Antiochus IV led an expedition into various territories of Parthia in an effort to raise much-needed funds. He is believed to have been killed in 164 BC (fighting in the east against Parthia), although the Jewish struggle against the Seleucids for political freedom continued.[569] In 164 BC Judas was able

568. Heard, "The Maccabean Martyr's Contribution to Holy War," 315.

569. Although Antiochus IV's death is commonly given as 164 BC, some would advocate that he died in 163 BC. Y. Ben-Dor, "A Note on the Two Seleucid Eras," https://www.academia.edu/14202011/A_Note_on_the_Two_Seleucid_Eras (accessed 25 April 2016), 3, for instance, writes, "Antiochus IV died in SE 149 (Babylonian) according to 1 Macc. 6:16–17 and his son and successor Antiochus V Eupator was just nine years old at the time. Indeed, in order for Antiochus IV to have heard about the altar he erected in Jerusalem being torn down by Yehuda 'the hammer' on

to hold off the Seleucid commander, Lysias, as the latter led a large army to attack Jerusalem. Judas was then able to regain control of all of Jerusalem except for a Seleucid fortress known as the Akra, which had long been a thorn in their side (1 Macc 1:33–36).[570] Yet Judas and his followers did regain the temple mount, destroyed the Olympian Zeus, built a new altar, renovated the temple, and selected a faithful priest. Then on December 14 of 164 BC they rededicated the Jerusalem temple, and the daily sacrifices were restored (1 Macc 4:36–59; 2 Macc 10:1–8; Josephus *Ant.* xii.7.6f). On account of this, the Feast of Dedication, or Lights (Hanukkah), was instituted to commemorate the occasion (cf. John 10:22).

After Judas was killed in battle in 160 BC (1 Macc 9:3, 15–18), his brother Jonathan (already serving as high priest) continued the struggle. He, in turn, was succeeded by another brother, Simon, who was finally able to win political independence for Judah about 142 BC (1 Macc 13:10–53). With this, the Jews were freed of the burden of paying tribute, and the Seleucid garrison stationed at the Akra citadel in Jerusalem was removed. The Hasmonean dynasty inaugurated by Simon lasted until 37/36 BC, when (following Pompey's conquest of Syria and Palestine for Rome in 64/63 BC) Herod the Great was appointed by Rome to rule Judah.

Biblical Theology Comments

As a biblical *type*, Antiochus IV illustrates the evil and sinister persona that will characterize the future antichrist. Chisholm has written,

> Most likely Antiochus is a type of Antichrist, just as his abominable altar (11:31; see 1 Macc. 1:54, 59) foreshadowed a future desecration of the temple (Matt. 24:15). His disrespect for God

---

Kislimu 25 (Dec 13, 164 BCE), as plainly stated in 1 Macc. 6, he must have lived well beyond this date." In footnote 16, Ben-Dor adds, "Appian also writes that Antiochus IV died just shy of 12 full years. Combined with the king list this means he died in the common SE 149 (Babylonian) prior to the month of Arahsamnu. The window is Apr 16 to Oct 10, 163 BCE." (For Appian, see *History of Rome: The Syrian Wars*, §66.) Nevertheless, most scholars go with a date of 164 BC for Antiochus' death.

570. In contrast to Y. Tsafrir, "The Location of the Seleucid Akra in Jerusalem," *RB* 82 (1975): 501–21, who located the Akra within the courtyard east of the al-Aqsa mosque (near Solomon's Stables), B. Bar-Kochva, "Appendix D: The Location and History of the Seleucid Citadel (the Akra) in Jerusalem," in *Judas Maccabaeus: The Jewish Struggle Against the Seleucids*, 461–62, insists that the Akra was located neither on the Temple Mount or the Ophel but rather in the City of David. Significantly, current excavations in Jerusalem since 2007 by Israeli archaeologist D. Ben-Ami have uncovered the probable Greek ruins of the Akra which tend to confirm Bar-Kochva's thesis. See N. Hasson, "After 100-year Search // The Akra, Epiphanes' Lost Stronghold in Jerusalem, Is Found," *Haaretz Online*, Nov 3, 2015 (online: https://www.haaretz.com/archaeology/.premium-found-epiphanes-lost-stronghold-in-jerusalem-1.5416745).

foreshadowed the attitude of the lawless one described by Paul (see 2 Thess. 2:3–9).[571]

Antiochus' obvious hatred for the Jewish people, his disdain for their religion, and his efforts to persecute them speak volumes of what we can expect of the antichrist, the latter being intent that the whole world worship him (and consequently Satan). On the one hand, the character and actions of Antiochus IV are informative for eschatology in general, while on the other hand they are instructive for demonology (especially Satan's diabolical plotting to defeat God's plan by obliterating the Jewish people).

While the parallels between Antiochus IV and antichrist are numerous, one illustration worth mentioning is found in the very way that Antiochus IV came to power. The honor of kingship was not rightfully his, but he seized power "through intrigue" (Dan 11:21). Likewise, antichrist will use deceptive techniques and even miraculous powers to gain what is not rightfully his (i.e., rule of the world and the worship of its citizens). In reality, he is Satan's counterfeit messiah who cannot be trusted, for he is out to destroy!

Application and Devotional Implications

Throughout the ages, God's people have had to endure persecution. During such times, it is good to remember verses like Dan 11:33, "Those of the people with insight will give understanding to the many." There is a principle in this verse about being an encourager and an example to others in times of great difficulty. Such times may call for personal sacrifice to be made in order to obey God. In such moments, the immature and fainthearted among God's people need to be reminded to view things from God's perspective and to see an example of faithfulness that they can emulate. Those with insight—those having spiritual perception and who are strong in faith—need to encourage the fainthearted to remain true to the Lord and obey him. They do this both by words and by personal example. In doing so, they serve to remind others that faithfulness to the Lord and one's willingness to sacrifice for his sake will prove worthwhile in the final analysis, i.e., when we stand before him and give an account of our lives. This is how one's life is well spent. How we need more such brothers and sisters "with insight"!

3. Predictions of the Distant Future—Reserved for the "end times" (11:36–12:4)

Up to this point in Dan 11, the message revealed to Daniel has surveyed the historic struggles between the Ptolemaic rulers of Egypt and the Seleucid rulers of Syria, culminating in the atrocities of Antiochus IV. While critical scholars assume that Antiochus continues to be described in the remainder of the chapter, many evangelical scholars (both in the early church and in modern times) have rightly concluded that there is a leap forward in time beginning with v. 36, and a different ruler is in view. The message that the

571. Chisholm, *Handbook on the Prophets*, 323.

angel began to reveal in 11:2 is seen extending through 12:4. The opening words to chap. 12 ("Now at that time") indicate a clear link with the preceding material. The notice at 11:40, "at the end time," alerts us that the "end time" that had been anticipated in the days of Antiochus (see 11:35) has now come into view. The most sensible conclusion is that there has been a temporal shift from the days of Antiochus to the future "end time" when terrible warfare and distress will finally give way to resurrection.

a. The Antichrist of the "end times" (11:36–45)

Dan 11:36–45 has long been a hotbed of debate. Critical scholars (following the lead of the Neoplatonic philosopher and skeptic, Porphyry, of the third century AD) contend that this passage is about Antiochus IV Epiphanes, continuing the account of him begun in v. 21.[572] Conservative evangelicals, however, argue that the account of Antiochus IV concluded at v. 35, and now the author has moved on to discuss the antichrist of the end times (the one for whom Antiochus IV was but a type).

Critical scholars admit that the details given in vv. 36–45 do not correspond accurately with the life of Antiochus IV (for instance, Antiochus did not even die in the land of Judah), but they use this observation to conclude that this portion of Daniel was written shortly before Antiochus IV died, as though the author *thought* that Antiochus' life might end this way, even though it did not.[573] As pointed out before, it is their denial of the validity

---

572. R. J. Clifford, "History and Myth in Daniel 10–12," *BASOR* 220 (1975): 25, explains the reason for the exalted presentation of Antiochus IV in 11:36 according to the perspective of critical scholars: "In Dan 11:36, vocabulary resonances with other Danielic and OT passages portray Antiochus IV as the great tyrant bent on self-deification destined for cosmic conflict with the Most High God. ... Antiochus' raising of himself against the divine assembly and even the Most High God is a reuse of the old Canaanite myth of the rebellion in the heavens which finds its OT reflex in such passages as Isa 14:3–21 and Ezek 28:1–19."

573. Critical scholars are not shy of admitting that the details of Dan vv. 36–45 fail to match what is known of Antiochus IV (they readily deny the infallibility of the Scriptures). Hill (199) explains why these discrepancies are not more of a problem for them: "... scholars adhering to this interpretation tend to dismiss the discrepancies as 'polemical exaggeration' on the part of the author (e.g., Collins, *Daniel*, 386; cf. Lucas, 290)." A. S. van der Woude, "Prophetic Prediction, Political Prognostication, and Firm Belief: Reflections on Daniel 11:40–12:3," in *The Quest for Context and Meaning: Studies in Biblical Intertextuality in Honor of James A. Sanders*, ed. C. A. Evans and S. Talmon, 63–73 (Leiden: Brill, 1997), however, has attempted to provide a more sincere rationale for the account given in 11:40–12:3 as the result of contemporaneous political developments at that time (namely an anticipated third invasion of Antiochus IV against Egypt) combined with prophetic expectations of the Scriptures (particularly drawn from passages such as Isa 10:12–14, 23–25; 14:24–27; and 26:19).

of predictive prophecy that drives them to such unwarranted conclusions. Miller (306), however, is certainly far more correct when he writes,

> Interpreting this passage to foretell Antichrist has been a widely accepted view since ancient times (e.g., Chrysostom, Jerome, Theodoret), and Young rightly calls this "the traditional interpretation in the Christian Church." Almost sixteen hundred years ago Jerome declared: "Those of our persuasion believe all these things are spoken prophetically of the Antichrist who is to arise in the end time." Today the majority of both amillennial (e.g., Young) and premillennial (e.g., Archer) scholars interpret this king to be Antichrist.

While most critical scholars interpret this passage as Antiochus IV and most evangelicals interpret this as the future antichrist, there are others who take a mediating position. Baldwin, for instance, is hesitant to fully assign this passage to antichrist, since he is not formally introduced in Scripture (i.e., by use of the term itself) until the epistles of John (1 John 2:18, 22; 4:3; 2 John 7). Yet she realizes the passage does envision a time of history beyond that of the historic person of Antiochus (even one bringing the readers right up until the end). Hence, she concludes (220–21), "Nevertheless there are reasons for thinking that, although the chapter finds its first fulfilment in the character and reign of Antiochus IV, the matter does not stop there." In a similar vein, Hill (199–200) builds upon her approach:

> Yet the tendency of biblical prophecy to "telescope" future events (or the idea that "the more distant event appears to merge with the nearer so as to become indistinguishable from it" (Baldwin, 202) has already been noted in Daniel (cf. 7:23–25). Thus Longman, 282, concludes that in vv.36–45 "we see references to Antiochus Epiphanes taking on larger than life characteristics, which we, living in the light of the New Testament, might describe as anticipatory of a figure called the Antichrist."

Finally, mention should be made of alternative (but minority) evangelical views. Chisholm, for instance, attempts to interpret the whole passage in light of Antiochus IV, but then asserts that though the passage describes Antiochus, it is typologically a portrayal of antichrist.[574] Parry, on the other hand, has attempted to argue—in a far more radical view—that the material in Dan 11:36–12:3 concerns the fall of Jerusalem in the years AD 66–70, such that "the king" in Dan 11:36–39 is John of Gischala, a zealot leader during

---

As for the demise of Antiochus IV, 1 Macc 6:1 (as well as Josephus, *Ant.*, XII.9.1 §354) indicates that he died while plundering the city of Elymais (or a city in the region of Elymais). Second Macc 9:2, however, indicates that it was Persepolis. In either case, this took place in what is known today as southwest Iran.

574. Chisholm, *Handbook on the Prophets*, 322–27.

the Jewish revolt, and "the king of the north" (as well as the "little horn" of Dan 7) is the Roman Emperor Vespasian.[575]

The following chart shows four of the primary approaches that commentators have taken in regard to this passage:

575. J. T. Parry, "Desolation of the Temple and Messianic Enthronement in Daniel 11:36–12:3," *JETS* 54 (2011): 485–526. For Parry the fourth kingdom of Daniel is the Roman Empire, and he attempts to argue that chaps. 2, 7, and 11 can all be harmonized to show the transition as the Roman Empire of the first century gives way to the messianic kingdom of God upon the fall of Jerusalem in AD 70. Despite a lengthy, forty-two-page defense of his thesis, his view faces numerous problems: (1) the details of Dan 7 do not fit Vespasian as "the little horn," since Vespasian did not subdue three kings (v. 24) and Vespasian was not slain nor his body given to the burning fire (v. 11); (2) Parry has to treat the "ten horns" of v. 24 as the preceding Roman emperors, though Vespasian is the ninth, which leads him (524) to spiritualize the number; (3) he must inconsistently argue that the sacrificial system was ended by Jesus (9:27) in AD 31, yet later (525) at the time of the destruction of Jerusalem in AD 70; (4) he must admit (510) that there is no evidence of John of Gischala taking bribes according to 11:39; (5) though he regards 12:1 as depicting the AD 70 "time of distress," he is forced to argue (522) that 12:2–3 is not chronologically connected but is "a summary description of kingdom realities, with a focus on resurrection and the vindication of the fallen *maskilim*"; (6) he must argue (520) that Jesus' warning in Matt 24:15–16 of the "abomination of desolation" pertains only to AD 70 in spite of the reference in v. 21 to the "great tribulation" of which there will never again be anything like it; (7) he interprets (526) Jesus' "coming" in Matt 24:29–31 as the final stage of his enthronement in AD 70 (which forces him to spiritualize the darkened sky and cosmic disturbances as well as Jesus' appearance in the sky and coming on the clouds); and (8) his arguing (525) that the messianic kingdom is ushered in after the AD 70 events stands in tension with Jesus' heavenly enthronement (Acts 2) following his resurrection and ascension to the Father's right hand.

Antiochus IV (Entire passage concerns Antiochus without any relation to antichrist, though the author errs in some details.)	**Antiochus IV (but Typological)** (All can be explained of Antiochus, but he is typological of antichrist.)	**Both Antiochus and Antichrist** (Basically describes Antiochus, but some parts go beyond him to describe antichrist.)	**Antichrist** (The entire passage, Dan 11:36–45, concerns the antichrist only.)
Porphyry O. Zöckler J. A. Montgomery A. A. Di Lella J. Goldingay J. J. Collins E. C. Lucas C. L. Seow C. A. Newsom	R. B. Chisholm	A. R. Fausset C. F. Keil J. Baldwin T. Longman A. E. Hill E. Carpenter	Many early Ch. Fathers H. C. Leupold E. J. Young J. F. Walvoord L. Wood R. Wallace J. D. Pentecost G. Archer S. R. Miller E. Merrill[576]

The present author holds the antichrist interpretation.[577] While admitting that there are some statements in vv. 36–45 that could be understood in regard to Antiochus IV (e.g., "he will do as he pleases" or "he will enjoy success until *the time of* wrath is completed," and even that he makes an

576. Merrill, "A Theology of Ezekiel and Daniel," 395.

577. Regarding the historical development and interpretation of the concept of antichrist, see G. C. Jenks, *The Origins and Early Development of the Antichrist Myth*, BZAW 59 (Berlin: de Gruyter, 1991); B. McGinn, *Antichrist: Two Thousand Years of the Human Fascination with Evil* (San Francisco: Harper, 1994); L. J. L. Peerbolte, *The Antecedents of Antichrist: A Traditio-Historical Study of the Earliest Christian Views on Eschatological Opponents*, JSJSup 49 (Leiden: Brill, 1996); and G. W. Lorein, *The Antichrist Theme in the Intertestamental Period*, rev. ed., Library of Second Temple Studies 44 (London: Bloomsbury T&T Clark, 2003). In chap. 1 of Peerbolte's work, he provides a survey of the research up until the time of his writing (1996). Earlier classic treatments include W. Bousset, *The Antichrist Legend: A Chapter in Christian and Jewish Folklore* (London: Hutchinson, 1876); idem., "Antichrist," in *The Encyclopaedia of Religion and Ethics*, ed. J. Hastings, 1:578–81 (New York: Charles Scribner's Sons, 1908); and R. H. Charles, *A Critical and Exegetical Commentary on the Revelation of St. John*, ICC (Edinburgh: T&T Clark, 1920), 2:76–87.

invasion of Egypt), there are too many statements in this passage that contradict what we know of Antiochus IV to be able to even admit the mediating position of Baldwin and Hill (i.e., that both Antiochus and antichrist are in view). Furthermore, it seems a bit illogical for the author, having already introduced Antiochus in v. 21 and having described his career in vv. 22–35, to suddenly reintroduce him again in vv. 36–39. We might have expected comments like those in vv. 36–39 to have followed v. 21. Steinmann concurs:

> The description of the eschatological king in verses 36–45 is parallel to the description of Antiochus in verses 21–35. Both passages begin with a general description of their reigns and of events not related to warfare (vv. 21–24, Antiochus; vv. 36–39, eschatological king). This is followed by descriptions of warfare.[578]

Baldwin's concern about injecting the term antichrist before its formal introduction in the NT hardly seems to qualify as an objection. Regardless of what label you give him, this *personage* has already been introduced in Dan 7 as the "little horn" of the fourth beast (and again in 9:26–27 as "the ruler who is to come"). And if the "small horn" of Dan 8 represents Antiochus IV while being typological of antichrist, it really comes as no surprise if here, at the end of the book, we have a culminating account focusing exclusively upon antichrist.

A more commonly held objection to the antichrist interpretation is the lack of a clear transition from Antiochus IV in vv. 21–35 to the antichrist in v. 36. Hill (199) explains: "The chief problem in assigning an eschatological meaning to the passage is that, unlike the earlier portion of the chapter (e.g., vv.2, 7, 20–21), there is no clear grammatical marker or transitional language indicating a shift of subject between v.35 and v.36 or between v.39 and v.40 (cf. Goldingay, 305; Longman, 281)."

To understand the transition point at v. 36 where the ruler is simply called "the king" is a reasonable conclusion. The designation itself ("the king") is not found elsewhere in Dan 11. Rather, in this chapter a qualifier such as "South" or "North" is always included when the kings of the Seleucid period are being discussed (with the exception "both kings" in 11:27). A careful study of the context reveals that he must be a ruler in the far distant future, not in the second century BC. Verse 35 concluded the discussion of Antiochus by anticipating "the end time," and v. 40 indicates that this new ruler is operating in "the end time." Furthermore, 12:1–4, which begins with the words "Now at that time" (linking the opening of chap. 12 with the end of chap. 11), goes on to describe a terrible time of distress, using words similar to those uttered by Jesus in Matt 24:21 describing the great tribulation, and then stipulates that the time of resurrection for OT saints will shortly follow. Miller (305) underscores the importance of this observation: "the clearest

578. A. J. Steinmann, "Is the Antichrist in Daniel 11?" *BSac* 162 (2005): 208.

indication that this 'king' will live in the latter days is that the resurrection of the saints will take place immediately after God delivers his people from this evil individual's power (cf. 12:2)." Thus the time-setting for 11:36–12:4 must be in that critical period of time preceding Christ's return known as the great tribulation, which will be followed by resurrection. "The king" introduced in 11:36 must then be the future antichrist, the one already revealed in chap. 7 as "the little horn" and in 9:27 as the one enforcing a covenant with Israel. That this ruler cannot be Antiochus IV is evident from 11:45. Antiochus IV is known to have died in Persia (after attacking a city in present-day southwest Iran in a foiled attempt to pillage a temple), but "the king" will come to his end in Israel.

An examination of further details from vv. 36–39 supports the notion that Antiochus IV cannot be in view. For example, is it really true that Antiochus magnified himself above every god (v. 36) or that he had regard for no other god (v. 37)?[579] Archer (144) shows the fallacy of assuming that he did:

> Some writers have argued that since Antiochus entitled himself "God manifest" on his coins, this was tantamount to "magnifying himself above every god." But in point of fact he placed a statue, not of himself, but of Zeus Olympius (or possibly

---

579. Even Collins (387) admits there is a problem here and acknowledges that Antiochus did honor the gods of his fathers: "far from imposing a single cult on his empire, Antiochus celebrated the multitude of deities in his famous festival at Daphne, outside Antioch, in 166 B.C.E. According to Polybius, 'the vast quantity of images is nearly impossible to enumerate. For representations of all the gods and spirits mentioned or worshiped by men, and of all the heroes, were carried along.' Apollo, whose sanctuary stood at Daphne, was honored on the festival coinage. Antiochus also promoted the cult of Dionysus in Jerusalem (2 Macc 6:7). ... It is true that Antiochus especially favored and promoted the cult of Zeus, and this preference is reflected in the coinage."

In a separate study, K. J. Rigsby, "Seleucid Notes: I. Zeus Olympius," *TAPA* 110 (1980): 233–38, surveys various scholarly theories concerning Antiochus IV's relationship to Zeus Olympius and explains the reasons for the esteem of Zeus Olympius in the Seleucid empire, including that by Antiochus IV himself. Seleucia Pieria at the mouth of the Orontes had been the first city founded by Seleucus Nicator after the battle of Ipsus—even older than Antioch—and therefore remained at least of symbolic importance to the dynasty. Rigsby notes (237), "I would suggest that Antiochus Epiphanes' ostentatious devotion to Zeus Olympius reflects the fact that this was the patron of his native place and first city of his dynasty, truly the god of his fathers. If this is so, we can the more comfortably reject any scheme of Hellenization or syncretism. ... Antiochus' devotion seems intended to invoke the origins of his dynasty and its first patron—a gesture appropriate to this ambitious ruler."

> Jupiter Capitolinus) as the cult image in the Jerusalem temple, just as he represented Zeus enthroned on the reverse side of his coins, adorned with the title of *Nikēphoros* ("Victory-winner"). Antiochus was evidently loyal to the Greek religious tradition, which revered the entire Olympian pantheon; and so it is hardly justifiable to accuse him of such impiety as exalting himself above all the gods to whom he offered sacrifice on the altar.[580]

Furthermore, it is well known that Antiochus IV did what he could to compel his Jewish subjects to sacrifice and bow down to his heathen gods. Also Mercer has pointed out several benefactions Antiochus made to Zeus and other deities, showing the respect he had for them.[581]

The statement in v. 37 that "he will show no regard ... for that desired by women" likewise hardly fits Antiochus. A number of critical scholars assume that a pagan deity known as Tammuz is in view. Montgomery (462), for instance, wrote, "But Ew.'s *[Ewald's]* identification with Tammuz-Adonis

---

580. Goldingay (304) attempts to escape this criticism by arguing (unconvincingly) that the issue was one of showing contempt for some key gods, not that he had no regard for any other god. He writes, "Antiochus replaced Apollo by Zeus as *the* god of the Seleucid dynasty, apparently again for political purposes; it provided religious support for the irregularity involved in his accession. 'The one women love' is then plausibly taken as a god especially favored in Egypt, Adonis or Dionysus, who was slighted by Antiochus through his various encroachments on the southern kingdom. ... The point is that Antiochus had shown contempt for the key gods of both the Seleucid and the Ptolemaic dynasties." But this does not do justice to the text, for Antiochus did more than show contempt. Furthermore, there is no historical evidence for the claims that Goldingay has made.

Chisholm (322), who interprets vv. 36–39 of Antiochus IV, also attempts to dodge this difficulty, by assuming that this is a matter of hyperbole. Cf. Collins (388), "Daniel is probably indulging in polemical exaggeration." Yet the restatement of the king's self-exaltation in v. 37 rules out hyperbole. Steinmann, "Is the Antichrist in Daniel 11?", 202, rightly responds, "The attempt to rescue the Antiochene interpretation of verses 36–45 by resorting to a theory of extreme polemics that distorted the depiction of Antiochus is more special pleading than reasoned exegesis."

581. M. Mercer, "The Benefactions of Antiochus IV Epiphanes and Dan 11:37–38: An Exegetical Note," *MSJ* 12 (2001): 89–93. Cf. Mercer's Th.D. dissertation, "An Historical, Exegetical, and Theological Study of Daniel 11:26–12:4" (Th.D. diss., Dallas Theological Seminary, 1987).

has now, since Bev. *[Bevan]*, come to be generally adopted. *Cf.* Eze. 8[14] for a description of this passionate cult of women."[582]

In response, Archer (144) states,

> Some commentators have taken them *[these words]* to be an allusion to Tammuz or Adonis, the object of a special cult practiced by women from the second millennium B.C. and continued till the time of Antiochus. Yet there is no slightest evidence in the historical records that Antiochus ever opposed or forbade this ancient practice.

Finally, the descriptions of "the king" in vv. 36–39 are strikingly similar to things said elsewhere of the antichrist, especially 2 Thess 2:1–4 and Rev 13:1–10, which warrants the consideration of "the king" of Dan 11:36–45 being the antichrist.

i. A Description of the Antichrist (11:36–39)

Textual Notes

37.a-a. The phrase וְעַל־כָּל־אֱלוֹהַּ is lacking in 2 MSS and unattested in LXX^{O}. However, it is reflected in LXX$^{\theta}$ in addition to MT.

38.a. Rather than translating מָעֻזִּים as "strongholds," LXX$^{\theta}$ transliterated: καὶ θεὸν μαωζιν, "and the god Maōzin." LXX^{O} renders θεὸν ἰσχυρὸν, "a strong god." Cf. Jerome (*et*) *deum fortissimum*, "a strong god" (similarly Aquila and S, *'lh ' 'šjn*). The uniqueness of the expression easily accounts for the diverse renditions in the VSS.

39.a. The MT pointing מִבְצְרֵי assumes a plural noun construct of מִבְצָר ("fortification, fortress, stronghold"). Some commentators (e.g., Collins, 368 and Montgomery, 463), without emending the text, would repoint to מְבַצְּרֵי, a Piʿel ptc., "those who fortify."

39.b. Rather than the prep. עִם ("with"), the *BHS* editor has suggested reading as עַם ("people"), and this is followed by Montgomery (463) and Collins (368). Against this suggestion, however, both LXX^{O} and LXX$^{\theta}$ have the prep. μετὰ ("with").

39.c-c. הִכִּיר אֲשֶׁר is lacking in LXX$^{\theta}$, but is attested in MT, MS 88, and Syh (not extant in Pap. 967).

---

582. Even Chisholm, *Handbook on the Prophets*, 322, seems to follow this interpretation: "The reference to the 'one desired by women' (v. 37) is cryptic. Apparently it refers to a deity who was particularly attractive to women, perhaps the god Tammuz (see Ezek. 8:14)." Cf. Di Lella (301–2).

39.d. The Kethib reading is הִכִּיר (Hipʿil perf.), but the Qere reading is יַכִּיר (Hipʿil impf.). The latter is supported by a Cairo Geniza MS.

Translation

11:36 Then the king[583] will do as he pleases[584] and will exalt[585] and magnify himself above every god. He will even utter shocking things[586] against[587] the God of gods.[588] Yet he will enjoy success until *the time of* wrath is completed, for that which is decreed[589] will be done.[590] **37** He will show no regard[591] for

583. הַמֶּלֶךְ (*hammelek̲*) appears uniquely. In all previous instances in Dan 11, the word "king" is qualified by either the word "South" or "North."

584. Lit., "according to his will" (כִּרְצוֹנוֹ, *k̲irṣônô*). The same expression was used of the ram with two horns in Dan 8:4, of Alexander the Great in 11:3, and Antiochus III in 11:16. The point is that he has no formidable opposition.

585. See a similar expression in the Aram. text of Dan 5:23 (הִתְרוֹמַמְתָּ, *hit̲rômamtā*) for Belshazzar.

586. נִפְלָאוֹת (*nip̲lāʾôt̲*, Nipʿal ptc. from פָּלָא, *pālāʾ*, "be surpassing, extraordinary") means "extraordinary things." Yet the context has a negative tone and therefore "wondrous things" (Collins, 368) or "awesome statements" (Goldingay, 274) are too mild. Montgomery's (460) translation, "monstrous things," does more to capture the point. What "the king" says is more than "astonishing"; it is "shocking."

587. The verb דָּבַר (*dāb̲ar*) with prep. עַל (*ʿal*) can mean "speak concerning" (e.g., Josh 23:14; 2 Sam 7:25), but there are numerous instances where it means to "speak against" another (e.g., Deut 13:6; 1 Kgs 22:23; 2 Kgs 19:21; Isa 37:22; Dan 9:12). The latter is more appropriate to this context.

588. The form for "gods" (אֵלִים, *ʾēlîm*) is extremely rare. Of three other occurrences in the OT (Ps 29:1; 89:7; Job 41:17), it never refers to God himself, being translated either "mighty ones" or "heavenly beings." On the singular form אֵל (*ʾēl*), Daniel only uses this one other time (Dan 9:4).

589. Cf. the use of נֶחֱרָצָה (*neḥĕrāṣâ*) in Dan 9:27 where it was translated "predetermined."

590. Classifying the Nipʿal perf. verb נֶעֱשָׂתָה (*neʿĕśāt̲â*) as a perfect of certitude, emphasizing the certainty of fulfillment (so NET; Montgomery, 462; and Goldingay, 280).

591. The base meaning of בִּין (*bîn*) is "to discern." On the construction of the impf. form of *bîn* plus prep. עַל (*ʿal*) plus object, see Dan 11:30, where it has the sense "show regard for, favor, or honor." Most Eng. VSS reflect this nuance by translating "have no regard for" or "pay no respect to." However, the ESV's "pay no attention to" fails to capture this sense (as though he simply ignores the one[s] in view).

the God of his fathers[592] or for that desired by women.[593] He will have no regard for any *other* god, for he will magnify himself above all. **38** Rather, in its place[594] he will honor a god of strongholds.[595] A god whom his fathers[596] had not acknowledged,[597] he will honor with gold, silver, precious stones,

592. The proper translation of אֱלֹהֵי אֲבֹתָיו (*ʾĕlōhê ʾăḇōṯāyw*) is a *crux interpretum*. From a grammatical standpoint, the plural form אֱלֹהִים (*ʾĕlōhîm*) can be translated either "God" (i.e., the true God of the Bible) or "gods" (i.e., pagan deities). Hence, Dan 11:37 could be saying either (1) "he will show no regard for the God of his fathers" or (2) "he will show no regard for the gods of his fathers." Most Eng. VSS opt for the latter, but this ignores some hard data to the contrary. The evidence favors the translation "the God of his fathers." For support of this position, see the relevant section in "Additional Exegetical Comments" following the commentary.

593. The genitive construct חֶמְדַּת נָשִׁים (*ḥemdaṯ nāšîm*) can be understood in different ways. If נָשִׁים (*nāšîm*), "women," is classified as an objective genitive, this would mean he had no regard for desiring women. The NASB seems to imply this view: "the desire of women." Most commentators and Eng. VSS, however, take this as a subjective genitive (agency), implying he had no regard for that which women desired (or took delight in or treasured). Compare מַחְמַד עֵינֶיךָ (*maḥmaḏ ʿênêkā*), "that which your eyes desire," in Ezek 24:16. The NIV, for example, has "the one desired by women." Since the phrases before and after this pertain to the religious outlook of this person, this should be understood as a subjective genitive (not his personal view of women).

594. כֵּן (*kēn*) can mean either (1) base, pedestal, or (2) office, place (BDB, 487b). Here it means "place" (i.e., in place of another). Of the six times the word is used in the OT, four are in Dan 11 (cf. vv. 7, 20, 21), all of which have this same sense "in place of another." Collins (388) rightly concludes, "The idea is replacement, ... not 'on his stand.'" (The latter concerns the suggestion by some, mistakenly, that the king was placing his god on the other's "pedestal.") Notice that the NIV, ESV, and NRSV all correctly translate כֵּן (*kēn*) "instead of." The suffix, however, is technically singular, not plural.

595. The construct לֶאֱלֹהַּ מָעֻזִּים (*leʾĕlōah māʿuzzîm*) is lit., "a god of strongholds," i.e., military fortresses. If מָעֻזִּים (*māʿuzzîm*) is understood as a genitive of attribute, it could be translated "a strong god" as LXX^{O} rendered this (see textual note above). However, the frequent use of *māʿuzzîm* in Dan 11 (note vv. 7, 10, 19, 31, 39)—and especially v. 39 that immediately follows—suggests this be understood as "strongholds, fortresses."

596. Or "ancestors," which is the intended idea (so NIV, NRSV, and NLT).

597. Lit., "known" (so most Eng. VSS). For the verb יָדַע (*yāḏaʿ*) in the sense "recognize, admit, acknowledge, confess," see BDB (394a 1f). NET also translated v. 38, "did not acknowledge."

and desirable *treasures.*[598] **39** He will deal with[599] the mightiest of strongholds[600] with[601] *the help of* a foreign god. Whoever acknowledges[602] *him,*[603]

---

598. Lit., "desirable things" (חֲמֻדוֹת, *ḥămuḏôṯ*). NET: "treasured commodities"; NIV: "costly gifts."

599. The translation and interpretation of v. 39a is extremely difficult. The combination עָשָׂה (*ʿāśâ*) plus לְ (*lᵊ*) prep. (which opens the sentence) is a construction used over 500 times in the OT, but not translated elsewhere in the sense "against" (i.e., to act against). (Compare NASB, NIV, NET, NLT, and NKJV which translate to "act against" or "attack.") Most frequently this combination is used in the sense "to do something to or act for the benefit of another" (e.g., 2 Chr 9:19). Yet that does not seem to fit this context. An alternative translation would be to understand עָשָׂה (*ʿāśâ*) in the sense "to make," with לְ (*lᵊ*) prep. marking the object of the action (on the latter, see BDB, 511d 3). Understood this way, it would mean, "And he will make the mightiest fortresses." The problem, however, is that *in actual usage*, whenever עָשָׂה (*ʿāśâ*) means "make" and is followed by לְ (*lᵊ*) prep., the latter indicates the indirect object, not the direct object of the verb (e.g., Gen 40:20), or it has a reflexive nuance (e.g., 2 Kgs 17:16). Ultimately, one's understanding of the following two phrases will impact the translation, but "deal with" may be the best option. There are several times where עָשָׂה (*ʿāśâ*) plus לְ (*lᵊ*) prep. means to "deal with" (e.g., Exod 21:9; Num 11:15; Jer 18:6; Ezek 31:11), and both Goldingay (274) and Newsom (323) adopt this translation, as does the NRSV and ESV.

600. The construct מִבְצְרֵי מָעֻזִּים (*miḇṣᵊrê māʿuzzîm*) is lit., "fortifications of strongholds." If מִבְצְרֵי (*miḇṣᵊrê*) is repointed as a Piʿel ptc., מְבַצְּרֵי (*mᵊḇaṣṣᵊrê*), the meaning would be "those who fortify strongholds." (So Montgomery and Collins; see textual note above for discussion.) Several Eng. VSS understand מִבְצְרֵי (*miḇṣᵊrê*) as a genitive of attribute (NIV, "the mightiest fortresses"; Goldingay, 274 "a most secure stronghold").

601. MT points עִם (*ʿim*), "with." Some (e.g., Montgomery, Collins, and *BHS* editor) would repoint as עַם (*ʿam*), "people." (See textual note above.) Collins (368) translates, "the people of a strange god." For this, he is dependent on understanding the preceding מִבְצְרֵי (*miḇṣᵊrê*) as a Piʿel ptc. Hence, "those who fortify strongholds" are "the people of a strange god." Cf. Seow (184), who translates, "and he shall act for those who fortify the fortresses, people of a foreign god." Against עם (*ʿm*), as "people," both LXX^{O} and LXX$^{\theta}$ have the prep. μετὰ ("with").

602. The Hipʿil of נָכַר (*nāḵar*) can mean to "recognize or acknowledge" (Deut 21:17) or even "to recognize with honor" (Isa 61:9). The nuance of "acknowledging" fits the context nicely, assuming "the king" is the one being acknowledged. In Heb., "whoever" is normally expressed by כָּל (*kol*) plus a ptc. (or simply a ptc. alone). However, see Exod 30:33 for a case where אֲשֶׁר (*ʾăšer*) plus a verb in the impf. is rendered "whoever." See textual note above, where the Qere reading יַכִּיר (*yakkîr*, Hipʿil impf.) is preferred over the Kethib reading הִכִּיר (*hakkîr*, Hipʿil perf.).

603. Although the object "him" does not appear in the Heb. text, see 2 Sam 3:36, where the Hipʿil of the verb נָכַר (*nāḵar*) occurs with an implied object. Technically, however, this could be translated as "the king" being the one who regards (or

he will multiply honor *upon* and cause them to rule over many *others*. He will apportion land as a payoff.[604]

Commentary

11:36 The first thing we are told about this future king—"the king"—is that he will "do as he pleases," i.e., he will be in a position of incredible authority, facing little effective opposition. The same was said of Cyrus in Dan 8:4 and Alexander the Great in 11:3. Before coming to have absolute authority, he will share power with the "ten kings" who have banded together to form a confederacy-kingdom, but following his subduing of three of the "ten kings" he virtually gains world dominion (recall Dan 7:24 and compare Rev 17:11–13).

Rather than promoting the deities of the Greek pantheon (as Antiochus did), this future king will "exalt and magnify himself above every god." It is doubtful that he does this too early in his career, seeing that at the beginning of Daniel's seventieth week "he will enforce a covenant for the many for one 'week.'" At that point, he apparently presents himself as Messiah and does what the Jewish people would expect Messiah to do; he acts as an advocate and enforcer of the Mosaic law. (Compare the commentary at Dan 9:27 for a reasoned explanation of this interpretation.) Had he exalted and magnified himself above every god at the time of the covenant, the Jewish people would never have given him a hearing. The fact that he puts an "end to sacrifice and offering" after the first three and a half years (the middle of the "week") is a signal that he is making a bold move in his demonic strategy to secure world dominion. The reference to "sacrifice and offering" in Dan 9:27 is also a subtle suggestion that there will be a rebuilt temple in Jerusalem by this point (the reality of which is supported by the New Testament [see Matt 24:15; 2 Thess 2:4; Rev 11:1–2]). The remainder of Dan 9:27 suggests it is at this point that he commits the "abomination of desolation" by entering the Jewish temple and proclaiming himself to be God. (Again, see the commentary at Dan 9:27.) According to 2 Thess 2:4, he (the man of lawlessness) "opposes and exalts himself against every so-called god or object of worship, so that he takes his seat in the temple of God, proclaiming himself to be God" (ESV).

While exalting himself, "he will even utter shocking things against the God of gods." He obviously hates the true God of heaven and will thus blaspheme his name (Rev 13:6). For a season of time (the three and one-half years foretold in Dan 7:25), God will allow the antichrist to "enjoy success," but only until "*the time of* wrath is completed" (Dan 11:36). The source or nature of this "wrath" is not made clear. This may refer to God's wrath, as

---

recognizes) others. So Goldingay (274): "those he regards, he will honor." Most Eng. VSS, however, assume "the king" is the one being regarded/recognized by others.

604. מְחִיר (*mᵊḥîr*) means "price, hire," or (more rarely) even "wages" (Deut 23:18). Compare Collins (368): "as their wages"; Goldingay (274): "as payment." Notice, however, the use of מְחִיר (*mᵊḥîr*) in Isa 45:13 where it is used in parallel with שֹׁחַר (*šōḥar*), a present or bribe. So the context can give *mᵊḥîr* a negative connotation.

the Hebrew word translated "wrath" (זַעַם, *za ʿam*) normally denotes God's wrath, rarely that of man (e.g., Jer 10:10; Zeph 3:8). The time of the great tribulation is a time that antichrist is allowed to "enjoy success," but this is also a time known in the Old Testament as the "day of Yahweh" (in the New Testament, "day of the Lord") when God punishes the evil unbelieving world that has rebelled against him (1 Thess 5:2; 2 Thess 2:2; Rev 6:17). At that time God will exercise his wrath in a way not previously seen. Yet when this period has run its course (and all that God has "decreed" will have been accomplished), the antichrist will be judged and removed by the personal appearance of Jesus Christ (2 Thess 2:8; Rev 19:20–21).

11:37 Verse 37 focuses upon the religious outlook of antichrist.

No regard for the God of his fathers. First, we are told "he will show no regard for the God of his fathers." That is, he will have no respect for the true God nor will he honor him (see translation note for בִּין, *bîn*, translated here "show no regard for"). The expression "the God of his fathers" (אֱלֹהֵי אֲבֹתָיו, *ʾĕlōhê ʾăḇōṯāyw*) is a *crux interpretum*. Grammatically, the plural form אֱלֹהִים (*ʾĕlōhîm*) can be translated "God" (i.e., the true God of the Bible), or if pagan deities are in view, "gods."[605] Context determines the correct translation. If the phrase in Dan 11:37 is translated "the God of his fathers," this would imply that the antichrist will be ethnically Jewish, a view that some have taken.[606] This was also a view commonly found among early church fathers.[607]

605. L. Wood (306) objects that *ʾĕlōhîm* means "God" in this context on the basis that the singular forms אֱלוֹהַ (*ʾĕlôah*) and אֵל (*ʾēl*) are used twice in v. 36, once in v. 37, and three times in vv. 38–39, which (he claims) would support the idea of a true plural in v. 37 for the form אֱלֹהֵי (*ĕlōhê*). In response, however, the author clearly does use the plural form *ʾĕlōhîm* in v. 32 for the true God (i.e., אֱלֹהָיו, *ʾĕlōhāyw*).

606. Although most Eng. VSS translate the phrase "the gods of his fathers," we find it translated "the God of his fathers" in the KJV, NKJV, and Young's Literal Translation. Among modern commentators taking the Jewish view are Darby, 107–14; Gaebelein, 186–90; Ironside, 118–19; Strauss, 343; Young, 249; Culver, 797; Feinberg, 174–75; and Whitcomb, 154. Of those taking the Jewish view, Gaebelein (185) and Feinberg (173–75) hold that the antichrist is to be equated with the "false prophet" of Rev 13:11–18, not "the beast."

607. So R. J. Endresz, "Daniel: A Survey of Patristic Exegesis," *Phronema* 31 (2016): 123–52. The early church fathers who commented on the antichrist viewed him, not merely as a world ruler, but as one who would be embraced by the Jews as the Messiah (for which reason he would have to be of Jewish descent). Hence, he would be a *false messiah*. He was also commonly viewed as springing from the tribe of Dan in accordance with the prophecy in Gen 49:16–18. See Irenaeus, *Haer.* 5.30.2 in vol. 1, *The Ante-Nicene Fathers*. (Also see Irenaeus, *Haer.* 5.25.4 and 5.28.2 on antichrist being received by the Jews as Messiah.) Hippolytus made numerous statements in support of antichrist being Jewish, stemming from the tribe of Dan and even of restoring the kingdom to the Jews (*Antichr.* paras. 14, 15, 19, 39 in vol. 5, *The*

Of greater significance, however, is the phrase in which the term occurs, "the *ʾĕlōhîm* of his fathers." This is a common expression in the OT (used at least forty-five times) that is *always* for Yahweh God of the Bible.[608] When God was about to reveal himself as Yahweh to the nation, he said to Moses, "Thus you shall say to the sons of Israel, 'The LORD, the God of your fathers (אֱלֹהֵי אֲבֹתֵיכֶם, *ʾĕlōhê ʾăbōtêkem*), the God of Abraham, the God of Isaac, and the God of Jacob, has sent me to you'" (NASB). The kings of the Jewish people were also evaluated in terms of their faithfulness (or lack thereof) to "the God of their fathers." For instance, Amon, an evil king of Judah, was reprimanded because he "forsook the LORD God of his fathers (אֱלֹהֵי אֲבֹתָיו, *ʾĕlōhê ʾăbōtāyw*)" (2 Kgs 21:22 NASB). This is a significant observation, paralleling that of "the king" of Dan 11:37, who is evaluated (and rebuked), because he too will forsake "the God of his fathers."

Steinmann admits that the phrase is always a description of Yahweh, yet nevertheless contends that the antichrist need not be Jewish:

> Therefore this king will come from among the people of God. Some interpreters see this as an indication that the Antichrist will be Jewish. However, this phrase is a religious identification, not an ethnic one. It indicates that the eschatological king will come from those whose ancestral tradition is to worship the true God.[609]

The problem, however, with Steinmann's conclusion that the phrase "the God of his fathers" only pertains to his "religious identification" and not his ethnic background is that in each of the forty-five occurrences of the phrase, it was used of those whose ethnic background was Jewish. Hence Steinmann has no valid basis for dismissing the ethnic element.

The objection is often raised that even though the expression "the God of his fathers" (אֱלֹהֵי אֲבֹתָיו, *ʾĕlōhê ʾăbōtāyw*) is used in Dan 11:37, the fact that the antichrist has been identified earlier in the book in connection with the Roman Empire would argue that he must be a Gentile rather than a Jew. In Dan 7 the "little horn" is associated with the fourth beast, which has been

---

Ante-Nicene Fathers). One such example: "in naming the tribe of Dan, he declared clearly the tribe from which Antichrist is destined to spring. For as Christ springs from the tribe of Judah, so Antichrist is to spring from the tribe of Dan" (par. 14).

608. The expression of אֱלֹהֵי אֲבֹתָיו (*ʾĕlōhê ʾăbōtāyw*), "the God of his fathers" appears 45x in the OT: Exod 3:13, 15, 16; 4:5; Deut 1:11, 21; 4:1; 6:3; 12:1; 26:7; 27:3; 29:24; Josh 18:3; Judg 2:12; 2 Kgs 21:22; Dan 11:37; Ezra 7:27; 8:28; 10:11; 1 Chr 5:25; 12:18; 29:20; 2 Chr 7:22; 11:16; 13:12, 18; 14:3; 15:12; 19:4; 20:6, 33; 21:10; 24:18, 24; 28:6, 9, 25; 29:5; 30:7, 19, 22; 33:12; 34:32, 33; 36:15. In addition, we find "the God of his father (sg.)" (אלֹהֵי אָבִיו, *ʾlōhê ʾābîw*) three times: Gen 46:1; 2 Chr 17:4; 34:3; and "the God of your father" (אֱלֹהֵי אָבִיךָ, *ʾlōhê ʾābîkā*) four times: Gen 46:3; 50:17; Exod 3:6; 1 Chr 28:9. Cf. Gen 32:9 ("the God of my father"). The expression also occurs in the New Testament for the God of the Bible: Acts 3:13; 5:30; 7:32; 22:14; and 24:14.

609. Steinmann, "Is the Antichrist in Daniel 11?" 206.

identified in this commentary as the Roman Empire. Yet a closer look at the text does not prove this "little horn" (the antichrist) is a Gentile. What we are told is that "the ten horns" come out of this kingdom, i.e., out of the Roman Empire. In light of what is revealed in the book of Revelation (see esp. Rev 17:8–14), these "ten horns" represent ten kings who unite in forming a kingdom. In some way not totally explained, they share their authority as kings with the beast (the antichrist) for a short period (v. 12). Yet then they turn their power and authority over to the beast (v. 13), or as v. 17 says, they give their kingdom to the beast. The most likely explanation for this transfer of power to the beast is the fact that he first subdues three of them, so that the kings of this confederacy/kingdom all turn their authority over to him (Dan 7:24). So, what we learn from this is that the "ten kings" emerge from what was once the Roman Empire. Yet the "little horn" (= the beast, the antichrist) does not necessarily emerge from the Roman Empire. Dan 7:24 simply says that he "will arise after them," and he comes to possess their kingdom. Yes, the kingdom that the "little horn" gains is one that *territorially* was once the Roman Empire, but that does not make him a Roman (or even a Gentile). The "ruler to come" in 9:26 can be understood in much the same way. The Roman armies destroyed Jerusalem in AD 70, and they are "the people of the ruler who is to come." He is connected to the Roman armies of AD 70 in that he will one day come to rule over a "ten-nation" confederacy/kingdom comprising territory once part of the ancient Roman Empire. Furthermore, that territory was extensive, including most of the countries of the Mediterranean, other countries now making up Europe (e.g., France and Germany), and even at times countries now regarded as part of the Middle East (including Syria, Turkey, Iraq, and even Judah).

Yet even if someone insists the antichrist must be in some way "Roman" because of Dan 7:24, that still does not prove he is a Gentile. He could be ethnically Jewish and yet politically part of the revived Roman Empire of the future.[610] Finally, one should observe that the New Testament never asserts that the antichrist will be a Gentile, which should elicit an ounce of caution.

No regard for that desired by women. A second statement about his religious outlook is that he will also have no regard for "that desired by women,"

---

610. Archer (147) admits that the antichrist's connection with the ancient Roman Empire still leaves latitude for his place of origin: "the historical Roman Empire was mainly centered around the Mediterranean, with its capital in Italy, and so there is a good possibility that 'the ruler who will come' will be from Europe rather than from the Near East. This is not beyond dispute, however, since at least one emperor of Rome, Elegabalus, was a Syrian or Phoenician; he reigned AD 218–22 and was succeeded by his cousin Severus Alexander, who was also Syrian or Phoenician, having been born in Acre."

which is a genitive construct חֶמְדַּת נָשִׁים (*ḥemdaṯ nāšîm*) in the Heb. text.[611] (Contrast "for the desire of women," NASB, NKJV.) For discussion of options, see the translation note above. This is certainly not a comment about his sexual preferences, because both the preceding and following statements say something about his attitude toward God (or gods). Hence, this is not a reference to him disfavoring normal human marital relations or having a low regard for women.[612] Most Eng. translations take this as a *subjective genitive* (agency), implying he had no regard for that which women desired (or took delight in or treasured).[613] As for what this might be, most are non-committal, assuming that it must be some deity that women worshiped or highly esteemed.

As for what is meant by the noun חֶמְדָּה (*ḥemdâ*), the word itself basically means "desire." *HALOT* (325) indicates "desirable things, precious things, or what is delightful." *DCH* (3:248) suggests (1) desire; or (2) beauty, preciousness (treasure, wealth). In Hag 2:7 it means "wealth." Otherwise, it typically refers to that which is precious, desirable, or valuable. The context of Dan 11:37 concerns this person's religious outlook. For those espousing the Antiochene interpretation of vv. 36–45, they would understand this as a *god* that women delighted in. Hence Collins (368) renders this, "even to the [god] beloved of women" and NET, "not even the god loved by women" (cf. Goldingay, 274 "to the one women love"). Montgomery (460–62) translates, "the darling of women," by which he means specifically Tammuz-Adonis (cf. *HALOT*, 325; and in Ezek 8:14 a Tammuz-worshiping cult of women). Some have suggested that what is in view is the desire that Jewish women have had to be the mother of Messiah.[614] Feinberg (175) elaborates,

> He will have no room for that One who is preeminently the Desire of women, Messiah Himself. It was the fond hope and longing of Jewish women that they might be the channel through

611. The genitive construct חֶמְדַּת נָשִׁים (*ḥemdaṯ nāšîm*) cannot be translated "desirable women." When *ḥemdaṯ* is in the genitive position of a genitive construct chain, it modifies the word in the absolute (e.g., Jer 3:19, land of desire = desirable land). But in Dan 11:37 *ḥemdaṯ* is in the absolute position.

612. So Calvin (2:349–50), Keil (465), Young (249), and Leupold (515–16). Archer (144) offers a unique suggestion: "perhaps it simply points to the cruelty Antiochus showed toward the women he was sexually involved with."

613. The use of *ḥemdaṯ* in 1 Sam 9:20 is supportive of taking this as a subjective genitive: "And for whom is all the desire of Israel (חֶמְדַּת יִשְׂרָאֵל, *ḥemdaṯ yiśrāʾēl*), if not to you ... ?" Saul, the prospective king, was the one desired *by* the people of Israel. Note that *ḥemdaṯ* is feminine here, though the king is in view.

614. Among those taking the messianic interpretation are P. Mauro, *The Seventy Weeks and the Great Tribulation* (Swengel, PA: Herendeen, 1944), 145; Ironside (120–21), Walvoord (272), Pentecost (1371), Campbell (171), Feinberg (175), and Miller (306).

> whom Messiah would be born. The reason that antichrist has no respect for the Desire of women is that he will seek to take that place himself.

Miller (307) adds in support of the messianic interpretation, "On either side of the phrase are statements concerning Antichrist's contempt for God and religion. It would not be surprising to find a reference to the rejection of the Messiah in this setting."

The most sensible understanding of *ḥemdaṯ nāšîm* is as a symbol of the messianic hope in general. Yet, however this particular statement is understood, the point of v. 37 is that the antichrist will so exalt himself that he will tolerate no other rival on earth being worshiped. This is consistent with Rev 13:4 that says the people of the earth in those days will worship both the dragon (Satan) and the beast (the antichrist). Also, the latter will oppose every so-called god or object of worship (2 Thess 2:4). Not surprisingly, he will hate true believers and Jewish people who seek to worship Yahweh God.

11:38 In the place of Yahweh God, the antichrist will honor "a god of strongholds," that is, he will put his stock in military might. The word "strongholds" (מָעֻזִּים, *mā'uzzîm*) is commonly used in the Old Testament (and even Dan 11:7, 10, 19, 31, 39) of a fortified military defense. Some have attempted (in vain) to identify a specific god, as Hill (202) summarizes:

> Several suggestions have been made identifying this "god" with one of the numerous fortresses established by Antiochus IV Epiphanes: the god Jupiter Capitolinus, to whom Antiochus erected a great statue at Antioch; the god Zeus, based on an inscription found at Scythopolis; and the Jerusalem citadel, or Akra, where Antiochus profaned the temple precinct by erecting an image of Zeus (cf. Lucas, 290).

Hill concludes that the expression "simply symbolizes his own tyrannical rule over his kingdom," or as Keil (466) puts it, "the personification of war."

The same word (Heb. *mā'ôz*) is used metaphorically of Yahweh. David proclaimed, "God is my strong fortress" (2 Sam 22:33; cf. Ps 37:39). For the Jewish kings of old, their trust was to be first and foremost in Yahweh God, not military might (cf. Ps 20:6–7). The antichrist, however, will rely heavily on military might. This is "a god whom his fathers had not acknowledged," not that they did not have or utilize military armies and hardware, but that their trust was not in this alone. Precious resources like "gold, silver, precious stones, and desirable *treasures*" will mean nothing to this tyrant. He will readily pour them into procuring whatever military goods he can obtain, for he assumes that having a superior military machine will enable him to take over the world and rule it (so Young, 249). From the human standpoint, he will be successful in this quest until the Lord Jesus Christ puts a stop to his madness. Revelation 13:4 states, "Who is like the beast, and who is able to wage war with him?" Many will suffer at the hands of this godless man when such massive military resources are placed in his hands.

11:39 In his quest to rule the world, the antichrist will out of necessity need to deal with mighty strongholds in strategic locations. This he will do, aided by "a foreign god" (אֱלוֹהַּ נֵכָר, *ʾělôah nēkār*). This latter expression is commonly used in the Old Testament of foreign gods or idols associated with them (e.g., Gen 35:2). Psalm 81:9 declares, "There must be no other god among you. You must not worship a foreign god" (NET). This aid rendered the antichrist could look at that from Satan himself, for he is ultimately the one propagating false deities, and Rev 13:4 indicates that Satan gives his authority to the beast (cf. 2 Thess 2:9).

In addition to military force, the antichrist will use other tactics to create a loyal following. To those who acknowledge him, "he will multiply honor" upon them. That is, he will dole out favors on those who back him and join his crusade. These favors will take the form of granting political positions (to "rule over many *others*") and the allocation of key territories ("apportion land as a payoff"). The word "land" (Heb. אֲדָמָה, *ʾădāmâ*) can also mean "territories" or "countries" (e.g., Gen 47:20), and the word "payoff" (מְחִיר, *mᵊḥîr*) can have the connotation of a "present" or "payoff" (note its use in Isa 45:13 in parallel with שֹׁחַד, *šōḥad*, a "bribe").

Biblical Theology Comments

Dan 11:36–39 is probably the most instructive passage in the Old Testament about the nature and mindset of the future antichrist. In light of the view taken in this commentary, he will probably be ethnically Jewish. Judas, the famed betrayer of the Lord Jesus, was also Jewish. So, it is not too surprising that Satan would use someone who was Jewish to accomplish his purposes. If Satan's purpose is to dupe the Jewish people in general by means of a counterfeit messiah, then it is not surprising at all that antichrist would be Jewish. He would have to be in order to be welcomed by the Jewish people as their messiah.

This passage is also significant for what it teaches about the antichrist's attitude and commitment to military might. He will honor a god of fortresses, so that we read in Rev 13:4, "Who is like the beast, and who is able to wage war with him?" His war machine will appear to be humanly unstoppable.

Application and Devotional Implications

According to Dan 11:36, the antichrist "will even utter shocking things against the God of gods." To this, Rev 13:5–6 adds, "There was given to him a mouth speaking arrogant words and blasphemies, and authority to act for forty-two months was given to him. And he opened his mouth in blasphemies against God, to blaspheme His name and His tabernacle, *that is*, those who dwell in heaven" (NASB). The very idea that anyone would speak a word of contempt against God—much less "blasphemies"—is dumbfounding. Repeatedly in Scripture God is exalted as one who is good (e.g., Ps 136:1). He is not merely *good* as humans might think of good (e.g., "mostly good"), but 100 percent purely good. He can do no other! The fact that God is totally and purely good is something that we, as believers, need to cherish and cling tightly to. There is no reason to speak a word against God, because he is perfectly good and operates out of a heart that longs to bestow his goodness on us. Satan, however, relishes every opportunity to attack the character of God and therefore tempts all those he can to question God's goodness (just as he did with Eve). If we are not careful, we can be deceived and start to believe the lies of the evil one—the very one who has the audacity to "utter shocking things against" and blaspheme the name of our glorious and wondrously good God.

ii. The military campaigns of the antichrist leading up to Armageddon (11:40–45)

Scholars have tended to follow one of three approaches to this passage: (1) these verses describe the historical facts pertaining to the reign of Antiochus IV; (2) they describe, not real facts but merely the expectation of the author (who either erred or deliberately exaggerated); or, (3) these verses portray the end of the antichrist. As an example of the first approach, Porphyry (the third-century AD Neoplatonic philosopher) tried to explain all details in light of Antiochus. He even argued that the two seas in v. 45 represented the Tigris and Euphrates and regarded the word Apedno (אַפַּדְנוֹ, *ʾappadnô*) in v. 45 as a place name (rather than a word meaning "palace"). Porphyry also claimed that Antiochus launched another campaign against Philometor in the eleventh year of his reign (which history does not confirm), which supposedly corresponds to the invasion mentioned in vv. 42–43.

Modern-day critical scholars like Collins and Goldingay are typical of those taking the second approach. Collins (388) writes, "Modern scholarship marks the transition from *ex eventu* prophecy to real (and erroneous) prediction at this point." Goldingay (305) elaborates, "... v 40 marks the transition from quasi-prediction based on historical facts to actual prediction based on Scripture and on the pattern of earlier events; this continues into 12:1–3." He goes on to say, "In vv 40–43, then, the seer imagines Antiochus's deeds reaching even beyond anything we have already read." Goldingay rather flippantly dismisses the tension that what is portrayed here does not correspond to actual events: "It is not the nature of biblical prophecy to give a literal account of events before they take place."

Needless to say, conservatives who respect the inspiration and trustworthiness of Scripture strongly disagree with the critical perspective and point out the problems facing those taking the historicist approach with Antiochus IV: (1) there are no historical records reporting any further battles between the Seleucids and Ptolemies by Antiochus IV that would correspond to the details of these verses; and, (2) the death record at the end simply does not match that of Antiochus IV. Critical scholars, while acknowledging these problems, are not too troubled by them. Hill (202) explains: "The 'embarrassing inaccuracy' of the 'dating preview of the future' (ibid.) is excused on two counts: first, the biblical writer is assumed to engage in 'polemical exaggeration' (so Collins, *Daniel*, 386); and second, biblical prophecy is defined in such a way as to exclude the fulfillment of predictions down to the precise details (so Goldingay, 305)."

In light of the shift from Antiochus IV to antichrist at v. 36 (as previously argued and defended), the more plausible approach is to understand vv. 40–45 in regard to the antichrist. Having described, then, the general character, religious outlook, and militaristic commitment of the antichrist in vv. 36–39, the author now turns to highlight a few important developments of his military campaigns that will take place in and around the land of Israel.

The "end time"—anticipated earlier at v. 35—is now clearly in view and marks this passage as eschatological, especially in light of the further temporal notice in 12:1 and the subsequent reference to the great tribulation and resurrection. However, it is very difficult to know whether these military campaigns will occur in the first half, at the middle, or sometime in the latter half of Daniel's seventieth week. The reference to the antichrist coming to his end in 11:45 might suggest a time late in the great tribulation, but this is not conclusive. The opening verse to chap. 12 announces a "time of distress unlike any other," as though the great tribulation (the final three and one-half years of Daniel's seventieth week) has just arrived. It is possible, therefore, that 11:45 does not mean to convey that the events mentioned in vv. 40–44 occur in close proximity to the antichrist's death or even that he himself actually dies at this point, but only that the setting up of his royal tents at (or near) Jerusalem will not result in his ultimate victory. The main point is that he will come to his end here (without necessarily stipulating the timing of his end). So it is wise to exercise caution about the exact chronology concerning the details recorded in 11:36–12:4. We do well to keep in mind that these verses only provide a brief summary.

Finally, since this passage pertains to the antichrist and the "end time," it is only logical to attempt to correlate Dan 11:36–12:4 with other known eschatological passages, especially with those pertaining to the antichrist, the return of the Lord, and the establishment of the kingdom (e.g., Jer 30:1–11; Ezek 36–37; Joel 2:28–3:17; Zech 12–14; Matt 24; 2 Thess 2:1–12; and Rev 12–19). In light of the reference to "the north" in Dan 11:40–44, a number of scholars have speculated on the relationship of this passage to the great battle depicted in Ezek 38–39, both in terms of the identity of the foe from "the north" and the timing of end time events. Wood (308–9), for example, assumes that Ezek 38–39 is the same event as that in Dan 11:40, or at least closely related. Walvoord (1971: 277), on the other hand, puts the Ezek 38–39 event in the first half of Daniel's seventieth week and Dan 11:40–45 later in the second half (when there is a breaking up of the world government). Yet a correlation of Dan 11:40–45 with Ezek 38–39 is very doubtful. As I have argued elsewhere, the Ezek 38–39 passage probably does not pertain to the period of the great tribulation but comes much later, after the millennial reign of Christ.[615] (See further discussion under "Additional Exegetical Comments" at the end of this unit.)

Textual Notes

41.a. MT's רַבּוֹת is a fem. pl. adj. of רַב, meaning "much, many." Pointed this way, it would presumably refer to "countries" (אֲרָצוֹת) in v. 40. Symmachus, however (followed by Jerome, *et multa millia*, "and many thousands"), understands the pointing רִבּוֹת, a fem. pl. of the noun רִבּוֹ, meaning "ten thousand or myriad." The *BHS* editor favors the latter. Cf. Dan 11:12. Commentators and translations are split on this matter, as either is possible.

41.b. Rather than MT's רֵאשִׁית ("first, foremost"), S (*wšrkʾ*) apparently reads שְׁאֵרִית, "remnant." So the *BHS* editor. Yet most commentators and translations side with MT.

42.a. Rather than MS L's initial vowel pointing with a *pathach* (בַּאֲרָצוֹת), this should be a *qamets* (בָּאֲרָצוֹת) as a few MSS have. See Ezek 6:8 for a good example. אֶרֶץ is properly pl. (but note LXX[θ]'s sg. ἐπὶ τὴν γῆν, "against the land").

45.a. Rather than MT's וְיִטַּע (Qal impf. of נָטַע, "to plant"), the *BHS* editor proposes וְיֵטֶּה (Qal impf. of נָטָה, "to stretch out, spread out"). Yet see BDB (642c 2), as נָטַע can have a figurative meaning "to establish," and hence to "plant a tent" would mean to set it up. There is no need for an emendation. Most Eng. VSS translate as "pitch."

45.b. L's אָהֳלֶי is undoubtedly incorrect. The pl. construct form should be אָהֳלֵי (which reading is found in many MSS as well as Edd). Cf. Num 16:26.

Translation

11:40 Now at the end time, the king of the South will attack[616] him, and the king of the North will storm[617] against him with chariots, cavalry, and

---

615. See J. P. Tanner, "Rethinking Ezekiel's Invasion by Gog," *JETS* 39 (1996): 29–46. For further discussion about the relationship of Dan 11:40–45 to Ezek 38–39 (and the timing of these events) by one who favors including both passages in Daniel's seventieth week, see Miller (310–11).

616. The Hitpaʿel verb יִתְנַגַּח (*yiṯnaggaḥ*, from √ נגח, *nāgaḥ*) means to "push, thrust, gore." For the Hitpaʿel (only used here), BDB (618c) suggests "engage in thrusting with, wage war with." *HALOT* (667) is similar: "to join in combat with, to wage war." Collins (368) suggests "join in battle with." The NIV translates, "engage him in battle."

617. The verb שָׂעַר (*śāʿar*, only 4x in the OT) basically means to "sweep or whirl away" (BDB, 973). For the Hitpaʿel, *HALOT* (1343) suggests "to storm against" (so NET). At least two of the four occurrences have to do with wind swirling about, and as a rushing wind of a storm is destructive, so this word has a negative connotation (cf. M. Dreytza, "שׂער," *NIDOTTE*, 1263–64). The cognate noun שַׂעַר (*śaʿar*) means a

many ships. He will enter[618] countries and sweep through like an overflowing river.[619] **41** He will even enter the Beautiful Land.[620] Now[621] many *countries*[622] will fall,[623] but these will be delivered[624] from his power:[625] Edom, Moab,

---

"storm" (see esp. Isa 28:2), which suggests (in battle terms) that the king of the North's attack will resemble a raging storm bringing catastrophic destruction to everything in its path.

618. The Heb. verb בּוֹא (*bô'*) lit. means "to enter." The NET translates "he will invade lands" (similarly NIV), as contextually it seems that his purpose in entering these countries was to invade them. Note the use of בּוֹא (*bô'*) in Dan 11:10.

619. The final two words of the sentence (וְשָׁטַף וְעָבָר, *wᵉšāṭap̱ wᵉʿāḇār*) represent a hendiadys (so Di Lella, 272). The verb שָׁטַף (*šāṭap̱*), "to flow or overflow" is frequently associated with water, e.g., like an overflowing stream (Isa 66:12). Rather than "overflow and pass through," the translation "sweep through like an overflowing river" best captures the imagery (cf. Goldingay, 274, "sweep through like a flood").

620. For אֶרֶץ הַצְּבִי (*'ereṣ haṣṣᵉḇî*) as the "land of Judah," see commentary at Dan 8:9 (also note 11:16). The Syriac version here has "land of Israel." MS 88 and Syh have "my land" (though LXX$^{\theta}$ transliterates as σαβαιν, *Sabain*).

621. After the series of *waw*-consecutive clauses, וְרַבּוֹת (*wᵉrabbôṯ*) indicates a break in the sequence. I have chosen to regard this as a *waw*-disjunctive parenthetical clause which forms a contrast (note again a *waw*-disjunctive with וְאֵלֶּה, *wᵉ'ēlleh*). So NET, NIV, and ESV.

622. This would be "many (*countries*)" if MT's pointing is accepted (רַבּוֹת, *rabbôṯ*, from adj. רַב, *raḇ*), or "myriads/ten thousands (of people)" if the pointing רִבּוֹת (*ribbôṯ*) is accepted (from the noun רִבּוֹ, *ribbô*). See textual note above. Goldingay (274) argues for MT's adjectival form רַבּוֹת (*rabbôṯ*) as modifying אֲרָצוֹת (*'ărāṣôṯ*) in the previous verse (both fem. pl.), as did Keil (471). Also, "countries" are in view in the following verse. Assuming "many countries" rather than "many people" are NASB, NIV, and NKJV. In contrast, NRSV, ESV and Collins (368) have "tens of thousands or myriads." The fact that the author consistently uses רַבִּים (*rabbîm*) when he means "many people," as in Dan 11:44 and elsewhere (11:14, 18, 26, 33, 34, 39; 12:2, 3, 4, 10), argues for the notion of "many countries." Cf. אֲרָצוֹת רַבּוֹת (*'ărāṣôṯ rabbôṯ*) in Jer 28:8. LXX$^{\theta}$'s πολλοὶ (*polloi*), "many," is ambiguous.

623. In the Nipʿal stem, the verb כָּשַׁל (*kāšal*) can mean to literally "stumble," i.e., trip over something (Nah 3:3; Prov 4:12), to stumble morally in sin (Prov 4:19), to falter in action (Jer 20:11), to suffer or struggle in battle (Dan 11:33, 34), to perish as a result of God's punishment (Jer 6:15), or to fall *decisively* in battle (Dan 11:35). Most Eng. VSS translate יִכָּשְׁלוּ (*yikkāšᵉlû*) as "fall."

624. The verb מָלַט (*mālaṭ*), here in the Nipʿal, can mean "escape" or "be delivered/rescued." In the only other use in Daniel (namely 12:1), it means "be delivered/rescued."

625. Lit., "from his hand," understanding "hand" as a metonymy for one's power.

and the foremost part,[626] the Ammonite *territory*.[627] **42** Then he will exert his power[628] against[629] *these* countries, and the land of Egypt will not escape. **43** He[630] will gain control[631] of the hidden stores[632] of gold and silver and all the precious things of Egypt; and the Libyans and Cushites[633] *will be forced* into submission.[634] **44** Yet reports from the east and from the north

---

626. The noun רֵאשִׁית (*rēʾšîṯ*), commonly translated "first, beginning," can have the nuance of "finest" (e.g., Jer 49:35; Amos 6:6), "foremost" (e.g., Amos 6:1; Num 24:20), or "choicest, best part" (e.g., Exod 23:19; 1 Sam 2:29; 15:21). Goldingay (274) chooses to see this as a reference to the "leaders" of the Ammonite people, and similarly Collins (368), "the leadership." Yet the words "Edom" and "Moab" refer to territories (and figuratively for the people of those territories), but not restricted to their leaders. Of the three entities mentioned here, the Ammonite region is viewed as the foremost part (cf. Deut 33:21 for the use of *rēʾšîṯ* to a geographical territory), with *rēʾšîṯ* being in apposition to "the sons of Ammon."

627. The phrase "sons of Ammon" (בְּנֵי עַמּוֹן, *bᵊnê ʿammôn*) is a frequent expression in the OT and often refers to the territory inhabited by the Ammonite people (e.g., Num 21:24).

628. Lit., "stretch forth his hand."

629. For the prep. בְּ (*bᵊ*) meaning "against," see BDB (89b 4a) and observe Gen 30:2 and Exod 4:14.

630. This could be translated as a temporal dependent clause: "When he gains control ... , the Libyans and Cushites will be forced into submission."

631. The verb מָשַׁל (*māšal*) basically means "to rule, have dominion, reign." In this instance, LXX$^{\theta}$ translated with the verb κυριεύω (*kurieuō*), "to lord, gain possession of, seize." In MH מָשַׁל (*māšal*) is attested with the meanings "to attend, manage, control" (see Jastrow, *DTT*, 855). Hence, Goldingay (274) translates as "gain control of," and NET "have control over."

632. מִכְמָן (*mikmān*) is a hapax. BDB (485a) thinks this derives from a verb root כמן (*kāman*), meaning "be hidden." In MH, כָּמַן (*kāman*) means "to be hidden, lie in wait" (Jastrow, *DTT*, 646). Cf. Arabic كَمَنَ (*kamana*), "lie in ambush." LXX$^{\theta}$ translated as ἀποκρύφοις (*apokruphois*), from the root ἀπόκρυφος (*apokruphos*), "to be hidden, concealed."

633. The name כֻּשִׁים (*Kušîm*) was translated by LXX$^{\theta}$ as Αἰθιόπων (*Aithiopōn*), "Ethiopians," but that does not correspond to modern-day national boundaries. Geographically the territory of כּוּשׁ (*kûš*) referred to the region south of the first cataract of Egypt, i.e., below Aswān, or what today would be the southernmost portion of Egypt and upper Sudan (cf. Ezek 29:10). More exactly, this is a reference to Nubians (so Archer, 148). Goldingay (274) is closer to the idea with the translation "Sudanese" (but "Ethiopians" is preferred by NASB, NKJV, NRSV, NLT, NET, and Collins, 368).

634. The translation "will be forced into submission" is an effort to capture the sense of what is a single word in Heb., בְּמִצְעָדָיו (*bᵊmiṣʿāḏāyw*). Lit., "in his steps." Observe the literal use in Ps 37:23 and Prov 20:24. Here, however, "steps" may be used figuratively for a "procession." Compare NASB, "will follow at his heels." Note

will alarm[635] him, and he will go forth in tremendous rage to annihilate and utterly destroy many. **45** Then he will pitch[636] his royal tents[637] between the

---

the cognate noun צְעָדָה (*ṣᵊʿādâ*), "marching." *DBL* (#5202) indicates that what is in view is a "procession, i.e., a victory march which is headed by the victor, and has the conquered follow in a parade of victory." This could imply a position of submission. Hence, NIV "in submission" and NET "will submit to him."

635. In the Piʿel stem, בָּהַל (*bāhal*) means (1) "dismay, terrify"; or (2) "hasten, make haste, act hastily." Here, the idea of being "terrified" or "alarmed" is appropriate. The translation "trouble him" is almost too mild.

636. For וְיִטַּע (*wᵊyiṭṭaʿ*, Qal impf. of נָטַע, *nāṭaʿ*, "to plant"), see textual note above. The verb נָטַע (*nāṭaʿ*) has a figurative meaning "to establish" (e.g., Amos 9:15), and thus "to set up" or "erect." For a tent, "to pitch."

637. אָהֳלֵי אַפַּדְנוֹ (*ʾohŏlê ʾappadnô*), "royal tents." (See textual note regarding the correct pointing.) According to Goldingay (274), "אפדנו comes from a Pers. word for a colonnaded audience hall; it entered Aram. via late Babylonian." LXX$^{\theta}$ simply transliterated, τὴν σκηνὴν αὐτοῦ εφαδανω (*tēn skēnēn autou ephadanō*), and similarly Vg. *DCH* (1:356) and BDB (66) have "palace." Collins (389) acknowledges *Apadana* as a Persian term for "palace," but notes, "In conjunction with tents, it must mean 'pavilion.'" *HALOT* (78) suggests "his state-tents, the royal tent." Jerome (142–43) mentions the views of those who regarded this as a place name within Judea.

Sea[638] and[639] the beautiful[640] holy[641] mountain, but he will come to his end with no one to help him.[642]

Commentary

11:40 This verse clarifies that the following events take place at "the end time." For Collins (389), "'The time of the End' here has the same meaning as in 11:35: the period when the crisis comes to its resolution," which for him means later in the career of Antiochus IV (similarly Newsom, 357). The problem, however, is that Dan 12:1 ("at that time") continues describing this same period, though including the "time of distress such as never occurred" (a reference to the Great Tribulation) and the subsequent time of resurrection. Hence, this must refer to an eschatological time period far beyond the days of Antiochus IV.[643] By "the end time" the author means the events leading

---

638. While the noun יַמִּים (*yammîm*) is technically plural, there are several cases in the OT where the plural form refers specifically to the Mediterranean Sea (e.g., Jud 5:17; Ezek 27:4; 27:27; Jonah 2:4). Hence, Goldingay (280) takes "seas" as a plural of extension meaning "the Mediterranean"; cf. GKC, 397 (§124b). So Keil (473–74), Montgomery (467), Charles (322), Di Lella (273), Baldwin (224), and Collins (368); also observe the NRSV, ESV, and NLT. Jerome, however, translated the phrase "the two seas, upon the famous and holy mountain" (by which he meant the Dead Sea and the Mediterranean). The NET added a study note, "Presumably *seas* refers to the Mediterranean Sea and the Dead Sea," and translated the sentence, "between the seas toward the beautiful holy mountain." Cf. NIV "between the seas at the beautiful holy mountain."

639. The לְ (*lᵊ*) prep. on הַר (*har*) involves a special syntactical relationship with the preceding prep. בֵּין (*bên*). In cases where בֵּין (*bên*) is followed by לְ (*lᵊ*), the latter may be translated "and" (so Keil, 473). Examples are numerous; see esp. Num 26:56; 2 Sam 19:36; Ezek 18:8; 22:26; 34:17; 34:22; and 2 Chr 14:10. This is also reflected in LXX^{O} (καὶ, "and"). Most Eng. VSS translate לְ (*lᵊ*) as "and" (so NASB, NKJV, NRSV, ESV, and NLT; also Archer, 149, Collins, 368, and Goldingay, 274; but NET "toward;" and NIV "at").

640. LXX$^{\theta}$ transliterates, ὄρος σαβι ἅγιον (*oros sabi hagion*), "the holy mountain of Sabain." Similarly, v. 41.

641. Taking קֹדֶשׁ (*qōḏeš*) as a genitive of attribute = "holy mountain." The concept of "holy mountain" appears some 26x in the OT and is clearly identified with Jerusalem in Dan 9:16 as well as Isa 27:13; 66:20; Joel 4:17; and Zech 8:3. There are other similar phrases, such as "the mountain of the house of Yahweh" in Isa 2:2.

642. Lit., "and there is no helper for him."

643. J. J. Collins, "The Meaning of 'The End' in the Book of Daniel," in *Of Scribes and Scrolls: Studies on the Hebrew Bible, Intertestamental Judaism, and Christian Origins*, Presented to John Strugnell on the Occasion of his Sixtieth Birthday, ed. H. W. Attridge, J. J. Collins, and T. H. Tobin, 91–98 (Lanham, MD: University Press of America, 1990), who embraces the critical interpretation of Dan 11:36–45, is certainly aware that the author of Dan 10–12 portrays "the end" as going beyond

up to Messiah's kingdom at the end of the age (but not the end of human history). This has been a particular focus of the author throughout the book of Daniel (recall especially 2:41–45 and 7:24–27).

Sometime during Daniel's seventieth week, the antichrist will be drawn into military conflict with other countries of the Middle East. Daniel is obviously not shown all the details of this period of history, but he is provided a brief sketch of certain important developments. We learn, first of all, that "the king of the South will attack him." Throughout this chapter, the king of the South has consistently referred to Egypt, and that is the meaning it undoubtedly has here. Hence, Egypt (and possibly certain North African countries allied with her) will initiate the hostilities by launching an attack against the antichrist (so Keil, 470).

Identifying the "king of the North." The identity of "the king of the North" in this verse, however, is not quite so apparent. Is the king of the North distinct from the antichrist, or are the two one and the same? Evangelicals differ on this, and admittedly the use of the pronouns in the verse ("him" and "against him") allows for confusion. Hence, some see three characters involved (the antichrist, the king of the South, and the king of the North), whereas others see only two (the king of the South and the king of the North who is the antichrist). The following chart summarizes the views of conservative commentators:[644]

---

the rededication of the temple in the time of Antiochus IV to include the time of resurrection. In order to escape the implications this has for the meaning of "the end" in 11:40, he posits that the author is engaged in *recalculating* the end time, adjusting his expectations as the years in which he wrote passed by. He writes (97), "The epilogue in Dan 12:5–13 was apparently written after the rededication of the temple, but still awaits the coming of 'the end of the wonders.' It may be, then, that 'the end' took on new meanings in the light of new circumstances, and that the focus on the resurrection of the dead only emerged in the composition of the final major section, chaps. 10–12."

644. Critical scholars (e.g., Montgomery, Di Lella, Collins, Goldingay, and Newsom) have not been included on this chart. In their view, "the king" (= king of the North) is Antiochus IV, and thus they would hold to only two kings in this paragraph, yet for different reasons.

The Two-King Theory (The "king of the North" is the antichrist)	**The Three-King Theory** (The "king of the North" is distinct from antichrist)	**Other** (Takes a different view)
Jerome (139) Theodoret (309) C. F. Keil (469) E. J. Young (251) J. Baldwin (224) C. L. Feinberg (176) G. Archer (147) S. R. Miller (309–10)	Kliefoth (acc. to Keil, 469) H. C. Leupold (521) R. D. Culver (798) J. F. Walvoord (277) L. Wood (308) J. Whitcomb (155–56) J. D. Pentecost (1372) D. Campbell (171–72)	J. Calvin (357): "The king" is not the antichrist but a ref. to the Romans (distinct from both Syria & Egypt). Some are non-committal: A. E. Hill (203) E. Carpenter (453–54)

In favor of the "three-king" view, the way the kings of the North and South are introduced in vv. 11 and 25 when in conflict with one another is distinct from the way they are referred to in v. 40. In the earlier verses, the wording is clear as to who is invading and who is being attacked (without the kind of ambiguity that we find in v. 40). Second, if the author intended "the king" in v. 36 to mean "the king of the North," it is quite remarkable that the text identified him only as "the king" and not by the fuller designation. In the earlier part of the chapter tracing the hostilities between the Ptolemies and Seleucids (vv. 5–35), the word "king" is mentioned fourteen times. Everywhere else, the king is always specified as either "the king of the North" or "the king of the South" (except in v. 27 which refers to "both kings"). The shortened reference, "the king" in v. 36, is quite eye-catching and stands in sharp contrast with the full title "king of the North" found in v. 40—almost suggesting that these might be *two different persons*. Finally, the Theodotion version of the Septuagint (LXX^{θ}) does not have "the king of the South" as the subject of the first line of v. 40.[645] This may indicate the author(s) of LXX^{θ} understood the verse to refer to three separate kings. Admittedly this is a minor point, especially since LXX^{O} does have "the king of the South" as the subject.

On the other hand, the two-king theory has several arguments in its favor. First, Antiochus IV, the type of the antichrist, was portrayed as a "king of the North" in vv. 21–35, and one would logically expect the antitype (i.e.,

645. LXX^{θ} for Dan 11:40: *καὶ ἐν καιροῦ πέρατι συγκερατισθήσεται μετὰ τοῦ βασιλέως τοῦ νότου, καὶ συναχθήσεται ἐπ' αὐτὸν βασιλεὺς τοῦ βορρᾶ ἐν ἅρμασιν καὶ ἐν ἱππεῦσιν καὶ ἐν ναυσὶν πολλαῖς καὶ εἰσελεύσεται εἰς τὴν γῆν καὶ συντρίψει καὶ παρελεύσεται.* "And at the end time he will fight (lit., butt horns) with the king of the south, and the king of the north will be gathered against him with chariots and with horsemen and with many ships and he shall enter into the land and shatter (or 'crush') and pass on."

the antichrist) to be *cast in the same mold* rather than be found fighting against an unknown "king of the North" in v. 40. As Miller (310) notes, "It would be appropriate, therefore, to designate both the type and the antitype by the same phrase, 'the king of the North.'" Second, there is no emphasis in vv. 40–45 on the antichrist attacking northward, whereas there is significant emphasis upon him attacking southward. The question is significant: why does the text only emphasize the invasion and defeat of the king of the South? ("Rumors from the north" only draw him back to Judah; they do not indicate he attacks a "king of the North.") Third, the three-king view would, in effect, turn the kings of the North and South into *allies* against a common enemy, whereas they are pictured elsewhere in the chapter as enemies.

As to which view is correct, it is difficult to say with certainty, and we simply cannot be dogmatic on this point. Elsewhere I wrote slightly in favor of the three-king position that the antichrist is distinct from both the king of the South and the king of the North, and therefore he comes into conflict with both of them.[646] Upon further reflection, however, the arguments in favor of the two-king theory probably have more to commend them, especially the emphasis in the text upon the pursuit and defeat of the king of the South. Verses 40–45 would then be the final war between the kings of the North and South, a struggle traced throughout the chapter but now climaxed with the antichrist himself as the final "king of the North."

Certain amillennial commentators (but not all) follow a spiritualizing hermeneutic and thus come to slightly different interpretations. Ford (275), for example, understands the two kings to represent two powers opposed to the true church. Young (252) interprets the "king of the North" as the antichrist of v. 36 but spiritualizes the "king of the South" to be representative of the powers that will resist the antichrist. Leupold, on the other hand, interprets both kings as forces coming against the antichrist, and the invasion of the "Beautiful Land" (v. 41) symbolizes an invasion against "the church of God" (520–21).

The "king of the North's" political background. A second question has to do with the political background of the king of the North. A number of evangelicals have argued that the king of the North in vv. 40–45 represents Russia to the far north of Israel.[647] I have argued elsewhere that this is certainly not the case.[648] To be consistent with the chapter, the king of the North should

646. J. P. Tanner, "Daniel's 'King of the North': Do We Owe Russia An Apology?" *JETS* 35 (1992): 315–28.

647. Walvoord (277), for instance, writes, "The king of the north . . . probably includes all the political and military force of the lands to the north of the Holy Land; hence the term could include Russia as well as related countries."

648. Tanner, "Daniel's 'King of the North': Do We Owe Russia An Apology?" (see esp. 322–28). C. Armerding, "Russia and the King of the North," *BSac* 120 (1963): 50–55 also argues against equating the "king of the north" in Daniel with the invasion depicted in Ezek 38–39. Regarding the bearing of the latter passage on Dan

be related to countries that once comprised the ancient Seleucid Empire (e.g., Syria, Iraq, Turkey—and even Israel). If this is true and the antichrist is the "king of the North," then this would need to be reconciled with 7:23–24 that somehow connects him with the Roman Empire. As pointed out in the commentary at 11:37, however, the antichrist need not necessarily be a "Roman" himself. (The text only says that he takes over the confederacy/kingdom of the ten kings that arose out of the Roman Empire.) Yet even if he himself arises from what was once the Roman Empire, we must remember that most all the countries that comprised the ancient Seleucid Empire were also a part of the Roman Empire.

In conclusion, 11:40 seems to portray the rise of Egypt as a Middle Eastern power in the period of the Great Tribulation that will initiate an attack upon the antichrist. Just as Antiochus IV once bore the designation "king of the North," so in the end times the antitype, the antichrist, will be the final "king of the North." (This presumes that the "two-king theory" is correct.) In response, the antichrist will set out on an expedition to retaliate against "the king of the South," and his attack will resemble a raging storm bringing catastrophic destruction to everything in its path. He will pass through various countries, with his forces swelling up like a river overflowing its banks. Though the implements of warfare are expressed in ancient terms (chariots and cavalry), the fulfillment will undoubtedly be realized in more modern forms.[649] Archer (147) elaborates, "Presumably the warfare will be carried on by armored vehicles and missiles such as are used in modern warfare—though in order to communicate with Daniel's generation, ancient equivalents of these are used here" (similarly Miller, 309).

11:41 The military conflict with these Middle Eastern powers will also result in the antichrist and his forces entering "the Beautiful Land," i.e., Israel (compare Dan 8:9). This raises the question of where the antichrist was positioned prior to this moment and "when" this takes place. Earlier in the commentary, the argument was made that the antichrist will be a Jewish false messiah who will enforce a covenant with Israel that initiates Daniel's seventieth week (the final seven years prior to Christ's return). Unfortunately, this verse is too vague to clearly identify how this "entrance" relates to what we know elsewhere of him. A possibility is that although he poses as the messiah and enforces the Mosaic covenant with the Jewish people, his military concentration might be outside of Israel prior to the events in 11:40–45.[650] This would not be illogical, since he takes over the kingdom—territories once

---

11:40–45, see Tanner, "Rethinking Ezekiel's Invasion by Gog," 29–46. In this latter article, I have argued that Ezek 38–39 does not have Russia in view.

649. Other eschatological passages employ similar archaic terms in describing instruments of war, e.g., Isa 66:20 and Ezek 39:20.

650. Pentecost (1372) has suggested that this marks the move of the antichrist's army from Europe.

associated with the ancient Roman Empire—that had previously been ruled by the "ten kings" (7:24; Rev 17:12–13).

In the process of these movements and battles, many countries "will fall" (to the antichrist). In the providence of God, however, "Edom, Moab, and the foremost part, the Ammonite territory" (countries that now comprise the modern-day nation of Jordan) "will be delivered from his power." No reason is stated for this. Jerome (140) mentioned a view (though not his own) that these were spared because they lay in the interior, out of the way of the line of march, and Miller (311) seems to favor this view. Yet this seems doubtful that in such a succinct passage as we have here; why even mention such an insignificant detail at all? Collins (389) has argued their exemption from the perspective of the Antiochene theory:

> Edom, Moab, and Ammon were traditional enemies of Israel. They are aligned with Belial and the Sons of Darkness in 1QM 1:1. Judas Maccabee attacked the Edomites and Ammonites (1 Macc 5:1–8). In light of this we would not expect Antiochus to attack them. What is surprising is that they are not listed as allies.

Yet this passage does not pertain to the time of Antiochus. Keil (471) took a spiritualizing view that they are "by name representatives of all the hereditary and chief enemies of the people of God. … [I]n this enmity lies the reason for the people's being spared by the enemy of God." Young (252) took a similar view that these are "mentioned here as symbolic representatives of nations which are enemies of God's people and who will escape the wrath of the king of the North." Against Keil and Young, however, is the fact that there is nothing in the text that hints these three territories should be understood symbolically, especially since they are part of the general geographical area involved and that other countries mentioned in this context are taken literally. Indeed, the whole chapter has been very literal in terms of the countries and territories mentioned. A more plausible explanation for their deliverance is that God will sovereignly protect them at this time for reasons of his own choosing. This could be related to the fact that some of the Jews inhabiting Judah will heed the warning of Jesus in Matt 24:15–20 to "flee Jerusalem" and find places of safety in the wilderness of those regions (cf. Rev 12:13–17).[651] Jerome (140) apparently took this view: "The Antichrist also is going to leave

651. Interestingly, a precedent for this is found in the events preceding Jerusalem's destruction in AD 70. The city of Pella in present-day northern Jordan was a refuge for Jewish Christians fleeing Jerusalem ca. AD 67 during the First Jewish Revolt. Cf. C. R. Koester, "The Origin and Significance of the Flight to Pella Tradition," *CBQ* 51 (1989): 90–106; J. Verheyden, "The Flight of the Christians to Pella," *ETL* 66 (1990): 368–84; and P. H. R. van Houwelingen, "Fleeing Forward: The Departure of Christians from Jerusalem to Pella," *WTJ* 65 (2003): 181–200. On Josephus' evidence of people fleeing Jerusalem to safety, see Josephus, *J.W.* 2.538; 4:378–79; 4.410; 5.420–23; 6.111–20; 6.229–31; and *Ant.* 20.256.

Idumaea, Moab, and the children of Ammon (i.e., Arabia) untouched, for the saints are to flee thither to the deserts." If this is indeed the case, then it might be a clue that the events of Dan 11:40–41 take place about the midpoint of Daniel's seventieth week, in conjunction with the antichrist entering the rebuilt Jewish temple and proclaiming himself to be God (an event either synonymous or occurring simultaneously with the "abomination of desolation").

11:42–43 In the course of events, the antichrist will make a successful invasion of the land of Egypt (in contrast to the countries mentioned in v. 41, Egypt will not escape). This victory will yield great riches for him—"hidden stores of gold and silver and all the precious things of Egypt."[652] The antichrist's victorious campaign into Egypt will then extend to neighboring countries of North Africa, resulting in the forced submission of the Libyans and Cushites (לֻבִים וְכֻשִׁים, *lub̲îm wᵉk̲ušîm*). Regarding the translation "*will be forced* into submission" (Heb., בְּמִצְעָדָיו, *bᵉmiṣʿād̲āyw*, lit., "in his steps"), see the translation note above to this verse. The notion that they might be "camp followers" (so Keil, 472) or allies (in step with him?) is doubtful in light of the fact that vv. 40–44 have antichrist's conquests in the forefront.[653]

Pentecost—who dismisses the idea that Libyans and Cushites are North African nations—suggests (1371–72) that "it is more likely that Put refers to Arab nations in the Sinai area and Cush to nations in the Persian Gulf region (cf. Gen. 2:13 and comments there)." Yet this is very doubtful. The term "Cushites" is a translation of the Hebrew word כֻשִׁים (*k̲ušîm*), a people more accurately linked with ancient Nubia, which encompassed what we think of today as southern Egypt and northern Sudan. Also, in the three other places where the word *lub̲* is used (2 Chr 12:3; 16:8; Nah 3:9), it refers to the region of North Africa west of Egypt.

What vv. 42–43 do indicate is that these three people groups (the Egyptians, Libyans, and Cushites) are either conquered or forced into submission to the antichrist. Some among the early church fathers held that these three were the same as those mentioned in 7:24 (the three kings subdued by the little horn).[654] Though theoretically possible, there is no confirmation of that in 11:40–45.

11:44 The final glimpse of the antichrist revealed to Daniel has him drawing back to the land of Israel on account of reports from the east and from the

---

652. Egypt was famous in ancient history for her great treasures (Heb 11:26). Although Egypt does not currently have that reputation, this verse seems to suggest that by the time of the great tribulation she will once again be in possession of such riches and treasures.

653. Young (252) translates "in his train," understanding this to mean they joined his army.

654. See Jerome (139, 142) and Theodoret (313).

north that alarm him. As to how much time transpires between the initial assault against the antichrist in v. 40 and the time he receives these alarming reports, we are not told.

The geographical references here (east and north) are vague but most likely have to do with regions of the Middle East (not the Far East such as China). (Compare the sixth bowl judgment of Rev 16:12, in which the Euphrates is dried up so as to prepare a way for the "kings of the east".)[655] Dan 11:44 probably means regions to the *east of Israel*, in keeping with biblical usage (cf. Isa 41:2, 25; Matt 2:1–2, 9). In any case, the antichrist hears reports that alarm him. As to the nature of these "reports," we are not told. They could have to do with troop movements against him while he was very engaged in the Egyptian campaign (and here, a connection with Rev 16:12 is a strong possibility).[656] Keil (472) took them to be "reports of revolt and insurrections" (similarly, Young, 252).[657]

As a result of these reports, the antichrist feels obligated to return northward to Israel in preparation for battle. He is intent on waging war, for "he will go forth in tremendous rage to annihilate and utterly destroy many." Some scholars (e.g., Miller, 311–12) would take vv. 44–45 as the final battle of the eschaton, namely Armageddon. A number of relevant biblical passages would need to be correlated with this, including (but not limited to) Joel 3:2–16; Zech 12:2–9; 13:8–9; 14:1–21; and Rev 19:19–20.

11:45 Verse 45 depicts the antichrist back in the land of Israel, where "he will pitch his royal tents between the Sea and the beautiful holy mountain." It is here that he will come to his "end." This certainly cannot refer to Antiochus IV, for he did not die in the land of Israel. Collins (390) points out that there are three accounts of Antiochus' end recorded in the books of Maccabees, though they are agreed on his death being in Persia (1 Macc 6:1–17; 2 Macc 1:14–16; and 2 Macc 9:1–29). Apart from these resources, the Greek historian Polybius has provided an account of Antiochus IV's demise:

---

655. Walvoord (279) and Pentecost (1372) think the report from the east also includes a two-hundred-million-man army mentioned in Rev 9:14–16. Notice the reference to the Euphrates in v. 14. Yet this is highly questionable. Since the horses mentioned in vv. 13–19 are not literal horses (note esp. vv. 18–19), their riders are probably not human riders. This scene apparently depicts a very deadly demonic release, in contrast to 16:12–16.

656. If there is a connection between Dan 11:44 and Rev 16:12, then the drying up of the Euphrates is a divine act (coming as it does from the sixth angel) that helps precipitate the events that quickly escalate into what becomes the battle of Armageddon. Note the comments in Rev 16:13–16 that explain the demonic influence behind the battle of Armageddon.

657. Collins (389) points out that kings on campaign were vulnerable to rumors of rebellion at home (cf. Rabshakeh's taunt of King Hezekiah in Isa 37:7 and 2 Kgs 19:7).

> In Syria King Antiochus, wishing to provide himself with money, decided to make an expedition against the sanctuary of Artemis in Elymais. On reaching the spot he was foiled in his hopes, as the barbarian tribes who dwelt in the neighbourhood would not permit the outrage, and on his retreat he died at Tabae in Persia, smitten with madness, as some say, owing to certain manifestations of divine displeasure when he was attempting this outrage on the above sanctuary.[658]

The exact location where he "pitches his royal tents" is a bit vague. The Hebrew text may be translated "between the seas toward [or at] the beautiful holy mountain" (so NET, NIV), or "between the seas and the beautiful holy mountain" (NKJV, NASB). Taken this way, "between the seas" would refer to a place between the Dead Sea and the Mediterranean. Yet the option preferred in this commentary is to understand the reference to "seas" to mean the Mediterranean Sea (singular), as in Judg 5:17; Ezek 27:4; Jonah 2:3. (See translation notes above at v. 45 for discussion and defense.) Hence, the antichrist establishes his royal tents "between the Sea (i.e., the Mediterranean) *and* the beautiful holy mountain. Regardless of which translation is preferred, the "beautiful holy mountain" refers to Mt. Zion, i.e., Jerusalem (Dan 9:16, 20; and note 11:16, 41).

Regarding the "royal tents," Hill (204) notes that the context suggests a "portable palace," that is, a cluster of tents forming a "royal pavilion" (NASB). Apparently this is not a permanent structure, but something suitable for ease of migration. Rather than being in (or "at") the city of Jerusalem itself, this verse hints at his being located *outside* Jerusalem. Earlier he may have dwelt at Jerusalem itself, especially in his deceptive role as Israel's messiah.

No details of final battles or catastrophes are recorded here in v. 45, yet the previous verse ("he will go forth in tremendous rage to annihilate and utterly destroy many") implies that this is certainly what takes place. As the time of Daniel's seventieth week draws to a close, the antichrist clearly distances himself from Jerusalem with every intention of destroying her. (This is clear whether or not one agrees that the antichrist is both Jewish and a false messiah.) Although Zech 12–14 does not specifically refer to the antichrist, it is clear from these chapters that many nations will come against Jerusalem at this time to destroy her (12:3), and the preceding verses (11:15–17) provide a hint that the antichrist is behind this final assault.[659] These attacking

---

658. Polybius, *Hist.* 31.9, Loeb edition (cited in Baldwin, 223).

659. Although there is no direct mention of antichrist in Zech 12–14, the verses immediately before this section (i.e., 11:15–17) do predict that God is going to raise up a "foolish shepherd" (NRSV "worthless shepherd") who will "devour the flesh of the fat *sheep* and tear off their hoofs" (NASB). A number of evangelical commentators have rightly interpreted this "foolish shepherd" as the antichrist, including D. Baron, *The Visions and Prophecies of Zechariah* (London: Hebrew Christian Testimony to

nations are at least partially successful, as 14:2 confirms: "For I will gather all the nations against Jerusalem to battle, and the city shall be taken and the houses plundered and the women raped. Half of the city shall go out into exile, but the rest of the people shall not be cut off from the city" (ESV). Zechariah 14 goes on to describe the Lord's intervention that prevents them from completely destroying Jerusalem and annihilating her inhabitants.

In conjunction with these events, I submit that "Babylon the great" in Rev 16:17–19:5 is really a *code name* for apostate Jerusalem in the tribulation.[660] If indeed "Babylon the great" is a cryptic reference to apostate Jerusalem, then Rev 17:16 would be very applicable to the context of Dan 11:44–45: "the ten horns *[ten kings]* which you saw, and the beast *[the antichrist]*, these will hate the harlot *[Jerusalem]* and will make her desolate and naked, and will eat her flesh and will burn her up with fire" (NASB). Although the Lord is committed and faithful to his covenant people, he has ordained that they must first pass through the fires of refinement: "It is the time of Jacob's distress, but he will be saved from it" (Jer 30:7). Zech 13:8–9 adds,

> "It will come about in all the land," declares the LORD, "that two parts in it will be cut off and perish; but the third will be left in it. And I will bring the third part through the fire, refine them as silver is refined, and test them as gold is tested. They will call on my name, and I will answer them; I will say, 'They are my people,' and they will say, 'The LORD is my God.'"

The emphasis in Dan 11:45, however, is on the fact that the antichrist will meet his final fate in Israel: "but he will come to his end with no one to help him." Whatever battles he wages, this is not what brings about his end.

Israel, 1918; repr., Grand Rapids: Kregel, 1972), 416–18; M. F. Unger, *Zechariah: Prophet of Messiah's Glory* (Grand Rapids: Zondervan, 1963), 202–5; C. L. Feinberg, *God Remembers: A Study of Zechariah* (Portland: Multnomah, 1965), 165–66; K. L. Barker, "Zechariah," in *EBC*, ed. F. E. Gaebelein (Grand Rapids: Zondervan, 1985), 7:679–80; and E. H. Merrill, *An Exegetical Commentary: Haggai, Zechariah, Malachi* (Chicago: Moody, 1994), 302–3. Merrill (302) points out, "The term used to describe him (אֱוִלִי, *ʾĕwilî*) is commonly employed in the wisdom literature to designate the man without God."

660. For a defense of this position, see my paper, "Apostate Jerusalem as Babylon the Great: Another Look at Revelation 17–18," paper presented at the annual meeting of the SW Region of ETS, Fort Worth, TX, March 31, 2017 (available for download at www.academia.edu). This position is also affirmed by J. L. Burns, "The Biblical Use of Marriage to Illustrate Covenantal Relationships," *BSac* 173 (2016): 273–96. He writes (288), "Revelation reintroduces unbelieving Israel as an adulteress in chapters 17 and 18 in the imagery of the prophets. Just as the prophets juxtaposed adulterous Israel in lifeless idolatry with the covenantal children of the living God (Hos. 1:10–11), so John compared the fall of the wicked city with the new Jerusalem when 'God himself will be with them and be their God' (Rev. 21:3)."

(Compare 8:25, "But he will be broken without human agency.") The New Testament is quite clear that he is slain by the personal return of the Lord Jesus Christ (2 Thess 2:8; Rev 19:19–21; cf. Dan 7:11, 26). With the antichrist slain, the time will then come for the Lord Jesus to take up his kingdom rule in fulfillment of Dan 7:13–14, 27. "The Lord will then be king over all the earth" (Zech 14:9).

Biblical Theology Comments

Dan 11:40–45 makes a significant contribution to the biblical theology concerning antichrist. We already know from vv. 38–39 that he will honor a god of fortresses and that he will command a huge war machine. Verses 40–45 build on this by giving the reader a glimpse of the antichrist's military maneuvers in action as he counterattacks the "king of the South" (Egypt) and her allies. This victory over Egypt provides him with great financial resources. Yet there is some event that seriously disturbs him ("reports from the east and from the north") and draws him back to Israel. Here it is that he meets his final doom. The limited information provided in vv. 40–45 can be correlated with New Testament passages related to the great tribulation and the antichrist (such as Matt 24; 2 Thess 2; and Rev 13–19). The final showdown for the antichrist will be in the land of Israel.

If "Babylon" of Rev 17–18 is a reference to apostate Jerusalem during the period of Daniel's seventieth week, this would certainly help explain other biblical data. The antichrist apparently presents himself as messiah to the Jewish people. Hence, he is a false messiah. (This would explain Jesus' warnings about a false messiah in such passages as Matt 24:4–5, 11, 23–24. This would also shed light on Jesus' comment in John 5:43, "I have come in My Father's name, and you do not receive Me; if another comes in his own name, you will receive him."[661])

According to Dan 9:27, he will "make strong (the) covenant with the many (Jewish people) for one week (of seven years)."[662] Some have thought this to be a reference to a *peace agreement* that antichrist will make with Israel, but there is nothing in the context about a peace agreement. The word "covenant" (בְּרִית, *bᵊrîṯ*) normally means "the Mosaic covenant, the law," though it can (more rarely) refer to other covenants or agreements. What favors the interpretation that it should be understood as "the Mosaic covenant, the law"

661. Irenaeus, *Haer.* 5.25.4, identified the figure in John 5:43 as the antichrist, whom he believed (as did many of the early church fathers) would be of Jewish descent.

662. Some translations have "make a strong (or firm) covenant," as though the covenant itself is a strong or firm one. Yet the Hebrew text has וְהִגְבִּיר בְּרִית (*wᵊhigbîr bᵊrîṯ*). There is no adjective in the text, but rather the causative verb (make strong) indicates what he does in regard to the covenant. To make it strong would mean that he imposes it upon the people or enforces it, not necessarily against their will but perhaps with their support.

in Dan 9:27 is the fact that the same sentence goes on to say that he will put a halt to sacrifice and offering in the middle of the "week" (i.e., after three and one-half years). Sacrifices, of course, go hand in hand with the Mosaic law. The point of Dan 9:27, then, would be that he "makes strong" the ancient Mosaic covenant of the law, i.e., he enforces or rejuvenates it. If he were parading himself as the messiah, this would be perfectly understandable (it would appear he was reinvigorating the ancient Jewish faith). The reality, however, is that he is only doing this (as part of Satan's scheme) to lure them into his destructive trap in which he will attempt to destroy the covenant nation in the final analysis, and thereby nullify the promises of God.

In the middle of the "week," he begins to turn against them. He puts a halt to the sacrificial system, and he enters the (rebuilt) Jewish temple in Jerusalem to proclaim himself a divine being (2 Thess 2:4). (If he is going to be worshiped, this is a logical step.) This *may* coincide with the erection of the image to the beast (Rev 13:14–15) in the temple itself. This, then, would be the "abomination of desolation" mentioned by Jesus in Matt 24:15–16 that marks the onset of the Great Tribulation (the final three and one-half years): "Therefore when you see the abomination of desolation which was spoken of through Daniel the prophet, standing in the holy place [let the reader understand], then those who are in Judea must flee to the mountains" (NASB). Those Jews in Jerusalem who heed these words would of course be ones who believe in the true Messiah, the Lord Jesus. They flee Jerusalem at that time, an event that fulfils Rev 12:6, "Then the woman [of the Jewish line] fled into the wilderness where she had a place prepared by God, so that there she would be nourished for one thousand two hundred and sixty days."

With the *believing Jews* (faithful to Christ) having departed from Jerusalem, that leaves the remaining Jews (most of whom are probably in unbelief) at the mercy of the antichrist. By this point, he has made his move to gain the allegiance of the whole world he wants to worship him (Rev 13:4). He also has the military might to back up his power play, not to mention Satan's deceptive powers at work. "And the whole earth was amazed and followed after the beast" (13:3). Those who belong to the Lamb of God, however, will not be duped and will refuse to honor him—many of whom will pay for this with their blood. Once the "ten horns" give their authority to the antichrist (Rev 17:12–14), they will conspire against the "woman" (apostate Jerusalem) to destroy her (Rev 17:16–17). This leads to the siege of Judah and Jerusalem depicted in Zech 12–14. Yet the ultimate victory belongs to the Lord Jesus Christ who in the final analysis will be Jerusalem's faithful defender. The antichrist has no chance of succeeding. In the words of 2 Thess 2:8, the Lord Jesus "will slay *[him]* with the breath of His mouth and bring *[him]* to an end by the appearance of His coming" (NASB).

Application and Devotional Implications

Throughout most of this section "the king" (the antichrist) seems to advance at will, with no one being able to stand against him. How ironic, then, that in the tiny country in which is situated "the beautiful holy mountain," he would somehow be overpowered. The final clause reads, "with no one to help him." The verb of this clause is a participle form of עָזַר (*ʿāzar*), which simply means "to help." Yet it is a word used in other contexts where Yahweh God is the subject. In Ps 54:4, for instance, we read, "Behold, God is my helper (עֹזֵר, *ʿōzēr*); the Lord is the sustainer of my soul" (NASB). Psalm 46:5 speaks of God as the one who helps Jerusalem, "the city of God," so that she will not be moved.

The irony of the verse is that the antichrist (whose power comes from Satan) ultimately has no "helper." Tiny Israel, on the other hand, will experience great wrath but ultimately will discover God to be her "helper." Revelation 19 clarifies that the antichrist will be defeated by the personal return of the Lord Jesus Christ. When the remaining remnant of Israel turns in faith to him (Zech 12:10), he comes to her rescue as her mighty "helper."

The word *ʿāzar* is also used in Isa 41:10: "Do not fear, for I am with you; do not anxiously look about you, for I am your God. I will strengthen you, surely I will help you, surely I will uphold you with My righteous right hand" (NASB). Those who trust in the Lord know that they have a reliable "helper" in him. Whatever our predicament might be, if we would humbly call on him, we would discover that he is faithful to reveal himself as our "helper," and there is no one who can stand against him. How blessed are those who have such a helper!

Additional Exegetical Comments

The Invasion by Gog in Ezekiel 38–39

Note: The following comments are taken from the conclusion to a paper originally published in *JETS*.[663] In the article, I argued that (1) the passage does not concern Russia; and (2) the time of the battle is not in the period of the great tribulation but following the millennial reign of Christ.

Ezekiel 38–39 describes a fierce invasion against the land of Israel led by Gog of the land of Magog. A common premillennial interpretation is that this invasion is led by Russia and her allies during the tribulation preceding the second coming of Christ. This is quite doubtful in light of the descriptions given in these chapters. Israel is said to have been restored from the sword and "living securely in the land." She has also been regathered from the nations. A study of God's plan of restoration for Israel, with its foundation in Deut 30, helps to identify a corpus of restoration terminology associated with the effecting of the new covenant with Israel (see esp. Ezek 39:25–29). In particular, the "regathering" of the people and the "pouring out" of God's Spirit are key aspects to Christ's return at the conclusion of the tribulation in preparation for the millennium. Therefore this invasion is not during the tribulation period but sometime after the second coming of Christ.

663. Tanner, "Rethinking Ezekiel's Invasion by Gog," 29–46.

Furthermore, the primary antagonist is most likely not Russia. In Ezek 39:1, the name "Rosh" (NASB) is best understood as the descriptive adjective "chief" (note NIV's "chief prince of Meshek and Tubal"). The other proper names are linked with people groups in the territories north of Israel. The stipulation that this invasion originates from the "remote parts of the north" does not demand any place so remotely north as Russia.

The thrust of this paper has been to argue the thesis that the Old Testament has a significant corpus of material describing God's plan of restoration for Israel with distinctive terminology and that Ezek 38–39 is strongly cast in this terminology. An analysis of this material leads to the conclusion that Ezek 38–39 finds its fulfillment after the restoration of Israel and the second coming of Christ. This would not demand the conclusion that Rev 20:7–9 is the proper fulfillment, but since the details of the passage suggest a time after Israel's regathering when God has restored them through the new covenant, the most plausible time of fulfillment is at the end of the millennium when Satan has been released and allowed to deceive the nations one final time to strike Israel.[664] The battle of Gog mentioned in Rev 20:8 ought to be more seriously considered as the proper fulfillment of Ezek 38–39. Objections to this view are not so determinative as to militate against it. Since Rev 20:7–9 is only a brief summary of this significant event, we should not expect detailed correlation of these passages.

Since there is a significant battle at the end of the millennium that John refers to as Gog and Magog, why should this not be the same as in Ezek 38–39? One thing they share in common is that the attack is directed at Israel. This provides a fitting inclusio to biblical history. In Gen 15:18–21 God binds himself by covenant to make a nation of Israel and give them this special land. When Satan is released at the end of the millennium, he makes one last desperate effort to defeat Israel, the apple of God's eye. If he can break God's promise to Israel, he will have defeated God's purposes and thereby won the final victory.

But the Word of God assures us this will never happen. God allows this final attempt to eternally demonstrate his own character (cf. Ezek 39:7, 21–24). Ezekiel's account makes us conscious of who God is—"the God who does not abandon Israel to her own devices because he is jealous for the holiness of his name, who remains true to his people because he remains true to his name."[665] God's promises to Israel are unshakable.

---

664. Keil (180) concluded that the invasion of Ezek 38–39 was to be connected with that in Rev 20:7–9, though he spiritualizes the one-thousand-year period to essentially coincide with most of church history (414). For Keil, Gog of Magog represents the "last hostile phrase of world-power that will wage war on earth against the kingdom of God" (433).

665. W. Zimmerli, *Ezekiel 2: A Commentary on the Book of the Prophet Ezekiel, Chapters 25–48*, trans. J. D. Martin, Hermeneia (Philadelphia: Fortress, 1983), 324.

Passages like Zech 14:1–11 indicate that the Lord Jesus is going to personally return to defend and save Jerusalem (cf. Zech 12:8; Joel 2:32), especially after her inhabitants "look (*in faith*) to the One whom they have pierced" (Zech 12:10). Nevertheless, the destruction language found in Rev 17–18 is not completely incompatible with passages like Zech 12–14. There is no doubt from a reading of Zech 12:2 and 14:2 that Jerusalem is placed under a great siege and brought to the brink of destruction. So, even though the Lord returns to rescue the surviving remnant in the final analysis, that does not preclude the city suffering attack and near destruction before He does.

Whatever "Babylon the great" represents, it must be significant, because more than two full chapters are devoted to her role and destruction. It is very hard to escape the fact that a literal city is involved. Of greater importance, perhaps, is the contrast between "Babylon the great" and the New Jerusalem. There are some parallels between Babylon the great and the New Jerusalem that suggest that Babylon the great is something of a *counterpart* to the New Jerusalem. First, we notice how each is introduced with the words "Come here, I shall show you" (17:1; 21:9). Second, they are both described in feminine terms. Babylon is the *harlot* (17:1), whereas the New Jerusalem is the *bride* of the Lamb (21:9). Third, both the harlot and the bride are called a "city" (17:18; 21:10). Fourth, in both cases John is shown these "cities" following the introductory statement "carried me away in the Spirit" (17:3; 21:10). Fifth, emphasis is given to the clothing of each. Babylon is dressed in worldly luxury (17:4; 18:11–12, 16), whereas the bride is adorned with fine linen, the righteous acts of the saints (17:7–8). Sixth, he goes "into a wilderness" (17:3) to see the harlot, but (in contrast) upon a great and high mountain (21:10) to see the bride. Seventh, the harlot is actively involved with committing acts of immorality and abominations (17:2, 4), but in regard to the bride/New Jerusalem it is said, "nothing unclean and no one who practices abomination and lying, shall ever come into it" (21:27). Eighth, the harlot persecutes and kills the saints (17:6; 18:24), but into the New Jerusalem only the saints can enter, i.e., those "whose names are written in the Lamb's book of life" (21:27). All this highlights the fact that Babylon is to the antichrist (at least initially) what the New Jerusalem is to Christ. Babylon is the focus and epitome of the Beast's empire, a counterfeit of the New Jerusalem. Yet from God's perspective, she is a harlot.

Selected Bibliography (Daniel 11)

Armerding, C. "Russia and the King of the North." *BSac* 120 (1963): 50–55.

Austin, M. M. *The Hellenistic World from Alexander to the Roman Conquest.* Cambridge: Cambridge University Press, 1981.

Baker, D. W. "Kittim." In *The Anchor Yale Bible Dictionary*, ed. D. N. Freedman, 4:93. 6 vols. New York: Doubleday, 1992.

Bar-Kochva, B. "Appendix D: The Location and History of the Seleucid Citadel (the Akra) in Jerusalem." In *Judas Maccabaeus: The Jewish Struggle*

Against the Seleucids, 445–65. Cambridge: Cambridge University Press, 1989.

Barrett, D. S. "Patterns of Jewish Submission in the Hellenistic-Roman World." *Prud* 5 (1973): 99–115.

Ben-Dor, Y. "A Note on the Two Seleucid Eras." https://www.academia.edu/14202011/A_Note_on_the_Two_Seleucid_Eras (accessed 25 April 2016).

Bevan, E. R. *The House of Seleucus*. 2 vols. London: Arnold, 1902.

Bousset, W. "Antichrist." In *The Encyclopaedia of Religion and Ethics*, ed. J. Hastings, 1:578–81. New York: Charles Scribner's Sons, 1908.

———. *The Antichrist Legend: A Chapter in Christian and Jewish Folklore*. London: Hutchinson, 1896.

Charles, R. H. *A Critical and Exegetical Commentary on the Revelation of St. John*. ICC. Edinburgh: T&T Clark, 1920. 2:76–87.

Clifford, R. J. "History and Myth in Daniel 10–12." *BASOR* 220 (1975): 23–26.

Conrad, D. "On זְרוֹעַ = 'Forces, Troops, Army' in Biblical Hebrew." *TA* 3 (1976): 111–19.

Endresz, R. J. "Daniel: A Survey of Patristic Exegesis." *Phronema* 31 (2016): 123–52.

Erling, B. "Ezekiel 38–39 and the Origins of Jewish Apocalyptic." In *Ex orbe religionum*, FS G. Widengren, ed. S. Brandon, C. Bleeker, and M. Simon., 1:104–14. Leiden: Brill, 1972.

Gardner, A. E. "שׂכל in the Hebrew Bible: Key to the Identity and Function of the Maskilim in Daniel." *RB* 118 (2011): 496–511.

Grabbe, L. L. *A History of the Jews and Judaism in the Second Temple Period*. Vol. 2, *The Coming of the Greeks: The Early Hellenistic Period (335–175 BCE)*. London: Bloomsbury T&T Clark, 2011.

Hammond, N. G. L., and F. W. Walbank. *A History of Macedonia: 336–167 B.C.* Vol. 3. Oxford: Oxford University Press, 1988.

Harton, G. M. "An Interpretation of Daniel 11:36–45." *GTJ* 4 (1983): 205–31.

Hasson, N. "After 100-year Search // The Akra, Epiphanes' Lost Stronghold in Jerusalem, Is Found." *Haaretz Online*, Nov 3, 2015. Online: https://www.haaretz.com/archaeology/.premium-found-epiphanes-lost-stronghold-in-jerusalem-1.5416745.

Heard, W. J. "The Maccabean Martyr's Contribution to Holy War." *EvQ* 58 (1986): 291–318.

Hempel, C. "Maskil(im) and Rabbim: From Daniel to Qumran." In *Biblical Traditions in Transmission: Essays in Honour of Michael A. Knibb*, ed. C. Hempel and J. Lieu, 133–56. Leiden, Boston: Brill, 2006.

Hölbl, G. *A History of the Ptolemaic Empire*. London: Routledge, 2001.

Itō, G. "Old Persian a p[a] d[a] a n[a]." *Orient* 8 (1972): 46–51.

Jenks, G. C. *The Origins and Early Development of the Antichrist Myth*. BZAW 59. Berlin: de Gruyter, 1991.

Jones, B. W. "Antiochus Epiphanes and the Persecution of the Jews." In *Scripture in Context: Essays on the Comparative Method*, ed. C. D. Evans, et al., 263–90. PTMS 34. Pittsburgh: Pickwick Publications, 1980.

Koester, C. R. "The Origin and Significance of the Flight to Pella Tradition." *CBQ* 51 (1989): 90–106.

Kosmala, H. "*Maśkîl*." *JANESCU* 5 (1973): 235–41.

Leuchter, M. "From Levite to *Maśkîl* in the Persian and Hellenistic Eras." In *Levites and Priests in Biblical History and Tradition*, ed. M. A. Leuchter and J. M. Hutton, 215–32. Atlanta: SBL, 2011.

Lorein, G. W. *The Antichrist Theme in the Intertestamental Period*. Rev. ed. Library of Second Temple Studies 44. London: Bloomsbury T&T Clark, 2003.

Lust, J. "Cult and Sacrifice in Daniel: The Tamid and the Abomination of Desolation." In *The Book of Daniel: Composition and Reception*, ed. J. J. Collins and P. W. Flint, 2:671–88. Leiden: Brill, 2001.

Mauro, P. *The Seventy Weeks and the Great Tribulation: A Study of the Last Two Visions of Daniel, and of the Olivet Discourse of the Lord Jesus Christ.* Swengel, PA: Herendeen, 1944.

Meadowcroft, T. J. "History and Eschatology in Tension. A Literary Response to Daniel 11:40–45 as Test Case." *Pacifica* 17 (2004): 243–50.

McGinn, B. *Antichrist: Two Thousand Years of the Human Fascination with Evil.* San Francisco: Harper, 1994.

McHardy, W. D. "The Peshitta Text of Daniel xi. 4." *JTS* 49 (1948): 56–57.

Mercer, M. "The Benefactions of Antiochus IV Epiphanes and Dan 11:37–38: An Exegetical Note." *MSJ* 12 (2001): 89–93.

———. "An Historical, Exegetical, and Theological Study of Daniel 11:26–12:4." Th.D. diss., Dallas Theological Seminary, 1987.

Morgenstern, J. "The King-God among the Western Semites and the Meaning of Epiphanes." *VT* 10 (1960): 138–97.

Niskanen, P. "Daniel's Portrait of Antiochus IV: Echoes of a Persian King." *CBQ* 66 (2004): 378–86.

Parry, J. T. "Desolation of the Temple and Messianic Enthronement in Daniel 11:36–12:3." *JETS* 54 (2011): 485–526.

Peerbolte, L. J. L. *The Antecedents of Antichrist: A Traditio-Historical Study of the Earliest Christian Views on Eschatological Opponents.* JSJSup 49. Leiden: Brill, 1996.

Peters, F. E. *The Harvest of Hellenism: A History of the Near East from Alexander to the Triumph of Christianity*. New York: Simon & Schuster, 1970.

Redditt, P. L. "Daniel 11 and the Sociohistorical Setting of the Book of Daniel." *CBQ* 60 (1998): 463–74.

Rigsby, K. J. "Seleucid Notes: I. Zeus Olympius." *TAPA* 110 (1980): 233–38.

Rowley, H. H. "The 'Prince of the Covenant' in Daniel xi. 22." *ExpTim* 55 (1943–1944): 24–27.

Schäfer, P. "The Hellenistic and Maccabaean Periods." In *Israelite and Judaean History*, ed. J. H. Hayes and J. M. Miller, 539–604. Trans. F. C. Prussner. OTL. Westminster Press, 1977.

Scolnic, B. "Antiochus IV as the Man Who Will Overflow the Flood and Break its Arms (Daniel 11.22)." *BT* 65 (2014): 24–33.

———. "Antiochus IV as the Scorned Prince in Dan 11:21." *VT* 62 (2012): 572–81.

———. "Heliodorus and the Assassination of Seleucus IV according to Dan 11:20 and 2 Macc 3." *JAJ* 7 (2017): 354–84.

———. "Is Daniel 11:1–19 Based on a Ptolemaic Narrative?" *JSJ* 45 (2014): 157–84.

———. "The Milesian Connection: Dan 11:23 and Antiochus IV's Rise to Power." *VT* 63 (2013): 89–98.

———. "Seleucid Coinage in 175–166 BCE and the Historicity of Daniel 11:21–24." *JAH* 2 (2014): 1–36.

———. "The Sons of Seleucus II and the Historicity of Dan 11:10." *VT* 66 (2016): 304–15.

Scolnic, B., and T. Davis. "How *Kittim* Became 'Rome': Dan 11,30 and the Importance of Cyprus in the Sixth Syrian War." *ZAW* 127 (2015): 304–19.

Steinmann, A. E. "Is the Antichrist in Daniel 11?" *BSac* 162 (2005): 195–209.

Swain, J. W. "Antiochus Epiphanes and Egypt." *CP* 39 (1944): 73–94.

Tanner, J. P. "Daniel's 'King of the North': Do We Owe Russia An Apology?" *JETS* 35 (1992): 315–28.

———. "Rethinking Ezekiel's Invasion by Gog." *JETS* 39 (1996): 29–46.

Täubler, E. "Jerusalem 201 to 199 B.C.E.: On the History of a Messianic Movement." *JQR* 37 (1946–1947): 1–30, 125–37, 249–63.

Teeter, A. "Isaiah and the King of As/Syria in Daniel's Final Vision: On the Rhetoric of Inner-Scriptural Allusion and the Hermeneutics of 'Mantological Exegesis.'" In *A Teacher for All Generations: Essays in Honor of James C. VanderKam*, ed. E. F. Mason, S. I. Thomas, A. Schofield, and E. Ulrich, 169–99. Vol. 1. JSJSup 153. Leiden: Brill, 2012.

Thompson, S. "Those Who Are Wise: The *maskilim* in Daniel and the New Testament." In *To Understand the Scriptures: Essays in Honor of W. H. Shea*, ed. D. Merling, 215–20. Berrien Springs, MI: Institute of Archaeology, 1997.

Tsafrir, Y. "The Location of the Seleucid Akra in Jerusalem." *RB* 82 (1975): 501–21.

van der Kooij, A. "A Case of Reinterpretation in the Old Greek of Daniel 11." In *Tradition and Re-interpretation in Jewish and Early Christian Literature*. FS J. C. H. Lebram, ed. J. W. van Henten et al., 72–80. SPB 36. Leiden: Brill, 1986.

———. "The Concept of Covenant (*BERÎT*) in the Book of Daniel." In *The Book of Daniel in the Light of New Findings*, ed. A. S. van der Woude, 495–501. Leuven: Leuven University Press, 1993.

———. "Groups and Parties in Early Judaism: Daniel 11:14 and the Hasideans." *Semitica et Classica* 8 (2015): 45–51.

van der Woude, A. S. "Prophetic Prediction, Political Prognostication, and Firm Belief: Reflections on Daniel 11:40–12:3." In *The Quest for Context and*

Meaning: Studies in Biblical Intertextuality in Honor of James A. Sanders, ed. C. A. Evans and S. Talmon, 63–73. Leiden: Brill, 1997.
van Houwelingen, P. H. R. "Fleeing Forward: The Departure of Christians from Jerusalem to Pella." *WTJ* 65 (2003): 181–200.
Van Kooten, G. H. "The Desecration of 'The Most Holy Temple of all the World' in the 'Holy Land': Early Jewish and Early Christian Recollections of Antiochus' 'Abomination of Desolation.'" In *The Land of Israel in Bible, History, and Theology: Studies in Honour of Ed Noort*, ed. Jacques van Ruiten and J. Cornelis de Vos., 291–316. Leiden: Brill, 2009.
Verheyden, J. "The Flight of the Christians to Pella." *ETL* 66 (1990): 368–84.
Wacholder, B. Z. "The Beginning of the Seleucid Era and the Chronology of the Diadochoi." In *Nourished with Peace: S. Sandmel Memorial*, ed. F. E. Greenspahn et al., 183–220. Chico, CA: Scholars Press, 1984.
Will, E. "The Succession to Alexander." In *Cambridge Ancient History*. Vol. 7, Part 1, 23–61. Cambridge: Cambridge University Press, 1984.

b. Implications for the Jewish remnant living in the days of the Antichrist (12:1–4)

The opening words to Dan 12 ("now at that time") closely link 12:1–4 with the final paragraphs of chap. 11, especially the temporal notice in 11:40, "at the end time." Also, the mention of Michael connects 12:1–4 with chaps. 10–11, since he was first introduced in 10:13. Although critical scholars see a continuation at 12:1 with the period of Antiochus IV, evangelical scholars insist that the proper time period is that of the great tribulation when the antichrist will be active. Hence "the time of distress" in 12:1 is not a reference to the days of the Maccabean revolt but rather to the great tribulation preceding the second coming of Christ. The emphasis of these verses is not upon the details of the great tribulation but rather the outcome of this difficult time, namely the rescue of Daniel's people and more importantly the resurrection of the righteous.

Textual Notes

4.a. MT's יְשֹׁטְטוּ (Poʿlel impf. of שׁוּט) makes for an obscure statement (many will go about or roam about?). *BHS* editor proposes reading יִשְׂטְטוּ (from שׂוּט, "to swerve or fall away"; so Di Lella, 261) or perhaps יָסוּטוּ (MH, "to move about, be unsteady, go astray"; *DTT*, 962). Yet neither of these two verb roots is attested with a duplication of the letter ט. Furthermore, the Greek translations took it quite differently. LXX^{O} has *ἀπομανῶσιν* (aor. pass. subj. of *ἀπομαίνομαι*, "to go mad or recover from madness," perhaps "to rage violently"; cf. Lucian, *Dialogi Deorum*, 12.1), while LXX$^{\theta}$ has διδαχθῶσιν (aor. pass. subj. of *δῐδάσκω*, "to teach)" and hence "until many are taught." Both of these, however, are dependent on their understanding of the final word of v. 4 (see 4.b. below). LXX$^{\theta}$ seems to have chosen the word *δῐδάσκω* in light of הַדָּעַת in the final clause (assuming a logical connection), as there are no Hebrew words similar to שׁוּט translated by *δῐδάσκω* in the LXX. LXX^{O}

(apparently reading הָרָעָה instead of הַדָּעַת) translated יְשֹׁטְטוּ as ἀπομανῶσιν which would yield a translation of the Hebrew: "many will rage violently, and wickedness (or injustice) will increase." Yet שׁוּט is well-attested in the HB (13x, including 5x in the Poʿlel), and has a consistent meaning in the Poʿlel as "go about," or "roam to and fro." The reading יְשֹׁטְטוּ makes very good sense, once the contextual usage of the Poʿlel forms are carefully considered (this will be explained in the translation note to this verse).

4.b. LXX$^{\theta}$ agrees with MT's הַדָּעַת ("knowledge"). LXX^{O}, however, translated the final clause as καὶ πλησθῇ ἡ γῆ ἀδικίας, "and the earth is filled with wickedness (or injustice)," apparently reading הָרָעָה ("evil, misery, wickedness or injustice")—with only a slight emendation—instead of הַדָּעַת. Collins (369) follows LXX^{O}: "evil will increase." Daniel 12 does not occur in the Qumran fragments. Vg. reads *multiplex erit scientia*, in support of MT and LXX$^{\theta}$. For discussion of the complexity of how Jerome's translation was historically understood see Webb.[666] Most Eng. VSS have "knowledge," but note NRSV's "evil shall increase."

Translation

12:1 At that time Michael, the great prince who defends[667] your people,[668] will arise.[669] And there will be a time of distress[670] which has not been *seen* since[671] the nation's beginning[672] until that time. Yet at that time your people will

666. See J. R. Webb, "'Knowledge Will Be Manifold': Daniel 12.4 and the Idea of Intellectual Progress in the Middle Ages," in *History Faculty Publications,* paper 38 (2014), 307–57; accessed 3 May, 2016, online: http://vc.bridgew.edu/cgi/viewcontent.cgi?article=1037&context=history_fac.

667. The ptc. הָעֹמֵד (*hāʿōmēḏ*) with the preposition עַל (*ʿal*)—lit., "who stands over"—can have the sense of "defending, protecting" as in Esth 8:11; 9:16 (so Collins, 390).

668. Lit., "the sons of your people" (בְּנֵי עַמֶּךָ, *bᵊnê ʿammekā*). Yet this is an idiomatic expression that refers to all the Jewish people (e.g., Lev 19:18; Ezek 33:2).

669. Heb. יַעֲמֹד (*yaʿămōḏ*), lit., "will stand," but here in the sense of coming on the scene as was the case with *yaʿămōḏ* in Dan 8:23.

670. The expression "time of distress" (עֵת צָרָה, *ʿēṯ ṣārâ*) is used 8x in the HB. Sometimes this refers to a general time of distress that has come upon the nation (e.g., Neh 9:27). However, there is also a specific eschatological tribulation referred to in Jer 30:7 as "the time of Jacob's distress" (עֵת־צָרָה הִיא לְיַעֲקֹב, *ʿēṯ-ṣārâ hîʾ lᵊyaʿăqōḇ*). The contextual similarities demand our understanding Dan 12:1 in the latter sense.

671. See BDB, 583c 7c for the use of the prep. מִן (*min*) with a temporal force ("since, after").

672. With the inf. const. מִהְיוֹת (*mihyôṯ*) followed by the sg. noun גּוֹי (*gôy*), "nation," the latter could be either the subject or object of the inf. If "nation" is understood as the subject, then this would be a specific reference to Israel (= "since the nation was," i.e., since it began). This is how Goldingay (274), Collins (359), and the NET ("from the nation's beginning") understand the syntax. Goldingay translates, "since

be delivered, *that is*, everyone found written in the book. **2** And many[673] of those who sleep in the dusty[674] ground will awake, some[675] to everlasting[676] life but others to disgrace,[677] to everlasting abhorrence.[678] **3** Those with *spiritual*

---

they became a nation." Others (e.g., Miller, 314), however, would understand "nation" as the object of the inf., which would imply a comparative statement of all nations. Hence, NIV "from the beginning of nations" and NRSV "since nations first came into existence." Either option is possible, but the singular form גּוֹי (*gôy*) gives a slight preference to "nation" as the subject (i.e., Israel), and hence the translation "since the nation's beginning."

673. The interpretation of "many" (רַבִּים, *rabbîm*) depends in part on one's understanding of the following preposition מִן (*min*). G. F. Hasel, "Resurrection in the Theology of Old Testament Apocalyptic," *ZAW* 92 (1980): 267–84, discusses three options for *min*: (1) partitive force, (2) local force, and (3) explicative (or explanatory) sense. He concludes (277–78): "The explicative or explanatory sense would suggest that the 'many' consist of those who are asleep, i.e. all of them. This position is supported with the suggestion that *răbbîm* is here used inclusively in the sense of 'all'. This interpretation takes advantage of the fact that *răbbîm* is not always used with the exclusive sense of 'many' but may mean 'all' in the inclusive sense. The crucial phrase would accordingly mean that all who sleep will awake."

674. Lit., "the ground of dust" (אַדְמַת־עָפָר, *ʾadmaṯ-ʿāp̄ār*), but understanding עָפָר (*ʿāp̄ār*) as a genitive of attribute (hence, "dusty ground"). This is the only occurrence of these two words together. However, the main point in utilizing עָפָר (*ʿāp̄ār*)—in light of the reference to death—is to make an allusion to Gen 3:19 ("for you are dust [*ʿāp̄ār*], and to dust you shall return").

675. Regarding the repetition אֵלֶּה ... אֵלֶּה (*ʾēlleh* ... *ʾēlleh*), see BDB, 41 b: "these ... those." Note Josh 8:22 and Ps 20:8 for the idea "some ... some." In this context, "some ... others" is smoother English. Collins (393) notes, "It has been suggested that ... the construction 'some ... some' (אלה ... אלה) does not indicate a subdivision of the 'many' but contrasts the 'many' with others. It is surely more natural, with most commentators, to see two groups here who awake to contrasting destinies."

676. In the expression לְחַיֵּי עוֹלָם (*lᵉḥayyê ʿôlām*), עוֹלָם (*ʿôlām*) is a genitive of attribute = "everlasting life."

677. Even though there is no conjunction between לַחֲרָפוֹת (*laḥărāp̄ôṯ*) and לְדִרְאוֹן (*lᵉḏirʾôn*), there is no reason to regard the former as a gloss on the latter, as the *BHS* editor has proposed (and hence suggests deleting). Neither LXX tradition had a problem with this, but simply supplied καὶ (*kai*, "and") in their translation.

678. דֵּרָאוֹן (*dērāʾôn*) occurs elsewhere only in Isa 66:24 (where it apparently depicts the wicked in eternal fire). Both BDB (201b) and *HALOT* (230) give the lexical meaning "abhorrence."

insight[679] will shine like the brightness[680] of the *heavenly* firmament,[681] and those who turn the many to righteousness as the stars forever and ever. **4** But

679. "Those with spiritual insight" is an attempt to render the Hip῾il ptc. הַמַּשְׂכִּלִים (*hammaśkilîm*). Basically, the word means "be prudent," but see BDB, 968c3, for the nuance in the Hip῾il "have insight, comprehension." Other than the NASB ("those who have insight"), most Eng. VSS translate as "the wise." The same word was used in Dan 9:22 of the angel who had come to Daniel in order to *give him insight*. Also note the use of שָׂכַל (*śāḵal*) in Dan 11:33, 35; 12:10. If the translation "wise" is preferred, it must be understood that they are wise as a result of following God's Word and gaining spiritual insight from it.
680. The Heb. involves a cognate accusative: יַזְהִרוּ כְּזֹהַר (*yazhirû kᵊzōhar*), based on the root זהר (*zhr*, "to shine"). The idea is that "They will shine like the sheen of the *heavenly* firmament" (cf. Montgomery, 471). Contrast Charles (330) who argued that *zōhar* was the result of dittography and should be deleted. A. Wolters, "*Zōhar hārāqîa῾* (Daniel 12.3) and Halley's Comet," *JSOT* 61 (1994): 111–20, attempted to argue that the term *zōhar* should not be understood as "brightness" (so BDB, 264) but rather as a reference to a specific luminary, which he considers to be Halley's Comet. Despite his attempt to marshal evidence in support of his thesis, the only other biblical use of *zōhar* (Ezek 8:2) does not mean a specific luminary. Furthermore, the term *zōhar* is found at least five times in the Qumran sectarian MSS with the meaning "splendor, radiance" (4Q262 Frag. B, Frag. 1:4; 4Q286 Frag 1, ii:3 and ii:4; 4Q287 Frag. 2:5; and 4Q301 Frag. 4:4).
681. The word הָרָקִיעַ (*hārāqîa῾*), translated here "expanse," is the same word used in Gen 1:6–8 ("And God called the expanse heaven"). In Ps 19:1 we read, "The heavens are telling of the glory of God; and their expanse (הָרָקִיעַ, *hārāqîa῾*) is declaring the work of His hands." So the "expanse" is the visible part of the heavens showcasing the heavenly stars and celestial bodies. The word "heavenly" has been added in my translation to bring this out.

you, Daniel, close up these words and seal up the book until the end time. Many will go about[682] *seeking to understand*, and knowledge[683] will increase.

Commentary

12:1 The angel Michael had previously been introduced in 10:13 (see comments there). He is the archangel who has special responsibility for overseeing and protecting the Jewish people (cf. Jude 9). He is said to "arise,"

682. Although some prefer to emend the text (see textual note above), the reading יְשֹׁטְטוּ (*yᵉšōṭᵉṭû*, Poʿlel impf. of שׁוּט, *šûṭ*) is preferred, as is the final word of the sentence, הַדָּעַת (*haddāʿaṯ*, "knowledge"). Although יְשֹׁטְטוּ (*yᵉšōṭᵉṭû*)—"to go about, roam about"—may at first seem awkward in the context, careful study of the four other occurrences of שׁוּט (*šûṭ*) in the Poʿlel stem are insightful (cf. 2 Chr 16:9; Jer 5:1; Amos 8:12; Zech 4:10). Contextually, all involve "going about" for the purpose of observing or seeking insight. Especially helpful is Amos 8:12: "they shall run to and fro, to seek the word of the LORD, but they shall not find it" (ESV). For this reason, the words "seeking to understand" have been added (in italics) to my translation. Hence, Dan 12:4a speaks of the book being closed up until the end time, and then anticipating many who will go about seeking to gain an understanding of what had been revealed to Daniel.

683. Regarding the definite article on הַדָּעַת (*haddāʿaṯ*), it is not unusual for a non-material virtue to be expressed with the article. Compare הַחָכְמָה (*haḥoḵmâ*, "wisdom") in 1 Kgs 7:14. Hence, this is not to be translated "the knowledge." Cf. *IBHS*, 245–46 (§13.5.1g) regarding the article on abstract terms and attributes (e.g., "faithfulness" in Isa 11:5, הָאֱמוּנָה, *hāʾĕmûnâ*). D. W. Thomas, "Note on הַדָּעַת in Daniel XII.4," *JTS* 6 (1955): 226, has argued that הַדָּעַת (*haddāʿaṯ*) in Dan 12:4—supposedly from a second root *yāḏaʿ*, cognate with Arabic *waduʿa* "to be, to become still, quiet, submissive," does not mean "knowledge" but rather "humiliation," and this suggestion has been subsequently defended by J. Day, "*Daʿaṯ* 'Humiliation' in the Light of Isaiah LIII 3 and Daniel XII 4, and the Oldest Known Interpretation of the Suffering Servant," *VT* 30 (1980): 97–103. Yet Day's defense of the translation "humiliation" is dependent on his assumption that the verse has persecution in view. He writes (99), "it may be noted that Thomas's translation of *haddāʿaṯ* as 'humiliation' enables us to make excellent sense of the preceding words *yᵉšōṭᵉṭū rabbīm* 'many shall run to and fro', which would very naturally refer to the panic and fleeing in the face of the persecution, but were never quite satisfactorily resolved by commentators who understood *haddāʿaṯ* here to mean 'knowledge'." The weakness to Day's argument, however, is that of the 13x that the verb שׁוּט (*šûṭ*) is used in the HB, it is never used elsewhere of "panic and fleeing" in a context of persecution. Furthermore, Thomas' appeal to Arabic *waduʿa* has been refuted by W. Johnstone, "*ydʿ* II, 'be humbled, humiliated'?," *VT* 41 (1991): 49–62, and the suggested "humiliation" theory is rejected by J. A. Emerton, "A Further Consideration of D. W. Thomas's Theories about *yādaʿ*," in *Studies on the Language and Literature of the Bible*, ed. G. Davies and R. Gordon, 101–16 (Leiden: Brill, 2015).

suggesting that he *steps up to take action* at this time.[684] The Hebrew word translated "will arise" (יַעֲמֹד, *ya ʿămōḏ*)—normally "stand"—can be used in the sense of arising to confront another in hostile fashion (cf. 2 Kgs 18:28; Isa 50:8). Given the eschatological context of this verse, this may have reference to Rev 12:7–12 involving a colossal battle scene in heaven between Michael and his angels on the one hand and Satan and his evil angels on the other. The victory of Michael and his angels results in the expulsion of Satan and his angels from heaven. Revelation 12:12 indicates that it is this defeat of Satan that propels him to unleash his wrath on the earth: "He is filled with terrible anger, for he knows that he only has a little time." A careful study of the context of Rev 12 (note esp. vv. 13–14) suggests that Satan's expulsion from heaven occurs at the beginning of the great tribulation, and that he has 1260 days (= "time, times, and half a time") remaining, i.e., until he is personally defeated at the return of Christ.

That the great tribulation is in view is confirmed by the reference in Dan 12:1 to "the time of distress."[685] (Goldingay, 306, is correct in pointing out that "the 'time of trouble' is thus a resumptive summary reference to the troubles of 11:40–45, not a new event.") The Jewish people have experienced many *distressful times* in their long history, but this will be unlike any other. In fact, v. 1 further stipulates that it will be unlike any that has "been *seen* since the nation's beginning until that time." Jesus' prediction of the great tribulation in Matt 24:21 is so strikingly similar to the Greek Septuagint translation of Dan 12:1 that he must assuredly have had this verse in mind when he predicted the great tribulation that would precede his second coming. During this time, Satan's special hatred of both Christians and Jews will be unleashed. The Bible has much to say about Israel's sufferings at this time, referred to elsewhere as "the time of Jacob's distress" (Jer 30:7; cf. Deut 4:25–31; Zech 13:7–9). One thing that is clear from a study of these passages and the book of Revelation is that many will be martyred. From the divine perspective, however, this suffering of Israel serves a good purpose, namely to bring the nation that has long rejected her Messiah to her knees, until finally she looks (in faith) to the One whom she had pierced and embraces him as Messiah (cf. Zech 12:10).

After undergoing this deep time of distress—the great tribulation—Israel will finally experience God's deliverance: "at that time your own people will

---

684. See BDB, 764b 6a for the nuance "arise, appear, come on the scene." Collins (390) notes, "In post-exilic Hebrew, עמד is often used as a synonym for קום in the sense of 'come on the scene' (cf. notably CD 20:1: עד עמוד משיח מאהרון ומישראל, 'until a messiah arise from Aaron and one from Israel')." See Dan 8:23 for a similar example.

685. A. E. Gardner, "The Way to Eternal Life in Dan 12:1e–2 or How to Reverse the Death Curse of Genesis 3," *ABR* 40 (1992): 14, has concluded, "It is likely that the time of trouble in Dan 12: 1 should be understood as the Day of the Lord in that it is described as being 'such as there never was, since there was a nation unto that time.'"

be delivered." The word translated "be delivered" (יִמָּלֵט, *yimmālēṭ*) is the same word used in Joel 2:32 to speak of the nation's eschatological deliverance. The verb is in the passive voice, indicating what is done for her (not that she delivers herself). Yet there is a precondition for this deliverance, although it is not indicated in Dan 12. Other passages clarify that Israel must first repent and embrace the Lord Jesus as her Messiah (not every single individual but a turning to him at a national level). Zechariah 12–14, for instance, speaks about both the national repentance and the deliverance of Israel (cf. Joel 2:28–32). Zechariah 14:2–4 indicates that this divine deliverance occurs when the nation is at the brink of annihilation. This is the national salvation of Israel referred to in Rom 11:25–27, when at long last the nation's hardening of heart is lifted and she is brought into the bond of the new covenant.

This national deliverance, however, does not extend to every single member of the nation who remains alive until the end of the Tribulation. Rather it is for "everyone found written in the book." This is most likely a reference to the "book of life" which contains a list of the names of all the righteous belonging to God (cf. Exod 32:32–33; Ps 69:28; Isa 4:3; Luke 10:20; Phil 4:3; Rev 3:5; 20:12, 15).[686] Revelation 20:15 indicates that anyone not having their name in the book of life will be thrown into "the lake of fire."

12:2 Not all will live to see God's great deliverance at the end of the tribulation. Many of the righteous will perish in this tribulation, and scores of others will have died in preceding ages.[687] Yet for all Daniel's people who were truly numbered among "the righteous" (having a faith like unto Abraham in Gen 15:6), God will resurrect "the many."[688] (This is not to say, however, that *this*

---

686. So Collins (391). He adds, "A close parallel to this idea is found in the *Book of the Heavenly Luminaries* (4QDibHam), which was found at Qumran but is older than the Essene settlement. There a prayer similar to that in Daniel 9 concludes by asking God to 'deliver thy people Israel ... every man who is inscribed in the Book of Life.' 4QDibHam is dated by its editor to the mid-second century B.C.E. and may well be older than Daniel." Not all evangelical scholars agree that "the book" mentioned in Dan 12:1 is "the book of life." For discussion, see C. R. Smith, "The Book of Life," *GTJ* 6 (1985): 219–30. He argues (224) that in the OT passages in which names are mentioned or persons are in view (Exod 32:32–33; Ps 69:28; Isa 4:3; Ezek 13:9; and Dan 12:1), "the reference is to those who are the slated recipients of covenantal blessings," not necessarily *eternal life*, though he concedes that Dan 12:1 might be an exception.

687. Critical scholars often assume that "the many" is a reference to the Jews who have died in the Seleucid persecutions of Antiochus IV; so J. M. Lindenberger, "Daniel 12:1–4," *Int* 39 (1985): 183.

688. The word "many" ("many ... will awake") need not be understood to be too restrictive. Baldwin (225–26) explains, "Hebrew *rabbîm* 'many', tends to mean 'all', as in Deuteronomy 7:1; Isaiah 2:2, where 'all nations' becomes 'many peoples' in the parallel verse 3; and in Isaiah 52:14, 15; 53:11, 12, where this key-word occurs no fewer

resurrection is limited to Daniel's people, though the primary focus of this passage is upon them.) The term "sleep" is used frequently in Scripture as a euphemism for "death" (cf. John 11:11–14; Acts 7:60; 1 Cor 15:51; 1 Thess 4:13).[689] Correspondingly, the term "awake" (קִיץ, *qîṣ*) is used figuratively of resurrection, just as in Isa 26:19:[690]

than five times, with an inclusive significance. .... The emphasis is not upon many as opposed to all, but rather on the numbers involved." (Cf. the translation note at v. 2 for "many.") For a more thorough study of resurrection in early Jewish sources (including Daniel, nineteen writings from the Apocrypha and Pseudepigrapha, the Qumran Scrolls, the Septuagint, Philo, Josephus, the early rabbinic traditions, and the corpus of inscriptions from Israel and the diaspora), see H. C. C. Cavallin, *Life After Death: Paul's Argument for the Resurrection of the Dead in 1 Cor 15*, Part 1, *An Enquiry into the Jewish Background*, ConBNT 7 (Lund: CWK Gleerup, 1974); and J. F. Hobbins, "Resurrection in the Daniel Tradition and Other Writings at Qumran," in *The Book of Daniel: Composition and Reception*, ed. J. J. Collins and P. W. Flint, 2:395–420 (Leiden: Brill, 2001). For the period under consideration, Cavallin concludes that there is no uniform Jewish doctrine about life after death. Significantly, he finds (200) on the basis of his inductive study that statements positing an immortality of the soul which excludes the resurrection of the body are almost as common as those which explicitly state the resurrection of the body.

689. Collins (392) points out that the terms "sleep" and "awake" are also used for resurrection in the Pseudepigrapha and later tradition (e.g., *1 En.* 91:10; 92:3). Cf. J. F. A. Sawyer, "Hebrew Words for the Resurrection of the Dead," *VT* 23 (1973): 223–24. Sawyer notes (220) that the "technical term for the resurrection of the dead תחִיַּת המתים does not occur in Biblical Hebrew, but is attested 4x in the Mishna and 41x in the Talmud." He does conclude that both Dan 12:2 and Isa 26:19 are references to resurrection.

690. For a convincing defense of physical resurrection in Isa 26:19, see Hasel, "Resurrection in the Theology of Old Testament Apocalyptic." In regard to Isa 26:19, M. S. Moore, "Resurrection and Immortality: Two Motifs Navigating Confluent Streams in the Old Testament (Dan 12,1–4)," *TZ* 39 (1983): 26, reasons, "... this text posits a deliberate contrast between the wicked dead (26,14) and 'thy dead' (26,19). Logic demands that if one is to speak of the raising of the righteous dead in 26,19 as an Ezekiel-type metaphor for national restoration, then the wicked dead in 26,14 must be only metaphorically dead (cf. Ez 27,11). But if one agrees that the wicked dead in 26,14 are, in fact, the dead shades who inhabit Sheol (established via the parallel with *r^ephāʾîm*), then must not the righteous dead in 26,19 have been promised a physical resurrection?"

> Your dead will come back to life; your corpses will rise up. Wake up (הָקִ֫יצוּ, *hāqîṣû*) and shout joyfully, you who live in the ground. (NET)[691]

Baldwin (225) explains, "The reason for using 'sleep' here as a metaphor for 'die' is that sleep is a temporary state from which we normally awake, and so the reader is prepared for the thought of resurrection." Miller (316) wisely clarifies, though, that "sleep" refers to physical death *only* and does not imply an intermediate state that one passes through:

> When the spirit of the believer leaves the body, there is no intermediate state; rather, the spirit goes directly into the presence of the Lord (cf. 2 Cor 5:8; Phil 1:21–23). Likewise, when the spirit of an unbeliever departs, it goes immediately to a place of conscious torment (cf. Luke 16:22ff.). Daniel 12:2 lends no support to the theories of some groups that persons who die are annihilated or experience "soul sleep."

This verse in Daniel is regarded as the clearest reference (perhaps the closest to an undisputed one) in all the Old Testament to the doctrine of resurrection (cf. Job 19:26; Ps 17:15).[692] The "dusty ground" (אַדְמַת־עָפָר, *'aḏmaṯ-'āp̄ār*)—literally, "ground (or earth) of dust," a figurative expression for the

691. D. P. Bailey, "The Intertextual Relationship of Daniel 12:2 and Isaiah 26:19: Evidence from Qumran and the Greek Versions," *TynBul* 51 (2000): 305–8, argues that the author of Dan 12:2 has deliberately drawn his terms from the text of Isa 26:19. He contends that the correct reading in Isa 26:19 is not הקיצו (*hāqîṣû*, Hip'il impv.) as appears in the MT, but rather יקיצו (*yāqîṣû*, Hip'il impf.) as found in 1QIsa[a]. He comes to this conclusion as a result of examining the relationship between the Hebrew and Greek texts and the various translations of the Hebrew verbs in the LXX. In so doing, he finds support for Hengel's thesis about the popularity of a Qumran text-type underlying the book of Daniel; see M. Hengel, "Zur Wirkungsgeschichte von Jes 53 in vorchristlicher Zeit," in *Der leidende Gottesknecht: Jesaja 53 und seine Wirkungsgeschichte*, ed. B. Janowski and P. Stuhlmacher, FAT 14 (Tübingen: Mohr Siebeck, 1996), 49–91.

692. Despite what most would regard as clear in Dan 12:2, there are dissenters. Hill (206) points out that "Seow, 187, understands the verse as 'a metaphor for the restoration of the people of Israel after a time of destruction ... using the imagery of resurrection to convey hope in the revival of the Jewish people after a history of suffering and death.' Lucas, 294, however, finds this position untenable given the references to 'everlasting life' and 'everlasting contempt.'" Numerous older dispensationalists have rejected the idea of physical resurrection in Dan 12:2 in favor of Israel's national restoration. These include J. N. Darby, W. Kelly, A. C. Gaebelein, and H. A. Ironside; see J. F. Walvoord, "Contemporary Problems: The Resurrection of Israel," *BSac* 124 (1967): 6, for discussion. Walvoord (7) points out the fallacy of their view, in that the text also speaks of those awakened to everlasting contempt (which for premillennialists does not occur at the same time as Israel's restoration).

grave—reminds the reader that though God once judged man in the garden ("for you are dust [*ʿāp̱ār*], and to dust you shall return"), his grace of resurrection will reverse this—at least for the righteous who inherit "everlasting life." The connection of Dan 12:2 with Gen 3 is so strong that Gardner claims, "In the case of Dan 12:2 it will be shown that the core text is Genesis 3 where mankind is condemned to death and denied access to the tree of life while Dan 12:1 centres upon who will be saved upon the Day of the Lord."[693] This connection is even more obvious when reading the Hebrew text of Gen 3:19:

> until you return to <u>the earth</u> (הָאֲדָמָה, *hā ʾăḏāmâ*), for out of it you were taken;
> for dust you are, and to dust (עָפָר, *ʿāp̱ār*) you shall return.

Based on this observation, Gardner (6) points out: "It is noteworthy that here 'earth' precedes 'dust' as in Dan 12:2. Sleeping in the earth of dust and then awakening from it in Dan 12:2 suggests that Daniel is alluding to a reversal of the death pronouncement of Gen 3:19."

Dan 12:1–2, then, reveals that at the end of the Great Tribulation, God will bring about deliverance for Israel, following which there will be a resurrection of the dead. Though v. 2 does have bodily resurrection in view, this also stands as the culmination of other "resurrection-like" stories seen earlier in chaps. 3 and 6. Goswell explains:

> … the resurrection doctrine in 12:1–3 is framed in terms that pick up significant features of the earlier stories of dramatic rescue: Dan 12 involves the agency of an angelic figure (Michael), recounts another super-natural "deliverance," focuses on the experience of the "wise" who are God's "servants," picks up the motif of "falling," concerns the fate of the very good and the very bad, and includes a promotion to a higher position of authority. These thematic connections across the generic divide of chapters

---

Similarly, C. Armerding, "Dan 12:1–3: Asleep in the Dust," *BSac* 121 (1964): 153–58, also objected to the idea that physical resurrection is in view in Dan 12:2, opting instead for a *spiritual awakening* of the Jewish people. In defense of this, he writes (156), "The Hebrew word for sleep (*yashen*) which occurs in Daniel 12:2 is not the usual word for the sleep (*shakab*) of death which occurs in such passages as 1 Kings 2:10; 11:21, 43, *et al.* The word *shakab* is used about forty times in the Old Testament with reference to the physically dead. The word *yashen* is never so used in the historical books of the Old Testament." Yet his argument is not convincing. Of the 9x that יָשֵׁן (*yāšēn*) is used in the OT, it always refers to awakening from physical sleep. So for Armerding's argument to be consistent, he would have to insist on that meaning in Dan 12:2, but obviously awakening from physical sleep is not in view, as even Armerding himself acknowledges. Hence, this is a unique usage of the verb (figurative), and physical resurrection cannot be so readily dismissed.

693. Gardner, "The Way to Eternal Life in Dan 12:1e–2 or How to Reverse the Death Curse of Genesis 3," 1.

> 1–6 and 7–12 assist the reader's perception of the high degree of theological unity within the book of Daniel as a canonical whole.[694]

Verse 2 is not intended to provide a detailed description of God's plan for resurrection. A careful study of the New Testament (esp. Rev 20) indicates that not all are resurrected at the same time. The righteous are resurrected after the great tribulation but preceding the millennial reign of Christ, whereas the unrighteous of all ages are resurrected following the millennial kingdom at an event known as the great white throne judgment (Rev 20:5, 11–15).[695] Daniel 12:2 is simply declaring the fact of resurrection. Those who are resurrected to "everlasting life" are obviously the righteous, and they are the ones who are resurrected at this time, i.e., at the conclusion of the great tribulation.[696] The point in raising the righteous dead at the conclusion of the great tribulation (but not the unrighteous) is to allow the righteous dead of all ages to be present for and to participate in the millennial reign of Christ. But for others, their resurrection (after Christ's millennial reign) will be one of "shame" and "everlasting abhorrence" when they are made to appear before God to be judged for their wickedness and are subsequently consigned to the lake of fire.

12:3 In v. 3 a special promise is held out for "those with *spiritual* insight" and "those who turn the many to righteousness." The parallelism of this verse suggests that these commendations refer to the same people. "Those with spiritual insight" is a translation of a single word in Hebrew, the ptc. הַמַּשְׂכִּלִים (*hammaśkilîm*), from שָׂכַל (*śāḵal*). In the Hip'il stem it means "to have insight or comprehension" and was used in 9:22 of the *spiritual insight* that the angel Gabriel brought to Daniel. The same word was also used in 11:33 of the spiritual insight that some were able to offer to others in the nation during the time of the Maccabean persecution, thereby encouraging and strengthening them. Hence, they are "wise" (the translation used in most Eng. VSS) because they have set their minds on the Word of God and have learned to apply it to life's situations, especially in times of crisis. By their instruction they help bring many to righteousness, i.e., they instruct them about God's way of being righteous and point them to Messiah Jesus in

---

694. G. Goswell, "Resurrection in the Book of Daniel," *ResQ* 55 (2013): 151.

695. The typical dispensational position is that the righteous of the "church" have a separate resurrection from national Israel, the former being prior to Daniel's seventieth week (in a pretribulational rapture) and the latter at the end of the tribulation. For discussion, see Walvoord, "Contemporary Problems: The Resurrection of Israel," 3–15. Yet there is nothing in the details of Dan 12:2 that would be incompatible with a post-tribulational view of the rapture.

696. Interestingly the LXX translation of "everlasting life" is ζωὴν αἰώνιον, *zōēn aiōnion*, the same Greek phrase used for everlasting life in John 3:16 and numerous other NT passages (cf. *1 En.* 15:4; *Pss. of Sol.* 3:1).

whom one is made righteous by faith.[697] In light of the contextual focus on the great tribulation, this may have the 144,000 Jewish believers in view (cf. Rev 7:4; 14:1–5). As a result of these commendable actions, these believers will shine like the starry hosts of heaven. This looks at their state of elevation in the Lord's kingdom following the present age, in what can be termed a *humiliation/exaltation motif*. Though they may have suffered in the flesh (some even as martyrs), their hope is in being resurrected and thereby vindicated and exalted.

In the parable of the wheat and tares, the Lord Jesus clearly alluded to this verse as he described the fate of the wicked and the righteous at the end of the age (see Matt 13:43). The imagery of them shining like the stars in the heavenly firmament probably looks at the glory these resurrected righteous ones will have in the Lord's kingdom (cf. 1 Cor 15:40–42)—a glory they will enjoy not merely temporarily but "forever and ever."

12:4 At this point, the revelation of what awaited Daniel's people in the "end time" stops. Daniel is told to "close up these words" and "seal up the book until the time of the end." Presumably the "words" (הַדְּבָרִים, *haddᵊḇārîm*) and the "book" (הַסֵּפֶר, *hassēper*) refer to one and the same thing. If so, then the "book" is probably not a reference to "the book" mentioned in v. 1 that has the names of those destined to experience the Lord's deliverance (see above; the "book of life"). But is the "book" a reference to the entire book of Daniel (so Montgomery, 473) or only to what has been revealed in the final vision?[698] In support of the latter, we observe the way the angel introduced his revelation to Daniel in the final vision (see 10:11: "Understand the words (דְּבָרִים, *dᵊḇārîm*) which I am about to say to you"; and 10:21: "I will tell you what is inscribed in the reliable writing" (בִּכְתָב אֱמֶת, *biḵtāḇ ʾĕmeṯ*). Verse 4 seems to apply primarily to these matters that have been revealed in this final vision—matters affecting Daniel's people at the time of the end, that is, in the great tribulation. Yet Goldingay (309) extrapolates from this a principle in regard to the whole book: "Though 'these words' and 'the book' that records them denote the message(s) of the man in linen recorded in 10:11–12:3, placing this vision at the end of Daniel hints at applying them to the book as a whole."

The greater question is what 12:4a is saying about "these words"/"the book." Is it saying that this material is to be "preserved" or "kept secret"? The word translated "seal up" (from Heb. חָתַם, *ḥāṯam*) can mean to authenticate

697. Lacocque (230) has suggested that the influence of the *maśkilîm* is not one of instruction but making the "many" righteous by their death, i.e., by their martyrdom, which is propitiatory. Collins (393) has responded, "It is simpler, however, to suppose that the *maśkilîm* make the common people righteous by instructing them, and so that instruction rather than martyrdom is the means of justification."

698. The term "books" (סְפָרִים, *sᵊp̄ārîm*) was used in Dan 9:1 in reference to books of the Bible, and the book of Jeremiah in particular.

a decree or transaction (e.g., 1 Kgs 21:8; Jer 32:10). Some would conclude from this that the words of this book are to be *preserved* until the time of the end, just as ancient scrolls were "sealed" for the purpose of making a preserved record. Miller, for example, argues that the admonition in Dan 12:4 concerned the preservation of the document, not its being kept "secret" (so Hill, 207). He states (320),

> In the ancient Near east the custom was to "seal" an important document by impressing upon it the identifying marks of the parties involved and the recording scribe. A sealed text was not to be tampered with or changed. Then the original document was duplicated and placed ("closed up") in a safe place where it could be preserved.

Wood (320), who also defends the notion of preserving the record, even uses the word "preserve" in his translation of the first clause: "preserve the words and seal the book until the time of the end." The problem with this, however, is that the word that Wood translates as "preserve" (Heb. סָתַם, *sāṯam*) does not have this lexical meaning. (Neither NASB, NET, NIV, NRSV, ESV, or NKJV translates *sāṯam* as "preserve.") The verb *sāṯam* is used 13 times in the Hebrew Bible and means either "stop up" (for example, a water well, Gen 26:15), "to keep hidden" (Ps 51:8 [Eng. 6]), or to "keep secret" (Dan 8:26).[699] Just as springs of water may be closed up, thereby cutting off access to their contents (as in 2 Kgs 3:19), this verse is saying that the understanding of much of the prophetic revelation of the book of Daniel is going to be withheld until the time of the end. Hence, "to close up these words" means to keep their meaning secret.

Miller (320) admits that these two clauses at the beginning of Dan 12:4 are synonymous. If so, then the word חָתַם (*ḥāṯam*)—translated "seal up"—ought to have a similar nuance of meaning to סָתַם (*sāṯam*), and lexically, it does. Not only can *ḥāṯam* mean "authenticate," but it can also mean to "restrict something" (Isa 29:11; Song 4:12) or "keep closed" (Job 14:17). A good example of the "restricted" nuance is Isa 29:11, "The entire vision will be to you like the words of a sealed book, which when they give it to the one who is literate, saying, 'Please read this,' he will say, 'I cannot, for it is sealed'" (NASB).

In conclusion, since *sāṯam* does not mean to "preserve" but to "keep hidden/secret" and since *ḥāṯam* (to "seal up") can have this meaning, the point of Dan 12:4 is that a full understanding of what has been revealed is not going to be possible—at least until God is ready to allow this in the "end time."

This interpretation of withholding full comprehension until the "end time" has two further points in its favor: (1) first, there is a repetition of

---

699. *HALOT* (771) offers two basic definitions for the Qal stem: (1) to stop up the springs of water, disguise; or (2) to shut up words, be aloof, keep secret.

this idea in vv. 8–9 in response to Daniel's struggle to understand and his pleading to know more; and (2) the statement of a reverse command is found at the end of Revelation. In Rev 22:10 the apostle John is told, "Do not seal up the words of the prophecy of this book, for the time is near." In this case, *preservation* is not the idea behind the words "seal up." During the great tribulation, especially as events with the antichrist begin to unfold, this revelation will begin to make greater sense to those who know the Lord Jesus Christ and seek to faithfully follow him and his word. Having said that, this does not mean there is no comprehension of this revelation prior to the great tribulation. At the time Daniel wrote this verse, there was obviously no New Testament. With the first coming of Jesus, the further disclosure of New Testament revelation, and the ministry of the Holy Spirit, we would expect that there is a much greater understanding of the book of Daniel during the church age than could be had in the centuries immediately following its original inscription.

The idea of a hidden or restricted comprehension of the revelation to Daniel also helps to explain the otherwise obscure expression "many will go about" (יְשֹׁטְטוּ רַבִּים, *yᵊšōṭᵊṭû rabbîm*) in the latter part of Dan 12:4. As explained in the translation notes above, the verb יְשֹׁטְטוּ, *yᵊšōṭᵊṭû*, (Poʿlel impf. of שׁוּט, *šûṭ*) is used elsewhere in a context of seeking to observe and gain insight. People will go about trying to gain greater understanding, and yet they will not be able to overcome the fact that the book has been sealed up (at least to some). Nevertheless, the verse ends by stating that "knowledge will increase." Despite the sealing up of the book, in the course of time there will be a fuller comprehension of the prophetic knowledge connected with this final vision.[700] There will be an increase of understanding over time in light of the completion of the Old Testament (Zechariah had not been written at the time Daniel wrote), the teaching ministry of Jesus, and the completion

---

700. The interpretation expressed in this commentary stands in contrast to that of Jerome, who translated the final phrase *multiplex scientia*, indicating the diversity of opinions that would result from trying to read the sealed scroll. Webb, "'Knowledge Will Be Manifold': Daniel 12.4 and the Idea of Intellectual Progress in the Middle Ages," 312, explains: "According to Jerome, many will read this scroll in search of the 'truth of history' (*historiae veritas*), that is, its fulfillment in history, either in connection to events that have already come to pass or, more importantly, those yet to come. Their opinions will diverge greatly 'on account of the magnitude of the obscurity' of the vision. For Jerome, the *scientia* in Dan 12.4 was not objective truth or reality, but rather the interpretations and opinions that would be drawn from the prophetic message." In contrast to Jerome, Webb (309) explains that Gregory the Great "saw the passage as signifying the gradual increase from generation to generation of knowledge of divine matters."

of the New Testament Scriptures.[701] The clearest understanding will apparently come in the "end time" (i.e., during the great tribulation) when the antichrist is actively reigning. The statement, "many will go about *seeking to understand*" may, then, primarily refer to those who are in rebellion against God and do not have "ears to hear" (cf. Mark 4:21–22). If so, this would be parallel to Jesus' statement to his disciples: "To you it has been granted to know the mysteries of the kingdom of heaven, but to them it has not been granted" (Matt 13:11 NASB). Rather, "while seeing they do not see."

Biblical Theology Comments

Even though critical scholars generally agree that bodily resurrection is taught in Dan 12:2, there is considerable debate as to how extensively resurrection is revealed in the Old Testament and when such belief emerged.[702] Hill (205) summarizes the tension in this discussion:

> The extent to which the Hebrews had any understanding of life after death during OT times is a topic of considerable debate. The minimalist position denies any hope of afterlife among the Hebrews in OT times. The maximalist view reads a full-orbed doctrine of afterlife into the OT on the basis of the NT report that Abraham believed God could raise Isaac from the dead if necessary (Heb 11:19).

Addressing this topic, Smick underscores the skepticism of many when he writes, "The consensus of critical opinion still insists that emergent belief in the resurrection of the dead was a thing unattested in the literature of preexilic Israel."[703] Hence, an acknowledgment by critical scholars affirming bodily resurrection being expressed and believed in Dan 12:2 is essentially a denial of such belief prior to the second century BC.[704] To this, Bronner

701. Baldwin (228) points out how Jesus would sometimes teach kingdom truth in parables (e.g., Matt 13:14–15) and, in so doing, much that was of value was kept hidden from those who rejected him as Messiah.

702. For an introductory discussion concerning death, the afterlife, and resurrection in the OT, see W. Dyrness, *Themes in Old Testament Theology* (Downers Grove, IL: InterVarsity, 1979), 237–42; and B. K. Waltke, *An Old Testament Theology* (Grand Rapids: Zondervan, 2007), 964–69 ("Appendix IV: Realm of the Dead").

703. E. Smick, "The Bearing of New Philological Data on the Subjects of Resurrection and Immortality in the Old Testament," *WTJ* 31 (1969): 12.

704. G. W. E. Nickelsburg, in his comprehensive study of resurrection, *Resurrection, Immortality, and Eternal Life in Intertestamental Judaism*, HTS 26 (Cambridge, MA: Harvard University Press, 1972; expanded ed., 2007), assumes the position of critical scholarship of a second-century BC dating for Daniel and thus analyzes Dan 12:2 in terms of Antiochus' persecution. P. J. W. Schutte, "The Origin of the Resurrection Idea: A Dialogue with George Nickelsburg," *HTS* 64 (2008): 1076–77, summarizes Nickelsburg's understanding of Dan 12:2 in regard to the oppression of

responds, "We argue that the clear expression of a belief in bodily resurrection as described in Daniel (12:2–4), dated by critical scholarship to the Second Century BCE, could not have emerged spontaneously without significant precursors." Certainly this entails far more than Jesus' defense of the doctrine of resurrection from the text of Exod 3:6. Chase has correctly pointed out, "the logic of Jesus' use of Exod 3:6 suggests that resurrection hope can be present even if explicit expressions are absent."[705] He traces this hope back to God's creating man from the *dust* of the ground, a term that resurfaces later in both Isa 26:19 and Dan 12:2, until this hope becomes much more obvious in Abraham's offering of Isaac.

> Abraham spoke in the plural when he spoke of returning ("come again," *wĕnāšûbāh*). The best explanation of his words is confidence that God would not renege on the promise of multiplying offspring through Isaac. His plural statement, "I and the boy will ... come again to you," was an expression of resurrection faith. ... Isaac's near-death deliverance was a figurative resurrection from the dead! And according to Beale, God's preservation of Abraham's seed through the deliverance of Isaac was a "type" of the future resurrection.[706]

There is certainly a developing expectation of resurrection throughout the Old Testament, beginning with Genesis. The concern mentioned in Gen 3:22 that (sinful) man might take of the tree of life and "live forever"—and which factored into his expulsion from the garden—must surely have played upon the minds of Hebrew thinkers of old. If mankind is kept from the tree of life because eating from it would allow him to live forever, then obviously God must hold the key for man being able to live forever, thus engendering

---

that time: "On Daniel, Nickelsburg (2006:32) concluded that the theology which the book reflects is that of people whose life situation is one of oppression. The Danielic resurrection belief therefore answered a religious need in the Hasidic community in which the Book of Daniel arose. The political backdrop for the origin of this belief in Daniel was the persecutions of Antiochus and the death of many Hasidic Jews. These deaths presented a theological problem because the Jews who died, were those who were obedient to the Torah. Resurrection was the answer to this dilemma. ..."

"For Daniel resurrection was a means by which both the righteous and the wicked dead are enabled to receive their respective vindication or condemnation."

705. M. L. Chase, "The Genesis of Resurrection Hope: Exploring Its Early Presence and Deep Roots," *JETS* 57 (2014): 470.

706. M. L. Chase, "'From Dust You Shall Arise:' Resurrection Hope in the Old Testament," *SBJT* 18 (2014): 14–15. For G. K. Beale, see *A New Testament Biblical Theology: The Unfolding of the Old Testament in the New* (Grand Rapids: Baker Academic, 2011), 320. That Abraham's near-sacrifice of Isaac is a picture or type of resurrection from the dead is verified by the author of Hebrews (Heb 11:19).

hope of life after death that would find fulfillment by resurrection. Chase points out, "The tree of life indicated that another kind of bodily life was possible, a superior and immortal existence,"[707] to which Waltke adds, "This highest potency of life was available in the garden and ... will be experienced consummately in the resurrection of our bodies."[708] Job spoke of a "redeemer" who would establish his innocence after his death (Job 19:23–27). Even God's boast in Deut 32:39, "It is I who put to death and give life," is in this context a claim to being able to raise the dead (in contrast to the powerless idols). Greenspoon clarifies, "Since there is perhaps no other action of God's which displays the totality and uniqueness of His power more forcefully than the process by which He restores His dead to life, a reference to bodily resurrection is surely in keeping with the context at this point."[709] Certainly the psalmist affirmed a strong belief that a deep relationship with God was not something to be terminated at death (Pss 16:9–11; 49:15; 73:23–26). Finally, the hope of national restoration following God's judgment—especially the notion of the people of Israel coming out of their graves—would necessitate their resurrection (cf. Ezek 37:12–13; Hos 6:2).[710]

The revelation made to Daniel about resurrection is admittedly sparse. The exact form of resurrection is not made explicit (cf. 1 Cor 15:35–41; and *2 Bar.* 51:1–3), nor is it made clear if the resurrection state is on earth. Among the Dead Sea Scrolls from Qumran, we find evidence of a belief in the resurrection of the dead.[711] Somewhat noteworthy is a reference to double resurrection; of the righteous and the wicked (and a judgment of the dead) in the Aramaic fragments of *1 Enoch*. Collins (396) notes,

> *1 Enoch* 22 contains a description of the abodes of the spirits of the dead, where they are kept until the day of judgment. The

---

707. Chase, "From Dust You Shall Arise," 16.

708. Waltke, *Old Testament Theology*, 257.

709. L. J. Greenspoon, "The Origin of the Idea of Resurrection," in *Traditions in Transformation: Turning Points in Biblical Faith*, Festschrift to F. M. Cross, ed. B. Halpern and J. D. Levenson, 247–321 (Winona Lake, IN: Eisenbrauns, 1981), 312.

710. Other hints of resurrection are surely to be found in the OT. Hill (205) calls attention to "the statement by Isaiah that 'your dead will live' (Isa 26:19)," and that "both the prophets Elijah and Elisha were miracle workers who brought individuals back to life (cf. 1 Ki 17:19–23; 2 Ki 4:32–35)." Regarding Hos 6:1–2, Chase says of the promise to Israel: "their restoration would be like resurrection from the dead" ("From Dust You Shall Arise," 12).

711. For an overview and brief discussion of relevant passages from Qumran, see Collins (395–98). Critical scholarship has produced abundant literature on the subject of resurrection at Qumran. The problem, however, is that their dating of Daniel in the second century BC leads to erroneous conclusions as to which had more influence on the other, Daniel or other Qumran documents? For conservative scholars, Daniel antedated the Qumran documents by several centuries.

spirits are divided into different chambers. In chap. 27, Enoch sees the place of judgment, where sinners will be judged "before the righteous, for ever, for evermore."

Certainly the doctrine of resurrection was widespread in Judaism by the first century AD, though viewpoints varied from one Jewish sect to another. Acts 23:8 points out, "the Sadducees say that there is no resurrection, nor an angel, nor a spirit, but the Pharisees acknowledge them all" (NASB; cf. Matt 22:23).[712] Yet the New Testament has abundant teaching on bodily resurrection as well as the resurrection for both the righteous and the wicked.[713] Jesus not only taught that he had the authority to grant eternal life but that he also would have the authority to execute judgment on those who would be resurrected from the grave (John 5:24–30). Some would come forth to a resurrection of life and others to a resurrection of judgment (John 5:29).[714]

Concerning the resurrection of the righteous, the question remains as to whether there will be one resurrection event for the righteous or multiple events.[715] The answer to this question depends on one's view of the doctrine of the rapture of the church (1 Thess 4:13–18; 1 Cor 15:50–57), for the rapture by its very nature involves bodily resurrection. Those who hold to a pretribulational view of the rapture would see a resurrection of the "church" before Daniel's seventieth week, and a resurrection of the Old Testament saints and martyred saints of the Tribulation following Christ's return (Rev 20:4–6). Those who hold to a posttribulation view of the rapture (or a prewrath view) would see one general resurrection of the righteous in conjunction with Christ's return for the saints of all time.[716] For those holding a premillen-

712. Regarding possible influences on the Sadducees' theology of resurrection, see P. G. Bolt, "What Were The Sadducees Reading? An Enquiry into the Literary Background of Mark 12:18–23," *TynBul* 45 (1994): 369–94.

713. For a more detailed discussion of the meaning of bodily resurrection, see the series of review articles in *JETS* 33 (1990): F. Beckwith, "Identity and Resurrection: A Review Article," 369–73; G. R. Habermas, "The Recent Evangelical Debate on the Bodily Resurrection of Jesus: A Review Article," 375–78; and, S. McKnight, "The Nature of Bodily Resurrection: A Debatable Issue," 379–82.

714. For helpful treatments of resurrection and judgment in regard to the unrighteous, see R. L. Mayhue, "Hell: Never, Forever, or Just For a While," *MSJ* 9 (1998): 129–45; and D. J. MacLeod, "The Sixth 'Last Thing': The Last Judgment and the End of the World (Rev 20:11–15)," *BSac* 157 (2000): 315–30.

715. For an introductory discussion of the biblical teaching of resurrection and the order of events, see chap. 92 ("Resurrection and Eternal Destiny") in C. C. Ryrie, *Basic Theology* (Chicago: Moody, 1999), 603–9.

716. Regarding resurrection in the prewrath view, see A. Hultberg, "A Case for the Prewrath Rapture," in *Three Views on the Rapture*, 109–54 (Grand Rapids: Zondervan, 2010). In the prewrath view, the rapture (and hence the resurrection of the righteous) takes places in the latter half of Daniel's seventieth week but before

nial theology, there would also be the question of whether or not there is a resurrection—though unmentioned in the New Testament—at the end of the millennium (i.e., for those born during the millennium). Conservative amillennial scholars typically hold to one general resurrection for both the righteous and the wicked in conjunction with Christ's return. Whatever theological position one opts for, this must be made to reconcile with Paul's statement in 1 Cor 15:22–23: "For as in Adam all die, so also in Christ all will be made alive [*i.e., be resurrected*]. But each in his own order: Christ the first fruits, after that those who are Christ's at His coming [*παρουσίᾳ*, *parousiāi*]."

Finally, it is beneficial to consider the contribution the resurrection theme makes to the overall theology of the book of Daniel. Stele has provided the following insights:

> First of all, resurrection contributes to a better understanding of the theme of God's absolute power and sovereignty. Resurrection makes it very apparent that indeed God has absolute sovereignty and power. Not even death can frustrate his plans.
>
> In addition, resurrection contributes to a more advanced comprehension of the kingdom of God theme as presented in the book of Daniel. Without resurrection there cannot be a universal and everlasting kingdom for the "saints of the Most High."
>
> Resurrection also contributes to a better perception of the judgment theme. Resurrection makes it possible to execute judgment and to restore justice not only upon those who are alive but also upon those who are dead. Without resurrection, universal and final judgment is not possible.[717]

Application and Devotional Implications

Dan 12:3 commends those who are "wise" (having *spiritual* insight) and who "turn the many to righteousness." Their future is likened unto brightly shining stars—shining forever and ever. The metaphor of brightly shining stars is an apt way to describe what awaits them. Miller (319) comments, "Just as stars display their beauty and glory in the sky, a bright (glorious) future and a great reward (which includes God's blessings and great honor) awaits those who were wise enough to comprehend and obey spiritual truth and who led others to repent of their sins and live a righteous life." Though this will be especially true of those having "spiritual insight" and who can instruct others in the great tribulation, the principle is true for believers in every age. Baldwin (227) concludes, "Those who lead others to righteousness, then, are

---

the pouring out of God's wrath in the trumpet judgments (i.e., before Rev 8:1; see Hultberg, 144).

717. A. A. Stele, "Resurrection in Daniel 12 and Its Contribution to the Theology of the Book of Daniel" (Ph.D. diss., Andrews University, 1996), 266–67.

those who demonstrate their faith and encourage others to faith, and this the humblest believer can do."

There are multitudes of people in every age who walk in darkness—who don't perceive the spiritual realities around them and who consequently are living in the consequences of their darkened minds. Yet some can be reached for Christ, can be changed by the Holy Spirit, and can go on to walk in newness of life. This verse is essentially a call for those who do understand (who have had their eyes opened and have acquired spiritual understanding) to have compassion on those who have not yet been so blessed. To care about those who are "lost" and to reach out to them in hopes of seeing them come to faith in Christ and go on to live as a "new creation" is what God delights to see happen. Those who do so can be assured of his favor and of enjoying rich spiritual rewards "forever and ever."

4. The Question about the Duration of the "distress" (12:5–7)

The setting beside the banks of the Tigris River now comes back in view (recall 10:4–6), so that the final vision ends where it had begun.[718] Two unidentified individuals are seen standing on each side of the bank. They pose a question for "the man dressed in linen" concerning *how long* it will be until the astonishing things end. Since the preceding context highlighted the "time of distress such as never occurred" followed by the rescue of Daniel's people, the question no doubt pertains to these things.

Textual Notes

5.a-a. LXX^{O} omits the final two words, and so Collins (369) does not include them in his translation. Yet there is no variant reading in the Heb. MSS, and LXX^{θ} includes the words. Their repetition in v. 5 is not sufficient grounds for regarding them as an accidental duplication.

6.a. The MT has the 3ms verb form וַיֹּאמֶר, but the *BHS* editor proposes emending to וָאֹמַר (1cs) in light of LXX^{O}'s εἶπα (1st sg., aor. ind. act. of εἶπον) and similarly Vg. Note, however, that LXX^{θ} has the 3ms form εἶπεν, and S has "they said." Most commentators and Eng. VSS reject the emendation and take

718. Critical scholars raise questions about Dan 12:5–13 as an epilogue to the final vision, asserting that it may have been rearranged or contain later additions. P. L. Redditt, "Calculating the 'Times': Daniel 12:5–13," *PRSt* 25 (1998): 374, for example, concludes, "Dan 12:5–13 constitutes an epilogue to 10:1–12:4 and to the whole book of Daniel as well, but 12:13 was the original conclusion to the vision in 10:1–12:4," then later adds, "A source critical analysis of 10:1–12:13 suggests that the primary narrative was 10:(1)2–20 + 12:1–4a, 13." In his view, vv. 5–12 constitute a later addition (376). He concludes (379) that the author(s) mistakenly held out a false hope to the readers: "Verse 11 probably looked ahead to the fall of the world empires, and v. 12 to the inauguration of God's kingdom, with the righteous dead being resurrected to live in the faithful community" (which he admits never occurred).

the 3ms verb form וַיֹּאמֶר as an *indefinite subject* as in Gen 19:17 ("one said"). So Collins (369), Goldingay (274), and Di Lella (274). Cf. GKC, 460 (§144d).

7.a-a. The *BHS* editor proposes transposing from יַד נַפֵּץ to נַפֵּץ יַד. His proposal also involves repointing the verb from a Pi'el inf. const. (נַפֵּץ) to a Qal ptc. (נֹפֵץ). This would change the translation from "when the shattering of the power of the holy people is completed" to "when the power of the one who shatters the holy people has been exhausted" (so NET) or "at the end of the power of the shatterer of the holy people" (so Collins, 369). In support of the transposition is LXX^{O}'s word order (ἡ συντέλεια χειρῶν ἀφέσεως, "the consummation of the hands/power *for* release." However, MT's וּכְכַלּוֹת נַפֵּץ יַד־עַם־קֹדֶשׁ makes sense, and there is no need to change the word order (though one could legitimately repoint the verb from נַפֵּץ to a Qal ptc. נֹפֵץ, "one who shatters").

Translation

12:5 Then I, Daniel, looked and behold, two others were standing, one on this[719] bank of the river[720] and the other on that bank of the river. **6** One said to the man dressed in linen who was above[721] the waters of the river, "How long *will it be until* the end of *these* astonishing things?"[722] **7** Then I heard the man dressed in linen who was above the waters of the river, as He raised His right hand and His left to heaven and swore by Him who lives forever,

---

719. Regarding the construction הֵנָּה לְ ... הֵנָּה לְ (*hēnnâ lᵉ ... hēnnâ lᵉ*), see BDB (244d a[β]) = "*on this side* of ... *on that side* of ... ."

720. In the opening scene of the vision (Dan 10:4), Daniel was beside the river Tigris. In that instance, the term for river was נָהָר (*nāhār*). Daniel now sees two men by the bank of the river, but the term is יְאֹר (*yᵉʾōr*). Although the later term is frequently used of the Nile specifically, we do find it in the Qumran sectarian documents of a stream in general (so 4Q286 Frag 5:10 and 4Q381 Frag 1:4; cf. Isa 33:21). Hence, J. Peters', "Hellenistic Imagery and Iconography in Daniel 12.5–13," *JSP* 19 (2009): 129, suggestion that "the use of היאר of 12.5 may be recalling the immediately preceding historical résumé that places much of the action in Egypt" is rather unlikely. There is no reason to read the Nile of Egypt into this context. Also, there is no reason to assert (as Collins does, 399) that the reference in Dan 12:5 is to the Euphrates.

721. Rather than translating מַעַל (*maʿal*) "above," Goldingay (274) renders this "who was further upstream" (similarly Di Lella, 274). Collins (369) omits the phrase in v. 6 but translates the same phrase in v. 7, "who was further up by the waters of the river." Yet of the 27 times that *maʿal* occurs with the prep. מִן (מִמַּעַל, *mimmaʿal*), it always means "above, over, on top." Most all Eng. VSS translate "above," except for the NRSV ("who was upstream").

722. The word הַפְּלָאוֹת (*happᵉlāʾôt*), from פֶּלֶא (*peleʾ*), means "a wonder, something extraordinary or astonishing." See BDB (810c 2) for the nuance of "wonder" as applied to God's acts of judgment and redemption.

that *it would be* for a time,[723] times and half *a time*. When the shattering[724] of the power[725] of the holy people has been completed, all these things will be finished.

Commentary

12:5–6 Two unidentified individuals are seen standing on each side of the bank. One of them poses a question to the man clothed in linen, the same glorious one whom Daniel had seen in 10:4–6 and most likely the Lord Jesus Christ. The question has to do with the end of "*these* astonishing things." In the Hebrew text this is just one word (הַפְּלָאוֹת, *happᵊlāʾôṯ*), which means "things which are incredible, hard to imagine or believe." In this context it refers to the astonishing things that were announced for Israel in the future tribulation when the antichrist will have authority to afflict Daniel's people. The question is not when they will take place, but how long they will last. (A similar question was posed in 8:13, but there it pertained to the atrocities of Antiochus IV, a type of antichrist.)[726]

---

723. The Heb. מוֹעֵד (*môʿēḏ*) is used here in the same way as Aram. עִדָּן (*ʿiddān*) was in Dan 7:25, a "time" meaning one year, and "times" meaning two years (i.e., two times). Archer (155) points out that מְוֹעֲדִים (*môʿăḏîm*) "may originally have been intended as a dual" and pointed מוֹעֲדַיִם (*môʿăḏayim*). Augustine bears witness to this understanding: "The word *times* may seem an indefinite plural in our language [Latin], but the Greek texts (and, so I am told, the Hebrew texts as well) show that 'times' is written in the dual number and so means 'two times'" (*City of God*, 20.23; see *Fathers of the Church: A New Translation*, 24:315). Di Lella (274) understands the full expression to mean three and one-half years.

724. Rather than the Piʿel inf. const. form נַפֵּץ (*nappēṣ*) as MT has, the verb could be pointed as a Qal ptc., נֹפֵץ (*nōp̱ēṣ*). This would change the translation from "the shattering of the power of the holy people" to "the one who shatters the power of the holy people," the latter implying the antichrist. Either translation is possible, but the effect on the "holy people" is the same. Most Eng. VSS (except the NET) stick with MT's pointing. Collins (369, 399) opts for the ptc. form (though of course he understands the "shatterer" to be Antiochus IV).

H. Tawil, "Hebrew *nappēṣ yad* [in Dan 12:7] = Akkadian *qāta napāṣu*: A Term of Non-Allegiance," *JAOS* 122 (2002): 79–82, has argued (rather uniquely) that the Heb. phrase *nappēṣ yad* has an equivalent in the Akk. idiom for repudiation of treaty relations, *qāta napāṣu*, "to push back the hand." From this, he suggests (82) the rendering, "at the time of the termination of thrusting the hand [i.e., of the covenantal rejection] of the holy people all these things will come to an end." Yet the context of chap. 12 (note esp. v. 1, "a time of distress such as never occurred") stresses the suffering that the covenantal people will endure.

725. Lit., "hand" (metonymy for one's power).

726. "Gowan, 154, has noted the similarities between 12:5–8 and 8:13–14, including the riverbank setting, the portrayal of Daniel in the role of one overhearing a conversation between unnamed celestial beings raising the question of 'How long?'

12:7 Before giving the answer, the man dressed in linen raises both his hands to heaven in a gesture of making an oath (cf. Gen 14:22; Deut 32:40). Using both hands is quite emphatic, or as Driver (204) notes, "the more complete guarantee of the truth of what is about to be affirmed."[727] In doing so, he swears on oath to "Him who lives forever" (cf. Dan 4:34). In the Old Testament, God is "the living God" (Josh 3:10) and "the living LORD" (Ps 18:46). The word "forever" reminds us that God alone has absolute immortality (1 Tim 6:16). (Compare divine oath-making in Gen 22:15–18 and Ps 110:4.) Making the statement with an oath adds certainty (for man's sake) to the truth of what he was about to say.

His answer is that the duration of these astonishing events (i.e., the great tribulation) will be for "a time, times, and half *a time*," the same extent of time that was specified for the saints to be given into the power of the "little horn" in Dan 7:25. These obviously refer to the same period, because the "little horn" is the antichrist who will severely persecute the Jewish people in the great tribulation. Not surprisingly, the same reference is found in Rev 12:14 and is equivalent to the 1260 days or forty-two months that "the beast"—the antichrist—is allocated for having "authority to act" (Rev 13:5; cf. Rev 11:2–3; 12:6, 14). During this time, "the power of the holy people" will be shattered. In this context, "the holy people" refers to the Jewish people (cf. Deut 7:6; 14:2; Exod 19:6; Isa 63:18), although we know from the book of Revelation that many believing Gentiles will also be persecuted and martyred. (Those who wish to understand these verses in regard to Antiochus IV are at a loss to explain this statement, for Antiochus did not do this. The Maccabees overcame his assault against them.)[728] As for their power being shattered, Archer explains, "In other words (as in Zech 14:2), the brave defenders of Jerusalem will be overwhelmed by the irresistible forces of antichrist; and they will appear doomed to utter defeat and extinction." Rather obviously, it is only because of God's sovereignty that the "power of the holy people" is allowed to be shattered. Wood (324) notes, "As parallel passages indicate, this power and resulting sense of self-sufficiency will need to be broken so that the Jews will be willing to accept Christ as their rightful King." The positive side of this verse (and the probable reason for the oath) is that this horrible time of persecution at the hands of the antichrist will be limited to three and one-half years.

Biblical Theology Comments

One of the purposes of the great tribulation—though not the only purpose—is to humble the Jewish people, especially in the latter half of Daniel's seventieth "week," i.e., the final three and one-half years. There

---

and the report that Daniel eventually joins in the conversation" (cited in Hill, 208).

727. Cited in Baldwin, 229.

728. Collins seeks to avoid this problem by emending the text. For him, "the shatterer" (Antiochus) is finished. See translation note above for נַפֵּץ (*nappēṣ*), "shattering."

will be immense suffering for them, once the antichrist puts an end to sacrifice and offering (Dan 9:27) and proclaims himself as God (2 Thess 2:4). Elsewhere the Bible refers to this as "the time of Jacob's distress" (Jer 30:7), and Zech 13:8–9 indicates that the majority of the people perish during this time, with only a third surviving this ordeal. Yet in the end, the Lord will save the surviving remnant once they "look to Him whom they have pierced" (Zech 12:10). Zechariah goes on to say, "They will call on My name, and I will answer them; I will say, 'They are My people,' and they will say, 'The LORD is my God'" (Zech 13:9 NASB). The "time, times, and half a time" will be the period of greatest suffering that the Jewish people will ever experience (Dan 12:1), yet it will be brought to an end by Christ's personal return. The one with uplifted arms by the river announcing the length of the Great Tribulation surely ought to be the one who knows, for he is the very one who will bring it to an end.

Application and Devotional Implications

There is certainly no delight to be had in reading that the power of the holy people must be shattered at some point in history future. One need only think of all the saddening incidents that have befallen the Jewish people in the course of history to realize how astonishing these words of prophecy are. As Christians who believe the Scriptures, we cannot help but have a burden for them to know the Messiah, our Lord Jesus Christ. Thankfully, a "remnant" among them do believe, though for the majority of Jewish people today, their hearts are hardened against Jesus. Yet for the apostle Paul, he could say, "For I am not ashamed of the gospel, for it is the power of God for salvation to everyone who believes, to the Jew first and also to the Greek" (Rom 1:16 NASB). Like Paul, we today need to remember that the gospel is still "to the Jew first." Our witness to them is important—both in how we live and in the testimony to Christ we give. We can also be involved in helping support missions that focus on outreach to the Jewish people.

The day will come when "the nations … will tread underfoot the holy city for forty-two months" (Rev 11:2). That will be a terrible era in which to be living. The consolation is that once the power of the holy people has been shattered (i.e., they have been thoroughly humbled), many will finally turn to Jesus Christ in faith (Rom 11). Just as Joseph's brothers rejected and mistreated him (though he would become their "savior") only to discover later how much he loved and cared for them, so in the future the Jewish people will finally be reconciled with their Savior. At the time of his earthly rejection, Jesus prophesied, "Behold, your house is being left to you desolate! For I say to you, from now on you will not see Me until you say, 'Blessed is He who comes in the name of the Lord'" (Matt 23:38–39 NASB). In that day he will deliver them by the mighty hand of God, and their sufferings will be at an end at last.

5. Daniel's Concern about the Final Outcome (12:8–12)

Daniel "heard" the words of the man dressed in linen, yet "he did not understand." Certainly he would have understood much of what had been revealed, yet (from his sixth-century BC perspective and without New Testament revelation) there were still many questions puzzling his mind. Since the prophecies concerned Daniel's "people" (recall 12:1), we can understand why he would be anxious to fully comprehend and know as many details as possible, especially what would be the final outcome for his people. His question did result in a *bit* more revelation, though this final revelation was itself as baffling for Daniel as it is for readers today.

Textual Notes

10.a. Rather than MT's Nipʿal impf. form, יִצָּרְפוּ, a Cairo Geniza fragment (CD) has the Hitpaʿel form יתצרפו. We also find the form יצטרפו in 4QFlor (the more proper form for the Hitpaʿel). However, צָרַף is not otherwise attested in BH in the Hitpaʿel. More likely, CD and 4QFlor are attempting to conform צָרַף to the two preceding Hitpaʿel verbs. Yet this is not necessary, as Hitpaʿel verbs do not always have a *reflexive* meaning but can also take a *passive* nuance; see *IBHS*, 431–32 (§26.3.a,b). So, if the Hitpaʿel verbs יִתְבָּרְרוּ וְיִתְלַבְּנוּ have a *passive nuance*, then the Nipʿal form יִצָּרְפוּ is quite understandable. In light of the way all three verbs are used in 11:35 (actions done *to them*)—the parallel situation in 12:10 rather expects a *passive* nuance (contrast Goldingay, 275, who opts for the reflexive, adding "themselves" to each of the verbs).

11.a. Rather than MT's Qal inf. const. לָתֵת, the *BHS* editor proposes reading וְנִתַּן (Nipʿal perf.). In support of a Nipʿal reading, LXX$^{\theta}$ has a future passive form, δοθήσεται. (Although Rahlf's edition has τοῦ δοθῆναι in LXX$^{\theta}$, the Göttingen ed., on the basis of MS B, has δοθήσεται.) A Nipʿal reading would yield a passive translation, "and the abomination of desolation is set up," and most Eng. VSS render the sentence this way.

Translation

12:8 Now I heard but did not understand. So I said, "my lord, what will be the outcome[729] of these things?" **9** And he said, "Go *your way*,[730] Daniel, for

---

729. The noun אַחֲרִית (*ʾaḥărîṯ*) means the "after-part, end" (BDB, 31a), but it can also have the nuance of "outcome" as in Isa 41:22; 47:7. This is the translation given by NIV, ESV, NRSV. Daniel is not asking what will happen "after these things" (so NET)—as though he wants to know what happens next—but rather their outcome.

730. The Hebrew simply has the imperative לֵךְ (*lēḵ*), "go!" Several translations add the words "your way" (so NKJV, NIV, NRSV, and ESV). The point is that Daniel is not to make further inquiry. Nevertheless, a bit more insight is provided in vv. 10–12.

the words are closed and sealed up until the end time.[731] **10** Many will be purified,[732] made clean,[733] and refined, though *the* wicked[734] will act wickedly.[735] Yet none of the wicked will understand, while those having *spiritual* insight will understand. **11** From the time the regular sacrifice[736] is removed and the abomination causing desolation[737] is set up, *there will be* 1290 days. **12** Blessed[738]

---

731. Regarding the "end time" (עֵת קֵץ, *ʿēṯ qēṣ*), this is the same expression as found in Dan 8:17; 11:35, 40; 12:4. This is the time when the "time of distress" occurs (12:1) and the antichrist is active.

732. The three verbs at the beginning of Dan 12:10 should be translated as *passives*, not reflexives as Goldingay (275) has done: "purified themselves, etc." Cf. the textual note to v. 10 above.

733. The verb לָבֵן (*lāḇēn*) means to "be white," but it can also be used metaphorically in an ethical sense to convey "purity" (Ps 51:9 Heb.). There is no need to translate it "made white," as Collins (369) has done.

734. Although the noun רְשָׁעִים (*rᵊšāʿîm*, "wicked") only occurs here in Daniel, the cognate verb form רָשַׁע (*rāšaʿ*, "to be wicked, act wickedly") did occur in 11:32. There it was used of those who rebelled against God's covenant, i.e., the Mosaic covenant that was in force at that time. This may suggest that by "the wicked," 12:10 primarily has in mind those among the Jewish people who refuse to repent and believe in Messiah Jesus (i.e., they remain defiant against the God of heaven).

735. My punctuation of 12:10 and the choice of translation for the *waw*-disjunctives is based on my recognition of the chiastic structure of the verse. See commentary below for v. 10.

736. On the meaning of the "regular sacrifice" (הַתָּמִיד, *hattāmîḏ*), see translation note at Dan 8:11.

737. Here in 12:11, the "abomination causing desolation" (שִׁקּוּץ שֹׁמֵם, *šiqqûṣ šōmēm*) is the fulfillment of the "abomination *by* one who makes desolate" in 9:27 (שִׁקּוּצִים מְשֹׁמֵם, *šiqqûṣîm mᵊšōmēm*). Typologically, the "abomination of desolation" (הַשִּׁקּוּץ מְשׁוֹמֵם, *haššiqqûṣ mᵊšōmēm*) by Antiochus IV foreshadowed the greater abomination that will come at the hands of the antichrist. Regarding these expressions, see translation notes at both 9:27 and 11:31. LXX$^{\theta}$ rendered שִׁקּוּץ שֹׁמֵם (*šiqqûṣ šōmēm*) in 12:11 as βδέλυγμα ἐρημώσεως (*bdelugma erēmōseōs*), the same expression used by LXX^{O} in 11:31 (and similar to the LXX translation at 9:27).

738. This is the only use of the noun אַשְׁרֵי (*ʾašrê*) in Daniel and needs to be distinguished from the more common verb בָּרַךְ (*bāraḵ*), "to bless." The Aram. equivalent (בְּרַךְ, *biraḵ*) occurs in 2:19, 20; 3:28; 4:31. אַשְׁרֵי (*ʾašrê*) occurs most often in the Psalms (note Ps 1:1, "Blessed is the man ..."), and primarily indicates that one is fortunate or found in a happy state of bliss (cf. *TDOT*, 1:445–48). LXX used the translation μακάριος (*makarios*)—a word meaning "happy, fortunate"—to render אַשְׁרֵי (*ʾašrê*) in 12:10. (The LXX will typically use εὐλογέω, *eulogeō*, to translate בָּרַךְ (*bāraḵ*), as in Gen 12:3.)

is the one who waits and attains[739] to 1335 days.

Commentary

12:8 Despite hearing the conversation in his vision, Daniel did not fully grasp the meaning of all that he saw and heard. Collins (400) remarks, "As in 8:27, Daniel's failure to understand emphasizes the mysteriousness of the revelation." There is some debate as to what exactly Daniel was asking. The NET translates, "what will happen after these things?" (so Jerome, 150).[740] The question, however, is, "what will be the אַחֲרִית (*ʾaḥărîṯ*) of these things?" The word *ʾaḥărîṯ* has the meaning "outcome" in Isa 41:22 and 47:7, and this is the translation chosen by the NIV, ESV, and NRSV. In particular, he wanted to know what would be "the outcome of these things," i.e., what would the sufferings that his people would go through in the distant future result in? He would naturally be concerned, having heard that the power of his people was to be broken, and he would be eager to know about their survival and the role they would have from that point on. Finally, how would all this relate to God's kingdom program previously revealed to him?

12:9 The response to Daniel in v, 9 ("Go *your way*, Daniel") seems to suggest that he is not to ask further questions but be content with what has been revealed to him. The remainder of the verse recalls v. 4 (that the words must be closed and sealed up). There is to be a divine restriction on what can be comprehended about the prophetic visions revealed to Daniel.[741]

---

739. The verb נָגַע (*nāga*ʿ) commonly means "to touch, reach, strike" (BDB, 619c 2). Here, *nāga*ʿ is used in the Hipʿil with prep. לְ (*lᵊ*). This combination occurs 11x in the HB and can mean (1) "to touch" (2 Chr 3:11, 12); (2) "to cause to touch" (Exod 4:25); (3) "to draw near or approach" (Ps 88:4); (4) "to reach a level" (Job 20:6; 2 Chr 28:9); or (5) "to attain [a status]" (Esth 4:14). The translation "reach" or "attain" is most suitable in Dan 12:12.

740. Although Collins translates *ʾaḥărîṯ* as "outcome" (369), his commentary (400) implies that Daniel is wanting to know what will happen *after* the resurrection.

741. A similar motif is found in the *Pesher on Habakkuk* from Qumran: "God told Habakkuk to write down the things that are going to come upon the last generation, but the fulfillment of the end time he did not make known to him" (1QpHab 7:1–2; cited in Collins, 400).

12:10 In this future time of distress, Daniel's people will surely be shattered at the hands of the antichrist, yet the Great Tribulation will serve to ensure that the nation is "purified, made clean and refined." Regarding the latter word "refined," Baldwin's comments (230) are helpful:

> The refining process which improves the quality of gold and silver at the same time separates out the dross, that is *the wicked.* No longer are the two indistinguishable, but only by fire can the separation be made, and the metal's purity be assured.

Through all the sufferings that they will have to undergo, this will cause the people to seek God and his Word. This, together with the witness of faithful believers, will result in many coming to faith in the Lord Jesus, gaining true righteousness, and being prepared to be part of this wonderful kingdom over which the Son of Man will rule.

Verse 10 is cast in a chiastic structure that heightens the contrast between the "wicked" and "those having *spiritual* insight" (the wise):

> *a* Many will be purified, made clean, and refined,
>   *b* though *the* wicked will act wickedly.
>   *b'* Yet none of the wicked will understand,
> *a'* while those having *spiritual* insight will understand.

Not everyone among the Jewish people will respond positively. There will be certain wicked ones among them who will not desist from acting wickedly. These are the ones who will refuse to repent and turn in faith to Messiah Jesus. Remaining unregenerate, then, they will not understand the things that are happening in the world in the days of the great tribulation. They will also remain deceived by the antichrist and fail to perceive his diabolical agenda until it is too late. In contrast to these will be the wise ("those having *spiritual* insight") and who do understand. They understand because they will have turned in faith to Christ, been born again, received the Holy Spirit, and gained spiritual insight from the Word of God. From this verse we see that there will be Jews prepared for the return of Christ and others who will not be prepared. For those among the wicked that remain alive until the Lord returns, they will face his severe judgment and not be allowed to enter his kingdom (cf. Ezek 20:33–38; Zech 13:1–6; Matt 13:36–43, 47–50).

12:11–12 Verses 11–12 provide some chronological details to augment what had just been revealed in v. 7. According to v. 12, there will be 1,290 days from the removal of the regular sacrifice and setting up of the abomination that causes desolation. This is thirty days longer than the previously revealed "time, times, and half *a time*" of v. 7 (presumably 1,260 days). Then, according to v. 13, there will be an unexplained extension to 1335 days, for which those who reach that point will be "blessed." Scholars have postulated several different views on the meaning of these two extensions, which are summed up below:[742]

A. The Antiochene View

This view, mostly held by critical scholars, attempts to explain the extensions of time in regard to the reign of Antiochus IV Epiphanes in the second century AD. There are two variations to this view:

1. Recalibration View[743]

This view understands that a recalculation needed to be made of the time between the removal of the regular sacrifice by Antiochus Epiphanes and either the rededication of the temple or the death of Antiochus. Hill (211) clarifies,

> For some scholars, the two time periods represent glosses in the form of 'successive corrections' to the

---

742. Not included in this summary are the various views held by Jewish exegetes. For this, see Goldwurm (328–30). Opinions tend to go in one of two directions. Quite a few interpret the "days" as years, and in particular as the years leading up to Messiah's coming. In contrast are ones like Ibn Ezra who take the "days" literally but relate them to the period before the temple's destruction in AD 70. Hence, "the daily sacrifice will be removed for 1290 days before the destruction of the Temple" (Goldwurm, 328). Ibn Ezra (330) further postulates, "Verse 12 refers to the length of time allowed for *the time of trouble* mentioned above (*v.* 1). This would endure for approximately three-and-a-half years as told above (7:25 and 12:7). Here the angel was more precise and gave the exact amount of days." Among the early church fathers, Clement of Alexandria held that these temporal notices pertained to the period leading up to Jerusalem's destruction in AD 70 (see "The Stromata," Book 1, Ch. 21 in *Ante-Nicene Fathers*, 2:334). Also not included in this summary are the various Adventist views. For a helpful overview, description, and evaluation of Adventist views, see A. F. Hernandez, "Adventist Eschatological Identity and the Interpretations of the Time Periods of Daniel 12:11–12," *AUSSJ* 1 (2015): 65–84. Although some in Adventist circles have advocated a symbolic or futuristic approach, most adhere to the "traditional historicist view." Hernandez (71) explains, "the traditional Adventist interpretation argues that the prophecies of Dan 12 should be interpreted using the year by day principle and the historicist principle of hermeneutic. In this manner, the 1290 days and the 1335 days represent an equal amount of years starting in A.D. 508 and ending in A.D. 1798 and 1843 respectively." The year AD 508 marks the year in the reign of Clovis in which church and state merged, being the culmination of the union of the Franks and the Catholic Church. In defense of this, see J. C. Zukowski, "The Role and Status of the Catholic Church in the Church-State Relationship Within the Roman Empire from A.D. 306 to 814" (Ph.D. diss., Andrews University, 2009).

743. Collins (401) credits Gunkel for this explanation; see H. Gunkel, *Schöpfung und Chaos* (Göttingen: Vandenhoeck & Ruprecht, 1895), 269.

> 1,150 days mentioned in Daniel's vision of the ram and the goat (8:14). According to this view, a later writer (or writers) attempted to extend the time period for the fulfillment of the prediction of the rededication of the Jerusalem temple when that event did not occur within the time frame originally expected.[744]

Collins (401) adds, "It is a well-known fact that groups who make exact predictions do not just give up when the prediction fails to be fulfilled. Instead they find ways to explain the delay."

2. The Length of Persecution View
This view focuses on the number of days that the Jews suffered persecution. The first time period might be from December 7, 167 BC (the desecration of the Jerusalem temple) to June 21, 163 BC (the collapse of the Antiochene dynasty), which would be approximately 1290 days (based on a solar calendar).[745] The second time period of 1,335 days looks further to the "anniversary of the public reading of the Torah (August 5, 163 BC), some forty-five days after the collapse of the dynasty of Antiochus" (Hill, 211). Goldingay (309–10) holds to a slight variation of this view, understanding the two periods of days as approximations for the time frame in fulfillment of the question, "How long will the persecution last?" (Dan 12:6),

---

744. So Montgomery, 477.

745. B. Hunt, "A Short Note on Daniel 12:11–12," *Scr* 9 (1957): 84, has proposed a different calculation. He suggested that Antiochus' decree forbidding the sacrifices occurred in June 167 and that 1290 days later the rededication took place on 25 Chislev (Dec.) 164. Then there were forty-five more days following the rededication before persecution finally ceased. S. F. Mathews, "The Numbers in Daniel 12:11–12: Rounded Pythagorean Plane Numbers?" *CBQ* 63 (2001): 630–46, takes a different approach altogether. For her, the numbers are approximations and symbolic, and "must be read against the backdrop of the Pythagorean arithmology" (646). She takes the 1290 as a reference to the first "half" of Antiochus' reign of terror and the 1335 as the second "half." This supposedly justifies her in concluding that the 1,335-day "week"—the second half—is better: "The 'good' second half-week is represented by 1,335, which refers to the fulfillment of Jeremiah's prophecy and marks the 'end' period in which the people of the Most High will gain triumph after the desolation." Such extreme speculation is its greatest weakness.

though the terminal points could potentially refer to any one of several different events during the years 168–164 BC.[746]

B. The Symbolic View[747]

According to this view, the numbers are not to be taken literally, but are only used to teach a spiritual lesson in regard to perseverance under persecution. Baldwin (232), who holds this view, writes, "The addition of 1,290 days, or just over three and a half years, would complete the seventy sevens of years, so bringing persecution to an end. Even so there is need to persevere a little longer, till 1,355 days, another month and a half, have passed." Lucas (298) has suggested "the numbers may have some symbolic significance that is now lost to us."

Young follows a view held by Keil in taking the numbers symbolically, with the period of 1,290 days representing a period of severe persecution. The numbers apply both to the period of Antiochus as well as to that of antichrist, since one *typifies* the other.[748] Young (263) explains,

---

746. Goldingay (310) suggests, "The beginning point of v 11 could be the time of one of Antiochus's edicts, the actual desecration of the temple, or the enforcement of the ban on the regular sacrificial order (11:31–33). The beginning point of v 12 could be one of these, or an earlier event such as Apollonius's mission, though more likely vv 11–12 begin with the same event and v 12 terminates later, suggesting that the promised release will have successive stages during which a continuing faithful expectancy is required. Thus vv 11–12 could terminate with Judas's victories, the temple rededication, Antiochus's death, the arrival of news of his death, or the further events envisaged by 11:45–12:3."

747. In addition to the ones specifically mentioned here, others holding the symbolic view include Wallace (196–97) and Carpenter (461–62). Calvin was very emphatic about a symbolic view. Regarding the "time, times, and half a time," he wrote (2:383), "I have stated my objection to the opinion of those who think one year, and two, and a half, to be here intended. ... Its meaning is very simple, *time* means a long period, *times*, a longer period, and *a half* means the end or closing period. The sum of the whole is this: many years must elapse before God fulfils what his Prophet had declared." He went on to say that the whole expression simply meant "an indefinite period." For Calvin, the persecution was in regard to the church throughout history: "the Church should be a stranger in the world, and be dispersed throughout it" (384). One should note his rendering "dispersed" for the Hebrew verb נָפַץ, *nāp̱aṣ*, in Dan 12:7. Although BDB (659a) does list a root II נָפַץ, *nāp̱aṣ*, meaning "disperse, be scattered," most all modern translations opt for root I "shatter" (BDB 658d) in the case of Dan 12:7.

748. Chisholm (328–29) takes a similar position, in that he understands the passage to portray Antiochus but yet at the same time *typify* the future antichrist. For Chisholm, however, he takes the numbers more literally. The 1290 days pertain

> The 1335 days, therefore, have reference to the entire period of persecution, not only that under Antiochus, but the whole period of opposition to God's kingdom unto the consummation. The 1290 days, however, have reference not to the entire period of persecution, but only to the most severe phase of this period, namely the persecution under Antiochus and its antitype, that under the Antichrist. The 1290 days are little more than ½ of 7 years and 7 appears to be a figure denoting completeness.

C. The Futurist View

According to this view, the numbers are to be taken literally and explained in relation to the future antichrist during the time of the great tribulation. Most taking the futurist view see the two temporal references as extensions beyond the 1260 days, yet questions remain as to the timing of Christ's second coming and what purpose these extensions serve. Premillennialists typically explain them as necessary transition events (subsequent to the second coming) related to the inauguration of the millennial kingdom of Christ on earth. However, there are some who would understand Christ's physical return to earth at the 1335 days (so Jerome). Hence, there are several variations to the futurist position (which will be further explained below).

The Antiochene view obviously has no merit if this portion of Daniel (11:36–12:4) pertains to the future antichrist rather than Antiochus of the second century BC (as I have argued in this commentary). In addition, the recalibration view is even less convincing. Baldwin (231) explains,

> ... Porteous confesses to difficulty in seeing how urgent corrections could have been added to a book that had just been issued, even

---

to the period of persecution, but he equates these with the "time, times, and half *a time*" by including an intercalated month in his calculations. He writes, "If one uses a lunar calendar (thirty days per month for forty-two months), three and a half years would add up to 1,260 days ..., but the figure here may include an intercalated month, added to make the calendar correspond to the solar year." As for the 1,335 days, Chisholm explains, "the additional forty-five days is the time it would take for complete restoration and purification to occur." A problem for Chisholm, however, is that his explanation of 1290 days on account of an intercalary month fails to hold up in light of the book of Revelation. Young (262–63) pointed this out in criticizing J. D. Prince, *A Critical Commentary on the Book of Daniel* (Leipzig, 1899) over this same issue. In the book of Revelation, the 1,260 days are equivalent to the "time, times, and half *a time*." So you cannot have the latter mean 1260 days in one place and 1290 days in another.

> though in a limited number of copies. The numbers did not fit, and it is difficult to make them fit any scheme.[749]

The symbolic view may have some truth to it (certainly there are spiritual lessons to be gleaned from these statements), yet it raises hermeneutical questions. The numbers of Dan 9:24–27 have been shown to be literal and precise, and given that the 1290 and 1335 are related to the "time, times, and half *a time*" (1,260 days) and the final "week" of v. 27 that is divided into two parts (apparently three and a half years each), it seems most reasonable to take the extensions literally (whether or not we understand their precise function).

The futurist view, then, has the most to commend it, and this has been an age-old view going back to the early church fathers. Jerome (150), for instance, saw the 1290 days as essentially the same as the "time, times, and half *a time*" (terminating in the death of antichrist). Regarding the 1335 days, he wrote (151),

> He means that he is blessed who waits for forty-five days beyond the predetermined number, for it is within that period that our Lord and Savior is to come in His glory. But the reason for the forty-five days of inaction after the slaying of the Antichrist is a matter which rests in the knowledge of God; unless, of course, we say that the rule of the saints is delayed in order that their patience may be tested.

The time that is allocated to the antichrist for his reign of terror is "time, times, and half *a time*," i.e., three and a half years (Dan 7:25). (Note that some, including Jerome, equate "time, times, and half *a time*" with the 1290 days.) This would be equivalent to forty-two months, the figure specified in Rev 13:5 for him to "exercise ruling authority." In the Bible, time spans are sometimes reckoned according to lunar months of thirty days, though the Jewish system had a means of correcting the calendar to bring it in line with solar years of 365 ¼ days (compare Gen 7:11, 24 and 8:2–4).[750] Thus forty-two months having thirty days each would amount to 1260 days, and this latter figure is used interchangeably with forty-two months and "time, times, and half a time" in Rev 11:2–3 and 12:6, 14. In Dan 12:11, however, a figure of 1290 days is now introduced, which is thirty days *longer* than the 1260. Yet all we are told is that there are 1290 days following the removal of "the regular sacrifice" and setting up of "the abomination that causes

---

749. Baldwin cites Porteous, 172. Di Lella (314) concurs with the criticism of the recalibration view and then adds, "Nevertheless, since none of the predicted numbers in 7:25; 8:14; 9:27; and 12:7 were meant to be understood as being mathematically precise, it appears plausible that the calculations in 12:11 and 12:12, whatever the respective *terminus ad quem* may refer to, were also intended only as round numbers."

750. Collins (400) points out that K. Marti, *Das Buch Daniel*, HKAT 18 (Tubingen: Mohr, 1901), 92, views the 1290 days as being forty-two months of thirty days each, with an intercalated month of thirty days.

desolation" (no *terminus ad quem* is specified). The "regular sacrifice" is a reference to the sacrifice that was made twice daily in the temple, once in the morning and once at twilight (see comments at 8:11–12). According to 12:11 this sacrifice will be removed, presumably by the antichrist or at his instruction. This would imply, then, that there must be some kind of Jewish temple standing and in operation during the years leading up to the second coming of Christ (cf. Dan 9:27; 2 Thess 2:4; Rev 11:1–3).[751] The "daily sacrifice" of the temple (once sanctioned by God under the old covenant) is removed, and "the abomination that causes desolation" replaces it. Something similar had taken place in the days of Antiochus IV Epiphanes (note Dan 11:31), which is but a foreshadowing of what the antichrist will do in the future Great Tribulation. Apparently this corresponds to the halting of "sacrifice and offerings" mentioned in 9:27 (which takes place at the midpoint of the final "week" of seven years). So significant is this act that Jesus prophesied of it in Matt 24:15, viewing this event as the primary sign inaugurating the great tribulation (note Matt 24:21). When the Jews of that day see this happen—and note that Jesus indicated it will take place in the "holy place," i.e., the Jewish temple—they are to flee Judea for the mountains.[752] In fact Jesus' reference to this "abomination" (and he clearly links it to Daniel's prophecy) proves that this sacrilege cannot have been fulfilled in the days of Antiochus IV, since Jesus uttered this in the first century AD, long after the time of Antiochus.[753]

---

751. The idea of a Jewish temple standing at the "time of the end" implies that the Jews will rebuild their temple prior to the return of Christ. This does not mean, however, that God has sanctioned the rebuilding of that temple, since their motive—in view of Dan 9:27—appears to be the reestablishment of the sacrificial system of the Mosaic law, in disregard of Christ's perfect sacrifice (Heb 9). I presume, then, that the initiative to rebuild a temple prior to Christ's second coming comes at the hands of apostate Jews who stand outside the new covenant. This, however, still leaves open the possibility of a sanctioned temple *following* Christ's return that would exist for different purposes, namely the temple described in Ezek 40–48.

752. Apparently only a minority of the Jews living at the time of the great tribulation will heed Christ's warning (at that point in time, most of the nation is still in unbelief). Nevertheless some do, and this is probably the background for the events recorded in Rev 12:6, 13–17.

753. D. Graham, "Early Christian Understandings of the 'Abomination that Causes Desolation,'" *RTR* 74 (2015): 166, though acknowledging that many early church fathers saw the "abomination" as the work of the future antichrist, nevertheless follows R. A. Cole, *Mark*, TTNTC (Leicester: IVP, 1989), 277, in taking the "abomination" as "the Roman legionary standards, which held cult status among Roman armies, and which the Romans set up and worshiped in the temple after they had set fire to Jerusalem in AD 70 as described by Josephus." The problem I see with this view is that when Jesus mentions "the abomination of desolation" in Matt 25:15 (cf. Mark 13:14), he connects it with the great tribulation that will be shortly followed by

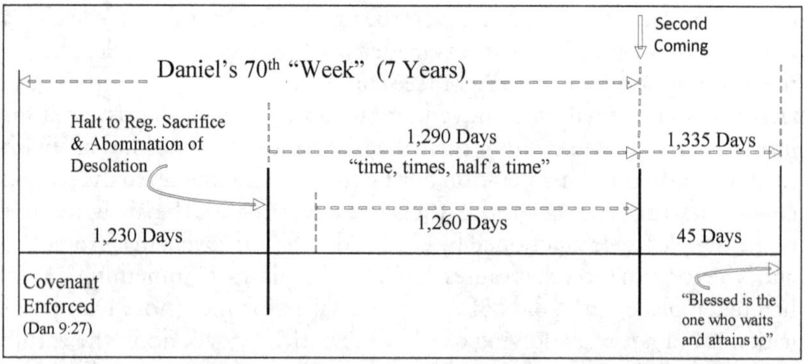

What then is "the abomination that causes desolation" that the antichrist will set up in the Jewish temple? We are not clearly told what it is, though it is certainly a fulfillment of the desolating sacrilege mentioned in Dan 9:27 (see discussion at that point). There is very good reason to think, however, that it is connected somehow with the prediction of the antichrist in 2 Thess 2:4, when "the man of lawlessness" (another title for the antichrist) "takes his seat in God's temple, displaying himself as God." Revelation 13:3–4 clarifies that the whole earth will follow after the beast and even worship him during the period of the great tribulation. Furthermore, the false prophet will have an image made of the beast that all are commanded to worship (Rev 13:15). Is this image of the beast placed in the rebuilt Jewish temple? And if so, could this be the "abomination" mentioned in Dan 12:11? This may very well be the case, since the image itself is to be worshiped on pain of death (Rev 13:15).

Whatever the "abomination" may be, we still are not told why there are 1290 days following its erection, i.e., thirty days longer than the 1260 days allocated for the antichrist's "authority to act." Then an additional numerical figure is mentioned in v. 12, as a special blessing for the one "who waits and attains to 1335 days." This would be forty-five days beyond the previously mentioned 1290 days. For both the 1290 days and the 1335 days, no event marking the *terminus ad quem* is stated. The reader is also not told how these temporal notices relate to Daniel's seventieth week (Dan 9:24–27) or at what point the second coming of Christ occurs. Based on the view taken in this commentary, the purposes of the seventy weeks' prophecy must extend to the second coming in light of statements made in Dan 9:24, e.g., "to bring in everlasting righteousness *[i.e., the messianic age when righteousness flourishes]*, to seal up vision and prophecy, and to anoint the most holy place." While a number of different variations of the futurist view are possible, the following discussion will consider three primary possibilities.

---

his return in glory. Thus, the AD 70 event (though it might *foreshadow* the "abomination") is not the ultimate fulfillment of what Jesus prophesies. Graham relies on Luke's account of the Olivet Discourse, which although including Jesus' comments on the AD 70 event (Luke 21:20–24) does not mention or refer to the "abomination" in association with the Roman destruction of AD 70.

A. View One: Christ Returns at the End of 1335 Days

The notion that the 1,335 days culminate with the second coming of Christ was held by some early church fathers (e.g., Jerome) and is found in the Pseudepigrapha (*Mart. Ascen. Isa.* 4:14).[754] Some, however, would equate the 1290 days with "time, times, half *a time*." Theodoret of Cyrus (323), commenting on the 1290 days, wrote, "Since he had said *a time, and times, and half a time,* and had seen that blessed Daniel did not understand, he clarified it for him in his ignorance by transposing the time into days while still leaving the statement obscure for the others." The problem with this, however, is that in Rev 12:6, 14, the 1260 days are apparently equated with the "time, times, and half *a time*."

There are difficulties with View One that must be considered. First, according to Dan 9:27, the antichrist puts an end to sacrifice and offering "in the middle (חֲצִי, *ḥăṣî*) of the week." If this means the exact middle (with two equal halves), then View One would not be possible. However, the word *ḥăṣî*, though it normally means "middle, a half," can mean "in the midst" (see Ps 102:25; Jer 17:11).[755] This is derived from the verb חָצָה (*ḥāṣâ*) meaning "to divide," regarding which Hess has noted, "*ḥṣh* refers to division, though not necessarily into two equal parts."[756] However, *ḥăṣî* in Dan 9:27 is not normally understood this way (i.e., "in the midst"). A second problem for View One is that according to Dan 9:7, the "time, times, and half *a time*" marks a point when "all these things will be finished." If "all these things" includes both the "time of distress" and "rescue" mentioned in 12:1–2 (as seems likely), this is hard to reconcile with the extended time periods that according to View One go beyond this. Other verses indicate that the antichrist has authority in which he afflicts God's people for "time, times, and half a time" (7:25) or "forty-two months" (Rev 13:5).

B. View Two: The 1290 Days Constitute the Second Half of Daniel's 70th "Week"

In this view, Dan 12:11 is understood as clarifying the meaning of "time, times, and half *a time*" in v. 7, i.e., they are one and the same.[757] In accordance with

---

754. Because *Mart. Ascen. Isa.* is a composite work, the section containing 3:13–4:22 is sometimes referred to as the *Testament of Hezekiah* or *T.Hez.*

755. Cf. Exod 12:29 and Judg 16:3, where instead of exactly "midnight" (in the middle of the night), *ḥāṣâ* could mean "in the midst of the night." Also see 1 Kgs 16:21, where *ḥāṣâ* could mean "part" rather than exactly "half."

756. R. Hess, "חצה," in *NIDOTTE*, 2:245.

757. The idea of the 1,290 days being a clarification of the more exact length of the "time, times, and half a time" was espoused in the early church by Hippolytus (see "Fragments," in *Ante-Nicene Fathers*, 5:184) and Theodoret of Cyrus (323), and has been embraced in more recent times by Archer (156) who writes, "it appears from v.11 that the interval between the setting up of the 'abomination that causes desolation' .... and the final deliverance of Jerusalem from his hosts will come out more exactly to ... a total of 1,290 days." Hippolytus also writes in the "Scholia on Daniel" (*Ante-Nicene Fathers*, 5:190–91) that the "time, times, and half a time" are 1290 days.

other eschatological data, the second coming would occur at the end of this period. This would imply (1) that the 1290 days begin slightly before the exact middle of Daniel's seventieth "week" (hence, 1230 plus 1290); and (2) that the 1260 days are not the full extent of the "time, times, and half *a time*." According to other verses, the 1260 days (beginning thirty days following the cessation of the regular sacrifice) would be the time the antichrist will be given "authority to act" (Rev 13:5), the time the nations would tread underfoot the city of Jerusalem (11:2), the time the "woman" would find refuge in the wilderness (12:6), and possibly the time when the "two witnesses" of 11:3 prophesy.[758] For the most part, this is the view held by Constable, who writes, "Antichrist will terminate the sacrifices and desecrate the temple 30 days before the middle of the seventieth 'week.'"[759] Pentecost takes a similar view, though he would have the 1,290 days beginning thirty days *before* the cessation of the regular sacrifice.[760] As for the 1335 days, they would be explained (by premillennialists) as a transition period in which certain necessary matters are taken care of in regard to the millennial rule of Christ (on this, see further comments under view three).

View Two has the same problem as View One in regard to the cessation of the sacrifice and offering in the "middle of the week" (see above), unless one regards the statement in Dan 9:27 as a *rough* approximation. Of greater difficulty, however, is reconciling the "time, times, and half a time" with 1290 days in light of the fact that the former expression is indicated as 1,260 days in Rev 12:6, 14.

C. View Three: Both Periods Extend Beyond the 2nd Half of Daniel's 70th "Week"

View three regards both extended periods as going beyond Daniel's seventieth "week," i.e., they would extend beyond the second coming of Christ. This is the more popular view among premillennial scholars.[761]

There are several factors in favor of this view. First, this satisfies the details in Dan 9:24–27 inferring that the seventieth "week" of Daniel will extend to

---

758. Among those interpreting the "two witnesses" as two literal individuals who prophesy during the great tribulation, not all assume their ministry is in the second half. Some hold they prophesy in the first half. For discussion, see J. A. McLean, "The Chronology of the Two Witnesses in Revelation 11," *BSac* 168 (2011): 460–71, though he concludes they do minister in the second half, as does C. J. Tan, "A Futurist View of the Two Witnesses in Revelation 11," *BSac* 171 (2014): 452–71.

759. T. L. Constable, "Notes on Daniel," 2015 ed., 150 (online: http://www.soniclight.com/constable/notes/pdf/daniel.pdf).

760. According to Pentecost (1374), "Another possibility is that the 1,290 days will begin 30 days before the middle of the 70th 'seven' of years when the world ruler will set up 'the abomination that causes desolation' (Matt. 24:15). The 1,290 days could begin with an announcement (about the abomination) made 30 days before the abomination is introduced."

761. So Walvoord (1971: 294–96), Wood (327–29), Feinberg (186–87), Campbell (183–83), and Miller (325–26).

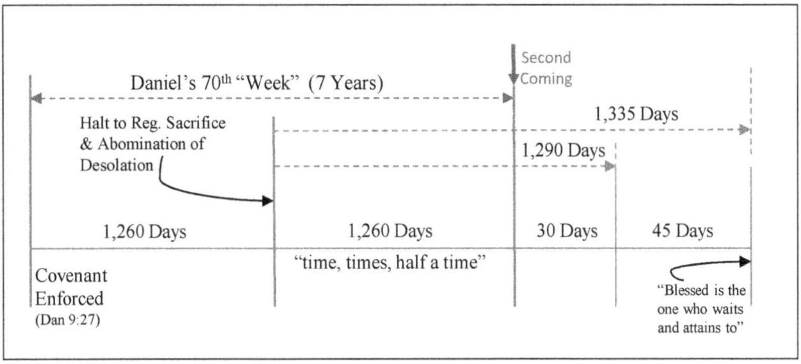

the second coming. Second, this better harmonizes with passages in Revelation that appear to equate the 1260 days with the "time, times, and half *a time*" (Rev 12:6, 14) and with the forty-two months (Rev 11:2–3). Also, the time that antichrist is "given authority" is forty-two months (Rev 13:5), which corresponds to the time of his power mentioned in Dan 7:25 of "time, times, and half a time." Third, 12:7 indicated that with the "time, times, and half *a time*," all "these things" (an apparent reference to both the "time of distress" and "rescue" mentioned in vv. 1–2) will be finished. Fourth, this view avoids any tension regarding the reference to *ḥăṣî* ("the *middle* of the week") mentioned in 9:27.

So the extra thirty days and the additional forty-five days seem to follow the second coming, and we can only speculate as to what they are for. The extra thirty days could be used for the Lord Jesus to carry out certain judgments on those who remain alive, clearing the world of the wicked who remained alive at his second coming (note Ezek 20:33–38; Matt 13:24–30, 36–43; 25:31–46).[762]

What is clear is that the one who attains to the 1335 days is considered "blessed" (אַשְׁרֵי, *ʾašrê*), a term emphasizing happiness (see translation note above). This obviously has "the righteous" in view. A very plausible suggestion is that this figure marks the wedding celebration of the Lamb mentioned in Rev 19:9, a verse in which the word "blessed" is used for those invited to this glorious event: "Blessed are those who are invited to the banquet at the wedding celebration of the Lamb!"[763] This is the grand and festive inaugural banquet at the onset of Christ's millennial kingdom on earth (cf. Isa 25:6; Luke 14:15–24; Rev 3:20). If the "judgment seat of Christ" takes place following the second coming of Christ (as I have argued for elsewhere), then it may be that the forty-five days preceding the banquet are used for the Lord

762. Wood (328) writes, "The cessation point in view, then, for the full 1,290 days may be the completion of this time of judgment." By this, he means Matt 25:31–46, "which describes a time of judgment by Christ immediately after He comes in power at the close of this period. The purpose of the judgment is to determine those who will be permitted to enter into and enjoy the blessedness of the millennial period."

763. The LXX translated אַשְׁרֵי (*ʾašrê*, "blessed") in Dan 12:12 as μακάριος (*makarios*), the same word that is used for "blessed" in Rev 19:9 for those invited to the "marriage supper of the lamb."

Jesus to judge/evaluate his children and give them their rewards.[764] This time may also be used for other preparations that need to be made before the kingdom is formally ushered in. Wood (328–29) reasons, "What will be the need of these forty-five days? It may be the time necessary for setting up the governmental machinery for carrying on the rule of Christ. The true and full border of Israel (from the River of Egypt to the Euphrates, Genesis 15:18) will have to be established, and appointments made of those aiding in the government."

In conclusion, the futurist view of the 1290 days and 1335 days has the best exegetical support in general. Since these temporal notices do not indicate a specific *terminus ad quem*, any one of the three futurist views presented above (or perhaps a variation of them) could conceivably be correct, though View Three has some slight advantages in reconciling with other temporal notices in Daniel and Revelation. However this eventually plays out, Carpenter (461) rightly points out, "The cryptic comments about certain time periods in 12:11–13 are given to encourage God's people to realize that God has placed a limitation on the desolation caused by the overspreading sacrilege."

Biblical Theology Comments

Determining the precise meaning of chronology related to prophetic events is admittedly a tenuous matter. Since Dan 12:5–7 had already indicated that the "time of distress" was limited to a period of "time, times, and half a time," i.e., three and one-half years, the two extensions of time mentioned in vv. 11–12 are not related to the nation's suffering. Whatever purpose they have, it is not one of more suffering at the hands of the antichrist. As clarified in the commentary above, the futurist interpretation of the 1290 years and 1335 years has the most to commend it. In light of the emphasis in the book on the kingdom to be given the Messiah (note especially Dan 2:44–45; 7:13–14; and 9:24), this will obviously be a grand event replacing the horrors of the great tribulation with the blessedness of Jesus' righteous rule. That there would be transitional events as history shifts from the great tribulation to Messiah's kingdom is quite plausible.

Application and Devotional Implications

For those of us living *on this side* of the great tribulation, the words of Dan 12:10 are still a consolation for us: "none of the wicked will understand, while those having *spiritual* insight will understand." We live in a fast-changing world in which many cultures are rapidly losing ground to forces of wickedness—perhaps more so than at any previous time. "Cultural, moral, and spiritual erosion" is disheartening to those who yearn for a righteous society.

---

764. J. P. Tanner, "The 'Marriage Supper of the Lamb' in Rev 19:6–10: Implications for the Judgment Seat of Christ," *TJ* 26 (2005): 47–68. Regarding the judgment seat of Christ (for believers only), see 2 Cor 5:9–10 and 1 Cor 3:10–17.

In the time of the great tribulation, the hearts of unbelievers will be even more hardened against the Lord and his truth, as the words of Rev 16:9 so poignantly remind us, "they blasphemed the name of God who has the power over these plagues, and they did not repent so as to give Him glory" (NASB). Their inner darkness will be matched by an inability to understand what will be taking place on the earth at that time, fanning the flames of hysteria, anger, and hatred. In contrast will be those who are wise, i.e., having *spiritual insight* as a result of worshiping the Lord Jesus and abiding in his Word. While we may presently be *on this side* of the great tribulation, there is much consolation in being able to "understand." That does not mean at all that we fully understand the things that are taking place, but we do understand enough to know that a fierce spiritual battle is raging in which Satan and his hordes are stepping up their hostilities—and all the more as the day of our Lord's glorious return draws near. We must not let the bereavement of today's cultural decline so overwhelm us that we fail to see what action we need to take. We need to step up to a greater level of spiritual commitment than ever before.

6. God's Special Promise for Daniel in the Resurrection (12:13)

The final verse of the book of Daniel is reserved for Daniel himself. Eternal reward awaited him for the life he lived, and his life serves as a model to those of us who would desire to live a consecrated life unto God. His faithfulness, courage, character, and love of God's Word summon each of us to follow in his steps. The final verse reminds us that God takes note of those who are faithful to him, and like Daniel, such people can anticipate being gloriously rewarded.

Textual Notes

13.a. The words "to the end" (לַקֵּץ) are omitted in LXX$^{\theta}$ and LXX^{O}. Consequently Montgomery (477–78), Di Lella (261), Goldingay (275), Collins (370), and Newsom (326) all omit לַקֵּץ, presuming a dittography with לְקֵץ later in the verse. Yet the Vg. and S have it. Furthermore, לַקֵּץ serves an important purpose here, as E. Carpenter (461) points out, "The word *laqqets* ... (end) refers back to and echoes the end or that time when even the dead will rise (11:40; 12:1) and is not a mere dittography of the second occurrence of the word in this verse."

Translation

12:13 Now *as for* you, go *your way* to the end. You will enter rest[765] and *then*

765. Daniel will "enter rest" (תָּנוּחַ, *tānûaḥ*). Here "rest" is a metaphor for resting in Sheol, the grave (cf. Job 3:17; Isa 57:2).

rise[766] for your allotted portion[767] at the end of days.

Commentary

12:13 The final verse of the book is reserved for Daniel himself. Given the date for this final vision mentioned in 10:1, Daniel would most likely be a man over eighty years of age at this point and not far from death. He would die soon and would not live to see the kingdom given to "One like a Son of Man" in his own lifetime (7:13–14). His only hope was to be resurrected in the distant future and enter Messiah's kingdom at that time. For now, he is told to go his way to the end, i.e., the end of his physical life when he would be placed in the grave and rest from his labors. Hill (212) elaborates, "The hortatory charge to 'go your way till the end' (v.13a) is not an admonition of rebuke, but rather an exhortation to the seer to persevere until his own death."

---

766. Here, the word translated "rise" is the verb עָמַד ('*āmaḏ*), normally meaning "stand." We might have expected the word קִיץ (*qîṣ*, "awake") as in Dan 12:2, or perhaps קוּם (*qûm*, "to arise, stand"). On עָמַד ('*āmaḏ*) as a term for resurrection, see Sawyer, "Hebrew Words for the Resurrection of the Dead," 223 (cf. 4Q Second Ezekiel 2.8). However, '*āmaḏ* is not a term used elsewhere for resurrection. (One might argue, as Goldingay, 281, does, that '*āmaḏ* is an equivalent term for קוּם (*qûm*) in late biblical Heb., and on this basis indicates "resurrection"; similarly Montgomery, 478. Another possibility is that '*āmaḏ* in Dan 12:13 has the sense "to appear, come on the scene" (BDB, 764b 6). The idea would be that of his standing before God for his "allotted portion" (this would imply he had first been resurrected, but the emphasis is on a subsequent moment when he will stand before God).

767. "Allotted portion" translates Heb. גּוֹרָל (*gôrāl*). Collins (402) understands it in the sense of "destiny" (so Goldingay, 275). He writes, "The use of the term גרל, 'lot' or 'destiny', is attested in the Hebrew Bible (Jer 13:25; Ps 125:3) and also in the Qumran texts, where people are assigned to the 'lot' of the Angel of Darkness (1QS 3:24) or of Melchizedek (11QMelch 1:8). ... Daniel's destiny is clearly with that of the *maśkîlîm*, who rise to eternal life." Yet most do not understand גּוֹרָל (*gôrāl*) as "destiny" in Dan 12:13. BDB (174d 3) indicates, "also עָמַד לְגֹ Dn 12:13, of *allotted portion, share* in the Messianic consummation." The more common meaning of גּוֹרָל (*gôrāl*) is of something that is *allotted* to one (their "portion"), esp. of land assigned by lot as one's inheritance (see NASB "allotted portion," and similarly the NET). Hence, the NIV, NLT, and NRSV translate *gôrāl* as "inheritance," while the NRSV translates as "reward"; Di Lella (261) also translates as "reward". In summary, גּוֹרָל (*gôrāl*) is not merely one's destiny (i.e., *where* one will ultimately be), but the inheritance or reward that one will have to enjoy. Although LXX[θ] translated *gôrāl* as κλῆρόν (*klēron* = lot, inheritance), MS 967 (a witness to LXX[O]) has "δόξα, *doxa*": ἀναστήσῃ ἐπὶ τὴν δόξαν σου (*anastēsēi epi tēn doxan sou*), "shall rise in your glory." F. Raurell, "The *Doxa* of the Seer in Dan-LXX 12,13," in *The Book of Daniel in the Light of New Findings*, ed. A. S. van der Woude, BETL 106, 520–32 (Leuven: Leuven University Press; Peeters, 1993), 529, suggests, "In addition to the idea of resurrection it seems as if it wishes to hint at the raising up of the seer in a shining eschatological dignity."

In the Old Testament, entering one's rest was a picture of believers who physically died and then found peace and rest from their struggles of life (cf. Job 3:17; Isa 57:2). Yet this would not be the end to his existence, for God promised him that he would "at the end of days ... rise," i.e., be resurrected in the distant future. He will awake to everlasting life, just as was promised the righteous in Dan 12:2, and we can safely conclude that he too will "shine like the brightness of the heavenly firmament." His resurrection will not simply be an awakening from the grave, but much more—to receive his "allotted portion." His "allotted portion" (a noun in the Heb. text—גּוֹרָל, *gôrāl*) is a word meaning a "lot" that is cast for determining a decision, from which it has the derived meaning of that which is obtained by a lot cast. The same word was used for the land inheritance that the tribes received upon entering the promised land (e.g., Josh 15:1). Hence, the word is used here for the inheritance that is in store for Daniel in the resurrection as his reward for a life of faithful service. This is what he will have to enjoy forever and ever in Messiah's kingdom. Such reward in the resurrection sets the stage and anticipates the doctrine of rewards that is developed more fully in the New Testament. Believers today can also hope to receive a future reward and inheritance, provided, that is, that they endure in a life of faithfulness with the Lord Jesus Christ (cf. Heb 10:35–36). For this, we have no greater model than Daniel. Amen.

Biblical Theology Comments

The doctrine of rewards, of which we are given a brief glimpse in Dan 12:13, is more fully developed in the New Testament. Those of us who are "in Christ" will one day stand before the Lord Jesus to give an account of ourselves (Rom 14:12). The Bible refers to this event as "the judgment seat of Christ" (2 Cor 5:9–10). The main purpose will be to examine our "works" to see what is rewardable and what is not (1 Cor 3:12–15). Earthly attainments will pale in comparison to the importance of what results from this scrutiny of our lives by the One with eyes of flaming fire. Each believer will enjoy the blessing of resurrection and being fully conformed to the image of Christ (1 John 3:1–2), and yet there will be individual rewards given to those who were faithful and served the Lord with pure motives during their time on earth.

Application and Devotional Implications

The apostle Paul understood the importance of faithful service, endurance, and rewards, likening them to an imperishable wreath: "Everyone who competes in the games exercises self-control in all things. They then *do it* to receive a perishable wreath, but we an imperishable" (1 Cor 9:25 NASB). God calls all of us who name the name of Jesus Christ to compete in the arena of the "spiritual Olympics." Living a sloppy, undisciplined life and failing to passionately serve the Lord Jesus with the time we have is not only sin but a sure path to "shrinking away from Him in shame at His coming" (1 John

2:28). Yet our destiny can be, like Daniel's, one of receiving our "allotted portion" when our Lord returns.

Selected Bibliography (Daniel 12)

Armerding, C. "Dan 12:1–3: Asleep in the Dust." *BSac* 121 (1964): 153–58.

Bailey, D. P. "The Intertextual Relationship of Daniel 12:2 and Isaiah 26:19: Evidence from Qumran and the Greek Versions." *TynBul* 51 (2000): 305–8.

Birkeland, H. "The Belief in the Resurrection of the Dead in the Old Testament." *ST* 3 (1949–1950): 60–78.

Bronner, L. "The Resurrection Motif in the Hebrew Bible: Allusions or Illusions?" *JBQ* 30 (2002): 143–54.

Cavallin, H. C. C. *Life After Death: Paul's Argument for the Resurrection of the Dead in 1 Cor 15*. Part 1, *An Enquiry into the Jewish Background.* ConBNT 7. CWK Gleerup, Lund, 1974.

Chase, M. L. "'From dust you shall arise': Resurrection Hope in the Old Testament." *SBJT* 18 (2014): 9–29.

———. "The Genesis of Resurrection Hope: Exploring Its Early Presence and Deep Roots." *JETS* 57 (2014): 467–80.

———. "Resurrection Hope in Daniel 12:2: An Exercise in Biblical Theology." Ph.D. diss., Southern Baptist Theological Seminary, 2013.

Clifford, R. J. "History and Myth in Daniel 10–12." *BASOR* 220 (1975): 23–26.

Collins, J. J. "The Meaning of 'The End' in the Book of Daniel." In *Of Scribes and Scrolls: Studies on the Hebrew Bible, Intertestamental Judaism, and Christian Origins*, Presented to John Strugnell on the Occasion of his Sixtieth Birthday, ed. H. W. Attridge, J. J. Collins, and T. H. Tobin, 91–98. Lanham, MD: University Press of America, 1990.

Day, J. "*Da ʿat* 'Humiliation' in the Light of Isaiah LIII 3 and Daniel XII 4, and the Oldest Known Interpretation of the Suffering Servant." *VT* 30 (1980): 97–103.

Doukhan, J. B. "From Dust to Stars: The Vision of Resurrection(s) in Daniel 12,1–3 and Its Resonance in the Book of Daniel." In *Resurrection of the Dead: Biblical Traditions in Dialogue*, ed. G. V. Oyen and T. Shepherd, 85–98. Leuven; Walpole, MA: Peeters, 2012.

Dubarle, A.-M. "Belief in Immortality in the Old Testament and Judaism." Trans. R. Ockenden. *Concilium* 10 (1970) 34–45.

Dyrness, W. *Themes in Old Testament Theology*. Downers Grove, IL: InterVarsity, 1979.

Emerton, J. A. "A Consideration of Some Alleged Meanings of ידע in Hebrew." *JSS* 15 (1970): 145–80.

———. "A Further Consideration of D. W. Thomas's Theories about *yādaʿ*." In *Studies on the Language and Literature of the Bible*, ed. G. Davies and R. Gordon, 101–16. Leiden/Boston: Brill, 2015.

Garcia, P. Z. "The Daniel and Qohelet Epilogues: A Similar Editorial Activity? (Qohelet 12:8–14 and Daniel 12:1–13)." In *The Bible as a Human*

Witness to Divine Revelation: Hearing the Word of God through Historically Dissimilar Traditions, ed. R. Heskett and B. Irwin, 202–22. London: T&T Clark, 2010.

Gardner, A. E. "The Way to Eternal Life in Dan 12:1e–2 or How to Reverse the Death Curse of Genesis 3." *ABR* 40 (1992): 1–19.

Ginsberg, H. L. "The Oldest Interpretation of the Suffering Servant." *VT* 3 (1953): 400–404.

Goswell, G. "Resurrection in the Book of Daniel." *ResQ* 55 (2013): 139–51.

Graham, D. "Early Christian Understandings of the 'Abomination that Causes Desolation.'" *RTR* 74 (2015): 162–75.

Greenspoon, L. J. "The Origin of the Idea of Resurrection." In *Traditions in Transformation: Turning Points in Biblical Faith*, Festschrift to F. M. Cross, ed. B. Halpern and J. D. Levenson, 247–321. Winona Lake, IN: Eisenbrauns, 1981.

Hasel, G. F. "Resurrection in the Theology of Old Testament Apocalyptic." *ZAW* 92 (1980): 267–84.

Hernandez, A. F. "Adventist Eschatological Identity and the Interpretations of the Time Periods of Daniel 12:11–12." *AUSSJ* 1 (2015): 65–84.

Hobbins, J. F. "Resurrection in the Daniel Tradition and Other Writings at Qumran." In *The Book of Daniel: Composition and Reception*, ed. J. J. Collins and P. W. Flint, 2:395–420. Leiden: Brill, 2001.

Hunt, B. "A Short Note on Daniel 12:11–12." *Scr* 9 (1957): 84–85.

Johnstone, W. "*yd*ʿ II, 'be humbled, humiliated'?" *VT* 41 (1991): 49–62.

Lindenberger, J. M. "Daniel 12:1–4." *Int* 39 (1985): 181–86.

Mathews, S. F. "The Numbers in Daniel 12:11–12: Rounded Pythagorean Plane Numbers?" *CBQ* 63 (2001): 630–46.

McGarry, E. P. "The Ambidextrous Angel (Daniel 12:7 and Deuteronomy 32:40): Inner-Biblical Exegesis and Textual Criticism in Counterpoint." *JBL* 124 (2005): 211–28.

Moore, M. S. "Resurrection and Immortality: Two Motifs Navigating Confluent Streams in the Old Testament (Dan 12,1–4)." *TZ* 39 (1983): 17–34.

Nickelsburg, G. W. E. *Resurrection, Immortality, and Eternal Life in Intertestamental Judaism*. *HTS* 26. Cambridge: Harvard University Press, 1972. Expanded ed., 2007.

Parry, J. T. "Desolation of the Temple and Messianic Enthronement in Daniel 11:36–12:3." *JETS* 54 (2011): 485–526.

Paul, S. M. "Daniel 12:9: A Technical Mesopotamian Scribal Term." In *Sefer Moshe: the Moshe Weinfeld Jubilee Volume: Studies in the Bible and the Ancient Near East, Qumran, and Post-Biblical Judaism*, ed. C. Cohen, A. Hurvitz, and S. Paul, 115–18. Winona Lake, IN: Eisenbrauns, 2004.

———. "Heavenly Tablets and the Book of Life." *JANESCU* 5 (1973): 345–53.

Peters, J. "Hellenistic Imagery and Iconography in Daniel 12.5–13." *JSP* 19 (2009): 127–45.

Raurell, F. "The *Doxa* of the Seer in Dan-LXX 12,13." In *The Book of Daniel in the Light of New Findings*, ed. A. S. van der Woude, 520–32. BETL 106. Leuven: Leuven University Press; Peeters, 1993.

Redditt, P. L. "Calculating the 'Times': Daniel 12:5–13." *PRSt* 25 (1998): 373–79.

Ryrie, C. C. *Basic Theology*. Chicago: Moody, 1999.

Sawyer, J. F. A. "Hebrew Words for the Resurrection of the Dead." *VT* 23 (1973): 218–34.

Schutte, P. J. W. "The Origin of the Resurrection Idea: A Dialogue with George Nickelsburg." *HTS* 64 (2008): 1075–89.

Smick, E. "The Bearing of New Philological Data on the Subjects of Resurrection and Immortality in the Old Testament." *WTJ* 31 (1969): 12–21.

Smith, C. R. "The Book of Life." *GTJ* 6 (1985): 219–30.

Spronk, K. *Beatific Afterlife in Ancient Israel and in the Ancient Near East*. AOAT 219. Neukirchen-Vluyn: Neukirchener Verlag, 1986.

Stele, A. A. "Resurrection in Daniel 12 and Its Contribution to the Theology of the Book of Daniel." Ph.D. diss., Andrews University, 1996.

Tanner, J. P. "The 'Marriage Supper of the Lamb' in Rev 19:6–10: Implications for the Judgment Seat of Christ." *TJ* 26 (2005): 47–68.

Tawil, H. "Hebrew *nappēṣ yad* [in Dan 12:7] = Akkadian *qāta napāṣu:* A Term of Non-Allegiance." *JAOS* 122 (2002): 79–82.

Thomas, D. W. "Note on הַדָּעַת in Daniel XII.4." *JTS* 6 (1955): 226.

Thomson, H. C. "Old Testament Ideas on Life after Death." *TGUOS* 22 (1967–68): 46–55.

Walvoord, J. F. "Contemporary Problems: The Resurrection of Israel." *BSac* 124 (1967): 3–15.

Waltke, B. K. *An Old Testament Theology*. Grand Rapids: Zondervan, 2007. Esp. "Appendix IV: Realm of the Dead," 964–69.

Webb, J. R. "'Knowledge Will Be Manifold': Daniel 12.4 and the Idea of Intellectual Progress in the Middle Ages." In *History Faculty Publications.* Paper 38 (2014) 307–57. Accessed 3 May, 2016. Online: http://vc.bridgew.edu/cgi/viewcontent.cgi?article=1037&context=history_fac.

Wolters, A. "*Zōhar hārāqîaʿ* (Daniel 12.3) and Halley's Comet." *JSOT* 61 (1994): 111–20.

Zamora, P. "The Daniel and Qohelet Epilogues: A Similar Editorial Activity? (Qohelet 12:8–14 and Daniel 12:1–13)." In *The Bible as a Human Witness to Divine Revelation: Hearing the Word of God through Historically Dissimilar Traditions*, ed. R. Heskett and B. Irwin, 202–22. LHBOTS 469. New York: T&T Clark, 2010.

Appendix

	NON-MESSIANIC VIEWS		
Name of view	**Roman Destruction View (AD 70)**	**Maccabean View (2nd Cent BC)**	**Maccabean Double Fulfillment View**
Adherents	Jewish Sources: Seder Olam Rabbah; Rashi (AD 1040–1105); Ibn Ezra (AD 1089–1164)	Porphyry (232–c.305 AD) Critical Scholars: Montgomery (ICC); Collins (Hermeneia); Hartman-DiL. – Anchor; Goldingay (WBC)	Robert B. Chisholm [He differs somewhat from T. McComiskey. The latter begins with Jer 29:10, with first 7 wks to Cyrus, and then 62 to Antichrist].
Descript.	The prophecy culminates with the destruction of the 2nd Temple in AD 70 (or possibly AD 135)	Most details fulfilled in the Maccabean era during the time of Antiochus Epiphanes (171–164 BC)	Same as the Maccabean view, except the final wk has a "double fulfillment." Antiochus foreshadows Antichrist.
Decree	Cyrus' decree – 538 BC	God's command – Jer 25:1	God's Announcement through Jeremiah (30:18)
1st 7 wks	1st exile until 538 BC (or 520)	587/86–538/36 BC	587/86–539 BC (Literal)

MESSIANIC VIEWS (Fulfilled with Jesus Christ)				
1st Century Messianic Symbolic View	**1st Century Messianic Literal View**	**Messianic Symbolic-Eschatological View**	**Messianic Postponement View**	
			Solar Year Calculation	***Prophetic Year Calculation***
Conservative Amillennial: E. J. Young, Meredith Kline, Anthony Hoekema	G. Hasel, J. Barton Payne, R. G. M. Gurney	Conservative Amillennial: T. Kliefoth, C. F. Keil, H. C. Leupold	Gleason Archer, Stephen R. Miller, Leon Wood	Sir Robert Anderson, Alva J. McClain, John Walvoord, J. Dwight Pentecost, Paul Feinberg, Harold Hoehner, J. Paul Tanner
The "anointed" of v. 26 is Christ who is crucified; and He makes a covenant with God's people in v. 27.	The 70 "weeks" are literal and all fulfilled in the 1st century, but extend beyond the crucifixion 3 ½ yrs.	70 "weeks" are symbolic of 3 periods. The 62 wks are the present age as "spir. Jer." being built. 70th wk is for Antichrist	First 69 weeks culminate with crucifixion of Christ, and 70th wk is still future with Antichrist. Calculations based on 365-day yr.	First 69 weeks culminate with crucifixion of Christ, and 70th wk is still future with Antichrist. Calculations based on 360-day yr.
Cyrus' decree – 538 BC	Artaxerxes' decree of 458–57 BC	Cyrus' decree – 538 BC	Artaxerxes' decree of 458–57 BC	Artaxerxes' authorization to Nehemiah, 444 BC
538/37 BC until completion by Ezra-Neh	458/57–ca. 409/08 BC	538 BC until the 1st Coming of Christ	458/57–ca. 409/08 BC	444–ca. 396 BC

	NON-MESSIANIC VIEWS		
Name of view	**Roman Destruction View (AD 70)**	**Maccabean View (2nd Cent BC)**	**Maccabean Double Fulfillment View**
2nd 62 wks	Time in land until first Jewish revolt (AD 60's)	538/36–171/70 BC	539–171 BC (Not literal)
3rd – 70th	Dest. of Jeru. in AD 70 (possibly to 135)	171/70–164 BC	539–164 BC (Literal)
Anointed of v. 25	Usually Cyrus the Great	Joshua the High Priest in Zerub.'s day	Cyrus the Great
Anointed of v. 26	King Agrippa II at time of AD 70 (so Rashi)	Onias III, the High Pr. assassinated in 171 BC	Onias III, the High Pr. assassinated in 171 BC
Prince to Come	Vespasian or Titus	Antiochus	Antiochus
One who Makes covenant (v. 27)	Romans with Jews in 1st century AD	Antiochus's alliance with Hellenizing Jews	Antiochus's alliance with Hellenizing Jews, but also a further fulfillment with the Antichrist

MESSIANIC VIEWS (Fulfilled with Jesus Christ)				
1st Century Messianic Symbolic View	**1st Century Messianic Literal View**	**Messianic Symbolic-Eschatolog-ical View**	**Messianic Postponement View** *Solar Year Calculation*	*Prophetic Year Calculation*
Completion of work by Ezra-Neh until 1st Advent of Christ	ca. 409/08 BC–ca. AD 26/27	After 1st Coming as "spiritual Jerusalem" (Church) is built	ca. 409/08 BC–ca. AD 26/27 (time of Christ's baptism)	ca. 396 BC–AD 33 (appr. time of Christ's crucifixion)
Most say 1st Century (mid. of wk = crucifixion)	ca. AD 26/27–ca. AD 33/34	Era of the Antichrist before the 2nd Coming	Future 7 years before the 2nd Coming of Christ	Future 7 years before the 2nd Coming of Christ
Christ Jesus (after the 1st 69 weeks)	Christ Jesus (time of His baptism)	Christ Jesus (after the 1st 7 weeks)	Christ Jesus (after the 1st 69 weeks)	Christ Jesus (after the 1st 69 weeks)
Jesus Christ ("cut off" = crucifixion; presum. AD 30)	Jesus Christ ("cut off" = crucifixion in AD 30/31)	Jesus Christ ("cut off" = His influence cut off by Antichrist)	Jesus Christ ("cut off" = crucifixion in AD 30)	Jesus Christ ("cut off" = crucifixion in AD 33)
Titus (so Young); or Jesus Christ (so Kline)	Titus (Hasel); but Christ acc. to Payne	The Antichrist	The Antichrist	The Antichrist
A covenant by Christ with the Church ("ratified" at the time of crucifixion)	Jesus Christ who makes the New Covenant, putting an end to the Jewish sacrificial system	1) Leupold – made in imitation of Christ and imposed on masses; or 2) Keil deceives people to follow him as God	A covenant made by the Antichrist with the Jews. Breaking the covenant starts the final 3 1/2 yrs of the Tribulation	A covenant made by the Antichrist with the Jews. Breaking the covenant starts the final 3 1/2 yrs of the Tribulation

	NON-MESSIANIC VIEWS		
Name of view	**Roman Destruction View (AD 70)**	**Maccabean View (2nd Cent BC)**	**Maccabean Double Fulfillment View**
Makes Desolation	Roman defilement of Temple in AD 70 and/or the establishment of Aelia on ruins of Jerus. by Hadrian	Pagan altar erected on top of Jewish altar (ca. 168/67 BC)	Apparently the same as the Maccabean view (but also Antichrist)
2nd Half of 70th Week	Events about AD 70 or 132–135	Antiochus' attempt to destroy Judaism (latter 3 ½ yrs of his rule)	Antiochus' attempt to destroy Judaism (latter 3 ½ yrs of his rule)

MESSIANIC VIEWS (Fulfilled with Jesus Christ)				
1st Century Messianic Symbolic View	**1st Century Messianic Literal View**	**Messianic Symbolic-Eschatological View**	**Messianic Postponement View**	
			Solar Year Calculation	***Prophetic Year Calculation***
Christ delegitimizes the sacrificial system; the Jewish temple is an abomin. to be destroyed later by Titus	Refers to the stoning of Stephen and scattering of early church from Jerusalem	The work of Antichrist in the Tribulation	The Antichrist halts sacrificial system and commits the "abom. of desolation" in the Jewish temple of Trib. (cf. Matt 24:15; 2 Thess 2:4)	The Antichrist halts sacrificial system and commits the "abom. of desolation" in the Jewish temple of Trib. (cf. Matt 24:15; 2 Thess 2:4)
(1) Young, Hoekema – work of Titus in AD 70 (2) Kline, West – an eschatological judgment	See above	The Antichrist's hatred for the city and temple	The 3 1/2 years of the Great Tribulation when the Antichrist is in power	The 3 1/2 years of the Great Tribulation when the Antichrist is in power

Scripture Index

Old Testament

Proverbs

Hosea

New Testament

CPSIA information can be obtained
at www.ICGtesting.com
Printed in the USA
BVHW032118131022
648805BV00008B/17/J

9 781683 593096